THE

PENSION ROLL OF 1835

Indexed Edition

In Four Volumes

With an Index to the Four Volumes
Compiled by Murtie June Clark

Volume IV

THE MID-WESTERN STATES

Illinois   *Michigan*

Indiana   *Missouri*

Ohio

Originally published in 1835 in three volumes as Senate Document 514,
Serial Nos. 249-51 (23rd Cong., 1st Sess.) under the title *Report from the
Secretary of War in Obedience to Resolutions of the Senate of the 5th and
30th of June, 1834, and the 3rd of March, 1835, in Relation to the Pension
Establishment of the United States*

Rearranged and reprinted in four volumes in 1968
by Genealogical Publishing Co., Inc.

Reprinted with a new index 1992
Genealogical Publishing Co., Inc.
Baltimore, Maryland

Contents

ILLINOIS PENSION ROLL.

Statement showing the Names, Rank, &c. of Invalid Pensioners residing in the State of Illinois.

NAMES AND COUNTIES.	Rank.	Annual allowance.	Sums received.	Description of service.	When placed on the pension roll.	Commencement of pension.	Laws under which they were inscribed, increased and reduced; and remarks.
ADAMS.							
John Fee	Lieut't	112 50	96 25	22d U. S. inf.	Mar. 12, 1816	June 16, 1815	Acts military establishment. Transferred from Pennsylvania.
Do	do	135 00	2,411 25	do	—	Apl 24, 1816	April 24, 1816.
Aaron Graham	Sergeant	48 00	97 46	1st U. S. rifles	Oct. 17, 1822	Aug. 24, 1822	Acts military establishment. Susp'd July 7, 1825.
Justice J. Perrigo	do	96 00	1,654 40	-	Mar. 10, 1818	June 10, 1815	Acts military estab. Paid in Missouri. Transferred from New York.
Israel Waters	Matross	48 00	788 26	U. S. I. artillery	Nov. 1, 1817	Oct. 2, 1817	Acts military estab. Paid in Missouri. Transferred from New York.
CLAY.							
Lina T. Helm	Captain	120 00	861 32	1st U. S. infantry	May 24, 1827	June 30, 1826	March 3, 1827. Transferred from Kentucky.
John Lewis	Private	96 00	193 84	U. S. riflemen	Dec. 7, 1820	Aug. 28, 1820	Acts military establishment.
John Myers	do	64 00	165 63	Indian wars	Mar. 22, 1817	Nov. 15, 1816	March 3, 1817. Died June 17, 1819.
CRAWFORD.							
Jacob Davis	do	72 00	149 20	19th U. S. infantry	Feb. 15, 1831	Feb. 8, 1831	Acts military establishment.
Samuel Jacqueway	do	48 00	624 00	U. S. rangers	Dec. 24, 1816	Jan. 9, 1814	April 30, 1816.
CALHOUN.							
John Patterson	Sergeant	48 00	890 13	-	Sep. 29, 1819	Sep. 18, 1815	April 30, 1816. Paid in Missouri.
FAYETTE.							
Henry Flesher	Ensign	156 00	204 00	Ohio volunteers	Feb. 10, 1831	Feb. 4, 1831	April 24, 1816. Transferred from Ohio.
Thomas Higgins	Private	32 00	375 86	Illinois rangers	Dec. 2, 1820	Mar. 17, 1820	April 10, 1812.
Do	do	72 00	164 20	do	Feb. 11, 1832	Nov. 23, 1831	Acts military establishment. Increased to this rate.

Name	Rank			Corps			Remarks
FULTON.							
Thomas Newill	do	96 00	900 00	U. S. artillery	Oct. 21, 1816	June 20, 1815	Acts mil. establishment. Transferred from New York.
GREEN.							
Thomas Richardson	do	48 00	342 93	6th U. S. infantry	Oct. 15, 1823	Aug. 2, 1822	Acts military establishment.
Do	do	96 00	506 66	do	-	Nov. 24, 1828	Acts military establishment. Paid in Missouri.
GALATIN.							
William Abney	do	48 00	883 60	24th U. S. infantry	Oct. 21, 1816	April 7, 1815	Acts military estab. Transferred from W. Tennessee.
William Bolton	do	96 00	1,225 60	U. S. rifles	Nov. 6, 1821	May 29, 1821	Acts military estab. Transferred from S. and N. Carolina.
John Barger	do	32 00	426 20	E. Tennessee mil.	Sept. 17, 1816	July 30, 1814	April 24, 1816. Transferred from W. Tennessee.
Tramel Ewing	2d lieut.	126 00	15 90	Illinois volunteers	Mar. 27, 1834	Jan. 20, 1834	April 24, 1816.
James Norton	Private	72 00	-	6th U. S. infantry	Mar. 22, 1834	Feb. 28, 1833	Acts military establishment.
HAMILTON.							
Henry J. Williams	do	96 00	1,369 60	11th U. S. infantry	Dec. 30, 1816	May 29, 1816	Acts military estab. Transferred from Virg. and W. Tennessee.
Do	do	96 00	288 00	do	-	Sep. 4, 1830	Acts military establishment.
JOHNSON.							
Samuel J. Chapman	do	64 00	1,193 95	23d U. S. infantry	Jan. 13, 1817	July 9, 1815	Acts military estab. Transferrred from New York.
Caleb Hayward	do	48 00	487 60	do	Aug. 5, 1816	July 8, 1815	Acts military estab. Transferred from New York.
LAWRENCE.							
James Gibson	do	96 00	672 00	Illinois militia	July 14, 1826	Sep. 4, 1825	May 16, 1826. Transferred from Indiana.
Edward Perdue	do	48 00	645 33	7th U. S. infantry	Feb. 12, 1821	Oct. 25, 1820	Acts military establishment. Transferred from Indiana.
John Rogers	do	96 00	267 73	Ind'a militia	Jan. 13, 1831	Dec. 21, 1830	April 24, 1816. Transferred from In.
Stephen Terry	do	64 00	340 97	do	Jan. 3, 1829	Dec. 17, 1828	April 10, 1812. Transferred from In.
Do	do	96 00		do	July 26, 1834	Apl 14, 1834	Acts military establishment.
James Thompson	do	96 00	-	Illinois militia	Sept. 28, 1833	Apl 23, 1833	April 24, 1816.
Thomas West	do	48 00	150 66	Ind'a mounted inf.	Nov. 25, 1828	Nov. 8, 1828	April 10, 1812.
Do	do	64 00	154 48	do	Dec. 20, 1831	Dec. 16, 1831	Acts mil. establishment. Transferred from Indiana.
Do	do	96 00	-	do	July 26, 1834	Apl 14, 1834	Acts military establishment.

Statement, &c. of Invalid Pensioners—Continued.

NAMES AND COUNTIES.	Rank.	Annual allowance.	Sums received.	Description of service.	When placed on the pension roll.	Commencement of pension.	Laws under which they were inscribed, increased and reduced; and remarks.
MADISON.							
Asa Brooks	Private	96 00	1,854 40	N. York volunteers	July 27, 1819	Nov. 10, 1814	Acts mil. establishment. Transferred from New York.
William Pruitt	do	96 00	1,808 52	U. S. rangers	July 1, 1816	Nov. 2, 1814	July 24, 1813.
William Richards	do	48 00	521 33	3d U. S. rifles	Jan. 2, 1818	Ap'l 24, 1815	Acts mil. establishment. Transferred from Virginia.
MONROE.							
John Birmingham	Corporal	96 00	67 46	6th U. S. infantry	Sep. 23, 1833	June 21, 1833	Acts military establishment. Paid in Missouri.
George Goble	Sergeant	96 00	354 66	3d U. S. infantry	June 26, 1830	June 24, 1830	Acts military establishment. Paid in Missouri.
William Howard	Private	48 00	176 53	do	June 30, 1830	June 30, 1830	Acts military establishment. Paid in Missouri.
John Jerrod	do	96 00	353 60	6th U. S. infantry	Sep. 29, 1830	June 28, 1830	Acts military establishment. Paid in Missouri.
MORGAN.							
John Seward	do	96 00	809 33	17th U. S. infantry	Dec. 6, 1825	Sep. 29, 1825	Acts mil. estab. Transf'd from Ohio.
George Saunders	do	96 00	435 73	Illinois militia	Feb. 11, 1818	Nov. 8, 1815	April 24, 1816. Died May 21, 1820.
Thomas Roberts	do	48 00	366 26	U. S. rangers	Sept. 27, 1826	Sept. 8, 1826	Acts military estab. Transferred from W. Tennessee.
Do	do	76 80	-	do	-	July 25, 1834	Acts military establishment. Paid in Missouri.
James Lammay	Corporal	32 00	488 44	23d U. S. inf.	June 9, 1818	May 30, 1815	Acts military estab. Transferred from N. York and Missouri.
POPE.							
Charles Dunn	Captain	240 00	88 66	Illinois volunteers	Dec. 13, 1833	Oct. 22, 1833	April 24, 1816.
Benjamin Glover	Sergeant	24 00	226 40	9th U. S. inf.	Feb. 17, 1817	Mar. 29, 1815	Acts military estab. Transferred from Massachusetts.
PIKE.							
David Callis	Private	57 60	1,031 36	35th U. S. infantry	Feb. 21, 1817	Ap'l 8, 1815	Acts mil. estab. Transf'd from Virg.

	Rank	Pay	Amount	Service	Date	Date	Remarks
RANDOLPH.							
Julian Bart	do	96 00	1,104 80	Illinois militia	Sep. 17, 1816	Sept. 1, 1815	April 24, 1816. Transferred from Virginia.
David Hoar	do	30 00	26 66	31st U. S. inf.	Mar. 29, 1816	June 4, 1816	Acts military estab. Transferred from Mass. and Ohio.
Do	do	48 00	809 33	do	Feb. 15, 1819	Ap'l 24, 1816	April 24, 1816.
William Henley	do	96 00	897 33	Dyer's reg. of mil.	–	Ap'l 28, 1815	April 24, 1816. Transferred from W. Tennessee.
Do	do	48 00	289 06	do	Sep. 11, 1830	Sept. 3, 1824	March 3, 1819. Reduced.
Do	do	96 00	238 13	do	Sep. 11, 1830	Sept. 11, 1830	Acts military establishment. Increased to this rate.
Armistead Jones	do	48 00	7 20	Illinois militia	Mar. 13, 1834	Jan. 9, 1834	April 24, 1816.
William Lippencott	do	72 00	838 98	2d U. S. inf.	Jan. 29, 1817	July 10, 1815	Acts military estab. Transferred from N. York.
William Lane	do	96 00	1,018 12	Tenn. volunteers	June 21, 1823	Jan. 27, 1823	April 24, 1816, and Feb. 4, 1822.
Eli Short	Assistant	45 00	93 13	Kentucky volunteers	–	Mar. 30, 1814	Mar. 3, 1815. Trans. from Kentucky.
Do	Forage	72 00	26 00	U. States service	–	Ap'l 24, 1816	April 24, 1816.
Do	Muster	117 00	457 15		Dec. 8, 1816	Sept. 4, 1816	Acts military establishment. Died May 21, 1820.
SANGAMON.							
Charles Revere	Private	60 00	80 66	U · S. rangers	Feb. 23, 1816	Dec. 20, 1814	Acts military establishment.
Do	do	96 00	1,090 66	do	–	Ap'l 24, 1816	April 24, 1816.
Do	do	48 00	-	do	–	Sept. 4, 1827	March 3, 1819. Reduced to this rate.
William Haile	do	20 00	88 61	Revolut'y army	–	Nov. 19, 1811	July 5, 1812.
Do	do	32 00	514 13	do	Dec. 20, 1824	Ap'l 24, 1816	April 24, 1816. Killed by Indians in 1832.
Joseph R. Young	do	96 00	66 66	Illinois volunt.	Sep. 25, 1833	June 20, 1833	April 24, 1816.
ST. CLAIR.							
John Appell	do	96 00	228 00	3d U. S. inf.	Oct. 11, 1831	Oct. 10, 1831	Acts military establishment. Paid in Missouri.
Abner Case	do	30 00	27 58	4th U. S. rifles	Dec. 29, 1815	May 23, 1815	Acts military estab. Transferred from N. York, Ohio and Pittsburg agency.
Do	do	48 00	401 86	do	Feb. 12, 1825	Ap'l 24, 1816	April 24, 1816.
Do	do	96 00	862 93	do	Sept. 8, 1824	Sept. 8, 1824	Acts military establishment'.
Daniel Kenney	do	60 00	308 50	U. S. army	Sept. 5, 1814	Mar. 3, 1811	March 16, 1802.
Do	do	96 00	1,714 66	do	April 24, 1816	April 24, 1816	April 24, 1816.
John Randleman	do	48 00	362 12	U. S. rangers	May 17, 1826	Feb. 16, 1826	February 25, 1813.

Statement, &c. of Invalid Pensioners—Continued.

NAMES AND COUNTIES.	Rank.	Annual allowance.	Sums received.	Description of service.	When placed on the pension roll.	Commencement of pension.	Laws under which they were inscribed, increased and reduced; and remarks.
Francis Valkmore	Private	64 00	442 66	5th U. S. inf.	Mar. 23, 1822	Aug. 1, 1821	Acts military establishment. Paid in Missouri.
Richard Windsor	do	64 00	775 28	8th do	Oct. 21, 1819	Jan. 24, 1819	Acts military establishment.
TAZEWELL. Earl Armstrong	do	48 00	889 60	9th U. S. inf.	Oct. 5, 1816	Aug. 23, 1815	Acts mil. estab. Transferred from N. York. Paid in Missouri.
UNION. James Campbell	do	30 00	57 00	16th do	July 13, 1814	May 31, 1814	Acts military estab. Transferred from Pennsylvania.
Do	do	48 00	68 80	do		Ap'l 24, 1816	April 24, 1816.
Do	do	72 00	444 80	do	Ap'l 16, 1819	Sep. 30, 1817	March 3, 1819. Died December 3, 1823.
Elias House	do	54 00	412 50	Revolutionary army	—	Sep. 4, 1808	Acts military estab. Transferred from N. Carolina.
Do	do	86 40	870 48	do	Sep. 27, 1824	Apr. 24, 1816	April 24, 1816. Died May 20, 1826.
WHITE. Daniel Chapman	do	24 00	222 46	Tenn. militia	Oct. 11, 1825	Nov. 17, 1824	April 24, 1816.
John Taylor	do	45 00	185 25	Army of the U. S.	—	Mar. 12, 1812	July 5, 1812. Transfered from West Tennessee.
Do	do	72 00	605 80	do	June 7, 1820	Ap'l 24, 1816	April 24, 1816.
Do	do	96 00	858 66	do	Oct. 14, 1825	Sep. 23, 1824	Acts military establishment.

Statement of the Names, &c. of the Heirs of non-commissioned Officers, Privates, &c. who died in the United States' service, who obtained five years' half pay in lieu of bounty land, under the second section of the act of April 16, 1816, and who resided in the State of Illinois.

Names of the original claimants.	Rank.	Description of service.	Time of decease.	Names of the heirs.	Annu'l allowance.	Sums received.	When placed on the pension roll.	Commencement of pension.	Ending of pension.
				JOHNSON COUNTY.					
Thomas F. Clark	Private	7th reg. inf.	Mar. 31, 1815	Gideon and William Clark	48 00	240 00	Sep. 4, 1814	Feb. 17, 1815	Feb. 17, 1820
				RANDOLPH COUNTY.					
Ephraim Carpenter	do	24th reg. inf.	March, 1814	William Carpenter	48 00	240 00	Ap'l 16, 1821	Mar. 13, 1821	Apr. 13, 1826

Statement showing the Names, Rank, &c. of persons residing in the State of Illinois, who have been inscribed on the Pension List under the act of Congress passed March 18, 1818.

NAMES AND COUNTIES.	Rank.	Annual allowance.	Sums received.	Description of service.	When placed on the pension roll.	Commencement of pension.	Laws under which they were formerly inscribed on the pension roll; and remarks.
ADAMS.							
Richard Rose	Private	96 00	467 47	Virginia cont'l	May 14, 1828	Ap'l 21, 1828	Transferred from Indiana and removed to Schuyler county.
John Cotton	do	96 00	-	S. Carolina cont'l	Sep. 5, 1819	July 13, 1818	Dropped.
CLINTON.							
Jacob Seagraves	do	96 00	1,043 20	N. Carolina cont'l	June 18, 1822	Ap'l 22, 1822	Transferred from W. Tennessee.
Moses Land	do	96 00	334 66	Virginia cont'l	May 15, 1820	Mar. 10, 1820	Removed from St. Clair county.
CRAWFORD.							
Willis Fellows	do	96 00	750 92	Mass. continental	Jan. 28, 1826	Nov. 8, 1825	Transferred from Indiana.
Daniel Kenney	do	96 00	377 33	Virginia cont'l	Nov. 15, 1820	Sep. 4, 1820	Died August 9, 1824.
FRANKLIN.							
John G. Simpkins	do	96 00	667 72	do	Jan 10, 1827	Sep. 20, 1826	
Samuel Gardner	do	96 00	698 10	N. York cont'l	July 20, 1826	May 27, 1826	
FAYETTE.							
Joseph Evans	do	96 00	169 87	Virginia cont'l	Mar. 5, 1819	May 28, 1818	Dropped under act May 1, 1820. Restored. Died September 4, 1832.
Do	do	96 00	581 33	do	-	Aug. 15, 1826	
FULTON.							
William Dollar	do	96 00	960 80	do	Jan. 16, 1824	Mar. 1, 1823	Transferred from Indiana.
Jonas Hobart	do	30 00	164 16	N. Hampshire cont.	July 5, 1812	Nov. 16, 1810	Transferred from Vermont, resided in Schuyler county, and died Decemb. 15, 1833. Invalid.
Do	do	48 00	92 13	do	-	Ap'l 24, 1816	April 24, 1816.
Do	do	96 00	1,434 66	do	Ap'l 26, 1819	Mar. 25, 1818	

Name	Rank	Annual	Amount	Line	Commenced	Certificate	Remarks
GREEN. Aaron Smith	do	96 00	1,333 60	N. Carolina cont'l	Jan. 13, 1819	Ap'l 13, 1818	Transferred from E. Tennessee, resided in Washington county.
Michael Baker	Sergeant	96 00	1,289 60	Pennsylvania cont'l	May 13, 1819	Ap'l 7, 1818	Transferred from Ohio. Died Sept. 13, 1831.
John Conelison	Private	96 00	119 72	N. Carolina cont'l	Jan. 26, 1832	Dec. 6, 1831	Died May 16, 1833.
Robert Lorton	do	96 00	1,331 20	Virginia cont'l	Oct. 12, 1819	July 5, 1819	
GALATIN. Lewis Howell	do	96 00	1,565 26	do	Feb. 15, 1820	Jan. 8, 1818	Transferred from Kentucky. Died April 27, 1834.
Jos. Minns, or Minzes	do	96 00	-	N. Carolina cont'l	Aug. 28, 1830	Aug. 28, 1830	Transferred from Kentucky.
JEFFERSON. George Roper	do	96 00	833 86	do	Mar. 11, 1825	Dec. 28, 1824	Transferred from W. Tennessee.
Thomas Williams	do	96 00	192 00	-	Oct. 21, 1819	Mar. 4, 1818	Suspended March 4, 1820.
LAWRENCE. William Milton	do	96 00	462 66	N. Carolina cont'l	Dec. 30, 1826	Nov. 9, 1826	
MADISON. Elihu Mather	Sergeant	96 00	1,120 26	Connecticut cont'l	July 23, 1821	Jan. 3, 1820	Died September, 1831.
MORGAN. Job Jenkins	Private	96 00	1,264 26	Virginia cont'l	June 3, 1819	Nov. 5, 1818	Transferred from W. Tennessee: Died January, 1832.
James McEver	do	96 00	1,026 40	Mass. continental	June 7, 1819	May 15, 1818	Transferred from Ohio. Died Jan'y 24, 1829.
Patrick Offing	Sergeant	96 00	312 00	N. H. continental	May 6, 1820	July 7, 1818	Transferred from Ohio. Died October 7, 1821.
POPE. David McNeely	Private	96 00	41 60	Virginia cont'l	Jan. 10, 1827	Nov. 9, 1826·	Died April 15, 1827.
Luke Devoir	do	96 00	40 52	New Jersey cont'l	June 6, 1820	Nov. 2, 1819	Died about March 4, 1820.
RANDOLPH. Charles McNabb	Pri. & f. m.	96 00	345 00	Maryland cont'l	June 24, 1819	June 27, 1818	Died February 1, 1822.
George Stamm	Private	96 00	609 06	do	June 14, 1820	Ap'l 28, 1819	

Statement, &c.—Continued.

NAMES AND COUNTIES.	Rank.	Annual allowance	Sums received.	Description of service.	When placed on the pension roll.	Commencement of pension	Laws under which they were formerly inscribed on the pension roll; and remarks.
SANGAMON.							
Absalom Baker	Private	96 00	544 80	Md continental	May 21, 1830	Jan. 1, 1828	Resided in Madison county.
Aquila Davis	do	96 00	811 68	Virg. continental	June 29, 1824	Mar. 1, 1823	Died August 15, 1831.
Robert Fisk	Sergeant	96 00	70 92	Mass. continental	Oct. 12, 1819	June 8, 1819	Suspended act May 1, 1820.
John Overstreet	Private	96 00	1,460 80	Virg. continental	June 9, 1819	June 16, 1818	Transferred from Ohio, Mar. 4, 1827.
James Thomas	do	96 00	1,320 53	Penn'a continental	Jan. 23, 1821	Feb. 1, 1820	Transferred from Kentucky. Died November 2, 1833.
ST. CLAIR.							
Eleazer Allen	do	96 00	469 60	Parson's cont'l	May 12, 1825	Ap'l 13, 1825	
Joseph Jones	do	96 00	329 33	Pulaski's legion	Mar. 3, 1824	Mar. 1, 1823	Died August 6, 1826.
SCHUYLER.							
William Kendrick	do	96 00	1,526 66	Virginia cont'l	July 21, 1819	May 29, 1818	Transferred from Kentucky.
WABASH.							
Job Pigsley	do	96 00	930 66	Mass. cont'l	Jan. 3, 1825	Dec. 15, 1823	
Alexander Stewart	do	96 00	1,482 92	N. Jersey cont'l	Mar. 31, 1818	Mar. 24, 1818	Transferred from N. Jersey.
Thomas Thompson	do	96 00	722 66	Virginia cont'l	Oct. 25, 1822	June 29, 1821	Died January 19, 1829.
WARREN.							
David Finley	do	96 00	1,469 80	Penn'a cont'l	Sept. 21, 1818	May 13, 1818	Transferred from Indiana.
WHITE.							
Clement Edelin	do	96 00	1,404 00	Maryland cont'l	May 21, 1819	July 20, 1818	Transferred from Kentucky.
William Hood	do	96 00	106 12	Virginia cont'l	Jan. 14, 1826	Dec. 10, 1825	Died January 18, 1827.

Statement showing the Names, Rank, &c. of persons residing in the State of Illinois, who have been inscribed on the Pension List under the act of Congress passed the 7th day of June, 1832.

NAMES AND COUNTIES.	Rank.	Annual allowance.	Sums received.	Description of service.	When placed on the pension roll.	Commencement of pension	Ages.	Laws under which they were formerly inscribed on the pension roll; and remarks.
ADAMS.								
Samuel Shaw	Private	30 00	69 91	Penn. continental	Feb. 9, 1833	Mar. 4, 1831	78	Died July 1, 1823.
Henry Covel	do	23 33	35 00	Connecticut cont'l	July 24, 1832	do	87	Residence unknown.
John Sowers	do	20 00	-	N. C. militia	June 19, 1834	do	74	
BOND.								
Hezekiah Row	do	24 44	-	S. C. continental	Ap'l 16, 1834	do	74	
CRAWFORD.								
George Baith	do	30 00	75 00	Penn. continental	Aug. 14, 1833	do	72	
William Dunlap	do	43 33	129 99	S. C. militia	Feb. 10, 1834	do	73	
Thomas Patten	do	40 00	120 00	N. C. continental	Sep. 25, 1833	do	98	
Asa Piper	do	30 00	90 00	Mass. continental	Ap'l 11, 1833	do	72	
James Ryan	Priv. &c.	85 00	255 00	N. C. continental	Aug. 13, 1833	do	78	
Silas Beckwith	Private	30 00	-	N. Hamp. militia	May 30, 1833	do	88	
CLARK.								
Thomas Boon	do	80 00	240 00	S. C. cont'l	July 16, 1833	do	73	
Nicholas Bean	Priv. &c.	100 00	300 00	Penn'a cont'l	May 3, 1834	do	70	
Peter Dozier	Private	23 33	-	Virginia contin'l	Oct. 31, 1832	do	72	
Samuel McClure	do	42 50	106 25	do	Aug. 14, 1833	do	86	
Frederick Unsell	do	80 00	240 00	Penn. militia	Feb. 11, 1834	do	70	
CLINTON.								
John King	do	23 88	71 64	S. C. cont'l	Feb. 25, 1834	do	67	
Michael Tedrich	Pri. of cav.	32 50	95 66	N. C. militia	do	do	81	Died February 10, 1834.
Elias Chaffin	Private	20 00	60 00	S. C. militia	Ap'l 21, 1834	do	71	

Statement, &c.—Continued.

Names and Counties.	Rank.	Annual allowance.	Sums received.	Description of service.	When placed on the pension roll.	Commencement of pension.	Ages.	Laws under which they were formerly inscribed on the pension roll; and remarks.
COLES.								
John Hart	Private	80 00	196 89	Va. continental	Jan. 6, 1834	Mar. 4, 1831	75	Died November 19, 1833.
John Parker	do	80 00	240 00	do	Oct. 22, 1833	do	75	
Joseph Painter	do	53 33	159 99	N. C. continental	Jan. 31, 1834	do	90	
EDGAR.								
Gurdin Burnham	Pri. dr. sea	85 77	-	Connecticut cont'l	June 4, 1834	do	78	
John Correy	Private	80 00	200 00	N. York cont'l	Aug. 14, 1833	do	74	
Elijah Clay	do	80 00	240 00	Va. militia	Mar. 4, 1834	do	75	
William Gannon, sen.	do	50 00	150 00	N. C. cont'l	July 3, 1833	do	75	
Ferrtl Hester	do	28 22	56 44	Md. continental	Aug. 22, 1833	do	83	
James Knight, sen.	Pri. & mar.	80 00	200 00	Penn'a continental	July 3, 1833	do	83	
William Means	Private	25 25	-	S. C. continental	Nov. 15, 1833	do	73	
Asa Moore	do	80 00	240 00	Md. militia	Jan. 23, 1834	do	69	
George Redman	do	30 00	75 00	N. C. continental	Aug. 22, 1833	do	77	
Abraham Wood	do	20 00	-	do	Aug. 14, 1833	do	81	
FRANKLIN.								
John Chandoin	do	32 34	97 02	Virg. continental	Ap'l 6, 1833	do	72	
John Duncan	do	21 66	54 15	do	Sep. 25, 1833	do	71	
Abel Dortch	do	33 33	99 99	do	do	do	73	
Archibald Daniel	do	20 00	60 00	N. C. militia	Mar. 21, 1833	do	69	
Benaijah Gill	Pri. &c.	100 00	-	N. J. militia	June 19, 1834	do	73	
Moses Jones	Private	30 00	90 00	N. C. continental	July 16, 1833	do	71	
Abel Man	do	30 00	75 00	Virg. do	Aug. 22, 1833	do	74	
William McElyra	do	40 00	120 00	N.C. do	Dec. 12, 1833	do	75	
Philip Russell	do	20 00	60 00	Virg. do	Dec. 17, 1833	do	69	
John Robinson	do	46 66	139 98	S. C. do	Ap'l 12, 1834	do	83	
Thomas Gill	Pri. l't. & captain	326 66	979 98	do	May 3, 1833	do	78	Removed to Crawford county.

Name	Rank	Annual allowance	Amount received	Line	Date		Age	Remarks
FAYETTE.								
John Diamond	Private	36 55	109 65	Penn'a continental	Ap'l 16, 1833	do	82	
Henry Ginger	do	80 00	240 00	do	Ap'l 11, 1833	do	67	
Mason Owens	do	76 66	229 90	Virg.	Sep. 25, 1833	do	74	Died September 30, 1832.
David Shipman	do	20 00	-	do	Ap'l 17, 1834	do	68	
Henry Walker	Spy	59 21	88 36	do	Ap'l 9, 1833	do	74	
GREEN.								
Daniel Allen	Private	30 00	90 00	N. C. cont'l	Oct. 23, 1833	do	71	
Joshua Armstrong	do	41 66	124 98	Penn'a cont'l	Jan. 31, 1834	do	79	
William Beeman	do	33 33	99 99	Connecicut cont'l	Jan. 9, 1834	do	75	
William Bates	do	80 00	240 00	N. C. continental	May 28, 1833	do	77	
Allen J. Bridges	do	23 33	69 99	do	Ap'l 8, 1834	do	77	
John Clarke	do	80 00	240 00	Virg. cont'l	Aug. 22, 1833	do	69	
Adonijah Griswold	do	80 00	240 00	Vermont cont'l	Nov. 15, 1833	do	74	
James Garrison	Pri. inf. & cavalry	22 50	67 50	N. C. continental	June 6, 1833	do	87	
John Huitt	Serg. &c.	101 55	304 65	do	do	do	73	
Caleb Post	Private	40 00	120 00	N. Jersey militia	Mar. 6, 1834	do	71	
Jonah Scoggins	Pri. & ser.	62 78	188 34	N. C. continental	June 6, 1833	do	70	
George Vinciner	Pri. of art.	100 00	300 00	Ky. continental	do	do	72	
John Thompson	Private	30 00	90 00	Virg. continental	Jan. 9, 1834	do	75	
Francis Miller	do	41 11	123 33	N. C. continental	May 13, 1834	do	80	
GALLATIN.								
William Allen	do	37 98	113 67	do	Ap'l 9, 1833	do	73	
Reuben Bramblet	do	30 00	90 00	Virg. cont'l	Ap'l 6, 1833	do	76	
John Lamb	do	45 00	135 00	N. C. continental	Ap'l 23, 1833	do	74	
William Sutton	do	26 66	79 98	Virg. continental	do	do	79	
HANCOCK.								
Charles Bettsworth	do	58 33	174 99	do	Aug. 22, 1833	do	71	Transferred from Kentucky, from March 4, 1834.
HAMILTON.								
Francis Dolahide	do	80 00	240 00	N. C. continental	Nov. 15, 1832	do	84	
Little Page Proctor	do	80 00	240 00	Virginia militia	Jan. 9, 1834	do	73	
Nicholas Proctor	do	80 00	-	do	May 3, 1834	do	78	
HARRISON.								
Joseph Morrison	do	30 00	90 00	do	Ap'l 9, 1833	do	73	

Statement, &c.—Continued.

NAMES AND COUNTIES.	Rank.	Annual allowance.	Sums received.	Description of service.	When placed on the pension roll.	Commencement of pension.	Ages.	Laws under which they were formerly inscribed on the pension roll; and remarks.
JACKSON.								
Daniel Banam	Private	53 33	-	Virginia militia	May 3, 1834	Mar. 4, 1831	76	
Robert Friatt	do	30 00	75 00	Virg'a cont'l	Oct. 2, 1833	do	74	
Zachariah Lyerly	do	43 33	129 99	N. C. cont'l	Aug. 14, 1833	do	78	
Ebenezer Pyott	Pri. & ser.	98 33	245 82	Penn'a cont'l	Oct. 9, 1833	do	79	
Thomas Sherley	Private	80 00	240 00	S. C. cont'l	Oct. 22, 1833	do	74	
Joshua Tyner	do	71 66	214 98	Georgia cont'l	Mar. 28, 1833	do	67	
Joseph J. Williams	Pri. & ser.	50 00	-	Penn'a cont'l	Mar. 24, 1834	do	77	Removed to Franklin county.
Hezekiah Davis	Pri. inf. & cavellry	25 83	-	S. C. continental	Oct. 2, 1833	do	73	
JEFFERSON.								
Daniel Chandler	Private	80 00	240 00	do	Oct. 22, 1833	do	72	
Samuel Little	Pri. of cav.	100 00	-	S. C. militia	July 12, 1833	do	68	
JOHNSON.								
Greenbury Choate	Private	20 00	60 00	Virg'a continental	Oct. 23, 1833	do	83	
Daniel Chapman	do	80 00	240 00	New York militia	Feb. 15, 1833	do	77	
Jacob Harwick	do	50 00	100 00		July 16, 1833	do	81	
William Wiggs	do	30 56	91 68	N. C. continental	July 18, 1833	do	77	
Hezekiah West	Pri. of inf. & cav.	24 17	72 51	do	do	do	70	
LAWRENCE.								
Isham Childers	Private	30 00	-		Apl 11, 1833	do	71	
Hezekiah Hardesty	do	33 33	83 33	Penn'a cont'l	July 16, 1833	do	71	
Adam Lackey	do	33 33	83 33	Virg'a cont'l	Oct. 22, 1833	do	79	
Benjamin Milton	do	60 00	150 00	N. C. cont'l	Sep. 28, 1833	do	67	
MONTGOMERY.								
Henry Briance, sen.	Private	62 22	153 13	do	Aug. 14, 1833	do	71	Died August 19, 1833

Name	Rank		Service	Date		Age	Remarks
Ezra Bostwick	do	50 00 / 150 00	do	Feb. 28, 1833	do	80	
Thomas Craig, sen.	do	48 84 / 146 52	do	do	do	71	
Benjamin Gordon	do	80 00 / 240 00	do	Sep. 25, 1833	do	71	
Wooton Harris	do	80 00 / 240 00	Virg'a cont'l	Dec. 1, 1832	do	76	
John Ligit	do	45 00 / 135 00	do	Feb. 28, 1833	do	71	
James Richardson	do	20 00 / 50 00	N. C. cont'l	do	do	76	
MADISON.							
Daniel Brown	Pri. & ser.	30 16 / 75 40	Virg'a cont'l	Oct. 14, 1833	do	75	
Jesse Conway	Private	80 00 / 240 00	do	Aug. 22, 1833	do	73	
Michael Deck	do	26 66 / 79 98	do	Ap'l 6, 1833	do	73	
John Gillham	do	80 00 / 240 00	S. C. continental	Aug. 22, 1833	do	77	
Isaac Gillham	do	80 00 / 240 00	do	do	do	74	
Anthony A. Harrison	do	26 66 / 79 98	Penn'a continental	Jan. 9, 1834	do	71	
William Hall	Pri. & ser.	65 00 / 195 00	S. C. continental	April 9, 1833	do	71	
John Long	Private	20 00 / 60 00	N. C. continental	Ap'l 23, 1833	do	71	
Joseph McAdams	Pri. of inf. and cav.	97 50 / 292 50	do	Aug. 14, 1833	do	76	Removed to Bond county.
William McAdams	Private	80 00 / 200 00	do	Aug. 22, 1833	do	74	Removed to Macoupin county.
Martin Pruitt	do	80 00 / 240 00	Virg'a continental	do	do	85	
John Robinson	do	80 00 / 240 00	N. C. continental	do	do	70	
Henry Revis	do	40 00 / 120 00	do	July 18, 1833	do	81	
Francis Roach	do	24 67 / 74 01	do	Jan. 29, 1834	do	94	
Harris Reavis	do	52 77 / 158 31	N. C. militia	Feb. 10, 1834	do	80	
Richard Randle	do	34 66 / 103 98	Virg'a cont'l	June 19, 1833	do	80	
Isham Randle	do	23 33 / 69 99	N. C. cont'l	Ap'l 6, 1833	do	74	
Laban Smart	do	20 00 / 60 00	do	Sep. 25, 1833	do	78	
Henry Thornhill	do	30 00 / 75 00	Virg'a continental	July 18, 1833	do	76	
Nathaniel West	do	30 00 / 75 00	do	June 25, 1834	do	83	
George Bridges	do	30 00 / -	N. C. militia		do	71	
MONROE.							
Ebenezer Bowen	do	48 33 / 144 99	Virginia cont'l	Dec. 17, 1833	do	81	
Andrew Hilton	do	30 00 / 90 00	Maryland cont'l	Oct. 23, 1833	do	77	
Michael Miller	do	30 00 / 90 00	Virginia cont'l	July 18, 1833	do	73	
James McRoberts	do	20 00 / 60 00	Pennsylvania cont'l	Apr. 28, 1834	do	71	
Joseph Wright	do	20 00 / 50 00	Virginia cont'l	May 2, 1833	do	74	
M'LEAN.							
Ebenezer Barnes	Pri. & ser.	98 33 / 294 99	Massachusetts con.	Feb. 7, 1834	do	74	

Statement, &c.—Continued.

NAMES AND COUNTIES.	Rank.	Annual allowance.	Sums received.	Description of service.	When placed on the pension list.	Commencement of pension.	Ages.	Laws under which they were formerly inscribed on the pension roll; and remarks.
M'LEAN—continued.								
Nathaniel Bell	Private	53 33	159 99	North Carolina mil.	Feb. 4, 1834	Mar. 4, 1831	79	
William Mc Ghe	do	80 00	240 00	Pennsylvania cont'l	Mar. 15, 1834	do	72	
Charles Moore	do	20 00	60 00	South Carolina mil.	Apr. 8, 1834	do	70	
Edward F. Patrick	do	20 00	60 00	North Carolina con.	Dec. 12, 1833	do	74	
John Scott	Pr. of cav.	50 00	125 00	Virginia cont'l	Sep. 25, 1833	do	71	
Thomas Sloan	Private	76 69	230 01	North Carolina con.	Dec. 12, 1833	do	73	
MORGAN.								
Isham Bobbit	do	47 50	142 50	do	May 29, 1833	do	79	
Martin Burris	do	20 00	60 00	Pennsylvania cont'l	do	do	78	
Samuel Caldwell	do	20 00	60 00	Virginia cont'l	Oct. 23, 1833	do	69	
Constantine Clarkson	do	40 00	120 00	do	Aug. 10, 1833	do	71	
Colbay Creed	do	23 88	71 64	North Carolina mil.	July 12, 1834	do	75	
John Dawson	do	60 00	180 00	Virginia militia	May 22, 1834	do	83	
Aaron Houten	do	56 66	169 98	New Jersey cont'l	Nov. 5, 1833	do	72	
Francis Haney	do	73 33	219 99	Virginia cont'l	July 16, 1833	do	79	
Joseph Jackson	do	36 66	109 98	South Carolina con.	do	do	73	
James Jordan	do	25 00	-	South Carolina mil.	July 30, 1834	do	78	
Lawrence Kellobrue	Pri. of inf. & cav.	75 83	227 49	North Carolina con.	July 18, 1833	do	70	
Henry Levins	Private	49 00	122 50	Pennsylvania cont'l	Sep. 25, 1833	do	89	
Edmund Moody	do	60 00	180 00	Virginia cont'l	Nov. 15, 1833	do	76	
Hugh McNary	do	34 00	102 00	North Carolina con.	Jan. 6, 1834	do	71	
David McPeters	Pri. of inf. & cav.	72 00	216 00	do	May 29, 1833	do	77	
John Robertson	Private	30 00	90 00	Delaware cont'l	Nov. 15, 1833	do	81	
Jesse Stout	do	33 33	99 99	New Jersey cont'l	Nov. 5, 1833	do	80	
David Strahan	do	37 50	112 50	North Carolina con.	June 6, 1833	do	79	
Augustus Sims	do	20 00		Virginia cont'l	Mar. 26, 1833	do	71	
William Scott	do	30 00	75 00	do	Apr. 16, 1833	do	79	

Name	Rank			Service	Date		Age	Remarks
Joseph Summers	do	32 77	98 31	North Carolina con.	do	do	84	
Andrew Turner	do	20 00	60 00	do	May 2, 1833	do	72	
James Wright	do	80 00	160 00	Virginia cont'l	do	do	71	
William Willard	do	31 67	95 01	-	do	do		
MARION.								
Samuel Eblin	do	20 00	60 00	Virginia cont'l	Apr. 12, 1834	do	79	
William Gaston	do	80 00	240 00	South Carolina con.	Oct. 22, 1833	do	75	
Michael Luttrell	do	20 00	60 00	Virginia militia	Apr. 12, 1834	do	82	
MACOUPIN.								
Thomas Moore	do	20 00	60 00	Virginia cont'l	Jan. 9, 1834	do	74	
POPE.								
Daniel Fox	do	40 00	120 00	North Carolina con.	Dec. 17, 1833	do	68	
PEORIA.								
James Harkness	Pri., &c.	86 00	258 00	Massachusetts con.	Feb. 10, 1834	do	74	
PERRY.								
Leonard Lipe	Private	33 34	100 02	South Carolina con.	Jan. 6, 1834	do	71	
PIKE.								
Uriah Gilmore	do	32 77	98 21	Virginia cont'l	July 16, 1833	do	84	
James McWithy	do	80 00	240 00	New York cont'l	Apr. 8, 1834	do	71	
Richard Taylor	do	20 00	60 00	Virginia cont'l	Oct. 2, 1833	do	78	
PALESTINE.								
Thomas Gill	Pri. lieut. & captain	326 66	978 98	South Carolina con.	May 3, 1833	do	78	Removed to Crawford county.
RANDOLPH.								
William Fowler	Private	20 00	-	South Carolina mil.	May 7, 1834	do	69	
Paul Harrolson	do	62 50	156 25	do	Sep. 28, 1833	do	73	
SANGAMON.								
John Burton	do	20 00	60 00	Virginia cont'l	May 3, 1834	do	72	
Michael Clifford	do	63 33	189 99	North Carolina con.	Dec. 12, 1833	do	74	
Peter Cutright	do	20 00	60 00	Virginia militia	May 3, 1834	do	74	
Christian Carver	do	30 00	60 00	North Carolina mil.	Apr. 23, 1833	do	74	

3

Statement, &c.—Continued.

NAMES AND COUNTIES.	Rank.	Annual allowance.	Sums received.	Description of service.	When placed on the pension roll.	Commencement of pension.	Ages.	Laws under which they were formerly inscribed on the pension roll; and remarks.
SANGAMON—Cont'd.								
Philip Crowder	Pri. & ser.	41 66	124 98	Virginia cont'l	Apr. 23, 1833	Mar. 4, 1831	73	
Edward Day	Private	43 33	129 99	Virginia militia	Feb. 15, 1834	do	73	
Lewis Ferguson	Pri. & ser.	110 00	330 00	Virginia cont'l	Dec. 17, 1833	do	74	
Ezekiel Harrison	Private	45 00	135 00	do	May 2, 1833	do	83	
James Haggard	do	20 00	60 00	do	do	do	77	
Joel Maxcey	do	23 33	58 33	do	Aug. 14, 1833	do	72	
Thomas Massee	do	21 55	63 88	do	Apr. 23, 1834	do	74	
Zachariah Nance	Pri. of art.	100 00	300 00	North Carolina con.	May 2, 1833	do	73	
John Purviance	Pr. of cav.	75 00	-	South Carolina con.	Oct. 23, 1833	do	71	
Howell Sellers	Private	30 00	90 00	Virginia militia	May 2, 1833	do	72	
James Turley	do	23 33	-	Virginia militia	Mar. 16, 1833	do	72	
John White, 1st	do	40 00	120 00	Pennsylvania cont'l	Oct. 23, 1833	do	92	
SCHUYLER.								
William Blair	do	46 66	139 98	do	Apr. 6, 1833	do	73	
Benjamin Carpenter	do	36 66	109 98	Virginia cont'l	Oct. 9, 1833	do	79	
Moses Justus	do	38 33	114 99	North Carolina con.	Aug. 14, 1833	do	79	
James Lauman	Pri. & ser.	28 50	71 25	South Carolina con.	Apr. 22, 1834	do	82	Died February 10, 1834.
George Taylor	Private	42 22	123 84	Pennsylvania cont'l	Oct. 9, 1833	do	72	
ST. CLAIR.								
Conrad Goodner	do	30 00	90 00	North Carolina con.	July 16, 1833	do	76	
Thomas Knighten	Pri. & ser.	31 67	79 16	South Carolina con.	July 18, 1833	do	81	
John Prime	Private	31 55	94 65	Virginia cont'l	Jan. 17, 1834	do	84	
Martin Randleman	do	26 66	79 98	S. Carolina cont'l	Ap'l 9, 1833	do	72	
Hosea Rigg	do	66 66	199 98	Pennsylvania cont'l	Feb. 9, 1834	do	72	
John Collinsworth	do	80 00	240 00	Virginia cont'l	Mar. 20, 1833	do	70	Transferred from E. Tennessee, from Sep. 4, 1833.
SHELBY.								
Obadiah Wade	do	21 66	64 98	N. Carolina cont'l	Oct. 23, 1833	do	73	

Name	Rank	Allowance	Amount	Service	Commenced		Age	Remarks
UNION.								
Alexander Beggs	do	70 44	211 32	Pennsylvania cont.	July 16, 1833	do	80	
Adam Clapp	do	26 66	79 98	N. Carolina cont'l	Ap'l 23, 1833	do	78	
John Ellis	do	80 00	240 00	Virginia militia	Feb. 25, 1834	do	98	
Jacob Frick	do	50 00	150 00	Pennsylvania mil.	July 16, 1833	do	83	
John Hargrave	do	28 22	70 55	S. Carolina cont'l	do	do	78	
Travis Morris	do	30 00	90 00	Virginia cont'l	Oct. 23, 1833	do	74	
Joshua Vick	do	20 00		do	Ap'l 23, 1833	do	71	
Peter Meisenheimer	do	21 11	63 33	N. Carolina cont'l	July 18, 1833	do	79	
VERMILLION.								
Robert Bailey	do	33 33	83 33	N. Carolina cont'l	Aug. 14, 1833	do	72	
James Huls	do	80 00	240 00	Virginia cont'l	Sep. 28, 1833	do	72	
Daniel Herrington	do	21 89	65 67	Pennsylvania con.	Ap'l 23, 1833	do	75	
Thomas Morton	Pri. & cap.	120 00	360 00	Virginia continental	Ap'l 17, 1833	do	81	
WHITE.								
John Childress	Private	37 00	111 00	N. Carolina militia	May 2, 1833	do	69	
James Clark	do	80 00	240 00	S. Carolina cont'l	Oct. 31, 1833	do.	78	
Robert Hawthorn	do	80 00	240 00	do	Aug. 14, 1834	do	80	
Joseph Hawthorn	do	60 00	180 00	do	Mar. 24, 1834	do	77	
Nathan Jaggors	do	76 55	229 65	do	July 16, 1833	do	73	
Randle McDaniel	do	23 33		do	July 18, 1833	do	79	Transferred from Tennessee.
Henry Morgan	do	80 00		N. Carolina cont'l	do	do	74	
Elias Veatch	do	60 00		S. Carolina militia	July 12, 1834	do	74	
Peter Shull	do	41 67	104 18	Pennsylvania cont'l	Ap'l 23, 1833	do	69	
Daniel Bidwell	Pri. & ser.	106 66	319 98	New York cont'l	June 11, 1833	do	73	
WASHINGTON.								
James Crabtree	Private	20 00	60 00	Virginia cont'l	Dec. 17, 1833	do	73	
WABASH.								
William Doughton	do	20 78	36 25	do	Oct. 23, 1833	do	72	Died December 1, 1833.
Jonathan Goss	do	28 33	84 99	Massachusetts con.	July 16, 1833	do	74	
Nathaniel Hendryx	do	50 00	150 00	N. York cont'l	do	do	81	
William Lawson	do	33 33	99 99	Virginia cont'l	Oct. 23, 1833	do	75	
Allen Ramsay	do	23 33	69 99	Pennsylvania con.	Feb. 15, 1834	do	70	
Benjamin Smith	do	80 00	240 00	R. Island cont'l	Aug. 14, 1833	do	73	
Stephen Simmons	do	26 22	78 66	Connecticut cont'l	do	do	69	
Andrew Tuttle	do	80 00	240 00	do	Nov. 5, 1833	do	75	

Statement, &c. —Continued.

NAMES.	Rank.	Annual allowance.	Sums received.	Description of service.	When placed on the pension roll.	Commencement of pension.	Ages.	Laws under which they were formerly inscribed on the pension roll; and remarks.
WABASH—Cont'd.								
John White, 2d	Private	60 00	180 00	Connecticut cont'l	Nov. 5, 1833	Mar. 4, 1831	72	
John Wood	Ensign	56 66	96 01	Marylan l cont'l	Mar. 23, 1833	do	79	Died November 4, 1832.
WAYNE.								
John Files	Private	80 00	240 00	S. Carolina cont'l	Aug. 14, 1833	do	73	
John Henson	do	43 33	129 99	Virginia cont'l	Oct. 31, 1833	do	68	
James Loek	do	20 00	60 00	do	May 2, 1833	do	71	
William Simpson	do	20 00		do	Oct. 31, 1833	do	78	
WATERLOO.								
Peter Rogers	Fife major	108 00		Pennsylvania cont'l	Mar. 26, 1834	do	77	

Statement showing the Names, Rank, &c. of persons residing in the State of Illinois, who have received the benefits of the act of Congress passed the 15th May, 1828.

NAMES AND COUNTIES.	Rank.	Annual allowance.	Sums received.	Description of service.	When placed on the pension roll.	Names of agents or representatives.	Remarks.
					Commencement of pay March 3, 1826.		
CLINTON.							
Peter Outhouse	Private	80 00	440 00	- reg. Md. line	Aug. 13, 1828	—	
FAYETTE.							
Matthias Parr	do	80 00	720 00	2d reg. N. Y. line	Dec. 11, 1830	Wm. H. Brown, ag't	Transf'd from Oldham county, Kentucky.
GALLATIN.							
Bennett Hancock	Matross	100 00	709 72	- reg. Virg. artil.	Oct. 22, 1828	Milley Hancock, widow	Died April 7, 1833.
RANDOLPH.							
John Edgar	Captain	480 00	2,291 33	U. S. navy	June 2, 1830	Hon. E. K. Kane, att'y for the adm'r	Admitted by special act of May 26, 1830.—Died December 19, 1830.
SCHUYLER.							
Henry Greene	Private	80 00	720 00	2d reg. Md. line	Oct. 22, 1828	A. W. Cavarly, ag't	
James Stewart	Matross	100 00	850 00	- Virginia artillery	May 23, 1829		

INDIANA PENSION ROLL.

Statement showing the Names, Rank, &c. of Invalid Pensioners residing in the State of Indiana.

NAMES AND COUNTIES.	Rank.	Annual allowance.	Sums received.	Description of service.	When placed on the pension roll.	Commencement of pension.	Laws under which they were inscribed, increased or reduced; and remarks.
ALLEN.							
Samuel Bird	Sergeant	96 00	425 33	3d reg. U. S. inf.	Dec. 10, 1824	Sep. 29, 1824	Acts military establishment. Died March, 1829.
Gaydon Branham	Private	45 00	84 25	Indiana militia	Jan. 28, 1815	June 10, 1814	April 10, 1812.
Do	do	72 00	175 60	do	-	Ap'l 24, 1816	April 24, 1816. Died October 1, 1818.
BARTHOLOMEW.							
David Bevens	do	48 00	625 60	New York militia	Jan. 22, 1818	Mar. 2, 1815	April 24, 1816.
Do	do	64 00	350 40	do	-	Mar. 14, 1828	Acts military establishment. Transferred from New York.
Samuel Colvin	do	72 00	183 20	U. States army	Dec. 2, 1831	Sep. 16, 1831	April 25, 1808.
Do	do	96 00	88 53	do	-	Ap'l 2, 1833	Acts military establishment.
BOONE.							
George Dye	do	72 00	791 80	Ohio militia	Oct. 30, 1823	Mar. 5, 1823	April 24, 1816. Transferred from Ohio, Pittsburg Agency.
CLARKE.							
Joseph Bartholomew	Lieut. col.	270 00	2,234 25	Indiana militia	Ap'l 12, 1814	Nov. 24, 1813	April 10, 1812.
Do	do	202 50	1,518 75	do	Not stated	Mar. 4, 1822	March 3, 1819.
Do	do	180 00	392 00	do	-	Sep. 4, 1829	do do
Do	do	270 00	627 00	do	Nov. 11, 1831	Nov. 8, 1831	Acts military establishment.
Samuel Carr	Private	24 00	-	Indiana dragoons	Mar. 4, 1834	Mar. 3, 1834	April 10, 1812.
John Norris	Captain	120 00	873 33	Indiana militia	Ap'l 12, 1814	Nov. 24, 1813	do do
Do	do	60 00	640 00	do	Papers lost	Mar. 4, 1821	March 3, 1819. Reduced. The exact time unknown.
Do	do	120 00	278 66	do	-	Nov. 8, 1831	Acts military establishment.
Humphrey Webster	1st lieut.	204 00	460 70	N. Y. militia	June 3, 1816	June 1, 1815	April 30, 1816. Transferred from New York.
CLAY.							
Daniel Minor	Private	60 00	115 50	Unknown	Unknown	Oct. 1, 1813	April 10, 1812.
Do	Jo	96 00	-	Papers lost	Papers lost	Ap'l 24, 1816	April 24, 1816.

Name	Rank	Pay	Amount	Service	Commenced	Date	Remarks
John Wheeler	do	32 00	403 02	Volunteer militia	Nov. 20, 1819	Nov. 24, 1811	April 10, 1812.
Do	do	48 00	313 73	do	do	June 28, 1824	April 24, 1816.
Do	do	72 00	226 80	do	do	Jan. 14, 1831	Acts military establishment.
CRAWFORD.							
Peter McMickle	do	30 00	76 92	Unknown	Unknown	Oct. 1, 1813	April 10, 1812.
Do	do	48 00	857 33	Papers lost	Papers lost	Ap'l 24, 1816	April 24, 1816.
William Samuels	do	32 00	653 06	Indiana militia	Jan. 16, 1818	Ap'l 7, 1813	do do
CASS.							
Joshua Shields	do	32 00	665 76	Indiana militia	Mar. 19, 1818	Nov. 24, 1811	do do
DEARBORN.							
Zachariah S. Conger	Lieutenant	168 00	1,037 40	15th reg. U. S. inf.	Nov. 1, 1830	Jan. 1, 1828	May 20, 1830.
Francis McDonough	Private	45 00	28 12½	U. States artillery	Mar 9, 1816	Sep. 9, 1815	Acts military establishment. Transferred from New York.
Do	do	72 00	1,286 00	do		Ap'l 24, 1816	April 24, 1816.
Thomas Piety	do	48 00	-	Indian war	Jan. 17, 1834	Jan. 1, 1834	April 25, 1808.
Thomas Porter	do	96 00	304 80	M'Clelland's vol.	May 17, 1832	Jan. 1, 1831	March 2, 1831.
Ebenezer Roberts	Sergeant	96 00	394 40	Hall's co. U. S. vol.	Feb. 3, 1830	Jan. 23, 1830	February 6, 1812.
William Ricketts	Private	96 00	112 80	Indian war 1791	Aug. 2, 1833	Jan. 1, 1833	March 2, 1833.
DAVIESS.							
Richard Holden	Sergeant	38 40	382 40	Kentucky militia	July 18, 1820	July 4, 1820	April 24, 1816. Died June, 1830. From Kentucky.
Daniel Rummer	Private	72 00	1,308 00	Tennessee militia	Nov. 9, 1824	July 4, 1815	April 30, 1816. Transferred from West Tennessee.
DECATUR.							
John Williams	do	32 00	280 00	Kentucky militia	June 20, 1825	June 4, 1825	April 25, 1808. Transferred from Kentucky.
EDWARDS.							
Robert Baird	Lieutenant	120 00	836 00	Wayne's campaign	Unknown: papers lost	May 6, 1809	April 27, 1810.
Do	do	156 00	134 33	do		Ap'l 24, 1816	April 24, 1816. Dead.
FRANKLIN.							
Daniel Budd	Corporal	64 00	172 95	N. York militia	June 22, 1831	June 22, 1831	April 24, 1816.
William Curry	Private	96 00	75 20	19th U. S. inf.	Dec. 3, 1825	Nov. 7, 1825	Acts military establishment. Died August 18. 1825.

Statement, &c.—Continued.

NAMES.	Rank.	Annual allowance.	Sums received.	Description of service.	When placed on the pension roll.	Commencement of pension.	Laws under which they were inscribed, increased and reduced; and remarks.
FOUNTAIN.							
Robert M'Intire	Sergeant	48 90	-	Kentucky rifles	Ap'l 14, 1834	Ap'l 10, 1834	April 10, 1812.
David Thompson	Private	48 00	118 13	Kentucky militia	Oct. 19, 1829	Sep. 18, 1829	April 24, 1816. Transferred from Kentucky. Died.
FLOYD.							
Jacob Keyser	do	48 00	624 40	N. York militia	Feb. 15, 1817	July 9, 1815	Acts military establishment. Transferred from N. York. Removed to N. York.
Matthew Byrnes	do	72 00	406 60	do	Feb. 7, 1816	July 12, 1828	Acts military establishment.
Do	do	30 00	26 35	17th U. S. inf.		June 8, 1815	April 10, 1812.
Do	do	48 00	372 26	do		Ap'l 24, 1816	April 24, 1816.
Do	do	64 00	582 93	do		Jan. 26, 1824	Acts military establishment. Reported December, 1833.
GIBSON.							
George Antis	do	30 00	74 16	United States army	May 13, 1819	Nov. 4, 1813	April 10, 1812.
Do	do	48 00	645 33	do		Ap'l 24, 1816	April 24, 1816.
James Evans	Sergeant	48 00	1,032 13	Indiana militia	June 6, 1818	Nov. 20, 1811	April 24, 1816. Died May 20, 1833.
Robert Skelton	Private	24 00	150 66	do	June 24, 1824	Nov. 1, 1823	April 24, 1816.
Do	do	48 00	195 46	do	Feb. 15, 1830	Feb. 6, 1830	Acts military establishment.
HARRISON.							
Samuel Little	2d lieut.	150 00	279 58	U. S. rangers	Dec. 14, 1815	June 13, 1814	Acts military establishment.
Do.	do	180 00	3,215 00	do		Ap'l 24, 1816	April 24, 1816.
Patrick McBride	Private	64 00	631 46	5th U. S. infantry	Nov. 14, 1821	Ap'l 22, 1821	Acts military establishment. Died.
Robert Briggs	Pr. & cor.	30 00	80 91	Indiana militia	Jan. 1, 1815	Aug. 13, 1814	April 10, 1812.
Do.	do	48 00	750 93	do		Ap'l 24, 1816	April 24, 1816.
Do.	do	64 00	147 37	de		Dec. 16, 1831	Acts military establishment.
Henry Bateman	Private	60 00	127 83	Indiana riflemen	Jan. 9, 1815	March 7, 1814	April 10, 1812.
Do.	do	96 00	1,487 60	do		Ap'l 24, 1816	April 24, 1816. Died Feb. 22, 1831.

Name	Rank	Rate	Amount	Service	Commencement	Placed on roll	Laws	Remarks
HAMILTON.								
Micah French	do	48 00	291 33	New York militia	Dec. 12, 1820	Feb. 6, 1828	April 24, 1816.	
HANCOCK.								
James Ryon	do	24 00	182 93	Kentucky militia	Feb. 11, 1823	Jan. 21, 1823	April 24 1816.	Transferred from Ky.
Do.	do	48 00	–	do	–	Mar. 25, 1833	Acts military establishment.	
James Wright	do	60 00	40 83	8th U. S. infantry	Dec. 11, 1815	Aug. 19, 1815	Acts mil. est.	Transf'd from Virginia.
Do.	do	96 00	1,714 66	do	–	Ap'l 24, 1816	April 24, 1816.	
JEFFERSON.								
George Burton	do	24 00	519 33	Revolutionary army	Unknown	Sept. 4, 1794	Acts mil est.	Trans'd from Penn.
Do.	do	38 90	549 97	do	June 21, 1822	Ap'l 24, 1816	April 24, 1816.	
Do.	do	57 60	184 64	do	Aug. 20, 1830	Aug. 20, 1830	Acts mil. est.	
Do.	do	96 00	23 73	do	Not stated	Dec. 6, 1833	Acts mil. est.	
Timothy Mallory	do	48 00	345 46	Kentucky militia	Oct. 10, 1823	Sep. 24, 1822	April 24, 1816.	Transf'd from Ky.
Do.	do	64 00	268 44	do	Jan. 13, 1830	Dec. 5, 1829	March 4, 1822.	
John McCammont	do	64 00	208 00	U. S. army	Feb. 25, 1831	Dec. 4, 1830	Feb. 6, 1812.	
David Sutton	do	48 00	237 03	1st U. S. infantry	Nov. 1, 1822	Sep. 30, 1822	April 25, 1808.	
Do.	do	72 00	61 00	do	–	Nov. 8, 1831	April 30, 1816.	
Samuel Welch	do	96 00	141 60	do	–	Sep. 13, 1832	Acts mil. est.	
Do.	do	72 00	265 80	Wayne's legion	May 30, 1888	Feb. 27, 1828	Acts mil. est.	
Do.	do	96 00	222 93	do	–	Nov. 8, 1831	Acts mil. est.	
KNOX.								
James Banks	do	24 00	76 53	Indiana militia	Jan. 14, 1830	Jan. 14, 1830	April 10, 1812.	
Do.	do	48 00	–	do	Mar. 19, 1834	Mar. 22, 1833	Acts mil. est.	Died: Rep'd June, 1838.
Samuel Potter	do	96 00	384 00	U. S. army	Oct. 18, 1816	Mar. 29, 1815	Acts mil. est.	Died.
John Parker	Sergeant	48 00	–	McClelland's vol's	May 30, 1834	May 9, 1834	April 25, 1808.	Died.
William Wilton	Private	48 00	94 80	Indiana militia	Mar. 31, 1832	Mar. 14, 1832	April 24, 1816.	
William Collins	do	48 00	294 26	do	June 19, 1817	Jan. 18, 1816	April 30, 1816.	
Do.	do	24 00	126 00	do	–	Mar. 4, 1822	Acts. mil. est.	Died June 3, 1827.
LAWRENCE.								
Leonard Houston	do	24 00	79 93	do	Nov. 10, 1828	Dec. 6, 1827	April 10, 1812.	
Do.	do	48 00	120 00	do	March 5, 1831	Mar. 4, 1831	Acts mil. est.	
John Thompson	do	96 00	–	17th U. S. infantry	July 28, 1818	June 10, 1815	Acts mil. est.	
MONROE.								
John V. Buskirk	do	60 00	151 16	Indiana riflemen	June 28, 1814	Oct. 19, 1813	April 10, 1812.	
Do.	do	96 00	1,714 66	do	–	April 24, 1816	April 24, 1816.	

Statement, &c.—Continued.

NAMES.	Rank.	Annual allowance.	Sums received.	Description of service.	When placed on the pension list	Commencement of pension.	Laws under which they were inscribed, increased or reduced; and remarks.
MONROE—cont'd.							
John Bradford	Private	48 00	45 83	6th U. S. infantry	June 10, 1822	Sep. 20, 1821	Acts mil. est.
George W. Hardin	do	96 00	438 40	Kentucky militia	Aug. 31, 1829	Aug. 11, 1829	April 24, 1816.
MARION.							
Stephen Collins	do	96 00	365 33	U. S. artillery	Feb. 21. 1817	Nov. 14, 1815	Acts mil. est. Transferred from New York and West Tennessee.
James Foster	Sergeant	48 00	616 40	Ohio volunteers	Feb. 22, 1817	May 8, 1813	April 24, 1816. Transferred from Ohio
Do	do	64 00	94 93	do	-	Mar. 11, 1826	Acts military establishment, Dead.
Nicholas Heanor	Private	72 00	163 20	Kenty. militia	Nov. 29, 1831	Nov. 28, 1831	April 24, 1816.
Daniel Smith	do	48 00	766 53	6. U. S, infantry	Sep. 22, 1818	Mar. 16, 1818	Acts military establishment.
Nathaniel Vice	Ensign	117 00	959 40	Kent'y militia	Jan. 27, 1826	Dec. 23, 1825	April 24, 1816. Transferred from Ky.
William Warren	Private	192 00	214 93	40 U. S. infantry	July 1, 1834	Jan. 22, 1833	June 30, 1834.
William Crist	do	30 00	44 25	Sholt's co. of rang's	Jan. 1, 1816	Nov. 3, 1814	February 2. 1812.
Do	do	48 00	454 13	do	-	Ap'l 24, 1816	April 24, 1816.
Do	do	72 00	605 00	do	-	Oct. 10, 1825	Acts military establishment
Stephen Pitts	do	48 00	887 60	10th U. S. infantry	-	Sep. 7, 1815	Acts military establishment. Paid in O.
MONTGOMERY.							
Jeremiah Douglas	do	96 00	1,805 86	17th U. S. infantry	June 17, 1816	May 13, 1815	Acts mil. est. Transferred from Ohio.
Barnes Bunn	do	24 00	969 60	Lamb's artillery	-	Dec. 31, 1775	April 23, 1782. Trans. from Sussex co.
Do	do	38 40	225 06	do	-	April 24, 1816	April 24, 1816. New Jersey in 1832.
MARTIN.							
John Smith	do	96 00	101 60	Indiana militia	Mar. 2, 1829	Sep. 10, 1828	April 24, 1816.
Do	do	72 00	183 80	do	-	Oct. 1, 1829	March 3, 1819.
Do	do	96 00	179 73	do	-	Apr'l 20, 1832	Acts military establishment.
Thomas Sedgwick	Corporal	72 00	-	Unknown	Mar. 20, 1829	Jan. 30, 1829	February 25, 1813.

OWEN. Hugh Barnes	Chaplain	60 00	162 87	4th Kentucky mil.	Dec. 5, 1816	June 15, 1813	April 18, 1814. Transferred from Kentucky.
Do	do	240 00	1,320 00	do	-	Mar. 4, 1816	
Do	do	120 00	366 00	do	-	Sep. 4, 1821	
Do	do	240 00	2,268 00	do	-	Sep. 22, 1824	
ORANGE. Zachariah Lindley	Sergeant	48 00	865 06	Not stated	Jan. 18, 1817	Nov. 24, 1811	Acts military establishment.
Do	do	96 00	408 53	do	Jan. 15, 1830	Dec. 2, 1829	do
Thomas Philips	Private	60 00	602 50	-	-	Ap'l 9, 1792	Acts military establishment. Transferred from Virginia.
Do	do	96 00	1,521 86	Darke's reg. 1792	Aug. 3, 1792	Ap'l 24, 1816	April 24, 1816.
Do	do	96 00	192 80	do	-	Mar. 1, 1832	March 2, 1833.
Isham Stroud	Musician	32 00	641 95	Indiana volunteers	Nov. 20, 1819	Nov. 24, 1811	April 10, 1812.
Do	do	48 00	-	do	-	Dec. 16, 1831	April 24, 1816.
Robert Worrell	Private	96 00	1,294 66	Kentucky militia	Mar. 21, 1817	Sep. 9, 1816	March 3, 1817. Transferred from Kentucky. Died.
James Wilson	do	48 00	56 93	Spence's rifles	Dec. 29, 1832	Dec. 28, 1832	April 24, 1816.
PERRY. John Russell	do	96 00	144 00	3d reg. U. S. inf.	Nov. 8, 1832	Sep. 3, 1832	Acts military establishment. Transferred from Louisiana.
Thomas Green Alvey	Pri & cor	22 00	597 05	Revolutionary army	Unknown.	Mar. 4, 1789	September 29, 1789.
Do	do	35 20	48 92	do	do	Ap'l 24, 1816	April 24, 1816. Pain in Maryland.
PIKE. Thomas White	Sergeant	48 00	985 73	Indiana militia	Ap'l 17, 1820	Nov 19, 1811	April 10, 1812.
Do	do	64 00	112 35	do	June 11, 1832	June 2, 1832	April 24, 1816.
RUSH. Alexander Irvine	Private	30 00	7,609 00	9th reg. U. S. inf.	Jan. 7, 1796	Mar. 5, 1795	Acts military establishment. Transferred from Pennsylvania. Suspended September, 1824.
Do	do	48 00	401 33	do	Sep. 4, 1821	Ap'l 24, 1816	April 24, 1816.
Charles Rumsey	Pri. & ser.	60 00	107 00	Kentucky militia	Jan. 9, 1816	July 12, 1814	March 3, 1815. Transferred from Kentucky.
Do	do	96 00	370 66	do	-	Ap'l 24, 1816	Ap'l 24, 1816.
Do	do	72 00	403 60	do	-	Mar. 4, 1820	March 3, 1819.
Do	do	36 00	806 13	do	-	Oct. 12, 1825	Acts military establishment.

Statement, &c.—Continued.

NAMES.	Rank.	Annual allowance.	Sums received.	Description of service.	When placed on the pension roll.	Commencement of pension.	Laws under which they were inscribed, increased or reduced; and remarks.
RIPLEY.							
Socrates Swift	Private	96 00	1,820 12	New York militia	July 29, 1816	Mar 18, 1815	April 30, 1816. Transferred from Kentucky.
John Ward	do	48 00	924 53	Kentucky militia	Jan. 9, 1816	Nov. 30, 1814	March 3, 1815. Transferred from Kentucky.
Do	do	72 00	–	do	Nov. 28, 1834	Oct. 8, 1834	Acts military establishment.
POSEY.							
Thomas Almon	do	30 00	66 33	Indiana militia	Unknown	Feb. 8, 1814	April 10, 1812.
Do.	do	48 00	200 94	do	Oct 1, 1817	April 24, 1816	April 24, 1816.
Do.	do	32 00	308 09	do	-	July 1, 1820	Acts military establishment.
Do.	do	48 00	170 00	do	-	Feb. 17, 1830	Acts military establishment.
Arza Lee	do	96 00	1,895 46	30th U. S. infantry	Aug. 23, 1816	June 6, 1814	Acts mil. est. Transf. from Illinois.
William Palmer	Corporal	50 00	1,356 80	Revolution'y army	Unknown	March 5, 1789	September 29, 1789. Transferred from Virginia and Kentucky.
	do	80 00	201 11	do	do	April 24, 1816	April 24, 1816.
Do.	do	96 00	129 60	do	Sept. 14, 1819	Oct. 29, 1818	March 18, 1818.
Do.	do	80 00	600 00	do	Sept. 19, 1820	March 4, 1820	May 1, 1820.
Samuel Scott	Private	96 00	1,034 13	Mounted voltr's.	April 12, 1823	May 27, 1815	April 30, 1816. Transferred from W. Tennessee.
Do.	do	72 00	432 00	do	-	March 4, 1826	March 3, 1819.
Do.	do	48 00	96 00	do	-	March 4, 1832	March 3, 1819.
PARKE.							
Samuel Scott	do	40 00	340 00	Rev'y army	Unknown	Sept. 4, 1791	June 7, 1785. Transf. from Penn.
David Blue	do	40 00	920 00	Darke's regiment	-	March 4, 1800	Acts military establishment. Transferred from Virginia and Kentucky.
Do.	do	64 00	704 00	39 U. S. infantry	May 10, 1816	March 4, 1823	April 24, 1816.
Adam Stropes	do	96 00	542 66	do	-	July 9, 1814	Acts military establishment.
Do.	do	72 00	848 40	do	-	March 4, 1820	March 3, 1819.
Do.	do	96 00	213 33	do	-	Dec. 16, 1831	Acts military establishment.

Name	Rank			Description			
SHELBY. Joseph Boone, sen.	do	64 00	43 55	Militia of 1790	Sept. 25, 1833	June 29, 1333	April 25, 1808.
SPENCER. Daniel Grass	1st lieut.	204 00	1,488 63	Indiana militia	Jan'y16, 1827	Nov. 13, 1826	April 24, 1816.
Silas Stansbury	Musician	48 00	830 40	U. S. artillery	Nov. 16, 1816	Nov. 16, 1816	Acts military establishment.
SWITZERLAND. James Pierce	Sergeant	60 00	76 83	New York vol.	Nov. 18, 1815	Mar. 13, 1814	Feb. 6, 1815. Transferred from N. Y.
Do	do	96 00	1,666 66	do	-	April 24, 1816	April 24, 1816.
Stephen G. Peabody	Private	48 00	666 13	do	Dec. 5, 1820	May 3, 1820	April 24, 1816. Transf. from N. Y.
Joseph Todd	do	24 00	102 80	Not stated	Unknown	Jan. 12, 1812	July 5, 1812. Transf. from Kentucky.
Do.	do	38 00	686 93	Papers lost	Feb. 12, 1820	April24, 1816	April 24, 1816.
Do.	do	48 00	686 93	do	Sept. 24, 1834	Sept. 11, 1834	Acts military estblishment. Increased.
TIPPECANOE. Elias Bedford	3d lieut.	84 00	1,535 33	11th U. S. infantry	Mar. 17, 1818	June 16, 1815	Acts mil. est. Transferred from N. Y.
Do.	do	126 00	55 30	do	-	Sept. 26, 1833	April 24, 1816.
VANDERBURG. George W. Jacobs	3d lieut.	168 00	2,156 46	9th U. S. infantry	July 22, 1816	Dec. 2, 1815	April 24, 1816. Transferred from Pennsylvania. Died Oct. 1828.
VIGO. John Coterin	Sergeant	48 00	835 20	23d U. S. infantry	Nov. 17, 1819	Ap'l 10, 1815	Acts mil. est. Transf'd from N, York.
John Hamilton*	Captain	120 00	669 72	Ohio militia	Feb. 7, 1821	Feb. 5, 1815	April 30, 1816.
Do.	do	78 00	591 72	do	-	Sept. 4, 1820	March 3, 1819. Reduced.
Do.	do	42 00	318 11	do	-	do	Arrears paid in 1828.
Do.	do	240 00	1,419 33	do	-	April 5, 1828	Acts mil. est.
VERMILLION. Isaac W. Taylor	Private	32 00	99 37	Kentucky militia	Feb. 3, 1830	Jan. 27, 1829	April 24, 1816.
WAYNE. Benjamin Bishop	do	24 00	651 33	Revolutionary army	Mar. 3, 1822	March 4, 1789	Sep. 28, 1789. Trans'd from N. Jersey.
Do.	do	38 40	685 87	do	Mar. 21, 1817	Ap'l 24, 1816	April24, 1816.
George Hendricks	do	48 00	729 20	Kentucky militia	Oct. 7, 1816	Oct. 7, 1816	March 3, 1817. Transf'd from Ky.
Do.	do	72 00	159 80	do	Dec. 20, 1831	Dec. 16, 1831	Acts military establishment.

*This pensioner was reduced to 6 dollars 50 cents per month, and restored to 10 dollars, from Sept. 4, 1820, and paid the arrears in 1828.

Statement, &c.—Continued

NAMES.	Rank	Annual allowance.	Sums received	Description of service.	When placed on the pension roll.	Commencement of pension.	Laws under which they were inscribed, increased or reduced; and remarks.
WAYNE—cont'd.							
Joseph Wasson	Private	60 00	1,268 33	Rev'y army	Unknown	Mar. 4, 1795	Acts mil. est. Transf'd from N. Car'a.
Do.	do	96 00	600 00	do	Papers lost	Ap'l 24, 1816	April 24, 1816. Died July 23, 1822.
William B. Welsh	Sergeant	24 00	325 20	U. S. artillery	April 8, 1817	Aug. 17, 1815	Acts mil. est.
Thomas Wyatt	Private	48 00	917 33	U. S. army	Oct. 17, 1821	July 24, 1811	July 5, 1812. Transferred from West Tennessee.
WARREN.							
Pollard Baldwin	do	64 00	800 00	3d U. S. infantry	Jan. 23, 1823	Ap'l 24, 1821	Acts military establishment.
WASHINGTON.							
Edward Emmery	do	32 00	533 25	Churchill's artillery	Aug. 10, 1817	July 6, 1817	April 24, 1816. Transf'd from Vt.
Robert McKinney	Lieut.	156 00	2,517 66	U. S. artillery	June	Mar. 4, 1800	Acts mil. est. Transf'd from Virginia, Pennsylvania, and Kentucky.
Do.	do	176 80	1,213 00	do	June 14, 1820	Ap'l 24, 1816	April 24, 1816.
Do.	do	102 00	48 16	do	–	Mar. 4, 1823	March 3, 1819. Died Aug. 24, 1823.
Julius Turner	Private	45 00	75 75	5th Ky. militia	Unknown	Aug. 18, 1814	March 3, 1815. Transf'd from Ky.
Do.	do	72 00	1,286 00	do	Papers lost	Ap'l 24, 1816	April 24, 1816.

Statement showing the Names, Rank, &c. of persons residing in Bartholomew county, in the State of Indiana, who have been inscribed on the Pension List under the act of Congress passed March 18, 1818.

NAMES.	Rank.	Sums received.	Annual allowance.	Description of service.	When placed on the pension roll.	Commencement of pension.	Ages.	Laws under which they were formerly inscribed on the pension roll; and remarks.
Job Hamblin	Private	703 51	86 00	Virginia line	Dec. 1, 1818	Oct. 12, 1818	72	Suspended under act May 1, 1820 Restored commencing act Sept. 12, 1827. Died Sept. 1, 1833.

Statement, &c. of Boone county, Indiana.

NAMES.	Rank.	Sums received.	Annual allowance.	Description of service.	When placed on the pension roll.	Commencement of pension.	Ages.	Laws under which they were formerly inscribed on the pension roll; and remarks.
Jonathan Davis	Private	1,561 60	96 00	New Jersey line	Mar. 20, 1819	May 29, 1818	73	

Statement, &c. of Carroll county, Indiana.

NAMES.	Rank.	Sums received.	Annual allowance.	Description of service.	When placed on the pension roll.	Commencement of pension.	Ages.	Laws under which they were formerly inscribed on the pension roll; and remarks.
James Shaw	Private	1,395 09	96 00	Virginia line	June 14, 1820	Aug. 24, 1819	91	Tranferred from Gallatin county, Kentucky.

Statement, &c. of Clarke county, Indiana.

NAMES.	Rank.	Annual allowance.	Sums received.	Description of service.	When placed on the pension roll.	Commencement of pension.	Ages.	Laws under which they were formerly inscribed on the pension roll; and remarks.
John Alstott	Private	96 00	791 88	Pennsylvania line	Feb. 26, 1825	Feb. 5, 1825	79	Died in 1831.
Robert Biggs	do	96 00	779 61	do	Feb. 12, 1824	Nov. 17, 1823	78	Transferred from Genessee co., New York. Died in 1832.
Isaac Bullard	do	96 00	1,323 42	Massachusetts line	May 3, 1819	May 9, 1818	72	
Samuel Calloway	do	96 00	298 09	Virginia line	Oct. 2, 1819	July 28, 1819	71	Transferred from Jefferson co., Kentucky, Mar. 4, 1820. Died in 1822.
Stephen Dolph	do	96 00	518 96	Connecticut line	Nov. 26, 1819	Aug. 27, 1818	70	Died June 22, 1824.
William Goben	do	96 00	1,064 99	Pennsylvania line	Nov. 29, 1819	Aug. 18, 1819	77	Suspended under act May, 1820. Restored commencing August 23, 1823.
Matthew McAfee	do	96 00	1,474 12	do	Oct. 31, 1818	Ap'l 27, 1818	70	Died in 1833.
Charles Pierce	do	96 00	1,515 61	Massachusetts line	Aug. 5, 1819	May 22, 1818	74	
Jacob Plough	do	96 00	1,514 83	New Jersey line	Sep. 16, 1819	May 25, 1818	81	
George Sparling	do	96 00	421 73	do	Dec. 1, 1818	July 20, 1818	78	Stricken from the roll January 18, 1823. [Deserter.]
Daniel Sullivan	do	96 00	397 70	Pennsylvania line	Jan. 2, 1819	July 13, 1818	82	Died in 1822.
Richard Sanborn	do	96 00	886 43	N. Hampshire line	June 1, 1830	Nov. 9, 1819	65	Died February 2, 1829.
James Taff	do	96 00	1,305 06	Virginia line	Mar. 5, 1819	Nov. 10, 1818	77	Died June 13, 1832.
Robert Wardell, alias Fowler	do	96 00	207 51	New Jersey line	May 17, 1820	July 7, 1818	75	

Statement, &c. of Daviess county, Indiana.

NAMES.	Rank.	Annual allowance.	Sums received.	Description of service.	When placed on the pension roll.	Commencement of pension.	Ages.	Laws under which they were formerly inscribed on the pension roll; and remarks.
Job Hammond	Private	96 00	1,421 93	Virginia line	Oct. 22, 1819	May 13, 1819	93	
Benjamin Peachy	do	96 00	1,517 41	New Jersey line	May 20, 1820	May 15, 1818	74	Transferred from Mason county, Kentucky.

Statement, &c. of Dearborn county, Indiana.

NAMES.	Rank.	Annual allowance.	Sums received.	Description of service.	When placed on the pension roll.	Commencement of pension.	Ages.	Laws under which they were formerly inscribed on the pension roll; and remarks.
John Able	Private	96 00	609 09	New Jersey line	Dec. 29, 1820	Sep. 23, 1820	69	Died January 27, 1827.
John Baker	do	96 00	1,029 06	Pennsylvania line	Sep. 10, 1823	June 12, 1823	82	
Charles Cook	do	96 00	595 66	Virginia line	Dec. 1, 1818	Oct. 23, 1818	65	Died January 7, 1825.
John Cooper	Drummer	96 00	713 53	Pennsylvania line	Ap'l 1, 1819	June 2, 1818	77	Transferred from Montgomery county, Virginia. Died Nov. 7, 1825.
John Campbell, 2d	Private	96 00	1,242 32	Virginia line	June 14, 1821	Mar. 27, 1820	77	Transferred from Kentucky.
John Demoss	do	96 00	1,368 25	do	Jan. 10, 1820	Dec. 4, 1819	79	
John O. Gullion	do	96 00	105 54	Pennsylvania line	Jan. 30, 1832	Jan. 30, 1832	74	

Statement, &c. of Dearborn county—Continued.

NAMES.	Rank.	Annual allowance.	Sums received.	Description of service.	When placed on the pension roll.	Commencement of pension.	Ages.	Laws under which they were formerly inscribed on the pension roll; and remarks.
David Haney	Private	36 00	488 75	Pennsylvania line	Jan. 6, 1804	Sep. 27, 1802	74	Acts mil. establishment. Transferred from Pennsylvania.
Do	do	57 60	183 48	do	–	Ap'l 24, 1816	–	Increased by act April 24, 1816.
Do	do	96 00	1,407 73	do	Sep. 27, 1819	July 6, 1819	–	Died March 10, 1834.
Thomas Johnston	do	96 00	466 31	do	July 22, 1818	July 18, 1818	68	Died May 26, 1823.
Moses Lindley	do	96 00	1,150 13	New Jersey line	July 20, 1819	Ap'l 25, 1818	79	Transferred from Cayuga county, New York. Died April 17, 1830.
Noah Miller	do	96 00	1,478 19	do	Dec. 1, 1818	Oct. 12, 1818	91	Transferred from Cumberland county, Maine.
William Meserve	do	96 00	1,524 64	Massachusetts line	Sep. 14, 1819	Ap'l 17, 1818	73	
Zebulon Pike	Captain	240 00	241 52	Pennsylvania line	Sep. 27, 1819	Ap'l 29, 1818	82	Suspended under act May 1, 1820. Restored, commencing September 6, 1824. Relinquished for benefit of act May 15, 1828.
David Porter	Private	96 00	161 03	Virginia line	do	July 1, 1818	84	Suspended under act May 1, 1820.
Samuel Stone	do	96 00	143 96	Massachusetts line	Ap'l 7, 1819	Sep. 5, 1818	61	Dropped under act May 1, 1820.
Daniel Shed	do	96 00	50 40	New Hamp. line	Dec. 13, 1819	Oct. 2, 1819	71	Died April 10, 1820.
Peter Saurman	do	96 00	835 46¾	Pennsylvania line	May 6, 1819	Dec. 22, 1818	82	Transferred from Bedford county, Pennsylvania.
John Six	do	96 00	732 90	Virginia line	Aug. 4, 1826	July 17, 1826	76	
John Shaver	do	96 00	658 89	do	May 12, 1827	Ap'l 24, 1827	68	
Daniel Welch	do	96 00	1,350 09	Connecticut line	July 29, 1819	June 12, 1819	72	
Robert Wright	do	96 00	1,474 19	New York line	Sep. 27, 1819	June 15, 1818	59	Died October 23, 1833.
David Hall	do	96 00	1,512 23	Pennsylvania line	Ap'l 18, 1821	June 4, 1818	74	

Statement, &c. of Decatur county, Indiana.

NAMES.	Rank.	Annual allowance.	Sums received.	Description of service.	When placed on the pension roll.	Commencement of pension.	Ages.	Laws under which they were formerly inscribed on the pension roll; and remarks.
Thomas Horton	Sergeant	96 00	1,478 19	South Carolina line	Feb. 3, 1819	Oct. 12, 1818	83	Transferred from Clay county, Kentucky.
Hugh Montgomery	Private	96 00	268 41	Virginia line	June 18, 1819	Feb. 1, 1819	79	Suspended under act May 1, 1820. Transferred from Butler county, Ohio. Dead.

Statement, &c. of Dubois county, Indiana.

NAMES.	Rank.	Annual allowance.	Sums received.	Description of service.	When placed on the pension roll.	Commencement of pension.	Ages.	Laws under which they were formerly inscribed on the pension roll; and remarks.
Lewis Powers	Private	96 00	1,444 37	Virginia line	Jan. 31, 1820	July 31, 1818	79	Transferred from Franklin county, Kentucky. Died Aug. 16, 1833.

Statement, &c. of Fayette county, Indiana.

NAMES.	Rank	Annual allowance	Sums received.	Description of service.	When placed on the roll.	Commencement of pension.	Ages.	Laws under which they were formerly inscribed on the pension roll; and remarks.
John Bayrd	Private	96 00	1,056 00	Virginia line	July 22, 1819	Mar. 30, 1819	75	
Nathaniel Farmer	do	96 00	606 96	Maryland line	Jan. 4, 1828	Oct. 9, 1823	77	
John Garretson	do	96 00	406 17	South Carolina line	Mar. 11, 1829	Feb. 11, 1829	77	Transferred from Jefferson county, Tennessee.
John Hubbell	Sergeant	96 00	1,536 53	New Jersey line	June 30, 1818	Ap'l 16, 1818	81	Transferred from Warren county, Ohio. Died April 17, 1834,
Nathaniel Richmond	Private	96 00	1,076 52	Massachusetts line	Mar. 7, 1819	June 15, 1818	66	Died September 1, 1829.
Samuel Seward	do	96 00	116 38	New Jersey line	Jan. 12, 1828	Dec. 19, 1827	77	Died March 4, 1829.
Othniel Johnson	do	96 00	1,480 26	do	June 3, 1818	Ap'l 3, 1818	80	Transferred from New Jersey March 4, 1820

Statement, &c. of Floyd county, Indiana.

NAMES.	Rank.	Annual allowance.	Sums received.	Description of service.	When placed on the pension roll.	Commencement of pension.	Ages.	Laws under which they were formerly inscribed on the pension roll; and remarks.
Benjamin Buckman	Sergeant	96 00	1,503 48	Massachusetts line	April 7, 1819	July 7, 1818	76	
Charles Boyll	Private	96 00	1,391 16	Virginia line	Nov. 30, 1819	Sep. 8, 1819	83	
John Chesshire	do	96 00	403 61	do	Dec. 31, 1829	Dec. 22, 1829	80	
John Russell	do	96 00	1,491 61	do	Oct. 17, 1821	Aug. 22, 1818	89	
Israel Ransom	do	96 00	1,516 64	Connecticut line	Mar. 22, 1822	May 18, 1818	75	

Statement, &c. of Fountain county, Indiana.

NAMES.	Rank.	Annual allowance.	Sums received.	Description of service.	When placed on the pension roll.	Commencement of pension.	Ages.	Laws under which they were formerly inscribed on the pension roll; and remarks.
Enos Davis	Private	96 00	464 00	Maryland line	June 13, 1829	May 4, 1829	73	

Statement, &c. of Franklin county, Indiana.

NAMES.	Rank.	Annual allowance.	Sums received.	Description of service.	When placed on the pension roll.	Commencement of pension.	Ages.	Laws under which they were formerly inscribed on the pension roll; and remarks.
Timothy Brown	Private	96 00	1,512 40	New Jersey line	June 1, 1820	June 2, 1818	72	
John Dickinson	do	96 00	309 41	Virginia line	Dec. 19, 1829	Dec. 15, 1829	80	
John Masters	do	96 00	1,498 06	do	Sep. 30, 1819	July 28, 1819	84	
Jacob Myers	do	96 00	1,356 41	North Carolina line	Oct. 1, 1819	July 19, 1819	90	
William Nithercut	do	96 00	183 76	do	Feb. 7, 1824	Oct. 6, 1823	74	
Timothy Brees	do	96 00	1,514 32	New Jersey line	Feb. 7, 1820	May 4, 1818	75	

3

Statement, &c. of Gibson county, Indiana.

NAMES.	Rank.	Annual allowance.	Sums received.	Description of service.	When placed on the pension roll.	Commencement of pension.	Ages.	Laws under which they were formerly inscribed on the pension roll; and remarks.
Arthur Johnson ·	Private	96 00	1,509 33	Virginia line	July 7, 1818	June 11, 1818	77	Dropped under act May 1, 1820. Restored commencing September 2, 1824.
Francis Lucas :	do	96 00	162 09	do	Mar. 20, 1819	June 27, 1818	67	Dropped under act May 1, 1820.
William M'Entire :	do	-96 00	122 83	Pennsylvania line	Jan. 4, 1821	Mar. 29, 1820	76	Died July 8, 1821.
John Pritchett :	do	96 00	1,116 51	N. Carolina line	Oct. 20, 1818	June 22, 1818	82	Suspended under act May 1, 1820. Restored commencing March 31, 1824.
David Stilwell ·	do	96 00	162 09	do	Sep. 15, 1819	June 27, 1818	65	Dropped under act May 1, 1820,

Statement, &c. of Greene county, Indiana.

NAMES.	Rank.	Annual allowance.	Sums received.	Description of service.	When placed on the pension roll.	Commencement of pension.	Ages.	Laws under which they were formerly inscribed on the pension roll; and remarks.
Cornelius Westfall -	Ensign	240 00	1,526 45	Virginia line	Sep. 29, 1819	May 30, 1818	70	Dropped under act May 1, 1820. Restored commencing Oct. 1, 1823. Dead.

Statement, &c. of Hancock county, Indiana.

NAMES.	Rank.	Annual allowance.	Sums received.	Description of service.	When placed on the pension roll.	Commencement of pension.	Ages.	Laws under which they were formerly inscribed on the pension roll, and remarks.
William Hatton	Private	96 00	1,516 12	Virginia line	June 6, 1820	May 20, 1818	69	Transferred from Champaign co., Ohio.

Statement, &c. of Harrison county, Indiana.

NAMES.	Rank.	Annual allowance.	Sums received.	Description of service.	When placed on the pension roll.	Commencement of pension.	Ages.	Laws under which they were formerly inscribed on the pension roll, and remarks.
John Cline	Private	96 00	1,395 35	Virginia line	Nov. 30, 1819	Aug. 23, 1819	82	Transferred from Madison county, Kentucky.
Christopher Coy	do	96 00	1,182 45	Maryland line	Ap'l 17, 1822	Nov. 6, 1821	67	
John Gardner	do	96 00	814 89	do	June 8, 1819	Sep. 9, 1818	64	Transferred from Hardin county, Kentucky. Dead.
Prosser Hogan]	do	96 00	1,185 86	N. Carolina line	Oct. 4, 1819	Ap'l 28, 1818	67	Transferred from Greene county, Kentucky. Dead.
John Long	do	96 00	875 56	Virginia line	July 22, 1819	Ap'l 7, 1819	74	Died May 20, 1828.
George Lefler	do	96 00	462 44	do	June 2, 1826	May 15, 1826	71	Died March 8, 1831.
Samuel Pendock	do	96 00	1,349 93	Rhode Island line	July 22, 1819	Feb. 10, 1819	68	Died July 20, 1833.
Joseph Reed	do	96 00	795 60	Pennsylvania line	Feb. 11, 1820	May 15, 1818	66	Transferred from Jefferson county, Ky. Died August 28, 1826.
John Thompson, 2d	do	96 00	443 87	Virginia line	May 31, 1824	Mar. 1, 1823	70	Died October 15, 1827.
Peter Vandeventer	do	96 00	178 09	do	Dec. 10, 1818	Ap'l 27, 1818	80	Suspended under act May 1, 1820.

Statement, &c. of Jackson county, Indiana.

NAMES.	Rank.	Annual allowance.	Sums received.	Description of service.	When placed on the pension roll.	Commencement of pension.	Ages.	Laws under which they were formerly inscribed on the pension roll; and remarks.
Charles Hagan	Private	96 00	271 48	Virginia line	May 11, 1831	May 7, 1831	73	
George Reiphart	do	96 00	532 89	Maryland line	Oct. 12, 1819	Jan. 31, 1819	70	Died August 18, 1824.
Asahel Phelps	do	96 00	1,510 70	Connecticut line	Ap'l 15, 1819	June 9, 1818	72	
Obadiah Walker	do	96 00	76 90	do	July 22, 1819	May 17, 1819	60	Suspended under act May 1, 1820.

Statement, &c. of Jefferson county, Indiana.

NAMES.	Rank.	Annual allowance.	Sums received.	Description of service.	When placed on the roll.	Commencement of pension.	Ages.	Laws under which they were formerly inscribed on the pension roll; andremarks.
Henry Cloyes	Private	96 00	200 58	Maryland line	March 5, 1819	Jan. 12, 1819	76	Died February 12, 1821.
Bartholomew Carroll	do	96 00	983 44	Virginia line	April 12, 1819	Sept. 5, 1818	106	Died Dec. 2, 1828.
Elias Edens	do	96 00	1,467 16	South Carolina line	June 15, 1819	Nov. 23, 1818	82	
John Field	do	96 00	147 09	Virginia line	Dec. 1, 1818	Aug. 24, 1818	68	Suspended under act May 1, 1820.
George Guess	do	96 00	155 35	Pennsylvania line	Dec. 5, 1818	June 22, 1818	58	Suspended under act May 1, 1820.
William Hood	do	96 00	1,035 73	North Carolina line	Dec. 21, 1818	June 23, 1818	74	Died April 6, 1829.
William Hall	do	96 00	1,507 43	Pennsylvania line	Nov. 11, 1822	June 23, 1818	81	
Emanuel Medok	do	96 00	1,013 23	New Jersey line	Dec. 7, 1818	do	71	Died Jan. 11, 1829.
John May	do	96 00	342 52	North Carolina line	Dec. 21, 1818	do	65	Died Jan. 16, 1822.
James McGill	Sergeant	96 00	1,513 03	Pennsylvania line	Mar. 18, 1819	June 1, 1818	79	Trans'd from Bracken co., Ky.
George Ryan	Private	96 00	1,089 78	Virginia line	Dec. 29, 1820	Nov. 4, 1819	75	Died March 10, 1831.
James Suggan	do	96 00	1,074 66	Maryland line	July 21, 1819	June 25, 1818	82	Transferred from Bourbon county, Ky. Died Sept. 4, 1830.
David Taylor	do	96 00	1,524 76	Virginia line	June 12, 1820	April 17, 1818	74	Trans'd from Henry county, Ky.
Joseph Wheatly	do	96 00	226 06	New Jersey line	Oct. 29, 1822	Oct. 28, 1830	59	

43

[514]

Statement, &c. of Jennings county, Indiana.

NAMES.	Rank.	Annual allowance.	Sums received.	Description of service.	When placed on the roll.	Commencement of pension.	Ages.	Laws under which they were formerly inscribed on the pension roll; and remarks.
Philip Conner	Private	96 00	541 40	Virginia line	July 1, 1828	June 20, 1828	80	Died February 19, 1834.
John Grinstead	do	96 00	1,472 51	do	June 12, 1819	Nov. 2, 1818	78	Transferred from Albermarle co., Virginia.
Evan Thomas	do	96 00	116 90	do	May 1, 1820	Dec. 17, 1818	64	Suspended under act May 1, 1820.

Statement, &c. of Johnson county, Indiana.

NAMES.	Rank.	Annual allowance.	Sums received.	Description of service.	When placed on the roll.	Commencement of pension.	Ages.	Laws under which they were formerly inscribed on the pension roll; and remarks.
John Barnett	Fifer	96 00	881 61	Virginia line	June 19, 1820	July 2, 1819	64	Transferred from Nicholas county, Kentucky. Died Sep. 8, 1828.
John Duke	Private	96 00	205 15	Pennsylvania line	Feb. 5, 1830	Jan, 16, 1830	79	Transferred from Alleghany county, Virginia.
Joshua Harris	do	96 00	1,410 36	Virginia line	Ap'l 20, 1820	June 26, 1819	75	Transferred from Shelby county, Kentucky.

Statement, &c. of Knox county, Indiana.

NAMES.	Rank.	Annual allowance.	Sums received.	Description of service.	When placed on the pension roll.	Commencement of pension.	Ages.	Laws under which they were formerly inscribed on the pension roll; and remarks.
Daniel Kenny	Private	96 00	96 51	Pennsylvania line	June 15, 1819	March 3, 1819	90	Suspended under act May 1, 1820.
Jesse McKensey	do	96 00	159 22	Maryland line	July 27, 1819	July 8, 1818	58	Suspended under act May 1, 1820.

Statement, &c. of Lawrence county, Indiana.

NAMES.	Rank.	Annual allowance.	Sums received.	Description of service.	When placed on the pension roll.	Commencement of pension.	Ages.	Laws under which they were formerly inscribed on the pension roll; and remarks.
Isaac Fleetwood	Private	96 00	856 54	Virginia line	Jan. 27, 1824	Oct. 3, 1823	83	Transf'd from Floyd county, Ky.
Isaac Herrin	do	96 00	1,438 44	South Carolina line	Feb. 2, 1819	Oct. 30, 1818	73	Transferred from Pulaski co., Ky. Died Oct. 23, 1833.
William Haggerty	do	96 00	1,487 16	Pennsylvania line	Feb. 3, 1819	Sept. 8, 1818	83	Transf'd from Mercer co., Ky.
Francis Lang	do	96 00	1,487 16	Maryland line	Nov. 27, 1819	Sept. 8, 1819	74	
Ebenezer Post	do	96 00	421 32	Connecticut line	Sep. 14, 1824	Apr'l 15, 1824	–	Died September, 1828.
Alexander Reid	do	96 00	1,421 35	Virginia line	May 7, 1822	Nov. 13, 1819	75	Transf'd from Estill county, Ky.
John Andrew Smith	do	96 00	1,078 85	do	May 3, 1819	Nov. 2, 1818	80	Transf'd from Blount co, Tenn.
Joshua Younger	do	96 00	302 70	do	Jan. 21, 1830	Jan. 11, 1830	79	Transferred from Nicholas county, Kentucky, March 4, 1833.

Statement, &c. of Madison county, Indiana.

NAMES.	Rank.	Annual allowance.	Sums received.	Description of service.	When placed on the pension roll.	Commencement of pension.	Ages.	Laws under which they were formerly inscribed on the pension roll; and remarks.
Mosby Childers	Private	96 00	1,506 36	Virginia line	June 9, 1819	June 26, 1818	79	
Philip Hobaugh	do	96 00	1,234 26	Pennsylvania line	May 3, 1818	Ap'l 7, 1810	64	Transferred from Madison co., O. Suspended under act May, 1820. Restored, commencing March 25, 1823.

Statement, &c. of Marion county, Indiana.

NAMES.	Rank.	Annual allowance.	Sums received.	Description of service.	When placed on the pension roll.	Commencement of pension.	Ages.	Laws under which they were formerly inscribed on the pension roll; and remarks.
Patrick Lynn	Private	96 00	1,047 02	Pennsylvania line	Nov. 25, 1819	May 12, 1818	76	Transferred from Bath co., Ky. Died April 7, 1829.

Statement, &c. of Montgomery county, Indiana.

NAMES.	Rank.	Annual allowance.	Sums received.	Description of service.	When placed on the pension roll.	Commencement of pension.	Ages.	Laws under which they were formerly inscribed on the pension roll; and remarks.
Alex. Montgomery	Private	96 00	1,507 43	Maryland line	Dec. 7, 1818	June 22, 1818	91	
Jacob Miller	do	96 00	1,381 67	Virginia line	May 6, 1820	Oct. 14, 1819	78	Transferred from Jefferson county, Kentucky. Died 4th Sept. 1829.

Statement, &c. of Monroe county, Indiana.

NAMES.	Rank.	Annual allowance.	Sums received.	Description of service.	When placed on the pension roll.	Commencement of pension.	Ages.	Laws under which they were formerly inscribed on the pension roll; and remarks.
David Boylls	Private	96 00	1,481 03	Virginia line	June 15, 1819	Oct. 1, 1818	81	
David Clements	do	96 00	1,381 15	North Carolina line	Oct. 5, 1822	Oct. 15, 1819	79	Died 12th November, 1828.
Thomas Ross	do	96 00	873 65	Virginia line	Nov. 29, 1819	Oct. 7, 1819	73	Transferred from Randolph county, N. C. Died Aug. 16, 1831.
Nathaniel Cunningham	do	96 00	1,272 82	Virginia line	Sep. 22, 1822	May 6, 1818	80	

Statement, &c. of Morgan county, Indiana.

NAMES.	Rank.	Annual allowance.	Sums received.	Description of service.	When placed on the pension roll.	Commencement of pension.	Ages.	Laws under which they were formerly inscribed on the pension roll; and remarks.
Charles Orme	Private	96 00	1,500 12	Maryland line	June 5, 1819	July 20, 1818	72	Transferred from Lewis county, Kentucky.

Statement, &c. of Orange county, Indiana.

NAMES.	Rank.	Annual allowance.	Sums received.	Description of service.	When placed on the pension roll.	Commencement of pension.	Ages.	Laws under which they were formerly inscribed on the pension roll; and remarks.
Joseph Bowling	Private	96 00	731 61	Virginia line	Jan. 29, 1827	July 22, 1826	81	
William Chandler	do	96 00	1,507 43	Virginia line	Feb. 5, 1819	June 22, 1818	89	
John Hopper	do	96 00	1,438 19	North Carolina line	Sep. 12, 1819	Mar, 12, 1819	83	Transferred from Madison county, Kentuky.
Patrick Hunter	do	96 00	318 36	Virginia line	Jan. 12, 1829	Nov. 11, 1829	74	Transferred from Madison county, Kentucky.
Alexander Keith	do	96 00	968 25	Virginia line	May 28, 1819	Apl 13, 1818	78	Transferred from Scott county, Kentucky. Died May 14, 1828.
James Jeffrey Murphey	do	96 00	97 03	Virginia line	July 22, 1819	March 1, 1819	75	Dropped under act May 1, 1820.
John Reily	do	96 00	1,515 61	Pennsylvania line	Mar. 5, 1819	May 22, 1818	75	Transferred from Clarke county, Kentucky.

4

Statement, &c. of Owen county, Indiana.

NAMES.	Rank.	Annual allowance.	Sums received.	Description of service.	When placed on the pension roll.	Commencement of pension.	Ages.	Laws under which they were formerly inscribed on the pension roll; and remarks.
James Blain -	Private	96 00	749 93	Virginia line	June 19, 1826	May 9, 1826	74	
John Carpenter	do	96 00	1,521 83	Virginia line	Sep. 6, 1819	April 28, 1818	80	Transferred from Green county, Kentucky.
John List -	do	96 00	1,501 31	New York line	Jan. 19, 1819	May 28, 1818	81	Transferred from Pickaway county, Ohio. Died Jan. 18, 1834.
Shadrach Pearson	do	96 00	1,496 11	Virginia line	Sept. 23, 1818	Aug. 3, 1818	80	Transferred from Bourbon county, Kentucky.
John Wallace	do	96 00	318 36	North Carolina line	Nov. 11, 1830	Nov. 11, 1830	84	

Statement, &c. of Parke county, Indiana.

NAMES.	Rank.	Annual allowance.	Sums received.	Description of service.	When placed on the pension roll.	Commencement of pension.	Ages.	Laws under which they were formerly inscribed on the pension roll; and remarks.
John Judd -	Private	96 00	659 00	Pennsylvania line	Nov. 27, 1819	June 19, 1818	72	Died April 30, 1825.

Statement, &c. of Perry county, Indiana.

NAMES.	Rank.	Annual allowance.	Sums received.	Description of service.	When placed on the pension roll.	Commencement of pension.	Ages.	Laws under which they were formerly inscribed on the pension roll; and remarks.
Richard Avit	Sergeant	96 00	677 00	Pennsylvania line	Sep. 16, 1819	May 24, 1819	87	Died June 12, 1826.
Thomas Green Alvey	Private	96 00	461 22	Maryland line	Sep. 29, 1819	do	79	Died February 12, 1824.
Terrence Conner	do	96 00	1,418 83	Virginia line	Sep. 10, 1819	May 25, 1819	82	
George Ewing	Ensign	240 00	546 93	New Jersey line	Jan. 31, 1820	Ap'l 20, 1818	80	Transferred from Ohio.

Statement, &c. of Pike county, Indiana.

NAMES.	Rank.	Annual allowance.	Sums received.	Description of service.	When placed on the pension roll.	Commencement of pension.	Ages.	Laws under which they were formerly inscribed on the pension roll; and remarks.
Josiah Arnold	Private	96 00	944 51	Virginia line	Sep. 22, 1819	May 3, 1819	80	Transferred from Muhlenburg co., Kentucky,
John Chambers	do	96 00	574 14	do	July 13, 1819	June 29, 1818	75	
Samuel Dedman	do	96 00	1,503 22	do	Nov. 27, 1819	July 8, 1818	86	Died June 22, 1834.

Statement, &c. of Posey county, Indiana.

NAMES.	Rank.	Annual allowance.	Sums received.	Description of service.	When placed on the pension roll.	Commencement of pension.	Ages.	Laws under which they were formerly inscribed on the pension roll; and remarks.
Cornelius Bradley	Private	96 00	1,249 31	Maryland line	May 23, 1822	Feb. 28, 1821	79	
John Scarborough	do	96 00	190 70	Virginia line	May 12, 1832	Mar. 10, 1832	72	

Statement, &c. of Putnam county, Indiana.

NAMES.	Rank.	Annual allowance.	Sums received.	Description of service.	When placed on the pension roll.	Commencement of pension.	Ages.	Laws under which they were formerly inscribed on the pension roll; and remarks.
Thomas Jones	Private	96 00	1,503 73	Virginia line	Feb. 15, 1819	July 6, 1818	89	Transferred from Mercer county, Kentucky.
William M'Gahey	do	96 00	1,076 67	Pennsylvania line	April 9, 1819	June 17, 1818	69	Transferred from Bath co., Kentucky. Died Sep. 4, 1829.
William Shepherd	do	96 00	1,400 77	Congress regiment	Sep. 15, 1819	Feb. 2, 1819	75	

Statement, &c. of Ripley county, Indiana.

NAMES.	Rank.	Annual allowance.	Sums received.	Description of service.	When placed on the pension roll.	Commencement of pension.	Ages.	Laws under which they were formerly inscribed on the pension roll; and remarks.
Ning Bell	Private	96 00	1,519 99	Maryland line	June 30, 1818	May 5, 1818	73	
John Boldery	do	96 00	1,525 29	Massachusetts line	Mar. 24, 1819	Ap'l 15, 1818	78	Transferred from Ontario county, New York.
Samuel Goskins	do	96 00	1,525 29	Connecticut line	Mar. 23, 1819	do	72	Transferred from Ontario county, New York.
Philip Johnson	do	96 00	1,486 09	Virginia line	Ap'l 25, 1820	Sep. 12, 1818	76	Transferred from Montgomery county, Kentucky.
James Rolf	do	96 00	1,524 76	New Hamp. line	June 7, 1819	Ap'l 17, 1818	80	Transferred from Windsor county, Vermont.
John Whitacer	do	96 00	1,403 86	Virginia line	Dec. 7, 1818	July 21, 1818	65	Died in 1833.

Statement, &c. of Rush county, Indiana.

NAMES.	Rank.	Annual allowance.	Sums received.	Description of service.	When placed on the pension roll.	Commencement of pension.	Ages.	Laws under which they were formerly inscribed on the pension roll; and remarks.
John Aldridge	Private	96 00	1,383 99	Virginia line	Nov. 4, 1819	Oct. 4, 1819	73	Transferred from Clermont county, Ohio.
Ebenezer Clark	do	96 00	1,525 15	Massachusetts line	Jan. 27, 1819	Ap'l 15, 1818	72	Transferred from Oneida, county, New York.
Matthew Gregg	do	96 00	1,143 69	Virginia line	Feb. 12, 1820	Ap'l 26, 1818	85	Transferred from Campbell county, Kentucky. Died Mar. 1830.
Daniel Grant	do	96 00	1,100 13	do	May 17, 1819	Sep. 8, 1818	71	Transferred from Washington county, Kentucky. Died Feb. 1831.
James Lane	Qr. master sergeant	96 00	870 35	do	May 31, 1819	Oct. 19, 1818	85	Transferred from Louis county, Kentucky. Died May, 1827.
John Legore	Private	96 00	1,008 50	Pennsylvania line	Ap'l 2, 1819	Jan. 6, 1819	73	Transferred from Washington county, Ohio. Died July 7, 1829.
John Riley	do	96 00	705 32	do	Dec. 20, 1820	Ap'l 30, 1818	85	Transferred from Campbell county, Kentucky.
Aaron Redman	do	96 00	289 25	Virginia line	Sep. 1, 1830	Aug. 31, 1830	-	Transferred from Kentucky.
John Yarbrough	do	96 00	1,502 70	do	Feb. 13, 1819	Jan. 8, 1818	79	Transferred from Nicholas county, Kentucky. Died March, 1834.
Benjamin Cruzan, alias Cruidson	do	96 00	851 96	do	May 12, 1825	Ap'l 18, 1825	76	
Michael Smith,	do	96 00	1,369 06	do	Feb. 7, 1820	Nov. 5, 1819	71	
Henry Smith, 2d	-	96 00	1,376 09	Pennsylvania line	Oct. 31, 1822	do	69	

53

Statement, &c. of Scott county, Indiana.

NAMES.	Rank.	Annual allowance.	Sums received.	Description of service.	When placed on the pension roll.	Commencement of pension.	Ages.	Laws under which they were formerly inscribed on the pension roll; and remarks.
Richard Kinney -	Private	96 00	1,490 83	Virginia line	-	Aug. 23, 1818	85	

Statement, &c. of Shelby county, Indiana.

NAMES.	Rank.	Annual allowance.	Sums received.	Description of service.	When placed on the pension roll.	Commencement of pension.	Ages.	Laws under which they were formerly inscribed on the pension roll; and remarks.
David Davis	Mar oss	96 00	1,036 00	Pennsylvania line	Ap'l 19, 1819	May 18, 1818	77	

Statement, &c. of Spencer county, Indiana.

NAMES.	Rank.	Annual allowance.	Sums received.	Description of service.	When placed on the pension roll.	Commencement of pensions.	Ages.	Laws under which they were formerly inscribed on the pension roll; and remarks.
Thomas Blair	Private	96 00	1,400 92	Pennsylvania line	June 9, 1819	May 29, 1818	76	Transferred from Nelson county, Kentucky. Died Jan. 1, 1833.
David Chancellor	do	96 00	188 64	Virginia line	Mar. 21, 1832	Mar. 17, 1832	87	Transferred from Fleming county, Kentucky. Died Feb. 1829.
Abraham Hornbeck	do	96 00	913 83	do	June 23, 1824	Feb. 26, 1824	76	
Henry Shaw	do	96 00	997 06	do	May 25, 1820	Sep. 12, 1818	71	
Thomas Turnham	do	96 00	1,453 96	do	Ap'l 5, 1819	July 13, 1818	84	Transferred from Wilson county, Tennessee,

Statement, &c. of Sullivan county, Indiana.

NAMES	Rank.	Annual allowance.	Sums received.	Description of service.	When placed on the pension roll.	Commencement of pension.	Ages.	Laws under which they were formerly inscribed on the pension roll; and remarks.
Mordecai Battison	Private	96 00	936 63	Virginia line	Dec. 23, 1818	Aug. 19, 1818	74	Transferred from Burton county, Kentucky. Died. Jan 6, 1829.
Thomas Flyn	do	96 00	1,027 91	Delaware line	Nov. 13, 1819	Feb. 19, 1819	89	Died September 4, 1830.
John Hopewell	do	96 00	740 53	Virginia line	May 31, 1819	Nov. 20, 1818	75	Transferred from Bullitt county, Kentucky. Died Aug. 6, 1826.
Micajah Mayfield	do	96 00	593 03	do	Feb. 1, 1831	Jan. 1, 1828	87	
Joseph Ransford	Gunner	96 00	1,348 78	Massachusetts line	Ap'l 19, 1822	Feb. 16, 1820	72	
James Spence	Private	96 00	1,506 09	North Carolina line	July 16, 1821	June 27, 1818	79	Transferred from Fayette county, Kentucky.

Statement, &c. of Switzerland county, Indiana.

NAMES.	Rank.	Annual allowance.	Sums received.	Description of service.	When placed on the pension roll.	Commencement of pension.	Ages.	Laws under which they were formerly inscribed on the pension roll; and remarks.
John Bray	Private	96 00	1,149 34	Virginia line	Aug. 9, 1819	June 20, 1818	70	Died June 10, 1832.
John Burns	do	96 00	806 65	do	Dec. 13, 1819	Feb. 12, 1819	65	Died July 7, 1827.
Joseph Bassett	do	96 00	190 93	Massachusetts line	July 17, 1822	Sept. 13, 1821	64	Died September 8, 1822.
Leman Deasky	do	96 00	1,024 28	New Jersey line	July 14, 1819	June 16, 1818	72	Died February 15, 1829.
Daniel Harris	do	96 00	291 40	Pennsylvania line	Ap'l 15, 1819	May 26, 1818	85	Died June 7, 1821.
Daniel Haycock	do	96 00	1,511 48	New Jersey line	Mar. 30, 1820	June 2, 1818		
Kimbrow Landres	do	96 00	172 38	Virginia line	Ap'l 19, 1819	May 19, 1818	67	Dropped under act May 1, 1820.
John Pennctent	do	96 00	277 67	do	June 17, 1819	Dec. 3, 1818	73	Died October 24, 1821.
Nathan Peak	Sergeant	96 00	538 31	Maryland line	Nov. 26, 1819	May 13, 1818	72	Died in 1824.
Stephen Rodgers	Private	96 00	1,202 30	Virginia line	Ap'l 26, 1819	May 30, 1818	70	Suspended under act May 1, 1820. Restored, commencing June 2, 1823.
Andrew Stepleton	do	96 00	1,519 99	do	Feb. 13, 1819	May 5, 1818	82	Suspended under act May 1, 1820. Restored, commencing June 5, 1823. Died March, 1831.
Smith Turner	do	96 00	916 58	do	Ap'l 19, 1819	May 20, 1818	89	
Michael Wilson	do	96 00	598 69	do	Feb. 13, 1819	June 2, 1818	63	Died August 27, 1824.
John Whittaker	do	96 00	693 32	do	July 22, 1819	June 23, 1818	65	Died September 12, 1825.

5

Statement, &c. of Union county, Indiana.

NAMES.	Rank.	Annual allowance.	Sums received.	Description of service.	When placed on the pension roll.	Commencement of pension.	Ages.	Laws under which they were formerly inscribed on the pension roll; and remarks.
James Colston or Colston	Private	96 00	1,031 69	New Jersey line	May 9, 1820	June 6, 1818	74	
Daniel Ward	do	96 00	563 89	New York line	Mar. 5, 1824	Oct. 21, 1823	71	

Statement, &c. of Vigo county, Indiana.

NAMES.	Rank.	Annual allowance.	Sums received.	Description of service.	When placed on the pension roll.	Commencement of pension.	Ages.	Laws under which they were formerly inscribed on the pension roll; and remarks.
Jacob Coleman	Lieut.	240 00	1,867 09	Virginia line	Aug. 13, 1819	May 25, 1818	72	Relinquished for benefit of act May 15, 1828.
John Hamilton	do	240 00	540 00	do	Jan. 10, 1820	do	66	Died in 1827.
Daniel Rhoads	Private	96 00	310 54	Pennsylvania line	May 5, 1830	May 3, 1830	79	
Isaac Stevens	do	96 00	1,029 56	New Jersey line	July 16, 1819	June 14, 1819	80	
Thomas Dample	do	96 00	548 29	S. Carolina line	July 7, 1819	June 19, 1818	87	
William Thomas	do	96 00	-	Virginia line	June 19, 1820	Feb. 29, 1820	65	Dropped under act May 1, 1820.

Statement, &c. of Warren county, Indiana.

NAMES.	Rank.	Annual allowance.	Sums received.	Description of service.	When placed on the pension roll.	Commencement of pension.	Ages.	Laws under which they were formerly inscribed on the pension roll; and remarks.
David Wilkerson -	Private	96 00	1,252 34	Virginia line	Feb. 11, 1819	July 1, 1818	67	Transferred from Clarke county, Kentucky. Died June 13, 1832.

Statement, &c. of Warrick county, Indiana.

NAMES.	Rank.	Annual allowance.	Sums received.	Description of service.	When placed on the pension roll.	Commencement of pension.	Ages.	Laws under which they were formerly inscribed on the pension roll; and remarks.
Jonah Frisbie - -	Private	96 00	136 25	Massachusetts line	Nov. 30, 1819	Oct. 4, 1819	54	Suspended under act May 1, 1820.
William Overlin - -	do	96 00	131 09	Virginia line	Mar. 5, 1819	Oct. 24, 1818	55	Suspended under act May 1, 1820.

Statement, &c. of Washington county, Indiana.

NAMES.	Rank.	Annual allowance.	Sums received.	Description of service.	When placed on the pension roll.	Commencement of pension.	Ages.	Laws under which they were formerly inscribed on the pension roll; and remarks.
Levi Bridgwater	Private	96 00	818 09	Virginia line	May 22, 1822	Mar. 1, 1823	73	Died in 1831.
William Case	do	96 00	751 48	Maryland line	Aug. 8, 1822	Jan. 3, 1820	75	Died November 1, 1827.
Michael Cooper	do	96 00	419 03	Pennsylvania line	Ap'l 6, 1827	Sep. 8, 1826	81	Died January 19, 1831.
John Deremiah	do	96 00	1,170 06	Virginia line	May 29, 1820	Aug. 23, 1819	87	Died December 30, 1831.
Thomas Flowers	do	96 00	1,481 29	Pennsylvania line	Ap'l 9, 1819	Sep. 30, 1818	73	Suspended under act May 1, 1820.
William Grace	do	96 00	133 15	Maryland line	June 21, 1820	Oct. 16, 1819	61	Transferred from Cayuga county, New York.
Philip Langdon	do	96 00	1,521 29	Rhode Island line	May 30, 1822	Ap'l 30, 1818	74	
James Mahoney	do	96 00	69 56	Virginia line	July 16, 1819	June 14, 1819	57	Suspended under act May 1, 1820.
Thomas Smith	do	96 00	996 92	do	July 12, 1819	Oct. 12, 1818	80	Died February 27, 1829.
William Stewart	do	96 00	1,122 66	Pennsylvania line	Ap'l 22, 1820	June 22, 1819	75	Died March 4, 1831.
Christopher Trinkle	do	96 00	69 03	Virginia line	July 16, 1819	June 16, 1819	68	Suspended under act May 1, 1820.
Abraham Wood	do	96 00	1,382 19	Pennsylvania line	Nov. 30, 1819	Oct. 12, 1819	76	

Statement, &c. of Wayne county, Indiana.

NAMES.	Rank.	Annual allowance.	Sums received.	Description of service.	When placed on the pension roll.	Commencement of pension.	Ages.	Laws under which they were formerly inscribed on the pension roll; and remarks.
William Alexander	Private	96 00	240 25	Pennsylvania line	Sep. 22, 1819	July 6, 1818	69	Died January 6, 1821.
Hugh Healy	do	96 00	1,561 03	New Jersey line	Jan. 9, 1820	May 28, 1818	67	Died August 31, 1834.
Joseph Hancock	do	96 00	530 83	Pennsylvania line	Nov. 29, 1828	Aug. 25, 1828	77	
Abraham Marlatt	do	96 00	984 25	Armand's legion	Aug. 12, 1818	Ap'l 28, 1818	67	Died July 23, 1828.
Jonathan Shaw	do	96 00	614 96	New Jersey line	Nov, 28, 1827	Oct. 9, 1827	75	
Barruch Webb	do	96 00	1,514 86	Maryland line	Oct. 4, 1819	May 25, 1818	74	

Names of Pensioners whose residence could not be ascertained.

NAMES.	Rank.	Annual allowance.	Sums received.	Description of service.	When placed on the pension roll.	Commencement of pension.	Ages.	Laws under which they were formerly inscribed on the pension roll; and remarks.
Samuel Ferguson	Private	96 00	605 44	Congress regiment	Ap'l 23, 1819	Ap'l 27, 1818	72	Transferred from Indiana county, Penn. Died August 17, 1824.
Seth Kinkley	do	96 00	408 78	Massachusetts line	Feb. 7, 1820	May 31, 1818	64	Transferred from Hamilton county. Ohio. Died September 2, 1822.
Joseph Hennegin	do	96 00	1,428 53	Congress regiment	May 23, 1818	Ap'l 14, 1818	74	Transferred from Onondago county, N. York. Died March 1833.
John Thompson	do	96 00	1,078 92	Virginia line	Jan. 27, 1820	June 9, 1819	78	Transferred from Mercer county, Kentucky. Died Sept. 1830.

Statement showing the Names, Rank, &c. of persons residing in Allen county, in the State of Indiana, who have been inscribed on the Pension List under the act of Congress passed June 7, 1832.

NAMES.	Rank.	Annual allowance.	Sums received.	Description of service.	When placed on the pension roll.	Commencement of pension.	Ages.	Laws under which they were formerly inscribed on the pension roll; and remarks.
James Ball -	Private	28 33	-	Maryland militia	Jan. 15, 1834	Mar. 4, 1831	68	
Michael Cronts -	do	40 00	120 00	N. Y. State troops	Oct. 26, 1833	do	72	
James Saunders -	do	21 66	-	Virginia St. troops	Jan. 3, 1834	do	78	

Statement, &c. of Bartholomew county, Indiana.

NAMES.	Rank.	Annual allowance.	Sums received.	Description of service.	When placed on the pension roll.	Commencement of pension.	Ages.	Laws under which they were formerly inscribed on the pension roll; and remarks.
George Alcorn -	Private	27 67	-	S. C. State service	Mar. 5, 1834	Mar. 4, 1831	74	
Richard Crittenden -	do	80 00	240 00	Virginia militia	June 13, 1833	do	72	
William Campbell -	do	43 33	129 99	Penn. militia	Oct. 15, 1833	do	69	
Stephen Goble -	do	80 00	240 00	Penn. State troops	July 15, 1833	do	75	
Thomas McQueen -	do	40 00	120 00	Virginia cont'l line	Dec. 21, 1835	do	69	

Statement, &c. of Boone county, Indiana.

NAMES.	Rank.	Annual allowance.	Sums received	Description of service.	When placed on the pension roll.	Commencement of pension.	Ages.	Laws under which they were formerly inscribed on the pension roll; and remarks.
Jacob Foreman	Private	20 00	60 00	N. C. militia	Nov. 29, 1833	Mar. 4, 1831	78	
William Gipson	Pri. & ser.	90 00	270 00	do	Aug. 27, 1833	do	81	
William Pawley	Private	20 00	-	S. C. do	June 20, 1834	do	74	
Harman Wyman	do	21 33	-	Virginia militia	Mag 16, 1834	do	68	

Statement, &c. of Carroll county, Indiana.

NAMES.	Rank.	Annual allowance.	Sums received.	Description of service.	When placed on the pension list.	Commencement of pension.	Ages.	Laws under which they were formerly inscribed on the pension roll; and remarks.
Willibe Nichols	Pri. & ser.	38 33	114 99	Virginia militia	Oct. 3, 1833	Mar. 4, 1831	85	

Statement, &c. of Cass county, Indiana,

NAMES.	Rank.	Annual allowance.	Sums received.	Description of service.	When placed on the pension roll.	Commencement of pension.	Ages.	Laws under which they were formerly inscribed on the pension roll; and remarks.
Alexander Scott -	Private	20 00	40 00	Virginia militia	Feb. 8, 1833	Mar. 4, 1831	70	
James Wiseman -	do	37 66	75 32	N. C. do	Feb. 5, 1833	do	72	
John Ward -	do	80 00	240 00	Virginia do	May 14, 1833	do	82	

Statement, &c. of Clarke county, Indiana.

NAMES.	Rank.	Annual allowance.	Sums received.	Description of service.	When placed on the pension roll.	Commencement of pension.	Ages.	Laws under which they were formerly inscribed on the pension roll; and remarks.
Joseph Alexander	Private	36 66	109 98	Penn. State troops	Nov. 12, 1833	Mar. 4, 1831	79	
Philip Austin	do	30 00	90 00	N. Y. do	Feb. 26, 1833	do	68	
John Brenton	do	23 33	70 09	Penn. militia	Dec. 18, 1832	do	72	
Robert Brenton	do	23 33	46 66	do	Dec. 28, 1832	do	75	
William Brenton	do	46 66	139 98	do	do	do	74	
Zalman Burrett	Pri. & ser.	45 00	112 50	Conn. State troops	May 29, 1833	do	81	
Peter Ditzer	Private	66 66	199 93	Penn. militia	Dec. 38, 1832	do	68	
Isaac Holman	do	23 33	—	N. H. do	June 6, 1834	do	79	
Ezekiel Jennings	do	80 00	240 00	Virginia State trp's	Dec. 28, 1832	do	70	
Elias Kelley	do	20 00	60 00	do	Dec. 18, 1832	do	72	
Frederick Kestler	do	66 66	199 98	Penn. militia	Dec. 28, 1832	do	74	
Moses Kelley	do	36 66	109 98	Virginia do	Dec. 13, 1832	do	84	
William McComb	do	50 00	150 00		Dec. 18, 1832	do	84	
Robert Patrick	do	80 00	240 00	Penn. line	do	do	77	
Joseph Robison	do	40 00	120 00	Virginia militia	Dec. 7, 1832	do	72	
Christian Shores	do	20 77	62 21	S. C. State troops	Oct. 1, 1832	do	91	
Enos Tuttle	do	50 00	150 00	Conn. militia	Sept. 7, 1832	do	97	
Jacob Teeple	Mus. & pr.	61 80	193 00	Penn. militia	Dec. 18, 1832	do	71	
Zebediah Ward	Pri. & ser.	100 00	300 00	Conn. do	do	do	78	
Barzilla Willey	Private	46 66	129 98	Conn. St. troops	do	do	70	
John Young	do	33 33	99 99	Virginia militia	do	do	77	

Statement, &c. of Clay county, Indiana.

NAMES.	Rank.	Annual allowance.	Sums received.	Description of service.	When placed on the pension roll.	Commencement of pension.	Ages.	Laws under which they were formerly inscribed on the pension roll; and remarks.
David Dannor -	Private	20 00	60 00	Maryland militia	Dec. 20, 1833	Mar. 4, 1831	86	
Lawrence Thompson -	do	21 55	64 65	N. C. militia	do	do	82	
Benjamin Wheeler -	do	20 00	60 00	Maryland militia	do	do	77	
John Williams -	do	30 00	90 00	N. Y. St. troops	Mar. 17, 1834	do	70	

Statement, &c. of Crawford county, Indiana.

NAMES.	Rank.	Annual allowance.	Sums received.	Description of service.	When placed on the pension roll.	Commencement of pension	Ages.	Laws under which they were formerly inscribed on the pension roll; and remarks.
Samuel Chapin -	Private	33 33	99 99	Virginia militia	Aug. 28, 1833	Mar. 4, 1831	82	
William Campbell -	do	40 00	120 00	N. C. State troops	Nov. 29, 1833	do	79	
Reuben Kemp -	do	80 00	240 00	Virginia cont'l line	Ap'l 10, 1833	do	80	
James Pierson -	do	20 00	60 00	N. C. militia	Oct. 21, 1833	do	77	
Thomas Reed -	do	26 66	-	do	June 25, 1834	do	69	
Constant Williams -	do	30 00	90 00	Mass. St. troops	Nov. 29, 1833	do	72	
Jeremiah Wright -	do	53 33	117 60	Virginia St. troops	Dec. 20, 1833	do	71	Died May 18, 1833.

Statement, &c. of Daviess county, Indiana.

NAMES.	Rank.	Annual allowance.	Sums received.	Description of service.	When placed on the pension roll.	Commencement of pension.	Ages.	Laws under which they were formerly inscribed on the pension roll; and remarks.
William Baldwin	Private	45 55	91 10	Virginia State tr.	May 29, 1833	Mar. 4, 1831	80	
Josiah Culberton	do	80 00	240 00	N. Carolina St. tr.	July 15, 1833	do	71	
James Cannon	do	50 00	150 00	S. Carolina militia	Oct. 18, 1833	do	79	
John Chumbley	do	30 88	77 20	Virginia militia	do	do	74	
William Harrall	do	60 00	180 00	Virginia cont'l line	Ap'l 6, 1833	do	77	
Moses Knight	Pri. of cav.	100 00	300 00	S. Carolina militia	Oct. 18, 1833	do	75	
Charles Kilgore	Private	36 00	108 00	Virginia militia	do	do	80	
James Kever	do	26 66	79 89	S. Carolina St. tr.	Dec. 11, 1833	do	75	
George Lashley	do	20 00	60 00	Maryland militia	Ap'l 11, 1833	do	97	
Joseph Reany	Pri. of inf. & cav'y	47 50	132 50	S. Carolina St. tr.	Oct. 29, 1833	do	81	
Cuthbud Tisdale	Private	44 88	134 64	Virginia St. troops	May 29, 1833	do	73	
James Carr Veale	do	80 00	-	S. Carolina militia	Dec. 19, 1832	do	71	

Statement, &c. of Dearborn county, Indiana.

NAMES.	Rank.	Annual allowance.	Sums received.	Description of service.	When placed on the pension roll.	Commencement of pension.	Ages.	Laws under which they were formerly inscribed on the pension roll; and remarks.
Charles Bisbee	Private	72 22	—	Mass. State troops	July 28, 1833	Mar. 4, 1831	73	
Peter Carbell	do	80 00	240 00	Pennsylvania mil.	Aug. 28, 1833	do	82	
Michael Ehler	do	40 00	100 00	do	June 17, 1833	do	75	
John Elliot	Pri. & ser.	113 11	282 77	N. Hamp. militia	Aug. 2, 1833	do	72	
Jacob Ellsbury	Private	60 00	180 00	N. Carolina militia	Mar. 22, 1834	do	72	
William Henderson	do	26 66	79 98	Pennsylvania mil.	Oct. 3, 1833	do	78	
Moses Hendrickson	do	20 00	60 00	Virginia State tr.	Feb. 25, 1834	do	80	
Job Judd	do	40 00	—	Continental militia	July 21, 1834	do	78	
Moses Lacey	do	30 45	91 62	Virginia militia	Nov 15, 1832	do	72	
Daniel Loder	do	26 66	—	N. Jersey militia	Oct. 26, 1833	do	75	Died May 14, 1833.
James Leedes	do	20 00	—	do	July 20, 1834	do	77	
Samuel Marsh	do	32 77	98 21	Massachusetts mil.	Aug. 2, 1833	do	70	
John Mead	do	60 33	180 99	New York militia	Oct. 26, 1833	do	71	
George Mason	do	60 00	180 00	Pennsylvania mil.	Dec. 31 1833	do	75	
Daniel Reddington	do	76 33	228 99	Mass. cont'l line	Ap'l 30, 1833	do	70	
David Reamer	Artificer	144 00	432 00	Pennsylvania militia	July 30, 1833	do	80	
Robert Rickett	Private	20 77	62 21	do	Aug. 20, 1833	do	72	
Henry Rander	do	56 66	169 98	Penn. State troops	Oct. 21, 1833	do	69	
Elijah Rich	do	30 00	90 00	Mass. State troops	Nov. 19, 1833	do	72	
Ezra Stanson	do	80 00	240 00	Connecticut St. tr.	Mar. 8, 1833	do	74	
William Smithers	do	20 00	—	Virginia militia	Ap'l 9, 1833	do	93	Died May 14, 1834.
Gideon Towers	Pri. & ser.	90 00	270 00	Connecticut militia	Ap'l 26, 1833	do	75	
Timothy Ward	Private	80 00	240 00	N. Jersey State tr.	Aug. 26, 1833	do	74	
Benjamin Walker	Pri. & ser.	90 00	270 00	Maryland State tr.	do	do	67	
Daniel Whetstone	Private	29 76	79 28	do	Oct. 21, 1833	do	81	
William White	do	30 00	—	Pennsylvania mil.	July 10, 1834	do	72	

Statement, &c. of Decatur county, Indiana.

NAMES.	Rank.	Annual allowance.	Sums received.	Description of service.	When placed on the pension roll.	Commencement of pension.	Ages.	Laws under which they were formerly inscribed on the pension roll; and remarks.
John Boyer - - -	Private	40 00	112 00	N. York State tr.	July 28, 1833	Mar. 4, 1831	73	
Josiah Collins - -	do	26 66	79 98	Maryland State tr.	Aug. 28, 1833	do	77	
Edward Dunham -	do	20 00	60 00	N. Carolina militia	Ap'l 6, 1833	do	70	
Jacob Falconbury -	do	60 00	180 00	N. Carolina St. tr.	Aug. 28, 1833	do	83	
Benjamin Gasnell -	do	30 00	75 00	Virginia militia	Aug. 27, 1833	do	73	
John Gray - - -	do	40 00	-	Virginia State tr.	Feb. 7, 1834	do	74	
George King - -	do	80 00	240 00	do	Ap'l 6, 1833	do	84	
Joseph Lee - -	do	46 66	139 98	New Jersey militia	Aug. 26, 1833	do	73	
Samuel Lloyd - -	do	80 00	200 00	N. Carolina militia	July 12, 1833	do	89	
Spencer Menefer -	do	60 00	180 00	Virginia State tr.	Feb. 16, 1833	do	71	
William McCoy -	do	80 00	240 00	do	Aug. 27, 1833	do	68	
Elijah Piles - -	do	80 00	240 00	do	Jan. 8, 1833	do	89	
John Prickard - -	do	40 00	120 00	Virginia militia	Feb. 14, 1833	do	76	
William Robins -	do	50 00	150 00	N. Carolina st. tr.	Jan. 8, 1834	do	74	

Statement, &c. of Delaware county, Indiana.

NAMES.	Rank.	Annual allowance.	Sums received.	Description of service.	When placed on the pension roll.	Commencement of pension.	Ages.	Laws under which they were formerly inscribed on the pension roll; and remarks.
William Dougherty -	Private	25 66	64 15	N. Carolina militia	Ap'l 11, 1834	Mar. 4, 1831	82	
William Polen - -	do	23 33	-	do	May 29, 1833	do	72	

Statement, &c. of Dubois county, Indiana.

NAMES.	Rank.	Annual allowance.	Sums received.	Description of service.	When placed on the pension roll.	Commencement of pension.	Ages.	Laws under which they were formerly inscribed on the pension roll; and remarks.
James Harbison	Private	20 00	40 00	Virginia militia	Feb. 22, 1833	Mar. 4, 1831	81	
John Hills	do	40 00	120 00	N. Carolina militia	July 11, 1833	do	75	

Statement, &c. of Fayette county, Indiana.

NAMES.	Rank.	Annual allowance.	Sums received.	Description of service.	When placed on the pension roll.	Commencement of pension.	Ages.	Laws under which they were formerly inscribed on the pension roll; and remarks.
Philemon Conner	Private	40 00	100 00	Virginia militia	Mar. 21, 1833	Mar. 4, 1831	71	
Benjamin Ellis	do	33 33	83 32	Mass. State troops	Dec. 19, 1832	do	84	
Jonathan Gilliam	do	80 00	240 00	Pennsylv'a militia	Ap'l 26, 1833	do	75	
Charles Harvey	do	43 33	108 32	Virginia militia	Dec. 18, 1833	do	73	
James Justice	do	80 00	240 00	Pennsylv'a militia	Feb. 28, 1832	do	73	
John McCormick	do	40 00	120 00	Virginia militia	Jan. 21, 1833	do	71	
Benjamin Pearce	do	20 00	60 00	New Jersey militia	Oct. 1, 1833	do	68	
Henry Vandalson	Pri. & ser.	100 00	300 00	N. Y. State troops	Mar. 21, 1833	do	72	
Dyer Woodworth	Private	60 00	180 00	do	do	do	85	

Statement, &c. of Floyd county, Indiana.

NAMES.	Rank.	Annual allowance.	Sums received.	Description of service.	When placed on the pension roll.	Commencement of pension.	Ages.	Laws under which they were formerly inscribed on the pension roll; and remarks.
William Bateman	Pri. of cav.	100 00	300 00	Maryland con. line.	Jan. 3, 1834	Mar. 4, 1831	78	
Daniel Deal	Private	26 66	79 98	Vermont militia	Ap'l 22, 1833	do	75	
Joshua Fowler	Pri. & ser.	45 00	135 00	Maryland militia	Feb. 4, 1833	do	75	
Joseph Ghormley	do	20 00	-	Pennsylv'a militia	Feb. 4, 1833	do	72	
Jacob Garneston or Garretson	do	20 00	60 00	N. Jersey militia	Mar. 20, 1834	do	81	
Epaphras Jones	do	80 00	240 00	Connecticut militia	Ap'l 26, 1833	do	75	
Andrew Ingram	Private of cav. & inf.	25 40	76 20	Virg'a State troops	Jan. 28, 1834	do	80	
Samuel Jackson	Private	33 33	83 32	do	Mar. 17, 1834	do	79	
John A. Miller	Pri. & ser.	76 66	229 98	Virginia militia	Feb. 4, 1833	do	69	
Samuel Ramsey	Private	20 00	60 00	Pennsylv'a militia	Jan. 22, 1834	do	75	
James Stephenson	Captain	439 99	1,099 97	Virg'a State troops	Nov. 29, 1832	do	71	
Reuben Smith	Corporal	88 00	264 00	do	Dec. 7, 1833	do	77	
Asa Smith	Private	30 00	90 00	do	Jan. 28, 1834	do	84	
John Steelman	do	26 66	79 98	N. J. State troops	Mar. 20, 1834	do	79	
Philo Stoddard	do	33 33	99 99	Mass. State troops	Mar. 22, 1834	do	70	

Statement, &c. of Fontaine county, Indiana.

NAMES.	Rank.	Annual allowance.	Sums received.	Description of service.	When placed on the pension roll.	Commencement of pension.	Ages.	Laws under which they were formerly inscribed on the pension roll; and remarks.
John Bake	Private	48 33	135 09	Virg'a State troops	Feb. 27, 1834	March 4, 1831	69	
Henry Balton	do	73 33	219 99	Penn'a State troops	Ap'l 18, 1834	do	85	
Jacob High	do	53 33	169 00	Virg'a State troops	Nov. 12, 1833	do	75	
Tobias Mozier	do	20 00	60 00	N. Carolina militia	June 22, 1833	do	81	
William Osborn	do	32 50	—	do	May 17, 1833	do	82	
John Osburn	do	80 00	240 00	do	Oct. 12, 1833	do	69	
Thomas Pearson	do	80 00	240 00	Pennsylv'a militia	Oct. 26, 1833	do	94	
Thomas Williams	do	20 00	50 00	Virginia militia	Oct. 29, 1833	do	80	
Jacob Youngblood	do	43 33	129 99	S. Carolina militia	Aug. 26, 1833	do	82	

Statement, &c. of Franklin county, Indiana.

NAMES.	Rank.	Annual allowance	Sums received.	Description of service.	When placed on the pension roll.	Commencement of pension	Ages.	Laws under which they were formerly inscribed on the pension roll; and remarks.
Samuel Alley	Private	20 00	60 00	Virginia cont'l line	Oct. 26, 1833	March 4, 1831	74	
Samuel Amburn	do	40 00	-	Virg'a State troops	Aug. 12, 1834	do	80	
John Burchfield	do	52 66	157 98	N. Carolina militia	May 14, 1833	do	69	
Zachariah Cooksey	do	22 33	56 32	Virginia militia	May 13, 1833	do	74	
John Colyer	Pri. & ser.	39 66	118 98	Virg'a State troops	Dec. 21, 1833	do	78	
William Cotten	Private	60 00	180 00	N. Carolina militia	Jan. 3, 1834	do	86	
Thomas Curry	do	80 00	240 00	Virg'a State troops	May 14, 1833	do	73	
James Deakins	do	20 00	-	do	June 5, 1834	do	81	
Henry Eads	do	80 00	240 00	Maryland militia	Feb. 7, 1834	do	80	
Henry Fordyce	do	80 00	240 00	New Jersey militia	Feb. 14, 1834	do	72	
James Fordyce	do	23 33	69 99	Virginia militia	Aug. 28, 1833	do	72	
Abraham Floyd	do	35 55	-	New Jersey militia	May 9, 1833	do	91	
Peter Griner	do	26 66	79 98	do	May 14, 1833	do	93	
James Guffy	Pri. & lieut.	136 66	-	Pennsylva'a militia	July 27, 1834	do	86	
William Logan, sen.	Private of cav. and inf.	25 88	77 54	S. Carolina militia	Dec. 11, 1833	do	68	
John Mann	Private	20 00	50 00	Mass. State troops	Aug. 26, 1833	do	82	
Joseph Reynolds	do	37 43	-	N. Carolina militia	June 15, 1834	do	73	
Richard Smith	Pri. of cav.	96 00	416 12	Virg'a State troops	Sep. 7, 1820	Oct. 14, 1818	-	March 18, 1818. Dropped under act May 1, 1820.
Do	do	100 00	300 00	do	Jan. 24, 1833	Mar. 4, 1831	72	
Lucas Slicer	Private	50 00	150 00	Pennsylva'a militia	Oct. 15, 1833	do	75	
William Sims, sen.	do	28 33	84 99	Virginia militia	Aug. 16, 1833	do	70	
James Trusler	do	20 00	60 00	do	Nov. 29, 1833	do	79	
Robert Templeton	do	23 88	71 54	N. C. State troops	Dec. 11, 1833	do	75	
John Vincent	Ser. and lt.	55 00	137 50	Virginia militia	July 10, 1833	do	78	
John Vanwinkle	Private	80 00	240 00	Virg'a State troops	Jan. 3, 1834	do	81	
William Wiggins	do	20 00	60 00	Pennsylva'a militia	Mar. 12, 1833	do	72	

7

Statement, &c. of Gibson county, Indiana.

NAMES.	Rank.	Annual allowance.	Sums received.	Description of service.	When placed on the pension roll.	Commencement of pension.	Ages.	Laws under which they were formerly inscribed on the pension roll; and remarks.
James Wheeler	Pri. of cav.	96 00	152 01	Virginia militia	Feb. 10, 1819	July 28, 1818	-	March 18, 1818. Dropped under act May 1, 1820.
Do	do	100 00	-	do	May 2, 1834	March 4, 1831	74	

Statement, &c. of Green county, Indiana.

NAMES.	Rank.	Annual allowance.	Sums received.	Description of service.	When placed on the pension roll.	Commencement of pension.	Ages.	Laws under which they were formerly inscribed on the pension roll; and remarks.
John Abbot	Private	40 00	-	Virginia militia	May 12, 1834	Mar. 4, 1831	84	
William G. Bryant	do	30 00	90 00	Virginia State tr'ps	July 12, 1834	do	84	
Abraham May	do	30 00	90 00	Virginia militia	Mar. 13, 1833	do	70	
Adam Rambolt	do	30 00	90 00	N. C. State troops	Jan. 25, 1834	do	76	
Daniel Solsby	do	80 00	200 00	Penn. militia	Oct. 21, 1834	do	79	

Statement, &c. of Hamilton county, Indiana.

NAMES.	Rank.	Annual allowance.	Sums received.	Description of service.	When placed on the pension roll.	Commencement of pension.	Ages.	Laws under which they were formerly inscribed on the pension roll; and remarks.
George Abney	Private	80 00	240 00	S. C. militia	Sep. 6, 1833	Mar. 4, 1831	83	
John Hair	do	24 44	61 10	Virginia militia	Aug. 27, 1833	do	77	
Samuel Torrens	do	20 00	60 00	do	Jan. 30, 1833	do	88	

Statement, &c. of Hancock county, Indiana.

NAMES.	Rank.	Annual allowance.	Sums received.	Description of service.	When placed on the pension roll.	Commencement of pension.	Ages.	Laws under which they were formerly inscribed on the pension roll; and remarks.
Robert Wilson	Private	31 33	93 99	Virginia militia	Oct. 26, 1833	Mar. 4, 1831	86	

Statement, &c. of Harrison county, Indiana.

NAMES.	Rank.	Annual allowance.	Sums received.	Description of service.	When placed on the pension roll.	Commencement of pension.	Ages.	Laws under which they were formerly inscribed on the pension roll; and remarks.
Garret Applegate	Private	40 00	120 00	Virginia State tr'ps	May 12, 1834	a r. 4, 1831	76	
Sherman, or Shermon Babcock	do	80 00	240 00	Conn. State troops	Oct. 26, 1833	do	81	
George Charles	do	80 00	193 00	Virginia cont'l line	Nov. 15, 1832	do	71	
John Cromer	do	33 33	83 32	Penn. militia	Ap'l 9, 1833	do	80	
James Case	do	35 64	106 92	do	do	do	69	
Alexander Gilmore	do	22 00	66 00	Virginia militia	Nov. 17, 1832	do	71	
Patrick Hunter	Ensign	170 00	510 00	Penn. militia	Mar. 16, 1833	do	69	
Henson Johnson	Private	20 00	60 00	Virginia militia	Nov. 15, 1832	do	70	
Mason Lunsford	do	80 00	240 00	Virginia State tr'ps	Nov. 12, 1833	do	70	
Joseph M'Clellan	do	40 00	120 00	Virginia militia	Mar. 9, 1833	do	69	
William Madden	do	20 00	60 00	do	June 22, 1833	do	73	
John Mannan	do	30 00	80 60	Virginia State tr'ps	June 29, 1833	do	81	
William Pell	do	40 00	120 00	Virginia militia	June 22, 1833	do	75	
Lewis Payton	do	23 33	69 99	do	Aug. 28, 1833	do	70	
Thomas Rencan	do	33 33	99 99	Penn. militia	Nov. 12, 1833	do	75	
Michael Sapplefield	Ser. & pri.	50 00	150 00	Virginia cont'l line	Mar. 16, 1832	do	71	
William Sampson	Private	26 66	53 32	Virginia militia	Ap'l 9, 1833	do	75	
David Sipes	do	33 33	-	Maryland militia	do	do	74	
Philip Stine	Drummer	44 00	132 00	Penn. militia	Aug. 26, 1833	do	67	
Stewart Sterret	Private	20 00	60 00	N. Carolina militia	Mar. 14, 1834	do	74	
Philip Shuck	do	20 00	-	Penn. militia	July 10, 1834	do	76	Died February 14, 1834.
An'hony D. Trout	do	20 00	240 00	N. Carolina militia	Aug. 27, 1833	do	67	
Isaac Williams	Pri. & ser.	113 70	190 12	Virginia militia	Nov. 12, 1832	do	81	

Statement, &c. of Hendricks county, Indiana.

NAMES.	Rank.	Annual allowance.	Sums received.	Description of service.	When placed on the pension roll.	Commencement of pension.	Ages.	Laws under which they were formerly inscribed on the pension roll; and remarks.
John Boyd	Private	30 00	75 00	Virginia State tr'ps	Jan. 3, 1834	Mar. 4, 1831	74	
David Erwin	Pri. of cav. and inf.	32 50	97 50	N. Carolina militia	May 1, 1834	do	76	
Edward Flathers	Private	20 00	50 00	Mass. cont'l line	Aug. 28, 1833	do	74	
William Florence	do	80 00	240 00	Virginia militia	Sep. 26, 1833	do	84	
Daniel Higgans	do	80 00	240 00	N. Carolina militia	Aug. 27, 1833	do	69	
Isaac Lawrence	do	37 10	92 75	S. C. State troops	Dec. 14, 1833	do	71	
William Ramsay	Pri. & ser.	29 44	73 60	N. C. State troops	Aug. 24, 1833	do	86	
William Wiley	Private	33 00	99 00	N. Carolina militia	June 29, 1833	do	77	

Statement, &c. of Henry county, Indiana.

NAMES.	Rank.	Annual allowance.	Sums received.	Description of service.	When placed on the pension roll.	Commencement of pension.	Ages.	Laws under which they were formerly inscribed on the pension roll; and remarks.
Richard Conway	Private	40 00	80 00	Virginia militia	Aug. 28, 1833	Mar. 4, 1831	72	
Thomas Hilman	do	75 55	226 65	N. J, State troops	Oct. 2, 1833	do	74	
Ebenezer Harper	do	20 00	—	Penn. State troops	Ap'l 9, 1834	do	96	
Andrew Ice	do	20 00	16 00	Virginia militia	Jan. 21, 1834	do	75	
John Lee, alias See	do	80 00		do	Mar. 13, 1833	do	73	
John M'Donald	do	30 00		Virginia State tr'ps	Nov. 12, 1833	do	68	
Joel Simmonds	do	33 33	99 99	Virginia militia	Aug. 26, 1833	do	76	
Jacob Winner	do	33 33	83 32	N. Jersey militia	Aug. 28, 1833	do	75	
William Wilson	Seaman	96 00	240 00	Continental navy	Oct. 21, 1833	do	78	

Statement, &c. of Jackson county, Indiana.

NAMES.	Rank.	Annual allowance.	Sums received.	Description of service.	When placed on the pension roll.	Commencement of pension.	Ages.	Laws under which they were formerly inscribed on the pension roll; and remarks,
Henry Boas	Private	20 00	60 00	Penn. State troops	Jan. 29, 1833	Mar. 4, 1831	74	
Christian Braneman	do	40 00	80 00	do	do	do	76	
David Benton	do	31 12	77 80	Mass. State troops	July 15, 1833	do	75	
William Chambers	do	30 00	90 00	N. Carolina militia	Feb. 4, 1833	do	70	
John Fisler	do	40 00	-	New Jersey militia	Dec. 14, 1833	do	67	
David Johnson	do	80 00	240 00	Virginia militia	Jan. 6, 1834	do	62	Died June, 1834,
Thomas Prather	do	80 00	240 00	N. Carolina militia	Aug. 27, 1833	do	81	
Leonard Shewmaker	do	80 00	240 00	Virginia St. troops	Ap'l 10, 1833	do	79	
Benjamin Scott	do	26 66	66 65	Virginia militia	Sept. 18, 1833	do	71	
James Sparks	do	40 00	-	Penn. State troops	Dec. 14, 1833	do	89	

Statement, &c. of Jefferson county, Indiana.

NAMES.	Rank.	Annual allowance.	Sums received.	Description of service.	When placed on the pension roll.	Commencement of pension.	Ages.	Laws under which they were formerly inscribed on the pension roll; and remarks.
Patrick Brown	Private	54 16	135 40	Virginia militia	July 15, 1833	Mar. 4, 1831	74	
George Burk	do	80 00	240 00	do	Oct. 10, 1833	do	75	
Jacob Chysman	do	20 00	-	Virginia St. troops	Ap'l 3, 1834	do	74	
John Conner	do	70 00	210 00	N. Carolina militia	Ap'l 11, 1834	do	79	
Ralph Griffin	do	43 33	-	S. Carolina militia	July 11, 1833	do	80	
David Jones	do	80 00	240 00	Virginia militia	July 9, 1833	do	74	
John Lott	Sergeant	42 00	126 00	do	Mar. 13, 1833	do	80	
Nicholas Lowber	Private	25 00	75 00	S. Carolina St. tr'ps	Oct. 18, 1833	do	74	
Jacob Mikesell	do	20 00	60 00	Virginia cont'l line	Dec. 3, 1832	do	71	
William McCausland	do	20 00	60 00	Penn. cont'l line	Feb. 26, 1833	do	76	
Joseph McCuen	do	30 00	75 00	Pennsylvania militia	May 29, 1833	do	75	
Robert McKay	do	30 00	90 00	Virginia militia	Sep. 9, 1833	do	81	
James McClelland	do	24 44	73 32	N. Carolina St. tr'ps	Mar. 17, 1833	do	77	
Robert Rea	do	79 66	238 98	do	Dec. 21, 1833	do	67	
Charles Stewart	do	80 00	240 00	Penn. cont'l line	Nov. 19, 1832	do	73	
William Tilford	do	20 00	60 00	Virginia St. troops	June 29, 1833	do	83	
Robert True	do	80 00	-	Virginia militia	July 15, 1833	do	76	
Joseph Tyler	do	36 66	109 98	Virginia cont'l line	Nov. 10, 1832	do	87	
William Wilson	do	20 00	60 00	Penn. State troops	Dec. 8, 1832	do	74	
John West	do	80 00	-	Virginia militia	June 29, 1833	do	75	Died August 14, 1833.

Statement, &c. of Jennings county, Indiana.

NAMES.	Rank.	Annual allowance.	Sums received.	Description of service.	When placed on the pension roll.	Commencement of pension.	Ages.	Laws under which they were formerly inscribed on the pension roll; and remarks.
John Carney	Private	40 00	120 00	Virginia militia	Feb. 4, 1833	Mar. 4, 1831	68	
Walter Carson	Pri. & capt.	123 33	-	Penn. State troops	Oct. 11, 1833	do	77	
William Elliott	Ensign	150 00	450 00	Virginia militia	June 29, 1833	do	81	
William Howlett	Private	76 66	229 98	Vt. State troops	Nov. 23, 1832	do	74	
Heth Kendrick	do	21 66	74 98	do	do	do	70	
Robert Magill	do	30 00	90 00	New Jersey militia	Aug. 27, 1833	do	74	
Harraway Owen	do	21 66	-	Virginia cont'l line	May 29, 1833	do	72	
John Stagg	do	80 00	240 00	N. Jersey St. troops	Nov. 23, 1832	do	74	
Amasa Spencer	do	31 88	95 54	Virginia militia	Mar. 15, 1833	do	72	
Samuel Smith	do	60 00	180 00	N. Y. State troops	Dec. 21, 1833	do	75	
Evan Thomas	do	80 00	240 00	Virginia militia	Mar. 15, 1833	do	78	

Statement, &c. of Johnson county, Indiana.

NAMES.	Rank.	Annual allowance.	Sums received.	Description of service.	When placed on the pension roll.	Commencement of pension.	Ages.	Laws under which they were formerly inscribed on the pension roll; and remarks.
James Carr	Private	30 29	75 72	Virginia militia	Nov. 29, 1833	Mar. 4, 1831	77	
Isaac Davidson	do	65 00	195 00	do	Ap'l 9, 1833	do	75	
Abner Hanks	do	20 00	60 00	Maryland militia	Ap'l 7, 1834	do	75	
John Israel	do	30 00	90 00	N. H. State troops	Aug. 27, 1833	do	69	
Matthias Parr	do	73 33	219 99	New Jersey militia	Aug. 28, 1833	do	77	
John Steel	do	20 00	50 00	Pennsylvania militia	Aug. 26, 1833	do	69	
Thomas Smith	do	30 00	-	N. C. cont'l line	Feb. 7, 1834	do	71	

Statement, &c. of Knox county, Indiana.

NAMES.	Rank.	Annual allowance.	Sums received.	Description of service.	When placed on the pension roll.	Commencement of pension.	Ages.	Laws under which they were formerly inscribed on the pension roll; and remarks.
James Anderson	Private	20 00	60 00	Virginia St. troops	Oct. 26, 1833	Mar. 4, 1831	75	
Thomas Baird	do	40 00	-	Pennsylvania militia	July 15, 1833	do	74	
Philip Catt	do	40 00	80 00	do	Nov. 12, 1832	do	84	
Frederick Claycomb	do	20 00	40 00	Virginia militia	Dec. 12, 1833	do	76	
Alexander Chambers	do	40 00	100 00	do	Sep. 26, 1833	do	70	
William Lindsay	do	80 00	240 00	Pennsylvania militia	Aug. 26, 1833	do	80	
Daniel Langdon	do	23 33	56 32	Conn. State troops	Dec. 9, 1833	do	75	
William McCord	do	30 00	90 00	Virginia militia	Nov. 12, 1832	do	72	
Robert McCoy	do	20 00	-	do	Jan. 10, 1833	do	78	
Peter McAnelly	do	30 00	90 00	do	June 15, 1833	do	71	
Cornelius Merry	do	40 00	100 00	Connecticut militia	do	do	77	
Frederick Mahl	do	40 00	120 00	N. J. cont'l line	Jan. 31, 1833	do	75	
Howard Putman	Pri. of art.	100 00	-	Virginia militia	Mar. 21, 1833	do	71	
Edward Purcell	Private	43 33	129 99	do	Oct. 10, 1832	do	73	
William Purcell	do	20 00	60 00	do	do	do	79	
William Sulcer	do	80 00	240 00	Virginia State tr.	Dec. 9, 1833	do	74	
John Thompson	do	41 10	123 30	Pennsylvania militia	July 15, 1833	do	85	
Michael Thorn	do	20 00	60 00	Pennsylvania militia	Nov. 12, 1832	do	72	
Jaret Young	do	20 00	60 00	N. C. militia	Dec. 12, 1833	do	72	

Statement, &c. of Lawrence county, Indiana.

NAMES.	Rank.	Annual allowance.	Sums received.	Description of service.	When placed on the pension roll.	Commencement of pension.	Ages.	Laws under which they were formerly inscribed on the pension roll; and remarks.
James Blevins -	Private	20 00	60 00	Virginia militia	Feb. 14, 1834	Mar. 4, 1831	84	
Ambrose Carlton	Ser. & pri.	104 33	-	N. C. militia	Oct. 29, 1833	do	71	
John Henderson	Private	30 00	90 00	Virginia militia	Ap'l 6, 1833	do	69	
Robert Hall -	do	30 00	90 00	do	May 29, 1833	do	81	
John Hamersly -	Pri. & corp.	87 66	-	Pennsylvania militia	do	do	75	
Abraham Michell	Private	26 66	79 98	N. C. State troops	Dec. 21, 1833	do	75	
Richard Ryan -	do	80 00	240 00	S. C. State troops	Jan. 31, 1834	do	79	
John Short -	do	36 00	108 00	Virginia militia	Ap'l 29, 1833	do	78	
John Thomas -	do	30 00	-	do	Jan. 7, 1834	do	80	
Aaron Watts -	Pri. of art.	100 00	-	Va. State troops	May 6, 1833	do	75	Transferred from Campbell county, Kentucky, Mar. 4, 1834.
James Wilson -	Private	25 66	63 90	do	May 29, 1833	do	63	

Statement, &c. of Madison county, Indiana.

NAMES.	Rank.	Annual allowance.	Sums received.	Description of service.	When placed on the pension roll.	Commencement of pension.	Ages.	Laws under which they were formerly inscribed on the pension roll; and remarks.
Aaron Dunn -	Private	23 33	56 32	N. Jersey militia	Oct. 15, 1833	Mar. 4, 1831	81	
John Keesling -	do	26 66	-	Pennsylvania militia	July 11, 1833	do	82	
John Scott -	do	47 00	141 00	Penn. State troops	Aug. 26, 1833	do	83	
William Wall -	do	80 00	200 00	Virginia militia	Ap'l 9, 1833	do	75	

Statement, &c. of Marion county, Indiana.

NAMES.	Rank.	Annual allowance	Sums received.	Description of service.	When placed on the roll.	Commencement of pension.	Ages.	Laws under which they were formerly inscribed on the pension roll; and remarks.
Robert Carr	Private	23 33	—	Virginia militia	Jan. 30, 1833	Mar. 4, 1831	75	Died July 4, 1833.
John Faucett	do	45 56	136 68	do	Oct. 26, 1833	do	74	
Edmund Hall	do	80 00	240 00	Va. State troops	Dec. 13, 1832	do	65	
Henry Harding, jr.	do	80 00	240 00	Virginia militia	Jan. 30, 1833	do	70	
Jeremiah Harrold	do	80 00	240 00	N. C. cont'l line	Feb. 27, 1833	do	74	
Ede Harding	do	33 33	99 99	Virginia militia	Dec. 21, 1833	do	77	
John Hume	do	24 66	73 98	N. Jersey St. troops	Ap'l 14, 1834	do	76	
Alexander Monroe	Sergeant	96 00	171 12	Virginia militia	Jan. 6, 1819	do	-	March 18, 1818. Dropped under act May 1, 1820.
Do	do	120 00	360 00	do	Aug. 26, 1833	do	79	
Harold Newland	Private	80 00	240 00	Penn. militia	July 11, 1833	do	69	
Jonathan Ray	do	20 00	60 00	Maryland militia	Ap'l 17, 1833	do	76	
Thomas Ragin	Pri. & cap.	180 00	540 00	Penn. militia	Dec. 2, 1833	do	70	
Jason Thurston	Private	44 44	133 32	N. York cont'l line	Jan. 1, 1834	do	73	
Obadiah Turpin	do	20 00	60 00	Penn. militia	Ap'l 7, 1834	do	74	
Robert White	do	80 00	240 00	Va. State troops	Mar. 5, 1834	do	76	

Statement, &c. of Martin county, Indiana.

NAMES.	Rank.	Annual allowance.	Sums received.	Description of service.	When placed on the pension roll.	Commencement of pension.	Ages.	Laws under which they were formerly inscribed on the pension roll; and remarks.
Josiah Hunt	Private	30 90	-	Penn. militia	June 22, 1833	Mar. 4, 1831	72	

Statement, &c. of Montgomery county, Indiana.

NAMES.	Rank.	Annual allowance.	Sums received.	Description of service.	When placed on the pension roll.	Commencement of pension.	Ages.	Laws under which they were formerly inscribed on the pension roll; and remarks.
Andrew Bower -	Fifer & pri.	31 00	83 00	Virginia militia	May 31, 1833	Mar. 4, 1831	75	
Alexander Foster -	Private	36 66	109 98	Penn. State troops	Nov. 12, 1833	do	74	
Presley Symmes -	do	80 00	240 00	Va. State troops	do	do	81	
Sebastian Stonebraker -	do	20 00	60 00	Penn. State troops	Nov. 29, 1833	do	76	
Jacob Westfall -	do	80 00	240 00	Virginia militia	Oct. 29, 1833	do	80	

Statement, &c. of Monroe county, Indiana.

NAMES.	Rank.	Annual allowance.	Sums received.	Description of service.	When placed on the pension roll.	Commencement of pension.	Ages.	Laws under which they were formerly inscribed on the pension roll; and remarks.
Alexander Armstrong	Private	41 66	-	Va. State troops	Ap'l 7, 1834	Mar. 4, 1831	75	
James Bryant -	do	30 00	90 00	do	do	do	68	
Aaron Buskirk -	do	80 00	240 00	do	June 11, 1834	do	80	
David Ephland -	do	80 00	240 00	do	Jan. 3, 1834	do	68	
Philip Greenwood -	do	26 66	79 98	Maryland militia	Ap'l 11, 1834	do	79	
Joseph Lawrence -	do	40 00	120 00	Virginia cont'l line	Ap'l 7, 1833	do	79	
William Moore, 2d -	do	36 66	109 98	N. Carolina militia	May 16, 1833	do	87	
Thomas Pearce -	do	30 00	90 00	Va. cont'l line	Ap'l 7, 1833	do	84	
Isaac Vanbuskirk -	do	40 00	-	Virginia militia	Aug. 27, 1833	do	80	

Statement, &c. of Morgan county, Indiana.

NAMES.	Rank.	Annual allowance.	Sums received.	Description of service.	When placed on the pension roll.	Commencement of pension.	Ages.	Laws under which they were formerly inscribed on the pension roll; and remarks.
George Baker	Private	47 77	119 42	N. C. cont'l line	July 28, 1833	Mar. 4, 1831	75	
Joseph Culton	do	23 33		Virginia militia	June 26, 1833	do	70	
William Jones	do	20 00	50 00	Virginia cont'l line	Aug. 26, 1833	do	74	
Cornelius King	Pri. & ser.	28 33		Virginia militia	do	do	82	
Alexander Kelso	Private	20 00		S. Carolina militia	do	do	77	
Devault Keller	do	20 00	240 00	do	May 29, 1834	do	87	
Mordecai Miller	do	80 00	150 00	do	Aug. 28, 1833	do	75	
William Townsend	do	50 00		N. Carolina militia	Aug. 26, 1833	do	82	
Sampson Tramel	do	43 33		S. Carolina militia	Jan. 30, 1833	do	75	
Benjamin Utterback	do	80 00	200 00	Virginia cont'l line	July 15, 1833	do	79	Transferred from Kentucky March 4, 1834.

Statement, &c. of Orange county, Indiana.

NAMES.	Rank.	Annual allowance.	Sums received.	Description of service.	When placed on the pension roll.	Commencement of pension.	Ages.	Laws under which they were formerly inscribed on the pension roll; and remarks.
Henry Brooks	Private	20 00	50 00	Virginia militia	May 29, 1833	Mar. 4, 1831	80	
George Duncan	do	23 33	70 00	do	Oct. 26, 1833	do	77	
William Irvine	Ser. & pri.	45 00	135 00	do	do	do	75	
William Moore, 1st	Private	20 00		N. Carolina militia	Mar. 13, 1833	do	80	
J.. .a Reed	do	30 00		N. Carolina St. tr'ps	Dec. 30, 1833	do	79	
Pe..r Urton	do	23 33	69 99	Virginia militia	May 29, 1833	do	70	

Statement, &c. of Owen county, Indiana.

NAMES.	Rank.	Annual allowance.	Sums received.	Description of service.	When placed on the pension roll.	Commencement of pension.	Ages.	Laws under which they were formerly inscribed on the pension roll; and remarks.
Bartlett Asher	Private	80 00	200 00	Kentucky militia	May 16, 1833	Mar. 4, 1831	70	
Thomas Ashbrook	do	50 00	150 00	Virginia militia	Mar. 8, 1834	do	78	
Andrew Evans	do	24 44	73 32	Va. State troops	Oct. 18, 1833	do	75	
Edward F. Fortner	do	20 00	60 00	N. Carolina St. tr'ps	May 9, 1833	do	81	
Elijah Lacy	do	33 33	99 99	Virginia militia	Oct. 18, 1833	do	69	
Adam Moderell	do	34 88	-	do	Ap'l 7, 1833	do	79	
Jacob Night	do	21 88	65 54	Pennsylvania militia	Mar. 4, 1833	do	74	
John Snoddy	do	80 00	200 00	N. Carolina St. tr'ps	Aug. 26, 1833	do	75	
Peter Witham	do	30 00	-	Virginia militia	July 10, 1834	do	74	

Statement, &c. of Parke county, Indiana.

NAMES.	Rank.	Annual allowance.	Sums received.	Description of service.	When placed on the pension roll.	Commencement of pension.	Ages.	Laws under which they were formerly inscribed on the pension roll; and remarks.
David Evins	Private	27 54	82 62	Virginia militia	Oct. 18, 1833	Mar. 4, 1831	77	
Jacob Hines	do	20 00	60 00	Maryland cont'l line	May 17, 1833	do	82	
Samuel Haslet	do	23 33	79 99	N. Carolina St. tr'ps	Mar. 14, 1834	do	72	
David Johnson	do	30 56	91 68	Virginia militia	May 13, 1833	do	71	
Larkin Lane	do	20 77	62 21	do	July 11, 1833	do	75	
William Mitchell	do	21 00	42 00	do	Mar. 26, 1833	do	72	
John Montgomery	do	80 00	240 00	do	Aug. 26, 1833	do	68	
Samuel Musgrace	do	40 00	120 00	do	Oct. 18, 1833	do	69	
William Oard	do	20 00	-	Maryland militia	July 11, 1833	do	74	
John Tucker	do	26 33	78 99	R. Island St. troops	Aug. 26, 1833	do	74	
John Vanzant	do	40 50	120 50	New York militia	Ap'l 26, 1833	do	71	
George Wilkins	do	40 00	120 00	N. Carolina militia	Dec. 21, 1833	do	69	

Statement, &c. of Perry county, Indiana.

NAMES.	Rank.	Annual allowance.	Sums received.	Description of service.	When placed on the pension roll.	Commencement of pension.	Ages.	Laws under which they were formerly inscribed on the pension roll ; and remarks.
Thomas Bolin	Private	60 00	180 00	N. Carolina militia	Oct. 15, 1833	Mar. 4, 1831	67	
Abraham Hiley	do	80 00	240 00	Penn. militia	Mar. 14, 1834	do	78	
Samuel Mallory	do	38 77	-	Conn. State troops	Oct. 18, 1833	do	85	
Joseph McReynolds	do	42 50	-	Virginia militia	Aug. 5, 1834	do	68	
Jeremiah York	do	80 00	220 00	Penn. militia	Aug. 27, 1833	do	70	

Statement, &c. of Pike county, Indiana.

NAMES.	Rank.	Annual allowance.	Sums received.	Description of service.	When placed on the pension roll.	Commencement of pension.	Ages.	Laws under which they were formerly inscribed on the pension roll; and remarks.
James Brenton	Private	23 33	58 32	Virginia militia	July 28, 1833	Mar. 4, 1831	70	
William Black	do	80 00	240 00	N. C. do	Jan. 3, 1834	do	77	
John Conrod	do	30 00	75 00	Penn. do	May 14, 1833	do	82	
John McManus	do	20 00	40 00	Virginia do	Mar. 13 1833	do	74	
Thomas Mead	do	80 00	240 00	do	Dec. 21, 1833	do	81	
John Palmer	do	20 00	60 00	S. C. militia	May 14, 1833	do	69	

Statement, &c. of Posey county, Indiana.

NAMES.	Rank.	Annual allowance.	Sums received.	Description of service.	When placed on the pension roll.	Commencement of pension.	Ages.	Laws under which they were formerly inscribed on the pension roll; and remarks.
David Gamble	Private	35 00	105 00	Virginia militia	Oct. 26, 1833	Mar. 4, 1831	82	

Statement, &c. of Putnam county, Indiana.

NAMES.	Rank.	Annual allowance.	Sums received.	Description of service.	When placed on the pension roll.	Commencement of pension.	Ages.	Laws under which they were formerly inscribed on the pension roll; and remarks.
William Banks	Private	30 00	90 00	Virgina militia	Oct. 29, 1833	Mar. 4, 1831	74	Transferred from East Tennessee, September 4, 1833.
Charles Bowen	do	80 00	240 00	do	Dec. 15, 1832	do	84	
John Buck, 2d	do	30 00	-	Penn. militia	July 23, 1834	do	80	
George Hammer	do	30 00	90 00	Maryland St. troops	Oct. 29, 1833	do	70	
Samuel Moore	do	23 33	79 99	Virginia militia	Feb. 22, 1833	do	73	
Benjamin Mahorney	do	60 00	180 00	Virginia St. troops	Oct. 12, 1833	do	75	
Andrew McPhester	do	48 33	-	Virginia militia	June 17, 1833	do	70	Transferred from East Tennessee, March 4, 1834.
John Norman	do	20 00	50 00	Delaware St. troops	Oct. 18, 1833	do	75	
Josiah Stephens	do	35 66	89 15	Virginia militia	Apl 29, 1833	do	72	
Thomas Tucker	do	43 33	129 99	N C. militia	May 29, 1833	do	82	
Robert Whitehead	do	80 00	200 00	do	July 11. 1833	do	81	
John Walls	Drummer	66 66	199 98	do	Aug. 26, 1833	do	82	
John Walden	Private	80 00	240 00	Virginia militia	Oct. 29, 1833	do	76	
Matthias Young	do	26 66	-	do	June 17, 1834	do	69	

Statement, &c. of Ripley county, Indiana.

NAMES.	Rank.	Annual allowance.	Sums received.	Description of service.	When placed on the pension roll.	Commencement of pension.	Ages.	Laws under which they were formerly inscribed on the pension roll; and remarks.
Robert Burchfield	Private	60 00	1830 00	N. Carolina militia	April 9, 1833	March 4, 1831	81	
Daniel Bumgardiner	do	30 00	—	N.C. State troops	Jan. 15, 1834	do	76	
William Bassett	Pri. of cav.	100 00	300 00	Penn. State troops	Feb. 4, 1834	do	81	
John Buskirk	Private	23 33	—	Virginia militia	July 16, 1834	do	69	
William Collins	do	20 22	—	Penn. militia	July 12, 1834	do	83	
Conrad Dowers	do	30 00	90 00	do	July 15, 1833	do	70	
James Delap	do	30 00	90 00	N. Jersey cont'l line	Nov. 29, 1833	do	80	
Philamore Davis	do	63 33	199 99	Md. State troops	March 6, 1834	do	77	
James Grimes	do	80 00	—	Virginia militia	Mar. 25, 1833	do	80	Died November 11, 1833.
Benjamin Hamilton	do	36 00	108 00	Penn. militia	June 29, 1833	do	75	
Benjamin Hall	do	80 00	—	R. I. State troops	Oct. 18, 1833	do	69	
William Lippard	do	80 00	200 00	Virginia militia	June 29, 1833	do	68	
Daniel McMillen	Pri. & ser.	86 66	259 98	Md. militia	June 15, 1833	do	75	
Joseph McDonald	Private	25 33	75 99	Va. State troops	Oct. 1, 1833	do	82	
Jacob Micheller	do	60 00	—	N. C. State troops	Feb. 7, 1833	do	71	
Henry Myers	do	80 00	184 98	Penn. cont'l line	July 12, 1834	do	87	
Peter Newcomer	do	61 66	76 30	Va. State troops	Oct. 29, 1833	do	77	
John O'Neal	do	46 66	120 00	do	Oct. 18, 1833	do	74	
Edward Pendegrast	do	40 00	240 00	Virginia militia	June 29, 1833	do	70	Died November 7, 1832.
John Parr	do	80 00	139 98	Penn. cont'l line	Aug. 26, 1833	do	69	
Ephraim Robbins	do	46 66	90 00	Conn. militia	April 9, 1833	do	75	
Samuel Stephens	do	30 00	69 99	Va. State troops	Oct. 1, 1833	do	69	
Henry Thomas	do	23 33	240 00	Penn. militia	Dec. 21, 1833	do	65	
Peter Vanbibber	do	80 00	66 65	Va. State troops	Jan. 8, 1834	do	78	
John Ward	do	26 66	120 00	N. C. militia	Nov. 20, 1832	do	74	
Isaac Way	do	40 00	70 99	Va. cont'l line	June 29, 1833	do	85	
Ephraim Wilson	do	23 33	240 00	Penn. militia	Oct. 3, 1833	do	75	
Isaac Wycoff	do	80 00	—	N. J. State troops	Feb. 4, 1834	do	76	

9

Statement, &c. of Rush county, Indiana.

NAMES.	Rank.	Annual allowance.	Sums received.	Description of service.	When placed on the pension roll.	Commencement of pension.	Ages.	Laws under which they were formerly inscribed on the pension roll, and remarks.
John Carson	Private	33 33	99 99	Virginia militia	Jan. 21, 1834	March 4, 1831	74	
Samuel Caswell	do	40 00	120 00	Mass. militia	June 22, 1833	do	75	
Isaac Cox	do	23 33	69 99	Md. cont'l line	Jan. 22, 1834	do	79	
Henry David	do	30 00	50 00	Virginia militia	Ap'l 13, 1833	do	74	
Jesse Duncan	do	36 66	109 98	N. Carolina militia	Aug. 28, 1833	do	80	
Leonard Edleman	do	30 00	90 00	Md. militia	Nov. 12, 1833	do	68	
John Finney	do	30 00	90 00	Penn. militia	Feb. 27, 1833	do	82	
John Hardy	do	80 00	240 00	Virginia militia	Feb. 26, 1833	do	73	
Jacob Hite	do	26 66	79 98	Va. State troops	July 15, 1833	do	68	
Thomas James	do	20 00	60 00	Md. militia	May 22, 1833	do	70	
John Lewis	Pri. ser. & musician	30 33	90 99	S. C. State troops	June 22, 1833	do	71	
William Mauzy	Private	20 00	60 00	Va. State militia	Feb. 18, 1833	do	81	
Henry Mezner	do	50 00	150 00	Penn. militia	June 15, 1833	do	82	
John Pollock	do	20 00	60 00	Virginia militia	Feb. 28, 1833	do	69	
John Watson, 1st	do	20 00	-	N. Carolina militia	Oct. 30, 1832	do	80	Transferred from Kentucky, Mar. 4, 1833.

Statement, &c. of Scott county, Indiana.

NAMES.	Rank.	Annual allow-ance.	Sums re-ceived.	Description of service.	When placed on the pen-sion roll.	Commencement of pension.	Ages.	Laws under which they were for-merly inscribed on the pension roll; and remarks.
John Burnside	Private	24 33	60 82	N. Carolina militia	July 15, 1833	March 4, 1831	81	
John Clark	do	80 00	240 00	Penn. militia	Aug. 28, 1833	do	75	
John Dean	do	20 00	60 00	Md. cont'l line	Feb. 6, 1833	do	74	
William Galbreath	Pri. & ser.	82 33	-	Penn. militia	May 29, 1833	do	77	Transferred from East Tennessee, March 4, 1831.
William Harrod	Private	20 00	50 00	do	June 29, 1833	do	82	
Solomon Jackson	do	60 00	180 00	N. Carolina militia	May 29, 1833	do	82	
Jacob Killion	do	40 00	120 00	do	April 29, 1833	do	70	
Hugh Parks	do	96 00	144 52	N. C. Cont'l line	Dec. 1, 1833	Aug. 28, 1818	-	March 18, 1818. Dropped under act May 1, 1820.
Do.	do	80 00	200 00	do	Dec. 6, 1833	Mar. 4, 1831	87	
Walter Spencer	do	80 00	240 00	Conn. militia	June 29, 1833	do	74	
Daniel Stringham	do	20 00	60 00	N. Y. State troops	Oct. 29, 1833	do	71	
Bergen Spader	do	23 33	69 99	New Jersey militia	Mar. 20, 1834	do	73	

Statement, &c. of Shelby county, Indiana.

NAMES.	Rank.	Annual allowance.	Sums received.	Description of service.	When placed on the pension roll.	Commencement of pension.	Ages.	Laws under which they were formerly inscribed on the pension roll; and remarks.
Lewis Barlow	Private	80 00	240 00	Virginia militia	April 9, 1833	Mar. 4, 1831	79	
Mathew Brown	do	30 00	75 00	S. Carolina militia	Oct. 12, 1833	do	81	
Allen Christian	do	20 00	60 00	Virginia militia	Nov. 29, 1833	do	75	
Mason Field	do	30 00	90 00	N. C. State troops	May 27, 1833	do	74	
Robert Gordon	do	23 33	-	Va. State troops	May 29, 1833	do	75	
John Gorsage	do	23 33	-	Virginia militia	May 13, 1833	do	70	
William Glidwill, 2d	do	44 33	-	Va. State troops	Oct. 29, 1833	do	81	
Nathaniel Goodrick, or Gootrick	do	53 33	-	Conn. militia	July 23, 1834	do	76	
Garret Harsin	Pri. & ser.	92 00	286 00	N. Y. State troops	July 15, 1833	do	69	
Edward Miller	Private	80 00	200 00	Virginia militia	Mar. 9, 1833	do	81	
Samuel Pope	do	40 00	120 00	New York militia	Mar. 5, 1833	do	74	

Statement, &c. of Spencer county, Indiana.

NAMES.	Rank.	Annual allowance.	Sums received.	Description of service.	When placed on the roll.	Commencement of pension.	Ages.	Laws under which they were formerly inscribed on the pension roll; and remarks.
Lodowick Davis	Private	80 00	240 00	Md. State troops	Nov. 29, 1833	Mar. 4, 1831	75	
James Pollard	do	80 00	200 00	Va. State troops	Oct. 1, 1833	do	73	

Statement, &c. of Sullivan county, Indiana.

NAMES.	Rank.	Annual allowance.	Sums received.	Description of service.	When placed on the pension roll.	Commencement of pension.	Ages.	Laws under which they were formerly inscribed on the pension roll; and remarks.
Alexander Armstrong	Pri. & ser.	23 33	46 66	Penn. militia.	Dec. 13, 1832	Mar. 4, 1831	78	
Levi Bemis	Private	30 00	75 00	Vt. State troops	Nov. 29, 1833	do	76	
Alexander Bailey	do	28 65	75 95	N. C. State troops	Jan. 8, 1834	do	83	
William Dougherty	do	30 00	90 00	N. C. militia	July 11, 1833	do	82	
Robert Beedwell	do	31 66	79 15	do	May 29, 1833	do	73	
Hardy Hanly	do	40 00	120 00	Md. continental line	July 11, 1833	do	75	
Abraham Johnson	Captain	140 00	420 00	Virginia militia	July 15, 1833	do	79	Died in 1834.
Matthew M'Cemmon	Private	53 33	159 99	S. Carolina militia	Mar. 21, 1833	do	70	
Joseph Neely	do	30 00	-	N. Carolina militia	Ap'l 18, 1833	do	76	
James Williams	do	40 00	120 00	N. Y. State troops	Ap'l 21, 1834	do	85	

Statement, &c. of Switzerland county, Indiana.

NAMES.	Rank.	Annual allowance.	Sums received.	Description of service.	When placed on the pension roll.	Commencement of pension.	Ages.	Laws under which they were formerly inscribed on the pension roll; and remarks.
Thomas Ayers	Private	80 00	240 00	New Jersey militia	July 31, 1833	Mar. 4, 1831	82	
William Coy	do	33 33	78 32	Maryland militia	Mar. 5, 1834	do	71	Died July 10, 1833.
William Dewit	do	30 00	75 00	Pennsylvania mil.	Ap'l 13, 1833	do	78	
William Davis	do	40 00	—	Virginia militia	Dec. 28, 1833	do	70	From Kentucky March 4, 1834.
Robert Gullion	do	20 00	60 00	Pennsylvania mil.	July 15, 1833	do	73	
Ebenezer Humphreys	Pri. & ser.	50 00	150 00	Connecticut St. tr.	Ap'l 26, 1833	do	71	
Daniel Heath	Private	95 00	237 50	New York militia	July 31, 1833	do	74	
Henry Harris	do	80 00	240 00	New York St. tr.	Oct. 18, 1833	do	81	
Robert Knox	do	30 00	86 53	S. Carolina militia	Dec. 25, 1832	do	81	
William Kelley	do	21 50	64 50	Virginia militia	July 31, 1833	do	75	
Thomas Lewis	do	80 00	240 00	do	Nov. 21, 1832	do	70	
Isaac Levi	do	30 00	60 00	do	Aug. 26, 1833	do	75	
William Lancaster	do	22 22	66 66	do	Mar. 13, 1833	do	87	
Norman B. Magruder	do	40 00	120 00	Pennsylvania St. tr.	Nov. 21, 1832	do	79	
Thomas Mounts	do	26 66	79 99	Connecticut militia	Mar. 26, 1833	do	74	
Roderick Moore	do	20 00	50 00	Virginia militia	June 31, 1833	do	82	
Nathan Morgan	do	30 00	90 00	do	do	do	74	
Thomas Porter	do	30 00	—	Connecticut militia	Ap'l 26, 1833	do	72	
Winthrop Robinson	Pr. dr. & ser	79 67	293 01	New Hamp. militia	July 31, 1833	do	69	
Nathan Ricketts	Private	37 22	111 66	Virginia State tr.	Oct. 3, 1833	do	81	
John Roberts	Ser. & lieut.	160 00	—	New Jersey St. tr.	Nov. 24, 1832	do	81	
John Shupe	Private	26 60	79 80	Pennsylvania mil.	Nov. 21, 1832	do	70	
John Shaddy	Pri. of inf & cav'y	50 83	152 59	N. Carolina mil.	July 31, 1833	do	82	

Statement, &c. of Tippecanoe county, Indiana.

NAMES.	Rank.	Annual allowance.	Sums received.	Description of service.	When placed on the pension roll.	Commencement of pension.	Ages.	Laws under which they were formerly inscribed on the pension roll; and remarks.
John Blue	Private	35 10	105 30	Pennsylvania mil.	Ap'l 9, 1833	Mar. 4, 1831	70	
Philip Crose	do	32 50	–	N. Carolina militia	May 23, 1834	do	81	
Jacob Dower	do	20 00	50 00	Virginia militia	Ap'l 29, 1833	do	74	
Henry Miller	do	56 66	141 65	Virginia State tr.	June 17, 1833	do	74	
Abraham Menneax	do	30 00	–	Pennsylvania mil.	Ap'l 6, 1834	do	72	
George Stingle	do	20 00	–	Virginia militia	May 10, 1834	do	73	
Nathaniel White	do	80 00	240 00	N. York State tr.	Mar. 14, 1834	do	77	

Statement, &c. of Union county, Indiana.

NAMES.	Rank.	Annual allowance.	Sums received.	Description of service.	When placed on the pension roll.	Commencement of pension.	Ages.	Laws under which they were formerly inscribed on the pension roll; and remarks.
Leonard Brackenbaugh	Private	20 00	60 00	Maryland militia	Oct. 12, 1833	Mar. 4, 1831	70	
Joel Garrison	do	50 00	125 00	New Jersey militia	do	do	75	
Richard Haynes	do	80 00	240 00	Virginia State tr.	Nov. 29, 1833	do	75	
Rawley McMullin	do	50 00	150 00	S. Carolina militia	Mar. 26, 1833	do	74	
Matthew McClurkin	–	30 00	–	do	Oct. 12, 1833	do	70	
Jedediah Ogden	–	30 00	90 00	N. Jersey cont'l line	Jan. 8, 1834	do	85	
George Renker	Pri. & ser.	95 66	286 98	Indiana militia	Oct. 12, 1833	do	76	
David Thomas	Private	40 00	120 00	N. Carolina St. tr.	do	do	68	

Statement, &c. of Vanderburgh county, Indiana.

NAMES.	Rank.	Annual allow-ance.	Sums re-ceived.	Description of ser-vice.	When placed on the roll.	Commencement of pension.	Ages.	Laws under which they were for-merly inscribed on the pension roll; and remarks.
William Mead	Pri ate	80 00	240 00	N. J. cont'l line	Mar. 6, 1833	Mar. 4, 1831	68	
Elijah Stinson	Pri. & ser.	85 00	255 00	N. Carolina St. tr.	Aug. 26, 1833	do	89	

Statement, &c. of Vermillion county, Indiana.

NAMES.	Rank.	Annual allow-ance.	Sums re-ceived.	Description of ser-vice.	When placed on the pen-sion roll.	Commencement of pension.	Ages.	Laws under which they were for-merly inscribed on the pension roll; and remarks.
Abraham Hamman	Private	60 00	180 00	Virginia St. troops	Nov. 12, 1833	Mar. 4, 1833	80	
William Hannaman	do	20 00	60 00	Virginia militia	Dec. 21, 1833	do	75	
Francis Malone	do	80 00	240 00	Pennsylvania mil.	Aug. 27, 1833	do	76	
Nimrod H. Stone	do	20 00	60 00	Virginia militia	Oct. 29, 1833	do	71	
Abraham White	do	41 12	123 36	Penn'a militia	Sep. 28, 1833	do	80	
James Williams	do	80 00	240 00	Virginia militia	Oct. 29, 1833	do	73	

Statement, &c. of Vigo county, Indiana.

NAMES.		Rank.	Annual allowance.	Sums received.	Description of service.	When placed on the pension roll.	Commencement of pension.	Ages.	Laws under which they were formerly inscribed on the pension roll; and remarks.
James Barnes	-	Private	20 00	-	Virginia State tr.	Feb. 5, 1833	Mar. 4, 1831	85	
John Colwell	-	do	20 00	50 00	Virginia militia	July 11, 1833	do	83	
Gowen Jeffries	-	Pri. of art.	100 00	300 00	Virginia State tr.	Dec. 24, 1833	do	76	
James Thompson	-	Private	40 00	120 00	Maryland cont. line	Oct. 29, 1933	do	72	

10

Statement, &c. of Warren county, Indiana.

NAMES.	Rank.	Annual allowance.	Sums received.	Description of service.	When placed on the pension roll.	Commencement of pension.	Ages.	Laws under which they were formerly inscribed on the pension roll; and remarks.
Samuel Bryan -	Private	30 00	90 00	Maryland State tr.	Nov. 18, 1832	Mar. 4, 1831	78	
Richard Biddlecomb	do	31 33	93 99	Vermont State tr.	May 1, 1834	do	76	
George Dixon :	do	80 00	240 00	Virginia militia	Aug. 28, 1833	do	76	
William Hough :	do	21 55	64 65	Virginia State tr.	May 6, 1834	do	81	
Matthew Jones :	do	28 00	-	do	Mar. 2, 1834	do	77	
James Kitchen :	do	80 00	200 00	Virginia cont'l	Mar. 10, 1834	do	69	
Henry Saunders :	do	80 00	-	S. Carolina militia	Ap'l 7, 1834	do	83	

Statement, &c. of Warrick county, Indiana.

NAMES.	Rank.	Annual allowance.	Sums received.	Description of service.	When placed on the pension roll.	Commencement of pension.	Ages.	Laws under which they were formerly inscribed on the pension roll; and remarks.
John Alexander :	Pr. of cav.	25 00	75 00	N. Carolina St. tr.	Nov. 23, 1833	Mar. 4, 1831	75	
John Baker :	Private	57 77	173 21	S. Carolina militia	do	do	73	
William Campbell :	do	30 00	75 00	do	do	do	85	
John Depositer :	do	33 33	99 99	Delaware militia		do	84	
Samuel Musgrave :	do	26 66	79 98	Penn'a State troops	Dec. 9, 1833	do	74	
Thomas Richardson -	do	30 00	90 00	Virginia State tr.	Nov. 23, 1833	do	73	
William Williams :	do	20 66	61 98	do	do	do	75	

Statement, &c. of Washington county, Indiana.

NAMES.	Rank.	Annual allowance.	Sums received.	Description of service.	When placed on the roll.	Commencement of pension.	Ages.	Laws under which they were formerly inscribed on the pension roll; and remarks.
Thomas Arbuckle	Private	41 66	104 15	Virginia militia	Aug. 1, 1833	Mar. 4, 1831	75	
William Bowman	do	51 66	164 98	do	July 11, 1833	do	72	
Benjamin Brewer	do	25 22	75 76	Pennsylvania mil.	July 11, 1833	do	80	
Micajah Caloway	do	80 00	240 00	Virginia militia	Feb. 4, 1833	do	76	
Nathaniel Chambers	do	30 00	90 00	S. Carolina militia	Oct. 2, 1833	do	74	
Adam Fiscus	do	80 00	240 00	Virginia militia	Feb. 4, 1833	do	73	
James Garrison	do	20 00	60 00	S. Carolina militia	do	do	70	
John Gould	do	100 00	300 00	R. Island State tr.	do	do	85	
John Gallimore	do	60 00	180 00	N. Carolina militia	Jan. 6, 1834	do	75	Died February 13, 1834.
William Hurst	do	60 00	180 00	Penn'a militia	Feb. 4, 1833	do	68	
Daniel Hole	do	51 33	153 99	N. Jersey militia	Oct. 2, 1833	do	68	
George Hall	do	20 00	50 00	S. Carolina militia	Oct. 26, 1833	do	75	
John Hicks	do	30 00	90 00	Virginia militia	do	do	76	
Philip Hignet	do	40 00	120 00	Georgia State tr.	Dec. 18, 1833	do	82	
Samuel Jacobs	do	80 00	240 00	Virginia State tr.	Feb. 4, 1832	do	74	
John Keyt	do	80 00	240 00	N. Jersey militia	Feb. 14, 1834	do	81	
Robert McWhortor	do	21 50	53 75	Penn'a militia	Feb. 4, 1833	do	87	
John McPheeters	do	21 66	64 98	Virginia militia	Aug. 1, 1833	do	73	
Joshua Nichols	do	56 66	169 98	Virginia State tr.	Nov. 12, 1833	do	76	
Richard B. Porter	do	40 00	120 00	N. C. continental	May 29, 1833	do	71	
Arthur Parr	do	80 00	240 00	S. Carolina militia	Feb. 2, 1833	do	74	
Calza Rubison	do	20 00	-	N. Carolina militia	Feb. 4, 1833	do	70	
Jacob Smith	do	20 00	60 00	Virginia militia		do	85	
John A. Scudder	Surgeon	480 00	1,440 00	Penn'a militia	July 15, 1833	do	68	
Samuel Vest	Private	25 00	62 50	Virginia militia	July 11, 1833	do	75	
William Wright	do	30 00	90 00	N. Carolina militia	July 4, 1833	do	81	
William Watts	do	80 00	240 00	Virgina cont'l	do	do	76	
Michael Weaver	do	20 00	60 00	Penn'a militia	Feb. 4, 1833	do	75	

Statement, &c. of Wayne county, Indiana.

NAMES.	Rank.	Annual allowance.	Sums received.	Description of service.	When placed on the pension roll.	Commencement of pension.	Ages.	Laws under which they were formerly inscribed on the pension roll; and remarks.
Christopher Bundy	Private	20 00	50 00	N. Carolina militia	Mar. 13, 1833	Mar. 4, 1831	76	
Samuel Boyd	do	80 00	240 00	S. Carolina militia	July 15, 1833	do	71	
John Burk	do	33 83	84 57	N. Carolina cont'l	do	do	75	
Benjamin Bishop	do	40 00	120 00	N. Jersey State tr.	Dec. 11, 1833	do	80	
Josiah Case	do	80 00	200 00	S. Carolina militia	Feb. 28, 1833	do	76	
John Carn	do	80 00	200 00	do	Aug. 28, 1833	do	74	
William Cook	Pri. of inf. & cav.	22 50	67 50	N. Carolina militia	Feb. 28, 1834	do	65	
William Carter	Private	20 00	-	Virginia militia	June 17, 1834	do	75	
John Dougan	Pri. of cav.	100 00	300 00	N. Carolina militia	Nov 29, 1833	do	75	
George Eperly	Private	24 66	73 98	Maryland militia	Dec. 11, 1833	do	74	
George Holman	do	80 00	200 00	Kentucky militia	Mar. 2, 1833	do	69	
Nimrod Jester	do	56 66	141 65	N. Carolina militia	Oct. 18, 1833	do	72	
Jacob Meek	do	39 00	97 50	Penn. militia	May 29, 1833	do	70	
Richard Rue	do	80 00	-	Kentucky militia	Mar. 2, 1833	do	74	
Samuel Walker	do	20 00	60 00	Virginia militia	June 29, 1833	do	76	

Statement showing the Names, Rank, &c. of persons residing in the State of Indiana, who have received the benefits of the act of Congress passed the 15th May, 1828.

NAMES AND COUN-TIES.	Rank.	Annual allow-ance.	Sums re-ceived.	Description of ser-vice.	When placed on the pen-sion roll.	Names of agents or representatives.	Remarks.
					Commencement of pay, March 3, 1826.		
BOONE. John Aldridge	Private	80 00	680 00	- reg't Penn. line	Ap'l 29, 1831	Major J. H. Hook, ag't	
DEARBORN. John Dixon	Dragoon	100 00	850 00	- reg't Penn. cav.	Oct. 21, 1828	-	
Zebulon Pike	Captain	600 00	4,554 99	- reg't Penn. drag.	Aug. 12, 1828		Died July 27, 1834.
FAYETTE. Nicholas Kimmer	Corporal	88 00	176 00	4th reg't Penn. line	Oct. 6, 1828	-	Transferred from Bracken co., Kentucky.
FLOYD. Adam Hart	Private	80 00	400 00	Lytle's N. O. line	May 2, 1830	Hon. A. C. Sheppord, agent	Transferred from Guilford co., North Carolina.
GIBSON. George Humphreys	Dragoon	100 00	850 00	Virginia dragoons	Sep. 9, 1828		
GREENE. John Storm	do	100 00	900 00	Washu's cavalry	June 8, 1832	Thomas F. G. Adams, Hon. W. Hendricks and Hon. J. Tipton, agents	
JACKSON. John Edwards	Musician	88 00	264 00	- reg't Penn. line	Oct. 21, 1829	-	Transferred from Pulaski co., Kentucky.
Obadiah Walker	Private	80 00	680 00	- reg't Conn. line	Oct. 6, 1828		
JOHNSON. William Morgan	do	80 00	40 00	1st reg't Va. line	Dec. 18, 1828	-	Transferred from Shelby co., Kentucky,

Statement, &c. of Indiana—Continued.

NAMES AND COUNTIES.	Rank.	Annual allowance.	Sums received.	Description of service.	When placed on the pension roll.	Names of agents or representatives.	Remarks.
						Commencement of pay, March 3, 1826.	
KNOX. Charles Fitzgerald	Private	80 00	640 00	- reg't Maryl'd line	Oct. 4, 1828	Hon. J. Ewing, ag't	
MARION. Robert Dickerson	do	80 00	240 00	2d reg't Va. line	Aug. 19, 1828	J. M. Ray, agent.	
ORANGE. Garret Voorhis	do	80 00	720 00	5th reg't N. J. line	Oct. 6, 1828	A. S. White, agent	
RUSH. William Smith	do	80 00	680 00	- reg't Virgina line	do	S. F. Hunt, agent	
UNION. Samuel Meredith	Dragoon	100 00	700 00	Lee's legion	do	Hon. J. Woods, agent	Transferred from Franklin co., Kentucky.
VERMILLION. Jacob Coleman	Lieutenant	320 00	1,120 00	7th reg't Va. line	Sep. 9, 1828	John M. Coleman, ag't	
Richard Mack	Musician	88 00	792 00	2d reg't Conn. line	Oct. 6, 1828	Amary Kinney, agent	
VIGO. George Jones	Private	80 00	680 00	- reg't Penn. line	Mar. 28, 1829	A. Kinney, agent	
WARRICK. William Overlin	do	80 00	720 00	7th reg't Va. line	Oct. 27, 1828		

MICHIGAN PENSION ROLL.

Statement showing the Names, Rank, &c. of Invalid Pensioners residing in the Territory of Michigan.

NAMES AND COUNTIES.	Rank.	Annual allowance.	Sums received.	Description of service.	When placed on the pension roll.	Commencement of pension.	Laws under which they were inscribed, increased or reduced; and remarks.
BERRIEN. Thomas Fitzgerald	Corporal	30 00	25 83	5th U. S. infantry	Dec. 14, 1815	June 14, 1815	Acts military establishment. Trans'd from N. York, and from Indiana. April 24, 1816.
Do	do	48 00	306 00	do	–	Apr. 24, 1816	
Do	do	96 00	1,097 33	do	–	Sep. 15, 1821	Acts military establishment.
CASS. John Silsbee	Captain	180 00	396 50	New York militia	–	Feb. 11, 1814	Acts mil. est. Trans'd from Albany.
Do	do	240 00	4,286 33	do	Feb. 6, 1817	Apr. 24, 1816	April 24, 1816.
CHICAGO. De La Fayette Wilcox	2d lieut.	180 00	463 20	25th U. S. infantry	June 18, 1828	June 18, 1828	Acts military establishment.
ERIE. William Griffith	1st lieut.	102 00	1,151 88	Kentucky volun'rs	Ap'l 3, 1818	Nov. 20, 1813	April 24, 1816.
IOWA. John McNair	Sergeant	72 00	–	Michigan militia	Mar. 10, 1834	Mar. 8, 1834	April 24, 1816.
KALAMAZOO. Joseph Clark	Ensign	78 00	109 84	New York militia	Ap'l 24, 1832	Apr. 7, 1832	April 24, 1816.
LENAWE: Jabez Fisk	Private	48 00	70 00	New York volun'rs	–	Nov. 9, 1814	Acts military establishment. Trans'd from New York.
Do	do	76 80	489 60	do	May 31, 1817	Apr. 24, 1816	April 24, 1816.
Do	do	96 00	1,102 66	do	–	Sep. 9, 1822	Acts military establishment.
MACOMB. Freeman Blakeley	do	96 00	1,751 68	31st U. S. infantry	Feb. 15, 1815	June 5, 1815	Acts military establishment.

Name	Rank	Rate per month	Arrears	Service	Date	Date	Remarks
William Letts	do	38 40	496 73	24th U.S. infantry	Jan. 10, 1817	Sep, 27, 1815	do — Trans'd
William Olds	do	32 60	198 13	Michigan militia	Sep. 19, 1825	Jan. 27, 1825	Acts military establishment. from New York.
Abel Warren	do	48 00	115 86	do		Apr. 5, 1831	April 24, 1816.
Do	Sergeant	48 00	948 40	23d U.S. infantry	July 28, 1818	Dec. 1, 1813	Acts military establishment. from New York. — Trans'd
Roswell Webster	do	96 00	-	do	Feb. 18, 1835	Feb. 4, 1835	Acts military establishment.
Do	Private	48 00	423 60	New Jersey militia	Sep. 17, 1820	Feb. 19, 1820	April, 1812. Trans'd from New York March 4, 1826. — Trans'd
John Walker	do	96 00	460 48	Revolutionary war		Dec. 18, 1828	March, 1819.
Do	do	96 00	489 60	Michigan cavalry	Dec. 31, 1822	Nov. 25, 1822	April 24, 1816. Died Dec. 31, 1825.
MONROE.							
John Francisco	do	48 00	173 73	New York militia	Feb. 3, 1830	Jan. 22, 1830	Acts military establishment. from New York. — Trans'd
Do	do	72 00	30 00	do		Oct. 4, 1833	Acts military establishment.
Lewis Jacob	do	48 00	466 66	Michigan volun'rs	Feb. 10, 1823	Dec. 16, 1822	do
Do	do	96 00	48 00	do	Sep. 13, 1852	Sep. 5, 1852	do
Martin Smith*	Pr. & cor.	72 00	915 12	25th U.S. infantry	Mar. 18, 1830	June 25, 1817	Act March 2, 1833.
Do	Private	48 00	167 60	-		Mar. 8, 1830	Acts military establishment.
MACKINAC.							
Nathan Puffer	do	96 00	1,183 44	U.S. army	Mar. 25, 1823	May 7, 1821	Acts military establishment. from New York.
John Reynolds	do	36 00	243 10	do		July 13, 1810	July 5, 1812.
Do	do	57 60	.			Apr. 24, 1816	April 24, 1816.
OAKLAND.							
James F. Chittenden	do	48 00	114 00	23d U.S. infantry	Jan. 11, 1830	Jan. 2, 1830	Acts military establishment. from Albany. — Trans'd
Do	do	96 00	124 80			May 17, 1832	Acts military establishment.
James A. Chadwick	Corporal	32 00	597 68	4th U.S. rifles	Aug. 1, 1817	Nov. 29, 1814	Acts military establishment. from New York. — Trans'd
Do	do	96 00	8 26	do		Aug. 3, 1833	Acts military establishment.
Richard Ferguson	Private	48 00	321 20	3d U.S. artillery	Apr. 28, 1832	Dec. 26, 1826	do — Trans'd
Elijah Measurell	de	72 00	245 00	2d U.S. infantry	Apr. 28, 1830	Apr. 9, 1830	Acts military establishment. from New York.
Oliver Jenks	do	72 00	828 00	27th U.S. infantry	Sep. 8, 1818	Sep. 4, 1818	Acts military establishment. from N. York. Resides in Huron co. See act March 2, 1833. — Trans'd

* This pensioner was allowed $6 00 per month, from June 25, 1817, until March 11, 1830, as arrears of pension. See act March 2, 1833.

Statement, &c. of Invalid Pensioners—Continued.

NAMES AND COUNTIES.	Rank.	Annual allowance.	Sums received.	Description of service.	When placed on the pension roll.	Commencement of pension:	Laws under which they were inscribed, increased or reduced; and remarks.
Henry Stevens	Private	64 00	874 66	New York militia	July 12, 1820	July 5, 1819	April 24, 1816. Trans'd from N. York
Henry Sutton	do	72 00	834 00	New York volun'rs	May 9, 1822	Feb. 4, 1822	April 24, 1816. Trans'd from Albany.
Thomas Watts	do	48 00	639 20	New York militia	May 11, 1820	May 11, 1820	April 24, 1816. Trans'd from N. York.
Leonard Witing	Corporal	96 00	586 08	19th U. S. infantry	June 18, 1818	Oct. 19, 1814	Acts military establishment.
ST. CLAIR.							
Richard Bean	Private	72 00	- -	17th U. S. infantry	Oct. 13, 1817	June 14, 1815	do
Do	do	96 00			Mar. 21, 1823	Jan. 17, 1823	do
Edward Locke	do	96 00	- -	5th U. S. infantry	Jan. 22, 1834	Ap'l 25, 1833	do
WAYNE.							
Robert Atkinson	do	72 00	1,288 00	3d U. S. infantry	Nov. 13, 1834	Oct. 15, 1815	April 24, 1816.
Henry T. Blake	Musician	72 00	86 20	19th U. S. infantry	May 3, 1831	Ap'l 26, 1831	Acts military establishment. Died July 7, 1832.
Aaron Brinck	Private	60 00	434 83	Revolutionary army	Feb. 29, 1820	Jan. 26, 1809	April 27, 1810. From New York.
Do	do	96 00	1,654 93	do	Ap'l 4, 1817	Ap'l 24, 1816	April 24, 1816. Died July 19, 1833.
George Best	do	72 00	1,229 00	3d U. S. infantry	Sep. 5, 1822	Feb. 7, 1816	Acts military establishment.
Abraham Cook	do	48 00	474 26	-		June 3, 1822	Acts 10, 1806.
Do	do	96 00	33 06	Michigan militia		Apr. 30, 1832	Acts military establishment.
Henry Cremer	do	48 00	714 53	29th U. S. infantry	May 3, 1816	July 1, 1815	Acts military establishment. Trans'd from N. York. Died May 20, 1830.
Alexander Campbell	do	72 00	325 38	5th U. S. infantry	Feb. 19, 1819	Jan. 18, 1818	Acts military establishment. Trans'd from Massachusetts.
Do	Pri. & ser.	96 00	222 40	do	-	Sep. 11, 1823	Acts military establishment. Died January 4, 1826.
Nathaniel Case	Captain	240 00	-	New York militia	Ap'l 1, 1834	Feb. 13, 1834	April 24, 1816.
Samuel Gray	Private	40 00	295 88	do	Jan. 11, 1816	Dec. 1, 1813	Acts military establishment. Trans'd from New York.
Do	do	64 00	218 81	-		Ap'l 24, 1816	April 24, 1816. Died Sep. 24, 1819.
John Heaton	do	96 00	1,083 72	3d U. S. infantry	Jan. 2, 1818	Nov. 25, 1817	Acts military establishment.

Name	Rank			Unit			Remarks
Jedediah Hunt	Captain	240 00	703 20	New York volun'rs	Oct. 2, 1830	Sep. 29, 1830	April 24, 1816. Trans'd from New York.
Thomas Johnson	Sergeant	72 00	62 80	2d U. S. infantry	June 25, 1833	Oct. 21, 1832	Acts military establishment.
Jonathan Kearsley	Major	360 00	6,558 00	4th U. S. rifles	Jan. 17, 1816	June 16, 1815	Acts military establishment. Trans'd from Pennsylvania.
Samuel McCrea	Private	72 00	150 60	5th U. S. infantry	Nov. 20, 1819	May 1, 1819	April 24, 1816. Died June 4, 1831.
Samuel McKee	do	32 00	300 88	3d U. S. rifles	Jan. 28, 1823	Oct. 30, 1822	April 25, 1808.
Do	do	96 00	138 66	do	-	Mar. 24, 1832	Acts military establishment.
John Martin	Captain	120 00	354 33	New York volun'rs	Sep. 22, 1830	Sep. 21, 1830	April 24, 1816.
Frederick Miller	Private	96 00	-	5th U. S. infantry	Nov. 13, 1819	Ap'l 29, 1819	Acts military establishment. Paid at Albany, N. Y. Died July 24, 1820.
Miles S. Miller	do	96 00	602 66	2d U. S. light drag.	Feb. 18, 1817	May 2, 1815	Acts military establishment. Died August 12, 1821.
Henry Myers	do	72 00	607 20	New York volun'rs	May 22, 1823	Mar. 29, 1823	Acts military establishment. Trans'd from New York.
Joseph G. Odall	Ensign	120 00	-	do	Nov. 4, 1833	Sep. 30, 1833	April 24, 1816.
Paul Parcels	Private	64 00	58 46	5th U. S. infantry	Ap'l 24, 1818	June 2, 1817	Acts mil. est. Died May 1, 1818.
James Randall	do	72 00	151 40	2d U. S. artilley	June 28, 1824	Jan. 28, 1824	Acts military establishment.
Do	do	48 00	204 26	do	Mar. 4, 1826	Mar. 4, 1826	do
Do	do	72 00	228 60	do	July 1, 1830	July 1, 1830	do
Jacob Rattaneur	do	60 00	1,628 33	New York militia	Mar. 4, 1789	Mar. 4, 1789	September 29, 1789.
Do	do	96 00	1,714 66	do	Ap'l 2, 1824	Ap'l 24, 1816	April 24, 1816. Trans'd from N. York.
Daniel Stevens	do	48 00	267 73	U. S artillery	Dec. 9, 1819	May 23, 1818	Acts military establishment.
Do	do	72 00	421 00	do	-	Dec. 20, 1823	do
Do	do	96 00	274 66	do	-	Oct. 25, 1819	do
Warren Stone	do	48 00	853 72	New York militia	July 12, 1820	Nov. 9, 1814	Acts military establishment. Trans'd from New York.
Do	do	72 00	104 54	do	-	Mar. 22, 1832	Acts military establishment.
Jonathan Thompson	do	48 00	36 92	3d U. S. infantry	Aug. 2, 1822	May 28, 1822	do
John M. Van Alstine	do	96 00	146 66	5th U. S. infantry	Ap'l 7, 1832	Feb. 22, 1832	do
John L. Shear	do	48 00	996 00	New York militia	June 18, 1817	Nov. 1, 1812	April 24, 1816. Trans'd from N. York.
WASHTENAW.							
Daniel French	do	96 00	1,768 00	11th U. S. infantry	Feb. 20, 1816	Apr. 4, 1815	Acts military establishment. Trans'd from Pennsylvania.

Statement showing the Names, Rank, &c. of persons residing in the Territory of Michigan, who have been inscribed on the Pension List under the act of Congress passed March 18, 1818.

NAMES AND COUNTIES.	Rank.	Annual allowance.	Sums received.	Description of service.	When placed on the pension roll.	Commencement of pension.	Ages.	Laws under which they were formerly inscribed on the pension roll; and remarks.
CASS.								
Lemuel Bolter	Private	96 00	720 00	Massachusetts con.	Sept. 24, 1825	Sep. 5, 1825	-	Trans'd from Ohio, Pittsburg, March 4, 1833.
Henry Massey	do	96 00	1,479 72	Maryland cont'l	Sep. 21, 1818	Apr. 5, 1818	34	Trans'd from Baltimore county, Maryland.
Amos Richards	do	96 00	1,430 92	Connecticut cont'l	Dec. 25, 1821	Apr. 8, 1818	77	Trans'd from Jefferson co, N. Y.
LENAWE.								
Moses B. Cook	do	96 00	1,460 08	New York cont'l	Ap'l 25, 1820	June 16, 1818	73	Trans'd to and from Albany.
Isaac W. Shumaway	do	96 00	1,475 44	Massachusetts con.	July 23, 1819	Apr. 21, 1818	73	Trans'd from Ontario co., N. Y.
Thomas Whipple	do	96 00	1,425 32	New Hamp. cont'l	May 3, 1819	do	80	Trans'd from Albany county.
MONROE.								
Gideon Badger	do	96 00	747 44	Massachusetts con.	Aug. 2, 1819	June 3, 1818	62	Trans'd to and from New York. Died March 26, 1826.
MACOMB.								
Levi Collins	do	96 00	1,425 32	New Hamp. cont'l	Nov. 30, 1810	Apr. 29, 1818	73	Trans'd from Niagara co., N. Y.
Asahel Haskins	do	96 00	1,240 26	Massachusetts con.	Oct. 17, 1822	Oct. 3, 1820	70	Trans'd from Crawford county, Illinois.
OAKLAND.								
Joshua Chamberlain	do	96 00	808 26	Revolutionary army	Nov. 27, 1818	Apr. 3, 1818	63	Trans'd from Niagara co., N. Y.
Benjamin Grace	do	96 00	1,473 33	New Hamp. cont'l	Apr. 13, 1819	Apr. 29, 1818	-	Trans'd from New York.
Silas Sprague	do	96 00	1,296 80	Massachusetts con.	June 13, 1820	Mar. 1, 1820	70	Trans'd from Broome co., N. Y.
WAYNE.								
Joseph Bates	do	96 00		Connecticut cont'l	May 1, 1820	July 19, 1819	71	
William Dunbar	do	96 00	388 00	New York cont'l	June 19, 1819	Feb. 17, 1819	60	
Ephraim Dains	do	96 00	1,474 40	Connecticut cont'l	July 16, 1819	May 26, 1818	73	Trans'd from Ontario co., N. Y.
Jonathan Dear	do	96 00	1,492 92	do	Apr. 23, 1819	Apr. 8, 1818	72	Trans'd from Jefferson co., N. Y,
Francis Gowen	do	96 00	1,425 33	Pennsylvania cont'l	Apr. 11, 1833	July 20, 1819	75	
Benjamin Knapp	do	96 00	954 40	New York cont'l	July 12, 1823	June 1, 1823	76	Died May 10, 1833.
Thompson Maxwell	do	240 00	3,435 33	New Hamp. cont'l	Oct. 9, 1818	July 1, 1818	90	Died October 24, 1832.

Name				Line			Age	Remarks
William Pangburn	do	96 00	1,079 20	New York cont'l	Nov. 30, 1821	Jan. 8, 1821	75	Trans'd from Clinton co., N. Y.
Robert Parker	do	96 00	1,479 73	Massachusetts con.	Sep. 22, 1818	Apr. 6, 1818	74	Trans'd from Seneca co., N. Y.
Levi Ross	do	96 00	1,423 44	New Jersey cont'l	Oct. 1, 1818	May 7, 1818	85	Trans'd from Erie co., Penn'a.
Jonathan Stratton	do	96 00	703 72	Massachusetts con.	Oct. 5, 1819	Apr. 24, 1818	60	Died August 18, 1823.
Jeremiah Stone	do	96 00	1,488 80	New Jersey cont'l	Apr. 14, 1818	Apr. 1, 1818	76	Trans'd from Saratoga co., N. Y.
Elisha Smith	do	96 00	1,425 32	Massachusetts cont.	Sep. 18, 1820	May 2, 1818	70	Trans'd from Seneca co., N. Y.
Darius Smead	do	96 00	1,522 66	New Hamp. cont'l	Mar. 25, 1819	Apr. 6, 1818	68	do
Aaron Thomas	do	96 00	638 12	Connecticut cont'l	Sep. 7, 1819	Mar. 23, 1819	72	Died October 15, 1825.
Joseph Van Atter	do	96 00	1,200 00	New York cont'l	May 22, 1822	Mar. 5, 1821	70	
WASHTENAW.								
Archibald Armstrong	do	96 00	1,474 00	do	Apr. 30, 1818	Apr. 25, 1818	69	Trans'd from Ontario co., N. Y.
Jotham Curtiss	do	96 00	459 72	Connecticut cont'l	June 6, 1828	May 21, 1828	-	Trans'd from Medina co., Ohio.
Asa Gillett	Pri. drag.	96 00	1,425 32	do	May 29, 1818	Apr. 27, 1818	-	Trans'd from Otsego co., N. Y.
Andrew Nichols	do	96 00	749 44	New Hamp. cont.	Dec. 10, 1825	Nov. 21, 1825	74	Trans'd from St. Lawrence co., New York.

Statement showing the Names, Rank, &c. of persons residing in the Territory of Michigan, who have been inscribed on the Pension List under the act of Congress passed 7th June, 1832.

NAMES AND COUNTIES.	Rank.	Annual allowance.	Sums received.	Description of service.	When placed on the pension roll.	Commencement of pension.	Ages.	Laws under which they were formerly inscribed on the pension roll; and remarks.
CASS.								
John Petticrew	Private	40 00	120 00	Pennsylvania cont'l	Mar. 4, 1834	Mar. 4, 1831	76	
Ebenezer Annable	Pri. & ser.	89 00	267 00	New York cont'l	Mar. 3, 1834	do	76	Trans'd from Onandaga co, N. Y.
JACKSON.								
Joseph Darling	Private	20 00	60 00	Massachusetts con.	Jan. 3, 1833	do	70	
Samuel Black	do	30 88	92 64	do	May 2, 1833	do	69	Trans'd from Wayne co, N. Y.
KALAMAZOO.								
Asa Briggs	Pri., &c.	66 66	166 65	Vermont cont'l	Oct. 9, 1833	do	79	
Abiel Fellows	do	70 00	210 00	Connecticut cont'l	Sep. 25, 1833	do	70	
LENAWE.								
Phineas Brown	Sergeant	105 00	315 00	Massachusetts cont'l	Aug. 9, 1833	do	79	
William Maples	Private	23 33	69 99	Connecticut cont'l	Oct. 3, 1833	do	74	
Thomas Nelson	do	26 66	79 98	Vermont militia	Mar. 3, 1834	do	77	
Daniel Olds	Pri. & ser.	105 66	266 65	Connecticut cont'l	Sep. 25, 1833	do	75	
MONROE.								
George Alfred	Private	40 00	120 00	Vermont cont'l	July 3, 1833	do	70	
Stephen Downing	do	70 00	210 00	Connecticut cont'l	Oct. 9, 1833	do	72	
MACOMB.								
Joseph Holland	do	50 00	150 00	Connecticut militia	Feb. 4, 1834	do	74	
Caleb Taft	do	20 00	-	Massachusetts mil.	July 23, 1834	do	82	
OAKLAND.								
Nathan Baldwin	do	20 00	60 00	Connecticut militia	Mar. 4, 1834	do	74	
John Blanchard	do	80 00	-	New Hamp. militia	July 30, 1834	do	71	

Name	Rank			Service	Date		No.	Remarks
James Graham	Corporal	44 00	132 00	Pennsylvania cont'l	Aug. 9, 1833	do	79	
Nathaniel Landon	Private	43 33	129 99	New Jersey militia	Feb. 10, 1834	do	77	
Joseph Todd	do	35 55	-	New York militia	July 23, 1834	do	69	
William N. Terry	do	80 00	240 00	Pennsylvania cont'l	Aug. 9, 1833	do	74	
ST. CLAIR.								
Jonathan Barron	do	57 22	171 66	New Hamp. cont'l	Apr. 15, 1833	do	74	Trans'd from Grafton co., N. H.
Thomas Fergo	do	40 00	120 00	Connecticut cont'l	Nov. 10, 1832	do	77	Trans'd from Cayuga co., N. Y.
Reuben Smith	do	80 00	240 00	do	Apr. 20, 1833	do	79	
'ST. JOSEPH'S.								
Mede Hurd	do	66 66	199 98	do	Aug. 10, 1832	do	77	Trans'd from Ulster co., N. Y.
Elisha Stanley	do	50 00	150 00	do	July 3, 1833	do	74	
WAYNE.								
George Horton	do	80 00	240 00	Pennsylvania cont'l	Dec. 15, 1832	do	73	Trans'd from Tioga co., N. Y.
Peter Lown	do	23 33	69 99	New York militia	Feb. 4, 1834	do	74	
William Patee	do	60 00	180 00	New Hamp. cont'l	Feb. 9, 1834	do	79	
John Walters	do	56 66	169 98	New Jersey militia	May 21, 1834	do	74	Trans'd from New York.
Benjamin Ellsworth	do	24 98	74 94	New York militia	June 7, 1833	do	80	Trans'd from Seneca co., N. Y.
WASHTENAW.								
David A. Coryell	do	80 00	240 00	New Jersey cont'l	Aug. 9, 1833	do	76	
Martin Dubois	do	30 00	90 00	New York cont'l	do	do	70	
Adam Overocker	do	80 00	240 00	do	do	do	73	
Jol'n Terhune	Ensign	240 00	720 00	New Jersey cont'l	do	do	76	
Samuel Waldron	do	80 00	-	do	July 1, 1834	do	73	

Statement showing the Names, Rank, &c. of persons residing in the Territory of Michigan, who have received the benefits of the act of Congress passed May 15, 1828.

NAMES AND COUN- TIES.	Rank.	Annual allow- ance	Sums re- ceived.	Descripion of ser- vice.	When placed on the pen- sion roll.	Names of agents or representatives.	Remarks.
					Commencement of pay, March 3, 1826.		
LENEWEE. John Bemis	Private	80 00	421 77	- reg. N. H. line	Oct. 21, 1828	Wonott Lawrence, ag.	Died June 10, 1831.
MONROE. Samuel Stone	do	80 00	320 00	3d reg. Conn. line	Sep. 10, 1828	‒	Transf'd from Onondago co., New York.
WAYNE. William McCoskey	Sur. mate	480 00	2,498 66	Penn'a artillery	Mar. 30, 1831	David Beard, ag't.— Felicity McCoskey, widow	Died May 16, 1820.
Jonathan Miller	Private	80 00	680 00	Col. Willy's reg't	Sep. 4, 1829	B. F. H. Witherill, ag. N. S. Sprague, Hon.	
James Witherell	Ensign	240 00	2,160 00	11th reg. Mass. line	Aug. 27, 1831	R. C. Mallory, and Hon. Lewis Cass, agents.	

MISSOURI PENSION ROLL.

Statement showing the Names, Rank, &c. of Invalid Pensioners residing in the State of Missouri.

NAMES AND COUNTIES.	Rank.	Annual allowance.	Sums received.	Description of service.	When placed on the pension roll.	Commencement of pension.	Laws under which they were inscribed, increased and reduced; and remarks.
BOONE.							
Abraham Grindstaff	Private	32 00	267 48	Kentucky militia	Jan. 18, 1833	Nov. 12, 1822	April 24, 1816.
Alexander Nairsmith	Conductor of pack horses	30 00	444 29	North West. army	Jan. 9, 1816	Aug. 20, 1816	March 3, 1815.
Do	do	48 00	131 33	do	June 10, 1830	June 10, 1831	Transferred from Kentucky.
CALLAWAY.							
Jesse D. Oldham	Private	72 00	292 19	Kentucky militia	Feb. 16, 1830	Feb. 13, 1830	April 24, 1816.
Henry Overly	do	60 00	504 00	U. States army	–	Dec. 1, 1808	March 3, 1809.
Do	do	96 00	1,618 63	do	–	Ap'l 24, 1816	April 24, 1816. Transferred from Virginia.
CAPE GIRARDEAU.							
John Leiper	do	48 00	174 88	Tennessee militia	July 21, 1830	July 19, 1830	Transferred from East Tennessee.
CLAY.							
Page Stanley	do	96 00	673 03	6th reg. U. S. inf.	Mar. 16, 1829	Mar. 1, 1827	March 2, 1821.
COLE.							
Michael Reynolds	do	96 00	904 02	6th reg. U. S. inf.	July 12, 1822	Oct. 5, 1820	Acts military establishment.
FRANKLIN.							
Sackett Davis	do	48 00	–	6th reg. U. S. inf.	Sep. 26, 1823	Ap'l 2, 1823	Acts military estab. Dropped from the roll, having recovered from his disabilities.
Patrick McMahon	do	96 00	–	do	Dec. 18, 1820	June 30, 1820	Acts military establishment. Dead.
John Prickett	do	48 00	814 59	24th reg. U. S. inf.	Jan. 8, 1816	Mar. 16, 1825	Transferred from Tennessee.
John Shuffield	do	48 00	869 51	44th reg. U. S. inf.	Mar. 21, 1816	Ap'l 25, 1815	Acts military establishment. Transferred from Kentucky.

Name	Rank		Amount	Unit			Remarks
John Spencer	do	48 00	877 82	1st reg. U. S. inf.	July 24, 1816	May 22, 1815	Ap'l 24, 1816. Died Dec. 20, 1826.
GASCONADE. John Estes	do	96 00	583 82	Tennessee militia	June 15, 1822	Nov. 21, 1820	
HOWARD. Robert Johnson	Corporal	48 00	157 43	6th reg. U. S. inf.	May 14, 1824	May 25, 1823	Acts military establishment.
Alphonso Whetmore	Ensign	156 00	2,433 99	23d reg. U. S. inf.	Mar. 11, 1828	Jan. 29, 1817	Acts military establishment.
JACKSON. Levi Arter	Corporal	72 00	237 17	6th reg. U. S. inf.	Apl 14, 1831	Nov. 19, 1830	Acts military establishment.
John Campbell	Captain	240 00	4,488 66	4th reg. U. S. inf.	Dec. 12, 1818	June 18, 1815	Acts military establishment.
JEFFERSON. Joseph Henderson	Lieut't	102 00	428 28	Missouri militia	Jan. 14, 1819	Dec. 24, 1814	April 30, 1816.
Do	do	76 50	276 23	do	–	Mar. 4, 1819	March 3, 1819.
Do	do	102 00	725 33	do	Nov. 8, 1822	Oct. 14, 1822	Died November 24, 1829.
LAFAYETTE. Andrew S. McGirk	Private	72 00	1,444 29	East Tennessee mil.	Jan. 17, 1818	Feb. 9, 1814	April 24, 1816.
LINCOLN. Robert Gilmore	do	72 00	217 38	Kentucky militia	Jan. 20, 1831	Jan. 18, 1831	April 24, 1816.
Peter Rebolt	do	96 00	576 25	Murrick's co, U. S. rangers	May 14, 1828	May 31, 1828	February 25, 1913.
MARION. Abraham Steyart	Sur. mate	180 00	974 05	U. S. army	Dec. 31, 1828	Oct. 7, 1828	Acts military establishment.
MONTGOMERY. Thomas Griffith	3d lieut.	168 00	1,023 75	17th reg. U. S. inf.	Feb. 2, 1828	Feb. 2, 1828	Acts military establishment. Trans-ferred from Kentucky.
James H. Osburn	Sergeant	96 00	1,206 09	6th reg. U. S. inf,	May 24, 1823	Aug. 13, 1821	Acts military establishment.
MORGAN. Thomas Roberts	Private	48 00	359 63	Tennessee rangers	Sept. 27, 1826	Sep. 8, 1826	April 24, 1816.
Do	do	72 00	–	do	–	July 25, 1834	

Statement, &c.—Continued.

NAMES AND COUNTIES.	Rank.	Annual allowance.	Sums received.	Description of service.	When placed on the pension roll.	Commencement of pension.	Laws under which they were inscribed, increased and reduced; and remarks.
PIKE.							
Horace S. Holliday	Private	64 00	669 25	6th reg. U. S. inf.	Nov. 5, 1823	Mar. 21, 1823	Acts military establishment.
Israel Waters	Matross	48 00	785 17	Leonard's c. U. S. ar.	Nov. 1817	Oct. 27, 1817	Acts military establishment. Transferred from Illinois.
ST. CHARLES.							
Nathan Heald	Major	240 00	4,261 91	1st reg't U. S. inf.	Jan. 27, 1817	June 2, 1814	Acts military establishment.
William Pennington	Private	96 00	1,846 44	28th reg't U. S. inf.	Dec. 29, 1815	Dec. 11, 1814	
George Shannon	Indian conductor	144 00	2,417 54	-	-	Sep. 11, 1816	March 3, 1817. Transferred from Kentucky.
William Tumey	Private	96 00	593 03	6th reg't U. S. inf.	Aug. 9, 1831	Jan. 1, 1828	May 20, 1830.
ST. FRANCIS.							
Isaac Burnham	do	48 00	639 20	Col. P. Douge's co.	-	Jan. 1, 1803	April 25, 1808.
Do	do	76 80	949 51	do	-	Ap'l 24, 1816	April 24, 1816. Transferred from Kentucky.
ST. GENEVIEVE.							
Benjamin Haile	do	48 00	-	Missouri rangers	Mar. 5, 1817	Dec. 5, 1815	March 3, 1817.
ST. LOUIS.							
Jeremiah Ball	do	96 00	611 09	8th reg't U. S. inf.	Ap'l 26, 1819	May 24, 1817	Acts military establishment.
Shephard Barrett	do	48 00	362 14	5th reg't U. S. inf.	Sep. 28, 1822	Aug. 1, 1821	Acts military establishment. Died February 15, 1829.
Arthur Barrett	do	96 00	394 12	do	Dec. 16, 1822	July 24, 1821	Acts military establishment.
Michael Chaptu	do	48 00	867 95	-	-	Feb. 5, 1816	Acts military establishment. April 30, 1816.
Jesse Colburn	Sergeant	72 00	1,353 28	Romayne's reg't art.	Dec. 1815	Mar. 9, 1815	Acts mil. establishment. Transferred from Pennsylvania.
James Callaghan	Private	96 00	142 47	6th reg't U. S. inf.	June 28, 1830	June 28, 1830	Acts military establishment.
John D. Doyle	do	96 00	304 80	3d reg't U. S. inf.	June 3, 1830	July 2, 1830	Acts military establishment.
John Debroskey	do	48 00	219 02	6th reg't U. S. inf.	Ap'l 30, 1825	Oct. 16, 1824	Acts military establishment.

James Fletcher	do	96 00	206 45	5th reg't U. S. inf.	Apr'l 23, 1825	Oct. 22, 1824	Acts military establishment. Died December 15, 1826.
Daniel Ferguson	do	84 00	144 19	2d reg't U. S. inf.	June 17, 1830	June 17, 1830	Acts military establishment.
George Gooding	2d lieut. & captain	90 00	779 87	5th reg't U. S. inf.	Feb. 17, 1824	July 22, 1831	April 12, 1808. Died March 20, 1830.
Stephen Hempstead	Sergeant	45 00	1,265 24	Connecticut militia	-	Sep. 30, 1788	April 24, 1816.
Do	do	72 00	873 80	do	-	Ap'l 24, 1816	
Do	do	96 00	261 83	do	-	June 13, 1828	
Daniel Kearney	Private	96 00	1,102 89	6th reg't U. S. inf.	June 2, 1823	Sep. 9, 1822	Acts military establishment.
Lawson Lovering	do	24 00	-	21st reg't U. S. inf.	Dec. 18, 1833	June 15, 1833	
Jean Baptiste La Taille	do	64 00	65 44	Missouri militia	Mar. 20, 1830	Feb. 25, 1830	April 24, 1816.
Joshua Miller	Corporal	96 00	-	1st reg't U. S. art.	Oct. 5, 1817	Jan. 1, 1814	Acts military establishment.
Vincent Morris	do	96 00	551 69	6th reg't U. S. inf.	Ap'l 19, 1825	June 6, 1821	do
John Maher	do	72 00	818 73	do	Jan. 17, 1823	Oct. 22, 1824	do
Milo Moses	Private	48 00	23 12	do		Sep. 25, 1822	Acts military establish't. Died March 18, 1823.
David Martin	do	48 00	394 96	U. S. rifle company	Feb. 2, 1826	Dec. 13, 1825	February 25, 1813.
John Putnam	Sergeant	48 00	782 57		Ap'l 19, 1822	Nov. 8, 1817	Acts military establishment and May 15, 1820.
William Richardson	Private	48 00	739 06	44th reg't U. S. inf.	Nov. 13, 1823	Ap'l 12, 1815	Acts military establishment.
John Rush	do	48 00		5th reg't U. S. inf.	Ap'l 19, 1824	Oct. 29, 1823	Transferred from Illinois.
James Rankin	do	30 00	545 66	19th reg't U. S. inf.	Jan. 2, 1816	June 7, 1815	Acts military establishment. Transferred from Michigan.
John Silvers	do	72 00	194 77	5th reg't U. S. inf.	Sep. 21, 1820	June 21, 1820	Acts military establishment.
Joseph Simmonds	do	48 00	695 22	6th reg't U. S. inf.	June 28, 1822	Dec. 8, 1821	do
John Smith	do	48 00	183 60	3d reg't U. S. inf.	May 8, 1830	May 8, 1830	do
George Thompson	do	96 00	600 51	7th reg't U. S. inf.	Oct. 22, 1817	Dec. 3, 1815	do
Jonathan Webber	Corporal	96 00	999 48	5th reg't U. S. inf.	Ap'l 30, 1824	Oct. 17, 1823	do
William G. Camp	Ensign	156 00	1,796 88	2d reg't U. S. rifl.	Aug. 2, 1816	July 16, 1815	Acts military establishment. By last report this pensioner resided at Fort Snelling, where he died Jan. 22, 1827.
SCOTT. Edward N. Matthews	do	48 00	169 41	Missouri rangers	Nov. 13, 1827	Aug. 25, 1827	July 2, 1812.

List of Invalid Pensioners who have been in the receipt of pensions at the Agency of St. Louis, in the State of Missouri, and whose residence cannot be ascertained in consequence of the destruction of the papers of the War Office in 1801 and 1814.

NAMES AND COUNTIES.	Rank.	Annual allowance.	Sums received.	Description of service.	When placed on the pension roll.	Commencement of pension.	Laws under which inscribed, increased and reduced; and remarks.
Daniel Kenny	Private	60 00	298 67	-	-	May 3, 1811	March 16, 1802.
Do	do	96 00	1,666 92	-	-	Apr'l 24, 1816	April 24, 1816.
Christopher Mourning	do	40 00	200 00	U. S. army	-	Mar. 4, 1809	Transferred from North Carolina.

Statement showing the Names, Rank, &c. of persons residing in the State of Missouri, who have been inscribed on the Pension List under the act of Congress passed the 18th day of March, 1818.

NAMES AND COUNTIES.	Rank.	Annual allowance.	Sums received.	Description of service.	When placed on the pension roll.	Commencement of pension.	Ages.	Laws under which they were formerly inscribed on the pension roll; and remarks.
BOONE.								
Isham Burks -	Private	96 00	1,392 23	Virginia cont'l line	Oct. 12, 1819	Sep. 4, 1819		
Benjamin Ethell or Athell -	Corporal	96 00	944 50	do	Sep. 7, 1820	Aug. 31, 1818	73	Died July 1, 1828.
CALLAWAY.								
Charles Colley -	Private	96 00	1,051 20	do	June 12, 1819	June 4, 1818	82	Died May 15, 1829.
Samuel Rhodes -	do	96 00	649 29	do	June 21, 1819	May 27, 1818	70	Died February 28, 1825.
CAPE GIRARDEAU.								
Uriah Brack -	do	96 00	68 49	do	Sep. 22, 1819	June 18, 1819	71	Dropped from the roll under act May 1, 1820.
Robert Chase -	do	96 00	737 80	N. York cont'l line	Dec. 2, 1823	Aug. 27, 1823	72	Died May 2, 1831.
James Cronister, or McCronister -	do	96 00	1,057 03	N. C. cont'l line	May 7, 1823	Mar. 1, 1823	81	
James Verden -	do	96 00	506 63	S. C. cont'l line	Jan. 14, 1829	Nov. 25, 1828		
Thomas Wrightington	do	96 00	436 12	Mass. cont'l line	Dec. 1, 1819	Aug. 20, 1819	79	Died March 20, 1824.
CLAY.								
William Rose -	do	96 00	1,391 16	Virginia cont'l line	do	Sep. 8, 1819	82	
COLE.								
Enoch Job -	do	96 00	503 99	Virginia cont'l line	Jan. 12, 1819	Dec. 5, 1828		
COOPER.								
William Campbell -	do	96 00	109 93	Virginia cont'l line	Jan. 13, 1830	Jan. 13, 1830		
Edward Robertson -	do	96 00	1,469 56	Houssegger's German regiment	Ap'l 24, 1819	Nov. 14, 1818		

Statement, &c.—Continued.

NAMES AND COUNTIES.	Rank.	Annual allowance.	Sums received.	Description of service.	When placed on the pension roll.	Commencement of pension.	Ages.	Laws under which they were formerly inscribed on the pension roll; and remarks.
FRANKLIN. George Miller	Private	96 00	680 64	Penn. cont'l line	June 9, 1823	May 14, 1823	74	Died June 15, 1830.
HOWARD. Henry Lynch	do	96 00	1,023 48	Virginia cont'l line	Sep. 19, 1823	July 7, 1823	70	
LAFAYETTE. John McLaughlin	do	96 00	973 92	Virginia cont'l	Oct. 2, 1819	May 26, 1818	79	Died July 17, 1828.
LINCOLN. John Barco	do	96 00	264 50	N. Carolina cont'l	Feb. 14, 1824	Dec. 2, 1823	90	
John Chambers	do	96 00	1,526 49	Virginia cont'l	June 9, 1820	Ap'l 13, 1818	94	
MONTGOMERY. Peter R. Feller	do	96 00	56 25	Washington's life guard	June 6, 1820	Aug. 4, 1819	-	Dropped from the roll under act May 1, 1820.
PIKE. Do	do	96 00	839 96	do	Ap'l 5, 1820	June 5, 1825	-	Restored under act March 1, 1823
William B. Rice	Sergeant	96 00	1,479 99	Virginia continental		Oct. 5, 1818	91	
ST. FRANCIS. Elijah Hendrick	Private	96 00	1,059 18	Virginia cont'l line	Mar. 23, 1822	Aug. 31, 1819	74	Died September 11, 1830.
ST. LOUIS. Thomas Arman	do	96 00	922 05	Virginia cont'l	Mar. 15, 1824	Jan. 5, 1824	83	Died August 12, 1833.
Daniel Applegate	Musician	96 00	643 14	New Jersey cont'l	Dec. 4, 1819	June 1, 1819	56	Died February 11, 1826.
Robert Blackwell	Private	96 00	1,483 69	Virginia cont'l	May 6, 1820	Sept. 21, 1818	73	
James Little	do	96 00	87 69	Pennsylvania cont'l	Oct. 7, 1819	Ap'l 6, 1819	80	
Thomas Wyatt	Ensign	240 00	218 24	do	do	do	80	
WAYNE. David Strickland	Sergeant	96 00	465 54	Connecticut cont'l	Oct. 12, 1819	July 26, 1819	65	Died May 31, 1824.

Statement showing the Names, Rank, &c. of persons residing in the State of Missouri, who have been inscribed on the Pension List under the act of Congress passed the 7th day of June, 1832.

NAMES AND COUNTIES.	Rank.	Annual allowance.	Sums received.	Description of service.	When placed on the pension roll.	Commencement of pension.	Ages.	Laws under which they were formerly inscribed on the pension roll; and remarks.
BOONE.								
William Bryant	Private	80 00	240 00	N. Carolina cont'l	Oct. 17, 1833	Mar. 4, 1831	90	
John Connelly	do	80 00	240 00	Maryland cont'l	May 2, 1833	do	72	
Benjamin Colvin	do	31 11	93 33	Virginia militia	Sept. 28, 1833	do	76	
Samuel Elgin	do	30 00	75 00	Maryland militia	do	do	75	
Reuben Hatton	Sergeant	48 33	123 32	Virginia militia	Feb. 20, 1834	do	72	
William Jones, 2d	Private	43 33	129 99	Virginia St. troops	Oct. 9, 1833	do	78	
Robert Lemon	Pr. & ser.	74 43	223 29	Pennsylvania militia	Sep. 28, 1833	do	79	
George Moore	Pri. of inf. & artlery	24 05	72 15	Virginia militia	July 2, 1834	do	73	
William Thompson	Private	23 33	69 99	do	Sep. 28, 1833	do	85	
CALLAWAY.								
William Armstrong	do	28 00	84 00	Pennsylvania militia	July 3, 1833	do	75	
Thomas Boyd, sen.	do	44 66	133 98	N. Carolina militia	Nov. 7, 1833	do	73	
Sylvester Baker, sen.	do	60 00	180 00	do	Feb. 8, 1833	do	80	
Reuben Clatterbuck	do	30 00	90 00	Virginia militia	Jan. 6, 1834	do	79	
Moses Ferguson	do	33 33	99 99	do	do	do	72	
David Henderson	do	23 33	58 32	do	Oct. 2, 1833	do	81	
George Key	do	80 00	240 00	Virginia cont'l	Oct. 17, 1833	do	81	
Josiah Ramsey	do	80 00	240 00	Virginia St. troops	Ap'l 12, 1834	do	81	
CAPE GIRARDEAU.								
Thomas Bull	do	80 00	240 00	Virginia cont'l	Sep. 18, 1833	do	81	
John Cockran	do	27 16	81 48	N. Carolina militia	June 5, 1833	do	79	
Mitchel Fleming	do	31 66	79 15	do	May 21, 1833	do	73	
Robert Green	Sergeant	120 00	300 00	Maryland cont'l	June 8, 1833	do	79	
Ithamar Hubbel	Private	56 66	169 98	N. York militia	Mar. 23, 1833	do	72	
Thomas Hill	Pri. of cav.	85 00	255 00	N. Carolina militia	Sep. 26, 1833	do	74	
Alexander McLane	do	63 33	189 99	N. Carolina St. tr'ps	do	do	78	

2

Statement, &c.—Continued.

NAMES AND COUNTIES.	Rank.	Annual allowance.	Sums received.	Description of service.	When placed on the pension roll.	Commencement of pension.	Ages.	Laws under which they were formerly inscribed on the pension roll; and remarks.
CHARITON.								
William Burton	Pri. & ser.	51 66	154 98	Virginia State tr.	June 3, 1834	Mar. 4, 1831	79	
Jonathan Elston	Private	20 00	60 00	N. Jersey militia	Jan. 6, 1834	do	71	
James Parks	do	39 56	98 90	N. Carolina St. tr.	Mar. 6, 1834	do	81	
Thomas Watson	do	20 00	60 00	Virginia State tr.	Feb. 11, 1834	do	80	
CLARKE.								
Thomas Holland	do	26 66	79 98	Virginia State tr.	Aug. 16, 1833	do	75	
CLAY.								
James Sewall	do	26 66	66 65	Virginia militia	Ap'l 2, 1833	do	76	
Richard Simms	do	80 00	200 00	Virginia continental	-	do	77	
Sabert Sollers	do	60 00	150 00	Virginia State tr.	May 13, 1834	do	76	
James Wills	do	26 55	79 65	do	May 13, 1834	do	71	
COLE.								
David Moore	do	30 00	90 00	Virginia militia	Ap'l 2, 1833	do	71	
William Powell	do	26 66	66 65	N. Carolina militia	Sep. 18, 1833	do	80	
John Roberts	do	23 33	69 99	Virginia militia	Ap'l 16, 1833	do	76	
Andrew Salisbury	do	80 00	240 00	S. Carolina State tr.	Nov. 8, 1832	do	80	
COOPER,								
David Allee	do	80 00	200 00	Virginia militia	Oct. 27, 1833	do	72	
George Carr	do	20 00	60 00	do	Oct. 17, 1833	do	87	
George Cathey	do	80 00	240 00	N. Carolina militia	Mar. 12, 1834	do	78	
John Chilcoat	do	63 33	189 99	Pennsylvania mil.	Mar. 14, 1834	do	75	
Josiah Dickson	do	80 00	200 00	Virginia continental	Feb. 8, 1833	do	82	
David Jones	Pri. & ser.	25 00	62 50	Virginia militia	Oct. 3, 1833	do	73	
Robert Kirkpatrick	Private	30 00	75 00	do	Oct. 17, 1833	do	70	
James Kelly	do	36 66	109 98	Virginia State tr.	Mar. 10, 1834	do	77	

Name	Rank			Service	Date		Age	Remarks
Benjamin Proctor	do	80 00	200 00	Virginia militia	Oct. 3, 1833	do	74	Died August 30, 1833.
Richard Westbrook	do	26 66	64 07	Penn. militia	Sep. 18, 1833	do	74	
CRAWFORD.								
Thomas Snelson	do	56 08	168 24	Virginia State tr.	Sep. 18, 1833	do	74	
William Wright	do	80 00	240 00	do	Jan. 31, 1834	do	75	
FRANKLIN.								
John Epperson	do	20 00	50 00	Virginia militia	Oct. 3, 1833	do	70	
Leonard Farrar	do	40 00	120 00	N. Carolina militia	Sep. 26, 1833	do	70	
Littlebury Hunt	do	40 00	100 00	Virginia militia	do	do	73	
William Mitchell	do.	20 00	50 00	do	Ap'l 2, 1833	do	70	
Hartly Sappington	do	40 00	-	Pennsylvania mil.	Ap'l 28, 1833	do	76	
Russel Twitty	do	30 00	90 00	N. Carolina militia	Sep. 26, 1833	do	70	
Charles H. Whittlesey	de	30 00	-	Connecticut St. tr.	June 19, 1834	do	63	Suspended.
HOWARD.								
Amos Ashcraft	do	80 00	193 54	Virginia militia	Aug. 29, 1833	do	77	Died August 5, 1833.
Abner Chappell	do	20 00	50 00	do	May 13, 1833	do	71	
James Callaway	do	80 00	240 00	Virg. continental	May 3, 1834	do	78	
Joseph Huges	do	27 43	82 29	Penn. militia	Ap'l 28, 1834	do	81	
Clabourn Johnson	do	50 00	150 00	Virginia S ate tr'p- do	May 28, 1834	do	74	
William Long	do	73 33	219 99	do	Feb. 6, 1833	do	74	
James Noble	do	80 00	240 00	Virg. continental	Jan. 29, 1834	do	73	
Samuel Tomlin	do	20 00	60 00	Virginia militia	Ap'l 28, 1833	do	79	
Edward Williams	Pri. & ser.	29 16	87 48	N. C. militia	Feb. 6, 1833	do	73	
Jesse Walker	Private	80 00	240 00	do	Jan. 29, 1834	do	86	
JACKSON.								
William Moore	do	80 00	200 00	Virginia cont'l	Oct. 17, 1833	do	77	
Ledston Noland	do	80 00	-	N. C. militia	Ap'l 8, 1834	do	84	
LAFAYETTE.								
James Demaster	do	80 00	240 00	Virg. cont'l	May 2, 1833	do	71	
Joshua Ferguson	do	20 00	-	S. Carolina St. tr.	July 16, 1834	do	80	
James Kincaid	do	58 11	174 33	Virginia militia	Ap'l 28, 1834	do	71	
LINCOLN.								
Joseph Brown	do	80 00	240 00	N. C. State troops	Oct. 17, 1833	do	77	
William Butler	do	20 00	60 00	Virg. State troops	Jan. 9, 1834	do	72	
James Cannon	Pr. of cav.	100 00	300 00	S. Carolina militia	Aug. 29, 1833	do	73	

Statement, &c.—Continued.

NAMES AND COUNTIES.	Rank.	Annual allowance.	Sums received.	Description of service.	When placed on the pension roll.	Commencement of pension.	Ages.	Laws under which they were formerly inscribed on the pension roll; and remarks.
LINCOLN—continued.								
Thomas Graves	Sergeant	96 66	241 66	Virginia militia	Sep. 18, 1833	March 4, 1831	87	
Michael Glass	Pr. of cav.	100 00	300 00	Virginia State tr.	Mar. 24, 1833	do	70	
Thomas Hampton	Private	80 00	240 00	do	Ap'l 2, 1833	do	74	
Hezekiah Murphey	do	40 00	100 00	Maryland militia	July 31, 1833	do	70	
Robert McNair	Pr. & art'r	112 00	280 00	Penn. militia	Jan. 9, 1834	do	77	
Adam Zumwalt	Private	80 00	240 00	Virginia State tr.	Oct. 9, 1833	do	78	
MADISON.								
William Boren	do	20 00	60 00	S. Carolina militia	Oct. 3, 1833	do	68	
Joham Harrison	Pr. & lieut.	50 00	150 00	Virginia militia	do	do	74	
John Reeves	Private	46 66	139 98	N. Carolina militia	do	do	74	
Jeremiah Robinson	do	40 00	100 00	Virginia militia	do	do	75	
Robert Sinc'air	do	33 33	99 99	do	do	do	80	
Jacob Stevens	do	30 00	90 00	do	do	do	75	
MARION.								
Michael Burchfield	Pri. of inf. and cavalry	69 72	209 16	N. Carolina milita	July 3, 1833	do	72	
Moses Gill	Private	80 00	240 00	M'd State troops	Sep. 28, 1833	do	77	
William Johnson, sen.	do	36 66	109 98	Virginia militia	July 3, 1833	do	72	
Anderson Long	do	60 00	180 00	do	Feb. 3, 1833	do	73	
William Montgomery	do	80 00	-	Virginia cont'l	April 2, 1833	do	77	
John Wash, sen.	Pri, lt, ass. com'y, & captain	158 65	475 95	Georgia militia	Feb. 20, 1833	do	82	Dead.
MONROE.								
Neilly Bybee	Private	60 00	180 00	Virginia continental	Nov. 14, 1832	do	71	Transferred from Kentucky.

Name	Rank			Service	Date		Age	Remarks
MONTGOMERY.								
Robert Baker	do	45 00	135 00	Virg'a State troops	Sep. 18, 1833	do	80	
Samuel Cobb	do	30 00	75 00	Virginia militia	Oct. 17, 1833	do	74	
William Hall	do	54 00	162 00	N. Carolina militia	Sept. 18, 1833	do	73	
Jacob Patton	do	36 66	91 65	S. Carolina militia	Oct. 2, 1833	do	84	
Daniel Taylor	do	40 00	120 00	Virg'a State troops	June 11, 1833	do	85	
MORGAN.								
Benjamin Letchworth	do	80 00	240 00	Virg'a continental	Feb. 8, 1833	do	77	
PERRY.								
John B. Gough	do	24 66	73 98	Maryland militia	Ap'l 12, 1833	do	70	
Casper Hinkle	do	20 00	60 00	N. Carolina militia	Mar. 12, 1834	do	72	
PIKE.								
Zachariah Burch	do	80 00	240 00	Maryland cont'l	Ap'l 2, 1833	do	77	
William Craig	do	30 00	90 00	Virginia militia	Nov. 28, 1833	do	76	
James McElwee	do	76 66	219 48	S. Carolina militia	May 28, 1833	do	76	
John Mulheren	do	30 00	-	do	Sep. 18, 1833	do	74	
James Mackey	do	53 33	133 32	N. Carolina cont'l	Sept. 26, 1833	do	76	
William McQuie	do	20 00	60 00	Virginia militia	Feb. 10, 1834	do	72	Transferred from New York.
George Reading	do	62 33	155 82	Pennsylv'a militia	Apr. 17, 1833	do	70	
David Tomb	Sergeant	80 00	200 00	S. Carolina militia	Sep. 18, 1833	do	80	Died January 3, 1834.
Samuel Watson	Pri. of cav.	95 00	285 00	do	Apr. 28, 1834	do	83	
PULASKI.								
John Vest	Private	35 31	88 27	Virginia militia	Sept. 18, 1833	do		
RALLS.								
Ignatius Greenwell	do	60 00	150 00	Maryland militia	Sept. 16, 1833	do	84	
Robert Jamison	do	32 22	80 55	Virginia militia	Oct. 2, 1833	do	73	
Rhodam Sims	do	30 00	90 00	do	Nov. 9, 1833	do	79	
Samuel Turner	do	20 00	50 00	do	Aug. 29, 1833	do	79	
RANDOLPH.								
Leonard Bradley	Lieutenant	176 59	529 79	Virginia State tr.	Sep. 18, 1833	do	78	
Edmund Bartlett	Private	49 33	123 32	Virginia militia	Oct. 17, 1833	do	74	
Edmund Chapman	do	20 00	50 00	do	Aug. 29, 1833	do	70	
James Davis	Sergeant	120 00	300 00	Virginia cont'l	Sep. 18, 1833	do	81	
James Fletcher	Private	22 33	66 99	Virginia State tr.	Oct. 17, 1833	do	76	

Statement, &c.—Continued.

NAMES AND COUNTIES.	Rank.	Annual allowance.	Sums received.	Description of service.	When placed on the pension roll.	Commencement of pension.	Ages.	Laws under which they were formerly inscribed on the pension roll; and remarks.
RANDOLPH—Continued.								
Charles Finnell -	Private	20 00	60 00	Virginia militia	Ap'l 3, 1834	Mar. 4, 1831	72	
Nicholas Tuttle -	do	80 00	240 00	Virginia contin'l	Sep. 18, 1833	do	75	
Bennet Tilley -	do	35 00	-	N. Carolina militia	July 10, 1834	do	77	
RAY.								
John Wallace -	do	80 00	240 00	S. Carolina militia	Dec. 12, 1833	do	88	
ST. FRANCOIS.								
James Cunningham -	do	40 00	120 00	Virginia militia	Oct. 17, 1833	do	78	
James Caldwell -	do	29 54	88 62	do	Jan. 29, 1834	do	71	
William Murphey, sen. -	Pri. & ser.	95 00	244 89	do	Oct. 17, 1833	do	75	Died November 2, 1833.
Joseph Murphey, sen. -	Private	23 33	58 32	do	do	do	73	
William Nicholson -	do	40 00	100 00	Penn. continental	do	do	79	
ST. LOUIS.								
William Berry -	Pri. & ser.	40 00	120 00	Virginia contin'l	Oct. 9, 1833	do	79	
John Cunningham -	Private	40 00	120 00	Penn. continental	Oct. 17, 1833	do	73	
Zachariah Cross -	do	40 00	120 00	N. Carolina militia	Jan. 2, 1834	do	81	Transferred from Tennessee.
Francis Hickman -	do	40 00	-	Penn. continental	June 23, 1834	do	71	
David Musick -	do	63 33	189 99	N. Carolina militia	Mar. 28, 1834	do	80	
Mathias Rose -	do	40 44	121 32	Virginia St. troops	Oct. 9, 1833	do		
SALINE.								
Isham Brown -	do	80 00	240 00	Virginia contin'l	May 30, 1833	do	84	
Benjamin Chambers -	Lieutenant	240 00	1,988 00	Pennsylvania cont'l	Feb. 21, 1823	Nov. 22, 1821	-	Act March 18, 1818. Relinquished for the benefits of the act of June 7, 1832.
Do. -	do	320 00	960 00	do	Aug. 31, 1832	do	72	
Benjamin A. Cooper -	do	320 00	960 00	Virginia State tr.	Ap'l 28, 1833	Mar. 4, 1831	78	

	Pri. & ser.							Transferred from Virginia.
ST. CHARLES. Matthew Farmer	Pri. & ser.	25 00	62 50	Virginia militia	Dec. 7, 1832	do		
WARREN. Benjamin Sharp	Private	35 97	89 92	Virginia militia	Sep. 18, 1833	do	73	
John Wyatt	do	80 00	240 00	N. C. State troops	Feb. 20, 1833	do	75	
William Ward	Pri. & ser.	117 50	352 50	Penn. State troops	Feb. 25, 1833	do	77	
WASHINGTON. Elijah Baker	Private	80 00	240 00	Virginia State tr.	Jan. 6, 1834	do	74	
John Hawkins	do	71 67	215 01	N. Carolina militia	Nov. 9, 1833	do	72	
James Johnson	do	33 08	82 70	Virginia militia	Sep. 18, 1833	do	74	
Joseph Moutry	do	60 00	180 00	Virginia contin'l	Ap'l 12, 1834	do	74	
Peter Pinnel	do	36 66	109 98	S. C. State troops	Jan. 6, 1834	do	74	

Statement showing the Names, Rank, &c. of persons residing in the State of Missouri, who have received the benefits of the act of Congress passed May 15, 1828.

NAMES AND COUNTIES.	Rank.	Annual allowance.	Sums received.	Description of service.	When placed on the pension roll.	Names of agents or representatives.	Remarks.
CAPE GIRARDEAU. Uriah Brock -	Musician	104 00	884 00	- reg. Virg. line	Oct. 6, 1828	J. Ranney, agent	
PIKE. John Allen -	Artificer	144 00	661 20	Corps artificers	Jan. 24, 1829	Sarah Allen, ext'x	Died October 5, 1830.
ST. CHARLES. Zachariah Moore -	Sergeant	120 00	960 00	2d reg. Md. line	Dec. 20, 1828	Hon. D. Barton, ag't.	

Commencem't of pay, Mar. 3, 1826.

OHIO PENSION ROLL.

Statement showing the names, rank, &c. of Invalid Pensioners residing in the county of Adams, in the State of Ohio.

NAMES.	Rank.	Annual allowance.	Sums received.	Description of service.	When placed on the pension roll.	Commencement of pension.	Laws under which they were inscribed, increased and reduced; and remarks.
John Symmonds Do	Private do	60 00 96 00	1,620 32 1,714 59	2d reg. U. S. inf. do	- -	Mar. 4, 1789 Ap'l 24, 1816	June 7, 1785. April 24, 1816. Increased by act April 24, 1816 to this rate. Transferred from Maryland,

Statement, &c. of Ashtabula county, Ohio.

NAMES.	Rank.	Annual allowance.	Sums received.	Description of service.	When placed on the pension roll.	Commencement of pension.	Laws under which they were inscribed, increased, and reduced; and remarks.
Enoch Barnum	Private	96 00	1,649 03	Bartholomew's co. militia.	Mar. 24, 1817	Jan. 1, 1817	March 3, 1817.

Statement, &c. of Athens county, Ohio.

NAMES.	Rank.	Annual allowance.	Sums received.	Description of service.	When placed on the pension roll.	Commencement of pension.	Laws under which they were inscribed, increased, and reduced; and remarks.
William Morrows	Private	96 00	2,028 38	Ohio volunteers	Dec. 5, 1817	Jan. 19, 1813	Acts military establishment.
John Rice	Corporal	45 00	105 55	4th reg. U. S. inf.	Dec. 4, 1815	Dec. 21, 1813	April 24, 1816. Increased to this rate by act April 24, 1816. Transferred from New York from Sept. 4, 1821. Died Feb. 4, 1823.
Do	do	72 00	591 77	do	-	April 24, 1816	
Samuel Taylor	Private	60 00	61 00	21st reg. U. S. inf.	Mar. 20, 1816	April 19, 1815	Acts military establishment. April 26, 1816. Increased to this rate by act April 24, 1816.
Do	do	96 00	1,714 63	do	-	April 24, 1816	

Statement, &c. of Belmont county, Ohio.

NAMES.	Rank.	Annual allowance.	Sums received.	Description of service.	When placed on the pension roll.	Commencement of pension.	Laws under which they were inscribed, increased and reduced ; and remarks.
Joseph Bggs	Ensign	108 00	2,140 80	Biggs' regiment	-	June 29, 1796	April 24, 1816. Increased by act April 24, 1816 to this rate. Transferred from Virginia from September 4, 1825. Died February 1, 1833.
Do	do	134 40	2,253 77	do	-	Ap'l 24, 1816	
William Broderick	Sergeant	40 00	1,060 00	-	-	Mar. 4, 1789	September 29, 1789. Died May 17, 1815.
David Kirkland	Sergeant	48 00	986 33	Ohio militia	Feb. 12, 1817	Aug. 18, 1813	Act April 30, 1816.

Statement, &c. of Brown county, Ohio.

NAMES.	Rank.	Annual allowance.	Sums received.	Description of service.	When placed on the pension roll.	Commencement of pension.	Laws under which they were inscribed, increased and reduced; and remarks.
Richard Harden	Sergt.	60 00	577 07	Revolutionary army	--	Sep. 11, 1806	March 3, 1807.
Do	do	96 00	1,198 69	do	--	Ap'l 24, 1816	Increased to this rate by act April 24, 1816. Transferred from Maryland, from March 4, 1820. Died October 10, 1828.

Statement, &c. of Butler county, Ohio.

NAMES.	Rank.	Annual allowance.	Sums received.	Description of service.	When placed on the pension roll.	Commencement of pension.	Laws under which they were inscribed, increased and reduced; and remarks.
William Smith	Private	96 00	603 96	26th reg. U. S. inf.	May 9, 1825	Nov. 20, 1824	Acts military establishment.
Hezekiah Seals	do	64 00	594 55	39th reg. U. S. inf.	Dec. 10, 1825	do	Acts military establishment. Transferred from East Tennessee from September 4, 1828.

Statement, &c. of Champaign county, Ohio.

NAMES.	Rank.	Annual allowance.	Sums received.	Description of service.	When placed on the pension roll.	Commencement of pension.	Laws under which they were inscribed, increased and reduced; and remarks.
Jonathan Burwell	Private	48 00	504 12	-	Feb. 12, 1824	Mar. 4, 1818	Transferred from Pennsylvania from September 4, 1822.
William Gutridge	do	72 00	517 78	19th reg. U. S. inf.	Jan. 24, 1822	Sep. 20, 1821	Acts military establishment.
Do	do	96 00	505 29	do	–	Nov. 29, 1828	
William Rhodes	Corporal	48 00	165 73	4th reg. U. S. inf.	Dec. 24, 1821	Nov. 3, 1814	April 30, 1816. Invalid pensioner under act April 30, 1816.
Do	do	96 00	181 03	do	-	Ap'l 15, 1818	March 18, 1818. Dropped from invalid roll and placed on revolutionary roll under act March 18, 1818.
Do	do	48 00	262 18	do	-	Mar. 4, 1830	May 1, 1820. Droppd from revolutionary roll under act May 1,1820, and replaced on inv. roll. Died Aug. 22,1825.
John Shery	Private	48 00	143 08	19th reg. U. S. inf.	Dec. 6, 1822	Oct. 15, 1822	Acts military establishment.
Do	do	72 00	166 91	do	–	Oct. 7, 1825	
Do	do	96 00	593 28	do	–	Jan. 30, 1828	
Jack M. Sally	do	48 00	366 54	17th reg. U. S. inf.	Dec. 31, 1824	July 27, 1824	
Do	do	72 00	141 37	do	-	Mar. 16, 1832	

Statement, &c. of Clark county, Ohio.

NAMES.	Rank.	Annual allowance.	Sums received.	Description of service.	When placed on the pension roll.	Commencement of pension.	Laws under which they were inscribed, increased, and reduced; and remarks.
Malyne Baker	Private	48 00	392 53	Little's com. art'y	Mar. 24, 1817	Jan. 1, 1817	March 3, 1817.
William G. Servess	2d lieut.	120 00	1,421 17	U. S. rangers	May 8, 1820	Mar. 28, 1815	Act June 2, 1812.
Do	do	180 00	1,277 50	do	-	Jan. 30, 1827	

Statement, &c. of Clermont county, Ohio.

NAMES.	Rank.	Annual allowance.	Sums received.	Description of service.	When placed on the pension roll.	Commencement of pension.	Laws under which they were inscribed, increased, and remarks.
George Barngrover	Private	96 00	1,999 22	1st reg. Ohio vol.	June 25, 181	May 8, 1813	April 24, 1816.
Frederick Bassee	do	96 00	1,816 51	Ohio militia	May 13, 182	Aug. 13, 1813	Died July 14, 1832.
Matthew Patterson	do	48 00	248 00	1st reg. U. S. inf.	Dec. 21, 1816	July 4, 1815	Acts mil'y estab. Died Oct. 1, 1823.
William Slye	do	40 00	685 72	Rev. army	-	Mar. 4, 1789	June 7, 1785.
Do	do	64 00	1,143 03	do	-	Apl 24, 1816	April 24, 1816.

Statement, &c. of Clinton county, Ohio.

NAMES.	Rank.	Annual allowance.	Sums received.	Description of service.	When placed on the pension roll.	Commencement of pension.	Laws under which they were inscribed, increased and reduced; and remarks.
Thomas Fugate	Private	96 00	601 31	22d reg. U. S. inf.	May 11, 1816	May 31, 1814	April 30, 1816.
Do	do	48 00	164 60	do	"	Sep. 4, 1820	March 3, 1819. Reduced to this rate by act March 3, 1819.
Do	do	72 00	211 48	do	"	Feb. 9, 1824	
Do	do	96 00	684 23	do	"	Jan. 19, 1827	
William Vineyard	do	48 00	448 32	Tupper's brigade	Feb. 9, 1822	Nov. 2, 1815	April 30, 1816.

Statement, &c. of Cuyahoga county, Ohio.

NAMES.	Rank.	Annual allowance.	Sums received.	Description of service.	When placed on the pension roll.	Commencement of pension.	Laws under which they were inscribed, increased and reduced; and remarks.
Benjamin Batchelor	Matross	32 00	571 70	Towson's artillery	Ap'l 25, 1820	Mar. 19, 1816	Acts military establishment. Transferred from Vermont from March 4, 1833.
John Burt	Sergeant	32 00	354 16	Pierce's artillery	Oct. 22, 1819	Dec. 5, 1818	Acts military establishment.
Moses Eldred	Private	64 00	1,345 53	Murray's co. militia	Feb. 25, 1817	Feb. 24, 1813	Acts military establishment.
Benjamin Johnston	do	96 00	1,495 99	3d reg. U. S. inf.	July 23, 1819	Aug. 5, 1818	
Ebenezer Maddox	Serge at	32 00	800 76	3rd reg. U. S. inf.	Nov. 18, 1825	Nov. 2, 1825	Acts military establishment. Transferred from Michigan from September 4, 1830.
Hiram Porter	Private	32 00	-	6th reg. U. S. inf.	Jan. 7, 1819	Mar. 17, 1818	July 5, 1812.

Statement, &c. of Columbiana county, Ohio.

NAMES.	Rank.	Annual allowance.	Sums received.	Description of service.	When placed on the pension roll.	Commencement of pension.	Laws under which they were inscribed, increased and reduced; and remarks.
William Snyder	Private	72 00	1,304 48	19th reg. U. S. inf.	Feb. 28, 1817	June 11, 1815	Acts military establishment.

Statement, &c. of Coshocton county, Ohio.

NAMES.	Rank.	Annual allowance.	Sums received.	Description of service.	When placed on the pension roll.	Commencement of pension.	Laws under which they were inscribed, increased, and reduced; and remarks.
Samuel Williams	Private	96 00	1,878 44	21st reg. U. S. inf.	Aug. 11, 1815	Aug. 12, 1814	Acts military establishment. Transferred from Penn. from March 4, 1825.

Statement, &c. of Crawford county, Ohio.

NAMES.	Rank.	Annual allowance.	Sums received.	Description of service.	When placed on the pension roll.	Commencement of pension.	Laws under which they were inscribed, increased and reduced; and remarks.
John Spitzer	Private	48 00	798 53	12th reg. U. S. inf.	May 20, 1817	Jan. 14, 1815	

Statement, &c. of Dark county, Ohio.

NAMES.	Rank.	Annual allowance.	Sums received.	Description of service.	When placed on the pension roll.	Commencement of pension.	Laws under which they were inscribed, increased and reduced; and remarks.
George Adams	Private	60 00	254 32	--		Jan. 29, 1812	July 5, 1812.
Do	do	96 00	1,593 33	--		Ap'l 24, 1816	April 24, 1816. Increased to this rate by act April 24, 1816. Died Nov. 28, 1832.

Statement, &c. of Delaware county, Ohio.

NAMES.	Rank.	Annual allowance.	Sums received.	Description of service.	When placed on the pension roll.	Commencement of pension.	Laws under which they were inscribed, increased and reduced; and remarks.
Oliver Bennett	Private	60 00	1,628 34	Revolutionary army	--	Mar. 4, 1789	June 7, 1785.
Do	do	96 00	1,714 56	do	--	Apr. 24, 1816	April 24, 1816. Transferred from Ky., from March 4, 1817. Dead.
Weeks Copeland	Corporal	72 00	200 66	30th reg. of U.S. inf.	Apl. 7, 1834	Feb. 18, 1834	January 29, 1813.
William Faucher	Private	38 40	490 56	Crane's regiment	-	Ap'l 24, 1816	Transferred from New York, from March 4, 1827. Died Feb. 3, 1829.
Lewis Hyatt	do	72 00	502 60	3d reg. of U. S. art.	Oct. 21, 1816	June 14, 1815	Acts military establishment. Transf'd from N. York, from March 4, 1820.
Benjamin Hillman	Lieutenant	120 00	974 00	Revolutionary army	--	Mar. 14, 1808	April 25, 1808.
Do	do	136 00	727 99	do	-	Ap'l 24, 1816	April 24, 1816. Increased to this rate by act April 24, 1816. Died June 7, 1822.
Richard Thompson	Musician	64 00	531 74	Sumner's militia	May 6, 1826	Nov. 13, 1825	Transferr'd from Pennsylvania, from September 4, 1820. Died August 31, 1821. April 24, 1816.

Statement, &c. of Fairfield county, Ohio.

NAMES.	Rank.	Annual allowance.	Sums received.	Description of service.	When placed on the sion roll.	Commencement of pension.	Laws under which they were inscribed, increased and reduced; and remarks.
Samuel Hawkins - -	Private	40 00	16 52	Mounted volunteers	Ap'l 3, 1824	Feb. 4, 1814	April 18, 1814.
Elijah Hedges - -	do	60 00	1,208 34	Revolutionary army	-	Mar. 4, 1796	March 23, 1796.
Do	do	96 00	1,714 63	do	-	Apl 24, 1816	April 24, 1816. Increased to this rate by act April 24, 1816. Transferred from Virginia, from Sep. 4, 1824.
Othias Miller - -	do	72 00	162 89	Ohio militia	Dec. 18, 1827	Nov. 12, 1827	April 24, 1827.
Do - -	do	96 00	387 31	do	-	Feb. 20, 1830	

Statement, &c. of Franklin county, Ohio.

Names.	Rank.	Annual allowance.	Sums received.	Description of service.	When placed on the pension roll.	Commencement of pension.	Laws under which they were inscribed, increased and reduced; and remarks.
David S. Chapin	Private	48 00	106 68	New York militia	Sep. 24, 1822	July 23, 1822	April 24, 1816. Transferred from N. York, from March 4, 1833.
Do	do	72 00	676 65	do	Oct. 29, 1824	Oct. 11, 1824	Transferred from N. York, from March 4, 1820.
John Dalzell	Corporal	32 00	558 53	23d reg. U. S. inf.	Oct. 14, 1816	Mar. 21, 1815	Acts military establishment.
Richard Fling	Private	64 00	533 78	Burd's co. lt. drag.	Mar. 22, 1816	May 2, 1815	March 3, 1819. Reduced by act Mar. 3, 1819.
Do	do	48 00	452 34	do	-	Sep. 4, 1823	Transferred from Virginia, from September 4, 1833.
Do	do	64 00	68 26	do		Feb. 7, 1833	Acts military establishment.
Cornelius McMahon	do	40 00	30 07	6th reg't U. S. inf.		July 25, 1815	April 24, 1816. Increased to this rate by act April 24, 1816.
Do	do	64 00	215 03	do		Ap'l 24, 1816	Mar. 3, 1819. Reduced by act March 3, 1819.
Do	do	48 00	353 39	do		Sep. 4, 1819	
Do	do	96 00	349 18	do	Sep. 26, 1788	Jan. 15, 1827	June 7, 1785. April 24, 1816. Increased to this rate by act April 24, 1816. Died August 10, 1824.
John Starr	do	40 00	1,385 39	Conn. militia	-	Sep. 6, 1781	
Do	do	64 00	530 72	do	-	Ap'l 24, 1816	
Tan-de-het-se	Seneca warrior	96 00	257 06	Late war	May 29, 1830	Jan. 1, 1828	May 20, 1830.
Ross Wallace	Private	48 00	-	3d reg't U. S. inf.	May 17, 1822	June 7, 1816	Acts military establishment.

Statement, &c. of Gallia county, Ohio.

NAMES.	Rank.	Annual allowance.	Sums received.	Description of service.	When placed on the pension roll.	Commencement of pension.	Laws under which they were inscribed, increased and reduced; and remarks.
William Butler	Private	78 00	990 66	Revolutionary army	--	Sep. 5, 1795	June 7, 1785.
Do	do	76 80	1,064 52	do	--	Ap'l 24, 1816	April 24, 1816. Increased to this rate by act April 24, 1816. Transferred from Virginia from September 4, 1821.
George Cress	do	30 00	199 52	do	--	Aug. 7, 1809	April 27, 1810.
Do	do	48 00	321 33	do	--	Ap'l 24, 1816	April 24, 1816. Increased to this rate by act April 24, 1816. Transferred from Virginia from Mar. 4, 1822
Moses Cremens	do	72 00	-	Ohio militia	Mar. 12, 1834	Jan. 1, 1832	Act March 2, 1833.

Statement, &c. of Geauga county, Ohio.

NAMES.	Rank.	Annual allowance.	Sums received.	Description of service.	When placed on the pension roll.	Commencement of pension.	Laws under which they were inscribed, increased and reduced; and remarks.
Amos Morse	Private	96 00	865 03	19th reg. of U. S. inf.	Mar. 2, 1825	Mar. 1, 1825	Acts military establishment.
Benjamin Mastick	do	40 00	926 19	Revolutionary army	Nov. 20, 1792	Mar. 17, 1786	June 7, 1785.
Do	do	60 00	417 04	do	-	May 11, 1809	March 3, 1811. Increased to this rate by act March 3, 1811.
Do	do	96 00	1,355 14	do	-	Ap'l 24, 1816	April 24, 1816. Increased to this rate by act April 24, 1816. Transferred from Massachusetts, from March 4, 1826. Died June 6, 1830.

Statement, &c. of Green county, Ohio.

NAMES.	Rank.	Annual allowance.	Sums received.	Description of service.	When placed on the pension roll.	Commencement of pension.	Laws under which they were inscribed, increased and reduced; and remarks.
Bartholomew Berry ·	Private	60 00	447 68	—	—	Nov. 7, 1808	March 3, 1809.
Do · ·	do	96 00	178 63	—	—	Ap'l 24, 1816	April 24, 1816. Increased to this rate by act April 24, 1816.
William Maxwell ·	do	48 00	488 76	M°Cormick's rang'rs	Mar. 24, 1817	Oct. 8, 1816	March 3, 1817.
Do · ·	do	72 00	376 25	do	—	Dec. 13, 1826	
Do · ·	do	96 00	191 73	do	—	Mar. 6, 1832	
Edward Warren ·	do	96 00	32 49	Revolutionary army	Nov. 5, 1819	Nov. 3, 1819	Act March 18, 1818. Dropped from revolutionary roll under act May 1, 1820, and placed on invalid roll.— Died August 5, 1824,
Do ·	do	96 00	424 25	do	—	Mar. 4, 1820	May 1, 1820.

Statement, &c. of Guernsey county, Ohio.

NAMES.	Rank.	Annual allowance.	Sums received.	Description of service.	When placed on the pension roll.	Commencement of pension.	Laws under which they were inscribed, increased and reduced; and remarks.
George Lantz ·	Private	72 00	421 59	Ohio militia	Dec. 12, 1827	Oct. 27, 1827	April 24, 1816.

Statement, &c. of Hamilton county, Ohio.

NAMES.	Rank.	Annual allowance.	Sums received.	Description of service.	When placed on the pension roll.	Commencement of pension.	Laws under which they were inscribed, increased, and reduced; and remarks.
John Arthur	Private	96 00	581 94	17th reg. U. S. inf.	Dec. 5, 1825	Oct. 11, 1825	Acts military establishment. Transferred from Kentucky from Sep. 4, 1826. Died November 2, 1831.
Thomas Auter	do	48 00	298 85	Ohio volunteers	Dec. 14, 1827	Dec. 14, 1827	February 6, 1825.
William Bowyer	do	96 00	1,477 92	1st reg. U.S. riflem.	Oct. 16, 1819	Oct. 10, 1815	April 30, 1816. Died March 1, 1831.
Joseph Cilley	1st lieut.	153 00	431 89	Ohio volunteers	Jan. 13, 1826	Nov. 8, 2825	April 24, 1816.
James Critchton	Private	60 00	68 80	1st reg. U. S. riflem.	Jan. 11, 1816	Mar. 10, 1815	Acts military establishment. April 24, 1816. Increased to this rate by act April 24, 1816.
Do	do	96 00	1,714 63	do	–	Ap'l 24, 1816	
Daniel C. Carter	do	30 00	17 16	17th reg.U. S. riflem.	Feb. 14, 1816	Sep. 28, 1815	Acts military establishment. April 24, 1816. Increased to this rate by act April 24, 1816. Died January 7, 1821.
Do	do	48 00	225 74	do		Ap'l 24, 1816	
Shubael Carpenter	do	72 00	1,343 14	5th reg. U. S. inf.	Jan. 8, 1816	July 7, 1815	Acts military establishment. Transferred from Vermont from March 4, 1825.
James Colburn	Artificer	96 00	1,810 89	Leonard's artillery	Mar. 19, 1816	Ap'l 24, 1815	Acts military establishment. Transferred from Kentucky from September 4, 1826.
Robert Curry	Private	96 00	593 03	1st reg. U. S. inf.	Aug. 30, 1830	Jan. 1, 1828	May 20, 1830.
David Corey	do	96 00	1,798 63	23d reg.U. S. inf.	Feb. 6, 1817	June 10, 1815	Acts military establishment. Transferred from Indiana from March 4, 1833.
James Dean	Sergeant	72 00	857 83	U. S. corps artill'y	Sep. 6, 1820	Oct. 2, 1819	Acts mil. est., & May 15, 1820.
Daniel Davis	do	64 00	1,198 94	17th reg.U. S. inf.	Oct. 21, 1816	June 10, 1815	Acts military establishment.
Stephen Enos	do	48 00	958 18	5th reg.U. S. inf.	Feb. 22, 1817	Mar. 19, 1814	Acts military establishment.
Do	do	96 00		do	–	May 17, 1834	Transferred from Delaware from Mar. 4, 1822.
Joseph Fiester	do	72 00	–	do	June 26, 1824	Sep. 26, 1823	Acts military establishment.
Isaac Freeman	Private	48 00	–	1st reg. U. S. inf.	July 28, 1834	May 6, 1834	

Name	Rank	Rate	Amount	Corps	Date	Date	Remarks
James Grigg	do	48 00	324 63	17th reg. U. S. inf.	July 12, 1827	May 31, 1827	Acts military establishment.
William Husted	do	48 00	88 53	5th reg. U. S. inf.	Feb. 4, 1824	Nov. 1, 1822	Acts military establishment.
John Hurd	do	96 00	1,052 47	40th reg. U. S. inf.	Mar. 30, 1818	Aug. 11, 1814	Acts military establishment.
Do	do	48 00	240 00	do	-	Sep. 4, 1825	March 3, 1819. Reduced by act March 3, 1819. Transferred from Massachusetts from March 4, 1824.
Andrew Lawson	do	96 00	1,797 56	25th reg. U. S. inf.	Jan. 6, 1816	June 14, 1815	Acts military establishment. Transferred from New York from September 4, 1820.
Charles Larrabee	1st lieut.	204 00	1,218 16	4th reg. U. S. inf.	Ap'l 22, 1828	Ap'l 13, 1824	Act April 12, 1818.
Do	do	300 00	983 01	do	-	Ap'l 2, 1830	
William Lever	Private	96 00	239 61	5th reg. U. S. inf.	June 20, 1823	July 22, 1821	Acts military establishment.
John R. Martin	Sur's mate	270 00	461 54	U. States navy	Dec. 30, 1815	June 16, 1815	Acts military establishment. Died.
Alexander McNutt	Private	96 00	672 25	4th reg. U. S. rifl'm	Oct. 16, 1827	Mar. 3, 1827	March 3, 1827.
Edmund Mayo	do	64 00	97 87	1st reg. U. S. inf.	Oct. 8, 1832	Aug. 25, 1832	Acts military establishment.
John McDonald	do	96 00		5th reg. U. infantry	June 20, 1823	July 3, 1821	do
William McGraw	do	48 00	185 84	do	do	Ap'l 21, 1821	March 3, 1811.
Edward Miller	Ser. major	60 00	428 48	Rev. army	Ap'l 20, 1821	May 3, 1809	April 24, 1816. Increased to this rate by act April 24, 1816.
Do	do	96 00	658 63	-	-	Ap'l 24, 1816	Acts military establishment.
Abraham Rigel	Private	48 00	484 28	19th reg. U. S. inf.	May 27, 1824	Feb. 7, 1824	Acts military establishment. Transferred from D. C. from Mar. 4, 1830.
Aaron Stewart	do	48 00	561 87	-	-	Oct. 4, 1815	Acts military establishment.
Do	do	96 00	644 49	-	-	June 17, 1827	do
John Sutton	do	48 00	909 80	6th reg. U. S. inf.	Feb. 17, 1818	Mar. 22, 1813	Acts military establishment.
Francis Saunders	Musician	72 00	-	7th reg. U. S. inf.	July 29, 1834	May 16, 1834	Acts military establishment.
William Taylor	Private	96 00	161 03	5th reg. U. S. inf.	Aug. 21, 1832	July 1, 1832	do
Earl D. Vinton	Sergeant	96 00	553 48	25th reg. U. S. inf.	Feb. 28, 1827	Jan. 31, 1827	Acts military establishment. Died November 4, 1832.
Benjamin Whetford	Private	48 00	591 86	do	Mar. 27, 1818	May 13, 1815	Acts military establishment.
Do	do	96 00	574 40	do	-	Sep. 10, 1827	
Robert Welsh	do	24 00	155 61	U. S. mt'd rangers	June 18, 1822	July 25, 1821	June 2, 1812, and May 15, 1820.
Do	do	48 00	294 18	do	Ap'l 16, 1828	Jan. 18, 1828	
Thomas Webster	do	48 00	1,016 51	Garrard's co. vol.	Jan. 1, 1813	Jan. 1, 1813	Transferred from Kentucky from Mar. 4, 1828.
Do	do	96 00		do	-	Feb. 19, 1834	
James C. Wingard	Sergeant	30 00	28 91	17th reg. U. S. inf.	Ap'l 16, 1816	May 7, 1815	April 24, 1816.
Do	do	48 00	29 80	do	-	Ap'l 24, 1816	March 3, 1819.
Do	do	96 00	516 00	do	-	Nov. 30, 1816	Died April 15, 1822.

Statement, &c. of Hocking county, Ohio.

NAMES.	Rank.	Annual allowance.	Sums received.	Description of service.	When placed on the pension roll.	Commencement of pension.	Laws under which they were inscribed, increased and reduced; and remarks.
Robert Williams	Private	60 00	1,468 33	21st reg. U. S. inf.	Nov. 17, 1791	Nov. 4, 1791	June 7, 1785.
Do	do	96 00	1,714 63	do	do	Ap'l 24, 1816	April 24, 1816. Increased to this rate by act April 24, 1816.

Statement, &c. of Huron county, Ohio.

NAMES.	Rank.	Annual allowance.	Sums received.	Description of service.	When placed on the pension roll.	Commencement of pension.	Laws under which they were inscribed, increased and reduced; and remarks.
George Bacon	Marine	48 00	1,445 02	Revolutionary army	July 9, 1786	Mar. 17, 1786	June 7, 1785.
Do	do	76 80	1,471 70	do	-	Ap'l 24, 1816	April 24, 1816. Increased to this rate by act April 24, 1816. Transferred from Mass. from Sept. 4, 1822.
John Brooks	Private	36 00	1,716 40	New York militia	-	Jan. 1, 1777	June 7, 1785.
Do	do	57 60	546 20	do	-	Sep. 4, 1824	April 24, 1816. Increased to this rate by act April 24, 1816.
Lewis Middleton	do	48 00	1,843 86	13th reg. of U. S. inf.	Oct. 21, 1816	Oct. 6, 1815	Acts military establishment. Transf'd from New York, from Mar. 4, 1825.
Alpheus McIntire	Sergeant	72 00	531 01	New York militia	May 13, 1826	Ap'l 14, 1826	April 24, 1816.
Do	do	96 00	-	do	-	Apr. 18, 1834	

Statement, &c. of Jefferson county, Ohio.

NAMES.	Rank.	Annual allowance.	Sums received.	Description of service.	When placed on the pension roll.	Commencement of pension.	Laws under which they were inscribed, increased and reduced; and remarks.
Alexander Patterson -	2d Lieut.	112 44	13 54	19th reg. of U.S. inf.	June 16, 1816	Mar. 12, 1816	Acts military establishment.
Do -	do	135 00	2,411 16	do	-	Ap'l 24, 1816	April 24, 1816.
Richard Smith -	Private	48 00	476 76	6th reg. of U. S. inf.	Mar. 31, 1824	Mar. 30, 1824	Acts military establishment.

Statement, &c. of Knox county, Ohio.

NAMES.	Rank.	Annual allowance.	Sums received.	Description of service.	When placed on the pension roll.	Commencement of pension.	Laws under which they were inscribed, increased and reduced; and remarks.
Joseph Cunningham -	Private	48 80	556 25	6th reg't U. S. inf.	July 8, 1823	Aug. 3, 1822	Acts military establishment.
Miller Mosier -	Corporal	86 00	1,913 54	21st reg't U. S. inf.	July 26, 1816	Mar. 30, 1814	Acts military establishment. Transferred from Vermont, from March 4, 1820.
William Marriott -	do	240 00	31 61	Maryland militia	Jan. 18, 1834	Jan. 18, 1834	April 24, 1816.

3

Statement, &c. of Lawrence county, Ohio.

NAMES.	Rank	Annual allowance.	Sums received	Description of service.	When placed on the pension roll.	Commencement of pension.	Laws under which they were inscribed, increased and reduced; and remarks.
George Sparling	Private	48 00	85 54	17th reg. of U. S. inf.	Mar. 16,	May 24, 1815	Acts military establishment. Transf'd from Virginia, from Sept. 4, 1833.

Statement, &c. of Licking county, Ohio.

NAMES.	Rank.	Annual allowance.	Sums received.	Description of service.	When placed on the pension roll.	Commencement of pension.	Laws under which they were inscribed, increased and reduced; and remarks.
John Blake	Sergeant	48 00	510 31	Heilman's co. 3d art.	July 18, 1821	July 18, 1821	Act May 15, 1820.
Isaiah Beaumont	Private	15 00	317 10	Revolutionary army	-	Mar. 4, 1795	June 7, 1785.
Do	do	24 00	261 93	do	-	Apl 24, 1816	April 24, 1816. Increased to this rate by act April 24, 1816.
Do	do	48 00	333 54	do		Mar. 23, 1827	Transferred from Connecticut, from March 4, 1827.
Israel W. Frisbee	Corporal	96 00	619 96	21st reg't U. S. inf.	Sep. 25, 1827	Sep. 20, 1827	Acts military establishment. Transferred from N. York, from Mar. 4, 1833.
George W. Parks	Private	72 00	1,364 48	do	Aug. 11, 1819	Mar. 21, 1815	Acts military establishment. Transferred from Maine, from March 4, 1829.
Jabez Smith	do	48 00	545 26	N. York volunteers	Jan. 14, 1819	Ap'l 6, 1814	April 24, 1816.
Do	do	72 00	1,335 55	do	-	Aug. 15, 1825	

Statement, &c. of Logan county, Ohio.

NAMES.	Rank.	Annual allowance.	Sums received.	Description of service.	When placed on the pension roll.	Commencement of pension.	Laws under which they were inscribed, increased and reduced; and remarks.
James Hayes	Private	96 00	761 03	Ohio militia	Ap'l 12, 1826	Ap'l 1, 1826	April 24, 1816.
Thomas Rothe	do	32 00	397 30	5th reg. of U. S. inf.	July 8, 1819	Feb. 16, 1816	Acts military establishment. Died July 20, 1828.

Statement, &c. of Medina county, Ohio.

NAMES.	Rank.	Annual allowance.	Sums received.	Description of service.	When placed on the pension roll.	Commencement of pension.	Laws under which they were inscribed, increased and reduced; and remarks.
Nebadiah Cass	Private	96 00	1,784 77		Oct. 21, 1816	Aug. 2, 1815	Acts military establishment. Transf'd from N. York, from Mar. 4, 1826.

Statement, &c. of Morgan county, Ohio.

NAMES.	Rank.	Annual allowance.	Sums received.	Description of service.	When placed on the pension roll.	Commencement of pension.	Laws under which they were inscribed, increased and reduced; and remarks.
Lloyd Piott	Private	48 00	909 80	1st reg. U. S. inf'y	Jan., 1817	May 22, 1815	Transferred from Pennsylvania from Sept. 4, 1821.

Statement, &c. of Miami county, Ohio.

NAMES.	Rank.	Annual allowance.	Sums received.	Description of service.	When placed on the pension roll.	Commencement of pension.	Laws under which they were inscribed, increased and reduced; and remarks.
John R. Bold	Private	72 00	745 67	New York militia	Nov. 14, 1823	Oct. 25, 1823	April 24, 1816.
Daniel Fielding	Sergeant	40 00	263 87	U. S. army	June 5, 1817	Sept. 19, 1809	March 3, 1811.
Do	-	64 00	611 93	do	-	April 24, 1816	April 24, 1816. Increased to this rate by act April 24, 1816.
Do	-	96 00	748 80	do	-	Nov. 16, 1825	

Statement, &c. of Mercer county, Ohio.

NAMES	Rank.	Annual allowance.	Sums received.	Description of service.	When placed on the pension roll.	Commencement of pension.	Laws under which they were inscribed, increased and reduced; and remarks.
Ira L. Foster	Private	30 00	26 41	19th reg. of U. S. inf.	Jan. 30, 1816	June 7, 1815	Acts military establishment.
Do	do	48 00	857 31	do	-	Apl 24, 1816	April 24, 1816. Increased to this rate by act April 24, 1816.
James Shoonover	do	96 00	1,298 83	New York militia	June 20, 1821	Aug. 25, 1820	April 24, 1816. May 15, 1820.

Statement, &c. of Montgomery county, Ohio.

NAMES.	Rank.	Annual allowance.	Sums received.	Description of service.	When placed on the pension roll.	Commencement of pension.	Laws under which they were inscribed, increased and reduced; and remarks.
James Gallespie	Private	48 00	376 87	Col. Crawford's reg.	-	June 18, 1808	March 5, 1809.
Do	do	76 80	1,332 94	do	-	Ap'l 24, 1816	April 24, 1816. Increased to this rate by act April 24, 1816.
Henry Houser	do	96 00	593 00	Ohio volunteers	Sep. 9, 1830	Jan. 1, 1828	May 20, 1830.
Robert Patterson	Colonel	300 00	4,820 50	1st reg't U. S. inf.	Oct. 16, 1823	July 11, 1811	July 5, 1812. Transferred from Kentucky, from September 4, 1817.
John Sprague	Private	72 00	1,388 30	19th reg't U. S. inf.	Oct. 21, 1816	Nov. 22, 1814	Acts military establishment.

Statement, &c. of Muskingum county, Ohio.

NAMES.	Rank.	Annual allowance.	Sums received.	Description of service.	When placed on the pension roll.	Commencement of pension.	Laws under which they were inscribed, increased and reduced; and remarks.
George Culins	Private	30 00	64 37	27th reg't U. S. inf.	Ap'l 25, 1816	Ap'l 3, 1814	Acts military establishment.
Do	do	48 00	857 34	do	-	Ap'l 24, 1816	April 24, 1816. Increased to this rate by act April 24, 1816.
Robert Cue	do	48 00	432 39	19th reg. U. S. inf.	Feb. 14, 1817	Sep. 6, 1813	Acts military establishment. Died Sept. 8, 1832.
Enos Devore	do	48 00	198 44	do	Jan. 15, 1830	Jan. 15, 1830	Acts military establishment.
Elisha B. Green	Sergeant	60 00	72 20	11th reg't U. S. inf.	Feb. 20, 1816	Feb. 3, 1815	Acts military establishment.
Do	do	96 00	1,714 63	do	-	Ap'l 24, 1816	April 24, 1816. Increased to this rate by act April 24, 1816.
William Gorman	Private	72 00	631 95	Taylor's company	June 20, 1825	May 25, 1825	April 25, 1828.
Isaac Green	do	48 00	-	27th reg't U. S. inf.	Feb. 22, 1817	Sep. 8, 1814	June 7, 1785.
Younger Grady	do	36 00	549 36	Revolutionary army	-	Mar. 4, 1796	August 2, 1813. Increased to this rate by act August 2, 1813.
Do	do	60 00	135 64	do	-	June 8, 1811	
Daniel Kirkpatrick	do	72 00	112 26	St. Clair's army	Feb. 18, 1832	Feb. 9, 1832	April 28, 1808.
Jacob Kendelsperyer	do	48 00	926 31	2d reg't Ohio vol.	-	Nov. 17, 1814	April 30, 1816.
William McIntosh	Private	32 00	113 35	6th reg't U. S. inf.	Jan. 4, 1817	Feb. 16, 1814	Acts military establishment.
Martin Rohrer	Sergeant	45 00	803 63	4th reg. U. S. rifle'n	Dec. 4, 1798	June 16, 1798	
Do	do	72 00	1,288 97	do	-	Ap'l 24, 1816	April 24, 1816. Increased to this rate by act April 24, 1816.
Joseph N. Ross	do	96 00	697 31	14th reg't U. S. inf.	July 7, 1816	May 31, 1815	Acts military establishment.
Do	do	72 00	224 67	do	-	Sep. 4, 1822	March 3, 1819. Reduced to this rate by act March 3, 1819.
Do	do	96 00	948 41	do	-	Oct. 18, 1825	Transf'd from Maryl'd Mar. 4, 1817.
Robert Smith	Private	96 00	516 02	27th reg. Md. militia	Ap'l 23, 1816	Ap'l 13, 1814	Acts military establishment. Transf'd from Maryland, from March 4, 1817. Died January 28, 1820.
James Taylor	Captain	240 00	2,541 93	Maj. M'Mahon's cav.	Aug. 28, 1823	Aug. 2, 1823	April 25, 1818 and May 15, 1820.

Statement, &c. of Ontario county, Ohio.

NAMES.	Rank.	Annual allowance.	Sums received.	Description of service.	When placed on the pension roll.	Commencement of pension.	Laws under which they were inscribed, increased and reduced; and remarks.
Ezekiel A. Turner -	Sergeant	48 00	820 89	5th reg't U. S. inf.	June 17, 1817	July 29, 1816	Acts military establishment. Transf'd from N. York, September 4, 1822.

Statement, &c. of Perry county, Ohio.

NAMES.	Rank.	Annual allowance.	Sums received.	Description of service.	When placed on the pension roll.	Commencement of pension.	Laws under which they were inscribed, increased and reduced; and remarks.
Robert Barron	Sergeant	60 00	1,484 32	Revolutionary army	Oct. 12, 1792	July 29, 1792	April 24, 1816. Increased to this rate by act April 24, 1816.
Do	do	96 00	322 66	do	-	Ap'l 24, 1816	March 3, 1819. Reduced by act Mar. 3, 1819.
Do	do	48 00	223 33	do	•	Sep. 4, 1819	
Do	do	72 00	552 35	do	-	Ap'l 28, 1824	Transferred from Kentucky from Mar. 4, 1817.
John King	Private	96 00	1,076 41	17th reg. U. S. inf.	Mar. 14, 1816	June 18, 1815	Died December 31, 1831. Acts military est.
Henry Stiers	do	72 00	94 61	Ohio militia	May 30, 1832	May 10, 1832	Transferred from Kentucky from September 4, 1820. April 24, 1816. Dead.

Statement, &c. of Pickaway county, Ohio.

NAMES.	Rank.	Annual allowance.	Sums received.	Description of service.	When placed on the pension roll.	Commencement of pension.	Laws under which they were inscribed, increased and reduced; and remarks.
Peter Dempsey	Corporal	48 00	504 13	U. States artillery	July 7, 1816	May 10, 1815	
Do.	do	96 00	20 05	do	Dec. 7, 1825	Nov. 9, 1825	Died January 25, 1826.
Alexander Foreman	Captain	120 00	2,249 68	Revolutionary army	-	Jan. 1, 1803	
Do.	do	180 00	339 68	do	May 4, 1822	Sep. 29, 1821	Transferred from Pennsylvania. Died December 25, 1831.
Do.	do	240 00	1,003 86	do	-	Aug. 19, 1823	Acts military establishment.
Samuel McKenney	Private	40 00	35 28	19th reg. U. S. inf	Jan. 4, 1816	Jan. 7, 1815	April 24, 1816. Increased to this rate by act April 24, 1816. Died August 31, 1829.
Do.	do	64 00	854 52	do	-	Ap'l 24, 1816	
Peter Perry	do	48 00	747 09	22d reg. U. S. inf.	Dec. 24, 1816	Aug. 12, 1815	Acts military establishment. Transferred from Pennsylvania from Sep. 4, 1821.

Statement, &c. of Pike county, Ohio.

NAMES.	Rank.	Annual allowance.	Sums received.	Description of service.	When placed on the pension roll.	Commencement of pension.	Laws under which they were inscribed, increased and reduced; and remarks.
Elijah Chinzaworth	Private	30 00	26 10	19th reg. U. S. inf.	Feb. 1, 1816	June 10, 1815	Acts military establishment April 24, 1816. Increased to this rate by act April 24, 1816.
Do	do	48 00	17 33	do	-	Ap'l 24, 1816	
Charles Cissna	2d lieut.	150 00	128 59	do	Mar. 7, 1816	June 16, 1815	Acts military establishment. April 24, 1816. Increased to this rate by act April 24, 1816.
Do	do	180 00	1,956 50	do	-	Ap'l 24, 1816	
Benjamin Daniels	Major	300 00	6,010 00		-	Feb. 22, 1814	April 18, 1814. Acts military establishment.
Charles Love	Private	72 00	868 60		-	Aug. 11, 1815	March 3, 1819. Reduced to this rate by act March 3, 1819.
Do	do	48 00	311 97		-	Sep. 4, 1827	

Statement, &c. of Portage county, Ohio.

NAMES.	Rank.	Annual allowance.	Sums received.	Description of service.	When placed on the pension roll.	Commencement of pension.	Laws under which they were inscribed, increased and reduced; and remarks.
Joseph Bowen	Corporal	24 00	76 34	1st reg. U. S. inf.	Ap'l 17, 1826	Mar. 16, 1826	Acts military establishment.
Do	do	72 00	344 13	do	-	May 23, 1829	
Ransom Isbel	Sergeant	32 00	431 73	N. York volunteers	June 18, 1814	Nov. 9, 1814	April 24, 1816.
Do	do	72 00	428 52	do	June 18, 1828	May 8, 1828	Transferred from New York September 4, 1822.
Andrews Stewart	Private	96 00	1,051 74	1st reg. U. S. drag.	Mar. 26, 1817	Oct. 2, 1814	Acts military establishment. Died September 15, 1825.
Ephraim Shaler	1st lieut. & adjt.	204 00	324 65	6th reg. U. S. inf.	Dec. 6, 1825	Sep. 29, 1825	Acts military establishment
Do	do	210 00	1,642 58	do	June 30, 1832	May 1, 1827	

4

Statement, &c. of Preble county, Ohio.

NAMES.	Rank,	Annual allowance.	Sums received.	Description of service.	When placed on the pension roll.	Commencement of pension.	Laws under which they were inscribed, increased and reduced; and remarks.
Jacob Clouse -	Private	32 00	608 88	22d reg't U. S. inf.	Oct. 7, 1816	Feb. 20, 1815	March 3, 1819.
Thomas Dowler -	do	32 00	594 72	-	-	Aug. 2, 1815	Acts military establishment.
Thomas Fleming -	do	96 00	593 03	Wayne's army	Jan. 23, 1832	Jan. 1, 1828	May 20, 1830.
Alexander C. Lanier -	Major	150 00	900 41	Ohio militia	Ap'l 17, 1818	Mar. 5, 1814	April 24, 1816.

Statement, &c. of Richland county, Ohio.

NAMES.	Rank.	Annual allowance.	Sums received.	Description of service.	When placed on the pension roll.	Commencement of pension.	Laws under which they were inscribed, increased and reduced; and remarks.
David Lee -	Private	48 00	460 25	Craig's co. U. S. art.	Feb. 18, 1818	Aug. 3, 1815	Acts military establishment.
Do -	do	96 00	863 22	do	-	Mar. 7, 1825	
Mordecai Lincoln -	do	72 00	1,059 32	3d reg, U. S. inf.	Sep. 29, 1820	June 18, 1819	Acts military establishment,
Samuel Mann -	do	48 00	494 05	Ohio militia	Feb. 2, 1826	Jan. 20, 1826	April 24, 1824.

Statement, &c. of Ross county, Ohio.

NAMES.	Rank.	Annual allowance.	Sums received.	Description of service.	When placed on the pension roll.	Commencement of pension.	Laws under which they were inscribed, increased and reduced; and remarks;
Charles Black	Private	48 00	698 86	1st reg. Ohio vols.	July 24, 1817	Ap'l 20, 1813	Act April 24, 1816.
Do	do	96 00	606 68	do	-	Nov. 9, 1827	
John Brown	do	40 00	41 17	Col. R. M. Johnson's regiment	Dec. 11, 1815	June 8, 1815	Acts military establishment.
Do	do	64 00	599 03	do	-	Ap'l 24, 1816	April 24, 1816. Increased to this rate by act April 24, 1816.
Francis Boyd	do	33 33	943 24	7th Virginia reg.	June 24, 1788	Jan. 1, 1788	June 7, 1785.
do	do	53 29	459 04	do	-	Ap'l 24, 1816	April 24, 1816. Increased to this rate by act April 24, 1816. Died December 17, 1824.
Willis Copelan	do	48 00	210 70	3d reg. U. S. inf.	Aug. 2, 1817	Aug. 2, 1817	Acts military establishment.
Do	do	72 00	347 49	do	-	Dec. 22, 1821	
Stephen Cissney	do	48 00	864 51	Ohio volunteers	Feb. 22, 1817	Oct. 28, 1812	Acts military establishment. Died October 31, 1830.
Jesse Downs	do	48 00	615 24	19th reg. U. S. inf.	July 20, 1816	May 10, 1814	Acts military establishment.
Joseph England	do	96 00	2,081 03	Ohio volunteers	Dec. 13, 1816	July 1, 1812	Acts military etsablishment.
George Hill	do	62 40	156 00	3d reg. of dragoons	-	Mar. 4, 1830	August 2, 1813: Transferred from Virginia from September 4, 1820.
Clayton Harper	do	64 00	-	19th reg. U. S. inf.	Aug. -, 1817	June 7, 1815	Acts military establishment.
George Hartsell	do	20 00	42 35	25th reg. U. S. inf.	Dec. 6, 1815	Mar. 9, 1814	Acts military establishment.
Do	do	32 00	267 00	do	-	Ap'l 24, 1816	April 24, 1816. Increased to this rate by act April 24, 1816.
Charles McMullin	do	48 00	410 71	3d reg. U. S. inf.	June 14, 1817	June 9, 1816	Acts military establishment.
Do	do	72 00	59 20	do	-	Dec. 30, 1824	
Edward Murphy	do	48 00	345 53	17th reg. U. S. inf.	Sep. 5, 1822	July 10, 1822	Acts military establishment.
Do	do	96 00	187 46	do	-	Sep. 22, 1829	do
Zebedee Smith	do	96 00	1,760 76	3d reg. U. S. inf.	July 7, 1816	Nov. 12, 1815	Acts military establishment.
Peter Shipley	do	72 00	556 97	19th reg. U. S. inf.	Sep. 11, 1816	June 7, 1815	do
John Williams	do	48 00	435 51	Ohio militia	Feb. 25, 1825	Feb. 8, 1825	April 24, 1816.

Statement, &c. of Sandusky county, Ohio.

NAMES.	Rank.	Annual allowance:	Sums received.	Description of service.	When placed on the pension roll.	Commencement of pension.	Laws under which they were inscribed, increased and reduced; and remarks.
Samuel Thompson -	Sergeant	72 00	1,307 32	6th reg't U. S. inf	May 13, 1816	Feb. 3, 1816	Acts military establishment. Transf'd from Vermont, from March 4, 1821.

Statement, &c. of Scioto county, Ohio.

NAMES.	Rank.	Annual allowance.	Sums received.	Description of service.	When placed on the pension roll.	Commencement of pension.	Laws under which they were inscribed, increased and reduced; and remarks.
James Munn -	Captain	120 00	2,999 03	-	Jan. 29, 1821	Mar. 18, 1809	April 27, 1810.
Daniel Rardon -	Private	96 00	298 16	-	"	Ap'l 19, 1816	Acts military establishment.
Do -	do	72 00	451 50	-	"	May 27, 1819	
Do -	do	64 00	544 00	-	"	Sep. 4, 1825	March 3, 1819.

Statement, &c. of Seneca county, Ohio.

NAMES.	Rank.	Annual allowance.	Sums received.	Description of service.	When placed on the pension roll.	Commencement of pension.	Laws under which they were inscribed, increased and reduced; and remarks.
William Sibberal	Private	60 00	52 83	19th reg't U. S. inf.	Dec. 30, 1815	June 7, 1815	Acts military establishment. April 24, 1816. Increased to this rate by act April 24, 1816.
Do	do	96 00	1,714 63	do	.	Apl 24, 1816	

Statement, &c. of Shelby county, Ohio.

NAMES.	Rank.	Annual allowance.	Sums received.	Description of service.	When placed on the pension roll.	Commencement of pension.	Laws under which they were inscribed, increased and reduced; and remarks.
Samuel Hall	Private	60 00	92 34	17th reg. U. S. inf.	Feb. 1, 1816	Oct. 11, 1814	Acts military establishment. April 24, 1816. Increased to this rate by act April 24, 1816.
Do	do	96 00	1,714 89	do	.	Ap'l 24, 1816	

Statement, &c. of Trumbull county, Ohio.

NAMES.	Rank.	Annual allowance.	Sums received.	Description of service.	When placed on the pension roll.	Commencement of pension.	Laws under which they were inscribed, increased and reduced; and remarks.
Andrew Bushnell -	2d Lieut.	45 00	167 35	19th reg. U. S. inf.	Jan. 8, 1817	June 16, 1815	
Do -	do	10 50	61 85	do	-	Mar. 4, 1819	March 3, 1819. Reduced to this rate by act March 3, 1819.
Do -	do	45 00	408 72	do	-	Feb. 2, 1825	Acts military establishment, April 24, 1816.
George Cassidy -	Private	60 00	47 20	22d reg. U. S. inf	Mar. 4, 1816	July 12, 1815	
Do -	do	96 00	1,714 63	do	-	Ap'l 24, 1816	Increased to this rate by act April 24, 1816.
Walter Dixon -	do	32 00	623 49	Ohio militia	Aug. 6, 1817	Sep. 8, 1814	Acts military establishment.
Jacob Frank -	do	32 00	632 32	do	Feb. 4, 1817	Dec. 1, 1812	Acts military establishment·

Statement, &c. of Tuscarawas county, Ohio.

NAMES.	Rank.	Annual allowance.	Sums received.	Description of service.	When placed on the pension roll.	Commencement of pension.	Laws under which they were inscribed, increased and reduced; and remarks.
Godfrey Westhaver -	Lieutenant	153 00	729 62	Ohio militia	June 12, 1829	May 29, 1829	April 24, 1816.

Statement, &c. of Warren county, Ohio.

NAMES.	Rank.	Annual allowance.	Sums received.	Description of service.	When placed on the pension roll.	Commencement of pension:	Laws under which they were inscribed, increased and reduced; and remarks.
Joseph Catherel	Private	48 00	926 13	Maryland militia	May 18, 1816	Nov. 19, 1814	April 24, 1816. Transferred from Maryland, from September 4, 1829.
Robert Doing	Corporal	96 00	1,784 77	1st reg't U. S. rifle.	May 6, 1817	Aug. 2, 1815	Acts military establishment.
James Elwell	do	30 00	103 92	3d reg't Ohio vol.	Mar. 14, 1816	Nov. 10, 1812	Acts military establishment.
Do	do	48 00	809 31	do	-	Ap'l 24, 1816	April 24, 1816. Increased to this rate by act April 24, 1816.
William Howell	do	96 00	445 93	Kiskling's company U. S. infantry	July 21, 1829	July 13, 1829	Acts military establishment.

Statement, &c. of Warran county, Ohio.

NAMES.	Rank:	Annual allowance.	Sums received.	Description of service.	When placed on the pension roll.	Commencement of pension.	Laws under which they were inscribed, increased and reduced; and remarks.
John Norton	Private	30 00	58 52	2d reg. U. S. art'y	-	May 11, 1814	March 3, 1815.
Do	do	48 00	420 80	do	-	Ap'l 24, 1816	April 24, 1816. Increased to this rate by act April 24, 1816. Died January 31, 1825.
Daniel Swyers	do	96 00	1,716 23	24th reg. U. S. inf.	Jan. 7, 1817	Ap'l 19, 1816	Acts military establishment. Transf'd from Penn. from March 4, 1817.
Samuel H. Steele	do	24 00	468 44	14th reg. U. S. inf.	Mar. 1, 1816	Sep. 14, 1814	Transferred from Connecticut, from Sep. 4, 1827.
Daniel Stagg	do	96 00	1,729 99	-	-	Feb. 26, 1816	Act April 30, 1816.

Statement, &c. of Washington county, Ohio.

NAMES.	Rank.	Sums received.	Annual allowance.	Description of service.	When placed on the pension roll.	Commencement of pension.	Laws under which they were inscribed, increased and reduced; and remarks.
David Hoor	Private	99 34	60 00	25th reg't U. S. inf.	Mar. 16, 1816	Aug. 28, 1814	Acts military establishment.
Do	do	562 68	96 00	do	-	Ap'l 24, 1816	April 24, 1816. Increased to this rate by act April 24, 1816. Died Sept. 23, 1824.
Faulkner Simons	do	54 51	32 00	19th reg't U. S. inf.	July 2, 1824	June 21, 1824	Acts military establishment.
George Wolf	do	1,063 46	45 00	Revolutionary army	-	Sep. 7, 1792	June 7, 1795.
Do	do	1,249 77	72 00	do	-	Ap'l 24, 1816	April 24, 1816. Increased to this rate by act April 24, 1826. Transferred from Pennsylvania from Sep. 4, 1826.

Statement, &c. of Wayne county, Ohio.

NAMES.	Rank.	Sums received.	Annual allowance.	Description of service.	When placed on the pension roll.	Commencement of pension.	Laws under which they were inscribed, increased and reduced; and remarks.
John Pierce	Private	508 92	32 00	Gibson's regiment	Feb. 28, 1823	Ap'l 24, 1816	Transferred from Pennsylvania.
Do	do	136 65	72 00	do	-	Ap'l 10, 1832	

Statement, &c. of Williams county, Ohio.

NAMES.	Rank.	Annual allowance.	Sums received.	Description of service.	When placed on the pension list.	Commencement of pension.	Laws under which they were inscribed, increased and reduced; and remarks.
Josiah B. Packard -	Private	96 00	1,739 61	-	July 29, 1816	Jan. 22, 1816	April 30, 1816. Transferred from N. York, from March 4, 1822.

Statement, &c. of Wood county, Ohio.

NAMES.	Rank.	Annual allowance.	Sums received.	Description of service.	When placed on the pension roll.	Commencement of pension.	Laws under which they were inscribed, increased and reduced; and remarks.
Elias G. Crego -	Private	72 00	1,201 42	6th reg't U. S. inf.	Jan. 31, 1818	June 27, 1817	Acts military establishment. Transferred from N. York from Mar. 4, 1832.

5

List of Invalid Pensioners who have been in the receipt of pensions at the agency of Cincinnati, in the State of Ohio, and whose residence cannot be ascertained in consequence of the destruction of the papers of the War Office in 1801 and 1814.

NAMES.	Rank.	Annual allowance.	Sums received.	Description of service.	When placed on the pension roll.	Commencement of pension.	Laws under which they were inscribed, increased and reduced; and remarks.
Abner Gage	Private	15 00	275 88	Revolutionary army		Sep. 4, 1789	June 7, 1785.
Do	do	60 00	494 67	do		Jan. 26, 1808	April 25, 1808. Increased to this rate by act April 25, 1808.
Do	do	96 00	418 60	do		Ap'l 24, 1816	April 24, 1816. Increased to this rate by act April 24, 1816.
Joseph Shaler	Captain	240 00	—	do		Feb. 12, 1809	April 27, 1810. Dead. Transferred from New Hampshire.
William Wells	do	240 00	2,520 00	Revolutionary army		Mar. 4, 1797	June 7, 1785.
*William Brinton	Private	72 00	—	2d reg. U. S. inf.	July 28, 1816	Mar. 19, 1816	Acts military establishment.

*This is an invalid pensioner on the roll of Ohio, whose residence in that State cannot be ascertained. No report in relation to him has been received at this office.

Statement of the names, &c. of the Heirs of non-commissioned Officers, Privates, &c. who died in the United States' service, who obtained five years' half pay in lieu of bounty land, under the second section of the act of April 16, 1816, and who resided in the State of Ohio.

Names of the original claimants.	Rank.	Description of service.	Time of decease.	Names of the heirs.	Annu'l allowance.	Sums received.	When placed on the pension roll.	Commencement of pension.	Ending of pension.
ADAMS COUNTY.									
John Cannon	Private	17th reg't inf.	Aug. 15, 1814	James Cannon	48 00	240 00	Ap'l 12, 1819	Feb. 17, 1815	Feb. 17, 1820
ATHENS COUNTY.									
Eleazer Kingsbury	do	19th	July 18, 1813	Hiram, Ira, Lyman and Hackley Kingsbury	48 00	240 00	May 21, 1819	do	do
BELMONT COUNTY.									
Henry Fryman	do	17th	Unknown	Catharine, George & Jacob Fryman	48 00	240 00	Aug. 21, 1817	do	do
Wm. Lansdown	do	20th	Mar. 11, 1815	Betsey, Fanny, John and William Lansdown	48 00	240 00	Nov. 3, 1817	do	do
Robert Morrison	do	19th	Nov. 2, 1813	John, Eleanor, Janoin & Esther Morrison	48 00	240 00	do	do	do
Joel Sherwood	do	29th	May 24, 1815	Joel, William and Philinia Sherwood	48 00	240 00	July 11, 1821	June 5, 1820	June 5, 1825
BROWN COUNTY.									
Wm. Thompson	do	19th	May 5, 1813	Susanna E., Betsey M. and William Harvey Thompson	48 00	240 00	Aug. 28, 1821	June 15, 1821	June 15, 1826
BUTLER COUNTY.									
John May	do	17th	Dec. 24, 1814	Elizabeth, Hannah and Isaac May	48 00	240 00	May 18, 1818	Feb. 17, 1815	Feb. 17, 1820

Statement of Heirs, &c.—Continued.

Names of the original claimants	Rank.	Description of service.	Time of decease.	Names of the heirs.	Annual allowance.	Sums received.	When placed on the roll.	Commencement of pension.	Ending of pension.
				CAMPBELL COUNTY.					
Th's W. Kesterson	Private	24th reg't inf.	Aug. 4, 1814	Nancy and Elizabeth Kesterson	48 00	240 00	Dec. 2, 1818	Feb. 17, 1815	Feb. 17, 1820
				CLERMONT COUNTY.					
Josiah Miller	do	23d do	In 1813	Sally, Roxey, Caroline, John & Leonora Miller	48 00	240 00	May 4, 1820	Ap'l 10, 1820	Ap'l 10, 1825
				COLUMBIANA COUNTY.					
William Davis	do	1st do	Feb. 15, 1821	William and George Davis [Paid at the Pittsburg agency.]	48 00	240 00	Sep. 25, 1821	Aug. 15, 1821	Aug. 15, 1826
				DELAWARE COUNTY.					
Jonathan Hatch	do	Corps artillery	Jan. 17, 1815	Barney Hatch	48 00	240 00	June 29, 1818	Feb. 17, 1815	Feb. 17, 1820
				FAIRFIELD COUNTY.					
Abijah Baker	Sergeant	22d reg't inf.	May 14, 1813	Abijah Baker	66 00	330 00	July 11, 1820	Ap'l 3, 1820	Ap'l 3, 1825
Rob't Cunningham	Private	19th do	May, 1813	Polly, James, Nancy, Samuel, John and Jane Cunningham	48 00	240 00	Mar. 21, 1820	July 8, 1818	July 8, 1823
Zachariah North	Corporal	do	May 5, 1813	John, Jacob and Sarah North	60 00	300 00	Aug. 9, 1817	Feb. 17, 1815	Feb. 17, 1820
				FRANKLIN COUNTY.					
Jacob W. Davis	Sergeant	do	Sept. 1, 1813	Henry D. G. Davis	66 00	330 00	Mar. 4, 1817	do	do

Name	Rank	Regiment	Date	Beneficiaries					
HAMILTON COUNTY.									
Jacob Burt	Private	25th reg't inf.	July or Aug. 1814	Ann, Isaac, Freeman, Manley, Jacob A., Abigail and James Mackey Bent	48 00	240 00	Nov. 21, 1818	do	do
Charles Boothe	do	19th	do	Aug. 31, 1813 Susannah, Eleanor and Henrietta Boothe	48 00	240 00	Aug. 28, 1821	Aug. 1, 1818	Aug. 1, 1823
Hugh Gaston	do	1st reg't rifle.	May 7, 1814	Sally, John, Rachel and Nancy Gaston	48 00	240 00	Dec. 22, 1817	Feb. 17, 1815	Feb. 17, 1820
John Hopwood	Sergeant	do	Nov. 23, 1813	James Hopwood	66 00	330 00	Aug. 27, 1818	do	do
Benjamin Leming	Private	17th reg't inf.	Jan. 12, 1815	Samuel, Robert C. and Benjamin Leming	48 00	240 00	Nov. 16, 1819	do	do
John Rerick	do	23d	Sep. 28, 1813	Martha, Henry, Elizabeth, Ann and Hannah Rerick	48 00	240 00	July 21, 1821	June 22, 1821	June 22, 1826
Jacob Slutz	do	19th	May 20, 1813	Henry, Adam and Lancy Shutz	48 00	240 00	June 15, 1818	Feb. 17, 1815	Feb. 17, 1820
JEFFERSON COUNTY.									
Philip Carroll	do	2d reg't art'y	Dec. 10, 1813	John, Mary, Margaret, Joseph, Armstrong, Catharine, Henry, Jane and Philip Carroll	48 00	240 00	Feb. 16, 1819	do	do
Robert Dixon	do	16th	Aug. 1, 1814	Daniel, Elizabeth and Abner Dixon	48 00	240 00	Oct. 26, 1319	do	do
John Eyres, or Ayres	do	12th reg't inf.	May 2, 1814	Thomas and George Eyres	48 00	240 00	Ap'l 12, 1813	do	do
William Gilliland	do	Corps of art'y	Aug. 7, 1813	Polly, John and David Gilliland	48 00	240 00	Mar. 5, 1819	do	do
Enos McClelland	do	22d reg't inf.	Feb. 22, 1814	Asa McClelland	48 00	240 00	May 26, 1821	May 4, 1821	May 4, 1826
LICKING COUNTY.									
Wm. Cunningham	do	17th	Mar. 25, 1814	John Cunningham	48 00	240 00	May 4, 1818	Feb. 17, 1815	Feb. 17, 1820
Jacob Stultz	do	19th	Nov. 29, 1814	Christiana and Susannah Stultz	48 00	240 00	Apr. 6, 1818	do	do
MONTGOMERY COUNTY.									
Joseph Dodds	do	7th	Sept. 4, 1812	Isabella and Lewis Dodds	48 00	240 00	Sep. 1, 1817	do	do
MUSKINGUM COUNTY.									
Robert Oliver	do	19th	Mar. 1, 1814	Samuel, William and Hetty Oliver	48 00	240 00	Aug. 13, 1817	do	do
Adam Stultz	do	do	May 5, 1813	Marshall and Elizabeth Stultz	48 00	240 00	Ap'l 14, 1818	do	do

Statement of Heirs, &c.—Continued.

Names of the original claimants.	Rank.	Description of service.	Time of decease.	Names of the Heirs.	Annu'l allowance.	Sums received.	When placed on the roll.	Commencement of pension.	Ending of pension.
				PICKAWAY COUNTY.					
John Letterell	Private	19th reg. inf.	May 15, 1813	John, Mahala, Archibald, Nancy and Levi Letterell	48 00	240 00	Jan. 17, 1820	Feb. 17, 1815	Feb. 17, 1820
				PORTAGE COUNTY.					
Asahel Blair	do	17th	Nov. 13, 1814	Aalina, Sally and Mary Blair	48 00	240 00	Ap'l 6, 1818	do	do
				ROSS COUNTY.					
Stephen Hallman	do	19th	Oct. 8, 1814	William, John, Philip, Conrad, Barbaras and Elizabeth Hallman	48 00	240 00	Dec. 13, 1816	do	do
John Rice	do	do	Oct. 5, 1813	Mary Ann, Charles, Henry, Betsey, Kitty and Matilda Rice	48 00	240 00	do	do	do
Eli Timmons	do	do	Feb. 24, 1815	Polly, Thomas, Jefferson, Betsey, Eliza, James Madison & Eli Timmons	48 00	240 00	Dec. 31, 1816	do	do
				STARK COUNTY.					
John Patterson	do	22d	In 1813	Mary S. and David Patterson	48 00	240 00	Sep. 23, 1819	do	do
				WARREN COUNTY.					
Samuel Everhart	do	Corps U.S. art.	Oct. 13, 1815	Catharine and Lydia Everhart	48 00	240 00	Jan. 2, 1817	do	do
William Marsh	do	17th reg't inf.	Jan. 1, 1815	Margarette, Nancy, Miria, Elizabeth and James Johnson Marsh	48 00	240 00	do	do	do
				COUNTY UNKNOWN.					
Abraham Kelly	do	26th	Feb. 23, 1814	Joseph Kelly	48 00	240 00	Mar. 14, 1822	Jan. 29, 1822	Jan. 29, 1827

Statement showing the Names, Rank, &c. of persons residing in the county of Adams, in the State of Ohio, who have been inscribed on the Pension List under the act of Congress passed the 18th day of March, 1818.

NAMES.	Rank.	Annual allowance.	Sums received.	Description of service.	When placed on the pension roll.	Commencement of pension.	Ages.	Laws under which they were formerly inscribed on the pension roll; and remarks.
Henry Aldred	Private	96 00	181 29	Virginia continental	Dec. 31, 1818	Ap'l 15, 1818	79	Dropped from the roll under act May 1, 1820.
Do	do	96 00	372 26	do	Sep. 18, 1819	Ap'l 10, 1818	91	Rest'd, comm'ng April 19, 1830.
John Alexander	do	96 00	1,041 63	Penn. continental	Feb. 2, 1819	June 13, 1818	69	
Henry Brewer	do	96 00	981 86	Congress regiment	July 2, 1819	Aug. 6, 1818	84	Died July 27, 1821.
Francis Costigan	Lieut.	240 00	713 54	N. Jersey cont'l	Nov. 14, 1818	Apl. 30, 1818	74	Died Feb. 7, 1832.
Daniel Copple	Private	96 00	1,322 26	Penn. continental	Nov. 3, 1820	Aug. 12, 1820	86	
Dennis Callahan	do	96 00	821 94	Maryland cont'l	May 21, 1819	Dec. 3, 1818	65	
James Ervin	Lieut.	240 00	2,338 70	Penn. continental	June 30, 1818	Ap'l 14, 1818	73	Dropped from the roll under act May 1, 1820.
Joseph L. Finley	Major	240 00	353 93	do				Restored under act Mar. 1, 1823.
Do	do	240 00	1,213 62	do	-	Aug. 14, 1823	-	Relinquished for benefit of act May 15, 1828.
William Flood	Private	96 00	1,476 80	Virginia continental	Mar. 23, 1819	Ap'l 16, 1818	94	
William Faulkner	do	96 00	1,519 23	Penn. continental	Ap'l 14, 1819	May 7, 1818	79	
Simon Fields	do	96 00	156 94	Virginia continental	Mar. 29, 1831	Mar. 26, 1831	77	Dead.
William Gates	do	96 00	1,072 25	Maryland cont'l	June 10, 1819	Aug. 28, 1818	74	Died Oct. 29, 1829.
Amos Gustin	do	96 00	23 49	Penn. continental	Ap'l 17, 1820	Dec. 2, 1819	68	Dropped from the roll under act May 1, 1820.
John Gordon	do	96 00	680 28	do	Mar. 4, 1826	Feb. 4, 1826	76	Dropped from the roll under act May 1, 1820.
Charles Hamilton	Corporal	96 00	133 06	Delaware cont'l	Feb. 4, 1819	Ap'l 16, 1818	-	Died August 8, 1831.
Thomas Jack	Sergeant	96 00	1,278 71	Penn. continental	Dec. 31, 1818	Ap'l 13, 1818	85	
Patrick McDaniel	Private	96 00	1,521 06	do	June 7, 1819	May 1, 1818	94	
Charles Magin	do	96 00	914 59	Maryland cont'l	Sept. 6, 1819	May 2, 1818	82	Died December 23, 1827.
Joseph McMahan	do	96 00	567 46	Virginia continental	Ap'l 10, 1828	April 7, 1828	73	
James Richardson	do	96 00	1,371 85	do	Mar. 23, 1819	Oct. 3, 1818	80	Died Jan. 16, 1833.
William Rogers	do	96 00	166 09	N. Jersey cont'l	April 1, 1819	June 12, 1818	66	Dropped from the roll under act May 1, 1820.

Statement, &c. of *Adams county*—Continued.

NAMES.	Rank.	Annual allowance.	Sums received.	Description of service.	When placed on the pension roll.	Commencement of pension.	Ages.	Laws under which they were formerly inscribed on the pension roll; and remarks.
William Rogers	Private	96 00	730 32	N. Jersey cont'l	May 1, 1819	July 27, 1826	66	Restored under act Mar. 1, 1823.
Daniel Rankins	do	96 00	179 43	Maryland cont'l		Apl. 22, 1818	80	Dropped from the roll under act May 1, 1820.
Do	do	96 00	828 38	do	April 1, 1819	July 19, 1824	-	Restored under act Mar. 1, 1823.
James Richards	do	96 00	-	Virginia continental		June 5, 1824	-	Dropped from the roll under act May 1, 1820.
Christopher Trotter	do	96 00	949 33	do	Dec. 30, 1818	Ap'l 17, 1818	75	Died March 6, 1828.
John Trotter	do	96 00	1,445 96	do	Jan. 28, 1820	Aug. 13, 1818	76	Transferred from Kentucky.
James Walsh	do	96 00	1,519 25	do	May 3, 1819	May 8, 1818	84	
Thomas Waters, sen.	do	96 00	1,286 32	do	July 21, 1819	Ap'l 15, 1818	81	
Richard Woodworth	do	96 00	1,518 96	Penn. continental	Oct. 23, 1819	May 9, 1818	79	
Peter Walker	do	96 00	169 03	do	May 24, 1820	June 1, 1818	65	Dropped from the roll under act May 1, 1820.
Do	do	96 00	344 54	do	-	Aug. 3, 1830	-	Restored under act Mar. 1, 1823,

Statement, &c. of *Allen county, Ohio.*

NAMES.	Rank.	Annual allowance.	Sums received.	Description of service.	When placed on the pension roll.	Commencement of pension.	Ages.	Laws under which they were merly inscribed on the pen roll; and remarks.
Simon Cochran	Private	96 00	1,426 63	Virginia cont'l	May 31, 1820	Ap'l 25, 1819	80	

Statement, &c., of Ashtabula county, Ohio.

NAMES.	Rank.	Annual allowance.	Sums received.	Description of service.	When placed on the pension roll.	Commencement of pension.	Ages.	Laws under which they were formerly inscribed on the pension roll; and remarks.
Josiah Atkins	Private	96 00	942 44	Connecticut cont'l	June 25, 1819	May 11, 1818	70	Died August 23, 1828.
Clement Andrus	do	96 00	1,522 89	do	Oct. 25, 1819	April 24, 1818	71	Transferred from Vermont. Died March 20, 1833.
Abraham Avmsden	do	96 00	1,437 16	Mass. continental	May 30, 1820	April 1, 1818	81	Transferred from N. York. Died July 9, 1831.
James Brown, 1st.	do	96 00	1,264 77	do	Oct. 16, 1818	May 6, 1818	69	
Asa Benjamin	do	96 00	161 03	do	May 24, 1820	July 1, 1818	67	Dropped from the roll under act May 1, 1820.
Benjamin Barrett	do	96 00	142 89	do	June 2, 1820	Sept. 9, 1818	74	Dropped from the roll under act May 1, 1820.
Do	do	96 00	992 23	do	-	Nov. 4, 1823	74	Restored under act March 1, 1823. Transferred from N. York.
Zacariah Burril	do	96 00	648 28	N. J. continental	Ap'l 28, 1819	May 26, 1818	70	Transferred from N. York. Died February 27, 1825.
Ebenezer Collins	do	96 00	1,527 20	Mass. continental	Sept. 25, 1818	April 7, 1818	72	Transferred from New York.
Charles DeMarianville	do	96 00	1,042 09	R. I. continental	Oct, 25, 1819	Ap'l 27, 1818		Transferred from N. York. Died November 24, 1830.
Noble Gunn	do	96 00	1,203 47	Mass. continental	Feb. 2, 1819	April 7, 1818	68	Transferred from N. York.
Arunah Judd	do	96 00	1,522 89	do	Dec. 28, 1818	Ap'l 24, 1818	86	
John Lamont	do	96 00	1,468 27	do	Ap'l 24, 1821	Nov. 18, 1818	69	
Jonathan Parker	Captain	240 00	447 32	Connecticut cont'l	April 1, 1819	Ap'l 24, 1818	86	Dropped from the roll under act May 1, 1820.
David Sackett	Lieut.	240 00	3,769 72	Mass. continental	Sept. 7, 1819	June 19, 1818	82	Dropped from the roll under act May 1, 1820.
Seth Thompson	Private	96 00	174 96	N. H. continental	May 12, 1819	May 9, 1818	74	Restored under act March 1, 1823.
Do	do	96 00	471,76	do	-	Oct. 6, 1823	74	Transferred from Pennsylvania.
Joseph Thayer	do	96 00	1,007 53	Connecticut cont'l	Oct. 16, 1823	Sept. 6, 1823	79	Dropped from the roll under act May 1, 1820.
Reuben W. Wilder	do	96 00	176 66	Mass. continental	May 12, 1819	May 2, 1818	72	

Statement, &c. of Ashtabula county—Continued.

NAMES.	Rank.	Annual allowance.	Sums received.	Description of service.	When placed on the pension roll.	Commencement of pension.	Ages.	Laws under which they were formerly inscribed on the pension roll; and remarks.
Reuben W. Wilder -	Private	96 00	991 96	Mass. continental	–	Nov. 5, 1823	72	Restored under act March 1, 1823.
Ezekiel Woodworth -	do	96 00	138 36	do	May 23, 1820	Sept. 26, 1818	74	Dropped from the roll under act May 1, 1820.
Do	do	96 00	294 20	do	–	Feb. 11, 1831		Restored under act March 1, 1823.
Noah Warner -	do	96 00	1,249 29	do	Oct. 10, 1818	May 1, 1818	70	Transferred from N. York. Died May 5, 1831.

Statement, &c. of Athens county, Ohio.

NAMES.	Rank.	Annual allowance.	Sums received.	Description of service.	When placed on the pension roll.	Commencement of pension.	Ages.	Laws under which they were formerly inscribed on the pension roll; and remarks.
Daniel Anderson	Lieutenant	240 00	1,008 98	Pennsylvania cont'l	Aug. 5, 1822	June 3, 1818	71	Died August 16, 1822.
Jeremiah Burnham	Private	96 00	174 19	Massachusetts cont'l	Oct. 13, 1818	May 12, 1818	74	Dropped [from the roll under act May 1, 1820.
Do	do	96 00	989 86	do	–	Nov. 13, 1823	–	Restored under act Mar. 1, 1823,
Benjamin Brown	Captain	240 00	827 97	do	Oct. 6, 1818	Ap'l 20, 1818	75	Died October 1, 1821.
William Bodwell	Private	96 00	465 29	do	Mar. 24, 1819	Ap'l 30, 1818	72	
William Buck	do	96 00	1,474 92	Pennsylvania cont'l	July 14, 1819	Ap'l 23, 1818	90	
Samuel Dunlap	do	96 00	650 86	Massachusetts cont'l	Oct. 14, 1820	Ap'l 22, 1818	67	Died February 4, 1825.
David Daily	do	96 00	863 74	Connecticut cont'l	Nov. 5, 1821	June 15, 1818	81	Died June 14, 1827.
Thaddeus Fuller	do	96 00	1,487 47	Massachusetts cont'l	Aug. 13, 1822	July 14, 1818	75	Died January 11, 1834.
Daniel Gill	do	·96 00	1,522 37	Pennsylvania cont'l	Oct. 29, 1818	Ap'l 25, 1818	89	
Thomas Hammond	do	96 00	–	Maryland cont'l	May 29, 1820	Nov. 10, 1819	58	Dropped from the roll under act May 1, 1820.
Thomas Hudnall	do	96 00	1,333 59	Virginia cont'l	Nov. 20, 1820	Ap'l 14, 1820	74	
Joel Lowther	do	96 00	1,508 79	do	do	June 18, 1818	78	
Moses Mingus, or Myngos	do	96 00	1,528 26	New York cont'l	Sep. 19, 1818	Ap'l 4, 1818	75	
Samuel Mansfield	Fifer	96 00	48 25	Maryland cont'l	May 1, 1819	May 16, 1818	80	Died November 16, 1819.
John Martin	Lieutenant	240 00	3,737 32	New Jersey cont'l	Mar. 5, 1819	Aug. 10, 1818	95	
Ephraim Pratt	Private	96 00	1,525 99	Massachusetts cont'l	June 12, 1819	Ap'l 20, 1818	70	Transferred from Pennsylvania.
Daniel Rowell	do	96 00	1,364 90	N. Hampshire cont'l	June 10, 1820	Dec. 17, 1820	71	Dropped from the roll under act May 1, 1820.
Jonathan Swett	do	96 00	171 89	Massachusetts cont'l	Mar. 24, 1818	May 21, 1818	74	Restored under act Mar. 1, 1823.
Do	do	96 00	761 31	do	–	Mar. 31, 1826	–	Restored under act Mar. 1, 1823.
Samuel Sage	Sergeant	96 00	809 83	Pennsylvania cont'l	May 10, 1818	Sep. 28, 1818	85	Dropped from the roll under act May 1, 1820.
John Simonton	Private	96 00	177 28	do	May 17, 1820	Ap'l 30, 1818	81	Dropped from the roll under act May 1, 1820.
Do	do	96 00	490 82	do	–	Aug. 20, 1823	–	Restored under act Mar. 1, 1823.
Robert Townsend	do	96 00	1,510 36	Rhode Island cont'l	Mar. 24, 1819	June 11, 1818	78	Died September 29, 1828.

Statement, &c. of Belmont county, Ohio.

NAMES.	Rank	Annual allowance.	Sums received.	Description of service.	When placed on the pension roll.	Commencement of pension.	Ages.	Laws under which they were formerly inscribed on the pension roll; and remarks:
Samuel Brown	Lieutenant	240 00	440 64	Mass. continental	Oct. 12, 1818	May 4, 1818	83	Dropped from the roll under act May 1, 1820
Roswell Beach	Private	96 00	1,521 06	Conn. continental	Sep. 14, 1818	May 1, 1818	76	
Edward Booth	do	96 00	1,471 76	Maryland cont'l	June 30, 1819	May 6, 1818	81	
William Chambers	do	96 00	-	Conn. continental	Sep. 30, 1818	Ap'l 2, 1818		
Jacob Dovenberger	do	96 00	739 43	Penn. continental	Ap'l 16, 1819	June 22, 1818	75	
John Edge	do	96 00	1,257 63	Virginia cont'l	Ap'l 8, 1819	May 6, 1818	78	Died June 11, 1831.
Arthur Gillis	do	96 00	177 87	Penn. continental	June 15, 1819	Ap'l 27, 1818	80	Dropped from the roll under act May 1, 1820.
Philip Hawkins	do	96 00	134 12	Maryland cont'l	Ap'l 18, 1832	Ap'l 12, 1832	78	
Jonathan Henderson	do	96 00	1,448 56	Mass. continental	Mar. 18, 1819	Ap'l 25, 1818	76	Died May 26, 1833.
Jacob Knight	do	96 00	533 93	Maryland cont'l	Nov. 27, 1819	Aug. 13, 1819	82	
William Lama	do	96 00	265 61	Penn. continental	Ap'l 16, 1819	July 3, 1818	64	Died April 8, 1821.
Alexander M'Ghoggan	do	96 00	1,478 14	do	June 22, 1819	Ap'l 11, 1818	86	
Francis M'Connel	do	96 00	1,321 28	N. J. continental	Sep. 22, 1819	May 31, 1818	80	
William Musgrove	do	96 00	1,439 25	Virginia cont'l	Dec. 27, 1819	Mar. 8, 1819	74	
William Paine	do	96 00	348 12	Maryland cont'l	June 25, 1818	July 20, 1818	81	Transferred from Virginia.
Amos Reed	do	96 00	1,474 66	N. J. continental	June 25, 1819	Ap'l 25, 1818	97	Died March 6, 1822.
Joseph Starkey	do	96 00	1,037 86	Virginia cont'l	Dec. 10, 1822	Nov. 13, 1822	62	Transferred from Virginia.
Joseph Thompson	do	96 00	1,467 89	Mass. continental	Nov. 13, 1818	May 21, 1818	72	
George Winham	do	96 00	1,244 89	Maryland cont'l	June 7, 1819	Aug. 15, 1818	71	Died August 2, 1831.

Statement, &c. of Brown county, Ohio.

NAMES.	Rank.	Annual allowance.	Sums received.	Description of service.	When placed on the pension roll.	Commencement of pension.	Ages.	Laws under which they were formerly inscribed on the pension roll; and remarks.
James Bonwell	Private	96 00	142 09	Virginia continental	July 22, 1819	Sep. 12, 1818	70	Dropped from the roll under act May 1, 1820.
Jesse Bayles, or Bales	do	96 00	1,150 42	do	Dec. 14, 1819	May 4, 1818	74	Transferred from Kentucky. Died April 27, 1830.
Thomas Cunningham	do	96 00	177 03	Pennsylvania cont'l	Sep. 30, 1819	May 1, 1818	78	Dropped from the roll under act May 1, 1820.
John Clark, 3d	do	96 00	349 00	do	Jan. 14, 1822	Oct. 25, 1821	77	Died June 12, 1825.
Michael Cowley	do	96 00	874 35	Maryland cont'l	Feb. 9, 1825	Jan. 27, 1825	84	
John Dye	do	96 00	1,487 46	Pennsylvania cont'l	July 22, 1819	Sep. 7, 1819	79	
William Dixon	do	96 00	41 03	Virginia continental	May 29, 1820	Oct. 1, 1819	68	Dropped from the roll under act May 1, 1820.
Do	do	96 00	574 22	do		Mar. 12, 1828	-	Restored under act March 1, 1823,
Valentine Fritts	do	96 00	151 99	do	Nov. 25, 1819	Aug. 5, 1818	62	Dropped from the roll under act May 1, 1820.
Stephen Fennell	do	96 00	1,523 43	Maryland cont'l	May 1, 1819	Ap'l 22, 1818	80	
Patrick Grogan	do	96 00	-	Virginia continental	Ap'l 2, 1831	Ap'l 1, 1831	94	
Samuel Jones	do	96 00	1,487 74	do	Sep. 6, 1819	Sep. 5, 1818	72	
Benjamin Leeton	do	96 00	932 05	do	June 19, 1819	Ap'l 10, 1819	68	Died December 25, 1828.
Patrick Lemrick	do	96 00	190 90	Pennsylvania cont'l	May 10, 1822	Aug. 4, 1820	82	Died July 30, 1822.
Connelly McFaden	do	96 00	156 64	N. J. continental	July, 1819	July 18, 1818	-	Dropped from the roll under act May 1, 1820.
Do	do	96 00	896 23	do		Nov. 4, 1824	-	Restored under act March 1, 1823.
George Marshall	do	96 00	1,397 18	Virginia continental	Oct. 1, 1819	Aug. 16, 1819	92	
William Printis	do	96 00	743 18	N. J. continental	July 21, 1819	May 13, 1818	85	Transferred from Kentucky. Died February 8, 1826.
Joseph Potter, 2d	do	96 00	1,497 83	Mass. continental	do	July 29, 1818	74	
James Rice	do	96 00	1,017 54	Virginia continental	Sep. 5, 1823	July 30, 1823	79	Transferred from Kentucky.
Richard Rilea	do	96 00	1,423 25	do	June 21, 1819	May 8, 1819	73	
James Rounds	do	96 00	954 86	Mass. continental	June 17, 1824	Mar. 25, 1824	74	
Lemuel Rounds	do	96 00	534 47	R. I. continental	Aug. 23, 1828	Aug. 11, 1828	78	

Statement, &c. of Brown county—Continued.

NAMES.	Rank.	Annual allowance	Sums received.	Description of service.	When placed on the pension roll.	Commencement of pension	Ages.	Laws under which they were formerly inscribed on the pension roll; and remarks.
Richard Spyers -	Private	96 00	1,516 67	Maryland cont'l	July 21, 1819	May 18, 1818	81	
John Thompson, 2d -	do	96 00	137 30	Virginia continental	June 9, 1819	May 29, 1818		Died November 2, 1819.
William White -	do	96 00	1,519 76	do	June 11, 1819	May 6, 1818	73	
Nicholas Wood -	do	96 00	848 00	do	May 18, 1825	May 5, 1825	73	
Thomas Woods -	do	96 00	177 29	Pennsylvania cont'l	June 5, 1820	Ap'l 30, 1818	75	Dropped from the roll under act May 1, 1820. Restored under act March 1, 1823.
Do	do	96 00	766 70	do	-	Dec. 26, 1825		Died December 20, 1833.

Statement, &c. of Butler county, Ohio.

NAMES.	Rank.	Annual allowance	Sums received.	Description of service.	When placed on the pension roll.	Commencement of pension.	Ages.	Laws under which they were formerly inscribed on the pension roll; and remarks.
Benjamin Applegate -	Private	96 00	1,211 12	N. Jersey cont'l	Nov. 9, 1819	July 20, 1819	71	
Herran Adams -	do	96 00	1,413 18	Mass. continental	May 31, 1820	Dec. 16, 1818	74	
Paul Bonnel -	do	96 00	139 61	Penn. continental	Nov. 22, 1819	Mar. 12, 1819	59	Died August 26, 1820.
Joshua Buckley -	do	96 00	314 09	Virginia continental	May 29, 1820	Nov. 27, 1819	74	
Benjamin Bridge -	do	96 00	1,468 67	Congress regiment	Sep. 18, 1819	May 18, 1818	81	
Michael Curts -	do	96 00	33 51	Penn. continental	Ap'l 15, 1819	June 5, 1818	66	Died Oct. 10, 1818.
Adam Deits -	Musician	96 00	1,522 39	Virginia continental	Oct. 23, 1818	Ap'l 24, 1818	70	

173 [514]

Name	Rank		Amount	Regiment	Date	Date	Age	Remarks
George Francis	Private	96 00	159 78	Penn. continental	Ap'l 15, 1819	June 5, 1818	75	Died Feb. 3, 1820.
John Haseltine	do	96 00	1,305 80	Mass. continental	Ap'l 29, 1819	July 29, 1818	78	Died Oct 13, 1831.
Gabriel Hutchings	do	96 00	1,289 54	N. J. continental	May 20, 1820	May 8, 1818	73	Died July 10, 1830.
Ebenezer Howe	do	96 00	324 86	Mass. continental	Feb. 27, 1827	Feb. 21, 1827	64	Dropped from the roll under act May 1, 1820.
Joseph Lummis	do	96 00	177 03	N. J. continental	May 12, 1820	May 1, 1818	75	Restored under act Mar. 1, 1823.
Do	do	96 00	860 41	do	Nov. 25, 1819	Mar. 19, 1825	-	
Charles McGuire	do	96 00	380 26	Penn. continental	June 18, 1819	Sep. 19, 1818	79	
John Phillips	do	96 00	1,305 06	Virginia continental	June 10, 1819	Feb. 1, 1819	79	
Joseph Potter, 1st	do	96 00	1,270 92	N. J. continental	Ap'l 15, 1819	June 9, 1818	86	
George Reed	do	96 00	1,512 79	do	May 1, 1819	June 2, 1818	80	
Leonard Rager	do	96 00	1,396 12	Virginia continental	May 31, 1820	Aug. 20, 1818	87	Dropped from the roll under act May 1, 1820.
Mathias Rall, or Roll	do	96 00	25 32	N. J. continental		Nov. 30, 1819	59	Dropped from the roll under act May 1, 1820.
Robert Rickey	Sergeant	96 00	-	Virginia continental	Oct. 6, 1820	Dec. 1, 1819	70	Dropped from the roll under act May 1, 1820.
George Sinclair	Private	96 00	1,366 39	N. J. continental	Ap'l 1, 1819	June 11, 1818	80	
Henry Symmond	do	96 00	792 00	Penn. continental	Ap'l 15, 1819	June 5, 1818	94	
Pardon T. Starks	do	96 00	1,507 96	Mass. continental	Sep. 30, 1819	June 20, 1818	70	
Elisha Stout	do	96 00	1,522 92	N. J. continental	Oct. 11, 1819	Ap'l 24, 1818	78	
John Thompson	do	96 00	1,518 22	New York cont'l	Jan. 18, 1819	May 12, 1818	97	
George Vannostran	do	96 00	143 43	N. J. continental	June 9, 1819	Sept. 7, 1818	69	Dropped from the roll under act May 1, 1820.
John Wilson	do	96 00	679 25	Virginia continental	Ap'l 29, 1819	Aug. 8, 1818	101	Dropped from the roll under act May 1, 1820.
Ichabod Wilkinson	do	96 00	122 35	Connecticut cont'l	July 14, 1819	May 27, 1818	66	
Ebenezer Wood	do	96 00	165 03	Virginia continental	July 31, 1819	June 16, 1818	74	Restored under act Mar. 1, 1823.
Do	do	96 00	667 35	Maryland cont'l	Oct. 18, 1819	Mar. 23, 1827	-	Restored under act Mar. 1, 1823.
James Warden	do	96 00	1,149 39	Conn. continental	Nov. 26, 1819	July 8, 1818	90	Died June 27, 1830.
William Wardwell	do	96 00	162 09			June 27, 1818	74	Dropped from the roll under act May 1, 1820.
Do	do	96 00	883 72	do		June 21, 1824	-	Restored under act Mar. 1, 1823.

Statement, &c. of Champaign county, Ohio.

NAMES:	Rank.	Annual allowance.	Sums received.	Description of service.	When placed on the pension roll.	Commencement of pension.	Ages.	Laws under which they were formerly inscribed on the pension roll; and remarks.
Robert Barnse	Private	96 00	8 38	Penn. continental	Ap'l 1, 1819	May 15, 1818	74	Died June 15, 1818.
John Burgess	do	96 00	1,520 77	N. York continental	Oct. 13, 1818	May 2, 1818	79	
George Bailitz	do	96 00	689 80	Penn. continental	Mar. 17, 1819	May 13, 1818	97	Died July 19, 1825.
Obadiah Beall	Corporal	96 00	419 73	Mass. continental	do	Ap'l 28, 1818	60	Died September 11, 1822.
David Bay	Private	96 00	241 55	Virginia cont'l	Sep. 6, 1819	Aug. 29, 1818	65	Dropped under act May 1, 1820.
John Bareth	do	96 00	–	do	Nov. 26, 1819	May 2, 1818	65	
William Colgan	do	96 00	1,516 12	do	Ap'l 1, 1819	May 20, 1818		
Thomas Edwards	Sergeant	96 00	1,032 49	Maryland cont'l	July 29, 1819	June 3, 1818	89	
James Irwin	Corporal	96 00	286 93	Mass. continental	July 21, 1819	Ap'l 22, 1818	80	Died April 17, 1821.
John Legg	Private	96 00	1,515 89	Virginia cont'l	July 14, 1819	May 21, 1818	80	
James Lindsey	do	96 00	551 07	do	Sep. 9, 1819	May 9, 1818	65	Died February 4, 1824.
William Mungee	Corporal	96 00	510 44	Mass. continental	Sep. 27, 1819	May 2, 1818	79	Died August 26, 1823.
Jacob Richards	Private	96 00	270 77	Virginia cont'l	Jan. 25, 1831	Jan. 14, 1831	73	Died November 8, 1833.
Beverly Spencer	do	96 00	172 64	N. H. continental	Sep. 27, 1819	May 18, 1818	72	Dropped under act May 1, 1820.
Benjamin Taylor	do	96 00	1,526 92	Mass. continental	Ap'l 9, 1819	Ap'l 9, 1818	76	Transferred from Maine.
Joshua Wyeth	do	96 00	1,029 93	do	June 17, 1819	Ap'l 30, 1818	76	
James Willard	do	96 00	1,517 72	do	Dec. 2, 1819	Ap'l 21, 1818	72	Died January 22, 1829.

Statement, &c. of Clarke county, Ohio.

NAMES.	Rank.	Annual allowance.	Sums received.	Description of service.	When placed on the pension roll.	Commencement of pension.	Ages.	Laws under which they were formerly inscribed on the pension roll; and remarks.
John Ayers	Private	96 00	774 12	Maryland cont'l	Ap'l 18, 1825	Feb. 22, 1825	80	Died March 16, 1833.
Timothy Bagley	do	96 00	583 12	N. Hampshire cont'l	Oct. 12, 1819	Aug. 24, 1819	76	Died September 19, 1825.
Elijah Beardsly	do	96 00	-	Conecticut cont'l	Ap'l 1, 1819	June 6, 1818	73	
Asaph Butler	do	96 00	602 35	N. Hampshire cont'l	Sep. 24, 1819	May 27, 1819	63	Died September, 1825.
James Craig	do	96 00	512 07	do	do	May 11, 1818	65	Died September 10, 1823.
John Craig	do	96 00	-	do	Nov. 9, 1819	May 18, 1818	68	
James Hopkins	do	96 00	523 76	Virginia cont'l	Sep. 27, 1819	Ap'l 13, 1818	75	Died September 27, 1823.
James Hunt	do	96 00	144 54	Maryland cont'l	Mar. 20, 1832	Mar. 3, 1832	79	
James Lee	do	96 00	471 76	Virginia cont'l	Feb. 2, 1819	Oct. 6, 1818	84	
Cornelius Morris	do	96 00	1,462 44	Maryland cont'l	Ap'l 27, 1819	May 13, 1818	76	Died August 6, 1833.
John Moreland	do	96 00	1,518 22	Virginia cont'l	Oct. 4, 1819	May 12, 1818	81	
Josiah Mott	Sergeant	96 00	593 06	-	Sep. 10, 1830	Jan. 1, 1828		
John Ross	Private	96 00	508 15	Pennsylvania cont'l	Ap'l 23, 1822	May 20, 1818	91	
William Rodgers	do	96 00	359 48	Virginia cont'l	Jan. 19, 1830	Jan. 7, 1830	73	
Cornelius Tollen	do	96 00	1,502 70	Pennsylvania cont'l	July 15, 1819	July 10, 1818		
Merifield Vicory	Musician	96 00	171 86	Congress regiment	July 21, 1819	May 21, 1818	72	Dropped from the roll under act May 1, 1820.
Do	do	96 00	1,041 03	do	do	May 1, 1823	-	Restored under act Mar. 1, 1823.
Jacob Waggoner	Private	96 00	527 36	German regiment		May 21, 1818	68	Died November 17, 1823.

7

Statement, &c. of Clermont county, Ohio.

NAMES.	Rank.	Annual allowance.	Sums received.	Description of service.	When placed on the pension roll.	Commencement of pension.	Ages.	Laws under which they were formerly inscribed on the pension roll; and remarks.
Ramoth Bunting	Private	96 00	175 22	N. J. continental	Mar. 29, 1819	May 8, 1818	86	Dropped from the roll under act May 1, 1820.
Do	do	96 00	818 40	do	–	Feb. 25, 1825	–	Restored under act March 1, 1823.
Lawrence Byrn	do	96 00	1,261 16	Penn. continental	Sep. 6, 1819	May 27, 1819	78	Died July 15, 1832.
James Chambers	do	96 00	1,461 25	N. J. continental	Mar. 29, 1819	May 8, 1818	72	
Andrew Chalmers	do	96 00	930 27	Penn. continental	June 17, 1824	Mar. 18, 1824	79	
Jeremiah Day	do	96 00	263 96	N. J. continental	July 28, 1819	June 5, 1818	81	
Benjamin Davis	do	96 00	288 26	Penn. continental	July 16, 1821	Sep. 4, 1818	82	
Benajah Hill	do	96 00	371 61	Mass. continental	Aug. 5, 1822	Mar. 22, 1822	70	
Hezekiah Lindsey	do	96 00	695 96	Virginia cont'l	June 5, 1819	June 5, 1818	87	
Mordecai Love	do	96 00	1,017 80	Penn. continental	May 16, 1822	July 29, 1818	81	
Neal Murry	do	96 00	1,332 38	do	Nov. 30, 1818	Ap'l 18, 1818	86	Died January 8, 1834.
John Miles	do	96 00	1,496 99	Virginia cont'l	July 7, 1819	June 5, 1818	95	Dropped from the roll under act May 1, 1820.
John M'Knight	do	96 00	178 09	Maryland cont'l	Jan. 7, 1819	Ap'l 25, 1818	76	Restored under act March 1, 1823
Do	do	96 00	1,032 77	do	–	June 2, 1823	76	
James Murphy	do	96 00	1,444 77	Penn. continental	June 10, 1819	Feb. 16, 1819	74	
John Mitchell or Mikle	do	96 00	1,509 32	do	May 6, 1820	June 15, 1818	76	
William Owen	do	96 00	216 79	dc	Ap'l 1, 1818	June 2, 1818	109	
Eli Porter	do	96 00	328 26	Virginia cont'l	Oct. 4, 1830	Oct. 4, 1830	71	Died October 3, 1831.
William Reddick	do	96 00	1,262 96	Penn. continental	Ap'l 29, 1819	Aug. 8, 1818	79	
Reuben Ross	do	96 00	1,510 92	Maryland cont'l	June 13, 1820	June 9, 1818	74	
Joshua Richardson	do	96 00	1,512 00	Mass. continental	Oct. 13, 1820	June 5, 1818	76	
Gideon Riggs	do	96 00	80 25	do	Oct. 27, 1828	Oct. 20, 1828	71	Died August 20, 1829.
Elnathan Sherwin	do	96 00	249 06	do	Ap'l 20, 1820	Jan. 31, 1820	75	Dropped from the roll under act May 1, 1820.
Obadiah Smith	do	96 00	172 38	N. Y. continental	Mar. 18, 1819	May 19, 1818		Restored under act March 1, 1823.
Do	do	96 00	172 89	do	–	Dec. 24, 1824	75	Died October 11, 1826.
Jesse Swem	do	96 00	167 16	N. J. continental	Sep. 8, 1819	June 8, 1818	79	Dropped from the roll under act May 1, 1820.
Do	do	96 00	319 19	do	–	Nov. 8, 1830	79	Restored under act March 1, 1823.

Statement, &c. of Clinton county, Ohio.

NAMES.	Rank.	Annual allowance.	Sums received.	Description of service.	When placed on the pension roll.	Commencement of pension.	Ages.	Laws under which they were formerly inscribed on the pension roll; and remarks.
Gordon Howard -	Private	96 00	250 09	Penn. continental	July 28, 1831	July 28, 1831	81	
Dennis O'Laughlin -	do	96 00	8 25	do	July 31, 1819	Aug. 4, 1818		
William Spencer -	do	96 00	1,452 22	Virginia continental	Nov. 26, 1819	July 27, 1818	104	Died Sept. 11, 1833.
Alexander Strickling -	do	96 00	877 96	do	April 8, 1825	Jan. 13, 1825	82	
Michael Wolf -	do	96 00	1,501 44	do	July 21, 1819	July 15, 1818	80	
Abraham Westfall -	do	96 00	482 36	N. York continental	Sept. 7, 1824	Aug. 28, 1824	71	
Thomas Wakle -	do	96 00	716 52	Conn. continental	Oct. 9, 1826	Sep. 18, 1826	70	Died Septi 5, 1829.

Statement, &c. of Columbiana county, Ohio.

NAMES.	Rank.	Annual allowance.	Sums received.	Description of service.	When placed on the pension roll.	Commencement of pension.	Ages.	Laws under which they were formerly inscribed on the pension roll; and remarks.
Jacob Bushong -	Private	96 00	168 49	Virginia continental	Nov. 10, 1818	June 3, 1818	66	Dropped from the roll under act May 1, 1820.
Isaac Brown -	do	96 00	-	do	Sep. 21, 1819	June 19, 1818	76	
Henry Fisher -	do	96 00	762 83	Pennsylvania cont'l	Jan. 19, 1819	May 22, 1818	62	Died May 1st, 1826.
William Huston -	do	96 00	1,254 44	do	Oct. 9, 1820	Aug. 15, 1820	72	Died June 17, 1824.
William Liggins -	do	96 00	558 33	do	Ap'l 30, 1818	Aug. 25, 1818	65	Died Jan. 6, 1828.
William Lee -	do	96 00	927 99	do	Mar. 18, 1819	May 7, 1818	85	Dropped from the roll under act May 1, 1820.
Mathias Shirts -	do	96 00	173 93	N. J. continental	Oct. 6, 1820	May 13, 1818	73	Dropped from the roll under act March 1, 1823.
Do			891 19	do	-	Nov. 23, 1824	-	Restored under act March 1, 1823.
James Smith -	do	96 00	365 44	Pennsylvania cont'l	May 19, 1830	May 15, 1830	78	
Michael Zane or Seyner	do	96 00	159 22	do	Oct. 6, 1320	July 8, 1818	89	Dropped from the roll under act May 1, 1820.

Statement, &c. of Coshockton county, Ohio.

NAMES.	Rank.	Annual allowance.	Sums received.	Description of service.	When placed on the pension roll.	Commencement of pension.	Ages	Laws under which they were formerly inscribed on the pension roll; and remarks.
John Bantham	Private	96 00	563 41	Maryland cont'l	Sep. 32, 1819	Ap'l 22, 1818	86	
Alexander Crawford Brown	do	96 00	895 22	Delaware cont'l	June 21, 1822	May 1, 1818	72	Died August 28, 1827.
William Speake	do	96 00	1,226 32	Virginia continental	Sep. 10, 1819	May 27, 1818	80	
Bartholomew Thayer	Lieutenant	240 00	1,913 33	Mass. continental	Sep. 30, 1818	Ap'l 22, 1818	69	Died April 11, 1826,
Solomon Vail	Private	96 00	734 78	Virginia continental	Dec. 8, 1818	do	89	Died December 17, 1825.
John Williams, 1st	Sergeant	96 00	179 16	do	Oct. 31, 1818	Ap'l 23, 1818		Dropped from the roll under act May 1, 1820.
James Williams, 2d	Private	96 00	624 59	Pennsylvania cont'l	May 24, 1819	May 8, 1818	79	Died November 9, 1824,
Samuel Wiley	do	96 00	1,491 86	Mass. continental	Oct. 12, 1819	Aug. 21 1818	77	Transferred from New York

Statement, &c. of Crawford county, Ohio.

NAMES.	Rank.	Annual allowance.	Sums received.	Description of service.	When placed on the pension roll.	Commencement of pension.	Ages.	Laws under which they were formerly inscribed on the pension roll; and remarks.
Nicholas Bergerhoff	Private	96 00	1,081 06	Virginia continental	June 31, 1819	June 1, 1819	78	Transferred from Virginia. Dead.
Daniel Canfield	do	96 00	386 60	New York cont'l	Sep. 15, 1828	Aug. 16, 1828	77	Transferred from Virginia.

Statement, &c. of Cuyahoga county, Ohio.

NAMES.	Rank.	Annual allowance.	Sums received.	Description of service.	When placed on the pension roll.	Commencement of pension.	Ages.	Laws under which they were formerly inscribed on the pension roll; and remarks.
Silvanus Burk	Private	96 00	1,464 26	Massachusetts cont'l	July 26, 1819	June 4, 1818	71	Transferred from New York.
Levi Brown	do	96 00	1,477 59	do	Oct. 24, 1820	Ap'l 4, 1818	62	
Seth Baldwin	do	96 00	977 32	Connecticut cont'l	Ap'l 14, 1820	Apr. 30, 1818	73	
John Crosier	Lieutenant	240 00	1,202 00	Massachusetts cont'l	Mar. 5, 1819	Ap'l 24, 1818	72	Died April 26, 1823.
Sergent Currier	Private	96 00	475 56	N. Hampshire cont'l		May 13, 1818	65	Died April 25, 1825.
Abner Cochrane	do	96 00	147 58	Massachusetts cont'l	July 26, 1819	June 4, 1818	62	Died December 17, 1819.
Jacob Coleman	do	96 00	917 15	Virginia cont'l	Feb. 16, 1825	Aug. 16, 1824	62	
Richard Cooper	do	96 00	1,514 32	New York cont'l	Ap'l 1, 1819	May 27, 1818	89	
Christopher Colson	do	96 00	58 84	Massachusetts cont'l	July 25, 1818	July 24, 1818	66	Transferred from Vermont.
Timothy Eggleston	do	96 00	1,434 06	Connecticut cont'l	Sep. 24, 1818	Mar. 28, 1818	76	Died December 18, 1825.
Samuel Eldred	Lieutenant	240 00	1,810 27	Massachusetts cont'l	Mar. 5, 1819	June 3, 1818	80	
William Fuller	Private	96 00	997 86	do	May 11, 1819	Ap'l 13, 1818	73	Dropped from the roll under act May 1, 1820.
Levi Hamblin	do	96 00	127 46	Connecticut cont'l	Mar. 5, 1819	Nov. 7, 1818	57	
Hezekiah Hall	do	96 00	522 60	do	Mar. 5, 1828	Mar. 26, 1828	77	Transferred from N. York.
James Jackson	do	96 00	417 32	Maryland cont'l	July 7, 1819	Ap'l 30, 1818	87	Transferred from Vermont.
Asa Jones	Sergeant	96 00	1,472 02	Connecticut cont'l	June 16, 1819	May 5, 1818	79	Died June 8, 1827.
Josiah Kellogg	Fifer	96 00	-	do	May 15, 1819	Ap'l 6, 1818	64	
John Murray	Private	96 00	368 32	do	May 24, 1824	Aug. 8, 1823	74	
James Nichols	do	96 00	1,024 25	Rhode Island cont'l	Oct. 20, 1819	July 4, 1818	79	Transferred from Vermont.
Daniel O'Brien	do	96 00	1,476 49	Maryland cont'l	July 7, 1819	Ap'l 18, 1818	84	
Simeon Powers	do	96 00	360 76	N. Hampshire cont'l	do	June 2, 1818	89	
Silvanus Smith	Sergeant	96 00	52 38	Connecticut cont'l	May 29, 1820	Aug. 20, 1819	61	Dropped from the roll under act May 1, 1820.
Ohimaas Sherwin	Private	96 00	1,478 66	do	Nov. 26, 1818	Ap'l 10, 1818	74	Transferred from Vermont.
Benjamin Sawtell	do	96 00	1,288 52	Massachusetts cont'l	Sep. 25, 1818	Ap'l 3, 1818	71	Transferred from N. York. Died December 28, 1831.
Peter Tuman	do	38 40	1,521 06	New York cont'l	Ap'l 28, 1819	May 1, 1818	63	Transferred from New York.
Benjamin Whitney, 3d	do	96 00	1,425 29	Massachusetts cont'l	Jan. 14, 1821	Ap'l 30, 1818	73	Transferred New York.

Statement, &c. of Delaware county, Ohio.

NAMES.	Rank.	Annual allowance.	Sums received.	Description of service.	When placed on the pension roll.	Commencement of pension.	Ages.	Laws under which they were formerly inscribed on the pension roll; and remarks.
Ephraim Ames	Private	96 00	610 92	Mass. continental	Mar. 22, 1819	Ap'l 24, 1818	74	Transferred from Pennsylvania.
Israel Clark	do	96 00	829 15	Connecticut cont'l	Jan. 28, 1819	May 20, 1818	77	Died September 19, 1834.
Roswell Caulkins	do	96 00	165 29	do	June 15, 1819	June 15, 1818	—	Died January 31, 1827. Dropped from the roll under act May 1, 1820.
Solomon Jones	Ensign	240 00	443 99	Mass. continental	Jan. 18, 1819	Ap'l 29, 1818	68	Dropped from the roll nnder act May 1, 1820.
Crocker Jones	Private	96 00	1,523 46	Connecticut cont'l	Mar. 24, 1819	Ap'l 22, 1818	86	Transferred from Pennsylvania.
Alexander Kingman	do	96 00	1,480 52	Mass. continatal	Aug. 2, 1819	Ap'l 4, 1818	69	Transferred from New York.
Edward Knapp	do	96 00	273 29	do	Ap'l 21, 1819	Ap'l 30, 1818		
James Landon	do	96 00	173 19	N. J. continental	July 21, 1819	May 12, 1818	94	Dropped from the roll under act May 1, 1820.
Do	do	96 00	1,051 83	do	-	Mar. 25, 1823	94	Restored under act March 1, 1823.
Leonard Munroe	do	96 00	894 77	Connecticut cont'l	June 21, 1819	Aug. 1, 1818	70	Died August 3, 1827.
Robert Porterfield	do	96 00	603 89	Mass. continental	Jan. 28, 1819	May 21, 1818	77	
Edmund Patee	Fifer	96 00	519 72	do	July 30, 1819	Ap'l 6, 1818	70	Transferred from New York.
Bixbee Rogers	Private	96 00	1,265 59	Connecticut cont'l	Ap'l 28, 1819	June 29, 1818	—	Died February 11, 1819.
John Shaw	do	96 00	71 67	Maryland cont'l	May 15, 1819	May 15, 1818		
Ebenezer Wood	do	96 00	1,298 46	Mass. continental	Nov. 5, 1819	Ap'l 14, 1818	80	Transferred from New York. Died October 23, 1831.
Ebenezer Welch	Fifer	96 00	463 22	Connecticut cont'l	Mar. 26, 1819	May 8, 1818		

Statement, &c. of Dark county, Ohio.

NAMES.	Rank.	Annual allowance.	Sums received.	Description of service.	When placed on the pension roll.	Commencement of pension.	Ages.	Laws under which they were formerly inscribed on the pension roll; and remarks.
William Dugan	Private	96 00	1,503 51	N. J. continental	May 10, 1819	July 7, 1818	71	
Stephen Fountain	do	96 00	1,219 69	Mass. continental	Aug. 9, 1819	June 21, 1818	80	
William Smith 2d	do	96 00	510 22	Delaware cont'l	June 28, 1819	May 12, 1818	83	
Samuel Satterly	do	96 00	542 73	N. J. continental	July 25, 1829	July 10, 1827	89	
John Tucker	do	96 00	941 08	Virginia continental	Dec. 4, 1819	Nov. 9, 1819	79	
James Wood	do	96 00	1,505 86	do	Aug. 2, 1819	June 28, 1818	73	Died August 28, 1829.

Statement, &c. of Fayette county, Ohio.

NAMES.	Rank.	Annual allowance.	Sums received.	Description of service.	When placed on the pension roll.	Commencement of pension.	Ages.	Laws under which they were formerly inscribed on the pension roll; and remarks.
Adam Allen	Private	96 00	883 72	Pennsylvania cont'l	July 2, 1825	June 21, 1825	79	Died December 17, 1824.
Francis Boyd	do	96 00	579 61	Virginia cont'l	May 21, 1819	Dec. 4, 1818	66	Dropped from the roll under act May 1, 1820.
John Buck	do	96 00	89 31	Pennsylvania cont'l	Sep. 10, 1819	Mar. 31, 1819	65	Died January 14, 1830.
Eben Clevenger	do	96 00	1,125 33	Virginia cont'l	Sep. 6, 1819	Ap'l 25, 1818	75	
Philip Fint	do	96 00	1,418 32	do	July 14, 1819	May 27, 1819	77	
Isaac Faucher	do	96 00	1,388 49	do	Nov. 8, 1819	Sep. 18, 1819	74	
Joseph Parret	Lieutenant	240 00	—	do	Aug. 14, 1827	July 23, 1827	68	Relinquished for the benefit of act May 15, 1828.
William Rankin	Private	96 00	31 76	do	June 10, 1823	May 6, 1823	86	Died December 31, 1828.]
Joh Fway	do	96 00	1,019 09	New Jersey cont'l	May 21, 1819	May 20, 1818	87	

Statement, &c. of Fairfield county, Ohio.

NAMES.	Rank.	Annual allowance.	Sums received.	Description of service.	When placed on the pension roll.	Commencement of pension.	Ages.	Laws under which they were formerly inscribed on the pension roll; and remarks.
Jonathan Burnside	Private	96 00	1,513 03	Virginia cont'l	June 15, 1819	June 1, 1818	73	
Joshua Burton	do	96 00	1,510 89	Maryland cont'l	July 21, 1819	June 9, 1818	84	
Jonathan Center	do	96 00	950 36	Penn. continental	July 24, 1819	Ap'l 11, 1818	90	
John Colman	do	96 00	1,057 60	do	Feb. 2, 1819	June 8, 1818	70	Died June 13, 1829.
Benjamin Carlisle	do	96 00	1,425 29	Virginia cont'l	May 25, 1821	Ap'l 30, 1818	73	March 3, 1817. Invalid pensioner.
Johnson Cook	Sergeant	48 00	89 82	Conn. continental	Mar. 24, 1817	Nov. 27, 1816	73	March 18, 1818. Relinquished for pension under act Mar. 18, 1818.
Do	do	96 00	134 70	do	Feb. 2, 1819	Oct. 10, 1818	-	May 1, 1820. Dropped from the roll under act May 1, 1820.
Do	do	48 00	240 00	do	-	Mar. 4, 1820	-	March 1, 1823. Restored to roll under act March 1, 1823.
Do	do	96 00	864 00	do	-	Mar. 4, 1825	-	
John Cross	Private	96 00	1,519 73	Virginia cont'l	Feb. 4, 1820	May 6, 1818	73	Transferred from Virginia.
William Davis	do	96 00	1,203 73	Conn. continental	May 12, 1820	May 1, 1818	69	Died Nov. 14, 1830.
Henry Fitzgerald	do	96 00	586 54	Penn. continental	Feb. 3, 1819	May 2, 1818	73	Died June 18, 1824.
William Johnson	Sergeant	96 00	460 41	Maryland cont'l	Feb. 2, 1819	May 16, 1818	75	Died February 20, 1823.
John G. King	Private	96 00	1,171 46	Penn. continental	do	June 22, 1818	73	
John Murphey	do	96 00	539 95	Virginia cont'l	Ap'l 21, 1819	July 10, 1818	74	Died February 22, 1824.
John Martin	do	96 00	842 87	Maryland cont'l	Nov. 5, 1821	May 12, 1818	71	Died February 20, 1827.
William Priest	do	96 00	280 80	Virginia cont'l	May 12, 1820	July 1, 1818	67	Died June 3, 1821.
William Rigby	Qr. m'r ser.	96 00	1,001 28	Maryland cont'l	Sep. 7, 1820	Oct. 18, 1819	77	Died March 12, 1830.
David Smith	Private	96 00	915 02	N. Y. continental	Feb. 2, 1819	May 12, 1818	66	Died November 22, 1827.
Jonathan Smith	Lieutenant	240 00	2,367 11	Virginia cont'l	July 13, 1819	Ap'l 14, 1818	71	Relinquished for benefit of act May 15, 1828.
John Sllife or Schlife	Private	96 00	1,421 43	Maryland cont'l	May 30, 1820	May 15, 1819	78	
Mathias Sheets	do	96 00	395 76	Virginia cont'l	Aug. 16, 1830	Aug. 16, 1830	81	Dropped from the roll under act May 1, 1820.
Jonathan Smith	do	96 00	67 43	Mass. continental	Nov. 30, 1819	June 22, 1819	65	
Thomas Torrence	do	96 00	948 49	do	Feb. 2, 1819	Ap'l 18, 1818	91	
Bernard Valentine	do	96 00	1,239 99	N. Y. continental	Feb. 11, 1819	Aug. 15, 1818	73	Died July 14, 1831.

NAMES.	Rank.	Annual allowance.	Sums received.	Description of service.	When placed on the pension roll.	Commencement of pension.	Ages.	Laws under which they were formerly inscribed on the pension roll; and remarks.
James Walters	do	96 00	141 03	Virginia cont'l	Ap'l 14, 1819	Sep. 16, 1818	79	Dropped from the roll under act May 1, 1820.
Do	do	96 00	831 51	do	-	Jan. 3, 1825	-	Restored under act March 1, 1823.
Christian Young	do	96 00	1,517 70	do	Feb. 3, 1819	May 14, 1818	81	

Statement, &c. of Franklin county, Ohio.

NAMES.	Rank.	Annual allowance.	Sums received.	Description of service.	When placed on the pension roll.	Commencement of pension.	Ages.	Laws under which they were formerly inscribed on the pension roll; and remarks.
John Anderson	Private	96 00	744 51	Virginia cont'l	May 19, 1819	Oct. 6, 1818	86	Transferred from Kentucky. Died July 7, 1826.
Adam Blain	do	96 00	1,473 06	Penn. continental	Sep. 10, 1819	May 1, 1818	75	
Henry Brumgarten	do	96 00	176 25	Congress regiment	Sep. 27, 1819	May 4, 1818	79	Dropped from the roll under act May 1, 1820.
Do	do	96 00	618 86	do	-	Mar. 25, 1823	-	Restored under act March 1, 1823.
James Curry	Captain	240 00	442 66	Virginia cont'l	Jan. 25, 1819	May 1, 1818	-	Dropped from the roll under act May 1, 1820.
Jacob Casey	Private	96 00	1,233 03	do	Sep. 28, 1819	do	79	
Roswell Cook	Drummer	96 00	35 86	Conn. continental	Nov. 25, 1819	Oct. 21, 1819	58	Dropped from the roll under act May 1, 1820.
James Cummings	Private	96 00	1,057 03	Penn. continental	June 12, 1823	Mar. 1, 1823	77	
John Denoon	do	96 00	1,520 80	Maryland cont'l	Sep. 24, 1819	May 2, 1818	58	
John Holton	do	96 00	1,137 03	Penn. continental	July 23, 1819	May 1, 1818	76	
Henry Hill	do	96 00	1,470 73	Virginia cont'l	June 10, 1819	May 10, 1818	83	
Ro..t Justice	do	96 00	1,520 00	Penn. continental	May 13, 1818	May 4, 1818	75	
Patrick Logan	do	96 00	50 32	Virginia cont'l	Oct. 2, 1819	Aug. 27, 1819	68	Dropped from the roll under act May 1, 1820.

Statement, &c. of Franklin county—Co...

NAMES.	Rank.	Annual allowance.	Sums received.	Description of service.	When placed on the pension roll.	Commencement of pension.	Ages.	Laws under which they were formerly inscribed on the pension roll; and remarks.
Joseph Lewis	Private	96 00	223 91	Penn. continental	June 12, 1820	Ap'l 11, 1818	77	Died August 10, 1820.
Josias Miller	do	96 00	853 03	Maryland cont'l	Ap'l 16, 1818	Ap'l 16, 1818	77	
John Montgomery	do	96 00	1,477 70	Penn. continental	Feb. 1, 1819	Oct. 14, 1818	79	
James M'Burney	do	96 00	1,521 32	N. J. continental	June 1, 1819	Ap'l 30, 1818	81	
Simeon Moore	do	96 00	684 86	Conn. continental	July 23, 1819	May 9, 1818	73	Died June 26, 1825.
Samuel M'Kee	do	96 00	494 96	Penn. continental	Ap'l 26, 1819	May 25, 1818	69	Died July 20, 1823.
William Manning	Sergeant	96 00	422 39	Conn. continental	May 13, 1819	Ap'l 11, 1818	80	Died May 8, 1825.
Jesse Menely	Private	96 00	673 80	N. J. continental	Sep. 24, 1819	May 2, 1818	75	Trans'd from Connecticut. Died September 29, 1831.
Lemuel Orton	do	96 00	1,290 66	Conn. continental	Sep. 21, 1818	Ap'l 20, 1818	74	Died January 21, 1828.
Francis Olmstead	do	96 00	921 41	do	June 10, 1819	June 16, 1818	64	
Elias Pegg	do	96 00	175 73	Penn. continental	Sep. 27, 1819	May 6, 1818	75	Dropped from the roll under act May 1, 1820.
Do	do	96 00	334 02	do	-	Mar. 5, 1830	-	Restored under act March 1, 1823.
Joseph Price	do	96 00	176 77	do	Sep. 27, 1819	May 2, 1818	80	Dropped from the roll under act May 1, 1820.
Do	do	96 00	97 06	do	-	Sep. 1, 1824	-	Restored under act March 1, 1823.
Moses Rugg	do	96 00	1,317 03	Mass. continental	Ap'l 15, 1819	June 16, 1819	76	Transferred from N. York. Died March 11, 1826.
Abijah Stow	Musician	96 00	762 83	Penn. continental	June 30, 1818	Ap'l 1, 1818	70	
Frederick Sprague	Private	96 00	1,519 76	Conn. continental	Aug. 2, 1820	May 6, 1818	71	
Thomas Smith	do	96 00	723 12	Maryland cont'l	Sep. 27, 1826	Aug. 24, 1826	74	
Thomas Sibliss	do	96 00	535 19	Mass. continental	May 13, 1819	Ap'l 11, 1818	98	Died November 7, 1823.
John Thompson	Colonel	240 00	3,827 09	Penn. continental	Mar. 30, 1819	Mar. 25, 1818	-	Transferred from D. Columbia.
John White	Private	96 00	95 86	do	Nov. 14, 1818	Mar. 21, 1818	93	
George Weightman	do	96 00	176 25	N. H. continental	Sep. 28, 1819	May 4, 1818	58	Dropped from the roll under act May 1, 1820.
Do	do	96 00	798 66	do	-	Nov. 10, 1825	-	Restored under act March 1, 1823.
Jenks Waits	do	96 00	564 68	R. I. continental	Sep. 27, 1819	Ap'l 7, 1815	79	
William Walcott	do	96 00	1,267 09	Maryland cont'l	May 12, 1820	Dec. 24, 1819	73	Died February 22, 1824.
Edward Whaley	do	96 00	1,526 66	Delaware cont'l	Ap'l 22, 1819	Ap'l 10, 1818	74	Transferred from N. Jersey.

Statement, &c. of Gallia county, Ohio.

NAMES.	Rank.	Annual allowance.	Sums received.	Description of service.	When placed on the pension roll.	Commencement of pension.	Ages.	Laws under which they were formerly inscribed on the pension roll; and remarks.
Henry Dike -	Private	96 00	1,207 06	Virginia cont'l	June 9, 1819	Feb. 8, 1819	75	Transferred from New York.
William Freehold -	do	96 00	625 06	do	Ap'l 23, 1823	Mar. 1, 1823	79	
John Graham -	do	96 00	695 72	Connecticut cont'l	May 1, 1819	June 6, 1818	75	Transferred from Pennsylvania.
Solomon Hayward -	do	96 00	1,989 86	Massachusetts cont'l	July 21, 1819	Ap'l 1, 1818	78	Transferred from Massachusetts. Died September 7, 1831.
Anthony Hailey -	do	96 00	1,516 38	Virginia cont'l	Ap'l 20, 1820	May 19, 1818	74	Transferred from Virginia.
Richard L. Jones	Fifer	96 00	315 46	Connecticut cont'l	Nov. 24, 1830	Nov. 23, 1830	67	
Elijah Knight -	Private	96 00	784 83	do	June 9, 1819	June 22, 1818	76	Died August 23, 1826.
Gains Niles -	do	96 00	1,306 39	N. Hampshire cont'l	do	June 26, 1818	87	
Daniel Polley -	do	96 00	1,171 19	Connecticut cont'l	do	June 23, 1818	74	
Thomas Prows -	do	96 00	972 38	N. Hampshire cont'l	Oct. 12, 1820	May 27, 1818	68	Died July 12, 1828.
Johnston Smith -	do	96 00	1,507 16	Virginia cont'l	June 9, 1819	June 23, 1818	69	
Oliver Scott -	do	96 00	1,522 12	Connecticut cont'l	Ap'l 22, 1819	Ap'l 27, 1818	70	Transferred from Pennsylvania.

Statement, &c. of Geauga county, Ohio.

NAMES.	Rank.	Annual allowance.	Sums received.	Description of service.	When placed on the pension roll.	Commencement of pension.	Ages.	Laws under which they were formerly inscribed on the pension roll; and remarks.
Stephen Ames	Private	96 00	170 32	N. H. continental	Jan. 20, 1820	May 27, 1818	70	Dropped under act of May 1, 1820.
Do	do	96 00	156 38	do	do	Mar. 17, 1824		Restored under act March 1, 1823. Died November 2, 1825.
James Blair	do	96 00	1,522 63	do	Oct. 26, 1818	Ap'l 25, 1818	71	Transferred from Pennsylvania.
William Branch	do	96 00	1,473 06	Connecticut cont'l	Oct. 8, 1819	May 1, 1818	73	Transferred from Pennsylvania.
Oliver Brown	do	96 00	1,448 02	do	Sep. 21, 1819	Aug. 5, 1818	78	
Philemon Church	do	96 00	1,517 67	do	Oct. 8, 1818	May 14, 1818	82	
Jonas Carter	do	96 00	1,526 66	Mass. continental	Ap'l 23, 1818	Ap'l 10, 1818	74	Transferred from Vermont
Caleb Fowler	do	96 00	175 22	Connecticut cont'l	March 5, 1819	May 8, 1818	65	Dropped from the roll under act May 1, 1820.
Parker Fellows	do	96 00	169 54	Mass. continental	July 27, 1819	May 30, 1818	57	Dropped from the roll under act May 1, 1820.
Joseph Fuller	Sergeant	96 00	153 03	do	Sep. 6, 1819	Aug. 1, 1818	62	Died May 2, 1827.
Nathan Ganson	Private	96 00	869 04	do	Oct. 28, 1818	Ap'l 14, 1818	71	
Libeus Herrick	do	96 00	315 89	Connecticut cont'l	Ap'l 29, 1819	May 21, 1818	84	
Benjamin Johnson	do	96 00	748 64	do	Ap'l 30, 1819	May 18, 1818	58	
Ebenezer Kentfield	do	96 00	1,477 06	Mass. continental	July 28, 1818	Ap'l 16, 1818	74	Transferred from Massachusetts.
Reuben Kidder	do	96 00	1,525 56	N. H. continental	Sep. 18, 1818	Ap'l 14, 1818	74	Transferred from New York.
Reuben Lake	do	96 00	1,519 19	Connecticut cont'l	June 19, 1822	May 9, 1818	68	
Frederick Loveland	do	96 00	1,516 15	Mass. continental	Ap'l 29, 1819	May 20, 1818	70	
John Moore 3d	do	96 00	1,514 66	N. Y. continental	May 30, 1820	May 26, 1818	80	Transferred from New York.
Jonathan Pratt	do	96 00	1,523 46	Mass. continental	Jan. 28, 1819	Ap'l 22, 1818	71	Transferred from Maine.
Oliver Robinson	do	96 00	159 22	do	July 27, 1819	July 8, 1818	68	Dropped from the roll under act May 1, 1820.
Do	do	96 00	253 41	do	-	July 15, 1827	68	Restored under act Mar. 1, 1823.
Samuel Moor Starr	do	96 00	1,495 73	Connecticut cont'l	Feb. 2, 1819	Aug. 6, 1818	61	Transferred from New York.
John Smith	do	96 00	170 32	Mass. continental	Ap'l 20, 1819	May 25, 1818	66	Dropped from the roll under act May 1, 1820.

NAMES.	Rank.	Annual allowance.	Sums received.	Description of service.	When placed on the pension roll.	Commencement of pension.	Ages.	Laws under which they were formerly inscribed on the pension roll; and remarks.
Isaac Thompson	Lieutenant	240 00	1,152 66	Pennsylvania cont'l	March 5, 1819	June 22, 1818	69	Died April 25, 1823.
Joseph Witter	Private	96 00	121 83	Mass. continental	June 12, 1819	Nov. 28, 1818	57	Dropped from the roll under act May 1, 1820.
Timothy Wells	Sergeant	96 00	158 19	Connecticut cont'l	Nov. 4, 1819	July 12, 1819	71	Dropped from the roll under act May 1, 1820.

Statement, &c. of Greene county, Ohio.

NAMES.	Rank.	Annual allowance.	Sums received.	Description of service.	When placed on the pension roll.	Commencement of pension.	Ages.	Laws under which they were formerly inscribed on the pension roll; and remarks.
Thomas Davis, 2d	Private	96 00	1,522 12	Virginia continental	Mar. 5, 1819	Ap'l 27, 1818	78	Transferred from Kentucky.

Statement, &c. of Guernsey county, Ohio.

NAMES.	Rank.	Annual allowance.	Sums received.	Description of service.	When placed on the pension roll.	Commencement of pension.	Ages.	Laws under which they were formerly inscribed on the pension roll; and remarks.
Morris Ader	Private	96 00	922 35	N. J. continental	July 9, 1819	Jan. 27, 1819	78	
Hollis Hutchins	do	96 00	402 83	Mass. continental	June 9, 1819	May 26, 1818	78	Died August 5, 1822.
William Lawrence	do	96 00	1,378 12	Maryland cont'l	July 30, 1821	Ap'l 27, 1818	76	Dead.
George Morgan	do	96 00	1,481 06	Penn. continental	June 15, 1819	Ap'l 1, 1818	65	
James M. Cann	do	96 00	1,439 76	do	June 1, 1822	Mar. 6, 1819	-	Transferred from Pennsylvania.
Mitchell L. K. Montgomery	do	96 00	1,507 99	do	July 15, 1819	June 20, 1818	81	
Hugh Porter	do	96 00	1,495 25	do	Sep. 6, 1819	Aug. 8, 1818	72	
Nathaniel Price	Gunner	96 00	1,257 83	N. York continental	Ap'l 28, 1819	July 29, 1818	76	
Amos Stackhouse	Private	96 00	174 96	N. J. continental	Feb. 11, 1819	May 9, 1818	76	Dropped from the roll under act May 1, 1820.
Do	do	96 00	573 70	do	- , 1819	Mar. 14, 1828	-	Restored under act March 1, 1823.
Peter Wynick	do	96 00	155 61	Penn. continental	Feb. 2, 1819	July 22, 1818	76	Dropped from the roll under act May 1, 1820.
John Watters	do	96 00	155 86	do	Feb. 11, 1819	July 21, 1818	56	Dropped from the roll under act May 1, 1820.
Christopher Waller	do	96 00	155 86	do	do	do	62	Dropped from the roll under act May 1, 1820.

Statement, &c, of Hamilton county, Ohio.

NAMES.	Rank.	Annual allowance.	Sums received.	Description of service.	When placed on the pension roll.	Commencement of pension.	Ages.	Laws under which they were formerly inscribed on the pension roll; and remarks.
John Burnham	Private	96 00	516 32	Massachusetts cont'l	Sep. 6, 1819	Ap'l 18, 1818	89	Transferred from Pennsylvania.
William Brown	do	96 00	1,228 75	New Jersey cont'l	Dec. 6, 1821	Feb. 25, 1819	94	Transferred from Indiania. Died December 14, 1831.
William Campbell	do	96 00	1,213 41	Pennsylvania cont'l	July 15, 1819	May 19, 1818	81	Died January 8, 1831.
Neviad Coleman	do	96 00	473 57	Virginia cont'l	Oct. 29, 1819	Sep. 29, 1818	88	Dropped from the roll under act May 1, 1820.
Philip Connor	do	96 00	-	do	Ap'l 5, 1820	June 12, 1818	68	
John Carle	do	96 00	957 72	New Jersey cont'l	Sep. 25, 1823	Ap'l 15, 1823	78	Died April 6, 1833.
Philip Coke, alias Cake	do	96 00	18 32	N. Carolina cont'l	Jan. 25, 1826	Dec. 27, 1825	79	
Christopher Cary	do	96 00	593 03	N. Hampshire cont'l	Sep. 15, 1830	Jan. 1, 1828	72	By the last returns this pensioner resides in Indiana, county not known.
Mosby Childers	do	96 00	1,506 06	Virginia cont'l	June 9, 1819	June 26, 1818	79	
Duncan Dunn	do	96 00	1,405 76	N. Hampshire cont'l	Ap'l 15, 1819	Aug. 6, 1819	83	Transferred from Kentucky.
Daniel Davis	do	96 00	1,520 28	New Jersey cont'l	Sep. 25, 1818	May 7, 1818	82	Transferred from Massachusetts.
Jesse Downs	do	96 00	847 44	Massachusetts cont'l	June 14, 1819	May 7, 1818	70	
Henry Dugan	do	96 00	1,320 44	Pennsylvania cont'l	Mar. 5, 1819	June 3, 1818	96	
Randall Douglass	do	96 00	867 06	S. Carolina cont'l	Ap'l 12, 1825	Feb. 22, 1825	71	Dropped from the roll under act May 1, 1820.
William Debzell	do	96 00	305 06	Pennsylvania cont'l	Aug. 12, 1831	Jan. 1, 1831	79	
Jonathan Emerson	do	96 00	172 38	N. Hampshire cont'l	Oct. 4, 1819	May 19, 1818	66	
Asa Foster	do	96 00	934 53	Connecticut cont'l	June 30, 1818	Ap'l 21, 1818	70	Died January 15, 1828.
Robert Faulkner	Ensign	240 00	3,695 99	Pennsylvania cont'l	June 24, 1819	Ap'l 11, 1818	78	Transferred from N. York.
Asa Gloyd	Private	96 00	1,421 67	Massachusetts cont'l	Jan. 25, 1819	May 14, 1818	77	
George Gwinup	Corporal	96 00	168 76	New Jersey cont'l	July 14, 1820	June 2, 1818	66	Dropped from the roll under act May 1, 1820.
William Gannon	Private	96 00	1,010 60	do	Jan. 20, 1824	Aug. 26, 1823	81	Dead.
James Gray, 2d	do	96 00	785 28	Pennsylvania cont'l	May 17, 1825	May 4, 1825	83	Died July 8, 1833.
William Grant	do	96 00	838 09	Virginia cont'l	June 23, 1819	May 15, 1818	76	Died February 6, 1827.
Edward Harvey	do	96 00	421 06	do	May 25, 1819	Ap'l 16, 1818	83	

Statement, &c. of Hamilton county—Continued.

NAMES.	Rank.	Annual allowance.	Sums received.	Description of service.	When placed on the pension roll.	Commencement of pension.	Ages.	Laws under which they were formerly inscribed on the pension roll; and remarks.
Richard S. Holden	Private	96 00	350 96	Massachusetts cont'l	June 17, 1820	May 5, 1818	59	Died Dec. 31, 1821.
James Hamer	do	96 00	1,474 12	New Jersey cont'l	Oct. 30, 1821	Ap'l 27, 1818	69	Transferred from New York.
John Hudson	do	96 00	970 35	New York cont'l	Feb. 9, 1824	Jan. 27, 1824	65	Transferred from N. York. Died July 14, 1823.
Matthew Jackson	do	96 00	506 27	Massachusetts cont'l	May 22, 1818	Ap'l 6, 1818	60	
George J. Isham	do	96 00	1,438 35	Connecticut cont'l	Oct. 2, 1819	Mar. 27, 1819	75	
Francis Kelsimere	do	96 00	135 48	Maryland cont'l	June 8, 1819	Oct. 7, 1818	90	Dropped from the roll under act May 1, 1820.
Do	do	96 00	317 41	do	-	Aug. 29, 1823	-	Restored under act March 1, 1823. Died Dec. 18, 1826.
Oliver Kelly	do	96 00	899 09	Connecticut cont'l	June 18, 1822	May 20, 1818	78	Died Sept. 30, 1827.
John Kitley	Musician	96 00	715 46	Massachusetts cont'l	Jan. 22, 1827	Sep. 22, 1826	71	
David Livingston	Private	96 00	1,208 02	Pennsylvania cont'l	Ap'l 10, 1819	June 27, 1818	97	Transferred from Indiana. Died Jan. 27, 1831.
Peter Lynch	do	96 00	1,041 03	do	Mar. 17, 1819	May 1, 1818	80	
John Lafler	Ensign	240 00	1,299 99	New York cont'l	June 5, 1819	May 31, 1818	73	Died Oct. 30, 1823.
Henry Loar	Private	96 00	167 16	Maryland cont'l	Dec. 1, 1819	June 8, 1818	62	Dropped from the roll under act May 1, 1820.
William Lemond	do	96 00	892 53	Pennsylvania cont'l	June 3, 1820	June 4, 1818	80	
Abraham Larew	do	96 00	502 70	Virginia cont'l	Jan. 17, 1829	Dec. 10, 1828	79	Died Sept. 20, 1827.
Alexander Lemmon	do	96 00	456 76	New York cont'l	July 19, 1821	June 2, 1818	85	
Daniel Moss	Private	96 00	1,472 80	Conn. continental	June 5, 1818	May 2, 1818	85	Transferred from New York. Re-linquished invalid pension for benefits of act March 18, 1818.
Robert McCollough	Sergeant	30 00	68 99	do	-	Feb. 14, 1814	-	April 18, 1814. Invalid.
Robert McCollough	do	30 00	120 79	Mass. continental	July 15, 1819	June 2, 1818	67	
Pelatiah Morgan	do	30 00	1,514 09	do	Sep. 29, 1819	May 28, 1818	72	Dropped from the roll under act May 1, 1820.
Jacob Morgan	do	30 00	1,390 39	do	Feb. 7, 1820	Sep. 11, 1819	75	

Name	Rank	Pay	Number	Organization			Age	Remarks
Moses Meddock, or Midagh	do	96 00	691 19	N. J. continental	Oct. 7, 1822	June 23, 1818	82	Transferred from Virgina.
Amasa Mitchell	do	96 00	1,056 28	Mass. continental	June 11, 1823	Mar. 4, 1823	82	Dropped from the roll under act May 1, 1820.
David Pierson	do	96 00	173 70	N. J. continental	Dec. 11, 1818	May 14, 1818	62	
Samuel Pierce	do	96 00	933 33	Conn. continental	Nov. 23, 1818	Sep. 23, 1818	69	Died June 12, 1828.
Osborn Parsons	do	96 00	757 03	do	June 13, 1818	Ap'l 16, 1818	72	Transferred from New York.
Abraham Pierson	do	96 00	982 70	Penn. continental	July 15, 1819	May 19, 1819	82	Died August 13, 1828.
Zephaniah Posey	do	96 00	804 87	Virginia cont'l	June 23, 1819	June 3, 1818	76	Died October 21, 1826.
John Robinson; 1st	do	96 00	1,462 92	do	Feb. 10, 1819	June 9, 1818	78	
John Robinson, 2d	do	96 00	101 76	Maryland cont'l	July 21, 1819	May 21, 1818	68	Died June 11, 1819.
Justus Reynolds	Musician	96 00	175 22	Conn. continental	June 12, 1819	May 8, 1818	74	Dropped from the roll under act May 1, 1820.
Do	do	96 00	980 93	do	-	Dec. 17, 1823	-	Restored under act March 1, 1823.
Jacob Richardson	Private	96 00	485 93	Penn. continental	July 19, 1821	July 29, 1818	67	Died August 20, 1823.
Henry Rogers	do	96 00	712 28	N. J. continental	Dec. 12, 1826	Oct. 4, 1826	82	
James Scates	Corporal	96 00	1,529 31	N. Y. continental	Aug. 18, 1818	Mar. 31, 1818	77	Transferred from Indiana.
Barnabas Strong	Private	96 00	285 15	Conn. continental	Jan. 25, 1819	May 18, 1818	61	Died May 6, 1821.
Nicholas Stephens	do	96 00	1,365 32	N. J. continental	June 23, 1819	June 15, 1818	73	
Patrick Sullivan	do	96 00	269 15	Penn. continental	do	May 14, 1818	81	Died March 30, 1821.
William Smith, 4th	do	96 00	17 54	Virginia continental	Feb. 7, 1820	Dec. 30, 1819	61	Dropped from the roll under act May 1, 1820.
Lemuel Snow	do	96 00	145 80	Mass. continental	June 15, 1820	Aug. 29, 1818	61	Dropped from the roll under act May 1, 1820.
Philip D. Smith	do	96 00	775 06	Maryland cont'l	May 26, 1826	Feb. 18, 1826	75	Transferred from Indiana.
Richard Sparr	do	96 00	1,518 22	Virginia cont'l	Mar. 20, 1819	May 12, 1818	76	Transferred from Pennsylvania.
Abraham Smith	do	96 00	549 31	N. J. continental	Ap'l 10, 1819	Ap'l 13, 1818	65	Transferred from N. Jersey. Died January 2, 1824.
Isaac Tibbetts	do	96 00	651 35	Mass. continental	June 15, 1820	May 23, 1818	75	
Michael Tull's	do	96 00	419 34	Virginia cont'l	Nov. 28, 1827	Oct. 21, 1827	78	Transferred from Indiana. Died March 2, 1832.
William Tucker	do	96 00	772 17	Penn. continental	Feb. 27, 1826	Feb. 11, 1826	77	Transferred from Kentucky.
John Williams	do	96 00	531 78	do	June 28, 1819	June 11, 1818	70	Died December 25, 1823.
Thomas Williams	do	96 00	733 91		Aug. 3, 1820	June 3, 1818	81	Died January 25, 1826.
Benjamin Williams	do	96 00	1,371 46	Maryland cont'l	June 12, 1820	Nov. 22, 1819	75	
Henry Willyard	do	96 00	580 12	Penn. continental	Dec. 12, 1826	Jan. 5, 1824	85	
Benjamin Wood	do	96 00	1,519 57	Conn. continental	Jan. 25, 1821	May 7, 1818	68	Died January 20, 1830.
William Worthington	do	96 00	167 72	Penn. continental	June 15, 1832	June 6, 1832	-	Transferred from New York.
Abraham Wellman	do	96 00	1,104 54	Mass. continental	Jan. 8, 1819	Ap'l 27, 1818	84	Died October 21, 1829.

9

Statement, &c. of Harrison county, Ohio.

NAMES.	Rank.	Annual allowance.	Sums received.	Description of service.	When placed on the pension roll.	Commencement of pension.	Ages.	Laws under which they were formerly inscribed on the pension roll; and remarks.
John Brannon	Private	96 00	462 44	Penn. continental	Ap'l 10, 1821	May 11, 1818	89	
Timothy Boyles	do	96 00	169 03	Delaware cont'l	Ap'l 19, 1820	June 1, 1818	96	Dropped from the roll under act May 1, 182
Thomas Haley	do	96 00	48 49	Maryland cont'l	Ap'l 11, 1820	Sep. 3. 1819	74	Dropped from the roll under act May 1, 1820.
Do	do	96 00	476 06	do		Mar. 17, 1827	-	Restored under act March 1, 1823.
Thomas Johns	do	96 00	519 22	Virginia cont'l	Nov. 6, 1819	Oct. 8, 1819	92	Transferred from Kentucky.
James Larkins	Sergeant	96 00	906 49	Penn. continental	June 9, 1819	Feb. 4, 1819	70	Died July 13, 1828.
Neal Peacock	Private	96 00	892 38	Maryland cont'l	June 8, 1819	May 1, 1818	74	Died August 17, 1827.
John Parker	do	96 00	1,048 80	Penn. continental	Nov. 9, 1822	Oct. 2, 1822	68	
Henry Rankin	do	96 00	1,035 44	Penn. continental	July 7, 1819	May 15, 1818	72	

Statement, &c. of Highland county, Ohio.

NAMES.	Rank.	Annual allowance.	Sums received.	Description of service.	When placed on the pension roll.	Commencement of pension.	Ages.	Laws under which they were formerly inscribed on the pension roll; and remarks.
Samuel Adkin	Private	96 00	727 06	Mass. continental	May 3, 1820	Feb. 8, 1819	103	
Azor Bagley	do	96 00	173 15	N. Y. continental	Mar. 20, 1819	May 16, 1818	77	Dropped from the roll under act May 1, 1820.
Do	do	96 00	345 83	do		July 29, 1830	-	Restored under act Mar 1, 1820.
Thomas Barnard	do	96 00	1,418 83	Virginia continental	Mar. 5, 1819	May 25, 1818	77	
Dempsey Capps	do	96 00	850 66	N. C. continental	June 10, 1825	Ap'l 2.5, 1825	74	
Jacob Fishback	do	96 00	675 86	Virginia continental	May 29, 1820	Mar. 16, 1819	77	
Andrew Pegan	Maine	96 00	706 12	Ship Montgomery	Feb. 1, 1819	Ap'l 27, 1818	77	Died March 30, 1826.
William Smith	Private	96 00	1,521 86	Virginia continental	Dec. 31, 1818	Ap'l 28, 1818	82	Transferred from Virginia.
Daniel Tyler	do	96 00	1,395 38	do	Oct. 18, 1819	Aug. 23, 1819	74	Transferred from Virginia.

Statement, &c. of Holmes county, Ohio.

NAMES.	Rank.	Annual allowance.	Sums received.	Description of service.	When placed on the pension roll.	Commencement of pension.	Ages.	Laws under which they were formerly inscribed on the pension roll; and remarks.
John Critchfield -	Private	96 00	1,390 63	Virginia continental	Dec. 28, 1820	Mar. 10, 1819	65	
John Davis, 2d -	do	96 00	596 44	Pennsylvania cont'l	Ap'l 20, 1824	Mar. 22, 1824	64	Died June 7, 1830.
Henry Dutcher -	do	96 00	788 12	N. Y. continental	July 25, 1825	May 17 1824	83	Transferred from N. York. Died August 1, 1832.
John Gwin -	do	96 00	1,508 79	Virginia continental	Jan. 11, 1821	June 17, 1818	62	
Isaac Munson -	do	96 00	1,094 70	Connecticut cont'l	Mar. 5, 1819	Oct. 10, 1818	72	
Jonathan Wheaton -	do	96 00	997 59	do	May 13, 1820	Ap'l 14, 1818	79	

Statement, &c. of Huron county, Ohio.

NAMES.	Rank.	Annual allowance.	Sums received.	Description of service.	When placed on the pension roll.	Commencement of pension.	Ages.	Laws under which they were formerly inscribed on the pension roll; and remarks.
James Brooks	Private	96 00	1,418 57	Washington's life guard	June 30, 1818	Mar. 21, 1818	75	Transferred from Connecticut,—Died December 30, 1832.
Jonah Barton	do	96 00	914 05	N. Y. continental	Nov. 20, 1819	May 26, 1818	66	Died December 2, 1827.
Amaziah Barber	do	96 00	1,025 29	Conn. continental	May 23, 1820	June 30, 1818	96	
Henry Cherry	do	96 00	180 26	N. J. continental	June 7, 1819	Ap'l 20, 1818	62	Died March 4, 1820.
David Carswell	do	96 00	497 03	N. Y. continental	Dec. 13, 1830	Jan. 1, 1888	70	
Daniel Carpenter	do	96 00	1,525 86	Conn. continental	Feb. 10, 1820	Ap'l 13, 1818	79	Transferred from N. York.
Michael Chapman	do	96 00	516 26	do	July 5, 1828	Ap'l 19, 1828	76	
John or Jonathan Church	do	96 00	1,495 22	Penn. continental	Oct. 18, 1819	Aug. 8, 1818	-	Transferred from N. York.
John Knapp	Fifer	96 00	1,385 86	Virginia cont'l	Nov. 4, 1819	Sep. 28, 1819	56	
John M'Millan	Private	96 00	1,526 63	N. J. continental	Sep. 18, 1818	Ap'l 10, 1818	73	Transferred from N. York.
Hieronimus Mingus	do	96 00	1,017 03	N. Y. continental	Sep. 6, 1823	Aug. 1, 1823	72	
Elijah Pollock	do	96 00	609 11	Conn. continental	Aug. 9, 1819	Ap'l 21, 1818	67	Died August 25, 1824.
Paul Pigsley	do	96 00	1,509 86	Mass. continental	Sep. 6, 1819	June 13, 1818	66	
Isaac Sampson	do	96 00	1,512 79	N. Y. continental	do	June 2, 1818	66	
Phinehas Stevens	do	96 00	1,519 22	Mass. continental	June 2, 1820	May 8, 1818	80	Transferred from N. York.
Benajah Wolcott	do	96 00	1,330 09	Conn. continental	Oct. 1, 1819	Ap'l 27, 1818	64	Died August 11, 1832.
Kenelm Winslow	do	96 00	1,422 63	Mass. continental	Sep. 10, 1819	June 10, 1819	-	Transferred from Vermont.

Statement, &c. of Jackson county, Ohio.

NAMES.	Rank.	Annual allowance.	Sums received.	Description of service.	When placed on the pension roll.	Commencement of pension.	Ages.	Laws under which they were formerly inscribed on the pension roll; and remarks.
George Anthony	Trumpeter	96 00	505 38	Penn. continental	May 22, 1828	May 12, 1828	71	Died August 16, 1833.
Thomas Craig, sen.	Private	96 00	1,313 29	Maryland cont'l	May 15, 1819	June 30, 1818	81	
William Clark	do	96 00	723 09	Virginia continental	Oct. 1, 1819	Aug. 24, 1819	76	
John Canter	do	96 00	726 47	do	Aug. 24, 1826	Aug. 10, 1826	80	
William Darby	Drummer	96 00	1,424 77	Penn. continental	Sept. 7, 1819	May 2, 1819	76	
Samuel Dailey	Private	96 00	200 02	Mass. continental	Sep. 22, 1819	Aug. 5, 1819	75	
James Dawson	do	96 00	1,334 99	Virginia continental	Nov 27, 1819	Oct. 9, 1819	75	
John Exline	do	96 00	803 06	do	Nov. 19, 1825	Oct. 24, 1825	75	
Henry Hughs	do	96 00	1,505 06	do	Ap'l 16, 1819	July 1, 1818	82	
John Hanna	do	96 00	835 46	do	July 6, 1825	June 22, 1826	77	
George Wealey	do	96 00	-	do	Oct. 8, 1821	June 27, 1821	90	Died January 27, 1821.

Statement, &c. of Jefferson county, Ohio.

Names.	Rank.	Annual allowance.	Sums received.	Description of service.	When placed on the pension roll.	Commencement of pension.	Ages.	Laws under which they were formerly inscribed on the pension roll; and remarks.
John Andrew	Private	96 00	562 86	Penn. continental	Nov. 27, 1819	Oct. 25, 1819	76	Transferred from Virginia.
Charles Brooks	do	96 00	1,344 80	Virginia cont'l	do	Sept. 2, 1819	74	
John Clancey	do	96 00	1,479 72	Maryland cont'l	April 7, 1819	April 6, 1818	72	Died Feb. 23, 1822.
John Davis	do	96 00	145 11	Penn. continental	July 20, 1822	Aug. 21, 1820	74	
George Evans	do	96 00	470 12	do	July 18, 1829	May 20, 1829	77	Died Feb. 3, 1822.
William Elkins	do	96 00	355 43	Maryland cont'l	May 17, 1819	May 22, 1818	89	Died May 9, 1826
John Evans	do	96 00	588 38	Penn. cont'l	Oct. 26, 1820	Mar. 24, 1820	77	Died March 31, 1823.
Jonas Grove	do	96 00	464 25	Virginia cont'l	July 21, 1819	May 1, 1818	78	
Bernard, or Barnardus Gordon	do	96 00	33 02	do		Aug. 21, 1820	63	Died Dec. 24, 1820.
Richard Jackson	Sergeant	96 00	1,290 66	N. J. cont'l	Oct. 13, 1820	Sept. 25, 1820	89	
John McElroy	Fife major	96 00	1,523 16	do	Nov. 16, 1820	Ap'l 23, 1818	66	
Thomas Minor	Private	96 00	912 26	Penn. cont'l	Oct. 29, 1818	Sep. 4, 1824	73	
John Potts	do	96 00	177 83	Virginia cont'l	Sep. 16, 1824	Ap'l 28, 1818	-	Dropped from the roll under act May 1, 1820.
Jonathan Potts	do	96 00	1,265 83	do	Jan. 8, 1819	do	76	Died July 4, 1831.
John Palmer	do	96 00	123 16	do	Mar. 17, 1819	Nov. 23, 1818	-	Dropped from the roll under act May 1, 1820.
William Roach	do	96 00	1,489 06	Penn. continental	Sep. 27, 1819	Sept. 1, 1818	76	
William Robins	do	96 00	1,359 25	N.-Jersey cont'l	May 1, 1819	Jan. 8, 1820	66	
Christian Shouse	do	96 00	1,292 69	Penn. cont'l	May 31, 1820	June 25, 1818	81	
Alexander Simrall	Lieutenant	240 00	999 99	do	July 15, 1819	Jan. 5, 1820	88	Died Dec. 12, 1831.

Statement, &c. of Knox county, Ohio.

NAMES.	Rank.	Annual allowance.	Sums received.	Description of service.	When placed on the pension roll.	Commencement of pensions.	Ages.	Laws under which they were formerly inscribed on the pension roll; and remarks.
Zerah Curtis	Private	96 00	-	Connecticut cont'l	Apl 19, 1819	June 11, 1818	72	
Do	do	96 00	-	do			69	
Lemuel Chapman	do	96 00	828 12	Mass. continental	July 6, 1819	July 20, 1818	81	
Levi Chadwick	do	96 00	957 67	N. J. continental	Sep. 23, 1824	Mar. 14, 1824	79	
Jonathan Davis, 2d	do	96 00	1,194 09	do	Sep. 21, 1819	Mar. 28, 1819	74	
Thomas Elwell	Matross	96 00	667 27	Pennsylvania cont'l	July 2, 1818	June 9, 1818	57	Died May 21, 1825.
Evan Holt	Private	96 00	154 83	do	Apl 30, 1819	July 25, 1818		Dropped from the roll under act May 1, 1820.
Andrew Kennedy	do	96 00	-	do	do	do	62	Dropped from the roll under act May 1, 1820.
George Kunsman	do	96 00	948 46	do	Mar. 22, 1825	Ap'l 22, 1824	77	
Thomas Laster	do	96 00	739 96	do	Ap'l 30, 1819	June 20, 1818	74	
Minard Lafever	do	96 00	255 51	N. J. continental	Jan. 25, 1831	Jan. 7, 1831	79	
Walter McFarland	do	96 00	816 90	Pennsylvania cont'l	Ap'l 30, 1819	Aug. 17, 1818	78	
John Mott	Lieut.	240 00	3,158 66	N. H. continental	Jan. 11, 1821	April 3, 1818	87	Died May 31, 1831.
Nathaniel Price, 2d	Private	96 00	929 02	Maryland cont'l	May 15, 1819	July 25, 1818	77	Died March 1, 1828.

Statement, &c. of Lawrence county, Ohio.

NAMES.	Rank.	Annual allowance.	Sums received.	Description of service.	When placed on the pension roll.	Commencement of pension.	Ages.	Laws under which they were formerly inscribed on the pension roll; and remarks.
Henry Anderson	Private	96 00	200 80	Virginia continental	Oct. 1, 1819	Aug. 2, 1819	85	
Robert Adams	do	96 00	1,496 51	do	do	Aug. 3, 1819	77	
Michael Bowen	do	96 00	165 03	Penn. continental	Feb. 3, 1819	June 16, 1818	79	Dropped under act May 1, 1820. Restored under act March 1, 1823.
Do	do	96 00	718 58	-		May 22, 1823	-	Died November 15, 1830.
Micajah Ballard	do	96 00	144 30	Virginia continental	Sep. 29, 1820	Dec. 6, 1819	84	Died June 6, 1821.

Statement, &c. of Licking county, Ohio.

NAMES.	Rank.	Annual allowance.	Sums received.	Description of service.	When placed on the pension roll.	Commencement of pension.	Ages.	Laws under which they were formerly inscribed on the pension roll; and remarks.
Squire Burnet	Private	96 00	1,203 06	N. J. continental	May 21, 1819	Aug. 19, 1818	81	Died February 27, 1831.
Samuel Ball	do	96 00	1,527 43	do	May 11, 1818	Apl 7, 1818	80	Transferred from N. Jersey.
Benjamin Critchard	do	96 00	357 16	N. Hamp. cont'l	May 21, 1819	Apl 30, 1818	70	Died January 19, 1822.
Samuel Carson	do	96 00	177 83	Penn. continental	do	Apl 28, 1818	-	Dropped from the roll under act May 1, 1820.
Patrick Cunningham	do	96 00	178 09	do	Sep. 23, 1819	Apl 27, 1818	81	Dropped from the roll under act May 1, 1820.
Do	do	96 00	282 85	do	-	Feb. 26, 1819	-	Restored under act March 1, 1823.
Mahlon Combs	do	96 00	889 03	Virginia cont'l	Jan. 3, 1824	Dec. 1, 1823	75	Died February 7, 1832.
James Devan or Devaun	do	96 00	968 02	Maryland cont'l	May 28, 1819	May 5, 1818	78	Died June 4, 1828.

Name	Rank	Allowance	Amount	Regiment	Date	Date	Age	Remarks
Gideon Daggett	do	96 00	1,527 43	Mass. continental	Mar. 8, 1819	Ap'l 8, 1818	74	Transferred from Vermont to Ohio, from Ohio to N. York, and from N. York to Ohio.
George Hill	do	96 00	416 02	Virginia cont'l	May 21, 1819	May 5, 1818	79	
Jacob Humphreys	do	96 00	1,310 44	do	do	May 9, 1818	85	Died January 2, 1832.
Simon Hill	do	96 00	207 76	do	Oct. 1, 1819	July 6, 1819	71	
Nathan Hartwell	do	96 00	370 09	Mass. continental	May 25, 1821	Ap'l 27, 1818	71	Dropped from the roll under act May 1, 1820.
Joseph Jackson	do	96 00	130 92	Penn. continental	May 21, 1819	Ap'l 24, 1818	-	
John Laws	do	96 00	1,485 32	Virginia cont'l	Feb. 19, 1818	Sep. 15, 1818	76	Transferred from Virginia.
John Larabee	do	96 00	1,521 56	Mass. continental	Sep. 15, 1819	Ap'l 29, 1818	83	
Samuel Lacey	do	96 00	-	N. J. continental	May 4, 1818	Ap'l 11, 1818	81	Transferred from N. Jersey.
John M'Quown	do	96 00	948 49	Virginia cont'l	May 21, 1819	Ap'l 18, 1818	84	
Joel Philbrook	Mariner	96 00	178 09	Ship Boston	June 6, 1820	Ap'l 27, 1818	-	Dropped from the roll under act May 1, 1820.
Phineas Pratt	Artificer	96 00	782 13	Mass. continental	do	Ap'l 17, 1818	72	Died June 9, 1826.
John Ridlin	Private	96 00	1,521 86	do	Feb. 11, 1819	Ap'l 28, 1818	72	
James Ranstead	do	96 00	1,514 83	Virginia cont'l	Ap'l 15, 1819	May 25, 1818	72	Transferred from Indiana.
Maximillian Robinson	do	96 00	1,244 82	Delaware cont'l	July 21, 1818	May 5, 1818	84	Died Ap'l 22, 1831.
William Smith, 3d	do	96 00	601 88	Virginia cont'l	July 7, 1819	Ap'l 29, 1818	71	Died July 13, 1825.
Lewis Stump	do	96 00	1,521 06	Virginia cont'l	Dec. 30, 1819	May 1, 1818	77	Dropped from the roll under act May 1, 1820.
Meshec Walker	do	96 00	170 57	N. J. continental	Sep. 17, 1819	May 26, 1818	69	
Thomas White	do	96 00	1,520 02	Virginia cont'l	Sep. 23, 1819	May 5, 1818	80	
Israel Wells	do	96 00	20 90	Conn. continental	May 30, 1820	Dec. 17, 1819	61	Dropped from the roll under act May 1, 1820.
Obadiah Wilson	do	96 00	799 76	Penn. continental	Jan. 19, 1822	May 6, 1818	76	
Eliel Wales	do	96 00	279 25	Conn. continental	Oct. 21, 1819	Ap'l 27, 1818	61	Died March 24, 1821.

10

Statement, &c. of Logan county, Ohio.

NAMES.	Rank.	Annual allowance.	Sums received.	Description of service.	When placed on the pension roll.	Commencement of pension.	Ages.	Laws under which they were formerly inscribed on the pension roll; and remarks.
Zachariah Griffey	Private	96 00	251 09	Virginia continental	Aug. 5, 1829	July 24, 1829	84	Placed on by act May 28, 1830.
Simon Kenton	General	240 00	1,242 58	do	June 5, 1830	Jan. 1, 1829	79	
Felix McIlhany	Private	96 00	1,435 72	Penn. continental	June 2, 1819	Sep. 21, 1818	78	Transferred from Kentucky.
John Tellis, sen.	do	96 00	30 92	Virginia continental	Feb. 8, 1820	Nov. 9, 1819	70	Dropped from the roll under act May 1, 1820.
Daniel Workman	do	96 00	474 66	do	do	Sep. 25, 1818	94	

Statement, &c. of Lorain county, Ohio.

NAMES.	Rank.	Annual allowance.	Sums received.	Description of service.	When placed on the pension roll.	Commencement of pension.	Ages.	Laws under which they were formerly inscribed on the pension roll; and remarks.
Thaddeus Gilbert	Private	96 00	9 28	Conn. continental	Ap'l 28, 1820	Jan. 31, 1820	89	Dropped from the roll under act May 1, 1820.
Do	do	96 00	468 79	do		Ap'l 17, 1829		Restored under act March 1, 1823.
Pliney Kellogg	do	96 00	1,478 66	Mass. continental	May 22, 1819	Ap'l 10, 1818	83	Transferred from New York.
Joseph Moore	do	96 00	1,527 69	do	Sep. 6, 1819	Ap'l 6, 1818	70	Transferred from New York.
Charles Rounes	do	96 00	1,522 12	do	Oct. 5, 1818	Ap'l 27, 1818	72	do do

Statement, &c. of Madison county, Ohio.

NAMES.	Rank.	Annual allowance.	Sums received.	Description of service.	When placed on the pension roll.	Commencement of pension.	Ages.	Laws under which they were formerly inscribed on the pension roll; and remarks.
Samuel Baskerville	Lieutenant	240 00	1,880 64	Virginia continental	Ap'l 19, 1819	May 4, 1818	80	Relinquished for the benefit of act May 15, 1828.
Samuel Bebee	Fifer	96 00	1,453 44	Mass. continental	June 6, 1820	July 15, 1818	69	Dropped from the roll under act May 1, 1820.
Andrew Cyprus	Private	96 00	183 69	Virginia continental	May 3, 1819	April 6, 1818	75	
Joel Coleman	do	96 00	1,310 44	do	Jan. 8, 1821	July 11, 1820	85	
Jedediah Geer	do	96 00	514 34	Conn. continental	Sep. 27, 1819	Oct. 27, 1818	76	
Stephen Jackson	do	96 00	-	N. H. continental	Mar. 1, 1826	Feb. 4, 1826	79	
Elias Laugham	Lieutenant	240 00	2,363 24	Virginia continental	Sep. 28, 1818	Ap'l 30, 1818	69	Relinquished for the benefit of act May 15, 1828.
Thomas McIntire	Private	96 00	1,513 83	Penn. continental	Oct. 4, 1819	May 29, 1818	84	
Tobias Shields	do	96 00	1,135 73	do	Sep. 29, 1819	May 6, 1818	84	
Isaac Tucker	do	96 00	511 30	Mass. continental	Ap'l 30, 1819	Ap'l 22, 1818	91	Died August 19, 1823.
Joel Wilcox	do	96 00	308 26	Conn. continental	June 25, 1819	July 1, 1818	58	Died Sep. 16, 1821.

Statement, &c. of Marion county, Ohio.

NAMES.	Rank.	Annual allowance.	Sums received.	Description of service.	When placed on the pension roll.	Commencement of pension.	Ages.	Laws under which they were formerly inscribed on the pension roll; and remarks.
David Potts	Private	96 00	1,523 46	Virginia continental	June 10, 1819	Ap'l 22, 1818	77	
James Swinnerton	do	96 00	172 15	Mass. continental	Jan. 28, 1819	May 20, 1818	64	Dropped from the roll under act May 1, 1820.

Statement, &c. of Medina county, Ohio.

NAMES.	Rank.	Annual allowance.	Sums received.	Description of service.	When placed on the pension roll.	Commencement of pension.	Ages.	Laws under which they were formerly inscribed on the pension roll; and remarks.
Solomon Goff	Private	96 00	1,526 66	Connecticut cont'l	July 14, 1819	Ap'l 10, 1818	70	Transferred from Pennsylvania.
Elisha Hinsdale	do	96 00	173 15	do	July 21, 1819	May 16, 1818	68	Dropped from the roll under act May 1, 1820.
Do	do	96 00	245 60	do	-	Dec. 2, 1824	-	Restored under act March 1, 1823. Died June 22, 1827.
Esbon Jennings	do	96 00	1,519 99	do	May 3, 1819	May 5, 1813	80	Transferred from New York.
Daniel Keyes	Sergeant	96 00	933 03	Mass. continental	May 21, 1819	June 16, 1818	74	Dead.
Robert McClung	Private	96 00	-	N. H. continental	May 31, 1820	May 14, 1818	79	
Philip Phillips	do	96 00	1,479 46	Connecticut cont'l	May 19, 1818	April 7, 1818	71	Transferred from Connecticut.
Samuel Phillips	do	96 00	1,474 66	do	Nov. 12, 1818	Ap'l 25, 1816	74	Transferred from Connecticut.
Stiles Parker	do	96 00	1,509 06	Mass. continental	June 7, 1820	June 16, 1818	69	Transferred from Kentucky.
Timothy Smith, 1st	do	96 00	176 77	do	Mar. 25, 1819	May 2, 1818	77	Dropped from the roll under act May 1, 1820.
Do	do	96 00	589 70	-	-	Jan. 14, 1828	-	Restored under act March 1, 1823. Transferred from New York.

Statement, &c. of Meigs county, Ohio.

NAMES.	Rank.	Annual allowance.	Sums received.	Description of service.	When placed on the pension roll.	Commencement of pension.	Ages.	Laws under which they were formerly inscribed on the pension roll; and remarks.
Luther Danielson -	Private	96 00	245 96	Mass. continental	Oct. 8, 1831	Aug. 13, 1831	77	
John Entsminger ·	do	96 00	48 02	Virginia continental	Mar. 5, 1830	Mar. 5, 1830	80	
James Graham ·	do	96 00	621 59	Pennsylvania cont'l	Sep. 27, 1819	Sep. 14, 1827	78	
Frederick Hisel ·	do	96 00	1,507 46	Virginia continental	June 9, 1820	June 22, 1818	77	
Daniel Harper ·	do	96 00	1,507 99	N. H. continental	June 2, 1820	June 20, 1818	69	
Robert Knowlton ·	do	96 00	1,270 39	Mass. continental	Mar. 24, 1819	June 11, 1818	86	Died May 11, 1826.
Andrew Kimball ·	do	96 00	756 96	N. H. continental	Sep. 22, 1819	June 23, 1818	83	
Roger McBride ·	do	96 00	547 16	Delaware cont'l	Ap'l 29, 1820	do	81	Died July 20, 1828.
Joseph Silvester ·	do	96 00	967 29	Mass. continental	June 9, 1819	do	73	Dropped from the roll under act May 1, 1820.
Josiah Simpson ·	do	96 00	163 16	N. H. continental	Sep. 14, 1819	do	68	Restored under act March 1, 1823.
Do	do	96 00	789 44	do	July 21, 1819	Dec. 15, 1825	-	Transferred from Virginia.
James Whaley -	do	96 00	1,522 63	Virginia continental	July 21, 1819	Ap'l 23, 1818	79	

Statement, &c. of Mercer county, Ohio.

NAMES.	Rank.	Annual allowance.	Sums received.	Description of service.	When placed on the pension roll.	Commencement of pension.	Ages.	Laws under which they were formerly inscribed on the pension roll; and remarks.
Amos Spencer -	Private	96 00	1,028 76	Virginia continental	Dec. 10, 1823	June 17, 1823	75	

Statement, &c. of Miami county, Ohio.

NAMES.	Rank.	Annual allowance.	Sums received.	Description of service.	When placed on the pension roll.	Commencement of pension.	Ages.	Laws under which they were formerly inscribed on the pension roll ; and remarks.
William C. Baily	Corporal	96 00	1,274 49	Virginia cont'l	Jan. 9, 1821	Nov. 27, 1820	80	
John Bottenhouse	Private	96 00	100 15	do	Dec 22, 1824	Aug. 20, 1824	73	
Joseph Conner	do	96 00	180 15	do	Dec. 19, 1827	Oct. 20, 1827	80	
John Gerrard	do	96 00	888 25	do	Ap'l 19, 1821	Dec. 4, 1819	78	
John W. Meredith	do	96 00	610 63	Delaware cont'l	Jan. 3, 1828	Oct. 26, 1827	74	
Benjamin Pegg	do	96 00	1,511 16	Pennsylvania cont'l	June 7, 1819	June 8, 1818	82	
Harmon Parsons	do	96 00	774 45	New Jersey cont'l	Dec. 1, 1819	Oct. 6, 1819	77	Died October 30, 1827.

Statement, &c. of Morgan county, Ohio.

NAMES,	Rank.	Annual allowance.	Sums received.	Description of service.	When placed on the pension roll.	Commencement of pension.	Ages.	Laws under which they were formerly inscribed on the pension roll; and remarks.
Asher Allen	Private	96 00	1,518 47	Conn. continental	Oct. 13, 1818	May 11, 1818	78	
Augustine Andersen	Lieutenant	240 00	3,692 66	N. J. continental	Ap'l 29, 1818	Ap'l 16, 1818	84	
Benjamin Dean	Private	96 00	1,520 02	Virginia cont'l	June 24, 1818	May 5, 1818	72	
Andrew Dennis	do	96 00	1,520 28	Penn. continental	Sep. 30, 1818	May 4, 1818	75	
William Harper	do	96 00	691 46	do	July 13, 1825	June 22, 1825	77	
John Mahana	do	96 00	838 63	Mass. continental	Jan. 1, 1825	June 10, 1824	66	
William M'Murray	do	96 00	1,521 86	Penn. continental	Nov. 9, 1819	Ap'l 28, 1818	81	
Hananiah Newton	do	96 00	744 76	Mass. continental	May 26, 1819	June 2, 1818	72	
Asher Russell	do	96 00	1,524 79	Conn. continental	July 10, 1818	Ap'l 17, 1818	80	Transferred from Connecticut.
Peter Shacklee	do	96 00	1,523 19	Pnne. continentai	Oct. 7, 1822	Ap'l 23, 1818	79	
John Springum	do	96 00	1,522 12	Virginia cont'l	Feb. 1, 1819	Ap'l 27, 1818	83	
Matthew Wilson	Sergeant	96 00	1,408 80	Penn. continental	Dec. 21, 1819	Jan. 2, 1819	72	

Statement, &c. of Monroe county, Ohio.

NAMES.	Rank.	Annual allowance.	Sums received.	Description of service.	When placed on the pension roll.	Commencement of pension.	Ages.	Laws under which they were formerly inscribed on the pension roll; and remarks.
Adam Crum	Private	96 00	1,228 58	Maryland cont'l	July 21, 1819	May 12, 1818	81	Died February 26,*1831.
John Derrough	do	96 00	237 31	Virginia continental	June 14, 1819	June 12, 1818	81	Died December 1, 1820.
Abner Goodrich	do	96 00	649 06	Conn. continental	Feb. 1, 1819	Feb. 1, 1819	90	Transferred from Virginia. Died November 4, 1825.
John Hicks	do	96 00	1,459 99	Virginia continental	June 25, 1819	June 20, 1818	80	
Arthur Hazzard	do	96 00	164 83	Delaware cont'l	June 20, 1820	June 13, 1818	59	Dropped from the roll under act May 1, 1820.
Elijah Hixon	do	96 00	806 12	Virginia continental	Feb. 5, 1825	Ap'l 12, 1824	66	
William McClain	do	96 00	1,504 54	Penn. continental	Sep. 6, 1819	July 3, 1818	80	Died June 27, 1822.
Benjamin Pearsall	do	96 00	369 78	do	do	Aug. 22, 1818	60	Transferred from Pennsylvania.
John Pratt	do	96 00	1,057 06	Virginia continental	Mar. 18, 1823	Mar. 1, 1823	75	Dropped from the roll under act May 1, 1820.
Lemuel Rucker	do	96 00	15 48	do	May 31, 1820	Jan. 7, 1820	80	
Do	do	96 00	303 25	do	-	Jan. 8, 1831	-	Restored, under act March 1, 1823.
Henry Smith	do	96 00	159 48	Mass. continental	Ap'l 22, 1819	July 7, 1818	66	Dropped from the roll under act May 1, 1820.
Richard Talbot	Lieutenant	240 00	413 24	Maryland cont'l	Ap'l 3, 1820	June 15, 1818	68	Dropped from the roll under act May 1, 1820.

Statement, &c. of Montgomery county, Ohio.

NAMES.	Rank.	Annual allowance.	Sums received.	Description of service.	When placed on the pension roll.	Commencement of pension.	Ages.	Laws under which they were formerly inscribed on the pension roll; and remarks.
John Bowers ·	Drummer	96 00	1,525 03	N. J. continental	June 13, 1818	Ap'l 16, 1818	74	
Anthony Chevalier ·	Private	96 00	1,249 83	Virginia cont'l	May 1, 1819	Aug. 29, 1818	79	
John Cunias ·	do	96 00	384 79	Penn. continental	Sep. 22, 1823	Sep. 2, 1823	69	Transferred from Pennsylvania.
William Manlove ·	do	96 00	-	Delaware cont'l	June 12, 1819	Aug. 22, 1818	72	
Daniel Pierson ·	Ser. major	96 00	1,060 67	N. J. continental	Ap'l 30, 1819	Aug. 18, 1818	82	
John Christopher Rudolph, or Christopher Rudolph ·	Lieutenant	240 00	50 22	do	Jan. 31, 1820	Dec. 20, 1819	70	Dropped from the roll under act May 1, 1820.
Peter Roaff ·	Private	96 00	489 31	N. Y. continental	Oct. 12, 1820	July 31, 1820	76	
Jacob Stump ·	do	96 00	1,210 86	Maryland cont'l	Nov. 4, 1822	July 25, 1821	73	
Conrad Witters ·	do	96 00	1,185 06	Virginia cont'l	Sep. 23, 1819	May 1, 1818	86	
	do	96 00	1,492 93	Penn. continental	June 2, 1820	Aug. 17, 1818	74	

Statement, &c. of Muskingum county, Ohio.

NAMES.	Rank.	Annual allowance.	Sums received.	Description of service.	When placed on the pension roll.	Commencement of pension.	Ages.	Laws under which they were formerly inscribed on the pension roll ; and remarks.
John Alford ·	Private	96 00	1,521 03	Pennsylvania cont'l	Sep. 10, 1819	May 1, 1818	83	
John Brown ·	do	96 00	1,504 25	Virginia cont'l	Ap'l 17, 1819	July 4, 1818	88	
William Bell ·	do	96 00	225 06	do	Sep. 10, 1819	May 1, 1818	102	
William Blunt ·	do	96 00	177 03	do	Sep. 15, 1819	do	64	
Samuel Baldwin ·	do	96 00	381 96	Mass. cont'l	May 25, 1820	Mar. 13, 1819	87	Dropped from the roll under act May 1, 1820.

Name	Rank			Line			Age	Remarks
Ralph Boon	do	96 00	1,160 17	Pennsylvania cont'l	Sep. 19, 1822	Feb. 4, 1822	-	Transferred from Pennsylvania.
John Campbell	do	96 00	1,521 06	Virginia cont'l	May 1, 1819	May 1, 1818	72	Died December 30, 1819.
John Clark, 1st	do	96 00	166 94	Pennsylvania cont'l	Oct. 31, 1818	Ap'l 4, 1818	62	
William Davis, 3d	do	96 00	920 54	do	Aug. 30, 1824	Aug. 3, 1824	82	Died February 28, 1821.
Robert Fleming	do	96 00	273 86	do	Ap'l 15, 1819	Ap'l 24, 1818	78	
John Green, 2d	do	96 00	1,521 06	Virginia cont'l	Sep. 10, 1819	May 1, 1818	91	
Isaiah Grovier	do	96 00	1,064 61	Mass. cont'l	Sep. 16, 1819	May 11, 1818	78	Trans'd from Pennsylvania. Died June 12, 1829.
John G. Holcomb	do	96 00	1,476 79	Connecticut cont'l	May 14, 1818	Ap'l 17, 1818	84	Tran-ferred from Connecticut.
Conrad Harman	do	96 00	395 46	Pennsylvania cont'l	Mar. 17, 1819	Ap'l 27, 1818	75	Died June 9, 1822.
Elijah Holcomb	do	96 00	368 25	do	Sep. 10, 1819	May 4, 1818	84	
Thomas Hawbeard	do	96 00	176 25	do	do	do	-	Dropped from the roll under act May 1, 1820.
Silas Johnson	do	96 00	1,269 06	Virginia cont'l	Ap'l 14, 1819	June 16, 1818	73	Dropped from the roll under act May 1, 1820.
John Kelley	do	96 00	1,508 79	do	Ap'l 17, 1819	June 17, 1818	78	Transf'd from Virginia. Died April 28, 1828.
Abraham Lyon	do	96 00	176 28	New Jersey cont'l	Sep. 10, 1819	May 4, 1818	71	
William Morris	do	96 00	965 06	Pennsylvania cont'l	Dec. 9, 1818	Ap'l 10, 1818	73	Died February 9, 1826.
Amos Mix	Musician	96 00	1,521 86	Connecticut cont'l	Ap'l 29, 1819	Ap'l 28, 1818	76	
William Mayberry	Private	96 00	731 63	Pennsylvania cont'l	June 9, 1819	June 27, 1818	69	
Richard Marshall	do	96 00	1,521 06	Virginia cont'l	Sep. 10, 1819	May 1, 1818	77	
Richard McHenry	do	96 00	687 20	Pennsylvania cont'l	do	do	89	Died June 27, 1825.
Robert McHenry	do	96 00	650 12	Virginia cont'l	Oct. 8, 1822	Nov. 27, 1820	83	Transferred from Virginia.
William Mayberry, sen.	do	96 00	1,391 69	Pennsylvania cont'l	Oct. 20, 1824	Sep. 6, 1819	96	
Alexander Moody	Surgeon	240 00	1,477 06	do	May 14, 1818	May 1, 1818		
William Pelham	Private	96 00	449 24	Virginia cont'l	Sep. 10, 1819	Ap'l 21, 1818	81	
John Remay	do	96 00	1,521 06	do	Feb. 16, 1819	May 1, 1818	80	Dropped from the roll under act May 1, 1820.
John Spicer	do	96 00	1,472 79	New Jersey cont'l	July 6, 1819	Nov. 2, 1818	69	Dropped from the roll under act May 1, 1820.
Jacob Shaffer	do	96 00	162 66	do		June 25, 1818		
James Sprague	do	96 00	170 83	Connecticut cont'l	Sep. 10, 1819	May 25, 1818	74	Dropped from the roll under act May 1, 1820.
Do	do	96 00	919 51	do		Aug. 7, 1824	-	Dropped from the roll under act May 1, 1820.
Thomas Simpson	Corporal	96 00	31 96	Maryland cont'l	Dec. 1, 1819	Nov. 5, 1819	65	Restored under act March 1, 1823.
Lewis Williams	Private	96 00	1,520 28	Pennsylvania cont'l	Sep. 10, 1819	May 4, 1818	92	Restored under act May 1, 1820.
Samuel Walker	do	96 00	1,400 80	New York cont'l	Sep. 22, 1819	Aug. 2, 1819	74	Dropped from the roll under act May 1, 1820.

Statement, &c. of Orange county, Ohio.

NAMES.	Rank.	Annual allowance.	Sums received.	Description of service.	When placed on the pension roll.	Commencement of pension.	Ages.	Laws under which they were formerly inscribed on the pension roll; and remarks.
John Brassbridge -	Private	96 00	-	N. Hampshire cont.	April 19, 1819	April 9, 1818	71	Transferred from New York.

Statement, &c. of Perry county, Ohio.

NAMES.	Rank.	Annual allowance.	Sums received.	Description of service.	When placed on the pension roll.	Commencement of pension.	Ages.	Laws under which they were formerly inscribed on the pension roll; and remarks.
John Faulkner -	do	96 00	1,510 36	Penn. continental	Sept. 6, 1819	June 11, 1818	79	Died July 14, 1823.
John Kennard -	do	96 00	501 21	N. J. continental	June 24, 1819	April 25, 1818	70	Died February 11, 1824.
Isaac Kent -	do	96 00	555 14	Md. continental	Nov. 26, 1819	May 1, 1818	68	Died February 16, 1825.
Samuel Lewis -	Corporal	96 00	634 76	Penn. continental	Feb. 1, 1819	July 8, 1818	78	Dropped from the roll under act May 1, 1820.
Peter Magee -	Lieutenant	240 00	447 24	N. Y. continental	Sept. 22, 1818	April 24, 1818	-	Dropped from the roll under act May 1, 1820.
James Rusk -	Private	96 00	164 36	Penn. continental	Jan. 25, 1819	June 11, 1818	73	Dropped from the roll under act May 1, 1820.
Do -	do	96 00	1,045 32	do		April 15, 1823	-	Restored under act March 1, 1823.
John Wimmer -	do	96 00	946 89	do	May 29, 1820	April 24, 1818	81	
Israel Wimmer, or Wiswell -	do	96 00	281 53	Mass. continental	June 1, 1820	Oct. 25, 1819	79	Died September 29, 1822.

Statement, &c. of Pickaway county, Ohio.

NAMES.	Rank.	Annual allowance.	Sums received.	Description of service.	When placed on the pension roll.	Commencement of pension.	Ages.	Laws under which they were formerly inscribed on the pension roll; and remarks.
Zachariah Burwell	Private	96 00	164 51	N. Y. continental	June 27, 1823	June 13, 1823	72	Died February 27, 1825.
William Champ	do	96 00	1,357 70	Virginia contin'l	Jan. 27, 1821	July 14, 1819	82	
Conrad Cline	do	96 00	474 57	Penn. continental	May 15, 1829	Mar. 26, 1829	77	
Joseph Clark	do	96 00	611 09	do	Mar. 19, 1828	Oct. 24, 1827	74	
John Clark, 2d	do	96 00	398 16	Virginia contin'l	June 21, 1819	June 4, 1818	75	Died July 27, 1822.
Hugh Huston	do	96 00	513 98	Penn. continental	Sept. 30, 1818	Ap'l 10, 1818	73	Died August 17, 1823.
Samuel Holam	do	96 00	1,134 22	do	Nov. 13, 1819	May 12, 1819	74	
Benjamin Hunter	do	96 00	-	do	Oct. 6, 1821	Ap'l 23, 1818	82	
Jacob Peter	do	96 00	989 18	Mass. continental	Feb. 3, 1819	May 16, 1818	84	
John Simpson	do	96 00	634 32	Virginia contin'l	April 28, 1819	July 27, 1818	82	
Harlehigh Sage	do	96 00	935 66	Conn. continental	Sept. 30, 1818	Ap'l 10, 1818	64	Died January 8, 1828.
William Subbuth, or Suddoth	do	96 00	1,134 19	Virginia contin'l	Feb. 3, 1819	May 12, 1818	81	Transferred from Virginia.
William Sandy	do	96 00	988 76	Virginia contin'l	March 6, 1819	Nov. 17, 1818	74	Dropped from the roll under act May 1, 1820.
Thomas Stothard	do	96 00	173 93	do	Sept. 15, 1819	May 18, 1818	62	Dropped from the roll under act May 1, 1820.
James Williams	do	96 00	173 41	Md. continental	Feb. 9, 1819	May 15, 1818	68	Restored under act Mar. 1, 1823.
Do	do	96 00	152 53	-	-	Ap'l 8, 1823	-	Died November 9, 1824.

Statement, &c. of Pike county, Ohio.

NAMES.	Rank.	Annual allowance.	Sums received.	Description of service.	When placed on the pension roll.	Commencement of pension.	Ages.	Laws under which they were formerly inscribed on the pension roll; and remarks.
Hugh Blackwell, alias Black	Private	96 00	1,503 51	Maryland contin'l	June 10, 1820	July 7, 1818	96	
Charles Barker	do	96 00	485 03	Virginia contin'l	Oct. 24, 1823	Mar. 1, 1823	84	
John Guthery	do	96 00	-	Pennsylvania cont'l	July 23, 1823	do	90	
John Halladay	do	96 00	105 60	N. C. continental	July 7, 1819	Feb. 27, 1819	65	Dropped from the roll under act May 1, 1820.
Thomas Sewall	do	96 00	1,381 93	Virginia contin'l	Dec. 1, 1819	Oct. 23, 1819	82	
Philip Wolfenbarger	do	96 00	1,447 06	do	Apl 29, 1820	Feb. 8, 1819	72	
John Walcott	do	96 00	1,384 80	Pennsylvania cont'l	Sept. 29, 1819	Oct. 2, 1818	75	Transferred from Kentucky.

Statement, &c. of Preble county, Ohio.

NAMES	Rank.	Annual allowance.	Sums received.	Description of service.	When placed on the pension roll.	Commencement of pension.	Ages.	Laws under which they were formerly inscribed on the pension roll; and remarks.
Thomas Beall	Private	96 00	-	Maryladd cont'l	Sep. 22, 1819	June 28, 1818	59	
Enos Campbell	do	96 00	1,417 06	N. J. continental	July 10, 1819	June 1, 1817	75	
Robert Craigs	do	96 00	1,509 86	Penn. continental	July 21, 1819	June 13, 1818	77	
Abijah Rowley	do	96 00	1,057 03	Mass. continental	Ap'l 24, 1823	Mar. 1, 1823	75	Transferred from New York.

Statement, &c. of Portage county, Ohio.

NAMES.	Rank.	Annual allowance.	Sums received.	Description of service.	When placed on the pension roll.	Commencement of pension.	Ages.	Laws under which they were formerly inscribed on the pension roll; and remarks.
Moses Adams	Private	96 00	1,507 46	Connecticut cont'l	Sept. 6, 1819	June 22, 1818	79	Dropped from the roll under act May 1, 1820.
Ebenezer Bostwick	do	96 00	176 25	do	Nov. 13, 1818	May 4, 1818	66	
Elijah Blackman	Captain	240 00	975 67	do	Sept. 26, 1818	Ap'l 22, 1818	82	Died May 15, 1822.
Stephen Butler	Private	96 00	181 29	do	Mar. 5, 1819	Ap'l 15, 1818	62	Dropped from the roll under act May 1, 1820.
Nathaniel Bettis	Ensign	240 00	179 43	Mass. continental	Sept. 24, 1818	Ap'l 22, 1818	86	Dropped from the roll under act May 1, 1820.
Do	do	240 00	893 70	do	-	May 14, 1824	.	Restored under act Mar. 1, 1823.
Elijah Burroughs	Private	96 00	11 61	N. H. continental	May 31, 1820	Jan. 22, 1820	61	Dropped from the roll under act May 1, 1820.
Stephen Baldwin	do	96 00	164 52	Mass. continental	Sept. 6, 1819	June 18, 1818	60	Dropped from the roll under act May 1, 1820.
Nehemiah Bacon	do	96 00	1,359 76	Connecticut cont'l	Sept. 24, 1819	July 6, 1818	97	Dropped from the roll under act May 1, 1820.
Benjamin Bixby	do	96 00	992 80	do	Sept. 27, 1819	May 2, 1818	75	
Gideon Crittenden	do	96 00	175 12	do	July 16, 1819	May 20, 1818	81	
Do	do	96 00	18 83	do	-	May 21, 1827	.	Restored under act Mar. 1, 1823. Died July 31, 1827.
Christopher Cackler	do	96 00	1,184 80	Pennsylvania cont.	Nov. 10, 1819	May 2, 1818	78	Transferred from N. Hampshire.
Clement Clark	do	96 00	1,392 49	N. H. continental	Ap'l 28, 1820	Sept. 3, 1819	82	Dropped from the roll under act May 1, 1820.
David Crocker	do	96 00	1,527 16	Connecticut cont'l	June 30, 1819	Ap'l 8, 1818	74	
Jacob Ettinger	do	96 00	161 03	Pennsylvania cont.	Dec. 4, 1819	July 1, 1818	76	
Do	do	96 00	828 89	do	-	May 15, 1823	.	Restored under act March 1, 1823. Died January 2, 1832.
Reuben Heart	do	96 00	577 29	Connecticut cont'l	June 22, 1819	May 2, 1818	61	Died May 6, 1824.
William Hobart	do	96 00	298 42	N. Hampshire cont.	Sept. 6, 1819	June 19, 1818	78	Died July 28, 1821.
Sylvanus Hulet	do	96 00	69 56	Mass. continental	June 15, 1820	June 14, 1819	63	Dropped from the roll under act May 1, 1820.

Statement, &c. of Portage county—Continued.

NAMES.	Rank.	Annual allowance.	Sums received.	Description of service.	When placed on the pension roll.	Commencement of pension.	Ages.	Laws under which they were formerly inscribed on the pension roll; and remarks.
Nathaniel Hardy	Private	96 00	321 93	Connecticut cont'l	July 6, 1820	Ap'l 16, 1818	62	Died August 23, 1821.
John Harrington	do	96 00	1,522 66	Mass. continental	Sept. 20, 1819	Ap'l 25, 1818	69	Transferred from New York.
Reuben Judd	do	96 00	1,517 18	do	Ap'l 30, 1819	May 16, 1818	73	Transferred from Massachusetts.
Jonathan Gaylord	Sergeant	96 00	456 83	Connecticut cont'l	Nov. 13, 1818	Ap'l 23, 1818	75	Died January 26, 1823.
John H. Goodrich	Private	96 00	160 25	do	July 21, 1819	July 4, 1818	59	Dropped from the roll under act May 1, 1820.
Nathaniel Gillet	Fife maj'r	96 00	1,520 80	do	Ap'l 29, 1819	May 2, 1818	76	Dropped from the roll under act May 1, 1820.
Ebenezer Goss	Private	96 00	158 44	Pennsylvania cont.	Nov. 4, 1819	July 11, 1818	70	
Do	do	96 00	815 01	do	-	Feb. 18, 1824	-	Restored under act March 1, 1823. Died August 15, 1832.
Thomas Granger	Private	96 00	1,515 64	Mass. continental	Feb. 2, 1819	May 21, 1818	70	Transferred from New York.
Benjamin Garrison	do	96 00	1,514 60	N-J. continental	Sep. 18, 1819	May 26, 1818	74	Transferred from Virginia.
John Gaylord	do	96 00	1,521 86	Mass. continental	Ap'l 28, 1818	Ap'l 28, 1818	73	Transferred from Massachusetts.
Gurdon Geer	do	96 00	1,057 60	Conn. continental	June 22, 1819	June 22, 1818	71	Died June 27, 1829.
Isaac Loveland	do	96 00	1,316 46	do	Mar. 17, 1819	June 18, 1818	72	Transferred from New York.
Samuel Mott, 1st	do	96 00	1,527 16	N. York continental	Jan. 19, 1819	Ap'l 8, 1818	-	do
Cato Meeds	do	96 00	1,436 49	Conn. continental	Mar. 5, 1819	Sep. 18, 1818	73	
Ezekiel Mott	do	96 00	644 46	N. York continental	Dec. 4, 1819	Ap'l 22, 1818	97	Died January 8, 1825.
Samuel McCloud	do	96 00	1,524 79	Mass. continental	Ap'l 28, 1820	Ap'l 17, 1818	74	Transferred from New York.
Abner Mather	do	96 00	1,524 79	Conn. continental	Dec. 2, 1818	do	82	do
James Moore	do	96 00	1,526 66	Mass. continental	Jan. 27, 1819	Ap'l 10, 1818	79	Transferred from Albany, N. Y.
Benjamin Prichard	do	96 00	162 09	Conn. continental	May 21, 1819	June 27, 1818	76	Dropped from the roll under act May 1, 1820.
David Preston	do	96 00	176 80	do	Nov. 30, 1819	May 2, 1818	62	Dropped from the roll under act May 1, 1820.
Jonathan Pike	do	96 00	1,416 26	do	Ap'l 28, 1821	June 4, 1818	84	
Thomas Richards	do	96 00	-	N. H. continental	Ap'l 25, 1826	Ap'l 20, 1826	81	Transferred from Albany.
John Seley	do	96 00	172 12	Mass. continental	May 21, 1819	May 20, 1818	63	Dropped from the roll under act May 1, 1820.

NAMES.	Rank	Annual allowance.	Sums received	Description of service.	When placed on the pension roll.	Commencement of pension.	Ages.	Remarks.
Aaron Smith, 2d	do	96 00	1,526 92	do	Sep. 9, 1819	Ap'l 9, 1818	74	Transferred from New York.
John Spencer	do	96 00	1,255 76	Conn. continental	Sep. 6, 1819	Aug. 6, 1819	76	Transferred from Connecticut.
John Leward	do	96 00	164 48	Mass. continental	Nov. 30, 1819	June 18, 1818	62	Dropped from the roll under act May 1, 1820.
Ebenezer Trowbridge	do	96 00	1,518 99	Conn. continental	Mar. 21, 1819	May 9, 1818	76	
John Tuttle	do	96 00	110 99	Mass. continental	Mar. 24, 1819	July 9, 1818	57	
Daniel Tilden	Lieutenant	240 00	3,540 07	Conn. continental	Mar. 5, 1819	Dec. 5, 1818	-	Transferred from Albany Agency.
William White	Private	96 00	1,476 79	do	June 30, 1819	Ap'l 17, 1818	74	
Joseph Wallace	do	96 00	1,041 29	R. I. continental	Nov. 30, 1819	Ap'l 30, 1818	79	
Hosea Wilcox	do	96 00	1,424 77	Conn. continental	Dec. 4, 1819	May 2, 1818	80	

Statement, &c. of Richland county, Ohio.

NAMES.	Rank	Annual allowance.	Sums received	Description of service.	When placed on the pension roll.	Commencement of pension.	Ages.	Laws under which they were formerly inscribed on the pension roll; and remarks.
James Baggs	Private	96 00	683 81	Pennsylvania cont'l	May 24, 1820	Nov. 29, 1819	74	Died February 1, 1827.
William Batchelder	do	96 00	694 39	N. H. continental	March 5, 1819	June 18, 1818	70	Transferred from Maine.
Stephen Crofford	do	96 00	653 12	Mass. continental	May 24, 1819	Nov. 12, 1818	65	
Jeremiah Conine	do	96 00	621 52	Virginia continental	Dec. 13, 1825	Nov. 19, 1825	70	Died May 9, 1832.
Massy Fleehart	do	96 00	1,510 89	Pennsylvania cont'l	Nov. 27, 1819	June 9, 1818	62	
Seth Holmes	do	96 00	704 80	Mass. continental	June 12, 1819	May 2, 1818	79	Transferred from Pennsylvania.
Moses Hadley	do	96 00	969 60	N. J. continental	Ap'l 20, 1819	do	83	Died June 7, 1828.
Jacob Heffier	do	96 00	1,446 48	Weltner Ger. reg't	July 29, 1819	Feb. 10, 1819	77	
John Jacobs	do	96 00	780 63	Pennsylvania cont'l	Jan. 27, 1819	May 20, 1818	71	Died July 6, 1826.
Joseph Jones, Jur.	do	96 00	1,509 86	Mass. continental	July 8, 1819	June 13, 1818	79	
George King	do	96 00	519 51	Virginia continental	Dec. 1, 1828	Oct. 7, 1828	73	
William C. Lee	do	96 00	349 18	Maryland cont'l	June 22, 1819	Jan 16, 1819	79	
William McKelvey	do	96 00	1,510 39	Pennsylvania cont'l	Sep. 6, 1819	June 11, 1818	74	
Daniel Prosser	do	96 00	611 08	Virginia continental	Oct. 23, 1825	Mar. 31, 1823	82	Died August 11, 1829.

Statement, &c. of Ross county, Ohio.

NAMES.	Rank.	Annual allowance.	Sums received.	Description of service.	When placed on the pension roll.	Commencement of pension.	Ages.	Laws under which they were formerly inscribed on the pension roll; and remarks.
John Briley	Private	96 00	-	Maryland cont'l	Sep. 20, 1819	June 27, 1818	74	
John Bodine	Sergeant	96 00	270 39	Washington's lf. gd.	June 9, 1820	Nov. 9, 1819	78	Died September 2, 1822.
John Blue	Private	96 00	169 80	N. York continental	Mar. 5, 1819	May 29, 1818	92	Dropped from the roll under act May 1, 1820.
Redman Coldon	do	96 00	1,124 99	Pennsylvania cont'l	Oct. 21, 1818	Ap'l 20, 1818	81	Died January 8, 1830.
Thomas Cliffton	do	96 00	1,267 87	Housegger's G. rgt.	Oct. 1, 1819	July 17, 1819	87	Died September 30, 1832.
John Clark, 4th	do	96 00	896 41	N. Carolina cont'l	Jan. 4, 1825	Oct. 19, 1824	81	
Stephen Cisna	do	96 00	453 20	Pennsylvania cont'l	Sep. 24, 1819	Nov. 23, 1818	68	Died August 15, 1823.
John Durham	do	96 00	1,516 67	N. Carolina cont'l	Mar. 24, 1819	May 18, 1818	79	
William Glover	do	96 00	780 41	Delaware cont'l	July 7, 1819	July 19, 1818	84	
Cornelius Hurley	do	96 00	1,177 83	Virginia cont'l	Feb. 2, 1819	May 29, 1818	78	
Richard Hardin	do	96 00	983 22	Pennsylvania cont'l	Ap'l 15, 1819	July 13, 1819	67	Died October 15, 1828.
James Hulse	do	96 00	909 86	Virginia cont'l	Nov. 9, 1819	Sep. 13, 1819	78	
Francis Jamison	do	96 00	475 22	Pennsylvania cont'l	Sep. 9, 1819	Ap'l 15, 1818	67	Transferred from Pennsylvania.
Thomas Miller	Ensign	96 00	770 31	Virginia cont'l	May 13, 1819	May 2, 1818	62	Died March 27, 1823.
Alexander McBride	Private	96 00	1,360 74	Pennsylvania cont'l	July 21, 1819	Feb. 2, 1819	80	Died July 17, 1821.
Robert Martin	do	96 00	1,516 67	Maryland cont'l	Mar. 22, 1819	May 18, 1818	79	Transferred from Pennsylvania.
John McMahon	do	95 00	1,521 86	Pennsylvania cont'l	Oct. 21, 1818	May 18, 1818	94	
William Nice	do	96 00	321 59	do	do	Ap'l 28, 1818	85	
John Newland	do	96 00	1,496 28	Virginia cont'l	Ap'l 28, 1819	Ap'l 29, 1818	96	
John Poe	do	96 00	1,486 12	do	June 23, 1819	Aug. 4, 1818	76	
Peter Prough	do	96 00	789 06	Pennsylvania cont'l	July 7, 1823	Sep. 12, 1818	77	
Adam Rider	do	96 00	729 09	Virginia cont'l	Ap'l 15, 1819	June 16, 1823	79	
Philip Raymer	do	96 00	1,458 60	Pennsylvania cont'l	May 21, 1819	July 20, 1818	76	Died February 21, 1826.
Paul Streve	do	96 00	1,028 95	do	Oct. 24, 1818	Dec. 26, 1818	74	Died January 12, 1829.
Nicholas Siprill	do	96 00	174 99	do	June 30, 1818	Ap'l 24, 1818	61	Dropped from the roll under act May 1, 1820.
Edward Sherlock	do	96 00	184 04	do	Oct. 22, 1823	Mar. 13, 1823	68	Died February 11, 1825.
Thomas Somersett	do	96 00	849 59	do	May 4, 1825	Ap'l 29, 1825	80	Dead.

Names	Rank.	Annual allowance.	Sums received.	Description of service.	When placed on the pension roll.	Commencement of pension.	Ages.	Remarks
Robert Timmons	do	96 00	1,366 92	Delaware cont'l	Sep. 6, 1819	June 9, 1818	78	Dropped from the roll under act May 1, 1820.
James Terney	do	96 00	157 93	Pennsylvania cont'l	Sep. 22, 1819	July 13, 1818	64	
Abraham Thompson	do	96 00	1,221 83	New Jersey cont'l	Sep. 20, 1819	June 13, 1819	80	
Nathan Ward	do	96 00	1,123 99	Massachusetts con.	Oct. 25, 1822	June 20, 1822	78	

12

Statement, &c. of Sandusky county, Ohio.

NAMES.	Rank.	Annual allowance.	Sums received.	Description of service.	When placed on the pension roll.	Commencement of pension.	Ages.	Laws under which they were formerly inscribed on the pension roll; and remarks.
Christian Crow	Private	96 00	1,516 12	Penn. continental	Dec. 1, 1819	May 20, 1818	72	

Statement, &c. of Scioto county, Ohio.

NAMES.	Rank.	Annual allowance.	Sums received.	Description of service.	When placed on the pension roll.	Commencement of pension.	Ages.	Laws under which they were formerly inscribed on the pension roll; and remarks.
Benjamin Burt	Private	96 00	872 17	Mass. continental	Ap'l 9, 1825	Feb. 4, 1825	73	
Christopher Crumb	do	96 00	896 00	N. Y. continental	July 10, 1819	Ap'l 30, 1819	66	Died August 30, 1828.
Southey Capes	Sergeant	96 00	1,451 12	Virginia cont'l	May 11, 1818	July 24, 1818	73	
William Connor	Ensign	240 00	1,738 71	do	Dec. 6, 1820	Dec. 6, 1820	77	
William Harbert	Private	96 00	1,581 22	do	Feb. 13, 1819	Sep. 30, 1818	84	Transferred from Kentucky.
George Hutton	do	96 00	1,493 96	Penn. continental	July 23, 1819	Aug. 13, 1818	80	
Josiah Haskinson	Ser. major	96 00	1,506 12	Maryland cont'l	Nov. 17, 1819	June 27, 1818	79	
Jacob Moore	Ensign	240 00	328 66	Virginia cont'l	July 14, 1823	Ap'l 22, 1823	84	
Samuel Salter	Private	96 00	1,057 03	do	May 7, 1823	Mar. 1, 1823	81	Transferred from Pennsylvania.
James Thompson	do	96 00	699 92	Penn. continental	Oct. 20, 1818	Ap'l 25, 1818	68	Died August 9, 1825.
Amos Wheeler	do	96 00	156 90	Mass. continental	May 1, 1819	July 17, 1818	58	Dropped from the roll under act May 1, 1820.
Henry Williamson	do	96 00	1,309 41	N. J. continental	Sep. 29, 1819	July 15, 1818	81	Transferred from N. Hampshire.
Nathan Wheeler	Ensign	240 00	939 99	Mass. continental	do	Aug. 16, 1819	72	Died July 15, 1823.
Isaac Wheeler	Private	96 00	1,366 39	N. Y. continental	July 22, 1819	June 11, 1819	71	Transferred from Pennsylvania.

Statement, &c. of Shelby county, Ohio.

NAMES.	Rank.	Annual allowance.	Sums received.	Description of service.	When placed on the pension roll.	Commencement of pension.	Ages.	Laws under which they were formerly inscribed on the pension roll; and remarks.
Elij. Pixley or Picksley	Musician	96 00	512 02	Connecticut cont'l	June 10, 1818	May 5, 1818	71	

Statement, &c. of Starke county, Ohio.

NAMES.	Rank.	Annual allowance.	Sums received.	Description of service.	When placed on the pension roll.	Commencement of pension.	Ages.	Laws under which they were formerly inscribed on the pension roll; and remarks.
John Albert	Private	96 00	901 86	Penns. cont'l	Mar. 22, 1819	Ap'l 13, 1818	77	Dropped from the roll under act May 1, 1820.
Jacob Bower	do	96 00	181 83	do	do	do	80	Restored under act March 1, 1823.
Do	do	–	133 32	do	–	Ap'l 15, 1824	–	
William Copis	do	96 00	1,522 09	Virginia cont'l	June 18, 1819	Ap'l 27, 1818	92	Transferred from Pennsylvania.
John Elliot	Lieut.	240 00	1,931 61	Penns. cont'l	Sep. 24, 1818	Aug. 21, 1818	81	Died August 29, 1826.
Peter France	Private	96 00	537 03	Maryland cont'l	Aug. 20, 1828	Aug. 1, 1828	83	
Martin Kephart	do	96 00	1,351 89	do	July 7, 1819	June 10, 1818	74	Died July 5, 1832.
Hugh McClelland	do	96 00	709 86	Penns. cont'l	Mar. 22, 1819	Ap'l 18, 1818	72	Died September 9, 1835.
Stephen Masters	do	96 00	1,499 64	N. Jersey cont'l	July 3, 1819	July 22, 1818	81	
James McGuinnes	do	96 00	977 32	Penns. cont'l	Sep. 27, 1819	June 30, 1818	87	
John Maxwell	do	96 00	664 50	Maryland cont'l	May 31, 1820	Jan. 15, 1820	80	Died December 16, 1826.
Thomas Simonton	do	96 00	1,103 57	Penns. cont'l	May 21, 1819	Dec. 14, 1818	75	Died June 11, 1830.
William Simmons	do	96 00	1,522 12	Maryland cont'l	July 9, 1819	Ap'l 27, 1818	61	Transferred from Maryland.
Casper Stoner	do	96 00	27 43	Penns. cont'l	Apr. 28, 1820	Nov. 22, 1819		Dropped from the roll under act May 1, 1820.
Andrew Shaffer	do	96 00	–	do	do	do	63	Dropped from the roll under act May 1, 1820.
Ebenezer White	do	96 00	559 48	Mass. cont'l	May 8, 1819	May 7, 1818	77	Transferred from Massachusetts.

Statement, &c. of Trumbull county, Ohio.

NAMES.	Rank.	Annual allowance.	Sums received.	Description of service.	When placed on the pension roll.	Commencement of pension.	Ages.	Laws under which they were formerly inscribed on the pension roll; and remarks.
Elihu Allen	Private	96 00	1,510 12	Mass. continental	Sept. 7, 1819	June 12, 1818	72	
John Brown	do	96 00	1,476 52	Conn. continental	Aug. 6, 1818	Ap'l 18, 1818	73	Transferred from New York.
Jedediah Burrell	do	96 00	1,053 59	N. Jersey contin'l	July 12, 1819	June 11, 1818	78	Died June 1, 1829.
Elihu Beach	do	96 00	1,253 02	Conn. continental	Aug. 2, 1821	Oct. 6, 1819	69	Died August 9, 1832.
Asa Bellamy	do	96 00	1,478 19	do	May 11, 1819	Oct. 12, 1818	82	
Joseph Badger	do	96 00	164 76	Mass. continental	Dec. 2, 1819	June 17, 1818	77	Dropped from the roll under act May 1, 1820.
Do	do	96 00	956 90	do	-	Mar. 17, 1824	-	Restored under act Mar. 1, 1823.
David Crosby	Corporal	96 00	1,507 46	Conn. continental	May 11, 1819	June 2, 1818	78	Died February 1, 1831.
John Cotton	Lieutenant	240 00	3,024 04	Mass. continental	June 10, 1819	June 26, 1818	85	
Elias Daily	Private	96 00	165 83	Penn. continental	Ap'l 1, 1819	June 13, 1818	71	Dropped from the roll under act May 1, 1820.
Asa Doty	do	96 00	1,464 80	Mass. continental	Ap'l 17, 1820	Dec. 2, 1818	68	
Solomon Durkee	do	96 00	1,475 72	Conn. continental	Dec. 2, 1822	Ap'l 21, 1818	63	
William Davidson	do	96 00	1,270 44	Penn. continental	Mar. 27, 1819	May 5, 1818	71	Transferred from Pennsylvania. Died July 29, 1831.
Friend Dickinson	do	96 00	58 12	Conn. continental	Jan. 31, 1832	Jan. 28, 1832	78	
John Delong	do	96 00	1,518 67	Penn. continental	Ap'l 28, 1819	May 9, 1818	89	
Luther Frisbie	do	96 00	162 89	Congress reg't.	Sept. 17, 1819	June 24, 1818	60	Dropped from the roll under act May 1, 1820.
Simon Fobes	do	96 00	593 03	—	Aug. 4, 1830	Jan. 1, 1828	78	
Eleazer Gilson	do	96 00	182 92	Conn. continental	Nov. 17, 1818	Ap'l 9, 1818	-	Dropped from the roll under act May 1, 1820.
John Gerrills	do	96 00	1,527 72	Mass. continental	Ap'l 1, 1819	Ap'l 6, 1818	66	Transferred from New York.
David Hickock	do	96 00	155 86	Conn. continental	July 12, 1819	July 21, 1818	63	Dropped from the roll under.act May 1, 1820.
Henry Hoston	do	96 00	1,527 72	do	May 20, 1818	Ap'l 6, 1818	68	Transferred from New York.
Jared Kimball	do	96 00	166 89	do	Dec. 14, 1819	June 9, 1818	67	Dropped from the roll under act May 1, 1820.

Names	Rank	Annual allowance	Amount received	Line	Commenced	Nov. 12, 1823	Age	Remarks
Do	do	96 00	781 89	do	—	Nov. 12, 1823	—	Restored under act Mar. 1, 1823.
Henry Lingo	do	96 00	1,427 16	Penn. continental	June 15, 1819	Ap'l 23, 1819	71	Died January 3, 1832.
Samuel Linscutt	do	96 00	1,349 18	Mass. continental	Sept. 29, 1818	Aug. 16, 1818	71	Dropped from the roll under act May 1, 1820.
Jonathan Mansfield	do	96 00	163 16	Mass. continental	July 12, 1819	June 23, 1818	82	
Do	do	96 00	954 83	do	—	Mar. 25, 1823	—	Restored under act Mar. 1, 1823.
Abner McMahan	do	96 00	1,037 96	New Jersey cont'l	Sept. 6, 1819	May 13, 1818	82	Died July 21, 1824.
Neil McMullen	do	96 00	600 61	Penn. continental	Sep. 17, 1819	Ap'l 20, 1818	71	Dropped from the roll under act May 1, 1820.
William Matthews	do	96 00	162 89	do	June 1, 1820	June 24, 1818	83	Restored under act Mar. 1, 1823.
John Morley	do	96 00	599 22	do	—	Dec. 8, 1827	.	Died January 27, 1825.
John Meloney	Musician	96 00	354 66	Conn. continental	July 31, 1823	June 25, 1823	76	Dropped from the roll under act May 1, 1820.
John Newell	Private	96 00	182 96	N. York contin'l	Mar. 18, 1823	Mar. 1, 1823	54	Transferred from Pennsylvania.
Abijah Perry	do	96 00	1,527 19	Penn. continental	Oct. 20, 1818	Ap'l 8, 1818	79	Dropped from the roll under act May 1, 1820.
Joel Pease	do	96 00	137 59	Conn. continental	July 26, 1819	Sept. 29, 1818	66	
Timothy Swan	do	96 00	1,506 89	do	do	June 24, 1818	74	Relinquished for benefit of act May 15, 1828.
William Smith, 2d	do	96 00	215 22	Penn. continental	Ap'l 19, 1821	Dec. 8, 1820	76	Dropped from the roll under act May 1, 1820.
James Tucker	do	96 00	1,235 96	Mass. continental	Dec. 23, 1820	Ap'l 20, 1818	76	
Do	do	96 00	178 63	Virginia contin'l	Ap'l 20, 1819	Ap'l 25, 1818	65	Restored under act Mar. 1, 1823.
William Taylor	Dragoon	96 00	—	do	—	June 27, 1823	—	Dropped from the roll under act May 1, 1820.
Do	do	96 00	177 83	Penn. continental	June 30, 1818	Ap'l 28, 1818	84	Restored under act Mar. 1, 1823.
William Wilson	Private	96 00	1,026 63	do	—	June 25, 1823	—	Dropped from the roll under act May 1, 1820.
Do	do	96 00	169 03	do	Dec. 4, 1819	June 1, 1818	68	

Statement, &c. of Tuscarawas county, Ohio.

NAMES.	Rank.	Annual allowance.	Sums received.	Description of service.	When placed on the pension roll.	Commencement of pension.	Ages.	Laws under which they were formerly inscribed, on the pension roll; and remarks.
John Barr	Private	96 00	180 76	Penn. continental	Feb. 2, 1819	Ap'l 17, 1818	71	Dropped from the roll under act May 1, 1820.
George Barnet	do	96 00	1,431 76	do	Sep. 15, 1819	Oct. 6, 1818	74	
William Gibbs	do	96 00	952 28	Virginia cont'l	Jan. 19, 1822	Oct. 4, 1820	66	
Matthew Organ	do	96 00	1,490 23	Penn. continental	Ap'l 18, 1820	Sept. 4, 1818		
Peter Shears or Sheese	do	96 00	495 76	German regiment	Mar. 16, 1819	July 6, 1818	85	Transferred from Pennsylvania.

Statement, &c. of Union county, Ohio.

NAMES.	Rank.	Annual allowance.	Sums received.	Description of service.	When placed on the pension roll.	Commencement of pension.	Ages.	Laws under which they were formerly inscribed on the pension roll; and remarks.
Thomas Orchead	Private	96 00	1,501 96	Penn. continental	June 24, 1819	July 13, 1818	77	

Statement, &c. of Warren county, Ohio.

NAMES.	Rank.	Annual allowance.	Sums received.	Description of service.	When placed on the pension roll.	Commencement of pension.	Ages.	Laws under which they were formerly inscribed on the pension roll; and remarks.
James Blackburn	Private	96 00	173 67	Pennsylvania cont.	July 29, 1818	May 14, 1818	82	Dropped from the roll under act May 1, 1820.
Do	do	96 00	313 83	do	-	May 29, 1823	-	Restored under act March 1, 1823.
Wyatt Ballard	do	96 00	899 08	N. Carolina cont'l	Aug. 7, 1819	Mar. 6, 1819	68	Transferred from Tennessee. Died July 17, 1828.
John Brant	do	96 00	1,127 43	N. Jersey cont'l	Mar. 20, 1819	May 22, 1818	79	Died February 17, 1830.
John Bodine	do	96 00	549 44	Virginia cont'l	Dec. 22, 1827	Dec. 15, 1827	70	
David Cornell	do	96 00	78 22	N. York cont'l	Aug. 14, 1818	May 12, 1818	62	
Patrick Connelly	do	96 00	837 03	Pennsylvania cont.	Oct. 9, 1820	June 16, 1818	80	
William Dougherty	do	96 00	747 86	do	Dec. 14, 1826	Nov. 28, 1826	69	
Jacob Earenfight	do	96 00	698 35		Nov. 24, 1818	May 27, 1818	90	
Anthony Geoghegan	do	96 00	1,552 66	Maryland cont'l	Jan. 7, 1819	Ap'l 25, 1818	70	
Robert Hunter	do	96 00	169 80	S. Carolina cont'l	Mar. 20, 1819	May 29, 1818	71	Dropped from the roll under act May 1, 1820.
Robert Hamilton	do	96 00	173 67	Pennsylvania cont'l	Feb. 1, 1819	May 14, 1818	-	Dropped from the roll under act May 1, 1820.
Thomas Keelor	do	96 00	1,512 79	N. J. continental	July 21, 1819	June 2, 1818	71	
Thomas Mason	do	96 00	1,517 06	Delaware cont'l	Ap'l 3, 1819	Ap'l 16, 1818	73	
Redmont McDonough	do	96 00	174 19	Virginia continental	Mar. 19, 1819	May 12, 1818	75	Dropped from the roll under act May 1, 1820.
Jonathan Moore	do	96 00	1,517 70	N. J. continental	Mar. 17, 1819	May 14, 1818	80	Dropped from the roll under act May 1, 1820.
Joseph Osborn	do	96 00	174 19	do	July 21, 1819	May 12, 1818	81	
Do	do	96 00	355 38	do	-	Dec. 23, 1825	-	Restored under act March 1, 1823.
Matthias Pearson	do	96 00	170 60	do	July 21, 1819	May 26, 1818	62	Dropped from the roll under act May 1, 1820.
Abraham Parmetter	do	96 00	1,518 99	Mass. continental	Oct. 8, 1818	May 9, 1818	74	Transferred from Pennsylvania.
Samuel Pierson	do	96 00	164 23	Connecticut cont'l	Sep. 27, 1819	June 19, 1818	59	Dropped from the roll under act May 1, 1820.

Statement, &c. of Warren county—Continued.

NAMES.	Rank.	Annual allowance.	Sums received.	Description of service.	When placed on the pension roll.	Commencement of pension.	Ages.	Laws under which they were formerly inscribed on the pension roll; and remarks.
Daniel Reddington -	Private	96 00	94 96	Mass. continental	Sep. 21, 1819	Mar. 9, 1819	-	Dropped from the roll under act May 1, 1820.
Benjamin Rice -	Ensign	240 00	310 58	Pennsylvania cont'l	Mar. 5, 1819	Nov. 19, 1818	69	Dropped from the roll under act May 1, 1820.
Samuel Richardson -	Private	96 00	399 78	Maryland cont'l	June 4, 1819	June 26, 1818	69	Died August 25, 1822.
Ephraim Stevens -	do	96 00	1,529 31	N. Hampshire cont.	Feb. 6, 1819	Mar. 31, 1818	75	Transferred from Maine.
Peter Sidle -	Musician	96 00	1,503 76	Pennsylvania cont'l	Ap'l 5, 1820	July 6, 1818	74	
Abraham Storms -	Private	96 00	1,512 49	N. Jersey cont'l	Ap'l 28, 1820	June 3, 1818	78	

Statement, &c. of Washington county, Ohio.

NAMES.	Rank.	Annual allowance.	Sums received.	Description of service.	When placed on the pension roll.	Commencement of pension.	Ages.	Laws under which they were formerly inscribed on the pension roll; and remarks.
Jesse Ballard -	Captain	240 00	320 07	R. Island cont'l	Aug. 15, 1818	May 5, 1818	57	Dropped from the roll under act May 1, 1820.
Robert Bradford -	do	240 00	1,050 66	Massachusetts con.	Ap'l 16, 1819	Ap'l 26, 1818	72	Died September 11, 1832.
Samuel Beaumont -	Private	96 00	1,413 83	Connecticut cont'l	Oct. 13, 1819	June 13, 1818	79	
John Broome -	Sergeant	96 00	684 06	Virginia cont'l	May 24, 1820	June 8, 1818	76	Died July 23, 1825.
George Canel -	Private	96 00	494 96	Maryland cont'l	Mar. 5, 1819	May 5, 1818	64	Died June 30, 1823.
Daniel Clay -	do	96 00	526 86	New Hamp. cont'l	Sep. 10, 1819	May 25, 1818	59	Died November 9, 1823.

Name	Rank	Annual allowance	Amount received	Line	Commenced	Certificate	Age	Remarks
Joseph Chandler	do	96 00	1,523 96	Connecticut cont'l	Sep. 16, 1819	Ap'l 20, 1818	90	Died August 19, 1824.
Thomas Corey	do	96 00	172 15	R. Island cont'l	May 23, 1820	May 20, 1818	56	Dropped from the roll under act May 1, 1820.
Chandler Dond	Private	96 00	1,244 41	Massachusetts con.	Ap'l 18, 1812	Mar. 19, 1821	79	Transferred from New York.
Jonathan Devol	Lieut.	240 00	1,509 66	R. Island cont'i	Nov. 4, 1819	May 5, 1818	69	Died October 13, 1825.
Thomas Dickerson	Private	96 00	177 86	Pennsylvania cont'l	Dec. 18, 1818	Ap'l 29, 1818	-	Dropped from the roll under act May 1, 1820.
William Davis, 2d	do	96 00	1,519 22	R. Island cont'l	Mar 18, 1819	May 8, 1818	73	
Dudley Davis	Corporal	96 00	710 92	Massachusetts con.	June 9, 1819	May 19, 1818	61	
Richard Done	Private	96 00	163 96	Connecticut cont'l	do	June 20, 1818	56	
Benjamin Ellinwood	Private	96 00	753 87	New Hamp. cont'l	Feb. 4, 1819	Ap'l 27, 1818	87	Died February 19, 1822.
Anthony Evans	Fife-maj.	96 00	364 64	Pennsylvania cont'l	Ap'l 15, 1819	May 4, 1818	67	
Peasley Eastman	Private	96 00	513 86	New Hamp. cont'l	June 2, 1820	Ap'l 28, 1818	72	
Sherebiah Fletcher	do	96 00	1,522 09	Massachusetts con.	June 30, 1818	Ap'l 27, 1818	72	
Ephraim Foster	do	96 00	517 59	New Hamp. cont'l	Oct. 10, 1818	Ap'l 14, 1818	85	Dropped from the roll under act May 1, 1820.
George Flake	do	96 00	509 70	Pennsylvania cont'l	Feb. 11, 1820	May 14, 1818	79	Restored under act March 1, 1823.
John Green	do	96 00	181 03	Massachusetts con.	Ap'l 17, 1819	Ap'l 16, 1818	76	Died November 11, 1832.
Do	do	96 00	558 02	do	-	Jan. 20, 1827	-	Relinquished for benefit of act May 15, 1828.
Jeremiah Greenman	Lieut.	240 00	2,372 58	R. Island cont'l	Ap'l 16, 1819	Ap'l 16, 1818	70	Died October 19, 1822.
Timothy Gates	Private	96 00	431 83	Massachusetts con.	May 31, 1819	Ap'l 20, 1818	75	Died March 29, 1819.
John Gosset	do	96 00	701 70	Virginia continental	Sep. 15, 1819	May 14, 1818	81	Transferred from Pennsylvania.
Moses Haskill	do	96 00	86 70	Massachusetts con.	Aug. 15, 1818	do	61	
Cornelius Haskins	do	96 00	1,287 72	do	Nov. 6, 1821	Ap'l 6, 1819	81	
Rufus Inman	do	96 00	1,436 67	do	Jan. 4, 1821	Mar. 18, 1820	72	Dropped from the roll under act May 1, 1820.
Henry Jolly	do	96 00	177 29	Pennsylvania cont'l	Dec. 18, 1818	Ap'l 30, 1818	77	Restored under act Mar. 1, 1823.
Do	do	96 00	830 92	do	-	June 9, 1835	-	
Thomas Johnson	do	96 00	755 69	do	Aug. 2, 1819	Ap'l 21, 1818	101	Died June 18, 1830.
James Knowles	do	96 00	1,161 44	do	Oct. 26, 1818	May 14, 1818	81	Died February 5, 1831.
John Liske	do	96 00	1,142 99	Virginia cont'l	Sep. 18, 1819	Oct. 9, 1818	77	Died December 20, 1821.
John Mills	do	96 00	348 12	Connecticut cont'l	Aug. 15, 1818	May 5, 1818	78	Died August 11, 1822.
Daniel Morley	do	96 00	409 79	do	June 30, 1818		57	
Nathaniel Mitchell	do	96 00	1,521 59	Pennsylvania cont'l	Dec. 18, 1818	Ap'l 29, 1819	94	
Isaac Moss	do	96 00	1,475 12	Mass. cont'l	May 21, 1819	Oct. 24, 1818	83	
William McGee	do	96 00	140 49	N. Hampshire cont'l	do	Sep. 18, 1818	87	Dropped from the roll under act May 1, 1820.
Do	do	96 00	-	do	-	Mar. 26, 1824	-	Restored under act March 1, 1823.

13

Statement, &c. of Washington county—Continued.

NAMES.	Rank.	Annual allowance	Sums received.	Description of service.	When placed on the pension roll.	Commencement of pension	Ages.	Laws under which they were formerly inscribed on the pension roll; and remarks.
Michael McClurie	Private	96 00	498 58	Pennsylvania cont'l	Sep. 10, 1819	May 22, 1818	71	Died July 31, 1823.
John Nestler	do	96 00	768 00	New Jersey cont'l	June 9, 1819	May 20, 1818	89	Died May 19, 1826.
Bazael Norman	do	96 00	1,133 67	Maryland cont'l	Mar. 5, 1819	May 14, 1818	77	
Gilbert Olds	do	96 00	1,520 28	Mass. cont'l	June 2, 1821	May 4, 1818	78	
Barnabas Otis	do	96 00	1,518 47	Connecticut cont'l	May 20, 1820	May 11, 1818	75	Transferred from New York
Benjamin Paine	do	96 00	938 32	Rhode Island cont'l	Oct. 30, 1821	May 27, 1818	72	
Oliver Rice	Lieutenant	240 00	434 19	Mass. cont'l	Oct. 13, 1818	May 14, 1818	67	Dropped from the roll under act May 1, 1820.
John McCrush Robert Ray	Private	96 00	699 60	Pennsylvania cont'l	Dec. 20, 1821	May 8, 1818	97	Died August 21, 1825.
Jacob Springer	do	96 00	1,178 06	New Jersey cont'l	Dec. 18, 1818	May 2, 1818	67	Died August 9, 1830.
Nicholas Smith	do	96 00	1,083 72	New York cont'l	June 9, 1819	May 22, 1818	97	
Abraham Saunders	do	96 00	42 66	Virginia cont'l	May 17, 1824	Nov. 17, 1823	75	Died April 26, 1824.
David Smith	do	96 00	511 25	Connecticut cont'l	July 22, 1819	May 8, 1818	88	
Timothy Sherman	do	96 00	171 86	Mass. cont'l	Sep. 16, 1819	May 21, 1818	62	Dropped from the roll under act May 1, 1820.
Joseph F. Trible	do	96 00	1,519 51	Virginia cont'l	Oct. 26, 1818	May 7, 1818	74	Dropped from the roll under act May 1, 1820.
John Turner	do	96 00	167 69	Delaware cont'l	Mar. 5, 1819	June 6, 1818	57	
Jonathan Thomas	do	96 00	460 64	N. Hampshire cont'l	May 21, 1819	Oct. 1, 1818	60	Died July 18, 1823.
Ignatius Waterman	do	95 00	1,516 67	Connecticut cont'l	June 9, 1819	May 18, 1818	76	
Oliver Woodward	do	96 00	1,509 32	do	do	June 15, 1818	90	

Statement, &c. of Wayne county, Ohio.

NAMES.	Rank.	Annual allowance.	Sums received.	Description of service.	When placed on the pension roll.	Commencement of pension.	Ages.	Laws under which they were formerly inscribed on the pension roll; and remarks.
John Burns	Private	96 00	161 83	Virginia cont'l	June 28, 1819	June 28, 1818	81	Dropped from the roll under act May 1, 1820.
John Critchfield	do	96 00	1,438 70	do	Mar. 28, 1821	Mar. 10, 1819	73	Transferred from Pennsylvania.
Richard Draught	Drummer	96 00	1,048 76	N. H. continental	Nov. 11, 1819	Aug. 26, 1818	64	Died July 28, 1829.
Stephen Fox	Private	96 00	1,464 73	Conn. continental	July 30, 1819	June 2, 1818	74	
James Gray	do	96 00	1,472 79	Mass. continental	Mar. 5, 1819	Nov. 2, 1818	59	
Thomas Gwin	do	96 00	154 26	Virginia cont'l	Jan. 11, 1821	June 30, 1818	80	Died February 7, 1820.
Jonathan Grant	do	96 00	1,479 96	do	Ap'l 23, 1822	Oct. 6, 1818	71	
Joel Isbel	do	96 00	1,467 99	Conn. continental	Nov. 29, 1819	Nov. 20, 1818	69	
Robert M'Curdy	do	96 00	433 22	Penn. continental	Sep. 23, 1819	June 8, 1819	69	Died December 12, 1824.
Conrad Mitsco	do	96 00	1,504 28	N. J. continental	Sep. 21, 1818	July 4, 1818	74	Transferred from Pennsylvania.
William Nixon	do	96 00	534 53	do	May 13, 1820	Feb. 22, 1820	70	Died September 17, 1825.
Conrad Peterson	do	96 00	1,419 72	Virginia cont'l	May 21, 1819	Nov. 21, 1818	74	
Isaac Starkey	do	96 00	893 83	do	Dec. 10, 1832	Nov. 13, 1822	73	Transferred from Virginia.
Ezra Tryon	do	96 00	1,472 79	Conn. con'inental	Mar. 5, 1819	Nov. 2, 1818	74	
Isaac Underwood	do	96 00	1,359 25	Mass. continental	May 23, 1820	July 8, 1818	69	

Statement showing the Names, Rank, &c. of persons residing in the county of Adams, in the State of Ohio, who have been inscribed on the Pension List under the act of Congress passed the 7th day of June, 1832.

NAMES.	Rank.	Annual allowance.	Sums received.	Description of service.	When placed on the pension roll.	Commencement of pension	Ages.	Laws under which they were formerly inscribed on the pension roll; and remarks.
John Baldwin	Private	20 00	60 00	Maryland militia	June 22, 1833	Mar. 4, 1831	77	
John Breedlove	do	23 33	69 99	Virginia militia	Oct. 18, 1832	do	82	Transferred from Madison county, Va. from March 4, 1833.
Samuel Cross	do	26 66	66 65	Pennsylvania mil.	June 11, 1832	do	79	
Zebediah David	do	20 00	60 00	do	May 28, 1833	do	76	
Jesse Edwards	do	33 33	99 99	do	Aug. 8, 1833	do	78	
Nathaniel Foster	do	30 00	75 00	New Jersey militia	do	do	74	
Abraham Grooms	do	20 00	—	Virginia militia	Nov. 16, 1833	do	94	
William Heddleson	do	23 33	58 33	Pennsylv'a militia	Aug. 24, 1833	do	77	
John Killing	Musician	88 00	264 00	do	May 24, 1833	do	77	
Thomas Malott	Pri. & ser.	57 50	172 50	Maryland militia	May 3, 1833	do	82	
John McPike	Private	70 00	210 00	Pennsylv'a militia	May 24, 1833	do	84	
John Mehaffey	do	60 00	180 00	do	Aug. 8, 1833	do	75	
Charles Osman	do	30 88	92 64	Virginia militia	Feb. 12, 1833	do	72	
Robert Simpson	do	80 00	240 00	N. Hamp. cont'l	do	do	71	
Charles Stevens	do	36 66	109 98	Pennsylv'a militia	Feb. 25, 1833	do	75	
John Stivers	do	29 16	87 48	Virginia militia	Aug. 8, 1833	do	69	
John Thompson	do	80 00	200 00	Pennsylv'a militia	Sep. 21, 1833	do	73	
Do	do	26 21	78 63	do	May 24, 1833	do	81	
Elijah Walden	do	80 00	156 37	Virginia cont'l	Feb. 12, 1833	do	72	Died February 17, 1833.
James Walker	do	40 00	120 00	N. Carolina militia	May 3, 1833	do	79	
James Williams	do	35 00	105 00	Pennsylv'a militia	Oct. 8, 1833	do	75	

Statement, &c. of Ashtabula county, Ohio.

NAMES.	Rank.	Annual allowance.	Sums received.	Description of service.	When placed on the pension roll.	Commencement of pension.	Ages.	Laws under which they were formerly inscribed on the pension roll; and remarks.
Nathaniel Austin	Private	23 33	69 99	Connecticut cont'l	July 20, 1833	Mar. 4, 1831	81	
David Andrews	do	40 00	120 00	Conn. State troops	Sept. 23, 1833	do	73	
Eliphalet Austin	do	36 66	109 98	Connecticut cont'l	Sept. 16, 1833	do	73	
Eli Baker	do	46 66	139 98	Mass. State troops	July 20, 1833	do	83	
Calvin Belknap	do	30 00	90 00	Vermont militia	July 24, 1833	do	69	
Hananiah Brooks	do	80 00	240 00	Conn. State troops	Aug. 8, 1833	do	77	
Ebenezer Buck	do	80 00	240 00	Mass. continental	Sep. 16, 1833	do	68	
Samuel Beebe	do	31 12	-	Conn. militia	Jan. 16, 1834	do	82	
Thomas Binham, Sen.	do	26 88	-	New York militia	Jan. 16, 1834	do	75	
Nathaniel Coleman	do	20 00	60 00	Mass. continental	Dec. 3, 1833	du	79	
Nathaniel Fobes	do	33 33	66 66	Cont'l State troops	Dec. 16, 1832	do	76	
John Fenn	do	80 00	240 00	Connecticut cont'l	Feb. 26, 1833	do	76	
Sinkler Fox	do	52 56	157 68	N. Hampshire cont.	July 20, 1833	do	75	
Christopher Ford	Pr. & artif.	39 33	98 33	Penn'a State troops	July 20, 1833	do	72	
Levi Gaylord	Artificer	144 00	360 00	Conn. State troops	Ap'l 13, 1835	cto	74	
Ebenezer Goodell	Private	30 00	-	Mass. State troops	July 24, 1833	do	79	
Solomon Griswold	Ser. & qr. master	303 33	909 99	Mass. militia	Aug. 1, 1833	do	76	
Joshua Giddings	Private	30 00	-	Conn. State troops	Nov. 1, 1833	do	79	
Ezra Griffin	do	43 33	108 32	do	Sep. 16, 1833	do	71	
Durlin Hickok	Sergeant	120 00	360 00	Mass. continental	Sep. 26, 1832	do	75	
Allen Hackett	Private	40 00	100 00	N. H. State troops	Ap'l 2, 1833	do	76	
Seth Hillyen	do	80 00	200 00	Connecticut cont'l	Aug. 8, 1833	do	76	
Thomas Holman	do	35 60	106 98	Conn. State troops	Sep. 23, 1833	do	79	
Moses Hall	do	20 00	50 00	Mass. continental	Ap'l 19, 1833	do	71	
Joseph M. Jewett	do	80 00	120 00	Conn. State troops	Ap'l 27, 1833	do	70	
Jacob Jenks	do	80 00	160 00	R. Island State	July 20, 1833	do	74	
Samuel Johnston	Pri. & ser.	39 66	118 98	Mass. continental	July 24, 1833	do	81	
Abijah Laned	Private	80 00	240 00	N. H. State troops	Ap'l 27, 1833	do	74	
Francis Lyman	do	40 00	120 00	Connecticut cont'l	Aug. 1, 1833	do	77	

Statement, &c. of Ashtabula county—Continued.

Names.	Rank.	Annual allowance.	Sums received.	Description of service.	When placed on the pension roll.	Commencement of pension.	Ages.	Laws under which they were formerly inscribed on the pension roll; and remarks.
Ebenezer Lamson	Private	40 00	120 00	Conn. continental	Nov. 21, 1833	Mar. 4, 1831	81	
Elijah Morse	do	20 00	50 00	Mass. militia	Ap'l 2, 1833	do	68	
John Macumber	do	43 33	129 99	Mass. State troops	Ap'l 10, 1833	do	74	
James Morrison	do	33 33	99 99	Conn. State troops	July 6, 1833	do	77	
Thomas Martin	do	43 33	108 32	do	Sep. 21, 1833	do	81	
Constantine Mills	do	20 00	50 00	Conn. militia	Oct. 9, 1833	do	71	
David Niks	do	63 33	199 99	New York militia	Sep. 17, 1833	do	74	
John Norris	do	60 00	-	Conn. continental	Sep. 16, 1833	do	69	
Dan Peck	do	80 00	200 00	Conn. State troops	Ap'l 13, 1833	do	72	
Samuel Parker	do	30 00	90 00	do	July 6, 1833	do	84	
John Pickett	do	40 00	120 00	do	July 24, 1833	do	82	
Elnathan Pratt	do	23 33	69 99	Mass. militia	July 24, 1833	do	76	
Joseph Rathbun	da	21 66	64 98	do	Ap'l 6, 1833	do	72	
Joseph Rogers	do	50 00	125 00	Mass. continental	Mar. 26, 1833	do	70	
S. Douglass Sacket	do	80 00	160 00	New York cont'l	Oct. 2, 1832	do	69	
Ezra Sexton	Pri. & ser.	83 33	249 99	Connecticut cont'l	Ap'l 2, 1833	do	76	
Paul Stephens	Private	60 00	180 00	Conn. State troops	July 20, 1833	do	74	
Matthew Talf	do	20 00	50 00	Mass. mil. & State	Mar. 21, 1833	do	72	
Rufus Thompson	do	20 00	50 00	Mass. militia	July 6, 1833	do	69	
Caleb Thomas	do	70 00	210 00	Connecticut militia	Sep. 16, 1833	do	70	
Clement Tuttle	do	80 00	-	do	Sep. 16, 1833	do	78	
Michael Webster	do	20 00	60 00	do	Mar. 11, 1833	do	86	
Obadiah Ward	do	33 33	66 66	do	Ap'l 2, 1833	do	81	
William Whitney	do	33 33	99 99	Mass. militia	Ap'l 13, 1833	do	71	
Ezra Woodworth	do	20 00	60 00	Mass. State troops	Ap'l 13, 1833	do	71	
Benjamin Watrous	do	43 33	86 66	Connecticut militia	July 6, 1833	do	69	
David Wood	Corporal	88 00	264 00	Connecticut State	July 24, 1833	do	73	
Stephen Winslow	Private	40 00	120 00	Connecticut militia	Oct. 2, 1833	do	86	
Benjamin Ward	Pri. & ser	95 00	285 00	Mass. State troops	Dec. 3, 1833	do	71	

Statement, &c. of Athens county, Ohio.

Names.	Rank.	Annual allowance.	Sums received.	Description of service.	When placed on the pension roll.	Commencement of pension.	Ages.	Laws under which they were formerly inscribed on the pension roll; and remarks.
Thomas Arnold	Private	46 66	139 98	R. Island militia	Ap'l 28, 1834	Mar. 4, 1831	73	
Hopson Beebe	do	30 00	60 00	Conn. continental & State troops	Ap'l 8, 1833	do	85	
Silas Bingham	do	41 11	123 33	N. H. continental	May 10, 1833	do	76	
Shepherd Collins	do	80 00	240 00	Delaware State tps.	Oct. 19, 1832	do	79	
Conner Dowd	do	43 33	129 92	Penn. militia	Ap'l 23, 1834	do	76	
James Fuller	do	23 33	69 99	Mass. State troops	July 4, 1833	do	74	
Aaron Fall	do	30 00	90 00	N. H. militia	Aug. 24, 1832	do	73	
Peter How	do	20 00	60 00	Vermont militia	Feb. 4, 1833	do	78	
William Howell	do	36 66	109 98	Virginia militia	Mar. 2, 1833	do	86	
Azel Johnson	do	30 00	90 00	Mass. militia	Feb. 4, 1833	do	71	
Joseph Lyons	do	30 00	90 00	N. H. continental	May 10, 1833	do	79	
Daniel Mosier	do	30 00	90 00	Mass. militia	Feb. 4, 1833	do	89	
Francis Munn	Pri. of art.	62 50	187 50	R. Island cont'l	June 26, 1833	do	71	
Robert Means	Private	53 33	159 99	N. J. militia	Aug. 9, 1833	do	76	
Thomas Mansfield	do	80 00	240 00	Maryland militia	Jan. 17, 1834	do	84	
Job Phillips	do	80 00	240 00	Penn. State troops	Sep. 21, 1834	do	93	
Samuel Risley	do	40 00	120 00	Conn. militia	Feb. 2, 1833	do	73	
Jason Rice	do	73 33	219 99	N. C. State troops	Sep. 21, 1833	do	78	
Daniel Stewart	do	80 00	240 00	Conn. State troops	July 27, 1833	do	72	
Samuel Sampson	do	50 00	150 00	Penn. militia & State troops	Aug. 24, 1833	do	72	
Charles Shepherd	do	26 66	79 98	Maryland militia	Dec. 27, 1833	do	77	
James Townsend	do	40 00	120 00	Virginia militia	Feb. 4, 1833	do	75	
Nathan Woodberry	do	66 66	199 98	Mass. militia	do	do	74	
Jonathan Watkins	do	40 00	120 00	Penn. militia	Aug. 9, 1833	do	73	
John White	Pri. & ser.	90 00	270 00	Conn. militia	Sep. 21, 1833	do	76	
John Wyman	Private	30 00	90 00	Mass. State troops	Dec. 27, 1833	do	71	

Statement, &c. of Allen county, Ohio.

NAMES.	Rank.	Annual allowance.	Sums received.	Description of service.	When placed on the pension roll.	Commencement of pension.	Ages.	Laws under which they were formerly inscribed on the pension roll; and remarks.
James Turner	Private	66 66	99 98	Maryland cont'l	Sep. 23, 1833	Mar. 4, 1831	78	

Statement, &c. of Belmont county, Ohio.

NAMES.	Rank.	Annual allowance.	Sums received.	Description of service.	When placed on the pension roll.	Commencement of pension:	Ages.	Laws under which they were formerly inscribed on the pension roll; and remarks.
Henry Aston	Private	30 00	90 00	Maryland militia	May 7, 1833	Mar. 4, 1831	79	
John Boyd	do	20 00	-	Maryland State	Nov. 30, 1832	do	78	
William Craig	do	20 00	60 00	Maryland militia	May 7, 1833	do	79	
Marmaduke Davis	do	28 33	184 99	Virginia State	Jan. 4, 1833	do	74	
Levi Davis	do	30 00	90 00	Mass. cont'l	June 20, 1833	do	69	
Daniel Farnsworth	do	65 86	164 65	New Jersey State	Sep. 17, 1833	do	72	
Jonathan Howell	do	56 66	169 98	Virginia State	Jan. 4, 1833	do	76	
Richard Hardesty	do	40 00	100 00	Pennsylvania militia	Aug. 20, 1833	do	80	
Thomas James	Pri. & mar.	20 00	60 00	do	Mar. 26, 1834	do	79	
Daniel Lockwood	Private	66 00	198 00	New York State	Sep. 21, 1833	do	72	
Eli McKnight	Private	20 00	60 00	Virginia militia	May 28, 1833	do	71	
William Perrine	do	23 33	69 99	New Jersey cont'l	May 7, 1833	do	69	
Hugh Pierce	do	30 00	90 00	Maryland militia	Nov. 21, 1833	do	77	
William Ramsey	Ensign	80 00	240 00	Pennsylvania militia	Mar. 15, 1834	do	79	

NAMES.	Rank.	Annual allowance.	Sums received.	Description of service.	When placed on the pension roll.	Commencement of pension.	Ages.
William Reneson	Private	21 66	64 98	do	Ap'l 13, 1833	do	77
Joseph Smith	do	30 00	90 00	Maryland militia	Nov. 27, 1832	do	81
Benjamin Shepard	do	26 66	79 98	New Jersey cont'l	Dec. 19, 1832	do	73
Robert Thompson	Sergeant	60 00	180 00	Pennsylvania militia	Jan. 4, 1833	do	75
Peter Tallman, guardian for Lewis Forman	Private	23 33	-	Virginia militia	Dec. 3, 1833	do	80
Charles Waterman	do	66 66	199 98	Connecticut State	Aug. 15, 1832	do	70
David Williams	do	80 00	240 00	Penn. State troops	Ap'l 16, 1833	do	87
Thomas White	Cap. & ens.	279 00	837 00	Virginia militia	May 3, 1834	do	79

14

Statement, &c. of Brown county, Ohio.

NAMES.	Rank.	Annual allowance.	Sums received.	Description of service.	When placed on the pension roll.	Commencement of pension.	Ages.	Laws under which they were formerly inscribed on the pension roll; and remarks.
Samuel Barr	Pri. & ser.	83 33	249 99	Pennsylvania mil.	June 6, 1833	Mar. 4, 1831	76	
John Blair	Private	80 00	240 00	New Jersey militia	Aug. 9, 1833	do	78	March 18, 1818.
John Cooper	Ensign	240 00	-	Pennsylvania cont'l	May 8, 1832	Ap'l 30, 1832	-	
Do	Pri. & ser.	240 00	720 00	do	Mar. 23, 1833	Mar. 4, 1831	77	
Thomas Cotterill	-	88 33	264 99	Virginia militia	Oct. 24, 1833	do	84	
James Cahill	Private	30 00	90 00	Maryland militia	Ap'l 22, 1833	do	85	
William Crosby	do	30 00	90 00	do	May 2, 1834	do	72	
Joshua Davidson	Ser. & en.	175 83	527 49	Pennsylvania con.	Aug. 21, 1833	do	81	
Gabriel Eakins, or Acron	Private	26 43	66 08	Virginia State tr'ps	Aug. 9, 1833	do	75	
Samuel Ellis	do	30 00	90 00	Pennsylvania mil.	Ap'l 17, 1834	do	81	
John Gunsauld	do	53 33	159 99	N. J. State troops	Nov. 8, 1832	do	80	
Benjamin Gardner	do	63 33	158 33	N. Y. State troops	Sep. 16, 1833	do	73	
Joseph Gould	do	26 66	79 98	Massachusetts mil.	Dec. 27, 1833	do	88	
Thomas Hetherly	do	80 00	240 00	Virginia continental	Feb. 25, 1833	do	79	

Statement, &c. of Brown county—Continued.

NAMES.	Rank.	Annual allowance.	Sums received.	Description of service.	When placed on the pension roll.	Commencement of pension.	Ages.	Laws under which they were formerly inscribed on the pension roll; and remarks.
Archibald Hopkins	Private	23 33	69 99	Virginia militia	Dec. 27, 1833	Mar. 4, 1831	74	
John Laney	do	24 44	73 32	do	July 27, 1833	do	75	
James Leonard	do	80 00	240 00	Pennsylvan a cont'l	Aug. 8, 1833	do	98	
Job Lecroy	do	80 00	226 67	New Jersey cont'l	Sep. 16, 1833	do	72	Died January 4, 1834.
Valentine McDaniel	do	20 00	60 00	Pennsylvania cont'l	June 6, 1833	do	74	
Walter McDaniel	do	40 00	120 00	Maryland cont'l	July 27, 1833	do	87	
Elijah Moore	do	31 33	-	New Jersey militia	Oct. 16, 1833	do	74	
Daniel Morford	do	43 33	129 99	do	Aug. 29, 1833	do	93	
Charles McManis	do	70 00	210 00	Pennsylvania mil.	Oct. 24, 1833	do	72	
Alexander McCoy	do	20 00	-	do	May 9, 1834	do	70	
Jacob Middleswart	do	60 00	-	do	May 30, 1834	do	73	
William Newberry	Pri & fifer	25 00	75 00	New Jersey militia	Dec. 2, 1833	do	74	
Samuel Pickerill	Drummer	88 00	264 00	Virginia State tr'ps	Oct. 19, 1832	do	74	
John Parke	Private	20 00	60 00	Virginia militia	Aug. 9, 1833	do	72	
Joab Reid	do	56 87	170 61	do	Oct. 18, 1832	do	72	
Thomas Rattan	do	80 00	240 00	Pennsylvania cont'l	Aug. 18, 1832	do	78	
Lawrence Ramey	do	23 33	69 99	Pennsylvania mil.	June 6, 1833	do	76	
William Rains	do	20 00	60 00	Virginia militia	do	do	70	
William Reeves	do	23 33	69 99	do	Aug. 9, 1833	do	69	
Benjamin Sutton	do	53 33	-	Pennsylvania mil.	Sep. 16, 1833	do	74	
Robert Stephenson	do	22 11	66 33	do	May 2, 1833	do	75	
Benjamin Wells	Mariner	20 00	-60 00	Mary'd State Navy	Oct. 18, 1832	do	79	
James Waits	Private	54 65	163 95	Pennsylvania mil.	Aug. 24, 1833	do	72	

Statement, &c. of Butler county, Ohio.

NAMES.	Rank.	Annual allowance.	Sums received.	Description of service.	When placed on the pension roll.	Commencement of pension.	Ages.	Laws under which they were formerly inscribed on the pension roll; and remarks.
John Ayers	Private	26 66	79 98	N. J. State troops	Nov. 8, 1832	Mar. 4, 1831	74	
Isaac Anderson	Pr. & lieut.	222 32	666 96	Penn. State troops	May 3, 1833	do	76	
James Arthur	Private	72 50	217 50	Va. militia	Oct. 8, 1833	do	70	
Thomas Berry	do	80 00	240 00	Va. continental	Nov. 1, 1832	do	72	
Joseph Braid	do	80 00	240 00	N. J. militia	do	do	72	
James Blackburn	Pri. of inf. and cav.	26 66	79 98	Penn. State troops	Nov. 8, 1832	do	76	
Jonathan Barrett	Private	70 70	212 10	Conn. State troops		do	72	
Elijah Barns	do	23 33	46 66	Md. continental	Feb. 20, 1832	do	79	
Jeremiah Brann	do	80 00	240 00	Va. militia	Mar. 27, 1833	do	72	
John Beckett	Pr. of cav.	20 00	50 00	Penn. militia	Ap'l 2, 1833	do	79	
Daniel Baker	do	100 00	300 00	N. J. militia	Aug. 8, 1833	do	79	
John Craig	do	76 66	229 98	do	Ap'l 8, 1834	do	72	
Joseph Compton	Private	100 00	300 00	do	Nov. 1, 1832	do	75	
John Carnes	do	20 00	60 00	N. J. continental	do	do	69	
William Caldwell	do	50 82	152 46	S. C. militia	Nov. 7, 1832	do	71	
Thomas Colyer	Lieutenant	320 00	960 00	N. J. continental	Dec. 29, 1832	do	90	
James Curry	Private	53 33	133 33	Penn. State troops	do	do	78	
William Cooley	do	49 33	98 66	N. York militia	May 3, 1833	do	78	
Walter Dickerson	do	20 00	40 00	N. J. State troops	Oct. 30, 1832	do	71	
William Davis	do	80 00	200 00	Virginia cont'l	Nov. 1, 1832	do	82	
James Deneen	do	21 98	65 94	N. J. militia	Nov. 8, 1832	do	78	
John Freeman	do	80 00	200 00	Mass. continental	Nov. 7, 1832	do	71	
Daniel Gray	do	60 00	180 00	N. J. militia	Nov. 4, 1832	do	85	
James Grimes	do	80 00	240 00	Virginia militia	Nov. 7, 1832	do	74	
John Grooms	Pri. & sea.	32 50	97 50	Continental navy	do	do	80	
David Griffith	Private	80 00	240 00	Mass. continental	Jan. 31, 1834	do	76	
Nathan Griffith	do	30 00	90 00	Md. State troops	Oct. 29, 1832	do	75	
John Hall	do	80 00	200 00	S. C. militia	Nov. 7, 1832	do	76	
Isaac Hull	do	30 00	90 00	Penn. continental	Nov. 7, 1832	do	74	
Daniel Higgins	do	53 33	159 99	Va. continental	Dec. 29, 1832	do	75	

Statement, &c. of Butler county—Continued.

NAMES.	Rank.	Annual allowance.	Sums received.	Description of service.	When placed on the pension roll.	Commencement of pension.	Ages.	Laws under which they were formerly inscribed on the pension roll; and remarks.
William Hutchings	Private	60 00	180 00	N. J. militia	May 3, 1833	Mar. 4, 1831	77	
Isaac Hammond	do	30 00	90 00	Va. continental	Mar. 27, 1833	do	72	
Mathias Handlin	do	80 00	240 00	N J. militia	Sep. 23, 1833	do	76	
Isaac Hoff	do	53 33	-	do	Nov. 25, 1833	do	76	
James Irwin	do	20 00	-	Penn. militia	Dec. 27, 1833	do	76	
John Lucas	do	33 33	66 66	Penn. State troops	Oct. 30, 1832	do	73	
Peter Lintner	do	20 00	60 00	Penn. militia	Mar. 27, 1833	do	74	
Hendrick Lane	do	40 00	80 00	N. J. militia	May 3, 1833	do	74	
J h. Lue	do	30 00	75 00	do	do	do	70	
Joshua Leach	Pri. & ser.	86 66	259 98	Md. militia	Sep. 21, 1833	do	78	
Robert Lytle	Private	20 00	50 00	Penn. militia	do	do	81	
Ichabod Miller	do	26 66	66 65	N. J. State troops	Dec. 29, 1832	do	75	
Elijah Mills	do	80 00	240 00	Md. militia	do	do	76	
Asahel Murdock	do	40 00	120 00	N. Hamp. cont'l	Mar. 27, 1833	do	79	
Michael Pearce	do	20 00	40 00	N. J. militia	Oct. 30, 1832	do	84	
John Patterson	do	61 25	183 75	S. C. militia	Aug. 24, 1833	do	71	
Martin Rienhart	do	40 00	120 00	Penn. continental	Oct. 27, 1832	do	75	
James Reily	do	80 00	240 00	Penn. continental	May 6, 1833	do	79	
Leonard Rickhart	do	36 63	91 58	N. C. militia	do	do	70	
Joseph Randall	do	80 00	240 00	N. York cont'l	Sep. 20, 1833	do	92	
Ezekiel Ross	do	80 00	240 00	N. J. militia	Mar. 24, 1834	do	77	
William Shepherd	do	80 00	180 22	do	Oct. 27, 1832	do	75	Died June 4, 1833.
Pierson Sayere	do	80 00	240 00	do	do	do	72	
Martin Stine	do	80 00	187 31	do	Dec. 29, 1852	do	79	
John Smith	do	70 00	175 00	do	May 25, 1833	do	72	
Robert Simmonds	Pri. & ser.	30 00	90 00	Md. militia	May 28, 1833	do	76	
Henry Taylor	Pri. & cor.	28 75	71 88	Va. militia	Oct. 29, 1832	do	82	
Mathew Vandyne	Pri. & ser.	83 33	249 99	N. J. militia	Aug. 8, 1833	do	82	
Garret Vanansdaller	Private	20 00	60 00	do	Feb. 11, 1834	do	81	
Thomas White	do	40 00	120 00	do	Oct. 27, 1832	do	78	

Names	Rank	Annual allowance	Sums received	Description of service	When placed on the pension roll	Commencement of pension	Ages	Laws under which they were formerly inscribed on the pension roll; and remarks
Andrew Wilson	do	20 00	—	Va. State troops	do	do	73	
Ashbel Waller	do	25 00	75 00	Conn. continental	do	do	74	
Jonathan Whitaker	Pri. & ser.	108 33	324 99	N. J. State troops	do	do	76	
William Wright	Private	20 00	60 00	Penn. militia	Oct. 12, 1833	do	72	
John Wilkinson	do	20 00	60 00	do	Mar. 8, 1834	do	73	

Statement, &c. of Carroll county, Ohio.

Names	Rank	Annual allowance	Sums received	Description of service	When placed on the pension roll	Commencement of pension	Ages	Laws under which they were formerly inscribed on the pension roll; and remarks
William English	Private	40 00	120 00	Virginia militia	Oct. 25, 1832	Mar. 4, 1831	71	
John Gribbon	do	43 33	129 99	Penn. continental	Sept. 16, 1833	do	82	

Statement, &c. of Champaign county, Ohio.

NAMES.	Rank.	Annual allowance.	Sums received.	Description of service.	When placed on the pension roll.	Commencement of pension.	Ages.	Laws under which they were formerly inscribed on the pension roll; and remarks.
John Davis	Private	21 67	65 01	N. H. State troops	Feb. 2, 1833	Mar. 4, 1831	77	
James Davis	do	34 66	103 98	N. H. cont. militia	June 25, 1833	do	72	
John Dawson	do	20 00	60 00	N. Jersey militia	May 3, 1833	do	89	
William Fuson	do	20 00	40 00	Virginia contin'l	Ap'l 20, 1833	do	72	
Daniel Hullinger	Pri. & ser.	56 66	141 65	Penn. continental	Feb. 2, 1833	do	78	
John Hamet	Private	36 66	109 98	Virginia militia	Sept. 21, 1833	do	74	
Benjamin Jones	do	56 66	169 98	Penn. continental	Feb. 2, 1833	do	71	
David Kirckwood	do	80 00	240 00	Md. militia	May 3, 1833	do	94	
James Largent	do	80 00	200 00	Virginia contin'l	Feb. 2, 1833	do	79	
Ezekiel Moses	do	50 00	150 00	Connecticut militia	May 10, 1833	do	72	
John McAdam	do	78 88	236 64	Penn. militia	May 27, 1833	do	71	
John McIntire	do	28 00	70 00	do	Sept. 21, 1833	do	75	
John Runyon	do	26 66	53 32	do	Feb. 2, 1833	do	77	
Henry Safely	do	36 00	108 00	Maryland militia	July 16, 1833	do	74	
William Wooley	do	80 00	240 00	N. Jersey militia	Mar. 2, 1833	do	79	
Stephen Wooley	do	80 00	240 00	do	do	do	76	
Jesse Welden	do	63 33	189 99	Deleware militia	May 28, 1833	do	74	
William Weaver	do	26 66	78 31	Virginia militia	Aug. 24, 1833	do	74	

Statement, &c. of Coshocton county, Ohio.

NAMES.	Rank.	Annual allowance.	Sums received.	Description of service.	When placed on the pension roll.	Commencement of pension.	Ages.	Laws under which they were formerly inscribed on the pension roll; and remarks.
Israel Baker	Sergeant	96 00	1,234 40	Mass. continental	Feb. 11, 1819	Ap'l 22, 1818	–	March 18, 1818.
Do	do	120 00	360 00	do	Nov. 9, 1832	Mar. 4, 1831	77	
Christian Messer	Private	23 33		Penn. militia	May 13, 1834	do	72	
William Norris	do	96 00	172 64	Virginia contin'l	Nov. 25, 1818	May 18, 1818	–	March 18, 1818.
Do	do	60 00	120 00	do	Nov. 3, 1832	Mar. 4, 1831	74	

Statemen', &c. of Clark county, Ohio.

NAMES.	Rank.	Annual allowance.	Sums received.	Description of service.	When placed on the pension roll.	Commencement of pension.	Ages.	Laws under which they were formerly inscribed on the pension roll; and remarks.
John Anderson	Private	50 00	130 00	N. H. continental	Nov. 27, 1832	Mar. 4, 1831	75	
John Bancroft	Ser. & lt.	106 66	319 98	Mass. State troops	Dec. 3, 1832	do	86	
Simeon Burdwell	Private	30 00	90 00	do	Ap'l 6, 1833	do	84	
William Brandenburg	do	20 00	50 00	Md. State troops	do	do	75	
William Davis	do	80 00	240 00	N. Jersey militia	Aug. 8, 1833	do	80	
Jacob Harris	do	30 67	92 01	do	Mar. 26, 1833	do	83	
James Kelly	do	80 00	240 00	Virginia contin'l	Ap'l 9, 1833	do	81	
John Kellar	do	20 00	50 00	Penn. militia	Oct. 24, 1833	do	76	
Robert Layne	do	46 66	130 98	Virginia militia	Dec. 26, 1832	do	76	
Samuel Lippincott	do	20 00	60 00	N. Jersey militia	May 10, 1833	do	74	
Jonathan Milkollin	do	74 17	185 43	Virginia militia	Aug. 8, 1833	do	70	

Statement, &c. of Clark county—Continued.

NAMES.	Rank.	Annual allowance.	Sums received.	Description of service.	When placed on the pension roll.	Commencement of pension.	Ages.	Laws under which they were formerly inscribed on the pension roll; and remarks.
Daniel Moore	Private	80 00	240 00	N. Jersey militia	Aug. 29, 1833	Mar. 4, 1831	80	
Moses Nelson	do	20 00	60 00	N. Carolina militia	Feb. 27, 1833	do	75	Died June 6, 1833.
Chester Pool	Pri. & cor.	80 27	181 24	Connecticut militia	July 27, 1833	do	73	
Jeremiah Priest	Private	80 00	240 00	Va. State troops	Dec. 12, 1834	do	75	
Andrew Ream	do	43 33	108 33	Penn. mil. & cont.	Dec. 3, 1832	do	77	
Henry Rudeailly	Pri. & ser.	36 66	73 32	Penn. State troops	Ap'l 6, 1833	do	78	
Joseph Sayre	Private	38 10	114 30	N. Jersey militia	July 27, 1833	do	77	
Daniel Wallen	do	80 00	240 00	N. York militia	May 3, 1833	do	85	
Peter Wakefield	Pri. & mar'r	41 66	124 98	Continental navy	May 10, 1833	do	85	
Isaac Wilson	Sergeant	120 00	360 00	Penn. militia	July 27, 1833	do	75	

Statement, &c. of Clinton county, Ohio.

NAMES.	Rank.	Annual allowance.	Sums received.	Description of service.	When placed on the pension roll.	Commencement of pension.	Ages.	Laws under which they were formerly inscribed on the pension roll; and remarks.
John Allen	Private	80 00	240 00	Va. State troops	Ap'l 15, 1833	Mar. 4, 1831	72	
Jacob Beard	do	20 00	60 00	Virginia militia	Nov. 27, 1833	do	72	
Asa Disbrow	do	21 66	64 98	Conn. State troops	Dec. 27, 1833	do	81	
Abraham Ellis	do	33 33	83 33	Penn. State troops	Sept. 20, 1833	do	81	
William Lloyd	do	30 00	75 00	Virginia contin'l	Ap'l 11, 1833	do	72	
Thomas Gaddis	Capt. & col.	538 32	1,616 46	Va. State troops	Ap'l 2, 1833	do	92	
Isaac Grant	Private	34 67	86 68	Virginia contin'l	Ap'l 11, 1833	do	75	
John Hall	do	45 00	135 00	Va. State troops	do	do	83	

NAMES.	Rank.	Annual allowance.	Sums received.	Description of service.	When placed on the pension roll.	Commencement of pension.	Ages.	Laws under which they were formerly inscribed on the pension roll; and remarks.
David Harwick	Pri. of cav.	100 00	300 00	Virginia contin'l	Ap'l 26, 1833	do	74	
Thomas Hardin	Private	47 50	142 50	Delaware militia	Mar. 19, 1834	do	79	
John Jones	do	27 11	54 22	Penn. militia	May 10, 1833	do	78	
Elijah Sabin	do	50 00	150 00	New York militia	Ap'l 11, 1833	do	79	
David Shields	do	25 55	76 65	Virginia militia	do	do	82	
James Spencer	do	80 00	240 00	do	May 2, 1834	do	72	
John Woollard	do	30 00	60 00	do	Ap'l 11, 1833	do	90	

15

Statement, &c. of Clermont county, Ohio.

NAMES.	Rank.	Annual allowance.	Sums received.	Description of service.	When placed on the pension roll.	Commencement of pension.	Ages.	Laws under which they were formerly inscribed on the pension roll; and remarks.
Joseph Alexander	Lt. & pri. lieut	140 00	420 00	S. Carolina militia	Aug. 8, 1833	Mar. 4, 1831	75	
David Brannen	Private	36 63	73 26	Penn. militia	May 18, 1833	do	83	
Adam Bicker	do	30 00	90 00	do	Mar. 6, 1834	do	79	
William Cowen	Pri. ser. & lieut	113 59	340 77	Penn. St. troops	Oct. 20, 1832	do	79	
Edward Coen	Private	43 33	108 33	Penn. militia	Aug. 9, 1833	do	79	
James Carter	do	30 00	90 00	Virginia militia	do	do	78	
John Dennie	do	33 78	191 34	N. Jersey militia	June 22, 1833	do	74	
Robert Dickey	do	20 00	50 00	N. Jersey militia	May 13, 1833	do	82	
Robert English	do	20 66	79 98	N. Jersey militia	May 3, 1833	do	78	
John Hulick	do	80 00	240 00	N. J. State troops	Dec. 5, 1832	do	79	
Christopher Hartman	do	80 00	162 82	N. Jersey militia	May 14, 1833	do	84	
James Johnson	do	46 66	116 65	Penn. militia	Aug. 29, 1833	do	83	
Thomas Jones	do	28 33	70 83	Maryland St. troops	June 22, 1833	do	77	
Ignatius Knott	do	80 00	240 00	Maryland militia	Sep. 24, 1833	do	87	
Robert Leeds	do	40 00	120 00	N. Jersey militia	July 25, 1833	do	77	
Barton Law	do	20 00	60 00	Penn. militia	Ap'l 28, 1834	do	72	

Statement, &c. of Clermont county—Continued.

NAMES.	Rank.	Annual allowance.	Sums received.	Description of service.	When placed on the pension roll.	Commencement of pension.	Ages.	Laws under which they were formerly inscribed on the pension roll; and remarks.
Thomas Manning	Private	80 00	240 00	Conn. continental	Dec. 13, 1832	Mar. 4, 1831	69	
Cornelius McCollum	Ensign	240 00	720 00	N. Jersey militia	June 22, 1833	do	85	
John Malott	Private	80 00	240 00	Maryland militia	June 26, 1833	do	76	
Dory Malott	do	80 00	240 00	do	do	do	79	
Hugh Mullay	Lieutenant	320 00	960 00	Mass. continental	Aug. 3, 1833	do	82	Died August 2, 1835.
James McKay	Private	23 33	56 32	Maryland militia	Sep. 16, 1833	do	81	
John Nelson	do	20 00	60 00	Penn. militia	Mar. 28, 1833	do	71	
Christian Plakard	do	23 33	69 99	do	June 11, 1833	do	78	
Josiah Prickett	do	36 66	109 99	do	July 27, 1833	do	71	
Nathaniel Reeven	do	39 43	118 29	New York militia	June 11, 1833	do	77	
John Smith	Pri. & ser.	80 00	240 00	Mass. continental	Oct. 26, 1832	do	77	
John Stewart	Private	35 00	105 00	Penn. militia	Mar. 28, 1833	do	79	
Ephraim Simpkin	do	48 33	144 99	N. Jersey militia	June 22, 1833	do	78	
Philip Stoner	do	50 00	125 00	Penn. militia	Aug. 24, 1833	do	70	
Elijah Sergeant	do	21 66	64 98	Maryland militia	Aug. 29, 1833	do	76	
Absalom Smith	do	40 00	120 00	N. Jersey militia	Sep. 23, 1833	do	78	
John Thomas	do	20 00	60 00	Virginia militia	Oct. 20, 1832	do	70	
Richard Taliaferro	do	80 00	240 00	Virginia St. troops	June 25, 1833	do	72	
John Wheeler	do	50 00	150 00	Mass. militia	Oct. 26, 1832	do	79	
Samuel Webster	Pri. & ser.	71 66	214 98	N. Hamp. cont'l	Dec. 18, 1832	do	85	
Samuel Wilson	Private	22 22	66 66	Penn. militia	May 13, 1833	do	78	
Nehemiah Ward	do	56 66	169 98	N. Jersey cont'l	June 25, 1833	do	78	
Samuel Walburn	do	80 00	240 00	Virginia St. troops	Aug. 24, 1833	do	72	

Statement, &c. of Columbiana county, Ohio.

NAMES.	Rank.	Annual allow-ance.	Sums re-ceived.	Description of ser-vice.	When placed on the pen-sion roll.	Commencement of pension.	Ages.	Laws under which they were for-merly inscribed on the pension roll; and remarks.
John Allerton	Private	43 33	129 99	N. Jersey militia	Jan. 3, 1833	Mar. 4, 1831	74	
Joseph Applegate	do	30 00	90 00	Pennsylvania militia	July 22, 1834	do	74	
Philip Bowman	Ensign	240 00	720 00	Maryland State tr.	Dec. 20, 1832	do	78	
Samuel Bunton	Private	20 00	40 00	N. Jersey State tr.	Jan. 3, 1833	do	75	
Barnhart Bothman	do	40 00	100 00	Virginia cont'l	Jan. 21, 1833	do	80	
Moses Blackburn	do	23 33	58 32	Pennsylvania mil.	Aug. 8, 1833	do	80	
James Boyd	do	28 33	84 99	Pennsylvania cont.	Sep. 21, 1833	do	74	
John Carmoody	do	80 00	240 00	Penn'a State troops	Dec. 3, 1832	do	85	
James Clark	do	25 55	76 65	Virginia State tr.	Dec. 20, 1832	do	91	
Stout Chamberlain	do	40 00	120 00	Penn'a State troops	Jan. 3, 1833	do	77	
John Crozer	Pri. & ser.	30 00	90 00	N. Jersey State tr.	May 9, 1833	do	81	
John Coburn	Private	20 00	60 00	Pennsylvania mil.	Oct. 25, 1833	do	79	
Reuben Howell	Sergeant	35 00	105 00	Virginia continenal	Mar. 1, 1833	do	72	
Jacob Johnston	Private	26 66	53 32	N. York State tr.	Jan. 21, 1833	do	89	
Thomas Kent	do	24 11	60 27	Virginia State tr.	Oct. 25, 1833	do	87	
Samuel Lyons	do	80 00	240 00	Pennsylvania mil.	Jan. 17, 1834	do	73	
David McKinsley	do	70 00	210 00	Penn'a State troops	Nov. 20, 1832	do	75	
William Murrel	do	33 33	66 66	N. Jersey State tr.	Nov. 24, 1832	do	75	
Andrew Milburn	do	40 00	120 00	Virginia State tr.	Jan. 3, 1833	do	71	
James McClellen	do	20 00	50 00	Virginia militia	Jan. 3, 1833	do	75	
William Mankin	do	30 00	90 00	Maryland militia	Jan. 26, 1833	do	74	
John Might	do	40 00	120 00	S. Carolina St. tr.	Jan. 3, 1833	do	77	
William Nicholas	do	46 66	139 98	Penn'a State troops	Feb. 9, 1833	do	75	
Samuel Quigley	do	26 66	79 98	Pennsylvania mil.	Dec. 18, 1832	do	77	
John Quin	do	40 00	120 00	do	Mar. 2, 1833	do	74	
Adam Rupart	do	66 66	199 98	Pennsylvania cont'l	Oct. 9, 1832	do	77	
Jacob Shawke	do	63 33	189 99	Flying camp Penn.	Nov. 27, 1832	do	76	
Amos Sharp	do	23 33	69 99	N Jersey State tr.	July 6, 1833	do	78	
William Sanders	do	20 00	-	Pennsylvania mil.	Sep. 28, 1833	do	88	
William Scheenhan	do	60 00	180 00	Virginia militia	Dec. 28, 1832	do	82	
Owen Thomas	do	23 86	71 58	Pennsylvania mil.	Feb. 9, 1833	do	80	
Jonathan Willington	do	60 00	163 60	Virginia militia	Jan. 3, 1833	do	97	Died February 26, 1834.

Statement, &c. of Cuyahoga county, Ohio.

NAMES.	Rank.	Annual allowance.	Sums received.	Description of service.	When placed on the pension roll.	Commencement of pension.	Ages.	Laws under which they were formerly inscribed on the pension roll; and remarks.
Ebenezer Abbott	Private	26 66	79 98	Mass. State troops	Nov. 14, 1832	Mar. 4, 1831	80	
Thomas Aiken	do	46 66	139 98	Connecticut cont'l	Apr. 27, 1833	do	86	
Amos Brainard	Pri. & cor.	82 66	218 65	Connecticut State	Oct. 23, 1832	do	76	
John Campbell	Private	80 00	240 00	N. Y. State troops	Nov. 14, 1832	do	72	
Nathan Cummins	do	80 00	240 00	Massachusetts con.	Mar. 28, 1833	do	76	
Samuel Copley	do	36 33	108 99	Connecticut mil.	July 6, 1833	do	76	
Jedediah Crocker	Pri. & ser.	32 76	—	Mass. State troops	Feb. 4, 1834	do	73	
Samuel Dean	Private	31 66	94 98	Mass. State	Mar. 28, 1833	do	79	
Calvin Dike	do	80 00	200 00	Vermont State	Aug. 1, 1833	do	73	
Adin Dike	do	80 00	240 00	do	do	do	76	
David Diller	Lt. & ser.	215 84	646 52	Virginia militia	Jan. 31, 1834	do	79	
William W. Ellsworth	Pri. & ser.	106 66	319 98	New York State	Mar. 28, 1833	do	71	
John Forgison	Private	80 00	240 00	New York militia	Aug. 20, 1833	do	77	
Jacob Gaudinier	do	60 00	180 00	Massachusetts mil.	Aug. 1, 1833	do	76	
Joshua Hudson	do	73 33	219 99	Conn. State troops	Oct. 18, 1832	do	74	
Roswell Humphrey	do	38 90	116 70	do	Nov. 14, 1832	do	69	
John Hall	Pri. & ser.	80 00	240 00	R. Island militia	Mar. 29, 1833	do	75	
Jacob Hutchinson	Private	80 00	240 00	Mass. State troops	do	do	75	
Abner Hull	do	43 89	131 67	Connecticut cont'l	May 7, 1833	do	75	
Pary Hardey	do	64 67	194 01	New Hamp. cont'l	July 6, 1833	do	76	
Edward Halstead	do	80 00	240 00	New York State	Oct. 2, 1833	do	83	
William Johnson	Sergeant	120 00	—	Massachusetts con.	Aug. 20, 1832	do	76	Transferred from New York, from March 4, 1834.
Elias Keys	Private	33 33	99 99	Mass. State	Apr. 27, 1833	do	71	
Andrew McIlrath	do	80 00	240 00	Conn. State	Oct. 23, 1832	do	76	
John Minar	do	80 00	240 00	Connecticut mil.	Feb. 5, 1834	do	71	
Joshua Palmitor	do	35 00	105 00	R. Island militia	Apr. 27, 1833	do	74	
David Perkins	do	20 00	50 00	Massachusetts mil.	Sep. 21, 1833	do	69	
John Palmiter	do	40 00	120 00	Connecticut cont'l	Nov. 5, 1833	do	80	
Daniel Richardson	do	38 21	114 63	New Hamp. cont'l	Apr. 10, 1833	do	70	
Edmund Rathbone	do	63 33	189 99	R. Island militia	Nov. 5, 1833	do	77	

Names	Rank.	Annual allowance.	Sums received.	Description of service.	When placed on the pension roll.	Commencement of pension.	Ages.
Hugh Stewart	do	36 66	109 98	Mass. State	Mar. 29, 1833	do	73
Phinehas Shepherd	do	80 00	240 00	Connecticut cont'l	Apr. 13, 1833	do	77
Claudius Stannard	do	50 00	150 00	Connecticut mil.	Oct. 9, 1833	do	70
Joseph Upson	do	22 50	56 25	Mass. mil. & State	May 7, 1833	do	85
Moses Warren	do	60 00	180 00	Mass. State troops	do	do	74
Josiah Wilcox	do	33 33	83 32	Massachusetts mil.	Aug. 1. 1833	do	81

Statement, &c. of Dark county, Ohio.

Names.	Rank.	Annual allowance.	Sums received.	Description of service.	When placed on the pension roll.	Commencement of pension.	Ages.	Laws under which they were formerly inscribed on the pension roll; and remarks.
William Brodrick	Pri. & ser.	33 33	99 99	N. J. militia	June 11, 1833	Mar. 4, 1831	74	
William Byers	Private	25 00	75 00	Virginia militia	Jan. 27, 1834	do	70	
Christopher Borders	do	20 00		do	May 30, 1834	do	71	
Jonathan Pearson	do	48 44	145 32	N. C, militia	May 6, 1833	do	77	
John Reed	do	26 66	79 98	Maryland militia	Ap'l 11, 1833	do	76	
William Walker	do	26 66	79 98	Virginia militia	Dec. 27, 1833	do	75	
David Ward	do	20 00	60 00	Penn. militia	Jan. 27, 1834	do	73	

Statement, &c. of Delaware county, Ohio.

NAMES.	Rank.	Annual allowance.	Sums received.	Description of service.	When placed on the pension roll.	Commencement of pension.	Ages.	Laws under which they were formerly inscribed on the pension roll; and remarks.
David Adams	Private	40 00	120 00	N. Jersey St. troops	Mar. 20, 1833	Mar. 4, 1831	73	
Ezekiel Brown	do	80 00	240 00	Penn. State troops	Mar. 22, 1833	do	74	
John Budd	do	36 66	109 98	do	do	do	84	
Thomas Beddo	do	30 00	90 00	Maryland St. troops	do	do	73	
Harman Coykendall	do	80 00	160 00	New York militia	do	do	78	
George Case	do	40 00	80 00	Connecticut militia	Mar. 23, 1833	do	75	
Benjamin Collins	do	80 00	240 00	New York militia	July 26, 1833	do	85	
Thomas DeFord	do	26 66	53 32	Maryland militia	June 22, 1833	do	98	
Alexander Dixon	do	23 33	55 33	Vermont militia	Aug. 8, 1833	do	69	
Jacob Fisher	do	23 33	69 99	Penn. State troops	Mar. 22, 1833	do	77	
Jacob Foust	do	30 00	60 00	Pennsylvania militia	June 22, 1833	do	77	
Joseph Gillett	do	23 33	58 33	Connecticut militia	Aug. 8, 1833	do	84	
James Gregory	do	80 00	200 00	Conn. State troops	Aug. 23, 1833	do	70	
Zinery Hills	do	26 66	79 98	Connecticut militia	Mar. 22, 1833	do	72	
Nathaniel Hawlen	do	20 00	40 00	New Jersey militia	Mar. 23, 1833	do	77	
Philo Hoadly	do	40 00	120 00	Connecticut militia	do	do	71	
John Hamlin	do	32 22	80 55	New Jersey militia	do	do	75	
Andrew Himrod	do	45 00	135 00	Pennsylvania militia	Mar. 21, 1833	do	71	
John Hoff	Sergeant	58 66	175 98	New Jersey militia	do	do	74	
Ebenezer Landon	Private	35 44	106 32	Connecticut militia	Mar. 22, 1833	do	74	
Simeon Linsly	do	29 00	58 00	. do	June 22, 1833	do	73	
James L. Moore	do	80 00	240 00	Pennsylvania militia	Mar. 20, 1833	do	78	
Peres Main	do	46 66	116 65	Connecticut militia	Oct. 24, 1833	do	71	
John Minter	do	120 00	360 00	Pennsylvania militia	Feb. 26, 1833	do	76	
Benjamin Newell	do	53 33	159 99	Rhode Island militia	Oct. 24, 1833	do	68	
Peleg Place	do.	80 00	200 00	Pennsylvania militia	July 25, 1833	do	73	
William Reed	do	20 00	40 00	do	Mar. 21, 1833	do	83	
Azariah Root	do	25 00	62 50	Mass. militia	Aug. 23, 1833	do	74	
Abel Spalding	do	23 33	46 66	Vermont militia	Mar. 22, 1833	do	70	
Silas Smith	do	80 00	240 00	Pennsylvania cont'l?	July 25, 1833	do	73	

NAMES.		Annual allowance.	Sums received.	Description of service.	When placed on the pension roll.	Commencement of pension.	Ages.	Laws under which they were formerly inscribed on the pension roll; and remarks.
Simeon Smith	do	80 00	200 00	Mass. militia & New York continental	Aug. 8, 1833	do	78	
John Williams	do	40 00	80 00	New York militia	Mar. 22, 1833	do	90	
Jehiel Wilcox	do	80 00	240 00	Conn. mil. & cont'l	do	do	76	
Christian Young	do	80 00	240 00	New York militia	Mar. 20, 1833	do	82	
Morgan Young	do	30 00	90 00	New Jersey militia	Mar. 22, 1833	do	82	

Statement, &c. of Fairfield county, Ohio.

NAMES.	Rank.	Annual allowance.	Sums received.	Description of service.	When placed on the pension roll.	Commencement of pension.	Ages.	Laws under which they were formerly inscribed on the pension roll; and remarks.
John Alspach	Private	80 00	240 00	Penn. State troops	May 10, 1833	Mar. 4, 1831	82	
Michael Alspach	Lieutenant	137 83	413 49	Penn. militia	May 27, 1833	do	86	
David Buffington	Private	76 66	229 98	Virginia cont'l	Jan. 8, 1833	do	72	
Charles Bowling	do	25 66	76 98	Virginia militia	Sep. 12, 1833	do	70	
William Bowling	do	25 33	63 33	do	do	do	75	
James Crawford	Pri. & sea.	44 00	132 00	Mass. State troops	Jan. 15, 1832	do	83	
Benjamin Cave	Private	70 00	210 00	Virginia State tr'ps	do	do	74	
Joshua Critchfield	Pri & art'r	124 67	374 01	Maryland cont'l	June 26, 1833	do	81	
Christopher Embrek	Private	40 00	120 00	Penn. State troops	Jan. 8, 1833	do	78	
Philip Ebright	do	80 00	240 00	Penn. continental	Jan. 15, 1833	do	80	
Henry Eyman	do	40 00	120 00	do	June 22, 1833	do	76	
Thomas Elsey	do	80 00	240 00	Maryland militia	Ap'l 8, 1833	do	74	
John Fisher	do	26 66	53 32	Maryland State tps.	Feb. 12, 1833	do	72	
William Hopwood	do	23 33	46 66	Virginia militia	Jan. 8, 1833	do	70	
Ef'aim Hubbert	do	37 32	111 96	N. Jersey militia	June 26, 1833	do	76	
Michael Hensel	do	60 00	180 00	Virginia militia	Aug. 23, 1833	do	80	
Edward Irvin	do	20 00	40 00	Penn. militia	June 22, 1833	do	85	
Daniel Lambrecht	do	33 33	99 99	do	Mar. 19, 1834	do	84	

Statement, &c. of Fairfield county—Continued.

NAMES.	Rank.	Annual allowance.	Sums received.	Description of service.	When placed on the pension roll.	Commencement of pension.	Ages.	Laws under which they were formerly inscribed on the pension roll; and remarks.
Robert McClelland	Private	20 00	60 00	Penn. militia	Jan. 8, 1833	Mar. 4, 1831	82	
James Morris	do	20 00	60 00	Virginia militia	Ap'l 11, 1833	do	77	
Walter Newman	do	80 00	240 00	Penn. militia	Jan. 8, 1833	do	73	
Jacob Ream	do	43 33	108 32	do	May 10, 1833	do	80	
John Reynolds	do	80 00	240 00	Penn. continental	Sep. 21, 1833	do	79	
Elijah Russell	do	80 00	240 00	Virginia cont'l	Nov. 16, 1833	do	76	
Peter Sturgeon	do	23 33	46 66	Penn. militia	Jan. 8, 1833	do	78	
William Shoemaker	do	80 00	240 00	do	Jan. 9, 1834	do	91	
Benjamin Turner	do	33 33	-	Maryland militia	Ap'l 8, 1834	do	71	
George Vallentine	do	60 00	-	Penn. militia	Aug. 8, 1833	do	84	
Peter Woodring	do	33 33	99 99	do	Jan. 8, 1833	do	77	
David Wright	do	46 66	116 65	Penn. continental	do	do	83	

Statement, &c. of Fayette county, Ohio.

NAMES.	Rank.	Annual allowance.	Sums received.	Description of service.	When placed on the pension roll.	Commencement of pension.	Ages.	Laws under which they were formerly inscribed on the pension roll; and remarks.
Sanford Carder	Pri. of cav.	75 00	225 00	Virginia St. troops	Jan. 16, 1832	Mar. 4, 1831	74	
John Priddy	Private	20 00	50 00	Virginia militia	Jan. 16, 1833	do	76	
George Rupert	do	80 00	240 00	Virginia St. troops	Ap'l 6, 1833	do	75	
Jesse Rowe	do	32 11	-	Virginia militia	Ap'l 2, 1833	do	79	
Charles Sexton	do	23 33	58 33	N. Jersey militia	Jan. 16, 1833	do	72	
Burnet Williams	do	80 00	240 00	N. J. continental	do	do	84	
James Wilty	do	80 00	240 00	N. C. continental	July 25, 1833	do	73	
Wm. Whicher	do	30 00	75 00	N. Carolina militia	Aug. 9, 1833	do	71	

Statement, &c. of Franklin county, Ohio.

NAMES.	Rank.	Annual allowance.	Sums received.	Description of service.	When placed on the pension roll.	Commencement of pension.	Ages.	Laws under which they were formerly inscribed on the pension roll; and remarks.
James Armstrong	Private	23 33	69 99	Penn. State troops	April 5, 1833	Mar. 4, 1831	73	
George Baughman	do	30 00	93 22	do	Ap'l 26, 1833	do	79	Died April 13, 1834.
Nathaniel Babcock	do	33 33	99 99	Conn. St. tr. & mil.	June 25, 1833	do	69	
Mathias Deagne	do	50 00	150 00	Pennsylvania militia	Oct. 12, 1833	do	79	
Henry Fix	do	60 00	180 00	do	do	do	83	
Isaac Fisher	do	20 00	60 00	New Jersey militia	Mar. 6, 1834	do	68	
Richard Gale	do	66 66	199 98	New York do	Sep. 21, 1833	do	76	
John Hoover	do	20 00	60 00	Pennsylvania do	April 5, 1833	do	79	
Joseph Ingalls	do	38 00	114 00	N. H continental	Mar. 15, 1834	do	82	
Joseph Mapes	do	50 00	150 00	New Jersey cont'l	April 5, 1833	do	73	
Henry Miller	do	80 00	200 00	Pennsylvania cont'l	Apr'l 11, 1833	do	76	
William McComb	do	23 33	58 33	Pennsylvania militia	Nov. 25, 1833	do	75	
William Patterson	do	20 00	50 00	do	May 6, 1833	do	72	
John Starrett	do	70 00	210 00	do	April 5, 1833	do	77	
Roger Smith	do	36 66	91 65	Connecticut militia	May 28, 1833	do	76	
John Trusler	do	30 00	90 00	Virginia militia	Oct. 12, 1833	do	76	
Isaiah Vory	do	80 00	282 00	N. J. militia	May 3, 1833	do	84	
John Whetherholt	do	80 00	240 00	N. J. continental	Oct. 8, 1832	do	88	Transferred from Washington co., D. C., from 4th March, 1833.

16

Statement, &c. of Gallia county, Ohio.

NAMES	Rank.	Annual allowance.	Sums received.	Description of service.	When placed on the pension roll.	Commencement of pension.	Ages.	Laws under which they were formerly inscribed on the pension roll; and remarks.
James Blakely	Private	34 66	103 98	Connecticut militia	May 28, 1833	Mar. 4, 1831	73	
William Carel	do	25 20	63 00	Maryland State tr.	Dec. 12, 1832	do	77	
Moses Gee	do	26 66	79 98	N. York State tr.	Dec. 5, 1832	do	74	
Abraham Haptinstall	do	60 00	180 00	N. York militia	May 28, 1833	do	73	
Jonathan Huges	do	45 66	136 98	Virginia militia	Ap'l 12, 1834	do	81	
David Keeton	do	60 00	180 00	do	Dec. 5, 1832	do	78	
William Loucks	do	80 00	240 00	Pennsylvania mil.	May 6, 1833	do	84	
Jacob Louts	do	20 00	50 00	Virginia militia	May 28, 1833	do	73	
Jordan Manning	do	53 32	159 96	Delaware militia	Ap'l 6, 1833	do	74	
James Martindale	Lieutenant	320 00	960 00	S. Carolina militia	July 27, 1833	do	81	
Henry McDaniel	Pri. of cav.	100 00	-	Virginia State tr.	Ap'l 3, 1834	do	71	
Adam Richabaugh	Private	40 00	120 00	Virgin a militia	Ap'l 15, 1833	do	73	
Charles Russell	do	30 00	75 00	do	Oct. 12, 1833	do	75	
Philip Switzon	do	60 00	180 00	do	Dec. 5, 1832	do	76	
David Sprouse	do	60 00	180 00	do	Ap'l 6, 1833	do	74	
John Strait	do	80 00	240 00	R. Island cont'l	June 25, 1833	do	76	
Gideon Viah	do	68 88	206 64	Virginia militia	Dec. 15, 1832	do	79	
Benjamin Viers	do	80 00	240 00	Virginia cont'l	May 28, 1833	do	82	
Daniel Wigner	do	70 00	210 00	Pennsylvania mil.	Dec. 5, 1832	do	79	
William Wass'n	do	26 66	66 65	do	July 27, 1833	do	82	
William Williams	do	60 00	-	Virginia militia	Nov. 13, 1833	do	74	
Benjamin Williams	do	80 00	240 00	N. Carolina militia	Jan. 9, 1834	do	72	

Statement, &c. of Geauga county, Ohio.

NAMES.	Rank.	Annual allowance.	Sums received.	Description of service.	When placed on the pension roll.	Commencement of pension.	Ages.	Laws under which they were formerly inscribed on the pension roll; and remarks.
John Abel	Pri & cor.	37 83	113 49	Conn. State troops	Ap'l 20, 1833	Mar. 4, 1831	76	
David Alden	Private	23 89	71 67	Mass. militia	July 20, 1833	do	76	
Thaddeus Bradley	do	66 66	199 98	Conn. militia	May 30, 1833	do	77	
Moses Barnes	do	20 00	60 00	N. J. State troops	June 6, 1833	do	89	
Zadock Benton	do	68 00	204 00		Aug. 1, 1833	do	74	
Elisha Bridgman	do	56 66	-	Mass. State troops	Jan. 12, 1833	do	74	Transferred from Massachusetts from March 4, 1834, June 1834.
Tracy Cleaveland	do	36 66	109 98	Conn. State troops	Nov. 28, 1833	do	84	
Samuel Cleaveland	do	30 00	90 00	Mass. State troops	Ap'l 27, 1833	do	81	
Merriman Cook	do	41 65	124 95	Conn. militia	May 30, 1833	do	73	
Abraham Daman	do	33 11	99 33	Mass. State troops	Ap'l 27, 1833	do	75	
Andrew Durand	do	66 66	199 98	Conn. militia	May 30, 1833	do	72	
Stephen Dunwell	do	80 00	240 00	Conr. continental	Sep. 13, 1832	du	71	Transferred from New York from September 4, 1833, December, 1833.
William R. Eddy	do	33 33	99 99	Mass. militia	Sep. 21, 1833	do	74	
John Elliott	do	80 00	240 00	Mass. continental	Nov. 23, 1832	do	83	
Joseph Emmerson	do	33 33	99 99	Mass. State troops	May 7, 1833	do	80	
Eliab Egleston	do	80 00	240 00	N. York militia	July 24, 1833	do	72	
Joshua Emmis	do	38 00	114 00	Mass. continental	Sep. 17, 1833	do	82	
Nathan French	do	40 00	120 00	Mass. State troops	Nov. 23, 1832	do	74	
Israel Fox	do	50 00	125 00	Conn. State troops	Ap'l 13, 1833	do	79	
Nathan Ford	do	24 74	74 22	Mass. militia	May 30, 1833	do	73	
Lemuel Fobes	do	40 00	120 00	Mass. militia	May 15, 1833	do	80	
Andrew Ford	do	26 66	66 65	Mass. State troops	Nov. 1, 1833	do	81	
Seba French	do	46 66	139 98	Mass. State troops	Sep. 17, 1833	do	73	
John Green	do	80 00	240 00	Mass. State troops	Dec. 26, 1832	do	78	
Jonathan Gardner	Pri. & ser.	35 55	106 65	N. J. State troops	Ap'l 20, 1833	do	87	
Daniel Gelson	Private	50 00	125 00	Mass. State troops	Nov. 5, 1833	do	72	
Samuel Heminway	do	24 33	72 99	do	July 24, 1832	do	78	

Statement, &c. of Geauga county--Continued.

NAMES.	Rank.	Annual allowance.	Sums received.	Description of service.	When placed on the pension roll.	Commencement of pensions.	Ages.	Laws under which they were formerly inscribed on the pension roll; and remarks.
Moses Hutchins	Private	80 00	240 00	Mass. St. troops	Aug. 1, 1833	Mar. 4, 1831	74	
Nathaniel Hickox	Pri. & drag.	58 80	176 40	Conn. continental	Dec. 5, 1832	do	76	Transferred from Pennsylvania from September 4, 1833; Dec. 1833.
Ebenezer Hopkins	Private	80 00	240 00	V't State troops	Feb. 9, 1834	do	71	
Samuel Hayden	do	30 00	75 00	Conn. State troops	Sep. 17, 1833	do	86	
Elijah Hanks	do	26 66	79 98	Conn. militia	Mar. 21, 1834	do	73	
Elkanah Jones	do	43 33	129 99	do	Sep. 16, 1833	do	73	
Ebenezer Joy	do	71 66	214 98	do	Sep. 17, 1833	do	70	
Benjamin King	do	20 00	60 00	do	Nov. 23, 1832	do	91	
Abel Kimball	do	20 00	60 00	N. H. State troops	Ap'l 2, 1833	do	72	
Joseph Lane	do	53 33	159 99	N. York militia	Sep. 21, 1833	do	73	
Thomas Morley	do	33 33	83 32	Connecticut militia	July 24, 1833	do	76	
Isaac Marlin	do	53 33	88 87	do	Sep. 12, 1833	do	75	
Peter Markell	do	43 33	129 99	N. York militia	Mar. 24, 1834	do	69	Died Nov. 6, 1832.
Ezekiel Morley	do	80 00	-	Mass. continental	May 2, 1833	do	75	Transferred from New York from March 4, 1834, June 1834.
Ichabod Pomery	do	60 00	180 00	Mass. State troops	Nov. 23, 1832	do	77	
Daniel Pomery	do	33 33	99 99	Connecticut militia	Nov. 23, 1833	do	82	
Edward Paine	Captain	480 00	1,440 00	do	Jan. 3, 1833	do	88	
Amaziah Pa k	Private	20 56	61 68	Conn. continental	May 7, 1833	do	75	
Isaac Pease	do	33 33	99 99	Connecticut militia	July 6, 1833	do	82	
Nathan Parks	do	66 66	199 98	Mass. continental	Sep. 24, 1833	do	76	
Gideon Russell	do	43 55	130 65	Connecticut cont'l	Ap'l 22, 1834	do	75	
John Reynolds	Sergeant	96 00	-	do	Ap'l 6, 1818	June 12, 1819	74	March 18, 1818. Suspended under the act May 7, 1820.
Do	do	120 00	300 00	do	Nov. 2, 1832	Mar. 4, 1831	-	Act June 7, 1832. Pens'd again.
Samuel Russell	Private	36 66	109 98	Mass. State troops	Oct. 23, 1832	do	77	
Benjamin Rider	do	74 55	223 65	do	Dec. 26, 1832	do	71	
Samuel Rogers	do	36 66	109 98	N. Hamp. State tr.	Dec. 10, 1832	do	68	Transferred from N. Hampshire from Mar. 4, 1833, Dec. 1833.

NAMES.	Rank.	Annual allowance.	Sums received	Description of service.	When placed on the pension roll.	Commencement of pension.	Ages.	Laws under which they were formerly inscribed on the pension roll ; and remarks.
David Smith	do	45 67	137 01	Connecticut militia	May 7, 1833	do	71	
Peter Thompson	do	20 00	60 00	N. Hamp. State tr.	Nov. 23, 1832	do	78	
Asa Turney	do	80 00	-	Connecticut St. tr.	May 3, 1833	do	75	
Retire Trask	do	30 00	90 00	Pennsylvania mil.	Ap'l 28, 1832	do	73	
Bartholomew Vrooman	do	80 00	240 00	N. York State tr.	Sep. 16, 1833	do	73	

Statement, &c. of Greene county, Ohio.

NAMES.	Rank.	Annual allowance.	Sums received	Description of service.	When placed on the pension roll.	Commencement of pension.	Ages.	Laws under which they were formerly inscribed on the pension roll ; and remarks.
Robert Cusbott	Private	80 00	240 00	Penn. continental	Sept. 27, 1832	Mar. 4, 1831	80	Transferred from Tioga county, Penn'a, from Sept. 4, 1833.
Richard Cunningham	do	80 00	240 00	Penn. militia	May 4, 1833	do	77	
James Campbell	do	74 43	-	N. York State tr.	Dec. 12, 1832	do	71	
George Deeds	do	26 66	79 98	Virginia cont'l	Ap'l 11, 1833	do	71	
Wm. F. R. Davis	do	33 33	83 33	Maryland militia	Aug. 23, 1833	do	71	
James Galloway	do	37 18	111 54	Penn. militia	May 23, 1833	do	84	
Robert Harbinson	do	56 67	170 01	do	July 27, 1833	do	76	
George Hiney	do	76 66	-	do	Oct. 12, 1833	do	79	
George Mallow	Ens. & pri.	92 22	276 66	Virginia militia	Ap'l 2, 1833	do	82	
John Musgrave	Private	36 66	109 98	Maryland militia	July 27, 1833	do	74	
Alexander McIlhatton	Maj. & lt. colonel	150 00	450 00	Pennsylvania mil.	Aug. 9, 1833	do	90	
Ashur Reaves	Private	43 33	129 99	Virginia militia	Aug. 8, 1833	do	77	
John Sanders	do	80 00	240 00	N. Jersey cont'l	May 6, 1833	do	81	
Samuel Snodgrass	do	29 11	87 33	Pennsylvania mil.	May 10, 1833	do	79	
James Small	do	40 00	120 00	do	May 23, 1833	do	77	
George Stepp	do	21 56	53 90	Virginia militia	Aug. 8, 1833	do	77	
Henry Seaman	do	80 00	240 00	do	May 3, 1833	do	76	
Thomas Townsley	do	80 00	60 00	Pennsylvania mil.	Mar. 25, 1833	do	79	
John Torrence	do	35 83	107 49	do	May 3, 1833	do	76	
Amos Thatcher	do	80 00	240 00	N. Jersey militia	Jan. 9, 1834	do	79	
Stephen Winter	do	29 44	88 32	Pennsylvania mil.	July 27, 1833	do	82	

Statement, &c, of Guernsey county, Ohio.

NAMES.	Rank.	Annual allowance.	Sums received.	Description of service.	When placed on the pension roll.	Commencement of pension.	Ages.	Laws under which they were formerly inscribed on the pension roll; and remarks.
James Bratten	Private	20 00	60 00	Penn. State troops	Ap'l 6, 1833	Mar. 4, 1831	77	
John Baird	do	20 00	60 00	Pennsylvania militia	May 9, 1833	do	75	
Robert Bay	do	60 00	180 00	do	May 13, 1833	do	74	
Jared Bailey	Pr. & cor.	81 67	245 01	Connecticut militia	Ap'l 28, 1834	do	76	
John Cummins	Private	80 00	240 00	New Jersey State	Ap'l 16, 1833	do	83	
Ephraim Dilley, sen.	do	20 00	60 00	New Jersey militia	July 6, 1833	do	79	
Joseph Eatton	do	80 00	142 39	Pennsylvania cont'l	Mar. 23, 1833	do	78	Died December 5, 1832.
Adam Linn	Sergeant	120 00	300 00	do	Jan. 4, 1833	do	85	
Garret Matthews	Private	50 00	150 00	New Jersey militia	Aug. 8, 1833	do	84	
Robert Porter	Pri. & ser.	56 66	169 98	Pennsylvania militia	Nov. 21, 1833	do	79	
Isaac Tobin	Private	23 33	69 99	New Jersey cont'l	Oct. 25, 1833	do	74	
Samuel White	do	37 44	-	N. Hampshire State	May 9, 1833	do	74	
William Waller	do	80 00	136 16	Virginia cont'l	-	do	79	Died September 21, 1832.

Statement, &c. of Hamilton county, Ohio.

NAMES.	Rank.	Annual allowance.	Sums received.	Description of service.	When placed on the pension roll.	Commencement of pension.	Age.	Laws under which they were formerly inscribed on the pension roll; and remarks.
Ebenezer Baldwin	Private	80 00	240 00	Conn. continental	Oct. 19, 1832	Mar. 4, 1831	69	
Aaron Bonnel	Pri. & artfi.	88 00	264 00	N. Jersey contin'l	May 10, 1833	do	75	
Jacob Broadwell	Private	40 00	120 00	N. J. continental	May 14, 1833	do	67	
Adam Boss	do	26 66	61 11	Maryland militia	June 26, 1833	do	71	
John Brasher	Pri. & mus.	80 33	240 99	New York militia	Sept. 21, 1833	do	70	Died June 19, 1833.
William Brewster	Private	80 00	240 00	N. Y. State troops	Oct. 19, 1833	do	71	
Jeremiah Bunores	Sergeant	60 00	180 00	Maryland militia	Ap'l 17, 1834	do	82	
John Cavender	Private	20 00	60 00	Del. State troops	Nov. 30, 1832	do	74	
Dannis Clark	Sergeant	60 00	87 76	Penn. State troops	Dec. 5, 1832	do	78	Diel August 20, 1832.
Nathaniel Clark	Private	73 33	118 31	Mass. continental	June 26, 1833	do	75	Diel October 14, 1832.
John Charlton	do	56 00	168 00	N. Jersey militia	Dec. 2, 1833	do	74	
Andrew Cox	do	80 00	240 00	Virginia militia	Feb. 4, 1834	do	74	
Jehiel Day	do	30 00	90 00	do	Ap'l 17, 1834	do	77	
John Campbell	do	20 00	40 00	N. Jersey militia	Ap'l 2, 1833	do	76	
Henry Deat	do	80 00	240 00	do	May 22, 1833	do	74	
Joshua Davis	do	80 00	240 00	do	Aug. 21, 1833	do	74	
Benjamin Enyart	do	33 33	83 33	do	May 28, 1833	do	74	
Jonas Frazee	do	80 00	240 00	do	Aug. 9, 1833	do	75	
William Finch	Pri. & ser.	80 00	240 00	Conn. continental	Oct. 8, 1833	do	71	
Benjamin Flinn	Private	115 00	345 00	N. Jersey militia	Jan. 6, 1834	do	68	
Reuben Gage	do	20 00	60 00	Virginia militia	Mar. 23, 1834	do	74	
Henry Gunsaluss	do	40 00	—	New York militia	July 16, 1834	do	73	
James Hillyer	do	45 00	135 00	N. J. State troops	Oct. 20, 1832	do	87	
James Harthorn	Lieutenant	160 00	480 00	Penn. continental	Oct. 24, 1832	do	80	
John Holstead	Private	80 00	240 00	N Jersey contin'l	Dec. 18, 1832	do	68	
Gershom Hubbell	do	30 00	75 00	N. Y. State troops	Mar. 5, 1833	do	76	
Oliver Hayes	do	33 33	99 99	Conn. militia	May 3, 1833	do	78	
Frederick Horn	do	40 00	120 00	Penn. continental	do	do	78	
Solomon Howard	do	43 33	129 99	Conn. State troops	do	do	73	
Ebenezer R. Hawley	do	80 00	240 00	Penn. militia	Jan. 27, 1834	do	74	

Statement, &c. of Hamilton county—Continued.

NAMES.	Rank.	Annual allowance.	Sums received.	Description of service.	When placed on the pension roll.	Commencement of pension.	Ages.	Laws under which they were formerly inscribed on the pension roll; and remarks.
Andrew Hipsher	Private	20 00	60 00	Va. State troops	Dec. 2, 1833	Mar. 4, 1831	71	
William Kelly	do	60 00	–	do	Feb. 28, 1833	do	76	Died April 24, 1834.
John Kerr	do	32 67	98 01	N. J. State troops	Ap'l 26, 1833	do	75	
James Lyon	Artificer	144 00	432 00	N. J. continental	Dec. 15, 1832	do	79	
Othniel Looker	Private	34 44	103 32	N. Jersey militia	May 6, 1833	do	76	
George Leiby	do	26 66	53 32	Penn. militia	May 10, 1833	do	80	
John W. Langdon	do	50 00	150 00	Mass. militia	July 19, 1833	do	75	
Isaac Lewis	do	80 00	240 00	Mass. continental	Aug. 24, 1833	do	79	
Thomas Lacy	do	80 00	240 00	N. Jersey militia	Jan. 9, 1834	do	75	
Francis McCormick	do	21 66	64 98	Virginia militia	Oct. 24, 1832	do	70	
Alexander Martin	Pri., artifi., & sailor	107 33	321 99	N. J. mil. & St. navy	May 6, 1833	do	74	
John Meeker	Private	46 66	139 98	New Jersey militia	Nov. 1, 1833	do	75	
William Neves	do	53 33	159 99	Virginia militia	Ap'l 2, 1833	do	83	
Bethnel Norris	do	23 33	69 99	New Jersey militia	Ap'l 26, 1833	do	76	
Abijah Phelps	do	23 66	70 98	Conn. St. tr. & con.	Ap'l 16, 1833	do	72	
William Pack	do	26 66	79 98	Maryland militia	Ap'l 18, 1833	do	76	
John Packer	do	80 00	240 00	New Jersey militia	Aug. 24, 1833	do	77	
Jonathan Pitman	Captain	480 00	1,440 00	do	do	do	86	
Joseph Ross	Private	40 00	100 00	N. J. mil. & contin'l	Dec. 15, 1832	do	84	
John Rase	do	80 00	240 00	New Jersey militia	Dec. 18, 1832	do	75	
Bethnel Riggs	Pri. & capt.	376 66	1,129 98	do	Aug. 8, 1832	do	76	
William Slaback	Private	80 00	200 00	do	Dec. 5, 1832	do	75	
Jedediah Sturges	do	80 00	240 00	do	Ap'l 16, 1833	do	76	
Thomas Stacy	do	60 00	180 00	Penn. militia	May 28, 1833	do	79	
John Schooly	do	40 00	100 00	New Jersey militia	Aug. 8, 1833	do	73	
Elisha Shepherd	Captain	480 00	1,440 00	do	Aug. 29, 1833	do	74	
Hezekiah Stiles	Sergeant	90 00	270 00	do	Jan. 4, 1833	do	72	
John Shipman	Private	63 33	189 99	do		do	74	Transferred from Northumberland county, in the State of Pennsylvania, from March 4, 1833.

NAMES.	Rank.	Annual allowance.	Sums received.	Description of service.	When placed on the pension roll.	Commencement of pension.	Ages.	Remarks.
Philip Sloate	do	60 00	180 00	do	Feb. 1, 1834	do	69	Died October 26, 1832.
William Travis	do	26 66	79 98	N. York St. troops	Oct. 28, 1833	do	70	
John B. Turner	do	80 00	-	New Jersey militia	Oct. 16, 1833	do	72	
Jonathan Waring	do	80 00	240 00	Conn. militia	Feb. 28, 1833	do	69	
Israel Ward	do	20 00	60 00	New Jersey militia	Ap'l 11, 1833	do	71	
Amos Ward	do	26 66	79 98	do	Ap'l 18, 1833	do	73	
Levi Wood	do	74 66	223 98	Vermont militia	May 3, 1833	do	75	
William Warrington	Pri. & ser.	93 33	279 99	Virginia militia	May 6, 1833	do	79	
Miles Williams	Private	80 00	240 00	New Jersey militia	Aug. 9, 1833	do	72	
Jacob White	Pri. & capt.	140 00	420 00	Penn. militia	Dec. 11, 1833	do	74	

Statement, &c. of Hancock county, Ohio.

NAMES.	Rank.	Annual allowance.	Sums received.	Description of service.	When placed on the pension roll.	Commencement of pension.	Ages.	Laws under which they were formerly inscribed on the pension roll; and remarks.
John Fox	Marine	96 00	103 03	Ship S. Carolina	Mar. 5, 1819	Feb. 8, 1819	-	Dropped from roll under act of March 18, 1818, August 16, 1820. Not continental.
Do	do	40 00	80 00	do	Jan. 9, 1832	Mar. 4, 1831	67	Transferred from Berks county, Penn. from March 4, 1833.
Jacob Shepherd	Private	80 00	240 00	New Jersey militia	Nov. 9, 1833	do	77	

17

Statement, &c. of Hocking county, Ohio.

NAMES.	Rank.	Annual allowance.	Sums received.	Description of service.	When placed on the pension roll.	Commencement of pension.	Ages.	Laws under which they were formerly inscribed on the pension roll; and remarks.
James Steel	Private	23 33	58 33	Pennsylvania militia	June 22, 1833	Mar. 4, 1831	81	

Statement, &c. of Harrison county, Ohio.

NAMES.	Rank.	Annual allowance.	Sums received.	Description of service.	When placed on the pension roll.	Commencement of pension.	Ages.	Laws under which they were formerly inscribed on the pension roll; and remarks.
Thomas Archibald	Private	53 33	159 99	Penn. militia	June 11, 1833	Mar. 4, 1831	80	
George Brokan	do	21 67	54 18	N. J. continental	May 3, 1833	do	80	
George Biner	do	42 66	127 98	Virginia State	Oct. 25, 1833	do	69	
Moses Beman	do	80 00	240 00	Penn. militia	Nov. 25, 1833	do	78	
Ephraim T. Carle	do	60 00	180 00	N. Jersey militia	Oct. 25, 1833	do	76	
George Dickson	do	20 00	50 00	Maryland militia	Sep. 21, 1833	do	76	
John Finney	do	20 00	–	Penn. continental	July 18, 1834	do	73	
John George	do	20 00	50 00	Penn. militia	June 11, 1833	do	82	
John Greery	do	20 00	–	do	do	do	74	
Nicholas Helmick	do	80 00	160 00	Virginia State	Ap'l 13, 1833	do	82	
Absalom Kent	do	22 53	50 00	Penn. militia	July 30, 1834	do	81	
Thomas Morgan	do	80 00	240 00	Virginia cont'l	May 10, 1833	do	82	
Hugh M'Donough	do	23 33	46 66	Flying camp Penn.	Ap'l 2, 1833	do	83	
Samuel Maholm	do	20 00	50 00	Penn. militia	Oct. 25, 1833	do	75	

Names	Rank	Annual allowance	Sums received	Description of service	When placed on the pension roll	Commencement of pension	Ages	Laws under which they were formerly inscribed on the pension roll; and remarks.
David Milligan	do	80 00	220 00	Penn. continental	Oct. 28, 1833	do	84	Died December 8, 1833.
Henry Martin	do	50 00	150 00	Penn. militia	Ap'l 12, 1834	do	77	
Robert Porter	do	21 33	53 32	Penn. State	Nov. 1, 1834	do	71	
Thomas Parkinson	do	46 66	116 65	Maryland militia	May 6, 1833	do	71	
James Russell	do	30 00	75 00	Penn. militia	May 13, 1833	do	90	
Jacob Ritchey	do	20 67	51 67	Penn. continental	Oct. 25, 1833	do	78	Died September 8, 1833.
John Ross	Ens. & lt.	130 66	326 65	Virginia militia	do	do	82	
William Wagstaff	Private	26 66	79 98	Virginia militia	May 10, 1833	do	82	
Charles D. Wells	do	33 22	83 10	Maryland State	Sep. 24, 1835	do	76	

Statement, &c. of Highland county, Ohio.

Names.	Rank.	Annual allowance.	Sums received.	Description of service.	When placed on the pension roll.	Commencement of pension.	Ages.	Laws under which they were formerly inscribed on the pension roll; and remarks.
James Anderson	Private	30 00	90 00	Penn. militia	May 3, 1834	Mar. 4, 1831	70	
Thomas Brady	do	21 67	43 34	Virginia cont'l	Ap'l 16, 1833	do	71	
John Beard	do	30 00	90 00	Penn. militia	Nov. 16, 1833	do	69	
John Crawford	do	80 00	240 00	Virginia cont'l	Dec. 15, 1832	do	85	
James Collier	Captain	430 00	1,440 00	Penn. militia	June 26, 1833	do	82	
Thomas Dickey	Private	30 00	90 00	Penn. cont'l	Dec. 15, 1832	do	76	
George Gall, sen.	do	20 00	60 00	Virginia State tr.	do	do	69	
Samuel Gibson	do	80 00	200 00	Virginia militia	May 10, 1833	do	72	
John W. Harper	Pri. & ser.	26 66	79 93	do	Nov. 16, 1833	do	74	
Joseph Horn	Private	26 67	80 01	Penn. militia		do	76	
John Halter	do	80 00	-	do	June 4, 1834	do	84	
Robert Moore	do	80 00	240 00	do	June 25, 1833	do	78	
William Morris	Sergeant	90 00	225 00	Maryland militia	Oct. 8, 1833	do	91	
William Manker	Private	20 00	60 00	Virginia militia	Nov. 16, 1833	do	69	

Statement, &c. of Highland county—Continued.

Names.	Rank.	Annual allowance.	Sums received.	Description of service.	When placed on the pension roll.	Commencement of pension.	Ages.	Laws under which they were formerly inscribed on the pension roll; and remarks.
John Middleton	Private	40 00	120 00	Virginia mil.	Nov. 16, 1833	Mar. 4, 1831	71	
William Morris, sen.	do	80 00	240 00	Maryland militia	Dec. 27, 1833	do	91	Died May 12, 1834.
Joseph Moler	do	80 00	240 00	do	Mar. 7, 1834	do	85	
John Peril	do	40 00	100 00	Virginia militia	Oct. 16, 1833	do	75	
Aaron Ruse	do	60 00	180 00	Virginia cont'l	Ap'l 20, 1833	do	70	
Lewis Robinson	do	61 56	184 68	Virginia militia	May 10, 1833	do	78	
John Ruble	do	33 33	99 99	do	Oct. 12, 1833	do	73	
John Richardson	do	23 33	69 99	do	Nov. 16, 1833	do	72	
Andrew Shafer	do	80 00	240 00	Maryland cont'l	Oct. 3, 1832	do	75	
John Smith	do	21 56	43 12	Virginia militia	Ap'l 16, 1833	do	92	
John Strange	do	32 50	97 50	do	do	do	75	
Thomas Strain	do	26 66	58 69	Penn. militia	Ap'l 18, 1833	Nov. 10, 1819	77	Died May 14, 1833.
George Spicard	do	96 00	-	Virginia cont'l	May 31, 1820		-	March 18, 1818. Suspended under act May 1, 1820.
Do	do	96 00		do	May 21, 1832	Ap'l 3, 1832	-	March 1, 1823. Restored.
Do	do	80 00	240 00	do	May 10, 1833	Mar. 4, 1831	75	Dropped from roll March 18, 1808.
Samuel Strain	do	88 33	220 83	S. Carolina militia	do	do	72	
Anthony Sonner	do	23 33	58 33	Virginia militia	do	do	73	
Philip Stoops	do	40 00	120 00	Delaware militia	June 26, 1833	do	80	
David Smalley	do	20 00	60 00	Virginia militia	Nov. 6, 1833	do	78	
Jacob Seerber	do	80 00	240 00	do	Nov. 8, 1833	do	90	
Andrew Shefer	do	96 00	-	Maryland cont'l	June 10, 1820	Jan. 22, 1820	-	March 18, 1818. Suspended under act May 1, 1820.
Do	do	80 00	200 00	do	Feb. 25, 1834	Mar. 4, 1831	74	
William Vanwinkle	do	34 89	87 22	N. Jersey militia	May 6, 1833	do	71	
Charles White	do	43 33	129 99	Virginia militia	Nov. 16, 1833	do	71	
Mathew Wilson	do	20 00	-	Maryland militia	July 20, 1834	d		
Benjamin Yeats	do	30 00	90 00	do	Ap'l 17, 1834	do	88	

Statement, &c. of Holmes county, Ohio.

NAMES.	Rank.	Annual allow- ance.	Sums re- ceived.	Description of ser- vice.	When placed on the pen- sion roll.	Commencement of pension.	Ages.	Laws under which they were for- merly inscribed on the pension roll; and remarks.
Arnold Carter	Private	20 00	60 00	Virginia militia	May 28, 1833	Mar. 4, 1831	75	
John Corbin	do	28 33	84 99	-	Oct. 9, 1833	do		
Peter Myers	do	40 00	120 00	Penn. continental	May 28, 1833	do	75	
Edward Otis	do	36 66	109 98	Connecticut cont'l	Oct. 2, 1833	do	68	
Jonathan Palmer	do	60 00	180 00	Virginia cont'l	Jan. 6, 1834	do	75	
Luke Tipton	do	60 00	180 00	Pennsylvania mil.	Jan. 9, 1834	do	73	
Samuel Williams	Corporal	88 00	264 00	N. H. continental	Ap'l 6, 1833	do	78	

Statement, &c. of Huron county, Ohio.

NAMES.	Rank.	Annual allow- ance.	Sums re- ceived.	Description of ser- vice.	When placed on the pen- sion roll.	Commencement of pension.	Ages.	Laws under which they were for- merly inscribed on the pension roll; and remarks.
Jonas Bemiss	Private	33 33	99 99	N. York State tr.	July 24, 1833	Mar. 4, 1831	69	
Nathaniel Burdue	do	80 00	240 00	Penn'a State tr.	Sep. 2, 1833	do	86	
John Brooks	do	80 00	240 00	N. York State tr.	Mar. 12, 1834	do	78	
Isaac Curtis	do	26 66	79 98	do	Sep. 16, 1833	do	80	
Benjamin Drake	do	80 00	240 00	do	May 13, 1833	do	63	
Charles Eastman	do	33 00	-	Mass. State troops	Ap'l 9, 1833	do	72	Transferred from Ohio from Mar. 4, 1834, April 1834.
Ti..thy Foot	do	35 00	50 00	Connecticut militia	Nov. 27, 1833	do	82	
Eli Haliday	do	66 66	199 98	do	Sep. 24, 1833	do	68	

Statement, &c. of Huron county—Continued.

NAMES.	Rank.	Annual allowance.	Sums received.	Description of service.	When placed on the pension roll.	Commencement of pension.	Ages.	Laws under which they were formerly inscribed on the pension roll; and remarks.
William Johnson	Private	59 83	-	Connecticut militia	July 8, 1834	Mar. 4, 1831	81	
Michael Mason	do	80 00	240 00	Mass. militia	Jan. 24, 1833	do	74	
Adam Myers	do	23 33	58 22	Pennsylvania mil.	Aug. 8, 1833	do	79	
Conrad Nessle	do	80 00	180 00	N. York State tr.	July 20, 1833	do	72	
Noah W. Norton	do	80 00	240 00	Connecticut cont'l	Aug. 20, 1833	do	70	
Solomon Parsons	do	60 00	180 00	Conn. State troops	Oct. 2, 1833	do	67	
Joseph Ransom	do	80 00	240 00	do	July 24, 1833	do	72	
Benjamin Reed	do	80 00	240 00	Mass. continental	Sep. 23, 1833	do	76	
Micah Skinner	do	80 00	240 00	N. Y. oontinental	Mar. 5, 1833	do	68	
Lambert Schaefer	do	80 00	240 00	N. Jersey cont'l	May 23, 1833	do	82	
Phineas Swartz	do	70 00	157 00	Pennsylvania mil.	Aug. 1, 1833	do	74	Died June 1, 1833.
Philip Stutton	do	23 33	-	N. Jersey State tr.	July 23, 1834	do	74	
John Taylor	Pri. & ser.	99 16	247 90	Flying Camp N. J.	Sep. 17, 1833	do	83	
Aaron Van Benschoten	Private	30 00	75 00	N. York militia	May 3, 1833	do	88	
Allen Watrous	do	30 00	-	Mass. State troops	Ap'l 16, 1833	do	77	
Josiah Ward	do	33 33	99 99	Pennsylvania mil.	Mar. 24, 1834	do	72	
Robert Wells	do	43 33	129 99	R. Island militia	Sep. 16, 1833	do	78	
Morgan Young	do	73 88	221 64	N. Jersey militia	May 13, 1833	do	72	

Statement, &c. of Jackson county, Ohio.

NAMES.	Rank.	Annual allowance.	Sums received.	Description of service.	When placed on the pension roll.	Commencement of pension.	Ages.	Laws under which they were formerly inscribed on the pension roll; and remarks.
Joel Arthur	Private	25 00	75 00	Virginia militia	Sep. 17, 1833	Mar. 4, 1831	83	
William Crow	do	44 64	133 92	do	Sep. 16, 1833	do	77	
Joseph Horton	Pri. of cav.	83 61	-	do	Dec. 27, 1833	do	75	
Thomas Jones	Private	30 00	75 00	Virginia State tr.	Ap'l 15, 1833	do	84	
William Owens	do	80 00	240 00	Penn. State troops	June 26, 1833	do	72	
Thomas Oliver	do	80 00	240 00	Virginia continental	Oct. 24, 1833	do	71	
Enoch Russell	do	20 00	-	Virginia militia	July 25, 1834	do	73	
George Weese	do	21 10	-	Pennsylvania mil.	May 3, 1834	do	70	

Statement, &c. of Jefferson county, Ohio.

NAMES.	Rank.	Annual allowance.	Sums received.	Description of service.	When placed on the pension list	Commencement of pension.	Ages.	Laws under which they were formerly inscribed on the pension list; and remarks.
George Alban	Private	80 00	240 00	Virginia continental	Dec. 28, 1833	Mar. 4, 1831	93	
Thomas Bryan	do	40 00	120 00	Maryland militia	Oct. 25, 1833	do	74	
James Barkers	do	20 00	60 00	do	Nov. 21, 1833	do	82	
Joseph Chambers	Sergeant	30 00	90 00	Penn. militia	May 28, 1833	do	80	
David Crawford	Private	38 00	114 00	do	do	do	70	
Jacob N. Clark	do	36 67	84 99	Maryland cont'l	Aug. 1, 1833	do	78	
John Dehuff	do	33 33	83 52	Penn. State troops	Feb. 25, 1833	do	76	

Statement, &c. of Jefferson county—Continued.

NAMES.	Rank.	Annual allow-ance.	Sums re-ceived.	Description of service.	When placed on the pension roll.	Commencement of pension.	Ages.	Laws under which they were formerly inscribed on the pension roll; and remarks.
James Glenn -	Private	40 00	120 00	Penn. militia	Oct. 25, 1833	Mar. 4, 1831	91	
Edward Greenelsh -	do	60 00	150 00	Virginia continental	do	do	87	
Reuben Hall -	Artificer	50 00	138 50	Penn. State troops	Mar. 2, 1833	do	79	
John Humphrey, sen. -	Pri. & ser.	96 66	289 98	Penn. militia	Jan. 6, 1834	do	82	
William Lock, *alias* Starr	Pri. of cav.	100 00	300 00	Virgin'a militia	Dec. 30, 1833	do	89	
Abraham Moore -	Private	29 76	89 28	Penn. militia	June 11, 1832	do	95	
Thomas Rouse -	do	40 00	80 00	Penn. State troops	July 20, 1833	do	72	
Jacob Ripley -	Pri & ser.	56 66	169 98	do	Ap'l 23, 1833	do	77	
William Taylor -	Seaman	96 00	288 00	U. States navy	Feb. 15, 1833	do	80	Transferred from Virginia from March 4, 1833, December, 1833.

Statement, &c. of Knox county, Ohio.

NAMES.	Rank.	Annual allow-ance.	Sums re-ceived.	Description of service.	When placed on the pension roll.	Commencement of pension.	Ages.	Laws under which they were formerly inscribed on the pension roll; and remarks.
John Ackerman -	Private	70 00	175 00	New Jersey cont'l	Aug. 8, 1833	Mar. 4, 1831	77	
Valentine Ball -	do	52 50	97 73	N. Jersey S. troops	Feb. 21, 1832	do	77	
Ellis Bower -	do	40 00	-	do	Mar. 14, 1833	do	78	
Abraham Blair -	do	30 00	75 00	N. Carolina militia	Ap'l 11, 1833	do	78	
William Beard -	do	30 00	75 00	New Jersey militia	May 29, 1833	do	74	Died February 23, 1833.
David Bryant -	do	40 00	120 00		Ap'l 8, 1834	do	78	

Name	Rank			Service	Date		Age
Nathaniel Critchfield	do	53 33	159 99	Virginia St. troops	Ap'l 11, 1833	do	73
William Critchfield	do	33 33	83 33	Pennsylvania cont'l	Sep. 20, 1833	do	70
Casper Clutter	do	80 00	-	Maryland cont'l	Nov. 6, 1833	do	88
Peter Doty	do	40 00	100 00	New Jersey militia	July 25, 1833	do	77
Jacob Dunham	do	80 00	240 00	do	May 13, 1833	do	77
Peter Fine	do	25 07	62 53	Maryland militia	do	do	84
Stephen Griffin	do	23 33	-	Pennsylvania militia	May 15, 1833	do	81
Solomon Hill	do	30 00	90 00	New Jersey cont'l	Mar. 14, 1833	do	75
Samuel Hofmire	do	23 33	-	N. Jersey St. troops	Ap'l 11, 1833	do	70
Lodowick Hardenbrook	do	20 00	50 00	New Jersey militia	Aug. 9, 1833	do	77
Daniel Jackson	do	43 33	-	do	Mar. 14, 1833	do	81
Benjamin Jackson	Sergeant	70 00	175 00	do	Sep. 23, 1833	do	82
Jacob Kline	Private	43 33	108 33	N. Jersey St. troops	Ap'l 26, 1833	do	78
John Harakin	do	23 33	58 33	Pennsylvania cont'l	May 3, 1833	do	74
John Kinny	do	80 00	240 00	Pennsylvania militia	Sep. 21, 1833	do	78
Henry Lewis	do	26 66	79 98	do	May 6, 1833	do	80
Edward Landon	do	33 33	99 99	New Jersey militia	Sep. 21, 1833	do	72
William Mc Williams	do	40 00	120 00	Pennsylvania cont'l	Mar. 14, 1833	do	75
Christopher Myers	do	20 00	50 00	Maryland militia	May 13, 1833	do	75
James McKown	do	43 33	108 33	Virginia militia	May 28, 1833	do	76
Robert McMillan	do	20 00	50 00	Pennsylvania militia	July 27, 1833	do	75
James McElroy	Pr. of cav.	100 00	-	New York cont'l	Mar 26, 1834	do	70
George McCreary	Sergeant	40 00	120 00	Pennsylvania militia	Ap'l 3, 1834	do	82
Cary McClelland	Private	70 00	-	Pennsylvania cont'l	July 12, 1834	do	80
George Stevenson	do	80 00	240 00	Pennsylvania militi	Mar. 14, 1833	do	78
William Spry	do	40 00	120 00	Maryland militia	June 25, 1833	do	77
William Stewart	Pri. & ser.	82 21	246 63	Connecticut militia	Sep. 21, 1833	do	82
Reuben Thornhill, sen.	Private	80 00	140 00	Virginia cont'l	Jan. 19, 1833	do	76
Nathan Terrill	do	73 33	183 33	Connecticut cont'l	July 27, 1833	do	79
Cornelius Vaunsdall	do	40 00	100 00	Virginia militia	Mar. 14, 1833	do	75
Joseph Vantresse	do	20 00	60 00	Maryland militia	Ap'l 16, 1833	do	83
Rufus Ward	do	40 00	100 00	Massachusetts mil.	June 25, 1833	do	75
David S. Welsh	do	80 00	200 00	N. Hampshire cont'l	Sep. 24, 1833	do	74

18

Statement, &c. of Lawrence county, Ohio.

NAMES.	Rank.	Annual allowance.	Sums received.	Description of service.	When placed on the pension roll.	Commencement of pension.	Ages.	Laws under which they were formerly inscribed on the pension roll; and remarks.
Humphrey Brumford	Private	80 00	-	Virginia militia	May 3, 1834	Mar. 4, 1831	82	
Anthony Clark	Pri. & ser.	26 66	79 98	Virginia State tr'ps	Mar. 23, 1833	do	76	
Zachariah Davis	Private	28 33	84 99	Penn. continental	Aug. 16, 1833	do	73	
John Ellison	do	50 00	150 00	Virginia milit a	Mar. 23, 1833	do	72	
Samuel Layne	do	43 33	86 66	do	do	do	75	
William Losey	do	26 66	79 98	N. Jersey militia	Sep. 16, 1833	do	71	
Joseph Lanebaugh	do	21 55	64 65	Virginia cont'l	Jan. 22, 1834	do	71	
Henry Mannon	do	45 97	137 91	Virginia militia	Sep. 16, 1833	do	74	
Robert M'Corkel	Pri. & ser.	110 00	-	Virginia cont'l	Feb. 4, 1834	do	74	
Nathaniel Prichard	Private	54 28	162 54	Conn. militia	Jan. 22, 1834	do	72	
Isaac Riall	do	43 33	129 99	N. Jersey militia	May 6, 1833	do	73	
Joseph L. Rowley	Pri, ser. & seaman	51 65	-	Conn. militia	July 18, 1834	do	83	

Statement, &c. of Licking county, Ohio.

NAMES.	Rank.	Annual allowance.	Sums received.	Description of service.	When placed on the pension roll.	Commencement of pension.	Ages.	Laws under which they were formerly inscribed on the pension roll, and remarks.
Zachariah Allbaugh	Private	80 00	-	Maryland militia	Nov. 6, 1833	Mar. 4, 1831	76	
Elijah Adams	Pri. & ser.	79 95	199 85	Conn. State troops	May 23, 1833	do	80	
Daniel Baker	Private	40 00	120 00	do	Ap'l 19, 1833	do	71	
Michael Beam	do	23 22	58 05	Va. State troops	Ap'l 26, 1833	do	76	
Jonathan Benjamin	do	80 00	160 00	Penn. militia	July 25, 1833	do	90	
Daniel Boyer	do	40 00	120 00	Del. State troops	June 22, 1833	do	79	
John Bower	do	33 33	82 44	N. Jersey militia	May 23, 1833	do	73	
Freegift Chamberlain	do	34 11	68 22	Penn. State troops	Mar. 2?, 1833	do	76	Died August 24, 1833.
John Coulter	do	43 33	108 33	Maryland cont'l	May 3, 1833	do	72	
James Colville	Pri. & ser.	55 00	165 00	Virginia militia	June 22, 1833	do	76	
Samuel Carpenter	Private	34 00	85 00	N. Y. continental	June 26, 1833	do	80	
Peter Danforth	do	80 00	240 00	Mass. continental	Mar. 23, 1833	do	71	
Richard Dove	do	80 00	200 00	Maryland militia	Aug. 9, 1833	do	89	
Samuel Edmund	do	80 00	240 00	N. Jersey militia	do	do	77	
John Feazle	do	70 00	175 00	Virginia cont'l	Mar. 28, 1833	do	82	
Jonathan French	Pri. & ser.	260 00	780 00	New York militia	Jan. 31, 1834	do	83	
Benjamin Green	Private	20 00	-	Va. State troops	Ap'l 26, 1833	do	79	
Amasa Hawe	do	80 00	240 00	Mass. continental	Ap'l 15, 1833	do	68	
Levi Hayes	Fifer	33 00	99 00	Conn. State troops	Ap'l 26, 1833	do	70	
William Harris	Private	33 33	83 33	Virginia militia	July 27, 1833	do	69	
Isaiah Hoskinson	do	23 33	-	do	Sep. 21, 1833	do	83	
Joseph Headley	do	46 66	139 98	New Jersey militia	Mar. 28, 1833	do	76	
George Horn	do	20 00	50 00	Virginia militia	do	do	69	
Caleb Hill	do	20 00	40 00	N.Y. State troops	do	do	78	
John Hoover	do	80 00	-	Penn. militia	July 8, 1834	do	80	
Joseph Linnell	do	20 00	57 21	Mass. militia	Ap'l 19, 1833	do	79	
Adam McKnight	do	80 00	240 00	Mass. continental	Nov. 23, 1832	do	71	
Jacob Martin	do	40 00	120 00	Mass. militia	Ap'l 26, 1833	do	90	
John Miles	do	40 00	80 00	Maryland cont'l	do	do	79	
Stephen Mead	do	40 00	120 00	Vermont militia	May 6, 1833	do	75	

Statement, &c. of Licking county—Continued.

NAMES.	Rank.	Annual allowance.	Sums received.	Description of service.	When placed on the pension roll.	Commencement of pension.	Ages.	Laws under which they were formerly inscribed on the pension roll; and remarks.
Charles Martin	Private	43 33	129 99	R. Island militia	May 30, 1833	Mar. 4, 1831	75	
Japat Mantzer	do	46 66	139 98	Penn. militia	Oct. 24, 1833	do	78	
Thomas Perkins	do	25 00	-	Virginia cont'l	Nov. 16, 1833	do	72	
John Priests	do	20 00	50 00	Virginia militia	May 6, 1833	do	83	
Lemuel Ro e	do	80 00	240 00	Mass. militia	July 27, 1833	do	71	
Aaron Searl	do	25 00	75 00	do	Mar. 23, 1833	do	73	
Daniel Shadley	do	21 66	54 15	Virginia militia	June 22, 1833	do	78	
Moses Scovell	do	46 66	139 98	Conn. militia	do	do	71	
Zebulon Sutton	do	46 66	116 65	Mass. militia	Sept. 16, 1833	do	31	
Lewis Sturges	Pri. & cor.	84 00	252 00	Conn. State troops	Aug. 20, 1833	do	79	
James Taylor	Ser. & pri.	23 33	69 99	Penn. militia	May 6, 1833	do	80	
Henry Trevitt	Private	37 21	111 63	N. H. milit'a	Sept. 24, 1833	do	74	
Samuel Wyckoff	do	33 33	99 99	Maryland cont'l	Ap'l 26, 1833	do	74	
Asa Woodward	do	37 55	112 65	Conn. continental	May 6, 1833	do	74	
Jacob Waters	do	37 50	112 50	Penn. ml. & St. trps.	June 22, 1833	do	77	
Samuel Wheeler	do	80 00	240 00	Va. State troops	Mar. 7, 1834	do	82	

Statement, &c. of Jefferson county, Ohio.

NAMES.	Rank.	Annual allowance.	Sums received.	Description of service.	When placed on the pension roll.	Commencement of pension.	Ages.	Laws under which they were formerly inscribed on the pension roll; and remarks.
Abel Armstrong	Private	80 00	240 00	Virginia continental	Nov. 10, 1832	March 4, 1831	76	
William Carrel	do	30 00	75 00	N. York militia	Ap'l 26, 1833	do	68	
James Coffel	do	40 00	100 00	Pennsylvania cont'l	May 28, 1833	do	90	
Michael Cox	do	28 33	-	Pennsylvania militia	Oct. 24, 1833	do	74	
Peter Howard	o	80 00	240 00	Virginia continental	April 2, 1833	do	89	
James L. New	do	25 55	76 65	Virginia militia	Sep. 21, 1833	do	70	
Jared Pichard	do	40 00	120 00	Connecticut cont'l	June 4, 1834	do	75	
Thomas Stennags	do	80 00	240 00	Virginia continental	May 10, 1833	do	75	

Statement, &c. of Lorain county, Ohio.

NAMES.	Rank.	Annual allowance.	Sums received.	Description of service.	When placed on the pension roll.	Commencement of pension.	Ages.	Laws under which they were formerly inscribed on the pension roll; and remarks.
Moses Allis	Sergeant	120 00	-	Mass. continental	July 29, 1834	Mar. 4, 1831	68	
Justus Battle	Private	80 00	240 00	do	May 4, 1833	do	73	
Aaron Burt	do	31 11	93 33	Mass. State	Oct. 25, 1833	do	75	
Jonathan Buck	do	20 78	62 34	Conn. militia	Dec. 3, 1833	do	83	
David Beebe	Pri. & ser.	40 00	120 00	Mass. continental	Sept. 16, 1833	do	87	
Eleazer Crawford	Pri. & ser.	90 00	-	Vermont militia	Dec. 30, 1833	do	73	
David Fox	Private	46 66	-	Connecticut State	Nov. 17, 1832	do	83	
Samuel J. Griffith	Pri. & ser.	53 33	-	New York State	Nov. 21, 1833	do	78	
Joseph Kingsbury	Private	24 09	60 22	Mass. continental	Nov. 8, 1832	do	73	

Statement, &c. of Lorain county—Continued.

NAMES.	Rank.	Annual allowance.	Sums received.	Description of service.	When placed on the pension roll.	Commencement of pension.	Ages.	Laws under which they were formerly inscribed on the pension roll; and remarks.
Oliver Lewis	Private	23 33	69 99	Mass. State	Nov. 8, 1832	Mar. 4, 1831	76	
Abner Loveland	do	25 78	64 45	Conn. continental	do	do	70	
Marshal Merrian	do	20 00	60 00	Connecticut militia	do	do	85	
Jesse Morgan	do	21 06	63 81	Conn. continental	Nov. 17, 1833	do	73	
Ashel Morgan	do	76 69	230 01	Penn. militia	Dec. 30, 1833	do	74	
Seth Morse	do	34 10	102 80	Mass. militia	Sept. 17, 1833	do	77	
Eli Pembor	do	80 00	240 00	Conn. continental	Nov. 17, 1833	do	78	
Samuel Pelton	do	80 00	240 00	Mass. State	Dec. 15, 1833	do	76	
Ben Rising	Pri. & ser.	91 66	-	do	Ap'l 17, 1834	do	85	
Ezra Squire	Private	80 00	240 00	Conn. State	Nov. 8, 1832	do	73	
Elihu Terrell	do	30 00	90 00	Penn. State	Oct. 25, 1833	do	75	
Thomas Williams	do	33 11	99 33	Conn. State	do	do	71	

Statement, &c. of Madison county, Ohio.

NAMES.	Rank.	Annual allowance.	Sums received.	Description of service.	When placed on the pension roll.	Commencement of pension.	Ages.	Laws under which they were formerly inscribed on the pension roll; and remarks.
Obil Beach	Private	80 00	200 00	Connecticut cont'l	Ap'l 15, 1833	Mar. 4, 1831	75	
David Colver	do	70 00	210 00	N. York State tr-	Aug. 24, 1833	do	70	
James Dockum	do	20 00	50 00	New York cont'l	Ap'l 9, 1833	do	73	
George Jones	do	36 65	91 65	Virginia cont'l	Ap'l 6, 1833	do	71	
Samuel Smith	Pri. & ser.	35 00	-	Massachusetts mil.	July 21, 1834	do	79	
Timothy Wale	Private	30 00	-	Virginia militia	July 8, 1834	do	71	

Statement, &c. of Medina county, Ohio.

NAMES.	Rank.	Annual allowance.	Sums received.	Description of service.	When placed on the pension roll.	Commencement of pension.	Ages.	Laws under which they were formerly inscribed on the pension roll; and remarks.
Josiah Brown	Private	34 89	60 00	New York militia	May 13, 1833	Mar. 4, 1831	71	
Phineas Bronson	do	20 00	60 00	Connecticut militia	May 28, 1833	do	70	
Ezra Brown	do	60 00	180 00	do	May 30, 1833	do	71	
Hinsdale Bates	do	40 00	120 00	Connecticut cont'l	Sep. 20, 1833	do	77	
Joshua Campbell	do	26 66	79 98	Mass. State	Feb. 27, 1834	do	73	
Solomon Deming	do	40 00	120 00	Massachusetts cont'l	Ap'l 6, 1833	do	71	
Deliverance Eastman	do	80 00	240 00	Pennsylvania mil.	Feb. 4, 1834	do	73	
Seth Goodwin	do	73 33	219 99	Connecticut State	Ap'l 2, 1833	do	71	
Jehiel Green	do	80 00	240 00	New York cont'l	July 25, 1833	do	74	Transferred from N. York on Feb. 8, 1834, from September 4, 1833.
John Hulet	Pri. & ser.	83 33	249 99	Mass. State	May 13, 1833	do	78	
Giles Hickcox	Private	30 00	90 00	do	May 30, 1833	do	69	
Asa Hubbard	do	21 32	63 96	Connecticut mil'.	do	do	76	
Israel Hubbard	do	21 67	65 01	Mass. militia	July 20, 1833	do	82	
Philemon Kirkum	do	80 00	200 00	Connecticut cont'l	July 2, 1832	do	71	
Eleazer Marsh	do	40 00	120 00	Vermont militia	Ap'l 2, 1833	do	78	
Adam Poe	do	80 00	240 00	Pennsylvania mil.	Sep. 21, 1833	do	86	
Edward Rogers	Seaman	96 00	240 00	U. S. Navy	May 30, 1833	do	80	
Joseph Riley	Private	21 55	59 15	Connecticut mil'a	Oct. 28, 1833	do	82	Died December 15, 1833.
John Stearns	do	23 33	69 99	Mass. continental	May 15, 1833	do	83	
Matthew Towsley	do	26 66	79 98	Vermont militia	Nov. 5, 1832	do	69	Transferred from Vermont from Sep. 4, 1833, Feb. 1834.

Statement, &c. of Meigs county, Ohio.

NAMES.	Rank.	Annual allowance.	Sums received.	Description of service.	When placed on the pension roll.	Commencement of pension.	Ages.	Laws under which they were formerly inscribed on the pension roll; and remarks.
David Cooper	Private	30 00	75 00	N. J. continental	Ap'l 2, 1833	Mar. 4, 1831	76	
Amos Carpenter	do	60 00	180 09	Virginia cont'l	June 25, 1833	do	79	
Joel Castle	do	30 00	90 00	Conn. continental	Mar. 4, 1834	do	83	
Asa Dains	do	50 00	150 00	Conn. State troops	Dec. 12, 1832	do	75	
Thomas Everton	do	50 00	150 00	Mass. continental	Nov. 27, 1832	do	72	
Joseph Griffin	do	40 00	80 00	N. Y. State troops	Nov. 13, 1832	do	74	
Peter Grow	Pri. & ser.	20 00	60 00	Mass. militia	July 25, 1833	do		
Daniel Gilleland	Private	119 16	357 48	N. Jersey militia	Jan. 9, 1834	do	69	
Freeman Hicox	Private	40 00	120 00	Conn. State troops	Nov. 13, 1832	do	69	
Brewster Higley	do	80 00	240 00	Conn. continental	Jan. 22, 1833	do	75	
George Harrell	do	20 00	60 00	Virginia State tr.	Mar. 2, 1833	do	79	
Abijah Hubbell	do	25 00	62 50	N. York militia	Sep. 11, 1833	do	71	
Samuel Kent	do	80 00	240 00	Conn. cont'l & mil.	July 27, 1833	do	77	
Thomas Love	do	53 33	133 33	Virginia militia	Sep. 16, 1833	do	79	
Josiah Osborn	do	36 22	108 66	Conn. militia	Oct. 28, 1833	do	73	
Miles Oakley	do	63 33	189 99	do	July 25, 1833	do	77	
John Pickens	do	60 00	180 00	Penn. State troops	Ap'l 28, 1834	do	82	
Charles Rice	do	50 00	150 00	Mass. continental	Ap'l 24, 1833	do	86	
George Rousk	do	23 33	69 99	Virginia militia	July 27, 1833	do	73	
Thaddeus Smith	do	23 33	58 33	N. Jersey militia	Aug. 24, 1833	do	92	

Statement, &c. of Mercer county, Ohio.

NAMES.	Rank.	Annual allowance.	Sums received.	Description of service.	When placed on the pension roll.	Commencement of pension.	Ages.	Laws under which they were formerly inscribed on the pension roll; and remarks.
William Berry -	Private	24 66	73 98	Virginia militia	June 25, 1833	Mar. 4, 1831	81	
John Latimer -	do	59 16	177 48	N. Jersey militia	May 6, 1833	do	83	
Robert M'Lumsey -	do	40 00	120 00	Penn. militia	do	do	78	

19

Statement, &c. of Miami county, Ohio.

NAMES.	Rank.	Annual allowance.	Sums received.	Description of service.	When placed on the pension roll.	Commencement of pension.	Ages.	Laws under which they were formerly inscribed on the pension roll; and remarks.
John Byrne	Private	50 00	150 00	Penn. State troops	Ap'l 9, 1833	Mar. 4, 1831	81	
Benjamin Brandon	do	80 00	-	N. Carolina militia	Nov. 25, 1833	do	75	
John Campbell	do	20 00	-	Pennsylvania militia	Sep. 20, 1833	do	77	
Thomas Edwards	do	30 00	60 00	Pennsylvania cont'l	Ap'l 5, 1833	do	70	
Ezekiel Farmer	do	80 00	200 00	S. Carolina militia	Sep. 20, 1833	do	70	
Patrick Heagan	do	80 00	240 00	Pennsylvania militia	Sep. 23, 1833	do	85	
Isaac Julin	do	23 33	57 55	do	Ap'l 5, 1833	do	93	
Alexander Jackson	do	33 33	99 99	do	do	do	75	
Thomas Kelsey	do	46 66	-	do		do	80	
David Lloyd	Pri. serg't & lieut.			New York militia				
Joseph I ine	Private	98 33	196 66	Pennsylvania militia	Ap'l 9, 1833	do	79	
Levi Munsell	do	80 00	240 00	do	Sep. 23, 1833	do	78	
Benjamin Morris	do	80 00	240 00	Connecticut cont'l	July 31, 1832	do	71	
David Munson	do	28 00	84 00	Virginia militia	Ap'l 11, 1833	do	71	
William Martin	do	23 33	58 33	Pennsylvania militia	June 3, 1833	do	81	
Levi Martin	do	24 00	60 00	do	June 11, 1833	do	78	
Samuel Mitchell	do	80 00	240 00	Virginia St. troops	June 22, 1833	do	69	
David H. Morris	do	63 33	189 99	Pennsylvania militia	July 25, 1833	do	75	
Henry Penney	do	80 00	240 00	S. Carolina militia	Jan. 17, 1834	do	65	
Edward Severns	do	24 66	61 65	New Jersey militia	Nov. 1, 1833	do	78	
Alexander Telford	do	20 00	50 00	Virginia militia	June 6, 1833	do	76	
Abraham Thomas	do	25 00	62 50	Pennsylvania militia	Ap'l 11, 1833	do	74	
Aaron Tullis	do	40 00	100 00	Virginia cont'l	Sep. 16, 1833	do	77	
Isaac Taylor	do	46 66	-	New Jersey militia	Oct. 12, 1833	do	81	
Samuel Wiley	do	23 33	69 99	Pennsylvania militia	July 8, 1834	do	77	

Statement, &c. of Monroe county, Ohio.

NAMES.	Rank.	Annual allowance.	Sums received.	Description of service.	When placed on the pension roll.	Commencement of pension.	Ages.	Laws under which they were formerly inscribed on the pension roll; and remarks.
Charles Atkinson	Private	80 00	240 00	Pennsylvania mil.	May 13, 1833	Mar. 4, 1831	74	
Ephraim Bates	do	40 00	100 00	Virginia State tr.	May 9, 1833	do	91	
James Craig	do	80 00	–	Penn. continental	Feb. 26, 1833	do		
William Gadd	do	54 77	64 31	Pennsylvania mil.	May 13, 1833	do		
Carey Headley	do	40 00	120 00	N. Jersey State tr.	Mar. 19, 1833	do	74	
Nathan Holister	do	46 22	138 66	Mass. continental	Nov. 4, 1833	do	74	
John Handershort	do	20 00	–	Pennsylvania mil.	May 22, 1834	do	72	
Bazil Morris	do	33 30	99 90	Virginia cont'l	May 6, 1833	do	74	
Benjamin McKay	do	40 00	120 00	Penn'a State troops	May 13, 1833	do	69	
Anthony Smith	do	80 00	240 00	N. Jersey militia	Feb. 6, 1833	do	92	
William Smith	do	80 00	–	Virginia militia	Ap'l 16, 1833	do	73	
Isaac Stackhouse	do	40 00	120 00	Virginia State tr.	May 23, 1833	do	83	
Ebenezer Tingley	do	43 65	76 28	N. Jersey militia	Feb. 25, 1833	do	73	Died December 1, 1832.
Robert Wilson, Sen.	do	80 00	240 00	do	Aug. 8, 1833	do	75	
John Walters	do	20 00	60 00	Pennsylvania mil.	Aug. 20, 1833	do	71	

Statement, &c. of Montgomery county, Ohio.

NAMES.	Rank.	Annual allowance.	Sums received.	Description of service.	When placed on the pension roll.	Commencement of pension.	Ages.	Laws under which they were formerly inscribed on the pension roll; and remarks.
Issachar Bates	Fifer & fife major	95 50	286 50	Mass. State troops	Ap'l 9, 1833	Mar. 4, 1831	77	
Benjamin Cox	Private	30 00	75 00	Alabama militia	May 3, 1833	do	82	
George Cloney	do	80 00	240 00	Virginia cont'l	Oct. 8, 1833	do	87	
John Grimes	do	20 00	50 00	Pennsylvania militia	Oct. 16, 1833	do	77	
Samuel Lusk	do	58 33	174 99	N. C. State troops	Ap'l 9, 1833	do	74	
Nathaniel Lyon	do	80 00	-	N. Jersey militia	July 25, 1833	do	74	Died September 2, 1833.
Jacob Larose	do	26 66	-	Pennsylvania mil.	Sep. 16, 1833	do	78	
Mordecai M'Llanan	do	80 00	240 00	N. Jersey militia	July 27, 1833	do	72	
John Ollinger	do	63 33	189 99	Penn'a State troops	Aug. 24, 1833	do	77	
Alexander Simpson	do	30 00	75 00	N. Jersey militia	May 6, 1833	do	71	
George Snyder	do	40 00	120 00	Maryland militia	May 14, 1833	do	80	
Charles Smith	do	80 00	240 00	N. Jersey militia	Sep. 23, 1833	do	74	
Andrew Small	do	79 33	237 99	Penn'a continental	Sep. 23, 1833	do	77	
Robert Strain	do	31 33	78 33	Pennsylvania mil.	Oct. 16, 1833	do	78	
Joseph Van Note	do	80 00	240 00	N. Jersey militia	Mar. 19, 1833	do	82	
Joseph Vandervier	Pri. inf. & artillery	85 77	-	do	June 26, 1833	do	74	
Peter Wise	Private	26 66	66 65	Pennsylvania mil.	Ap'l 26, 1833	do	81	
Samuel Woodward	do	29 66	88 98	Virginia militia	Sep. 23, 1833	do	74	

Statement, &c. of Morgan county, Ohio.

NAMES.	Rank.	Annual allowance.	Sums received.	Description of service.	When placed on the pension roll.	Commencement of pension.	Ages.	Laws under which they were formerly inscribed on the pension roll; and remarks.
Timothy Blackmore	Private	20 00	60 00	Vermont militia	May 7, 1833	Mar. 4, 1831	68	
William Beckwith	do	80 00	240 00	Maryland State tr.	Oct. 19, 1832	do	76	
Benjamin Beekwith	do	80 00	240 00	do	Oct. 19, 1832	do	79	
James Beer	do	21 66	44 32	Penn'a State troops	Jan. 3, 1833	do	76	
Phineas Coburn	Sergeant	80 00	240 00	Mass. continental	Nov. 9, 1832	do	68	
Jesse George	Private	26 66	79 98	Virginia State tr.	Apl. 19, 1833	do	76	
Nicholas S. Hoyt	do	32 36	97 08	N. H. State troops	Oct. 19, 1832	do	71	
William Hardin	Sergeant	60 00	180 00	Maryland militia	July 6, 1833	do	95	
William Jacobs	Private	80 00	240 00	do	May 28, 1833	do	79	
William Lyon	do	66 66	199 98	Pennsylvania mil.	May 4, 1833	do	77	
Gasper Moler	do	30 00	90 00	Virginia State tr.	Apl 20, 1833	do	75	
Christopher Mummy	do	20 00	60 00	Virginia militia	Sep. 21, 1833	do	80	
Thomas Nott	do	80 00	240 00	Connecticut St. tr.	Sep. 21, 1833	do	99	
Benjamin Severance	do	44 12	132 36	Mass. continental	Mar. 26, 1833	do	73	
Philip Sailor	Corporal	22 21	66 63	Pennsylvania mil.	Sep. 26, 1833	do	82	
John N. Smith	Private	60 00	180 00	N. Jersey militia	Sep. 23, 1833	do	70	
Edward Smith	do	20 00	-	Virginia State tr.	July 23, 1834	do	75	
Thomas Thorla	Pri. & cor.	81 24	243 72	Mass. continental	Mar. 2, 1833	do	81	
Peter Walters	Private	40 00	100 00	Virginia State tr.	Sep. 25, 1832	do	73	
Jesse Waller	do	20 00	60 00	Virginia militia	Apl 19, 1833	do	75	
Benjamin Worral	do	80 00	240 00	Penn. continental	May 7, 1833	do	90	
Thomas Wiley	do	21 10	-	Pennsylvania mil.	May 25, 1833	do	79	
John Wickham, Sen.	do	80 00	240 00	do	Mar. 21, 1834	do	100	

Statement, &c. of Muskingum county, Ohio.

NAMES.	Rank.	Annual allowance.	Sums received.	Description of service.	When placed on the pension roll.	Commencement of pension.	Ages.	Laws under which they were formerly inscribed on the pension roll; and remarks.
Jacob Addison	Private	20 00	60 00	Delaware State tr.	Aug 8, 1833	Mar. 4, 1831	74	
Samuel Beavers	do	20 00	50 00	Virginia State tr.	Ap'l 11, 1833	do	72	
Daniel Bean	do	60 00	150 00	Penn. militia	Aug. 24, 1833	do	69	
George Clapper	do	40 00	120 00	do	May 10, 1833	do	77	
Balsar Diterick	do	20 00	50 00	do	June 26, 1833	do	79	
John Forsyth	do	23 33	84 99	do	Sep. 20, 1833	do	83	
Thomas Forshey	Ensign	240 00	720 00	do	Sep. 24, 1833	do	83	
David Jemison	Private	23 33	69 99	N. Hampshire cont'l	Feb. 5, 1833	do	75	
Philemon Johnson	do	70 00	210 00	Virginia continental	Mar. 23, 1833	do	72	
Charles King	Ser. & maj.	180 00	540 00	N. Jersey militia	Jan. 18, 1833	do	78	
Jacob Kreager	Pri. & ser.	41 66	104 15	Penn. continental	Sep. 24, 1833	do	81	
Thomas Leedom	Sergeant	120 00	360 00	Virginia militia	June 26, 1833	do	80	
Alexander McQueen	Pri. & ens.	173 33	519 99	Penn. militia	Oct. 8, 1833	do	83	
John Richey	Private	40 00	100 00	Virginia militia	Feb. 5, 1833	do	79	
William Riley	do	20 00	60 00	Connecticut mil.	Ap'l 11, 1833	do	74	
Jesse Richardson	do	80 00	240 00	Continental navy	June 5, 1833	do	75	
James Reynolds	Pri. of mar.	80 00	240 00	Penn. militia	Nov. 9, 1833	do	84	
John Slack	Private	40 00	120 00	Penn. militia	June 26, 1833	do	80	
Benjamin Walker	do	50 00	150 00	N. Jersey militia	Dec. 27, 1833	do	75	

Statement, &c. of Perry county, Ohio.

NAMES.	Rank.	Annual allowance.	Sums received.	Description of service.	When placed on the pension roll.	Commencement of pension.	Ages.	Laws under which they were formerly inscribed on the pension roll; and remarks.
Lawrence Allwin	Private	80 00	200 00	New Jersey militia	June 22, 1833	Mar. 4, 1831	78	
James Crosby	Pr. & ser.	28 33	84 99	Maryland militia	Aug. 8, 1833	do	92	
Jacob Custard	Private	30 00	-	Virginia militia	Sep. 16, 1833	do	84	
William Dusinberry	do	58 22	174 66	New Jersey militia	Jan. 6, 1834	do	76	
Thomas Davis	do	80 00	...	Maryland cont'l	May 28, 1833	do	84	
Thomas Moore	do	30 00	90 00	Mass. continental	Mar. 27, 1833	do	73	
John Melish	do	66 66	199 98	N. Jersey militia	Jan 6, 1834	do	79	
Jacob Martin	do	20 00	60 00	Maryland militia	do	do	75	
John Myers	do	23 33	69 99	Pennsylvania militia	do	do	82	
Daniel Parkinson, Sen.	do	26 66	79 98	Penn. State	July 6, 1833	do	80	
Samuel Parrot	do	20 00	50 00	Virginia militia	Aug. 8, 1833	do	77	
Christian Randolph	do	43 33	129 99	Penn. militia	June 22, 1833	do	75	
Philip Spoken	Lieut.	106 66	319 98	Penn. State	Mar. 26, 1833	do	79	
Rauel Sayre	Pr. & lt.	70 00	210 00	New Jersey militia	Nov. 21, 1833	do	79	
Edward Wards	Private	20 00	60 00	Maryland militia	Jan. 6, 1834	do	77	

Statement, &c. of Pike county, Ohio.

NAMES.	Rank.	Annual allowance.	Sums received.	Description of service.	When placed on the pension roll.	Commencement of pension.	Ages.	Laws under which they were formerly inscribed on the pension roll; and remarks.
Reuben Bristol	Private	40 00	100 00	Connecticut militia	Nov. 8, 1833	March 4, 1834	78	
William Beekman	do	80 00	240 00	S. Carolina militia	Mar. 7, 1834	do	78	
Samuel Ridgeway	do	61 67	185 01	do	Nov. 16, 1834	do	78	
John Stewart	do	80 00	240 00	Pennsylvania militia	June 25, 1833	do	77	

Statement, &c. of Pickaway county, Ohio.

NAMES.	Rank.	Annual allowance.	Sums received.	Description of service.	When placed on the pension roll.	Commencement of pension.	Ages.	Laws under which they were formerly inscribed on the pension roll; and remarks.
William Ballard	Private	80 00	240 00	Virginia cont'l	Oct. 18, 1832	Mar. 4, 1831	74	
Anthony Bowsher	do	20 00	40 00	Penn. State troops	Oct. 25, 1832	do	79	
William Brown	do	26 66	53 32	do	Ap'l 11, 1833	do	75	
Humphrey Beckett	do	96 00	1,031 96	Virginia cont'l	May 7, 1819	June 5, 1818		March 18, 1818.
Do	do	80 00	-	do	Dec. 5, 1832	Mar. 4, 1831	75	Transferred from Kentucky from September 4, 1833.
John Davis	do	73 33	219 99	do	Oct. 25, 1832	do	77	
Peter Dingman	do	63 33	-	N. Jersey militia	Aug. 8. 1833	do	76	
Charles Duryea	do	80 00	240 00	do	Oct. 8, 1833	do	80	
Anthony S. Davenport	do	20 00	-	Virginia militia	July 8, 1833	do	76	
John Fisher, Sen.	do	20 00	60 00	Virginia State tr'ps	Nov. 8, 1832	do	73	
Jacob Grim	Pri. & ens.	60 00	180 00	do	Mar. 12, 1832	do	90	
Ferdinand Gulick	Private	26 66	79 98	N. Jersey militia	Ap'l 11, 1833	do	77	
George Hill	Pri. of cav.	100 00	300 00	Virginia militia	Nov. 16, 1833	do	80	
John Judy	Private	33 33	99 99	Penn. State troops	Ap'l 18, 1833	do	75	
John Maurer	do	53 33	-	Penn. militia	Dec. 26, 1832	do	69	
George Phebus	do	33 33	99 99	Maryland State t'ps	Oct. 19, 1832	do	72	Died February 26, 1833.
John O. C. Smith	do	33 33	-	Penn. militia	Dec. 3, 1833	do	73	
Jacob Try	do	50 00	40 00	do	Dec. 18, 1832	do	77	
John Toland	Pri. of cav.	20 00	300 00	Virginia cont'l	July 28, 1833	do	72	
William Williams	Private	100 00	210 00	Maryland militia	Sep. 24, 1833	do	85	

Statement, &c. of Portage county, Ohio.

279   [514]

NAMES.	Rank.	Annual allow-ance.	Sums re-ceived.	Description of ser-vice.	When placed on the pen-sion roll.	Commencement of pension.	Ages.	Laws under which they were for-merly inscribed on the pension roll; and remarks.
Samuel Austin	Private	48 33	94 81	Connecticut cont'l	Oct. 2, 1833	Mar. 4, 1831	86	Died February 20, 1833.
Andrew D. Austin	do	66 66	199 98	Connecticut mil.	Oct. 25, 1833	do	82	
George Allen	Pri. & ser.	36 66	109 98	N. Jersey cont'l	Nov. 21, 1833	do	77	
Philip Baker	Private	70 00	210 00	N. Jersey State	Mar. 1, 1833	do	69	
Eleazer Bostwick	do	43 33	129 99	Connecticut cont'l	Ap'l 2, 1833	do	77	
William Bierce	Sergeant	120 00	360 00	do	Ap'l 16, 1833	do	81	
Jonathan Baldwin	Private	38 21	114 63	Penn. militia	Sep. 2, 1833	do	76	
Doctor Bostwick	do	30 00	90 00	Conn. continental	Feb. 25, 1833	do	99	Transferred from Ohio from Mar. 4, 1833.
John Bancroft	Pri. & ser.	40 00	120 00	Mass. State troops	Nov. 1, 1833	do	84	
Daniel Bunnoughs	Private	40 00	120 00	N. Hamp. cont'l	June 18, 1834	do	78	
Valentine Coosard	do	30 00	90 00	N. Jersey State	Feb. 28, 1833	do	89	
Elijah Canfield	do	80 00	240 00	Conn. continental	July 16, 1832	do	83	
Constant Chapman	Sergeant	96 00	-	do	June 11, 1819	Ap'l 14, 1818	-	Act April, 1818. Suspended under the act May 1, 1820. June 7, 1832. Pensioned again under act June 7, 1832.
Do	do	120 00	360 00	do	Aug. 2, 1832	Mar. 4, 1831	79	
Zelotes Clark	Private	44 10	132 20	do	Feb. 24, 1833	do	86	
Isaac Dudley	do	33 33	99 99	Vermont State	May 9, 1833	do	72	
Lewis Day	Pri. & ser.	56 63	141 57	Mass. State troops	May 13, 1833	do	80	
Phineas Downing	Private	40 00	120 00	Connecticut mil.	Sep. 21, 1833	do	73	
Oliver Dewey	do	20 00	60 00	Mass. State	Mar. 24, 1834	do	71	
Darius Ely	do	46 66	139 98	Massachusetts cont'l	July 20, 1833	do	73	
John Ellsworth	do	29 88	89 64	Conn. State troops	Dec. 12, 1832	do	71	
Elias Farnam	do	70 00	210 00	Massachusetts mil.	July 6, 1833	do	77	Transferred from Connecticut from March 4, 1833.
Nowell Furman	do	60 00	150 00	New York militia	July 20, 1833	do	83	
Truman Gilbert	do	43 33	129 99	Conn. State	July 6, 1833	do	77	
Ozias Hawley	do	31 00	93 00	Connecticut cont'l	Mar. 4, 1833	do	70	
Ashbel Hoskins	do	40 00	120 00	do	Sep. 24, 1833	do	73	

20

Statement, &c. of Portage county—Continued.

NAMES.	Rank.	Annual allowance.	Sums received.	Description of service.	When placed on the pension roll.	Commencement of pension.	Ages.	Laws under which they were formerly inscribed on the pension roll; and remarks.
Ebenezer Hickox	Drum. & pr.	24 26	72 78	Connecticut mil.	Oct. 28, 1833	Mar. 4, 1831	79	
Francis Hardesty	Private	20 00	60 00	Penn. militia	May 2, 1834	do	77	
Nathaniel Kelly	do	33 33	99 99	N. Hamp. mil.	Sep. 23, 1833	do	68	
Paul Larcum	do	80 00	240 00	Massachusetts cont'l	Mar. 1, 1833	do	70	
Asa Loomis	do	29 00	87 00	Mass. State	Ap'l 10, 1833	do	77	
John Lane	Pri. &	20 33	60 99	N. Hamp. State	May 27, 1833	do	80	
Ichabod Lord	Private	20 00	60 00	N. Jersey State	Nov. 1, 1833	do	71	
Josiah Mix	do	47 22	141 66	Connecticut mil.	May 13, 1833	do	80	
Bille Messinger	do	80 00	240 00	Massachusetts cont'l	May 14, 1833	do	77	
Ebenezer Mather	Sergeant	45 00	135 00	Connecticut mil.	Sep. 21, 1833	do	78	
Nathan Muzzy	Private	45 44	136 32	Massachusetts mil.	do	do	72	
William Neal	do	36 66	109 98	Connecticut mil.	Ap'l 13, 1833	do	70	
Ozias Norton	do	20 00	60 00	do	Aug. 20, 1833	do	73	
Stephen Pitkin	do	26 41	70 27	Connecticut cont'l	May 27, 1833	do	79	Died November 23, 1833.
Simeon Prior	do	30 00	90 00	do	Nov. 21, 1833	do	81	
Solomon Payne	Pri. & ser.	100 00	300 00	Connecticut mil.	Jan. 14, 1834	do	73	
Richard Rogers	Private	50 00	240 00	do	May 9, 1833	do	80	
Christopher Riddin	Pri. & cor.	29 83	89 49	N. Jersey cont'l	Dec. 3, 1833	do	81	
John Shreve	Lieutenant	320 00	960 00	do	Feb. 23, 1833	do	73	
John Steward	Private	46 66	139 98	Massachusetts cont'l	May 4, 1833	do	76	
Samuel Sandford	do	26 66	79 98	Connecticut cont'l	May 9, 1833	do	66	
Obadiah Stevenson	do	43 33	129 99	Massachusetts mil.	Feb. 28, 1833	do	78	Transferred from Ohio September 4, 1833 December 1833.
Noah Shirtliff	do	23 33	-	New York militia	July 30, 1834	do	74	
Amos Thurber	do	80 00	240 00	Rhode Island cont'l	Sep. 21, 1833	do	71	
Elisha Taylor	do	40 00	120 00	Connecticut cont'l	Aug. 20, 1833	do	72	
Daniel Tilden	Captain	480 00	-	Conn. State troops	Nov. 25, 1833	do	90	
Job Thompson	Private	40 64	121 92	N. Hampshire cont'l	Feb. 28, 1833	do	76	Transferred from Ohio from September 1833 December 1833.
William Tuffs	do	50 00	150 00	Massachusetts mil.	Ap'l 12, 1834	do	84	

Names	Pri. & sea.	Annual allowance	Sums received	Militia & navy	When placed on pension roll	Commencement	Ages
Gladding Watterman	Pri. & sea.	92 00	276 00	Militia & navy	July 6, 1833	do	74
Zebulon Whipple	Private	32 77	98 31	Continental militia	July 20, 1833	do	70
John Weston	do	70 83	212 49	do	Aug. 1, 1833	do	79
John Walker	do	26 66	-	Virginia militia	Aug. 20, 1833	do	69

Statement, &c. of Preble county, Ohio.

NAMES.	Rank.	Annual allowance.	Sums received.	Description of service.	When placed on the pension roll.	Commencement of pension.	Ages.	Laws under which they were formerly inscribed on the pension roll; and remarks.
Charles Armontrout	Private	20 00	60 00	Virginia cont'l	May 3, 1833	Mar. 4, 1831	70	
Francis Beard	do	26 66	79 98	Pennsylvania militia	Oct. 16, 1833	do	91	
Daniel Cawgill	do	80 00	240 00	Virginia St. troops	Feb. 22, 1833	do	78	
John Curry	do	50 00	150 00	Penn. St. troops	Aug. 24, 1833	do	84	
John Cailes	do	33 33	99 99	Virginia militia	Dec. 27, 1833	do		
William Decoursey	do	28 33	84 99	N. Carolina militia	Mar. 5, 1833	do	78	
James Fleming	Pr. & cor.	25 00	75 00	N. C. State troops	Feb. 22, 1833	do	72	
William Gray	Cap. of cav.	300 00	900 00	N. Carolina militia	May 30, 1833	do	78	
Eber Homan	Private	20 00	60 00	New Jersey militia	Nov. 1, 1833	do	71	
Gamaliel Jagua	do	40 00	120 00	Conn. St. troops	Feb. 4, 1834	do	70	
Jacob Kester	do	33 33	99 99	Pennsylvania militia	May 30, 1833	do	77	
Philip Clinger	do	80 00	240 00	Pennsylvania cont'l	May 7, 1833	do	80	
Elijah Mitchell	do	30 00	90 00	N. Carolina militia	Feb. 22 1833	do	73	
Frederick Miller	do	44 33	132 99	Virginia militia		do	74	
David McDill	do	20 66	61 98	S. Carolina militia	Feb. 25, 1833	do	71	
Matthew McClung	do	33 33	99 99	Pennsylvania militia	Aug. 24, 1833	do	77	
Thomas Morgan	do	80 00	240 00	Penn St. troops	Sep. 21, 1833	do	85	
Samuel Mitchell	Pri. & ser.	76 66	229 98	do	Sep. 24, 1833	do	83	
Jeremiah Piles	Private	26 66	79 98	Virginia militia	May 13, 1833	do	72	

Statement, &c. of Preble county—Continued.

NAMES.	Rank.	Annual allowance.	Sums received.	Description of service.	When placed on the pension roll.	Commencement of pension.	Ages.	Laws under which they were formerly inscribed on the pension roll; and remarks.
Casper Potter	Private	30 00	75 00	Maryland militia	Aug. 9, 1833	Mar. 4, 1831	75	
John Runyan	do	31 12	93 36	N. Carolina militia	Mar. 5, 1833	do	71	
Michael Sheverdecker	do	21 25	43 50	Virginia militia	do	do	71	
David Truax	do	33 33	99 99	do	do	do	78	Died March 3, 1833.
Tobias Tillman	Pr. of cav.	27 04	81 12	N. Carolina militia	May 30, 1833	do	82	
Richard Taylor	Pr. & cor.	32 00	96 00	Maryland militia	Aug. 24, 1833	do	78	
Carey Toney	Private	28 33	70 83	Virginia militia	Sep. 16, 1833	do	71	
Barnabas Vandevender	do	23 33	69 99	do	Mar. 5, 1833	do	73	
William Williams	Ser. & fifer	62 29	186 87	do	Dec. 2, 1833	do	73	

Statement, &c. of Richland county, Ohio.

NAMES.	Rank.	Annual allowance.	Sums received.	Description of service.	When placed on the pension roll.	Commencement of pension.	Ages.	Laws under which they were formerly inscribed on the pension roll; and remarks.
Luke Allen	Private	29 32	87 96	Conn. militia	Sep. 17, 1833	Mar. 4, 1831	77	
Frederick Bumpus	do	33 33	83 32	New York State	Nov. 9, 1832	do	69	
William Bodley	do	56 66	141 65	Virginia State	Jan. 3, 1833	do	70	
Abraham Bennett	do	30 00	90 00	N. Y. continental	Oct. 25, 1833	do	70	
George Coffenbery	do	20 00	60 00	Virginia militia	Feb. 4, 1834	do	73	
John Collins	Sergeant	31 50	94 50	Maryland State	Ap'l 10, 1833	do	72	

Names	Rank	Annual allowance	Amount received	Description of service	Commencement of pension		Ages	Remarks
Noah Cook	Pri. & ser.	26 23	78 69	Penn. State	Ap'l 20, 1833	do	76	
Solomon Culver	Private	27 77	83 31	New York militia	July 6, 1833	do	73	
Jonas Clinc	do	53 33	159 99	New York State	Sep. 24, 1833	do	72	
Adam Clark	do	43 33	129 99	Conn. militia	Dec. 30, 1833	do	73	
John Camp	do	80 00	240 00	Penn. continental	Feb. 28, 1833	do	79	
John Campbell	Sergeant	21 25	42 50	Virginia State tr'ps	Mar. 5, 1823	do	73	
Abraham Decker	Private	120 00	300 00	New Jersey	Aug. 1, 1833	do	94	
Christian Fast	Sergeant	80 00	240 00	Virginia militia	do	do	72	
Samuel Ferguson	Pri. & ser.	120 00	-	Conn. militia	Jan. 31, 1834	do	70	
George Gibney	Corporal	37 43	112 29	Penn. State	Dec. 1, 1832	do	80	
James Gamble	Private	58 64	175 92	New York militia	Sep. 17, 1833	do	75	
William Hendrickson	do	24 43	61 07	Maryland militia	May 28, 1833	do	76	Died August 20, 1833.
Stephen Harrison	do	80 00	193 25	N. H. militia	July 6, 1833	do	81	
Thomas Herbert	do	40 00	120 00	N. Jersey militia	July 20, 1833	do	76	
Jonah Hanchet	do	43 33	129 99	Conn. militia	Dec. 30, 1832	do	76	
John Hellen	Sergeant	80 00	240 00	Penn. State	Ap'l 12, 1834	do	82	
William Johnston	Private	120 00	360 00	do	Jan. 31, 1834	do	72	
Adam Link	do	60 00	180 00	do	Ap'l 17, 1834	do	75	
Benjamin Mellott	Sergeant	20 00	60 00	do	Dec. 3, 1833	do	76	
James M'Durmut	Private	120 00	-	do	Feb. 10, 1834	do	70	
William Mathews	do	60 00	-	New York militia	July 23, 1834	do	84	
William Oldfield	do	73 33	-	N. J. militia	Nov. 21, 1833	do	74	
David Post	Pri. & ser.	50 00	125 00	Conn. continental	July 6, 1833	do	79	
Ezra Pope	Private	80 00	240 00	Vermont State	Jan. 6, 1833	do	82	
Samuel Poppleston	do	56 67	94 50	Penn. militia	Mar. 15, 1834	do	86	Died November 9, 1832.
Joseph Rickey	Private	20 00	50 00	do	Ap'l 18, 1833	do	73	
Christian Riblet	do	23 33	-	N. Jersey militia	June 26, 1834	do	72	
David Swaze	do	46 66	116 65	Maryland militia	Jan. 15, 1833	do	74	
Peter Snyder	do	23 33	69 99	Mass. militia	May 9, 1833	do	74	
David Snell	do	66 66	166 65	Penn. continental	July 6, 1833	do	7	
Frederick Selcer	do	80 00	-	N. Jersey militia	May 20, 1834	do	76	
Joseph Strickland	do	58 77	-	N. York militia	July 23, 1834	do	73	
Phineas Thompkins	do	80 00	-	N. Jersey militia	Mar. 7, 1834	do		
John Tilton	Pri. & ser.	90 00	270 00	Conn. militia	Sep. 17, 1833	do	74	
Amariah Watson	Private	80 00	200 00	Penn. militia	Mar. 13, 1833	do	82	
Adam Wolfe	do	29 33	87 99		Ap'l 19, 1833	do	74	

Statement, &c. of Ross county, Ohio.

NAMES.	Rank.	Annual allow-ance.	Sums re-ceived.	Description of service.	When placed on the pension roll.	Commencement of pension.	Ages.	Laws under which they were formerly inscribed on the pension roll; and remarks.
William Christian	Captain	240 00	2,238 58	Virginia cont'l	May 21, 1822	Nov. 7, 1821	84	March 18, 1818.
Do	do	320 00	800 00	do	Oct. 20, 1832	Mar. 4, 1831	72	
Christopher Depoy	Private	30 00	60 00	Virginia militia	May 10, 1833	do	72	
Isaac Dukes	do	57 98	173 94	Maryland militia	May 25, 1833	do	72	
Reuben Elliott	do	30 00	90 00	Virginia militia	May 13, 1833	do	74	
John Emmitt	do	21 66	64 98	Maryland militia	Sep. 17, 1833	do	78	
John Freshour	do	43 33	129 99	Virginia militia	Oct. 24, 1833	do	76	
John Goldsbury	do	60 00	180 00	Virginia cont'l	Feb. 12, 1833	do	70	
John Gates	do	20 00	50 00	Pennsylvania mil.	May 13, 1833	do	70	
John Hutt	do	80 00	-	Virginia State tr.	Aug. 9, 1833	do	70	
Adam Howard	Pri. & ser.	20 00	60 00	Virginia militia	Feb. 27, 1834	do	85	
Caleb Johnson	Private	68 33	204 99	N. Jersey militia	Nov. 1, 1833	do	77	
Peter Jackson	do	29 28	87 84	Pennsylvania mil.	May 25, 1833	do	71	
William Kent	do	20 00	-	do	Feb. 25, 1833	do	71	
David Kehr	do	80 00	240 00	do	Oct. 8, 1833	do	89	
James McCartney	do	21 66	64 98	do	Ap'l 19, 1833	do	87	
Jacob Metzger	do	41 66	-	do	Ap'l 8, 1834	do	74	
Dan'l James McMullen	Drummer	30 00	90 00	Maryland militia	June 26, 1834	do	73	
Arnold Norris	Private	30 00	-	Pennsylvania mil.	July 27, 1833	do	74	
Joseph Parker	do	28 00	-	Virginia militia	Dec. 27, 1833	do	72	
Sampson Price	do	20 00	199 98	N. Jersey militia	July 21, 1834	do	78	
Hendrick Rosebrom	Pri. & ser.	66 66	-	Virginia militia	Dec. 27, 1833	do	69	
William Roberts	Private	30 00	114 99	do	July 21, 1834	do	74	
Peter Sperry	do	38 33	79 98	N. Jersey militia	Ap'l 19, 1833	do	73	
James Stinson	do	25 66	90 00	Pennsylvania mil.	Oct. 16, 1833	do	73	
William Smith	do	30 00	-	do	Dec. 27, 1833	do	77	
John Vandeman	do	80 00	1,440 00	do	April 8, 1834	do	77	
Eleazer Williamson	Captain	480 00	-	Connecticut militia	Nov. 8, 1832	do	71	
Joseph Waugh	Private	50 00	243 00	Mass. continental	July 25, 1833	do	71	
Benning Wentworth	Pri. & dr.	81 00	-		July 27, 1833	do		

Statement, &c. of Sandusky county, Ohio.

NAMES.	Rank.	Annual allowance.	Sums received.	Description of service.	When placed on the pension roll.	Commencement of pension.	Ages.	Laws under which they were formerly inscribed on the pension roll; and remarks.
Daniel Brainard	Private	36 44	109 32	Connecticut State	Ap'l 27, 1833	Mar. 4, 1831	79	
Daniel Bates	do	40 00	120 00	New Jersey militia	July 20, 1833	do	71	
John Davenport	do	37 77	94 42	Massachusetts mil.	Sep. 23, 1833	do	73	
Jacob Dagget	do	80 00	240 00	Massachusetts cont'l	Sep. 16, 1834	do	74	
Reuben Patterson	do	40 00	-	Massachusetts mil.	May 30, 1834	do	74	

Statement, &c. of Scioto county, Ohio.

NAMES.	Rank.	Annual allowance.	Sums received.	Description of service.	When placed on the pension roll.	Commencement of pension.	Ages.	Laws under which they were formerly inscribed on the pension roll; and remarks.
Uuriah Barber	Private	80 00	240 00	Pennsylvania militia	Sep. 20, 1833	Mar. 4, 1831	73	
William Brady	do	80 00	-	do	Jan. 31, 1834	do	73	
Joseph Concklin	do	46 66	116 65	New Jersey cont'l	Sep. 24, 1833	do	82	
Job Foster	do	60 00	180 00	Virginia cont'l	May 10, 1833	do	78	
Isaac Hull	do	66 66	166 65	New Jersey militia	Jan. 31, 1834	do	94	

Statement, &c. of Seneca county, Ohio.

NAMES.	Rank.	Annual allowance.	Sums received.	Description of service.	When placed on the pension roll.	Commencement of pension.	Ages.	Laws under which they were formerly inscribed on the pension roll; and remarks.
William Campbell	Private	80 00	—	Penn. militia	Nov. 13, 1833	Mar. 4, 1831	70	
Francis Campbell	do	80 00	—	Penn. continental	Jan. 14, 1834	do	76	
William Harris	Pri. & fifer.	34 33	85 82	Penn. State	Feb. 13, 1853	do	72	
Jedediah Holmes	Private	50 00	—	N. York militia	May 9, 1833	do	71	Transferred from New York from Mar. 4, 1831, on Feb. 17, 1834.
Ezekiel Lane	do	60 00	—	N. Jersey militia	Nov. 5, 1833	do	79	
Henry Myers	do	50 00	—	Penn. State	Feb. 25, 1834	do	77	
Matson Paterson	do	20 00	50 00	N. Jersey militia	Feb. 13, 1833	do	69	
Joel Scott	Pri. & corp.	37 66	112 98	Mass. State	do	do	82	
Frederick Shawn	Private	80 00	—	Penn. militia	Dec. 30, 1833	do	74	

Statement, &c. of Shelby county, Ohio.

NAMES.	Rank.	Annual allowance.	Sums received.	Description of service.	When placed on the pension roll.	Commencement of pension.	Ages.	Laws under which they were formerly inscribed on the pension roll; and remarks.
Benjamin Blackenship	Pri. of art.	100 00	300 00	Virginia cont'l	Sept. 29, 1832	Mar. 4, 1831	74	
Peter L. Hall	Private	80 00	240 00	N. Jersey militia	Aug. 9, 1833	do	69	
John Line	Pri. & capt.	124 88	374 64	Penn. militia	July 25, 1833	do	76	

Statement, &c. of Union county, Ohio.

NAMES.	Rank.	Annual allowance.	Sums received.	Description of service.	When placed on the pension roll.	Commencement of pension.	Ages.	Laws under which they were formerly inscribed on the pension roll; and remarks.
John Burdick -	Private	20 00	-	R. Island militia	May 12, 1834	Mar. 4, 1831	80	
Ozias Hebbard -	do	23 33	69 99	Conn. State troops	Feb. 22, 1833	do	71	
Robert Snodgrass	do	20 00	40 00	Penn. militia	May 28, 1833	do	76	
James Thompson	do	80 00	240 00	Va. State troops	Oct. 16, 1833	do	75	

Statement, &c. of Stark county, Ohio.

NAMES.	Rank.	Annual allowance.	Sums received.	Description of service.	When placed on the pension roll.	Commencement of pension.	Ages.	Laws under which they were formerly inscribed on the pension roll; and remarks.
Henry Bagum -	Private	56 66	169 98	Maryland militia	Nov. 8, 1833	Mar. 4, 1831	73	
Joseph Croninger -	do	80 00	240 00	Penn. State	Dec. 20, 1833	do	80	
Leonard Drury -	do	20 00	50 00	Maryland State	Jan. 26, 1833	do	75	
John Henry -	do	26 66	79 98	Penn. State	Feb. 25, 1833	do	75	
Ludwick Houser -	do	80 00	200 00	Penn. continental	May 28, 1833	do	89	
Michael Hahn -	do	80 00	240 00	Maryland militia	Jan. 17, 1834	do	86	
Adam Hock -	do	60 00	180 00	Penn. State troops	Oct. 16, 1833	do	78	
Joshua Knapp -	do	80 00	240 00	Penn. militia	Feb. 27, 1834	do	78	
Jacob Nagle -	Pri. & sea.	32 46	81 15	U. States navy	Sep. 16, 1833	do	73	
Benjamin Page -	Lieut.	240 00	600 00	do	Mar. 2, 1833	do	82	
Cornelius Rickey -	Private	69 43	215 57	N. Jersey cont'l	Sept. 21, 1833	do	73	
Jonathan Wood -	do	80 00	240 00	Vermont militia	Sep. 13, 1832	do	73	
William Watson -	do	30 00	75 00	Virginia militia	Aug. 9, 1833	do	74	Died April 11, 1834.
Jonathan W. Winter -	do	26 66	66 65	Conn. militia	do	do	69	

Statement, &c. of Sussex county, Ohio.

NAMES.	Rank.	Annual allowance.	Sums received.	Description of service.	When placed on the pension roll.	Commencement of pension.	Ages.	Laws under which they were formerly inscribed on the pension roll; and remarks.
James Headley -	Sergeant	111 66	334 98	N. Jersey militia	Sep. 18, 1833	Mar. 4, 1831	78	

Statement, &c. of Trumbull county, Ohio.

NAMES.	Rank.	Annual allowance.	Sums received.	Description of service.	When placed on the pension roll.	Commencement of pension.	Ages.	Laws under which they were formerly inscribed on the pension roll; and remarks.
William Anderson	Private	26 66	79 98	Penn. militia	Ap'l 10, 1833	Mar. 4, 1831	87	
Alhira Ackley	do	40 00	120 00	Conn. militia	May 13, 1833	do	73	
James Allen	do	20 22	60 66	Penn. militia	Sep. 24, 1833	do	97	
Joseph Bartholomew	do	26 66	79 98	Conn. State	Ap'l 10, 1833	do	76	
John Barnes	Artificer	144 00	432 00	N. Y. State troops	Nov. 2, 1832	do	75	
Timothy Bigelow	Private	80 00	240 00	Conn. State troops	Dec. 18, 1833	do	73	
Oliver Brooks	do	80 00	240 00	N. Jersey militia	May 14, 1833	do	75	
Ezekiel Beach	do	48 88	146 64	Conn. State troops	July 24, 1833	do	83	
Edraund Burnett	do	43 33	129 99	N. J. continental	Oct. 24, 1833	do	78	
David Brook	do	77 22	231 66	Mass. militia	Oct. 28, 1833	do	79	
Benjamin Belden	do	43 33	129 99	Conn. militia	Ap'l 28, 1834	do	77	
Peter Bellesfelt	do	23 33	69 99	Penn. continental	Sep. 16, 1833	do	77	
Samuel Backus	do	40 00	120 00	Conn. State	do	do	71	
McDonald Cambell	Ex. rider	240 00	720 00	Ex. rider Penn. line	Mar. 1, 1833	do	80	
Samuel Calhoon	Private	23 33	69 99	Penn. State troops	Ap'l 6, 1833	do	80	
Robert Caldwell	do	50 00	115 90	Penn. militia	July 20, 1833	do	70.	

Name	Rank			Organization	Date		Age	Remarks
James Cook	do	20 00	60 00	N. Y. State troops	Nov. 1, 1833	do	71	
Peter Dewolf	do	26 66	179 98	Conn. militia	July 20, 1833	do	80	
William Dunlap	Pri. & ser.	36 66	109 98	Penn. militia	Aug. 1, 1833	do	81	
Joseph Dewolf	Pri. & cor.	83 00	249 00	Mass. continental	Oct. 9, 1833	do	72	
Isaac Fithain	Private	80 00	200 00	N. J. State troops	Ap'l 27, 1833	do	77	
William French	Pri. & ser.	48 33	120 82	Mass. militia	Sept. 18, 1833	do	90	
Windle Grove	Private	40 00	120 00	Penn. State troops	May 9, 1833	do	79	
John Gordon	do	23 00	69 00	Penn. militia	Ap'l 6, 1833	do	75	
Thomas Holt	do	40 00	120 00	Penn. State troops	Ap'l 20, 1833	do	73	
Jacob Halstead	do	80 00	240 00	N. Hampshire State	Oct. 21, 1833	do	76	
Joel Humason	do	60 00	81 00	Conn. militia	Mar. 19, 1834	do	80	
Jacob Harroff	do	23 33	69 99	Penn. State troops	Ap'l 27, 1833	do	72	Died July 8, 1832.
Silas Jones	do	80 00	240 00	Mass. continental	July 20, 1833	do	74	
William C. Jones	do	20 00	40 00	Conn. State troops	Aug. 1, 1833	do	79	
Stewart Key	do	30 00	—	Mass. State troops	Sep. 21, 1833	do	74	
George Loveless	do	26 66	—	Virginia militia	Nov. 28, 1832	do	71	
Amos Loveland	do	80 00	240 00	Connecticut cont'l	Dec. 12, 1833	do	73	
Stephen Linsley	do	26 66	79 98	Conn. State troops	Feb. 26, 1834	do	86	
Abner Leach	do	50 00	150 00	N. Jersey militia	Ap'l 10, 1833	do	80	
Reuben Mowry	do	46 66	139 98	Mass. State troops	Ap'l 20, 1833	do	86	
John McGill	do	20 00	40 00	Penn. militia	Nov. 21, 1833	do	84	
Benjamin Mallbie	do	26 66	66 65	Conn. militia	Mar. 23, 1833	do	79	
John B. Miller	Trumpeter	120 00	360 00	Penn. continental	July 6, 1833	do	84	
William Netterfield	Private	26 66	53 32	Flying camp Penn.	July 24, 1833	do	72	
Ethan Newcomb	do	40 00	120 00	N. Jersey militia	July 6, 1833	do	73	
Joshua Osborn	do	80 00	120 00	Conn. continental	Aug. 6, 1833	do	77	
George Owrey	Ensign	250 00	600 00	Penn. militia	Ap'l 13, 1833	do	73	
James Riley	Private	70 00	202 00	Pennsylvania cont'l	May 7, 1833	do	72	
William Robert	do	40 00	80 00	Conn. State troops	July 6, 1833	do	78	
Joseph Reeves	Ser. & pri.	110 00	330 00	N. Jersey militia	Sep. 13, 1833	do	77	
James Reed	Private	80 00	200 00	Penn. militia	Oct. 2, 1833	do	71	
Isaac Rice	do	57 33	—	Conn. State troops	Ap'l 20, 1833	do	78	
James Stevenson	Pri. & ser.	50 66	141 65	Penn. militia	May 9, 1833	do	82	Died February 5, 1834.
William Slater	Private	80 00	240 00	Pennsylvania cont'l	July 20, 1833	do	86	
Samuel Snead	Pri. & ser.	27 44	67 99	Mass. State troops	July 24, 1833	do	72	
Martin Smith	Private	27 44	67 99	Conn. State troops	do	do	76	
Amasa Scovill	Pri. & mus	55 33	105 99	Conn. militia	Aug. 8, 1833	do	78	
Isaac Scott	Pri. & capt.	256 66	641 65	Maryland State	Aug. 20, 1833	do	70	
Naphtali Streeter	Private	80 00	240 00	R. Island State	Sep. 13, 1833	do	83	
George Stump	do	80 00	240 00	Penn. continental	Sep. 13, 1833	do	83	

Statement, &c. of Trumbull county—Continued.

NAMES.	Rank.	Annual allowance.	Sums received.	Description of service.	When placed on the pension roll.	Commencement of pension.	Ages	Laws under which they were formerly inscribed on the pension roll; and remarks.
Joseph Shepard	Private	70 00	210 00	N. Jersey militia	Sept. 23, 1833	Mar. 4, 1831	85	
Michael Scoville	do	40 00	-	Conn. militia	July 8, 1834	do	72	
Tryall Sanner	Adjutant	320 00	765 35	Conn. State	Aug. 4, 1832	do	82	
Jonathan Trescott	Private	26 66	79 98	Mass. militia	May 9, 1833	do	74	
Henry Taylor	do	76 66	229 98	N. Jersey State	July 20, 1833	do	77	
Eleazer Talcott	do	70 00	219 00	Conn. State troops	Sept. 20, 1833	do	74	
William Tanner	do	80 00	240 00	R. Island State	Nov. 25, 1833	do	73	
Gideon Vanaker	do	53 33	133 32	New York State	Sept. 17, 1833	do	78	
John Williams	do	20 00	60 00	Penn. militia	Ap'l 10, 1833	do	76	
Simeon Wheeler	do	20 00	60 00	Conn. militia	do	do	73	
Daniel William	do	39 00	117 00	Conn. militia	Ap'l 18, 1833	do	77	
Josiah Webb	do	26 66	79 98	New York militia	May 7, 1833	do	83	
Abner Waters	do	39 22	117 66	Mass. militia	do	do	76	
James Wilson	do	80 00	180 00	New Jersey State	May 13, 1833	do	85	
James Wilson	Ensign	240 00	720 00	Penn. continental	Jan. 9, 1834	do	87	Died June 26, 1833.
William Wick	Private	23 36	58 40	New Jersey militia	Sept. 17, 1833	do	74	

Statement, &c. of Warren county, Ohio.

NAMES.	Rank.	Annual allowance.	Sums received.	Description of service.	When placed on the pension roll.	Commencement of pension.	Ages.	Laws under which they were formerly inscribed on the pension roll; and remarks.
Lewis Anderson	Private	80 00	-	New Jersey militia	June 21, 1833	Mar. 4, 1831	78	Transferred from Middlesex co., New Jersey, June, 1834.
Francis Bedle	Pr. & ser.	33 33	99 99	Penn. State troops	Mar. 26 1833	do	76	
Charles Brooks	Private	23 33	58 33	do	Ap'l 6, 1833	do	78	

Name	Rank			Service	Date		Age
Job Borden	do	73 33	219 99	New Jersey militia	May 24, 1833	do	74
Abner Bonnell	do	80 00	240 00	N. J. State troops	July 27, 1833	do	73
Daniel Bonta	do	80 00	240 00	New Jersey militia	May 13, 1833	do	72
Richard Bennett	do	60 00	180 00	Virginia Tt. troops	Nov. 9, 1833	do	71
Anthony Brandenburg	do	30 00	90 00	Virginia militia	Jan. 14, 1834	do	72
Benjamin Cox	Pri. & ser.	57 22	171 66	New York militia	Mar. 26, 1833	do	74
William Cummins	Private	23 88	59 70	N. J. State troops	Ap'l 2, 1833	do	72
Elijah Carle	do	80 00	240 00	New Jersey militia	May 24, 1833	do	72
Uzzial Carter	do	46 66	139 98	Connecticut militia	Sep. 17, 1833	do	70
Moses Crosley	do	30 00	90 00	Maryland militia	Sep. 24, 1833	do	70
John Clark	do	40 00	120 00	Maryland St. troops	Oct. 12, 1833	do	80
Burgum Coovert	do	80 00	240 00	New Jersey militia	Nov. 9, 1833	do	74
Francis Dunlary	do	35 27	88 18	Penn. militia	Mar. 21, 1833	do	72
Frederick Drullinger	do	71 54	214 62	New Jersey militia	Aug. 17, 1833	do	80
Richard Davis, sen.	do	80 00	240 00	Pennsylvania militia	Jan. 14, 1834	do	87
Benajah Gustin	do	26 66	-	New Jersey militia	Mar. 6, 1834	do	68
John Houston	Pr. of cav.	90 00	270 00	N. Carolina militia	May 24, 1833	do	71
Matthew Huxson	Private	40 00	120 00	New Jersey militia	July 25, 1833	do	77
Jonathan Holcomb	Musician	66 00	198 00	Pennsylvanin militia	Feb. 5, 1834	do	72
James Howe	Private	26 22	78 66	Virginia miltia	Ap'l 21, 1834	do	72
James Johnson	do	20 00	40 00	Pennsylvania militia	Ap'l 20, 1833	do	85
Ezekiel Irwin	do	33 33	69 99	do	Sept. 20, 1833	do	73
Stephen Kenney	do	80 00	200 00	Conn. State troops	Feb. 20, 1833	do	72
Peter Kesling	do	30 00	90 00	Virginia militia	Sep. 20, 1833	do	77
John Lake	db	80 00	240 00	New Jersey militia	June 26, 1833	do	74
William Marts	do	31 98	95 94	do	May 30, 1833	do	70
Reuben Morris	do	80 00	-	Virginia cont'l	Dec. 30, 1833	do	78
James Piper	do	80 00	240 00	Pennsylvania militia	May 24, 1833	do	72
Abijah Pelham	Fifer	88 00	264 00	New York cont'l	June 2,6 1833	do	76
Mahlon Pierson	Private	67 77	203 31	S. Carolina militia	Sep. 28, 1833	do	74
Joseph Stont	Corporal	88 00	264 00	New Jersey cont'l	Mar. 26, 1833	do	76
Garret G. Schennack	Private	85 00	255 00	New Jersey militia	July 25, 1833	do	76
Elijah Stiles	do	80 00	240 00	New Jersey cont'l	Oct. 12, 1833	do	75
Francis Turft	do	34 40	86 00	Mass. militia	Feb. 20, 1833	do	91
Thomas Venard	do	39 41	118 23	Pennsylvania militia	Ap'l 7, 1834	do	78
Thomas Wilkerson	Prn. & artfr	74 66	224 01	Virginia continental	May 3, 1833	do	75
William Whicker	Pri & ser.	55 00	165 00	N. Carolina militia	Nov. 9, 1833	do	74

Statement, &c. of Washington county, Ohio.

NAMES.	Rank.	Annual allowance.	Sums received.	Description of service.	When placed on the pension roll.	Commencement of pension.	Ages.	Laws under which they were formerly inscribed on the pension roll; and remarks.
Samuel Brown	Private	20 00	60 00	Mass. State troops	May 3, 1833	Mar. 4, 1831	76	
Eddy Burch	do	23 33	69 99	Vermont militia	Aug. 9, 1833	do	73	
James Bailey	do	80 00	240 00	Virginia State tr.	Nov. 9, 1833	do	83	
Asa Cheadle	do	80 00	200 00	Vermont State tr.	July 27, 1833	do	72	
William Dunbar	do	20 00	60 00	Virginia cont'l	Nov. 13, 1832	do	73	
Ephraim Ellis	do	80 00	240 00	Massachusetts cont'l	Mar. 23, 1833	do	69	
William French	do	40 00	120 00	Pennsylvania mil.	July 27, 1833	do	93	
John Floyd	do	20 00	–	Virginia militia	Mar. 15, 1834	do	87	
Henry Franks	do	40 00	–	Pennsylvania mil.	July 21, 1834	do	83	
Duty Green	do	30 00	75 00	Massachusetts cont'l	Ap'l 16, 1833	do	73	
John Hill	do	30 00	90 00	Penn. State troops	Nov. 13, 1832	do	74	
William Hovey	Pri. & ser.	57 50	172 50	Massachusetts cont'l	Ap'l 6, 1833	do	85	
John Hair	Private	26 66	79 98	Pennsylvania mil.	Ap'l 15, 1833	do		
Thomas Hawkins	do	26 66	42 21	Virginia militia	Sep. 23, 1833	do	73	Died November 8, 1832.
Nathaniel Hinkley	Pri. qr. m. & ens.	168 33	504 99	Massachusetts cont'l	Dec. 2, 1833	do	78	
Thomas Perry	Private	80 00	240 00	Penn. State troops	Ap'l 16, 1833	do	78	
Benjamin Paine	Ser. & cor.	100 00	300 00	R. Island cont'l	Oct. 24, 1833	do	77	
John Pain	Private	30 00		R. Island militia	May 3, 1833	do	73	
William Plumer	Pri. & lieut.	46 66	109 51	Pennsylvania mil.	Ap'l 26, 1833	do	77	Died July 8, 1833.
Nathan Rice	do	30 00	90 00	Massachusetts cont'l	Nov. 8, 1833	do	72	
Simeon Wright	Private	30 00	90 00	Massachusetts mil.	Nov. 13, 1833	do	74	
Andrew Webster	do	40 00	120 00	Massachusetts cont'l	Mar. 23, 1833	do	73	
David White	do	20 00	50 00	Vermont militia	July 27, 1833	do	68	

Statement, &c. of Wayne county, Ohio.

Names.	Rank.	Sums received.	Annual allowance.	Description of service.	When placed on the pension roll.	Commencement of pension.	Ages.	Laws under which they were formerly inscribed on the pension roll; and remarks.
Andrew Anderson	Private	120 00	40 00	Pennsylvania militia	May 20, 1834	Mar. 4, 1831	73	
John Bivins	Pr. & fifer	249 00	83 00	Massachusetts state	July 6, 1833	do	74	
Michael Brouse	Private	50 00	20 00	Pennsylvania militia	Oct. 28, 1833	do	79	
William Campbell	do	120 00	40 00	do	Mar. 12, 1834	do	75	
Augustus Case	do	-	40 00	N. York militia	May, 3, 1834	do	75	
William Ewing	Pr. & d'r	210 00	35 00	Pennsylvania militia	May20, 1834	do	70	
Henry Franks	Private	60 00	70 00	do	Oct. 25, 1833	do	70	
Rufus Freeman	do	150 00	20 00	N. II. militia	Feb. 25, 1834	do	71	
John Jeffrey	Pr. & m'e	99 99	50 00	Pennsylvania militia	Ap'l 10, 1833	do	78	
John Luke	Private	-	33 33	N. J. continental	Nov. 21, 1833	do	72	
Peter Lash	do	50 00	40 00	Vew Jersey militia	July 8, 1834	do	70	
William Miller	do	-	20 00	N. H. continental	Ap'l 10, 1833	do	89	
Reuben Martin	do	-	64 88	N. Jersey militia	July 8, 1834	do	87	
David Powell	do	-	30 00	Pennsylvania militia	do	do	77	
Frederick Piper	do	60 00	20 00	do	Dec. 30, 1833	do	86	
Jesse Richards	do	240 00	20 00	Pennsylvania cont'l	Ap'l 13, 1833	do	78	
Frederick Rice	do	-	80 00	Pennsylvania militia	Ap'l 20, 1834	do	80	
John Shiner	do	90 00	33 33	do	July 8, 1833	do	81	
Peter Smith	do	167 62	30 00	do	May 9, 1833	do	77	
Alexander Shankland	do	-	56 66	N. Y. militia	Feb. 25, 1834	do	78	
Edward Taylor	do	-	38 00	New Jersey militia	July 8, 1834	do	72	
Tragift Taylor	do	-	28 77	do	July 23, 1834	do	74	
Andrew Wonder	do	-	26 66	Pennsylvania militia	July 8, 1834	do	72	

[514]   294

Statement, &c. of Wood county, Ohio.

NAMES.	Rank.	Annual allow-ance.	Sums re-ceived.	Description of ser-vice.	When placed on the pen-sion roll.	Commencement of pension.	Ages.	Laws under which they were for-merly inscribed on the pension roll ; and remarks.
Robert Dunlap	Private	20 00	-	Pennsylvania mil.	July 18, 1834	Mar. 4, 1831	84	

Statement showing the Names, Rank, &c. of persons residing in the State of Ohio, who have received the benefits of the act of Congress passed the 15th May, 1828.

NAMES AND COUNTIES.	Rank.	Annual allowance.	Sums received.	Description of service.	When placed on the pension roll.	Names of agents or representatives.	Remarks.
ASHTABULA.							
Luther Reeves	Sergeant	120 00	1,020 00	3d reg. Conn. line	Sept. 9, 1828		
ADAMS.							
Joseph L. Finley	Captain	480 00	3,840 00	2d reg. Penn. line	Aug. 29, 1828	Wesley Lee, agent.	
BELMONT.							
Obadiah Hardesty	Private	80 00	352 66	1st reg. Penn. line	Sept. 9, 1828	James Caldwell, ag't, Crawford Welsh, executor.	Died 29th July, 1830
John Williams	do	80 00	680 00	1st reg. M'd line	Feb. 2, 1833	Hon. W. Kennon, ag't.	
BUTLER.							
Matthias Rall or Roll	do	80 00	447 78	1st reg. N. J. line	Oct. 6, 1828	Hon. John Woods, agent, Israel and Isaac Roll, exec'rs	Died 7th October, 1831.
BROWN.							
James Erwin	Lieut.	320 00	2,280 00	3d reg. Penn. line	Dec. 10, 1828	Wesley Lee, att'y.	
CHAMPAIGN.							
John Bareth	Dragoon	100 00	900 00	Armand's corps	Jan. 8, 1829	John H. James, ag't.	
COLUMBIANA.							
James Figgins	Private	80 00	720 00	— reg. Virg'a line	Feb. 20, 1830	John Thurman, ag't.	
Isaac Jackson	Sergeant	120 00	1,080 00	3d reg. Penn. line	Dec. 22, 1829	T. J. Hodson, agent.	

Commencement of pay, March 3, 1826.

Statement, &c.—Continued.

Commencement of pay, March 3, 1826.

NAMES AND COUNTIES.	Rank.	Annual allowance.	Sums received.	Description of service.	When placed on the pension roll.	Names of agents or representatives.	Remarks.
COSHOCTON.							
James Pierce	Private	80 00	363 33	— reg. Virg'a line	Oct. 2, 1829	W. Silliment, agent, and W. Pierce, administrator	Died 17th September, 1830.
John Williams	Sergeant	120 00	901 66	13th do	Sept. 12, 1828	Elizabeth Williams, widow	Died 17th September, 1833.
DELAWARE.							
Jacob Rose	Private	80 00	40 00	— reg. N. Y. line	July 17, 1828	Silas Bowker, agent	Transferred from Tompkins county, New York.
FAIRFIELD.							
Low Courts	do	80 00	720 00	— reg. Penn. line	Mar. 11, 1829		
FAYETTE.							
Joseph Parret	Lieut.	320 00	2,733 33	8th reg. Virg'a line	Dec. 18, 1828		
FRANKLIN.							
Samuel Meredith	Dragoon	100 00	200 00	Lee's legion	Oct. 6, 1828	Hon. John Woods, agent	Transferred to Union county, Indiana.
Stephen R. Price	Sergeant	120 00	746 66	2d reg. M'd line	Sept. 1, 1828	Elizabeth Price, wid.	Died 22d May, 1832.
GEAUGA.							
Joseph Fuller	do	120 00	1,080 00	4th reg. Mass line	Aug. 13, 1828	Sam'l Wheeler, ag't.	
Benjamin Johnson	do	120 00	300 00	2d reg. Conn. line	Aug. 19, 1828	Peter Hitchcock, ag't.	
GREENE.							
John Gregg	Lieut.	320 00	2,560 00	13th reg. Penn. line	Oct. 17, 1831	A. Ogden, J.R. Nourse, Joseph Watson, Hon. J. Vance, and Sam. Newell, agents.	
Nathan Lamme	Captain	480 00	3,773 33	do	March 6, 1832	Hon. Jos. Vance, ag't	Died 15th January, 1834.

Name	Rank			Regiment	Commencement of pay	Agent / Executor	Remarks
John Scott	Matross	100 00	900 00	Crane's Mass. reg.	Mar. 11, 1829	Jos. Watson, agent.	
Nicholas Rhoads	Dragoon	100 00	389 44	Lee's legion	June 13, 1829	Hon. Joseph Vance, agent, Geo. Shaw, administrator	Died 24th January, 1830.
GUERNSEY.							
Thomas Cooke	Captain	480 00	2,724 00	8th reg. Penn. line	Nov. 17, 1828	James M. Bell, agent, Ebenezer Smith, executor	Died 5th November, 1831.
Josiah Thomas	Private	80 00	680 00	—— do	Feb. 20, 1830	Hon. W. Kennon, ag't.	
Christopher Walter	do	80 00	640 00	Butler's Penn reg.	Aug. 13, 1828		
William Waterhouse	do	80 00	720 00	Rhode Island line	Sept. 30, 1831		
John Walters	do	80 00	240 00	—— reg. Penn. line	Aug. 25, 1828		
HAMILTON.							
David Black, sen.	Private	80 00	530 22	2d reg. N. Y. line	Dec. 22, 1829	D. Black, jun., agent, Catharine Black, widow	Died 18th October, 1832.
George Gwinnup	Sergeant	120 00	1,080 00	2d rég. N. J. line	Aug. 23, 1828	S. F. Hunt, agent.	
Henry Laws or Loar	Private	80 00	720 00	—— reg. M'd line	May 23, 1829	Sam. F. Hunt, agent.	
Samuel Lining	do	80 00	680 00	—— reg. Virg'a line	Aug. 19, 1828	Sam. F. Hunt, agent.	
Samuel Pearson	do	80 00	680 00	—— reg. N. J. line	Aug. 13, 1828		
Price Thompson	Corporal	88 00	748 00	1st do	Oct. 22, 1828	Sam. F. Hunt, agent.	
George Turner	Captain	480 00	2,160 00	1st reg. S. C. line	July 14, 1828		
Peter Walker	Musician	88 00	792 00	8th reg. Mass. line	Sept. 1, 1828		Transferred to Campbell county, Kentucky.
HANCOCK.							
Jacob Fox	Dragoon	100 00	900 00	Van Heer's cav'ry	Aug. 6, 1828	P. Beecher, agent.	
HIGHLAND.							
Jacob Nicely	Sergeant	120 00	479 66	8th reg. Virg'a line	June 19, 1829	H. Phelps and W. Lougborough, agt's, and J. Nicely, adm'r	
HURON.							
Joseph Strong	Corporal	88 00	792 00	3d reg. Mass. line	July 3, 1829		Died 1st March, 1830.
KNOX.							
Evan Holt	Private	80 00	680 00	1st reg. Penn. line	Sept. 9, 1828	H. B. Curtis, attor'y.	

Commencement of pay, March 3, 1826.

Statement, &c.—Continued.

NAMES AND COUNTIES.	Rank.	Annual allowance.	Sums received.	Description of service.	When placed on the pension roll.	Names of agents or representatives.	Remarks.
					Commencement of pay, March 3, 1826.		
LICKING.							
Samuel Carson	Private	80 00	373 55	5th reg. Penn. line	Sept. 9, 1828	–	Died November 3, 1830.
Peter Stevens	do	80 00	680 00	1st reg. N. H. line	July 1, 1829	Wm. Stanbery, ag't.	
Mashah Walker	Corporal	88 00	792 00	1st reg. N. J. line	Sept. 11, 1828		
MADISON.							
Samuel Baskerwell	Lieut.	320 00	957 33	3d reg. Virg'a line	July 17, 1828	Wm. B. Baskerwell, executor	Died 29th August, 1830.
Solomon Brittenham	Private	80 00	720 00	2d reg. M'd line	Apr. 25, 1832	Hon. W. W. Irwin, agent.	
Andrew Cypress	do	80 00	720 00	3d reg. Virg'a line	July 17, 1828	Sam. N. Kerr, adm'r	Died April 3, 1830.
Elias Langham	Lieut.	400 00	1,154 44	— reg. Virg'a art.	do		
MEDINA.							
John Farnum	Corporal	88 00	704 00	2d reg. Conn. line	July 23, 1828		
MIAMI.							
Lewis Boyer	Dragoon	100 00	900 00	Von Heer's cavalry	Sept. 1, 1828	Wm. McLean, agent.	
MONTGOMERY.							
Matthias Pearson	Private	80 00	720 00	--- reg. N. J. line	Aug. 13, 1828		
MONROE.							
Philip Hupp	do	80 00	440 00	— reg. Virg'a line	May 8, 1829	Robert F. Naylor, ag't.	Died 16th August, 1833.
John Turner	do	80 00	596 44	Delaware line	Aug 20, 1828	Mary Turner, widow.	
MUSKINGUM.							
Jonathan Cass	Captain	480 00	1,936 00	--- reg. N. H. line	July 23, 1828	A. Ogden and J. R. Nourse, attys, G. W. Cass, executor	Died 14th August, 1830.

Name	Rank	Annual allowance	Amount received	Regiment and line	Commencement of pay, March 3, 1826.	Agent or attorney	Remarks
Philip Richcreek	Private	80 00	680 00	2d reg. Penn. line	Nov. 18, 1828	R. Stillwell, agent.	
Isaac Van Horne	Captain	480 00	3,800 00	do	June 17, 1828	A. Ogden and Gen. Reed, attorneys, Dorothy Van Horne, widow.	Died 2d February, 1834.
PERRY.							
Stephen Owens	Private	80 00	720 00	3d reg. M'd line	Sept. 11, 1828		
PORTAGE.							
Reuben Beach	Sergeant	120 00	1,020 00	3d reg. Conn. line	Aug. 19, 1828		
Ebenezer Bostwick	do	120 00	1,080 00	2d do	July 15, 1828		Transferred from Delaware county, New York.
Elijah Bryan	Private	80 00	80 00	3d do	Aug. 6, 1828		
Amariah Daniels	Musician	88 00	792 00	6th reg. Mass. line	Aug. 8, 1831	Hon. E. Whittlesey, agent.	
Joel Gaylord	Private	80 00	271 55	-- reg. M'd line	Oct. 4, 1828	A. Ogden and J. R. Nourse, attorneys C. B. Thompson, ag't.	Died 24th July, 1829.
John Seeley	do	80 00	720 00	-- reg. Mass. line	Aug. 8, 1828		
PIKE.							
Joshua Brooks	do	80 00	720 00	9th reg. Mass. line	Mar. 31, 1831	Hon. Robert Lucas, agent.	
John Violet	do	80 00	720 00	9th reg. Virg'a line	Sep. 1, 1828	Hon. Robert Lucas, agent.	
ROSS.							
William Collins	Dragoon	100 00	900 00	Lee's legion	Nov. 18, 1828		
Samuel Finley	Major	600 00	5,400 00	-- reg. Virg'a line	July 14, 1828		
Caspar Plyley	Private	80 00	720 00	-- reg. Penn. line	July 15, 1829		
Peter Thum	Dragoon	100 00	900 00	Von Heer's cavalry	Sept. 9, 1828		
SENECA.							
Jeremiah Williams	Private	80 00	720 00	-- reg. M'd line	Aug. 19, 1828	A. Rawson, agent.	
Ely Wright	do	80 00	720 00	1st reg. N. H. line	May 23, 1829		
SANDUSKY.							
John Waggoner	Dragoon	100 00	900 00	Von Heer's corps	Jan. 19, 1832	W. P. Darst and Hon. W. W. Irwin, ag'ts.	

Statement, &c.—Continued.

Names and counties.	Rank.	Annual allowance.	Sums received.	Description of service.	When placed on the pension roll.	Names of agents or representatives.	Remarks.
TRUMBULL.							
Luther Frisbie	Artificer	144 00	1,296 00	Patten's artillery	Sept. 17, 1828	J. R. Nourse, attorney.	
Eleazar Gillson	Private	80 00	720 00	2d reg. Conn. line	Aug. 5, 1828	Hon. E. Whittlesey, agent.	
Jonathan Smith	Lieut.	320 00	2,406 00	5th reg. Virg'a line	Sept. 1, 1828	Hon. E. Whittlesey, agent.	
Timothy Swan	Private	80 00	440 00	Col. Brodhead's reg.	Sept. 12, 1828	Abm. Griswold, ex'r.	
David Webb	Sergeant	120 00	368 00	3d reg. Conn. line	Oct. 22, 1828		Died 26th March, 1829.
TUSCARAWAS.							
George Palmer	Private	80 00	248 22	2d reg. M'd line	May 23, 1829	J. W. Hayt and B. M. Atherton, agents, J. Paulmore, ext'r	
Caleb Stark	Lieut.	320 00	1,440 00	— reg. N. H. line	Aug. 6, 1828	-	Died 9th April, 1829. Transferred from Merrimack county, New Hampshire.
John Weaver	Private	80 00	200 00	— reg. Virg'a line	Sept. 11, 1828	J. D. Wynns, agent	Transferred from Hertford county, North Carolina.
UNION.							
James Curry	Captain	480 00	4,004 00	4th reg. Virg'a line	Sept. 1, 1828	Jas. A. Curry and others, representatives	
WARREN.							
Benjamin Baldwin	Sergeant	120 00	1,080 00	— reg. Virg'a line	Feb. 14, 1829	B. Baldwin and Hon. W. McLean, ag'ts.	
Moses Easton	Private	80 00	720 00	1st reg. N. J. line	Oct. 22, 1828	G. Kesling, agent.	
Robert Hamilton	Corporal	88 00	792 00	9th reg. Penn. line	Feb. 12, 1829	Geo. Kesling and Hon. W. McLean, ag'ts.	
John Scott	Private	80 00	720 00	— reg. Virg'a line	Oct. 24, 1829	James Taylor, agent.	Died 5th July, 1834.
William Simpson	do	80 00	720 00	— reg. Del line.	Nov. 18, 1828	Benj. Baldwin, agent.	

Commencement of pay March 3, 1826.

WASHINGTON.							
Jeremiah Greenman	Lieut.	320 00	2,400 00	Rhode Island line	Aug. 12, 1828		
Oliver Rice	do	320 00	2,880 00	— reg. Mass. line	Aug. 19, 1828		Died 12th November, 1830.
WILLIAMS.							
John Butler	Private	80 00	379 44	2d reg. Penn. line	Sept. 11, 1828	Wm. L. Bellinger, agent, Wm. Preston, administrator	

March 3, 1826.

Aaron, William III:161
Aarons, Abraham III:253
Abbe, Juduthan I:37
Abbe, Mason I:472
Abbe, Thomas I:53
Abbee, Ichabod I:739
Abbee, Obadiah I:261
Abbee, William II:283
Abbey, Edward III:120
Abbey, Hezekiah I:974
Abbey, Horrace B. II:128
Abbey, Samuel II:549
Abbot, Aaron I:488
Abbot, Abigail I:686
Abbot, Benjamin I:697
Abbot, Caleb I:409
Abbot, Daniel H. I:686
Abbot, Daniel L. I:686
Abbot, David I:705
Abbot, Elijah III:225
Abbot, Enoch I:675
Abbot, George I:389
Abbot, Hannah I:686
Abbot, Isaac I:281
Abbot, James I:389
Abbot, Jeremiah I:690
Abbot, John IV:72
Abbot, John, 2d I:202
Abbot, Jonthan I:178
Abbot, Joseph I:281, 982
Abbot, Josiah I:998
Abbot, Moses I:690
Abbot, Nathan I:511
Abbot, Nathaniel I:178
Abbot, Olive I:686
Abbot, Philip I:281
Abbot, Richard I:686
Abbot, Thomas I:686
Abbot, Timothy I:886
Abbott, Aaron I:30
Abbott, Abner I:213
Abbott, Abraham I:439
Abbott, Ameline I:686
Abbott, Amos I:511, 763
Abbott, Beriah I:697
Abbott, Cato I:495
Abbott, Daniel I:304
Abbott, David I:472
Abbott, Ebenezer IV:242
Abbott, Elias I:715
Abbott, Ezra I:715, 748
Abbott, George I:686
Abbott, Hannah I:683
Abbott, Henry I:202
Abbott, Isaac I:409
Abbott, James I:82
Abbott, John I:304, 683;
    II:68, 365, 527; III:544
Abbott, Joseph I:763; II:403
Abbott, Joshua I:763
Abbott, Josiah I:879
Abbott, Louisa I:683
Abbott, Maria I:686
Abbott, Mary I:683
Abbott, Moses I:763
Abbott, Nehemiah I:511
Abbott, Pardon I:45

Abbott, Peter I:705
Abbott, Reuben I:763
Abbott, Ruth I:683
Abbott, Samuel I:737; II:365
Abbott, Silas I:233
Abbott, Stephen I:82
Abbott, Susan I:683
Abbott, Thomas L. I:686
Abbott, William I:705, 969;
    III:782
Abbree, William I:302
Abeel, David II:43
Abel, Azel II:400
Abel, David II:359
Abel, Garrett II:116
Abel, John III:198; IV:249
Abell, Abel I:115
Abell, Elijah I:115
Abell, Stanfield III:19
Aber, Morris II:80
Abercombie, James I:478
Abernathey, Robert III:428
Abernathy, David III:582
Abers, Hezekiah II:27
Abers, Jerusha II:27
Abers, Silas II:27
Abers, Susanna II:27
Able, John IV:35
Abney, George IV:73
Abney, William III:244; IV:3
Aborn, Ebenezer I:389
Aborn, Samuel I:73
Abraham, James II:70
Abraham, Woodward I:495
Abro, Benijah I:45
Absalom, Edmund III:663
Abshier, Josiah III:340
Abshire, Abraham III:774
Achmet, Hamet I:53
Acillis, John A. III:541
Acker, Benjamin II:546
Acker, Christian II:730
Acker, Daniel II:104
Acker, George II:129
Acker, Jacob II:128
Acker, Jacob, 2d II:177
Acker, Peter II:492
Ackerman, Isaac II:166
Ackerman, John IV:262
Ackerman, William II:210
Ackerson, Cornelius II:210
Ackerson, Derick II:498
Ackerson, John II:477
Ackler, John II:245
Ackler, Leonard II:413
Ackley, Abraham II:223
Ackley, Ahira IV:288
Ackley, Edward II:513
Ackley, Elihu II:304
Ackley, Isaac C. I:115
Ackley, Ithamer II:397
Ackley, Joel II:55
Ackley, Simeon I:345
Ackley, Stephen I:115
Ackley, Thomas I:53, 156
Acklye, Thomas II:560
Ackuberger, David II:583

Acock, Robert III:248
Acor, Jacob III:562
Acorn, George Michael I:202
Acre, Cronamus III:556
Acre, William III:329
Acree, James III:549
Acree, John III:620
Acron, Gabriel IV:231
Acton, Smallwood III:269
Adair, James III:498
Adair, John III:305, 329
Adair, Mary II:625
Adair, William II:625
Adams, Aaron II:426; III:194
Adams, Abijah I:797
Adams, Abner I:511
Adams, Abraham I:82
Adams, Adam III:49
Adams, Alanson I:842
Adams, Almira I:862
Adams, Alpheus I:174
Adams, Amos I:261; II:194
Adams, Andrew I:747
Adams, Ansell I:326
Adams, Asa I:511; II:749
Adams, Bartholomew II:8
Adams, Benjamin I:947;
    III:229
Adams, Charles I:998
Adams, Charlotte II:194
Adams, Daniel I:409, 658, 737
Adams, David I:690, 748;
    II:304, 321; III:120, 290;
    IV:244
Adams, Deliverance II:336
Adams, Dudley G. I:728
Adams, Ebenezer I:76, 728,
    862; II:395
Adams, Eber II:194
Adams, Edward I:941
Adams, Elias I:632
Adams, Elijah II:395, 492;
    IV:265
Adams, Elisha II:146; III:774
Adams, Elizabeth I:174
Adams, Ellison C. III:713
Adams, Emanuel II:202
Adams, Enoch I:763
Adams, Ezekiel II:538
Adams, Francis III:166, 305
Adams, George III:506; IV:135
Adams, Gideon II:276
Adams, Heman IV:172
Adams, Henry III:752
Adams, Isaac I:739, 913;
    II:591
Adams, James I:294, 511,
    862, 955; II:180, 544;
    III:160, 460
Adams, Jedediah I:202; II:684
Adams, Jeremiah III:431
Adams, Jesse I:615
Adams, Joel I:202, 705
Adams, John I:337, 409, 488,
    542, 632, 655, 719, 789,
    955; II:128, 239, 468, 556,
    675; III:226, 328, 601, 770

Adams, John, 2d III:237
Adams, John W. I:174
Adams, Jonas I:853, 913
Adams, Jonathan I:511, 632;
III:706, 850
Adams, Joseph I:146, 495,
632, 896
Adams, Joseph, 2d I:213
Adams, Joseph, 1st I:202
Adams, Joshua I:82, 896
Adams, Josiah I:409
Adams, Lemuel I:542
Adams, Levi I:913; II:372, 557
Adams, Luke I:37
Adams, Luther I:862
Adams, Lyman II:194
Adams, Marg't III:850
Adams, Mark II:39
Adams, Martin I:955
Adams, Mary I:174; II:194
Adams, Matthew II:40, 155
Adams, Micajah III:620
Adams, Moses IV:211
Adams, Nancy I:174
Adams, Nathan I:974
Adams, Nathaniel I:389, 821
Adams, Nehemiah I:530
Adams, Obadiah I:534
Adams, Olive I:174
Adams, Oliver I:862; II:503
Adams, Paul I:409
Adams, Peter I:361; II:288
Adams, Peter B. F. III:275
Adams, Phebe II:194
Adams, Philemon I:958
Adams, Philip I:907; III:460
Adams, Rebecca I:862
Adams, Reuben I:632, 948
Adams, Richard III:14
Adams, Robert IV:198
Adams, Ruth II:557
Adams, Samuel I:167, 202,
273, 690, 886, 923, 974;
II:402
Adams, Samuel C. I:146
Adams, Seth II:701
Adams, Silas II:503
Adams, Solomon I:261, 763
Adams, Stephen I:409; II:288
Adams, Theophilus B. I:662
Adams, Thomas I:775; II:245,
434; III:160
Adams, Thomas F. G. IV:99
Adams, Timothy I:146, 983
Adams, Walter III:282
Adams, William I:131, 174,
495, 511, 715; II:214, 481,
591; III:195, 290
Adams, William, 2d III:216
Adams, Zanin I:671
Adams, Zebediah I:345
Adcock, John III:542
Adcock, Joshua III:774
Adcock, Thomas III:608
Adcock, William III:696
Addams, Jonas II:558
Addis, Richard III:515

Addis, Simon II:70
Addison, D. D. I:xii
Addison, George M. III:337
Addison, J. I:xiii
Addison, Jacob IV:276
Addison, Richard III:704
Addison, William III:300
Addison, Wm. M. I:xiii
Additon, Thomas I:261
Ader, Morris IV:188
Adkin, Samuel IV:192
Adkins, Charles, Sen. III:182
Adkins, Isaiah II:666
Adkins, Jabez I:453
Adkins, James III:269
Adkins, Luther I:460
Adkins, William, Sen. III:408
Adkinson, James III:317, 390
Adkinson, William III:663
Adley, Peter I:223
Adlington, John I:557
Adlum, John III:14
Adye, Caleb II:403
Adye, John I:983
Agard, Hezekiah II:468
Agard, Joseph II:216
Agard, Noah II:337
Agee, Jacob III:758
Agens, James II:35
Ager, Hugh II:46
Agle, Philip III:387
Agnew, John III:677
Ahart, Jacob III:408
Ahl, John Peter III:45
Aiken, James II:384; III:611
Aiken, John III:663
Aiken, Samuel I:705
Aiken, Solomon I:865
Aiken, Thomas IV:242
Aiken, William III:501
Aikin, Eliakim I:896
Aikin, Israel I:983
Aikin, James I:983
Aikin, Jonathan I:929
Aikins, Matthew I:389
Aikins, Nathaniel II:500
Ailesworth, George III:563
Ainger, Jesse I:873
Aingur, Justus I:907
Ainsworth, Amaziah I:948
Ainsworth, Moses I:969
Ainsworth, Welcome I:851
Akaley, John II:671
Ake, William II:8
Akeley, Francis I:907
Akeley, John II:216
Akeley, Thomas I:974
Akely, Francis I:37
Akely, Jacob II:329
Aker, John II:389
Akerd, Andrew III:805
Akerman, Peter I:675
Akers, John III:774
Akers, William II:757
Akin, Andrew I:715
Akin, James III:163
Akin, Thomas I:82

Akins, John I:775
Akins, Samuel II:327
Akins, William III:174
Akley, Samuel I:213
Alban, George IV:261
Albarty, Frederick III:391
Albee, Asa I:439
Albee, Caleb I:632
Albee, Eleazer I:896; II:216
Albee, John I:896
Albee, Jonathan I:223
Albee, Reuben I:429
Albee, Salathel II:397
Albert, Jacob III:58
Albert, John IV:217
Albert, William I:817; III:697
Albertson, Abraham II:67
Albertson, Early III:609
Albertson, Edward II:128
Albertson, Jacob I:822
Albertson, Richard II:473
Albott, Benjamin II:384
Albright, Adam II:523
Albright, Henry III:438
Albright, John II:554
Albright, William III:418
Albritton, John III:161
Albro, Andrew II:321
Albro, Job II:321
Albro, John II:503
Albro, Stephen II:283
Alcock, David II:245
Alcock, Robert II:61
Alcock, Thomas III:838
Alcorn, George IV:60
Alden, Bartlett R. I:556
Alden, Benjamin I:903
Alden, Benjamin R. I:556
Alden, David IV:249
Alden, Ebenezer I:337
Alden, Eliab II:409
Alden, Elijah I:478
Alden, Humphrey I:557
Alden, Isaiah I:569
Alden, John A. II:376
Alden, Judah I:658
Alden, Moses I:739
Alden, Nathan I:569
Alden, Oliver I:870
Alden, Roger II:473
Alden, Samuel I:556
Alden, Samuel G. I:556
Alden, Silas I:281
Alden, Simeon I:542
Alder, George III:715
Alder, James L. III:66
Aldermain, Ephraim II:304
Alderman, Gad I:472
Alderson, Thomas III:810
Aldreck, Rufus I:632
Aldred, Henry IV:165
Aldredge, William III:182
Aldrich, Asquire I:932
Aldrich, Gustavus I:603
Aldrich, James I:557
Aldrich, Jesse I:478
Aldrich, Joshua II:376

Aldrich, Noah I:983
Aldrich, Solomon II:523
Aldrick, Abel I:804
Aldrick, Caleb I:763
Aldrick, David I:14
Aldrick, Elisha I:804
Aldrick, Henry I:213
Aldrick, Joel I:822
Aldrick, Joseph I:821
Aldrick, Noah I:95
Aldrick, Phineas I:615
Aldrick, Richard I:821
Aldrick, Simon I:822
Aldrick, William I:690
Aldricks, Nathaniel I:244
Aldridge, Francis III:243
Aldridge, John IV:52, 99
Aldridge, Luke I:609
Aldridge, William III:259
Aldrish, Caleb I:662
Aldrlck, John I:831
Aleshite, Henry III:824
Aleshite, John C. III:805
Alexander, Abraham I:495;
III:410
Alexander, Asa III:81
Alexander, Benjamin II:449
Alexander, Charles III:431
Alexander, D. III:635
Alexander, Dan III:586, 603
Alexander, Elijah III:604
Alexander, Eliphas II:365
Alexander, Elisha I:439
Alexander, Henry I:821
Alexander, Isaac III:305, 431
Alexander, Jabez I:782
Alexander, James I:146, 802;
III:403, 424, 713
Alexander, James R. III:254
Alexander, Jeremiah III:89
Alexander, John I:865; IV:96,
165
Alexander, John, Sen. III:269
Alexander, Jonathan S. II:478
Alexander, Joseph II:755;
IV:63, 239
Alexander, Matthew III:590
Alexander, Nathan'l II:255
Alexander, Philip I:880
Alexander, Quartus I:983
Alexander, Robert II:701
Alexander, Rufus II:288
Alexander, Samuel III:399
Alexander, Silas II:152
Alexander, Simeon I:439
Alexander, Thomas I:37, 609;
III:431
Alexander, William I:697;
II:735; III:235, 431, 458,
527, 595, 604; IV:59
Alexander, M. III:851
Alfin, William, Sen. III:413
Alford, Alexander I:876
Alford, Asahel II:248
Alford, Eber I:95
Alford, Jacob III:663

Alford, John II:640; III:575;
IV:206
Alfred, George IV:108
Alfred, John II:568
Alger, David II:170
Alger, James I:xv, 337
Alger, Jonathan I:812
Algood, William III:391
Alkissor, Ellis III:301
Allan, John II:327
Allay, Samuel III:622
Allbaugh, Zachariah IV:265
Allcox, Asa II:321
Allds, Benjamin I:705
Allee, David IV:120
Allembaugh, Peter III:233
Allen, Abel I:690; II:235
Allen, Abiel II:228
Allen, Abijah I:937
Allen, Abner I:632, 932
Allen, Abraham II:111
Allen, Adam IV:181
Allen, Alice II:28
Allen, Amasa II:239
Allen, Amos I:273, 886; II:346
Allen, Andrew II:193, 607
Allen, Anna II:200
Allen, Arnold I:95
Allen, Asahel I:141, 969
Allen, Asher IV:204
Allen, Azor II:376
Allen, Barnabas III:234
Allen, Barnett I:802
Allen, Barsham I:304
Allen, Benjamin I:30; III:385
Allen, Benjamin P. I:471
Allen, Berthett III:460
Allen, Caleb I:632
Allen, Charles II:625; III:250,
631
Allen, Daniel I:76, 122, 261;
II:625; III:734; IV:13
Allen, Daniel, 2d I:202
Allen, David I:37, 155, 345;
II:235, 666, 727; III:216
Allen, David O. I:26
Allen, David Osborn I:26
Allen, David S. II:704
Allen, Diarca I:748
Allen, Ebenezer I:30, 228, 948
Allen, Edmund I:460
Allen, Edward I:876, 997;
III:82
Allen, Eleazer I:368; IV:10
Allen, Electa I:155
Allen, Elihu IV:218
Allen, Elijah I:534, 955; II:481
Allen, Eliza II:28
Allen, Elizabeth II:200
Allen, Elvira I:471
Allen, Enos I:122
Allen, Ephraim I:202
Allen, Ezekiel II:113
Allen, Ezra I:865; II:481
Allen, Gabriel I:122
Allen, George I:37, 903;
II:147, 527; III:424; IV:279

Allen, Gideon II:276, 365
Allen, Heman I:xiv, 998
Allen, Henry I:584; II:193
Allen, Hezekiah II:389
Allen, Hezekiah P. I:202
Allen, Howard II:245
Allen, Hugh II:586
Allen, Ira II:113
Allen, Ira H. I:998
Allen, Isaac I:45, 244, 409
Allen, Isham III:207
Allen, Israel I:632
Allen, Jabez I:821
Allen, Jacob I:244, 632; II:9,
46, 216, 651, 686; III:50
Allen, Jacob, 2d I:304
Allen, James I:233, 609;
II:503; III:112; IV:288
Allen, Jane I:471
Allen, Jared I:146
Allen, Jeffrey I:809
Allen, Jeremiah II:251
Allen, Job I:244
Allen, Joel II:111
Allen, John I:45, 95, 155,
161, 169, 233, 261, 304,
389, 697, 873; II:35, 321,
428, 708, 712; III:331, 498,
542, 552, 684; IV:126, 238
Allen, John, 2d II:200, 318
Allen, Jonathan I:146, 842;
II:337, 468
Allen, Jonathan, 2d II:318
Allen, Joseph I:178, 368, 429;
II:197, 523
Allen, Joseph, 2d I:233
Allen, Josiah I:697
Allen, Lathrop II:223
Allen, Levi II:462
Allen, Luke I:95; IV:282
Allen, Lyman I:842
Allen, Malicah I:609
Allen, Maria II:28, 197
Allen, Moses II:88; III:632
Allen, Moses, 2d III:737
Allen, Nathan I:937; II:276
Allen, Nathaniel I:389
Allen, Nathaniel, 2d I:495
Allen, Nehemiah I:244
Allen, Noah I:337, 471
Allen, Othniel I:37
Allen, Parley II:365
Allen, Paul III:397
Allen, Peter I:202; II:701
Allen, Philip II:119, 434;
III:156
Allen, Phineas I:697; II:449
Allen, Phinehas I:542
Allen, Reuben II:124, 477
Allen, Richard II:31; III:458,
611
Allen, Robert III:77
Allen, Samuel I:671, 947;
II:22, 350; III:438, 810
Allen, Samuel, 2d II:35
Allen, Samuel, Sen. III:318
Allen, Samuel, 1st II:53

Allen, Samuel G. I:913
Allen, Sarah I:155; II:28; IV:126
Allen, Seth I:329; II:481
Allen, Silas II:28
Allen, Sluman I:948
Allen, Stephen I:82, 429; II:353, 517
Allen, Sybil II:200
Allen, Timothy I:460, 557; II:538
Allen, Titus II:654
Allen, Vincent III:428
Allen, William I:82, 244, 291; II:168; III:141, 304, 421, 529, 687, 814; IV:13
Allen, William Cornelius II:344
Allen, Wright I:213
Allen, Zoeth II:397
Aller, Conrad II:755
Allerton, John IV:241
Alley, Abraham III:827
Alley, Isaiah III:327
Alley, James III:611
Alley, Samuel IV:71
Alley, Shadrach III:424
Allgaier, Sebastian II:702
Allgood, John III:262, 606
Allin, Thomas III:305
Alling, Abel I:37
Alling, Joseph II:35
Alling, Stephen I:59
Allis, Aaron II:312
Allis, Charles Henry II:625
Allis, Henry II:625
Allis, Lemuel I:472
Allis, Margaret II:625
Allis, Moses IV:267
Allis, Russell I:439
Allis, Stephen I:439
Allison, James III:438
Allison, John II:297, 631, 755; III:249, 313, 629
Allison, Joseph B. II:498
Allison, Richard II:180
Allison, Robert II:317, 631, 657
Allison, Thomas II:726
Allison, William S. I:xii
Allman, Edward III:433
Allmond, Thomas III:636
Allphin, Ransom III:212
Allred, Elias, Sen. III:165
Allstock, Absalom III:831
Allwin, Lawrence IV:277
Allyn, Charles I:95
Allyn, David I:460
Allyn, John II:339
Allyn, Jonathan I:955
Allyn, Timothy I:657
Allyn, Walcott I:948
Almon, Thomas IV:30
Almond, John III:837
Almond, Nathan III:433
Almond, William III:760
Almy, John I:817

Almy, Peleg I:817
Almy, Sanford I:817
Alpin, Stephen A. I:821
Alsdorph, Lawrence II:510
Alshouse, David II:642
Alshouse, Henry II:758
Alsobrook, Jesse III:83
Alsop, Benjamin III:837
Alsop, James III:305
Alsop, John III:36
Alsop, Samuel II:607
Alspach, John IV:245
Alspach, Michael IV:245
Alstott, John IV:34
Alsworth, Andrew II:708
Altherton, Philip I:361
Altigh, Michael III:58
Altorn, James III:503
Alverson, George I:632
Alverson, James III:478
Alverson, John I:822; III:486, 663, 755
Alverson, John S. III:298
Alvey, Josias III:56
Alvey, Thomas Green IV:29, 49
Alvis, Elijah III:726
Alvis, Jesse III:247
Alvis, Zachariah III:791
Alvond, Thomas G. II:554
Alvord, Daniel II:258
Alvord, Eleazer I:478
Alvord, Eliab I:472
Alvord, Elijah I:472
Alvord, Phineas I:478, 982; II:428
Alvord, Seth I:115
Alvord, Timothy I:472
Alworth, James II:699
Amadon, Jonathan I:948
Amaker, John III:509
Amam, John II:35
Amberson, William II:670
Ambler, James I:937
Ambler, John II:389
Ambler, Moses I:958
Ambler, Peter I:154
Ambler, Squire I:30
Ambler, Stephen I:30
Ambreister, Matthias II:676
Ambrose, David III:140
Ambrose, Stephen I:789
Amburn, Samuel IV:71
Ament, George II:758
Ament, Henry III:728
Ament, Philip III:260
Amerman, Powell J. II:365
Ames, Amos I:728
Ames, Anne II:187
Ames, Asa I:748
Ames, Asahel II:239
Ames, Burpee I:748
Ames, Daniel I:131
Ames, David II:503
Ames, David A. II:119
Ames, Eleazer I:190
Ames, Elijah II:500

Ames, Elisha II:666
Ames, Ephraim IV:180
Ames, Everett I:30
Ames, Jacob I:261
Ames, James III:354
Ames, John I:281; II:216
Ames, Joseph I:131, 728
Ames, Joshua II:231
Ames, Josiah II:187
Ames, Nathaniel II:449
Ames, Peter I:958
Ames, Robert I:584
Ames, Samuel I:7, 122, 281
Ames, Smith I:6
Ames, Solomon I:697
Ames, Spafford I:675, 748
Ames, Stephen IV:186
Ames, Zebulon I:896
Amesbury, Brownwell I:368
Amey, George I:748
Amicks, Mathew III:191
Amicks, Matthew III:642
Amidon, Jacob II:462
Amidon, Jedediah I:146
Amidon, Moses II:538
Aminet, John III:88
Amis, John I:172
Amis, Lydia I:172
Amis, William I:172
Amlin, Charles II:220
Ammerman, Albert III:199
Ammidon, Jacob I:739
Ammidon, Titus I:460
Ammon, Christopher III:832
Ammonet, Charles III:825
Ammons, Joshua III:507
Amos, Charles III:359
Amos, Isaac I:326
Amos, James III:359
Amos, John III:396
Amos, Martha III:359
Amos, Mordecai III:65
Amsden, Adam I:870
Amsden, Benjamin I:782
Amsden, John I:615
Amsden, Silas I:609
Amy, Heman I:865
Anders, James III:401
Andersen, Augustine IV:204
Anderson, Adam II:692
Anderson, Alexander II:216, 510; III:619
Anderson, Allen I:769
Anderson, Andrew IV:293
Anderson, Armstead III:326
Anderson, Asa I:958
Anderson, Bailey III:114
Anderson, Daniel I:82; III:735; IV:169
Anderson, David I:439; II:304; III:506, 826
Anderson, Elijah II:341
Anderson, Enoch III:671
Anderson, Enoch, 1st II:676
Anderson, Francis I:817
Anderson, George II:60, 692; III:416, 591

Applegate, Garret IV:74
Applegate, James III:194
Applegate, John II:70
Applegate, Joseph II:70; IV:241
Applegate, Moses II:263
Applegate, Robert II:43
Applegate, William II:76
Appleton, Nathaniel I:xiv
Appleton, Thomas I:609
Appling, John I:569
Arbagust, Ludwig II:591
Arboghart, Adam III:824
Arbour, Michael I:223
Arbuckle, James III:261
Arbuckle, Thomas IV:97
Archdeacon, John III:2
Archer, Albert II:288
Archer, Amasa I:115
Archer, Crippen I:65
Archer, Edmund III:314
Archer, Evan III:377
Archer, Isaac III:559
Archer, Jeremiah II:580
Archer, Michael I:886
Archer, Moses III:190
Archer, Obadiah II:538
Archer, Stephen III:720
Archer, W. S. III:852
Archibald, John I:719
Archibald, Thomas IV:256
Arcules, James I:429
Ares, William I:59
Arey, Cornelius I:804
Argor, Leven III:509
Argubright, George III:832
Argubute, Jacob III:810
Arickson, Samuel C. I:671
Armable, John, Jr. I:409
Arman, Thomas IV:118
Armitage, Shubert II:676
Armontrout, Charles IV:281
Armsburg, John I:800
Armsbury, John I:792; II:492
Armsbury, Thomas II:312
Armsden, Abraham IV:167
Armsden, Isaac I:907
Armstead, William III:806
Armstrong, Abel IV:267
Armstrong, Adam II:248
Armstrong, Alexander IV:82, 91
Armstrong, Ambrose III:275
Armstrong, Archibald IV:107
Armstrong, Bela II:426
Armstrong, Benjamin II:109
Armstrong, Charles W. I:28
Armstrong, Daniel I:65
Armstrong, Diah I:28
Armstrong, Dyer I:28
Armstrong, Earl IV:6
Armstrong, Ebenezer II:288
Armstrong, Edward II:2, 128
Armstrong, Elias I:326
Armstrong, Elijah II:129
Armstrong, George I:28; II:166, 549

Armstrong, Henry III:253
Armstrong, Isaac II:503; III:565
Armstrong, James III:466, 604; IV:247
Armstrong, James, Sr. II:733
Armstrong, Jeremiah I:958
Armstrong, Jesse I:821
Armstrong, John II:210, 392, 555; III:558, 769
Armstrong, Joseph II:712
Armstrong, Joshua IV:13
Armstrong, Lydia I:28
Armstrong, Matthew III:428
Armstrong, Nancy I:28
Armstrong, Nathan II:517
Armstrong, Solomon II:523
Armstrong, Thomas II:527; III:598
Armstrong, Timothy I:439
Armstrong, William I:28; III:199, 264, 494, 750; IV:119
Arnaud, John P. III:158
Arnel, William II:8
Arnett, David III:256
Arnett, John III:179
Arney, Christian III:428
Arn_ld, John I:821
Arno, John I:190
Arnold, Aaron I:804
Arnold, Abraham II:731
Arnold, Alexander II:538
Arnold, Alfred I:804
Arnold, Amelia I:26
Arnold, Anthony I:814
Arnold, Benedict I:26
Arnold, Benjamin III:626
Arnold, Caleb I:814; II:376
Arnold, David I:821; III:378
Arnold, Edward I:569; II:248
Arnold, Edy I:195
Arnold, Elisha I:345, 822; III:792
Arnold, Fenner I:345
Arnold, Francis III:563
Arnold, George II:683
Arnold, Henry II:755
Arnold, Hezekiah III:451
Arnold, Isaac I:141
Arnold, Jabez II:478
Arnold, James II:70; III:331
Arnold, Jesse II:195
Arnold, Job II:413
Arnold, John III:269
Arnold, Jonathan II:228, 691
Arnold, Joseph I:814
Arnold, Joseph H. II:98
Arnold, Josiah IV:49
Arnold, Lewis B. I:26
Arnold, Lindsey III:388
Arnold, Nathaniel I:146, 261
Arnold, Nicholas I:814
Arnold, Oliver I:821, 958
Arnold, Remington I:814
Arnold, Reuben III:441
Arnold, Richard I:814

Arnold, Robert I:223
Arnold, Sally I:26
Arnold, Samuel B. P. I:115
Arnold, Seth I:974
Arnold, Solomon III:434
Arnold, Stephen II:55
Arnold, Susan I:26
Arnold, Thomas I:792; III:78; IV:229
Arnold, Timothy I:345
Arnold, William I:821; III:152, 193
Arnot, Henry III:810
Arnsdale, Abner II:274
Arnsden, Isaac II:468
Arnsden, Noah II:288
Arnsden, Simeon II:468
Array, James II:40
Arrington, Adler III:760
Arrington, John III:782
Arrowsmith, Edmond II:503
Arrowsmith, John T. II:128
Arskine, Alexander I:202
Arter, Levi IV:113
Artherton, Joel I:213
Artherton, Jonathan I:690
Arthur, James III:822; IV:233
Arthur, Joel IV:261
Arthur, John II:637; IV:140
Arthur, Richard, Sen. III:411
Arthur, William III:752
Artis, Isaac II:655
Artiss, John III:484
Arundall, John III:693
Arwood, John III:399
Asbury, George III:696
Asbury, Henry III:195
Ash, Charles II:621
Ash, John II:403
Ash, Joshua I:621
Ash, Thomas II:621
Ash, William I:715
Ashbrook, Thomas IV:84
Ashburn, Luke III:797
Ashby, Albert II:625
Ashby, Daniel, Sr. III:293
Ashby, Fielding III:314
Ashby, George II:625
Ashby, Joseph II:625
Ashby, Mary II:625
Ashby, William II:625
Ashby, Zebulon II:376
Ashcraft, Amos IV:121
Ashcraft, William I:65
Ashcroft, Daniel III:283
Ashcroft, John III:788
Ashe, Samuel III:463
Asher, Bartlett IV:84
Asher, Canada I:557
Asher, Charles III:305
Asher, Frederick II:625
Asher, Gad I:12
Asher, George II:625
Asherst, William III:264
Ashley, Abner I:141
Ashley, Barnabas I:557
Ashley, Daniel I:146; II:255

Ashley, Elisha I:115, 937
Ashley, John I:460
Ashley, Joseph I:146
Ashley, Martin I:958
Ashley, Noah I:368
Ashley, Percival I:557
Ashley, Peter III:293
Ashley, Samuel I:146
Ashley, Thomas III:206
Ashley, William III:476
Ashley, Zena II:426
Ashlock, James III:560
Ashlock, Jesse III:609
Ashlock, William III:312
Ashman, Samuel II:382
Ashmead, John II:625
Ashmead, Margaretta II:625
Ashmead, William II:625
Ashmore, Jabesh II:60
Ashton, Andrew II:625
Ashton, George II:712
Ashton, J. N. I:xii
Ashton, John III:711
Ashton, Judith II:625
Ashton, Mary II:625
Ashton, Samuel II:625
Ashton, Silas II:625
Ashton, Thomas G. II:538
Ashworth, Joel III:780
Ask, Samuel II:444
Askew, James III:663
Askew, William III:457
Askins, George III:557
Aslin, Thomas III:551
Aspenwall, Samuel I:948
Aspinwall, Aaron II:210
Aspinwall, Thomas I:488
Aspley, John III:560
Asselin, Thomas III:551
Aster, Abraham II:128
Aston, Henry IV:230
Atcherson, Thomas I:907
Atchley, Thomas III:616
Athell, Benjamin IV:117
Atherton, B. M. IV:300
Atherton, Caleb I:358
Atherton, Joel II:517
Atherton, John I:281, 913
Atherton, Joseph I:439, 763
Atherton, Mathew I:983
Atherton, Thomas I:439
Athey, William III:42
Athy, Thomas III:704
Atkens, Ambrose III:830
Atkins, Alexander III:245
Atkins, Chauncey II:473
Atkins, David I:7; II:263, 523, 558
Atkins, Edward III:205
Atkins, John III:726
Atkins, Joshua I:594
Atkins, Josiah IV:167
Atkins, Julia Ann S. III:668
Atkins, Lewis III:590
Atkins, Seth II:523
Atkins, Thos. B. III:668
Atkinson, Amos III:427

Atkinson, Charles IV:273
Atkinson, David III:230
Atkinson, Elisha III:311
Atkinson, Isaac II:39
Atkinson, Jehu III:494
Atkinson, John I:478; III:631, 708
Atkinson, Joshua III:253
Atkinson, Nathaniel I:763
Atkinson, Reuben III:769
Atkinson, Richard T. III:720
Atkinson, Robert IV:104
Atkinson, Samuel II:67
Atkinson, Theodore I:728, 789
Atkinson, Thomas III:767
Atkinson, William I:202; II:591
Attender, George II:607
Attwater, John II:365
Attwood, Amos II:297
Attwood, Elijah II:645
Atwater, Benjamin II:437
Atwater, Holbrook I:59
Atwater, Ichabod I:345
Atwater, Russell II:165
Atwater, Stephen II:714
Atwell, Charles III:644
Atwell, John I:697
Atwell, Joseph II:428
Atwell, Oliver I:472
Atwell, Paul II:362
Atwell, Samuel I:131
Atwill, Peter II:468
Atwood, Ebenezer II:500
Atwood, Gideon I:329
Atwood, Isaac I:958
Atwood, Jabez II:473
Atwood, James I:821
Atwood, Jesse II:513
Atwood, Joshua I:756
Atwood, Moses I:748
Atwood, Nathan I:187
Atwood, Philip I:439, 739
Atwood, Samuel II:538
Atwood, Thomas I:880, 942
Atwood, Wait I:337
Atwood, Zaccheus I:632
Atys, London I:302
Auchmuty, Samuel II:675
Audebert, Philip I:609
Augur, Felix II:477
Auld, James II:710
Aumock, Abraham II:437
Aumock, John II:76
Aumock, Tunis II:76
Aunes, Stephen I:304
Aunin, Daniel II:395
Auriganson, Resolv_nt II:58
Ausburne, Robert III:631
Ausley, Jesse III:407
Austin, Aaron I:10, 45
Austin, Abiather I:969
Austin, Amos II:428
Austin, Andrew D. IV:279
Austin, Apollos I:958
Austin, Benjamin I:233; III:399

Austin, Benjamin, Jr. I:xiv
Austin, Caleb I:59, 670
Austin, Dan. I:345
Austin, David II:686
Austin, Ebenezer II:346
Austin, Edward II:223
Austin, Elias II:449
Austin, Eliphalet IV:227
Austin, Eusebius II:297
Austin, Ezekiel I:831
Austin, George I:804, 907; II:544
Austin, Holmes II:350
Austin, Isaac I:409; II:392
Austin, Isaiah III:780
Austin, James I:844; II:239
Austin, Jedediah I:831
Austin, Jeremiah I:942
Austin, Job II:490
Austin, John I:190, 831, 942, 982; II:288; III:314, 560
Austin, John A. II:84
Austin, Jonah I:244
Austin, Joseph I:937
Austin, Joshua I:913
Austin, Moses I:719
Austin, Nathaniel I:6, 923; IV:227
Austin, Noah II:176
Austin, Percis I:831
Austin, Philip IV:63
Austin, Phineas II:321, 563
Austin, Polepus I:831
Austin, Richard III:752
Austin, Samuel II:365; IV:279
Austin, Solomon I:763
Austin, Stephen I:261
Austin, Walter III:705
Austin, William I:409
Austin, Zephaniah II:365
Auter, Thomas IV:140
Averell, Ezekiel I:202
Averil, Daniel I:122
Averil, Ira II:94
Averil, Nathaniel II:437
Averill, C. K. II:553
Averill, Daniel I:756, 849
Averill, Ebenezer II:517
Averill, Jesse II:346
Averill, Jonathan II:248
Averill, Moses I:190
Averill, Robert I:876
Averill, Thomas II:434
Averill, Wyman I:937
Avery, Abner I:478
Avery, Abraham II:376
Avery, Amos I:14, 345; III:112
Avery, Benjamin II:350
Avery, Caleb I:131
Avery, Christopher I:131; II:640
Avery, Constant II:428
Avery, Daniel I:18; II:302
Avery, David I:131
Avery, Deneson I:141
Avery, Ebenezer I:14, 131
Avery, Gardiner II:276

310

Bagby, John III:164
Bagg, Oliver I:461
Baggel, James III:555
Baggs, James IV:213
Bagley, Aaron I:948
Bagley, Asher III:101
Bagley, Azor IV:192
Bagley, Barnard II:409
Bagley, Benjamin II:198
Bagley, Horace II:198
Bagley, John I:479; II:409;
  III:256
Bagley, Jonathan I:896
Bagley, Mary Ann II:198
Bagley, Philip I:411
Bagley, Samuel I:948
Bagley, Thomas I:984
Bagley, Timothy II:198; IV:175
Bagley, Winthrop I:748
Bagum, Henry IV:287
Bagwell, Isaiah III:745
Bagwell, John III:494
Bailance, Leven III:411
Bailes, Robert II:334
Bailey, Abijah I:994
Bailey, Absalom III:723
Bailey, Alexander IV:91
Bailey, Amasiah II:492
Bailey, Benjamin I:617; II:105
Bailey, Callow III:256
Bailey, Christopher I:115
Bailey, Daniel I:756; II:473;
  III:19
Bailey, Dudley I:763
Bailey, Ebenezer II:346
Bailey, Eliakim I:115
Bailey, Eliphalet I:190, 262,
  496
Bailey, Elisha III:253
Bailey, Elizabeth III:535
Bailey, Enoch II:462
Bailey, Ephraim I:381
Bailey, George I:671, 818;
  II:760
Bailey, Gordon I:698
Bailey, Henry III:840
Bailey, Hezekiah I:83
Bailey, Hiram III:535
Bailey, Ichabod I:115
Bailey, Isham III:795
Bailey, Israel I:178
Bailey, J. W. II:553
Bailey, Jacob I:949
Bailey, James I:122; II:304;
  III:335, 391; IV:292
Bailey, James, 2d II:310
Bailey, Jared IV:252
Bailey, Jerem'h II:563
Bailey, Jesse I:948
Bailey, Job I:756
Bailey, John I:214, 391, 472,
  748; II:742; III:535
Bailey, John, 2d I:178
Bailey, John, Jr. I:21
Bailey, John M. I:749
Bailey, Jonas I:603, 615
Bailey, Jonathan I:512

Bailey, Jos. II:560
Bailey, Joseph I:337, 814;
  II:318; III:45
Bailey, Joseph, 2d II:226
Bailey, Joshua II:392
Bailey, Josiah I:203
Bailey, Lowden I:53
Bailey, Luther I:933
Bailey, Maria I:452
Bailey, Mary III:535
Bailey, Moses I:683
Bailey, Mountjoy III:16
Bailey, Noah III:451
Bailey, Orsamas I:941
Bailey, Peter I:452
Bailey, Philip I:683; III:752
Bailey, Prince I:190
Bailey, Richard III:256
Bailey, Robert II:686; IV:19
Bailey, Robert (2) II:686
Bailey, Samuel I:220, 543,
  907, 975
Bailey, Silas I:634
Bailey, Sylvester II:601
Bailey, Tabitha III:535
Bailey, Thaddeus I:262
Bailey, Thomas III:52, 661,
  732
Bailey, Thompson B. III:535
Bailey, Timothy II:255, 389
Bailey, William I:46; II:173;
  III:515, 694, 795
Bailey, William, Jr. I:21
Baileys, James III:839
Bailie, John II:742
Bailis, Eldridge III:88
Bailitz, George IV:174
Baily, Israel I:633
Baily, Luther I:557
Baily, Moses III:88
Baily, Noah I:495
Baily, Reuben III:76
Baily, Robert I:802
Baily, Stephen III:387
Baily, Thomas III:517
Baily, William C. IV:204
Bain, Casparus II:539
Bain, Casprus III:463
Bain, John II:742
Bain, Martin III:19
Baird, Francis II:707
Baird, John II:84, 173; IV:252
Baird, Robert II:719; IV:25
Baird, Thomas IV:79
Bairsher, Philip II:702
Baith, George IV:11
Bake, George II:68
Bake, John IV:70
Baker, Abel II:403
Baker, Abel, Jr. II:113
Baker, Abijah IV:162
Baker, Abner II:226
Baker, Abraham II:190
Baker, Absalom IV:10
Baker, Amos I:176, 513
Baker, Anna II:625
Baker, Anthony I:28

Baker, Asa I:164; II:521
Baker, Athony III:787
Baker, Beal III:165
Baker, Benjamin I:706
Baker, Benoni I:633
Baker, Bowling III:271
Baker, Bradford I:570
Baker, Caleb II:26
Baker, Caty II:190
Baker, Charles II:538
Baker, Claiborne III:359
Baker, Daniel II:107, 382,
  520, 578; IV:233, 265
Baker, David II:67; III:399,
  408
Baker, Delia I:176
Baker, Eleazer II:528
Baker, Eli IV:227
Baker, Elias III:164
Baker, Elijah II:231; IV:125
Baker, Elsha II:503
Baker, Enoch I:132
Baker, Ephraim II:274
Baker, Esther I:28
Baker, Ezekiel II:462
Baker, George IV:83
Baker, Glover III:680
Baker, Gurdon M. I:28
Baker, Henry B. III:557
Baker, Henry K. I:176
Baker, Isaac III:372
Baker, Israel IV:237
Baker, J. C. II:500
Baker, Jacob II:130, 591, 625
Baker, James II:190, 283, 631
Baker, Jeremiah I:822
Baker, Joel II:258
Baker, John I:233, 391;
  II:538, 760; III:191, 271,
  434, 542; IV:35, 96
Baker, John, 2d I:453
Baker, John H. III:52
Baker, Jonathan I:28; II:35,
  119, 283
Baker, Joseph I:176, 281, 542;
  II:288; III:281
Baker, Joshua I:132; II:362,
  409
Baker, Joshua L. I:28
Baker, Judah II:528
Baker, Justus II:521
Baker, Lewis II:190, 462
Baker, Lovel I:46
Baker, Lucretia III:359
Baker, Lyman II:450
Baker, Malyne IV:132
Baker, Maria III:359
Baker, Mary I:176; II:26, 190
Baker, Mary Ann II:625
Baker, Michael IV:9
Baker, Morris II:395
Baker, Nathan II:251, 434,
  557
Baker, Nathaniel I:584
Baker, Nicholas III:252
Baker, Peter I:896; II:491;
  III:629

312

Bancroft, Jonathan I:512
Bancroft, Joseph I:633
Bancroft, Nathaniel I:592
Bancroft, Oliver I:84
Bancroft, Robert I:390
Bancroft, Sarah Ann I:592
Bancroft, Thaddeus II:365, 544
Bancroft, William I:495, 635
Bandfield, James, Sen. II:339
Bandy, Epperson III:530
Bandy, Thomas III:622
Bangs, Adnah I:975
Banister, Jason I:983
Banister, Jesse I:870
Banister, Levi II:239
Banister, Thomas I:870; III:494
Banker, E. A. II:560
Banker, Frederick II:395
Banker, John I:896
Banker, Nicholas II:177
Banker, Stephen II:492
Banker, William II:220
Bankroft, Timothy I:739
Banks, Abraham D. II:444
Banks, Andrew II:746
Banks, Benjamin I:84
Banks, Ebenezer I:82
Banks, Edward III:562
Banks, Ezekiel O. I:83
Banks, Gershom I:82
Banks, Hyatt I:84
Banks, Jacob III:758
Banks, James IV:27
Banks, John I:233; II:267; III:777
Banks, John, Sen. III:701
Banks, Joseph I:84; III:385
Banks, Moses I:178
Banks, Moses O. I:83
Banks, Nathan I:83
Banks, Nehemiah I:84
Banks, Obadiah II:129, 444
Banks, Peter III:409
Banks, Thomas II:341
Banks, William IV:86
Bankston, Andrew III:449
Bannell, Amos I:37
Banner, Benjamin III:451
Banner, Ephraim III:451
Banner, Joseph, Sen. III:451
Bannerman, George III:437
Bannister, Andrew I:635
Bannister, Solomon I:635
Bantham, John IV:178
Bantham, Perigrine III:45
Baptist, John I:903
Baptiste, John II:591
Bar, John II:669
Barbarick, John I:164
Barbee, Daniel III:305
Barbee, Elias III:284
Barber, Abraham I:342; II:229
Barber, Amaziah IV:194
Barber, Bela I:141

Barber, Benjamin I:831; III:663
Barber, Benjamin, 2d I:831
Barber, Charles II:576
Barber, Charlotte II:622
Barber, Daniel I:831; III:62
Barber, David I:840; II:538
Barber, Euphemia II:622
Barber, George III:61
Barber, Gray III:643
Barber, Henry II:622
Barber, James I:924
Barber, Jethro I:763
Barber, Job I:943; II:462
Barber, John I:788; II:473, 538; III:12
Barber, Jonathan I:832
Barber, Joseph I:832
Barber, Joshua III:305
Barber, Michael I:95
Barber, Mons I:831
Barber, N. I:156-57
Barber, Nathan I:831
Barber, Obadiah I:933
Barber, Peter I:748
Barber, Reuben II:523
Barber, Reynolds I:831
Barber, Robert II:752
Barber, Silas I:180
Barber, Simeon I:106
Barber, Smith II:539
Barber, Solomon I:187
Barber, Thomas II:397
Barber, Timothy I:123
Barber, Uuriah IV:285
Barber, William II:312; III:454
Barbey, Elijah III:208
Barbour, J. S. III:848-49, 853
Barbour, James M. II:622
Barbour, James S. III:186
Barbour, P. P. III:851-52
Barcalow, Cornelius II:321
Barce, Josiah II:434
Barckert, Christian II:702
Barclay, John III:614
Barclay, Michael II:353
Barclay, Stephen II:604
Barclay, Thomas III:14
Barco, John IV:118
Barco, Thomas II:29
Bardean, Moses II:549
Bardeen, Aaron I:805
Bardeen, Stephen II:321
Barden, Benjamin I:472
Barden, Ichabod I:558
Barden, James I:690
Barden, Lemuel I:959
Barden, Samuel I:453
Barden, Timothy I:453
Bardine, James II:71
Bardsley, William II:321, 563
Bardwell, Obadiah I:346
Bardwell, Reuben I:440
Bardwell, Samuel I:440
Bardwin, Samuel I:18
Bare, Edward II:350
Bareth, John IV:174, 295

Barfield, George I:949
Barfield, James III:522
Bargenhoff, William II:693
Barger, John III:118; IV:3
Barham, Benjamin III:737
Barham, Hartwell III:390
Barham, John III:265
Barheydt, Jerome II:510
Bark, James III:19
Barkelew, Runyan II:71
Barkelow, James II:752
Barker, Abijah I:756
Barker, Barnabas I:932
Barker, Benjamin I:282, 739
Barker, Charles IV:210
Barker, Daniel I:214; II:398
Barker, Daniel, 2d I:191
Barker, Edward III:842
Barker, Elijah I:749
Barker, Ethan I:95
Barker, Ezra I:460
Barker, Francis I:691
Barker, George III:310, 605
Barker, Hannaniah I:914
Barker, Hezekiah II:373
Barker, Isaac III:188
Barker, Isaac Bowen I:571
Barker, J. N. II:560
Barker, James I:178
Barker, Jesse I:282
Barker, John I:410, 691, 788; III:318
Barker, Jonathan I:179
Barker, Levi II:449
Barker, Nathan I:874
Barker, Nathaniel III:770
Barker, Oliver II:235
Barker, Peleg I:818
Barker, Peter I:407, 706
Barker, Sally I:788
Barker, Samuel I:178, 214; II:376
Barker, Simeon I:477; II:346
Barker, Stephen III:222
Barker, Theodore I:948
Barker, Thomas I:390, 410
Barker, William II:239; III:216
Barker, Zenas II:397
Barkers, James IV:261
Barkley, James III:626
Barkley, Robert II:715
Barkley, Robert (2) II:715
Barkley, William III:174
Barkman, Jacob II:468
Barksdale, Samuel III:746
Barlee, Michael I:46
Barley, Jacob I:73
Barleys, James III:832
Barlison, Edward II:129
Barlow, Abner II:214, 469
Barlow, George I:558
Barlow, Henson III:525
Barlow, John I:46
Barlow, Joseph III:207
Barlow, Lewis IV:90
Barlow, Moses II:362
Barlow, Obed I:817

313

Barlow, Samuel II:389
Barmer, John III:433
Barnabe, James I:73
Barnaby, Henry II:147
Barnaby, Jonathan I:369
Barnard, Benjamin I:929
Barnard, Dan I:983
Barnard, Daniel I:179
Barnard, Edmund I:757
Barnard, Elisha I:440
Barnard, Grove I:38
Barnard, John II:426
Barnard, Jonathan I:616;
  III:541
Barnard, Joseph I:617
Barnard, Nathan I:203
Barnard, Richard I:347
Barnard, Rufus I:924
Barnard, Stephen I:846
Barnard, Thomas IV:192
Barnard, Timothy II:434
Barnard, William II:481
Barnard, William L. III:313
Barndollar, Frederick II:591
Barnes, Abel II:288
Barnes, Abraham I:233
Barnes, Ambrose II:207
Barnes, Amos I:728; II:276
Barnes, Benjamin I:460, 570;
  III:280
Barnes, Benjamin C. II:189
Barnes, Calvin II:101
Barnes, Canterbury I:571
Barnes, Chesley III:448
Barnes, Corban I:570
Barnes, Daniel I:804; II:372
Barnes, David I:123
Barnes, Dennis II:189
Barnes, Ebenezer IV:15
Barnes, Elijah I:95, 853;
  II:189, 413
Barnes, Eliphalet I:46
Barnes, Elisha I:763
Barnes, Enos II:226
Barnes, George III:267
Barnes, Heartwell II:283
Barnes, Henry II:329
Barnes, Hephsiba I:123
Barnes, Hugh IV:29
Barnes, Israel I:96
Barnes, Ithiel I:896, 999
Barnes, J., Jr. I:156
Barnes, James II:655; III:558,
  575; IV:95
Barnes, Jared I:123
Barnes, Jeremiah I:739
Barnes, John I:886; II:267,
  365, 521, 758; III:225, 622;
  IV:288
Barnes, John C. II:366
Barnes, Jonah I:106
Barnes, Jonathan II:276
Barnes, Jonathan, 2d III:216
Barnes, Jonathan, Jr. I:156
Barnes, Joseph I:231
Barnes, Joshua I:123
Barnes, Josiah I:38

Barnes, Lemuel II:226
Barnes, Moses IV:249
Barnes, Nathan I:95, 616;
  II:276
Barnes, Nehemiah II:684
Barnes, Orange I:46
Barnes, Reuben I:511; II:413
Barnes, Sally II:189
Barnes, Samuel I:46, 123;
  II:742; III:3
Barnes, Shadrach III:280
Barnes, Silas I:346
Barnes, Simeon I:37
Barnes, Solomon III:122
Barnes, Sophia Ann II:189
Barnes, Thomas I:390, 496
Barnes, Thompson S. II:189
Barnes, Warner II:353
Barnes, William I:617; II:276,
  638; III:620
Barnet, Andrew III:284
Barnet, Benjamin I:880
Barnet, Daniel III:252
Barnet, George IV:220
Barnet, John II:276
Barnet, John, 2d II:245
Barnet, Joseph III:788
Barnet, Michael III:594
Barnet, Robert II:758; III:29
Barnet, Thomas III:91
Barnet, William III:284
Barnett, Ambrose III:313
Barnett, Carter III:611
Barnett, Charles III:421
Barnett, James III:336
Barnett, James P. III:298
Barnett, John II:231, 556;
  IV:43
Barnett, Lance James III:543
Barnett, Moses I:937
Barnett, Robert I:679
Barnett, Sion III:170
Barnett, Thomas I:410; III:431
Barnett, William III:600
Barney, Asa II:346
Barney, Benjamin II:321
Barney, John I:782
Barney, Jonathan I:368; II:104
Barney, Joseph I:959
Barney, Martin I:956
Barney, William II:274
Barney, William, 2d II:251
Barney, William, 3d II:329
Barngrover, George IV:132
Barnham, Caleb II:122
Barnham, Rufus I:389
Barnhardt, George III:410
Barnhart, Cornelius II:510
Barnhart, Jeremiah II:531
Barnheiser, John III:58
Barnhill, Henry III:442
Barnhill, John III:166
Barnhill, Samuel III:320
Barnitz, Jacob II:605
Barnover, George III:20
Barns, Armstead III:717
Barns, Burwell III:447

Barns, Elijah IV:233
Barns, Jacob I:896
Barns, Josiah I:633
Barns, Samuel I:633
Barns, William I:822
Barnse, Robert IV:174
Barnthisler, Christopher III:12
Barnum, Amos I:45
Barnum, Charles II:196
Barnum, Daniel I:876; II:196
Barnum, Enoch IV:128
Barnum, Ezbon I:83
Barnum, Jehiel II:238
Barnum, John P. II:196
Barnum, Joshua II:162
Barnum, Noah I:30; II:196
Barnum, Samuel II:346
Barnum, Stephen I:333, 923;
  II:667
Barnum, Thomas I:923; II:462
Barnwell, James III:694
Barnwell, John II:697
Barott, Hezekiah II:478
Barr, Alexander I:896
Barr, Hugh III:11
Barr, Isaac III:390
Barr, James II:591; III:169,
  529, 775
Barr, John III:324; IV:220
Barr, Philip III:735
Barr, Robert II:608
Barr, Samuel IV:231
Barr, William II:631
Barrackman, William III:19
Barrage, Charles III:738
Barram, Fielding III:113
Barratt, William III:434
Barrel, Alfred I:849
Barremore, Marshall II:403
Barren, James III:14
Barret, Benjamin II:365
Barret, Joel I:983
Barret, Wait II:202
Barrett, Abraham II:546
Barrett, Alexander III:2
Barrett, Arthur IV:114
Barrett, Bartholomew II:288
Barrett, Benjamin I:635;
  IV:167
Barrett, David II:123
Barrett, Edmund II:129
Barrett, Elizab'h I:1000
Barrett, Francis III:271
Barrett, Henry II:585; III:846
Barrett, Isaac III:415
Barrett, Israel II:276
Barrett, Jacob II:365
Barrett, James I:178
Barrett, Jeremiah I:37, 907
Barrett, John I:223
Barrett, Jonathan I:511;
  III:415; IV:233
Barrett, Lemuel I:749
Barrett, Lewis III:182
Barrett, Nathaniel I:223
Barrett, Oliver I:346, 914,
  1000; II:318

Bassett, Abel II:251
Bassett, Abraham I:123
Bassett, Benjamin I:337
Bassett, Burwell III:847
Bassett, Caleb I:571
Bassett, Cornelius I:345
Bassett, David I:203
Bassett, Edward I:122
Bassett, Henry II:147
Bassett, Howard I:913
Bassett, Isaac I:76, 122, 635
Bassett, James I:123
Bassett, Jonathan I:326
Bassett, Joseph IV:55
Bassett, Lot I:440
Bassett, Nathan I:329
Bassett, Nathaniel I:345
Bassett, Samuel I:123, 263, 739
Bassett, William IV:87
Bassett, Zachariah I:913
Bassford, Dorcas I:861
Bassford, James I:861; III:527
Bassford, Jane I:861
Bassford, Mary I:861
Bassford, Thomas I:861
Bassham, Obadiah III:209
Bastedo, James II:71
Basteen, Joseph I:231
Bastian, Jacob II:733
Baston, Jonathan I:234
Bastow, William I:797, 804
Baswell, David III:631
Bat, Abraham II:607
Batchelder, John I:769
Batchelder, Josiah I:769
Batchelder, Mark I:763
Batchelder, Ruppe I:923
Batchelder, Simon I:769
Batchelder, William I:190; IV:213
Batcheldor, Gideon I:233
Batchelder, James I:610
Batchellor, John P. I:495
Batchelor, Archelaus I:706
Batchelor, Benjamin IV:133
Batchelor, Enoch I:633
Batchelor, Jeremiah I:635
Batchelor, Joseph II:428
Batchelor, Joshua F. III:20
Batchelor, Peter III:682
Bateman, Daniel II:61
Bateman, Henry IV:26
Bateman, Joseph I:958
Bateman, Moses II:61
Bateman, Thomas III:228
Bateman, William II:33, 61; IV:69
Bateman, Zadock II:366
Bates, Aaron I:479
Bates, Amason I:346
Bates, Ambrose I:543
Bates, Asa I:146
Bates, Barnabas I:571
Bates, Benjamin I:571; II:67, 395
Bates, Benoni I:804

Bates, Benony II:676
Bates, Carver I:903
Bates, Christopher I:959
Bates, Clement I:571
Bates, Cornelius I:571
Bates, Daniel IV:285
Bates, Doughty I:262
Bates, Edward I:609; II:180
Bates, Eleazer I:453
Bates, Elisha I:543
Bates, Elizabeth II:187
Bates, Ephraim IV:273
Bates, Ezra I:83
Bates, Francis I:870
Bates, Hinsdale IV:269
Bates, Humphrey III:319
Bates, Isaac III:529
Bates, Issachar IV:274
Bates, J. C. I:657
Bates, Jabez I:262
Bates, Jacob I:245, 472
Bates, James I:832; III:282, 620, 782
Bates, John I:46
Bates, John, 2d II:344
Bates, Jonathan I:584
Bates, Jonathan, 2d I:534
Bates, Joseph I:557; II:187; IV:106
Bates, Josiah I:914
Bates, Lemuel I:479
Bates, Libbeus I:345
Bates, Moses I:886
Bates, Noah I:634
Bates, Oliver II:251
Bates, Phineas II:753
Bates, Robert I:543
Bates, Rufus II:536
Bates, Samuel I:542, 804; II:239
Bates, Thaddeus I:542
Bates, Thomas I:262; III:208
Bates, William II:549; III:230; IV:13
Bathrick, Jason I:615
Bathurst, Lawrence II:709
Batson, James III:663
Battan, John I:676
Battean, Christian III:19
Batten, Ebenezer I:391
Battenby, John II:607
Batterman, George III:49
Batterson, Abijah II:523
Batterson, George I:45
Batterson, James I:31
Batterson, Joseph II:304
Batterson, Stephen I:30
Battey, William I:823
Battist, John I:903
Battle, James II:276
Battle, Justus IV:267
Battles, Asa I:281
Battles, Jared I:571
Battles, John II:274, 659
Battles, Noel III:93
Battles, Shadrach III:674
Battson, Mordecai IV:54

Bauer, William III:19
Baugh, Henry III:318
Baughman, George IV:247
Bauldwin, Edward III:293
Baum, Frederick II:437
Baum, John II:709
Baumgardner, Henry II:760
Baurer, Frederick II:702
Bavor, Edward III:217
Baw, David II:709
Baw, Jacob II:723
Baw, Robert II:725
Bawcott, William III:849
Bawyer, Philip III:677
Baxter, Aaron I:73; II:517
Baxter, Benjamin I:223; II:331
Baxter, Cornelius I:326
Baxter, David I:326
Baxter, Ebenezer I:804
Baxter, Francis I:21
Baxter, John I:223; II:96, 418; III:72, 127
Baxter, John, 2d II:129
Baxter, John, 3d II:382
Baxter, Malachi I:558
Baxter, Nathan II:392
Baxter, Stephen II:130
Baxter, William I:342; II:302; III:756
Bay, Andrew III:632
Bay, David IV:174
Bay, Joseph III:198
Bay, Robert IV:252
Bayan, John III:641
Bayles, Jesse IV:171
Bayley, Daniel II:231
Bayley, David II:513
Bayley, Elijah II:235
Bayley, Elijah, 2d II:277
Bayley, Frye I:886
Bayley, Henry II:11
Bayley, Jonathan II:122
Bayley, Peter I:948
Bayley, Solomon I:748
Bayley, Thomas I:390
Baylies, Hodijah I:655
Baylis, Elias II:231
Baylis, Elijah III:622
Baylis, Henry III:849
Baylis, Hezekiah III:88
Baylis, Nehemiah II:312
Baylis, William III:249, 326
Bayliss, John III:549
Baylor, George II:663
Baylor, Michael II:71
Baylor, Walker III:663
Baynton, Jonathan I:389
Bayrd, John IV:38
Baytop, James III:700
Beabe, Richard II:331
Beabout, John II:755
Beach, Adnah III:490
Beach, Asa II:366, 503
Beach, Ashbel II:450
Beach, Daniel I:106
Beach, David I:876; II:555
Beach, Dorothy II:193

Beach, Edmund II:403
Beach, Elihu IV:218
Beach, Eliza II:193
Beach, Elnathan II:428
Beach, Ezekiel IV:288
Beach, Francis I:106
Beach, Harriet II:193
Beach, Henry II:604
Beach, Israel II:468
Beach, Jabez I:83
Beach, Jedediah II:482
Beach, Jesse II:129
Beach, John I:937; II:409, 714
Beach, Jonathan II:426
Beach, Julius I:107
Beach, Nathan II:731
Beach, Nathaniel III:336
Beach, Obil IV:268
Beach, Reuben IV:299
Beach, Robert I:937
Beach, Roswell IV:170
Beach, Samuel I:453, 997;
  II:193
Beach, Sarah W. II:193
Beach, Stephen II:418
Beach, Susanna II:193
Beach, Thaddeus I:46
Beach, Thomas I:96
Beacroft, John III:45
Beadles, Ann III:671
Beadles, Edmund III:762
Beadles, Har'n D. III:671
Beadless, Joel III:796
Beadsley, Orra I:7
Beagle, John II:327
Beakley, Christopher II:444
Beakman, Michael III:243
Beal, Azariah I:542
Beal, Ben. III:836
Beal, Daniel I:178
Beal, Jarvis I:160
Beal, Job I:245
Beal, John II:566
Beal, Joseph I:228, 542, 802
Beal, Joshua I:542
Beal, Noah I:571
Beal, Samuel I:570
Beal, Shadrach III:836
Beal, Shadrach (2) III:836
Beal, Thomas I:634
Beale, Jonathan I:543
Beale, Robert III:853
Beale, William III:140
Beale, William D. III:70
Beales, Isaac I:262
Beall, E. L. I:xii, xiv
Beall, Benjamin I:203
Beall, Christopher III:43
Beall, John II:331; III:836
Beall, Obadiah IV:174
Beall, Robert L. III:14
Beall, Thomas IV:210
Bealle, Richard E. III:771
Bealmear, Daniel V. III:201
Bealor, George II:748
Beals, Adam I:880
Beals, Enoch I:880

Beals, Jonathan I:441
Beals, Joshua I:337
Beals, Levi I:584
Beals, Levi, Jr. I:584
Beals, Uriah I:429
Beam, John II:58
Beam, Michael IV:265
Beam, Peter II:130
Beaman, Gideon I:633
Beaman, Joseph I:870
Beaman, Josiah I:440
Beaman, Lemuel I:45
Beamont, Caesar I:65
Beamont, Deodate I:123
Bean, Anthony II:80
Bean, Benjamin I:697
Bean, Conrad III:328
Bean, Daniel I:282, 715, 782;
  IV:276
Bean, Ebenezer I:233, 775,
  903
Bean, James I:671; II:742
Bean, James, Jr. I:671
Bean, James R. I:169
Bean, Jeremiah I:670, 769
Bean, John I:885; III:36
Bean, Jonathan I:213
Bean, Joseph I:728
Bean, Josiah I:261
Bean, Josiah (2) I:262
Bean, Leonard III:234
Bean, Nathaniel II:239
Bean, Nicholas IV:11
Bean, Peter II:81
Bean, Richard III:297; IV:104
Bean, Richard (2) III:297
Bean, Samuel I:203
Bean, Thomas I:812
Bean, William I:410; II:437
Beans, John I:161
Beans, John J. II:588
Beans, William II:735
Bearce, Benjamin I:571
Bearce, Elemezer I:203
Bearce, Gideon I:281
Bearce, Levi I:214
Beard, Andrew I:123
Beard, David IV:110
Beard, Ebenezer I:513
Beard, Francis IV:281
Beard, Frederick II:696
Beard, Henry II:289
Beard, Jacob IV:238
Beard, John IV:257
Beard, Jonathan I:635
Beard, Moses III:156
Beard, Nathaniel I:31
Beard, Robert III:166, 624
Beard, Samuel III:591
Beard, William I:763; III:622;
  IV:262
Bearden, John III:566
Beardslee, Abijah I:59, 82
Beardslee, Joseph I:83
Beardslee, Thaddeus I:83
Beardsley, Ashley II:625
Beardsley, Barnard II:625

Beardsley, Benjamin II:366
Beardsley, Gersham II:277
Beardsley, Horace II:625
Beardsley, James I:82
Beardsley, John I:2, 83; II:625
Beardsley, Salmon W. II:234
Beardsley, Whitmore I:943
Beardsly, Elijah IV:175
Beardsly, Josiah II:482
Beares, Judah I:329
Bears, Foard I:880
Bears, Joseph I:82
Bearse, David I:329
Bearse, Prince I:329
Beaseley, William III:370
Beasley, Leonard III:506
Beasley, Smith III:673
Beasly, John III:673
Beaster, William II:67
Beatly, Isaac II:297
Beatly, James III:719
Beatman, William II:216
Beatty, Arthur II:523
Beatty, Daniel III:308
Beatty, Henry III:775
Beatty, Hugh II:752
Beatty, James II:692, 715;
  III:36, 614
Beatty, John II:17, 737;
  III:192, 308
Beatty, John, 2d II:693
Beatty, John, 1st II:635
Beatty, Joseph II:473; III:222
Beatum, Jacob II:602
Beaty, Andrew III:579
Beaty, David III:424
Beaty, John II:473, 531;
  II:356
Beaty, Samuel III:50
Beaty, Walter III:546
Beaty, William II:473; III:321
Beaumont, Daniel II:346
Beaumont, Isaiah IV:144
Beaumont, Oliver II:223
Beaumont, Samuel IV:222
Beaver, Adam II:752
Beaver, Benjamin II:657
Beaver, George II:657
Beaver, Jeremiah II:408
Beaver, Martin III:45
Beavers, John III:256
Beavers, Samuel IV:276
Beavert, John III:614
Beazley, Benjamin III:668
Beazley, Cornelius III:697
Beazley, Edmund III:668
Beazley, Elizabeth III:668
Beazley, Ephraim III:769
Beazley, Marshall III:668
Beazley, Sophia III:668
Beazley, Susanna III:668
Beazley, Thomas III:668
Bebe, Joseph II:376
Bebee, Aurora III:194
Bebee, Daniel II:194
Bebee, David I:45
Bebee, Ezra I:337

Bebee, Paul I:65
Bebee, Peter II:403
Bebee, Phebe II:194
Bebee, Samuel IV:201
Becher, John II:638
Beck, Andrew III:91
Beck, George I:675
Beck, Jeoffrey III:510
Beck, Jesse III:748
Beck, John III:415
Beck, Jonathan I:411
Beck, Thomas I:719; II:742; III:264
Beck, William III:451
Beckarth, John F. II:638
Becker, Abraham II:500
Becker, Barnet II:513
Becker, Henry I:169
Becker, Jacob II:513
Becker, Philip II:513
Becker, William II:503, 513
Beckett, Humphrey IV:278
Beckett, John IV:233
Beckey, Magnus I:223
Beckford, Samuel II:339
Beckford, William I:305
Beckham, William III:677
Beckler, Daniel I:213
Beckley, Daniel II:376
Beckley, Richard I:46
Beckley, Zebedee I:969
Beckman, James III:697
Beckman, Robert III:663
Becktel, Borick II:710
Becktel, George III:663
Becktel, Philip II:746
Beckwith, Abner I:132
Beckwith, Amos I:874
Beckwith, Ansel II:147
Beckwith, David II:210
Beckwith, George III:65
Beckwith, Ichabod I:453
Beckwith, Jesse I:131
Beckwith, Job II:527
Beckwith, John II:395
Beckwith, Joseph I:65
Beckwith, Nathan I:66
Beckwith, Nehemiah III:64
Beckwith, Phineas I:66
Beckwith, Rice II:382
Beckwith, Roswell II:428
Beckwith, Samuel II:527
Beckwith, Seth I:132
Beckwith, Silas IV:11
Beckwith, Thomas II:403
Beckwith, Timothy I:65
Beckwith, William IV:275
Becraft, Abraham II:531
Beddo, Thomas IV:244
Bedel, Ann I:683
Bedel, Jane I:683
Bedel, Joshua I:697
Bedel, Timothy I:683
Bedell, David III:462
Bedell, Isaac II:80
Beden, Wesson I:361
Beden, William II:329

Bedford, Elias IV:31
Bedford, Stephen II:80
Bedient, Mordecai II:481
Bedinger, Christopher III:697
Bedinger, Henry III:848
Bedle, Francis IV:290
Bedon, William I:21
Bedsell, John III:479
Bedunah, Moses II:312
Bedwell, Eleazer I:106
Beebe, Alexander II:302
Beebe, Asahel I:866
Beebe, David IV:267
Beebe, Ezekiel I:896
Beebe, Gideon II:538
Beebe, Hopson IV:229
Beebe, Joel I:59
Beebe, Joseph I:82
Beebe, Pater II:562
Beebe, Paul I:14
Beebe, Philo II:384
Beebe, Richard J. II:517
Beebe, Roderick II:384
Beebe, Ruel II:538
Beebe, Samuel IV:227
Beebe, Solomon I:866
Beebe, William C. I:14
Beebee, Amon II:214
Beebee, Asa II:312
Beebee, David II:258
Beebee, Guy I:843
Beebee, Reuben II:749
Beebee, Seba I:994
Beebee, Zaccheus I:994
Beech, Asa III:207
Beecher, P. IV:297
Beecher, Wheeler I:106
Beedle, Henry I:304
Beedle, Thomas I:933
Beedwell, Robert IV:91
Beedy, Rosiah I:886
Beeker, John P. II:538
Beeker, Martinus II:437
Beekman, William IV:277
Beekwith, Benjamin IV:275
Beekwith, Niles I:690
Beel, Henry II:297
Beeler, Jacob III:620
Beeman, Daniel I:107
Beeman, Ebenezer II:640
Beeman, Friend I:876, 937
Beeman, Isaac II:384
Beeman, Josiah II:289
Beeman, Matthias I:46
Beeman, Samuel II:538
Beeman, Simon II:384
Beeman, Tracey I:106
Beeman, Truman II:428
Beeman, William IV:13
Beemis, John I:615
Beemont, Benjamin I:122
Beer, Gershom (heirs) I:83
Beer, James IV:275
Beer, Robert II:699
Beers, Daniel II:527
Beers, David I:31, 83
Beers, Ezra II:365

Beers, Fanton I:31
Beers, Isaac I:31; II:365
Beers, Jabez II:527
Beers, James I:53, 84
Beers, John I:123
Beers, Josiah II:527
Beers, Lewis I:107
Beers, Matthew I:84
Beers, Nathan I:59, 123, 156
Beers, Phineas I:107
Beers, Samuel I:83
Beers, Silas I:96
Beers, Zachariah II:462
Beeson, Edward III:93
Beetman, Jacob II:688
Beetom, Adam III:290
Beeton, William II:677
Begeant, John III:697
Begeant, William III:800
Beggs, Alexander IV:19
Beggs, Moore III:225
Behway, Peter II:729
Belanger, Julian II:220
Belar, John II:159
Belcher, Bartlet III:587
Belcher, Jacob I:513
Belcher, Jonathan II:329
Belcher, Joseph I:513
Belcher, Nathan I:132
Belcher, Robert III:490
Belcher, Samuel I:542
Belcher, Supply I:262
Belden, Benjamin IV:288
Belden, Bildad I:66
Belden, Charles III:437
Belden, Ezekiel P. I:38
Belden, John I:96
Belden, Othniel I:461
Belden, Richard I:38
Belding, John I:441
Belding, Jonathan I:865; II:462
Belding, Selah II:468
Belew, Solomon III:242
Belger, James II:147
Belknap, Abel II:434
Belknap, Calvin IV:227
Belknap, Ebenezer II:444
Belknap, Ezekiel I:769
Belknap, Francis I:141
Belknap, John II:297
Belknap, Jonas II:152; III:224
Belknap, Josiah I:983
Belknap, William II:297, 561
Bell, Andrew II:397-98
Bell, Arthur II:372
Bell, Bazzel I:77
Bell, Benjamin I:885; III:433
Bell, Elizabeth III:9
Bell, Ezekiel III:19
Bell, George II:130
Bell, George H. II:180
Bell, Israel I:619
Bell, James I:65; II:39, 619; III:444
Bell, James M. IV:297
Bell, James R. II:712

Bennett, Deliverance I:361
Bennett, Ebenezer II:392
Bennett, Eleazer I:775
Bennett, Elias II:684
Bennett, Elisha II:223
Bennett, Elizabeth II:625
Bennett, Ephraim II:523
Bennett, Ezekial II:304
Bennett, George III:19
Bennett, George W. II:625
Bennett, Godfrey I:818
Bennett, Henry II:206, 331
Bennett, Isaac II:21, 202, 263
Bennett, Jacob II:310
Bennett, James I:513, 937; II:226, 625
Bennett, James A. I:841
Bennett, Jedediah II:289
Bennett, Jeremiah I:763; II:288
Bennett, Jesse II:492
Bennett, John I:95, 146, 342, 426, 983; II:151, 180, 604; III:149
Bennett, John L. II:76
Bennett, Joseph I:66, 369, 479, 903; II:151, 751; III:807
Bennett, Joseph D. II:538
Bennett, Joshua I:453
Bennett, Josiah I:83
Bennett, Margaretta II:625
Bennett, Mary Ann II:625
Bennett, Matthew II:234
Bennett, Micajah II:304
Bennett, Moses I:179
Bennett, Nathan I:822; II:321, 395
Bennett, Oliver III:3; IV:135
Bennett, Richard III:245, 803; IV:291
Bennett, Roland I:594
Bennett, Rufus II:667
Bennett, Samuel I:223, 959, 974-75, 983
Bennett, Stephen I:77, 805; II:691
Bennett, Stephen, 2d I:510
Bennett, Thomas II:450, 527
Bennett, Timothy II:334
Bennett, William I:76, 983; II:365, 403; III:842
Bennett, William P. II:625
Benningfield, Henry III:237
Bennings, Daniel III:744
Bennington, Job III:734
Bennis, Henry I:749
Bensley, David II:413
Benson, Abel I:495
Benson, Asa I:570
Benson, Barak I:147
Benson, Daniel I:975
Benson, Ellis I:861
Benson, Enoch III:164
Benson, Fanny I:861
Benson, Francis I:390
Benson, Ichabod I:282
Benson, Isaac I:558

Benson, Joel II:373
Benson, John II:331, 640; III:375, 401
Benson, Jonah I:570
Benson, Levin III:598, 798
Benson, Maria I:861
Benson, Matthew II:498
Benson, Meriamna I:861
Benson, Nehemiah I:861
Benson, Perry III:34
Benson, Peter I:949; II:600
Benson, Reuben III:375
Benson, Robert I:305
Benson, Sally I:861
Benson, Seth I:896
Benson, Spencer III:610
Benson, Thomas III:444
Benson, Traverse III:19
Benson, Trevor III:19
Bent, Abigail IV:163
Bent, Ann IV:163
Bent, Freeman IV:163
Bent, Isaac IV:163
Bent, Jacob A. IV:163
Bent, James Mackey IV:163
Bent, Lemuel III:849
Bent, Manley IV:163
Bent, Nathan I:690
Bent, Prince I:809
Bentley, Azel II:362
Bentley, Benjamin II:478
Bentley, Charles I:346
Bentley, Ezekiel I:132
Bentley, Henry II:649
Bentley, James III:397
Bentley, Jeremiah III:544
Bentley, John II:346
Bentley, Margarette III:9
Bentley, Sally III:9
Bentley, Susanna III:9
Bentley, Thomas III:442
Bentley, William II:418, 492; III:728
Bently, Efford III:88
Bently, George II:321
Bently, Gideon II:478
Bently, Jonas III:9
Benton, Abijah I:728
Benton, Adoniram I:690
Benton, Bethel II:468
Benton, David III:561; IV:76
Benton, Edward II:180
Benton, Elisha I:688
Benton, Elkanah III:385
Benton, Felix I:923
Benton, Jacob I:141
Benton, Joel I:955
Benton, Jonas I:617
Benton, Jonathan I:346, 460
Benton, Joseph, Sen. III:154
Benton, Nathaniel W. II:288
Benton, Noah I:122
Benton, Selah I:181
Benton, Warren III:357
Benton, Zadock IV:249
Benton, Zebulon I:429
Bentzinger, Daniel II:746

Beran, Nicholas II:607
Bereman, Thomas III:305
Bergerhoff, Nicholas IV:178
Bergh, Abraham II:513
Bergin, John I:688
Bergmeyer, Daniel II:676
Berkley, John III:320
Berkley, William III:269
Berlin, Isaac II:648
Berlin, Jacob III:775
Bernard, Benjamin III:765
Bernard, John II:676
Bernard, Walter III:774
Bernhurt, Daniel II:638
Berray, Seth II:468
Berrey, Samuel II:382
Berry, Asahel I:942
Berry, Barnabas II:402
Berry, Bartholomew IV:139
Berry, Bayne S. III:2
Berry, Benjamin I:609; III:304, 833
Berry, Benjamin, 2d I:390
Berry, Caleb III:341
Berry, Charles I:809
Berry, Daniel II:712
Berry, Doct'r Kellog I:106
Berry, Enock III:626
Berry, George I:262; II:232
Berry, Jabez II:490
Berry, James I:495, 775; II:607, 649; III:197, 733, 811
Berry, Jeremiah I:326
Berry, Joel III:316
Berry, John I:584; II:39; III:315, 367, 489, 527, 659, 708
Berry, Jonathan I:305
Berry, Joseph I:233; II:202
Berry, Josiah I:202, 245
Berry, Lemuel I:106
Berry, Ludford III:492
Berry, Michael I:607
Berry, Nathaniel I:190, 775
Berry, Nicholas I:460; II:395
Berry, Pelatiah I:178
Berry, Robert III:428
Berry, Sandford III:580
Berry, Thomas I:203, 282, 775; III:223, 269, 693; IV:233
Berry, Timothy I:214
Berry, William II:40, 353; III:199, 483, 784; IV:124, 271
Berry, Zebulon I:245
Berryhill, Alexander III:580
Berryman, L. H. I:xiv
Berryman, Newton I:xii
Bert, Reuben I:472
Bertholf, Crymes II:473
Bertoff, John S. II:58
Bertrugg, Peter III:808
Beshaw, Thomas III:663
Bess, Edward II:689
Besse, Jabez I:262
Besse, Joseph I:213

Besse, Silas I:570
Bessee, Ebenezer I:294
Bessent, John III:106
Bessom, Nicholas I:410
Bessor, John II:68
Best, Abraham II:607
Best, George IV:104
Best, James III:215
Best, John II:752
Best, John J. II:384
Bethea, Elisha III:813
Bethel, John J. III:594
Bets, Peter III:249
Betsell, John III:479
Bett, Amzi I:281
Betterley, Thos. I:907
Betterley, William II:667
Betterson, Naboth I:690
Bettersworth, Rich'd III:250
Betterton, Joshua III:494
Bettes, Leonard I:337
Bettis, Jeremiah I:304; II:130
Bettis, Nathaniel IV:211
Betton, Thomas II:62
Betts, Aaron I:84
Betts, Charles II:638
Betts, Charles J. II:124
Betts, Daniel I:83
Betts, David I:30
Betts, Hezekiah I:84
Betts, Isaiah I:82; II:263
Betts, Jacob II:635
Betts, James II:202
Betts, Peter II:492
Betts, Reuben II:503
Betts, Ruth I:154
Betts, Stephen I:66, 154
Betts, Uriah II:384
Betts, William II:676
Bettsworth, Charles III:253; IV:13
Betty, William II:276
Betz, Peter II:651
Bevan, William III:401
Bevans, Henry I:31
Bevens, David IV:24
Bever, Charles III:250
Beveridge, Matthew I:299
Bevermore, Lewis II:71
Bevers, James III:76
Bevier, Conrad II:531
Bevier, Jacob I. II:366
Bevier, Simon II:754
Beville, Edward III:88
Bevington, Thomas II:635
Bevins, Wilder II:608
B_ggs, Joseph IV:129
Bibb, Benjamin III:802
Bibb, Henry III:802
Bibb, James III:256
Bibb, Thomas III:798
Bibber, James I:245
Bibee, Thomas III:574
Bice, Dennis III:290
Bickell, Jacob II:752
Bickell, John II:729
Bicker, Adam IV:239

Bicker, Walter II:267
Bicker, William I:174
Bickers, Nicholas III:819
Bickford, Andrew I:728
Bickford, Benjamin I:262
Bickford, Dunlis I:719
Bickford, Eli I:932
Bickford, John I:233, 769, 846
Bickford, Samuel I:720
Bickham, Abner III:114
Bickly, William III:304
Bickman, John R. I:769
Bickmore, John I:228
Bicknall, Joshua I:812
Bicknall, Sinsfield III:191
Bicknell, Abner I:299
Bicknell, Esau III:58
Bicknell, Josiah I:37
Biddle, Richard III:45
Biddle, Thomas I:xvi
Biddlecomb, Richard IV:96
Bidlock, Benjamin II:667
Bidwell, Allen I:690
Bidwell, Daniel IV:19
Bidwell, Elisha II:500
Bidwell, Ozias I:38
Bidwell, Phineas II:372
Bidwell, Thomas I:38
Bierce, James I:106
Bierce, William IV:279
Biers, Nathan I:82
Biffle, Jacob III:605
Bigbie, William III:848
Bigelow, Abijah I:147
Bigelow, Alpheus I:512
Bigelow, Andrew I:616
Bigelow, Eli I:684
Bigelow, Elnathan I:684
Bigelow, Ephraim I:513
Bigelow, Eunice I:684
Bigelow, Fanny I:27
Bigelow, Frederick I:46
Bigelow, Humphrey I:633
Bigelow, Jabez II:339
Bigelow, James II:691
Bigelow, John I:27, 634
Bigelow, Jonas I:634
Bigelow, Josiah I:949
Bigelow, Noah II:327
Bigelow, Polly I:27
Bigelow, Samuel I:496, 635
Bigelow, Sarah I:684
Bigelow, Sophia I:27
Bigelow, Timothy II:62; IV:288
Bigelow, William I:615, 684
Bigford, Samuel II:437
Bigge, David I:132
Bigger, Robert III:601
Bigger, William II:146
Biggs, John III:333
Biggs, Robert IV:34
Bigham, Andrew III:600
Bigham, William III:566
Biglow, Barna I:948
Biglow, Noah II:426
Biglow, Simeon I:958
Bilbrey, Nathaniel III:416

Bilbury, Wooldrick II:40
Biles, Thomas III:433
Bill, Abiel I:132
Bill, Azariah I:133
Bill, Benaijah I:132
Bill, Benjamin, Jr. I:21
Bill, Daniel I:14, 96
Bill, Eleazer I:131
Bill, Elijah II:403
Bill, Jabez I:342
Bill, Jarv_s II:312
Bill, Jonathan II:276, 331
Bill, Joshua I:133
Bill, Phineas II:544
Bill, William II:312
Billeu, Stephen III:431
Billing, Leavett II:283
Billing, Matthew II:289
Billinger, Emanuel II:651
Billings, Benjamin I:369, 533; II:544
Billings, Ebenezer I:913
Billings, Enoch I:880
Billings, Ephraim I:512
Billings, Isaac I:851, 880
Billings, James I:533; II:239
Billings, Jasper III:458
Billings, Jesse I:441
Billings, John I:983
Billings, Joseph II:462
Billings, Lemuel I:542
Billings, Samuel I:534, 802
Billings, Silas I:880
Billings, William I:533
Billingsby, John III:327
Billington, Elisha I:802
Billington, Ezekiel III:566
Billington, Francis I:609
Billington, Isaac I:190
Billington, John II:239
Billington, Thomas I:809
Bills, Ebenezer I:706
Bills, Elisha II:481
Bills, Jabez E. I:997
Bills, John E. III:787
Bills, Nathaniel I:534
Bills, Sylvanus I:122
Bills, William II:76
Bilman, Duvalt II:687
Bilson, William II:329
Binchley, Joseph II:413
Biner, George IV:256
Binger, Nicholas III:326
Bingham, Aaron II:220
Bingham, Abel I:53
Bingham, Benjamin III:569
Bingham, Calvin I:840
Bingham, Chester I:77
Bingham, Elias I:893
Bingham, Gurdon I:76
Bingham, Jeremiah I:146, 924
Bingham, Johnson II:389
Bingham, Joseph III:517
Bingham, Leonard P. I:862
Bingham, Louisa Ann I:862
Bingham, Ozias II:704
Bingham, Ralph I:20, 862

Bingham, Samuel II:449
Bingham, Silas IV:229
Bingham, Thomas I:886; II:670
Binham, Thomas, Sen. IV:227
Binkerhoff, Garret II:58
Binkley, Adam III:575
Binkley, Frederick III:451
Bintzal, John III:31
Birch, Jeremiah I:488
Birch, John III:206
Birch, Thomas II:719
Birchard, Daniel I:83
Birchard, Elias II:468
Birchfield, Thomas II:727
Bircki, Peter II:414
Bird, Andrew II:649
Bird, Edmund II:350
Bird, Herman III:126
Bird, Isaac II:92
Bird, John II:731; III:491
Bird, Joseph I:923
Bird, Joshua III:239
Bird, Michael II:591
Bird, Nathaniel II:214
Bird, Reuben III:728
Bird, Samuel IV:24
Bird, Thomas I:534
Bird, William III:701
Birdseye, Victory II:555, 561
Birdsley, Ezra I:82
Birge, David I:876
Birge, Hosea II:384
Birge, James I:106
Birge, John I:107
Birges, John II:392
Birmingham, John IV:4
Birmingham, Patrick II:608
Birth, Archibald II:667
Bisbee, Charles IV:66
Bisbee, Ebenezer I:479
Bisbee, Elisha I:214
Bisbee, George I:569
Bisbee, Isaac I:983
Bisbee, John I:570
Bisbee, Jonah I:571
Bisbee, Luther II:359
Bisbee, Noah, Jr. I:682
Bisbee, Samuel I:361
Bisbee, Seth II:601
Bisbee, William Bradford I:682
Bisby, Benjamin I:542
Bisby, Joseph II:248
Bisby, Noah I:739
Biscoe, James III:279
Bish, Frederick II:723
Bishop, Abraham II:403
Bishop, Austin I:95
Bishop, Benjamin IV:31, 98
Bishop, Benoni II:346
Bishop, Caroline II:190
Bishop, Charles I:862
Bishop, Comfort I:797
Bishop, David II:450
Bishop, Eleazer I:862
Bishop, Elisha II:400; III:290
Bishop, Enos I:245

Bishop, Ezekiel I:822
Bishop, Golden III:148
Bishop, Harriet II:190
Bishop, Henry III:777
Bishop, Hooper II:462
Bishop, Isaac II:239
Bishop, Jacob I:82
Bishop, James I:115, 123, 887; II:339; III:768
Bishop, James, 1st II:321
Bishop, Jeremiah III:768
Bishop, Jesse I:866
Bishop, Joel II:544
Bishop, John I:76, 749; II:283, 310; III:498
Bishop, Joseph II:462
Bishop, Joshua II:350
Bishop, Lawrence III:262
Bishop, Lemuel I:929
Bishop, Levi I:983; II:151, 561
Bishop, Lyman I:862
Bishop, Maria I:862
Bishop, Moses II:312
Bishop, Newman I:460
Bishop, Rhoda I:862
Bishop, Richard II:304; III:240
Bishop, Rich'd W. II:190
Bishop, Robert I:1000
Bishop, Seth I:106
Bishop, Simeon I:12
Bishop, Solomon II:450; III:312
Bishop, Squire, Jr. I:161
Bishop, Stephen I:31; III:684
Bishop, Sylvanus II:478
Bishop, Thomas III:36
Bishop, Thomas F. I:96
Bishop, William III:513, 646, 839
Bishop, Wyatt III:82
Bishop, Zadock I:262
Bishop, Zepheniah I:369
Bison, Charles II:672
Bissel, John I:38
Bissell, Annis II:197
Bissell, Archelaus I:46
Bissell, Benjamin I:46, 924
Bissell, Calvin I:106
Bissell, Charles D. I:592
Bissell, Charlotte C. I:592
Bissell, Clark I:154
Bissell, Daniel II:288
Bissell, David I:832
Bissell, Ebenezer F. I:95
Bissell, Emeline A. I:592
Bissell, Ezekiel I:107
Bissell, Geo. C. I:592
Bissell, George I:107
Bissell, Jerijah I:95
Bissell, John II:197
Bissell, Jonathan M. I:984
Bissell, Josiah I:346
Bissell, Lemuel I:96
Bissell, Moses I:592
Bissell, Noadiah I:749
Bissell, Oliver II:346
Bissell, Ozias I:73

Bissell, Polly II:197
Bissell, Return I:106
Bissell, Samuel I:809; II:304
Bissell, Thomas I:96
Bissey, Nehemiah II:403
Bisson, Charles II:672
Biswell, John III:229
Biteley, John II:504
Biter, Peter I:190
Bitgood, John I:147
Bitten, John I:720
Bitting, Joseph II:752
Bittle, Samuel II:717
Bitz, Michael II:663
Bivins, Abner II:210
Bivins, John IV:293
Bixbey, Aaron I:146
Bixbey, Moses I:146
Bixby, Aaron I:907
Bixby, Adonijah I:914
Bixby, Benjamin IV:211
Bixby, Daniel I:947
Bixby, David I:749
Bixby, Elias II:276
Bixby, Jacob I:697
Bixby, John I:617
Bixby, Jonathan I:698
Bixby, Nathaniel I:974
Bixby, Samson II:517
Bixby, Samuel I:632, 749
Blachard, Will-you-be III:846
Black, Catharine IV:297
Black, Cato I:38
Black, Charles IV:153
Black, D., Jun. IV:297
Black, Daniel II:667
Black, David, Sen. IV:297
Black, Ezekiel III:431
Black, George I:458; II:304, 742; III:646, 775
Black, Henry I:233; II:696
Black, Hugh IV:210
Black, Jacob I:969; III:516
Black, James II:716; III:83, 478
Black, Joab I:178
Black, John III:143
Black, John, 2d III:516
Black, John, 1st III:495
Black, Joseph I:999; III:495
Black, Josiah I:305
Black, Martin III:387
Black, Moses I:187
Black, Robert III:331
Black, Rudolph III:261
Black, Samuel I:794; II:544; IV:108
Black, Thomas II:717
Black, William I:782, 975; III:182; IV:85
Black, William, 2d II:657
Blackburn, Benjamin III:74
Blackburn, James III:536; IV:221, 233
Blackburn, John II:608; III:290
Blackburn, Moses IV:241

Blackburn, Samuel III:240
Blackburn, William III:264
Blackenship, Benjamin IV:286
Blackford, Anthony II:288
Blackford, David I:326
Blackford, Jacob II:719
Blackington, James I:203
Blackleach, John I:31
Blackledge, Ichabod III:243
Blacklee, Samuel I:106
Blackman, Dan. II:276
Blackman, Daniel II:413
Blackman, David I:2
Blackman, Elijah IV:211
Blackman, Elisha II:731
Blackman, Enoch II:389
Blackman, Jacob I:146
Blackman, James I:84
Blackman, Jonathan I:337
Blackman, Kemar I:497
Blackman, Sampson I:30
Blackman, Samuel I:30, 542; II:255
Blackman, Zachariah II:288
Blackmer, Abner I:870
Blackmer, Solomon I:633
Blackmore, George III:598
Blackmore, George D. III:598
Blackmore, Jas. A. III:637
Blackmore, John I:76, 886; III:322
Blackmore, Timothy IV:275
Blackner, Godfrey II:35
Blackshire, Ebenezer III:851
Blackslee, Caleb I:429
Blacksley, Caleb I:656
Blacksley, Enos I:21
Blackston, William I:262
Blackstone, John I:123, 203
Blackwelder, Charles III:410
Blackwell, Abraham III:497
Blackwell, David III:611, 771, 786
Blackwell, Elijah II:89
Blackwell, Hugh IV:210
Blackwell, James III:374
Blackwell, John III:322
Blackwell, Joseph III:694
Blackwell, Judith III:338
Blackwell, Robert IV:118
Blackwell, Thomas III:249, 338, 421
Blackwood, James I:231
Blaikey, William III:481
Blain, Adam IV:183
Blain, James II:503, 741; IV:48
Blair, Aalina IV:164
Blair, Abraham IV:262
Blair, Allen III:748
Blair, Asahel IV:164
Blair, James I:203; II:428; IV:186
Blair, John I:461; II:297; III:36, 530, 635; IV:231
Blair, John, 2d III:36
Blair, John Neal III:702

Blair, Joseph I:616
Blair, Mary IV:164
Blair, Reuben I:635
Blair, Robert II:565
Blair, Sally IV:164
Blair, Samuel III:275, 600
Blair, Seth II:428
Blair, Solomon I:635
Blair, Thomas II:58, 607-8; III:604; IV:54
Blair, Timothy I:453
Blair, William I:706; IV:18
Blair, Wm. K. I:xvi
Blairvelt, Cornelius II:498
Blairvelt, John A. II:444
Blairvelt, John G. II:498
Blairvelt, John J. II:498
Blaisdell, Levi II:353
Blake, Benjamin I:213
Blake, Beverly A. III:202
Blake, Braxton III:203
Blake, Christopher I:720
Blake, Cordelia III:202
Blake, David II:409
Blake, Dearborn T. I:176
Blake, Ebenezer II:226
Blake, Eleazer I:690, 788
Blake, Elijah I:106; II:478
Blake, Elvira III:203
Blake, George I:461
Blake, Henry I:592, 873
Blake, Henry T. IV:104
Blake, Isaac I:748
Blake, Jacob I:543; III:60
Blake, James I:245, 496; II:202
Blake, Jane III:202
Blake, Jason I:361
Blake, Jeremiah I:635
Blake, John I:178, 263, 291, 937; IV:144
Blake, John P. I:739
Blake, Jonathan I:440
Blake, Joseph I:176, 179
Blake, Joshua I:413
Blake, Josiah I:983
Blake, Lucy III:202
Blake, Reuben I:31
Blake, Robert I:262
Blake, Robert Henry I:592
Blake, Seth I:691
Blake, Thomas I:658; III:433, 781
Blake, Timothy I:886
Blake, William I:176; II:239, 645
Blake, Willing I:273
Blakeley, Freeman IV:102
Blakely, Aquilla III:79
Blakely, James IV:248
Blakely, Moses II:544
Blakely, Thomas III:506
Blakely, William III:506
Blakely, Zealous I:37
Blakeman, George III:775
Blakeman, Zachariah I:83
Blakeney, William II:631

Blakesle, Abel III:62
Blakeslee, James II:714
Blakeslee, Jesse I:59
Blakeslee, Philip I:59
Blakeslee, Samuel II:257
Blakesley, Jared II:231
Blakesley, Obed II:210
Blakey, George III:300
Blalack, Charles III:632
Blalack, Daniel III:578
Blalock, Jeremiah III:516
Blalock, John III:572
Blanchar, Amos I:389
Blanchard, Aaron I:914
Blanchard, Abner I:543; II:686
Blanchard, Andrew II:667
Blanchard, Benjamin II:258
Blanchard, Caleb I:958
Blanchard, Daniel I:543
Blanchard, David I:956
Blanchard, Elias I:146; II:226
Blanchard, Ephraim II:258
Blanchard, Francis I:594
Blanchard, Hastings I:842
Blanchard, Isaac I:706; II:43
Blanchard, Jacob I:30
Blanchard, Jedediah II:362
Blanchard, John I:635, 929; IV:108
Blanchard, John, 2d II:226
Blanchard, John, 1st II:245
Blanchard, Jonathan I:543
Blanchard, Joseph I:782, 873; II:321
Blanchard, Josiah I:542
Blanchard, Lysias I:497
Blanchard, Nathaniel I:496; II:337, 402
Blanchard, Peter II:220
Blanchard, Seth I:245
Blanchard, Simon I:616, 865
Blanchard, Solomon I:273
Blanchard, Timothy I:273
Blanchard, Timothy (2) I:273
Blanchard, Willard I:6
Blanchard, William I:21, 511, 603, 947
Blancher, Theophilus I:203
Blanck, Peter II:712
Bland, Jesse III:810
Blanden, Elisha I:616
Blanden, Francis I:617
Blanden, Jonas I:617
Blanden, Lamech I:975
Blanden, Samuel II:482
Blander, John II:365
Blandford, Ricahrd III:312
Blandin, Jonathan I:749
Blane, John II:68
Blaney, Samuel I:534
Blank, Cornelius II:263
Blankenship, Abraham III:752
Blankenship, Henry III:760
Blankenship, John III:822
Blankenship, Josiah III:764
Blankenship, Reuben III:93

Blankenship, Wommock III:119
Blanton, Thomas III:557
Blanvelt, Abraham II:58
Blanvelt, Harman II:58
Blanvelt, James J. II:58
Blasdell, Daniel I:203, 748
Blasdell, E. I:789
Blasdell, Ebenezer I:684
Blasdell, Ezra I:948
Blasdell, Isaac I:684
Blasdell, James W. I:684
Blasdell, John I:719; II:749
Blasdell, Loel I:684
Blasdell, Lydia I:684
Blasdell, Nancy I:684
Blasdell, Parrit I:903
Blasdell, Philip I:769, 880
Blasdell, Samuel I:684, 763
Blasdell, William I:870
Blassdell, John I:411
Blatchford, John C. III:701
Blaucet, Joel III:820
Blauvelt, Cornelius II:165
Blauvelt, Frederick II:29
Blazar, Anthony III:58
Blazeur, Lawrence II:449
Bleakley, Robert III:329
Bleakly, George II:689
Blechhynden, Charles III:821
Bledsoe, George III:348
Bledsoe, Jacob III:571
Bledsoe, Lewis III:421
Bledsoe, Miller III:177
Bleecker, Leonard II:267, 558
Blenn, Justus I:38
Blesdell, Henry I:495
Bletcher, Jacob III:537
Blethen, Increase I:223
Blevens, Daniel III:608
Blever, James III:29
Blevin, James III:310
Blevins, James IV:80
Blevins, Nathan III:398
Blew, David III:641
Blew, Sealey II:61
Blick, James III:757
Blick, John III:264
Blimby, William II:384
Blin, Simeon II:258
Blin, William I:876
Bling, Silas II:321
Blinn, George I:534
Blish, Ezra I:37
Bliss, Asa I:368
Bliss, Calvin I:924
Bliss, Dan I:131
Bliss, Daniel II:758
Bliss, David II:426
Bliss, Ebenezer II:276
Bliss, Eli I:595
Bliss, Francis I:450
Bliss, Gaines I:461
Bliss, Isaac I:95
Bliss, Isaiah I:748
Bliss, Jacob I:461
Bliss, Jane Reuben I:452

Bliss, John II:712
Bliss, Jonathan I:805
Bliss, Joshua I:903
Bliss, Louisa I:452
Bliss, Mariett I:452
Bliss, Moses I:461
Bliss, Nathan I:633
Bliss, Noah I:923
Bliss, Reuben I:452
Bliss, Russell I:27
Bliss, Samuel I:141, 361, 452; II:513
Bliss, Sears I:452
Bliss, Timothy I:27
Bliss, William I:368
Bliss, Zenas II:462
Bliven, William I:831
Blivin, Henry III:587
Blivin, Nathan I:831
Blizzard, Burton III:821
B_llings, Abel I:259
Blodget, Abisha III:818
Blodget, Admatha II:339
Blodget, Amos I:510
Blodget, Artemas II:302
Blodget, James I:495
Blodget, Jonas I:488, 491
Blodget, Jonathan I:282
Blodget, Ludin II:468
Blodget, Rufus II:331
Blodget, Salmon I:908
Blodget, Silas II:321
Blodget, Solomon II:468
Blodgett, Amos I:728
Blodgett, Benjamin I:949
Blodgett, Elijah I:879
Blodgett, Henry I:949
Blodgett, Jacob I:739
Blodgett, James I:662
Blodgett, Joshua I:715; II:382
Blodgett, Josiah I:715
Blodgett, Nathan II:389
Blodgett, Samuel I:923
Blodgett, William I:513
Blodjet, James I:994
Blomkenbaker, Nic'las III:322
Blood, Abel I:715
Blood, Amos I:756
Blood, Asa II:263
Blood, Caleb I:496
Blood, David I:975; II:321
Blood, Edmund I:513
Blood, Ephraim I:999
Blood, Francis I:670
Blood, George I:469
Blood, Isaac II:468
Blood, Israel M. II:469
Blood, John I:983
Blood, Jonas I:495
Blood, Josiah I:496
Blood, Lemuel I:782
Blood, Levi I:739, 782
Blood, Moses I:513
Blood, Nathaniel I:937
Blood, Phineas I:865
Blood, Reuben I:616
Blood, Simeon I:691

Blood, Thaddeus I:511
Blood, Thomas I:705
Bloodgood, John II:413
Bloom, Daniel II:637
Bloom, Peter C. II:473
Bloomer, William II:267
Bloomfield, Aaron II:71
Bloomfield, James II:71
Bloomfield, Thomas II:43, 71
Bloss, Joseph II:434
Bloss, Samuel II:450
Bloss, Valentine III:759
Bloss, William II:384
Blossom, Benjamin I:896
Blossom, Peter I:959
Blott, Andrew II:608
Blount, Nathaniel III:682
Blowers, Ephraim I:870
Blowers, Robert II:48
Blowers, Samuel II:437
Bloxom, Scarborough III:816
Blucher, Zost II:665
Blue, David IV:30
Blue, Frederick II:712
Blue, John III:444; IV:93, 214
Blue, Michael II:712
Blum, John Henry III:390
Blumer, Gilbert III:297
Blundin, John II:642
Blundon, Elijah III:725
Blunt, Asher II:538
Blunt, John I:609
Blunt, Jonathan II:239
Blunt, William II:478; III:113; IV:206
Blurton, Edward III:564
Bly, John I:932; III:735
Bly, Moses I:769
Bly, Oliver I:823
Bntts, Thomas I:369
Boafoy, Benanuel I:53
Boaraem, Jacob II:71
Board, Patrick III:845
Board, Philip III:305
Boardman, Amos I:948
Boardman, Backus I:337
Boardman, Benjamin I:748
Boardman, Elias II:477
Boardman, James I:497; II:129
Boardman, Jehiel II:364
Boardman, John H. I:410
Boardman, Jonathan II:255
Boardman, Rebecca I:387
Boardman, Richard I:387
Boardman, Seth I:6
Boardman, Thomas I:609
Boardman, Timothy I:958
Boardman, William I:886
Boas, Henry IV:76
Boas, James I:178
Boatwright, John III:826
Boaz, James III:820
Bobbit, Isham IV:16
Bobbit, William III:498
Bo_ce, Peter, 2d II:288
Bock, George II:728
Bock, Michael III:788

324

Bockus, Jacob II:258
Boden, James II:14
Bodg, Meshac III:684
Bodine, Isaac II:384
Bodine, John IV:214, 221
Bodle, Charles II:564
Bodley, Andrew II:341
Bodley, Thomas II:710
Bodley, William IV:282
Bodly, John III:84
Bodwell, Ebenezer I:166
Bodwell, John II:239
Bodwell, William IV:169
Boekieus, George II:117
Bogardus, Henry II:202, 462
Bogart, Henry II:418
Bogart, John II:353
Bogert, David R. II:503
Bogert, Hester II:193
Bogert, James II:193
Bogert, James J. II:193
Bogert, John G. II:498
Bogert, Peter II:193
Bogge, John II:180
Boggs, David II:676
Bogle, Thomas I:886
Bogle, William I:511
Bogman, Charles I:804
Bogue, John II:180
Bogue, Publius V. II:450
Bohan, Joseph III:152
Bohem, Joseph II:591
Bohor, John III:305
Bohoron, Ananiah I:886
Bohoron, Stephen I:705
Boice, James I:233
Boies, James I:719
Boileau, Abraham II:220
Boileau, Amable II:553
Boin, Reuben III:587
Bointon, Joseph I:213
Bointon, Pelatiah I:191
Bois, John I:223
Boisseau, John III:617
Bold, John R. IV:146
Bolden, Barbara I:176
Bolden, Jemima I:176
Bolden, John I:176, 203
Bolden, Mary I:176
Bolden, Samuel I:176
Bolden, William I:176
Boldery, John IV:51
Boldman, John II:517
Bole, James III:614
Bole, Peter II:607
Bolen, John III:620
Bolener, Adam III:787
Boley, Eliza II:622
Boley, Priestley III:680
Boley, Thomas II:622
Bolick, Casper III:428
Bolin, Thomas IV:85
Boling, Edmund III:545
Bolles, Asa I:345
Bolles, James I:66
Bolles, Joseph I:66
Bolling, Robert III:768

Bolster, Baruch I:907
Bolster, Joel I:974
Bolster, Nathan I:737
Bolt, Abraham, Sen. III:506
Bolter, Lemuel IV:106
Bolton, Aaron I:635
Bolton, Alexander II:366
Bolton, Benjamin III:75, 343
Bolton, David I:190
Bolton, Ebenezer I:634
Bolton, John I:513, 558; II:55
Bolton, Joseph I:557; II:297
Bolton, Matthias II:35
Bolton, Philip I:557
Bolton, Solomon I:220
Bolton, Timothy I:907
Bolton, William IV:3
Boman, John III:820
Boman, John, Sr. III:289
Bomgardner, George II:692
Bomgardner, William III:58
Bompus, Morris I:213
Bonar, Henry III:575
Bond, Adonijah II:428
Bond, Asa I:907
Bond, Bailey I:461
Bond, Bethuel II:373
Bond, David I:975
Bond, Elial I:848
Bond, Elisha II:62
Bond, Gilbert I:720
Bond, Israel II:428
Bond, Jacob I:517
Bond, James I:231
Bond, John III:704
Bond, Joseph I:511, 657; II:329
Bond, Phinehas I:974
Bond, Richard III:161
Bond, Samuel I:715
Bond, Thomas III:607
Bond, William I:697; III:2, 219, 626
Bond, Wright III:587, 752
Bonds, John III:315
Bonds, William I:782
Bondy, John III:463
Bone, Archibald III:371
Bone, John, 2d III:292
Bone, John, 1st III:311
Bonett, Joseph I:876
Bonfoy, Henry II:413
Bonistale, Philip II:531
Bonnall, Alexander III:663
Bonnel, Aaron IV:253
Bonnel, Gilbert II:35
Bonnel, Paul IV:172
Bonnell, Abner IV:291
Bonnell, John II:757
Bonner, Archibald II:622
Bonner, Elizabeth II:622
Bonner, Isabella II:622
Bonner, Jeremiah II:129
Bonner, John III:436, 632
Bonner, Joseph III:720
Bonner, Margaret II:622
Bonner, Rebecca II:622

Bonner, William II:622; III:751
Bonner, Wm. III:590
Bonnett, Jacob III:798
Bonnett, Lewis III:798
Bonnett, Peter III:798
Bonney, Alexander III:663
Bonney, Ezekiel I:571
Bonney, Joseph I:569
Bonney, Thomas I:825
Bonneys, Isaac I:281
Bonny, John II:510
Bonsall, Benjamin II:742
Bonta, Daniel IV:291
Bonton, Moses II:546
Bonton, Samuel I:84
Bonwell, James IV:171
Booden, Ebenezer I:187
Booden, Theodore I:220
Booffee, Thomas I:203
Booker, Aaron I:305
Booker, Abraham II:631
Booker, Isaiah I:223
Booker, Josiah I:190
Boom, John II:339
Boom, Nicholas II:202
Boomer, Ephraim I:361
Boomer, James I:635
Boon, Betsey III:360
Boon, Cynthia III:360
Boon, Elisha III:205
Boon, Jesse III:174
Boon, John II:653; III:418, 810
Boon, Martha III:360
Boon, Mary III:360
Boon, Moses III:719
Boon, Patterson III:360
Boon, Rackford III:407
Boon, Ralph II:655; IV:207
Boon, Rhoderick III:360
Boon, Samuel III:275
Boon, Thomas IV:11
Boon, Willis III:368
Boone, John III:63
Boone, Joseph, Sen. IV:31
Boone, Squire III:197
Booth, Beverly III:839
Booth, David I:38, 82
Booth, Edward IV:170
Booth, Erastus II:229
Booth, George III:614
Booth, Isaac II:468
Booth, Isaiah I:907
Booth, James III:331
Booth, John I:123; III:74, 508
Booth, Joseph III:3
Booth, Nathaniel II:503
Booth, Reuben I:154
Booth, Samuel I:492
Booth, Silas II:353
Booth, Stoten I:369
Booth, Thomas I:96; III:645
Boothby, William I:233
Boothe, Charles IV:163
Boothe, Eleanor IV:163
Boothe, Henrietta IV:163

Boothe, John H. III:670
Boothe, Nathan'l III:670
Boothe, Nath'l III:670
Boothe, Sally III:670
Boothe, Susannah IV:163
Boothe, Thomas III:670
Boothe, Walter I:59
Bootle, Thomas II:312
Bootman, Nathaniel I:706
Bootwright, Samuel III:431
Booty, Joseph I:941
Booz, Jacob II:738
Booz, John III:252
Boozer, Jacob II:31
Borah, Jacob III:263
Boran, Henry III:40
Boran, John III:40
Boran, Mary III:40
Boran, Rebecca III:40
Borden, Elijah I:534
Borden, Gideon I:369
Borden, Job IV:291
Borden, John I:823
Borden, Josiah I:817
Borden, Selden II:686
Borden, Thomas II:163
Borden, William I:817
Borders, Christopher IV:243
Borders, Peter III:254
Boren, William IV:122
Borer, Charles III:821
Bornhumen, Jacob I:273
Boroughs, Stephen II:428
Borres, John Procter I:886
Borrow, John II:733
Borry, John II:670
Borst, John II:513
Borst, Martines II:513
Borst, Peter J. II:564
Bortel, Philip II:504
Bortfield, Samuel II:591
Bortle, Andrew II:478
Borum, Edmund III:73
Boss, Adam IV:253
Boss, Benjamin I:822
Boss, Daniel C. II:568
Boss, Jabez I:809
Boss, Joseph II:68
Bostain, Andrew III:444
Boston, Andrew III:444
Boston, Christopher III:541
Boston, Elijah I:305
Boston, Gershom I:879
Boston, Jacob III:424
Boston, Peter I:529
Boston, Reuben III:255
Boston, Shebruel I:305
Boston, Thomas I:305
Bostwick, Amos II:302, 304
Bostwick, Andrew I:59
Bostwick, David I:46
Bostwick, Doctor IV:279
Bostwick, Ebenezer IV:211, 299
Bostwick, Eleazer IV:279
Bostwick, Elisha I:106
Bostwick, Ezra IV:15

Bostwick, John II:359
Bostwick, Jonathan I:107
Bostwick, Nathan II:640
Bostwick, Oliver I:7
Boswell, Jesse III:493
Boswell, Reuben III:431
Boswell, William I:804; III:386
Bosworth, Benjamin I:984; II:640
Bosworth, Daniel I:231; II:35
Bosworth, Elisha I:369
Bosworth, Isaac I:369
Bosworth, Jacob I:157; III:186
Bosworth, John II:226
Bosworth, Jonathan I:223, 698
Bosworth, Nathaniel I:903
Bosworth, Richard I:558
Bosworth, Zadock I:478
Bothel, James II:538
Bothman, Barnhart IV:241
Botsford, Samuel I:123
Bott, Frederick III:811
Bottenhouse, John IV:204
Bottom, Abel II:210
Bottom, Asahel I:131
Bottom, Darius I:123
Bottom, Jabez L. II:365
Bottom, John I:999
Bottom, Miles III:626
Botts, Joseph III:36
Botts, Moses III:258
Botts, Seth III:214
Bouce, Henry II:180
Boucher, Richard III:234
Bouck, Peter II:327
Boudy, John III:439
Boughman, John II:11
Boughton, Asa II:202
Boughton, Daniel II:172
Boughton, David II:288
Boughton, Eleazer II:468
Boughton, Matthew II:409
Boughton, William II:492
Boughum, Paul II:4
Bouker, Ithamer II:267
Boulder, James III:40
Boulton, George II:327
Bound, William II:642
Bouney, Joseph III:218
Bourdman, Elijah I:21
Bourke, William I:610
Bourn, James III:308
Bourn, John I:558; III:726
Bourn, Shearjashab I:557
Bourn, Shubael II:403
Bourn, Zuriel I:329
Bourne, Aaron I:832
Bourne, John I:304
Bourne, Nathaniel I:329
Boutard, Joseph II:591
Boutell, John I:633
Bouton, Avery II:130
Bouton, Azor I:997; II:552
Bouton, Daniel I:2
Boutwell, Asa I:903
Bovee, Jacob II:492
Bovee, Nicholas II:372

Bovee, Philip II:124
Bovie, Nicholas II:180
Bow, Edward II:304
Bow, Thaddeus I:472
Bowan, Benjamin III:41
Bowars, Leonard III:572
Bowden, Amos I:187
Bowden, Elias III:590
Bowden, Matthias II:35
Bowden, Samuel I:411
Bowden, Thomas I:391
Bowden, William III:605
Bowdish, Joseph I:880
Bowels, Samuel III:260
Bowen, Aaron II:365
Bowen, Amos I:336
Bowen, Asa II:239
Bowen, Beauajah I:37
Bowen, Benjamin I:929; III:494
Bowen, Bracy III:449
Bowen, Charles IV:86
Bowen, Christopher I:337
Bowen, Consider I:958
Bowen, Daniel II:712
Bowen, Daniel (2) II:712
Bowen, Ebenezer IV:15
Bowen, Eleazer I:146
Bowen, Elijah III:180
Bowen, Elkanah II:304
Bowen, Enoch I:887
Bowen, Ephraim I:814, 841
Bowen, Isaac I:896
Bowen, Jabez I:xiv
Bowen, Jacob Gibson I:595
Bowen, James I:822, 929; II:40
Bowen, Jeremiah I:749, 948
Bowen, Joel I:369
Bowen, John I:481; III:164
Bowen, John, 3d I:595
Bowen, John P. III:795
Bowen, Joseph I:346, 822; IV:151
Bowen, Mary Ann III:41
Bowen, Micajah III:746
Bowen, Michael IV:198
Bowen, Nancy I:336
Bowen, Nathan I:410
Bowen, Nathaniel I:609
Bowen, Samuel I:369; II:699; III:160
Bowen, Stephen I:361; III:151
Bowen, Stephen Lewis III:50
Bowen, Timothy II:180
Bowen, William I:698; II:262; III:18
Bowen, William, Sr. III:766
Bowen, Zadock II:67
Bower, Andrew IV:82
Bower, Ellis IV:262
Bower, Jacob II:638; IV:217
Bower, John IV:265
Bower, William III:58
Bowers, Alpheus I:147
Bowers, Benajah I:27
Bowers, Benjamin I:220, 513

326

Bowers, Brittain III:440
Bowers, Chauncy I:27
Bowers, Ephraim I:46, 53
Bowers, Erin I:27
Bowers, George II:662
Bowers, George, 2d II:631
Bowers, James I:999; III:601
Bowers, Jerameel I:698
Bowers, Jeremiah I:698
Bowers, Joab II:336
Bowers, John I:496; IV:206
Bowers, Jonathan I:10
Bowers, Josiah I:634
Bowers, Lucretia I:27
Bowers, Mary I:27
Bowers, Michael I:123
Bowers, Milton II:794
Bowers, Milton C. II:197
Bowers, Oliver II:318
Bowers, Otis I:27
Bowers, Sebastian II:634
Bowers, Zephaniah II:336
Bowing, Jabish I:223
Bowker, Edmund I:635
Bowker, Ezekiel I:633
Bowker, Ishmael I:461
Bowker, John I:513; II:500
Bowker, Levi I:231
Bowker, Samuel W. I:739
Bowker, Silas II:365, 565;
 IV:296
Bowland, Thomas II:649
Bowles, Benjamin III:381
Bowles, Charles I:887
Bowles, John II:312
Bowles, Matthew III:283
Bowles, Thomas III:786
Bowles, Zachariah III:705
Bowley, John I:749
Bowling, Charles IV:245
Bowling, Edward III:156
Bowling, James III:748
Bowling, Jarret III:841
Bowling, Jesse III:271
Bowling, Joseph IV:47
Bowling, Richard III:111
Bowling, William IV:245
Bowling, William I. III:56
Bowman, Abiatha I:782
Bowman, Abraham III:334
Bowman, Adam II:413
Bowman, Albert I:20
Bowman, Andrew II:43
Bowman, Daniel III:614
Bowman, Elijah II:676
Bowman, Elisha II:714
Bowman, Francis I:686
Bowman, George H. III:334
Bowman, John I:635; III:556
Bowman, Luke II:563
Bowman, Macness III:764
Bowman, Marshall III:795
Bowman, Michael II:608
Bowman, Nancy I:686
Bowman, Philip IV:241
Bowman, Samuel II:147;
 III:726

Bowman, Sherwood III:399
Bowman, Sparling III:584
Bowman, William III:595;
 IV:97
Bowmon, Solomon I:495
Bownd, Obadiah II:719
Bowne, Henry II:321
Bowne, W. J. II:91
Bowner, John II:696
Bowsher, Anthony IV:278
Bowtell, Joseph I:497
Bowtelle, Ebenezer I:440
Bowyer, Agatha III:848
Bowyer, Henry III:848
Bowyer, Laban II:22
Bowyer, William IV:140
Box, Daniel I:794
Box, Edward III:610
Box, Joshua II:129
Box, Samuel III:594
Boxwell, Joseph III:42
Boxwell, Robert III:42
Boy, Jacob III:620
Boyce, Abraham II:444
Boyce, David I:410
Boyce, James II:129
Boyce, Peter, 1st II:129
Boyce, Thomas II:177
Boyd, Alexander II:608
Boyd, Benjamin III:55
Boyd, Conrad II:625
Boyd, Daniel I:xii; III:378
Boyd, David I:174
Boyd, Ebenezer II:181
Boyd, Francis III:663; IV:153,
 181
Boyd, George II:481
Boyd, Hannah I:174
Boyd, Henry II:9; III:325
Boyd, James II:289, 473;
 III:820; IV:241
Boyd, John I:633; II:35
 III:367, 533; IV:75, 230
Boyd, Joseph II:276
Boyd, Mary I:174
Boyd, Patrick III:810
Boyd, Peggy I:174
Boyd, Richard II:267
Boyd, Robert II:735
Boyd, Samuel I:262, 679;
 II:568; IV:98
Boyd, T. J. III:853
Boyd, Thomas, Sen. IV:119
Boyd, Valentine II:625
Boyd, Washington I:174
Boyd, William I:880; II:312,
 503, 710; III:188, 217, 256,
 498, 611, 746
Boyden, Ames I:429
Boyden, John I:441
Boyden, Josiah I:440
Boyden, Justus II:258
Boyden, Thomas I:616
Boydston, Samuel III:91
Boydston, Wm. III:574
Boyer, Daniel IV:265
Boyer, Frederick II:682, 693

Boyer, Henry II:742
Boyer, John IV:67
Boyer, John G. III:275
Boyer, Lewis IV:298
Boyer, Peter III:849
Boyer, Yost II:666
Boyers, Jacob II:234
Boyers, Michael III:573
Boyes, James I:720
Boyington, Jewett I:983
Boykin, John III:455
Boyle, Andrew III:189
Boyle, Daniel II:634
Boyle, James II:676
Boyle, John II:660
Boyle, Robert I:584; III:752
Boyles, Daniel II:4
Boyles, George II:207
Boyles, Timothy IV:192
Boyles, Walter II:473
Boyll, Charles IV:38
Boylls, David IV:46
Boylston, William I:513
Boynton, Andrew II:359
Boynton, Bela I:141
Boynton, Daniel I:849
Boynton, David E. I:739
Boynton, Elias I:756
Boynton, Isaac II:289
Boynton, Jane I:175
Boynton, Joseph I:322
Boynton, Moses I:757
Boynton, Richard I:698
Boynton, Roxanna I:175
Boynton, Royal I:175
Boynton, Samuel I:175
Boynton, Solomon II:346
Boynton, Thomas I:410
Boyt, Jacob B. III:401
Bozworth, Ichabod I:534
Bozworth, Jonathan III:222
Brace, David I:141
Brace, Jeffery I:880
Bracey, James I:233
Brack, Uriah IV:117
Brackenbaugh, Leonard IV:93
Bracket, John II:239
Bracket, Joshua I:305
Bracket, Josiah I:179
Bracket, Peter I:245
Bracket, William I:282
Brackett, Benjamin I:440
Brackett, Daniel II:288
Brackett, Heard I:162
Brackett, Hezekiah II:216
Brackett, James I:281
Brackett, John I:244
Brackett, Nathan I:282
Brackett, Samuel I:441
Bracy, Cornelius I:870
Bradan, Robert I:304
Bradbury, Ammiruhama II:341
Bradbury, Daniel I:390
Bradbury, James I:390
Bradbury, Paul I:263
Braddish, Edmund I:169
Bradeen, Joseph I:390

Bradenburg, Batus II:117
Bradfield, Elzey II:623
Bradfield, Joseph II:623;
III:670
Bradfield, Julian K. III:670
Bradfield, Rebecca II:623
Bradfield, Samuel II:623
Bradfield, William II:623
Bradford, Alden I:656, 658-59;
II:560
Bradford, Andrew I:569, 914
Bradford, Baxter II:195
Bradford, Benjamin I:671
Bradford, C. A. I:xiv
Bradford, Charles III:191
Bradford, Daniel II:195
Bradford, David I:558
Bradford, Elijah I:203
Bradford, Elisha II:220
Bradford, George I:794
Bradford, Israel I:570
Bradford, James I:570; II:653;
III:40, 410
Bradford, Joel I:823
Bradford, John I:756; IV:28
Bradford, Josiah I:558
Bradford, Lucy II:195
Bradford, Marian II:195
Bradford, Nathaniel I:570
Bradford, Noah I:570
Bradford, Oliver I:369
Bradford, Patty II:195
Bradford, Peabody I:244
Bradford, Perez I:554
Bradford, Peter I:263
Bradford, Robert IV:222
Bradford, Samuel I:739
Bradford, T. G. I:xii
Bradford, Timothy II:195
Bradford, William I:769;
III:560
Bradford, William J. III:40
Bradish, Daniel II:500
Bradish, Samuel I:853
Bradley, Aaron I:107
Bradley, Alling I:59
Bradley, Aner I:10
Bradley, Austin III:766
Bradley, Benjamin I:763
Bradley, Burrel III:416
Bradley, Cornelius IV:50
Bradley, Daniel I:30, 59, 154;
III:822
Bradley, David I:337, 655;
II:220
Bradley, Dimond I:337
Bradley, Ebenezer II:195
Bradley, Eber I:937
Bradley, Elihu II:478
Bradley, Elijah I:123
Bradley, Francis III:510
Bradley, George II:195
Bradley, George A. II:195
Bradley, George W. III:449
Bradley, Gilead I:122
Bradley, James II:304, 625;
III:762

Bradley, John I:907; II:625;
III:614
Bradley, Joshua I:513
Bradley, Lemuel I:123
Bradley, Lent II:372
Bradley, Leonard IV:123
Bradley, Mary II:625
Bradley, Nathan I:84; II:181
Bradley, Peter I:840
Bradley, Philbrick I:763
Bradley, Richard III:560
Bradley, Robert II:607
Bradley, Samuel I:262, 411,
937
Bradley, Stephen I:123
Bradley, Susan II:625
Bradley, Susanna II:195
Bradley, Thaddeus IV:249
Bradley, William III:132, 658,
822
Bradpick, John II:180
Bradshard, Jas. III:337
Bradshaw, Claiborne III:305
Bradshaw, George III:58
Bradshaw, John III:779, 824
Bradshaw, Jonas III:428
Bradshaw, Jonathan I:799
Bradshaw, Larner III:235
Bradshaw, Nathaniel I:542
Bradt, Aceneth II:187
Bradt, Frederick S. II:187
Bradt, Garret T. II:492
Bradt, Peter II:187
Bradt, Sam'l A. II:187
Bradt, Samuel II:187
Brady, Benjamin III:61
Brady, Catherine II:189
Brady, Christopher I:60
Brady, George II:193
Brady, John III:221
Brady, Lewis II:231
Brady, Robert II:189
Brady, Roger II:608
Brady, Sally Cordelia II:193
Brady, Thomas IV:257
Brady, William III:207; IV:285
Braford, Robert II:210
Brag, Nicholas I:178
Bragdon, Aaron I:220
Bragdon, Amos I:775
Bragdon, Arthur I:282
Bragdon, Daniel I:233
Bragdon, Ezekiel I:233
Bragdon, John I:233, 305
Bragdon, John, 2d I:179
Bragdon, Jotham I:166, 588
Bragdon, Samuel II:302
Bragdon, Solomon I:775
Bragg, Benjamin I:263
Bragg, Joab I:190
Bragg, John I:615
Bragg, Moses I:886
Bragg, Robert I:390
Bragg, William I:983; III:146,
803
Bragg, Wm. III:574
Bragman, Joseph I:831

Braid, Joseph IV:233
Brainard, Amos IV:242
Brainard, Buckley II:558
Brainard, Church I:263
Brainard, Daniel IV:285
Brainard, Elijah III:355
Brainard, Jabez I:782
Brainard, Othniel II:258, 558
Brainard, Simon I:115
Brainerd, Timothy I:461
Braithwaith, William III:697
Brake, John III:788
Braley, Gideon II:398
Braman, Benjamin I:369
Braman, Daniel I:38
Braman, James I:969
Bramble, Hackett III:371
Bramble, Robert I:131
Bramble, William II:392
Bramblet, Reuben IV:13
Bramblett, James III:262
Bramin, Benjamin II:625
Bramin, Isaac II:170
Bramin, John II:625
Bramin, Sarah II:625
Bramin, William II:625
Branan, Sylvanus I:369
Branch, Aholiab I:804
Branch, Almond I:859
Branch, Awilla I:859
Branch, Burrell III:413
Branch, David I:859
Branch, Elijah I:859, 865
Branch, Olive III:758
Branch, Samuel II:366
Branch, William IV:186
Branch, Zepheniah II:289
Brand, Amos II:341
Brand, Jeremiah I:273
Brand, William III:184
Brandenburg, Anthony IV:291
Brandenburg, William IV:237
Brandon, Benjamin IV:272
Brandon, Charles III:566
Brandon, Christopher III:515
Brandon, Josiah III:598
Brandon, Peter III:241
Brandon, Thomas III:807
Braneman, Christian IV:76
Brangton, William III:663
Branham, Gaydon IV:24
Branham, William III:260
Brank, Robert III:281
Brann, Jeremiah IV:233
Brann, William, Sen. III:844
Brannan, James III:607
Brannan, John II:607
Brannan, Thomas III:537
Brannen, David IV:239
Brannon, Adam II:210
Brannon, Jeremiah II:635
Brannon, John II:130; IV:192
Branscum, Charles I:187
Brant, Christian II:223
Brant, John II:21; IV:221
Brantley, Amos III:143
Brare, Elijah II:239

Brasfield, James III:190
Brashears, Ignatius III:66
Brashears, Morris III:611
Brasher, John IV:253
Brasier, Daniel B. II:193
Brasier, Eliza H. II:193
Brass, Thomas II:444
Brassbridge, John IV:208
Braswell, Henry III:508
Braswell, Jacob III:416
Braswell, Richard III:397
Bratcher, Charles III:570
Bratcher, Samuel III:492
Bratcher, William III:553
Bratherton, Thomas III:458
Bratten, James IV:252
Brawley, William III:605
Brawn, Daniel I:610
Braxton, James III:649
Bray, Andrew II:68
Bray, Christopher II:738
Bray, David III:454
Bray, John II:71; IV:55
Bray, Joseph I:223
Bray, Samuel I:543
Bray, Timothy III:645
Bray, William II:331
Brayton, Borden I:818
Brayton, Francis I:822
Brayton, James W. I:818
Brazil Byrd III:167
Breakill, Peter III:606
Breast, John III:260
Brechal, Martin II:673
Brechen, William, Sen. III:566
Breck, Daniel I:543, 983;
    III:335-36
Breck, Jonas I:429
Breckenridge, Jas. D. III:335
Breckenridge, Robert III:335
Brecker, Peter II:660
Breckett, Daniel I:411
Breden, Charles III:632
Breden, John III:573
Breed, Allen II:437
Breed, Frederick I:389
Breed, Jesse I:66
Breed, John II:478
Breed, Joseph II:389, 753
Breed, Oliver II:478
Breed, Stephen II:428
Breeding, John III:815
Breedlove, John IV:226
Breedlove, Major III:199
Breedlove, William III:324
Breedon, Enoch III:837
Brees, Henry II:523
Brees, Samuel II:731
Brees, Timothy IV:39
Breese, Garrett II:85
Breeze, Henry II:71
Breeze, John III:234
Breidegam, John II:702
Breiner, Philip II:607
Breman, Aaron I:245
Brenesholtz, George II:25
Brenesholtz, Henry II:25

Brenesholtz, John II:25
Brenesholtz, Maria II:25
Brenesholtz, Sarah Ann II:25
Brennman, Henry II:604
Brennon, John III:692
Brent, John III:558
Brenton, James IV:85
Brenton, John IV:63
Brenton, Robert IV:63
Brenton, William IV:63
Brest, John III:189
Brett, Daniel I:571
Brett, John I:411
Brevard, Alexander III:463
Brevard, Benjamin III:322, 592
Brevoort, John II:25
Brevoort, Samuel II:25
Brewer, Barnet III:90
Brewer, Benjamin IV:97
Brewer, Daniel I:38
Brewer, David I:513
Brewer, Eliab I:983
Brewer, Elisha I:594; II:376
Brewer, Elizabeth III:669
Brewer, Henry II:207; III:213;
    IV:165
Brewer, Isaac I:346
Brewer, James I:739
Brewer, John II:376, 675;
    III:669
Brewer, Moses I:706, 933
Brewer, Peter II:346
Brewer, Samuel III:305
Brewer, Thomas S. III:43
Brewer, William III:290, 569
Brewer, Zach. III:669
Brewers, Abraham J. II:58
Brewster, Baniel II:573
Brewster, Caleb II:129
Brewster, Darius I:273
Brewster, David II:409
Brewster, Elias I:132
Brewster, Elisha I:472, 657
Brewster, Frederick I:132
Brewster, Henry I:155
Brewster, Hezekiah I:66
Brewster, Hugh III:164
Brewster, J. W. II:561
Brewster, James I:757; II:704
Brewster, Jesse II:366
Brewster, John I:728
Brewster, Joseph II:503
Brewster, Joshua I:570
Brewster, Joshua, Jun. I:558
Brewster, Samuel II:503
Brewster, Sarah I:657
Brewster, Sheriff III:184
Brewster, William I:558;
    III:378, 494; IV:253
Brezerdine, Reuben III:763
Brian, Daniel III:710
Briance, Henry, Sen. IV:14
Briant, Betsey I:686
Briant, David I:633
Briant, Diana I:686
Briant, Isaac I:632
Briant, Jeremiah I:686

Briant, Jeremiah S. I:686
Briant, Priscilla I:686
Briant, Sally I:686
Briant, Timothy I:410
Briant, Zachariah III:273
Brickley, William III:844
Bridge, Benjamin IV:172
Bridgeham, John I:245
Bridges, Allen J. IV:13
Bridges, Benjamin III:211
Bridges, Daniel I:233
Bridges, Edmund I:187
Bridges, George IV:15
Bridges, Hackaliah I:880
Bridges, Ivory I:176
Bridges, John III:259, 305
Bridges, Joseph I:176; III:407
Bridges, Joshua, Jr. I:176
Bridges, Ransom III:718
Bridget, James III:658, 734
Bridgewater, William III:814
Bridgham, Samuel I:214
Bridgham, William I:245
Bridgman, Elisha I:487;
    IV:249
Bridgman, Gideon I:748
Bridgwater, Levi IV:58
Bridwell, Benjamin III:620
Bridwell, Simon III:324
Brierly, George III:304
Briggs, Aaron II:468
Briggs, Abiezer I:368
Briggs, Abner I:245, 358
Briggs, Abraham II:492
Briggs, Aden I:223
Briggs, Alpheus W. II:116
Briggs, Anderson I:800
Briggs, Arnold I:557
Briggs, Asa II:318; IV:108
Briggs, Benjamin I:346, 570;
    III:298
Briggs, Burton I:800
Briggs, Daniel I:800
Briggs, Darius I:409
Briggs, David III:300
Briggs, Edmund I:369
Briggs, Elisha I:570-71
Briggs, Enos I:958
Briggs, Ephraim I:896; III:397
Briggs, Ezra I:31
Briggs, Gideon I:907
Briggs, Henry II:238
Briggs, Isaac I:31, 814
Briggs, Jabez I:337
Briggs, Jacob I:429, 697, 797
Briggs, Jacob, Jun. I:429
Briggs, James I:369; II:276
Briggs, Jeremiah II:258
Briggs, Jesse I:213, 571
Briggs, Job I:800, 817
Briggs, John II:245, 312, 428,
    462; III:584, 699
Briggs, John, Jr. I:794
Briggs, Jonathan I:528, 800,
    805; II:312
Briggs, Joseph I:975; III:642
Briggs, Joshua II:258

329

Briggs, Lemuel I:607
Briggs, Leonard I:557
Briggs, Nathaniel I:698
Briggs, Owen I:923
Briggs, Paul I:361, 369
Briggs, Perez I:571
Briggs, Phinehas II:413
Briggs, Richard I:479
Briggs, Robert IV:26
Briggs, Rufus II:481
Briggs, Samuel I:294, 570;
II:568
Briggs, Solomon I:914
Briggs, Sweet I:831
Briggs, Thomas I:818
Briggs, William I:190, 814,
831; II:29
Briggs, Zephaniah I:83
Brigham, Abel II:478
Brigham, Abraham I:886
Brigham, Amariah I:616
Brigham, Don C. I:95
Brigham, Edward I:937
Brigham, Elnathan I:141
Brigham, Henry I:617
Brigham, Jesse I:595
Brigham, John I:512, 782
Brigham, Paul I:887, 942
Brigham, Stephen II:450
Brigham, Warren I:511
Brigham, Winslow I:634
Bright, James III:559
Bright, Simon III:412, 655
Bright, Willis III:367
Bright, Wyndle III:284
Brightman, Israel I:369
Brightman, Johnson II:397
Brightman, Peleg I:369
Brightman, Thomas I:831
Brightwell, Anderson III:688
Brightwell, Charles III:826
Briley, John IV:214
Briley, William III:690
Brillifont, James III:688
Brim, Henry II:657
Brimer, William III:616
Brimhall, Gideon I:908
Brimhall, Sylvanus I:633, 728
Brimigion, Thomas I:203
Brimley, William II:76
Brimmage, John III:282
Brinck, Aaron IV:104
Brinckley, John I:495
Bringham, Jonas II:130
Bringman, Daniel III:3, 19
Bringman, Thomas II:568
Brink, Adam II:531
Brink, Albert II:625
Brink, George II:523
Brink, Henry II:516
Brink, Hoses II:523
Brink, Jacob II:531
Brink, John II:625
Brink, John C. II:531
Brink, Peter II:531
Brink, Peter C. II:531
Brink, Rebecca II:625

Brink, William II:625
Brinker, Henry III:784
Brinkerhoff, Henry II:395
Brinsmade, Mrs. Cyrus I:83
Brinson, Hilira III:413
Brintnal, Peter II:418
Brinton, William IV:160
Brisban, John II:651
Briscoe, Henry III:294
Briscoe, Philip III:121
Brisler, John I:542
Brister, Aaron II:288
Brister, John I:46
Brister, Stephen I:46
Bristol, Benjamin II:403
Bristol, David I:122
Bristol, Gideon I:123
Bristol, John S. II:98
Bristol, Jonathan I:123
Bristol, Nathaniel II:365
Bristol, Reuben IV:277
Bristol, Samuel II:500
Bristol, Thomas I:20
Britain, James I:969
Britchett, James I:769
Britt, Ann E. II:189
Britt, Edmund I:609
Britt, John I:190
Britt, John W. II:189
Britt, Obed III:610
Britt, Richard II:484
Britt, Robert II:189
Brittain, Jeremiah III:338
Brittain, Philip III:537
Brittain, Samuel III:235
Brittain, William III:403
Brittan, Luther I:584
Britten, John, 2d II:331
Britten, John, 1st II:283
Britten, William I:368
Brittenham, Solomon IV:298
Brittin, Joseph II:687, 742
Britton, Asa I:739
Britton, Bartholomew II:631
Britton, Daniel II:46
Britton, Elias II:216
Britton, Gersham H. II:129
Britton, James II:362
Britton, Job I:679
Britton, John I:320, 739
Britton, John, 3d II:274
Britton, Joseph II:43, 80;
III:546, 635, 788
Britton, Michael III:423
Britton, Samuel II:418
Britton, William II:40, 235
Britton, Zachariah I:543
Brizendine, Bartlett III:692
Brizendine, Leroy III:622
Brizendine, Wm., Sr. III:774
Broach, Charles III:713
Broaders, Pryor III:795
Broadhead, Daniel II:676
Broadhead, Luke II:607
Broadrick, John I:440
Broadus, William III:851
Broadus, Wm. III:851

Broadwater, Chas. L. III:770
Broadway, John III:561
Broadway, Samuel III:435
Broadwell, Jacob IV:253
Brobst, John II:752
Brocas, John I:994
Broch, Reuben III:494
Brochus, John III:544
Brock, Bezzant III:413
Brock, Henry III:228
Brock, John I:896
Brock, Uriah IV:126
Brockett, Giles I:122
Brockett, Isaac I:59
Brockett, Joel I:122
Brockett, John I:461
Brockham, Pheneas R. II:104
Brockington, John III:504
Brocklebank, Job I:390
Brocklebank, Joseph I:245
Brockman, Joseph III:674
Brockway, Asa I:106
Brockway, Benjamin I:66
Brockway, Enoch II:413
Brockway, Ephraim II:437
Brockway, Gideon II:462
Brockway, John I:132
Brockway, Martin II:500
Brockway, Russell II:302
Brockway, Zebulon I:131
Broderick, William IV:129
Brodhead, Gawett II:745
Brodhead, Samuel II:531
Brodrick, William IV:243
Broga, Andrew I:337
Broile, Philip II:311
Brokan, George IV:256
Brokaw, Abraham II:516
Brokaw, Isaac II:71, 84
Brokaw, Jasper II:84
Brokaw, Peter II:40
Brokaw, Richard II:84
Bromigin, Jarvis III:258
Bromley, William I:958
Bronk, J. L. II:556
Bronson, Abraham II:564
Bronson, Isaac I:122; II:558
Bronson, Jabez I:141
Bronson, Joel I:96
Bronson, Joseph II:251
Bronson, Phineas IV:269
Bronson, Reuben I:106
Bronson, Selah I:123
Brook, David IV:288
Brook, Dudley III:612
Brook, George II:717; III:708
Brook, Humphrey III:775
Brook, Jesse III:287
Brook, John III:254, 411
Brook, Peter, Jr. II:558
Brooke, Edmund III:16
Brooke, Francis III:848
Brooke, Francis T. III:853
Brooker, Benj. D. I:595
Brooker, Isaac I:346
Brooker, Samuel I:346
Brookfield, Jacob II:62

330

Brookfield, Job II:80
Brookins, Artemus II:267
Brookins, Reuben II:263
Brookever, John III:845
Brooks, Abraham III:358
Brooks, Almarin II:33
Brooks, Alpheus I:924
Brooks, Amos I:690
Brooks, Asa II:239; IV:4
Brooks, Azariah II:402
Brooks, Charles IV:196, 290
Brooks, Daniel I:775
Brooks, David II:187, 558;
  III:573
Brooks, Ebenezer I:634
Brooks, Edward I:461
Brooks, Eli III:358
Brooks, Elias, Jr. III:765
Brooks, Elizabeth II:187
Brooks, Hananiah IV:227
Brooks, Henry IV:83
Brooks, Jabez I:345
Brooks, James II:40; III:239,
  760; IV:194
Brooks, James G. II:558
Brooks, Job I:739
Brooks, John I:83, 615, 756;
  II:187, 463, 478, 481;
  III:578; IV:142, 259
Brooks, Jonas I:749
Brooks, Jonathan II:283;
  III:418
Brooks, Joseph III:528, 645
Brooks, Joseph R. III:19
Brooks, Joshua IV:299
Brooks, Josiah I:95
Brooks, Levi I:633
Brooks, Littleton III:587
Brooks, Michael II:113
Brooks, Middleton III:169
Brooks, Nathan I:472
Brooks, Nathaniel I:77
Brooks, Nelson III:760
Brooks, Oliver IV:288
Brooks, Peter I:187
Brooks, Reuben I:345, 984
Brooks, Robert III:173
Brooks, Ruthy III:358
Brooks, Samuel I:234; II:478
Brooks, Samuel, 2d I:214
Brooks, Samuel Lewis II:262
Brooks, Shadrach II:449
Brooks, Silas II:228, 554
Brooks, Simon I:460
Brooks, Solomon I:304
Brooks, Thaddeus II:210
Brooks, Thomas II:180, 187,
  481; III:587, 779
Brooks, Thomas, 2d II:289
Brooks, William I:305, 756;
  II:607; III:420, 763, 773
Brooks, Zachariah S. III:501
Brookshire, John III:503
Brookshire, Manning III:447
Broom, John III:501
Broom, Mason III:376
Broome, John IV:222

Broozman, Jesse III:373
Brosins, Abraham III:677
Bross, Benjamin II:625
Bross, Garret II:625
Bross, Hermanus II:58
Bross, Lucy II:625
Bross, Mary II:625
Brotherton, Wm. III:584
Brothwell, Benjamin I:84
Brothwell, Joseph F. I:106
Brothwell, Thomas I:83
Broughton, Ebenezer I:893
Broughton, Job III:296
Broughton, Thomas III:342
Broun, Jeremiah III:748
Brounson, Leeman I:865
Brouse, Michael IV:293
Brow, Peter I:534
Brower, Jacob II:737
Brower, John II:353
Brower, John C. II:395
Brown, Aaron I:77; II:27, 384;
  III:606
Brown, Abel I:495, 728; II:500
Brown, Abiel I:804
Brown, Abijah I:870
Brown, Abraham I:617
Brown, Alexander II:657
Brown, Alexander Crawford
  IV:178
Brown, Amasa I:59
Brown, Ambrose I:76
Brown, Amos I:214, 558;
  III:435
Brown, Amos, 2d I:214
Brown, Andrew I:203, 245,
  615
Brown, Ann II:27
Brown, Arabia III:281
Brown, Archibald III:478
Brown, Arthur III:539
Brown, Asa I:958; II:473
Brown, Asenath I:685
Brown, Austin II:289, 557
Brown, Barnabas III:376
Brown, Barron II:216
Brown, Basel III:645
Brown, Bazel III:580
Brown, Benjamin I:513, 595,
  728; II:545; III:161, 600,
  629; IV:169
Brown, Benjamin, 2d I:728
Brown, Benjamin A. II:71
Brown, Betsey III:203
Brown, Caleb I:764
Brown, Charles I:634, 775;
  III:227
Brown, Charles, 2d III:235
Brown, Charles F. II:202
Brown, Chistopher I:831
Brown, Christopher I:132;
  III:35
Brown, Clark I:800
Brown, Cyril I:259
Brown, Cyrus II:481
Brown, D. I:xii

Brown, Daniel I:472, 497,
  775, 853; II:48, 389, 428,
  527; III:766; IV:15
Brown, David I:203, 329, 369,
  495; II:129, 199, 304, 704
Brown, David E. III:542
Brown, Dexter I:161
Brown, Ebenezer I:411, 496,
  657; II:173, 527
Brown, Ebenezer, 2d I:38, 635
Brown, Ebenezer, 1st II:251
Brown, Edward I:20, 410, 728
Brown, Eleazer I:886
Brown, Eli II:274
Brown, Eliada I:969
Brown, Elias I:38, 66
Brown, Eliezer I:822
Brown, Elihu I:635
Brown, Elijah I:974; II:318;
  III:448
Brown, Elisha II:216
Brown, Elkanah I:337
Brown, Enoch I:220
Brown, Enos II:731
Brown, Ensley I:691
Brown, Ephraim I:7, 479;
  III:174
Brown, Esek I:633
Brown, Ezekiel I:187, 190;
  IV:244
Brown, Ezra II:48; IV:269
Brown, Fanny I:685
Brown, Francis I:698
Brown, Frederick II:129, 625
Brown, George I:817; II:68,
  337; III:624
Brown, Gershom I:472
Brown, Gunsbury II:3
Brown, Hamilton III:83
Brown, Harmon III:203
Brown, Henry I:66; III:45,
  203, 245, 752, 760, 847
Brown, Hiram III:535
Brown, Humphrey II:504
Brown, Ichabod II:478
Brown, Ira II:199
Brown, Irvine III:194
Brown, Isaac I:512, 662, 818;
  II:428, 546, 687, 749;
  III:688; IV:177
Brown, Isacher III:800
Brown, Isaiah I:441; III:611
Brown, Isham III:544; IV:124
Brown, Jabez II:116
Brown, Jacob I:203, 213, 346,
  409, 495, 907; II:68, 71,
  473, 728; III:624
Brown, James I:203, 305, 411,
  609, 634, 763, 769; II:568;
  III:31, 329, 460, 489, 494,
  558, 575, 798
Brown, James, 1st IV:167
Brown, James, 2d I:233;
  II:207, 327, 666
Brown, James, 3d II:226, 645
Brown, James, Sen. II:634
Brown, James B. III:3

Brundage, Israel II:62
Bruner, Jacob III:207, 584
Brunner, Valentine III:64
Brunson, Asa I:37
Brunson, John III:56
Brunson, Levi II:731
Brunson, Stout III:254
Brunthefer, Adam II:692
Brunthever, Adam II:692
Brus, Edward III:562
Brush, Benjamin I:84
Brush, David II:341
Brush, Gilbert II:312
Brush, John Cicero III:12
Brush, Nathaniel I:xiv
Brush, Thomas I:853
Bruster, James III:305
Brusus, Jacob II:574
Bruton, Benjamin III:94
Bruton, George III:329
Bryam, Jonathan I:245
Bryams, James III:682
Bryan, Barich III:226
Bryan, Benajah I:106
Bryan, Charles II:669
Bryan, Daniel III:321
Bryan, Elijah II:229, 554;
  IV:299
Bryan, Jehiel I:123
Bryan, Jn. III:462
Bryan, John I:122; III:372,
  458
Bryan, John H. III:463
Bryan, Joseph II:651
Bryan, Michael III:557
Bryan, Mrs. Oliver I:122
Bryan, Reuben III:391
Bryan, Samuel IV:96
Bryan, Thomas III:172; IV:261
Bryan, William III:401, 832
Bryan, Zephaniah II:697
Bryant, Abijah I:281
Bryant, Alexander II:482
Bryant, Amasa I:914
Bryant, Amos I:691
Bryant, Benjamin III:101, 327
Bryant, Billey I:557
Bryant, Caleb I:440
Bryant, Charles III:483
Bryant, Daniel I:233
Bryant, Daniel C. I:739
Bryant, David IV:262
Bryant, Ebenezer I:95
Bryant, Elias I:512
Bryant, Ephraim III:672
Bryant, George II:195; III:313
Bryant, Hezekiah II:195
Bryant, Israel I:706
Bryant, Jacob I:52
Bryant, James II:248; III:583;
  IV:82
Bryant, Jesse III:460, 540
Bryant, John I:302, 450, 790;
  II:43; III:221, 281, 646, 738
Bryant, John (2) III:221
Bryant, Jonathan II:40
Bryant, Joseph I:245

Bryant, Joseph, 2d I:169
Bryant, Joseph H. I:843
Bryant, Levi I:790
Bryant, Louisa III:672
Bryant, Lydia II:195
Bryant, Mary II:195
Bryant, Moses I:790
Bryant, Patrick I:478
Bryant, Peter III:322
Bryant, Randolph II:22
Bryant, Reuben I:76
Bryant, Robert III:458
Bryant, Samuel II:195
Bryant, Sarah II:195
Bryant, Solomon I:513; II:195
Bryant, Stephen I:233
Bryant, Sylvanus I:782
Bryant, Thomas III:290, 454
Bryant, William III:146, 481,
  542; IV:119
Bryant, William G. IV:72
Bryant, Zenas I:570
Brydia, David I:865
Bryley, Zadock III:673
Bryne, Richard I:534
Bryson, Andrew II:642
Bryson, Samuel III:633
Buchan, David III:660
Buchanan, Alexander II:682
Buchanan, George I:851;
  III:173
Buchanan, James II:643
Buchanan, John II:180, 657;
  III:518
Buchanan, Richard I:851;
  III:640
Buchanan, Robert II:649;
  III:702
Buchannan, James III:148
Buchanon, Hiram II:166
Buchanon, John III:621
Buchanon, Joseph III:621
Buchanon, Thomas II:649
Buchanon, William II:297
Buchans, John II:304
Bucher, Jonathan I:46
Bucher, Nathan I:941
Buck, Aaron I:76; II:413
Buck, Abel II:346
Buck, Abner II:228
Buck, Amasa I:748
Buck, Asaph II:482
Buck, Benton I:937
Buck, D. A. A. I:998
Buck, Daniel I:996; II:450
Buck, Ebenezer IV:227
Buck, Elijah I:974
Buck, Francis II:262
Buck, George II:428
Buck, Isaac I:616; II:500;
  III:403
Buck, Israel II:359
Buck, Joel II:220
Buck, John I:440; IV:181
Buck, John, 2d IV:86
Buck, Jonathan IV:267
Buck, Joseph II:321

Buck, Leonard II:647
Buck, Levi II:539
Buck, Michael II:329
Buck, Michel II:329
Buck, Samuel II:258
Buck, Thomas II:517
Buck, William I:440; IV:169
Buck, Zebediah I:146
Buckalew, Frederick II:71
Buckalew, John II:71
Buckanan, Henry III:744
Buckhanan, William III:495
Buckhart, Henry III:841
Buckingham, Reuben II:216
Buckland, George I:95
Buckland, Jonathan I:96
Buckland, Joshua I:95
Bucklew, Peter II:675
Buckley, Daniel I:73
Buckley, Elizabeth III:668
Buckley, J. I:157
Buckley, James III:628
Buckley, John III:668
Buckley, Joshua IV:172
Buckley, Solomon I:95
Bucklin, Rufus I:958
Bucklup, Charles III:36
Buckman, Benjamin IV:38
Buckman, Elias I:748
Buckman, Joses I:705
Buckman, Reuben I:346
Buckman, Samuel II:206
Bucknam, William I:495
Buckner, Philip P. III:775
Buckner, William III:742
Bucknor, R. A. III:333
Buckter, Matthias II:638
Budd, Bristoll II:684
Budd, Daniel IV:25
Budd, John II:704; IV:244
Budd, Nathaniel II:58
Budlong, Benjamin II:413
Budlong, Rhodes I:814
Budlong, Samuel I:823
Budlong, Stephen I:814
Buel, Alexander M. II:197
Buel, Asa II:239
Buel, Augustus II:197
Buel, Cyrus II:549
Buel, Ezra II:503
Buel, Joseph I:346
Buel, Nathan II:749
Buel, Oliver II:481
Buel, Solomon I:95, 937
Buell, Daniel I:958
Buell, David I:45, 115
Buell, Gideon I:958
Buell, Isaac II:449
Buell, James I:115
Buell, John II:413
Buell, Josiah II:239
Buell, Levi I:959
Buell, Martin I:123
Buell, Salmon I:20
Buell, Timothy II:468
Buferd, Simeon III:256
Buff, Michael III:177

333

Buffington, David IV:245
Buffington, Samuel I:472, 657
Buffum, Samuel I:817
Buford, Abraham III:337
Buford, John III:281
Bugan, John II:742
Bugbee, Benjamin I:76, 914
Bugbee, George II:376
Bugbee, Hannah S. J. I:493
Bugbee, James I:77
Bugbee, Josiah II:312
Bugbee, Nathaniel I:698
Bugbee, Peletiah II:346
Bugbee, Peter I:782
Bugbee, Rufus I:460
Bugbee, Sally Ann D. I:493
Bugbee, Stephen D. I:493
Bugbee, Sylvester I:949
Bugbey, John I:73
Buker, Zebulon I:943
Buley, George III:64
Bulkeley, John I:132
Bulkley, Abraham I:83
Bulkley, Charles I:132
Bulkley, Eleazer I:83
Bulkley, Joseph I:82
Bulkley, Nathan I:82
Bull, Curtis III:745
Bull, Daniel III:745
Bull, Edmund III:331
Bull, Henry I:59
Bull, John I:106; II:503
Bull, Jonathan I:xiv
Bull, Reuben I:115
Bull, Thomas IV:119
Bullard, Aaron II:276
Bullard, Aden I:849
Bullard, Asa I:633
Bullard, Baruch I:635
Bullard, Benjamin I:496, 543
Bullard, Elisha I:543
Bullard, Isaac IV:34
Bullard, Joel I:609
Bullard, John I:429, 542;
    III:614
Bullard, John, 2d I:595
Bullard, Joseph I:461
Bullard, Luther I:682
Bullard, Lyman I:682
Bullard, Nathan I:763; II:336
Bullard, Rufus I:682
Bullard, Thomas III:401
Bullard, Tho's G. I:682
Bullin, Isaac III:390
Bullock, Charles III:421
Bullock, Comfort II:384
Bullock, Darius I:975
Bullock, David III:802
Bullock, David (2) III:802
Bullock, E. D. I:xii
Bullock, Ebenezer II:403
Bullock, Hawkins III:172
Bullock, Israel I:974
Bullock, James III:837
Bullock, James P. III:191
Bullock, John II:760
Bullock, Simeon I:812

Bullock, William II:304
Bully, Benjamin II:531
Bulson, Henry II:353
Bulson, John II:353
Buman, John I:190
Bumf, Bethuel II:604
Bumfries, Stephen I:453
Bumgardiner, Daniel IV:87
Bumgarner, David III:805
Bump, Aaron II:503
Bump, Isaac I:876
Bump, John II:289
Bump, Joseph II:503
Bumpass, William III:786
Bumpers, Asa I:558
Bumpus, Daniel I:558
Bumpus, Edward I:558
Bumpus, Frederick IV:282
Bumpus, Joseph I:570
Bumpus, Reuben II:704
Bumpus, Shubael I:228
Bunce, Daniel II:283
Bunce, Isaiah I:20
Bunch, Jeremiah III:499
Bunch, Richard III:328
Bundy, Christopher IV:98
Bundy, Elijah I:8
Bundy, Francis III:690
Bundy, Gurdon I:29
Bundy, Numan I:29
Bundy, Stephen I:29
Bundy, William II:122
Bune, Ellis II:755
Bunker, Richard I:380
Bunker, Zachariah I:675
Bunn, Barnes IV:28
Bunn, John II:67
Bunn, Samuel II:239
Bunnel, Enos I:122
Bunnel, Joel I:95
Bunnel, John I:123
Bunnell, Frederick II:231
Bunnell, Jehiel II:426
Bunnell, John III:706
Bunnell, Joseph I:30, 123
Bunnell, William I:123
Bunnoughs, Daniel IV:279
Bunores, Jeremiah IV:253
Bunten, John I:763
Bunting, Ramoth IV:176
Bunting, Solomon III:673
Bunting, Thomas II:350
Bunting, William III:673
Bunton, Alex. III:663
Bunton, Samuel IV:241
Bunton, William III:782
Burbage, Thomas III:499
Burbank, David I:769
Burbank, Eleazer I:261
Burbank, Isaac II:538
Burbank, Joel I:983
Burbank, John I:305
Burbank, Jonathan I:715
Burbank, Nathaniel I:874
Burbank, Thomas I:615
Burbank, Wells I:874
Burbank, William I:675

Burbeck, Henry I:66, 157
Burbeck, James I:748
Burbeck, John I:594
Burbeck, Joseph I:595
Burbeck, Thomas I:595
Burbeck, William II:98
Burbridge, Charles I:6
Burbridge, George III:320
Burbridge, James I:10
Burbridge, Limfield III:269
Burch, Benjamin III:337
Burch, Ebenezer II:312
Burch, Eddy IV:292
Burch, Francis III:686
Burch, Hendly III:337
Burch, Henry III:9
Burch, Isaiah II:231
Burch, James II:33
Burch, John III:9, 256
Burch, Joseph III:320
Burch, Rebecca III:9
Burch, Theoph. Y. III:9
Burch, Thomas II:372
Burch, William III:391
Burch, Zachariah IV:123
Burchard, Jonathan II:450
Burchard, Nathaniel II:304
Burchel, Daniel III:709
Burchett, John III:271
Burchett, Robert III:647
Burchett, William III:271
Burchfield, John IV:71
Burchfield, Michael IV:122
Burchfield, Robert IV:87
Burchure, Samuel II:4
Burckdorff, John II:248
Burd, Benjamin II:637
Burdeen, Timothy I:233
Burden, Abraham II:288
Burden, Nathaniel I:635
Burdge, Michael II:365
Burdick, Adam II:413
Burdick, Elisha II:228, 554
Burdick, Francis II:492
Burdick, Gideon I:809; II:373
Burdick, Hazard II:481
Burdick, Henry II:228
Burdick, Isaiah I:831
Burdick, John IV:287
Burdick, Robert II:113
Burdick, Silvester I:831
Burdick, Thompson II:283
Burdick, Walter I:18
Burdin, John III:808
Burdine, Reuben I:xii
Burdoo, Silas I:983
Burdsall, Bennett II:19
Burdue, Nathaniel IV:259
Burdwell, Simeon IV:237
Burford, John, Sen. III:84
Burford, Martha III:337
Burford, Philip T. III:578
Burfu, Nathan I:763
Burgdoff, Conrad II:428
Burge, Lathrop II:536
Burge, Lott II:403
Burgen, Christopher II:426

Burger, Zachariah II:531
Burges, Abial I:391
Burges, Asahel II:105
Burges, Edward III:230
Burges, John I:571
Burges, William I:571; III:701
Burgess, Asa I:147
Burgess, Bangs II:312
Burgess, Benjamin I:886
Burgess, David I:294
Burgess, Edward I:190; III:695
Burgess, Ephraim I:326
Burgess, Ichabod I:558
Burgess, Jacob I:557
Burgess, James II:267
Burgess, John III:407, 772;
IV:174
Burgess, Jonathan I:262
Burgess, Joseph I:617
Burgess, Joshua III:336
Burgess, Josiah III:170
Burgess, Michael II:267
Burgess, Nathaniel I:983
Burgess, Stephen I:557
Burgess, Thomas I:609
Burgess, Vachel III:45
Burgess, William II:581
Burgett, Lambert II:517
Burghardt, John I:346
Burgis, John II:283
Burhans, Tierck II:531
Burhart, Jacob II:748
Burhaus, Edward II:392
Burk, George IV:77
Burk, James III:36
Burk, John I:887; II:591;
IV:98
Burk, Jonathan I:907
Burk, Joseph I:706, 955, 958;
III:574
Burk, Malchijah III:19
Burk, Michael III:301
Burk, Patrick II:689
Burk, Robert III:611
Burk, Samuel III:295
Burk, Silas II:561
Burk, Silvanus IV:179
Burk, Thomas II:693; III:36
Burk, William II:657
Burkard, Frederick II:742
Burke, Elisha III:552
Burke, Isham III:602
Burke, James III:769
Burke, John I:477; II:510;
III:742
Burke, Mathew III:663
Burke, Nathan I:603; III:45
Burke, Robert III:315
Burke, William III:697
Burke, William, 2d III:690
Burkes, Samuel III:614
Burkett, Frederick III:584, 587
Burkman, Thomas I:187
Burks, Isham IV:117
Burland, Allen W. I:857
Burland, Belus H. I:857
Burland, Bradford I:857

Burland, John I:857
Burleigh, William I:697
Burley, Ebenezer II:751
Burley, Joseph I:763, 994
Burley, Stephens I:728
Burlingame, Daniel I:896
Burlingame, Nathan II:376
Burlingame, Pardon I:822
Burlingame, Solomon II:329
Burlingame, Wanton II:403
Burlinggame, Nathan II:318
Burlingham, Hopkins II:481
Burlinson, John I:880
Burlison, John II:163
Burman, Henry III:33
Burn, David III:503
Burn, Thomas II:645
Burnam, Israel II:255
Burnam, Jonathan I:923
Burnam, William I:959
Burnam, Zadock I:914
Burnap, Abijah I:633
Burnap, Edward I:616
Burnap, Jeriah I:141
Burnap, John I:147
Burnap, Joseph I:763
Burnee, John II:648
Burnell, Ephraim I:478
Burnell, John I:223
Burnell, Joseph I:479
Burnell, Samuel I:959
Burner, Abraham III:732
Burner, Joseph I:513
Burnes, James II:22
Burnes, Philip III:305
Burnes, Samuel II:672
Burnet, Aaron II:62
Burnet, Jacob II:557
Burnet, Josiah II:22
Burnet, Squire IV:198
Burnet, Thomas II:469
Burnett, Andrew I:818
Burnett, David II:80
Burnett, Ebenezer II:297
Burnett, Edmund IV:288
Burnett, James I:146
Burnett, John II:327
Burnett, Joseph II:727
Burnett, Robert II:561
Burnett, Rodney I:193
Burnett, Samuel II:193
Burnett, William I:440
Burnham, Abner I:880
Burnham, Ammi I:706
Burnham, Amos I:410
Burnham, Andrew I:756
Burnham, Asa I:365
Burnham, Asahal II:337
Burnham, Benjamin I:411
Burnham, Charles I:391
Burnham, David I:391
Burnham, Ebenezer I:983
Burnham, Gurdin IV:12
Burnham, H. N. II:562
Burnham, Ira I:682
Burnham, Isaac I:390; II:318;
III:2; IV:114

Burnham, James I:146, 479,
728, 769-70
Burnham, Jeremiah I:381,
391; IV:169
Burnham, John I:76, 146,
410, 682, 720, 789, 907;
II:403; IV:189
Burnham, Jonathan I:390
Burnham, Joseph I:132, 141,
390, 682
Burnham, Joshua I:512, 706
Burnham, Josiah I:147; II:503
Burnham, Mary I:682
Burnham, Nathan, 2d I:76
Burnham, Nathan, 1st I:53
Burnham, ___nezer I:409
Burnham, Oliver I:7
Burnham, Orrin II:409
Burnham, Pike G. I:747
Burnham, Roger I:95
Burnham, Stephen I:38
Burnham, Sylvester I:132
Burnham, Thomas I:390, 411
Burnham, Timothy D. I:682
Burnham, Wailliam II:326
Burnham, Wesley I:411
Burnham, Wolcott I:865
Burnhart, George P. II:701
Burnhart, Henry II:672
Burnhart, John II:655
Burnitt, William III:614
Burnley, Henry III:183
Burnley, James III:677
Burns, Andrew III:317
Burns, David II:231
Burns, James III:119, 207,
407
Burns, Jeremiah III:223
Burns, John I:688; II:130,
579; III:40, 51, 240, 506,
524, 566; IV:55, 225
Burns, Laird III:611
Burns, Luke III:36
Burns, Michael III:792
Burns, Robert II:267
Burns, Samuel I:876; III:517
Burns, Thomas III:19
Burns, Walter I:802
Burns, William I:73; III:271
Burnside, John IV:89
Burnside, Jonathan IV:182
Burnside, Robert III:301
Burnsides, Andrew III:506
Burpee, Elijah I:633
Burpee, Isaac I:757
Burpee, Nathan II:426
Burpee, Nathaniel I:410
Burpie, Nathaniel I:769
Burr, Aaron II:444
Burr, Asa II:434
Burr, Cushing I:512
Burr, Daniel I:261
Burr, Edmund III:740
Burr, Hezekiah I:83
Burr, Joel I:503
Burr, Jonathan I:599
Burr, Joseph I:190

335

Burr, Joshua I:805
Burr, Levi I:570
Burr, Mrs. Daniel I:261
Burr, Nathaniel I:115
Burr, Roger I:896
Burr, Semo I:534
Burr, Seth I:543
Burr, Sylvanus I:994
Burr, William I:123
Burrall, Jonathan II:444
Burrell, Alden I:391
Burrell, Humphrey I:294
Burrell, Isaac I:571
Burrell, James I:557
Burrell, Jedediah IV:218
Burrell, John I:220, 557
Burrell, Joseph I:411
Burrell, Noah I:558
Burrett, Anthony I:123
Burrett, Nathan I:82
Burrett, Zalman IV:63
Burridge, John I:495
Burril, Zacariah IV:167
Burrill, Benjamin I:804
Burrill, Ebenezer I:390; II:444
Burrill, Noah I:294
Burris, Jacob III:618
Burris, Martin IV:16
Burris, Nathaniel III:305
Burris, Solomon III:433
Burrit, Charles II:276
Burritt, Eben I:106
Burritt, William II:180
Burronough, John II:462
Burroughs, Eden II:673
Burroughs, Elijah IV:211
Burroughs, John II:52, 68;
    III:653
Burroughs, Josiah I:994
Burroughs, Matthew II:206
Burroughs, Zebulon I:873
Burrow, William III:389
Burrows, Elisha II:175
Burrows, Ezekiel III:720
Burrows, Giles I:389
Burrows, Hubbard II:654
Burrows, John II:304
Burrows, Joseph I:77; II:267,
    608
Burrows, Nathaniel II:707
Burrows, Paul I:132
Burrows, Robert II:492
Burrows, William I:19, 705;
    II:400
Burrows, William, 2d I:705
Burseil, James I:670
Burseil, Moses I:671, 769
Burt, Aaron IV:267
Burt, Alvin II:398
Burt, Benjamin IV:216
Burt, D. II:555
Burt, David I:616
Burt, Edward II:113
Burt, Henry II:318
Burt, Jacob IV:163
Burt, Joel I:478
Burt, John II:359; IV:133

Burt, Samuel II:122
Burt, Stephen II:492
Burt, W. B. III:186
Burtch, Billings I:132
Burter, Michael III:318
Burton, Asa I:429
Burton, Benjamin I:955
Burton, David I:914; II:462
Burton, Elijah I:929
Burton, Elizabeth III:852
Burton, George IV:27
Burton, Henry III:547
Burton, James III:852
Burton, John II:21; III:649;
    IV:17
Burton, Joshua IV:182
Burton, Lewis I:82
Burton, Marshall III:699
Burton, Nathan I:107
Burton, R. M. III:637
Burton, Richard III:481
Burton, Robert III:448
Burton, Sam'l III:676
Burton, Seley III:313
Burton, Simon II:101
Burton, Thomas I:273; III:674
Burton, William I:273; IV:120
Burton, William H. III:460
Burts, James II:473
Burwell, Jere I:59
Burwell, Jonathan IV:131
Burwell, Zachariah IV:209
Burwill, Daniel I:106
Bury, Conrad II:607
Burzett, Charles II:216
Busby, Isham III:618
Busby, James III:208
Busby, Nedom III:507
Busby, Robert III:253
Busby, William III:263
Bush, Abijah II:492
Bush, Charles III:290
Bush, Conrad II:561
Bush, Daniel I:346; II:758
Bush, Dennis III:697
Bush, Drury III:317
Bush, Enoch III:611
Bush, Frederick II:531
Bush, George I:xv, 115; II:482
Bush, Henry II:739
Bush, Hezekiah I:478
Bush, Jacob III:798
Bush, Jacobus H. II:389
Bush, James III:269
Bush, John I:947; II:245
Bush, John D. II:231
Bush, Jonathan I:634
Bush, Richard I:817
Bush, Rufus I:96
Bush, Samuel I:30
Bush, Solomon II:607
Bush, Stephen II:372
Bush, William III:194
Bush, Zachariah II:481
Bush, Ziba I:337
Bushee, Consider III:405
Bushee, James I:812

Bushee, Jonathan I:812
Bushee, Samuel II:503
Bushnell, Andrew IV:156
Bushnell, Daniel I:8, 115
Bushnell, Doud I:923
Bushnell, Elisha I:115
Bushnell, Ephraim II:450
Bushnell, Jason II:449
Bushnell, John I:948
Bushong, George III:529
Bushong, Jacob IV:177
Buskill, John III:195
Buskirk, Aaron IV:82
Buskirk, John IV:87
Buskirk, John V. IV:27
Buss, Ephraim II:450
Buss, John I:633
Buss, Joseph I:665
Buss, Samuel I:690
Bussell, Isaac I:231, 321
Bussell, Jonathan I:263
Bussell, Matthew III:573
Bussell, William III:587
Bussey, Enos II:231
Bussey, John I:543
Bussing, William II:444
Bussle, Vincent III:740
Buster, Claudius III:750
Buswell, Daniel I:706
Buswell, Elias I:756
Buswell, Noah I:728
Buswell, Richard I:748
Butcher, Benjamin, 2d I:876
Butcher, Benjamin, 1st I:843
Butcher, John III:36
Butcher, William III:20
Butland, Jesse I:305
Butland, Nathaniel I:233
Butler, Allen II:517
Butler, Asaph IV:175
Butler, Azariah I:461
Butler, Benjamin I:59; III:591
Butler, Calvin I:155
Butler, Charles I:27; II:555;
    III:366
Butler, Charles J. II:625
Butler, Charles T. III:130
Butler, David I:147, 492
Butler, Easton I:329
Butler, Edward II:625
Butler, Ezekiel III:554
Butler, Ezra I:60, 969
Butler, George I:346
Butler, Ira II:113
Butler, Isaac I:880
Butler, Israel II:288, 625
Butler, Jacob III:800
Butler, James III:160, 610
Butler, Jethro III:363
Butler, John I:390, 411, 749;
    II:180, 312, 392; III:2, 310,
    363, 412, 486, 796; IV:301
Butler, Jonathan I:756
Butler, Joseph I:885; III:807
Butler, Josiah II:403
Butler, Leonard II:105
Butler, Lydia II:554

Cain, John III:798
Cain, Nicholas I:203, 599
Cain, Patrick III:299
Cain, Peter Warren II:510
Cain, William III:557
Caine, John II:450
Caines, Richard III:218
Cake, Philip IV:189
Calder, James I:823
Calder, Robert I:528
Calder, William II:312
Calderwood, John I:299
Calderwood, Thomas I:204
Caldwell, George III:569
Caldwell, James I:706; III:509;
    IV:124, 295
Caldwell, John I:441; II:284;
    III:498, 526, 664, 818
Caldwell, John T. II:523
Caldwell, Joseph II:478
Caldwell, Medford I:893
Caldwell, Moses I:392
Caldwell, Nicholas II:608
Caldwell, Orvin C. I:334
Caldwell, Philip II:321
Caldwell, Robert III:240;
    IV:288
Caldwell, Samuel III:428;
    IV:16
Caldwell, Thomas, Jun. I:392
Caldwell, William II:346, 424;
    III:513, 594, 5809; IV:233
Caldwell, William, 2d III:204
Calebs, Elijah II:107
Calender, Samuel II:667
Calhoon, George III:273
Calhoon, Hugh II:39
Calhoon, Samuel IV:288
Calhoun, Benjamin I:8
Calhoun, James II:350
Calhoun, John I:554; III:475
Calhoun, Samuel I:938
Calif, Joseph I:770
Calkin, Eli I:897
Calkin, Nathaniel II:504
Calkin, Nathaniel S. I:480
Calkin, Solomon II:418
Calkins, Daniel II:248
Calkins, Dennis II:667
Calkins, Matthew II:377
Calkins, Moses II:705
Call, John I:430
Call, Nathaniel I:994
Call, Thomas M. III:798
Callaghan, Daniel II:669;
    III:21
Callaghan, Edward II:181
Callaghan, James IV:114
Callahan, Daniel II:586
Callahan, Dennis IV:165
Callahan, Joel III:503
Callahan, John III:582
Callahan, Patrick II:609
Callander, William I:599
Callaway, James IV:121
Callaway, Lowder II:8
Callender, John II:662

Callender, John R. III:463
Callender, Silas I:338
Callender, Thomas III:463
Callett, John III:247
Calley, Edward I:866
Calley, Jonathan I:775
Calligan, Richard III:3
Callis, David III:642; IV:4
Callis, George III:806
Callis, Thomas I:783
Calloway, Chesley III:313
Calloway, Samuel IV:34
Calmes, Marcus III:331
Calmes, William III:509
Calnan, Thomas I:729
Caloway, Micajah IV:97
Calvert, Spencer III:264
Calvert, Willis III:189
Calvin, Benedict I:814
Calvin, Benoni I:823
Calvin, David I:97
Cam, Daniel I:559
Cambe, James II:231
Cambell, McDonald IV:288
Cambridge, John I:691
Camer, Abraham II:385
Cameron, Alexander II:48,
    737; III:133
Cameron, John III:405
Cameron, Murdoch I:655
Cameron, Murdock II:552, 558
Camfield, John II:81
Cammell, George I:426
Cammett, Samuel I:234
Camp, Abel I:984
Camp, Amos II:305
Camp, Benjamin II:483
Camp, Caspar II:648
Camp, Elias I:124
Camp, Ephraim I:107
Camp, Ezra I:107
Camp, Hosea III:128
Camp, Israel I:775
Camp, Joel I:21
Camp, John I:47, 107; III:684;
    IV:283
Camp, Manoah I:116
Camp, Morris D. II:35
Camp, Nicholas II:482
Camp, Rejoice I:116
Camp, Samuel I:46; II:240
Camp, Sharp I:39
Camp, Thomas III:737
Camp, William G. IV:115
Campbell, Abraham III:494
Campbell, Alexander I:179;
    II:592, 670, 675; IV:104
Campbell, Amelia A. III:202
Campbell, Andrew I:729; II:31
Campbell, Anthony III:752
Campbell, Archibald I:107;
    II:226, 434
Campbell, Benj. II:558
Campbell, Charles II:187;
    III:87
Campbell, Christopher II:741
Campbell, Daniel I:691, 706

Campbell, David II:705; III:83,
    602
Campbell, Duncan II:181
Campbell, Enos IV:210
Campbell, Eve II:187
Campbell, Francis IV:286
Campbell, Frederick II:21
Campbell, Geo. K. III:202
Campbell, George III:174, 444
Campbell, Henry III:814
Campbell, Isaac I:358; II:434
Campbell, Jacob II:482
Campbell, James I:264, 274,
    450, 617, 662, 757, 783;
    II:123, 450; III:54, 308, 517,
    572, 595, 641; IV:6, 251
Campbell, James, 2d I:874
Campbell, Jeremiah I:617;
    III:572
Campbell, Jesse I:782
Campbell, John I:148, 479;
    II:6, 131-32, 444, 482, 675,
    711; III:197, 230, 321, 574,
    697, 748, 775; IV:113, 207,
    242, 253, 272, 283
Campbell, John, 2d IV:35
Campbell, John W. II:131
Campbell, Joseph III:585
Campbell, Joshua IV:269
Campbell, Jotham II:107
Campbell, Kenneth II:558
Campbell, Kennett II:326
Campbell, Lawrence III:284
Campbell, Lewis II:22
Campbell, Louisa S. III:202
Campbell, Owen III:824
Campbell, Peter II:187
Campbell, Phebe II:187
Campbell, Robert I:707, 915;
    II:33, 223, 359, 669; III:295,
    587
Campbell, Robert, 2d II:675
Campbell, Robert, 3d II:689
Campbell, Samuel II:672, 674
Campbell, Solomon III:537
Campbell, Thomas II:605,
    692; III:410, 678, 725
Campbell, William I:160, 757;
    II:76, 498, 549, 677;
    III:189, 241, 760, 774; IV:60,
    64, 96, 117, 189, 286, 293
Campen, Joseph, Sen. III:403
Camper, John III:755
Camper, Tilman III:275
Campernell, David I:671
Campernell, William I:234
Campfield, Jabez II:48
Campfield, Nathaniel II:35
Campin, James III:356
Compton, Archibald III:657
Camron, James III:277
Camron, William III:772
Canady, John III:771
Canady, William III:486
Canafax, William III:810
Cancannon, John II:132
Candee, Job I:124

338

339

Carner, Philip II:510
Carnes, Ephraim II:81
Carnes, John IV:233
Carnes, Philip III:602
Carney, James II:166
Carney, John II:609; III:558; IV:78
Carney, Patrick II:692
Carney, Thomas II:569; III:49
Carney, William III:715
Carnine, Peter III:322
Carothers, James II:608; III:295
Carothers, John II:643; III:99
Carothers, Thomas III:245
Carpenter, Abel I:933
Carpenter, Abiel II:419
Carpenter, Albion I:175
Carpenter, Allen II:226
Carpenter, Amos IV:270
Carpenter, Barnard II:451
Carpenter, Benjamin I:370, 740, 814; III:396; IV:18
Carpenter, Comfort I:77, 142
Carpenter, Daniel IV:194
Carpenter, David I:461, 740
Carpenter, Ebenezer I:740
Carpenter, Elias I:603, 887, 949
Carpenter, Eliphalet I:943
Carpenter, Eliza I:175
Carpenter, Ephraim I:782; IV:7
Carpenter, Ezra I:544
Carpenter, Greenwood II:211
Carpenter, Guy II:132
Carpenter, Isaac II:101; III:397
Carpenter, Isaiah II:450
Carpenter, Israel I:461
Carpenter, Jesse II:513; III:815
Carpenter, John I:544, 815, 949, 975; IV:48
Carpenter, Jonathan I:949
Carpenter, Joseph I:823; II:132, 398
Carpenter, Joshua A. II:289
Carpenter, Lewis I:348
Carpenter, Matthew II:524
Carpenter, Nathan II:400
Carpenter, Nathaniel I:430, 698
Carpenter, Philip II:418
Carpenter, Rufus I:347
Carpenter, Samuel I:175; IV:265
Carpenter, Shubael IV:140
Carpenter, Simeon I:637
Carpenter, Thomas I:306
Carpenter, William I:31, 370; II:500; III:329; IV:7
Carper, John III:721
Carr, Amos I:333
Carr, Ballart Decatur II:626
Carr, Benjamin II:117, 400
Carr, Caleb I:799
Carr, Candy II:193
Carr, Clement I:46

Carr, Ebenezer I:818; II:302
Carr, George IV:120
Carr, Gideon III:577
Carr, Hezekiah III:689
Carr, Jacob I:757
Carr, James I:688, 707, 789; II:366, 626; III:582; IV:78
Carr, Jesse I:764
Carr, John I:818; II:523; III:58, 731
Carr, John F. III:605
Carr, Jonathan II:418
Carr, Joseph I:381; II:313, 504
Carr, Levi II:367
Carr, Margaret II:193
Carr, Mary II:193
Carr, Meckins III:746
Carr, Moses III:417
Carr, Nathan I:782
Carr, Oliver P. I:789
Carr, Robert I:757, 794; II:277, 743; IV:81
Carr, Samuel II:578; IV:24
Carr, Selia II:193
Carr, Solomon III:385
Carr, Thomas I:691
Carr, Thomas, 2d I:904
Carr, William I:228, 757; II:223, 469; III:165, 413, 532, 549, 620
Carr, William, 2d III:549
Carr, William, Jr. II:473
Carragan, Thomas II:608
Carrall, Jesse I:805
Carraway, William III:182
Carrel, William IV:267
Carrell, Aaron I:783
Carrell, Benjamin I:264
Carrell, Daniel III:551
Carrell, James III:427
Carrell, James P. III:853
Carrent, James III:32
Carrick, Patrick III:12
Carrico, Alexander I:391
Carrier, Amaziah II:493
Carrier, Jonathan D. II:98
Carrigan, James III:356
Carrigan, Peter II:644
Carrigan, William III:410
Carringer, Martin II:670
Carrington, Clement III:848
Carrington, George III:439
Carrington, Gilbert II:162
Carrington, Joseph II:29
Carrol, Dumpsey III:95
Carrol, John III:295
Carrol, William III:428
Carroll, Armstrong IV:163
Carroll, Bartholomew IV:42
Carroll, Catherine IV:163
Carroll, Daniel III:627
Carroll, Dennis III:714
Carroll, Ebenezer I:204
Carroll, Hardy III:372
Carroll, Henry IV:163
Carroll, Isaac II:3

Carroll, Jane IV:163
Carroll, John IV:163
Carroll, Joseph IV:163
Carroll, Margaret IV:163
Carroll, Martin II:132
Carroll, Mary III:9; IV:163
Carroll, Perry III:692
Carroll, Philip IV:163
Carroll, Sinclair III:9
Carroll, William II:175, 206; III:611
Carrolls, Malachi III:825
Carrothers, John III:431
Carry, William III:271
Carsly, Ebenezer I:320
Carson, Andrew III:424
Carson, Benjamin II:644
Carson, Henry III:628
Carson, James I:231; II:267; III:267, 593
Carson, John III:224; IV:88
Carson, Robert III:626
Carson, S. P. III:462
Carson, Samuel II:216; IV:198, 298
Carson, Thomas III:263, 580
Carson, Walter IV:78
Carson, William II:635; III:327, 760
Carswell, Abner II:539
Carswell, David IV:194
Carswell, John III:609
Carswell, Joseph I:729
Cart, John III:499
Cart, William III:702
Carte, John II:609
Carter, Abijah I:247
Carter, Andrew I:858
Carter, Anthony II:210
Carter, Arnold IV:259
Carter, Asahel Elisha II:27
Carter, Bame Roberts II:27
Carter, Barnabas III:239
Carter, Benjamin II:424; III:338, 519
Carter, Braxton III:342
Carter, Charles III:177, 271, 618
Carter, Charles, Sen. III:600
Carter, Daniel I:764; III:605
Carter, Daniel C. IV:140
Carter, David III:161
Carter, Edward I:73, 187
Carter, Elihu I:97
Carter, Elijah II:214
Carter, Elisha II:27
Carter, Elizabeth I:858
Carter, Ephraim III:451
Carter, Frederick I:853
Carter, George II:41
Carter, Gideon I:392
Carter, Halsey III:758
Carter, Heman II:216
Carter, Henry III:220, 256, 390
Carter, Isaac I:347; III:122
Carter, Isam III:477

Carter, Ithiel I:39
Carter, Jabez II:277
Carter, Jacob I:770
Carter, James I:514; II:33;
III:425, 439, 510, 816;
IV:239
Carter, James M. III:807
Carter, Jared I:6
Carter, Jirah II:159
Carter, Job II:31
Carter, Joel I:97
Carter, John I:234, 959;
II:305, 648; III:213, 293,
519, 680, 762
Carter, John, Sen. III:584
Carter, John B. III:331
Carter, Jonah I:897
Carter, Jonas IV:186
Carter, Joseph I:858; III:328,
724
Carter, Joshua I:635
Carter, Josiah, Sen. III:455
Carter, Landon III:390
Carter, Lewis Basmont II:27
Carter, Martin III:305
Carter, Michael I:707
Carter, Moses III:391
Carter, Nathan I:764
Carter, Ned I:73
Carter, Nicholas III:336
Carter, Obadiah III:216
Carter, Philip III:256, 782
Carter, Poval III:826
Carter, Richard II:22, 482
Carter, Richard, 1st II:248
Carter, Robert III:156
Carter, Rufus II:463
Carter, Russel P. I:858
Carter, Sally I:858
Carter, Samuel I:147; III:356
Carter, Samuel, Sr. III:606
Carter, Solomon I:924
Carter, Stephen I:124; II:590
Carter, Sybele Riggs II:27
Carter, Thaddeus I:191
Carter, Thomas II:753; III:448,
549, 714
Carter, Timothy I:858
Carter, Uzzial IV:291
Carter, William I:637; II:27,
424; III:199, 313, 810, 820;
IV:98
Carter, William (2) III:820
Carthill, Pelutiah I:299
Cartinton, John III:798
Cartmill, Henry III:755
Cartwright, Aaron II:173
Cartwright, Christopher II:257
Cartwright, Cyrus II:210
Cartwright, Gideon III:524
Cartwright, Joseph III:412
Cartwright, Justinian III:211
Cartwright, Solomon II:528
Cartwright, Thomas II:22
Carty, Daniel II:52
Carty, Isaac II:39
Carty, John II:52

Carty, Thomas II:592
Cartz, Thomas II:733
Carull, Isaac II:4
Caruthers, Hugh III:88
Caruthers, James III:569
Caruthers, Robert III:566
Carver, Aldrich I:73
Carver, Asa I:959
Carver, Christian IV:17
Carver, Henry I:358
Carver, Isaac I:488
Carver, Jabez I:361
Carver, James III:301
Carver, John I:370
Carver, Richard III:510
Carver, Rufus I:959
Carver, William, Sen. III:405
Carvil, Zachariah III:495
Cary, Ason II:377
Cary, Christopher IV:189
Cary, John III:3
Cary, Jonathan I:572
Cary, Michael I:812; III:706
Cary, Peter I:617
Cary, Recompense II:404
Caryell, David I:299
Case, Abel I:96-97; II:337
Case, Abner IV:5
Case, Adam II:255
Case, Asahel I:107
Case, Augustus IV:293
Case, Clark I:334
Case, George IV:244
Case, Giles II:463
Case, Gillum II:334
Case, Henry II:26
Case, Hosea I:97
Case, Isaac I:264
Case, James I:975; IV:74
Case, Jesse II:104
Case, John I:81
Case, John M. I:96
Case, Joseph III:370
Case, Josiah IV:98
Case, Julian II:26
Case, Micah I:96
Case, Nathan I:924
Case, Nathaniel IV:104
Case, Oliver I:97
Case, Richard I:38
Case, Roswell I:38
Case, Timothy I:866
Case, Tunis II:68
Case, Walter II:561
Case, William II:289; IV:58
Casewell, Simeon I:179
Casey, Archibald III:225, 689
Casey, Charles III:322
Casey, Edward III:677
Casey, Hugh I:27
Casey, Hugh (2) I:27
Casey, Jacob IV:183
Casey, James III:793
Casey, John II:586, 677;
III:219, 575, 664, 795
Casey, Joseph III:266
Casey, Mary II:626

Casey, Morris II:609
Casey, Nathaniel II:626
Casey, Nicholas III:828
Casey, Oliver II:206
Casey, Patrick I:609
Casey, Robert II:558
Casey, Wanton I:814
Casey, William III:78, 457
Cash, Bartlett III:748
Cash, George I:392
Cash, James III:161
Cash, John I:234, 247; III:166
Cash, Peter III:421
Cash, Samuel I:179, 329
Cash, Warren III:286
Cash, William III:319
Cashart, Robert II:68
Cashin, David III:628
Cashman, Daniel II:111
Cashman, Eliphalet II:277
Cashone, Burwell III:431
Cashone, Thomas III:431
Cashwell, Henry III:748
Cashwell, William III:748
Casler, John II:419
Casler, Nicholas II:438
Casler, Richard II:414
Casner, Adam III:756
Cason, Cannon III:502
Cason, Edward III:837
Cason, John III:397, 401
Cason, Thomas III:837
Cason, William III:183, 837
Cass, G. W. IV:298
Cass, Jonathan IV:298
Cass, Lewis IV:110
Cass, Moses I:223
Cass, Nebadiah IV:145
Cass, Theophilus I:764
Cassel, Abraham III:295
Cassel, James I:600
Cassel, Thomas III:370
Cassiday, Nicholas II:692
Cassidy, George IV:156
Cassino, Paul III:192
Casten, John II:398
Caster, Adam II:438
Casterer, John II:478
Casterline, Jacob II:81
Casterline, Joseph II:81
Casterline, Loammi II:517
Castile, Samuel II:632
Castle, Bazle III:297
Castle, Gideon II:389
Castle, Joel IV:270
Castle, John II:384
Castle, Robert II:444
Castle, William II:341
Castleberry, William M.
III:293
Castlebury, Paul III:513
Castor, Dryer I:xiii
Castor, Dyer I:xii
Castor, Isaac II:664
Castor, William I:943
Caswell, Abraham I:361
Caswell, Barnabas I:985

Caswell, Edwin I:27
Caswell, Elijah I:559
Caswell, Ezra I:337
Caswell, Henry I:27
Caswell, Jedediah I:915
Caswell, Job III:45
Caswell, John I:67
Caswell, John, Jr. I:391
Caswell, John N. I:27
Caswell, Jonathan I:559
Caswell, Joshua II:210
Caswell, Lemuel I:27, 73
Caswell, Maria I:27
Caswell, Mary Ann I:27
Caswell, Nancy I:27
Caswell, Nathan I:995
Caswell, Richard I:600
Caswell, Samuel IV:88
Caswell, Squire I:214
Caswell, William I:391
Catchum, Hugh III:86
Cate, Andrew I:721
Cate, Elisha I:933
Cate, Enoch I:970
Cate, Neal I:776
Cate, Robert III:384
Cate, Samuel W. I:413
Caten, Richard II:283
Cater, Edward I:729
Cater, John II:326
Caters, Abraham II:513
Cathcart, James L. III:14
Cathcart, Joseph III:606
Cathcart, Thomas II:403-4
Catherel, Joseph IV:157
Cathey, Alexander III:431
Cathey, George IV:120
Catlett, David III:812
Catlett, Jonas II:67
Catlin, David I:107
Catlin, Eli II:684
Catlin, Hezekiah I:47
Catlin, Isaac I:107
Catlin, Roswell I:880
Catlin, Simeon II:404
Catlin, Timothy I:441
Cator, John III:21
Catron, Peter III:329
Catt, Philip IV:79
Catter, Stephen II:216
Catterlin, Jonathan II:524
Caughey, John III:240
Caul, Alexander II:609
Caulder, Meriman II:133
Caulk, Jacob III:557
Caulkins, James I:462
Caulkins, Joel II:418
Caulkins, Roswell IV:180
Caustlen, Isaac III:62
Cavanaugh, Edward II:649
Cavanaugh, John II:605
Cavance, Joseph II:712
Cavarly, A. W. IV:21
Cave, Benjamin IV:245
Cave, Reuben III:824
Cave, William III:309
Cavenaugh, Patrick II:689

Cavender, Charles I:757
Cavender, John IV:253
Cavender, Joseph III:219
Cavenough, John II:693
Caverley, John I:414
Cavil, David II:216
Cavil, Sanford I:833
Caviller, John II:53
Cavin, John III:424
Cavin, William II:657
Cawada, David I:78
Cawgill, Daniel IV:281
Cawood, Berry III:287
Cawthorn, Richard III:772
Cay, John I:246
Caycaux, Joseph II:220
Caywood, John II:516
Ceasy, John III:328
Ceater, William II:297
Cecil, William III:841
Center, Jonathan IV:182
Cezar, Solomon II:312
Chace, Ebenezer I:870
Chace, Eseek I:610
Chace, Ezekiel I:370
Chace, Isaac I:938
Chace, Jacob II:451
Chace, James I:685
Chace, Jared I:370
Chace, Lucinda I:685
Chace, Mary I:685
Chace, Nancy I:685
Chace, Nathaniel I:685
Chace, Nathaniel L. I:413
Chace, Samuel I:876
Chace, Sarah Ann I:685
Chace, Simon I:685
Chace, Theophilus I:685
Chadbourne, Cummon I:306
Chadbourne, Silas I:179
Chadbourne, Simeon I:306
Chadbourne, Timothy I:168
Chadd, Samuel III:287
Chadoin, Andrew III:284
Chadsey, Benjamin II:563
Chadsey, Rowland I:797
Chadwell, Harris I:412
Chadwich, Bowman I:956
Chadwick, Benjamin I:493
Chadwick, Caleb I:610
Chadwick, Charles W. I:493
Chadwick, Elias I:28
Chadwick, Elihu II:735
Chadwick, Eliza I:493
Chadwick, Erastus I:28
Chadwick, Hamet I:28
Chadwick, Horace I:28
Chadwick, Isaac I:637
Chadwick, James I:191
Chadwick, James A. IV:103
Chadwick, John I:392, 493,
  706, 887
Chadwick, Joseph I:707
Chadwick, Joshua I:740
Chadwick, Julianna I:28
Chadwick, Levi IV:197
Chadwick, Mary W. I:493

Chadwick, Nathan II:477
Chadwick, Richard I:133
Chadwick, Roxa I:28
Chadwick, Sarah Ann I:493
Chadwick, Sylvanus I:915
Chadwick, Thomas I:338
Chadwick, William II:424, 677
Chaffee, Abiel I:77
Chaffee, Carill I:96
Chaffee, Chester I:148
Chaffee, Ephraim I:461
Chaffee, Frederick I:97
Chaffee, Joel I:107
Chaffee, Josiah II:478
Chaffee, Leonard II:147
Chaffee, Nathaniel I:866
Chaffee, Thomas I:78
Chaffee, William I:38
Chaffer, Comfort I:880
Chaffin, Christopher III:841
Chaffin, David I:782, 915
Chaffin, Elias IV:11
Chaffin, Joseph I:514
Chaffin, Phineas I:783
Chaffin, Samuel I:975
Chaffin, Stephen I:497
Chaffin, Tilla I:636
Chaffy, Thomas II:46
Chalffin, Solomon III:808
Chalfinch, Hiram III:132
Chalk, John III:20
Chalker, Jabez I:116
Chalker, Moses I:116
Chalker, Oliver I:116
Challer, Henry II:131
Challis, Christopher I:720
Challis, Ephraim I:720
Challis, Nathaniel I:737
Chalmers, Andrew IV:176
Chalmers, James III:21
Chamberlain, Aaron I:179;
  II:77, 229
Chamberlain, Anna I:171
Chamberlain, Benjamin I:975;
  II:245
Chamberlain, Charles II:426
Chamberlain, Daniel II:684
Chamberlain, David II:289
Chamberlain, Ebenezer I:881,
  908
Chamberlain, Elias II:426
Chamberlain, Elisha I:740
Chamberlain, Ephraim I:215,
  245, 729
Chamberlain, Freegift IV:265
Chamberlain, Isaac I:107
Chamberlain, James I:691
Chamberlain, Jason I:729
Chamberlain, Jeremiah I:204
Chamberlain, Jireh I:924
Chamberlain, John I:246, 572
Chamberlain, Jonathan I:171
Chamberlain, Joseph I:847,
  887; II:568
Chamberlain, Joseph S. I:54
Chamberlain, Joshua IV:106

Chapman, Joseph I:133, 675;
II:582, 667; III:458, 511
Chapman, Joshua I:347
Chapman, Lemuel I:897;
IV:197
Chapman, Libbeas I:54
Chapman, Michael IV:194
Chapman, Nathaniel I:223
Chapman, Peter I:370
Chapman, Plumbs I:832
Chapman, Richard I:783
Chapman, Robert I:107;
III:557
Chapman, Rufus II:277
Chapman, Salathiel I:97
Chapman, Samuel J. IV:3
Chapman, Silas I:39
Chapman, Smith I:770
Chapman, Stephen I:749
Chapman, Valentine I:776
Chapman, William II:240,
723; III:387
Chappal, Amaziah II:346
Chappel, Curtis II:284
Chappel, Daniel I:933
Chappel, Hiram II:539
Chappel, Noah II:305
Chappel, Samuel III:374
Chappell, Abner IV:121
Chappell, Amaziah I:8
Chappell, Benjamin III:723
Chappell, Hicks III:512
Chappell, James I:793
Chappell, John I:21; III:770
Chappell, Reessell II:181
Chappell, Thomas I:832;
II:743
Chappell, William III:263, 840
Chapu, Michael IV:114
Chard, Caleb I:572
Chariton, James II:623
Chariton, James Washington
II:623
Chariton, John II:623
Chariton, Mary II:623
Chariton, Peggy II:623
Charity, Charles III:487
Charles, George IV:74
Charles, Thomas I:461
Charlick, Henry II:546
Charlton, Charles II:48
Charlton, Francis III:811
Charlton, Jacob III:587
Charlton, John III:575; IV:253
Charmichael, John III:656
Charnock, John III:673
Charthie, Joseph II:289
Chartier, John I:866
Chartier, Peter I:866
Chase, Aaron I:881
Chase, Amariah II:339
Chase, Anne II:189
Chase, Aquilla I:391
Chase, Asa I:635
Chase, Benjamin I:191, 721
Chase, Charles I:585
Chase, David II:147, 189

Chase, Dean II:504
Chase, Deborah II:189
Chase, Ebenezer I:274, 326;
II:474
Chase, Enoch I:392
Chase, Ezekiel I:220, 321
Chase, Ezra I:358
Chase, Gadeliah I:108
Chase, Gideon I:31
Chase, Grindal I:812
Chase, Henry II:189
Chase, Isaac I:60, 245, 273
Chase, Isaiah I:329
Chase, Jacob I:840
Chase, James I:412, 976;
II:189
Chase, Jarahmeel II:377
Chase, Jeremiah II:389
Chase, Joel II:346
Chase, John I:617, 783, 985
Chase, Jonathan I:728
Chase, Joseph I:783; II:302
Chase, Josiah I:716
Chase, Lemuel I:924
Chase, Lot I:107
Chase, Maria II:189
Chase, Moses I:392, 498, 770,
904, 985
Chase, Nathan I:592
Chase, Nathan (2) I:592
Chase, Nathaniel I:282
Chase, Oliver I:147
Chase, Parker I:749
Chase, Perley I:770
Chase, Reuben, 2d I:326
Chase, Reuben, 1st I:528
Chase, Richard I:333, 347
Chase, Robert I:204; III:745;
IV:117
Chase, Samuel I:329, 392,
915; II:558, 657
Chase, Simeon I:370
Chase, Stephen I:162, 908
Chase, Thomas I:282
Chase, Timothy I:381; II:341
Chase, William II:373
Chasey, John II:46
Chasteen, James III:244
Chatfield, Dan I:60
Chatfield, Isaac I:60
Chatfield, Joel II:210
Chatfield, John III:144
Chatfield, Jonathan II:202
Chatfield, Josiah I:54
Chatfield, Levi I:47
Chatham, John III:386
Chatlin, William III:36
Chatterton, Nathaniel II:553
Chatterton, Wait I:959
Chauncey, Daniel H. I:861
Chauncey, Joel B. I:861
Chauncey, John I:859
Chauncey, Nathaniel W. I:116
Chaves, Lazarus III:510
Cheadle, Asa IV:292
Cheadle, Elijah II:438
Cheaney, Nathaniel I:805

Cheatham, Benjamin III:582
Cheek, Ellis III:506
Cheek, James III:439
Cheek, William III:161
Cheeny, Jonathan I:412
Cheeny, William I:497
Cheesman, Benjamin II:718
Cheesman, Stephen I:534
Cheesman, William II:76
Cheever, Abijah I:391, 656
Cheever, Bartholomew I:637
Cheever, Ebenezer II:366
Cheever, James I:412
Cheever, Joseph I:497
Chelton, George III:331
Chelton, Stephen III:331
Chenault, James III:684
Chenault, John III:137
Cheney, Benjamin I:897
Cheney, Daniel I:749
Cheney, Ebenezer I:770
Cheney, Eliphalet II:251
Cheney, Enoch I:887
Cheney, Joseph I:543, 707;
II:210
Cheney, Moses I:412
Cheney, Nathaniel I:716, 749,
975
Cheney, Samuel II:101
Cheney, Thomas I:770
Cheney, Waldo I:985
Cheney, William II:469
Cherry, Henry IV:194
Cherry, Joshua III:566
Cherry, Peter III:493
Cherry, Robert II:608
Cherry, Samuel II:258
Cheseborough, Perez I:133
Chesebra, Christopher II:353
Chesebrough, James I:67
Chesebrough, Nathan'l I:67
Cheshire, Richard III:401
Chesley, Corydon I:729
Chesley, James I:842
Chesley, John I:770
Chesley, Joshua I:671
Chesley, Sawyer I:191
Chesley, Simon II:667
Chesly, James I:775
Chesman, Benjamin II:718
Chesney, Benjamin III:720,
851
Chesney, Thomas E. III:20
Chesnut, Benjamin III:755
Chesshire, John IV:38
Chester, Christopher I:810
Chester, Giles I:67
Chester, John I:54, 599;
III:559, 628
Chetham, William III:271
Chevalier, Anthony IV:206
Chevers, William II:267
Chew, John III:664
Cheyney, Richard II:645
Chichester, Henry I:84
Chichester, Nathan I:84
Chick, Isaac I:306

Chick, James III:296
Chick, John I:204
Chickering, Nathaniel I:543
Chickering, Oliver I:617
Chidsey, Ephraim I:133
Chieves, Joel III:827
Chieves, William R. III:644
Chilcoat, Isaac II:62
Chilcoat, John IV:120
Chilcott, Elihu III:708
Child, Abiathar I:636
Child, Abijah I:497
Child, Amos I:263
Child, Cephas I:949
Child, Cromwell II:705
Child, Elias I:147
Child, Isaac I:956
Child, John I:534
Child, Lyman I:984
Child, Penuel I:959
Child, Salmon II:504
Child, Stephen I:915
Child, Willard I:147
Child, William, I:636
Child, Zachariah I:637
Childe, Obadiah I:78
Childers, David III:559
Childers, Goolsberry III:281
Childers, Henry III:282
Childers, Isham IV:14
Childers, Miller III:394
Childers, Mosby IV:45, 189
Childes, Timothy I:338
Childres, Pleasant III:218
Childress, Alexander III:708
Childress, John III:595, 614;
IV:19
Childress, Mitchel III:595
Childress, Thomas III:598
Childress, William III:629
Childrey, William III:782
Childs, Abraham I:513
Childs, Calvin II:94
Childs, Ebenezer I:162, 480
Childs, Enoch I:295
Childs, Jonathan I:908
Childs, Reuben I:441
Childs, Thomas III:340
Chiles, Henry III:804
Chiles, Hezekiah III:598
Chiles, James III:819
Chillson, Reuben I:805
Chilner, Christopher II:251
Chilson, Ezra I:924
Chilson, John I:21
Chilson, Joseph I:441
Chilton, Andrew III:714
China, John, Sen. III:512
Chiney, Jonathan I:716
Chinn, Peter III:454
Chinzaworth, Elijah IV:151
Chipman, Jesse II:402
Chipman, John I:997
Chipman, Nathaniel I:959
Chipman, Thomas II:210
Chipman, Timothy I:38
Chipman, William I:283

Chisham, James III:321
Chism, George III:245
Chit_enden, Solomon I:897
Chittenden, Abraham I:124
Chittenden, Benjamin I:60
Chittenden, Calvin I:348
Chittenden, Cornelius I:116
Chittenden, James I:985
Chittenden, James F. IV:103
Chittenden, Jared II:277
Chittenden, John I:54, 116
Chittenden, Levi I:124
Chittenden, Nathan I:124
Chittenden, Reuben II:305
Chittenden, William I:337
Chittim, John III:347
Chitwood, James III:570
Chivers, William II:268
Choat, Benjamin I:721
Choat, James I:770
Choate, Christopher III:602
Choate, David I:699
Choate, Ebenezer I:246
Choate, Greenbury IV:14
Choate, Jonathan I:729
Choate, Simeon I:392
Chockley, Thomas II:655
Chodel, John I:823
Chouteau, Auguste I:xvi
Chrisholme, Walter III:786
Christ, Adam II:609
Christ, Philip III:755
Christeyance, Isaac II:510
Christian, Allen IV:90
Christian, Andrew III:275
Christian, Charles II:132
Christian, Charles P. II:20
Christian, Daniel III:67
Christian, James III:344
Christian, James, 2d III:354
Christian, John I:453; II:366;
III:275, 558, 806
Christian, Levi H. II:132
Christian, Rawleigh C. III:725
Christian, Robert III:795
Christian, Valentine II:712
Christian, William III:216;
IV:284
Christian, Zachariah II:267
Christiance, Isaac II:504
Christiance, John II:504
Christie, Alexander II:609
Christie, Christopher II:133
Christie, Daniel II:132
Christie, James III:322
Christie, John I:592
Christie, Margaret G. I:592
Christie, Wm. T. III:636
Christman, Felix I:645
Christman, Jacob II:478
Christman, Nicholas II:263
Christmas, Richard III:439,
501
Christy, John II:622
Christy, Martha II 622
Christy, Sarah II:622
Christy, Susannah II:622

Chriswell, Samuel II:438
Chubb, Joseph II:202
Chubb, Silas I:637
Chubb, Thomas I:497
Chubback, Ebenezer II:705
Chubbs, William II:609
Chubbuck, Levi I:688
Chubbuck, Simeon II:258
Chumbley, John IV:65
Chumley, Daniel III:633
Chun, Sylvester III:553
Church, Abigail I:176
Church, Alexander II:238
Church, Amos II:482; III:458
Church, Anthony I:347
Church, Benjamin I:176, 461
Church, Caleb I:430; II:376
Church, Charles I:294, 975
Church, Constant II:531
Church, Daniel II:404
Church, Drusilla I:176
Church, Earl I:571
Church, Ebenezer II:384
Church, Eber I:430
Church, Eleazer II:377
Church, Elihu II:251
Church, Fairbanks I:133
Church, Gideon I:818
Church, Greenleaf I:176
Church, Harriet I:176
Church, Isaac I:887
Church, Jabez I:665
Church, James C. II:216
Church, Joel W. II:231
Church, John I:108, 294, 924;
III:458; IV:194
Church, Jonathan IV:194
Church, Joseph I:67, 818
Church, Joshua I:809, 915,
985; II:477
Church, Nathaniel I:8, 675
Church, Philemon IV:186
Church, Polly I:176
Church, Reuben I:908, 999
Church, Samuel I:264; II:451
Church, Samuel, 2d I:880
Church, Samuel, 1st I:870
Church, Silas I:637
Church, Simon II:353
Church, Thomas I:116, 559,
812
Church, Uriah I:39, 473
Church, Willard II:289
Churchfield, John II:692
Churchill, Caleb I:959
Churchill, Elijah I:472
Churchill, Isaac II:414
Churchill, Jabez I:215
Churchill, Jabish I:215
Churchill, James I:191
Churchill, Jonas II:414
Churchill, Jonathan I:887
Churchill, Joseph I:299, 617
Churchill, Joshua I:214
Churchill, Josiah I:246
Churchill, Nathaniel I:959
Churchill, Oliver I:960

345

346

Clark, Lee III:418
Clark, Lemuel I:107, 970;
  II:751
Clark, Levi I:39
Clark, Lewis III:700
Clark, Lyman I:46
Clark, Maltiah I:572
Clark, Mary Ann I:171
Clark, Matthew I:441, 479;
  II:277
Clark, Micajah III:327
Clark, Moses I:391, 413;
  II:377, 434, 520, 551
Clark, Nabby I:325
Clark, Nathan I:142; II:400,
  546
Clark, Nathaniel I:10, 54, 691,
  770; III:407; IV:253
Clark, Nathaniel S. I:749
Clark, Obadiah III:322
Clark, Obedience III:470
Clark, Oliver I:84
Clark, Oren I:897
Clark, Osborn III:385
Clark, Parnal I:556
Clark, Patrick III:305
Clark, Paul I:479, 915, 1000
Clark, Peter II:608
Clark, Reuben I:133; II:283
Clark, Richard II:483
Clark, Richard, 2d II:35
Clark, Robert I:54, 720;
  III:624
Clark, Roger II:214
Clark, Rufus I:115
Clark, Sally I:556
Clark, Samuel I:124, 392,
  514, 556, 610, 790, 933,
  994; II:424, 626, 688; III:810
Clark, Samuel, 2d II:329
Clark, Samuel, 3d II:259
Clark, Samuel, 1st II:251
Clark, Samuel S. I:585
Clark, Selah II:277
Clark, Seth I:473, 933; II:686
Clark, Silas II:609
Clark, Solomon I:847
Clark, Stephen I:116, 764
Clark, Sylvanus I:124, 441
Clark, Thaddeus II:259
Clark, Theophilus I:370
Clark, Thomas I:204, 347,
  430; III:161, 191, 692
Clark, Thomas F. IV:7
Clark, Ward I:870
Clark, Waters I:915
Clark, Watson II:193
Clark, Wells II:434
Clark, William I:6, 54, 124,
  147, 171, 306, 370, 381,
  441, 480, 514, 559, 740;
  II:63, 377, 712; III:21, 299,
  517; IV:7, 195
Clark, William, 1st II:283
Clark, William, 2d II:245
Clark, William, 3d II:223
Clark, Zelotes IV:279

Clarke, Amos, Jr. I:60
Clarke, Arnold I:147
Clarke, Benjamin I:171; II:398
Clarke, Benoni II:366
Clarke, Charles II:609
Clarke, Edward I:832
Clarke, Elias I:832
Clarke, Elijah II:763
Clarke, Eliza III:671
Clarke, Ethan I:814
Clarke, Fanny III:671
Clarke, George III:577
Clarke, Hemel III:671
Clarke, Isaac II:546
Clarke, James II:463
Clarke, Jesse II:389
Clarke, John I:430; III:232,
  436, 614, 671, 712; IV:13
Clarke, John, 3d I:47
Clarke, Josiah III:671
Clarke, Lemuel I:636
Clarke, Leonard III:657
Clarke, Lewis III:84
Clarke, Mark Fernald I:171
Clarke, Moses I:832
Clarke, Nicholas I:832
Clarke, Peter I:391
Clarke, Randall III:671
Clarke, Randolph III:671
Clarke, Rebecca I:171
Clarke, Richard I:823
Clarke, Richard, 1st II:105
Clarke, Robert III:644, 663
Clarke, Sally I:171; III:671
Clarke, Samuel II:463; III:679
Clarke, Simeon II:429
Clarke, Spencer III:719
Clarke, Stephen III:780
Clarke, Thankful I:171
Clarke, Thomas II:638; III:94,
  644, 760
Clarke, Turner III:701
Clarke, Wedon I:832
Clarke, Weston I:802
Clarke, William II:131, 155;
  III:168, 671, 690, 798
Clarke, William C. I:833
Clarke, Winslow II:99
Clarkson, Constantine IV:16
Clarkson, David III:259
Clarkson, Matthew I:xv
Clarkson, Randolph II:18, 85
Clary, Charles III:33
Clary, Daniel II:339
Clary, David I:441
Clary, J. II:555
Clary, James II:317
Clary, Phineas I:441
Claspy, John III:327
Clatterbuck, Reuben IV:119
Claud, Jeptha II:592
Claughbaugh, Martin II:660
Clawson, Ezra II:202
Clawson, Garret II:659
Claxton, Samuel I:47
Clay, Benjamin I:234
Clay, Daniel IV:222

Clay, Elijah IV:12
Clay, John I:770; III:614
Clay, Samuel I:879
Clay, Thomas III:783
Clay, William III:583
Clayborn, John III:595
Claycomb, Frederick IV:79
Clayes, Francis I:997
Clayes, Peter I:866, 997
Clayton, Augustine III:327
Clayton, Coleman III:441
Clayton, Elijah II:697
Clayton, Elisha III:808
Clayton, Henry II:46
Clayton, Jehu II:71
Clayton, Job D. II:76
Clayton, John II:76; III:441
Clayton, Jonathan II:438
Clayton, Lambert III:363
Clayton, Noah II:723
Clayton, Peter II:263
Clayton, Zebulon II:76
Claywell, Shadrach III:272
Clear, Philip I:721
Clearwater, Jacob II:531
Clearwater, Martin II:342
Clearwater, Matthew II:474
Clearwaters, Benjamin III:552
Cleasby, Joseph I:715
Cleaveland, Augustus II:111
Cleaveland, Ebenezer I:392
Cleaveland, Gardner II:373
Cleaveland, Isaac II:418
Cleaveland, John III:287
Cleaveland, Johnson I:39
Cleaveland, Joseph I:908
Cleaveland, Josiah I:67
Cleaveland, Nehemiah II:463
Cleaveland, Samuel IV:249
Cleaveland, Silas I:148
Cleaveland, Solomon I:897;
  II:418
Cleaveland, Solomon, 2d
  II:226
Cleaveland, Stephen II:277
Cleaveland, Tracy IV:249
Cleaveland, William II:504;
  III:316
Cleaver, William III:283
Cleaves, Abraham I:263
Cleaves, Edmund I:179
Cleaves, William I:179
Cleer, Peter III:12
Clefford, John I:956
Cleland, John II:214
Clemence, Ebenezer I:637
Clemence, Peter II:687
Clemens, John III:593
Clement, Augustus Hazen
  II:625
Clement, Edmund III:513
Clement, Ira Thomas II:625
Clement, Isaac I:893; II:226
Clement, John I:749
Clement, Joseph T. II:625
Clement, Lambert II:438
Clement, Moses I:514

Clement, Reuben I:887
Clement, Roger III:309
Clement, Sarah Belknap II:625
Clement, Simeon I:749
Clements, Benjamin III:451
Clements, Charles III:772
Clements, David IV:46
Clements, Jacob II:414
Clements, John III:779
Clements, Thomas I:729;
III:695
Clements, William I:783;
II:223
Clemins, Henry II:660
Clemmens, John III:446
Clemments, Cornelius III:450
Clemments, Timothy I:691
Clemmons, Richard I:823
Clemmons, Thomas III:633
Clemons, Benjamin I:747
Clemons, Bernard III:219
Clemons, Jonathan II:289
Clemons, Patrick II:677
Clendennin, James II:728
Clendinnin, James II:632
Cleveland, Amsa I:480
Cleveland, Chester II:434
Cleveland, Enoch I:887
Cleveland, Henry I:348
Cleveland, Ichabod II:58
Cleveland, Jacob I:77
Cleveland, John II:346
Cleveland, Joseph II:216, 362
Cleveland, Josiah II:202, 277
Cleveland, Nehemiah I:412
Cleveland, Roswell II:258
Cleveland, Samuel I:77, 984
Cleveland, Squier I:985
Cleveland, Stephen I:984
Clevenger, Eben IV:181
Clever, Anthony I:610
Clevidence, John II:632
Clevinger, Isaiah II:659
Clewley, Isaac I:220
Cl_fton, William III:460
Clibourn, William III:807
Clicke, Henry III:530
Clifford, David I:204
Clifford, Isaac I:764
Clifford, John II:68
Clifford, Michael IV:17
Clifford, Nathan I:380
Clifford, William I:715
Clifford, Zachariah I:933
Cliffton, George III:186
Cliffton, Thomas IV:214
Clifton, John II:4
Clifton, Joshua II:8
Clifton, Whitenton II:8
Cline, Andrew III:842
Cline, Conrad III:58; IV:209
Cline, Henry II:353
Cline, John IV:41
Cline, Jonas IV:283
Cline, Michael III:428
Cline, William II:693
Clinger, Philip IV:281

Clinkenbeard, Isaac III:260
Clinton, Allen I:84
Clinton, Isaac II:424
Clinton, James II:31; III:264
Clinton, Joseph II:229
Clinton, Matthew II:609
Clinton, Peter II:22
Clinton, Thomas III:42
Clock, John I:108
Clodfelter, George III:444
Cloes, Charles II:289
Cloney, George IV:274
Clontier, Charles II:321
Clontz, George III:399
Clontz, Jeremiah III:431
Clopton, Thomas III:791
Clopton, Walter III:633
Close, Abraham I:85
Close, Benjamin II:99
Close, Henry II:748
Close, Solomon I:85
Closs, Charles II:289
Clossen, William II:626
Closser, Christopher II:263
Closson, Nathan I:788, 837
Closson, Nehemiah II:517
Closson, Zachariah II:738
Clothur, Jesse II:718
Clotterback, Henry II:609
Cloud, Ezekiel III:166
Cloud, Forest I:949
Cloud, John III:114
Cloud, William III:820
Clough, Aaron I:904
Clough, Abner I:764
Clough, Benjamin I:246, 264;
II:240
Clough, Daniel I:412
Clough, David I:776, 866
Clough, Gilman I:941
Clough, John I:223; II:240
Clough, Joseph I:729
Clough, Oliver I:729
Clough, William I:497
Clouse, Jacob IV:152
Clouts, Jacob II:592
Clower, Daniel III:142
Clower, George III:735
Clower, Jonathan III:79
Clower, William III:119
Clowerd, Abraham II:43
Cloyd, William III:624
Cloyes, Henry IV:42
Cluff, Isaac I:38
Cluff, John I:729
Cluff, Noah I:234
Clung, Henry II:657
Clutch, John II:76
Clute, Bartholomew II:510
Clute, Jacob B. II:510
Clute, Jacob J. II:438
Clutter, Casper IV:263
Clutterbook, Joseph II:608
Clutterbuck, James III:804
Coal, Willis III:579
Coalden, James III:12
Coambs, John I:191

Coan, John I:124
Coan, Peter II:336
Coan, William II:274
Coas, William I:411
Coates, Christopher II:362
Coates, Reuben I:472
Coates, Robert II:353
Coates, William III:542, 762
Coatney, James III:584
Coats, Amos I:147
Coats, Benjamin II:463
Coats, Daniel III:3
Coats, Edward I:133
Coats, John I:472
Coats, Zebulon II:448
Cobb, Abel II:216
Cobb, Benjamin I:370
Cobb, Binney I:985
Cobb, Daniel I:245, 706, 800
Cobb, David I:320, 655
Cobb, Ebenezer I:214, 324;
II:99
Cobb, Ethelred III:526
Cobb, Francis I:783
Cobb, George II:289
Cobb, Isaiah I:572
Cobb, Jacob I:949
Cobb, James I:572
Cobb, John I:329, 370, 535,
876; II:251
Cobb, Mallatiah I:294
Cobb, Mallatiah (2) I:295
Cobb, Mason I:370
Cobb, Matthias II:235
Cobb, Meletiah II:706
Cobb, Nathan I:985; II:255
Cobb, Nathaniel I:247
Cobb, Nehemiah I:571
Cobb, Pharaoh III:587
Cobb, Roland I:204
Cobb, Salmon I:370
Cobb, Salter I:160
Cobb, Samuel I:956; IV:123
Cobb, Silas I:637
Cobb, Silvanus I:179
Cobb, Simeon I:67, 933
Cobb, Sylanus I:637
Cobb, Sylvester I:994
Cobb, Thomas II:48
Cobb, William I:283
Cobbs, John III:760
Cobby, James I:679
Cobleigh, Eleazer I:908
Cobleigh, Reuben II:398
Cobler, Frederick III:575
Coblidge, Joseph I:283
Coburn, Asa I:949
Coburn, Charles I:174
Coburn, Daniel I:498
Coburn, Hezekiah II:400
Coburn, James II:339
Coburn, Jeptha I:191, 510
Coburn, John I:174; III:16;
IV:241
Coburn, Jonathan I:862
Coburn, Josiah II:469
Coburn, Justice I:174

Coburn, Leah I:862
Coburn, Lemuel I:949
Coburn, Mary P. I:174
Coburn, Miles B. I:488
Coburn, Moral I:678
Coburn, Morril I:783
Coburn, Moses I:214, 510
Coburn, Nathaniel II:655
Coburn, Nehemiah I:862
Coburn, Phineas IV:275
Coburn, Primas III:45
Coburn, Prudence I:862
Coburn, Reuben I:174
Coburn, Saul I:497
Coburn, Titus I:392
Coburn, Zebediah II:226
Cochran, Blaney II:675
Cochran, Cornelius II:195
Cochran, David III:20
Cochran, Edward II:677
Cochran, Hannah II:195
Cochran, James III:706
Cochran, John I:xv; II:211, 586, 717; III:686
Cochran, Robert II:632; III:501
Cochran, Samuel III:622
Cochran, Simon IV:166
Cochran, Thomas III:253
Cochran, William III:75
Cochran, Wm. R. II:195
Cochrane, Abner IV:179
Cochrane, James I:392
Cock, Charles III:408
Cock, Jacob II:366
Cock, John III:626
Cocke, Anderson III:826
Cocke, William III:614
Cockenbough, John II:720
Cockerel, Peter III:208
Cockerell, John III:234
Cockerham, Daniel III:454
Cockerham, David III:454
Cockle, John I:691
Cockle, Robert I:843
Cockley, John II:283
Cocklin, John II:608
Cockran, Elijah I:757
Cockran, James I:757
Cockran, John IV:119
Cockran, Matthew III:174
Cockrane, Thomas I:426
Cockrell, William III:478
Cockrem, Daniel II:48
Cockrem, Squire II:35
Cockrum, William III:292
Cocks, Benj. III:739
Codding, Abijah I:691
Codding, Robert I:356; II:493
Coddington, Enoch II:474
Coddington, Robert II:18
Coddrington, Benjamin III:18
Code, Patrick II:132
Cody, Samuel II:450
Coe, Abner I:933
Coe, Ebenezer I:2; II:81, 654
Coe, Ichabod II:554

Coe, Jedediah I:933
Coe, John II:373, 498
Coe, Peter II:755
Coe, Richard III:66
Coe, Samuel II:207
Coe, Seth I:107
Coe, Thomas I:60
Coe, Timothy I:96
Coe, William III:62
Coe, Zachariah II:482
Coen, Edward IV:239
Coen, James II:723
Coff, William III:682
Coffel, James IV:267
Coffenbery, George IV:282
Coffey, Benjamin III:587
Coffey, James III:566
Coffey, Osbourne III:267
Coffey, Reuben III:329
Coffield, Owen III:36
Coffin, Alexander II:445
Coffin, Enoch I:764
Coffin, George I:636
Coffin, Isaac I:306
Coffin, J. N. I:xiv
Coffin, James Josiah I:529
Coffin, Lemuel I:391
Coffin, Nathaniel I:228
Coffin, Nicholas I:228
Coffin, Obed I:326
Coffin, Peter I:214
Coffman, Jacob III:212
Coffren, Robert I:263
Coffroth, Conrod II:657
Cofran, Joseph I:670
Cogan, Richard II:4
Cogburn, Henry III:515
Coger, Enoch II:258
Coger, Peter III:798
Coggeshall, Gideon I:361
Cogghill, Thomas III:769
Coghill, James III:220
Cogswell, Amos I:141, 728
Cogswell, Asahel I:610
Cogswell, James I:514
Cogswell, Jesse I:949
Cogswell, John III:539
Cogswell, Jos. B. I:789
Cogswell, Northend I:306
Cogswell, Reuben II:321
Cogswell, Rufus II:414
Cogswell, William I:789
Cohoon, Joel III:326
Cohoon, John II:493
Coil, William II:619
Coile, James III:165
Coins, Dominick III:53
Coit, Farewell I:67
Coit, Isaac I:479
Coit, Richard I:107
Coke, Philip IV:189
Coker, William I:204
Colamy, Richard I:679
Colbath, Joseph I:671
Colbath, Leighton I:381
Colbert, John III:775
Colbeth, Peter I:302

Colbey, Salem I:887
Colbourn, John I:881
Colbreath, Dependence II:448
Colbroth, Lemuel I:264
Colbry, Moses I:764
Colbura, James I:707
Colburn, Charles I:764
Colburn, David I:985
Colburn, Ebenezer I:299
Colburn, James IV:140
Colburn, Jesse IV:114
Colburn, Joseph I:514
Colburn, Josiah I:514
Colburn, Lewis I:543
Colburn, Nathan I:636
Colburn, Robert II:748
Colburn, Thomas I:191
Colburn, William I:291
Colby, Benjamin I:264
Colby, Ebenezer I:306, 776
Colby, Ezekiel II:398
Colby, Ichabod I:776
Colby, James I:263
Colby, Judith I:387
Colby, Nicholas I:387
Colby, Polly I:387
Colby, Samuel, 2d I:204
Colby, Stephen I:707
Colby, Sylvanus I:204
Colby, Theophilus I:720
Colby, Thomas I:715, 933
Colby, William II:302
Colchard, Thomas I:691
Colcord, John I:698
Colcord, Joseph I:770
Colcord, Josiah I:306
Coldon, Redman IV:214
Coldwater, Philip II:677
Cole, Abel I:273
Cole, Abijah I:259
Cole, Abner I:54
Cole, Amos II:377
Cole, Andrew I:571; II:438
Cole, Asa I:347
Cole, Aschah I:172
Cole, Azer II:426
Cole, Barnabas II:717
Cole, Barnabus II:277
Cole, Barnet I:191
Cole, Benjamin I:263, 812, 985; II:289, 418; III:234
Cole, Benjamin, 2d II:240
Cole, Charles I:572; III:383
Cole, Daniel I:783; II:463, 720
Cole, David I:46; II:321, 563
Cole, Ebenezer II:132
Cole, Eleazer I:283
Cole, Eli I:305
Cole, Eliphalet I:707
Cole, Ephraim I:799
Cole, Ezra I:172
Cole, Francis II:263; III:768
Cole, George I:172; III:21, 45, 396
Cole, Hamblin III:689
Cole, Hendrick I:116
Cole, Henry II:426; III:490

349

Cole, Henry, 2d I:169
Cole, Hutchinson I:832
Cole, Ichabod I:812
Cole, Isaiah I:204
Cole, Jabez II:463
Cole, Jacob I:347
Cole, Jacob P. II:395
Cole, Jacobus II:346
Cole, James I:338; II:500; III:571
Cole, James, 2d I:342; II:257
Cole, Job I:571; III:458
Cole, John I:191, 893; II:398, 463; III:256, 691
Cole, John, 2d II:206
Cole, John, 1st II:297
Cole, Joseph I:370, 559; II:117
Cole, Lemuel I:571
Cole, Levi III:43
Cole, Martin III:490
Cole, Nathan I:749
Cole, Nathaniel I:572, 908; II:362
Cole, Parker I:678, 783
Cole, Richard III:751
Cole, Royal II:751
Cole, Rufus II:400
Cole, Samuel I:204, 412, 832, 995; II:211, 429, 709
Cole, Seth I:812
Cole, Simeon I:411
Cole, Sisson II:483
Cole, Solomon I:38, 450, 698
Cole, Stephen III:612
Cole, Thomas I:797; III:489
Cole, Tobias II:640
Cole, William III:331; III:689
Cole, Zephaniah II:482
Colebath, George I:770
Colegate, Asaph III:720
Colegrove, Jeremiah I:347
Colegrove, Stephen II:482
Colehammer, Andrew II:493
Coleman, Charles P. III:83
Coleman, Eliza III:470
Coleman, Hardy III:622
Coleman, Jacob IV:56, 100, 179
Coleman, James I:729; III:664
Coleman, Job I:535
Coleman, Joel IV:201
Coleman, John I:142; II:39, 339, 662, 699; III:559
Coleman, John M. IV:100
Coleman, Mahala III:470
Coleman, Nathan I:73
Coleman, Nathaniel IV:227
Coleman, Neviad IV:189
Coleman, Niles I:342; II:274
Coleman, Noah III:470
Coleman, Patrick II:584
Coleman, Philip II:132
Coleman, Robert III:305, 758
Coleman, Solomon I:985
Coleman, Spencer III:606
Coleman, Theophilus III:412

Coleman, Thomas II:725; III:252, 256
Coleman, William III:719
Coleman, Wm. III:574
Coles, James I:823
Coles, Jesse II:546
Coles, John II:483
Coles, Thomas I:837
Coley, Francis III:618
Coley, James III:592
Coley, Mainyard III:76
Coley, Samuel II:223
Colfax, Robert II:48
Colfax, William II:29, 90
Colfex, Samuel II:373
Colfix, John II:119
Colgan, William IV:174
Colgroove, William I:823
Colgrove, Caleb I:823
Colgrove, Christopher II:493
Colhoun, John III:506
Colkins, Jonathan II:289
Coll, Daniel II:604
Collamer, Samuel I:876
Collamore, Anthony I:866
Collamore, Benjamin I:610
Collamy, Daniel I:675
Collamy, Isaac I:164
Collar, Hezekiah I:823
Collar, Jason I:636
Collar, John I:38
Collater, Jacob II:39
Collember, Thomas III:36
Coller, Narvis II:482
Collester, James II:429
Collester, John I:480
Collett, Isaac III:290
Colley, Azariah I:430
Colley, Charles III:822; IV:117
Colley, George I:124
Colley, Henry II:81
Colley, Richard I:246
Collier, James III:196; IV:257
Collier, Joseph II:240
Collier, Oliver I:943
Collier, William III:719
Collings, William II:68
Collins, Alexander III:9
Collins, Ambrose I:107
Collins, Andrew I:860
Collins, Ann Maria III:9
Collins, Anthony II:71
Collins, Asael I:805
Collins, Bartlett III:193
Collins, Benjamin I:223; IV:244
Collins, Caleb III:395
Collins, Chandra II:305
Collins, Charles I:847
Collins, Charles W. II:119
Collins, Daniel I:66, 223, 294-95
Collins, E. II:557
Collins, Ebenezer IV:167
Collins, Ebenezer, 1st II:132
Collins, Eleazer I:823
Collins, Elisha I:400; III:83

Collins, Ely III:86
Collins, George III:21, 798
Collins, Henry I:943; II:133
Collins, Isaac I:413
Collins, Jacob III:45
Collins, James II:46; III:36, 417, 436, 603, 808
Collins, Jeffrey III:835
Collins, John I:846, 860, 959; II:197, 434, 632; III:9, 217, 379, 513, 664, 712, 746; IV:282
Collins, John, Sen. III:165
Collins, Jonathan II:424
Collins, Joseph I:246; II:52, 263
Collins, Joshua III:14, 258
Collins, Josiah IV:67
Collins, Judith III:197
Collins, Knowlton I:860
Collins, Lemuel I:264
Collins, Levi IV:106
Collins, Louisa III:9
Collins, Margaret II:197
Collins, Mason III:712
Collins, Moses I:413
Collins, Nathaniel I:96
Collins, Oliver II:277, 366, 560
Collins, Patrick II:609
Collins, Philemon I:295
Collins, Richard I:302
Collins, Samuel I:770; II:450, 523; III:428
Collins, Shepherd IV:229
Collins, Solomon I:187, 897; III:715
Collins, Stephen II:46; IV:28
Collins, Stephens III:266
Collins, Susan III:9
Collins, Thomas I:897; II:580
Collins, Timothy II:692
Collins, William II:151, 251, 651; III:20, 688; IV:27, 87, 299
Collins, William Lock I:31
Collinsworth, John IV:18
Colly, Benjamin I:764
Colly, Enoch I:749
Colman, John IV:182
Colman, Solomon I:392
Colony, Isaac II:504
Colquett, Ransom III:388
Colson, Bolton I:514
Colson, Christopher IV:179
Colson, Hateevil I:187
Colston, James IV:56
Colt, John I:970
Colter, John III:119
Colton, Alpheus I:453
Colton, Charles I:975
Colton, Enoch I:949
Colton, Frederick I:454
Colton, Harman I:453
Colton, James IV:56
Colton, John I:949
Colton, Julius I:915

351

Corey, Ebenezer II:640
Corey, Gideon I:809
Corey, Isaac I:479
Corey, James II:500
Corey, Joseph I:814
Corey, Josiah I:147
Corey, Martin I:6
Corey, Philip II:240
Corey, Samuel I:740, 818; III:756
Corey, Stephen II:531
Corey, Thomas IV:223
Cork, William II:677
Corkins, John I:870
Corl, John II:510
Corl, Leonard II:637
Corl, William II:510
Corle, Samuel II:68
Corless, Emerson I:887
Corless, Samuel I:887
Corless, Timothy I:887
Corlew, Edward I:984
Corley, Abner III:501
Corley, Austin III:633
Corley, William III:633
Corley, Zaccheus III:79
Corliss, Bliss I:949
Corliss, Elisha I:749
Corms, Hosea I:187
Corn, William II:671
Cornegys, John II:6
Cornelison, Conrad III:301
Cornelius, Ann III:40
Cornelius, Charles III:779
Cornelius, Dolly III:40
Cornelius, Elizabeth III:40
Cornelius, Henry II:640
Cornelius, John II:223; III:40
Cornelius, Joseph III:601
Cornelius, Margaret III:40
Cornell, David II:283; IV:221
Cornell, Joseph I:802
Cornell, Oliver I:823
Cornell, Richard II:366
Cornell, William II:720
Cornet, Jesse III:788
Cornett, William III:317
Corneyle, Jacob III:760
Corning, Allen I:31
Corning, Amas I:28
Corning, Amasa I:28
Corning, Clara I:28
Corning, David I:28
Corning, Hannah I:28
Corning, Sally I:28
Corning, Uriah I:133
Corningore, Henry III:305
Corningore, John III:305
Cornish, Eber II:116
Cornish, Gabriel II:238
Cornish, George I:97
Cornish, Joel II:463
Cornish, John I:179
Cornish, Stephen II:450
Cornish, William I:571
Cornue, Wessel II:544
Cornwall, Isaac II:419

Cornwall, Richard I:999
Cornwall, William III:594
Cornwell, Ashbel II:438
Cornwell, Avery II:11
Cornwell, Benjamin II:226
Cornwell, John I:115
Cornwell, Samuel II:327
Cornwell, William II:723; III:210
Corret, Ebenezer I:326
Correy, John IV:12
Corriell, Elisha II:71
Corrington, Benjamin II:85
Corse, John II:7
Corson, Abel II:33
Corson, David I:776
Corthell, Robert I:559
Corthell, Sherebiah I:572
Cortleyon, Hedrich II:71
Cortwite, Charles I:845
Corwen, Samuel II:336
Corwin, Amaziah II:520
Corwin, Joseph II:81
Corwin, Selah II:339
Corwine, Samuel II:68
Cory, Amos G. I:589
Cory, Benjamin I:370
Cory, Elnathan II:699
Cory, Gabriel II:745
Cory, Nathan I:497
Cory, Oliver II:482
Cory, Thomas III:73
Cory, William I:370
Coryell, David A. IV:109
Coryell, Emanuel II:523
Cosart, John II:277
Cosby, Zaccheus III:750
Cosleman, Christian II:248
Cosper, David II:601
Cosper, John II:647
Cosselman, Pardel II:450
Cossit, Timothy II:463
Costen, Stephen III:441
Costigan, Francis IV:165
Costigin, Lewis J. II:267
Costner, Thomas III:428
Costur, Bishop II:274
Cotby, Eben I:716
Coteral, Thomas III:798
Coterin, John IV:31
Cotheal, Isaac II:22
Cott, Jabez II:258
Cotten, William IV:71
Cotter, John II:609
Cotterill, Thomas IV:231
Cottle, Peter II:409
Cottle, Robert I:380
Cottman, James III:643
Cotton, Benjamin I:665; II:226
Cotton, Bibye L. I:984
Cotton, Caleb I:904
Cotton, Elias I:595
Cotton, James III:88
Cotton, John I:204; IV:8, 218
Cotton, Josiah I:559
Cotton, Rowland II:109

Cotton, William I:338, 370; II:720
Cottrell, Asa I:480
Cottrell, Nicholas I:473
Cottrill, John III:706
Couch, Abraham I:31
Couch, Amos I:38
Couch, Ebenezer I:39
Couch, Ely III:74
Couch, John, Jr. I:162
Couch, Samuel I:347
Couch, Stephen I:347
Coudon, John I:161
Cough, John II:181
Coughey, James II:609
Coulder, John III:176
Coulson, David III:629
Coulter, John IV:265
Coulter, Martin III:428
Coulter, Matthew III:305
Coulter, Nathaniel II:669
Coulter, Samuel III:682
Counce, Nicholas III:583
Council, Jesse III:836
Countryman, Frederick II:248
Countryman, Jacob II:327
Countryman, John II:304
Counts, William I:610
Courier, Amme II:500
Courrier, Asa I:729
Courrier, Thomas I:698
Courson, James III:90
Courter, Aaron Burr II:198
Courter, Betsey C. II:198
Courter, Henry II:434
Courter, James II:198
Courter, Jane II:198
Courter, John Sherburn II:198
Courter, Joseph II:198
Courter, Warner II:198
Courtner, Anthony III:781
Courtney, Francis II:181
Courtney, James III:122
Courtney, Michael III:549
Courtney, Samuel III:694
Courts, Low IV:296
Couse, Hontice H. II:107
Couse, Jacob II:395
Cousens, Ebenezer I:234
Cousins, Nathaniel I:306
Cousins, Samuel I:228
Covall, Judah I:299
Covel, Ebenezer I:147, 559
Covel, Henry IV:11
Covel, James II:359
Covel, Thomas II:152
Covell, Benjamin II:214
Covell, Eliphalet II:414
Covell, Ephraim II:451
Covell, Richard II:493
Covenhoven, Abraham II:438
Covenhoven, Albert II:41
Covenhoven, Isaac II:438
Covenhoven, Jacab II:76
Covenhoven, Lewis II:77
Covenhoven, William II:498
Covenhover, Peter II:125

Covenhover, Robert II:733
Coverly, Thomas III:640
Covert, Burgun II:85
Covert, Ellison II:77
Covert, Jacob II:71
Covert, Jeremiah I:348
Covert, Luke P. II:516
Covert, Peter II:301
Covey, Samuel III:595
Covill, Ebenezer II:463
Covill, Joseph B. II:400
Covinger, Higgins III:562
Covington, Matthew III:571
Covington, Robert III:329
Cowan, Isaac I:192
Cowan, John II:209
Cowan, Jonathan II:418
Cowan, Joseph III:377
Cowan, William I:191
Coward, Adam II:132
Coward, Joseph II:46
Cowden, James I:635; II:377
Cowden, Robert III:566
Cowdery, Ambrose I:97
Cowdery, Asa I:97
Cowdery, Edward I:887
Cowdrey, Benjamin II:268
Cowdrey, John II:444
Cowdry, Nathaniel I:514
Cowell, Isaac II:723
Cowell, Samuel II:353
Cowen, David II:544
Cowen, Joseph II:539
Cowen, William II:758; IV:239
Cowgill, Ralph III:255
Cowherd, Francis III:852
Cowherd, James III:284
Cowherd, Jonathan III:284
Cowherd, Lucy III:852
Cowing, Calvin I:204
Cowing, Gatheleus I:472
Cowing, Job I:572
Cowing, John II:373
Cowl, Benjamin II:490
Cowles, Adonijah II:463
Cowles, Asa I:47; II:385
Cowles, Ezekiel I:97
Cowles, Isaac I:97
Cowles, Jabez I:97
Cowles, Nathaniel II:469
Cowles, Phineas I:956
Cowles, Solomon I:97
Cowles, Timothy II:216
Cowley, Michael IV:171
Cowley, Robert III:478
Cowpland, Christian II:608
Cox, Andrew IV:253
Cox, Ann II:626
Cox, Bartlett III:767
Cox, Benj. III:739
Cox, Benjamin I:214; III:430; IV:274, 291
Cox, Bray I:234
Cox, Caleb III:299
Cox, Curd III:595
Cox, Ebenezer I:984
Cox, Edward III:620

Cox, Eliza II:626
Cox, George I:984; III:756
Cox, Hugh I:264
Cox, Isaac II:798; IV:88
Cox, James I:559; II:626; III:452
Cox, Javan III:602
Cox, John II:317; III:229, 366, 397, 430, 816
Cox, Joseph I:497-98; II:626; III:20, 392, 620
Cox, Mary II:626
Cox, Michael IV:267
Cox, Moses III:184
Cox, Philip III:798
Cox, Phineas III:327
Cox, Robert II:321, 341
Cox, Samuel III:507, 697
Cox, Solomon III:324
Cox, Stewart II:626
Cox, Thomas II:132; III:164, 620
Cox, Tunis II:707
Cox, William II:297, 626, 745; III:297, 507
Coxe, Bartlett III:654
Coxe, John III:611
Coxe, Phineas II:181
Coy, Christopher IV:41
Coy, David II:226
Coy, Edee I:342; II:262
Coy, Elisha II:528
Coy, Ephraim I:108
Coy, Joseph II:283
Coy, William IV:92
Coy, Willis I:473
Coye, Nehemiah II:216
Coye, Vine II:429
Coykendall, Harman IV:244
Coykendoll, Benjamin II:524
Coyle, Jacob II:619
Coyle, James II:619
Coyle, Manasseh II:735
Coyle, Mark III:58
Coyle, Mary II:619
Coyle, Patrick II:329
Coyle, William II:619
Cozby, Robert III:73
Cozens, George III:21
Cozzens, Richard I:805
Crab, Benjamin III:561, 564
Crabb, Abijah II:211
Crabb, James II:22
Crabb, Jarrott III:394
Crabtree, Isaac III:609
Crabtree, Jacob III:797
Crabtree, James IV:19
Crabtree, Newman II:170
Crabtree, William III:439
Craddock, Eleazar III:456
Craddock, Robert III:338
Craddock, William I:21
Cradlebaugh, Wm. III:301
Crafford, Alexander III:605
Crafford, Elijah II:755
Crafford, John I:870
Craft, Achilles III:317

Craft, Benjamin II:263
Craft, Ezekiel III:88
Craft, James II:14
Craft, Mary Ann I:862
Craft, Samuel I:862
Crafts, Graves I:441
Crafts, Joseph II:562
Crafts, Samuel I:306
Crafts, William I:802
Craig, Abijah I:635
Craig, Alexander III:590
Craig, David II:504; III:649
Craig, Elias I:263
Craig, Enoch I:264
Craig, Gerrard II:608
Craig, James II:76; IV:175, 273
Craig, John II:92, 504, 673, 698; III:31, 86; IV:175, 233
Craig, John H. III:259
Craig, Moses I:543
Craig, R. III:851
Craig, Samuel I:291
Craig, Thomas I:985; II:673; III:774
Craig, Thomas, Sen. IV:15, 195
Craig, William II:92; III:256, 319; IV:123, 230
Craige, Frazee II:85
Craige, Nathan I:636
Craige, Robert III:216
Craige, Thomas I:984
Craighead, Robert III:526
Craighton, Samuel I:174
Craigs, Robert IV:210
Craigue, William I:956
Crail, John II:635
Crain, Amos I:984
Crain, Daniel I:142
Crain, Jonathan II:216
Crain, Roger II:389
Crain, Stephen III:498
Crain, Thomas III:305
Cram, Ephraim I:729
Cram, Humphrey I:915
Cram, John S. I:234
Cram, Samuel S. I:770
Cram, Theophilus I:715
Cram, Tristram I:228
Cram, Zebulon I:959
Cramer, Andrew II:642
Cramer, Helfer II:760
Cramer, Henry II:521
Cramer, Jacob II:418, 694
Cramer, John II:181
Cramer, Joseph II:248
Crampersey, John I:381
Crampton, Elon I:107
Crampton, Jonathan I:124
Crampton, Thomas III:58
Crandal, Benjamin II:510
Crandal, Joseph I:810
Crandall, Abner II:492
Crandall, Amherst I:810
Crandall, Azel II:377
Crandall, Barney I:833

Crandall, Cary II:359
Crandall, Christopher II:389
Crandall, Elisha I:809
Crandall, Ethan I:832
Crandall, Ezekiel II:377
Crandall, Ezra II:429
Crandall, Gideon I:985; II:493
Crandall, Isaiah II:359
Crandall, James I:810
Crandall, Jesse I:833
Crandall, Jonathan I:870
Crandall, Joseph II:493
Crandall, Levi I:461
Crandall, Peter II:359
Crandall, Richmond I:949
Crandall, Simeon I:133
Crandell, Edward II:302
Crandell, Hosea II:331
Crandell, Jeremiah II:463
Crandell, John I:810
Crandell, Luke II:274
Crane, Aaron II:181
Crane, Abijah I:263
Crane, Amariah II:263
Crane, Ambrose II:155
Crane, Asa I:866
Crane, Benjamin I:770; II:62
Crane, Caleb II:132
Crane, David I:337
Crane, David D. II:63
Crane, Elihu II:718
Crane, Elijah II:62, 377
Crane, Elisha II:429
Crane, Enos II:277
Crane, Henry II:181, 608
Crane, J. II:553
Crane, Jabez II:163
Crane, James I:924
Crane, Joel III:586
Crane, John I:610, 866; II:63, 240, 389, 437; III:619
Crane, Jonathan II:48, 490
Crane, Jonathan E. II:62
Crane, Joshua II:22
Crane, Mayfield III:92
Crane, Nathaniel I:47
Crane, Obadiah II:63
Crane, Peter I:534
Crane, Rufus I:274
Crane, Samuel I:715
Crane, Simeon II:392
Crane, Timothy II:504
Crane, William II:22, 62; III:449, 503, 586
Crane, Zebulon I:887
Crannel, Isaac II:312
Crannel, Martin II:513
Cranson, Asa II:428-29
Cranston, Charles I:28
Cranston, Eliza I:28
Cranston, Hannah I:28
Cranston, James I:28
Cranston, Richmond I:28
Cranston, Samuel II:229
Crantz, Mark II:556
Crapo, Jonathan II:418
Crapo, Peter II:312

Crary, Archibald C. II:147
Crary, Joseph I:299
Crary, Nathan II:500
Crass, Abraham III:620
Crass, Elijah III:620
Cratin, Eunice I:174
Cratin, Henry I:174
Cratin, James I:174
Cratin, Jane I:174
Cratin, Samuel I:174
Cratin, William I:174
Craton, Anthony III:324
Craven, Andrew III:53
Craven, John II:758
Craven, Joseph II:35
Craw, David II:429
Craw, Reuben I:880
Crawford, Abigail I:683
Crawford, Absalom II:193
Crawford, Andrew II:258, 677
Crawford, Ann I:683
Crawford, Arthur III:165
Crawford, Benjamin I:683
Crawford, Daniel II:521
Crawford, David I:849; IV:261
Crawford, Deborah II:193
Crawford, Eleazer IV:267
Crawford, Eliza II:193
Crawford, Hannah II:193
Crawford, Henry II:181
Crawford, Isaac II:209
Crawford, James III:52, 277, 527, 589; IV:245
Crawford, James L. III:527
Crawford, Jason II:226
Crawford, John I:671; II:474, 531, 632; III:173, 491, 585, 849; IV:257
Crawford, Joseph I:637, 683
Crawford, Nehemiah III:49
Crawford, Peter II:638; III:448
Crawford, Phoebe II:193
Crawford, Polly I:683
Crawford, Richard II:76
Crawford, Robert I:683; III:605
Crawford, Samuel L. I:683
Crawford, Samuel S. II:474
Crawford, Spencer II:104
Crawford, Susanna I:683
Crawford, Thomas I:274; II:97, 181; III:305, 697
Crawford, W. III:96
Crawford, William I:263, 665
Crawford, Wm. II:483
Crawley, James I:392
Crawley, Thomas III:629
Crawley, William III:399
Crawsman, James I:757
Crawston, John I:832
Creamer, Daniel III:584
Creamer, Jacob II:9
Creamer, John I:274
Creasey, Jacob I:164
Creasey, John III:272
Crecy, Manuel III:111
Cree, Asa I:274

Cree, Mrs. Asa I:274
Creed, Colbay IV:16
Creegan, Henry III:3
Creekbaum, Philip II:655
Creell, John III:766
Creemer, James, Sen. III:403
Creery, William III:62
Cregkendall, Martin III:366
Crego, Abraham II:451
Crego, Elias G. IV:159
Cremens, Moses IV:138
Cremer, David II:630
Cremer, Henry IV:104
Cremer, Leach II:630
Cremer, William II:43
Crenshaw, John III:611
Cress, George III:658; IV:138
Cressey, Benjamin I:716
Cressey, Jonathan I:430
Cresson, Andrew III:364
Cressy, Benjamin I:631
Cressy, Gould I:97
Creswell, Andrew III:616
Cresy, Benjamin I:179
Cresy, John I:721
Creushaw, William III:817
Crew, Isaac II:490
Crew, Robert III:556
Crews, Gideon III:549
Crews, Joseph III:680
Crews, Reuben III:539
Crider, David II:649
Criggins, Patrick III:3
Criley, Ishmael III:684
Crill, Joseph II:21
Crilly, Peter II:229
Crim, Harman III:788
Crippen, Alpheus II:402
Crippen, Joseph II:539
Crise, Barnet II:366
Crisp, John III:614
Crissey, Moses II:131
Crist, William IV:28
Criswell, David III:290
Criswell, Henry III:633
Criswell, Richard III:756
Criswell, Samuel III:230
Critchard, Benjamin IV:198
Critchet, Caleb III:190
Critchfield, John IV:193, 225
Critchfield, Joshua IV:245
Critchfield, Nathaniel IV:263
Critchfield, William IV:263
Critchton, James IV:140
Crittenden, Amos I:347
Crittenden, Ann II:669
Crittenden, Catherine III:669
Crittenden, Ebenezer II:289
Crittenden, Gideon IV:211
Crittenden, Jared II:669
Crittenden, Jas. III:669
Crittenden, Levi I:348
Crittenden, Nancy III:669
Crittenden, Nathaniel I:31
Crittenden, Richard IV:60
Crittenden, Sarah III:669
Critzer, Leonard III:788

Croat, John II:312
Croaxall, Charles III:45
Crocker, Ansel I:329
Crocker, Anthony III:513
Crocker, Benjamin I:220; II:329
Crocker, Bursely I:329
Crocker, David IV:211
Crocker, Dyer II:749
Crocker, Ephraim II:539
Crocker, James I:426
Crocker, Jedediah IV:242
Crocker, John I:46
Crocker, Jonathan II:202
Crocker, Josiah I:326
Crocker, Noah I:984
Crocker, Oliver II:113
Crocker, Peter I:959
Crocker, Richard I:412
Crocker, Rolon I:776
Crocker, Solomon III:513
Crocker, Theophilus II:404
Crocket, Asha III:759
Crocket, Jesse III:836
Crockett, Anthony III:279
Crockett, Ephraim I:246
Crockett, Joseph III:335
Crockett, Robert I:xv; III:272
Crockett, Samuel I:179
Croddy, John III:831
Croes, John II:81
Croes, Joseph III:481
Crofford, Stephen IV:213
Crofoot, Benjamin II:353
Crofoot, Ephraim I:54
Croft, James II:490
Croft, John II:366
Croft, Joseph II:760
Croggin, Robert III:373
Croker, Jeremiah I:764
Cromelt, Jeremiah I:204
Cromer, John IV:74
Cromlin, Caleb II:655
Cromlin, Cutlip II:655
Crommitt, James I:675
Cromwell, Christopher II:474
Cromwell, John I:xii, xiii
Cromwell, Joseph I:204
Cromwell, Oliver II:31
Croninger, Joseph IV:287
Cronk, Daniel II:546
Cronk, Garret II:552
Cronk, John II:152, 699
Cronmeller, Martin II:752
Cronnell, Ann C. II:197
Cronnell, Cornelius II:197
Cronnell, Daniel II:197
Cronnell, Elizabeth II:197
Cronnell, Harvy II:197
Cronnell, Sophia II:197
Cronster, James IV:117
Cronts, Michael IV:60
Crook, Andrew I:749
Crook, Charles II:398
Crook, Henry III:661
Crook, Jeremiah III:282
Crook, John III:301

Crook, Joseph II:418
Crook, Martin II:341
Crook, Thomas II:398
Crooker, Almira I:175
Crooker, Benjamin I:740
Crooker, Calvin I:175
Crooker, Deborah I:175
Crooker, Doras I:175
Crooker, James I:558
Crooker, Joshua I:179
Crooker, Rhoda I:175
Crooker, Tilden I:559
Crooker, Turner III:468
Crookshanks, Jno. III:702
Croosman, Asahel I:823
Cropper, James III:744
Cropsey, Nathan II:103
Crosby, Benjamin I:493
Crosby, Charles I:220
Crosby, David II:711; IV:218
Crosby, Eben I:291
Crosby, Enoch II:469, 490
Crosby, Esther I:493
Crosby, Florilla I:493
Crosby, James I:493; IV:277
Crosby, Jesse II:509
Crosby, Joel I:659
Crosby, John I:513
Crosby, Jonathan I:617
Crosby, Joseph I:707
Crosby, Joshua I:479
Crosby, Malinda I:493
Crosby, Nathan I:324, 493
Crosby, Rebecca I:493
Crosby, Rhoda I:493
Crosby, Simeon II:214
Crosby, Simon I:450
Crosby, Sparrow I:636
Crosby, Stephen I:191; II:259
Crosby, Timothy II:389
Crosby, William I:321; II:57; IV:231
Crose, Philip IV:93
Crosford, Daniel I:775
Crosham, Mary II:25
Crosham, Rebecca II:25
Crosham, William II:25
Crosier, John IV:179
Crosley, Moses IV:291
Crosly, Alpheus I:740
Cross, Abijah I:413
Cross, Caleb I:264
Cross, Daniel II:677
Cross, David I:897
Cross, James II:760
Cross, John I:764; II:131, 463; IV:182
Cross, Joseph I:179; II:220, 240; III:70
Cross, Joshua I:391
Cross, Michael II:321
Cross, Moses I:715
Cross, Nathan I:893
Cross, Nero I:887
Cross, Othniel I:585
Cross, Reuben II:451
Cross, Samuel I:73; IV:226

Cross, Solomon II:500
Cross, Stephen I:461
Cross, Thomas II:402
Cross, Timothy II:362
Cross, Uriah II:429
Cross, William I:749; III:565
Cross, Zachariah IV:124
Crossan, John II:637
Crossby, Nelson I:720
Crossfield, Tim. Adams I:497
Crossley, James II:181
Crossman, Elijah II:235
Crossman, Eliza I:360
Crossman, Isaac I:381
Crossman, Joseph A. I:179
Crossman, Melvin I:360
Crossman, Noah I:637
Crossman, Samuel, Jr. I:607, 794
Crossman, Seth I:360
Crossman, Simeon I:361
Crossman, Thomas II:531
Crossman, Velecia Ann I:360
Crossman, William I:959
Crosson, John III:152
Crosson, Robert III:364
Crosston, Gustavus III:849
Crosswell, James I:361
Crostick, Edward III:765
Croston, Gustavus III:704
Croswell, Benjamin I:559
Croswell, John I:929
Crouch, Christopher I:142
Crouch, Richard I:610
Crouch, Robert III:45
Crouch, William III:680
Croukhite, Francis II:258
Crouse, Christian III:812
Crout, Matthias II:694
Crow, Abraham III:513
Crow, Christian IV:215
Crow, Dennis III:717
Crow, George II:609, 642
Crow, Jeremiah II:85
Crow, Thomas III:550
Crow, William IV:261
Crowder, Philip IV:18
Crowder, Sterling III:295
Crowell, David I:770; II:226
Crowell, Edward I:116
Crowell, Enoch I:191
Crowell, George, Sen. III:433
Crowell, Joseph II:71
Crowell, Manoah I:264
Crowell, Michael I:191
Crowell, Samuel I:116
Crowell, Sylvanus II:76
Crowell, Thomas I:610
Crowley, David II:608
Crowley, John III:20
Crowley, Miels II:645
Crowley, Royall I:959
Crowninshield, Benj. I:412
Crowninshield, William I:391
Crownover, Daniel III:515
Crownover, Joseph III:580
Croxall, Charles III:69

Currier, Hannah I:685
Currier, Hazen I:685
Currier, John I:956
Currier, Jonathan I:685, 721
Currier, Joseph II:263
Currier, Louisa I:685
Currier, Mary I:685
Currier, Moses I:776
Currier, Richard I:749
Currier, Samuel I:764, 904;
    II:717
Currier, Sergent IV:179
Currier, Theophilus I:749
Currier, Thomas I:764
Currier, Toppan I:685
Currier, William I:720
Currin, Edward II:258, 669
Curry, Aaron II:193
Curry, Baldwin II:193
Curry, Catherine Cromwell
    II:193
Curry, Edward III:326
Curry, James II:632, 717;
    III:20; IV:183, 233, 300
Curry, Jas. A. IV:300
Curry, John I:938; II:48;
    III:446, 575; IV:281
Curry, Robert IV:140
Curry, Samuel II:193, 743
Curry, Thomas II:193; IV:71
Curry, William II:523; IV:25
Curtcher, John III:219
Curtes, Jonathan III:399
Curtice, Isaac Palmer I:698
Curtice, Jacob I:740
Curtice, Stephen I:707
Curtis, Abner I:572
Curtis, Amos I:39
Curtis, Asahel II:450
Curtis, Benjamin II:76
Curtis, Caleb I:204; II:450
Curtis, Chancey I:879
Curtis, Charles I:204
Curtis, Daniel II:239
Curtis, David B. I:452
Curtis, Ebenezer I:637
Curtis, Eli I:39
Curtis, Elijah II:504
Curtis, Eliza B. I:452
Curtis, Felix II:248
Curtis, Gideon I:938
Curtis, H. B. IV:297
Curtis, Henry II:691
Curtis, Hull I:929
Curtis, Isaac I:38; II:544;
    IV:259
Curtis, James II:377; III:195
Curtis, Japhet II:123
Curtis, Joel II:268, 344, 362
Curtis, John I:473, 740; II:22;
    III:568, 818
Curtis, Jonah II:277
Curtis, Jonathan I:497, 933
Curtis, Joseph I:234, 929, 956
Curtis, Leonard I:603
Curtis, Marmaduke II:654
Curtis, Martin I:924

Curtis, Michael III:693
Curtis, Nehemiah II:339
Curtis, Oliver I:637
Curtis, Peter III:231
Curtis, Philip I:544
Curtis, Russel III:326
Curtis, Samuel I. II:277
Curtis, Silas II:231-32
Curtis, Simeon I:572, 887
Curtis, Solomon II:377
Curtis, Thomas I:544; II:41,
    373; III:629
Curtis, Vinson I:479
Curtis, William I:664; II:267
Curtis, Zachariah I:866
Curtis, Zerah IV:197
Curtiss, Agur I:84
Curtiss, Agur, Jr. I:85
Curtiss, Andrew I:84
Curtiss, Augustine I:107
Curtiss, Benjamin I:228; II:277
Curtiss, David I:224; II:259
Curtiss, Ebenezer I:85
Curtiss, Enoch I:47
Curtiss, Everard I:85
Curtiss, Fielding U. III:308
Curtiss, Frederick II:226
Curtiss, Giles I:155, 655
Curtiss, Hannah I:655
Curtiss, Jacob I:124
Curtiss, James III:551
Curtiss, John III:45
Curtiss, Joseph I:107
Curtiss, Joshua III:542
Curtiss, Jotham IV:107
Curtiss, Lemuel I:707
Curtiss, Lysander I:107
Curtiss, Philip I:124
Curtiss, Samuel I:706
Curtiss, Stephen I:214
Curtiss, William I:559
Curts, Michael IV:172
Curvan, Gersham II:158
Cusbott, Robert IV:251
Cuser, Henry III:39
Cushing, Abel I:473
Cushing, Adam I:559
Cushing, Charles I:823
Cushing, Daniel I:776
Cushing, Ebenezer I:593
Cushing, Er I:534
Cushing, Ezekiel I:347
Cushing, Isaac I:593
Cushing, John I:757
Cushing, John W. I:847
Cushing, Jonathan I:572
Cushing, Joshua I:559
Cushing, Loring I:179
Cushing, Nathaniel I:559
Cushing, Reg. I:593
Cushing, Regemelick I:534
Cushing, Sarah I:593
Cushing, Seth II:389
Cushing, William I:554
Cushman, Andrew I:263
Cushman, Benjamin I:572;
    II:482

Cushman, Caleb I:282-83
Cushman, Caroline I:861
Cushman, Catherine I:861
Cushman, Daniel I:21; II:235
Cushman, Daniel S. I:861
Cushman, David II:404
Cushman, Ephraim I:473
Cushman, Frederick I:943
Cushman, George I:559
Cushman, Gideon I:283
Cushman, Holmes I:985
Cushman, Isaac I:282; II:720
Cushman, Isaiah I:246, 282
Cushman, Jacob I:572
Cushman, John I:263
Cushman, Jonah I:347
Cushman, Jonathan I:263
Cushman, Joseph I:370, 915
Cushman, Joshua II:344
Cushman, Nathaniel I:866
Cushman, Obed I:366
Cushman, Peres II:463
Cushman, Ralph I:656
Cushman, Silvanus I:274
Cushman, William I:283
Cushman, Zebedee I:215
Cushwa, David III:35
Cusick, Nicholas II:274, 560
Cussard, Philip II:720
Custard, Conrad II:707
Custard, Jacob IV:277
Custer, Jacob II:624
Custer, Richard III:833
Custer, Sarah II:624
Cuter, John I:764
Cuthbert, William II:403
Cuthright, John III:798
Cutler, Abner II:350
Cutler, Andrew III:12
Cutler, Charles I:600
Cutler, Ebenezer I:970
Cutler, Elias II:437
Cutler, Isaac I:897
Cutler, John I:764
Cutler, Jonathan I:148
Cutler, Joseph I:740; II:130,
    444
Cutler, Joseph, 2d II:277
Cutler, Josiah I:871
Cutler, Nathaniel II:516
Cutler, Oliver I:544
Cutler, Seth II:418
Cutright, Peter IV:17
Cutter, Benjamin II:346
Cutter, Charles I:514
Cutter, Ebenezer I:392
Cutter, Hodges I:783
Cutter, Josiah I:908
Cutter, Nathaniel I:908
Cutter, Seth I:757
Cutter, Thomas I:707
Cutter, William I:497, 706
Cutting, Aaron I:361
Cutting, Benjamin I:737
Cutting, Bille I:749
Cutting, Earl I:637
Cutting, Eliphalet II:216

Cutting, John Brown III:16
Cutting, Jonas I:914
Cutting, Jonathan I:636
Cutting, Moses I:740
Cutting, Silas I:497
Cutting, Zebedee I:749
Cutts, R. I:xii
Cutts, William, Sen. III:405
Cuyler, Jos. II:557
Cylder, John II:336
Cypher, Jacob II:546
Cypher, Peter II:211
Cypress, Andrew IV:298
Cyprus, Andrew IV:201
Cyrus, Bartholomew III:684
Cyrus, Exeter I:77

Dabbs, John III:159
Dabell, John, 2d II:226
Dabney, Austin III:126
Dabney, George III:329
Dabney, John O. III:321
Daboll, John I:15
Dacon, Jonathan III:680
Dacus, Nathaniel III:503
Dacy, John I:180
Dade, Isaac I:393
Dadge, Reuben II:305
Dadman, Jonathan I:515
Daffendorf, John II:438
Daffron, Rody III:329
Dagar, Robert III:713
Dager, Joseph I:387
Dager, Lucy I:387
Dager, Nancy I:387
Dager, Sally I:387
Dager, Warren I:387
Dagger, Peter III:682
Daggert, John II:718
Dagget, Jacob IV:285
Daggett, Daniel I:805
Daggett, Darius I:740
Daggett, Elijah I:362
Daggett, Gideon IV:199
Daggett, Henry I:156
Daggett, Henry, Jr. I:60
Daggett, Joseph, Senr. I:960
Daggett, Mahu II:510
Daggett, Reuben II:524
Daggett, Samuel I:535
Daggett, Tristram I:224, 321
Daggett, William I:371
Dahoney, William III:199
Dail, John III:443
Dailey, Bennet III:303
Dailey, Dennis III:243
Dailey, Elijah III:21
Dailey, Giles I:60
Dailey, James, 1st II:229
Dailey, Jesse III:801
Dailey, John II:89, 337;
   III:704
Dailey, Samuel IV:195
Dailly, Nezer I:302
Daily, David IV:169
Daily, Dennis II:689

Daily, Elias IV:218
Daily, London I:721
Daily, William J. II:377
Daimwood, Boston III:614
Dain, John I:274
Daines, Castle II:566
Dains, Asa IV:270
Dains, Ephraim IV:106
Dains, Jesse II:549
Dake, John M. II:359
Dakin, Elisha II:359
Dakin, Thomas I:231
Dale, Archelaus I:392
Dale, John III:629
Dale, Richard III:774
Dale, Samuel I:21, 699; III:73
Dale, William III:252
Daley, John II:670
Daley, Silas II:332
Dallaby, George II:278
Dallas, Robert III:822
Dalliver, Peter I:187
Dalrymple, Albert I:493
Dalrymple, David II:544, 754
Dalrymple, Edmund II:68
Dalrymple, Henry I:493
Dalrymple, James I:515
Dalrymple, James T. I:493
Dalrymple, Thomas II:720
Dalrymple, William I:493;
   III:21
Dalton, Isaac I:764
Dalton, James II:31
Dalton, John III:568
Dalton, Samuel I:729
Dalton, Thomas II:181
Dalton, William III:450
Dalzell, John IV:137
Daman, Abraham IV:249
Damans, Abiah I:302
Damard, Edmund I:74
Dame, Edward I:737
Dame, Jonathan I:306
Dame, Joseph I:776
Dameron, George III:380
Dameron, Joseph III:408
Damon, Benjamin I:515, 757
Damon, Chandler II:187
Damon, Daniel I:515
Damon, Edward I:560
Damon, Evelina II:187
Damon, Isaac I:480
Damon, Isaiah I:480
Damon, Jason I:429
Damon, John II:187
Damon, Joseph I:515
Damon, Oliver I:740
Damon, Reuben I:573
Damon, Stephen I:441, 573
Damon, William I:530
Damon Julia II:187
Dample, Frederick I:202
Dample, Thomas IV:56
Damron, Charles III:130
Dan, Henry Bar II:58
Dan, James II:546
Dan, Jonathan II:377

Dan, Samuel II:546
Dana, Benjamin I:658
Dana, Daniel II:404
Dana, David I:960
Dana, Ezra II:302
Dana, Josiah I:915
Dana, Luther I:179, 510
Dana, Samuel I:657
Danbury, Nicholas II:41
Danbury, William II:41
Dance, Etheldred III:383
Dane, Benjamin I:441
Danford, James III:4
Danford, Job I:823
Danford, Prince II:298, 561
Danforth, Abner I:205
Danforth, Asa II:284
Danforth, Elkanah I:699
Danforth, Henry I:721
Danforth, Jedediah I:750
Danforth, John I:498
Danforth, Jonathan I:881
Danforth, Joshua I:338, 393,
   655
Danforth, Moses I:721
Danforth, Peter I:881; IV:265
Danforth, Samuel II:322
Danforth, Thomas I:362, 729
Danforth, William I:764
Danforth, William B. I:593
Danf_rd, Joshua II:220
Daniel, Archibald IV:12
Daniel, Benjamin W. III:619
Daniel, Beverly III:309
Daniel, Buckner III:415
Daniel, Christopher III:439
Daniel, Ezekiel III:508
Daniel, H. III:333
Daniel, James III:523
Daniel, Jesse III:526
Daniel, John I:783; III:161
Daniel, Richard III:760
Daniel, William I:559
Daniell, Joseph I:729
Danielly, Daniel II:31
Daniels, Albert J. I:857
Daniels, Amariah I:618;
   IV:299
Daniels, Asa E. I:857
Daniels, Benjamin II:165;
   IV:151
Daniels, Charles III:118
Daniels, Daniel II:290
Daniels, Ezekiel I:74; II:229
Daniels, Henry R. I:857
Daniels, Herman I:857
Daniels, James III:819
Daniels, Jesse I:544
Daniels, Job I:133
Daniels, Joel I:544
Daniels, John I:348, 897;
   II:400
Daniels, Jonathan I:441, 721
Daniels, Joseph I:747
Daniels, Nathan I:544; II:451,
   546
Daniels, Nehemiah II:483

Daniels, Pelatiah I:98
Daniels, Reuben I:39
Daniels, Samuel I:124, 857, 933; II:500
Daniels, Solomon I:995
Daniels, Starling I:338
Danielson, Altamont II:390
Danielson, Luther IV:203
Danielson, Timothy II:483
Danks, Eliakim I:462
Danks, John III:300
Danks, Zadock I:480
Danley, James II:220
Dann, Abijah II:513
Dannels, James II:438
Danner, Frederick III:454
Danner, Jacob III:682
Danning, David I:665
Dannor, David IV:64
Dansdill, George II:701
Darbe, Asa I:960
Darbee, Jedediah II:234
Darby, Benjamin III:80
Darby, John II:505
Darby, Moses II:731
Darby, Richard III:163
Darby, Samuel I:515; II:410, 505
Darby, William IV:195
Darden, George III:94
Dardin, John III:122
Dare, Philip II:61
Darley, Elijah II:500
Darling, Aaron I:915, 1000
Darling, Benjamin I:573; II:284, 301
Darling, David I:595
Darling, Jewett B. I:618
Darling, Job I:618
Darling, John I:26, 847, 908, 986; II:414
Darling, Joseph IV:108
Darling, Levi I:867
Darling, Maria I:26
Darling, Montgomery I:676
Darling, Moses I:874
Darling, Oliver I:850
Darling, Peletiah I:639
Darling, Richard II:223
Darling, Samuel I:545
Darling, Solomon II:392
Darling, Thomas II:133
Darling, Zelek I:638
Darlington, John II:711
Darnaby, John III:275
Darnall, Joseph III:452
Darnan, Luther I:573
Darnel, Cornelius III:598
Darnell, Adam, Jun. III:250
Darnell, John II:578
Darnell, Spencer III:192
Darnell, William III:593
Darrach, John III:401
Darrah, Robert III:343, 655
Darrell, William I:530
Darrin, Daniel II:451
Darrow, Benjamin I:32; III:635

Darrow, Daniel I:32; II:510
Darrow, Ebenezer I:97, 133
Darrow, George II:373
Darrow, James II:524
Darrow, Jedediah II:429
Darrow, John II:749
Darrow, Nathan I:133
Darrow, Samuel I:924
Darrow, William I:133
Darrow, Zaccheus II:404
Darst, W. P. IV:299
Dart, Abel I:97
Dart, David I:133
Dart, Dolphin I:54
Dart, Jonathan I:142
Dart, Levi I:462
Darten, Edward III:277
Dartt, Justus II:751
Dascomb, David I:707
Dasham, William I:32
Dashiel, Ann III:41
Dashiel, Betsey III:41
Dashiel, Hensau III:41
Dashiel, John III:41
Dashiel, Levi III:41
Dashiel, Levin III:41
Dashiel, Sally III:41
Daskam, John II:337
Datamar, John II:760
Daub, Dilman II:729
Daubert, Peter II:610
Daud, Isaac II:684
Daud, John II:592
Daulton, Michael I:770
Davenport, Addington I:595
Davenport, Adrian III:216
Davenport, Anthony S. IV:278
Davenport, Caleb I:362
Davenport, Claiborne III:742
Davenport, Eliphalet II:429
Davenport, Ephraim I:283
Davenport, Henry II:474
Davenport, Humphrey II:203
Davenport, Ira II:564
Davenport, Jacobus II:522
Davenport, James I:535; III:275
Davenport, Joel III:682
Davenport, John II:329; IV:285
Davenport, Jonathan I:794
Davenport, Moses I:413
Davenport, Noah II:392
Davenport, Reuben III:713
Davenport, Richard II:217; III:763
Davenport, Samuel I:818
Davenport, Squire II:329
Davenport, Thomas I:265
Davenport, William I:617; III:430, 752
Daver, Solomon I:559
David, Azariah III:610
David, Francis I:15
David, Henry IV:88
David, John II:229
David, Jonathan II:245

David, Michael III:304
David, Peter III:491
David, Zebediah IV:226
Davidhiser, Henry II:638
Davidson, Abraham III:592
Davidson, Alexander I:205
Davidson, Barnabas I:898
Davidson, Daniel I:672, 956
Davidson, David III:703
Davidson, Francis I:672
Davidson, George III:577
Davidson, Giles III:749
Davidson, Isaac IV:78
Davidson, Jacob II:46
Davidson, James II:445; III:21, 61
Davidson, James, 2d III:43
Davidson, John I:338, 904; II:305, 517; III:4, 170, 566, 657, 831
Davidson, Jonah III:788
Davidson, Joseph I:148; III:150, 473, 730
Davidson, Joshua III:192, 277; IV:231
Davidson, Josiah III:788
Davidson, Nelson, 1st III:4
Davidson, Stephen III:758
Davidson, W. S. III:463
Davidson, William IV:218
Davidson, Zachariah I:125
Davie, Solomon I:573
Davies, Daniel II:689
Davies, Isaac II:619
Davis, Aaron I:274, 283, 437; III:384
Davis, Abel I:515, 943
Davis, Abner I:771
Davis, Abraham I:707; III:652, 716
Davis, Adeline II:619
Davis, Albert III:670
Davis, Alden I:686
Davis, Allen I:247
Davis, Amos I:393; II:438
Davis, Andrew III:568
Davis, Andries II:531
Davis, Anna III:535
Davis, Ann Eliza II:619
Davis, Anthony III:56
Davis, Apheus I:740
Davis, Aquila IV:10
Davis, Aquilla I:765
Davis, Asa III:605
Davis, Benjamin I:228, 407, 413, 515, 749, 908; IV:176
Davis, Bennett I:617
Davis, Burrell III:457
Davis, Chapman II:334
Davis, Charles III:452, 664
Davis, Clement III:404
Davis, Comfort II:305
Davis, Cornelius I:943
Davis, Cyrus I:299; III:374
Davis, Daniel I:67, 986; III:759; IV:140, 189

362

Dehart, Winant II:71
Dehaven, Edward III:209
Dehaven, Isaac III:774
De Haven, Jonathan II:592
Dehuff, John IV:261
Deiley, Daniel II:666
Deirl, Jacob II:730
Deis, John II:694
Deits, Adam IV:172
Deitz, John II:739
Deitz, John Joast II:354
Delamater, Isaac II:546
Delamater, John S. II:268
Delamater, Samuel II:445
Delancy, Abram II:298
Deland, Jacob II:322
Delaney, Nathan I:192
Delaney, Sharp I:xv
Delano, Aaron I:47
Delano, Alpheus I:205
Delano, Amaziah I:265
Delano, Isaac I:595
Delano, Jabez I:215
Delano, Jeptha I:559
Delano, Jesse I:560
Delano, Jonathan I:205, 904
Delano, Malachi I:573
Delano, Nathan I:517
Delano, Oliver I:573
Delano, Philip I:559, 638
Delano, Reuben I:573
Delano, Seth I:295
Delano, Thomas II:419
Delany, Frances II:220
Delany, John II:622; III:849
Delany, Martin III:702
Delap, Henry, Sen. III:448
Delap, James IV:87
Delapierre, Barthol II:133
Delauy, Esther II:622
De Lavan, Daniel II:351
Delaway, John I:881
Delesdernier, Lewis F. I:302
Delezeene, Christopher II:268
Delezenne, Christo'er II:559
Delezenne, J. B. II:559
De Ligney, Peter III:50
Delleber, John I:148
Dellica, Godfrey II:571
Delong, Daniel II:377
Delong, John IV:218
Delong, Joseph II:290
De Longe, John II:133
De Long Francis II:159
Demaree, John III:306
Demarest, Peter D. II:125
Demarest, Samuel II:504
DeMarianville, Charles IV:167
Demary, Thomas I:750
Demass, Peter II:211
Demaster, James IV:121
Demasters, Edward III:847
Demelt, Barnet II:438
Dement, Jarret III:280
De Meranville, Simeon I:371
DeMerritt, Robert I:750
Demfrey, Patrick II:592

Demick, Elias I:929
Demick, Joseph I:915
Deming, Abiel I:683
Deming, Andres II:245
Deming, Benjamin I:934
Deming, Daniel II:373
Deming, Dolly I:683
Deming, Ebenezer I:683
Deming, Elijah I:39
Deming, Gideon I:348
Deming, John I:348, 683;
II:483
Deming, Jonathan I:897, 999
Deming, Julius I:108
Deming, Lucy I:683
Deming, Mehitabel I:683
Deming, Nancy I:683
Deming, Simeon II:510
Deming, Solomon IV:269
Deming, Stephen I:60
Deming, Theron I:97
Demmick, Braddock I:329
Demming, Daniel II:451
Demming, Davis II:284
Demming, Elisha I:603
Demming, William II:400
Democh, Jeduthun I:74
Demock, David II:684
Demons, Gamaliel I:302
Demony, Henry II:513
Demoss, John IV:35
Demoss, Peter III:316
Demott, Hans Mark II:181
Demott, Peter III:306
Demott, Richard II:211
Demott, William II:245
Dempsey, Isaac II:133
Dempsey, John III:43
Dempsey, Peter IV:150
Dempsey, Sampson III:682
Dempsy, Dennis II:645
Denbo, Cornelius I:776
Deneen, James IV:233
Deneger, George II:223
Denel, Benjamin II:544
Denham, Benajah I:348
Denham, Harden III:593
Denick, Ephraim II:274
Denight, James II:34
Denike, Davis II:743
Denike, Samuel II:72
Denis, Aaron I:929
Denison, Beebee II:544
Denison, David I:441
Denison, George II:429
Denison, James I:15, 55
Denison, James P. II:483
Denison, Jedediah I:116
Denison, Joseph II:504
Denison, Nathan I:960
Deniston, William II:755
Denkins, Joshua III:590
Denman, Isaac II:474
Denman, Matthias II:63
Denmark, Burnardus II:339
Denn, Patrick II:133
Dennett, Ebenezer I:265

Dennett, Joseph I:307
Denney, Elijah III:319
Dennie, John IV:239
Dennie, William III:529
Denning, Lemuel, Jr. I:6
Denning, William II:649
Dennis, Adonijah I:638
Dennis, Andrew IV:204
Dennis, Benjamin I:393
Dennis, Jacob III:46
Dennis, James I:909
Dennis, John I:610; II:305
Dennis, Moses I:757
Dennis, Philip II:385
Dennis, Russel I:133
Dennis, Thomas II:322
Dennis, William III:714, 724
Dennison, Amos I:908
Dennison, Andrew II:707
Dennison, Chauncey I:108
Dennison, David I:247
Dennison, E. II:563
Dennison, Emeline I:29
Dennison, George I:133
Dennison, Henry II:353
Dennison, Isaac I:413
Dennison, James II:313
Dennison, Joseph I:29
Dennison, Lucius I:29
Dennison, Prince I:21
Dennison, Robert I:265
Dennison, William I:29
Denniss, Samuel I:67
Denniston, Daniel II:29
Denniston, John II:22
Denn_s, Jonas I:413
Denny, Absalom II:463
Denny, Charles II:373
Denny, James III:720
Denny, Joseph III:419
Denny, Richard II:513
Denoon, James S. III:649
Denoon, John IV:183
Denslow, Benjamin II:117
Denslow, Eli I:60
Denston, Elijah I:97
Dent, George III:56
Dent, John III:36, 808
Denton, Amos II:329
Denton, Daniel II:298
Denton, David III:256
Denton, James II:196
Denton, John III:388, 607
Denton, Thomas II:196
Denton, William III:695
Dentzler, Christian II:665
Deon, Jabez II:483
Depass, Ann III:40
Depass, George III:40
Depass, John III:40
Depass, Margaret III:40
Depass, Mary III:40
Depew, Cornelius III:498
Depew, David II:516
Depew, Henry II:268
Depositer, John IV:96
Depoy, Christopher IV:284

Depp, William III:256
Depreist, William III:450
Depriest, Robert III:541
Depue, John II:336
Deputron, William I:498
Depuy, Benjamin II:463
Depuy, Isaac II:716
Depuy, John II:463
Depuy, John, Jr. II:532
Derby, Edward II:211
Derby, Jonathan II:400
Derby, Samuel I:740
Derby, Simeon I:750
Deremiah, John IV:58
Dermis, Enos III:50
Derr, Christian II:687
Derr, John II:752
Derr, Matthias II:729
Derrance, David II:336
Derrick, Joseph I:610
Derrickson, Joseph II:626
Derric, Frederick II:419
Derrough, John IV:205
Derry, Peter I:908
Dersham, Ludwig II:752
De Russy, Thomas II:268
Dervey, Barzilla I:960
Desbrow, Henry II:284
Desbrow, Joshua I:32
Desbrow, Justus I:32
Desbrow, William II:101
Desburn, Simon II:240
Desforges, Lewis III:111
Deshay, William II:398
Deshazure, Henry III:306
Deshler, Charles II:739
Deshon, James I:235
Deshon, Moses I:307
Deskins, Daniel III:206
Desmont, Amelia II:621
Desmont, Benjamin II:621
Desmont, Elizabeth II:621
Desmont, Henry II:621
Desmont, Joseph II:621
Desmont, Maria II:621
Desmont, Martha II:621
Desnoyers, Louis III:3
De Spain, Peter III:284
Despervine, John C. I:867
Dessasure, A. A. III:518
Dester, Nathan I:74
Determore, Robert II:659
Detrick, George II:665
Deusenbury, Gabriel II:517
Deusenbury, William II:367
Devan, James IV:198
Devane, James III:436
Devault, John II:590
Devaun, James IV:198
Devaux, Peter III:137
Deveney, John II:694
Devenny, Daniel II:727
Devenny, James II:727
Devenport, Franklin II:63
Devens, John II:55
Deveraux, John I:938
Devereaux, William III:60

Devericks, John III:821
Devers, James III:808
Devin, Robert III:822
Devin, William II:584
Devine, William III:304
Devlin, James III:476
Devoe, Anthony II:414
Devoe, David II:546
Devoe, Eliza II:193
Devoe, Isaac II:193, 505
Devoe, Jeremiah II:342
De Voe, John II:133
Devoe, William II:539
Devoir, Luke IV:9
Devol, Jonathan IV:223
Devons, Leonard II:731
Devore, Cornelius II:55
Devore, Enos IV:148
Devore, John II:53
Devouriex, James III:200
Dew, John H. III:635
Dewall, Thomas II:48
Dewalt, Michael III:696
De Waltz, Peter II:654
Deweberry, Andrew III:610
Dewees, Isaac II:7, 10
Dewees, Samuel III:46
Dewey, Abijah II:410
Dewey, Abraham I:142
Dewey, Amos I:794
Dewey, Daniel I:133
Dewey, Darius I:986
Dewey, Elijah II:362
Dewey, Gideon II:289
Dewey, Harmon I:15
Dewey, Isaac I:98
Dewey, Jeremiah II:402
Dewey, John W. II:516
Dewey, Josiah II:424
Dewey, Oliver IV:279
Dewey, Peleg II:539
Dewey, Russell I:454
Dewey, Samuel II:220
Dewey, Silas I:97
Dewey, Timothy I:888
Dewing, Elijah I:544
Dewing, Henry I:530
Dewing, John I:515
Dewing, Nathan I:535
Dewire, James II:592
Dewise, Hezekiah III:431
Dewit, John C. II:410
Dewit, William IV:92
Dewitt, Abraham II:518, 532
De Witt, Cornelius D. II:367
DeWitt, Egbert II:367
De Witt, Garret I:124
Dewitt, Henry II:133
Dewitt, Jacobus II:532
DeWitt, James II:172
Dewitt, John II:268
Dewitt, John A. II:531
Dewitt, Paul II:705
De witt, Peter III:269
DeWitt, Simeon II:353
Dewitt, William II:337, 531
Dewitter, John II:577

DeWolf, Benjamin II:248
De Wolf, Edward II:435
Dewolf, Joseph IV:289
Dewolf, Peter IV:289
De Wolf, Samuel II:451
De Wolfe, Elisha I:442
Dewry, Martin I:750
Dews, William III:822
Dexter, Arathusa I:614
Dexter, Benjamin I:823
Dexter, Caleb I:749
Dexter, Daniel S. I:361, 656, 837
Dexter, David I:976
Dexter, Eleazer I:614
Dexter, Eleazer (2) I:614
Dexter, Elisha I:573; II:445
Dexter, John I:985
Dexter, John S. I:837
Dexter, Joseph I:380
Dexter, Nathan I:639
Dexter, Stephen I:934
Dexter, Thankful I:614
Dexter, Thomas I:78, 231; II:217
Dexter, William II:248
Dey, John Ogden II:552
Dey, Josiah II:72
Deyo, Abraham II:532
De Young, Isaac II:592
Dezern, Frederick III:546
Dial, Jeremiah III:566
Diall, Daniel III:392
Diamond, John IV:13
Diamond, William I:707
Dias, George II:677
Dibbel, Asa II:278
Dibble, Armena II:200
Dibble, Bartlett II:200
Dibble, Benjamin I:97
Dibble, Daniel I:97
Dibble, Hezekiah II:274
Dibble, Israel I:8
Dibble, John I:85, 867
Dibble, Mary II:200
Dibble, Sally Ann II:200
Dibble, Silas II:200
Dibble, Thompkins II:200
Dibol, Moses I:98
Dibrell, Charles III:575
Dice, George II:677
Dicher, Godfried II:746
Dick, Charles III:492
Dick, Henry II:385, 414
Dick, Jacob II:702
Dick, William II:581
Dickason, Samuel II:698
Dicken, Ephraim III:308
Dicken, John III:284
Dicken, Richard III:156
Dicken, William III:422
Dickens, James II:667
Dickens, Thomas III:367
Dickenson, Griffith III:822
Dickenson, Jesse II:667
Dickenson, Thomas I:925
Dickerman, Enoch I:765

Dickerman, John II:536
Dickerman, Joseph II:347
Dickerman, Peter I:535
Dickerson, Abraham II:445
Dickerson, Benj. II:155
Dickerson, Betsy II:188
Dickerson, Clarissa II:188
Dickerson, David II:336
Dickerson, Elijah III:777
Dickerson, Elisha II:188
Dickerson, Jonas I:595
Dickerson, Moses II:63
Dickerson, Robert IV:100
Dickerson, Solomon III:308
Dickerson, Thomas IV:223
Dickerson, Villetta II:188
Dickerson, Walter IV:233
Dickerson, William III:664
Dickery, John II:619
Dickeson, Isham III:458
Dickey, Adam I:887
Dickey, Charles II:672
Dickey, David III:425, 503
Dickey, Ebenezer III:324
Dickey, Eleazer I:228
Dickey, Elias I:757
Dickey, Horace W. I:173
Dickey, Horatio G. I:173
Dickey, James I:618; II:705
Dickey, John I:173; II:619, 701
Dickey, Mary E. I:173
Dickey, Newton II:619
Dickey, Peter II:749
Dickey, Robert III:306; IV:239
Dickey, Thomas IV:257
Dickey, William I:707, 757
Dickins, Richard II:498
Dickins, William II:350
Dickinson, Asahel II:451
Dickinson, Charles II:493, 498
Dickinson, Cotton I:473
Dickinson, David I:39
Dickinson, Ebenezer I:480
Dickinson, Edward III:45
Dickinson, Elijah III:716
Dickinson, Francis II:483
Dickinson, Friend IV:218
Dickinson, Gideon I:888
Dickinson, Heman W. II:158
Dickinson, Ichabod I:134
Dickinson, James I:515
Dickinson, Joel I:691
Dickinson, John I:480; II:60, 377; IV:39
Dickinson, Jonathan I:480
Dickinson, Josiah II:451
Dickinson, Justin II:165
Dickinson, Levi I:480
Dickinson, Nathaniel I:98; III:610
Dickinson, Oliver I:108
Dickinson, Reuben I:442
Dickinson, Samuel I:638; II:344
Dickinson, Seth II:483
Dickinson, Silvanus I:60

Dickinson, Simeon I:117, 480
Dickinson, Solomon II:389
Dickinson, Vacarious III:705
Dickinson, Waitstill II:289, 561
Dickinson, Warsal II:240
Dickinson, William III:802
Dickisson, Isaac II:55
Dickman, John I:515
Dicks, David II:207
Dicks, Isaac III:46
Dickson, Abner III:72
Dickson, Benjamin II:714
Dickson, George IV:256
Dickson, Henry I:10
Dickson, James III:718
Dickson, Jesse III:619
Dickson, Joel III:369
Dickson, John III:392
Dickson, Joseph III:380
Dickson, Josiah IV:120
Dickson, Robert II:373
Dickson, Thomas I:885
Dickson, William I:514; III:618
Dickson, Wm. II:677
Diddle, John III:750
Diddleston, Thomas III:221
Didson, Seth I:498
Diefendorf, Jacob H. II:438
Diefendorff, John Jacob II:438
Diehl, Jacob II:730
Dietrich, John B. II:133
Diffenderfer, David II:728
Diffenderffer, Richard III:21
Digges, Dudley III:802
Diggins, Martin I:986
Diggs, William III:806
Dike, Adin IV:242
Dike, Calvin I:849; IV:242
Dike, Daniel I:342, 867
Dike, Henry IV:185
Dike, Nathan II:251
Dike, Nicholas I:638
Dike, Samuel I:986
Dike, William II:402
Dikeman, Daniel I:85
Dikeman, Eliphalet I:85
Dikeman, Frederick I:897
Dikeman, Levi I:85
Dilday, Joseph III:423
Dildee, Amos III:420
Dildine, Jonathan III:608
Dill, Archibald III:593
Dill, George II:524
Dill, John II:367; III:408
Dill, Lemuel I:559
Dill, Richard III:633
Dill, Thomas I:326; II:635
Dillard, Benjamin III:584
Dillard, James III:139, 506
Dillard, John III:603
Dillen, Benjamin III:415
Diller, David IV:242
Dilley, Ephraim, Sen. IV:252
Dillingham, Elisha I:599, 805
Dillingham, John I:180, 247

Dillingham, Lemuel I:299
Dillingham, Nathan I:348
Dillingham, Paul I:904
Dilman, Andrew III:209
Diman, David I:560
Dimkinson, Thomas III:267
Dimmick, Amassa I:73
Dimmick, Benjamin II:322, 563
Dimmick, Edward II:749
Dimmick, John I:142
Dimmick, Moors II:516
Dimmick, Samuel I:750
Dimmick, Shubel II:392
Dimmick, Sylvanus I:348
Dimon, William I:812
Dimond, Benjamin I:833
Dimond, Isaac I:764
Dimpsey, Richard II:39
Dingee, Elijah I:85
Dingham, Abraham II:326
Dingley, Levi I:247
Dingman, Geradas II:147
Dingman, Gerardus II:560
Dingman, Peter IV:278
Dingman, Rudolphus II:438
Dinguid, George III:760
Dinsmore, Abraham II:390
Dinsmore, Elijah I:776
Dinsmore, John I:716
Dinsmore, Samuel I:716
Dinsmore, Thomas I:167, 477, 692, 788; II:445
Dinwiddie, John III:231
Dinyman, Andrew II:745
Disbrow, Asa IV:238
Disbrow, Erastus II:133
Disbrow, John D. II:71
Dishman, William III:256
Dishon, Lewis III:439
Dishong, Lewis III:439
Dismuches, Paul III:593
Dispair, Benjamin II:503
Ditcher, Robert II:694
Diterick, Balsar IV:276
Ditson, Thomas I:498
Ditts, William II:68
Ditty, John III:629
Ditzer, Peter IV:63
Divin, James III:298
Divine, John II:336
Dix, Benjamin I:904
Dix, Jonathan I:909
Dix, Joseph II:214
Dix, Thomas III:692
Dix, William I:192
Dixon, Abner IV:163
Dixon, Alexander IV:244
Dixon, Amos II:546
Dixon, Archibald III:335
Dixon, Curtis II:419
Dixon, Daniel IV:163
Dixon, David II:217
Dixon, Elizabeth IV:163
Dixon, George I:21; III:546; IV:96
Dixon, Henry I:10

Dixon, Jacob II:632
Dixon, James II:651
Dixon, Jared I:876
Dixon, John II:610; IV:99
Dixon, Joseph II:377
Dixon, Marshall II:181
Dixon, Nathaniel III:774
Dixon, Patrick II:677
Dixon, Robert II:451; IV:163
Dixon, Thomas II:561
Dixon, Walter IV:156
Dixon, William III:527, 822; IV:171
Dixon, Wm. II:677
Dixon, Wynne III:335
Dixson, Patrick II:699
Doack, Robert II:700
Doak, Benjamin I:413
Doan, Josiah II:409
Doane, Amos I:220
Doane, Joel I:54
Doane, Oliver I:291
Doane, Prince I:326
Doane, Seth I:970
Dobb, Chesley III:573
Dobbin, Hugh W. II:169
Dobbin, John I:393
Dobbins, David III:605
Dobbins, James I:179; II:758; III:450
Dobbins, John III:702
Dobbins, William III:530
Dobbs, Nathan III:164
Dobel, John I:348
Dobkins, Jacob III:573
Dobson, John I:393; II:202
Dobson, John, Sen. III:778
Dobson, Joseph III:399
Dobson, Richard III:815
Doby, John III:170
Docherty, John II:22
Docker, John II:202
Dockham, James I:729
Dockum, James IV:268
Dodd, Bishop I:60
Dodd, Daniel II:268
Dodd, David III:551
Dodd, Ebenezer II:419
Dodd, Jesse III:76
Dodd, Robert III:396
Dodd, Stephen I:205
Dodd, Timothy II:36
Dodd, William III:494, 600
Doddridge, Jacob II:638
Dodds, Isabella IV:163
Dodds, Joseph IV:163
Dodds, Lewis IV:163
Dodds, Zachariah II:395
Dodge, Abner I:180
Dodge, Abraham I:393
Dodge, Amos I:683; II:217
Dodge, Benjamin II:226
Dodge, Brewer I:699
Dodge, Daniel II:556
Dodge, Ebenezer I:970
Dodge, Edward I:950
Dodge, Francis II:259

Dodge, Ira II:404
Dodge, Israel I:393
Dodge, James I:860
Dodge, Joel II:419
Dodge, John I:515; II:556
Dodge, John, 2d II:297
Dodge, John, 3d II:240
Dodge, John, 1st II:277
Dodge, John T. I:413
Dodge, Josiah I:863
Dodge, Levi II:268, 561
Dodge, Lydia I:860
Dodge, Nathaniel II:474
Dodge, Nathaniel B. I:904
Dodge, Nicholas I:192
Dodge, Paul I:205
Dodge, Phinehas II:404
Dodge, R. II:558
Dodge, Richard II:558
Dodge, Robert I:707
Dodge, Rufus II:410
Dodge, Samuel I:392
Dodge, Sarah II:556
Dodge, Shadrack I:915
Dodge, Simon I:707
Dodge, Smith I:860
Dodge, Stephen II:133
Dodge, Thaddeus I:638
Dodge, Thankful I:863
Dodge, Thomas I:413; II:284
Dodge, William I:393, 683, 863; II:251, 445
Dodge, Wm. J. II:558
Dodge, Zimner I:860
Dodson, John III:587
Dodson, Michael II:637
Dodson, Thomas III:735
Dodson, William III:312
Doe, Henry I:162
Doe, James I:228
Doe, Sampson I:192
Doe, Simon I:224
Dogan, Jeremiah J. III:290
Dogan, Lovel H. III:318
Doherty, George, Senr. III:594
Doherty, John III:247
Doing, Robert IV:157
Doke, Immanuel II:500
Dolahide, Francis IV:13
Doland, John III:758
Dolbear, Benjamin I:224
Dolbear, James I:638
Dolbear, Jesse II:71
Dolbee, Jonathan II:329
Dolbee, Pardon II:331
Dolby, William III:21
Dole, Amos I:220
Dole, Benjamin II:327
Dole, David I:413
Dole, James II:313
Dole, Richard I:215
Doleber, Thomas I:393
Dolhagin, Frederick II:268
Dolin, Michael II:689
Doll, Henry II:694
Doll, Martin II:694
Dollar, William III:439; IV:8

Dollard, Peter II:71
Dollars, Elijah III:439
Dollas, Jacob II:14
Dollaway, Andrew II:232
Dolley, John III:439
Dollif, Noah I:228
Dolliff, Thomas I:729
Dollinger, John II:746
Dollins, Presley III:598
Dolliver, Joseph II:483
Dolliver, William I:393
Dolloff, Miles I:676
Doloff, Richard I:283
Dolph, Stephen IV:34
Dolsbury, Lyles III:841
Dolson, John II:524
Dominick, Henry III:509
Don, Squire I:85
Donaho, James II:10
Donald, William II:758
Donaldson, James II:48
Donaldson, John II:669
Donaldson, Lothario I:541; II:435
Donaldson, William II:647; III:159
Donalson, Matthew I:441
Donavan, John II:609
Dond, Chandler IV:223
Dond, Richard I:54
Done, Richard IV:223
Done, Thomas II:163
Donel, Ezekiel I:815
Donelson, Robert III:631
Doney, William II:513
Dongan, James III:580
Donita, Francis I:925
Donley, Stephen II:423
Donnell, Andrew III:419
Donnell, Daniel III:419
Donnell, George III:633
Donnell, John III:686
Donnell, Joshua P. I:488
Donnell, Jotham I:235
Donnell, Nathaniel II:677
Donnell, Obadiah I:235
Donnell, William III:633
Donnelly, James II:181
Donnelly, John II:692
Donnelly, Thomas II:367; III:647
Donnison, William I:600
Donoho, James II:7
Doobler, Abraham II:729
Dooley, Jacob III:233
Doolittle, Charles I:124
Doolittle, David II:731
Doolittle, Eber I:47
Doolittle, George II:278
Doolittle, Hackaliah II:181
Doolittle, Joseph I:55
Doolittle, Nathaniel II:528
Doolittle, Obed I:125
Doolittle, Uri II:451
Doolittle, W. II:558
Door, Allen I:173
Door, Clarissa I:173

367

Door, Margaret I:173
Door, Martha Ann I:173
Doran, James II:610
Doran, Myles I:393
Dorand, Richard II:353
Dorch, William III:230
Dorchester, Alexander II:251
Dorchester, Reuben II:463
Dore, Benaiah I:729
Dore, Jonathan I:750
Dorey, Bartlett II:108
Dorey, James II:317
Dorgin, John III:67
Dorland, Lambert II:642
Dorman, Gershom I:19
Dorman, Israel I:307
Dorman, John I:234
Dorman, Ludwig II:687
Dorman, Timothy I:413
Dorn, Abraham II:377
Dornbimch, John II:647
Dorney, John I:672
Doron, Terence III:742
Dorothy, Charles I:915
Dorr, Edward I:413, 805
Dorr, Melcher III:416
Dorr, Samuel I:338, 655
Dorr, William I:192
Dorrah, Arthur I:943
Dorsett, Dudley F. I:171
Dorsett, Edmund I:171
Dorsett, James I:171
Dorsett, Jedediah I:171
Dorsett, John I:171
Dorsett, Salome I:171
Dorsett, Thomas I:171
Dorsett, William I:171
Dorsey, Bartlett II:108
Dorsey, Catherine I:174
Dorsey, Danie II:289
Dorsey, Honour I:174
Dorsey, James II:268
Dorsey, John I:174
Dorsey, Margaret I:174
Dorsey, Mary I:174
Dorsey, Patrick I:174
Dortch, Abel IV:12
Dorton, Henry III:808
Dorvill, John II:743
Doss, John III:552, 758
Doss, John C. II:119
Doss, William III:579
Dossett, Thomas III:293
Dossey, John III:252
Dota, John II:364
Doten, Edward I:560
Doten, James I:430
Doten, Samuel I:247
Doton, Ephraim I:729
Dotson, Esau III:121
Dotson, Richard III:842
Dotter, Sam. Solomon II:731
Dotty, Isaac III:555
Dotty, Moses II:216
Doty, Asa IV:218
Doty, Azariah III:584
Doty, Benjamin II:245, 385

Doty, Danforth II:451
Doty, Daniel I:750
Doty, Ellis I:xvi; II:214
Doty, Ezra II:684
Doty, Isaac II:350, 539
Doty, Jacob II:528
Doty, James I:430; II:63
Doty, Jerathmiel I:335, 897
Doty, John I:179; II:147, 493
Doty, Joseph II:63
Doty, Nathaniel I:180; II:712
Doty, Peter IV:263
Doty, Samuel II:223
Doty, Thomas I:554
Doty, William II:313; III:21
Doty, Zebulon II:758
Douberman, Henry III:727
Doubleday, Asahel I:986
Doubleday, Joseph I:637, 915
Doubleday, Seth II:483
Doud, Benjamin II:424
Doud, Jesse I:897
Doud, Solomon I:60
Doud, William II:342
Doudeen, Thomas III:730
Doudon, Clementius III:260
Dougan, John IV:98
Douge, Peter III:370
Dougherty, Andrew II:698
Dougherty, Archibald II:579
Dougherty, Barnabas III:36
Dougherty, George III:702
Dougherty, Hannah II:622
Dougherty, Henry II:587;
   III:194
Dougherty, James II:644;
   III:189, 649
Dougherty, John II:622, 683,
   733; III:247, 478
Dougherty, Matilda II:622
Dougherty, Patrick III:664
Dougherty, Samuel II:622
Dougherty, Sarah II:622
Dougherty, William II:41, 735;
   III:21, 298; IV:67, 91, 221
Doughton, William IV:19
Doughty, Benjamin I:247
Doughty, Christopher II:697
Doughty, Elias II:232
Doughty, Ichabod I:180
Doughty, Jacob II:52
Doughty, James I:205, 247
Doughty, James, 2d I:180
Doughty, Joseph I:247
Doughty, Linton II:77
Doughty, Nathaniel, I:180
Doughty, Thomas II:39
Douglas, Edward III:594
Douglas, Jeremiah IV:28
Douglas, John III:625
Douglas, Joseph II:211
Douglas, Nathaniel II:202
Douglas, Thomas III:137, 575,
   742
Douglass, Abigail I:174
Douglass, Alexander II:60
Douglass, Andrew II:692

Douglass, Charles I:833
Douglass, David I:573; II:451
Douglass, Elijah I:174
Douglass, Elisha I:168
Douglass, James I:21, 172;
   II:522
Douglass, Jane I:174
Douglass, Jas. II:560
Douglass, John I:172, 215;
   II:728, 743
Douglass, Phineas I:707
Douglass, Randall IV:189
Douglass, Robert II:663;
   III:67, 600
Douglass, William II:181;
   III:542
Douthit, Silas III:279
Dove, Richard IV:265
Dove, Thomas III:595
Dove, William III:822
Dovenberger, Jacob IV:170
Dover, Andrew II:677
Dover, John II:677
Dovey, Peter II:715
Dow, Benjamin I:167, 934
Dow, Fuleard III:734
Dow, Henry I:205
Dow, James I:665
Dow, Jesse I:750
Dow, Joseph I:765
Dow, Joshua I:165
Dow, Moses I:924
Dow, Nathan I:721; II:483
Dow, Nathaniel I:934
Dow, Reuben I:665
Dow, Salmon I:750
Dow, Samuel I:600, 740
Dow, Stephen I:757
Dow, Zebulon I:771
Dowd, Conner IV:229
Dowd, Daniel II:483
Dowd, Michael II:609
Dowden, James III:302
Dowden, Moses III:110
Dowderman, Jacob II:677
Dowdle, William III:58
Dowdney, Samuel II:22
Dowe, William I:960
Dowen, Anne II:191
Dowen, John II:191
Dowen, Oliver II:191
Dowen, Sarah II:191
Dower, Jacob IV:93
Dowers, Conrad IV:87
Dowler, George II:277
Dowler, Thomas IV:152
Dowlf, Ellis I:205
Dowling, James I:960; III:201
Down, Jabez I:691
Down, John I:393
Down, William III:21
Downe, Nathaniel H. I:602
Downer, Cushman I:949
Downer, Eliphalet I:611
Downer, James I:950
Downer, Jason I:750
Downer, John, 2d I:160

Dudley, John I:909; II:435
Dudley, Mahala I:682
Dudley, Mehitabel I:682
Dudley, Nathan I:180, 283, 515
Dudley, Paul I:638
Dudley, Roswell II:377
Dudley, Samuel I:176; III:808
Dudley, Thomas I:176, 924
Dudley, Trueworthy I:176
Dudley, William I:176
Due, James III:50
Duesler, John II:414
Duesler, Marcus II:438
Dufault, Michael II:553
Duff, Henry II:593
Duff, James II:689
Duffey, Edward II:133
Duffey, Michael II:592
Duffield, Abraham III:815
Duffield, J. M. I:xii
Duffield, James II:592
Duffy, Henry III:21
Dugan, Daniel II:733
Dugan, George II:604
Dugan, Henry IV:189
Dugan, William IV:181
Duggan, William III:527
Dugger, John III:622
Duke, Clevears III:716
Duke, Hardeman III:439
Duke, Hardin III:802
Duke, Henry III:233
Duke, James III:433
Duke, John IV:43
Duke, Matthew III:269
Duke, William III:439
Dukes, Isaac IV:284
Dulany, Benjamin III:620
Dulin, Jane III:535
Dulin, Jefferson III:535
Dulin, John II:755; III:694
Dulin, Sally III:535
Dulin, William III:535
Dull, Christian II:666
Dulton, Abel I:970
Dulvis, John II:326
Dumaresque, Ebenezer II:347
Dumas, H. I:xiii
Dumbleton, Abigail Brised II:187
Dumbleton, Benj. II:187
Dumbleton, Benjamin II:187
Dumbleton, Betsy II:187
Dumbleton, James II:187
Dumbleton, Polly II:187
Dumbolton, Benj. II:187
Dummer, Jeremiah I:265
Dummer, Rich'd (heirs) I:265
Dumont, John II:81
Dunavant, Josiah III:817
Dunaway, Samuel III:290
Dunbar, Abner I:638
Dunbar, Amos I:47; II:735
Dunbar, Catherine II:553
Dunbar, David I:187, 259
Dunbar, Ebenezer I:560

Dunbar, Elijah I:274
Dunbar, Eliza I:171
Dunbar, Enoch I:573
Dunbar, George II:479
Dunbar, Jacob I:283
Dunbar, Jesse I:573
Dunbar, Joel II:278
Dunbar, John II:483
Dunbar, Jonathan III:815
Dunbar, Joseph I:15
Dunbar, Josiah I:473
Dunbar, Melzar I:559
Dunbar, Miles II:302
Dunbar, Muril I:171
Dunbar, Nancy Morse I:171
Dunbar, Nathaniel I:371
Dunbar, Nehemiah II:553
Dunbar, Obed I:302
Dunbar, Olive I:171
Dunbar, Peter I:171
Dunbar, Prince I:171
Dunbar, Robert I:915
Dunbar, Samuel I:171, 995
Dunbar, Thomas I:462; III:301
Dunbar, William IV:106, 292
Duncan, Alexander II:657
Duncan, Charles III:699
Duncan, David I:721
Duncan, Elijah III:618
Duncan, Francis I:338
Duncan, Gabriel III:301
Duncan, George III:386; IV:83
Duncan, J. M. I:xiii
Duncan, James II:660, 755; III:135, 470
Duncan, Jared II:105
Duncan, Jesse IV:88
Duncan, John I:783; II:117; III:39, 470, 569, 777; IV:12
Duncan, Joseph III:625
Duncan, Rebecca III:470
Duncan, Robert II:660
Duncan, Samuel III:298
Duncan, Simeon I:638
Duncan, Thomas II:181; III:607
Duncan, William III:483
Duncombe, Edward I:32
Dunden, Mills III:386
Dunfee, Cornelius I:192
Dunham, Abisha II:483
Dunham, Ammi I:180
Dunham, Azariah II:71
Dunham, Calvin II:451
Dunham, Cornelius II:181, 516
Dunham, Daniel II:346
Dunham, Ebenezer I:881
Dunham, Edward II:477; IV:67
Dunham, Elijah I:559
Dunham, Elisha I:867
Dunham, Ephraim II:245
Dunham, George I:559
Dunham, Gershom I:986
Dunham, Gideon II:404
Dunham, Holton II:322
Dunham, Jacob IV:263

Dunham, James I:142; II:284
Dunham, Jehu II:71
Dunham, Jeremiah II:284, 561
Dunham, John II:63
Dunham, Joseph I:338
Dunham, Moses I:283
Dunham, Obadiah I:929
Dunham, Robert I:559; II:688
Dunham, Sally II:561
Dunham, Samuel I:361; II:322, 469, 479, 640
Dunham, Simeon II:483
Dunham, Solomon I:783
Dunham, Stephen I:142
Dunham, Timothy II:289
Dunham, William I:371
Dunhane, Richardson II:565
Dunikin, Daniel III:545
Dunkill, George II:125
Dunkin, Anthony III:584
Dunkle, George II:439
Dunkle, Nicholas II:438
Dunkleberger, Peter II:733
Dunkley, John III:783
Dunkley, Moses III:783
Dunlap, Andrew I:849
Dunlap, James I:205; II:181; III:237, 527
Dunlap, John I:205
Dunlap, Joseph III:545
Dunlap, Robert IV:294
Dunlap, Samuel II:659; III:592; IV:169
Dunlap, Thomas II:263
Dunlap, William III:475, 506; IV:11, 289
Dunlary, Francis IV:291
Dunlop, George I:473
Dunn, Aaron IV:80
Dunn, Alexander III:290
Dunn, Andrew II:643
Dunn, Carey II:445
Dunn, Charles IV:4
Dunn, Christopher I:264
Dunn, Duncan IV:189
Dunn, George III:387
Dunn, Isaac II:85, 659
Dunn, James II:373; III:746
Dunn, James F. II:72
Dunn, Joel II:72
Dunn, John I:639; II:532; III:214
Dunn, Joseph III:264
Dunn, Joshua I:180; III:692
Dunn, Nicholas III:416
Dunn, Patrick II:4
Dunn, Philip II:714
Dunn, Samuel II:544
Dunn, Thomas III:177
Dunn, Timothy II:217
Dunn, William I:618; III:45, 595
Dunnavant, William III:817
Dunnehill, Frank I:585
Dunnells, John I:169
Dunning, Abram I:925
Dunning, Butler III:56

Dunning, David I:85
Dunning, Dennis II:677
Dunning, Ebenezer II:504
Dunning, James II:504
Dunning, John I:247, 960
Dunning, Josiah II:544
Dunning, Michael II:339, 565
Dunning, Stephen II:402
Dunnington, William III:232
Dunsett, Cato I:338
Dunsmoor, James III:89
Dunston, Almon III:778
Dunston, John II:263
Duntlen, Nathaniel I:393
Dunton, David II:322
Dunton, James I:618
Dunton, Joseph I:976
Dunton, Levi I:618
Dunton, Samuel I:618
Dunton, Silas I:638
Dunton, William I:929
Dunwell, Stephen IV:249
Dunwell, William I:338
Dunworth, George I:148
Dupee, John I:638
Dupelle, Antonie III:50
Du Peron, Jean III:111
Dupey, John III:826
Duplex, Prince II:337
Dupuy, Daniel II:172
Dupuy, William III:267
Durand, Alexander I:877
Durand, Andrew IV:249
Durand, Ebenezer I:10
Durand, Eleazer II:305
Durand, Fish II:373
Durand, Isaac I:2
Durand, John I:60
Durand, Joseph II:400
Durand, Lemuel I:125
Durand, William I:124
Durant, Allen II:354, 395
Durant, David I:934
Durant, Isaac I:498
Durant, Joshua I:960
Durant, Reuben I:488
Durell, Peter I:215
Durfee, Benjamin I:371
Durfee, Ebenezer I:924
Durfee, Joseph I:371
Durfee, Richard I:818
Durfee, Robert I:823
Durfee, Walter I:960
Durfey, John II:362
Durgen, John I:307
Durgin, John I:729
Durgin, Joseph I:776
Durgin, Josiah I:676
Durgin, Richard I:776
Durham, Asa II:390
Durham, Charnel III:502
Durham, Enoch II:43
Durham, James II:568; III:231, 648
Durham, John III:254; IV:214
Durham, Mastin III:329
Durham, Matthew III:173

Durham, Stephen II:255
Durham, Washington III:524
Durkee, Asahel I:950
Durkee, Benjamin I:887, 998
Durkee, John I:750
Durkee, Lydius II:539
Durkee, Marshall S. I:450
Durkee, Moses II:539
Durkee, Nathan II:539
Durkee, Nathaniel III:137
Durkee, Solomon IV:218
Durkee, William I:148
Durland, Thomas II:133
Durney, James II:163
Durney, Philip II:758
Durnham, James III:196
Durossett, Samuel II:119
Durow, William I:205
Durphey, James II:500
Durrell, David I:306
Durrett, Claiborne III:687
Durrill, Benjamin I:192
Durturff, Philip II:550
Duryea, Charles IV:278
Duryee, John II:63
Dusenbury, John II:211
Dusett, John II:289
Dusinberry, William IV:277
Dusky, John II:649
Dustin, John I:783
Dustin, Moses II:718
Dustin, Stephen I:721
Duston, Amos II:183
Duston, Chandler R. I:175
Duston, Ezekiel I:175
Duston, Ezekiel W. I:175
Duston, Hannah I:175
Duston, John I:175
Duston, Leander G. I:175
Duston, Perigrine I:175
Duston, York I:175
Duston, Zacheus II:220
Dutcher, Abraham II:223
Dutcher, Barnet II:310
Dutcher, Charles II:195
Dutcher, Henry IV:193
Dutcher, Jacob II:445
Dutcher, Marvin II:195
Dutcher, Simeon II:414
Dutcher, Solomon II:479
Duttar, Oliver I:39
Dutton, Amasa I:133
Dutton, Asa I:67, 976
Dutton, Ephraim I:915
Dutton, John I:707
Dutton, Joseph I:97
Dutton, Oliver I:462
Dutton, Thomas I:741
Dutton, Timothy I:498
Dutton, Titus II:232
Dutton, William I:960
Duval, Joseph III:12
Duval, Samuel III:12
Duvall, Benjamin III:55
Duvall, William III:758
Duvey, Emanuel II:716
Duzey, Thomas II:8

Dwelley, Allen I:220
Dwelly, Jeremiah I:818
Dwelly, John I:299
Dwelly, Joseph I:638
Dwelly, Pearce II:513
Dwinel, Archelaus I:904
Dwinel, Solomon I:618
Dwinell, Amos I:950
Dwinnell, Jonathan I:740
Dwinnell, Thomas I:740
D'Wolf, Daniel I:98
D'Wolf, John I:812
D'Wolf, Stephen I:67
Dyal, John III:297
Dych, Peter II:692
Dyche, Charles III:584
Dyckman, Benjamin II:546
Dyckman, Richard II:268
Dyckman, William N. II:546
Dycus, Edward III:593
Dye, Daniel II:113
Dye, George IV:24
Dye, John IV:171
Dyer, Alexander III:9
Dyer, Amherst II:539
Dyer, Baldy III:533
Dyer, Bickford I:179
Dyer, David III:533
Dyer, Eleanor III:9
Dyer, Eliab I:142
Dyer, Elisha III:162
Dyer, Emanuel II:728
Dyer, Ephraim I:187
Dyer, Ezeck I:824
Dyer, Francis III:717
Dyer, Ichabod I:888
Dyer, Isaac I:306
Dyer, Isaac, 1st I:205
Dyer, James I:480; II:353; III:21, 533
Dyer, John B. III:9
Dyer, Jonathan III:657
Dyer, Joseph I:39
Dyer, Manoah III:570
Dyer, Mary III:533
Dyer, Moses I:691
Dyer, Paul I:180
Dyer, Simpson III:533
Dyer, Stephen I:986
Dyer, Susanna III:533
Dyer, Walter II:677; III:3-4
Dyer, William III:9, 533
Dyer, Willie III:533
Dygert, Peter II:438
Dygert, Severenus II:517
Dyke, John III:269
Dykee, Daniel I:611
Dykeman, Benjamin II:490
Dyre, Joseph II:743
Dyre, Solomon I:544
Dysart, James III:199
Dysart, John III:566
Dyson, John III:765
Dyson, Robert III:730

Eads, Charles III:300
Eads, Henry IV:71
Eaerl, James III:52
Eagar, Archibald II:53
Eager, George II:284
Eager, Haron I:618
Eager, James II:400
Eager, Jason I:840
Eager, Noah I:431
Eager, Oliver I:639
Eager, Peter II:181
Eagle, John II:72
Eagle, William III:727
Eagles, Michael I:498
Eaker, George II:439
Eakin, Samuel III:627
Eakins, Gabriel IV:231
Eakins, John II:755
Eakins, Wm. III:566
Eames, Ebenezer I:215
Eames, Gershum I:639
Eames, James I:284; II:451
Eames, Jonathan I:516
Eames, Jotham I:741
Eames, Samuel I:265, 595
Earenfight, Jacob IV:221
Earl, Amarilla I:614
Earl, Amasa I:614
Earl, Camilla H. I:614
Earl, Dominy I:134
Earl, Eliza II:193
Earl, Israel II:55
Earl, James II:193
Earl, Jonathan II:392
Earl, Julia I:614
Earl, Mary II:193
Earl, Moses II:385
Earl, Peter II:193
Earl, Philip II:193
Earl, Richard II:193
Earl, Stephen II:322
Earl, William I:585; II:193
Earle, David I:915
Earle, Joel I:960
Earle, John I:639; II:77
Earle, Robert I:824
Earle, Samuel III:95
Earles, Joseph II:439
Earll, Jonas II:561, 564
Earnest, Charles III:21
Earnest, George II:593; III:175
Earnest, William III:21
Earp, Edward III:379
Earp, Josiah III:318
Earthen, Reuben III:664
Earthforth, Samuel I:824
Earthman, Isaac III:575
Easby, Benj I:530
Easely, Drury III:529
Easland, James II:410
Easland, John I:349
Easley, Daniel III:433
Eason, Jacob III:382
Easor, Aaron II:8
East, Isham III:820
East, John I:805
Eastabrook, John I:499

Eastabrook, Nehemiah I:499
Eastabrooks, Benj. II:514
Eastbrook, Warren I:976
Eastburn, Betsey I:593
Eastburn, John I:593
Eastburn, John H. I:593
Eastburn, Mary I:593
Easter, John III:812
Easterbrook, Joel I:771
Eastin, William III:674
Eastis, Elisha III:214
Eastlick, Alexander II:332
Eastman, Amelia I:683
Eastman, Asahel I:442
Eastman, Benjamin I:771
Eastman, Charles IV:259
Eastman, Clark II:539
Eastman, Daniel I:284, 307
Eastman, Deliverance IV:269
Eastman, Ebenezer I:699
Eastman, Eli I:960
Eastman, Henry I:683, 757
Eastman, Jacob I:235, 716
Eastman, James I:284, 721,
  750
Eastman, John I:215
Eastman, Joseph I:451
Eastman, Josiah I:888
Eastman, Nathaniel I:765
Eastman, Obadiah I:699
Eastman, Peasley IV:223
Eastman, Reuben Kimball
  I:683
Eastman, Sally I:683
Eastman, Samuel I:765, 888
Eastman, Thomas I:665, 750;
  III:647
Eastman, William I:382, 717
Eastman, Zachariah I:180
Easton, Ashbel I:657
Easton, Eliphalet I:13
Easton, Henry I:60
Easton, Julian I:47
Easton, Moses IV:300
Easton, Obadiah I:824
Easton, Richard II:708
Easton, Samuel II:564
Easton, Theophilus I:148
Easton, W. C. I:xiii
Eastwick, John II:9
Eastwood, Daniel II:484
Eastwood, Israel III:163
Easty, Benj I:530
Eaton, Aaron II:700
Eaton, Abiathan II:240
Eaton, Abijah I:771, 909
Eaton, Abram I:960
Eaton, Benjamin I:295, 771;
  II:298
Eaton, Betsey I:174
Eaton, Brigham II:344
Eaton, Christopher III:454
Eaton, Cyril II:464
Eaton, Daniel I:960
Eaton, David I:771
Eaton, Ebenezer I:265, 320,
  516, 665; II:377

Eaton, Eleazer II:464
Eaton, Eliab I:295
Eaton, Eliah I:224
Eaton, Enoch I:960
Eaton, Ephraim II:284
Eaton, Ezra II:305
Eaton, Giles III:65
Eaton, Henry III:220
Eaton, Isaiah I:976
Eaton, Israel I:574
Eaton, John I:717, 783; II:414
Eaton, Jonathan I:721
Eaton, Joseph I:515, 757;
  III:331
Eaton, Joseph J. I:970
Eaton, Josiah I:148
Eaton, Lemuel I:783
Eaton, Levi I:771
Eaton, Lot II:313
Eaton, Luther I:516, 867
Eaton, Maverick I:976
Eaton, Moses I:741
Eaton, Nathan I:174, 929
Eaton, Nathaniel I:498
Eaton, Nathaniel, 2d I:454
Eaton, Noah I:611
Eaton, Origen II:561
Eaton, Orrigen II:151
Eaton, Pearson I:595
Eaton, Peter II:165
Eaton, Peter, 1st II:159
Eaton, Ruth I:174
Eaton, Samuel I:180, 414,
  881; II:419
Eaton, Solomon I:74
Eaton, Stephen II:464
Eaton, Sylvanus I:771
Eaton, Timothy I:498
Eaton, Uriah I:618
Eaton, William I:307, 600,
  688, 776; III:353
Eatton, Joseph IV:252
Eaty, William III:650
Ebb, Emanuel II:671
Ebbs, Emanuel III:46
Eberhart, Jacob III:177
Eberle, Henry I:593
Ebitz, William I:560
Eblin, Samuel IV:17
Ebner, Caspar II:692
Ebright, Philip IV:245
Ebzey, William III:543
Eccleston, Betty I:29
Eccleston, David II:377
Eccleston, Erastus I:29
Eccleston, Giles I:29
Eccleston, Ichabod I:29
Eccleston, Nabby I:29
Eccleston, Wilcox I:29
Echard, Charles I:469
Echert, John II:532
Echols, William III:364
Eck, Samuel II:14
Eckels, Arthur II:635
Eckerson, Cornelius II:58, 439
Eckerson, Teunis II:514
Eckert, Stephen II:342

Elwell, Luther I:333
Elwell, Robert I:393, 611
Elwell, Thomas IV:197
Elwell, Zebulon I:393
Elwood, Abram II:211
Elwood, Isaac II:181, 211
Ely, Andrew II:342
Ely, Daniel I:98
Ely, Darius IV:279
Ely, Enoch I:462
Ely, Gurdon I:117
Ely, Jabez II:240
Ely, Jacob I:108
Ely, John II:743
Ely, John Edwards I:454
Ely, Joseph I:462
Ely, Jube I:462
Ely, Michael III:50
Ely, Moses II:63
Ely, Wells II:334
Ely, William III:714
Emberson, William II:52
Embrek, Christopher IV:245
Embry, Abraham III:540
Emerick, John II:571
Emerick, Matthias II:105
Emerick, Philip II:738
Emerick, Wilhelmus II:532
Emerson, Amos I:722
Emerson, Benjamin I:393
Emerson, Charles I:692
Emerson, Elias I:639
Emerson, Enoch I:986
Emerson, Ephraim I:367
Emerson, Harriet I:686
Emerson, Henry III:381, 513
Emerson, James I:499, 686
Emerson, John I:639, 692,
   741; III:223, 334
Emerson, Jonathan I:493;
   IV:189
Emerson, Mark I:765
Emerson, Mary I:493, 656
Emerson, Michael I:722
Emerson, Nehemiah I:656
Emerson, Oliver II:133
Emerson, Parker I:595
Emerson, Peter I:757
Emerson, Sam. T. I:686
Emerson, Samuel I:161, 307,
   414
Emerson, Samuel F. I:686
Emerson, Samuel M. I:757
Emerson, Stephen II:745
Emerson, Thomas I:413
Emerson, Timothy I:686
Emerson, William I:516
Emerton, Thomas I:750
Emery, Daniel I:193, 235, 717
Emery, Ephraim I:393
Emery, Isaac I:307
Emery, Jacob I:235
Emery, James I:307
Emery, Job I:307
Emery, Joel I:950
Emery, John I:224
Emery, Joseph I:162

Emery, Joshua I:180
Emery, Nathaniel I:224
Emery, Peter II:551
Emery, Ralph I:235
Emery, Rama I:729
Emery, Samuel I:295
Emery, Stephen I:639
Emery, Thomas I:757
Emery, William I:741
Emes, Alexander I:757
Emes, Charles I:430
Emes, Jonathan I:498
Emes, Luther I:595
Emmel, George II:48
Emmerson, Ephraim II:206
Emmerson, George I:722
Emmerson, John I:515
Emmerson, Joseph IV:249
Emmerson, Nehemiah I:394
Emmerson, Reuben III:275
Emmerton, Ephraim I:393
Emmery, Edward IV:32
Emmes, Nathaniel I:600
Emmest, George III:540
Emmis, Joshua IV:249
Emmitt, John IV:284
Emmonds, Joseph II:133
Emmons, Arthur II:483
Emmons, Daniel S. I:117
Emmons, Horatio II:175
Emmons, James III:778
Emmons, John II:524; III:851
Emmons, Jonathan I:909
Emmons, Noah II:419
Emmons, Pendleton I:307
Emmons, Phineas I:47
Emmons, Samuel I:117
Emmons, Solomon I:986;
   II:539
Emmory, Peter III:679
Emonons, John I:699
Emory, Eliphalet II:528
Emory, William III:55
Empie, John F. II:439
Enders, Jacob III:514
Endicott, Moses III:260
Endicott, Samuel I:737
Enekes, Jesse I:824
Engal, George II:752
England, John III:834
England, Joseph III:565;
   IV:153
Engle, Adam III:625
Engle, Jacob II:743
Engle, John III:562
Engle, Michael II:81
Engler, Leonard II:739
Engletraupt, John II:714
Englis, Andrew II:337, 561
Englis, Rachel II:561
English, Alvah I:864
English, Charles III:724
English, George II:610
English, James II:578, 669
English, John I:864; II:337,
   669
English, Joseph II:626

English, Mehitable I:864
English, Robert II:392; IV:239
English, Thomas II:626
English, William II:351, 626;
   III:194; IV:235
Engly, Timothy I:639
Engram, Timothy I:481
Enlow, Deason III:489
Ennis, Abraham I:833
Ennis, Eliza II:193
Ennis, Paul I:833
Ennis, Sylvanus II:193
Ennis, William I:837
Eno, Levi I:142
Eno, Reuben I:39
Enos, Alexander II:464
Enos, David I:39, 898
Enos, Elisha II:414
Enos, Matthias II:354
Enos, Nathaniel II:146
Enos, Stephen IV:140
Ensign, Daniel II:469
Ensign, Edward F. I:655
Ensign, Eliphalet I:108
Ensign, James I:39
Ensign, Otis II:373
Ensminger, Henry II:649
Ensworth, Jesse I:148
Ensworth, Samuel I:489
Ent, Daniel, Senr. II:68
Ent, John III:4
Entrot, Henry II:310, 562
Entsminger, John IV:203
Entwisle, Thomas I:585
Enyart, Benjamin IV:253
Eoff, Isaac III:614
Eperly, George IV:98
Ephland, David IV:82
Eply, John II:651
Epperson, Francis III:275
Epperson, John IV:121
Epperson, Thomas III:587
Eppes, Peter III:768
Epposon, Thompson III:162
Epps, Moses III:783
Epps, Richard III:541
Erb, Henry II:738
Erdman, Andrew II:738
Ernest, Felix III:584
Errickson, Thomas II:77
Erskine, David I:274
Erskine, John I:741
Erven, John II:72
Ervin, Charles III:245
Ervin, David II:94, 112
Ervin, James I:672; III:54;
   IV:165
Erwin, A. III:635
Erwin, David IV:75
Erwin, Hen. II:647
Erwin, Jacob II:610
Erwin, James II:342; IV:295
Erwin, John II:133; III:582
Erwin, John, 2d II:298
Erwin, William II:298, 677;
   III:404
Esbridge, William III:678

375

Eschleman, Abraham II:728
Esher, Frederick II:625
Esher, George II:625
Eskridge, Elizabeth III:849
Eskridge, George III:704
Eskridge, Wiliam III:849
Esler, Conrad II:48
Esley, Moses II:743
Espey, Samuel III:347, 429
Espy, George II:714
Espy, James III:156
Espy, John III:156
Esselstyn, J. B. II:557
Esseltine, Jacob II:385
Essender, John III:21
Esser, Jacob II:702
Essick, Joseph III:415
Essig, Joseph III:415
Essix, Joseph III:415
Estabrook, Nathan IV:235
Estabrook, Nehemiah II:274
Estell, William III:217
Esten, John I:824
Estes, Abraham III:190, 298
Estes, Clement III:189
Estes, Elijah III:660, 738
Estes, George III:783
Estes, John III:583, 803;
    IV:113
Estes, Rowland III:695
Estes, Thomas III:597
Estill, Samuel III:302
Estill, Wallace, Sen. III:580
Estin, Thomas III:190
Estler, John II:81
Esty, Edward I:265
Esty, Moses II:68
Etchberger, William III:46
Etchberger, Wolfgang III:46
Etchison, Edmund III:444
Ethell, Anthony III:771
Ethell, Benjamin IV:117
Etheridge, John III:538
Etherington, John III:738
Ethridge, Stephen I:776
Etter, John III:636
Ettick, George I. II:414
Etting, Henry II:532
Etting, John II:385
Ettinger, Jacob IV:211
Etz, William II:463
Eubank, Royal III:687
Euler, Conrad III:21
Eustice, Jacob I:187
Eustis, Cyprus I:175
Eustis, Hannah I:175
Eustis, John C. I:175
Eustis, Mary I:175
Eustis, Minerva I:175
Eustis, Soton I:175
Eustis, Thomas I:175
Evans, Abel II:677
Evans, Abiathar I:898
Evans, Allen I:55
Evans, Andrew II:220; III:610;
    IV:84
Evans, Anthony III:847; IV:223

Evans, Asa II:385
Evans, Barnabas II:305
Evans, Batte III:481
Evans, Benjamin I:307, 824
Evans, Catherine II:194
Evans, Colton I:976
Evans, Cornelius III:622
Evans, Daniel I:871
Evans, David I:98; II:377
Evans, E. T. II:552
Evans, Echisa I:683
Evans, Edith I:683
Evans, Edward I:665
Evans, Eldad II:419
Evans, Elisha, Sen. III:408
Evans, Eliza I:683
Evans, Evan II:645
Evans, Frederick I:171
Evans, F.S. I:xii
Evans, George IV:196
Evans, Gettrel III:584
Evans, Gilbert III:584
Evans, Hannah I:683
Evans, Henry III:831
Evans, Isaac II:227
Evans, J. III:334
Evans, Jacob I:683
Evans, James I:162; III:2, 677;
    IV:26
Evans, James Pratt I:291
Evans, Jenkins II:4
Evans, John I:295; II:419,
    435, 674; III:296, 318, 808;
    IV:196
Evans, Joseph I:192, 915;
    II:262; IV:8
Evans, Josiah I:171; II:259
Evans, Laura II:194
Evans, Leonard I:362
Evans, Lewis I:595
Evans, Mary I:171, 683
Evans, Moses I:39, 874
Evans, Nathan II:248
Evans, Nathaniel I:187, 741
Evans, Obadiah II:41
Evans, Ordin III:611
Evans, Osgood I:683
Evans, Owen III:76
Evans, Perry III:492, 519
Evans, Philip III:503
Evans, Randall II:505
Evans, Reuben III:396
Evans, Robert I:171; III:4
Evans, Sally I:171
Evans, Samuel II:414; III:441,
    556
Evans, Shirebiah II:284
Evans, Silas II:223
Evans, Simeon I:688
Evans, Thomas I:414; II:22,
    133, 569; III:46
Evans, William I:283, 362,
    371, 683; II:194, 464; III:36,
    529, 806, 840, 848
Evans, William, Sen. III:181
Evans, Wm. R. II:194
Evans, Zachariah III:122

Evarts, Eber I:925
Evarts, Ezra I:925
Evarts, Reuben I:943
Evarts, Stephen II:240
Eveland, Daniel II:741
Eveland, Peter II:713
Eveleth, Aaron I:414
Eveleth, Isaac I:248
Eveleth, John I:473
Eveleth, Joseph I:413
Eveleth, Joseph (2) I:414
Eveleth, Mrs. James I:265
Evens, Isaac II:172
Everest, Benjamin I:867
Everest, Daniel I:47
Everest, Elisha II:337
Everett, Andrew II:451
Everett, Daniel II:255
Everett, Jeremiah II:223
Everett, Josiah I:224
Everett, Levi I:716
Everett, Nathaniel III:461
Everett, Oliver II:278
Everett, Pelatiah I:618
Everett, Samuel III:571
Everett, William III:603
Everhart, Catherine IV:164
Everhart, George III:754
Everhart, John II:677, 702
Everhart, Lawrence III:29
Everhart, Lydia IV:164
Everhart, Peter III:415
Everhart, Samuel IV:164
Everingham, William II:31
Everit, Abner I:108
Everit, Ebe I:108
Everitt, Daniel II:518
Everitt, James II:41
Everitt, John II:36, 426
Everitt, Robert III:538
Everitt, Thomas III:446
Everly, Simeon III:808
Evers, Andrew II:754
Evers, Sampson III:760
Eversole, Peter III:853
Everson, George R. II:638
Everson, Joseph I:574
Everson, Samuel I:574
Everton, Benjamin I:535
Everton, Thomas IV:270
Everton, Zephaniah I:205
Everts, Daniel II:528
Everts, Nathaniel I:108
Everts, Solomon II:445
Everts, Stephen II:108
Every, Miles I:337
Evins, Benoni II:290
Evins, David IV:84
Ewell, Charles III:336
Ewell, Maria D. III:336
Ewer, Jonathan I:192
Ewer, Paul II:528
Ewers, Rufus I:765
Ewing, Alexander III:566
Ewing, Bennington II:22
Ewing, George III:569; IV:49
Ewing, J. IV:100

380

Fite, Leonard III:618
Fithain, Isaac IV:289
Fitts, John III:703
Fitts, Samuel I:248
Fitz, Abraham I:193
Fitz, Robert W. III:807
Fitzer, Jacob II:694
Fitzgerald, Aaron III:4
Fitzgerald, Benj. III:722
Fitzgerald, Benjamin III:234
Fitzgerald, Charles IV:100
Fitzgerald, Daniel III:279
Fitzgerald, David I:235
Fitzgerald, George III:141, 562
Fitzgerald, Harvey III:820
Fitzgerald, Henry IV:182
Fitzgerald, James II:9
Fitzgerald, John I:205; III:74
Fitzgerald, Nicholas III:58
Fitzgerald, Patrick II:632
Fitzgerald, Thomas IV:102
Fitzgerald, William I:481;
    III:419
Fitzhugh, Daniel III:844
Fitzhugh, William III:557
Fitzimmons, William II:733
Fitzpatrick, Jacob III:203
Fitzpatrick, James III:203, 240
Fitzpatrick, Nathan III:62
Fitzpatrick, Peggy III:203
Fitzpatrick, Sally III:203
Fitzpatrick, Samuel III:203
Fitzsimmins, John II:354
Fitzsimmons, George II:179
Fitzsimmons, John II:610
Fitzsimmons, Thomas III:247
Fitzsimmons, Tho's III:337
Fix, Henry IV:247
Fix, Philip III:831
Flack, James, 1st III:325
Flagg, Asa I:221
Flagg, Ebenezer I:877
Flagg, Eleazer I:640
Flagg, Elijah II:500
Flagg, Gershom I:758
Flagg, Hiram I:517
Flagg, Isaac I:299
Flagg, Jonathan I:639
Flagg, Josiah I:950
Flagg, Nathaniel I:516
Flagg, Samuel A. I:205
Flagg, William I:970
Flagge, Abijah I:98
Flake, George IV:223
Flamming, James I:193
Flanagan, William III:165
Flanders, Abner I:765
Flanders, Alice I:683
Flanders, Benjamin I:683
Flanders, Daniel I:414
Flanders, David I:717
Flanders, Dennis A. II:439
Flanders, Ezekiel I:879, 995
Flanders, Henry II:439
Flanders, Jacob I:888; III:224
Flanders, John I:193; III:768
Flanders, Joseph I:683

Flanders, Josiah I:751
Flanders, Levi I:699
Flanders, Moses I:783
Flanders, Onesiphus I:751
Flanders, Philip I:228
Flanders, Polly I:683
Flanders, Stephen II:500
Flanders, Susan I:683
Flannagan, David III:349
Flaridy, John III:731
Flatford, Thomas III:731
Flathers, Edward IV:75
Flecharty, Stephen III:706
Fleck, Peter II:660
Fleece, John III:231, 338
Fleehart, Massy IV:213
Fleenor, Michael III:842
Fleet, William III:198
Fleetwood, Benjamin III:22
Fleetwood, Isaac IV:44
Fleisher, Jacob II:702
Fleisher, Jacob (2) II:702
Fleming, Asa I:944
Fleming, Benoni II:452
Fleming, James III:788; IV:281
Fleming, John II:182
Fleming, Michael II:36
Fleming, Mitchel IV:119
Fleming, Robert IV:207
Fleming, Samuel III:78, 614
Fleming, Thomas IV:152
Fleming, William III:165
Flemming, Allison III:444
Flemming, James III:490
Flemming, Robert III:165
Flenner, Elizabeth III:670
Flenner, Emanuel III:670
Flenner, John III:670
Flenner, Washington III:670
Flesher, Adam III:798
Flesher, Henry IV:2
Fleshman, Moses III:773
Fletch, Edward I:666
Fletcher, Archelaus II:290
Fletcher, Benjamin II:322
Fletcher, C. I:xiv
Fletcher, Chester II:96
Fletcher, Daniel I:987
Fletcher, Ebenezer I:668
Fletcher, George III:835
Fletcher, Isaac I:893
Fletcher, James I:640, 987;
    II:284; III:216; IV:115, 123
Fletcher, Jeremiah I:266
Fletcher, John I:284; II:217,
    528; III:105, 214
Fletcher, Jonathan I:898
Fletcher, Joshua I:639
Fletcher, Josiah I:517
Fletcher, Levi I:517
Fletcher, Luke II:318
Fletcher, Nathan I:619
Fletcher, Oliver II:290
Fletcher, Peter I:741
Fletcher, Philip III:46
Fletcher, Reuben III:404
Fletcher, Richard III:757

Fletcher, Sherebiah IV:223
Fletcher, Silas II:445
Fletcher, Simeon I:758
Fletcher, Simon II:643
Fletcher, Thomas III:458, 783,
    834
Fletcher, William III:84
Fleuman, Thomas III:709
Flewellen, William III:571
Flick, James, 2d III:302
Flin, Daniel III:690
Flin, Thomas I:32
Fling, Abel I:986
Fling, James III:65
Fling, Lemuel II:318
Fling, Richard IV:137
Fling, William II:743
Flink, Benjamin I:692
Flink, Luke II:278
Flinn, Benjamin IV:253
Flinn, John III:390
Flinn, William III:501
Flint, Aaron I:148
Flint, Austin I:639
Flint, Benjamin I:414, 618
Flint, Daniel I:516, 888
Flint, Davis II:469
Flint, Dolly I:387
Flint, Ebenezer I:499
Flint, Edmund I:516
Flint, Eunice I:788
Flint, Henry I:387, 499
Flint, Jabez II:395
Flint, Jacob I:777
Flint, John I:517
Flint, Jonas I:758
Flint, Jonathan I:950
Flint, Joshua I:40
Flint, Lavinia I:387
Flint, Nathaniel I:707, 888
Flint, Robert II:359
Flint, Surrell I:387
Flint, Thomas I:180, 618;
    III:659
Flint, Tilly I:640
Flint, William I:415
Flint, Zaccheus II:484
Flints, Benjamin I:788
Flippin, Joseph III:822
Flipse, Homanus II:419
Flonagan, Dennis III:37
Flood, Alexander II:298
Flood, Amos II:264
Flood, Henry I:235
Flood, James I:180
Flood, Joseph II:240
Flood, Richard I:55
Flood, Thomas I:589; II:134
Flood, William IV:165
Florence, Thomas I:394
Florence, William IV:75
Flory, Peter II:644
Flournoy, Jacob III:765
Flower, Abdiel II:565
Flower, Zebulon I:640
Flowers, Abraham III:840
Flowers, Benjamin II:584

Flowers, Thomas II:743; IV:58
Flowers, William II:36
Floyd, Abraham IV:71
Floyd, Andrew III:517
Floyd, Benjamin I:500
Floyd, C. A. II:564
Floyd, George III:281
Floyd, Henry III:326
Floyd, Henry F. III:720
Floyd, John III:281, 509, 851;
 IV:292
Floyd, Matthew III:745
Floyd, Perry III:562
Floyd, Samuel II:593
Floyd, William I:619
Fluker, George III:95
Fluker, John III:157
Fly, William I:274
Flyn, Thomas IV:54
Flynn, Joshua II:187
Flynn, Peter II:187
Flynn, Simon II:651
Foard, Bille I:574
Foard, Hezekiah III:69
Fobes, Daniel II:479
Fobes, Edward I:442
Fobes, John II:469, 500
Fobes, Jotham II:426
Fobes, Lemuel IV:249
Fobes, Nathaniel IV:227
Fobes, Robert I:574
Fobes, Simon IV:218
Fobs, Jonah I:215
Focht, George II:746
Fodrell, Charles III:727
Fog, Joseph III:394
Fogas, John II:610
Fogat, John III:574
Fogg, Aaron I:235
Fogg, Caleb I:265
Fogg, Charles I:215
Fogg, George I:274
Fogg, Jeremiah I:758
Fogg, Jonathan I:765
Fogg, Samuel I:295
Fogg, Stephen I:776
Foggerson, Francis III:782
Foggett, Richard III:61
Foght, John Morris II:559
Fogler, Simon III:37
Folansbee, James I:414
Folansbee, Nehemiah I:415
Folck, Daniel III:794
Folger, Thomas II:505
Folk, Simon II:716
Folker, Ebenezer I:47
Follensbee, William I:758
Follet, Abel II:152
Follet, Benjamin I:950
Follet, Frederick I:611
Follet, Samuel I:481
Follett, Robert I:371
Follett, William I:824
Folliard, John II:313
Follinsbee, Abigail I:683
Follinsbee, David I:683
Follinsbee, James I:683

Follinsbee, Sam'l I:683
Follock, Adam II:248
Follonsbee, John I:751
Follonsbee, Nathan I:751
Folsom, Jeremiah I:776
Folsom, Moses I:308
Folson, Asa I:722
Folson, John I:215
Folts, George II:464
Foltz, George II:663
Foltz, John Jost II:163
Foltz, Joshua III:835
Fonda, Abraham II:439
Fonda, Jacob II:439
Fonda, Jellis A. II:429
Fonda, Jellis J. II:510
Fonis, William II:398
Fons, John III:277
Fontain, Caroline C. III:671
Fontain, Fanny C. III:671
Fontain, Harriet III:671
Fontain, James III:671
Fontain, Mary Ann III:671
Foord, Hezekiah I:699
Foord, Joseph I:750
Foos, Matthias II:645
Fooshee, John III:407
Foot, Beeri II:544
Foot, Bronson II:451
Foot, Daniel I:925
Foot, David I:2
Foot, Ebenezer II:227
Foot, Freeman I:925
Foot, Jehiel II:284
Foot, Jesse II:439
Foot, Martin I:925
Foot, Rowell I:394
Foot, Samuel I:722
Foot, Simeon II:749
Foot, Ti__thy IV:259
Foote, Ambrose I:134
Foote, Amos I:108
Foote, Asahel I:349
Foote, Darius I:108
Foote, Elihu I:125
Foote, Fenner I:349
Foote, Isaac I:758; II:211
Foote, Joseph II:224
Foote, Stephen I:134
Foote, Thomas I:611
Forbes, Aaron II:207
Forbes, Alexander II:181;
 III:598, 758
Forbes, Daniel II:610
Forbes, Edward I:867
Forbes, Eli I:125
Forbes, Elisha II:175
Forbes, Hugh III:755
Forbes, James II:264
Forbes, John I:639, 939;
 II:367; III:296
Forbes, Jonathan I:639
Forbes, Joseph III:450
Forbes, Nathan II:667
Forbes, Samuel II:402
Forbes, William I:220; II:632
Forbis, William III:678

Forbs, James I:68
Forbus, Hugh III:432
Forbush, Aaron W. I:603
Forbush, David I:618
Forbush, William III:678
Force, Amariah I:499
Force, Baldwin II:194
Force, Ebenezer I:535
Force, Henry II:269
Force, Jeremiah I:805
Force, Jesse III:314
Force, Joseph II:49; III:322
Force, Lydia Ann II:194
Force, N. II:194
Force, Peter III:290
Force, William II:269
Forcett, Rob't III:387
Ford, Abel II:313, 354
Ford, Amos I:78, 125
Ford, Andrew IV:249
Ford, Ann III:40
Ford, Asher II:536
Ford, Benjamin II:52, 329
Ford, Caleb I:308
Ford, Charles I:284
Ford, Christopher IV:227
Ford, Cromwell III:535
Ford, Dabney III:706
Ford, David II:645
Ford, Elisha III:322
Ford, Hannah III:535
Ford, Isaac II:640; III:535
Ford, Jacob II:385
Ford, Jesse III:299
Ford, John I:499; II:452;
 III:721
Ford, John, Sen. III:568
Ford, John C. D. III:535
Ford, John Dye III:535
Ford, Jonathan II:313, 404
Ford, Joseph III:37, 46, 317
Ford, Joshua I:284; III:614
Ford, Jotham I:960
Ford, L. II:556
Ford, Loyd III:625
Ford, Mahlon II:134
Ford, Martin I:60
Ford, Miles I:193
Ford, Nathan I:848; IV:249
Ford, Nathaniel I:266;
 II:451-52
Ford, Nicholas II:134
Ford, Phinehas I:78
Ford, Prince I:481
Ford, Richard I:750
Ford, S. II:556
Ford, Sanburn II:505
Ford, Stephen I:125
Ford, Thomas I:560; II:648;
 III:535
Ford, Thomas, 2d I:431
Ford, Timothy II:134
Ford, William III:40, 264, 413,
 809
Fordham, Nathan II:520
Fordyce, Henry IV:71
Fordyce, James IV:71

Fowler, Nathaniel I:125
Fowler, Nehemiah I:21
Fowler, Patrick II:610
Fowler, Phebe II:626
Fowler, R. I:xiii
Fowler, Robert I:414; IV:34
Fowler, Robert H. II:622
Fowler, Sherwood III:566
Fowler, Silas II:749
Fowler, Theodosius II:91, 559
Fowler, Thomas II:626
Fowler, William IV:17
Fowler, William M. II:196
Fowler, William W. II:176
Fowles, Albert I:585
Fowles, Henry III:804
Fowlkes, James III:822
Fox, Aaron II:654
Fox, Alleyn II:554
Fox, Amos I:40
Fox, Andrew II:638
Fox, Augustus C. II:135
Fox, Benjamin I:777; II:200
Fox, Catherine II:200
Fox, Charlotte II:200
Fox, Chrispus I:40
Fox, Christian W. II:125
Fox, Christopher W. II:439
Fox, Consider II:505
Fox, Daniel IV:17
Fox, David II:200, 514, 638;
    IV:267
Fox, Ebenezer I:545, 877, 971
Fox, Edward I:776
Fox, Elijah II:252
Fox, Elisha I:777; II:735
Fox, Ezekiel I:134
Fox, Francis III:395
Fox, Isaac I:67
Fox, Israel IV:249
Fox, Jabez I:149
Fox, Jacob I:142; II:305, 572;
    IV:297
Fox, Jedediah II:248
Fox, Jeremiah II:469
Fox, Jesse I:134
Fox, Joel I:516; II:124, 435
Fox, John I:149, 284, 874;
    II:200, 305, 689; IV:255
Fox, John, Sen. III:399
Fox, John B. II:200
Fox, Joseph II:36, 232, 723
Fox, Lemuel I:40
Fox, Mary Ann II:200
Fox, Nathaniel III:740
Fox, Olive II:200
Fox, Oliver II:200
Fox, Peter I:961; II:12, 439
Fox, Robert II:200
Fox, Samuel II:339, 565
Fox, Samuel, 2d II:217
Fox, Silas I:699, 998
Fox, Simeon II:313
Fox, Sinkler IV:227
Fox, Stephen IV:225
Fox, Thomas I:39, 458; II:705
Fox, Uriah I:995

Fox, Venia II:214
Fox, William W. II:439
Fox, Zibla II:200
Foxworthy, John III:287
Foy, Darby III:134
Foy, Heman A. II:94
Foy, James I:235
Foy, John I:265
Foy, Joseph I:676
Foy, Moses I:308
Foy, Peggy III:134
Foy, Samuel III:22
Fradenburgh, John II:313
Fradenburgh, Peter II:322
Frailey, John II:743
France, Adam II:532
France, Jacob II:514
France, John III:732
France, Peter IV:217
France, Wilhelmus II:532
Frances, David II:410
Franciosi, F.S. I:xii
Francis, Aaron I:394; II:429
Francis, Charles II:677
Francis, Elijah I:98
Francis, George IV:173
Francis, Jacob II:68
Francis, James I:39, 117;
    II:720
Francis, Job II:452
Francis, John I:382; II:593
Francis, John, 2d I:326
Francis, Jonathan II:278
Francis, Robert I:98, 349
Francis, Samuel III:491
Francis, Thomas I:394, 656;
    II:217; III:801
Francis, Titus I:125
Francis, William I:39; III:640,
    678
Francisco, Cornelius II:414
Francisco, Henry II:347
Francisco, Israel II:194
Francisco, John II:469; IV:103
Francisco, Levi II:469
Francisco, Margaret II:194
Francisco, Mary Ann II:194
Francisco, Michael II:550
Francisco, Peter III:649
Francisco, Stephen II:194
Francisco, William II:194
Franciscus, Jacob II:398
Francum, Francis III:479
Frank, Adam II:439
Frank, Andrew I:825; II:182
Frank, Henry II:364; III:710
Frank, Jacob IV:156
Frank, James I:248
Frank, Joshua I:40
Frank, Michael II:227
Frank, Thomas I:180
Frankfort, Henry II:651
Franklin, Abel I:78
Franklin, Absalom III:267
Franklin, Arnold II:705
Franklin, Benjamin I:462
Franklin, Dean II:424

Franklin, Elisha II:41
Franklin, Ezra I:148
Franklin, Henry III:548
Franklin, James II:364
Franklin, James M. III:322
Franklin, Jehiel II:290
Franklin, John II:195; III:250,
    827
Franklin, John (2) II:195
Franklin, John, 2d III:694
Franklin, John, Sen. III:827
Franklin, Jonathan I:751
Franklin, Joseph II:593;
    III:209
Franklin, Joshua I:833
Franklin, Lewis III:792
Franklin, Moses II:484
Franklin, Nathan II:479
Franklin, Reuben III:269
Franklin, Samuel I:47; III:752
Franklin, Squire I:824
Franklin, Stephen III:255
Franklin, Thomas III:760
Franklin, Thomas P. III:760
Franks, Henry IV:292-93
Franks, Isaac II:677
Franks, John II:334; III:46
Franks, Samuel III:506
Frans, Conrad II:248
Frantz, Conrad II:560
Frary, Eleazer I:442
Frary, Julius C. II:224
Frary, Nathaniel I:481
Frary, Seth I:442
Fraseur, John III:278
Frasier, James A. II:536
Fratt, Henry II:642
Frazee, Jonas IV:253
Frazee, Joseph Reading I:360
Frazee, Matthias II:63
Frazee, Samuel W. I:360
Frazer, Alexander II:134
Frazer, Christian II:63
Frazer, Daniel I:987
Frazer, Donald II:134
Frazer, Jeremiah II:500
Frazer, Robert II:610
Frazer, Zebedee II:36
Frazie_, Adam E. III:134
Frazie_, Narcissey J. III:134
Frazier, Alexander III:601
Frazier, Charles I:362
Frazier, Duncan II:182
Frazier, Elijah III:134
Frazier, James III:61, 495
Frazier, Jeremiah I:563
Frazier, John III:348, 831
Frazier, Levin III:64
Frazier, Lowell II:452
Frazier, Thomas III:547
Frazier, William III:760
Frazzle, Nathan III:566
Freame, Thomas III:118
Freame, William II:748
Freaze, Martin II:677
Fredenburgh, James II:203
Frederick, Betsey III:360

Frost, Mark I:193
Frost, Micajah III:319
Frost, Moses I:284
Frost, Nathaniel I:235, 528
Frost, Phineas I:166
Frost, Richard I:394
Frost, Samuel I:193
Frost, Stephen I:235
Frost, Thomas II:367
Frost, William I:235
Frost, Zepheniah I:516
Frothingham, Jane Ann II:558
Frothingham, Samuel I:117
Frutchman, Elias II:674
Fruthy, Joseph I:187
Fry, Allen I:815
Fry, Benjamin III:130
Fry, Christopher II:395
Fry, Conrad II:674
Fry, Cynthia I:428
Fry, Earl I:428
Fry, Gabriel III:554
Fry, George II:589
Fry, Henry II:645
Fry, Jacob II:674
Fry, John I:428
Fry, Joseph I:815
Fry, Joshua III:281
Fry, Lawrence II:651
Fry, Nathan III:709
Fry, Nicholas III:715
Fry, Philip II:674
Fry, Rozier II:310
Fry, William I:428
Fry, Windsor I:800
Frye, Anna I:857
Frye, Benjamin I:394, 819
Frye, Dolly I:321
Frye, Ebenezer I:188
Frye, Frederick I:408; II:298
Frye, Gatesford I:387
Frye, Isaac I:857
Frye, John I:338, 857
Frye, Joseph I:857
Frye, Joshua I:394
Frye, Luther I:857
Frye, Nathaniel I:321
Frye, Nathaniel, Sr. I:215
Frye, Owin I:387
Frye, Peter I:414
Frye, Theophilus I:387
Fryer, John III:781
Fryer, Leonard II:603
Fryman, Catharine IV:161
Fryman, George IV:161
Fryman, Henry IV:161
Fryman, Jacob IV:161
Fugard, Samuel I:679
Fugate, Jeremiah III:770
Fugate, John H. III:199
Fugate, Randall F. III:321
Fugate, Thomas IV:133
Fuhr, John C. II:224
Fujeley, John II:738
Fulcher, Richard III:256
Fulford, James III:411
Fulford, John I:21

Fulford, Stephen III:411
Fulk, David III:727
Fulkerson, Caleb II:550
Fulkerson, Henry II:85
Fulkerson, John III:283
Fulkerson, Joseph II:332
Fulkerson, William II:134
Fulkinson, John II:700
Fulkison, John III:625
Fullam, Jacob I:640
Fuller, Aaron I:284
Fuller, Abiah I:976
Fuller, Abijah I:78
Fuller, Abraham I:934
Fuller, Alexander III:404
Fuller, Amasa I:961
Fuller, Andrew I:206
Fuller, Arthur III:506
Fuller, Arum II:148
Fuller, Asa II:452
Fuller, Asahel I:858
Fuller, Azariah I:619
Fuller, Bartholomew I:976
Fuller, Barzilla I:215, 321
Fuller, Benajah II:731
Fuller, Benjamin I:148, 367,
  382, 489, 800, 970; II:451,
  536
Fuller, Consider II:684
Fuller, Daniel I:333, 777, 934;
  II:404, 493
Fuller, David II:400, 426
Fuller, Dayton I:349
Fuller, Ebenezer I:134, 371
Fuller, Edward I:47, 640
Fuller, Eleazer I:338, 595
Fuller, Elisha I:500, 640
Fuller, Elkanah II:284
Fuller, Ely I:40
Fuller, Enoch I:193
Fuller, Ezekiel I:462
Fuller, Ezra I:78
Fuller, Florilla I:858
Fuller, Frederick I:846
Fuller, George III:556
Fuller, George A. I:682
Fuller, Gershom II:354
Fuller, Helsey II:194
Fuller, Hubble I:858
Fuller, Hubble S. I:858
Fuller, Ichabod II:718
Fuller, Isaac I:193; II:419, 484
Fuller, Isaiah I:431
Fuller, James I:40, 415;
  II:464; III:525; IV:229
Fuller, Jason I:934
Fuller, Jedediah I:530
Fuller, Jefferson II:194
Fuller, Jeremiah I:682
Fuller, John I:108, 142, 394,
  489, 898, 929, 999; II:194,
  240, 398
Fuller, John, 2d II:318
Fuller, John B. II:152
Fuller, Jonathan I:78, 545,
  640; II:364

Fuller, Joseph I:326, 639;
  II:655; IV:186, 296
Fuller, Joshua II:211
Fuller, Josiah I:143; II:290
Fuller, Josiah, 2d I:442
Fuller, Josiah, 3d I:326
Fuller, Josiah, 1st I:560
Fuller, Lemuel I:699
Fuller, Littleton III:94
Fuller, Lot II:452
Fuller, Mary I:321
Fuller, Meshac III:489
Fuller, Nathan I:148, 499;
  II:404
Fuller, Nathaniel I:407
Fuller, Noah I:326, 783
Fuller, Permit II:194
Fuller, Peter II:484
Fuller, Robert I:215
Fuller, Rufus I:717
Fuller, Samuel I:877; II:484
Fuller, Samuel, Jr. II:206
Fuller, Seth I:916
Fuller, Silas I:18
Fuller, Simeon II:451
Fuller, Stephen I:463, 668;
  II:322; III:488
Fuller, Thaddeus IV:169
Fuller, Theodore I:771
Fuller, Thomas I:722, 874
Fuller, Varsell II:536
Fuller, W. K. II:558, 560
Fuller, William I:265; IV:179
Fullerton, James I:777
Fullerton, John II:593
Fullerton, Thomas II:648
Fullilove, Anthony III:302
Fullington, Ezekiel I:943
Fullum, Oliver I:619
Fulmer, Jacob II:505; III:507
Fulmore, Joseph III:14
Fulp, Michael, Sen. III:452
Fulper, William II:41
Fulton, David II:196; III:435
Fulton, James II:622, 711;
  III:22
Fulton, James B. III:517
Fulton, Jesse II:698
Fulton, Nancy II:193
Fulton, Polly II:622
Fulton, Robert III:750
Fulton, Susan II:196
Fulton, Thomas II:196
Fultz, Frederick II:575
Fultz, Joshua III:835
Fuman, Jack I:90
Funk, Adam III:194
Funk, Daniel II:624
Funk, George II:663
Funk, Jacob Swisher II:624
Funk, John II:624
Furbeck, John II:354
Furbee, Richard I:776
Furbush, Aaron I:442
Furbush, Benjamin I:193
Furbush, Simeon I:415
Furgason, James III:610

386

Furgason, John II:134
Furgason, William II:134
Furgurson, Isaac III:631
Furguson, Caleb III:493
Furguson, John I:765; II:546
Furguson, Josiah II:72
Furguson, Robert III:822
Furguson, William III:218
Furgusson, Moses III:765
Furman, Abraham II:491
Furman, John II:134
Furman, Joshua II:68
Furman, Nowell IV:279
Furnald, Amos I:777
Furnald, Nicholas I:215
Furness, Thomas III:11
Furnham, Ralph I:308
Furnish, James III:287
Furnish, Thomas III:287
Furniss, Benjamin I:976
Furniss, William II:259
Furrar, John II:290
Furrer, Henry III:410
Fury, John III:196
Fuson, William IV:236
Fussel, Wm. III:114
Fyler, John I:108
Fyler, Orris II:714
Fyler, Stephen I:108
Fysel, Wm. III:114

Gabbert, George III:306
Gabbert, Michael III:306
Gable, Joseph W. III:114
Gabriel, James III:411
Gaby, George I:871
Gadd, Thomas III:46, 319
Gadd, William IV:273
Gaddis, Anna II:622
Gaddis, Hannah II:622
Gaddis, Henry II:720
Gaddis, James II:622
Gaddis, Priscilla II:622
Gaddis, Samuel II:611
Gaddis, Sarah II:622
Gaddis, Thomas IV:238
Gaddy, Joseph III:760
Gadeau, Cornelia II:192
Gadeau, Lewis II:192
Gaff, Daniel III:259
Gaff, James I:812
Gaff, John III:237
Gaffitt, John II:269
Gage, Aaron III:602
Gage, Abel I:708
Gage, Abijah I:415
Gage, Abner I:679; IV:160
Gage, Alden II:415
Gage, Amos I:285
Gage, Asa II:214
Gage, Daniel I:285
Gage, David II:435
Gage, Ebenezer I:327
Gage, John I:415; II:72
Gage, Jonathan I:415, 431
Gage, Nathaniel II:464

Gage, Phineas I:758
Gage, Reuben IV:253
Gage, Thaddeus I:765
Gage, Zenas I:327
Gager, Samuel R. I:109
Gailer, William II:445
Gailor, William II:269
Gaine, William I:611
Gaines, Ambrose II:620
Gaines, James I:916
Gaines, James, Sen. III:434
Gaines, Madison III:203
Gaines, Richard III:746
Gaines, Robert III:331
Gaines, Thomas III:203, 284
Gaines, William III:161, 203
Gains, Anthony III:564
Gains, Josiah II:310
Gains, Jude I:339
Gains, Thomas III:486
Gaithritt, John II:36
Gaitskill, William I:193
Galbraith, Alexander II:650
Galbrath, James II:611
Galbreath, William IV:89
Gale, Adam I:387
Gale, Asa I:976
Gale, Bartholomew I:676
Gale, Daniel I:296, 641, 676
Gale, Edmund I:395
Gale, Eli I:961
Gale, Henry II:306
Gale, Jacob I:387
Gale, James H. III:32
Gale, John I:387
Gale, John C. I:751
Gale, Jonathan I:619
Gale, Joseph II:31
Gale, Joseph (2) II:31
Gale, Paul I:875
Gale, Richard IV:247
Gale, Robert F. III:322
Gale, William B. I:387
Gall, George, Sen. IV:257
Gallagher, Ebenezer II:697
Gallagher, Francis II:575
Gallagher, James III:22
Gallagher, Michael II:593
Gallant, James II:610
Gallegher, John III:683
Gallespie, James IV:147
Gallimore, John IV:97
Gallinger, John II:593
Gallop, Enos I:415
Gallop, Isaac III:367
Galloway, Ann II:192
Galloway, Benjamin III:682
Galloway, Delilah II:192
Galloway, Elizabeth II:192
Galloway, Harriet II:192
Galloway, James III:306; IV:251
Galloway, John II:192; III:233
Galloway, Michael III:559
Galloway, William II:192
Gallup, Amos I:134
Gallup, Andrew I:134

Gallup, John I:149
Gallup, Joseph I:135, 916
Gallup, Levi II:514
Gallup, Nehemiah I:134
Gallup, Robert II:103
Gallup, Rufus II:493
Gallup, William I:149; II:159
Gallut, James I:604
Galpin, Abel II:718
Galpin, Amos I:108
Galpin, Samuel I:117
Galtry, David III:494
Galusha, Abram II:344
Galusha, Jacob II:306
Galusha, Samuel II:203
Galusha, Thomas II:540
Galwicks, Daniel II:593
Galworth, Gabriel III:65
Gamage, Joshua I:285
Gambare, John III:29
Gambel, John I:987
Gamber, John II:743
Gamble, Abraham III:37
Gamble, Archibald I:758
Gamble, David IV:86
Gamble, James IV:283
Gamble, Joseph II:344
Gamble, Thomas III:544
Gamble, William III:14
Gambleton, Robert II:135
Gamblin, Joshua III:301
Gambling, James III:622
Gammon, Benjamin I:560
Gammon, David I:284
Gammon, Harris III:595
Gammon, Jesse III:594
Gammon, Joseph I:285
Gammon, Joshua I:292
Gammon, Moses I:216, 285
Gammon, Samuel I:284
Gammons, John I:561
Gammut, Paul II:484
Gander, Jacob II:723
Gandy, Enoch II:743
Gann, Nathan III:625
Gann, Samuel, Sen. III:449
Gann, Thomas III:585
Gann, William III:528
Gannett, Deborah I:536
Gannett, Joseph II:464
Gannon, William IV:189
Gannon, William, Sen. IV:12
Gano, Daniel III:321
Ganong, Reuben II:490
Gansey, Seth I:898
Ganson, Nathan I:437; IV:186
Gapen, Stephen III:809
Garabrants, Garabrant N. II:58
Garberich, John II:578
Garbey, John II:692
Garden, Alexander III:518
Garden, Andrew II:645
Gardenier, Gilbert II:224
Gardenier, Jacob II:182
Gardenier, Samuel II:182
Gardiner, Abiel II:528
Gardiner, Abraham II:439

Gardiner, Benjamin I:815, 833
Gardiner, Charles I:206
Gardiner, Cornelius II:36
Gardiner, Daniel II:593
Gardiner, Elijah I:231
Gardiner, Ezekiel I:708
Gardiner, Gideon I:833
Gardiner, James I:833; II:659
Gardiner, John I:216; II:528
Gardiner, Nathaniel B. II:718
Gardiner, Richard I:815
Gardiner, Silas I:833
Gardiner, Thomas III:802
Gardiner, Townsend S. II:378
Gardiner, William I:672
Gardner, Abiel I:708
Gardner, Abijah II:211
Gardner, Alexander I:604
Gardner, Allen II:190
Gardner, Andrew I:443; II:224
Gardner, Andris II:224
Gardner, Benjamin IV:231
Gardner, Benoni II:313
Gardner, Caleb I:560
Gardner, Caswell II:711
Gardner, Christopher I:784
Gardner, David I:61, 68, 574
Gardner, Diark II:190
Gardner, Elias III:446
Gardner, Elijah II:217
Gardner, Elizabeth III:202
Gardner, George II:190;
   III:808
Gardner, Isaac I:134
Gardner, Jack I:619
Gardner, James III:202
Gardner, John I:327, 833;
   II:190, 334, 734; III:14, 202,
   432; IV:41
Gardner, John F. III:569
Gardner, Jonathan I:284;
   II:313; IV:249
Gardner, Joseph III:665
Gardner, Josiah II:405
Gardner, Perez I:560
Gardner, Samuel I:560; IV:8
Gardner, Seth II:217
Gardner, Sherman I:469
Gardner, Silas T. II:175
Gardner, Thomas I:473;
   II:306, 731; III:202
Gardner, Timothy II:190
Gardner, William I:xiv; II:269,
   337, 424; III:202
Garey, Elisha II:241
Garey, Seth II:257
Garey, William II:89
Garfield, Jesse II:249
Garfield, John I:349
Garfield, Joseph I:641
Garfield, Nathaniel II:540
Garfield, Reuben I:619
Garfield, Samuel I:784
Gargy, Enos II:360
Garlach, Elias II:191
Garlach, Nancy II:191
Garland, D. S. III:847

Garland, Elisha III:575
Garland, Jacob I:881
Garland, James I:221
Garland, John I:730; III:229
Garland, Moses I:765
Garland, Richard I:747
Garlands, Humphrey III:540
Garlinghouse, Benj. II:290
Garlington, Christopher III:121
Garlough, Adam II:440
Garlow, John II:146
Garmond, Jacob II:269
Garnage, Samuel II:224
Garnar, Thomas II:55
Garnel, James II:224
Garnell, William I:758
Garner, Andrew II:514
Garner, Charles III:138
Garner, James II:31
Garner, John III:72, 711
Garner, Joseph III:77
Garner, Samuel III:481
Garner, Sturdy III:88
Garneston, Jacob IV:69
Garnett, Daniel I:231
Garnett, John II:155; III:315
Garnsey, David I:751; II:393
Garnsey, Joel II:362
Garnsey, Samuel II:424
Garnwell, James I:339
Garrard, William III:87
Garratt, Joseph II:594
Garrel, John III:717
Garret, William III:435
Garretson, Jacob IV:69
Garretson, John IV:38
Garretson, Richard II:85
Garretson, Samuel II:22
Garrett, Alexander II:611
Garrett, Andrew I:327, 655
Garrett, David III:491
Garrett, Francis II:367
Garrett, Henry III:631
Garrett, John II:278, 474
Garrett, Thomas III:491
Garrigues, John II:81
Garris, Bedford III:432
Garris, Sikes III:311
Garrish, Joseph II:72
Garrison, Aaron II:58
Garrison, Abraham II:34, 58,
   317, 469, 498
Garrison, Benjamin IV:212
Garrison, Bennet II:49
Garrison, Dennis II:547
Garrison, Harvey II:562
Garrison, James IV:13, 97
Garrison, Joel IV:93
Garrison, John II:516, 644;
   III:633
Garrison, Jonah II:49
Garrison, Leonard II:723
Garrison, Matthias II:34
Garrison, Richard II:182
Garrison, Samuel III:327
Garrison, Stephen III:96
Garriss, Henry III:438

Garrit, John II:336
Garrott, John III:245
Garrott, Robert III:309
Garter, Nathaniel III:810
Garth, James III:37
Garth, John III:321
Gartsee, John II:217
Garven, Isaac III:298
Garvey, Francis II:203
Garvey, Job III:220
Garwood, Samuel II:580
Gary, Jonas I:741
Gary, Josiah I:78
Gary, Moses I:619
Gase, Clark I:15
Gashkobigh, Jean II:165
Gaskins, Herman III:342
Gaskins, Jesse III:720
Gaskins, Thomas II:611
Gaslee, Solomon I:48
Gasnell, Benjamin IV:67
Gaspenson, John III:565
Gasper, Peter II:305
Gass, John III:584
Gass, Patrick III:642
Gassaway, James III:487
Gassaway, John III:43
Gassett, John I:500
Gaster, Jacob III:434
Gaston, Daniel II:741
Gaston, Hugh IV:163
Gaston, John IV:163
Gaston, Joseph III:467, 499
Gaston, Nancy IV:163
Gaston, Rachel IV:163
Gaston, Sally IV:163
Gaston, William IV:17
Gatchell, Benjamin I:180
Gatchell, James I:843
Gatchell, Samuel H. III:46
Gates, Amos I:692
Gates, Asa I:463, 819
Gates, Benjamin II:101
Gates, Cyrus I:962
Gates, Edward I:395
Gates, Ezra I:699, 853; II:385
Gates, Freeman II:240
Gates, George I:758
Gates, Henry I:604
Gates, James A. II:245
Gates, Jehiel II:332
Gates, John I:944; III:631;
   IV:284
Gates, Jonas I:888
Gates, Jonathan I:619; II:419
Gates, Joseph I:117
Gates, Luther II:306
Gates, Marvin II:469
Gates, Mary I:117
Gates, Micah I:463
Gates, Nathan I:956; II:135
Gates, Nathaniel II:677
Gates, Nehemiah I:117, 962
Gates, Oldham II:354
Gates, Oliver I:517; II:705
Gates, Paul I:641
Gates, Peter I:431

388

Gates, Samuel I:758, 941, 961
Gates, Silas II:419
Gates, Simon I:641
Gates, Solomon I:443
Gates, Sylvanus II:757
Gates, Timothy IV:223
Gates, William I:517; II:104, 278 IV:165
Gatewood, Dudley III:408
Gatewood, Edmund III:762
Gatewood, John III:254, 321
Gatewood, William III:762, 795
Gathre, Joseph II:553
Gatliff, Charles III:330
Gatlin, Edward III:737
Gattchell, Nathaniel I:249
Gattchell, William I:249
Gatten, Jesse III:389
Gattis, Alexander III:439
Gattis, James III:598
Gaudinier, Jacob IV:242
Gaudy, David II:61
Gaudy, Ephraim III:500
Gauf, John II:677-78
Gaul, John F. II:743
Gaulden, William III:822
Gauley, John II:553
Gault, James II:594, 735
Gault, John I:596
Gault, Robert III:505
Gauss, Benjamin II:469
Gautt, Erasmus III:754
Gavett, Samuel II:36
Gavit, Edward I:795
Gay, Allen III:155
Gay, Asahel I:134
Gay, Ebenezer I:546
Gay, Edward II:393
Gay, James II:240, 435
Gay, James, Sen. III:269
Gay, Jason II:298
Gay, John I:692; II:439
Gay, Jonathan II:252
Gay, Richard I:99
Gay, Stephen I:619
Gay, Thomas I:431
Gaylord, Ambrose II:667
Gaylord, Chauncey II:464
Gaylord, Deodate I:86
Gaylord, Elijah II:362
Gaylord, Harvey I:451; II:105
Gaylord, Jedediah II:393
Gaylord, Joel IV:299
Gaylord, John I:458; IV:212
Gaylord, Jonathan II:332; IV:212
Gaylord, Joseph I:109
Gaylord, Levi IV:227
Gaylord, Robert I:454
Gaynn, William II:696
Gazlay, Jonathan II:390
Gearhart, Jacob II:741
Gearson, Thomas II:77
Geary, Gilbert II:484
Geary, Ichabod I:619
Geary, Joshua I:888

Geasey, Henry III:64
Geddes, Joseph II:661
Gedding, Samuel I:216
Geddings, Isaac I:415
Geddings, Isaac, 2d I:415
Geddings, John I:98
Gee, David II:686
Gee, Ebenezer I:481
Gee, Ezekiel II:229
Gee, John II:207
Gee, John, 2d II:227
Gee, Moses IV:248
Geer, Allen II:484
Geer, Benajah II:278
Geer, Benjamin II:322
Geer, Charles II:313
Geer, Ebenezer S. I:641
Geer, George II:269
Geer, Gurdon IV:212
Geer, Jedediah IV:201
Geer, Nathaniel I:109
Geer, Richard II:493
Geer, Robert II:536
Geer, Walter III:12
Geeslin, Charles III:77
Geiger, Jacob II:665
Geip, Henry II:760
Geise, Jeremiah II:675
Gelat, George II:749
Gelat, John I:372
Gellon, John III:344
Gelson, Daniel IV:249
Gelston, William I:117
Genat, Thomas III:709
Genningson, Samuel I:382
Gent, Charles III:613
Gent, Jesse III:618
Genter, John H. II:306
Genthner, Andrew I:275
Gentry, Claiborn III:575
Gentry, George III:746
Gentry, James III:746
Gentry, Richard III:302, 319
Gentry, William III:705
Genung, Isaac II:20
Genung, Jacob II:49
Geoghagen, Thomas III:22
Geoghan, John III:240
Geoghegan, Anthony IV:221
George, Amos II:306
George, Benjamin I:950
George, Britton III:558
George, David III:881
George, Francis I:193
George, Jesse IV:275
George, John I:500, 708, 806; III:306; IV:256
George, Jorden III:320
George, Joseph III:787
George, Michael I:881
George, Moses II:146
George, Moses S. I:888
George, Prince II:232
George, Reuben III:727
George, Samuel I:771, 784
George, Thomas I:221; III:314
George, William II:667; III:598

Gerald, Gamaliel I:909
Geren, Solomon III:611
Gerlack, George II:576
Gerlock, John II:610
German, Betsey III:360
German, Fanny III:360
German, James II:528
German, John III:360
German, Levi III:360
Gerock, Samuel III:409
Gerolman, Henry II:310
Gerould, Samuel I:692
Gerrald, Edward II:195
Gerrald, Joanna II:195
Gerrald, Phoebe II:195
Gerrald, Sally II:195
Gerrald, William II:195
Gerrard, John IV:204
Gerrills, John IV:218
Gerrish, Edward III:50
Gerrish, John I:415
Gerrish, Thomas I:722
Gerrish, Timothy I:309
Gerry, Jonathan I:619
Getchell, Jeremiah I:415
Getchell, Nathaniel I:300
Getchell, Seth I:193
Getman, Conrad II:415
Getman, Peter II:439
Gettchell, Joseph I:302
Gettey, Christopher II:611
Gettys, Joseph II:588
Getzendamier, Solomon III:29
Gevedann, John III:290
Geyer, George I:596
Geyer, John II:657
Gherkins, Zachariah III:105
Gholson, William III:211
Ghormley, Joseph IV:69
Gibbes, William Hasell III:499
Gibbon, James III:850
Gibboney, Alexander II:737
Gibbons, Bildad I:463
Gibbons, Isaac III:736
Gibbons, John II:7
Gibbons, Peter II:279
Gibbons, Philip II:575
Gibbons, Timothy I:463
Gibbs, Benjamin III:439
Gibbs, Churchill III:851
Gibbs, Cornelius I:898
Gibbs, David I:99, 881
Gibbs, Edward III:760
Gibbs, Elijah I:909
Gibbs, Elisha I:292
Gibbs, Frederick II:279
Gibbs, Gershom I:109
Gibbs, Isaac I:944
Gibbs, Ithamar II:279
Gibbs, Jabez II:264
Gibbs, James I:500
Gibbs, John I:819; III:752
Gibbs, Joseph I:574; II:705
Gibbs, Joshua I:574; II:634
Gibbs, Josiah I:987
Gibbs, Julia I:154
Gibbs, Julius III:321

Gibbs, Luman III:805
Gibbs, Moore I:47, 155
Gibbs, Pelatiah I:285
Gibbs, Samuel I:3, 33, 154, 339
Gibbs, Simeon I:47; II:152, 290
Gibbs, Solomon I:109, 848, 962
Gibbs, Spencer I:48
Gibbs, Stephen I:40, 987
Gibbs, Sylvanus I:109
Gibbs, Thomas I:327
Gibbs, Thomas, 2d I:898
Gibbs, Thomas, 1st II:319
Gibbs, William I:109; IV:220
Gibby, John III:566
Gibhart, Adam III:491
Gibney, George IV:283
Gibs, Ebenezer I:898
Gibson, Alexander III:316
Gibson, Bellingsby III:625
Gibson, Charles III:393
Gibson, Elisha III:322
Gibson, Erasmus III:510
Gibson, George III:325
Gibson, Henry II:298
Gibson, Jacob III:256
Gibson, James I:221, 741; II:337; III:22; IV:3
Gibson, Joel III:226
Gibson, John I:302, 916; II:306, 632; III:254, 272, 321, 515, 564, 633, 774, 802
Gibson, Joseph III:444
Gibson, Nathaniel I:692
Gibson, Nicholas III:798
Gibson, Roger I:463
Gibson, Samuel IV:257
Gibson, Thaddeus I:717
Gibson, Thomas I:640; III:728
Gibson, William I:987; II:290; III:547, 802
Giddings, Benjamin I:40
Giddings, John I:987
Giddings, Joseph I:68
Giddings, Joshua IV:227
Giddings, Niles II:405
Giddis, Azariah II:27
Giddis, Charity II:27
Giddis, Jeremiah II:27
Giddis, Mary II:27
Giddis, Thomas II:27
Gideon, George II:677
Gideon, Jacob III:12
Gideon, Peter III:801
Gideon, Richard III:122
Gidleman, John III:27
Gier, Asa II:688
Gier, John II:657
Giffin, Simon I:40
Giffins, Joshua II:39
Gifford, Absalom II:415
Gifford, Elisha I:819; II:490
Gifford, Gideon I:819
Gifford, James I:372
Gifford, Jeremiah II:453

Gifford, John II:135, 439
Gifford, Lewis I:372
Gifford, Lot I:330
Gifford, William I:372; II:654
Gigher, Jacob II:665
Gilbert, Aaron B. I:26
Gilbert, Allen II:302
Gilbert, Amos II:290
Gilbert, Asa I:109
Gilbert, Asahel II:313
Gilbert, Benedict III:203
Gilbert, Benjamin I:117; II:306
Gilbert, Bradley I:26
Gilbert, Burr II:182
Gilbert, Butler I:305
Gilbert, Charles III:282
Gilbert, Charlotte I:26
Gilbert, Daniel II:474
Gilbert, David I:85
Gilbert, Ebenezer I:78
Gilbert, Elam II:235
Gilbert, Gardner II:257
Gilbert, Gershom II:264
Gilbert, Henry I:619
Gilbert, Isaac I:26, 125
Gilbert, Jesse I:47; II:393
Gilbert, Joel I:641
Gilbert, John I:372, 751; II:182, 604
Gilbert, Jonas I:640
Gilbert, Jonathan II:415
Gilbert, Joseph II:290, 505
Gilbert, Josiah I:443
Gilbert, Justis II:135
Gilbert, Lemuel I:125
Gilbert, Lewis I:443
Gilbert, Moses I:86
Gilbert, Nathan I:86
Gilbert, Obadiah I:881
Gilbert, Peter II:203
Gilbert, Richard M. III:203
Gilbert, Samuel I:285; II:227, 464; III:203, 797
Gilbert, Sewell II:426
Gilbert, Simeon I:961
Gilbert, Solomon II:313
Gilbert, Stephen II:547, 638
Gilbert, Thaddeus I:473; IV:200
Gilbert, Theodore II:302, 429
Gilbert, Thomas I:125; II:148, 290
Gilbert, Truman IV:279
Gilbert, William II:360; III:203
Gilbreath, Alexander III:458
Gilbreath, Thomas III:548
Gilbreath, William III:458
Gilbreth, Benjamin I:162
Gilchrist, John II:611
Gilchrist, Richard I:741
Gilchrist, Samuel I:206
Gilderslean, Benjamin II:63
Gile, Asa II:493
Gile, Benjamin I:415
Giles, Aquila II:269
Giles, George III:822
Giles, James II:414

Giles, John I:236; III:308
Giles, Joseph I:236
Giles, Josiah III:826
Giles, Samuel I:78; II:439
Giles, Thomas II:429
Giles, Wm. B. III:848
Gilford, John, Jr. I:235
Gilgo, Faber III:384
Gili, Benaijah IV:12
Gilkey, James I:236
Gilkey, William I:961
Gill, Daniel IV:169
Gill, George III:498, 561
Gill, Henry II:484
Gill, Hugh II:670
Gill, James III:83
Gill, John I:916; III:827
Gill, Moses IV:122
Gill, Obadiah I:909
Gill, Silas I:611
Gill, Thomas IV:12, 17
Gill, William I:898; II:736
Gillam, Ezekiel II:367
Gillan, Thomas II:298
Gillaspie, Jacob III:595
Gillaspie, John III:325
Gillaspie, William III:751
Gillaspy, William II:647
Gillehan, William III:558
Gilleland, Daniel IV:270
Giller, George II:683
Gilles, Joseph II:440
Gillespie, Andrew II:493
Gillespie, George III:826
Gillespie, James III:432
Gillespie, John II:645
Gillespie, William III:589
Gillet, Alpheus II:640
Gillet, Benoni I:61
Gillet, Jabez II:518
Gillet, Jeremiah I:40, 699
Gillet, John I:40
Gillet, Luther II:415
Gillet, Nathaniel IV:212
Gillet, Noadiah II:385
Gillet, Othniel I:48
Gillet, Reuben I:925
Gillet, Simon I:889
Gillet, Stephen II:439
Gillet, William II:227
Gillett, Asa IV:107
Gillett, Benjamin I:125
Gillett, Benoni I:99
Gillett, Elijah I:98
Gillett, Ephraim I:40
Gillett, Isaac I:135
Gillett, Joel I:47
Gillett, John I:155
Gillett, Jonathan I:109
Gillett, Joseph I:134; II:170; IV:244
Gilley, Richard III:792
Gillham, Isaac IV:15
Gillham, Jacob III:605
Gillham, John IV:15
Gilliam, John III:300, 415
Gilliam, Jonathan IV:68

Gillian, Archilaus III:749
Gilligan, Thomas II:322
Gilliham, Clammaus III:338
Gilliham, Mark H. III:338
Gilliland, David IV:163
Gilliland, James III:843
Gilliland, John IV:163
Gilliland, Polly IV:163
Gilliland, William IV:163
Gilliland, William, Sen. III:163
Gillingwater, James III:686
Gillis, Arthur IV:170
Gillis, John II:505
Gillman, Anth_ny I:395
Gillman, Calvin II:419
Gillman, Charles II:445
Gillman, Ezekiel I:224
Gillman, Jonathan I:676
Gillman, Moses I:676
Gillmore, Adam I:925
Gilloch, John III:229
Gillpatrick, James I:308
Gillpatrick, Joseph I:309
Gillpatrick, Joshua I:309
Gillpatrick, Nathaniel I:308
Gillson, Eleazar IV:300
Gilman, Andrew I:771
Gilman, Benjamin I:777
Gilman, Caleb I:784
Gilman, Daniel I:784
Gilman, Ezekiel I:730
Gilman, Israel I:491; II:148
Gilman, James I:758
Gilman, Jeremiah I:730, 784
Gilman, John I:730; III:705
Gilman, Jonathan I:300
Gilman, Joseph II:332; III:42
Gilman, Joshua I:846
Gilman, Mrs. Peter I:275
Gilman, Peter I:296
Gilman, Philip II:152
Gilman, Samuel II:580
Gilman, Samuel T. I:995
Gilman, Zebulon I:843
Gilmer, Thomas II:674
Gilmon, Edmond III:786
Gilmore, Alexander IV:74
Gilmore, Charles II:73
Gilmore, Daniel I:545; III:493
Gilmore, David II:429
Gilmore, James II:453; III:165,
184, 267
Gilmore, John I:372; II:99,
429; III:831
Gilmore, Joseph III:523
Gilmore, Robert I:74, 458;
IV:113
Gilmore, Samuel I:291; II:580
Gilmore, Samuel (2) I:292
Gilmore, Uriah IV:17
Gilmore, William II:540
Gilner, Henry I:15
Gilpatrick, Nathaniel I:206
Gilpin, William III:710
Gilson, Eleazer I:758; IV:218
Gilson, Jacob I:909
Gilson, John I:758

Gilson, Peter I:987; II:493
Gilson, Solomon I:517, 909
Ginger, Henry IV:13
Ginnett, Thomas III:709
Gipson, Henry II:298
Gipson, William IV:61
Girardeau, John III:499
Girdler, James III:243
Girton, Belala III:27
Girton, Hannah II:27
Girton, James II:27
Girton, Temperance II:27
Girton, Thomas II:27
Gist, Joseph III:308
Gist, Thomas III:629
Gitchel, Zebulon I:951
Gitz, John, Sr. II:728
Given, Dickson III:335
Given, John I:248
Givens, James III:581
Givens, Patrick III:548
Givens, Robert, 2d III:298
Givens, Robert, 1st III:298
Givens, Samuel III:432
Givens, William III:326
Gladden, Azariah I:481
Gladden, Major III:383
Gladden, Solomon II:720
Gladding, James II:290
Gladding, Jedediah I:40
Gladding, William I:799
Glading, Joseph I:55
Gladsom, William II:49
Glasgo, William III:172
Glasgow, Cornelius III:628
Glasgow, James II:737
Glasgow, Lemuel III:447
Glasgow, Richard III:421
Glass, Alexander II:439
Glass, Charles III:760
Glass, Consider I:221
Glass, James III:299
Glass, John I:619
Glass, John, 2nd I:561
Glass, Michael IV:122
Glass, Seraiah I:560
Glass, William O. III:655
Glasscock, Robert III:719
Glassmeyer, Jacob III:638
Glasson, Patrick III:651, 654
Glaves, Michael III:199
Glazebrook, Julius III:267
Glazer, Aaron I:916
Glazier, Asa II:159
Glazier, Benjamin I:871
Glazier, Ebenezer II:344
Glazier, John III:46
Glazier, Jonathan I:443
Glazier, Moses II:157
Glazier, Oliver I:640
Glazier, Wm. II:347
Glean, Anthony II:505
Gleason, Benjamin I:909
Gleason, Caleb II:207
Gleason, Daniel I:961
Gleason, Ebenezer II:400
Gleason, Isaac I:851

Gleason, James II:393
Gleason, John I:149, 619
Gleason, Jonathan I:611
Gleason, Patrick III:712
Gleason, Thomas I:909
Gleason, Timothy I:722
Gleason, Windsor I:662
Gledden, Andrew I:300
Gleeson, Thomas I:500
Gleeson, William I:454
Glen, John III:543
Glendy, William II:635
Glenn, Andrew III:311
Glenn, James III:517; IV:262
Glenn, John II:574
Glenton, John III:633
Glentworth, James III:593
Glidden, Arnold I:221
Glidden, Comfort I:173
Glidden, Daniel I:173
Glidden, David II:544
Glidden, Gideon I:193
Glidden, Joseph I:173
Glidden, Lois I:173
Glidden, Winthrop I:173
Glidwill, William, 2d IV:90
Glines, Eli I:730
Glines, Israel I:284, 730
Glines, Nathaniel I:874
Glines, William I:717
Glinn, John III:316
Glinney, Isaac I:916
Gload, Eliza II:188
Gload, Elnathan II:188
Gload, Jane II:188
Glode, John I:500
Glontz, John II:699
Glossom, Abel I:160
Gloucester, James III:770
Glover, Alexander I:536
Glover, Benjamin I:590; III:88;
IV:4
Glover, Caesar I:596
Glover, Eliza S. I:533
Glover, Hannah I:533
Glover, James II:610
Glover, John I:531, 765;
III:481
Glover, Joseph III:265
Glover, Joshua I:533
Glover, Lemuel I:32
Glover, Nancy H. I:533
Glover, Nathaniel I:596
Glover, Peter I:395
Glover, Richard III:620
Glover, Samuel K. I:545
Glover, Susanna I:533
Glover, Thomas II:306
Glover, William IV:214
Gloyd, Asa IV:189
Gloyd, James II:419
Gloyd, Joseph I:481
Glozen, Phineas I:741
Goans, Blair III:202
Goans, James III:202
Goans, Mary III:202
Goans, Patrick III:202

391

Goans, Sophia III:202
Goatley, John III:209
Goatly, John III:334
Gobble, Christian III:843
Goben, William IV:34
Goble, George II:298; IV:4
Goble, Stephen IV:60
Godby, George III:445
Goddard, Abial I:585
Goddard, Barton III:658, 671
Goddard, Charles III:22
Goddard, Ebenezer I:99, 135
Goddard, Ed. Burton III:56
Goddard, Edward II:259
Goddard, Isaac I:98
Goddard, John I:98; III:12, 671
Goddard, Joseph III:278
Goddard, Josiah I:206
Goddard, Nancy III:671
Goddard, Rufus I:99
Goddard, Samuel I:657
Godden, John II:278
Godding, John I:962
Godenberger, Adam II:611
Godfrey, Caesar I:596
Godfrey, George II:674
Godfrey, Isaac I:85
Godfrey, John II:203
Godfrey, Jonathan I:86, 810
Godfrey, Rufus I:372
Godfrey, Seth I:443
Godfrey, Stephen I:85
Godfrey, Zachariah I:589; III:528
Godfry, George I:871
Goding, Spencer I:193
Godley, George III:445
Godman, William III:681
Godphrey, Jonathan I:722
Godsey, William III:448
Godsey, Wm. III:559
Godwin, Abraham A. II:559
Godwin, David II:559
Goens, David III:585
Goes, Lawrence M. II:385
Goewey, Garret II:354
Goff, Abel I:372
Goff, Abraham III:680
Goff, Adam III:715
Goff, Amos I:349
Goff, Comfort II:435
Goff, David, 2d II:259
Goff, David, 1st II:306
Goff, Gideon I:40, 155
Goff, Hezekiah I:881
Goff, Isaac II:264
Goff, Israel I:362
Goff, James I:249
Goff, Job III:788
Goff, John I:372; II:415
Goff, John, Jun. I:604
Goff, Nathan II:22
Goff, Nathaniel I. III:170
Goff, Richard II:377
Goff, Samuel I:55; I:390; III:414

Goff, Samuel D. II:640
Goff, Simeon I:349
Goff, Solomon IV:202
Goff, Wm. B. II:556
Goff, Zachariah III:680
Goforth, Cornelius III:534
Goforth, John III:534
Goforth, Miles III:351
Goforth, Nancy III:534
Goforth, Preston III:534
Goforth, Sally III:534
Goggin, Richard III:318
Gohn, Philip II:760
Goine, Joseph III:233
Going, Daniel III:539
Going, Edward III:421
Going, Sherard III:674
Going, William III:454
Goings, William III:546
Gold, John I:173
Gold, Joseph I:74
Gold, Mary Ann I:173
Gold, Tolent II:206
Golden, David II:63, 626
Golden, Walter III:22
Golden, Windsor II:318
Golding, Amos II:505
Golding, Reuben III:506
Golding, William III:259
Goldsberry, Charles III:56
Goldsbury, John IV:284
Goldsmith, James II:214
Goldsmith, Jeremiah II:342
Goldsmith, John III:155, 210
Goldsmith, Josiah III:367
Goldsmith, Zaccheus I:395
Goldthwait, James I:395
Goldthwait, M. I:322
Goldthwait, Philip I:236, 322
Goldthwaithe, Timothy I:266
Goldy, John II:669
Goldy, Nicholas II:44
Gollentine, Abraham II:720
Gollentine, Jacob II:720
Golloday, Joseph III:736
Gollyhorn, Thomas III:838
Gomsanlis, James III:287
Gonsalas, James II:731
Gonsowe, John I:825
Gooch, James I:771
Gooch, Jedediah I:309
Gooch, John I:889
Good, John III:267
Good, Solomon III:399
Good, William III:620
Goodale, Chester I:349
Goodale, Ebenezer I:416
Goodale, Eli II:490
Goodale, Ezekiel II:252
Goodale, Isaac II:524
Goodale, Samuel I:395
Goodale, Zachariah I:236
Goodall, Albert II:188
Goodall, Alvin I:875
Goodall, James II:351
Goodall, John II:188
Goodall, Lorin Shaw II:188

Goodall, Nathan II:284
Goodall, Prentice II:188
Goodard, Ebenezer I:619
Goode, Thomas III:75
Goode, William III:514
Goode, William, Sr. III:765
Goodel, James II:398
Goodell, Asa I:149
Goodell, Ebenezer IV:227
Goodell, Ezra II:211
Goodell, Jacob I:722
Goodell, Josiah I:971
Goodell, Richard III:819
Goodell, Silas I:68
Goodell, William I:500
Gooden, George II:313
Goodenough, Adino II:278
Goodenough, Ellsworth I:682
Goodenough, H. I:682
Goodenough, Joseph I:682
Goodenough, Mercy I:682
Goodenough, Moses I:682
Goodenough, Nancy I:682
Goodenow, Asaph I:593
Goodenow, Daniel I:961
Goodenow, Eben I:925
Goodenow, Hez. I:593
Goodenow, Isaac I:501
Goodenow, John I:285
Goodenow, Jonas II:165
Goodenow, Nacey I:593
Goodenow, Nahum I:977
Goodenow, William I:517
Goodfaith, David I:68
Goodhue, Phineas I:395
Goodin, Isaac III:286
Goodin, Lewis III:256
Gooding, George II:135; IV:115
Gooding, James II:659
Gooding, Thaddeus I:708
Goodlett, John III:503
Goodloe, Henry III:252
Goodman, Ansel III:320
Goodman, Elihu I:443
Goodman, Henry III:565
Goodman, Jacob III:308
Goodman, Moses I:40
Goodman, Thomas III:333, 850
Goodner, Conrad IV:18
Goodnight, Christo'r III:787
Goodnight, Henry III:544
Goodno, Calvin I:867
Goodnough, Calvin I:867
Goodnough, Ebenezer I:904
Goodnow, Abner I:443
Goodnow, Eli I:630; II:269
Goodnow, Elisha I:493
Goodnow, Ephriam I:500
Goodnow, Harriet I:493
Goodnow, John I:517
Goodnow, Margaret I:493
Goodnow, Rufus I:382
Goodrich, Abel II:452
Goodrich, Abner IV:205
Goodrich, Allen I:961; II:199

Goodrich, Bethuel, Jr.   I:840
Goodrich, Bethuel, Sen.   I:867
Goodrich, Charles   II:269
Goodrich, David   II:377
Goodrich, Deborah   I:155
Goodrich, Elisha   II:227
Goodrich, George   I:431
Goodrich, Gideon   I:98
Goodrich, Ichabod   I:40
Goodrich, Isaac   II:393
Goodrich, Jacob   II:464
Goodrich, James   I:125
Goodrich, Jared   I:155
Goodrich, Jemima   II:199
Goodrich, John   I:917
Goodrich, John, Sen.   III:575
Goodrich, John H.   IV:212
Goodrich, John M.   I:849
Goodrich, Joseph   I:679
Goodrich, Josiah   I:771
Goodrich, Levi   II:269
Goodrich, Micah   I:349
Goodrich, Michael   II:229
Goodrich, Noah   I:339
Goodrich, Peter   II:101
Goodrich, Roswell   I:99; II:452
Goodrich, Samuel   I:395;
   II:227
Goodrich, Simeon   I:962
Goodrich, Solomon P.   II:344
Goodrich, Stephen   I:867
Goodrich, Thomas   I:961
Goodrich, Zenos   II:484
Goodrick, Nathaniel   IV:90
Goodridge, Abijah   I:641
Goodridge, Benjamin   I:236
Goodridge, Francis   I:944
Goodridge, John   I:641
Goodridge, Joshua   I:881
Goodridge, Thomas   I:741
Goodrige, Oliver   I:415
Goodrum, John, Sr.   III:782
Goodrum, Thomas   III:345
Goodsell, Charles   I:2
Goodsell, Samuel P.   II:148
Goodsell, Thomas   II:453
Goodsey, Wm.   III:559
Goodson, Benjamin   III:121
Goodson, Joshua   III:414
Goodson, Thomas   III:500, 777
Goodson, William   III:272
Goodspeed, Elisha   I:904
Goodspeed, Gardner   II:104
Goodspeed, Nathaniel   I:443
Goodspread, Sympson   II:235
Goodwill, Damaris   II:189
Goodwill, James   II:189
Goodwill, Susanna   II:189
Goodwin, Aaron   I:236
Goodwin, Abigail   I:685-86
Goodwin, Abraham   II:90
Goodwin, Adam   I:309
Goodwin, Altuzah   I:685
Goodwin, Amaziah   I:309, 685
Goodwin, Amos   I:309; III:294
Goodwin, Benjamin   I:236,
   309, 395, 686; III:119

Goodwin, Daniel   I:771
Goodwin, Daniel S.   I:686
Goodwin, David   III:629
Goodwin, Edward   III:789
Goodwin, Elijah   I:898
Goodwin, George   I:193
Goodwin, Hezekiah   I:155
Goodwin, Jacob   I:206, 510
Goodwin, James   I:666, 676
Goodwin, James M.   I:686
Goodwin, John   I:284; III:121,
   789
Goodwin, John, Sr.   III:443
Goodwin, John M.   I:686
Goodwin, Jonathan   I:847
Goodwin, Joseph   I:296, 686
Goodwin, Julius C.   III:266
Goodwin, Lemuel   III:421
Goodwin, Levi   I:98
Goodwin, Moses   I:99
Goodwin, Paul   I:236
Goodwin, Pierce   III:412
Goodwin, Polly   I:155
Goodwin, Reuben   I:236, 309
Goodwin, Reuben, Jr.   I:236
Goodwin, Richard   I:249
Goodwin, Robinson   III:429
Goodwin, Sally   I:686
Goodwin, Samuel   I:686, 765
Goodwin, Seth   IV:269
Goodwin, Simeon   I:303
Goodwin, Solomon   II:453
Goodwin, Theophilus   III:75
Goodwin, Thomas   I:473, 517;
   III:814
Goodwin, Tristram   I:686
Goodwin, Uriah   I:500; II:453
Goodwin, Wells   I:842
Goodwin, Wiley   III:135
Goodwin, William   I:500, 611
Goodwin, Willowby   I:685
Goodwin, Zebedee   I:871
Goodyear, Edward   II:328, 558
Goodyear, George   II:760
Goodyear, Stephen   I:99
Goodyear, Theophilus   I:21
Googins, David   I:309
Googins, Stephen   I:236
Gookin, Abigail   I:322
Gookin, Daniel   I:322, 722
Goold, Daniel   I:236
Goold, James   I:717
Goold, John   I:977
Goold, Joseph   I:249
Goold, William   II:360
Goolsbury, Mark   III:221
Goolsby, Reuben   III:128
Goothery, Adam   I:611
Gootrick, Nathaniel   IV:90
Gorden, David   II:81
Gorden, James   III:415
Gorden, Kenneth   II:505
Gordin, Isaac   III:514
Gordon, Abel   I:765
Gordon, Albion   III:655
Gordon, Alfred   I:174
Gordon, Archibald   III:50

Gordon, Barnardus   IV:196
Gordon, Benjamin   I:228; IV:15
Gordon, Bernard   IV:196
Gordon, Caleb   I:193
Gordon, Catherine   II:626
Gordon, Charles   III:376, 631
Gordon, David   II:298
Gordon, Eliphalet   II:274
Gordon, Elizabeth   I:174
Gordon, Freelove   I:174
Gordon, George   III:726
Gordon, Hugh   I:174
Gordon, Isaac   II:192
Gordon, James   I:193; II:206;
   III:148
Gordon, James F.   III:177
Gordon, Jane   I:174
Gordon, John   I:174, 585;
   III:269; IV:165, 289
Gordon, John, 2d   II:650
Gordon, John, Jr.   I:174
Gordon, John, 1st   II:577
Gordon, Joseph   I:188, 321;
   II:259
Gordon, Joshua   III:351
Gordon, Josiah   I:174, 266
Gordon, Justin   I:174
Gordon, Lawrence   III:279
Gordon, Maria   II:27
Gordon, Peter   II:469
Gordon, Richard   III:593
Gordon, Robert   II:662; IV:90
Gordon, Samuel   II:313; III:325
Gordon, Solomon   III:394
Gordon, Sophia   II:192
Gordon, Thomas   II:27, 674
Gordon, Timothy   I:415; II:424
Gordon, William   I:174, 362,
   656, 730; II:27, 626; III:605
Gordon, Wm.   I:xiii
Gore, Isaac   III:283
Gore, Jacob   I:231
Gore, John   II:731
Gore, Joseph   I:536
Gore, Levi   I:771
Gore, Notley   III:292
Gore, Obadiah   II:640
Gore, Samuel   II:705
Gore, Simon   II:610
Gore, Thomas   III:537
Gorforth, Zachariah   III:627
Gorham, Daniel   I:109
Gorham, George   I:61, 454
Gorham, James   I:13
Gorham, John   I:641
Gorham, Joseph   I:327
Gorham, Josiah   I:206
Gorham, Nathan   I:86
Gorham, Nehemiah   I:154
Gorham, Phinehas   I:48
Gorham, Seth   I:961
Gorham, Silas   I:874
Gorill, Andrew   III:31
Gorin, John   III:256
Gorman, Archibald   III:278
Gorman, James   II:182
Gorman, John   II:4

393

Gorman, Joseph II:57
Gorman, William IV:148
Gorrell, John III:206
Gorsage, John III:620; IV:90
Gorsline, Samuel II:323
Gorton, Benjamin I:815; II:493
Gorton, Joseph I:135
Gorton, Prosper I:806
Gorton, Samuel II:429
Goskins, Samuel IV:51
Goslin, Lewis II:220
Gosline, Catherine II:192
Gosline, David II:192
Gosline, Richard II:192
Gosline, William L. II:192
Gosling, George III:477
Gosling, Samuel II:85
Goss, Abraham II:712
Goss, Andrew I:454
Goss, Comfort II:540
Goss, Ebenezer IV:212
Goss, Ephraim I:708, 765
Goss, Jacob III:415
Goss, John A. I:708
Goss, Jonathan IV:19
Goss, Philip I:443
Goss, Samuel I:723
Gossage, Jared III:22
Gosset, John IV:223
Gossom, Joseph I:595
Gotman, Henry II:252
Gott, John II:385
Gott, Joshua I:415
Gott, Story II:385
Gough, Ignatius III:262
Gough, John B. IV:123
Gould, Abigail I:174
Gould, Abraham I:596
Gould, Alexander I:309
Gould, Amos I:751
Gould, Asa I:977; II:146
Gould, Benjamin I:415, 611,
   708, 864; II:217
Gould, Carbaralzaman I:500
Gould, Daniel I:236, 266, 284;
   II:731
Gould, David I:517
Gould, Ebenezer I:481
Gould, Edmund II:405
Gould, Eli I:431
Gould, Elijah I:641; II:323,
   334
Gould, Harriet I:452
Gould, Henry I:593
Gould, Hiram I:174
Gould, Hosea I:864
Gould, Isaac I:174; II:398
Gould, Jabez I:193
Gould, Jacob I:898
Gould, James I:666, 751;
   II:187
Gould, Jeremiah I:688
Gould, Jesse I:266
Gould, John I:174, 236, 452,
   589, 676, 864, 889; II:81,
   445; IV:97
Gould, Jonas I:224

Gould, Jonathan I:593, 641
Gould, Joseph IV:231
Gould, Josiah II:68
Gould, Lavinia I:174
Gould, Levi I:168; II:187
Gould, Mary I:174
Gould, Moriah I:224
Gould, Noah II:313
Gould, Noah M. I:193
Gould, Peter I:929
Gould, Polly I:864
Gould, Robert II:58
Gould, Sally II:187
Gould, Samuel I:174, 415
Gould, Samuel, 2d I:431
Gould, Samuel, 1st I:395
Gould, Seth I:909
Gould, Silas I:193
Gould, Simeon II:207
Gould, Stephen I:758, 864
Gould, Thomas I:961; II:187
Gould, Timothy II:63
Gould, Willard II:536
Gould, William I:452, 723;
   II:63, 220, 290
Gould, William, 2d II:347
Gouldman, Francis III:692
Gove, Ebenezer I:751
Goves, Ezekiel II:464
Gow, Eleazor III:249
Gowan, Ezekiel I:619
Gowan, Hugh II:675
Gowdy, Alexander I:99
Gowdy, Hill I:99
Gowdy, John II:479
Gowdy, Samuel II:424
Gowell, Benjamin I:309
Gowell, Timothy I:676
Gowen, Francis IV:106
Gowens, Charles III:280
Gower, Abel III:164
Gower, George II:740
Gowey, Thomas III:372
Gowin, Charles I:585
Graber, Valentine II:637
Grace, Benjamin IV:106
Grace, Charles B. I:771
Grace, George II:611
Grace, Jacob II:677
Grace, John I:309; II:33;
   III:180
Grace, Lawrence II:313
Grace, Patrick I:206
Grace, William IV:58
Gracey, Robert III:425
Grady, William III:736
Grady, Younger III:665;
   IV:148
Graff, Philip II:439
Graff, Samuel II:714
Graffham, Enoch I:180
Graft, Philip II:696
Gragg, George I:881
Gragg, Samuel I:517
Gragg, William III:399
Graham, Aaron IV:2
Graham, Amos III:328

Graham, Andrew III:82
Graham, Benjamin I:27
Graham, Daniel II:643
Graham, E. A. II:563
Graham, Edmund I:27
Graham, Francis II:722
Graham, George II:723;
   III:849
Graham, Henry II:741
Graham, Hugh II:700
Graham, Isaac III:629
Graham, Isaac G. II:351, 566
Graham, James III:444, 499;
   IV:109, 203
Graham, Jesse I:55
Graham, John II:737; III:447,
   590; IV:185
Graham, Joseph I:22; III:429
Graham, Michael III:752
Graham, Nehemiah I:32
Graham, Roswell II:405
Graham, Stafford III:511
Graham, Thomas III:306, 683
Graham, William I:98; II:211,
   322; III:450, 555, 565
Gramlin, Adam II:703
Grammar, Jacob III:631
Grammer, F. L. I:xiv
Gramps, Henry II:439
Granberry, Thomas III:375
Grandison, Simeon I:560
Grandy, Asa II:235
Grandy, Bezaleel II:347
Grandy, Eri II:194
Graney, William III:455
Granger, Andrew II:740
Granger, Bildad I:40
Granger, D. I:322
Granger, Ebenezer II:306
Granger, Frederick I:596
Granger, George II:730
Granger, Ithamar I:454
Granger, Jacob II:290
Granger, John II:347
Granger, Justin I:454
Granger, Sebe II:305
Granger, Thomas IV:212
Granger, Zaccheus III:772
Grangwer, George II:730
Grannis, David II:364
Grannis, Ello I:125
Grannis, Enos II:692
Grannis, Jared I:125
Grant, Abel I:976
Grant, Alexander III:5809
Grant, Andrew I:961
Grant, Azariah I:904
Grant, Benjamin I:812
Grant, Benoni I:881
Grant, Beriah I:536
Grant, Charles H. II:255
Grant, Daniel IV:52
Grant, David I:99; III:540
Grant, Drury III:669
Grant, Edmund I:236
Grant, Edward II:593
Grant, Elisha III:393

Grant, Eliza III:669
Grant, Elnathan I:143
Grant, Gideon, Jr. I:40
Grant, Gilbert I:806
Grant, Godfrey II:192
Grant, Gustavus I:98
Grant, Hamilton I:19
Grant, Hezekiah I:349
Grant, Isaac IV:238
Grant, James III:539
Grant, Jeremiah III:74
Grant, John I:236; III:189,
    306, 425
Grant, Jonathan IV:225
Grant, Joseph II:274; III:167
Grant, Joshua I:162, 236
Grant, Margaret II:192
Grant, Martin I:206
Grant, Oliver I:134
Grant, Peter I:309
Grant, Reuben I:751
Grant, Richard I:795
Grant, Robert III:669, 749
Grant, Robert H. III:669
Grant, Roswell I:99, 109
Grant, Samuel II:611
Grant, Silas I:309
Grant, Thomas I:206; II:364
Grant, William I:236, 308;
    IV:189
Grantham, Richard III:583
Grapevine, Catherine III:40
Grapevine, Elizabeth III:40
Grapevine, Fred'k III:40
Grapevine, Mary Ann III:40
Grapevine, Rebecca III:40
Grapevine, Sarah III:40
Grass, Daniel IV:31
Grass, Frederick III:678
Grass, Peter III:795
Grasty, John III:326
Grater, Francis I:758
Gratton, Crary II:405
Gratton, Thomas II:479
Grauf, John II:677-78
Grave, Timothy I:125
Graves, Abner I:619
Graves, Abraham II:119
Graves, Allen I:871
Graves, Amos II:718
Graves, Asa I:939; II:278
Graves, Benjamin II:220
Graves, Boston III:595
Graves, Chauncey I:939
Graves, Daniel II:443
Graves, David I:961; III:774
Graves, Ebenezer II:290
Graves, Edmund III:322
Graves, Elijah II:278, 415
Graves, Eliphalet II:550
Graves, Gideon I:454, 657;
    II:323
Graves, Gilbert I:61
Graves, Hobart II:414
Graves, James III:295
Graves, Job I:443

Graves, John I:415; III:275,
    762
Graves, John B. II:151
Graves, Jonathan II:235
Graves, Joshua II:111
Graves, Josiah I:443
Graves, Levi I:619
Graves, Oliver I:443
Graves, Peter II:306
Graves, Ralph III:695
Graves, Reuben I:443; II:390;
    III:593
Graves, Richard III:397
Graves, Samuel I:206
Graves, Selah I:431
Graves, Seth II:332
Graves, Simeon II:238
Graves, Stephen III:549
Graves, Thadeus I:939
Graves, Thomas II:107; III:4,
    320; IV:122
Graves, Thomas H. III:199
Graves, Timothy II:493
Graves, Whitney I:149
Graves, William I:784, 961;
    III:135
Gravitt, John III:269
Graw, Ebenezer I:78
Gray, Aaron I:236
Gray, Alexander I:266; II:569,
    632
Gray, Alexander M. III:659
Gray, Amos I:976
Gray, Cato I:338
Gray, Daniel I:415; III:736;
    IV:233
Gray, David I:871
Gray, Dominicus I:934
Gray, Ebenezer I:481
Gray, Elijah II:240
Gray, Elliott I:481
Gray, Francis III:665, 686
Gray, Frazier II:8
Gray, Frederick III:495
Gray, Gabriel III:766
Gray, George III:228
Gray, Henry II:55; III:479
Gray, Isaac II:701; III:188
Gray, Jabesh II:344
Gray, Jacob II:53; III:100
Gray, James I:722; II:203,
    439, 661, 751; III:450, 458,
    633, 779; IV:225
Gray, James, 2d IV:189
Gray, Joel II:290, 694
Gray, John I:206, 730, 971;
    II:522, 540, 723; III:511,
    598; IV:67
Gray, Joseph I:85-86, 758;
    II:68, 112, 400 669, 713;
    III:324, 620
Gray, Josiah II:63
Gray, Lynch III:46
Gray, Matthew II:540
Gray, Robert I:481, 730;
    II:716

Gray, Samuel I:149; II:232;
    III:227, 566; IV:104
Gray, Shared III:100
Gray, Silas II:203
Gray, Solomon I:730
Gray, Thomas I:395; II:347
Gray, William III:22, 267,
    309, 367, 633; IV:281
Gray, Zerobabel III:575
Graydon, Alexander II:651
Greacey, John III:582
Greanleaf, Israel II:751
Grear, Thomas III:419
Greathouse, John III:789
Greeg, John II:611
Greely, John II:235
Greely, Jonathan I:395
Greely, Joseph I:668, 758
Greely, Noah I:266
Greely, Sally II:188, 192
Greely, Samuel II:188, 192
Greeman, John II:550
Greeming, Nehemiah III:674
Green, A. M. III:336
Green, Abel II:211
Green, Abner I:149
Green, Allen I:833, 961;
    II:174
Green, Amasa I:40
Green, Amos I:149, 463
Green, Andrew III:193, 690
Green, Archer II:173
Green, Asa I:987
Green, Asahel I:99
Green, Benjamin I:180, 630,
    815, 917; III:133; IV:265
Green, Bradbury I:722, 995
Green, Calvin I:850
Green, Chaffer II:435
Green, Charles III:245
Green, Cleophas I:500
Green, Coggishall I:825
Green, Daniel I:193, 249;
    II:306, 453, 474
Green, Dexter II:493
Green, Dorastus I:32
Green, Dorothy II:134
Green, Duty IV:292
Green, Ebenezer I:149; II:405
Green, Edward II:360
Green, Edward I. II:359
Green, Eleazer I:500
Green, Elias I:944
Green, Elijah III:731
Green, Eliphalet II:454
Green, Elisha B. IV:148
Green, Ezra I:777
Green, Fortunatus III:786
Green, Francis I:510, 658, 741
Green, George II:550; III:422,
    495
Green, Gerard III:287
Green, Henrich II:415
Green, Henry I:349, 815;
    II:469
Green, Irijah I:889

395

Green, Isaac I:640, 916, 987; II:377; IV:148
Green, Jabez II:414
Green, Jack II:351
Green, Jacob II:269
Green, James I:99, 668, 815, 852; II:38, 395, 474, 688
Green, James, 1st II:688
Green, James, 2d II:27
Green, James S. II:92
Green, Jehiel IV:269
Green, Jeremiah I:517; III:398
Green, Jesse III:427
Green, Jesse P. III:191
Green, Job II:493
Green, John I:47, 619; II:317, 367, 439, 493, 611, 643; III:133-34, 245, 286, 399, 460, 572, 664, 734; IV:223, 249
Green, John, 2d IV:207
Green, John R. III:134
Green, Jonathan I:229, 330
Green, Joseph I:206, 679, 723; II:63; III:696
Green, Joseph J. III:394
Green, Josiah II:182
Green, Lemuel I:603-4
Green, Lewis III:287
Green, Lodowick II:453
Green, Lucy III:134
Green, Malachi I:825
Green, Mark I:723
Green, Mrs. E. I:109
Green, Nathan II:290; III:591
Green, Noah I:349
Green, Obadiah I:99
Green, Paul III:331
Green, Peleg I:961
Green, Peter I:134, 431
Green, Pierson II:36
Green, Prince I:800
Green, Rebecca III:134
Green, Reuben II:419
Green, Richard I:561, 722
Green, Richard D. I:585
Green, Robert I:561; III:229; IV:119
Green, Rufus II:124
Green, Russell I:349
Green, Samuel I:125, 443; II:337, 426, 429
Green, Silas II:306
Green, Simon III:12, 806
Green, Stephen II:547
Green, Thomas I:853; II:362; III:133, 170, 186, 256
Green, Timothy II:214, 439, 667
Green, Uzziah I:962
Green, Wardwell III:159
Green, William I:517, 679, 692; II:85; III:28, 134, 284, 633
Green, William R. I:833
Green, Zachariah II:171, 520
Green, Zera I:850

Greene, Cato I:806
Greene, Charles I:800
Greene, Cuff I:806
Greene, David I:833
Greene, Henry IV:21
Greene, John Hayes II:7
Greene, Mansier II:313
Greene, Marcer II:313
Greene, Philip I:815
Greene, Stephen I:815, 833
Greene, Willard II:705
Greene, William I:800, 833; III:751
Greenelsh, Edward IV:262
Greenewalt, Nicholas II:657
Greenfield, Charles I:708
Greenfield, Enos II:284
Greenfield, James I:134
Greening, James III:269
Greenland, James II:692
Greenlaw, John I:216
Greenleaf, Benjamin I:206
Greenleaf, Caleb I:415
Greenleaf, Daniel I:216
Greenleaf, David I:688
Greenleaf, Enoch I:206
Greenleaf, John I:295
Greenleaf, Nathan I:708
Greenleaf, Samuel I:656
Greenleaf, Sophia I:656
Greenleaf, William I:395, 656
Greenman, Gideon I:833
Greenman, Jeremiah IV:223, 301
Greenman, Job I:795
Greenough, John I:395
Greenough, Jonathan I:224
Greenough, Manuel I:395
Greenough, William I:751
Greenslet, Benjamin I:68
Greenslet, John I:68
Greenslit, Joel II:453
Greenslit, John I:971
Greenwald, Jacob II:703
Greenwalt, Abraham II:694
Greenway, William III:625
Greenwell, Bennett III:321
Greenwell, Ignatius IV:123
Greenwood, Aaron I:619
Greenwood, Abel I:517
Greenwood, Bartlee III:231
Greenwood, Enoch I:619
Greenwood, Joseph III:265
Greenwood, Moses I:517
Greenwood, Philip IV:82
Greenwood, Thomas I:619
Greer, Amos I:149
Greer, George I:149; III:22
Greer, James I:229
Greer, Mesheck III:608
Greer, Moses I:60, 78
Greer, Richard III:629
Greer, Samuel III:562
Greer, Walter III:609
Greery, John IV:256
Greesham, Robert III:73
Gregg, David I:300

Gregg, Isaac I:881
Gregg, John II:429; IV:296
Gregg, Matthew IV:52
Gregg, Peter III:730
Gregg, Samuel III:85
Greggs, Hezekiah II:55
Greggs, Robert III:591
Gregorry, Spittsby III:324
Gregory, Abigail I:26
Gregory, Abraham III:386
Gregory, Asahel I:749
Gregory, Benjamin H. III:361
Gregory, Bry III:618
Gregory, Christian III:678
Gregory, Daniel I:85
Gregory, Elias I:86
Gregory, Eliza I:26
Gregory, Elnathan I:349
Gregory, Esbon II:373
Gregory, Ezra I:86
Gregory, George III:525, 594, 742
Gregory, Hannah I:26
Gregory, Isaac III:361, 483
Gregory, James III:781; IV:244
Gregory, John I:85, 554; II:645, 703; III:331
Gregory, Joshua III:490
Gregory, Josiah I:86
Gregory, Luther I:168
Gregory, Matilda I:26
Gregory, Matthew II:552
Gregory, Moses I:86
Gregory, Nathan I:85
Gregory, Nehemiah II:393
Gregory, Noah III:361
Gregory, Read I:26
Gregory, Richard III:177
Gregory, Sally I:26
Gregory, Samuel I:85; III:361
Gregory, Stephen II:493, 705
Gregory, Thomas II:344; III:361, 370, 391, 765
Gregory, Uriah II:505
Gregory, Walter III:738
Gregory, William II:435; III:429, 618
Greider, John, Sen. III:253
Greiger, John L. II:739
Greir, Moses III:774
Grelick, Henry III:197
Greman, Patrick II:135
Greninger, Henry II:709
Grennell, Amasa II:322
Grennell, Michael II:757
Grennell, Owen I:819
Grennell, William I:442
Gresham, David III:180
Gresham, George II:743
Gresham, John III:511
Gresham, Littlebury III:180
Grettin, George G. III:2
Grey, Jonathan II:673
Grey, Samuel II:135
Gribbon, John IV:235
Grice, William III:405
Grider, Henry III:327

Grider, John III:201
Gridley, Asahel II:429
Gridley, Ashbel I:99
Gridley, Coert H. II:555
Gridley, Elijah II:464
Gridley, Elisha II:367
Gridley, Giles II:171
Gridley, Hosea II:279
Gridley, John II:232, 555
Gridley, Obadiah II:224
Gridley, Seth I:40, 458
Gridley, Silas I:109
Gridley, Thomas II:524
Gridsby, Benjamin III:322
Grier, George II:604
Griffer, Andrew II:493
Griffer, Thomas II:429
Griffey, Zachariah IV:200
Griffin, Amos III:388
Griffin, Benjamin I:395, 708;
  II:310
Griffin, Charles III:62
Griffin, Daniel I:55
Griffin, David I:117
Griffin, Edward III:133
Griffin, Ezra IV:227
Griffin, George II:4
Griffin, Gordon III:206
Griffin, Ira I:685
Griffin, James III:170, 783
Griffin, James, Jun. I:395
Griffin, Jeremiah I:708
Griffin, Jesse III:478
Griffin, John I:55; III:377
Griffin, Joseph I:995; II:484;
  IV:270
Griffin, Joshua II:667
Griffin, Kirkland II:279
Griffin, Martin II:306; III:665
Griffin, Moses III:592
Griffin, Nathan III:64
Griffin, Nathaniel I:765
Griffin, Obadiah III:791
Griffin, Philip I:810
Griffin, Pierce II:135
Griffin, Ralph IV:77
Griffin, Reuben III:228
Griffin, Richard III:432
Griffin, Samuel II:484
Griffin, Sherrod III:284
Griffin, Stephen IV:263
Griffin, Susannah I:685
Griffin, Theophilus I:685, 708
Griffin, Thomas I:722; III:437
Griffin, William III:228
Griffin, Zachariah III:766
Griffing, Samuel R. II:378
Griffing, Stephen II:536
Griffis, Abner II:484
Griffis, Reuben III:422
Griffis, Southward I:825
Griffis, Stephen II:749
Griffith, Barnabas I:327
Griffith, Chrisholm III:774
Griffith, David IV:233
Griffith, Elijah II:8
Griffith, Elisha II:720

Griffith, Ellis I:976
Griffith, Evan III:62
Griffith, George II:227
Griffith, Griffin III:650
Griffith, Isaac III:439
Griffith, Jeremiah II:214
Griffith, John I:806; II:73,
  653; III:607
Griffith, Joseph III:608
Griffith, Levi II:655
Griffith, Nathan I:867; IV:233
Griffith, Philemon III:64
Griffith, Samuel III:65, 646
Griffith, Samuel J. IV:267
Griffith, Thomas II:540;
  III:801; IV:113
Griffith, Wiliam II:701
Griffith, William IV:102
Griffith, Wm. II:484
Griffith, Zaddock III:445
Griffiths, Abraham III:702
Griger, Cato II:278
Grigg, Henry I:85
Grigg, James II:182; IV:141
Grigg, Josiah III:768
Grigg, Lewis III:614
Griggs, Benjamin II:72
Griggs, Charles III:411
Griggs, Ephraim I:917
Griggs, Gideon I:846
Griggs, John II:18
Griggs, Joseph I:463
Grigsby, Aaron III:582
Grigsby, Moses III:369
Grill, Thomas II:249, 556
Grim, Jacob IV:278
Grim, John III:776
Grim, Peter III:736
Grimes, Abraham I:929
Grimes, Andrew I:909
Grimes, James IV:87, 233
Grimes, John III:4, 598;
  IV:274
Grimes, Leonard III:226
Grimes, William III:12
Grimnit, Josiah III:592
Grimsley, Joseph III:620
Grimsley, Thomas III:147
Grindle, William I:188
Grindstaff, Abraham IV:112
Grindstaff, Jacob III:295
Grindstaff, Michael III:229
Griner, Peter III:162
Grinnell, Bailey I:275
Grinnell, George II:284
Grinnell, Richard I:454
Grinnell, Robert I:819
Grinnell, Royall I:275
Grinnell, William I:819
Grinnell, Wise I:722
Grinstead, John IV:43
Grinstead, William III:779
Grinter, John III:232
Grisham, James, Sen. III:421
Grisham, Moses III:498
Grissom, Richard III:345
Grist, Benjamin III:511

Griswold, Aaron I:971
Griswold, Abm. IV:300
Griswold, Adonijah IV:13
Griswold, Albert II:187
Griswold, Andrew I:68
Griswold, Ann II:187
Griswold, Asa I:48
Griswold, Avery I:6
Griswold, Benjamin I:881
Griswold, Chester II:148
Griswold, Constant I:99
Griswold, D. J. I:156
Griswold, Daniel II:415
Griswold, David I:962; II:524
Griswold, Ebenezer I:61
Griswold, Edmund II:423
Griswold, Edward II:528
Griswold, Elijah I:40, 99
Griswold, Elisha I:857
Griswold, Francis II:415
Griswold, George I:117; II:187
Griswold, Harriet II:187
Griswold, Hiram II:187
Griswold, Huldah I:857
Griswold, Jabez II:323
Griswold, Janna II:415
Griswold, Joel I:117
Griswold, John II:278, 757
Griswold, John, 2d II:249
Griswold, Joseph II:290
Griswold, Josiah II:187
Griswold, Midian I:47
Griswold, Nathaniel I:117
Griswold, Samuel I:961; II:344
Griswold, Sarah II:187
Griswold, Selah I:117
Griswold, Simeon II:313, 493
Griswold, Solomon IV:227
Griswold, William II:187
Griswold, Zenos I:117
Gritton, John III:306
Griwold, Ahua I:857
Griwold, Betsy I:857
Groat, Abraham S. II:354
Groat, Isaac II:354
Groat, Peter II:385
Groat, William I:300
Groessel, John III:744
Grogan, Patrick IV:171
Groom, Jonathan III:752
Groom, Major III:264
Grooms, Abraham IV:226
Grooms, John IV:233
Groot, Derick II:510
Groot, Derick C. II:510
Groot, Simon A. II:510
Groover, Peter III:162
Grose, Deborah I:658
Grose, Elisha I:560, 658
Grosh, Michael III:693
Gross, Alexander I:327
Gross, Benjamin I:259
Gross, David I:249
Gross, Ebenezer H. I:216
Gross, John I:751, 806
Gross, Jonah I:454
Gross, Peter II:269, 562

397

Gross, Samuel I:78
Grossman, Eliza II:626
Grossman, Mary II:626
Grossman, Samuel II:626
Grossman, Sarah II:626
Grosvenor, Asa I:517
Grosvenor, Joshua I:149
Grosvenor, Samuel I:149
Grosvenor, Thomas I:78
Grotecloss, Gilbert II:559
Grout, Amasa I:784
Grout, Demil I:862
Grout, Elias I:517
Grout, Elihu I:944
Grout, Hilkiah I:961
Grout, Joel I:481
Grout, Jonathan I:862
Grout, William II:360
Grove, David III:58
Grove, John II:72; III:697
Grove, Jonas IV:196
Grove, Philip II:733; III:771
Grove, Windle IV:289
Grover, Amasa I:889
Grover, Amaziah I:950
Grover, Benjamin I:619, 841
Grover, Clemenia II:195
Grover, David I:362
Grover, Dwight II:195
Grover, Eben I:143
Grover, Elisha II:195
Grover, Jabez I:117
Grover, Jacob I:917
Grover, James II:195
Grover, Jonathan M. III:297
Grover, Joseph II:640
Grover, Luther I:987
Grover, Nehemiah II:536
Grover, Peter II:195
Grover, Stephen II:63
Grover, Velency II:195
Grover, Zalman II:195
Groves, Jacob II:125
Groves, Stephen III:172
Groves, Thomas III:694
Groves, William III:42
Grovesnor, Richard III:240
Grovier, Isaiah IV:207
Grow, Abrose II:464
Grow, Ebenezer I:78
Grow, John II:435
Grow, Peter IV:270
Grownhart, John II:259
Grubb, Jacob II:663
Grubb, John II:29
Grubbs, Hensley III:705
Grubbs, Nathan III:826
Gruber, Philip III:505
Grummun, Ebenezer II:393
Grumph, Christopher II:728
Grundy, Edmund I:867
Grush, Thomas I:395
Gryder, Martin III:272
Gryder, Valentine III:272
Gualtney, Nathan III:380
Guard, Daniel II:49
Guechen, Peter II:610

Guellow, Francis I:362
Guess, Benjamin III:82
Guess, George IV:42
Guess, Joseph III:264
Guest, James II:711
Guest, John I:47
Guest, William III:511
Guffin, John II:611
Guffy, James IV:71
Guice, John, Sen. III:171
Guild, Amos I:545
Guild, Elias I:546
Guild, Jacob I:545
Guild, Jesse I:976
Guild, John I:951
Guild, Joseph I:473, 657
Guild, Napthali II:505
Guild, Richard I:806
Guild, Samuel I:546; II:453
Guile, Abraham II:439
Guile, Holly II:148
Guiles, Joseph II:135
Guilford, Joseph III:403
Guilford, Samuel I:443
Guilford, Simeon I:473
Guilford, Timothy I:473
Guill, John III:245
Guill, William III:783
Guillion, John O. IV:35
Guines, James III:202
Guion, Isaac II:269
Gulick, Abraham II:405, 429
Gulick, Abraham I. II:72
Gulick, Ferdinand IV:278
Gulick, John II:72
Gulick, Peter II:72
Gulley, John III:593
Gulley, Richard III:139
Gullion, Robert IV:92
Gulliver, Lemuel I:545
Gulliver, Reuben I:929
Gulpin, Daniel I:98
Gump, Frederick II:723
Gundeway, Richard I:561
Gunison, Samuel III:233
Gunn, Aaron I:33
Gunn, Abel II:232
Gunn, Alexander I:339
Gunn, Daniel II:211
Gunn, Eli I:443
Gunn, Gabriel III:176
Gunn, Jeremiah II:611
Gunn, John III:633
Gunn, Moses I:443
Gunn, Noble IV:167
Gunn, Salmon I:443
Gunn, Starling III:408
Gunnell, John II:637
Gunnell, William III:142
Gunney, Timothy III:579
Gunnison, Josiah I:309
Gunnison, William I:530-31
Gunsalus, Daniel II:336
Gunsaluss, Henry IV:253
Gunsanlies, Richard II:709
Gunsauld, John IV:231
Gunston, James III:425

Gunter, Charles III:169
Gunter, Henry III:484
Gunter, Joel III:561
Gunter, John III:490
Gunter, William III:193
Gurley, Jeremiah III:88
Gurner, Samuel II:99
Gurney, Asa I:481, 574
Gurney, Bazaleel II:278
Gurney, Benjamin I:560
Gurney, Eliab I:180
Gurney, Francis II:439
Gurney, Jacob I:284
Gurney, Jonathan I:216
Gurney, Joseph I:443
Gurney, Joseph P. I:574
Gurney, Lemuel I:249
Gurney, Levi I:561
Gurney, Zachariah I:574
Gurnsey, Chauncey I:109
Gushan, Joseph I:611
Gushe, Elijah I:372
Gushee, Samuel I:372
Gushert, Dietrich II:722
Gust, Matthias II:716
Gustin, Amos IV:165
Gustin, Benajah IV:291
Gustin, Thomas I:180
Gustine, Edward I:741
Gustine, Elisha II:419
Gustine, Joel III:14
Guthery, James III:515
Guthery, John IV:210
Guthery, William III:226
Guthrey, John III:783
Guthrie, Abraham II:279
Guthrie, Daniel II:99
Guthrie, James I:48
Guthrie, John III:357
Guthrie, Nathaniel III:302
Guthrie, Robert II:593; III:631
Guthrie, William II:692;
    III:642
Guthry, John III:678
Gutridge, William IV:131
Gutterson, William I:777
Guy, James III:405
Guy, John II:31, 540
Guy, William II:360; III:421
Guyant, Luke I:135
Guynip, Benjamin II:55
Guynn, John III:190
Guyton, Aaron III:494
Gwin, Andrew III:704
Gwin, Humphrey III:718
Gwin, John III:571; IV:193
Gwin, Thomas IV:225
Gwinn, Jesse III:822
Gwinn, Samuel III:781
Gwinnup, George IV:297
Gwinup, George IV:189

Haas, Christian III:785
Haas, John II:69
Haas, Robert II:337
Haaze, Leonard II:674

399

Hall, Benjamin, 2d II:494
Hall, Caleb I:771; II:367
Hall, Calvin I:266; II:453
Hall, Charles I:181; II:494
Hall, Clement III:542
Hall, Cyrus II:179
Hall, Daniel I:171, 350, 765;
II:252, 479
Hall, David I:55, 311, 709;
II:73; III:462, 565, 699; IV:36
Hall, David, Jr. II:152
Hall, Ebenezer I:110, 171,
709, 777
Hall, Edmund IV:81
Hall, Edward I:xv; III:269
Hall, Elias I:875, 962
Hall, Elijah I:730
Hall, Elisha I:562; II:415
Hall, Enoch I:285, 296, 330;
II:454
Hall, Enos I:126
Hall, Ephraim I:672, 977;
II:464
Hall, Farnham I:416
Hall, Gad II:453
Hall, George II:405; IV:97
Hall, Gershom I:925
Hall, Hananiah I:995
Hall, Hannah I:171; II:622
Hall, Henry I:330, 988; II:135
Hall, Herbert III:669
Hall, Hezekiah IV:179
Hall, Hubbard III:669
Hall, Isaac I:275, 300, 742,
833; II:594
Hall, Isham III:760
Hall, Jabez I:194
Hall, Jacob I:988; II:31
Hall, James I:536, 785, 917;
II:31, 203, 622; III:107, 123,
287, 379, 802, 825
Hall, Jeremiah I:126; II:494
Hall, Jesse I:463; III:511, 811
Hall, Job I:194, 372
Hall, John I:110, 266, 373,
473, 643; II:319, 474, 622;
III:273, 320, 746, 766, 786;
IV:233, 238, 242
Hall, John, 2d II:217
Hall, John B. II:390
Hall, John Y. III:23
Hall, Jonathan I:463, 987;
II:303
Hall, Joseph I:194, 611;
II:291, 516; III:298, 706
Hall, Josiah I:641
Hall, Josiah, 2d I:546
Hall, Jotham II:259
Hall, Jude I:723
Hall, Justus II:494
Hall, Laban I:432
Hall, Levi I:118, 207, 784,
934
Hall, Luther I:180
Hall, Lyman I:109, 350, 833
Hall, Malinda II:622
Hall, Mordecai II:177

Hall, Moses I:125, 709; IV:227
Hall, Moses, 2d II:323
Hall, Moses, 1st II:291
Hall, Nancy II:622
Hall, Nathan III:746
Hall, Nathaniel, Jr. I:810
Hall, Nicholas II:238
Hall, Noah I:260
Hall, Obed I:688
Hall, Oliver I:286
Hall, Peleg I:825
Hall, Percival I:596
Hall, Peter I:963
Hall, Peter L. IV:286
Hall, Recompence I:917
Hall, Reuben I:723; IV:262
Hall, Rhodes II:485
Hall, Richard I:709; III:69
Hall, Robert I:426; II:203;
III:324; IV:80
Hall, Samuel I:61, 925; II:405;
IV:155
Hall, Sarah II:622
Hall, Seth I:86; III:669
Hall, Silas I:833; II:524
Hall, Solomon, Sen. III:496
Hall, Stephen I:33, 86, 363,
641, 905; II:474
Hall, Susan II:622
Hall, Sylvanus I:731
Hall, __thaniel II:245
Hall, Thomas I:350, 723, 810,
934; II:354; III:309, 595,
669
Hall, Timothy I:99, 717;
III:802
Hall, Titus I:61
Hall, Wakeman II:691
Hall, Wildman I:87
Hall, William I:207, 237;
II:23, 291, 368, 494; III:93,
350, 447, 669, 713, 786,
841; IV:15, 42, 123
Hall, William W. III:23
Halladay, John IV:210
Halladay, Roger II:540
Hallady, Jonah II:479
Hallam, John I:135
Hallam, Robert I:135
Hallet, Solomon I:194, 266
Hallet, Thomas I:69
Hallet, William II:298, 611
Hallett, Benjamin I:330
Hallett, Jonathan I:249
Hallett, Solomon II:217
Hallett, Thomas I:157
Hallman, Barbaras IV:164
Hallman, Conrad IV:164
Hallman, Elizabeth IV:164
Hallman, George II:673
Hallman, John IV:164
Hallman, Philip IV:164
Hallman, Stephen IV:164
Hallman, William IV:164
Hallock, Daniel II:520
Hallock, Joseph II:298
Hallock, Moses I:482

Hallow, Richard P. I:18
Halloway, James III:649
Halloway, Taylor III:437
Halloway, William I:194
Hallowell, Henry I:396
Hallowell, Richard II:594
Halls, Timothy II:684
Hallstead, Richard II:241
Hally, Benjamin III:269
Haloy, Morris III:245
Halsey, Andrew II:187
Halsey, Elias II:187
Halsey, Henry III:413
Halsey, Hezekiah II:187
Halsey, John I:925
Halsey, Luther II:298, 557
Halsey, Malache III:413
Halsey, Margaret II:187
Halsey, Matthew II:518
Halsey, Philip I:100
Halsey, Sylvanus II:520
Halsinger, Abraham II:153
Halstead, Edward IV:242
Halstead, Jacob IV:289
Halstead, John I:xv; II:291
Halsted, Joseph II:453
Halsted, Matthias II:36
Halsted, Thomas II:506
Halter, John IV:257
Ham, Benjamin I:777
Ham, Drury III:298
Ham, Ephraim I:700
Ham, John I:176, 194, 777;
III:602
Ham, Mary I:176
Ham, Nathaniel I:250
Ham, Robert I:162
Ham, Sarah I:176
Hambell, John II:574
Hambin, David II:399
Hamblet, Jonathan I:501
Hamblet, Phineas I:692
Hamblet, William I:894
Hambleton, James III:752
Hambleton, Thomas III:622
Hamblin, America I:286
Hamblin, Daniel I:925
Hamblin, Job IV:33
Hamblin, John I:482, 925,
963
Hamblin, Levi IV:179
Hamblin, Pierce Dant III:296
Hamblin, William I:207
Hamblin, Zacchia II:373
Hambright, Davis II:624
Hambright, Elizabeth II:624
Hambright, Henry II:728
Hambright, Henry, Jr. II:624
Hambright, Maria II:624
Hamburgh, Francis I:793
Hamby, William III:569
Hamer, James IV:190
Hamersly, John IV:80
Hames, John, Sen. III:165
Hames, Samuel I:110
Hames, Simeon I:229
Hamest, John IV:236

Hamilton, Abner III:256
Hamilton, Adam I:473
Hamilton, Alexander III:750
Hamilton, Andrew II:645
Hamilton, Andrew, Sen.
III:512
Hamilton, Ann III:668
Hamilton, Asa I:659
Hamilton, Barton III:74
Hamilton, Benjamin II:49;
III:310; IV:87
Hamilton, Charles IV:165
Hamilton, Daniel II:332, 755
Hamilton, David II:99, 368;
III:502, 511, 581
Hamilton, Davis III:668
Hamilton, Eliakim I:349
Hamilton, Eliphalet I:620
Hamilton, Elizabeth I:659
Hamilton, Frederick I:815
Hamilton, Geo_ge II:569
Hamilton, George III:668
Hamilton, James I:930; II:657;
III:275, 318, 410, 518, 640,
668, 697, 797
Hamilton, James (2) III:640
Hamilton, John I:310; II:342,
661; III:261, 264, 333, 668;
IV:31, 56
Hamilton, John, 2d II:662
Hamilton, John, Sen. III:143
Hamilton, Joseph I:620, 904
Hamilton, Joshua II:279;
III:621
Hamilton, Mustoe III:668
Hamilton, Osbourne III:668
Hamilton, Reuben II:291
Hamilton, Richard I:229
Hamilton, Robert I:431;
IV:221, 300
Hamilton, Samuel II:506
Hamilton, Silas II:368
Hamilton, Thomas II:651;
III:310, 437, 610
Hamilton, William I:249, 643;
II:49, 654, 726; III:4, 259
Hamlet, John III:265
Hamlet, William III:763
Hamlin, Amos II:410
Hamlin, Asa II:279
Hamlin, Benjamin I:109
Hamlin, Cornelius I:48
Hamlin, Elisha I:109
Hamlin, Europe I:709
Hamlin, James II:419
Hamlin, John I:74, 117, 459;
III:309; IV:244
Hamlin, Joseph I:86
Hamlin, Mark I:99
Hamlin, Prince I:180
Hamlin, Samuel II:323
Hamlin, Seth II:207
Hamm, John I:xv; III:244, 300
Hamma, William II:135
Hamman, Abraham IV:94
Hammell, Hugh II:758
Hammell, Robert II:758

Hammer, George IV:86
Hammer, Palser III:821
Hammer, Peter III:809
Hammerly, James III:315
Hammet, Caleb II:291
Hammill, William II:440
Hammock, William III:326
Hammon, Henry II:627
Hammon, Jonathan II:627
Hammon, Obadiah III:296
Hammon, Philip III:237
Hammon, Thomas III:587
Hammond, Abbey II:197
Hammond, Abijah II:559
Hammond, Abner II:197
Hammond, Catherine II:197
Hammond, Daniel II:171
Hammond, David I:723, 789;
II:401, 611
Hammond, Elisha II:547
Hammond, Elizabeth II:197
Hammond, Experience I:561
Hammond, Gardner I:596
Hammond, Gideon I:575
Hammond, Hinsdel II:518
Hammond, Isaac II:291;
IV:234
Hammond, Jason II:524
Hammond, Job IV:35
Hammond, John II:229;
III:278
Hammond, Joshua III:174
Hammond, Lewis II:197
Hammond, Margaret II:559
Hammond, Maria II:197
Hammond, Moses I:260
Hammond, Noah I:575
Hammond, Paul II:262
Hammond, Paulipus I:194
Hammond, Peter III:52, 317
Hammond, Roger I:310
Hammond, Samuel III:501
Hammond, Shubel I:561
Hammond, Staats II:177
Hammond, Stephen II:415
Hammond, Thomas I:962;
II:310; IV:169
Hammond, Titus II:550
Hammods, Edmond I:310
Hammons, Absalom III:520
Hammons, Benjamin III:458
Hammons, Joseph III:392
Hamond, John I:825
Hampton, Jacob III:5
Hampton, John II:18; III:169
Hampton, Thomas IV:122
Hampton, Wm. III:600
Hampton, Wm. Dennis III:714
Hamrick, Benjamin III:815
Hamrick, Henry II:678
Hamrick, Siras III:785
Hamrickhouse, Peter III:67
Hamson, Edson II:292
Hamson, John I:397
Hamson, William II:651
Han, David III:52
Hanchet, Jonah IV:283

Hanck, George M. III:830
Hanckett, Ezra I:100
Hancock, Austin III:802
Hancock, Bennett IV:21
Hancock, Cutlope II:699
Hancock, Edward III:752
Hancock, Isaiah III:311
Hancock, James III:783
Hancock, Joel II:107
Hancock, Joseph III:565; IV:59
Hancock, Levi I:742
Hancock, Martin III:633
Hancock, Milley IV:21
Hancock, Moses I:455
Hancock, Nathan I:207
Hancock, Samuel III:433, 752
Hancock, Stephen III:611
Hancock, Thomas I:537
Hancock, William I:237, 454
Hancox, Edward I:135
Hand, Aaron II:63
Hand, Abraham III:350
Hand, Christopher III:810
Hand, Darius II:306
Hand, Ichabod II:126
Hand, John III:316
Hand, Joseph II:484; III:166
Hand, Josiah II:520
Hand, Samuel III:626
Handcock, John III:411
Handell, John II:678
Handershort, John IV:273
Handerson, Timothy I:481
Handford, Ebenezer I:87
Handley, Charles I:518
Handley, James H. III:643
Handley, Samuel III:580
Handlin, Mathias IV:234
Handlin, Patrick III:23
Handlin, Stephen III:555
Hands, James I:181
Hands, John I:117
Handy, Benjamin I:286
Handy, E. W. I:xiii
Handy, Ebenezer I:825
Handy, Edward I:575
Handy, Elnathan I:188
Handy, Gamaliel I:363
Handy, John I:802
Handy, John L. II:9
Handy, Joseph II:207
Handy, Levi I:327
Handy, Russell I:799
Handy, Samuel I:362; II:566
Handy, Silas I:575
Handy, Thomas I:362
Hanes, Benjamin III:622
Hanes, John I:xvi; III:705
Hanes, Robert I:620
Haney, Charles III:399
Haney, Daniel I:249
Haney, David IV:36
Haney, Francis IV:16
Haney, James III:819
Haney, John III:698
Haney, Robert III:450
Haney, William III:218

Hanford, Levi II:393
Hanford, Ozias II:182
Hanies, Thomas I:766
Hankerson, William I:194
Hankins, Abraham III:596
Hankins, James III:600
Hankins, John III:293
Hanks, Abner IV:78
Hanks, Abraham III:598
Hanks, Ebenezer I:482
Hanks, Elijah IV:250
Hanks, Levi I:925
Hanks, William II:398
Hanley, Mathew I:795
Hanlin, Patrick III:741
Hanlon, James III:706
Hanly, Hardy IV:91
Hanmor, Jabez II:528
Hanmore, David II:332
Hanna, James P. III:40
Hanna, John II:9, 524; III:40, 240; IV:195
Hanna, Nancy III:40
Hanna, Robert III:517
Hanna, Thomas III:514
Hanna, William III:40
Hannaford, Thomas I:777
Hannah, Andrew III:625
Hannah, Daniel II:159
Hannah, James II:252
Hannah, John II:632
Hannah, Robert II:720, 758
Hannaman, William IV:94
Hannan, Esom III:755
Hannegan, James III:129
Hanness, William II:328
Hannewell, William I:224
Hannon, William II:611
Hannum, Moses I:482
Hannum, William II:241
Hanor, Philip II:494
Hanpt, John M. III:46
Hans, William I:181
Hanscom, Gideon I:237
Hanscom, Humphrey I:250
Hanscom, Nathan I:266
Hanscom, Reuben I:237
Hanscomb, John, 2d I:207
Hanscomb, John, 1st I:237
Hanscomb, Nathaniel I:237
Hansel, George II:151
Hansell, Anthony II:73
Hansford, Charles III:312
Hansford, William III:243
Hansicum, Robert I:237
Hansil, Isaac II:153
Hansley, Robert III:587
Hanson, Charles I:879
Hanson, Christian I:61
Hanson, Isaac I:397
Hanson, John II:536
Hanson, Jonthan I:237
Hanson, Nathan I:777
Hanspan, Cutlip III:43
Hant, Asa I:501
Happes, Michael, Sen. II:747
Happy, John G. II:532

Happy, William III:22
Haptinstall, Abraham IV:248
Haraden, John I:988
Harakin, John IV:263
Harbaugh, Jacob II:655
Harbert, Edward III:789
Harbert, Samuel III:789
Harbert, William IV:216
Harbeson, David II:11
Harbeson, John II:603
Harbeson, William II:708
Harbinson, Robert IV:251
Harbison, Francis II:662
Harbison, James III:499; IV:68
Harbison, John III:538
Harbolt, Adam III:637
Harbour, Jeremiah III:188
Harbour, Noah III:783
Hard, Zadock III:197
Hardee, Thomas III:184
Hardee, William III:484
Harden, Richard IV:130
Hardenbrook, Lodowick IV:263
Harder, Peter II:540
Hardesty, Francis IV:280
Hardesty, Hezekiah IV:14
Hardesty, Obadiah IV:295
Hardesty, Richard IV:230
Hardey, Pary IV:242
Hardiman, John III:613
Hardin, Benjamin III:99, 290
Hardin, Cato II:580
Hardin, George W. IV:28
Hardin, Henry III:184
Hardin, James II:326
Hardin, John II:720
Hardin, Joseph III:94
Hardin, Lewis III:478
Hardin, Mark III:328
Hardin, Richard IV:214
Hardin, Samuel I:561
Hardin, Thomas III:220; IV:239
Hardin, William II:720; IV:275
Harding, Abiel II:477
Harding, Abijah I:431
Harding, David I:181
Harding, Ede IV:81
Harding, Fielding III:665
Harding, George II:419; III:746
Harding, Henry, Jr. IV:81
Harding, Hezekiah I:181
Harding, Israel II:667
Harding, Jeremiah I:135
Harding, John II:55
Harding, Joshua I:620
Harding, Nathan I:330
Harding, Oliver II:332
Harding, Robert II:611
Harding, Samuel II:751
Harding, Seth I:300
Harding, Stephen I:546
Harding, Thomas III:284
Harding, Vachel III:294
Harding, William I:825

Hardison, James III:605
Hardison, Stephen I:229, 237
Hardman, Michael II:36
Hardwick, George III:297
Hardy, Barbara III:671
Hardy, Benjamin I:765, 893
Hardy, Caroline III:359
Hardy, Daniel I:898
Hardy, Elias II:655
Hardy, Fanny III:359
Hardy, Henrietta III:359
Hardy, Isaac I:765
Hardy, Jesse I:730
Hardy, John III:359, 671; IV:88
Hardy, Joshua I:596
Hardy, Lavinia III:359
Hardy, Louisa III:359
Hardy, Moody I:759
Hardy, Nathaniel IV:212
Hardy, Noah I:741
Hardy, Phineas I:759
Hardy, Thomas III:573
Hardy, Whitwell III:359
Hardy, William I:194; II:306
Hare, Michael II:654
Hare, Richard, Sen. III:814
Hare, Robert I:431
Hare, Thomas II:224
Harford, Peter II:155-56
Hargan, Michael III:286
Hargate, Peter III:304
Hargis, Thomas III:441
Hargis, William III:629
Hargrave, Hezekiah III:814
Hargrave, John IV:19
Hargrave, William III:77
Hargrove, Alexander III:122
Hargrove, John III:739
Hargus, John III:240
Haring, Garrett F. II:58
Haring, John A. II:445
Haring, John D. II:498
Haring, John F. II:58
Haring, Samuel II:95
Harisbrough, John III:785
Harker, Joseph II:182
Harkerider, John II:846
Harkeshimer, John III:58
Harkness, James IV:17
Harkness, John II:705
Harlan, George III:306
Harlew, George III:319
Harley, Solomon I:502
Harlow, Alexander C. I:863
Harlow, Alonzo B. I:863
Harlow, Ansel I:575
Harlow, Ataline I:173
Harlow, Catherine I:173
Harlow, Dolly I:173
Harlow, Eliza I:173
Harlow, Jabez I:173
Harlow, James I:575, 893
Harlow, John III:267
Harlow, Joseph I:173
Harlow, Josiah I:207, 863
Harlow, Josiah W. I:863

Harlow, Maria I:173
Harlow, Moses H. I:173
Harlow, Nathaniel I:221; III:695
Harlow, Sylvanus I:292
Harlow, William I:988
Harman, Charles III:609
Harman, Conrad IV:207
Harman, Edward II:8
Harman, John II:720; III:745
Harman, Lazarus III:60
Harman, Martin II:654
Harman, Moses I:777
Harman, Pelatiah I:259
Harman, Thomas I:285
Harman, William I:181
Harmon, Abner I:236
Harmon, Adam III:625
Harmon, Jehiel I:99
Harmon, Joel I:310
Harmon, John II:385; III:429, 584
Harmon, Josiah I:229
Harmon, Lazarus III:70
Harmon, Pelatiah I:216
Harmon, Samuel I:221
Harmon, Seth I:930
Harmon, Thomas II:58
Harmony, Nicholas II:269
Harnden, Benjamin I:518
Haroll, Thomas II:611
Harp, Frederick II:731
Harpel, John II:673
Harper, Clayton IV:153
Harper, Daniel II:670; IV:203
Harper, Ebenezer IV:75
Harper, Henry III:814
Harper, James II:655
Harper, John I:777; III:238, 422
Harper, John W. IV:257
Harper, Joseph II:183
Harper, Josiah III:618
Harper, Nathan III:311
Harper, Richard III:573
Harper, Samuel A. III:60
Harper, Thomas III:92, 548
Harper, Wiley V. III:523
Harper, William II:582; IV:204
Harradan, Elisha I:360
Harradan, Elisha Zerviah I:360
Harradan, Polly I:360
Harraden, John I:806
Harrall, William IV:65
Harrell, George IV:270
Harrell, John III:397, 813
Harrell, Josiah III:402
Harrell, Kidder III:414
Harrell, Reuben III:742
Harrell, Simon III:698
Harrer, Daniel II:738
Harriet, Reuben II:257
Harriman, Benjamin F. I:387
Harriman, Joab I:194
Harriman, Moses I:387, 692
Harriman, Simon I:292
Harrington, Abiel I:194

Harrington, Abraham II:494
Harrington, Ahab II:291
Harrington, Andrew I:68
Harrington, Anthony III:302
Harrington, Asa I:692
Harrington, Benjamin I:454
Harrington, Drury III:515
Harrington, Ebenezer II:279
Harrington, Ester H. II:148
Harrington, James I:455, 604, 825
Harrington, Job I:815
Harrington, John I:825; III:655; IV:212
Harrington, Jonas I:846
Harrington, Jonathan I:641
Harrington, Joshua I:742
Harrington, Josiah I:825
Harrington, Lemuel I:641
Harrington, Levi I:518
Harrington, Loammit I:501
Harrington, Moses II:174
Harrington, Nathan I:905
Harrington, Nathaniel II:364
Harrington, Noah I:621, 643
Harrington, Parley II:306
Harrington, Randall I:826
Harrington, Samuel I:621, 988; II:236
Harrington, Simeon I:917
Harrington, Thomas I:642
Harrington, Uriah I:962
Harrington, William I:641; II:344
Harriott, Ephraim II:73
Harriott, Israel II:351
Harris, Abijah II:547
Harris, Andrew II:332
Harris, Asa II:419
Harris, Benjamin I:806; III:184, 629, 746
Harris, Charles I:193
Harris, Cyrus III:716
Harris, Daniel I:350, 643, 857, 910; IV:55
Harris, David I:55; III:542
Harris, Edward III:689
Harris, Edwin III:613
Harris, Eliza I:189-90
Harris, Ezekiel II:506, 547
Harris, Fieldman III:419
Harris, Francis II:190
Harris, George II:77
Harris, Goodman III:476
Harris, Henry II:291; III:77, 302; IV:92
Harris, Herman II:99
Harris, Hiram I:857
Harris, Hugh III:562
Harris, Israel II:540
Harris, Ithran I:604
Harris, Jacob IV:237
Harris, James I:350; II:189, 249; III:277, 694
Harris, James, 2d II:688
Harris, Jedediah I:118
Harris, Jesse III:396

Harris, Job II:189
Harris, John I:55, 207, 741, 784, 857, 917, 977; II:189, 611, 663; III:494, 734, 822
Harris, John, 2d II:646; III:741
Harris, John, 3d III:730
Harris, John, 4th III:697
Harris, John C. III:814
Harris, Jonathan I:397, 759; III:629
Harris, Joseph II:182; III:169
Harris, Joseph, 2d II:224
Harris, Joshua I:751; II:540; IV:43
Harris, Luda I:501
Harris, Luke I:988
Harris, Mason I:416
Harris, Matthew III:163
Harris, Moses II:536
Harris, Nathan II:135
Harris, Nathaniel III:331, 841
Harris, Oliver I:642, 825
Harris, Oliver, 2d I:537
Harris, Overton III:325
Harris, Paul I:149
Harris, Pearly I:875
Harris, Philip II:485
Harris, Polly I:857
Harris, Richard III:88
Harris, Roben III:457
Harris, Robert II:183; III:356
Harris, Salathiel I:977
Harris, Sally I:857
Harris, Samuel III:32, 306
Harris, Simon III:829
Harris, Squire II:36
Harris, Stephen I:825; III:164
Harris, Thomas I:910; II:23; III:215, 346, 581, 730
Harris, Walter I:765
Harris, Waterman II:168
Harris, William I:160, 416, 709, 910; II:190, 207, 234, 518; III:257, 260, 274, 395, 732, 746, 762, 766, 814; IV:265, 286
Harris, William, 2d I:455, 871
Harris, William, 3d I:431
Harris, Winans III:474
Harris, Wooten IV:15
Harrison, Aaron II:64
Harrison, Abraham II:64
Harrison, Anthony A. IV:15
Harrison, Benjamin III:15
Harrison, Burdett III:804
Harrison, Daniel I:109
Harrison, David II:63
Harrison, Dempsey III:367
Harrison, Ezekiel IV:18
Harrison, George II:573, 594
Harrison, Gideon III:614
Harrison, Henry III:813
Harrison, Isaac II:36
Harrison, Jairus I:61
Harrison, James III:609, 682, 749

403

Harrison, Jesse III:387
Harrison, Job II:544
Harrison, Joham IV:122
Harrison, John III:374, 804
Harrison, John, 2d III:370
Harrison, Joseph III:557
Harrison, Kinsey III:43
Harrison, Leonard II:594
Harrison, M. III:333
Harrison, Matthew II:390
Harrison, Moses II:64
Harrison, Nathan I:126
Harrison, Nathaniel III:569
Harrison, Reuben III:831
Harrison, Richard III:254, 746
Harrison, Robert III:332
Harrison, Silas II:429
Harrison, Solomon I:110
Harrison, Stephen IV:283
Harrison, Theodore I:100
Harrison, Thomas I:592; II:82, 440; III:5, 580
Harrison, William III:374, 546, 557, 660, 758
Harrison, William B. III:851
Harrison, Wm. B. III:851
Harrod, Noah I:621
Harrod, William IV:89
Harroff, Jacob IV:289
Harrold, Jeremiah IV:81
Harrolson, Paul IV:17
Harrow, Jacob III:789
Harrup, Joseph I:3
Harry, Francis II:190
Harry, John I:810
Harsin, Garret IV:90
Hart, Aaron II:506
Hart, Adam III:462; IV:99
Hart, Anthony III:783
Hart, Benjamin I:48
Hart, Bliss I:41
Hart, Charles III:306
Hart, Christopher II:701
Hart, Cyrus D. II:36
Hart, Daniel II:64
Hart, Ebenezer I:396, 656
Hart, Elias I:109
Hart, Elisha II:241
Hart, Elizabeth II:627
Hart, Frederick A. I:790
Hart, George II:506, 686
Hart, Gilbert II:430
Hart, Henry III:83
Hart, Hezekiah I:99
Hart, Ithuriel I:100
Hart, Jacob I:221, 397
Hart, James I:236; III:439
Hart, John I:55, 292, 657; II:627; III:264; IV:12
Hart, John, 2d I:225
Hart, John R. II:69
Hart, Joseph II:627
Hart, Lent I:99
Hart, Mark III:111
Hart, Martin I:349; II:647
Hart, Mary Ann II:627
Hart, Munson I:99

Hart, Nicholas II:678
Hart, Patrick II:595
Hart, Pharo II:41
Hart, Phineas I:48
Hart, Reuben I:109
Hart, Robert III:644
Hart, Samuel I:22, 100; III:378, 776
Hart, Sandford I:799
Hart, Sanford I:367
Hart, Sarah II:627
Hart, Selah I:109
Hart, Seth I:917
Hart, Simeon I:155
Hart, Stephen II:69
Hart, Thomas, Sen. II:378
Hart, Titus I:110
Hart, Zachariah I:939
Hartchy, John II:678
Harter, Adam II:556
Harter, Lewis II:669
Harter, Nicholas II:454
Hartgrove, Howell III:452
Harthorn, James IV:253
Hartles, William III:749
Hartless, Peter III:749
Hartley, Daniel III:247
Hartline, Jacob II:657
Hartman, Adam II:148, 575, 722
Hartman, Christopher IV:239
Hartman, Jacob II:594
Hartman, John II:713; III:828
Hartman, Michael II:634
Hartman, Tandy III:215
Hartner, Patrick II:594
Hartsell, George IV:153
Hartsfield, John III:430
Hartshell, Peter II:594
Hartshorn, David I:546
Hartshorn, Jacob II:440
Hartshorn, Jeremiah I:518, 547
Hartshorn, Jesse I:546
Hartshorn, John I:537
Hartshorne, Silas I:537
Hartt, West III:713
Hartung, Christopher II:747
Hartwell, Benjamin I:518
Hartwell, Daniel I:561
Hartwell, Edward I:266; III:642
Hartwell, Ephraim I:643
Hartwell, Isaac I:561
Hartwell, John II:262
Hartwell, Nathan IV:199
Hartwell, Oliver I:221; II:217
Hartwell, Samuel II:485
Hartwell, Solomon II:485
Hartwell, Thomas II:453
Hartwick, Barent II:44
Hartwick, Lawrence III:306
Hartzell, Jacob III:828
Harvay, Thomas I:723
Harvest, John A. I:229
Harvey, Archibald I:875
Harvey, Charles IV:68

Harvey, Daniel I:751
Harvey, Edward I:810; IV:189
Harvey, Elisha I:363
Harvey, James I:292, 852
Harvey, John II:217; III:85
Harvey, Jonathan II:415
Harvey, Kimber I:693
Harvey, Moses II:540
Harvey, Nathan I:143
Harvey, Nathan B. I:841
Harvey, Norment III:705
Harvey, Robert II:453
Harvey, Samuel II:611
Harvey, Silas I:833
Harvey, Thomas II:367; III:761
Harvey, Timothy I:693
Harvey, William I:309, 875; II:574; III:611
Harvey, Zadock III:51
Harville, William III:408
Harvin, Edward III:801
Harvy, George I:135
Harvy, Jonathan I:620
Harwell, Andrew III:317
Harwick, David IV:239
Harwick, Jacob IV:14
Harwood, Benjamin I:xv
Harwood, Daniel I:643
Harwood, Ebenezer I:910
Harwood, Gershom I:620
Harwood, Jacob I:444
Harwood, Jesse I:41
Harwood, John I:473, 709
Harwood, Jonathan I:395
Harwood, Marville I:350
Harwood, Osborn J. III:61
Harwood, Peter I:620
Harwood, Thomas I:xv; II:651
Hasbronck, Solomon II:532
Hasbrook, A. B. II:565
Hasbrouck, Abraham II:589
Hase, Robert I:951
Haseltine, John IV:173
Haseltine, Thomas I:875
Hasey, Ebenezer I:292
Hasey, John I:910
Hashfield, Henry III:262
Haskall, Moses II:390
Haskel, John I:988
Haskell, Benjamin, 2d I:362
Haskell, Charles I:806
Haskell, David II:319
Haskell, Greenleaf I:173
Haskell, Job I:951
Haskell, John II:249
Haskell, Philip I:455
Haskell, Prince I:988
Haskell, Samuel I:825
Haskell, Simeon II:249
Haskell, Simon II:249
Haskell, Stephen I:181, 216
Haskell, William I:173, 194
Hasket, John III:594
Haskew, John III:508
Haskill, Benjamin, 1st I:382
Haskill, Caleb I:397
Haskill, Jacob I:987

Haskill, Jarius I:382
Haskill, Job I:575
Haskill, John I:489
Haskill, Joseph I:642
Haskill, Josiah I:207, 642;
II:217
Haskill, Moses I:904; IV:223
Haskill, Nathaniel II:430
Haskill, Philip I:463
Haskill, Roger I:350
Haskill, Samuel II:445
Haskill, Solomon I:642
Haskill, William I:416
Haskin, Jacob I:362
Haskings, Eli I:751
Haskins, Aaron I:604; III:765
Haskins, Abraham II:279
Haskins, Achilles III:291
Haskins, Asahel IV:106
Haskins, Cornelius IV:223
Haskins, David II:113
Haskins, Elijah I:373
Haskins, Enoch, Jr. II:494
Haskins, Henry I:373
Haskins, James III:290, 421
Haskins, Joseph I:428
Haskins, Joshua I:575
Haskins, Lemuel II:518
Haskins, Levi I:428
Haskins, Luther I:428
Haskins, Nathaniel II:540
Haskins, Richard I:962
Haskins, William I:416
Haskinson, Josiah IV:216
Haslet, Samuel IV:84
Haspin, John Wm. II:552
Hassell, Joseph III:393
Hastin, Absalom III:514
Hastin, William III:450
Hastings, Abijah I:596
Hastings, Ann Maria I:174
Hastings, Benjamin I:741
Hastings, Benj'n I:174
Hastings, Charles I:642
Hastings, David I:642
Hastings, Elihu II:453
Hastings, Eliphalet I:501
Hastings, James I:772
Hastings, John I:320, 519,
620, 657; II:36
Hastings, John, 2d I:621
Hastings, Jonas I:641
Hastings, Jonathan I:619
Hastings, Moses I:930
Hastings, Neverson I:643
Hastings, Oliver II:550
Hastings, Robert III:481
Hastings, Samuel I:518
Hastings, Silvanus I:692
Hastings, Theophilus I:620
Hastings, Thomas III:119
Hastings, Timothy II:332
Hastings, William I:668
Hastings, Zaccheus II:328
Hastings, Zachariah III:408
Hasty, David I:250
Hasty, James, Sen. III:446

Hasty, John II:206
Hasty, Samuel I:310
Hasty, William I:181
Haswell, N. B. II:555
Hatch, Abel II:469
Hatch, Adrian I:987
Hatch, Alexander III:439
Hatch, Anthony E. I:575
Hatch, Asa I:951
Hatch, Barney IV:162
Hatch, Benjamin II:429
Hatch, Betsy I:856
Hatch, Caleb II:405
Hatch, David I:310
Hatch, Ebenezer I:856
Hatch, Ede II:339
Hatch, Eliakim I:225
Hatch, Elihu I:267
Hatch, Elijah I:237
Hatch, Estes I:904
Hatch, Ezekiel I:310
Hatch, Gilbert I:971
Hatch, Heman II:241
Hatch, Ichabod I:917
Hatch, James I:382
Hatch, Jeremiah I:997
Hatch, John I:109
Hatch, Jonathan IV:162
Hatch, Joseph I:33
Hatch, Joseph, 2d I:327
Hatch, Josiah I:463, 575, 988
Hatch, Luther I:575
Hatch, Martin I:840
Hatch, Micah I:905
Hatch, Moses I:48
Hatch, Nathan II:373, 540
Hatch, Obed S. I:666
Hatch, Oliver II:529
Hatch, Philip I:275
Hatch, Prince I:330
Hatch, Samuel I:181, 309,
800
Hatch, Seth I:575
Hatch, Shubael I:327
Hatch, Sylvanus I:300
Hatch, Thomas I:777
Hatch, Timothy I:41, 856,
971; II:378
Hatch, Walter I:300
Hatch, William II:453
Hatch, Wm. I:856
Hatch, Zaccheus I:275
Hatcher, Henry III:284
Hatcher, John III:767
Hatcher, Samuel III:309
Hatcher, Seth III:767
Hatcher, William III:175, 369
Hatchman, John I:501
Hatfield, Aaron II:63
Hatfield, Elias III:721
Hathaway, Abner II:347
Hathaway, Abraham I:373
Hathaway, Arthur I:561
Hathaway, Benoni II:20
Hathaway, Ebenezer II:568
Hathaway, Elisha I:373
Hathaway, Ephraim I:285

Hathaway, Erastus I:944
Hathaway, Guilford I:481
Hathaway, Jabez I:372
Hathaway, James I:898
Hathaway, Jeremiah I:643
Hathaway, John I:373; II:536
Hathaway, Joshua II:454
Hathaway, Josiah I:431
Hathaway, Levi I:604
Hathaway, Nathan II:540
Hathaway, Peleg II:529
Hathaway, Philip I:373
Hathaway, Robert I:643
Hathaway, Seth I:930
Hathaway, Silas I:806
Hathaway, Theophilus II:49
Hathaway, Thomas I:630;
II:319
Hathaway, Timothy I:643
Hathaway, Zenos II:558
Hatherly, Thomas I:621
Hatheway, Abraham II:170
Hathiway, Arthur II:342
Hathorn, Nathaniel I:275
Hathorn, William III:701
Hathpenny, John III:214
Hathway, Zenus II:323
Hatler, Michael III:254
Hatman, Daniel II:119
Hatton, Basil III:66
Hatton, N. I:655
Hatton, Reuben IV:119
Hatton, William IV:41
Hatz, John II:728
Haught, Peter III:809
Haughtaling, Betsey II:197
Haughtaling, David II:197
Haughtaling, Hiram II:197
Haughton, Lebbeus I:69
Hause, Leonard II:740
Hauson, Isaac I:777
Havely, Jacob III:212
Haven, John I:362
Haven, Joseph II:332
Havenor, Charles I:207
Havens, Cornelius I:78
Havens, James I:889
Havens, John I:68; II:400
Havens, Nathaniel II:485
Havens, Peleg II:454
Havens, Peter II:211
Havens, Samuel II:382
Havens, William II:306
Haveracker, Gotl'b II:594
Haviland, John II:395
Haviland, Samuel I:842
Haward, Benjamin, 2d I:700
Hawawas, Nicholas I:302
Hawbeard, Thomas IV:207
Hawe, Amasa IV:265
Hawe, William III:558
Hawes, Abijah I:275
Hawes, Benjamin I:642
Hawes, David I:546
Hawes, Elijah I:143
Hawes, Ezekiel III:412
Hawes, George I:547

405

Hawes, Jason I:641
Hawes, Joel I:643
Hawes, John I:481
Hawes, Jonathan I:194
Hawes, Joseph I:330
Hawes, Pelatiah I:619
Hawes, Thomas III:280
Hawes, Zenos I:79
Hawk, Isaac III:824
Hawk, Jacob III:620
Hawk, James II:720
Hawkenberry, Hermany II:722
Hawkenburg, John II:642
Hawkins, Alfred III:668
Hawkins, Amaziah I:925
Hawkins, Bartlett III:655, 814
Hawkins, Benj. III:722
Hawkins, Benjamin I:825
Hawkins, Benoni I:871
Hawkins, Christopher II:415
Hawkins, Darius I:825-26
Hawkins, David II:169
Hawkins, Ebenezer II:382
Hawkins, Elisha III:279
Hawkins, Ephraim III:441
Hawkins, Eveline III:668
Hawkins, George III:322
Hawkins, Giles III:295
Hawkins, Henry III:195-96
Hawkins, Isaac I:126
Hawkins, James II:506, 518;
    III:695
Hawkins, James M. III:672
Hawkins, Jeremiah III:683
Hawkins, Job I:655; II:559
Hawkins, John III:672, 785;
    IV:125
Hawkins, Joseph I:962, 988;
    II:485; III:593
Hawkins, Joshua III:490
Hawkins, Moses I:962
Hawkins, Nathan III:306
Hawkins, Parke III:668
Hawkins, Philip III:668;
    IV:170
Hawkins, Robert I:777
Hawkins, Rodolphus II:405
Hawkins, Samuel I:125;
    II:490; III:585; IV:136
Hawkins, Sarah III:668
Hawkins, Stephen I:825;
    II:419
Hawkins, Thomas II:731;
    IV:292
Hawkins, Uriah II:415
Hawkins, William I:825;
    II:326; III:805
Hawkins, Zachariah II:77, 224
Hawkins, Zapher II:564
Hawkley, James I:668
Hawks, Frederick III:172
Hawks, Jotham II:393
Hawks, Reuben I:971
Hawks, Thomas III:768
Hawlen, Nathaniel IV:244
Hawley, Abel I:126; II:454
Hawley, Abraham II:485

Hawley, Chapman II:448
Hawley, Daniel III:121
Hawley, David I:22
Hawley, David W. II:109
Hawley, Ebenezer R. IV:253
Hawley, Elijah I:86
Hawley, Elisha I:86
Hawley, Francis III:620
Hawley, Gad I:99
Hawley, Henry II:505
Hawley, Hezekiah I:33
Hawley, Israel I:86
Hawley, James I:48
Hawley, Joseph II:323
Hawley, Joseph C. II:307
Hawley, Nathan I:9; II:393
Hawley, Nero I:3
Hawley, Ozias IV:279
Hawley, Peter III:811
Hawley, Robert I:87
Hawley, Samuel III:119
Hawley, Seth I:455
Hawley, Talcot I:22
Hawley, Thomas I:86
Hawley, Zadoch II:229
Haws, Joseph I:181
Hawthorn, John III:282
Hawthorn, Joseph IV:19
Hawthorn, Robert IV:19
Hay, Alexander II:440
Hay, Daniel I:xvi, 501
Hay, David I:493; II:77
Hay, Elizabeth Finley I:493
Hay, John I:493; II:703
Hay, Peter I:493
Hay, Susan C. I:493
Hay, Thomas III:324
Hay, William I:493; III:455
Haycock, Daniel IV:55
Haycraft, Samuel, Sen. III:224
Hayden, Abel I:600
Hayden, Benjamin III:290
Hayden, Caleb I:531
Hayden, Charles II:302
Hayden, Daniel I:537; II:291
Hayden, David I:519
Hayden, Ezra I:562
Hayden, Jacob I:536; II:211
Hayden, Jesse I:963
Hayden, Joel I:349
Hayden, Josiah I:194
Hayden, Levi I:537
Hayden, Lewis I:621
Hayden, Moses I:536
Hayden, Philip I:531
Hayden, Samuel IV:250
Hayden, Silas II:291
Hayden, William I:596
Hayden, William, 2d I:517
Hayden, Ziba I:546
Haydon, John II:720; III:725
Haydon, Jonathan I:267
Haye, Asa I:41
Hayens, Walter I:310
Hayes, Aaron I:349
Hayes, Amos II:506
Hayes, Barney II:577

Hayes, Benajah II:360
Hayes, Benjamin II:259
Hayes, Dudley I:7
Hayes, Elijah II:400
Hayes, Enoch I:109, 751
Hayes, George III:587
Hayes, Hugh III:531
Hayes, James I:397, 784;
    II:581; IV:145
Hayes, Jesse I:109
Hayes, Joseph I:86
Hayes, Levi IV:265
Hayes, Nathaniel I:730; II:378
Hayes, Oliver IV:253
Hayes, Seph I:100
Hayes, Thomas I:777
Hayes, William A. I:322
Hayes, Wm. I:731
Hayes, Zenas II:259
Hayford, Daniel I:825
Hayford, Ira II:494
Hayford, Nathaniel I:731
Hayford, William I:286
Haygood, Buckner III:201
Haygood, William III:575
Hayl, Stephen I:33
Hayles, Chapman III:427
Hayley, Daniel III:698
Haymond, Edward III:720
Hayne, R. T. III:518
Hayner, William II:415
Haynes, Aaron I:620
Haynes, Alexander III:474
Haynes, David II:518
Haynes, Eli I:846
Haynes, Elisha I:765
Haynes, Ephriam I:188
Haynes, George III:540
Haynes, James I:207, 621;
    III:590
Haynes, James, Sr. III:320
Haynes, John III:582, 752
Haynes, Jonas I:977
Haynes, Jonathan I:853
Haynes, Joseph III:605
Haynes, Parley I:188
Haynes, Reuben I:641
Haynes, Richard IV:93
Haynes, Samuel I:765
Haynie, William III:149
Hays, Amos M. I:250
Hays, David III:400
Hays, Edmund III:447
Hays, George S. I:777
Hays, Hezekiah I:33
Hays, Israel I:930
Hays, James II:743
Hays, John III:159, 266, 548
Hays, John Hawkins III:56
Hays, Jonathan I:899
Hays, Robert II:63; III:542
Hays, Samuel III:653
Hays, Stephen II:63
Hays, Thomas III:260, 374
Hays, William II:77; III:318,
    327, 548, 849
Hays, Zebedee I:765

Hayse, David I:751
Hayslet, Thomas III:734
Hayt, J. W. IV:300
Hayt, Stephen II:562
Hayward, Caleb IV:3
Hayward, Daniel I:546
Hayward, Ebenezer II:529
Hayward, Edward I:267
Hayward, Ephraim II:235
Hayward, George III:41
Hayward, Isaiah I:194
Hayward, Jacob I:784
Hayward, James I:643; II:241
Hayward, John I:944
Hayward, Joshua I:501
Hayward, Levi I:977
Hayward, Nathaniel I:934
Hayward, Robert III:41
Hayward, Samuel I:951, 977
Hayward, Seth I:547
Hayward, Simeon I:443;
  II:540
Hayward, Solomon I:988;
  IV:185
Hayward, Solomon, 2d I:367
Hayward, Waldo I:575
Hayward, Ziba II:506
Haywood, Eleazar I:700
Haywood, John I:xv
Haywood, Josiah II:332
Haywood, Lemuel I:641
Haywood, Nathaniel I:641
Haywood, Samuel I:641
Haywood, Sherwood I:xv
Haywood, Solomon I:611
Hazard, Charles II:41
Hazard, George W. I:833
Hazard, John I:833
Hazard, Levi II:347
Hazard, London I:833
Hazard, Thomas I:518
Hazelet, Rinley III:532
Hazeltine, Elijah I:397
Hazeltine, Jonas I:397
Hazeltine, William I:851
Hazelton, Manzel I:847
Hazelton, Solomon II:557
Hazen, Abraham II:89
Hazen, Charlt'e II:94
Hazen, Jacob I:135, 181
Hazen, Solomon I:988
Hazlet, Rinley III:5
Hazletine, John I:417
Hazletine, Prince I:621
Hazletine, Richard I:700
Hazletine, Thomas I:275
Hazletine, William I:699
Hazleton, John I:699
Hazleton, Jonathan I:806
Hazleton, Nathaniel I:709
Hazlett, Robert II:693
Hazlewood, Luke III:298
Hazzard, Arthur IV:205
Hazzard, Cord II:3
Hazzard, James I:784
Hazzard, Jason I:772
Hazzard, Steward II:550

Head, Britin II:529
Head, David I:777
Head, James I:237, 286
Head, John II:351
Head, Joseph II:430
Head, Moses I:221, 848
Head, Richard M. III:493
Heading, Amos II:200
Heading, Esther II:200
Heading, Hannah II:200
Heading, Polly II:200
Headley, Carey IV:273
Headley, Jacob II:705
Headley, James IV:288
Headley, John II:298
Headley, Joseph IV:265
Headley, Stephen II:69
Headley, William I:784
Headrick, Peter III:415
Heady, Daniel I:48
Heady, Jacob III:324
Heagan, Patrick IV:272
Heald, Asa II:235
Heald, Ephraim I:988
Heald, Nathan IV:114
Heald, Oliver I:225
Heald, Thomas I:267
Healey, Mrs. Eliphaz I:275
Healy, Comfort I:742
Healy, Hugh IV:59
Healy, John I:175, 894; II:440
Healy, Lemuel I:642
Healy, Mehitabel I:175
Healy, Sally I:175
Healy, Stephen I:642
Healy, Thomas I:149
Healy, William I:175
Heanor, Nicholas IV:28
Heap, John III:65
Heaps, Archibald III:65
Heard, Amos I:700
Heard, James II:44, 91
Heard, Jeremiah I:686
Heard, John II:44; III:777
Heard, Nathaniel I:417
Heard, Richard I:518
Heard, Timothy I:686
Heard, Tristram I:296
Hearl, John I:310
Hearn, Drury III:501
Hearn, Ephraim III:700
Hearn, John III:590
Hearne, Ebenezer III:433
Hearne, James III:373
Hearsay, James I:286
Hearsay, Noah I:275
Hearsay, Zadock I:302
Hearsey, Bela I:533
Hearsey, David I:620
Hearsey, Hannah I:533
Hearsey, James B. I:533
Hearsey, Jonathan I:537
Hearsey, Lewis G. I:533
Hearsey, Mary I:533
Hearsey, Peter I:561
Hearsey, William I:501
Heart, Job I:342; II:292

Heart, Reuben IV:211
Heath, Aaron I:350
Heath, Abial I:772
Heath, Amos I:176
Heath, Anna I:859
Heath, Benjamin I:731; II:367
Heath, Daniel I:700, 751;
  IV:92
Heath, Editha III:533
Heath, Emma I:858
Heath, Enoch I:784
Heath, Eunice I:176
Heath, Isaac I:275, 951
Heath, James I:772, 934
Heath, Jane I:859
Heath, Jesse I:875
Heath, John I:176, 772;
  II:207; III:533
Heath, John W. I:859
Heath, Jonathan I:893
Heath, Joseph II:207
Heath, Joseph W. I:859
Heath, Josiah II:529
Heath, Lifkin I:859
Heath, Lydia I:859
Heath, Nancy III:533
Heath, Polly I:859; III:533
Heath, Reuben I:963
Heath, Richard I:771; II:69
Heath, Sally I:176
Heath, Samuel I:723
Heath, Samuel C. II:238
Heath, Starling I:875
Heath, Thomas I:109, 858;
  III:121
Heath, William I:161, 320,
  350, 859, 881; III:243, 787
Heath, William L. II:101
Heathcock, James III:407
Heaton, James II:638
Heaton, John IV:104
Heaton, Nathaniel I:13
Heavener, Christopher III:327
Heavenor, Charles I:275
Hebard, Asa I:431
Hebard, Diah I:951
Hebard, Jabez I:149
Hebard, Jedediah II:203
Hebard, Vird Timothy II:241
Hebb, William III:729
Hebbard, Jacob I:397, 899
Hebbard, Oliver II:269
Hebbard, Ozias IV:287
Hebberd, Bushnell I:149
Hebberd, John I:216
Heberly, Frederick II:651
Hebert, James II:77
Heblinger, Peter II:638
Hebron, William II:594
Heck, Youst III:720
Hecktor, William I:339
Hecock, Aaron I:125
Hecox, Freeman IV:270
Hecox, Samuel II:454
Hector, Monday I:620
Hedden, Amos II:200
Hedden, James II:63

407

Hedden, Job II:511
Hedden, Jonas II:82
Hedden, Obadiah II:64
Hedden, Simon II:64
Hedden, Zadock II:445
Heddleson, William IV:226
Hedge, Asa II:518
Hedgepeth, Arcadia III:361
Hedgepeth, Chilly III:361
Hedgepeth, Henry III:361
Hedgepeth, Noah III:361
Hedger, Edward II:390
Hedger, Thomas III:306
Hedger, William II:474
Hedges, Abigail II:27
Hedges, Benjamin II:63
Hedges, Christopher II:524
Hedges, Eleazer II:385
Hedges, Elijah III:642; IV:136
Hedges, Joseph II:49
Hedges, Reuben II:334
Hedges, Robert III:279
Hedges, Samuel II:27
Hedgfroth, John III:614
Hedrick, William III:616
Heeler, John II:594
Heeter, George III:254
Heeth, Samuel I:699
Heffer, Andrew II:611
Hefferlin, John III:697
Hefflish, Melchior II:647
Heffner, Jacob IV:213
Heffron, Edward I:531
Hefler, John II:707
Hegin, Edward II:634
Hegnight, James III:797
Heiler, George II:665
Heimmons, James I:790
Heir, Hendrick II:46
Heiskell, Christ'r III:849
Heisy, John C. III:4
Heitrick, Jacob II:727
Helgar, Henry II:665
Heliker, John II:518
Hellegas, John II:187
Hellen, John IV:283
Heller, John II:674
Heller, John, 1st II:674
Helligas, Jacob II:187
Helligas, Joham II:187
Helligas, John II:187
Helligas, Joshua II:187
Helligas, Rebecca II:187
Helligas, Yost II:187
Helm, Daniel II:522
Helm, George III:543
Helm, John III:429
Helm, Lina T. IV:2
Helm, Samuel II:445, 745
Helmage, John II:291
Helme, Miles II:454
Helme, Peleg II:274
Helme, Robert H. III:463
Helme, William I:810
Helmer, George II:117
Helmer, John F. II:249
Helmer, John G. II:360

Helmer, John W. III:58
Helmer, Philip II:264
Helmershausen, Hy. F. I:207
Helmick, John III:846
Helmick, Nicholas IV:256
Helms, Leonard III:682
Helphinstine, Philip III:217
Helpoman, Stephen I:833
Helsey, Jacob III:835
Helsinger, Jacob II:514
Helsinger, Michael II:485
Helton, Abraham, Sen. III:567
Helyard, Peter II:740
Hembree, Abraham III:540
Hemenway, James I:428
Hemenway, Jeffrey I:621
Hemenway, Jonathan I:501
Hemenway, Manford I:428
Hemenway, Maria I:428
Hemenway, Phineas II:249
Hemenway, Rufus II:274
Heminger, John II:683
Heminger, John (2) II:683
Hemington, Azariah I:135
Hemingway, Jacob I:110
Hemingway, Stephen F. I:846
Heminway, Samuel IV:249
Hemmenway, Ebenezer I:741
Hemmenway, Elias I:741
Hemmenway, Peter I:585
Hemmenwrey, Asa I:267
Hemmingway, Daniel I:531
Hemmingway, Enos I:126
Hemphill, Joseph III:541
Hemphill, Samuel II:624
Hempstead, Stephen IV:115
Hemstrought, David II:525
Hendee, Caleb I:149
Henderliter, Michael III:721
Hendershott, William J. II:109
Henderson, Abigail I:683
Henderson, Alexander III:367
Henderson, Arthur I:683
Henderson, Benjamin I:275,
    416; III:261
Henderson, Daniel I:672;
    II:319
Henderson, David I:683;
    III:526, 837; IV:119
Henderson, Edward III:783
Henderson, Ezekiel III:503
Henderson, Isaac III:541
Henderson, James II:420;
    III:419
Henderson, John I:683; II:734;
    III:602, 717; IV:80
Henderson, Jonathan IV:170
Henderson, Joseph II:344,
    667, 713; IV:113
Henderson, Meshach III:611
Henderson, Pleasant III:571
Henderson, Richard III:132
Henderson, Robert III:169
Henderson, Sampson III:704
Henderson, Samuel I:971;
    III:517
Henderson, Thomas III:511

Henderson, Timothy B. I:604
Henderson, William I:620;
    II:182; III:522, 693, 837;
    IV:66
Henderson, Wm. II:647
Hendley, Elkana III:191
Hendley, William I:596
Hendrake, Andrew II:684
Hendrick, Abijah I:463
Hendrick, Coe I:126
Hendrick, Daniel III:763
Hendrick, Elijah IV:118
Hendrick, George III:194
Hendrick, Moses II:494
Hendrick, Obadiah III:688
Hendricks, Albert III:622
Hendricks, George IV:31
Hendricks, Hillary III:85
Hendricks, Moses III:300
Hendricks, Solomon III:572
Hendricks, W. IV:99
Hendricks, Zachariah III:727
Hendrickson, Cor. II:594
Hendrickson, Daniel II:77
Hendrickson, Garretson II:22
Hendrickson, Hendrick II:77
Hendrickson, James II:77
Hendrickson, Moses IV:66
Hendrickson, Peter II:430
Hendrickson, William IV:283
Hendrix, David I:33
Hendrix, Nathaniel I:33
Hendrixen, Isaac III:402
Hendry, Samuel II:31
Hendryx, Isaiah I:930
Hendryx, Nathaniel IV:19
Hendy, John II:525
Heneberger, John II:722
Henegan, Conrad III:329
Henesy, John II:657
Hening, John II:655
Henley, Charles I:593
Henley, Edward I:593
Henley, Henry I:709
Henley, John I:593
Henley, Peter II:135
Henley, Samuel I:593
Henley, William IV:5
Hennance, John II:494
Hennegin, Joseph IV:59
Hennen, Matthew II:724
Hennen, Thomas II:635
Hennenger, Caleb III:5
Hennigan, John III:841
Hennion, Cornelius II:23
Hennis, Benjamin III:217
Hennon, Abel II:635
Henrick, Ephraim II:395
Henry, Adam II:484
Henry, Andrew I:443
Henry, Benjamin II:274
Henry, David II:494; III:613
Henry, Francis I:742
Henry, George II:665
Henry, Hugh III:613
Henry, Jacob III:225

Henry, James II:518; III:94, 429
Henry, John I:125, 165; II:430; III:313, 574, 594, 627; IV:287
Henry, Joseph I:742; III:404
Henry, Michael I:537
Henry, Moses III:835
Henry, Nathaniel III:697-98
Henry, Nicholas III:812
Henry, Peter II:748
Henry, Philip II:611
Henry, Robert III:625
Henry, Samuel I:825, 956
Henry, Silas I:621
Henry, Thomas I:825
Henry, Tobias II:582
Henry, William III:616, 755
Hensdale, Hiram I:856
Hensdale, Jane I:856
Hensdale, Miriam I:856
Hensdale, Sally I:856
Hensdale, Strong I:856
Hensdale, William I:856
Hensel, Michael IV:245
Hensel, William II:728
Hensell, George III:776
Henshaw, Benjamin I:55
Henshaw, Thomas I:643; III:133
Henson, Elijah III:404
Henson, Jesse, Senr. III:265
Henson, John IV:20
Henson, William II:246, 556; III:229, 362, 702
Henwood, Robert III:559
Heppard, William III:322
Heppener, John II:252
Herald, Henry II:55
Heralson, Herndon III:589
Herbaugh, David II:673
Herbert, James I:751
Herbert, Jeremiah III:328
Herbert, Josiah, Sr. III:266
Herbert, Samuel II:77
Herbert, Thomas IV:283
Herbest, Peter II:728
Herd, Eleazer II:398
Hereden, James III:626
Hereford, Jesse II:183
Hereford, John III:805
Herendeen, Hezekiah I:79
Hergan, John II:135
Herin, Gersham II:741
Herin, William III:785
Herinden, Joseph I:759
Herington, Peter II:390
Herman, Frederick W. I:956
Hermitty, Henry II:611
Herndon, Edward III:760
Herndon, George III:300
Herndon, Joseph III:184
Herod, William III:618
Herrendeen, Reuben I:806
Herrick, Andrew I:407
Herrick, Asa I:396
Herrick, Charles I:709

Herrick, Daniel II:393
Herrick, Ebenezer I:742; II:323
Herrick, Elijah II:440
Herrick, Ephraim II:373
Herrick, George I:684
Herrick, Hezekiah II:390
Herrick, Israel II:405
Herrick, Jacob I:250
Herrick, John I:848
Herrick, Joseph I:135, 700
Herrick, Joshua I:396
Herrick, Josiah I:759
Herrick, Lemuel II:323
Herrick, Libeus IV:186
Herrick, Martin I:501
Herrick, Oliver I:165
Herrick, Richard I:397
Herrick, Samuel I:684
Herrick, Simeon II:367
Herrick, Stephen I:951
Herriman, Jacob II:703, 734
Herriman, Jonathan II:241
Herriman, Joseph I:944
Herriman, Moses I:676
Herrin, Isaac IV:44
Herrin, John III:293
Herring, Daniel I:292
Herring, E. II:560
Herring, George III:322
Herring, James III:746
Herring, Jesse III:164
Herrington, Bezelah II:252
Herrington, Daniel IV:19
Herrington, Eber II:484
Herrington, Isaac III:367
Herrington, John II:378
Herrington, Jonathan II:291
Herrington, Joseph I:596
Herron, Allen III:432
Herron, David II:629
Herron, James III:23
Herron, John I:55; II:514
Herron, Luke II:594
Hersey, Ezekiel I:575
Hertshoy, Valentine II:594
Hertz, Conrad II:703
Hervard, James III:761
Hervey, Benjamin II:415
Hervey, John III:80
Hescock, Samuel I:977
Hess, George II:729
Hess, Han Jost II:249
Hess, Hezediah III:798
Hess, Johannis II:183
Hess, John II:182-83
Hess, John Jost II:556
Hess, Michael II:385
Hess, Peter, Sen. II:743
Hesselton, David I:917
Hesser, Frederick II:746
Hester, Abraham III:503
Hester, Benjamin III:421
Hester, Ferrtl IV:12
Hester, Robert III:174
Hester, Thomas III:401
Hester, William III:528

Hester, Zechariah III:421
Hestey, Clement III:690
Hetfield, Daniel II:63
Hetfield, Stephen II:659
Heth, William I:xv
Hetherly, Thomas IV:231
Hethner, Nicholas III:5
Hetsler, George F. II:124
Heurilow, Reuben II:11
Heuston, William I:575
Hewell, Wiatt III:176
Hewes, Benjamin II:429
Hewes, George R. T. II:485
Hewet, Andrew I:962
Hewet, Gideon I:962
Hewett, Ebenezer III:365
Hewett, Israel II:684
Hewett, James II:505
Hewett, John III:755
Hewett, Nathaniel I:846
Hewins, Joseph I:350
Hewit, Asa II:291
Hewit, Joseph II:323
Hewit, Randal II:352
Hewit, William I:207
Hewitt, Daniel I:3; II:158
Hewitt, Ebenezer III:462
Hewitt, Edward II:506
Hewitt, Elisha II:368
Hewitt, Elkanah II:454
Hewitt, Ephraim II:464
Hewitt, Gershom I:110
Hewitt, Henry II:367
Hewitt, John II:279
Hewitt, Lewis II:368
Hewitt, Patrick III:629
Hewitt, Phipps W. II:157
Hewitt, Richard II:323
Hewitt, Robert II:689
Hewitt, Simeon I:135
Hewitt, Sterry II:494
Hewitt, Thomas II:373
Hewlett, Aaron I:871
Hewlett, Joseph B. II:174
Hewlit, Lemuel III:195
Hews, Alpheus II:63
Heydon, David II:313
Heymer, David II:192
Heymer, Gabriel D. II:192
Heymer, Mary T. II:192
Heysham, David III:842
Hiatt, Shadrach III:309
Hibard, Aaron I:751
Hibbard, Arunah II:146
Hibbard, David I:941
Hibbard, Ebenezer II:514, 524
Hibbard, Israel II:241
Hibbard, Joseph II:279
Hibbard, Rufus II:435
Hibbard, Thomas II:554
Hibbard, Timothy II:699
Hibbard, Uriah II:274
Hibbard, William I:143
Hibbert, Jonathan I:225
Hice, George II:726
Hichcock, Aaron I:463
Hick, Joshua II:430

Hickcox, Asher II:556
Hickcox, Giles IV:269
Hickcox, S. II:556
Hickey, Daniel III:216
Hickey, David II:611
Hickey, James III:629
Hickle, Samuel III:697
Hickman, Adam III:706, 831
Hickman, Benjamin III:630
Hickman, Edwin III:452
Hickman, Francis IV:124
Hickman, George II:647
Hickman, Jacob III:376
Hickman, James III:322
Hickman, Joel III:269
Hickman, John III:324, 733
Hickman, John B. III:745
Hickman, Salsbury I:562
Hickman, Samuel III:412
Hickman, Sotha III:789
Hickman, Thomas III:193, 575
Hickock, Asa II:705
Hickock, Daniel I:86
Hickock, David IV:218
Hickock, Ichabod I:339
Hickok, Aaron H. I:26
Hickok, Amos I:26
Hickok, Caroline M. I:26
Hickok, Durlin IV:227
Hickok, Ebenezer III:749
Hickok, William T. I:26
Hickox, Ebenezer IV:280
Hickox, James I:125
Hickox, Nathaniel IV:250
Hickox, Stephen I:350
Hicks, Abraham I:819
Hicks, Alice Burger II:192
Hicks, Benj. II:562
Hicks, Benjamin I:688; II:562
Hicks, Catherine II:192
Hicks, Daniel I:825; II:399
Hicks, Daniel, Sr. III:807
Hicks, David I:630, 807
Hicks, Durfee II:292
Hicks, Farthing III:820
Hicks, Harris III:421
Hicks, Isaac III:148
Hicks, James I:930
Hicks, Jesse III:500
Hicks, Joel III:587
Hicks, John I:554; II:378;
   III:155; IV:97, 205
Hicks, Joseph II:659
Hicks, Micajah III:376
Hicks, Miles III:417
Hicks, Nathan I:372
Hicks, Samuel I:126, 181,
   249, 812; II:49
Hicks, Simeon I:930
Hicks, Solomon III:299
Hicks, Thomas II:192
Hicks, Thos. II:562
Hicks, William III:75, 216,
   221, 779
Hickworth, Daniel II:183
Hicock, Samuel II:313
Hidden, Samuel I:777

Hidecker, John A. III:78
Hier, Jacob II:310
Hier, Josiah II:135
Higbe, Elnathan I:939
Higbee, Hendrick II:285
Higby, Samuel I:126
Higden, Charles III:795
Higdon, Joseph III:257
Higgans, Daniel IV:75
Higgason, Samuel III:622
Higgason, Thomas III:322
Higginbotham, Wm. III:636
Higginbothom, Benj. III:749
Higgins, Andrew II:646
Higgins, Benjamin I:339;
   II:440
Higgins, Cornelius I:118
Higgins, Daniel IV:233
Higgins, Ebenezer II:368
Higgins, Hawes I:118
Higgins, Henry I:643
Higgins, Ichabod I:910
Higgins, Isaac I:22
Higgins, John I:163; III:633
Higgins, Josiah I:596
Higgins, Moses II:547
Higgins, Nathaniel II:323
Higgins, Patrick II:580
Higgins, Philip I:275
Higgins, Solomon I:463
Higgins, Thomas II:135, 378;
   IV:2
Higgins, Timothy I:61, 395
Higgins, Uriah I:844
Higginson, William II:611
Higgs, Samuel II:232
High, Gardner III:397
High, George II:752
High, Jacob IV:70
Highfield, Leonard III:199
Highfield, William II:569
Highsmith, Moses III:442
Hight, George III:831
Hight, Matthew III:814
Hightower, Thomas III:665
Higley, Brewster IV:270
Higley, Obed I:99
Higley, Roswell II:362
Higley, Seba II:536
Higley, Seth II:211
Hignet, Philip IV:97
Higqy, Betsey I:656
Hilary, Ashburn II:720
Hilbert, William I:396
Hilborn, Robert I:250
Hildreath, Abel I:939
Hildreth, Jesse I:431
Hildreth, John I:864
Hildreth, Jonathan I:501;
   II:529
Hildreth, Reuben II:249
Hildreth, Susan I:864
Hildrith, Abijah I:765
Hildrith, Simeon I:784
Hiler, Jacob I:600
Hiles, Conrad II:655
Hiles, John III:321

Hiley, Abraham IV:85
Hill, Abner I:41
Hill, Abraham I:977; III:425
Hill, Abram I:126
Hill, Alpheus II:99
Hill, Amelia II:190
Hill, Asa I:621; II:306-7
Hill, Benajah II:540; IV:176
Hill, Benoni II:214
Hill, Bernard II:378
Hill, Betsey I:686
Hill, Caleb I:833; IV:265
Hill, Christopher I:806
Hill, Clem III:256
Hill, Cyrus I:904
Hill, Daniel I:249, 759; II:430,
   464; III:602
Hill, David I:600; II:190
Hill, Ebenezer I:758-59;
   II:217, 279
Hill, Edmund E. I:396
Hill, Edward I:686
Hill, Eleazer II:368
Hill, Elisha II:275
Hill, Erastus II:291
Hill, Erastus Greenleaf II:194
Hill, Frederick II:669, 701;
   III:250
Hill, Geo. I:686
Hill, George III:648; IV:153,
   199, 278
Hill, Hannah II:190
Hill, Harry II:194
Hill, Henry I:135; II:264, 741;
   IV:183
Hill, Hiram II:194
Hill, Hiram Kirkland II:194
Hill, Horace Putnam II:194
Hill, Humphrey III:766
Hill, Ichabod II:453
Hill, Isaac I:126, 930; III:156
Hill, James I:518, 825, 944;
   II:306; III:429, 569, 739
Hill, Jasper Clark II:194
Hill, Jehiel I:881
Hill, Jeremiah I:237
Hill, Jesse I:784
Hill, Joel I:977; III:86
Hill, John I:600, 643, 686,
   825; II:190, 279, 705, 738;
   III:43, 167, 293, 723, 786;
   IV:292
Hill, John, 1st I:586
Hill, John, 2d I:501
Hill, John B. I:723
Hill, Jonas III:580
Hill, Jonathan I:562, 723, 799
Hill, Joseph II:734
Hill, Joseph, 2d I:327
Hill, Joseph, 1st I:561
Hill, Joshua III:403
Hill, Josiah I:349
Hill, Leonard I:561
Hill, Levi I:930
Hill, Lewis I:554
Hill, Lowry II:190
Hill, Michael III:311

Hill, Miranda II:194
Hill, Moses I:741
Hill, Nathaniel I:898
Hill, Nicholas II:558
Hill, Nicholas D. I:771
Hill, Noah I:641
Hill, Peter I:620
Hill, Primus II:279
Hill, Reuben II:328
Hill, Richard I:917; II:105;
III:819
Hill, Robert II:525; III:260,
555
Hill, Robert, Sen. III:452
Hill, Sally I:686
Hill, Samuel I:237, 621, 877,
899, 934; III:449
Hill, Shadrach I:686
Hill, Simeon II:470
Hill, Simon IV:199
Hill, Solomon I:443
Hill, Stukely I:833
Hill, Thomas I:61, 518, 934;
II:292; III:27, 629; IV:119
Hill, Thomas, 2d II:241
Hill, Uri I:944
Hill, Uriah II:342
Hill, William I:396, 686;
III:250, 765, 826
Hill, William, 2d I:596
Hill, Zimra II:101
Hillan, James III:742
Hillard, David II:511
Hillard, John I:68
Hillen, George III:327
Hiller, Thomas I:529
Hiller, Timothy I:575
Hillhouse, William III:87
Hilliard, Azariah I:135
Hilliard, John III:715
Hilliard, Jonathan I:731
Hilliard, Joseph III:688
Hilliard, Thomas, 2d III:457
Hilliard, Thomas, 1st III:457
Hilliard, Thurston I:22
Hillier, David II:611
Hillman, Benjamin IV:135
Hillman, William III:57
Hills, Asahel I:910
Hills, Ebenezer II:354
Hills, Guy II:494
Hills, Jacob I:463
Hills, John IV:68
Hills, Joseph I:41, 100; II:561
Hills, Nathaniel I:416, 693
Hills, Samuel II:485
Hills, Seth II:259
Hills, Solomon II:560
Hills, Stephen I:709
Hills, Thomas I:416, 765
Hills, Zinery IV:244
Hillyen, Seth IV:227
Hillyer, Asa I:41
Hillyer, James IV:253
Hillyer, Theodore I:41
Hilman, Thomas IV:75
Hilsabeck, Jacob III:452

Hilton, Andrew IV:15
Hilton, Derrick II:354
Hilton, Dudley I:309
Hilton, Ebenezer I:225, 310
Hilton, Edward I:310; III:629
Hilton, Isaac I:250
Hilton, Jacob W. II:410
Hilton, James II:354
Hilton, John II:183
Hilton, Joseph I:310, 672
Hilton, Morrill I:206
Hilton, Richard II:354
Hilton, William, 2d I:296
Hilton, William, 1st I:296
Hilyard, Daniel II:382
Hilyard, Joshua II:382
Hilyard, Minor I:962
Hilyard, Peter III:501
Himdley, John III:314
Himrod, Andrew IV:244
Hinard, Michael II:547
Hincher, Isaac I:988
Hinchson, John III:189
Hinckley, Abner I:330
Hinckley, David I:143
Hinckley, Ebenezer I:118
Hinckley, Heman II:435
Hinckley, Jared I:854; II:217
Hinckley, John II:291
Hinckley, Joshua II:291
Hinckley, Nehemiah I:260
Hinckley, Nymphas I:330
Hinckley, Philip I:327
Hinckley, Prince I:330
Hinckley, Samuel I:643
Hinckley, Silvanus I:330
Hinckley, Wiat III:342
Hind, Dennis II:31
Hind, John II:636
Hindman, James II:697
Hinds, Bartlett II:684
Hinds, Benjamin I:225
Hinds, Eli I:846
Hinds, Esau II:81
Hinds, James III:672
Hinds, Jesse II:378
Hinds, John III:137
Hinds, Kesiah III:672
Hinds, Nancy III:672
Hinds, Nimrod I:296
Hinds, Samuel I:207; II:672
Hinds, Sarah III:672
Hinds, Seth II:347
Hinds, Thomas II:182
Hinds, William III:672
Hine, Benjamin II:410
Hine, Conrad II:682
Hine, Hezekiah I:61
Hine, Hollingworth I:126
Hine, Richard I:285
Hine, Samuel I:125
Hinery, Francis II:689
Hines, Hardy III:238
Hines, Henry III:716
Hines, Jacob IV:84
Hines, James III:206, 544
Hines, Richard I:431

Hines, Titus I:61
Hines, William, Sen. III:826
Hiney, George IV:251
Hink, John II:182
Hinkle, Casper IV:123
Hinkle, Henry III:831
Hinkley, Josiah II:354
Hinkley, Nathaniel IV:292
Hinkley, Samuel I:482
Hinkley, Seth I:643
Hinkley, Shubel I:330
Hinkson, Samuel I:877
Hinley, William II:77
Hinman, Benjamin II:279
Hinman, Enoch I:351
Hinman, Isaac I:956
Hinman, Joel I:22
Hinman, Jonas II:378
Hinman, T. I:998
Hinman, Timothy I:xxv, 893
Hinnis, Samuel III:37
Hinsdale, Abel I:109
Hinsdale, Elisha IV:202
Hinsdale, Jacob I:109
Hinshaw, Josiah I:620
Hinson, Charles III:397
Hinson, Daniel III:424
Hinson, Lazarus III:158
Hinton, Hale I:397
Hinton, Lewis III:797
Hinton, Priscilla III:40
Hinton, Rezin III:40
Hiott, John, Sen. III:498
Hipp, Valentine III:432
Hipple, Conrad II:738
Hipple, John II:755
Hipple, Lawrence II:575
Hipsher, Andrew IV:254
Hirley, William III:37
Hiscock, Richard II:464
Hiscox, Clarke I:833
Hiscox, Edward I:833
Hiscox, Ephraim I:810
Hise, Leonard III:400
Hisel, Frederick IV:203
Hiser, John III:256
Hisle, Benjamin III:690
Hisle, Samuel III:290
Hisrott, John II:135
Histut, Thaddeus II:718
Hitchcock, Aaron I:910
Hitchcock, Abijah II:306
Hitchcock, Abraham II:547
Hitchcock, Ashbel II:485
Hitchcock, Chileob II:360
Hitchcock, Daniel I:61, 156
Hitchcock, Ebenezer II:405,
440
Hitchcock, Eli II:378
Hitchcock, Eliada I:61
Hitchcock, Gad I:561, 576
Hitchcock, Jared II:245
Hitchcock, John I:962
Hitchcock, Jonathan I:74;
II:525
Hitchcock, Joshua III:277
Hitchcock, Lemuel II:246

Hitchcock, Levi I:49, 155; II:453
Hitchcock, Luke I:455, 944
Hitchcock, Luke, 2d I:455
Hitchcock, Luther I:463
Hitchcock, Lyman II:221
Hitchcock, Mary I:155
Hitchcock, Moses II:148
Hitchcock, Nathaniel I:917
Hitchcock, Oliver II:540
Hitchcock, Peter IV:296
Hitchcock, Phineas III:347
Hitchcock, Reuben I:463
Hitchcock, Samuel I:99; II:203
Hitchens, Major II:8
Hitchens, Nathan I:397
Hitchings, Nathan'l, 1st I:396
Hitchings, Thomas I:416
Hitchman, Salsbury I:562
Hite, Abraham III:335
Hite, Conrad II:748
Hite, George III:665
Hite, Isaac III:849
Hite, Jacob IV:88
Hite, Julius III:851
Hite, Matthias III:706
Hix, Daniel I:373
Hix, Stephen II:420
Hixon, Amos II:89
Hixon, Elijah IV:205
Hixon, Elkanah I:917
Hixon, James III:801
Hixon, John III:681
Hixon, Jonathan II:41
Hixon, Joseph I:889
Hixson, James II:755
Hoadley, Ebenezer I:41
Hoadley, Thomas I:917
Hoadly, Philo IV:244
Hoag, Hussey I:723
Hoagland, Derrick II:69
Hoagland, John II:44, 328
Hoagland, Richard II:85
Hoagland, Tunis II:85
Hoar, Braddock I:562
Hoar, David I:590; IV:5
Hoar, Edmund II:241
Hoar, Jeptha II:98
Hoar, Leonard I:519
Hoard, Jonathan II:314
Hoardley, Ebenezer I:155
Hoardley, Silas II:757
Hoare, Leonard II:306
Hoats, Beltzer II:752
Hobart, Edmund I:575
Hobart, Isaac I:708
Hobart, Jacob I:708
Hobart, Jeremiah I:758
Hobart, John I:951
Hobart, Jonas IV:8
Hobart, Jonathan I:759
Hobart, Joseph I:904
Hobart, Mason I:125
Hobart, Nathaniel I:575, 759
Hobart, Noah I:417
Hobart, Solomon I:939
Hobart, William IV:211

Hobaugh, Philip IV:45
Hobbey, William I:181
Hobbie, S. R. II:554-55
Hobbs, Benjamin, 2d I:397
Hobbs, Benjamin, 1st I:397
Hobbs, Elisha III:730
Hobbs, John I:501
Hobbs, Joseph I:723
Hobbs, Josiah I:249
Hobbs, Morrell I:181
Hobbs, Thomas III:573
Hobbs, William III:455
Hobby, Hezekiah I:87
Hobson, Jeremiah I:708
Hobson, Moses I:416
Hobson, William I:236
Hock, Adam IV:287
Hockstrasser, Paul I. II:354
Hodg, Philo I:48
Hodgden, Hanson I:723
Hodgdon, Alonzo I:686
Hodgdon, George I:686
Hodgdon, Harriet I:686
Hodgdon, Jeremiah I:216
Hodgdon, John I:867
Hodgdon, Joseph I:747, 777
Hodgdon, Lydia I:686
Hodgdon, Molly I:686
Hodgdon, Richard I:686
Hodgdon, Samuel I:162
Hodgdon, Supply I:686
Hodge, Abraham, 2d II:252
Hodge, Abraham, 1st II:252
Hodge, Alexander III:432
Hodge, Asahel II:323
Hodge, Benjamin I:867; III:512
Hodge, David II:217
Hodge, George III:400
Hodge, James II:314
Hodge, John III:515
Hodge, Levi I:431
Hodge, Thomas I:700
Hodge, William III:172
Hodge, Wm. I:709
Hodgeman, Abel I:759
Hodgeman, Thomas I:759
Hodges, Abednego III:696
Hodges, Benjamin I:825
Hodges, Daniel II:494
Hodges, Edmund III:609
Hodges, Elijah I:373
Hodges, Eliphalet II:405
Hodges, Ephraim II:378
Hodges, Ezra I:194
Hodges, Isaac I:372
Hodges, James II:454
Hodges, Jesse III:302
Hodges, Job I:33
Hodges, John III:496
Hodges, Joseph III:401
Hodges, Leonard I:939
Hodges, Philemon III:174
Hodges, Rufus I:372
Hodges, Seth I:988
Hodges, Timothy II:506
Hodges, William I:547; III:508

Hodges, Willis III:618
Hodges, Zebulon I:742
Hodggets, Emanuel I:339
Hodgkins, Emeline I:387
Hodgkins, Jacob I:416
Hodgkins, John I:387, 784
Hodgkins, Joseph I:397
Hodgkins, Lydia I:387
Hodgkins, Nathaniel I:149
Hodgkins, Thomas I:988
Hodgkins, Thomas, 2d I:216
Hodgkins, Timothy I:397
Hodgkins, William II:382
Hodgman, Asa I:518
Hodgman, John I:206
Hodgman, Joseph I:917
Hodkins, Thomas, 1st I:207
Hodsdon, Samuel I:237
Hodsdon, Stephen I:216
Hodskings, Samuel I:432
Hodson, T. J. IV:295
Hodson, Thos. J. II:553, 559; III:853
Hodson, Tho's J. III:16
Hodston, Jacob I:731
Hody, Josiah I:296
Hoevenbergh, Henry V. II:505
Hoevenburgh, Eggo J. H. II:535
Hoff, Henry II:760
Hoff, Isaac IV:234
Hoff, Jacob II:641
Hoff, John IV:244
Hoff, Nicholas II:169
Hoff, William III:314, 395
Hoffains, Adam I:397
Hoffman, Ambrose III:256
Hoffman, Christian III:727
Hoffman, Cornelius II:682
Hoffman, Evert II:532
Hoffman, Henry I:934; II:746; III:69
Hoffman, John II:69, 707; III:818
Hoffman, Ludwick II:697
Hoffman, Michael II:556
Hoffman & Hunt II:556
Hoffner, Martin III:445
Hoffstaden, Christian II:249
Hofmire, Samuel IV:263
Hofner, Nicholas III:429
Hofstalar, George III:79
Hogaboon, Peter II:125
Hogaboone, Benjamin II:197
Hogaboone, Elisha II:197
Hogaboone, Henry II:197
Hogaboone, John II:197
Hogal, Barnabas II:195
Hogal, Bithah Ann II:195
Hogan, Benoni II:291
Hogan, David III:544
Hogan, Edward III:590
Hogan, John I:909
Hogan, Pat II:342
Hogan, Patrick II:183
Hogan, Prosser IV:41
Hogan, William III:502, 665

Hogdon, Caleb I:275
Hogdon, Phinehas I:688
Hoge, John II:700
Hogeboom, James II:440
Hogeboom, John II:354
Hogeboom, Peter C. II:385
Hogeland, James III:801
Hogeland, Joseph II:707
Hogeman, Nathan II:540
Hogenkamp, Martines II:445
Hogg, Abner I:758
Hogg, Ebenezer I:723
Hogg, James II:694
Hogg, Samuel III:558
Hogg, Thomas III:778
Hogg, William I:709; III:700
Hogg, Wm. I:709
Hogge, James II:642
Hogh, Gideon III:543
Hogins, Abram III:577
Hogsdon, Benjamin I:180
Hogue, Andrew III:212
Hoisington, Ebenezer I:987
Hoisington, Isaac I:899
Hoisington, Velina II:544
Hoit, Arteban I:844
Hoit, Benjamin I:777, 917
Hoit, Elisha I:501
Hoit, Ephraim II:252
Hoit, Jeremiah I:963
Hoit, Joseph I:765
Hoit, Moses I:672
Hoit, Nathan I:699, 730
Hoit, Reuben I:700
Hoit, Richard I:731
Hoit, Robert I:699
Hoit, Samuel I:61
Hoit, Warren I:126
Hoitt, Stephen I:772
Holam, Samuel IV:209
Holansby, Jacob M. I:166
Holben, Lorentz II:730
Holbert, Aaron III:798
Holbert, Robert III:649
Holbrook, Abel I:126
Holbrook, Amos I:546, 910
Holbrook, Caleb I:692
Holbrook, Calvin I:149
Holbrook, Chandler I:657
Holbrook, Daniel I:546
Holbrook, Darius I:642
Holbrook, David I:292, 537; II:464
Holbrook, Ebenezer I:531, 934
Holbrook, Eddy III:141
Holbrook, Henry I:547
Holbrook, Ichabod I:536
Holbrook, James I:546
Holbrook, Jesse III:162
Holbrook, John I:275, 643, 784
Holbrook, Nathan III:137
Holbrook, Nathaniel I:61, 536
Holbrook, Peter I:296
Holbrook, Reuben II:207
Holbrook, Samuel I:723
Holbrook, Seth I:546; II:430

Holbrook, Silas I:181; II:405
Holbrooks, David I:657
Holcomb, Abel II:410
Holcomb, Abner II:401
Holcomb, Abram I:109
Holcomb, Apollos II:153
Holcomb, Asahel I:40, 100
Holcomb, Azariah II:494
Holcomb, Dose I:463
Holcomb, Elijah I:455; IV:207
Holcomb, Ezekiel II:506
Holcomb, Increase I:100
Holcomb, John I:110; III:643
Holcomb, John G. IV:207
Holcomb, Jonathan IV:291
Holcomb, Joseph I:350
Holcomb, Levi II:751
Holcomb, Nahum I:99
Holcomb, Obed II:401
Holcomb, Peter I:99
Holcomb, Phineas I:99
Holcombe, Philomel III:578
Holden, Abel II:269
Holden, Abraham I:917, 925
Holden, Amos I:339
Holden, Asa I:737
Holden, Benjamin I:537
Holden, Daniel I:216, 321
Holden, Darius II:351
Holden, Ebenezer M. II:217
Holden, Ephraim I:977
Holden, Henry II:55
Holden, Isaac I:881
Holden, Jacob II:638
Holden, James II:405
Holden, John I:181, 620, 806
Holden, Jonas II:236
Holden, Joseph I:917
Holden, Lemuel I:692
Holden, Levi II:36
Holden, Moses II:166
Holden, Nathaniel I:784
Holden, Nehemiah I:501
Holden, Phineas I:759
Holden, Richard IV:25
Holden, Richard S. IV:190
Holden, Robert I:619
Holden, Samuel I:221
Holden, Sartill II:705
Holden, Timothy I:784
Holder, Daniel III:515
Holder, James III:845
Holder, Jesse III:471
Holder, Jesse (2) III:471
Holdridge, Amasa II:203
Holdridge, Ephraim I:867
Holdridge, John II:332, 564
Holdridge, Robert I:74
Holdridge, Rufus I:69
Holdridge, Wm. R. II:564
Holdston, Thomas II:7, 10
Holdway, Henry III:395
Holdway, Timothy III:594
Hole, Daniel IV:97
Hole, James II:269
Holey, John I:55
Holgate, William II:678

Holister, Nathan IV:273
Holladay, Amos II:518
Holladay, Zacharias III:253
Holland, Henry III:180
Holland, Hugh III:141
Holland, Isaac III:43
Holland, Ivory II:306
Holland, J. I:xiii
Holland, Jacob III:809
Holland, James III:414
Holland, James M. III:322
Holland, Joab I:620
Holland, John III:94
Holland, John F. III:53
Holland, Joseph I:267; II:395; III:52; IV:108
Holland, Park I:221, 321
Holland, Reuben I:917
Holland, Thomas II:637; III:86; IV:120
Holland, William III:450, 608
Hollard, Charles III:94
Hollaway, Thomas III:840
Hollenback, John I:877
Hollenbeck, Jacob II:203
Holley, Benjamin I:925
Holley, Daniel III:194
Holley, Elijah I:339
Holley, John I:33
Holley, Jonathan II:454
Holley, Joseph II:227
Holley, Rawleigh III:740
Holley, Robert I:925
Holley, Samuel III:337
Holley, Stephen I:925
Holley, William I:759
Holliday, Benjamin III:315
Holliday, Elias II:564
Holliday, Horace S. IV:114
Holliday, Is'l Ellsworth III:15
Holliday, James III:818
Holliday, John II:661; III:617
Holliday, Robert II:246
Holliday, Stephen III:269
Holliman, James III:505
Hollingshead, Benjamin III:79
Hollingsworth, H. Sen. III:455
Hollingworth, Zebedee III:455
Hollinshead, James II:701
Hollis, Adam I:546
Hollis, David I:501
Hollis, Elijah II:291
Hollis, James III:515
Hollis, John III:219, 502, 614
Hollis, Stephen I:194
Hollis, William III:614
Hollister, Asa II:529
Hollister, Asahel I:930
Hollister, Ashbel I:963
Hollister, Clarissa I:998
Hollister, David II:393, 525
Hollister, Elijah II:364
Hollister, Ephraim II:454
Hollister, Innett I:962
Hollister, Jesse I:877, 998
Hollister, Joseph I:109
Hollister, Josiah I:100

413

414

417

Hubble, Nathan II:611
Hubbs, Alexander II:440
Hubbs, David II:44
Hubbs, Jacob III:263
Hubbs, John III:296
Hubbs, Samuel II:440
Huber, Christian II:730
Huber, Daniel II:626
Huber, Dorothea II:626
Huber, George II:665
Huber, John II:626
Huber, Nancy II:626
Huber, Susan II:626
Hubner, Frederick II:694
Hucans, Abiah III:234
Huchins, William I:723
Huckins, Israel I:731
Huckstep, Charles III:746
Huddleston, John III:532
Huddleston, Robert III:432
Hudgeons, Samuel III:613
Hudgins, Anthony III:806
Hudgins, Hugh III:806
Hudgins, John III:439
Hudgins, William III:523
Hudnall, Thomas IV:169
Hudson, Abraham II:291
Hudson, Benoni II:221
Hudson, Charles III:783, 807
Hudson, David III:161
Hudson, Eleazer I:15
Hudson, Elijah I:604
Hudson, Elisha I:593
Hudson, Enos II:259
Hudson, James III:9, 564
Hudson, John I:905; II:498;
    III:381, 620, 850; IV:190
Hudson, Joshua IV:242
Hudson, Peter III:803
Hudson, Rush III:694
Hudson, Samuel I:620, 751,
    826; III:46
Hudson, Sarah I:593
Hudson, Seth I:910
Hudson, Stephen I:501
Hudson, Thomas III:12, 582,
    835
Hudson, Timothy I:194
Hudson, Uriah III:354
Hudson, Vincent III:700
Hudson, William I:593
Hudspeth, Carter III:454
Hudwell, John III:752
Hues, James III:605
Huey, George II:580
Huey, John III:264
Huey, Lewis III:292
Hufacre, George III:595
Huff, Benjamin II:688
Huff, Daniel I:206, 309
Huff, Isaac II:85
Huff, Israel I:310
Huff, James II:25; III:91
Huff, John I:310; III:774
Huff, Johnson II:25
Huff, Jonathan II:25
Huff, Moses I:275

Huff, Peter III:306
Huff, Stephen III:503
Huffey, James II:575
Huffman, Christian II:638
Huffman, George III:198
Huffman, Henry III:821
Huffman, John III:481
Huffman, Joseph III:804
Huffman, Reuben III:702
Huffman, William II:368
Huffnagle, Michael II:632
Hufnagel, Christian II:440
Hufnagle, Christian II:752
Hugeley, Charles III:290
Hugeman, John II:752
Hugens, Edmund I:249
Huges, Jonathan IV:248
Huges, Joseph IV:121
Hugg, Isaac II:525
Huggins, James III:463
Huggins, John III:542
Huggins, Robert II:405
Huggins, Samuel III:27
Huggins, Zenos III:367
Hugh, Moses III:324
Hughes, Absalom III:256
Hughes, Benjamin III:761
Hughes, Camden Riley III:9
Hughes, David III:621
Hughes, Dyer I:998
Hughes, Edward III:746
Hughes, Gabriel III:806
Hughes, Isaac Riley III:9
Hughes, James II:659; III:460
Hughes, Jesse III:772
Hughes, John II:577; III:16,
    226, 665, 831
Hughes, Joseph III:83
Hughes, Parley III:632
Hughes, Peter III:620
Hughes, Richard I:699
Hughes, Robert II:470
Hughes, Thomas I:800; II:269;
    III:830
Hughes, William I:61; III:93,
    530
Hughes, Zachariah III:9
Hughlett, William III:694
Hughs, Francis III:584, 726
Hughs, Henry IV:195
Hughs, John I:941; III:600
Hughs, William III:298
Hughy, John II:697
Huitt, John IV:13
Hukill, Abiah III:234
Hukins, Daniel III:234
Hulbert, Amos I:110
Hulbert, Asher I:777
Hulbert, Daniel I:688
Hulbert, Elizabeth II:199
Hulbert, Jemima II:199
Hulbert, Juliana II:199
Hulbert, Louisa II:199
Hulbert, Lucius I:857
Hulbert, Lydia I:857
Hulbert, Silas II:199
Hulbert, Simeon I:857; II:291

Hulburt, Elijah II:224
Hulburt, Gideon II:410
Hulet, James M. III:230
Hulet, John II:73; IV:269
Hulet, Phineas II:55
Hulet, Sylvanus IV:211
Hulett, Joseph I:988
Hulett, Nehemiah II:540
Hulfish, John II:73
Hulick, John IV:239
Huling, Andrew III:833
Huling, John I:930; II:506
Huling, Jonathan III:266
Hull, Abner IV:242
Hull, Agrippa I:339, 655
Hull, Asa II:241
Hull, Asahel II:410
Hull, Benjamin I:109
Hull, C. Jr. II:556
Hull, Chester II:246, 556
Hull, Daniel III:594
Hull, David I:339; II:3, 245
Hull, David, 2d II:485
Hull, Eli II:235
Hull, Elias I:784
Hull, Ezra I:87
Hull, George II:337; III:781
Hull, Henry III:665, 778
Hull, Isaac I:100; IV:233, 285
Hull, James I:99, 672; II:73
Hull, James W. I:621
Hull, Jeremiah I:36
Hull, John I:231, 806; II:153;
    III:381, 584, 690
Hull, Joseph I:784; III:586
Hull, Josiah II:314, 453
Hull, Pomeroy II:469
Hull, Prince I:41
Hull, Samuel II:23, 246, 525
Hull, Solomon IV:263
Hull, Stephen I:22
Hull, Warren II:399
Hull, William III:809
Hull, Zephaniah I:100
Hullinger, Daniel IV:236
Hulme, George III:631
Huls, James IV:19
Hulse, Jacob II:470
Hulse, James IV:214
Hulse, Matthias II:77
Hulsiger, Christopher II:41
Hults, Stephen II:490
Hum, Henry II:727
Human, Alexander III:172
Humason, Joel IV:289
Humastow, Jesse I:110
Humble, Michael III:776
Humble, Robert III:331
Hume, John III:716; IV:81
Humes, Josiah I:619
Humes, Stephen I:349
Humeston, David I:126
Humewell, Richard I:181
Humfres, John III:294
Hummel, Frederick II:741
Hummell, Elijah II:69
Hummell, Henry II:645

418

419

Hunton, Moses I:751
Hunton, Reuben II:221
Huntoon, Aaron I:723
Huntoon, Charles I:854
Huntoon, George I:664
Huntoon, Joseph I:679, 853
Huntoon, Willard I:850
Huntsley, Nicholas II:405
Huntt, Julius III:766
Hupp, Philip IV:298
Huppull, Adam II:678
Hurd, Aaron I:951
Hurd, Abijah II:269
Hurd, Adam I:930
Hurd, Benjamin I:118
Hurd, Calvin III:658
Hurd, Cooley II:367
Hurd, Crippen, Jr. I:55
Hurd, David I:3; II:49
Hurd, Ebenezer I:692
Hurd, Elijah I:930
Hurd, Elnathan I:118
Hurd, Isaac I:518; II:252
Hurd, Jacob I:117
Hurd, John I:590; IV:141
Hurd, Lewis I:930
Hurd, Mede IV:109
Hurd, Philo I:48
Hurd, Robert L. II:360
Hurd, Thomas I:444
Hurd, Wilson I:126
Hurd, Wyal I:784
Hurdle, Lawrence III:11
Hurdle, Robert III:54
Hurlbert, Alfred I:68
Hurlbert, John II:285
Hurlbert, William I:69
Hurlburt, Abiram II:501
Hurlburt, David II:207
Hurlbut, Amos I:110
Hurlbut, Eliphalet I:350
Hurlbut, Elisha I:867
Hurlbut, Gideon I:33
Hurlbut, John II:285
Hurlbut, Jubilee A. II:319
Hurlbut, Seymour I:118
Hurlbut, Silas I:99
Hurlbut, Simeon II:291
Hurlbut, Stephen II:169
Hurlbut, Thaddeus I:339
Hurlbut, Wait I:881
Hurley, Cornelius IV:214
Hurley, David III:137
Hurley, John I:596
Hurley, Joseph III:152
Hurley, Joshua III:433
Hurley, Salem III:15
Hurst, Henry III:317, 321, 665
Hurst, Kemp W. III:534
Hurst, Richard III:806
Hurst, Sally III:534
Hurst, Samuel III:51
Hurst, Smith W. III:534
Hurst, William IV:97
Hurt, Benjamin III:762
Hurt, James III:553
Hurt, William III:253

Husam, John II:632
Husband, James III:681
Husbands, J. B. III:336
Husbands, William III:83
Huse, Isaac I:759
Huse, John I:777
Huse, Samuel I:396, 772
Huse, William I:777
Husled, Thaddeus I:86
Hussey, Betsey I:173
Hussey, Experience I:173
Hussey, John I:173
Hussey, Polly I:173
Hussey, Theodore I:173
Hussey, Zachariah I:173
Husstead, Moses III:789
Husted, David II:453
Husted, Hosea II:34
Husted, John II:34
Husted, Reuben II:34
Husted, Robert II:720
Husted, William IV:141
Hustler, Thomas II:146
Huston, Daniel II:755
Huston, Hugh IV:209
Huston, James II:726, 755
Huston, John, Jr. I:237
Huston, Philip II:689
Huston, William II:291;
  IV:177
Hutcheons, Simeon I:237
Hutcherson, James III:825
Hutcherson, John III:748
Hutcherson, William III:738
Hutchings, Benjamin I:207
Hutchings, Eastman I:237
Hutchings, Gabriel IV:173
Hutchings, Hezekiah I:473
Hutchings, John I:194
Hutchings, Moses III:822
Hutchings, Thomas I:275
Hutchings, William IV:234
Hutchins, Bulkely I:899
Hutchins, Charles II:291
Hutchins, Edward III:145
Hutchins, Enoch I:237
Hutchins, Hollis IV:188
Hutchins, Jacob II:506
Hutchins, James I:717; II:27
Hutchins, Joseph I:216
Hutchins, Levi I:237, 717
Hutchins, Maria II:27
Hutchins, Moses I:286; IV:250
Hutchins, Nathan I:947
Hutchins, Nathaniel I:216,
  321
Hutchins, Noah II:419
Hutchins, Shubael I:149
Hutchins, Simon I:939
Hutchins, Solomon I:777
Hutchins, Thomas III:450
Hutchins, Thomas S. III:661
Hutchins, William I:260, 741;
  II:27
Hutchins, Zadoc I:149
Hutchinson, Abijah I:951
Hutchinson, Asa I:266

Hutchinson, Cor. II:662
Hutchinson, Cor. (2) II:662
Hutchinson, Drury III:514
Hutchinson, Ebenezer I:143
Hutchinson, Elisha I:889
Hutchinson, Elizabeth II:28
Hutchinson, Francis III:32
Hutchinson, Israel I:266, 416
Hutchinson, Jacob IV:242
Hutchinson, James II:28;
  III:553
Hutchinson, Job I:925
Hutchinson, John I:988; II:28,
  291, 405, 611, 661
Hutchinson, John, Sr. III:810
Hutchinson, Jonathan I:463;
  II:28
Hutchinson, Joseph III:262
Hutchinson, Levi I:731
Hutchinson, Nehemiah I:207
Hutchinson, Oliver I:684
Hutchinson, Orlando W. I:862
Hutchinson, Phebe I:684
Hutchinson, Philip I:684
Hutchinson, Rufus I:862
Hutchinson, Saml., 2d I:917
Hutchinson, Samuel I:207,
  917; II:259
Hutchinson, Stephen I:181;
  III:481
Hutchinson, Thomas I:899;
  III:693
Hutchinson, William I:684;
  III:432
Hutchison, David III:590
Hutchison, Samuel III:517
Hutchkins, Edmund I:237
Hutinack, Francis II:382
Huting, Augustus I:833
Hutson, Thomas III:756
Hutson, William III:228
Hutt, Gerard III:844
Hutt, John IV:284
Hutto, Henry III:136
Hutton, Christopher II:554
Hutton, Christopher, 2d II:224
Hutton, George IV:216
Hutton, James II:650; III:306
Hutton, John II:498
Hutton, N., Jr. II:552
Hutton, Timothy II:81
Hutton, William II:445
Hutts, Leonard III:696
Huxford, John I:143
Huxley, James II:269
Huxson, Matthew IV:291
Huxworth, Edward II:738
Huyck, William II:705
Huzzey, James I:910
Hyatt, Abraham II:547
Hyatt, Alvan I:87
Hyatt, Isaac I:87
Hyatt, Jose III:29
Hyatt, Lewis IV:135
Hyatt, Samuel II:306
Hyatt, Stephen I:86
Hyde, Agur I:33

Hyde, Alexander I:69
Hyde, Andrew I:135
Hyde, Azel I:135; II:554
Hyde, Benjamin II:453
Hyde, Clarke II:314
Hyde, Ebenezer I:126
Hyde, Elihu I:135
Hyde, Elijah I:463
Hyde, Elisha I:126
Hyde, Ephraim II:501
Hyde, Gershom I:501, 519
Hyde, Ichabod I:951
Hyde, Irvine III:605
Hyde, James I:889, 998
Hyde, Jedediah I:893
Hyde, Joel I:135
Hyde, John I:86, 350
Hyde, Jonathan II:430
Hyde, Joseph I:956
Hyde, Joshua I:643
Hyde, Oliver II:284
Hyde, Phineas I:68
Hyde, Zenas I:977
Hyden William III:611
Hyer, Conrad I:207
Hyer, Walter II:23
Hylanc, Henry II:46
Hylanc, Samuel I:561
Hylanc, William I:575
Hyler, John II:746
Hymer, David II:192
Hyre, Jacob III:798
Hyre, Philip I:22
Hyslop, Levin III:673
Hyzer, Christian II:95

Ice, Andrew IV:75
Iddings, William II:708
Ide, Jacob I:373
Ide, James II:326
Ide, Joseph I:807
Ide, Nathan I:363
Ide, Oliver I:963
Iden, John III:801
Ides, Reuben I:644
Idle, Earney II:639
Idol, Jacob III:452
Illson, Oliver I:807
Ilsley, Isaiah I:397
Imeson, John III:49
Imhoff, Frederick III:698
Imlay, Isaac II:73
Imlay, Wiliam I:xiv
Imman, Henry II:700
Immel, Leonard II:729
Impson, Henry II:55
Ingalls, Caleb II:401
Ingalls, Ebenezer II:401
Ingalls, Edmund I:977
Ingalls, Jacob II:354
Ingalls, Joseph IV:247
Ingalls, Luther I:700
Ingalls, Moses I:747
Ingalls, Nathan I:250
Ingalls, Nathaniel I:502
Ingalls, Phineas I:250

Ingalls, Solomon II:420
Ingals, James I:502
Ingalsbie, John II:465
Ingbe, Ebenezer I:302
Ingell, Jonathan I:373
Ingell, Zadock I:482
Ingersol, Artemadores II:667
Ingersol, Justis II:113
Ingersoll, Abraham I:597
Ingersoll, Andrew I:398
Ingersoll, Briggs I:49
Ingersoll, Ebenezer II:454
Ingersoll, Francis I:683; II:211
Ingersoll, George I:683
Ingersoll, John I:417; II:67,
  211, 479
Ingersoll, Jonathan I:988
Ingersoll, Mrs. N'l I:250
Ingersoll, R. J. I:156
Ingersoll, Zebulon I:398
Ingerson, Richard I:237
Ingham, Benjamin I:541
Ingham, Daniel I:267
Ingham, David I:237
Ingham, Isaac II:279
Ingham, Samuel II:232
Ingham, Solomon I:482
Ingham, Thomas III:633
Inghram, David I:195
Ingle, John III:552
Ingle, Michael III:562
Ingraham, Amos II:214
Ingraham, Benjamin I:807
Ingraham, Hezekiah I:69
Ingraham, Holladay II:249
Ingraham, James I:118
Ingraham, Job I:276
Ingraham, John I:351
Ingraham, Jonathan I:351
Ingraham, Samuel I:925
Ingraham, Simeon I:826
Ingraham, William II:328
Ingram, Abel II:580
Ingram, Andrew IV:69
Ingram, Edwin III:446
Ingram, Jeremiah III:253
Ingram, John I:482
Ingram, Melinda III:672
Ingram, Philip I:944
Ingram, Seth I:854
Ingram, Valentine III:672
Inlo, Thomas III:481
Inlow, John III:487
Inman, Rufus IV:223
Innes, Jacob II:136
Innis, John II:506
Innman, Elias I:167
Innois, Jacob II:760
Inskeep, John II:743
Ipoch, Samuel III:409
Iradon, Henry III:563
Irby, Douglas III:682
Ireland, Alin II:26
Ireland, David II:26
Ireland, Dayton II:61
Ireland, Esther II:26
Ireland, Hezekiah II:26

Ireland, Joel I:166
Ireland, John II:713
Ireland, Judah II:26
Ireland, Rebecca II:26
Ireland, Reuben II:26
Irick, Abraham III:445
Irish, Isaac I:250
Irish, Thomas I:250
Irons, Garrett II:77
Irons, Jeremiah I:826
Irvin, Edward IV:245
Irvin, James I:669; III:229,
  450
Irvin, William II:332
Irvine, Alexander III:133;
  IV:29
Irvine, James II:595, 722;
  III:253
Irvine, Jno. III:734
Irvine, John, 2d II:661
Irvine, William IV:83
Irving, John, 1st II:652
Irvy, David III:822
Irwin, Ezekiel IV:291
Irwin, Hen. II:647
Irwin, James IV:174, 234
Irwin, Jno. III:734
Irwin, John II:133, 612
Irwin, Nathan II:711
Irwin, Robert I:363
Irwin, Thomas III:410
Irwin, Thomas H. III:114
Irwin, W. W. IV:298-99
Isaacs, Isaac II:351
Isaacs, James III:37
Isaacs, Samuel III:598
Isaac Vertrees III:224
Isbel, Joel IV:225
Isbel, Ransom IV:151
Isbell, Benjamin III:779
Isbell, Christopher III:749
Isbell, Garner II:749
Isbell, Henry III:210, 779
Isbell, James III:327
Isbell, Pendleton III:488
Iseley, Philip III:164
Iseman, Christian II:758
Iseman, Michael II:758
Isenhoar, Philip II:670
Isham, Daniel I:939
Isham, George J. IV:190
Isham, Jehiel I:877
Isham, Jirah I:939
Isham, John I:100
Isham, Joshua I:998
Isham, William I:881, 998
Ishmael, Benjamin III:240
Israel, John II:351; IV:78
Israel, William III:189
Itnise, Daniel III:67
Ittig, Conrad I:556
Ittig, Conradt II:249
Ittig, Jacob C. II:415
Ivers, Samuel I:597
Ivery, James II:336
Ives, Amasa II:374
Ives, Amos II:415

Ives, Charles I:127
Ives, Ichabod I:127
Ives, Joel, Jr. I:22
Ives, John II:285
Ives, John P. III:409
Ives, Lent I:963; II:148
Ives, Levi II:514
Ives, Thomas III:411, 549
Ivey, David III:542
Ivey, Elijah III:85
Ivington, Jeremiah III:55
Ivins, John III:631
Ivory, James II:171
Ivy, David III:631
Ivy, Henry III:594

Jack, James III:584
Jack, John I:41
Jack, Matthew II:604, 758
Jack, Robert I:207
Jack, Thomas IV:165
Jacklin, Ebenezer I:339
Jackman, Benjamin I:398
Jackman, Richard I:195
Jackman, Samuel I:717
Jackson, Aaron I:717
Jackson, Abednego III:15
Jackson, Alexander IV:272
Jackson, Anthony II:612
Jackson, Archibald II:385
Jackson, Asa I:473; II:238
Jackson, Barnabas I:225
Jackson, Bartholomew I:276
Jackson, Benjamin III:499;
IV:263
Jackson, Caleb I:417
Jackson, Churchwell III:607
Jackson, Daniel I:33, 87, 502,
657; IV:263
Jackson, David II:270, 611
Jackson, Drury III:736
Jackson, Ebenezer I:156, 597;
II:751
Jackson, Edward III:164
Jackson, Eleazer I:785
Jackson, Eli I:181
Jackson, Elias II:279
Jackson, Elijah I:22
Jackson, Eliza III:669
Jackson, Enoch I:296; II:475
Jackson, Ephraim I:910
Jackson, Francis III:331
Jackson, George III:221, 669
Jackson, George Washington
III:533
Jackson, Henry III:825
Jackson, Isaac I:286; III:416,
718; IV:295
Jackson, James III:317, 531,
717; IV:179
Jackson, James W. II:173
Jackson, Jeremiah II:464
Jackson, John I:267; II:9, 717;
III:76, 533
Jackson, John A.H. I:685
Jackson, John C. III:279

Jackson, John Henry I:685
Jackson, Jonas I:432
Jackson, Jonathan I:899;
III:562, 807
Jackson, Joseph I:217, 327;
II:544; III:260; IV:16, 199
Jackson, Joseph, 2d I:207
Jackson, Joshua II:684
Jackson, Joshua J. III:481
Jackson, Josiah III:269, 590
Jackson, Louisiana III:533
Jackson, Lyman II:718
Jackson, Mark III:605
Jackson, Matthew IV:190
Jackson, Michael II:299
Jackson, Moses I:693
Jackson, Nathan I:868
Jackson, Nathaniel I:217
Jackson, Obadiah III:590
Jackson, Oliver I:502
Jackson, Patton II:317
Jackson, Peter IV:284
Jackson, Polly I:657
Jackson, Reuben III:709
Jackson, Richard IV:196
Jackson, Robert I:731; III:533
Jackson, Royal I:670
Jackson, Samuel I:155, 286;
III:452, 625; IV:69
Jackson, Solomon IV:89
Jackson, Stephen IV:201
Jackson, Thomas I:267;
III:114
Jackson, William II:667;
III:183, 533, 538, 580, 680
Jackson, Wm. III:633
Jackson, Wm. 2d III:633
Jackson, Wm. Henry Harrison
III:669
Jackson, Zebulon I:22
Jackway, Daniel I:49
Jackway, William I:351
Jaco, William III:209
Jacob, John J. III:704, 850
Jacob, Lewis IV:103
Jacob, Z. III:852
Jacobs, Asa I:149
Jacobs, Asahel I:143
Jacobs, Benjamin III:719
Jacobs, David III:741
Jacobs, Edward G. III:633
Jacobs, Enoch I:22
Jacobs, Ezekiel I:127
Jacobs, Francis II:95
Jacobs, George I:237
Jacobs, George W. IV:31
Jacobs, Gershom II:310
Jacobs, Isaiah I:899
Jacobs, James II:671
Jacobs, John I:195, 519; II:37,
275, 307, 760; III:321;
IV:213
Jacobs, Jonathan II:694
Jacobs, Joseph III:567
Jacobs, Lemuel I:576
Jacobs, Lewis I:926
Jacobs, Nathaniel I:905; II:479

Jacobs, Primus III:382
Jacobs, Roby III:218
Jacobs, Samuel IV:97
Jacobs, Simeon II:454
Jacobs, Thomas III:351
Jacobs, William I:611; II:183;
III:214; IV:275
Jacobs, Zachariah III:437
Jacoby, Nicholas III:631
Jacoby, Philip II:666
Jacocks, Joshua II:292
Jacox, Bowers II:498
Jacques, Daniel I:519
Jacques, William II:292
Jacquette, Peter II:12
Jacqueway, Samuel IV:2
Jaggers, Jeremiah III:77
Jaggor, Abraham I:100
Jaggors, Nathan IV:19
Jagua, Gamaliel IV:281
Jameison, John III:208
James, Aaron III:577
James, Abner III:439
James, Amos II:495
James, David II:61
James, Ebenezer I:177; II:334
James, Elijah II:163
James, Elisha I:576
James, Eliza I:177
James, George I:834
James, Isaac III:785
James, Jabez I:778
James, Jamaica II:299
James, James III:497
James, John I:177, 195; II:69,
299
James, John H. IV:295
James, Jonathan II:711
James, Joseph III:245
James, Joshua I:807
James, Nathan II:707
James, Paul II:217
James, Rolling III:570
James, Silas I:815
James, Thomas I:482; III:195;
IV:88, 230
James, William I:49; II:183;
III:253, 523, 778
Jameson, David III:260, 766
Jameson, John III:257
Jameson, Samuel I:700
Jameson, William III:258
Jamieson, Benoni III:194
Jamieson, James III:499
Jamieson, John III:649
Jamieson, Joseph III:517
Jamieson, Thomas I:759
Jamison, Francis IV:214
Jamison, John II:518, 643;
III:315, 583
Jamison, Robert IV:123
Jams, John Frederick III:583
Janes, Almirah II:191
Janes, Alphileda II:191
Janes, Damaris B. I:27
Janes, Diantha II:191
Janes, Eliza I:27

Janes, Emeline II:191
Janes, Jonathan I:881
Janes, Louisa II:191
Janes, Lowis II:109
Janes, Lucinda I:27
Janes, Mary II:191
Janes, Rachel L. I:27
Janes, Thomas I:27, 79
Janes, William I:464
Jansen, Benjamin II:532
Jansen, Matthew H. II:529
Jansom, Matthew II:183
Japson, William I:621
Jaqua Asahel II:224
Jaques, Nathan I:398, 810, 868
Jaques, Parker I:417
Jaques, Richard I:188
Jaques, William II:566
Jaquins, John II:224
Jaquish, John II:229, 554
Jaquith, Ebenezer I:742
Jarman, Azariah II:84
Jarman, William III:462
Jarrel John III:717
Jarrel Solomon III:721
Jarrel, William III:819
Jarvis Bill II:529
Jarvis Edward I:596; III:311
Jarvis Elisha III:511
Jarvis Field III:810
Jarvis James III:648
Jarvis John I:343; II:328
Jarvis L. I:320-21
Jarvis Robert II:292
Jarvis Thomas III:411
Jaseph, Joseph I:432
Jasksen, Benjamin II:16
Jay, Joseph II:57
Jayne, Ebenezer III:199
Jayne, Samuel II:550
Jean, Nathan III:374
Jean, Philip III:419
Jean, William III:454
Jeannerel, Claude F. III:698
Jeannret, Elias III:412
Jeems, Vachel III:87
Jefferd, Samuel M. I:311
Jefferies, William III:281
Jeffers, Allen III:512
Jeffers, Francis II:19
Jeffers, Jacob III:55
Jeffers, Joseph II:255
Jeffers, William III:335
Jefferson, George II:454
Jefferson, Russell I:840
Jeffery, Charles I:135
Jeffords, William I:881
Jeffrey, Garrett II:77
Jeffrey, John IV:293
Jeffreys, James I:61
Jeffreys, John II:67; III:439
Jeffreys, William III:823
Jeffries, Alexander III:771
Jeffries, Gowen IV:95
Jeffries, John III:314; III:646
Jeffries, Reuben III:830

Jeffries, William I:807
Jeffry, Humphrey II:46
Jeliff, James I:87
Jemison, David IV:276
Jenckes, Jediah I:826
Jencks, Dickinson II:332
Jenison, Joseph B. II:218
Jenison, Robert I:910
Jenison, William I:977
Jenkens, John III:388
Jenkins, Aaron III:445
Jenkins, Abraham III:363
Jenkins, Absalom III:786
Jenkins, Alvan I:330
Jenkins, Anthony III:306
Jenkins, Benjamin I:672
Jenkins, Caleb III:778
Jenkins, Calvin I:33, 576
Jenkins, Charles III:364
Jenkins, David I:693; II:101
Jenkins, Enoch I:889, 998; II:555
Jenkins, James III:512, 616
Jenkins, Job IV:9
Jenkins, Joel II:310-11
Jenkins, John I:237; II:667; III:86, 287, 708
Jenkins, Joseph I:951; II:374
Jenkins, Lemuel I:207, 276, 934
Jenkins, Lewis III:164
Jenkins, Nathaniel I:330; II:393
Jenkins, Obadiah I:693
Jenkins, Richard III:824
Jenkins, Robert III:35
Jenkins, Samuel I:286, 688
Jenkins, Solomon II:136
Jenkins, Stephen I:889
Jenkins, Thomas II:595; III:15, 416
Jenkins, William I:417; II:758; III:84, 153, 225, 454
Jenkins, Zacheus I:330
Jenks, Adam II:368
Jenks, Anthony II:227
Jenks, Bromer I:977
Jenks, Jacob IV:227
Jenks, Levi II:485
Jenks, Lory II:485
Jenks, Oliver IV:103
Jenks, Prince I:795
Jenne, George I:861
Jenne, George (2) I:861
Jenne, Prince I:868
Jenness, John I:875
Jenning, Peter III:615
Jennings, Aaron I:87
Jennings, Abel I:464
Jennings, Abner II:405
Jennings, Abraham I:87
Jennings, Benjamin I:621
Jennings, Burritt I:49
Jennings, Charles I:22
Jennings, Daniel I:79, 611
Jennings, Ebenezer I:679
Jennings, Edmund III:575

Jennings, Eliphalet I:87, 194
Jennings, Esbon IV:202
Jennings, Ezekiel IV:63
Jennings, James III:211, 404
Jennings, Jonathan I:644, 868; II:691
Jennings, Jonathan S. II:270
Jennings, Joseph I:600; II:279
Jennings, Justus I:22; II:323
Jennings, Nathan I:143
Jennings, Nathan B. II:678
Jennings, Peter I:87
Jennings, Royal III:583
Jennings, Solomon III:241
Jennings, Stephen I:612, 917
Jennings, Thomas II:612
Jennings, William I:33, 351; II:477; III:598, 769
Jennins, Thomas III:385
Jennis, George I:861
Jennison, Joseph B. I:630
Jennison, Moses I:519
Jennison, Samuel I:207
Jennison, William I:597
Jenville, Alexis II:221
Jepherson, Jedediah I:917
Jepherson, John I:643
Jepson, David I:871
Jepson, John I:474
Jepson, Joseph I:482
Jeralemon, Nicholas II:355
Jeremiah, John II:203
Jeriner, Samuel II:95
Jernigan, George III:459
Jerolman, James II:14
Jerome, David I:41
Jerome, Isaac I:611
Jerrald, Hugh Pugh III:385
Jerrod, John IV:4
Jervin, Robert I:22
Jesse, William III:826
Jessup, Ebenezer I:87
Jessup, Jonathan I:33
Jessup, Joseph II:494
Jester, Daniel II:11
Jester, James F. III:404
Jester, Nimrod IV:98
Jeter, Fielding III:216
Jeter, James III:515
Jeter, Littleton III:216
Jett, William S. III:844
Jewel, Ephraim I:944
Jewel, Seth II:688
Jewel, William II:736
Jewell, Benjamin I:910
Jewell, Elisha III:7709
Jewell, Fielder III:645
Jewell, Jacob III:338
Jewell, James I:759
Jewell, John I:586; II:547
Jewell, John, 2d I:217, 237
Jewell, John, 1st I:237
Jewell, John M. II:307
Jewell, Jonathan II:351
Jewell, Joseph III:272
Jewell, Samuel I:286

Jewell, William I:917; II:44; III:575, 587
Jewet, Moses I:207
Jewett, Benjamin I:731, 789
Jewett, Caleb I:9
Jewett, David I:339, 655
Jewett, Elisha II:379
Jewett, Enoch I:709
Jewett, Epes I:398
Jewett, Gibbons I:22
Jewett, Jedediah I:519
Jewett, John II:525
Jewett, Jonathan I:752
Jewett, Joseph I:644
Jewett, Joseph M. IV:227
Jewett, Nathaniel I:772
Jewett, Oliver I:621
Jewett, Samuel I:778
Jewetts, Zebulon I:963
Jewitt, David I:296
Jewitt, Ezekiel II:146
Jewitt, John I:267
Jewitt, Nathan H. I:135
Jewitt, Noah I:311
Jillson, David I:977
Jincks, Benjamin II:241
Jinks, Thomas III:396
Job, Enoch IV:117
Job, Robert II:736
Jobbs, William II:23
Joel, Richard I:562
Johannett, Prince I:759
John, Thomas III:52
Johns, George III:11
Johns, Jacob II:724
Johns, Samuel I:621
Johns, Stephen I:351
Johns, Thomas IV:192
Johns_n, Joseph I:250
Johnson, Abner III:527, 605
Johnson, Abraham I:61; III:152, 312; IV:91
Johnson, Abraham, 2d II:339
Johnson, Abram III:436
Johnson, Adrian II:41
Johnson, Alexander III:405
Johnson, Alonzo II:200
Johnson, Amos I:621; II:479
Johnson, Andrew I:216; II:211, 605, 612; III:828
Johnson, Archibald III:49
Johnson, Arthur IV:40
Johnson, Asa I:250, 621; II:113-14
Johnson, Azel IV:229
Johnson, B. P. II:558, 560
Johnson, Barnabas III:626
Johnson, Barney II:31, 678
Johnson, Benedict III:37
Johnson, Benjamin I:229, 398; II:67, 362, 678; III:555, 773; IV:186, 296
Johnson, Benoni I:110
Johnson, Bulkley II:329
Johnson, Caleb II:501; III:122; IV:284
Johnson, Calvin I:988

Johnson, Cave III:259
Johnson, Charles II:200, 252; III:245, 779
Johnson, Chauncey II:200
Johnson, Christopher II:752
Johnson, Clabourn IV:121
Johnson, Clarissa II:200
Johnson, Comfort II:501
Johnson, Dalmath III:268
Johnson, Daniel I:41, 229; II:41, 195, 236, 379
Johnson, Daniel, 2d II:323
Johnson, David I:351, 905; II:193, 270, 368, 410, 559, 700; III:340; IV:76, 84
Johnson, Dennis I:237
Johnson, Ebenezer I:397
Johnson, Edmund III:115
Johnson, Edward I:621; II:207, 479
Johnson, Eleazer I:87
Johnson, Elias I:464
Johnson, Elijah I:693; II:470
Johnson, Elijah, Sen. III:512
Johnson, Elisha I:482, 977; II:337
Johnson, Elisha E. III:544
Johnson, Ellis III:514
Johnson, Enos III:587
Johnson, Ephraim I:709
Johnson, Ezekiel I:815
Johnson, F. R. III:335
Johnson, Francis III:340
Johnson, George II:41, 748
Johnson, George, Sen. III:458
Johnson, Gideon I:127; III:631
Johnson, Giles III:688
Johnson, Gulcon II:573
Johnson, Hardy III:167
Johnson, Harriet II:189
Johnson, Henry I:611; II:46, 109, 224, 399
Johnson, Henson IV:74
Johnson, Hezekiah II:424
Johnson, Howell III:514
Johnson, Hugh II:650; III:234
Johnson, Isaac I:118, 547, 597, 978; II:189, 292, 368; III:210, 571, 633
Johnson, Isaac, 2d I:432
Johnson, Isaiah II:454
Johnson, Israel II:236, 555
Johnson, J. T. III:334
Johnson, Jacob II:69; III:310, 665
Johnson, James I:118, 195, 766, 917; II:84, 203, 612, 697, 700, 724; III:111, 232, 363, 596, 608, 793; IV:125, 239, 291
Johnson, James, 1st II:46, 332; III:247
Johnson, James, 2d II:34, 337; III:237, 247
Johnson, James, Sr. III:778
Johnson, Jane II:193

Johnson, Jedediah I:143; II:485
Johnson, Jeremiah I:917
Johnson, Jesse I:759; III:564
Johnson, Jeter III:536
Johnson, Jno II:630
Johnson, Jno. Jacob II:713
Johnson, John I:118, 597, 759, 772, 881; II:82, 374, 470, 494, 555, 559, 653, 724; III:23, 245, 705, 812
Johnson, John, 1st II:177
Johnson, John (2) I:597
Johnson, John, 2d II:269; III:223
Johnson, John, 3d II:314; III:226
Johnson, John, Sen. III:291
Johnson, John, 4th II:224; III:221
Johnson, John, 5th II:323
Johnson, John A. I:807
Johnson, John R. II:77
Johnson, Jonah I:944
Johnson, Jonas I:621
Johnson, Jonathan I:181, 373, 502, 717, 910; III:164
Johnson, Joseph I:605, 700; II:328, 655; III:367, 422
Johnson, Joseph, 1st II:77
Johnson, Joseph, 2d I:408, 701; II:67
Johnson, Joseph Payne III:152
Johnson, Joshua I:417, 957
Johnson, Josiah I:118
Johnson, Julia II:193
Johnson, Julian II:189
Johnson, Justus I:13; II:465
Johnson, Lavinia II:195
Johnson, Lawrence II:529
Johnson, Levi I:127
Johnson, Libeus II:319
Johnson, Luther II:405
Johnson, Miles I:785
Johnson, Moses I:742; II:193, 360; III:241, 587
Johnson, Nahum III:763
Johnson, Nathan I:181, 502, 644
Johnson, Nathaniel I:127; II:259; III:567
Johnson, Nathaniel, 2d I:502
Johnson, Nathaniel, 3d I:398
Johnson, Obadiah III:779
Johnson, Orange II:207
Johnson, Othniel IV:38
Johnson, Ozias I:963
Johnson, Peleg I:800
Johnson, Peter I:79, 679; III:850, 853
Johnson, Peter, 2d I:398
Johnson, Peter W. III:23
Johnson, Phebe II:189, 195
Johnson, Philemon IV:276
Johnson, Philip II:440; IV:51
Johnson, Phineas I:777
Johnson, Phinehas I:61

Johnson, Phoebe II:559
Johnson, R. M. III:334, 337-38, 853
Johnson, Reuben I:127; III:518
Johnson, Richard I:576; III:83, 96, 522, 746, 837
Johnson, Richard M. III:200, 333
Johnson, Robert II:183; III:204, 312, 681; IV:113
Johnson, Rowland III:514
Johnson, Rufus I:149; II:426, 494
Johnson, Sampson II:200
Johnson, Samuel I:143, 537, 700, 951; II:77, 229, 475, 525; III:355, 692, 843
Johnson, Samuel, 2d II:241
Johnson, Samuel, 3d II:298
Johnson, Samuel, Sen. III:273
Johnson, Samuel, 4th II:285
Johnson, Samuel C. II:227
Johnson, Sarah II:193
Johnson, Seth I:537, 605
Johnson, Shadrach I:41
Johnson, Silas I:482; IV:207
Johnson, Simon I:795
Johnson, Solomon III:119
Johnson, Stephen I:644, 978; II:420
Johnson, Stephen W. II:354
Johnson, Sylvester I:834
Johnson, Theodate II:485
Johnson, Thias II:347
Johnson, Thomas I:195; II:73, 195, 612; III:319, 375, 750; IV:105, 223
Johnson, Thomas, 1st II:53; III:711
Johnson, Thomas, 2d II:31; III:674
Johnson, Timothy I:62, 778, 899; II:399
Johnson, Turner II:211
Johnson, Uriah I:917
Johnson, Uzal I:135
Johnson, Vixon II:189
Johnson, William I:237, 644, 826; II:12, 21, 193, 195, 232, 379, 396, 454, 743; III:274, 282, 326, 397, 458, 508, 546, 779; IV:182, 242, 260
Johnson, William (2) II:454; III:458
Johnson, William, 1st I:79; II:229
Johnson, William, 2d I:69, 519; II:55, 207; III:329
Johnson, William, 3d I:33; II:285
Johnson, William, Sen. IV:122
Johnson, Windsor I:857
Johnson, Witter II:393
Johnson, Wm. Sen. III:287
Johnson, Zapher III:584

Johnston, Andrew II:77, 620, 630
Johnston, Benjamin IV:133
Johnston, Crawford III:394
Johnston, David I:250; II:745
Johnston, Francis III:398
Johnston, Frederick III:395
Johnston, George III:711
Johnston, Gideon III:694
Johnston, Harvey I:843
Johnston, Jacob II:595, 738; IV:241
Johnston, James I:250; III:291, 698, 851
Johnston, Jno II:630
Johnston, John I:292, 302; II:643, 758; III:618
Johnston, Joseph II:611, 635; III:226, 447
Johnston, Lewis II:73
Johnston, Margaret II:630
Johnston, Martin III:214
Johnston, Mary II:630
Johnston, Michael I:751
Johnston, Nathaniel, 1st I:562
Johnston, Nicholas III:55
Johnston, Peter II:77
Johnston, Richard III:720
Johnston, Robert III:402, 596
Johnston, Samuel II:319; IV:227
Johnston, Thomas III:93; IV:36
Johnston, William I:875; II:603, 631; IV:283
Johnston, William, 2d I:875
Johnstone, George II:332
Johnton, Archibald III:323
Johonnet, Gabriel I:221
Johonnet, Oliver I:601
Joiester, George II:711
Joiner, Jonathan III:586
Joiner, Moses III:417
Joiners, Michael II:678
Jolley, Lewis II:73
Jolly, Henry IV:223
Jonah, Jacob I:502
Jonas, John III:18
Joner, Jacob I:502
Jones, Aaron III:51
Jones, Abel I:621
Jones, Abiah II:197
Jones, Abraham II:61; III:848
Jones, Abraham P. III:149
Jones, Alexander II:52; III:55
Jones, Ambrose III:218
Jones, Amos I:229, 519; II:197, 435
Jones, Anna II:199
Jones, Armistead IV:5
Jones, Arthur I:174
Jones, Asa I:510, 742; II:378; IV:179
Jones, Asaph II:731
Jones, Augustus I:118
Jones, Barnabas I:807

Jones, Benjamin I:87, 807; II:218, 241, 752; III:292, 452, 618; IV:236
Jones, Berryman III:781
Jones, Brittain III:385
Jones, Cadwallader III:633
Jones, Charles II:170, 259; III:204, 455
Jones, Consider I:562
Jones, Cornelius I:286; II:475
Jones, Cotton III:57
Jones, Crocker IV:180
Jones, Daniel II:82, 314; III:66, 587
Jones, David I:181; II:307, 475, 514; III:590, 596, 613; IV:77, 120
Jones, Deborah II:621
Jones, Dennis II:659
Jones, Deodate P. I:61
Jones, Eaton I:110
Jones, Ebenezer III:390
Jones, Edmund III:407
Jones, Edward III:452, 622
Jones, Elias I:978
Jones, Elijah III:813
Jones, Elisha III:414, 823
Jones, Elizabeth II:25
Jones, Elkanah IV:250
Jones, Enoch I:174; II:77
Jones, Epaphras IV:69
Jones, Ephriam I:87
Jones, Ethel I:356
Jones, Ezekiel I:644; II:347, 454
Jones, Ezra II:211
Jones, Francis II:197; III:396
Jones, Freeman III:92
Jones, Gabriel III:218
Jones, George I:110; III:291, 563; IV:100, 268
Jones, Gideon I:455
Jones, Giles II:31
Jones, Gray III:752
Jones, Griffin II:323
Jones, Hannah II:621
Jones, Hardy III:380
Jones, Harris I:49
Jones, Harrison III:131, 665
Jones, Henry III:670, 787
Jones, Henry, 1st I:840
Jones, Henry, 2d I:840
Jones, Herman II:249
Jones, Horatio II:426
Jones, Incomes I:977
Jones, Isaac I:135, 276; II:232, 378
Jones, Israel I:944, 978
Jones, Jacob II:199; III:511
Jones, James I:62, 195, 597; II:12, 197, 586, 621, 625, 731; III:232, 273, 321, 329, 603, 613, 670, 740, 796, 810, 830
Jones, James, 1st III:369
Jones, James, 2d III:378
Jones, Jane III:670

425

Jones, Jason III:61
Jones, Jennet E. II:25
Jones, Jeremiah I:537; III:510
Jones, Jesse III:433, 687
Jones, Jethro I:455
Jones, Joel II:347; III:850
Jones, John I:118, 207, 250,
363; II:241, 355, 385, 393,
525, 627; III:73, 89, 265,
281, 551, 603, 605, 670,
783, 804; IV:239
Jones, John, 1st III:687
Jones, John, 2d III:692
Jones, John, 3d III:674
Jones, Jonathan I:759, 988;
III:172
Jones, Jones II:104
Jones, Joseph I:110; II:197,
454, 525, 627; III:315, 545,
582; IV:10
Jones, Joseph, Jur. IV:213
Jones, Joshua I:250; III:23,
269, 282, 670, 789
Jones, Josiah I:351; II:15
Jones, Josiah, 2d I:324
Jones, Lazarus I:225
Jones, Lemuel I:162
Jones, Leroy III:189
Jones, Lewellen III:686
Jones, Lewis I:537
Jones, Lydia B. II:25
Jones, Martin III:580
Jones, Mary II:199, 621
Jones, Mary C. II:25
Jones, Matthew IV:96
Jones, Meriwether I:xv
Jones, Michael II:41
Jones, Morris I:127
Jones, Moses II:199; IV:12
Jones, Moses E. II:25
Jones, Musgrove III:401
Jones, Nathaniel III:504
Jones, Neals II:9
Jones, Nehemiah II:454
Jones, Nicholas III:269, 425
Jones, Noah I:925
Jones, Oliver I:143, 910
Jones, Peregrine II:667
Jones, Peter II:199; III:394
Jones, Peter S. II:25
Jones, Philip II:646; III:12, 55,
300
Jones, Phineas I:644; II:211
Jones, Prudence III:670
Jones, Rebecca II:627
Jones, Reuben II:731
Jones, Richard I:174; II:23;
III:257, 557, 582, 615, 628
Jones, Richard, 2d III:706
Jones, Richard, 1st III:689
Jones, Richard L. IV:185
Jones, Robert III:235
Jones, Sally II:197
Jones, Sally C. II:25

Jones, Samuel I:195, 519,
644; II:23, 25, 136, 347,
379, 385, 465, 495, 621;
III:268, 504; IV:171
Jones, Samuel, 2d II:167
Jones, Samuel, 3d II:298
Jones, Samuel J. II:625
Jones, Samuel P. I:562
Jones, Samuel Z. III:798
Jones, Sarah II:621
Jones, Seth II:148, 197, 269,
435
Jones, Silas I:963; II:495;
IV:289
Jones, Silvester I:267
Jones, Simeon I:135, 174
Jones, Simpson I:537
Jones, Solomon I:181, 339;
III:147; IV:180
Jones, Squire II:241
Jones, Stephen I:971; II:37,
197, 232; III:287, 752
Jones, Susan C. II:25
Jones, Tabathy II:199
Jones, Taverner III:804
Jones, Thomas I:237, 339,
709; II:193, 307; III:43, 143,
192, 260, 337, 452, 621,
781, 814, 823; IV:50, 239,
261
Jones, Thomas, 1st II:595
Jones, Thomas, 2d I:229;
II:342, 632; III:447
Jones, Thomas C. III:79
Jones, Tim III:846
Jones, Timothy I:464
Jones, Vincent III:93
Jones, William I:62, 363, 709,
868, 899; II:44, 430, 589,
697; III:11, 130, 144, 197,
212, 292, 417, 618, 665,
823; IV:83
Jones, William, 2d II:264;
IV:119
Jones, William C. IV:289
Jones, Zebulon I:926
Jones, Zenas I:841
Jones, Zimri II:378
Jonnson, Philip II:95
Jon_s, Thomas I:905
Jopling, Thomas III:722
Jordan, Abner I:207
Jordan, Abraham I:181
Jordan, Benjamin I:747
Jordan, Charity A. III:669
Jordan, David I:216-17, 562
Jordan, Dempsey III:181
Jordan, Eleazer I:693
Jordan, Elijah I:195
Jordan, Freeman III:757
Jordan, George III:255
Jordan, Hezekiah I:181;
III:598
Jordan, Humphrey I:181
Jordan, James IV:16
Jordan, Jesse III:41

Jordan, John I:62, 250;
III:847-48
Jordan, Josiah I:988
Jordan, L. III:852
Jordan, Leroy III:847
Jordan, Leroy (2) III:847
Jordan, Martin I:611
Jordan, Michael II:678
Jordan, Peter III:235
Jordan, Pleasant III:669
Jordan, Pleasants III:463
Jordan, Richard III:442
Jordan, Robert II:726; III:41
Jordan, Samuel I:250
Jordan, Simon III:41
Jordan, Thomas I:181; II:323;
III:645
Jordan, William III:669, 746,
830
Jorden, John II:84
Jordon, Amanda I:858
Jordon, Betsy I:858
Jordon, David I:858
Jordon, Dearborn I:858
Jordon, Ebenezer I:826
Jordon, Edmund I:815
Jordon, Fountain III:139
Jordon, James II:697
Jordon, Jeremiah I:858
Jordon, Jesse I:537
Jordon, John III:54, 538, 675
Jordon, Mahala III:134
Jordon, Miles III:134
Jordon, Platt I:858
Jordon, Robert III:41
Jordon, Sylvia I:858
Jordon, William I:79; III:669,
814
Joseph, Jared III:593
Joseph Wadsworth I:654
Josiah, James II:678
Joslin, David I:693; II:522
Joslin, Hezekiah II:465
Joslin, John I:742, 834
Joslin, Nathaniel I:742
Joslin, Peter I:742
Joslin, Reuben II:241
Josselyn, Francis I:562
Josselyn, Jabez II:292
Josselyn, John I:417
Josselyn, Nathaniel I:250
Jotham, Calvin I:195
Jotham, Luther I:195
Jourdon, John III:189
Jourdon, William I:840
Jowett, Thomas II:454
Joy, Abiather II:415
Joy, Amos I:978
Joy, Asa II:153
Joy, Benjamin I:882
Joy, Bennett II:153
Joy, Ebenezer IV:250
Joy, Edward III:23
Joy, Gershom II:691
Joy, Irad II:565
Joy, Jedediah I:576
Joy, Jesse I:482

Kehr, David IV:284
Keiphart, George IV:42
Keirns, Thomas II:136
Keison, John I:957
Keith, Alexander IV:47
Keith, Asa I:644
Keith, Barak II:465
Keith, Caleb I:752
Keith, Daniel III:734
Keith, Grindell I:911
Keith, Ichabod I:742
Keith, Isaac I:562
Keith, James I:231; II:415
Keith, John III:149
Keith, Peter II:218
Keith, Ruel I:944
Keith, Simeon I:989
Keith, Unite I:944
Kelan, James III:146
Kelch, John II:430
Kelch, Philip II:279
Keler, Henry I:161
Kelham, William I:398
Kelkner, Henry III:721
Kell, Allen II:595
Kell, Christopher II:264
Kell, James III:179
Kell, Robert II:612; III:179
Kellam, Honsten III:745
Kellar, John IV:237
Kellee, Jeremiah M. I:127
Keller, Conrad III:23
Keller, Devault IV:83
Keller, Edward II:612
Keller, Frederick II:671
Keller, George II:743; III:809
Keller, Jacob II:728
Keller, John II:259
Keller, Simon II:740
Keller, William II:571
Kelley, Alexander I:605
Kelley, Charles II:241, 584
Kelley, David I:xxv, 330, 778
Kelley, Edward I:866; II:136
Kelley, Elias IV:63
Kelley, Hugh III:37
Kelley, James I:672
Kelley, Jared II:49
Kelley, John I:875; IV:207
Kelley, Jonathan I:731
Kelley, Joseph I:195
Kelley, Joshua I:217
Kelley, Lloyd III:167
Kelley, Micajah I:778
Kelley, Moses IV:63
Kelley, Nathaniel I:723
Kelley, Patrick III:23
Kelley, Samuel I:726
Kelley, Timothy I:752
Kelley, William I:195; II:663;
    III:139; IV:92
Kelley, William, 1st II:136
Kellobrue, Lawrence IV:16
Kellock, David I:207
Kellock, Ebenezer I:251
Kellock, Matthew I:207
Kellog, Daniel I:101

Kellog, Helmont I:110
Kellog, Medad I:143
Kellogg, Aaron I:474
Kellogg, Benjamin II:430
Kellogg, Ebenezer I:351
Kellogg, Eldad II:236
Kellogg, Elijah I:251; II:401,
    405
Kellogg, Eliphalet II:757
Kellogg, Elisha II:114
Kellogg, Ellazer II:148
Kellogg, Enoch I:234
Kellogg, Enos I:971
Kellogg, Ezekiel I:752
Kellogg, Ezra I:351
Kellogg, Horace II:292
Kellogg, Jason II:347
Kellogg, John I:351
Kellogg, Joseph I:459; II:314
Kellogg, Josiah I:911; IV:179
Kellogg, Levi II:455
Kellogg, Loomis II:455
Kellogg, Martin I:971; II:415
Kellogg, Nathaniel I:483;
    II:379
Kellogg, Noah II:279
Kellogg, Phineas I:951; II:279
Kellogg, Pliney IV:200
Kellogg, Preserved I:963
Kellogg, Samuel II:641
Kellogg, Seth II:332
Kellogg, Silas I:351
Kellogg, Solomon I:868
Kellogg, Stephen I:351; II:183,
    495
Kellogg, Thomas II:415
Kellogg, Titus I:872
Kellogg, William I:840; II:236
Kell_r, Christian II:109
Kelly, Abraham II:724; III:485;
    IV:164
Kelly, Allen III:525
Kelly, Anthony I:772
Kelly, Barney II:136
Kelly, Beal III:327
Kelly, Charles I:685; III:548
Kelly, David I:826; II:420
Kelly, Dennis III:633
Kelly, Edmund II:229
Kelly, Edward I:489; II:612
Kelly, Eliza II:627
Kelly, George II:627
Kelly, Isaac I:169
Kelly, James I:693; III:273,
    592; IV:120, 237
Kelly, Jeremiah II:490
Kelly, Johanna I:685
Kelly, John II:137, 627; III:41,
    205, 242, 324
Kelly, Joseph I:685; IV:164
Kelly, Joshua II:229
Kelly, Lavinia B. I:684
Kelly, Levi I:331
Kelly, Louisa III:41
Kelly, Mary I:685
Kelly, Matthew II:23
Kelly, Maurice I:502

Kelly, Michael III:41
Kelly, Nathaniel IV:280
Kelly, Oliver IV:190
Kelly, Peter I:612; III:95
Kelly, Richard III:572
Kelly, Robert II:232
Kelly, Samuel III:191, 310
Kelly, Stephen I:300; II:390
Kelly, Thomas II:612; III:208
Kelly, Thomas, 2d III:228
Kelly, William I:684; II:49,
    709; III:306, 600; IV:254
Kelly, William, 2d I:882
Kelly, William D. II:627
Kelsey, Aaron I:23
Kelsey, Benjamin I:56
Kelsey, Ezra I:118
Kelsey, Giles I:905
Kelsey, Heath II:379
Kelsey, Joel I:785
Kelsey, John I:978; II:355
Kelsey, Reuben II:415
Kelsey, Samuel II:405
Kelsey, Stephen I:118
Kelsey, Thomas IV:272
Kelsey, Zachariah I:731
Kelsimere, Francis IV:190
Kelso, Alexander IV:83
Kelso, David II:445
Kelso, James III:831
Kelso, Thomas III:323
Kelton, Ammi I:531
Kelton, Amos I:373
Kelton, Arden I:864
Kelton, Benjamin I:444
Kelton, Charles I:593
Kelton, Delinda I:864
Kelton, Ebenezer I:864
Kelton, Edward I:537, 593
Kelton, Henry I:593
Kelton, James I:593
Kelton, John I:474
Kelton, Sarah I:593
Kelty, John II:259
Kemball, Jesse I:752
Kemp, Asa I:709
Kemp, Benjamin I:742
Kemp, Dudley I:502
Kemp, Ebenezer I:182
Kemp, Jonas I:502, 519
Kemp, Joseph I:502
Kemp, Reuben I:79; IV:64
Kemp, Simon I:709
Kemp, Thomas I:701
Kemper, Charles III:771
Kemper, Daniel II:73
Kemper, John II:385
Kemplin, William III:696
Kempton, Peter II:15
Kempton, Samuel I:432
Kendall, Aaron III:261, 838
Kendall, Asa I:519
Kendall, Chever I:300
Kendall, Clayton II:32
Kendall, Eleazer I:978
Kendall, Francis III:830
Kendall, Isaac I:432, 989

428

430

432

Lambert, Charles III:753
Lambert, Christopher III:24
Lambert, Chrst'phr, 2d III:47
Lambert, Cornelius II:547
Lambert, David I:110
Lambert, George III:753
Lambert, Jacob II:703
Lambert, James II:64
Lambert, John III:157, 328, 387
Lambert, Matthias III:302
Lambert, Samuel II:88
Lambert, William II:547
Lamberton, James I:483
Lamberton, Obed I:737
Lambertson, Simon II:342
Lambeth, Moses III:415
Lambrecht, Daniel IV:245
Lamkin, John III:690
Lammas, Dyre I:225
Lammay, James IV:4
Lamme, Nathan IV:296
Lamoigne, Joseph III:5
Lamon, Moses II:420
Lamont, John I:208; IV:167
Lamper, Benjamin I:731
Lamphaer, Abel II:751
Lampher, Amos II:541
Lamphier, Benjamin II:379
Lamphier, James I:69
Lamphier, Wheeler II:137
Lamphire, Fitch II:246
Lamphun, Samuel II:705
Lampman, Abraham II:148
Lampman, Jacob II:470
Lampman, Peter II:183
Lamprey, Daniel I:772
Lampson, Joseph I:760
Lampson, Thomas II:82
Lampson, William I:208
Lamson, Benjamin II:465
Lamson, Daniel I:111
Lamson, David I:939
Lamson, Ebenezer IV:228
Lamson, Thomas II:49
Lamungon, Thomas II:430
Lancaster, Catherine I:176
Lancaster, Ezekiel I:268
Lancaster, Henry III:417
Lancaster, John I:276
Lancaster, Joseph I:208
Lancaster, Mary I:176
Lancaster, R. III:338
Lancaster, Samuel I:418
Lancaster, Thomas I:176, 890
Lancaster, William I:176; IV:92
Lancer, Abraham II:647
Lancert, Abraham II:647
Lancistus, Jacob III:13
Lanckton, Matthias R. II:430
Lancy, Samuel I:297
Land, John III:233
Land, Lewis III:503
Land, Moses IV:8
Land, Reuben III:419
Landengham, G. Van III:699

Lander, Charles I:593; III:260
Lander, James I:593
Lander, Peter II:740
Landerkin, Daniel I:208
Landers, Aquilla II:477
Landers, Asael I:351
Landers, Ebenezer II:379
Landers, John III:159
Landers, Joseph II:379
Landman, Newman III:690
Landon, Alban I:27
Landon, Anna I:27
Landon, Benjamin II:55
Landon, Daniel I:27
Landon, Ebenezer IV:244
Landon, Edward IV:263
Landon, Erastus I:27
Landon, James I:88; IV:180
Landon, John, Jr. I:27
Landon, Laban II:641
Landon, Maria I:27
Landon, Nathaniel IV:109
Landon, Orlando I:27
Landon, Rufus I:111
Landres, Kimbrow IV:55
Landrum, James III:585
Landrum, Thomas III:177, 245, 321, 596
Lands, Ephraim III:452
Lane, Abiel II:328
Lane, Abraham II:77, 85
Lane, Alexander II:705
Lane, Asa I:333
Lane, Asaph I:743
Lane, Benjamin I:645
Lane, Caleb I:418, 577
Lane, Cornelius II:441
Lane, Dan I:111
Lane, Daniel III:409
Lane, David I:519
Lane, Derick II:562
Lane, Drury III:615
Lane, Ebenezer II:562
Lane, Ephraim I:612
Lane, Ezekiel IV:286
Lane, Francis I:217
Lane, Gilbert II:533
Lane, Hendrick IV:234
Lane, Henry II:64
Lane, Hezekiah II:507
Lane, Isaac I:312; II:307; III:600
Lane, Isham III:302
Lane, Jabez I:88, 163, 238
Lane, Jacob II:569; III:386
Lane, James I:772; III:583; IV:52
Lane, Job I:612
Lane, John II:613, 632, 701; III:395, 689; IV:280
Lane, Joseph II:411; III:611; IV:250
Lane, Joshua II:533
Lane, Larkin IV:84
Lane, Leavitt II:386
Lane, Levi II:153
Lane, Living I:166

Lane, Matthias II:364
Lane, Michael II:270
Lane, Nathaniel I:49
Lane, Prince I:731
Lane, Samuel I:251, 743; III:5
Lane, Tidence III:594
Lane, Turner III:630
Lane, William II:293, 485, 533, 537; III:689; IV:5
Lane, William, 2d II:342
Lanebaugh, Joseph IV:264
Laned, Abijah IV:227
Laney, John IV:232
Laney, Thomas I:710
Laney, William III:288
Lanfair, Leonard I:444
Lanfair, Roswell I:464
Lanfear, Ezra II:479
Lanford, Richard I:612
Lang, Francis IV:44
Lang, John I:300
Lang, Thomas I:807
Lang, William I:957
Langdale, James B. II:589
Langdon, Benjamin II:293
Langdon, Daniel IV:79
Langdon, John II:347, 423
Langdon, John W. IV:254
Langdon, Lewis II:328
Langdon, Martin II:455
Langdon, Paul II:242
Langdon, Philip IV:58
Langfit, Philip III:731
Langfitt, Francis III:743
Langford, Jonathan I:69
Langham, Elias IV:298
Langham, James III:151
Langley, Benjamin I:772, 995
Langley, Eli I:252
Langley, John I:533; III:180, 535, 605
Langley, Newell I:533
Langley, Shadrach III:417
Langley, Thomas I:533; III:535
Langley, William III:535
Langley, Winthrop I:752
Langly, David I:731
Langsdon, Charles III:210
Langstaff, James II:73
Langstaff, John II:73
Lanham, John III:665
Lanier, Alexander C. IV:152
Laning, Ralph II:69
Lankford, Elijah III:57
Lankford, William III:765
Lanman, Philip II:632
Lanman, Thomas I:622
Lanning, John III:404
Lannum, Joseph III:565
Lanpher, Paul II:424
Lanphese, Shubael I:918
Lanphier, Arnold I:859
Lanphier, Fortuna I:859
Lanphier, John I:859
Lanphier, Moses I:859
Lans, Jacob II:729
Lansdale, Isaac III:96

435

Lenox, James III:47
Lent, Elias II:351
Lent, Hermanus II:547
Lent, Isaac II:323, 547
Lent, Jacob II:351, 406, 498
Lent, James W. II:137
Lent, John II:718
Lent, Philip II:333
Lent, William III:312
Lents, Benjamin III:567
Lentz, Henry III:86
Leonard, Amos II:280
Leonard, Archippus I:563
Leonard, Asa II:525
Leonard, Benijah II:344
Leonard, Caleb I:268
Leonard, Cuff I:363
Leonard, David II:446, 529
Leonard, Elias II:60
Leonard, Elijah I:339
Leonard, Elisha I:939
Leonard, Enoch I:569, 918
Leonard, Ephraim I:339
Leonard, Ezekiel II:705
Leonard, Frederick III:559
Leonard, George I:868; II:728
Leonard, Henry III:661
Leonard, Isaac II:570
Leonard, Jacob I:562, 658; III:415
Leonard, James II:613; III:58; IV:232
Leonard, John II:37; III:546
Leonard, Josiah I:577
Leonard, Justin I:468
Leonard, Moses I:939
Leonard, Nathan B. I:826
Leonard, Nathaniel I:374
Leonard, Nehemiah I:374
Leonard, Noah II:280
Leonard, Patrick II:137; III:224
Leonard, Robert II:314; III:661
Leonard, Rowland I:576
Leonard, Samuel I:577; II:20
Leonard, Seth I:363
Leonard, Silas I:110; II:525
Leonard, Simeon I:900
Leonard, Solomon I:374; II:545
Leonard, Stephen II:285
Leonard, Thomas II:700
Leonard, William III:235, 417
Leonard, Ziba I:444
Leonardson, John T. II:440
Lepper, Jacob II:440
Lepper, John II:264
Lepper, Wynant II:441
Leppinwell, Reuben I:978
Leray, John I:136
Le Roye, Simon II:368
Lesh, Philip II:679
Lesley, Peter III:575
Lesley, Samuel II:612
Lesley, William III:177
Leslie, Alexander I:890; III:621
Leslie, William II:726

Lesly, Thomas III:600
Lesperance, Joseph I:xxv
Lesseur, Joseph II:368
Lessig, David II:707
Lessley, Betsy I:387
Lessley, Edward I:387
Lessley, John III:681
Lessley, Lucy Ann I:387
Lessley, Mary Stone I:387
Lessley, Samuel I:387
Lessley, Swain I:387
Lesson, George I:622
Lester, Alexander III:631
Lester, Amos I:23
Lester, Asa I:136
Lester, Bennett II:199
Lester, Caigill III:672
Lester, Ebenezer I:56
Lester, Francis I:432
Lester, Guy II:224
Lester, Jeremiah II:393
Lester, John II:292
Lester, Julian H. II:199
Lester, Nathan I:339
Lester, Phebe S. II:199
Lester, Thomas III:220
Lester, William III:672
Lestor, Elihu I:333
Lesuer, John II:215
Lesuer, William II:44
Lesueur, Martel III:774
Lesure, Levi I:622
Lesure, Samuel I:432
Leswitt, Francis II:697
Letcher, R. P. III:335, 337
Letchworth, Benjamin IV:123
Leterell, Archibald IV:164
Leterell, John IV:164
Leterell, Levi IV:164
Leterell, Mahala IV:164
Letford, Robert II:612
Letson, John II:73
Letson, William II:399
Lett, James III:490
Letterell, John IV:164
Letterell, Nancy IV:164
Lettice, James II:441
Letts, Francis II:73
Letts, William IV:103
Leture, Harmon III:621
Levalley, William I:815
Levally, Cook II:486
Levally, Peleg II:514
Levengood, Peter II:659
Lever, William IV:141
Leverick, Gabriel II:311
Levering, John III:39
Levet, John I:590
Levett, Abigail I:175
Levett, Elijah I:175
Levett, Jonathan I:175
Levett, Joseph I:175
Levett, Samuel I:175
Levett, Sarah I:175
Levi, Henry I:27
Levi, Isaac IV:92
Levi, Judah III:665

Levi, Rice III:565
Levi, Theodore I:27
Levick, Robert II:34
Levinbery, Frederick II:668
Levingood, Peter II:724
Levins, Henry IV:16
Levinus, Thomas II:319
Levisey, George III:587
Leviston, David I:xxv
Levy, Abraham II:613
Levy, Judah III:197
Lewallen, Richard III:565
Leward, John IV:213
Lewes, Samuel I:459
Lewes, William I:622
Lewin, Thomas I:374
Lewis, Aaron I:363; III:80
Lewis, Aaron, Sen. III:402
Lewis, Abel I:41, 88, 963
Lewis, Abigail I:175
Lewis, Abijah I:34, 217
Lewis, Abner I:978
Lewis, Abraham II:495
Lewis, Alexander I:175
Lewis, Ambrose III:13
Lewis, Amos III:373
Lewis, Andrew I:88, 119; III:653, 811
Lewis, Anthony III:5
Lewis, Archelaus I:252
Lewis, Augustus I:119
Lewis, Augustus J. I:834
Lewis, Avery II:212
Lewis, Bazzel III:336
Lewis, Benjamin II:218, 705
Lewis, Chaney I:41
Lewis, Daniel I:175; II:46, 307; III:425
Lewis, Darius I:351
Lewis, Doughty II:627
Lewis, Dyer II:280
Lewis, Ebenezer II:280
Lewis, Eleazer I:331
Lewis, Eli I:926
Lewis, Elijah I:101; II:718
Lewis, Elisha I:351, 597; III:120
Lewis, Elizabeth II:627
Lewis, Enoch I:834
Lewis, Ezekiel II:699
Lewis, Fabius III:693
Lewis, Frederick II:137
Lewis, George I:331; III:673
Lewis, Goodall II:191
Lewis, Hannah I:175
Lewis, Henry II:126, 326; IV:263
Lewis, Herbert III:407
Lewis, Isaac I:88, 455; II:242, 573; IV:254
Lewis, Jabez I:41; II:293, 557
Lewis, Jacob II:627, 642; III:842
Lewis, James II:221, 323; III:133, 250, 437, 580
Lewis, James M. II:191
Lewis, Jesse III:746

Livingston, Daniel II:709
Livingston, David II:748; IV:190
Livingston, Gilbert J. II:455
Livingston, Henry III:496
Livingston, Isaac I:49
Livingston, James II:554, 558
Livingston, Joseph II:137
Livingston, Robert II:203, 557
Livingston, Samuel III:89
Livingston, William I:760
Lloyd, David II:190; IV:272
Lloyd, Edward III:133
Lloyd, Electa II:190
Lloyd, Geo. E., Sen. III:694
Lloyd, James I:110
Lloyd, John I:451, 852; II:673
Lloyd, Joseph II:560; III:210
Lloyd, Martin I:601
Lloyd, Perry III:5
Lloyd, Phoebe II:560
Lloyd, Releva II:190
Lloyd, Sally II:190
Lloyd, Samuel IV:67
Lloyd, Silas II:190
Lloyd, Thomas II:679
Lloyd, Thompson C. III:188
Lloyd, William II:78; III:229; IV:238
L_nton, Joseph I:380
Loar, Henry IV:190, 297
Lobdell, Isaac II:355
Lobdell, Jacob II:547
Lobdell, Joseph II:420
Lobdell, Josiah I:88
Lochenour, George III:452
Lochenour, Jacob III:452
Lock, Ayres II:323
Lock, Benjamin I:519, 760
Lock, Charles III:633
Lock, Ebenezer I:680
Lock, Edward I:772
Lock, James IV:20
Lock, James, Sen. III:423
Lock, John II:57, 749; III:375
Lock, Joseph I:483
Lock, Richard I:723
Lock, Thomas I:502
Lock, William II:670; IV:262
Lockard, Philip III:680
Lockard, William III:677
Lockart, Aaron III:706
Lockarty, John II:183
Locke, Edward IV:104
Locke, Elijah I:766
Locke, Francis I:723
Locke, Frederick I:766
Locke, Jonas I:502
Locke, Joseph III:714
Locke, Nicholas III:46
Locke, Simon I:772
Locker, John A. II:195
Locker, Roderick II:195
Locker, Sally II:195
Lockerman, Jacob III:456
Lockert, John II:694
Locket, Edmund III:765

Lockett, Benjamin III:214
Lockett, James III:161
Lockett, Royall III:807
Lockhart, James III:689
Lockhart, John III:397
Lockhurt, John III:626
Lockman, John II:679
Lockman, Matthias II:673
Lockrey, Michael II:333
Lockridge, James III:605
Lockridge, John III:309
Lockridge, Robert III:23
Lockwood, Charles I:88
Lockwood, Daniel IV:230
Lockwood, Daniel, 2d I:34
Lockwood, David I:49; II:411
Lockwood, Drake I:88
Lockwood, Ebenezer II:440
Lockwood, Enos I:88
Lockwood, Gilbert II:533
Lockwood, Isaac I:88; II:299
Lockwood, Israel II:446
Lockwood, James I:88
Lockwood, John II:37
Lockwood, Joseph II:406
Lockwood, Messenger I:88
Lockwood, Moses II:177
Lockwood, Nathan II:107, 137, 351
Lockwood, Samuel III:260
Lockwood, Timothy I:74
Lockwood, William I:41, 155; II:522
Loder, Daniel IV:66
Loder, Jacob I:101
Loder, Zenos II:34
Lofton, Thomas III:92
Lofty, William III:574
Logan, Alexander II:697; III:749
Logan, Andrew III:496
Logan, David II:675
Logan, Drury III:450
Logan, James III:291, 293
Logan, John I:359; II:632; III:291
Logan, Patrick IV:183
Logan, Philip III:135
Logan, Samuel II:299, 755
Logan, Timothy III:281
Logan, William III:313
Logan, William, Sen. IV:71
Logsden, Edward III:61
Logsden, James V. III:289
Logue, Eliza II:621
Logue, George II:621
Logue, Jane II:621
Logue, Joseph II:621
Lohner, John III:507
Lohnes, Adam II:495
Lohr, Beltzer III:54
Lohr, Peter III:750
Lomack, William III:371
Lomax, John III:49
Lomax, William III:387
Lombard, Butler I:225
Lombard, Jedediah I:160

Lombard, John I:251, 287
Lombard, Jonathan I:455
Lombard, Justin I:464
Lombard, Nathaniel I:297
Lombard, Solomon II:545
Lombard, Stephen II:368
Lombard, Thomas I:276, 287
Lonas, George III:776
London, Archibald II:715
London, George III:278
Long, Alexander II:700
Long, Anderson IV:122
Long, Andrew II:707
Long, Benjamin II:657; III:408, 762
Long, Daniel III:88
Long, David II:405, 630; III:605
Long, Elial II:724
Long, Gasper III:439
Long, George I:772; II:630, 754; III:588
Long, Gideon II:721
Long, Henry III:31, 584, 641
Long, Jacob II:630; III:801
Long, Jacob, Sr. II:728
Long, James I:612
Long, John III:219, 373, 660; IV:15, 41
Long, John P. III:727
Long, Jonathan III:588
Long, Joseph I:772; II:753
Long, Levi I:963
Long, Matthew II:697
Long, Moses I:766
Long, Nathaniel I:399
Long, Nicholas III:266, 596
Long, Paul I:723
Long, Reuben III:519
Long, Richard III:567
Long, Robert II:183, 541; III:506
Long, Stephen I:398, 963
Long, William I:444; II:717; III:337; IV:121
Longby, James I:644
Longby, Nathaniel I:645
Longedyck, Cornelius II:533
Longee, John I:752
Longest, Richard III:712
Longfellow, Samuel I:229
Longfellow, William I:408, 701
Longley, Asa I:296
Longley, Edmund I:444
Longley, Ezekiel I:963
Longley, Jonathan I:217
Longley, Joseph I:432
Longley, Zachariah I:221
Longly, William III:600
Longsthreth, John II:701
Longsthreth, Martin II:701
Longsthreth, Philip II:701
Longstreet, Aaron II:137
Longworthy, Southcot I:795
Longworthy, William I:802
Longyear, William II:533

441

Loofborrow, David II:721
Loofborrow, Isaac II:270
Look, Cheeney II:455
Look, Elijah II:374
Look, John I:563
Look, Jonathan I:380
Lookebee, David III:415
Looker, Eleazer II:64
Looker, John I:926
Looker, Othniel IV:254
Lookingbill, Daniel III:72
Loomis, A. II:556
Loomis, Andrew I:351
Loomis, Asa IV:280
Loomis, Benaiah II:379
Loomis, Benjamin I:41
Loomis, Daniel I:143
Loomis, Elijah II:465
Loomis, Epaphras II:479
Loomis, Ezra I:926; II:465, 550
Loomis, George II:705
Loomis, Hezekiah I:464
Loomis, Israel I:143; II:215
Loomis, Jacob I:79, 464; II:203
Loomis, Jerome II:470
Loomis, Jesse I:930
Loomis, John I:136; II:705
Loomis, Joseph I:788
Loomis, Lebbeus II:562
Loomis, Lebbius II:270
Loomis, Oliver I:964; II:411
Loomis, Roger I:195
Loomis, Samuel I:15; II:238, 455
Loomis, Simon I:136; II:249, 529
Loomis, Thomas II:486
Looney, John III:466, 494
Loper, Abraham II:649
Lopez, Isaac II:270
Lorah, Jacob II:703
Lorance, Michael III:615
Lorance, William III:315
Lord, Aaron I:418
Lord, Abner I:69
Lord, Amos I:23
Lord, Andrew III:47
Lord, Asa I:444; II:430
Lord, Benjamin I:217
Lord, Daniel I:188, 717
Lord, Daniel, 2d I:239
Lord, Daniel, 3d I:239
Lord, Daniel, Jr. I:156; II:559
Lord, David I:399
Lord, Dolly I:177
Lord, Dominicus I:311
Lord, Ebenezer I:160
Lord, Elias I:195
Lord, Elijah I:69
Lord, Eliphalet I:731; II:246
Lord, Elisha I:239
Lord, Frederick I:101
Lord, George I:23
Lord, Henry III:51
Lord, Ichabod I:312; IV:280

Lord, Jacob I:177
Lord, James I:208, 267
Lord, Jeremiah I:56
Lord, John I:119
Lord, John J. II:137
Lord, Jonathan II:344
Lord, Joseph I:101, 239; II:379
Lord, Nathan I:311
Lord, Richard I:311
Lord, Robert I:418
Lord, Samuel I:56, 312
Lord, Theophilus I:69
Lord, Thomas I:778
Lord, Timoth II:203
Lord, William I:56, 963; II:479
Lord, Wintworth I:238
Lore, Joseph III:64
Lore, Michael III:833
Loree, Job II:82
Lorentz, Joseph II:675
Loring, Benjamin II:270
Loring, Christopher III:722
Loring, Daniel I:537
Loring, David I:331
Loring, Jacob I:576
Loring, Jonathan I:760
Loring, Joseph I:503
Loring, Richard I:398
Loring, Samuel II:522
Loring, Simeon I:576
Loring, Solomon I:136
Lorrain, John II:636
Lorton, Robert IV:9
Lose, George II:759
Losee, Abraham I:474
Losee, John II:420
Losey, Abraham II:340
Losey, William IV:264
Lot, Jeremiah II:55
Lothrop, Barnabas I:576
Lothrop, Daniel I:268
Lothrop, Jacob I:287
Lothrop, John I:374
Lott, John II:441; IV:77
Lott, Nicholas II:572, 703
Lott, Philip Jacob II:663
Lotz, Henry II:639
Loucks, George II:441
Loucks, Henry II:255
Loucks, Peter H. II:441
Loucks, William IV:248
Loud, David I:547
Loud, Eliphalet I:547
Loud, Silvanus I:547
Loud, William I:547
Loudeback, John H. II:270
Loudon, John II:393
Lougee, John I:677
Loughborough, W. IV:297
Loughgaski, Matthias III:23
Loughton, David II:506
Louk, David II:114
Loundsbury, David I:455
Lounsbery, Nathan M. I:900
Lounsbery, Stephen II:547

Lounsbury, Epinetus II:522
Lounsbury, Jarius I:127
Lounsbury, Linus I:127
Lounsbury, Walker II:52
Louts, Jacob IV:248
Love, Charles III:242, 653; IV:151
Love, David III:337, 671
Love, Edmund III:610
Love, Elias III:836
Love, Henry II:612; III:836
Love, Hezekiah III:611
Love, Jane III:671
Love, John III:458
Love, Mark III:206
Love, Mary Ann III:671
Love, Mordecai IV:176
Love, Robert II:430; III:424, 805
Love, Samuel III:505
Love, Thomas III:152; IV:270
Love, Thomas C. II:109
Love, William II:259
Loveborough, William II:137
Lovejoy, Abner II:242
Lovejoy, Andrew II:385
Lovejoy, Asa II:445
Lovejoy, Daniel I:989
Lovejoy, Henry I:760
Lovejoy, Ira I:684
Lovejoy, Isaac I:398
Lovejoy, Jesse I:503
Lovejoy, Joshua I:677
Lovejoy, Nathan II:307
Lovejoy, Obadiah III:303
Lovejoy, Samuel I:710
Lovejoy, Susanna I:684
Lovejoy, William I:684
Lovelace, David II:668
Lovelace, Elias III:301
Lovelace, Philip III:770
Lovelace, Vachel III:283
Loveland, Abner IV:268
Loveland, Amos IV:289
Loveland, Charles I:156
Loveland, Chester C. II:199
Loveland, Frederick IV:186
Loveland, George I:432
Loveland, Isaac IV:212
Loveland, James I:225
Loveland, John I:119
Loveland, Maria II:199
Loveland, Mary I:156
Loveland, Nathan II:275
Loveland, S. C. I:1000
Loveland, Samuel W. I:663
Loveland, Truman I:62
Loveless, George IV:289
Loveless, Joshua II:323
Lovell, Caleb I:577
Lovell, David I:374
Lovell, James I:658
Lovell, Joshua I:483
Lovell, Josiah I:182
Loven, James III:588
Loverin, Samuel I:710
Loverin, Simeon I:989

Lovering, Benjamin I:772
Lovering, Ebenezer I:772
Lovering, Isaac I:622
Lovering, John I:772
Lovering, Lawson IV:115
Lovering, Nathaniel I:267
Lovering, Richard I:399
Lovering, Samuel I:911
Lovering, Theophilus I:772
Lovering, Thomas I:772
Lovern, Christopher III:687
Lovett, Ebenezer I:398
Lovett, John I:56, 343; II:95, 137
Lovett, Joseph III:376
Lovett, Moses I:622
Lovett, Samuel II:649
Lovewell, Joseph B. I:854
Lovewell, Robert I:882
Loving, Richard III:791
Lovis, John I:408, 718
Low, Aaron I:418
Low, Abraham I:644
Low, Alexander II:78
Low, Asa I:701
Low, Bazaleel I:225
Low, Cornelius P. II:522
Low, Henry III:742
Low, Hooker II:470
Low, Jacob I:701
Low, Jacob G. II:285, 465
Low, John I:160, 239; III:490
Low, John, 2d I:383
Low, John, 1st I:597
Low, John J. II:533
Low, Phineas I:238
Low, Robert I:268
Low, Simon I:760
Low, Thomas I:911
Low, Wilson II:236
Lowber, Nicholas IV:77
Lowden, William II:445
Lowe, Abraham D. II:533
Lowe, Basil III:481, 518
Lowe, Cornelius D. II:85
Lowe, Dennis III:481
Lowe, Jonathan I:267
Lowe, Thomas I:851; III:449
Lowe, William III:324
Lowell, Benjamin I:188, 320
Lowell, Ezra I:989
Lowell, Isaac II:448
Lowell, John I:276; II:249
Lowell, Paul I:217
Lowell, Peter I:785
Lowell, Thomas I:221
Lowell, Timothy II:242
Lowell, William I:680, 995
Lowman, Emery III:23
Lown, Peter IV:109
Lownsberry, Henry II:475
Lownsberry, Samuel II:707
Lowrey, Levi III:169
Lowrie, Jas. III:16
Lowrie, Walter I:ix, x, xi
Lowring, Nathaniel I:519
Lowry, Daniel III:113

Lowry, Giles III:766
Lowry, Jacob II:748
Lowry, John III:37, 580, 753
Lowry, John, 2d III:37
Lowry, Michael II:748
Lowry, Robert J. III:118
Lowry, Thomas III:269
Lowry, Thornton III:779
Lowry, William II:700
Lowther, Joel IV:169
Loyd, James III:703
Loyd, John III:843
Loyd, Nicholas III:567
Loyd, William III:703
Loyer, Christopher II:224
Lozea, Henry II:299
Lozelton, Freeman II:554
Lozey, Jesse II:686
Lozier, Helebrant II:270, 559
Lozier, John II:58
Lozier, Martha II:627
Lozier, Nicholas II:627
Lozier, Peter II:270
Lucardo, Isaac III:772
Lucas, Abijah I:576
Lucas, Amaziah I:127
Lucas, Asahel I:872
Lucas, Ashel I:541
Lucas, Barnabas I:562
Lucas, Basil II:776
Lucas, Bela I:563
Lucas, Consider II:293
Lucas, Ephraim I:576
Lucas, Francis IV:40
Lucas, George II:637; III:111
Lucas, George W. I:664
Lucas, Ichabod I:56
Lucas, James I:359, 747
Lucas, John I:778; III:12, 43, 811; IV:234
Lucas, Parker III:778
Lucas, Robert IV:299
Lucas, Samuel I:576
Lucas, Thomas I:56; II:657
Lucas, William I:335, 576; II:172; III:297, 450, 700
Lucas, William B. II:183
Luce, Benjamin I:351
Luce, Crosby I:612
Luce, David I:339
Luce, Ebenezer I:732
Luce, Ephraim II:479
Luce, Ivory I:405
Luce, John II:344
Luce, Jonathan I:74, 157, 989
Luce, Luke I:101
Luce, Malachi I:380
Luce, Noah I:358
Luce, Parnel I:157
Luce, Rowland I:563
Luce, Samuel I:380
Luce, Seth I:276
Luce, Shubael I:195
Luce, Thomas I:380
Luce, Timothy I:74
Luce, Uriah II:485
Luce, Vinal I:xii

Luck, John III:425
Luckett, Samuel III:205
Luckey, Hugh III:578
Luckey, Robert III:260
Luckie, William III:445
Lucy, Nathaniel I:150
Ludden, Benjamin I:483
Ludden, Beza I:383
Ludden, Enos II:465
Ludden, Samuel I:547
Ludden, Sylvanus I:548
Luddington, Jude I:464
Luddington, Lemuel I:868
Luddon, Daniel I:995
Ludington, Jesse I:127
Ludington, Stephen II:249
Ludington, William II:751
Ludlum, Jacob II:64
Ludwick, John M. II:612
Luellin, John II:5
Lufberry, Abraham II:44
Lufkin, Isaac I:537
Lufkin, Levi I:890
Lufkin, Moses I:399, 612
Lufkin, Samuel I:785
Lufman, John II:224
Luke, John IV:293
Luke, Solomon II:355
Lukre, David II:759
Lull, Asa I:989
Lull, David I:760
Lum, Israel II:82
Lumb, James I:267
Lumbard, Aaron I:455
Lumbard, Caleb I:217
Lumbard, David I:483, 989
Lumbard, John I:989
Lumkin, Moore III:852
Lummis, Joseph IV:173
Lumpkin, Wilson III:712
Lumpkins, Philip III:155
Lumsden, Charles III:774
Lumsden, John III:405
Luna, Peter, Sr. III:598
Lund, Stephen I:752
Lung, Joseph II:336
Lunsford, Mason IV:74
Lunsford, Rodham III:298
Lunt, Amos I:252
Lunt, Daniel I:182, 238, 251
Lunt, John I:160
Lunt, Thomas I:398
Lunt, Timothy I:399
Lunt, William I:797, 834
Lupardus, William II:73
Lupkin, Benjamin I:287
Lurvey, Jacob I:188
Lurvey, Moses I:918
Luscombe, Francis I:374
Lush, Stephen, Jr. II:137
Lushbaugh, Henry II:669
Lusher, Thomas S. I:826
Lusk, John II:697; III:561
Lusk, Joseph III:600
Lusk, Michael II:544
Lusk, Patrick II:587
Lusk, Samuel IV:274

Luther, Aaron I:374
Luther, Amos I:363
Luther, Benjamin I:374, 826
Luther, Caleb I:785
Luther, Cromwell I:343; II:234
Luther, Elisha II:486
Luther, Ellis I:483
Luther, Frederick I:812
Luther, George III:447
Luther, James I:826, 879
Luther, John II:203; III:111
Luther, Levi I:136
Luther, Martin I:812; II:218
Luther, Michael III:447
Luther, Stephen I:374
Luther, Theophilus II:406
Luther, Thomas I:826
Luther, Thomas S. I:807
Luther, Wheaton I:374
Luther, William II:605
Luttrell, Michael IV:17
Lutz, Joseph III:23
Luyster, John P. II:77
Lyberger, Nicholas II:718
Lydstow, William I:267
Lyerly, Zachariah IV:14
Lyford, Fifield I:935
Lyman, Benjamin II:420
Lyman, Benjamin F. II:197
Lyman, Caty I. II:197
Lyman, Dan I:995
Lyman, Daniel I:837
Lyman, Eleazer I:963
Lyman, Elihu I:432
Lyman, Elisha I:136
Lyman, Ezekiel II:255
Lyman, Francis IV:227
Lyman, Giles I:449, 483
Lyman, H. B. I:837
Lyman, Hill II:197
Lyman, John I:939, 952; II:242
Lyman, Josiah I:474
Lyman, Philomela E. II:197
Lyman, Richard I:905
Lyman, Samuel I:464
Lyman, Susan II:197
Lyman, Thomas I:483
Lynch, Elijah III:449
Lynch, Henry IV:118
Lynch, Hugh III:47
Lynch, John I:899; III:37
Lynch, Joshua III:396
Lynch, Michael II:653
Lynch, Peter IV:190
Lynch, Thomas III:56
Lynch, William III:23
Lynd, John II:495
Lynde, Benjamin I:918
Lynde, Cornelius I:952
Lynde, Jonathan II:236
Lyndes, Ebenezer J. I:998
Lynds, Betsey G. I:26
Lynds, Cinderella I:26
Lynds, David I:26
Lynds, Dennis W. I:26
Lynds, Mariam I:26

Lynds, Nathaniel B. I:26
Lynds, Sally M. I:26
Lyne, David II:411
Lynes, Ignatius II:486
Lynes, John I:9
Lynn, David I:118; III:69
Lynn, Israel III:257
Lynn, James III:89
Lynn, John II:465; III:37
Lynn, Patrick IV:45
Lynn, William T. III:301
Lyon, Abraham IV:207
Lyon, Benjamin II:671, 724
Lyon, Chittenden III:338
Lyon, David II:64, 613
Lyon, Ebenezer I:688
Lyon, Edward I:918; III:476
Lyon, Eleazer I:432
Lyon, Enos II:29
Lyon, Jacob I:537; III:395
Lyon, James I:446; III:694; IV:254
Lyon, Jediah II:653
Lyon, Job I:88
Lyon, John II:687
Lyon, Jonas II:49
Lyon, Jonathan I:841
Lyon, Joseph II:64
Lyon, Matthew III:211
Lyon, Moses II:362, 368
Lyon, Nathan I:88
Lyon, Nathaniel IV:274
Lyon, Nehemiah Webb I:88
Lyon, Robert II:99, 675
Lyon, Samuel II:553
Lyon, Thomas I:537; II:385, 426, 579
Lyon, William II:177; III:297; IV:275
Lyons, Edward II:613
Lyons, Hosea II:307
Lyons, Joseph IV:229
Lyons, Michael II:174
Lyons, Samuel IV:241
Lyons, William II:44; III:168
Lyport, Jacob II:511
Lyster, Thomas II:584
Lyster, William III:672
Lytle, Robert IV:234
Lytle, William II:726; III:636
Lyttle, John I:267

Maben, Henry III:325
Mabin, John III:577
Mabry, David III:460
Mabry, John III:326
Mabry, Reps III:394
Maccoun, James III:215
Mace, Andrew I:268
Mace, Isaac III:799
Mace, John III:799
Machin, Thomas II:126
Mack, Andrew I:101
Mack, Archibald I:979
Mack, Benjamin I:890
Mack, Bezaleel I:693

Mack, D., Jun. I:657
Mack, David I:905
Mack, Gurdon II:470
Mack, Hezekiah I:119
Mack, Jeremiah II:259
Mack, Jesse II:533
Mack, John I:911; II:470
Mack, Joseph II:314
Mack, Ralph II:420
Mack, Richard IV:100
Mack, Stephen II:564
Mack, Zebulon II:470
Mackall, Benjamin II:636
Mackay, Thomas III:734
Mackel, Jacob P. II:533
Mackeon, John III:47
Mackerell, James III:665
Mackey, Alexander II:355
Mackey, Benjamin II:580
Mackey, James IV:123
Mackey, Thomas III:505
MacKey, William II:614
Mackey, William III:538
Mackie, Samuel III:162
Macklin, John II:614
Macknet, Charles II:744
Maclean, William III:463
Macomber, Abiather I:363
Macomber, Elijah I:375
Macomber, Ephraim I:819
Macomber, Job I:905
Macomber, John I:877
Macomber, Jonathan II:293
Macomber, Josiah I:363
Macomber, Lemuel I:432
Macomber, Samuel II:424
Macomber, Seth I:363
Macomber, Southworth I:182
Macomber, William II:420
Macomber, Zenas II:694
Macomer, Ebenezer II:557
Macrae, John III:853
Macumber, Abner I:175
Macumber, Conrad I:175
Macumber, Gideon I:175
Macumber, James I:175
Macumber, John IV:228
Macumber, Joseph I:175
Macumber, Pitts I:175
Macumber, Sophronia I:175
Madden, David I:520
Madden, John I:188
Madden, Michael I:597
Madden, William IV:74
Maddin, Joseph III:278
Madding, Chapness III:603
Maddock, Henry I:239
Maddocks, Samuel I:189
Maddox, Ebenezer IV:133
Maddox, Jacob III:594
Maddox, John III:696, 849
Maddox, Matthew III:743
Maddox, Sherwood III:315
Maddox, Wilson III:323
Madeira, Michael II:703
Madera, Casper II:703
Madera, Christian III:720

444

Mading, Daniel III:531
Madison, Ambrose III:325
Madison, John III:73
Madison, Peyton III:73
Madison, William III:762
Madon, Joseph II:647
Maer, Henry I:503
Maeyer, John III:559
Maffett, John III:288
Maffett, Zebulon II:285
Maffit, David II:679
Maffit, Eli II:333
Maffit, Robert II:614
Maffitt, William III:248
Magahan, Michael II:46
Magar, James I:911
Magarvy, Francis II:736
Magaw, William II:657
Magawren, Henry III:24
Magee, J. II:557
Magee, James III:594
Magee, John II:486, 561, 564
Magee, Peter IV:208
Magee, Samuel II:386
Magee, Thomas, 2d III:592
Mager, Michael II:138
Magert, Henry, Sen. III:621
Magher, Michael II:137
Magie, John II:475
Magill, James III:585
Magill, John III:279
Magill, Robert IV:78
Magill, William I:183
Magin, Charles IV:165
Maginnis, Daniel III:851
Magner, Henry III:476
Magner, Martin I:586
Magoon, Edward I:875
Magoon, Joseph I:995
Magoon, Josiah I:778; II:615
Magoon, Joshua I:577
Magrath, Henry I:7
Magregory, John I:785
Magruder, Nathaniel B. III:42
Magruder, Norman B. IV:92
Maguire, Hugh II:393
Maguire, Peter I:42
Magus, Pomp I:503
Mahaffey, Samuel II:759
Mahan, James III:330
Mahan, Samuel II:406
Mahana, John IV:204
Mahanas, Tapley III:429
Mahanna, John J. III:200
Mahemson, John III:159
Maher, John IV:115
Mahl, Frederick IV:79
Maholland, John III:634
Maholm, Samuel IV:256
Mahoney, Daniel II:653
Mahoney, James II:673; IV:58
Mahony, Edward III:55
Mahorney, Benjamin IV:86
Mahorney, Thomas III:731
Mahurin, Jonathan I:945
Maib, John, Sen. III:453

Maiden, Lawrence, Sen.
III:425
Mail, William III:704
Main, Amos I:313
Main, David I:137
Main, Ezekiel II:749
Main, Henry II:406; III:395
Main, Peres IV:244
Main, Philip II:700
Maine, Stephen II:386
Maine, William II:369
Maines, George III:209
Mainor, Josiah III:391
Mains, Samuel III:153
Mains, Williams II:722
Mairs, Elias III:626
Maize, William II:259
Major, Alexander III:293
Major, Humphrey III:804
Major, Samuel III:768
Majors, John III:329
Majors, Robert III:567
Majory, John II:334
Makepeace, Jason I:911
Makepeace, William I:548
Maker, Borden I:327
Maker, Joseph I:88
Makins, Samuel II:614
Malaby, John III:568
Malbeuf, Baptiste II:554
Malcolm, Henry II:679
Malcom, Richard M. III:6
Malcome, Hugh II:46
Males, John III:721
Maley, Ebenezer III:285
Malick, John II:514; III:785
Mallaby, Thomas II:42
Mallard, John I:918
Mallard, Lawson III:428
Mallbie, Benjamin IV:289
Mallery, David I:49
Mallery, John III:86
Mallet, Miles I:127
Mallet, Thomas I:710
Mallet, William I:196, 268
Mallett, John I:127
Mallin, William I:732
Mallison, Benjamin I:70
M'Allister, John III:248
Mallory, Asa I:128
Mallory, Benaijah I:128
Mallory, Benajah II:448
Mallory, Dan I:111
Mallory, Gideon I:89
Mallory, Gill II:465
Mallory, Jacob I:127
Mallory, James II:364
Mallory, John III:701, 786
Mallory, R. C. IV:110
Mallory, Roger III:631
Mallory, Samuel IV:85
Mallory, Timothy III:532;
IV:27
Mallory, William III:634
Mallow, George IV:251
Mallows, Henry III:821
Malone, Cornelius III:89

Malone, Deloney III:622
Malone, Francis IV:94
Malone, Hugh III:704
Malone, John III:252
Malone, Mullins III:167
Malone, Thomas III:720
Malone, William III:86
Maloney, Archibald III:741
Maloney, John II:299, 584
Maloney, Michael II:184
Maloney, Robert III:294
Malony, Jeremiah III:24
Maloon, Sam'l I:203
Malord, Thomas I:432
Malott, Dory IV:240
Malott, John IV:240
Malott, Thomas IV:226
Malpass, James III:437
Man, Aaron I:827
Man, Abel IV:12
Man, Asa II:435
Manadier, Henry III:61
Manan, John II:700
Manchester, Abraham I:819
Manchester, Barzella I:375
Manchester, Edward I:374
Manchester, Ellery I:333
Manchester, Gideon I:815
Manchester, Giles I:819
Manchester, Israel I:826
Manchester, Jeremiah I:802
Manchester, John I:464, 802
Manchester, Joseph I:815;
II:430
Manchester, Nathaniel I:813
Manchester, Stephen II:203
Manchester, Thomas II:345
Manderville, Matthew II:355
Mandeville, James II:547
Mandigo, Jeremiah II:411
Manerson, John II:614
Mangum, John III:92
Mangum, Lewis III:190
Manhall, Samuel B. I:62
Manheart, John II:333
Manier, David III:829
Mank, Andrew III:621
Manker, William IV:257
Mankin, William IV:241
Manley, Ancil III:565
Manley, Micajau III:772
Manley, Thomas II:139
Manley, William I:931
Manlove, William IV:206
Manly, Moses III:378
Mann, Abel I:826
Mann, Abraham II:64
Mann, Amos I:293
Mann, Andrew I:143; II:456
Mann, Benjamin II:314;
III:242
Mann, Bille I:979
Mann, Catherine I:171
Mann, Daniel I:171
Mann, David I:292, 577;
III:850
Mann, Ebenezer I:419; III:546

445

Marsh, James Johnson IV:164
Marsh, Jason I:852
Marsh, Jasper II:215
Marsh, Jesse I:979
Marsh, Job I:111
Marsh, John I:101, 111, 761; II:69, 486
Marsh, John L. II:470
Marsh, Jonathan I:711
Marsh, Joseph I:483, 623, 733
Marsh, Joseph, 2d I:773
Marsh, Joseph C. II:382
Marsh, Lot I:577
Marsh, Margarette IV:164
Marsh, Miria IV:164
Marsh, Nancy IV:164
Marsh, Nathan II:456
Marsh, Noah I:225, 673
Marsh, Obed II:280
Marsh, Reuben I:352; II:456
Marsh, Robert III:493
Marsh, Roswell I:111
Marsh, Samuel II:253; IV:66
Marsh, Samuel, Jr. II:139
Marsh, Seymour II:126
Marsh, Silas I:646; II:212
Marsh, Stephen I:313, 646
Marsh, Thomas III:673
Marsh, William I:622, 979; II:82; III:407; IV:164
Marshall, Aaron, Sen. II:8
Marshall, Abel I:747
Marshall, Amon II:547
Marshall, Andrew I:165
Marshall, Antipas I:747
Marshall, Benj. III:763
Marshall, Benjamin I:165, 188; III:52, 452, 787
Marshall, Daniel II:455
Marshall, David II:649, 653
Marshall, Dixon III:394, 558
Marshall, Elisha I:49
Marshall, Ezekiel III:623
Marshall, Francis III:623
Marshall, George IV:171
Marshall, Humphrey III:279
Marshall, Isaac I:760; III:378
Marshall, Jacob I:520
Marshall, James M. III:776
Marshall, Jesse III:162
Marshall, John II:314, 689; III:297, 791
Marshall, Joseph I:537; II:369
Marshall, Mead II:183
Marshall, Nathaniel I:761
Marshall, Perez I:464
Marshall, Purnell III:441
Marshall, Richard IV:207
Marshall, Robert I:773; II:138; III:266
Marshall, Samuel I:693
Marshall, Simeon II:324
Marshall, Thomas I:69; II:541; III:852
Marshall, Timothy I:646
Marsters, Edward I:597
Marston, Abraham I:778

Marston, Asa I:773
Marston, Benjamin I:677
Marston, David I:268, 313, 399
Marston, James III:212
Marston, John I:601, 753, 778
Marston, Joseph I:268
Marston, Levi I:773
Marston, Matthias I:724
Marston, Nathaniel I:195
Marston, Samuel I:231
Marston, Thomas I:773
Martague, Jonathan I:41
Martens, John I:16
Martenson, John III:312
Martenus, Goddard I:70
M'Arthur, Peter II:441
Martiacy, John III:24
Martin, Aaron I:911
Martin, Abel I:646
Martin, Absolam III:369
Martin, Albro I:339
Martin, Alexander II:679; III 665; IV:254
Martin, Amasa I:150; II:495
Martin, Amos I:374, 711
Martin, Andrew I:778; III:88
Martin, Anthony II:507
Martin, Asa I:455
Martin, Ashbel I:935
Martin, Azariah III:271
Martin, Baltzer II:728
Martin, Baptiste II:554
Martin, Benjamin I:813, 952; III:257
Martin, Charles IV:266
Martin, Christopher I:919; II:158
Martin, Claudius II:642
Martin, Comfort I:623
Martin, Daniel I:979; III:852
Martin, David I:183, 935; IV:115
Martin, David Williams II:668
Martin, Ebenezer II:435
Martin, Edward I:400
Martin, Eleazer I:845
Martin, Ennalls III:67
Martin, Ephraim I:918; III:432
Martin, George I:918; II:614
Martin, George, 2d I:905
Martin, Gideon III:327
Martin, Henry III:376; IV:257
Martin, Hudson III:814
Martin, Isaac I:935
Martin, Jacob I:872; II:744; IV:265, 277
Martin, James I:399, 900; II:655; III:83, 145, 295, 452, 517, 698
Martin, Jesse I:971
Martin, Jirah I:752
Martin, Job III:795

Martin, John I:182, 856, 877, 890, 971; II:73, 293, 658; III:150, 214, 270, 466, 532, 564, 643, 797; IV:105, 169, 182
Martin, John, Sr. III:779
Martin, John R. IV:141
Martin, Jonathan I:408, 711
Martin, Joseph I:79; II:415, 501, 554; III:709
Martin, Joseph P. I:229
Martin, Joshua I:952; III:376
Martin, Josiah III:567
Martin, Kinchen III:397
Martin, Leonard II:69
Martin, Levi IV:272
Martin, Lewis II:724
Martin, Lucas I:856
Martin, Luther II:319
Martin, Margery I:856
Martin, Maria I:856
Martin, Martha I:856
Martin, Martin III:490
Martin, Mary II:554
Martin, Matt III:567
Martin, Moses III:318
Martin, Nathan II:338
Martin, Nathaniel I:167, 293, 710
Martin, Nathaniel F. I:150
Martin, Oliver I:399
Martin, Patrick II:659
Martin, Peter I:890; II:693
Martin, Philip II:184; III:57
Martin, Pleasant III:634
Martin, Rebecca I:856
Martin, Reuben I:111, 952; IV:293
Martin, Rhodeham III:581
Martin, Richard I:419; III:408, 523
Martin, Robert I:183, 753; III:369, 604; IV:214
Martin, Roger II:713
Martin, Samuel I:879, 926; III:34, 429, 574
Martin, Scott III:722
Martin, Seth I:964
Martin, Solomon I:900
Martin, Stephen II:427
Martin, Thomas II:396; III:517; IV:228
Martin, Thomas N. I:868
Martin, William I:856; II:215, 671; III:214, 270, 331, 481, 532, 789, 814
Martin, Wm. I:753
Martin, Zachariah III:783
Martindale, Ebenezer II:293
Martindale, James IV:248
Martindale, John III:37
Martindale, Samuel III:435
Martindale, Stephen I:931
Martindale, Uriah I:445
Martine, William II:137
Martling, Abraham II:351
Martling, Abraham B. II:446

447

Marts, William IV:291
Martz, George II:759
Marvell, John I:760
Marvin, Benjamin I:885;
  II:507
Marvin, Jonathan I:926
Marvin, Matthew II:227
Marvin, Ozias II:455
Marvin, Richard I:807
Marvin, Seth I:34
Marvin, William D. II:104
Marvine, Matthew II:555
Marwin, John C. II:221
Marx, William II:639
Mase, Samuel II:57
Mason, Aaron I:503
Mason, Abel I:646
Mason, Alexander I:375
Mason, Arthur II:9
Mason, Ashbel II:260
Mason, Broadstreet I:229
Mason, Caleb III:577
Mason, Daniel I:520; II:369
Mason, Ebenezer I:268
Mason, Edward I:778; III:596
Mason, Elijah I:150; II:406
Mason, Elisha I:111
Mason, George III:475; IV:66
Mason, Henry I:137
Mason, Hugh I:743
Mason, Isaac II:714
Mason, James I:813; II:259;
  III:241
Mason, John I:183, 710;
  III:16, 511
Mason, Jonathan I:732, 752
Mason, Joseph I:49, 374, 743;
  III:262
Mason, Lemuel B. I:789
Mason, Lewis III:24
Mason, Luther II:362
Mason, Matthew I:926
Mason, Michael III:62; IV:260
Mason, Moses I:287, 321
Mason, Nathan II:541
Mason, Nathaniel II:351
Mason, Noah II:491
Mason, Pardon I:827
Mason, Patrick III:386
Mason, Peter I:663, 680;
  III:266, 666, 717
Mason, Philip III:419
Mason, Rober I:399
Mason, Robert I:701
Mason, Rufus II:401
Mason, Samuel B. I:732
Mason, Simeon I:646, 732
Mason, Smith III:837
Mason, Thomas III:380;
  IV:221
Mason, Tilly I:297
Mason, William II:644; III:425
Mass, Samuel III:815
Massee, Thomas IV:18
Massengill, Michael III:583
Masser, John III:841
Massey, Edmond III:266

Massey, Henry III:505, 633;
  IV:106
Massey, Jessey III:58
Massey, John III:212, 424,
  630
Massey, Peter II:95
Massie, Thomas III:814
Masso, Francis II:138
Masten, Jacob I:766
Masten, Matthew II:342
Masters, Clement II:655, 724
Masters, Enoch III:409
Masters, James II:369
Masters, John II:56; IV:39
Masters, Stephen IV:217
Masters, Thomas III:483
Masters, William II:701
Masterson, James I:287;
  III:275
Mastic, Benjamin I:590
Mastick, Benjamin IV:138
Masuere, Peter I:689
M'Atee, Walter III:312
Matheny, Jane III:9
Matheny, John III:9
Matheny, Wm. III:590
Mather, Abner IV:212
Mather, Ebenezer IV:280
Mather, Elihu IV:9
Mather, Increase I:101
Mather, John I:137
Mather, Joseph I:88, 101;
  II:379
Mather, Nathaniel I:136
Mather, Phinehas I:979
Mather, Reuben II:456
Mather, Samuel I:89, 101,
  137
Mather, Stephen II:486
Mather, Sylvanus II:486
Mathers, William, 2d I:455
Mathers, William H. III:105
Mathews, Aaron II:170
Mathews, Abner I:520
Mathews, Amos V. III:280
Mathews, Asahel I:645
Mathews, Benjamin III:84
Mathews, Daniel, 2d I:183
Mathews, Francis III:678
Mathews, Hardy III:405
Mathews, James III:793
Mathews, John III:184
Mathews, John, 1st I:217
Mathews, Philip III:826
Mathews, Richard III:756
Mathews, Timothy I:868
Mathews, William III:626;
  IV:283
Mathews, William, 1st I:399
Mathewson, Richard I:815
Mathins, John III:408
Mathiot, George II:721
Mathis, Thomas I:724
Matley, Ann III:670
Matley, Francis III:670
Matley, Jas. III:670
Matley, Rosetta III:670

Matlock, Francis III:670
Matlock, Henry III:527
Matlock, Jacob II:67, 744
Matlock, John III:388
Matrick, Quorck I:548
Matsinger, Adam II:744
Matsinger, Frederick II:596
Matson, John I:952
Matson, Joseph I:23
Matteson, Benjamin I:815
Matteson, Caleb II:319
Matteson, David II:654
Matteson, Obadiah I:815
Matteson, Samuel II:406
Matteson, Stephen I:815
Matthews, Atkins I:352
Matthews, Benjamin II:204
Matthews, Daniel I:226; II:260
Matthews, David II:541
Matthews, Ebenezer II:218
Matthews, Edward N. IV:115
Matthews, Elisha I:646
Matthews, Garret IV:252
Matthews, George III:673
Matthews, Gilbert III:382
Matthews, Giles III:443
Matthews, Hugh I:701
Matthews, Isaac III:169, 828
Matthews, Jabez II:262
Matthews, James II:55, 679;
  III:389
Matthews, Jesse I:42
Matthews, John I:62, 694;
  II:78; III:37
Matthews, John, 2d I:239
Matthews, Joseph III:814
Matthews, Moses I:101
Matthews, Peter H. III:293
Matthews, Samuel III:761
Matthews, Thomas II:435
Matthews, William III:169;
  IV:219
Matthewson, Alex. II:614
Matthewson, Charles I:785
Matthewson, Daniel II:545
Matthewson, William II:363
Matthias, James II:614
Mattingley, John III:731
Mattingly, James III:693
Mattison, Dyer II:430
Mattison, Hezekiah II:456
Mattison, James II:379
Mattison, Jonathan II:420
Mattison, Roswell II:393
Mattock, Nathaniel III:299
Mattocks, Caroline II:621
Mattocks, Daniel II:621
Mattocks, Isaiah II:621
Mattocks, James II:621
Mattocks, Richard II:736
Mattoon, Abel II:215
Mattoon, Ebenezer I:483
Mattoon, Sylvanus I:911
Mattox, James II:621
Mattson, Elias II:26
Mattson, Eliza II:26
Mattson, John II:26

448

449

McBride, Daniel C. II:577
McBride, James II:759
McBride, John II:73; III:419
McBride, Josiah III:419
McBride, Patrick IV:26
McBride, Peter II:646
McBride, Roger IV:203
McBride, William III:515
McBroom, Andrew III:440
McCabe, Hugh III:605
McCaffery, James II:39
McCain, John III:432
McCaity, Daniel III:645
McCall, John III:86
McCallister, James III:51
McCallister, John II:44
McCallister, Randall I:669
McCallister, Wm. III:600
McCallon, James III:569
McCalvin, John II:627
McCalvin, Mary Ann II:627
McCam, Michael III:52
McCammont, John IV:27
McCampbell, Solomon III:596
McCan, Patrick III:799
McCance, David III:166
McCandless, John III:224
McCane, Samuel, Sr. III:750
McCanless, John III:582
McCanley, John III:47
McCann, Daniel II:633
McCann, John III:597
McCarr, John II:658
McCarrol, John III:619
McCarroll, John III:558
McCarter, James III:83, 807
McCarter, Robert II:541
McCarthy, John II:299
McCartney, Henry II:669
McCartney, James IV:284
McCartney, John III:88
McCarty, Andrew III:711
McCarty, Daniel II:229; III:309
McCarty, Dennis II:721
McCarty, Isaiah II:613-14
McCarty, John II:119
McCarty, Thomas II:299, 707; III:226
McCarty, William III:430
McCary, Richard III:75
McCasland, John III:576
McCauley, James II:29
McCauley, John III:843
McCauley, Thomas III:288
McCausland, Andrew III:709, 751
McCausland, Robert I:167
McCausland, William IV:77
McCaw, Francis III:701
McCaw, James III:499
McCay, John III:47
Mccay, John II:317
McChan, John III:52
McChesney, Charles G. II:91
McChesney, James II:73
McChesney, John III:641
McChesney, Robert II:73

McChristy, James III:215
McClain, Abijah II:721
McClain, Charles III:351
McClain, Daniel III:245
McClain, James III:474
McClain, John III:831
McClain, William IV:205
McClanahan, William III:645
McClanahan, Wm. III:771
McClanning, John II:336
McClanning, Plato I:795
McClary, James I:601
McClean, Alexander II:721
McClean, Andrew II:756
McClean, Hugh II:614
McClean, Jacob II:694
McClean, John II:78
McClease, Betsy II:188
McClease, Catherine II:188
McClease, Charles II:188
McClease, Cornelius II:188
McClease, John II:188
McClease, Polly II:188
McClease, Thomas II:188
McCleiver, Richard III:450
McClellan, Malcom III:405
McClellan, Prince I:183
McClellan, Samuel I:826
McClellan, Thomas II:756
McClelland, Asa IV:163
McClelland, Cary IV:263
McClelland, David III:120
McClelland, Enos IV:163
McClelland, George II:721
McClelland, Hugh IV:217
McClelland, James IV:77
McClelland, Joseph II:711
McClelland, Robert IV:246
McClellen, James IV:241
McClenachan, Blair I:xv
McClenan, John III:655
McClenden, Shadrack III:119
McClennen, William I:658
McClennen, Wm. I:658
McCleran, Daniel III:371
McCleskey, James III:165
McCleur, John III:86
McClintock, John I:432
McClister, James III:636
McClosky, John III:111
McClosky, Samuel III:111
McCloud, Anguish I:331
McCloud, Samuel IV:212
McCluer, John I:760
McClung, James III:516
McClung, John III:619
McClung, Matthew IV:281
McClung, Robert IV:202
McClunie, Michael IV:224
McClure, Alexander III:654
McClure, Andrew II:2, 668
McClure, David I:711
McClure, John II:15
McClure, Samuel IV:11
McClure, William II:697
McClurken, Thomas III:499
McClurkin, Matthew IV:93

McCockle, Samuel III:284
McCollister, Reuben I:918
McCollock, Joseph II:697
McCollom, David II:689
McCollough, Robert IV:190
McCollough, Robert (2) IV:190
McCollum, Cornelius IV:240
McCollum, Patrick II:67
McComas, John III:759
McComb, John II:23
McComb, William IV:63, 247
McComber, Ebenezer II:270
Mccomber, John I:631
McConaghy, John II:655
McConehy, John II:580
McConemy, John II:627
McConemy, Julianna II:627
McConemy, Mary Ann II:627
McConn, James II:613
McConnally, Michael II:613
McConnel, Hugh II:299
McConnel, Samuel I:900
McConnell, Jonathan II:654
McConnell, Manuel III:605
McConnell, Matthew II:596
McConnell, Ware I:666
McConnell, William II:634
McCord, Alex'r III:203
McCord, Eleanor III:203
McCord, John II:533
McCord, Josiah III:613
McCord, William II:636; IV:79
McCorkle, Archibald III:619
McCormack, Benjamin III:91
McCormick, Archibald I:978
McCormick, Charles II:615
McCormick, Francis IV:254
McCormick, George III:236
McCormick, Hugh III:245
McCormick, James II:700
McCormick, John I:773; IV:68
McCormick, Robert III:600
McCormick, Thomas II:614
McCoskey, Felicity IV:110
McCoskey, William IV:110
McCowan, Archibald II:614
McCowan, John II:613
McCowan, Patrick III:679
McCoy, Alexander II:183; III:217; IV:232
McCoy, Angus II:756
McCoy, Charles II:633, 676
McCoy, Daniel II:584; III:221
McCoy, David I:29
McCoy, Ephraim II:586
McCoy, John I:29, 503; II:123, 333, 654; III:37, 594
McCoy, Jonathan I:718
McCoy, Kenneth II:614
McCoy, Mary I:29
McCoy, Nancy I:29
McCoy, Neil I:280
McCoy, Paul I:433
McCoy, Redden III:513
McCoy, Robert III:569; IV:79
McCoy, Samuel III:710

452

453

McNeill, Thomas I:868; II:563
McNelly, Henry I:989
McNemara, Patrick I:597
McNemara, Peter I:597
McNiel, Henry II:456
McNish, Alexander II:175
McNitt, John II:420
McNorton, Patrick III:110
McNutt, Alexander IV:141
McNutt, John II:379
McNutty, John II:138
M'Collough, William II:89
M'Collum, Thomas II:475
M'Conn, Alexander III:312
M'Connel, Francis IV:170
M'Connell, John II:692
M'Connell, Jonathan III:212
M'Connell, Joseph III:190
M'Connell, Samuel III:50
M'Corkel, Robert IV:264
M'Cormick, David II:525
M'Cormick, Dennis II:441
M'Cormick, James I:183
M'Cormick, Joseph III:604
M'Cowan, James III:232
M'Coy, Daniel II:662; III:580
McPeatz, Jonathan II:88
McPeters, David IV:16
McPeters, Jonathan III:461
McPheeters, John IV:97
McPherson, Alexander III:207
McPherson, Andrew II:661
McPherson, Hugh I:538
McPherson, Mark III:335
McPherson, Matthew III:425
McPherson, Robert H. II:596
McPhester, Andrew IV:86
McPike, John IV:226
McQuay, John II:33
McQueen, Alexander IV:276
McQueen, Joshua III:233, 335
McQueen, Thomas IV:60
McQueston, Hugh N. I:669
McQuie, William IV:123
McQuinn, John II:656
McQuinney, James III:58
M'Crackin, David, Jr. II:153
McRaimey, Francis III:567
M'Crary, John III:580
M'Cready, Daniel II:700
McRee, William III:789
M'Creery, William II:579
McReynolds, Joseph IV:85
McRoberts, David III:556
McRoberts, James IV:15
M'Crosky, John III:616
M'Crum, William II:707
McSpadden, Archibald III:607
McSpadden, Samuel III:595
McSpeddin, Thomas III:634
McStewart, John II:198
McSwaine, Hugh II:614
McSwine, George II:679
McTeer, William II:78
M'Cullen, Alexander III:602
M'Culley, James III:237
M'Culloch, James W. III:25

M'Cullough, James III:237
M'Curda, Thomas I:163
M'Curdy, Alex. II:692
M'Curdy, Robert IV:225
McVancy, Christop'r III:799
McVaugh, John II:738
McVay, Hugh III:264
McWain, Andrew I:989
McWhiter, James III:516
McWhorter, George III:432
McWhorter, Henry III:799
McWhorter, John III:85
McWhortor, Robert IV:97
McWilliams, James III:286, 853
McWilliams, John III:750
McWilliams, William IV:263
McWithey, Silas I:883
McWithy, James IV:17
M'Daniel, James III:608
M'Donald, John II:579; III:548; IV:75
M'Donald, Joseph II:699
M'Donnough, Andrew III:568
M'Donough, Hugh IV:256
M'Dowell, James III:275
M'Dowell, Michael III:573
M'Durmut, James IV:283
Meach, Jacob I:16
Meacham, Elijah III:722
Meacham, Ichabod III:722
Meacham, Jeremiah II:307
Meacham, Jonathan I:445
Meacham, Joseph III:268
Meacham, Simeon III:253
Meachum, Benj'n I:27
Meachum, Mary Ann I:27
Mead, Abijah I:646
Mead, Alfred II:99-100
Mead, Amos II:525
Mead, Andrew I:3
Mead, Benjamin I:645, 868
Mead, Calvin I:89
Mead, David II:355, 406
Mead, Ebenezer II:547
Mead, Israel I:520; II:369, 525
Mead, James II:50, 533
Mead, Jeremiah I:34
Mead, John III:226, 678; IV:66
Mead, Joseph II:393
Mead, Lemuel III:96
Mead, Levi I:89
Mead, Lewis II:525
Mead, Libbeus II:183
Mead, Minor III:158
Mead, Peter I:88
Mead, Samuel II:218
Mead, Silas II:448
Mead, Stephen IV:265
Mead, Thaddeus I:89
Mead, Thomas IV:85
Mead, Thornton III:716
Mead, Tilley I:623
Mead, Truman II:293
Mead, Uriah I:34, 154

Mead, William II:529; III:556; IV:94
Mead, Zaccheus I:89
Meade, Jason I:623
Meade, Levi I:693
Meade, William II:326; III:800
Meaden, Andrew III:595
Meader, Francis I:226
Meader, Isham III:618
Meader, Joel III:618
Meader, Stephen I:732
Meaderis, John III:635
Meaders, Daniel III:567
Meadow, Benjamin III:753
Meadow, Josiah III:778
Meadows, Francis III:721
Meadows, Israel III:215
Meadows, Jacob III:778
Meadows, James III:833
Meadows, John III:514
Meaker, Ephraim II:307
Meanley, James III:779
Meanly, John III:712
Means, James I:182, 320
Means, Philip II:635, 700
Means, Robert II:737; IV:229
Means, Thomas, 1st I:196
Means, William IV:12
Mears, Daniel I:400
Mears, Hillary III:745
Mears, James II:139
Mears, John I:363
Mears, Russel I:503
Mearse, Samuel, Jr. I:503
Mearse, William I:503
Measurell, Elijah IV:103
Mebane, John III:407
Mebrard, George I:399
Mebrard, John I:399
Mecham, Paul III:356
Medaris, Massy C. III:419
Medbury, Abel I:374
Medbury, Benjamin I:827
Medbury, John I:363
Medbury, Joseph II:379
Medcalf, Jane III:41
Medcalf, John D. III:41
Medcalf, Rebecca III:41
Meddack, Frederick III:59
Meddock, Moses IV:191
Medford, James III:436
Medlar, Boston III:711
Medley, Bryant III:452
Medley, John III:630
Medlin, Bradley III:633
Medlin, Shadrach III:396
Medlock, Richard III:588
Medok, Emanuel IV:42
Meech, Cynthia I:29
Meech, Elijah I:455
Meech, Elisha I:939
Meech, Ephraim I:29
Meech, John G. I:29
Meech, Joshua I:29
Meech, Louisa I:29
Meech, Lucy I:29
Meech, Maria I:29

454

Meech, Martha I:29
Meechum, Philip I:483
Meecker, Elizabeth II:90
Meecker, Uzal II:90
Meed, Stephen I:785
Meeder, Edward S. I:847
Meeds, Cato IV:212
Meek, Basil III:291
Meek, Jacob IV:98
Meek, John III:37
Meekeer, Michael II:37
Meeker, Carey II:708
Meeker, Ichabod II:525
Meeker, John I:23; IV:254
Meeker, Jonathan II:514
Meeker, Obadiah II:64
Meeker, Robert II:362
Meeker, Timothy II:64
Meeks, Alexander III:599
Meeks, Austin III:696
Meeks, Brittain III:175
Meeks, John III:716
Meers, Moses III:284
Meese, Baltzer II:683
Mefford, Jacob III:212
Meggs, Richard II:673
Megregory, Joel I:737
Mehaffey, John IV:226
Meharin, Isaac I:287
Mehren, Jonathan I:597
Meigs, Abel I:127
Meigs, Benjamin S. I:882
Meigs, Daniel B. I:945
Meigs, John I:49
Meigs, Phineas II:285
Meigs, Stephen I:62
Meisenheimer, Peter IV:19
Melam, John III:88
Melcoy, John I:399
Meldrum, John I:239
Melency, James I:645
Melency, John I:941
Melency, Thomas I:760
Melfartrick, Hector II:621
Melish, John IV:277
Mellen, Atcheson II:285
Mellen, Casper II:225
Mellen, Ebenezer I:593
Mellen, James I:847
Mellen, John I:971
Mellen, Joshua I:593
Mellen, Matthew II:265
Mellen, Sarah I:593
Mellen, Thomas I:890
Mellen, William II:225
Mellin, Hugh II:569
Mellin, Thomas II:596
Mellog, Andrew III:476
Mellon, Samuel II:639
Mellott, Benjamin IV:283
M'Elnay, John II:696
Melone, Andrew III:265
Melone, John II:689
Meloney, John IV:219
Melroy, Bartholomew II:759
M'Elroy, Daniel III:546
M'Elroy, Hugh II:579

M'Elroy, Micajah III:598
Melsom, James II:39
Melson, Charles III:680
Melson, Samuel III:503
Melton, Charles III:224
Melton, Isham III:481
Melton, Jonathan III:384
Melton, Pearce W. III:772
Melton, Thomas III:214
Melton, William III:184
Melville, Thomas I:601
Melvin, David I:188
Melvin, James I:455, 657
Melvin, John I:196, 685
Melvin, John F. I:685
Melvin, Jonathan II:470
Melvin, Luther I:685
Melvin, Lydia I:685
Melvin, Thomas S. I:685
Menably, Michael III:538
Mendenhall, Joseph II:721
Mendenhall, Nathan III:430
Mendum, William I:239
Menefer, Spencer IV:67
Menely, Jesse IV:184
Menimon, Israel II:435
Menius, Frederick III:445
Mennear, Abraham IV:93
M'Entire, William IV:40
Mentor, Thomas II:311
Mercer, C. F. III:851
Mercer, Joshua III:129
Merchant, Thomas I:49
Mercoreau, Francis II:29
Mercy, John III:212
Meredith, Henry III:506
Meredith, James III:786
Meredith, Jesse III:75
Meredith, John W. IV:204
Meredith, Samuel IV:100, 296
Meredith, Thomas II:634
Meredith, William III:338
Meredith, William L. III:338
Merewether, William III:294
Meriam, David I:964
Meriam, Ezra I:710
Meriam, Jesse I:445
Meriam, John I:646
Meriam, Josiah I:520
Merian, John II:253
Meriman, Francis III:549
Merithew, William I:807
Meriwether, James III:186
Mero, Amariah I:277
Mero, Josiah I:277
Merony, Alexander II:227
Merrel, Dan I:447
Merrell, Andrew III:269
Merrell, Benjamin III:404
Merrell, William II:420
Merrells, Reuben II:225
Merret, James III:494
Merret, Levi II:659
Merrett, Daniel III:455
Merriam, Amos I:127
Merriam, Christopher I:111
Merriam, Ephraim I:62

Merriam, Ichabod II:379
Merriam, John I:957
Merriam, Jonathan II:401
Merriam, Joseph I:645
Merriam, Timothy I:520
Merrian, Isaac I:747
Merrian, Marshal IV:268
Merrick, Constant I:743
Merrick, John I:297
Merrick, Luther I:143
Merrick, Peter I:62
Merrick, Samuel F. I:464
Merrick, William III:64
Merricle, Henry II:314
Merricle, Samuel II:340
Merrifield, Ithamar I:646
Merrifield, Robert I:445
Merril, John III:122
Merrill, Aaron I:49, 773; II:293
Merrill, Abel I:313
Merrill, Abner I:169
Merrill, Amos I:253
Merrill, Benj. I:656
Merrill, Benjamin I:605
Merrill, Caleb II:285
Merrill, Daniel I:760
Merrill, Enoch I:773
Merrill, Hosea I:352
Merrill, Hugh II:596
Merrill, Jacob I:253, 313
Merrill, James I:677, 931; II:507
Merrill, Jared I:13
Merrill, Jesse II:688
Merrill, John I:252, 785, 941; III:404
Merrill, Jonathan I:964
Merrill, Joseph I:789
Merrill, Joshua II:138
Merrill, Levi I:766
Merrill, Mead II:227
Merrill, Medad II:227
Merrill, Moses I:183, 253, 778
Merrill, Nathan I:253, 761
Merrill, Nathaniel I:710
Merrill, Nathaniel, 2d I:50
Merrill, Nathaniel, 1st I:42
Merrill, Nehemiah I:688
Merrill, Noah II:215
Merrill, Phineas I:701
Merrill, Roger I:268; II:280
Merrill, Samuel I:119, 313, 419
Merrill, Simeon II:545
Merrill, Simon I:773
Merrill, Stephen I:872
Merrils, Jephtha I:111
Merrils, Kzekiel II:386
Merrils, Noah II:406
Merriman, Asaph I:127
Merriman, George I:127; II:386
Merriman, Josiah I:23
Merriman, Murcus I:127
Merriman, Samuel S. I:964
Merris, John III:538

Merriss, Thirsa F. II:197
Merriss, William II:197
Merrit, Daniel III:408
Merrit, Stephen III:254
Merritt, Amos I:645
Merritt, Archelaus III:228
Merritt, Daniel I:577
Merritt, Ezekiel II:259
Merritt, Isaac B. II:149
Merritt, John I:399
Merritt, Jonathan I:277
Merritt, Major III:680
Merritt, Noah I:964
Merritt, Samuel III:682
Merritt, Shadrach III:422
Merritt, Thomas II:705; III:329
Merritt, William I:232; III:452
Merrow, David I:733
Merrow, William I:183
Merry, Cornelius IV:79
Merry, Jacob O. III:403
Merry, John II:456
Merry, Jonathan I:597
Merry, Philip III:771
Merry, Samuel I:343; II:303
Merryfield, Abraham I:854
Merryman, Thomas III:691
Mershon, Henry II:69
Mershon, Joab II:368
Mervin, Joseph I:136
Merwin, Andrew I:89
Meseroe, Solomon I:183
Meserve, Nathaniel I:239
Meserve, William I:531; IV:36
Mesler, Peter II:82
Messellier, Lewis II:139
Messenger, Abner III:828
Messenger, Joel II:328
Messenger, Lemuel I:101
Messenger, Reuben I:49
Messer, Christian IV:237
Messer, Ebenezer I:701
Messer, Jeremiah III:397
Messer, Simon II:85
Messeroll, Abraham II:73
Messeroll, Peter II:73
Messeroll, William II:73
Messhew, Jesse III:292
Messinger, Bille IV:280
Messinger, John I:352
Messowey, Charles I:175
Messowey, Harriet I:175
Messowey, Robert I:175
Messowey, Sel'n I:175
Metcalf, Benjamin I:911
Metcalf, Danza III:450
Metcalf, Ebenezer I:137
Metcalf, Elias I:905
Metcalf, James I:548
Metcalf, Luther I:548
Metcalf, Philemon I:926
Metcalf, Samuel I:989
Metcalf, Timothy I:694, 743
Metcalf, Titus I:300
Metcalf, Warner III:450
Metcalf, William III:604
Metcalf, William M. I:548

Methany, William III:750
Metheany, Luke III:236
Metz, John II:682
Metzger, Jacob IV:284
Meyer, John II:658
Meyer, Leonard II:682
Meyers, Lewis II:613
Meyers, Michael II:183
Mezner, Henry IV:88
M'Fadden, Mannasseh II:574
M'Fall, Patrick II:386
M'Farland, Alexander II:605
M'Farland, Benjamin I:277
M'Farland, James I:165, 196
M'Farland, Joseph II:345
M'Farling, Andrew II:342
M'Farling, John Bennet III:11
M'Farran, John II:550
M'Gahey, William IV:50
M'Gee, James II:688
M'Gee, John III:295
M'Gee, Neil I:189
M'Gee, Samuel III:331
M'Ghoggan, Alexander IV:170
M'Gill, Peggy II:200
M'Gill, William II:200
M'Ginnis, Andrew III:257
M'Glasson, John III:190
M'Goldsmith, Pelatiah I:79
M'Gonigal, Edward III:25
M'Graw, John II:441
M'Gregor, David II:215
M'Guire, Daniel III:257
M'Hatton, James III:199
M'Henry, John II:525
M'Henry, Thomas II:713
Michael, John II:694
Michals, William I:300
Michell, Abraham IV:80
Micheller, Jacob IV:87
Mick, Philip II:665, 728
Micker, Usal II:29
Mickle, Reuben II:659
Micon, Henry III:711
Midagh, Moses IV:191
Middaugh, Daniel II:525
Middaugh, Solomon III:529
Middlebrook, John II:465
Middleswart, Jacob IV:232
Middlesworth, John N. II:69
Middleton, Benjamin II:204
Middleton, John III:789; IV:258
Middleton, Lewis IV:142
Middleton, Theodore III:66
Middletown, Peter I:49
Middough, Henry C. T. II:745
Middough, John II:727
Midge, Abraham, Jr. II:246
Midkiff, Isaiah III:583
Midkiff, John III:820
Miel, Charles III:293
Miers, Daniel II:475
Mifflin, Jonathan II:760
Migate, Jonathan I:49
Mighal, Moses II:348
Mighell, Asahel I:861

Mighell, Elias I:861
Mighell, Hannah I:861
Mighell, John W. I:861
Mighell, Randall I:861
Might, John IV:241
Mikesell, Jacob IV:77
Mikle, John IV:176
Milam, Jordan III:592
Milbourn, Thomas III:623
Milburn, Andrew IV:241
Milburn, Nicholas III:50
Milburn, William III:585
Milcham, William II:652
Miles, Caleb II:641
Miles, Charles III:766
Miles, Daniel I:101
Miles, Edward III:15
Miles, Ephraim II:501
Miles, Isaac II:518
Miles, Jacob III:613, 661
Miles, Jesse III:263, 508
Miles, Joab I:645
Miles, Joel I:693
Miles, John I:62, 156; III:226, 730; IV:176, 265
Miles, John, 2d III:223
Miles, Joseph III:661
Miles, Leonard III:599
Miles, Simon I:127
Miles, Thomas III:749
Miles, Thomas, Sen. III:633
Miles, William II:285, 718; III:216
Miley, Jacob II:663
Milford, John III:494
Miligan, Joseph III:312
Milirons, William III:153
Milkollin, Jonathan IV:237
Millam, Rush III:795
Millan, Thomas II:430
Millard, Joseph I:42
Millard, Levitt I:144
Millard, Loudon II:431
Millard, Nathaniel III:72
Millard, Noah I:826
Millard, Samuel II:293
Millard, Stephen II:537
Millen, Richard I:854
Millen, William I:483
Miller, Abner II:533
Miller, Adam II:441; III:612
Miller, Alexander II:525
Miller, Ann II:627
Miller, Anthony II:613
Miller, Asa I:229
Miller, Barney III:262
Miller, Benjamin I:79; II:212
Miller, Betsey T. I:593
Miller, Betsy I:858
Miller, Caleb I:62, 156; II:249
Miller, Caroline IV:162
Miller, Charles I:42
Miller, Christian II:668; III:835
Miller, Christian, 2d II:639
Miller, Clark II:64
Miller, Conrad II:635

Miller, Consider I:807
Miller, Daniel II:323, 529;
III:698, 811
Miller, David I:952; III:347
Miller, David B. II:424
Miller, Ebenezer I:111
Miller, Edward III:324; IV:90,
141
Miller, Eleazer II:411
Miller, Eliakim II:456
Miller, Elizabeth II:627
Miller, Farrar I:710
Miller, Fleeting II:622
Miller, Francis II:188; III:295;
IV:13
Miller, Frank I:277
Miller, Frederick II:730;
III:294, 329, 571; IV:105,
281
Miller, George II:582, 724,
753; III:47, 269; IV:118
Miller, Giles II:441
Miller, Godfrey II:664
Miller, H. I:xiii
Miller, Henry II:627, 650,
700, 721; III:593; IV:93, 247
Miller, Ichabod IV:234
Miller, Isaac I:743; II:627
Miller, Jacob I:483; II:614,
675; III:288, 410, 415; IV:46
Miller, Jacob, 2d II:644
Miller, Jacob P. II:495
Miller, James I:785, 815, 883;
II:299, 411; III:573, 727
Miller, Jason II:431
Miller, Jeremiah II:105
Miller, Jesse II:317
Miller, Joanna II:627
Miller, Job I:520
Miller, John I:239, 483, 490;
II:203, 399, 416, 525, 730;
III:204, 208, 244, 263, 272,
278, 321, 399, 479, 572,
581, 623, 812; IV:162
Miller, John, 1st II:156, 674
Miller, John, 2d II:159, 663
Miller, John, 3d II:342, 668
Miller, John A. IV:69
Miller, John B. IV:289
Miller, John H. III:595
Miller, John P. II:441
Miller, John V. I:964
Miller, Jonathan IV:110
Miller, Joseph II:78, 123, 620
Miller, Joseph, Sr. III:253
Miller, Joshua IV:115
Miller, Josiah IV:162
Miller, Josias IV:184
Miller, Lawrence III:114
Miller, Lemuel I:313
Miller, Leonard I:593; III:84
Miller, Leonora IV:162
Miller, Levi II:486
Miller, Lewis III:736
Miller, Lucy J. I:593
Miller, Ludwick II:715
Miller, Luke II:82

Miller, Mark III:524
Miller, Martin II:694, 703;
III:573
Miller, Martin, 2d II:639
Miller, Mary I:593
Miller, Michael IV:15
Miller, Miles S. IV:105
Miller, Mordecai IV:83
Miller, Nathan I:815
Miller, Nathaniel II:252, 401
Miller, Nelson I:813
Miller, Nicholas II:750; III:240
Miller, Noah II:420; IV:36
Miller, Othias IV:136
Miller, Peleg II:393
Miller, Peter II:465, 518, 641,
728; III:809
Miller, Philip II:689, 760;
III:445
Miller, Richard II:708
Miller, Robert I:858, 911;
II:622; III:488
Miller, Rosewell I:101
Miller, Roxey IV:162
Miller, Sally IV:162
Miller, Samuel I:503, 945;
II:178, 343, 547, 570, 622;
III:72, 532, 756
Miller, Sarah II:627
Miller, Sarah R. I:593
Miller, Smith II:206
Miller, Solomon I:939
Miller, Stephen II:714
Miller, Thaddeus I:979; II:547
Miller, Thomas II:246; IV:214
Miller, Valentine II:641
Miller, William II:390, 425;
III:37, 169, 185, 278, 831;
IV:293
Miller, William, 2d II:246
Miller, William C. II:386
Miller, Wm. I:xii, xiii
Millerd, Samuel I:815
Millet, John I:239
Millet, Thomas I:196
Millet, Zebulon I:399
Millett, Benjamin I:807
Millett, James I:418
Millett, Nathaniel I:400
Millican, James III:327
Milligan, Cookson II:119
Milligan, David IV:257
Milligan, Hugh III:708
Milligan, John III:245
Milligan, Moses III:484
Milligin, Joel I:183
Milliken, James III:574
Milliken, Joshua I:253
Milliken, Lemuel I:253
Millikin, Abner I:188
Millikin, Josiah I:183
Millikin, Samuel I:760
Millikin, William I:352
Milliman, George III:314
Milliner, Moses II:32
Milling, Hugh III:518
Millingan, John III:818

Millington, Samuel II:345
Milliway, Isaac III:675
Milner, Luke, Sen. III:288
Milner, Nicholas III:288
Mills, Aaron II:379
Mills, Alexander I:34; II:183
Mills, Amasa I:42
Mills, Betsey I:862
Mills, Constantine IV:228
Mills, Cornelius II:50
Mills, Daniel Hellyard III:669
Mills, Edward II:50
Mills, Elijah IV:234
Mills, Elisas II:721
Mills, Francis II:614; III:735
Mills, Gabriel I:34
Mills, George III:827
Mills, George, 2d II:323
Mills, George, 1st II:270
Mills, Gideon III:523
Mills, Handy III:588
Mills, Henry III:669
Mills, James II:456
Mills, Je_se I:862
Mills, Jesse III:450
Mills, John I:732, 766, 862,
957; II:334; III:412, 669,
852; IV:223
Mills, John, 1st I:69
Mills, John, 2d I:34
Mills, Jonathan I:862; II:547
Mills, Joseph I:34
Mills, Josiah I:684
Mills, Menan III:255
Mills, Morgan III:96
Mills, Moses III:163
Mills, Naaman III:460
Mills, Nasby III:443
Mills, Peter II:139; III:13
Mills, Philip I:287; III:669
Mills, Richard II:41
Mills, Robinson III:669
Mills, Roxana I:862
Mills, Ruth III:852
Mills, Samuel I:790, 939;
II:311
Mills, Samuel, Jr. II:103
Mills, Samuel F. II:456
Mills, Sarah III:669
Mills, Solomon II:351, 547
Mills, Stephen II:525, 547
Mills, Thomas III:818
Mills, Timothy II:73
Mills, William I:597; II:639
Mills, Zachariah III:43
Millson, James III:34
Millspaugh, John II:183
Miloy, John R. III:706
Milspaugh, Christian II:299
Milstead, John III:462
Milstead, Zelus III:598
Milton, Benjamin IV:14
Milton, Elijah III:331
Milton, Nathaniel III:608
Milton, Robert I:537, 541
Milton, Thomas III:214
Milton, William II:204; IV:9

458

M'Lain, Uriah II:212
M'Lane, Alexander II:693
M'Lardy, Alexander III:232
M'Laughton, James I:785
M'Lean, James I:101
M'Llanan, Mordecai IV:274
M'Lumsey, Robert IV:271
M'Lure, James I:300
M'Mahan, Andrew III:564
M'Mahon, Daniel III:631
M'Manis, Christopher II:553
M'Manners, Daniel I:277
M'Manning, George III:192
M'Manus, Christopher II:215
M'Master, James II:699
M'Math, Daniel II:693
M'Meehan, Alex'r II:475
M'Michael, Daniel II:441
M'Michael, John II:475
M'Mickle, Robert III:193
M'Millan, Archibald I:680
M'Millan, John II:581; IV:194
M'Minn, Robert III:588
M'Mulin, William II:299
M'Mullen, Archibald I:188
M'Mullen, John II:671
M'Mullen, Michael II:671
M'Mullen, William II:671
M'Murphy, Daniel I:680
M'Murray, William IV:204
M'Murtry, James II:196
M'Murtry, John III:560
M'Natt, John III:612
M'Naughton, Alexander II:541
M'Neal, James III:24
M'Neal, John II:324
M'Near, Robert II:550
M'Neary, Martin II:232
M'Nelly, Nathaniel I:163
M'Nutt, Andrew II:265
Moart, John II:665
Mobley, Clement III:99
Mobley, Isaiah III:99
Moderell, Adam IV:84
Modewell, John II:603
Moffat, Alexander II:689
Moffett, Daniel II:21
Moffett, Lewis II:333
Moffit, Bazaleel II:338
Moffit, Jesse III:771
Moffit, John II:627
Moffit, Judah I:964
Moffit, Thomas II:627
Moffith, Mathew I:79
Mohon, John III:803
Moler, Gasper IV:275
Moler, Joseph IV:258
Molesby, William III:588
Molott, John II:701
Molton, Michael I:802
Monday, Thomas II:595-96
Monday, William III:573
Money, Dennis II:679
Money, Enoch III:671
Money, John III:412, 671
Money, Thos. M. III:671
Monger, Jonathan II:303

Monier, John II:471
Monjoy, James II:271
Monk, Christopher II:465
Monk, Elias I:287
Monk, George I:352
Monk, John II:501; III:173
Monk, Joseph III:689
Monks, Daniel I:795
Monro, John I:150
Monroe, Abel II:547
Monroe, Abijah I:217
Monroe, Abraham II:456
Monroe, Alexander IV:81
Monroe, Amasa I:29
Monroe, Augustus I:842
Monroe, Cornelius I:29
Monroe, George III:445, 771
Monroe, Hugh I:208
Monroe, Isaac II:218
Monroe, John I:127; II:323;
  III:215, 313
Monroe, John Beckwith I:29
Monroe, Joseph I:34
Monroe, Joshua II:525
Monroe, Josiah I:964; II:299
Monroe, Samuel I:29
Monroe, William II:379;
  III:776
Montague, John I:483
Montague, Medad I:445
Montague, Nathaniel II:456
Montague, Peter III:726
Montague, Rice D. III:811
Montague, Rufus I:945
Montague, Seth I:339
Montague, Thomas III:767
Montague, William I:483, 548
Montawney, Isaac II:82
Monteath, Samuel III:424
Montey, Amable II:221
Montey, James II:221
Montey, John II:221
Montey, Joseph II:221
Montey, Placid II:221
Montford, Peter II:85
Montgomery, Alex. IV:46
Montgomery, Alexander
  III:238
Montgomery, Alex'r I:419
Montgomery, Burnett II:78
Montgomery, David III:400
Montgomery, Ezekiel II:529
Montgomery, Henry III:369
Montgomery, Hugh I:49;
  III:710; IV:37
Montgomery, James II:78;
  III:527
Montgomery, John II:662;
  III:195, 309, 419, 458; IV:84,
  184
Montgomery, Jonathan III:601
Montgomery, Josiah I:931
Montgomery, Mitchell L. K.
  IV:188
Montgomery, Richard III:843
Montgomery, Robert II:582
Montgomery, Thomas III:312

Montgomery, William III:571;
  IV:122
Month, Ambrose III:596
Montrose, Elijah I:42
Montross, Abraham II:547
Monty, Cloud I:885
Monty, Francis II:184
Moody, Abigail I:686
Moody, Abner I:778
Moody, Alexander IV:207
Moody, Asa I:686
Moody, Benj. I:753
Moody, Benjamin I:666
Moody, Bishop I:686
Moody, Blanks III:665
Moody, Clement I:701
Moody, Deborah I:686
Moody, Edmund IV:16
Moody, Edward I:297
Moody, Enoch I:419
Moody, George I:239
Moody, Gideon W. I:900
Moody, John I:167, 277, 387,
  918; II:165
Moody, John S. I:387
Moody, Joshua I:183
Moody, Josiah I:686, 743
Moody, Nathaniel P. II:686
Moody, Oliver I:686
Moody, Polly I:686
Moody, Samuel I:268
Moody, Thomas III:177, 371
Moody, William I:387; II:139;
  III:696
Moody, William, 2d III:734
Mooers, Benjamin II:554
Mooers, David I:419
Mook, Gerradus II:184
Moon, James II:655
Moon, Paul II:328
Moon, Peleg I:800
Mooney, Artis II:721
Mooney, Barnet II:562
Mooney, Martin III:675
Mooney, Nicholas I:64
Mooney, Patrick II:138
Mooney, Richard III:675
Mooney, William II:351;
  III:37, 388
Moor, Daniel I:724
Moor, John, 3d II:255
Moor, John, Jun. I:918
Moor, Josiah I:673
Moor, Moses I:701
Moor, Perez II:323
Moor, Thomas, 3d II:293
Moor, Timothy I:760
Moor, William I:761; II:486;
  III:356
Moore, Abel II:151
Moore, Abraham II:420;
  III:323; IV:262
Moore, Alexander II:642;
  III:429, 837
Moore, Alexander C. III:15
Moore, Amos L. III:779
Moore, Andrew II:650

459

Morgan, Nicholas I:137
Morgan, Parker I:732
Morgan, Pelatiah IV:190
Morgan, Reuben I:778
Morgan, Richard III:446
Morgan, Simon III:666
Morgan, Skiff I:868
Morgan, Thomas III:314, 585; IV:256, 281
Morgan, Valentine III:583
Morgan, William I:612, 760; II:369; III:247, 337, 365, 417, 640, 666, 806, 826; IV:99
Morgan, William, 2d III:366
Morgan, William A. I:137
Morgert, Peter II:701
Morgon, Caleb I:964
Mo_rill, Israel I:419
Morin, Edward III:266
Moring, John III:407
Morison, Jonathan I:666
Morison, Morris III:435
Morley, Abner I:356
Morley, Daniel IV:223
Morley, Ezekiel IV:250
Morley, Herrick II:406
Morley, Isaac II:641
Morley, John IV:219
Morley, Thomas IV:250
Morphis, John III:384
Morrell, Benjamin III:275
Morrell, Betsey I:387
Morrell, Clarissa I:387
Morrell, Harriet I:387
Morrell, Isaac II:311
Morrell, Jane I:387
Morrell, Jesse II:491
Morrell, John II:311
Morrell, Jonathan I:419
Morrell, Jos. II:561
Morrell, Joseph I:673; II:299
Morrell, Nathan I:753
Morrell, Polly I:387
Morrell, Ruth I:387
Morrell, Samuel I:673
Morrell, Stephen I:163
Morrell, Susan I:387
Morrell, Thomas II:64; III:621
Morrice, Peter II:627
Morrill, Asa II:285
Morrill, Amos I:419
Morrill, Annis I:753
Morrill, David I:711
Morrill, Elizabeth II:193
Morrill, Enoch I:387
Morrill, Hebard I:926
Morrill, Jacob I:188
Morrill, Jeremiah I:935
Morrill, John I:701, 711
Morrill, Jos. II:193
Morrill, Joseph I:935; II:193, 561
Morrill, Joshua I:971
Morrill, Julian I:683
Morrill, Juliann II:193
Morrill, Madeline II:193

Morrill, Nathaniel I:778, 952
Morrill, Samuel I:683, 711
Morrill, Sargent II:364
Morrill, William I:419, 732
Morrill, Wm. II:193
Morris, Adeline II:627
Morris, Amos III:809
Morris, Bazil IV:273
Morris, Benjamin IV:272
Morris, Charles III:65
Morris, Charlotte II:627
Morris, Chester II:402
Morris, Clairbourne III:796
Morris, Cornelius IV:175
Morris, D. I:111
Morris, Daniel III:289
Morris, David H. IV:272
Morris, Dennis II:85
Morris, Dinah I:111
Morris, Elisha II:73
Morris, George II:633
Morris, Henry, Jun. III:118
Morris, Isaac III:91
Morris, Jacob II:379; III:261
Morris, James I:952; II:650; IV:246
Morris, Jesse III:284
Morris, John II:420, 533, 663; III:84, 111, 508, 665, 743, 802
Morris, Jonathan II:689, 724
Morris, Lester III:582
Morris, Micajah III:388
Morris, Nathaniel III:171
Morris, Nathaniel G. III:209
Morris, Peter II:627
Morris, Reuben IV:291
Morris, Robert II:275
Morris, Stayton II:9
Morris, Thomas III:144, 302, 304
Morris, Thornis III:240
Morris, Travis IV:19
Morris, Vincent IV:115
Morris, William I:239, 612; II:69, 613, 717; III:98, 622; IV:207, 257
Morris, William, Sen. III:142, 400; IV:258
Morris, William W. II:270, 559
Morris, Zadock III:720, 851
Morrison, Abraham I:400
Morrison, Alexander II:595; III:357
Morrison, Archibald III:201
Morrison, Benjamin I:701
Morrison, David I:445, 732
Morrison, Edward III:771
Morrison, Eleanor IV:161
Morrison, Ephraim II:360
Morrison, Esther IV:161
Morrison, Ezra III:298
Morrison, Hugh III:204
Morrison, James I:313; II:225, 754; III:326, 588; IV:228
Morrison, Janoin IV:161

Morrison, John I:773; II:95, 153, 595; III:425, 567, 585, 802; IV:161
Morrison, Jonathan I:778-79
Morrison, Joseph IV:13
Morrison, Larkin II:613
Morrison, Moses I:208
Morrison, R. N. II:557, 566
Morrison, Richard III:204
Morrison, Robert IV:161
Morrison, Roderick II:455
Morrison, Samuel I:732, 789; II:293
Morrison, Thomas II:596
Morrison, Thomas D. I:677
Morrison, William I:269; II:280; III:37, 577
Morriss, Edmond I:128
Morriss, Henry III:671
Morriss, James III:671
Morriss, John III:671
Morrissit, Joseph III:525
Morriston, James III:546
Morrow, David I:733; III:85
Morrow, Isaac III:24
Morrow, John III:288, 523
Morrow, Joseph III:499
Morrow, Samuel II:56; III:82, 514
Morrow, Thomas III:212
Morrow, William III:509
Morrows, William IV:129
Mors, Mark I:239
Morse, Abiel I:989
Morse, Alexander III:323
Morse, Amos I:400; IV:138
Morse, Artemas II:215
Morse, Asaph II:280
Morse, Benjamin I:400, 623, 659, 724
Morse, Benjamin, 2d I:732
Morse, Charles II:424
Morse, Chester I:455
Morse, Cornelius I:538
Morse, Daniel I:277, 939
Morse, Ebenezer I:418; II:336; III:742
Morse, Elihu II:470
Morse, Elijah I:363, 680, 979; IV:228
Morse, Eliphalet I:287
Morse, Eliphalet L. I:670
Morse, Enoch I:253
Morse, Enos II:435
Morse, Isaac I:196; II:401, 470
Morse, Jacob I:196
Morse, James II:242
Morse, Jesse I:623
Morse, Joel I:503
Morse, John I:503, 646, 971; II:293
Morse, Jonathan I:277, 753
Morse, Joseph I:400, 483, 548, 747, 890
Morse, Josiah I:221; II:215
Morse, Levi I:252, 645

461

Morse, Levi, 2d I:277
Morse, Mark I:399
Morse, Micah II:360
Morse, Moses I:101, 952
Morse, Nathan II:470
Morse, Noble II:149
Morse, Obadiah I:548, 623, 666, 905
Morse, Philip I:268
Morse, Rufus II:486
Morse, Samuel I:490, 645, 718, 753, 766
Morse, Samuel, 2d I:623
Morse, Seth I:287; IV:268
Morse, Simeon I:646
Morse, Stephen I:701
Morse, Stephen, 2d I:753
Morse, Thomas I:548
Morse, William I:269
Morseman, Oliver II:420
Morss, David II:238
Mortimer, James III:40, 780
Mortimer, Margaret III:40
Morto, Henry I:537
Morton, Abner I:563
Morton, Archibald II:9
Morton, Benjamin I:160
Morton, David I:183; II:340
Morton, Ebenezer I:483
Morton, Edward III:821
Morton, Elizabeth I:175
Morton, Ezra I:577
Morton, Hannah I:175
Morton, Hezekiah III:852
Morton, Isaac I:694
Morton, James I:175, 252; III:852
Morton, John I:577
Morton, Josiah I:577; III:449
Morton, Levi I:577
Morton, Magnes I:175
Morton, Mary I:175
Morton, Oliver III:171
Morton, Priscilla I:175
Morton, Samuel III:302
Morton, Samuel G. I:433
Morton, Silas I:658
Morton, Susanna I:175
Morton, Thomas I:252; IV:19
Morton, William III:581
Mory, John I:433
Mory, Samuel I:375
Mosby, Joseph III:275
Mosby, Wade III:825
Mosby, William III:204
Moseley, Joseph, Sen. III:496
Moseley, Thomas I:548
Mosely, Arthur III:825
Mosely, James III:537
Mosely, James, Sen. III:515
Mosely, Peter III:765
Mosely, Robert III:241
Mosely, Samuel III:162
Moser, Christian II:738
Moser, Henry II:679
Moser, John II:708; III:841
Moses, Abraham I:900

Moses, Ashbel I:111
Moses, Daniel I:183, 971
Moses, Enan II:242
Moses, Ezekiel IV:236
Moses, John I:939
Moses, Joshua III:330
Moses, Josiah I:253
Moses, Martin I:101
Moses, Milo IV:115
Moses, Seba II:386
Mosher, Aaron I:989
Mosher, David II:396
Mosher, Jabez II:399
Mosher, Jeremiah II:664
Mosher, Joel I:34
Mosher, John II:183, 314
Mosher, Joseph II:396
Mosher, Josiah II:456
Mosher, Moses III:62
Mosher, Reuben II:56
Mosher, Stephen I:79
Mosher, William II:547
Mosier, Abraham III:565
Mosier, Daniel IV:229
Mosier, Francis III:607
Mosier, Miller IV:143
Mosley, Hezekiah III:825
Mosley, Leonard III:252
Mosley, Thomas III:309
Mosman, Ezra I:520
Moss, Benoni I:49
Moss, Daniel IV:190
Moss, David II:554
Moss, Icaiah II:310
Moss, Isaac IV:223
Moss, James III:826
Moss, John II:541; III:289, 309
Moss, Joseph I:680; III:517
Moss, Philip II:333
Moss, Simeon II:541
Moss, Solomon II:641
Mosser, George II:666
Mosser, Jonathan I:645
Mossman, Jesse I:911
Mosyer, John D. III:24
Motes, James III:487
Motherall, Samuel III:633
Mothershead, Nathaniel III:200
Mott, Benjamin III:463
Mott, Edgerton III:382
Mott, Ezekiel IV:212
Mott, John IV:197
Mott, Josiah IV:175
Mott, Lyman I:352
Mott, Noah II:317
Mott, Samuel, 2d II:293
Mott, Samuel, 1st IV:212
Moul, Jacob II:386
Moul, John II:386
Moulten, Garden II:207
Moulton, Charles I:686
Moulton, Chase I:686
Moulton, Daniel I:313, 732, 752
Moulton, David I:287, 313

Moulton, Edward B. I:778
Moulton, James II:348
Moulton, Job I:753
Moulton, John I:646
Moulton, Jonathan I:753
Moulton, Joseph I:253, 753
Moulton, Josiah I:677
Moulton, Mahala I:686
Moulton, Nancy I:686
Moulton, Nathaniel I:879
Moulton, Noah I:753
Moulton, Reuben I:778
Moulton, Richard I:686
Moulton, Sally I:686
Moulton, Salmon II:455
Moulton, Simeon I:313
Moulton, Solomon I:964
Moulton, Stephen II:455
Moulton, Thomas I:686
Moulton, William I:724, 785; II:329, 566
Moulton, Wm. B. II:566
Moultroup, Moses II:285
Mount, Ezekiel III:801
Mount, John II:416, 441
Mount, Joseph II:73
Mount, Matthias II:340
Mount, Richard II:270
Mount, Samuel II:78
Mountain, James II:619
Mountain, Mich'l B. II:619
Mountford, Joseph I:601
Mountfort, Ebenezer I:601
Mountjoy, Alven III:242
Mountjoy, John III:242
Mounts, Thomas IV:92
Mour, George II:118
Mour, Jacob II:396
Mour, John II:82
Mouris, Daniel II:173, 529
Mouris, Peter II:533
Mourning, Christopher IV:116
Moutry, Joseph IV:125
Mowen, Samuel I:268
Mower, Conrad II:441
Mower, John I:268
Mower, Peter II:456
Mower, Peter A. II:561
Mowland, Richard II:9
Mowry, John I:795
Mowry, Pero I:807
Mowry, Peter III:596
Mowry, Reuben IV:289
Moxley, George III:239
Moxley, Joseph I:16
Moy, Gardner III:385
Moyer, Christopher II:430
Moyer, Frederick II:716
Moyer, George I:88
Moyer, Jacob II:730
Moyer, Jacob, 2d II:661
Moyer, John Jacob II:441
Moyer, Lodowick II:456
Moyer, Nicholas II:753
Moyers, Peter III:598
Moylan, Stephen I:xv
Mozier, Ebenezer I:363

Murphy, Pierce I:239
Murphy, Richard III:122
Murphy, Samuel II:699
Murphy, Thomas I:313
Murphy, Thomas, 1st I:232
Murphy, William III:594
Murrah, Joshua III:300
Murray, Alexander I:919; II:511
Murray, Amasa I:62
Murray, Andrew II:203
Murray, Barnabas II:330; III:318
Murray, Benjamin II:455
Murray, Daniel I:34; II:360
Murray, David II:280
Murray, Edward II:139
Murray, Elihu II:218
Murray, Ichabod II:255
Murray, Jacob II:653
Murray, James II:633; III:216, 417
Murray, Jasper II:537
Murray, Jeremiah I:642
Murray, John II:32, 575; III:37; IV:179
Murray, Matthew II:635
Murray, Solomon II:225
Murray, Stephen I:964
Murray, Thomas II:658; III:157, 218
Murray, William I:313; II:265, 613, 669
Murray, William H. III:24
Murrel, Merrit III:414
Murrel, William IV:241
Murrell, Benjamin III:628
Murrell, Samuel, Sen. III:257
Murrey, Anthony II:583
Murrow, Bryant II:32
Murry, Alexander I:607
Murry, Charles III:693
Murry, Nathan I:883
Murry, Neal IV:176
Murry, Richard III:665, 698
Murry, Robert II:42
Murtle, Benjamin III:766
Murvin, Patrick III:286
Muse, Fauntley II:697
Muse, George III:217
Muselwhite, Milbed III:448
Musgrace, Samuel IV:84
Musgrave, John IV:251
Musgrave, Samuel IV:96
Musgrove, William IV:170
Mushellee, Peter II:50
Mushler, Adam II:656
Musick, David IV:124
Musketmuss, Adam III:664
Musselwhite, Nathan III:448
Mussey, John, Jr. I:xiv
Mustain, Avery III:823
Muterspaw, Philip III:831
Muxan, Reuben I:563
Muzzey, Benoni I:548
Muzzy, Amos II:242
Muzzy, Joseph I:978

Muzzy, Nathan IV:280
Muzzy, Robert II:303
M'Vaugh, Jacob II:744
M'Vay, Daniel III:216
M'Vay, Eli III:546
M'Whater, Aaron III:598
M'Whorter, John III:267
Myat, John Baptist II:29
Myer, Ephraim II:533
Myer, Frederick II:533
Myer, Henry II:53
Myer, Jacob II:661
Myer, John II:486
Myer, Peter L. II:533
Myer, William II:533
Myers, Adam II:249; IV:260
Myers, Albertus II:69
Myers, Andrew II:514, 724
Myers, Chloe I:856
Myers, Christopher IV:263
Myers, Conrad II:728
Myers, Conrad (2) II:729
Myers, Cornelius II:69, 495
Myers, Gideon I:872
Myers, Henry IV:87, 105, 286
Myers, Jacob IV:39
Myers, John I:856; II:69, 314, 545; III:445; IV:2, 277
Myers, Lewis II:95
Myers, M. & Co. II:558, 560
Myers, Michaes II:89
Myers, Mordecai II:138
Myers, Moses II:386
Myers, Peter II:694; IV:259
Myers, Philip II:732
Myers, Stephen II:533
Myers, Thomas III:598
Mygatt, Elisha I:56
Mynard, Lemuel II:209
Myngos, Moses IV:169
Myre, John III:62
Myrick, Asel III:358
Myrick, Azel III:358
Myrick, Bezaleel I:926
Myrick, Elizabeth III:358
Myrick, John I:327
Myrick, Joseph I:930; II:399
Myrick, Joshua II:547
Myrick, Mathew III:590
Myrick, Samuel I:918, 1000

Nabois, Nathan III:250
Nacross, John II:293
Nadeau, Basil II:221
Naffee, Garrit II:50
Nagel, Philip II:658
Nagle, Jacob IV:287
Nagle, Peter II:703
Nagle, Philip II:639
Nagle, Richard II:644
Nail, Matthew III:88
Nailor, Isaac III:216
Nailor, Joshua III:381
Nails, John I:34
Nairsmith, Alexander IV:112
Nall, Richard III:592

Nance, Frederick III:328
Nance, James, Sen. III:460
Nance, Sherwood III:516
Nance, William M. III:837
Nance, Zachariah IV:18
Nango, Deergoodfor I:427
Nanny, David II:475
Napier, William P. III:762
Naramore, A. I:861
Naramore, Asa I:939
Naramore, Joel I:861
Naramore, Joshua D. I:861
Narcross, John II:114
Narmil, John H. II:204
Narramore, Joseph I:483
Nash, Bartlett I:427
Nash, Benjamin I:538
Nash, Caleb I:877
Nash, Daniel II:486
Nash, Elisha I:427
Nash, Jacob I:483
Nash, James I:694; II:249
Nash, Job I:548
Nash, Joel I:425
Nash, John I:743; II:363, 420; III:724
Nash, Jonathan I:253, 375; II:507
Nash, Joseph, 2d I:549
Nash, Joseph, 1st I:446
Nash, Luke I:563
Nash, Michael III:397
Nash, Noah I:89
Nash, Samuel I:646
Nash, Silas II:374
Nash, Tho. I:883
Nash, Thomas I:577
Nash, Timothy I:548
Nash, William III:578
Nason, Benjamin I:779
Nason, Edward I:314
Nason, John I:300, 995
Nason, Jonathan I:239
Nason, Nathaniel I:7, 239
Nason, Stephen I:733
Nason, Willoby I:549
Nassall, Benjamin I:652
Natham, Noah III:443
Nathway, Ozias II:286
Naughton, Solomon I:926
Nay, John III:789
Nay, Samuel I:773
Nayle, Christian II:615
Naylor, Robert F. IV:298
Neagus, Benjamin I:375
Neal, Andrew I:877
Neal, Benjamin III:300
Neal, Charles III:245
Neal, Isaac I:605
Neal, James I:363; II:646; III:480, 743
Neal, John I:208; II:330; III:25
Neal, Jonathan I:419
Neal, Joseph I:549, 779; II:581
Neal, Joshua I:733

Neal, Lawrence II:615
Neal, Micajah III:323
Neal, Stephen III:516
Neal, Walter I:314
Neal, William IV:280
Neal, Zephaniah III:634
Neale, Thomas I:269
Nealey, Andrew I:971
Nealey, Joseph I:724
Neall, John III:823
Nealy, Abraham II:118
Nealy, Benjamin I:673
Nealy, John III:155
Nealy, William I:673
Near, Charles II:396
Near, John III:715
Nearing, John II:286
Nearing, Joseph II:486
Nearings, Henry I:111
Nease, George III:440
Nease, Martin III:440
Nebinger, Andrew II:596
Nedson, James I:70
Needar, Toney I:42
Needham, Benjamin I:964
Needham, Daniel I:419, 593
Needham, Francis II:369
Needham, George I:593
Needham, James I:593
Needham, John I:287; II:242
Needham, William A. III:32
Neel, John III:569
Neel, Wm. III:778
Neels, John II:105
Neely, George III:631
Neely, Jacob III:121
Neely, John III:549, 799
Neely, Joseph IV:91
Neely, Nicholas III:73
Neese, George III:419
Neese, Lawrence II:533
Negro, Caesar I:67
Negus, Isaac I:819
Negus, Noles II:545
Neider, Henry II:639
Neil, Charles III:112
Neil, Harriet III:41
Neil, James III:326
Neil, Jeremiah III:41
Neil, Margaret III:41
Neil, Martha III:41
Neil, Robert III:73
Neile, Andrew I:779
Neill, Gilbreath III:425
Neill, Lewis III:291
Neilson, John II:82
Neilson, Joseph II:673
Nelems, John E. III:586
Nell, Jacob II:606
Nellis, John L. II:441
Nellis, Joseph II:441
Nelms, Charles III:753
Nelson, Admiral II:629
Nelson, Alexander III:678
Nelson, Allen II:242
Nelson, Andrew III:89
Nelson, Arthur II:629

Nelson, Benjamin II:406
Nelson, Daniel I:226
Nelson, David I:419
Nelson, Edward III:409
Nelson, Eli II:411
Nelson, Francis II:204
Nelson, George I:144
Nelson, Giles III:443
Nelson, Hanse III:596
Nelson, James III:819
Nelson, James, Sen. III:502
Nelson, Jaratt III:542
Nelson, John II:416, 629;
    III:216, 334-35, 596, 626,
    635; IV:240
Nelson, Joseph III:88
Nelson, Martha II:26
Nelson, Moses I:905; II:456;
    III:258; IV:238
Nelson, Nathan I:287
Nelson, Nathan, Jr. II:97
Nelson, Paul II:541
Nelson, Philip I:766
Nelson, Reuben II:396
Nelson, Robert II:26
Nelson, Roger III:29
Nelson, Samuel II:629; III:440
Nelson, Thomas I:xv; IV:108
Nelson, William I:352; II:605,
    670; III:530, 588
Nemblett, Robert I:400
Nephew, Matthias II:713
Nesbett, John III:577
Nesbit, Robert III:830
Nesbit, Samuel II:615
Nesmith, James I:711, 761
Nessle, Conrad IV:260
Nestel, George II:184
Nestle, Martin II:265
Nestler, John IV:224
Nestor, Frederick III:570
Nestor, Michael II:85
Netherland, Benj., Sen. III:295
Netherton, John III:314
Nethrew, Adam I:590
Netterfield, William IV:289
Nettles, Abraham III:666
Nettles, William III:504
Nettleson, Josiah I:50
Nettleton, Caleb I:128
Nettleton, John I:128
Nettleton, Nathan I:128
Neufas, John II:615
Neufville, Isaac I:xv
Neufville, John I:xv
Nevelle, Jesse III:511
Nevens, Nehemiah II:293
Neves, Daniel III:240
Neves, William IV:254
Nevil, Henry II:673
Nevil, Thomas II:615
Nevill, James III:257
Nevill, Yelverton III:593
Neville, John III:829
Nevins, Andrew II:621
Nevins, David I:70; II:446,
    621

Nevins, Garret II:44
Nevins, George II:621
Nevins, John II:621
Nevins, Martha II:621
Nevins, Mary II:621
Nevins, Thomas II:621
Nevitt, Joseph III:15
Nevius, Peter II:18
New, Christopher II:694
New, Jacob III:282
New, James I:521
New, James L. IV:267
New, John III:847
New, Thomas III:713
New, William III:437, 634,
    783
Newbegin, George I:314
Newberry, Amasa II:456
Newberry, James II:675
Newberry, William IV:232
Newbit, Christopher I:163
Newbury, James III:529
Newbury, Jeremiah II:348
Newbury, Stedman I:137
Newby, Francis III:386
Newby, John III:318
Newby, Levi III:765
Newby, Thomas III:765
Newcomb, Bryant I:548
Newcomb, Charles I:538
Newcomb, Eleazer I:34
Newcomb, Ethan IV:289
Newcomb, Henry Oliver I:593
Newcomb, James I:331
Newcomb, Jeremiah I:331
Newcomb, Kinner II:554
Newcomb, Lemuel I:327, 331
Newcomb, Luther I:926
Newcomb, Oliver I:593
Newcomb, Rem'r I:593
Newcomb, Reuben II:23
Newcomb, Simon III:382
Newcomb, Stillman B. I:593
Newcome, Samuel II:662
Newcomer, Peter IV:87
Newell, Anne I:171
Newell, Barstow I:171
Newell, Benjamin IV:244
Newell, Daniel I:743
Newell, Ebenezer II:236
Newell, James I:419; II:78;
    III:35
Newell, John II:465; IV:219
Newell, Jonathan I:239
Newell, Joseph I:623, 964
Newell, Josiah III:362
Newell, Julia I:171
Newell, Mark I:42
Newell, Nathaniel I:939
Newell, Norman II:265
Newell, Revirius I:900
Newell, Sam. IV:296
Newell, Samuel I:646; III:199
Newell, Samuel, Sen. III:318
Newell, Stephen I:647
Newell, Sullivan III:357
Newell, Theodore I:964

465

Nickle, John III:50
Nicklisson, Israel II:416
Nicknolls, John I:613
Nickol, William III:85
Nickols, Ephraim F. II:108
Nicolle, Simon II:260
Nieves, William III:197
Night, Jacob IV:84
Nightingale, Samuel I:538
Nightingale, Timothy II:727
Niks, David IV:228
Niles, Dan I:989
Niles, Elisha I:56, 119; II:280
Niles, Ephraim I:935
Niles, Gains IV:185
Niles, Jehiel II:330
Niles, Jeremiah I:811
Niles, John I:601
Niles, Nathan I:947
Niles, Nathaniel I:79
Niles, Peter I:785
Niles, Robert III:765
Niles, Samuel I:883
Niles, William I:926
Nimes, Eliakim I:743
Nimley, Henry III:565
Nims, Daniel II:537
Nims, Ebenezer I:446
Ninemaster, Michael II:85
Nipper, George III:708
Nipple, Frederick II:727
Nisbet, Alexander II:711
Nithercut, William IV:39
Nithington, Jeremiah III:55
Nitz, Philip II:753
Nivington, Jeremiah III:55
Nix, George III:454
Nix, James III:168
Nixon, Absalom III:213
Nixon, Isaac III:42
Nixon, John I:854; III:549
Nixon, Joseph I:538
Nixon, Richard II:446
Nixon, Thomas I:521
Nixon, William IV:225
Noble, Aaron I:333
Noble, Anthony I:183
Noble, Elijah I:42
Noble, Enoch II:153
Noble, Goodman II:411
Noble, James I:965; IV:121
Noble, John I:232, 689, 964;
III:111
Noble, Luke II:541
Noble, Mark I:11
Noble, Nathan II:207
Noble, Oliver II:435
Noble, Stephen I:314
Noble, Tahan I:455
Noble, William I:964; III:477
Noble, Wm. II:348
Nobles, Asa II:751
Nobles, Isaac I:807
Nobles, John III:403
Nobles, Jonathan I:503
Nobles, Rozwell I:101
Noblit, Samuel III:514

Nock, Drisco I:773
Nock, Jonathan I:313
Nock, Stephen I:163
Nocke, Sylvanus I:239
Noe, Amos II:74
Noe, James II:50
Noe, John II:316
Noe, Marsh II:74
Noel, Taylor III:281
Noel, Thomas III:280
Nogle, John II:597
Noland, James III:274
Noland, Jesse III:274
Noland, Ledston IV:121
Nolen, Ezekiel III:419
Nolen, Shadrack III:586
Noline, James II:603
Nollner, Jacob III:849
Nolton, H. II:556
Nolton, Hiram II:556
Nolton, Nathan II:324
Nolton, Robert II:416
Noon, Darby II:121
Norcutt, Ephraim I:577
Norcutt, Zenas I:577
Norman, Bazael IV:224
Norman, Benjamin II:74
Norman, John I:239; IV:86
Norman, Lyman B. II:196
Norman, Obadiah II:74
Norman, Stokely III:33
Norman, Thomas III:766
Norman, William III:342, 601
Norris, Abner III:630
Norris, Arnold IV:284
Norris, Benjamin I:753
Norris, Bethnel IV:254
Norris, Daniel W. III:25
Norris, Edward II:114
Norris, Eliphalet II:501
Norris, George II:32
Norris, Henry I:70
Norris, James F. I:163
Norris, John II:212, 369;
III:799; IV:24, 228
Norris, Jonathan I:894
Norris, Luther A. III:25
Norris, Moses I:894
Norris, Nathaniel I:846
Norris, Patrick III:35, 83
Norris, Peter II:82
Norris, Samuel II:293
Norris, Shadrach I:333
Norris, Theophilus I:773
Norris, William III:544; IV:237
Norris, Ziba II:85
Norsworthy, James III:537
North, Abijah III:280
North, Daniel I:623
North, Jacob IV:162
North, John IV:162
North, Levi I:101
North, Sarah IV:162
North, Seth I:50
North, Simeon I:926
North, Thomas III:764
North, William I:157; II:559

North, Zachariah IV:162
Northam, Timothy I:605
Northern, Reuben III:263
Northern, Solomon III:538
Northey, Eliphalet I:733
Northorp, Angelina I:28
Northorp, David T. I:28
Northorp, Gers'm I:28
Northrop, Amos II:705
Northrop, Elisha I:50
Northrop, Gideon II:754
Northrop, Isaac I:62
Northrop, Lemuel I:935
Northrop, Nathaniel I:34
Northrup, Elijah II:242
Northrup, Ichabod I:800
Northrup, Stephen II:431
Northrup, Thomas II:456
Northrup, William II:324
Northum, John I:144
Northum, Samuel II:425
Northup, Asa II:541
Northup, David II:399
Northup, Henry I:811, 834;
III:336
Northup, John I:834
Northup, Joseph II:486
Northup, Nicholas I:834
Northup, Stephen I:811
Northup, Stukely I:811
Northup, Sylvester I:811
Northup, William I:834
Northup, Zebulon I:834
Northway, George I:939
Northway, Zenas II:465
Norton, Abel II:379
Norton, Abraham I:999
Norton, Alexander III:569
Norton, Amos I:419
Norton, Asahel II:293
Norton, Benjamin II:249, 556
Norton, Christopher II:465
Norton, David I:144
Norton, Elihu, 1st I:167
Norton, Elijah I:277, 919;
II:541
Norton, Elisha I:854
Norton, Elnathan I:23
Norton, Elon II:286
Norton, Freeman II:286
Norton, George II:271; III:546
Norton, Giles II:427
Norton, Hugh II:189
Norton, Isham, Sen. III:446
Norton, Jabez I:42
Norton, James II:664; III:297;
IV:3
Norton, Jared II:705
Norton, Jedediah I:23
Norton, John I:647; II:56;
IV:157
Norton, Jonathan II:541
Norton, Joseph I:196, 952;
II:541
Norton, Josiah I:229
Norton, Levi I:42
Norton, Martin I:931

467

468

Palmer, Nathan II:308
Palmer, Nathaniel I:209, 278, 811
Palmer, Nehemiah II:380
Palmer, Noah II:545
Palmer, Osias II:457
Palmer, Param I:80
Palmer, Philip II:42
Palmer, Reuben I:111
Palmer, Richard I:161
Palmer, Samuel I:57, 137
Palmer, Samuel, 2d II:204
Palmer, Samuel, 1st II:140
Palmer, Simeon I:197
Palmer, Smith I:35
Palmer, Solomon II:393
Palmer, Stephen I:137; II:363
Palmer, Thomas I:43; II:319, 431; III:574
Palmer, Thos. II:563
Palmer, Timothy I:402
Palmer, W. R. I:xii
Palmer, Walter I:1000
Palmer, William III:444; IV:30
Palmer, Wyatt II:406
Palmes, Andrew II:294
Palmeteer, John II:158
Palmeter, Phineas II:374
Palmeton, Benjamin I:901
Palmeton, John II:324
Palmetter, Jesse II:260
Palmiter, John IV:242
Palmiter, Jonathan II:360
Palmiter, Joseph II:487
Palmiter, William II:294
Palmitor, Joshua IV:242
Palmore, David III:35
Pamphilion, Thomas III:47
Pamphlin, William III:599
Pampilly, Bennet I:218
Pander, Thomas III:503
Pangborn, David II:190
Pangborn, David (2) II:190
Pangborn, Elijah II:190
Pangborn, Jason II:190
Pangborn, Joseph II:37
Pangborn, Miron II:190
Pangburn, Adonijah I:50
Pangburn, John II:204
Pangburn, Richard II:525
Pangburn, Samuel II:236
Pangburn, William IV:107
Pannel, John III:527
Pano, Lawrence I:843
Pano, Loran I:843
Panter, Edom III:625
Papple, George I:795
Parcels, Paul IV:105
Parcher, George I:197
Parcher, Henry I:773
Parchment, Peter II:633; III:666
Pardea, Nathaniel II:249
Pardee, Aaron I:656
Pardee, Abijah I:128
Pardee, Charles II:466
Pardee, Daniel I:102

Pardee, Eli I:102
Pardee, Joseph I:128
Pardee, Lemuel II:352
Pardee, Silas II:471
Pardee, Thomas II:457
Pardie, Chandler I:13
Pardoe, Joseph II:56
Pardy, Samuel II:490
Parent, William II:78
Parham, Drury III:514
Parham, Thomas III:303, 421
Paris, Robert III:323
Parish, Ephraim I:484
Parish, Frederick III:768
Parish, Humphrey III:451
Parish, John II:541; III:757
Parish, Moses III:719
Parish, Silas II:153
Parish, Stephen III:431
Parish, William III:233
Park, Ebenezer I:150
Park, Jacob I:340
Park, Jonas II:229
Park, Joshua I:505
Park, Matthias I:352
Park, Thomas I:625
Park, William I:625, 931
Parkard, James I:217
Parke, Daniel II:457
Parke, Jacob I:785
Parke, John I:286; IV:232
Parke, Thomas II:573
Parke, Zebulon II:759
Parker, Aaron I:254, 522, 798, 957
Parker, Abel I:945
Parker, Abraham I:446; III:266, 606
Parker, Alexander III:738
Parker, Amasa II:338
Parker, Amos II:281
Parker, Asa I:144
Parker, Asaph III:121
Parker, Barnabas I:197
Parker, Benjamin I:269, 493, 521; II:208; III:286
Parker, Benjamin W. I:711
Parker, Charles I:931; III:25
Parker, Dan I:702; II:369
Parker, Daniel I:209, 401, 767; II:67
Parker, David I:521-22, 965
Parker, E. I:789
Parker, Ebenezer I:226, 522, 980
Parker, Edmund I:63, 297
Parker, Edward I:431; III:258
Parker, Eldridge I:137
Parker, Elijah I:712; III:813
Parker, Elisha I:712
Parker, Ephraim I:965
Parker, Ezra II:457
Parker, Farewell I:593
Parker, Francis I:815
Parker, Freegrove I:260
Parker, George I:383, 492, 625; II:88, 615

Parker, Humphrey III:429
Parker, Imla I:505
Parker, Isaac I:327, 659
Parker, Isaiah I:383
Parker, J. C. II:565
Parker, Jacob I:538
Parker, James I:990; II:348, 457; III:785
Parker, Jane C. I:28
Parker, Jesse III:767
Parker, Jesse, 2d I:455
Parker, Jesse, 1st I:624
Parker, John I:57, 161, 724, 931; II:208; III:276, 402; IV:12, 27, 192
Parker, Jonathan I:711, 801; IV:167
Parker, Jonathan, 2d I:694
Parker, Joseph II:78, 253, 271, 679; III:694
Parker, Joseph U. II:253
Parker, Joshua I:504
Parker, Josiah I:297, 300
Parker, Kedar III:438
Parker, Kider III:420
Parker, Levi I:128, 711
Parker, Marion I:593
Parker, Martin I:178
Parker, Mary L. I:28
Parker, Matilda I:494
Parker, Moses I:494
Parker, Nahum I:743
Parker, Nathan II:448
Parker, Nehemiah I:648
Parker, Noah I:494
Parker, Peter I:900; II:421; III:619
Parker, Philemon I:694, 919
Parker, Phineas II:519
Parker, Reuben II:541
Parker, Richard J. II:348, 565
Parker, Robert I:624, 972; IV:107
Parker, Rufus I:848
Parker, Sally I:593
Parker, Samuel I:28, 593, 702, 965, 979; II:406; IV:228
Parker, Sarah Ann I:798
Parker, Silas I:421, 919
Parker, Simon I:521
Parker, Solomon I:753
Parker, Stephen I:128, 624, 868
Parker, Stiles IV:202
Parker, Thaddeus II:246
Parker, Thomas I:493, 827, 891, 995; II:172; III:294, 586, 687
Parker, Thos. I:593
Parker, Timothy III:615
Parker, William I:167, 297, 522, 743, 761, 795; II:110, 227; III:74, 408
Parker, William, 2d I:402; II:307
Parker, William, 3d I:504

Patch, Joseph I:420
Patch, Reuben I:711
Patch, William I:89
Patchen, Azor II:303
Patchen, Daniel II:486
Patchen, Samuel II:537
Patchin, Ebenezer II:338
Patchin, Elijah I:35
Patchin, Isaac II:515
Patchin, Jacob I:35
Patchin, Walter II:519
Patee, Edmund IV:180
Patee, Eliphalet I:965
Patee, James P. I:753
Patee, William IV:109
Pater, Robert III:208
Paterson, Matson IV:286
Patrick, Ebenezer II:507
Patrick, Edward F. IV:16
Patrick, Jacob II:545
Patrick, James II:212; III:277
Patrick, John I:919
Patrick, Joshua II:586, 732
Patrick, Reuben II:140, 406
Patrick, Robert IV:63
Patrick, William III:750
Patridge, Ozias II:431
Patridge, Timothy I:648
Pattee, Asa I:684
Pattee, Dummer I:684
Pattee, Elba I:684
Pattee, John I:684
Pattee, Moses I:733
Pattee, Polly I:684
Pattee, William I:773
Patten, David I:724
Patten, Edward II:271
Patten, James I:321; III:285
Patten, Jonathan I:761
Patten, Joseph III:608
Patten, Nathaniel I:221
Patten, Thomas II:78; IV:11
Pattengell, Jacob II:275
Pattengill, Joseph I:401
Patterson, Adam I:189
Patterson, Alex., Sen. III:496
Patterson, Alexander I:302;
  II:674; IV:143
Patterson, Ansel I:883
Patterson, Arthur II:615
Patterson, David IV:164
Patterson, Ebenezer II:399
Patterson, Hezekiah II:225
Patterson, Isaac I:711
Patterson, Jacob II:525
Patterson, James II:324, 761;
  III:453
Patterson, John III:245, 346;
  IV:2, 164, 234
Patterson, John, 1st II:140
Patterson, John, 2d II:140,
  351
Patterson, Jonathan II:253,
  271
Patterson, Joseph I:613, 670,
  990, 999
Patterson, Luther H. I:336

Patterson, Mark I:336
Patterson, Mark O. I:336
Patterson, Mary S. IV:164
Patterson, Matthew IV:132
Patterson, Michael II:229
Patterson, Poindexter III:761
Patterson, Reuben II:84;
  IV:285
Patterson, Robert I:23; III:159;
  IV:147
Patterson, Samuel I:905;
  II:570
Patterson, Sherman II:457
Patterson, Thomas I:357;
  II:525, 759; III:440
Patterson, Tilman III:374
Patterson, William I:278, 340;
  II:100; III:229, 608; IV:247
Patteson, Thomas III:576
Pattilo, William III:300
Pattin, Benjamin I:226
Pattin, John I:221
Pattison, David I:900
Pattison, Robert III:582
Pattison, Sunderland II:350
Pattison, William II:541
Patton, Alexander III:694
Patton, Isaac I:521
Patton, Jacob III:607; IV:123
Patton, James II:18
Patton, John II:642; III:567,
  789
Patton, Matthew III:268, 516
Patton, Samuel III:286, 404
Patton, William I:144; II:727;
  III:260
Patts, David I:504
Patty, John I:563
Paugh, Young III:604
Paul, Benjamin I:364
Paul, David I:209
Paul, Ebenezer I:375
Paul, Frederick I:597
Paul, George III:262
Paul, Hugh II:345
Paul, James I:433; II:249, 556
Paul, John I:613
Paul, Kiles I:919, 990
Paul, Sarah II:556
Paul, William I:80
Paulding, John II:548
Paulding, Peter II:548
Paulent, Amable II:554
Paulent, Amiable II:221
Paulin, Nathan I:297
Paull, Benjamin I:375
Paull, James II:721
Paull, Samuel I:375
Paulling, William III:510
Paulmore, J. IV:300
Paulshamus, Abraham II:734
Pawlett, Richard III:186
Pawley, William IV:61
Pawling, Albert II:495
Pawling, Henry II:265, 563
Pawns, James III:623
Paxton, Joseph III:190

Paxton, Samuel III:831
Paxton, William III:831
Payne, Augustine III:771
Payne, Benjamin I:521
Payne, Charles III:626
Payne, D. McC. III:334
Payne, Elisha II:140
Payne, George III:704
Payne, Isaac II:521
Payne, John I:315, 408;
  II:316; III:623, 738
Payne, John, Jr. III:193
Payne, Joseph I:869; III:679
Payne, Ledford III:320
Payne, Nehemiah III:165
Payne, Noah II:541
Payne, Rufus I:50
Payne, Samuel L. II:577
Payne, Solomon IV:280
Payne, Stephen I:885
Payne, Thomas III:404
Payne, William I:226; II:386;
  III:771
Paynton, William II:78
Payson, Asa I:549
Payson, Ephraim I:229
Payson, George I:549
Payson, Samuel I:209
Payton, Henry III:759
Payton, Lewis IV:74
Payton, Yelverton III:303
Peabody, Amos I:402
Peabody, Andrew I:957
Peabody, Charles I:167
Peabody, Ebenezer I:605
Peabody, Francis I:401
Peabody, John I:420, 647
Peabody, Jonathan I:420
Peabody, Joseph I:613
Peabody, Keziah I:684
Peabody, Mary Jane I:684
Peabody, Moses I:684, 990
Peabody, Phineas I:357
Peabody, Phinehas I:364
Peabody, Samuel I:401
Peabody, Seth I:197
Peabody, Stephen G. IV:31
Peabody, Thomas I:505, 711
Peace, John III:146, 490
Peach, John I:421
Peachy, Benjamin IV:35
Peacock, Isam III:180
Peacock, James II:507
Peacock, Neal IV:192
Peacock, Richard III:837
Peacock, Uriah III:184
Peagan, Joseph I:624
Peak, Jesse III:231
Peak, Nathan IV:55
Peak, Rich'd III:764
Peake, John III:300
Peake, Thomas I:597
Peake, William III:291, 660
Peale, James II:679
Pea_ley, David II:206
Peallar, Jacob II:265
Peallar, Joseph II:265

474

Pelton, Stephen II:495
Pelton, Thomas I:455
Pelts, James I:737
Pemberton, Christian II:679
Pemberton, John II:5; III:298
Pemberton, John B. III:849
Pemberton, Thomas III:849
Pembleton, Jabez II:486
Pembleton, Jebez II:160
Pembor, Eli IV:268
Pembroke, David II:153, 471
Pembrook, David II:271
Pence, John, Sen. III:833
Pendegrast, Edward IV:87
Pendel, Thomas III:6
Pendell, Jonathan II:545
Pendelton, Philip C. III:848
Pender, John I:34
Pender, Thomas III:241
Pendergrass, Job III:364
Pendergrass, John, Sen. III:367
Pendergrass, Michael I:586
Pendergrass, Thomas II:23
Penderick, William I:613
Pendleton, Benjamin III:327
Pendleton, David I:4
Pendleton, Hiram III:429
Pendleton, Micajah III:814
Pendleton, Stephen II:260
Pendock, Rufus I:801
Pendock, Samuel IV:41
Penefill, Thomas III:54
Penfield, Isaac II:411
Penfield, James I:90
Penfield, Jesse II:281
Penfield, Nathaniel I:102
Penfield, Phineas I:102
Penfield, Samuel II:374
Penfield, Simeon I:119
Pengree, Stephen I:287
Penhallow, Benj. I:790
Penhallow, Nathan II:101
Penigo, Frederick II:382
Peniose, Reuben III:397
Penley, Joseph I:254
Penn, Benjamin III:228
Penn, Joseph II:541
Penn, Stephen III:85
Pennel, Reuben III:397
Pennell, Clement I:183
Pennell, Joseph I:254
Pennell, Robert I:940
Pennetent, John IV:55
Penney, Henry IV:272
Penney, John I:197
Penney, Salathiel I:197
Penniman, Ebenezer I:538
Penninger, Martin III:370
Pennington, James III:294
Pennington, John II:86
Pennington, Kinchen III:434
Pennington, William IV:114
Pennock, Human I:753
Pennoyer, William I:4
Penns, Peter I:807
Pennsinger, Henry II:658

Penny, Benjamin I:314
Penny, John I:168; III:255
Penny, Joshua II:140
Penny, Peletiah I:733
Pennyman, Adna I:733
Pennyman, James I:538
Penticost, William III:130
Pentiscoste, William III:666
Pentland, John II:569
Pentland, Thomas II:310
Penton, James II:23
Penton, William III:628
Penwell, Aaron II:615
Peonix, Overton III:454
Peppen, Richard III:417
Pepper, John I:965
Pepper, William III:789
Perady, Emanuel II:204
Peran, Henry II:29
Percil, John II:756
Percival, John II:380
Perdue, Edward IV:3
Perham, Ezekiel I:911
Perham, Joel W. I:883
Perham, Joseph I:919
Perham, Oliver I:761
Peril, John IV:258
Perin, Daniel II:293
Perin, Edward II:293
Perine, John, Jr. II:91
Perine, William II:557
Perkens, Isaac III:366
Perkings, James III:212
Perkins, Aaron II:668
Perkins, Abiezer II:260
Perkins, Abner I:278, 891;
   II:360
Perkins, Abraham I:71, 402
Perkins, Amos II:308
Perkins, Anthony III:303
Perkins, Archelaus III:849
Perkins, Benjamin I:779
Perkins, Christian III:193
Perkins, Daniel I:556, 883,
   953
Perkins, Daniel, 2d I:883
Perkins, Daniel S. I:862
Perkins, David IV:242
Perkins, Ebenezer I:70, 166,
   563, 712
Perkins, Edmund I:767
Perkins, Eliab II:225
Perkins, Elias I:128; III:781
Perkins, Enoch I:258
Perkins, Ezekiel III:802
Perkins, Francis I:901
Perkins, Gaines P. I:862
Perkins, George I:685
Perkins, Hannah I:862
Perkins, Hector III:25
Perkins, Henry I:375
Perkins, Isaac I:402, 577
Perkins, Israel I:753
Perkins, James I:209, 597,
   685
Perkins, Jason II:256
Perkins, Jesse I:9, 711

Perkins, Joel I:990
Perkins, John I:862, 990;
   III:580
Perkins, John, 2d I:401
Perkins, John, Jr. I:862
Perkins, John, 1st I:421
Perkins, Jonathan I:578, 702
Perkins, Joseph I:287, 712,
   995
Perkins, Joshua I:446
Perkins, Leonard II:406
Perkins, Lucy S. I:862
Perkins, Lyman I:27
Perkins, Mary I:685
Perkins, Mary Ann I:27
Perkins, Mila I:862
Perkins, Moses I:785; III:626
Perkins, Nancy S. I:556
Perkins, Nathaniel I:315, 402,
   935; II:360
Perkins, Nimrod III:745
Perkins, Obadiah I:23
Perkins, Pelatiah I:314
Perkins, Rachel I:27
Perkins, Reuben II:431
Perkins, Richard I:689
Perkins, Rizpah I:27
Perkins, Russell Lyman I:27
Perkins, Samuel II:363; III:303
Perkins, Solomon I:23
Perkins, Theodore III:113
Perkins, Thomas I:xiv, 712;
   III:509; IV:266
Perkins, Timothy I:433
Perkins, Timothy E. I:862
Perkins, William I:240, 455,
   995; III:422, 635
Perkins, Zilpha I:862
Perkinson, James III:691
Per Lee, Abraham II:108
Perley, Daniel I:254
Perley, Eliphalet I:625
Perley, Henry I:401
Perley, Stephen I:420
Perre, Joshua III:631
Perrigin, Holliston III:563
Perrigo, David I:883
Perrigo, Joseph II:541
Perrigo, Justice J. IV:2
Perrigo, Rufus I:945
Perrigo, William II:345
Perrin, Jesse II:294
Perrin, John I:827
Perrin, Nathan III:621
Perrine, James II:78
Perrine, James D. II:86
Perrine, Peter II:756
Perrine, William IV:230
Perrini, William II:736
Perrit, Needham III:492
Perry, Abel I:522
Perry, Abijah IV:219
Perry, Abner I:919, 979
Perry, Abraham II:225; III:80
Perry, Almon II:324
Perry, Arthur II:479
Perry, Benjamin III:291

477

Phelps, Oliver I:102, 935; II:380
Phelps, Putnam I:883
Phelps, Roger I:144
Phelps, Samuel I:70, 218, 631, 879; II:431
Phelps, Silas II:471
Phelps, Timothy I:102
Phelteplace, John II:537
Phielding, Wm. D. III:650
Phifer, Martin III:410
Philbrick, Danel I:767
Philbrick, Daniel I:890
Philbrick, David I:686
Philbrick, Eliphalet I:673
Philbrick, Lyman I:673
Philbrick, Nathaniel I:166
Philbrick, Samuel I:686, 779
Philbrook, Abigail H. I:175
Philbrook, Almari I:175
Philbrook, David I:197
Philbrook, Elisha I:175
Philbrook, Joel IV:199
Philbrook, Jonathan I:733
Philbrook, Jon'n I:175
Philbrook, Lucy H. I:175
Philbrook, Phoebe I:175
Philbrook, Samuel I:747
Philbrook, Thomas I:827
Philbrook, William I:300
Philbrooks, William I:189
Phile, George II:650
Phile, Philip II:615
Philip, Hugh III:510
Philips, Aaron II:218
Philips, Abraham II:441
Philips, Adam II:457
Philips, Amos I:945
Philips, Bennett III:615
Philips, Clemmon III:608
Philips, David III:593
Philips, Elisha I:953
Philips, Evan II:95
Philips, George III:307
Philips, Isaac III:62
Philips, James II:184
Philips, Jeruel I:50
Philips, Job I:150
Philips, John III:11, 268, 421, 686, 703
Philips, John, 2d II:140
Philips, Jonathan I:625
Philips, Joseph III:573
Philips, Joshua I:631
Philips, Levi III:488
Philips, Matthias III:673
Philips, Michael I:71
Philips, Mitchel III:367
Philips, Nehemiah I:875
Philips, Newton III:740
Philips, Norton I:314
Philips, Philip II:184; III:14
Philips, Philo I:807
Philips, Samuel H. I:90
Philips, Thomas II:15; IV:29
Philips, William III:688
Phillips, Abiezer II:421

Phillips, Adeline I:863
Phillips, Andrew III:92
Phillips, Asa I:364
Phillips, Barzilla I:901
Phillips, Benjamin I:331
Phillips, Caroline I:863
Phillips, Charles II:253
Phillips, Daniel II:294
Phillips, David II:56
Phillips, Ebenezer I:647; II:253
Phillips, Ebenezer H. I:647
Phillips, Eli II:498
Phillips, Elkanah I:753
Phillips, Elvira I:682
Phillips, Esquire II:754
Phillips, Geo. W. I:682
Phillips, George III:636
Phillips, Gideon I:111, 743
Phillips, G.W.A. I:682
Phillips, Henry W. II:386
Phillips, Ichabod I:197
Phillips, Irby III:449
Phillips, Isaac II:721
Phillips, Israel I:965
Phillips, Jacob I:375; II:441; III:236
Phillips, James I:901; II:380
Phillips, James, 2d I:811
Phillips, James, 1st I:811
Phillips, Jarius I:197
Phillips, Jedediah I:549
Phillips, Job IV:229
Phillips, John I:75, 293, 563, 743, 807, 901, 979; II:42, 382, 732; II:271, 550; IV:173
Phillips, John, 2d I:364
Phillips, John, 3d II:281
Phillips, Joshua I:863, 920; II:299
Phillips, Levi III:158
Phillips, Luke I:827
Phillips, Maria I:682
Phillips, Mark III:382
Phillips, Mary I:863
Phillips, Nathan II:334
Phillips, Nathaniel I:743, 799, 837
Phillips, Nehemiah I:997
Phillips, Oliver I:979
Phillips, Pelatiah I:900
Phillips, Philip IV:202
Phillips, Richard I:743
Phillips, Roby I:837
Phillips, Samuel II:351; IV:202
Phillips, Seth I:353
Phillips, Silas I:364
Phillips, Solomon I:869
Phillips, Spencer II:212
Phillips, Sylvester II:380
Phillips, Thomas I:23; II:431, 495; III:656
Phillips, Timothy I:421
Phillips, Turner I:521
Phillips, William I:80, 815; III:776

Phillips, Zachariah III:215
Phillpott, Charles III:792
Philo, Azor II:732
Philpot, John I:779
Philpot, Warren III:100
Phinney, Ithamar I:287
Phinney, Jno. I:869
Phinney, John I:240
Phinney, Joseph I:80, 184
Phinney, Zenas I:647
Phipney, Nehemiah II:369
Phipps, Benjamin III:780
Phipps, Daniel Goffee I:128
Phipps, Jason I:150
Phipps, Jedediah I:601
Phipps, John I:504; III:293
Phipps, Joshua III:223
Phipps, Samuel II:208
Phoenix, Matthew III:13
Piatt, John D. II:59
Piatt, William III:7
Pickard, Adolph II:160, 421
Pickard, Jacob I:421
Pickell, Matthias II:83
Pickens, Andrew III:578
Pickens, Benjamin II:537
Pickens, John I:563; IV:270
Pickens, William III:606
Pickerill, Samuel IV:232
Pickering, Benjamin I:648
Pickering, David I:625
Pickering, Winthrop I:733
Picket, John I:401
Picket, Thomas I:23
Pickett, Henry III:292
Pickett, John IV:228
Pickett, Phineas I:102
Pickett, Robert II:23
Pickett, Samuel I:446
Pickett, William I:254
Pickford, Daniel III:254
Pickham, Daniel I:819
Pickins, Alexander I:785
Picksley, Elij. IV:216
Pidgeon, John III:25
Piegon, John II:141
Pier, Abner II:184
Pier, John Earnest II:265
Pier, Solomon II:333
Pierce, Abel I:505
Pierce, Amos I:647; II:541
Pierce, Augustus II:333
Pierce, Benjamin I:314, 789, 919, 980; II:393, 495
Pierce, Charles IV:34
Pierce, Daniel I:74, 801
Pierce, David I:226
Pierce, Ebenezer II:330
Pierce, Edward I:792
Pierce, Eli II:227
Pierce, Eliab II:416
Pierce, Ephraim II:421
Pierce, Ezekiel I:911; II:457
Pierce, Francis III:272
Pierce, Hugh IV:230
Pierce, Ichabod I:819
Pierce, Israel III:403

479

Place, Simeon I:827
Place, Stephen I:29
Plaisted, John I:253-54
Plakard, Christian IV:240
Plank, Asa I:80
Plank, Isiah I:80
Plank, John I:80
Plant, Ethel II:229
Plant, William III:716
Plantt, William, Sen. III:487
Plass, Peter II:225
Plato, Thomas II:221
Platt, Daniel I:965
Platt, Ebenezer I:89-90
Platt, Gideon I:128
Platt, Isaac I:34
Platt, James I:353
Platt, John I:50
Platt, Joseph I:90
Platt, Richard II:559
Platt, Samuel I:50
Platt, Sarah II:559
Platt, Truman I:927
Platt, William II:149, 457
Platts, Dan I:57
Platts, James I:773
Pleasant, William III:408
Pleasants, Arch. III:779
Pleasants, B. F. I:xiii
Pleasants, Robert III:779
Pledger, John III:816
Plemline, Charles II:597
Plimly, Hendrick II:343
Plimpton, Oliver I:625
Ploss, Michael II:534
Plotts, George II:748
Plough, Jacob IV:34
Plugh, Henry II:514
Plum, John II:706
Plumb, Elish II:175
Plumb, George I:119
Plumb, Isaac II:501
Plumb, Jared II:265
Plumb, Joseph I:119
Plumb, Nathaniel II:253
Plumb, Stephen II:184
Plumb, William I:57
Plumbe, Daniel I:70
Plumbe, William I:156
Plumbley, Levi I:840
Plumer, Stephen I:773
Plumer, William IV:292
Plumer, William, Jr. I:xiv
Plumley, Benjamin I:869
Plumley, Ebenezer II:369
Plumley, George II:621
Plumley, John II:621
Plumley, Jonathan I:869
Plumley, Nathan II:621
Plumley, Samuel I:953; II:621
Plummer, Daniel I:184
Plummer, Edward I:197
Plummer, Elisha II:724
Plummer, Geo. I:155
Plummer, Isaac I:167, 184
Plummer, John I:218, 229
Plummer, Joseph II:120

Plummer, Nathan I:724
Plummer, Richard III:405
Plummer, Simeon II:374
Plummer, Thomas I:421, 724
Plummer, William I:183
Plunk, Jacob III:429
Plunket, Reuben III:643
Plunket, Thomas III:734
Plunkett, Reuben III:192
Plutt, Frederick I:24
Plyley, Caspar IV:299
Plympton, Ebenezer I:522
Poak, James S. II:753
Poe, Adam IV:269
Poe, Benjamin III:254
Poe, David III:367
Poe, John IV:214
Poe, Virgil III:219
Poge, William III:755
Poindexter, David III:453
Poindexter, Thomas I:169
Pointdexter, Chapman III:583
Pointer, Elizabeth III:471
Pointer, Fleming III:471
Pointer, Jackson III:471
Pointer, John III:471
Pointer, Katy III:471
Pointer, Leanna III:471
Pointer, Levin II:5
Pointer, Lucinda III:471
Pointer, Melinda III:471
Pointer, Polly III:471
Pointer, Thomas III:471
Poke, Geo. II:328
Poland, Abner I:402, 702, 789
Poland, Asa I:905
Poland, John II:47
Poland, Moses I:217
Poland, Sarah I:789
Poland, Seward I:209
Poland, William I:648
Polen, William IV:67
Poleresky, John I:209
Polhelmus, Cornelius II:369
Polhemus, John II:679
Polhemus, Joseph III:37
Polk, J. K. III:635-36
Polk, Job II:9
Polk, William III:460
Pollard, Absalom III:335
Pollard, Andrew II:5
Pollard, Barton I:197
Pollard, Braxton III:316
Pollard, Chatlen III:775
Pollard, Edmund III:288
Pollard, Edward I:875
Pollard, Jacob III:409
Pollard, James III:227; IV:90
Pollard, John I:504; II:569
Pollard, John, 2d I:340
Pollard, Jonathan I:184; II:123
Pollard, Joseph III:796
Pollard, Robert III:791, 815
Pollard, Samuel II:658
Pollard, Seth I:872
Pollard, Solomon, Jr. I:613
Pollard, Timothy I:226

Pollard, Walter I:990
Pollard, William III:255, 514
Poller, John III:307
Pollet, John III:252
Polley, Daniel IV:185
Polley, John II:486
Polley, Samuel II:550
Pollock, David II:718
Pollock, Elias II:679
Pollock, Elijah IV:194
Pollock, Geo. II:328
Pollock, James II:140
Pollock, John II:597; IV:88
Polly, Edward III:242
Polly, John II:165, 501; III:320
Polly, Jonathan II:541
Polly, Joseph I:34
Pomeray, Phineas II:208
Pomeroy, Daniel II:328
Pomeroy, Ebenezer I:484
Pomeroy, Gad I:484
Pomeroy, Ira II:466
Pomeroy, Jacob I:484
Pomeroy, Luther I:469
Pomeroy, Pliney I:854
Pomeroy, T. S. I:655; II:559
Pomery, Daniel IV:250
Pomery, Ichabod IV:250
Pompilley, Bennet I:288
Pomroy, Gaius I:474
Pomroy, Luther I:474
Pomroy, Medad II:718
Pomroy, Ralph I:43
Pomroy, Simeon I:484, 990
Pond, Abijah I:550
Pond, Barnabas II:457
Pond, Benjamin I:522
Pond, Beriah II:281
Pond, Dan I:927
Pond, Elias I:63
Pond, Elihu I:549
Pond, Ezekiel I:945
Pond, Ezra II:401
Pond, Jabez I:549
Pond, John H. III:836
Pond, Josiah I:926
Pond, Oliver I:538
Pond, Pallu I:549
Pond, Paul I:869
Pond, Phineas II:218, 553
Pond, Zebulon I:900
Pool, Anna I:683
Pool, Charles I:493
Pool, Chester IV:238
Pool, Eleanor I:683
Pool, Ephraim III:601
Pool, Garrit J. II:191
Pool, George II:191
Pool, George W. III:104
Pool, Henry II:191
Pool, Jacob I:578; II:605
Pool, James, Sen. III:506
Pool, Jepthali II:431
Pool, Job I:184
Pool, John II:83, 191, 357; III:91, 214, 440

Pool, Joshua I:288
Pool, Lana Maria II:191
Pool, Leonard I:493
Pool, Luke I:493
Pool, Peter II:191, 689
Pool, Samuel I:63, 269;
III:182
Pool, Susan I:493
Pool, Thomas I:70, 184, 683
Poole, Abijah I:197
Poole, David I:16
Poole, John I:694
Pooler, George II:479
Pooler, Isaac I:807
Pooler, John I:xv
Poor, Benjamin I:421
Poor, Daniel I:753
Poor, George I:761
Poor, John III:722
Poor, Jonathan I:34
Poor, Samuel I:767
Poor, Thomas III:779
Poor, Timothy I:421
Poor, William II:664
Poore, Thomas III:547
Poorman, Christian II:577
Pope, Adam II:761
Pope, Christopher II:545
Pope, Elisha III:460
Pope, Elnathan I:578
Pope, Ezra IV:283
Pope, Isaac I:239
Pope, James III:37
Pope, Jeremiah III:455
Pope, John I:401, 549; II:299;
III:52
Pope, Le Roy I:xvi
Pope, Richard III:407
Pope, Samuel II:86; IV:90
Pope, Seth I:578
Pope, Simeon I:894
Pope, Thomas I:364; III:490,
737
Pope, William III:119
Popham, Benjamin III:61
Popham, William II:566
Popkin, Benjamin I:455
Poplin, George III:400
Poplin, William III:434
Poppino, Daniel II:475
Poppino, William II:475
Poppleston, Samuel IV:283
Popst, Christian II:664
Porch Henry III:330
Porrage, Jabez I:74
Porter, Aaron I:401
Porter, Abel II:457
Porter, Abijah I:102
Porter, Alexander II:242
Porter, Amos II:250
Porter, Asa I:743; II:293
Porter, Benjamin I:433; II:406
Porter, Benjamin J. I:209
Porter, Benj'n Jones I:321
Porter, Charles III:397, 625
Porter, Charles T. I:xv
Porter, Daniel I:42

Porter, David II:411; IV:36
Porter, Edward I:446
Porter, Eldad II:271
Porter, Eleazer II:260
Porter, Eli IV:176
Porter, Elijah I:102, 459
Porter, Eliphalet II:281
Porter, Emeline I:26
Porter, Ephraim III:325
Porter, Ezekiel II:271, 380
Porter, Ezra I:26, 57
Porter, Ezra C. I:26
Porter, F. D. III:334
Porter, Frederick I:197
Porter, George I:980
Porter, Hancock III:516
Porter, Hiram IV:133
Porter, Hugh IV:188
Porter, Ira G. I:4
Porter, Ira Jones I:26
Porter, Isaac I:102
Porter, James I:761; III:72,
558
Porter, Joel I:663
Porter, John I:521, 538, 753;
II:348, 386; III:263, 277,
668, 716
Porter, Jonathan I:421
Porter, Joseph I:62, 433;
II:243, 597
Porter, Joshua B. I:26
Porter, Martin II:457
Porter, Mary Ann III:668
Porter, Mitchell III:616
Porter, Moses I:197, 408;
II:293
Porter, Nancy III:668
Porter, Nathan III:67
Porter, Nathaniel I:747; II:328
Porter, Nehemiah I:254
Porter, Oliver III:163
Porter, Philo II:153
Porter, Polly I:26
Porter, Richard B. IV:97
Porter, Robert I:549; IV:252,
257
Porter, Samuel I:102; II:380;
III:496
Porter, Silas I:484
Porter, Simeon II:399
Porter, Stephen II:541
Porter, Thomas III:802; IV:25,
92
Porter, Tho's III:334
Porter, Truman I:128
Porter, Tyler I:254
Porter, William I:578, 753,
905; III:211, 334, 668
Porter, William, 2d II:265
Porter, William, 1st II:246
Porter, William M. III:725
Porterfield, John I:254
Porterfield, Richard III:545
Porterfield, Robert III:847;
IV:180
Portman, John II:633
Portwood, Page III:565

Posey, Benjamin III:11
Posey, Harrison III:523
Posey, Thomas I:xvi
Posey, Zephaniah IV:191
Poss, Nicholas II:281
Post, Abraham II:69
Post, Anthony II:560
Post, Betsey Ann II:196
Post, Caleb IV:13
Post, Christopher II:196
Post, Cornelius H. II:59
Post, David IV:283
Post, Ebenezer IV:44
Post, Elias I:965
Post, Ezra II:411
Post, Gideon II:668
Post, Hendricus II:534
Post, Henry II:44
Post, Henry, 2d II:52
Post, Jacob I:927
Post, Jedediah II:88
Post, Jimmy I:119
Post, John C. II:59
Post, John H. II:65
Post, John P. II:59
Post, Martin II:534
Post, Samuel II:534
Post, Simeon I:965
Post, Stephen I:137
Post, William II:53, 196
Pottage, Jabez I:74
Potter, Aaron I:111, 877
Potter, Abel II:421
Potter, Abijah I:689
Potter, Amos II:65
Potter, Benjamin I:50, 155
Potter, Borden II:457
Potter, Caleb I:965; II:466
Potter, Casper IV:282
Potter, Cyrus II:416
Potter, Daniel I:965; II:307
Potter, David I:128; II:208,
416
Potter, Ebenezer I:743
Potter, Edmund I:613
Potter, Edward I:102
Potter, Elisha II:495
Potter, Ephraim I:504; II:253
Potter, Ezra I:57
Potter, George I:815
Potter, Gideon II:507
Potter, Holliman I:807
Potter, Hugh I:197
Potter, Jacob II:65
Potter, James I:209, 353, 624;
III:574
Potter, Jeremiah II:487
Potter, Joel I:50
Potter, John I:128, 773, 965;
II:487
Potter, Jones I:815
Potter, Joseph II:427, 732,
750
Potter, Joseph, 2d IV:171
Potter, Joseph, 1st IV:173
Potter, Lemuel II:243
Potter, Levi I:128

Potter, Medad I:57, 156
Potter, Milton I:965
Potter, Moses I:63
Potter, Nicholas II:369
Potter, Noel I:945
Potter, Platt II:558
Potter, Reuben I:815
Potter, Robert II:641
Potter, Samuel I:670, 789; II:355; IV:27
Potter, Samuel B. I:834
Potter, Silas I:150
Potter, Thaddeus I:935
Potter, William I:209, 811, 827; II:495; III:429
Potter, Zebedee II:466
Pottle, Dudley I:667
Pottle, Loring II:140
Potts, Benjamin II:243
Potts, David II:386; IV:201
Potts, Elizabeth III:359
Potts, Francis III:359
Potts, Francis (2) III:359
Potts, Isaac II:208
Potts, Jacob III:9
Potts, James III:346, 632
Potts, Jesse III:107
Potts, John IV:196
Potts, Jonathan IV:196
Potts, Lenan III:359
Potts, Mary III:9
Potts, S. J. I:xii
Potts, Thomas II:548; III:397
Potts, William II:78; III:169
Potts, Wm. III:590
Pottsgrove, Henry II:738
Potwine, George I:945
Poulk, Ammi I:144
Poulson, John III:50
Pounds, Hezekiah III:294
Pousland, John I:421
Powe, William II:281
Powell, Aaron II:26; III:753
Powell, Abigail II:26
Powell, Abner III:449
Powell, Abraham A. III:634
Powell, Absalom III:412
Powell, Alfred H. III:849
Powell, Ambrose III:274
Powell, Asahel I:352
Powell, Benjamin I:701; III:804
Powell, Charles III:423
Powell, David IV:293
Powell, Felix II:253
Powell, Francis III:161
Powell, Frederick II:664
Powell, George III:422
Powell, Jeremiah II:457
Powell, John I:953; III:488, 645
Powell, John, 2d III:694
Powell, Joseph II:26
Powell, Leven H. III:715
Powell, Levi II:8
Powell, Lewis III:160, 400
Powell, Lloyd II:615

Powell, Nathaniel III:300
Powell, Peyton III:96
Powell, Richard III:221
Powell, Stephen II:184, 518
Powell, Thomas II:15, 184, 234
Powell, Truman I:945
Powell, William I:474, 877; II:441; III:458; IV:120
Powels, Jacob II:59
Powelson, Henry III:785
Power, David I:455
Power, Robert II:615
Powers, Aaron II:656
Powers, Asahel I:919, 990
Powers, Augustus II:149
Powers, Charles I:779
Powers, David II:457
Powers, Eliza Ann II:195
Powers, Ephraim II:257; III:437
Powers, Henry, Sen. III:453
Powers, Isaac II:255
Powers, James I:42; II:212; III:724
Powers, Jeremiah III:321
Powers, Jesse III:56, 330
Powers, John I:63, 433, 648; II:44, 537, 624
Powers, Jonathan I:935
Powers, Joseph I:597, 869; II:486
Powers, Justus I:844
Powers, Lewis IV:37
Powers, Mannasseh II:751
Powers, Mary Ann II:195
Powers, Moses III:378
Powers, Nathan II:324
Powers, Nicholas II:421; III:500
Powers, Oliver II:250
Powers, Peter I:901
Powers, Pierce I:613
Powers, R. V. II:195
Powers, Robert II:624
Powers, Samuel S. II:195
Powers, Simeon IV:179
Powers, Stephen I:433
Powers, Stephen, 2d I:433
Powers, Thomas I:56, 990; II:293
Powers, Vancia E. II:195
Powers, William I:666; II:195, 260; III:799
Poyner, Thomas III:411
Poyton, James II:615
Prastee, Jonathan I:278
Prater, Jonathan III:774
Prather, Thomas IV:76
Pratt, Aaron I:549
Pratt, Abel II:319
Pratt, Abigail I:155
Pratt, Abijah I:549
Pratt, Alonzo II:193
Pratt, Amos II:165
Pratt, Asa I:990; II:110
Pratt, Augustus II:411

Pratt, Benjamin I:197, 564
Pratt, Caleb I:601; II:466
Pratt, Cary III:15
Pratt, Chalker II:281
Pratt, Charles II:120
Pratt, Cushing I:254
Pratt, Cyrus I:538
Pratt, Dan I:287
Pratt, David I:667, 702
Pratt, Dier I:375
Pratt, Ebenezer I:711
Pratt, Edmund II:448
Pratt, Edward II:486
Pratt, Elam I:269
Pratt, Elias II:208
Pratt, Elijah I:883
Pratt, Elnathan IV:228
Pratt, Ephraim I:433, 564; II:236; IV:169
Pratt, George I:226
Pratt, Gideon I:57
Pratt, Isaac I:550, 911
Pratt, Isaiah I:625
Pratt, Ivory II:193
Pratt, Jabez I:795
Pratt, Jacob III:259
Pratt, James I:965; II:243, 647; III:297
Pratt, Jasper I:50, 155
Pratt, Jeremiah I:920
Pratt, Jesse I:446
Pratt, Joel I:624, 659
Pratt, John I:34, 433, 504, 694; II:436; IV:205
Pratt, Jonathan II:246, 471, 514; III:819; IV:186
Pratt, Joseph I:269, 624, 803
Pratt, Joseph, 2d I:474
Pratt, Josiah I:xxv
Pratt, Laban I:549
Pratt, Lemuel I:343, 901
Pratt, Levi I:744, 843
Pratt, Mary I:xxv
Pratt, Mathew I:890
Pratt, Matthew I:549
Pratt, Nathan I:647, 990
Pratt, Nathaniel I:504
Pratt, Noah II:242, 435
Pratt, Paul I:505
Pratt, Phineas IV:199
Pratt, Robert II:401
Pratt, Seth I:197
Pratt, Seth, 2d I:189
Pratt, Silas I:872
Pratt, Simeon I:578
Pratt, Solomon I:297; II:218
Pratt, Stephen I:931; II:260, 374, 399; III:329
Pratt, Sylvanus I:549, 578, 827
Pratt, Thaddeus I:217
Pratt, Thomas I:724; II:399; III:546
Pratt, Whitcom I:484
Pratt, William I:102, 364, 656, 872, 927
Pratt, Zadoc II:246

Pritchard, William I:761; II:597
Pritchart, John II:740
Pritchett, James III:208
Pritchett, John IV:40
Pritchett, Stephen III:153
Privit, John III:378
Probasco, Gerrit II:86
Probsman, Peter II:729
Probst, Geo. II:628
Probst, George II:628
Probst, Jacob II:628
Probst, William II:628
Procter, Silas I:965
Proctor, Abel I:504
Proctor, Benjamin IV:121
Proctor, George III:276, 319
Proctor, John III:666
Proctor, Joseph I:712; III:274
Proctor, Josiah I:287
Proctor, Levi I:505
Proctor, Little Page IV:13
Proctor, Micajah III:499
Proctor, Nathaniel I:827
Proctor, Nicholas IV:13
Proctor, Samuel I:919
Proctor, Simeon I:522
Proctor, Timothy I:990
Proctor, William III:278, 623
Profit, James I:801
Proove, John II:140
Propest, Geo. II:628
Prosser, Daniel IV:213
Prosser, William I:421
Proud, Charles II:615
Proudfoot, James II:756
Prough, Peter IV:214
Prout, James I:50
Prout, Oliver I:119
Prouty, Amos I:979
Prouty, Bela I:743
Prouty, Burphy I:919
Prouty, Caleb I:578
Prouty, Daniel I:785
Prouty, Eli I:624
Prouty, Johnson I:648
Prouty, John W. II:516
Prouty, Joshua I:647
Prouty, Stephen II:319
Provandie, Louis II:554
Province, Joseph Y. II:721
Provost, Daniel I:3
Provost, David II:59, 74
Provost, Samuel I:90
Provost, Thomas I:90
Prows, Thomas IV:185
Prowtt, Degorey II:330
Prudden, Adoniram II:338
Pruet, Ransom III:564
Pruett, John III:244
Pruett, Joshua III:476
Pruett, Samuel III:496
Pruitt, Martin IV:15
Pruitt, William IV:4
Prutt, Levi I:474
Pryor, Matthew, Sen. III:604
Pryor, Thomas III:50

Pryor, William III:749
Puce, Ebenezer II:522
Puckelt, Jacob III:761
Puckett, Josiah III:555
Puckitt, Nathaniel III:765
Pudding, Conrad II:695
Puffer, Amos I:911
Puffer, Daniel II:204
Puffer, Isaac II:425
Puffer, John I:564
Puffer, Nathan IV:103
Puffer, Simeon I:433; II:204
Pugh, James III:826
Pugh, John III:814
Pugh, Josiah III:806
Pugh, Richard III:696
Pulcifer, Joseph I:197
Pulcifer, Nathaniel I:421
Pulford, Elisha I:877, 998
Pulford, Joseph II:380
Pulis, John II:65, 328
Pulleam, Mosby III:791
Pullen, John III:623
Pullen, Joseph I:738
Pullen, Oliver I:229
Pullen, Robert III:163
Pullen, Thomas III:753
Pullen, William I:197; III:252
Pulley, John III:349
Pulliam, Richard III:441
Pulliam, Thomas III:766
Pullim, George III:209
Pullin, William III:75
Pullins, Loftus III:303
Pulman, Salter III:204, 552
Pulver, Jacob II:225
Pulver, John J. II:495
Pumphrey, Henry III:319
Punchard, Samuel I:402
Punderson, John II:218
Purbeck, Aaron I:402
Purcell, Edward IV:79
Purcell, George III:644
Purcell, John II:615
Purcell, William IV:79
Purdour, Thomas III:736
Purdy, Daniel II:548
Purdy, James II:280
Purdy, Jeremiah II:218
Purdy, Jonathan II:184; III:818
Purdy, Josiah II:431
Purdy, Justus II:229
Purdy, Obadiah II:548
Purdy, Solomon II:156
Purgett, Henry III:785
Purham, Peter I:293
Purkison, Jackman III:634
Purkitt, Henry I:658
Purnall, John II:606
Purnell, John III:34
Purple, John I:711
Purrenton, Joseph I:446
Purrington, Sylvanus II:204
Purtle, John II:615
Purviance, John IV:18
Purvis, George III:814

Purvis, William III:206
Puryear, Jesse III:223
Puryear, Reuben III:684
Pushee, David I:753
Pushee, John I:522
Pusley, Peter II:7, 10
Putman, Francis II:441
Putman, Howard IV:79
Putman, John III:751
Putman, Peter II:333
Putnam, Aaron I:753
Putnam, Asa I:522
Putnam, Daniel I:26, 80
Putnam, Elijah II:686
Putnam, Ezra I:990
Putnam, Francis I:648; II:265
Putnam, Israel I:953
Putnam, Jacob I:402
Putnam, Jane I:26
Putnam, Jesse II:754
Putnam, John I:743, 891, 972; II:641; IV:115
Putnam, Joseph I:421
Putnam, Levi I:26
Putnam, Nathan I:383, 402
Putnam, Reuben II:243
Putnam, Seth I:972
Putnam, Stephan I:911
Putnam, Thomas I:785
Putnam, Timothy I:421
Putney, Asa I:670, 767
Putney, Caleb II:21
Putney, Edward II:151
Putney, James I:269
Putney, John I:712
Putney, Jonathan I:711
Putney, Joseph I:505, 767
Putney, Samuel II:441
Putney, Stephen I:767
Putney, Thomas I:718
Putney, William I:995
Putrin, William I:965
Putty, William III:634, 719
Pyatt, Joseph III:400
Pyatt, Robert III:818
Pyke, Abraham II:586
Pyles, Joseph II:756
Pyon, Jacob II:421
Pyon, Pierre II:554
Pyott, Ebenezer IV:14
Pyron, Allen III:118
Pytts, Jonathan III:277

Qeary, Elisha III:682
Quack, Peter II:86
Quackenboss, Isaac II:393
Quackenboss, John II:511
Quackenbush, Cornelius II:59
Quackenbush, Daniel II:507
Quackenbush, David II:466
Quamtanee, John II:711
Quarles, Francis III:596
Quarles, William I:402
Quarterman, John II:756
Quas, Gideon I:71
Quash, Quomony I:564

Quasha, Cato I:24
Quay, John II:47
Queen, John III:785
Queen, Thomas III:89
Queen, William L. III:435
Queener, John III:601
Quern, Christopher II:247
Quick, Cornelius II:343
Quick, Henry II:682
Quick, Jacob II:343
Quick, John II:56, 184, 448, 548; III:715
Quicknell, Adam III:747
Quigg, John II:615
Quigley, Edward II:644
Quigley, James I:343; II:286
Quigley, Samuel IV:241
Quigley, Thomas II:212
Quigley, William II:343
Quigly, Cary II:756
Quillin, John III:453
Quimby, Benjamin I:173, 197, 779
Quimby, Celia I:173
Quimby, Dennis I:184
Quimby, Eliphalet I:173
Quimby, Jacob I:773
Quimby, James I:733
Quimby, John I:173; II:407
Quimby, Jonathan I:733
Quimby, Joseph I:173
Quimby, Josiah II:83
Quimby, Love I:173
Quimby, Lucinda I:173
Quimby, Moses I:942
Quimby, Vienna I:173
Quimby, Zachariah I:702
Quimley, Daniel I:875
Quimley, Thomas I:71
Quin, John IV:241
Quinby, John II:50
Quinby, Samuel II:736
Quinn, Daniel III:517
Quinn, David III:414
Quinn, John III:728
Quint, Benjamin I:702
Quint, Thomas I:702
Quintard, Everet I:90
Quintard, Isaac I:90
Quintard, James I:35
Quirk, Timothy II:141
Quont, Frederick II:458
Quy, Libbeus I:71

Rabbe, Samuel II:294
Rabenstine, Dewalt II:761
Raber, John II:747
Race, Andrew II:315
Race, Benjamin II:387
Race, Philip II:387
Racket, Noah II:521
Rackley, Jeremiah III:402
Rackley, Micajah III:558
Rackliff, Joseph C. I:184
Radcliff, Minus III:315
Radcliffe, William III:799

Radeer, Conrad III:833
Radeer, Henry III:833
Rader, Michael III:793
Radford, Benjamin I:184
Radford, James III:272
Radford, John II:326
Rady, Daniel III:666
Raffsnyder, Joseph II:294
Ragains, Thomas III:632
Ragan, Bartholomew III:678
Rager, Leonard IV:173
Ragin, Owen III:623
Ragin, Thomas IV:81
Ragland, David L. II:446
Ragland, Dudley III:779
Ragland, Evan III:666
Ragland, Finch III:779
Ragland, John III:250, 758
Ragsdale, Baxter III:567
Ragsdale, Benjamin III:632
Ragsdale, Godfrey III:323
Rahn, Jonathan III:160
Rahn, Philip II:696
Raidinger, Samuel III:627
Railey, James II:184
Raine, Nathaniel III:208
Raines, Anthony III:447
Raines, John III:568
Rainey, James III:243
Rainey, John III:567
Rainey, Stephen I:57, 156
Rains, Henry III:286
Rains, James III:236
Rains, John III:572, 721, 799
Rains, Robert III:72
Rains, William IV:232
Raleigh, William III:674
Raley, Charles III:89
Rall, Mathias IV:173
Rall, Matthias IV:295
Ralph, Jonathan I:63
Ralph, Thomas III:678
Ralston, Andrew II:693
Ralston, John II:736; III:288
Ralyea, John II:340
Ramage, John II:734
Ramble, Samuel II:695
Rambolt, Adam IV:72
Ramer, John II:294
Ramey, Lawrence IV:232
Ramsay, Allen IV:19
Ramsay, Andrew III:426
Ramsay, Daniel III:593
Ramsay, David II:695
Ramsay, Francis III:337
Ramsay, James I:702; III:50, 303
Ramsay, Joel III:733
Ramsay, John III:133, 359
Ramsay, Mary III:359
Ramsay, Robert III:590
Ramsay, Thomas III:221, 359
Ramsay, William III:359; IV:75
Ramsdale, Betsey I:387
Ramsdale, Catherine P. I:387
Ramsdale, John II:281
Ramsdale, Moses II:120

Ramsdale, Peggy I:387
Ramsdale, Sally I:387
Ramsdale, Silas I:598
Ramsdale, William I:387
Ramsdell, Aquilla I:744
Ramsdell, Betsy I:856
Ramsdell, Cassand I:856
Ramsdell, Ezra I:71
Ramsdell, Harthan I:63
Ramsdell, James I:232; II:218
Ramsdell, Joel I:856
Ramsdell, John I:579
Ramsdell, Joseph I:564
Ramsdell, Lot I:564
Ramsdell, Lydia Maria I:856
Ramsdell, Saul I:625
Ramsdill, Nehemiah I:649
Ramsey, James III:636
Ramsey, Jeremiah II:751
Ramsey, Jesse II:141
Ramsey, John I:356; III:289
Ramsey, Josiah IV:119
Ramsey, Samuel IV:69
Ramsey, Seth II:501
Ramsey, Thomas I:754
Ramsey, William IV:230
Ramsey, Willis III:659
Rand, Artemas I:995
Rand, Israel II:383
Rand, Jack I:891
Rand, James I:184
Rand, Jasper I:648
Rand, John I:210, 891
Rand, Michael I:240
Rand, Reuben I:198
Rand, Stephen N. I:677
Rand, Thomas I:278, 773
Rand, William II:141
Randal, Eneas I:91
Randal, Phineas I:91
Randale, Avery II:253
Randall, Abraham I:550
Randall, Amariah I:862
Randall, Amia I:862
Randall, Amos I:119, 862
Randall, Benjamin I:605-6
Randall, Charles I:112
Randall, Chloe I:862
Randall, Daniel I:862
Randall, David II:396
Randall, Elijah I:578
Randall, Elisha I:364
Randall, G. Jethro I:364
Randall, Gersham I:485
Randall, Hannah I:862
Randall, Jack I:57
Randall, Jacob I:345; III:787
Randall, James III:789; IV:105
Randall, Job I:288
Randall, John I:564, 828, 966; II:243
Randall, Jonas II:431
Randall, Jonathan I:935
Randall, Joseph I:883, 967; II:526; IV:234
Randall, Joshua I:901; II:495
Randall, Mark I:773

485

Raymond, Zaccheus II:754
Raymond, Zadoc I:90
Raymond, Zuriel II:227
Raymonds, Lemuel III:556
Raynes, Benjamin III:197
Raynes, John I:725
Raynes, Lawrence III:833
Raynor, Willet II:561
Rayzor, Paul III:323
Raze, Antoine III:7
Razey, Joseph II:356
Razey, Pelatiah II:281
Rea, Benjamin I:260
Rea, David III:433
Rea, Henry III:517
Rea, Pierce R. I:523
Rea, Robert IV:77
Reab, George II:348, 565
Read, Abijah I:505
Read, Abraham III:813
Read, Betsey I:172
Read, Charles I:172
Read, David I:695; II:744
Read, Edmund III:745
Read, Eleanor II:620
Read, Eleazer I:505
Read, Ephraim I:523
Read, Francis I:172
Read, George I:269
Read, Giles III:707
Read, Isaac I:433
Read, Jacob I:403
Read, Jesse II:243
Read, John I:376, 613, 677;
    II:620; III:226, 570, 789
Read, John P. I:165
Read, Jonathan I:891
Read, Robert III:203
Read, Samuel I:523
Read, Samuel M. II:620
Read, Thomas B. II:146
Read, William I:550, 803;
    II:519; III:518
Read, William M. II:598
Reading, George IV:123
Reading, John III:279
Reading, Ramnel III:335
Reading, Robert III:666
Reading, William III:666
Ready, Dennis III:699
Ready, John Abm. II:730
Ready, Shadrack III:77
Reagan, Darby III:607
Reagan, Michael III:243
Reagan, William III:841
Reager, Larkin III:580
Reager, Michael II:713
Real, David III:787
Ream, Andrew IV:238
Ream, Henry III:729
Ream, Jacob IV:246
Ream, John F. II:710
Reamer, David IV:66
Reams, Anna III:534
Reams, Bartley III:534
Reams, David III:534
Reams, Elizabeth III:534

Reams, Jaers III:534
Reams, Jesse III:619
Reams, John III:192
Reams, Joshua III:481
Reams, Obadiah III:534
Reams, Richard D. III:534
Reary, Joseph IV:65
Reardon, Eleanor II:624
Reardon, James II:406
Reardon, John III:316, 734
Reardon, Paul II:624
Reasor, Michael III:325
Reaves, Ashur IV:251
Reaves, John III:445
Reaves, Zachariah III:371
Reavis, Harris IV:15
Rebeck, William II:23
Rebolt, Peter IV:113
Reckey, David II:603
Record, Jonathan I:288
Record, Nathan I:945
Record, Samuel II:431
Record, Simon I:288
Records, Owen I:869
Rector, Benjamin III:425
Rector, Maximilian III:554
Rector, Uriah III:556
Redd, John III:792
Reddick, William IV:176
Reddin, William II:5
Redding, Anne III:203
Redding, John III:395
Redding, William III:203
Reddington, Daniel IV:66, 222
Redenour, Jacob III:29
Redfern, James III:340
Redfield, Ambrose I:695
Redfield, Constant I:119
Redfield, Levi II:487
Redfield, Martin I:119
Redfield, Nathan I:129
Redfield, Peleg II:471
Redfield, Roswell I:119
Redin, Timothy II:340
Redington, Asa I:270
Redington, Jacob II:319
Redlion, Henry II:597
Redlon, Ebenezer I:184
Redlon, Ephraim I:240
Redlow, Matthias I:269
Redman, Aaron IV:52
Redman, Barnabas II:26
Redman, George IV:12
Redman, John II:271, 615;
    III:708
Redman, Jonathan I:673
Redman, Joseph II:26; III:190
Redman, Rachael II:26
Redman, Richard III:708
Redman, Robert II:26
Redoubt, Giles III:782
Redway, Comfort II:253
Redway, Joel I:353
Redway, Preserved II:421
Reed, Aaron II:78
Reed, Abraham I:184; III:607

Reed, Amos I:138; II:421;
    IV:170
Reed, Artemas III:683
Reed, Bailey II:515
Reed, Benjamin I:43, 980;
    III:10, 375; IV:260
Reed, Christopher III:38, 666
Reed, Daniel I:71, 851; II:271
Reed, David I:550; II:458
Reed, David, 2d I:278
Reed, E. C. I:157
Reed, Ebenezer I:376; II:364
Reed, Elihu I:505
Reed, Elijah I:364
Reed, Eliphalet I:670
Reed, Elisha I:786
Reed, Elizabeth Jane I:494
Reed, Elnathan I:920
Reed, Ezra I:550, 786
Reed, Frederick I:980; II:348,
    723
Reed, Garrett II:380
Reed, Gen. IV:299
Reed, George I:364, 376;
    III:262; IV:173
Reed, Henry II:47
Reed, Hezekiah II:236
Reed, Hinds I:879
Reed, Howard I:738
Reed, Isaac I:523, 966; III:10,
    809
Reed, Isaiah III:606
Reed, Issachar I:966
Reed, Ithel I:112
Reed, Jacob II:165, 560
Reed, James I:613, 680, 694;
    II:74, 690, 700, 727, 744;
    IV:289
Reed, James (2) II:690
Reed, Job I:953
Reed, Joel I:694, 827
Reed, John I:607, 649, 655,
    657; II:78, 160, 308, 425,
    471, 740; III:82, 314, 567;
    IV:243
Reed, John, 1st III:25
Reed, John, 2d I:505; III:53
Reed, John M. II:458
Reed, Jonathan I:184
Reed, Joseph I:71; II:69, 689;
    III:526; IV:41
Reed, Joseph, 2d II:345
Reed, Joshua I:505, 695
Reed, Josiah I:254, 523;
    II:114, 308
Reed, Joshua IV:83
Reed, Juliana III:10
Reed, Justus I:103
Reed, Kitchel II:541
Reed, Lemuel I:376
Reed, Leonard II:407
Reed, Lorin I:29
Reed, Lovett III:568
Reed, Lura I:29
Reed, Mary I:360
Reed, Mary Ann III:10
Reed, Moses I:360, 905

Reed, Nathan I:649; III:91
Reed, Noah I:550, 673
Reed, Peter I:972
Reed, Philip III:70
Reed, Richard II:74, 286
Reed, Robert III:93, 203
Reed, Samuel I:144, 365, 494;
  II:311, 431; III:400
Reed, Samuel, 1st I:505
Reed, Samuel, 2d I:474
Reed, Samuel, 3d I:433
Reed, Silas II:471
Reed, Simeon I:967
Reed, Solomon I:29
Reed, Stephen I:991; II:338
Reed, Supply I:786
Reed, Thomas I:334, 912;
  II:700; IV:64
Reed, Thomas, 2d I:912
Reed, Uriah I:376
Reed, Ward I:293
Reed, William I:422, 538,
  761; II:714; III:441; IV:244
Reed, Zachariah III:207
Reed, Zalmon I:91
Reeder, William II:69
Reep, Adam III:429
Reep, Michael III:347
Rees, George II:680
Rees, Griffith II:589
Rees, Jonathan III:197
Rees, Thomas II:719
Reese, Alexander II:628
Reese, Charles T. III:523
Reese, George II:628; III:495
Reese, Harriet II:628
Reese, James E. III:518
Reese, John III:25
Reese, Peter II:652
Reetan, Samuel II:690
Reeve, William III:496
Reeven, Nathaniel IV:240
Reeves, David II:56
Reeves, Elisha II:475
Reeves, Israel II:100
Reeves, James II:156
Reeves, John IV:122
Reeves, John D. III:455
Reeves, Joseph III:195; IV:289
Reeves, Luther I:71; IV:295
Reeves, Puryer II:369
Reeves, Richard III:417
Reeves, Robert II:42
Reeves, Samuel III:551
Reeves, William II:324; III:47;
  IV:232
Reewark, James III:44
Regan, Charles III:429
Regan, Philip II:759
Regar, Philip III:799
Regem, Samuel III:193
Register, John III:455
Register, John, Jr. III:456
Rehern, Joseph II:184
Reichart, Charles II:759
Reichwick, Conrad II:647

Reid, Alexander III:15, 281;
  IV:44
Reid, David III:601
Reid, Joab IV:232
Reid, Jonathan II:628
Reid, Nathan III:847
Reid, Rachel II:628
Reid, Richard III:495
Reid, Thomas III:404
Reid, Zadock I:712
Reigel, Michael II:671
Reigleman, Conrad II:703
Reiley, John I:51
Reilly, Christopher III:216
Reilly, Jacob H. II:2
Reilly, John II:576
Reilly, William III:13
Reily, Francis I:598
Reily, James IV:234
Reily, John IV:47
Reily, John, 2d III:223
Reinehardt, Matthias II:515
Reiner, Jacob II:747
Reinick, Frederick II:606
Reins, John II:271
Reintzel, A. I:xiii
Reintzel, George III:25
Reiter, Jacob II:740
Reizer, John III:485
Relly, Henry I:613
Relph, Thomas I:827
Relyea, Henry II:534
Relyea, Jacob II:204
Relyea, Peter II:355
Remay, John IV:207
Remick, James I:779
Remick, Samuel I:241, 725
Remington, Anthony I:456
Remington, Benedict I:801
Remington, Caleb I:828
Remington, David II:542
Remington, Elisha II:281
Remington, Ira I:848
Remington, Jabez I:795
Remington, John I:353, 819
Remington, Jonathan I:966
Remington, Joseph I:991
Remington, Joseph N. II:294
Remington, Joshua I:940
Remington, Simeon II:416
Remington, Teddeman I:819
Remington, Thomas I:819
Renan, John II:184
Rencan, Thomas IV:74
Rendall, Daniel I:779
Rendall, James I:240
Rendall, John I:673
Renels, Benjamin I:641
Reneson, William IV:231
Renfro, John III:257
Renich, James III:298
Reniff, Charlos II:253
Renker, George IV:93
Rennison, John II:643
Reno, Zela III:288
Renol, Christopher III:38
Renolds, James III:813

Renway, Peter II:554
Requa, Abraham II:548
Requa, Gilbert II:141
Requa, John II:178
Requa, Joseph II:411
Rerick, Ann IV:163
Rerick, Elizabeth IV:163
Rerick, Hannah IV:163
Rerick, Henry IV:163
Rerick, John IV:163
Rerick, Martha IV:163
Resa, Storm II:411
Resimer, Johannes II:341
Ressequie, Abraham II:351
Ressiquie, John II:515
Retherford, William III:596
Reuchart, Thomas III:828
Reuger, Conrad II:721
Reveau, Daniel II:141
Revel, Holiday III:737
Revell, Holiday III:836
Revell, Michael III:459
Revere, Charles IV:5
Reves, Joshua II:61
Revis, Henry IV:15
Rewey, Thomas II:466
Rex, Daniel II:696
Rex, William II:740
Rexford, Benjamin I:995
Rexford, Ensign II:487
Rexford, Isaac I:878
Rexrode, Zachariah III:821
Reynolds, Aaron III:582
Reynolds, Abijah II:686
Reynolds, Albrow I:649
Reynolds, Alexander III:753
Reynolds, Alfred III:534
Reynolds, Allen II:141, 225
Reynolds, Ann Elizabeth
  II:628
Reynolds, Benedict II:756
Reynolds, Benjamin II:411
Reynolds, Bernard III:834
Reynolds, Calvin III:534
Reynolds, Cynthia III:534
Reynolds, Daniel I:198; II:548
Reynolds, David I:151, 232,
  270
Reynolds, David, 3d I:112
Reynolds, Eliphalet I:232
Reynolds, Elisha I:845, 947;
  III:458
Reynolds, Ephraim III:137
Reynolds, Ezekiel III:567
Reynolds, Ezra I:564; II:387
Reynolds, Fielding III:81
Reynolds, Gamaliel II:706
Reynolds, George I:835;
  II:732; III:13
Reynolds, Henry III:585
Reynolds, Hezekiah II:501
Reynolds, Isaac II:324
Reynolds, Jacob II:380;
  III:523, 534
Reynolds, James I:827, 834;
  II:236; IV:276
Reynolds, Jeremiah II:458

488

Reynolds, Jesse III:753
Reynolds, Jethro III:534
Reynolds, Joel II:374
Reynolds, John I:165, 364;
II:628, 750; III:388, 669;
IV:103, 246, 250
Reynolds, Jonathan I:813,
920, 966; II:184, 542
Reynolds, Joseph I:80, 767;
II:554; IV:71
Reynolds, Justus IV:191
Reynolds, Keziah III:534
Reynolds, Michael I:xvi;
IV:112
Reynolds, Nancy II:199;
III:534
Reynolds, Nathaniel III:257
Reynolds, Peter I:966
Reynolds, Polly III:534
Reynolds, Richard D. III:311
Reynolds, Robert I:451, 835
Reynolds, Samuel I:813;
III:580
Reynolds, Sarah III:669
Reynolds, Shubel II:448
Reynolds, Silas I:945
Reynolds, Simeon I:340;
II:680
Reynolds, Solomon I:112
Reynolds, Temperance Anna
I:29
Reynolds, Thomas I:138, 845;
III:530
Reynolds, Timothy II:351
Reynolds, Tobias III:44
Reynolds, Trueman II:199
Reynolds, William I:29, 835;
II:185, 199, 753; III:13, 577,
762
Reynolds, Zachariah II:542
Rhea, David II:47
Rhea, Elizabeth III:534
Rhea, Jenney III:534
Rhea, John III:534
Rhea, Lunar III:529
Rhea, Nancy III:534
Rhea, Robert III:527, 596
Rhea, Sarah III:534
Rhea, William II:575
Rheams, Barclay III:534
Rhesa, Oliver III:105
Rhinchard, Jacob II:471
Rhinehart, George S. II:650
Rhinehart, William II:265
Rhoades, Ezekiel II:526
Rhoades, Jacob I:240
Rhoades, Joseph II:421
Rhoades, Moses I:241
Rhoades, Samuel, Sen. II:348
Rhoads, Daniel IV:56
Rhoads, David II:369
Rhoads, Eliphalet I:550
Rhoads, John II:565
Rhoads, Nicholas IV:297
Rhodan, Thomas III:278
Rhodes, Anthony II:416

Rhodes, Benjamin I:816;
III:283
Rhodes, Bristol I:795
Rhodes, Charles III:121
Rhodes, Cornelius III:444
Rhodes, George III:696
Rhodes, Hezekiah III:454
Rhodes, James I:816
Rhodes, John II:324, 507;
III:460
Rhodes, Joseph II:343
Rhodes, Josiah I:422
Rhodes, Mark II:680
Rhodes, Nathan III:392
Rhodes, Nicholas II:598
Rhodes, Richard I:801
Rhodes, Samuel IV:117
Rhodes, Thomas III:842
Rhodes, William I:835; IV:131
Rhodes, Zachariah I:601
Rhodes, Zebulon I:485
Rhone, Saml. II:122
Rhyer, Peter II:597
Riall, Isaac IV:264
Ribbet, Abraham II:665
Ribbet, William II:91
Ribert, John II:718
Riblet, Christian IV:283
Rice, Abiah I:1000
Rice, Abiram II:253
Rice, Abner II:501
Rice, Abraham I:151
Rice, Achsee I:428
Rice, Allen III:759
Rice, Amos I:649
Rice, Andrew I:175
Rice, Asa II:537
Rice, Asahel I:428
Rice, Ashbell I:303
Rice, Bailey III:743
Rice, Benjamin I:649; IV:222
Rice, Betsey IV:164
Rice, Charles I:119, 663;
II:176; IV:164, 270
Rice, Chauncey I:129
Rice, Danel II:401
Rice, Daniel I:523, 816
Rice, David I:175, 184, 744
Rice, Eber II:458
Rice, Edmund I:523
Rice, Eliakim I:991
Rice, Elisha I:587
Rice, Ephraim I:980
Rice, Ezekiel I:523
Rice, Ezra I:626
Rice, Frederick II:652; IV:293
Rice, Gideon I:254
Rice, Henry IV:164
Rice, Holman III:258
Rice, Isaac I:920; IV:289
Rice, Israel II:431
Rice, Jacob II:243, 387
Rice, Jacob, Sen. III:437
Rice, James II:330; IV:171
Rice, Jason I:991; IV:229
Rice, Jesse I:369; III:761

Rice, John I:269, 607, 891;
II:265, 345, 411, 664;
III:307, 443, 686; IV:129,
164
Rice, John P. II:151
Rice, Jonas I:648, 966
Rice, Jonathan I:523
Rice, Joseph I:198, 816
Rice, Josiah I:446, 626, 744
Rice, Kitty IV:164
Rice, Lemuel I:184
Rice, Leonard II:619; III:161
Rice, Luther I:218
Rice, Martin I:626; II:421
Rice, Mary Ann IV:164
Rice, Matilda IV:164
Rice, Merrick I:891
Rice, Nathan I:xii, 649, 998;
IV:292
Rice, Nathaniel I:523; II:569
Rice, Naum I:433
Rice, Oliver IV:224, 301
Rice, Peggy II:619
Rice, Pelatiah II:374
Rice, Philip III:261
Rice, Phineas I:523
Rice, Randolph III:284
Rice, Reuben I:648
Rice, Sally I:175
Rice, Samuel I:51, 175, 446,
801; III:295
Rice, Thaddeus I:63
Rice, Thomas III:588
Rice, Uriah I:523
Rice, Wait I:51
Rice, William I:144, 649, 801;
II:519, 545, 597, 616
Rice, William B. IV:118
Rice, William H. III:449
Rich, Amos II:229
Rich, Barnabas I:456
Rich, Calneh I:856
Rich, Elijah IV:66
Rich, Jacob III:580
Rich, Joel I:229
Rich, John I:856
Rich, Jonas I:966
Rich, Jonathan I:953
Rich, Lemuel I:334
Rich, Lot III:456
Rich, Samuel I:57
Rich, Stephen I:972
Rich, Thaddeus I:128
Rich, Thomas I:11
Rich, William II:407
Rich, Zachias I:625
Richabaugh, Adam IV:248
Richard, Erastus I:859
Richard, John III:415
Richard, John J. I:859
Richard, Silas II:348
Richards, Abigail I:686
Richards, Alvin II:141
Richards, Ambrose III:804
Richards, Amos I:712; IV:106
Richards, Boswell III:657
Richards, Bradley I:198

Richards, Daniel I:422; III:41
Richards, David II:597
Richards, Edward III:734
Richards, Elijah I:786
Richards, Geo. III:851
Richards, George III:219, 799
Richards, Isaac II:141; III:789
Richards, Jacob II:507; IV:174
Richards, James I:484; III:229, 531; IV:166
Richards, Jesse I:90; IV:293
Richards, Joel I:786
Richards, John I:240, 340; III:41, 779
Richards, Jonathan I:301, 465, 550, 677
Richards, Joseph I:315, 353
Richards, Joseph, 2d I:226
Richards, Joshua III:323, 514
Richards, Josiah I:550
Richards, Lemuel I:920
Richards, Lewis III:326
Richards, Mark I:980
Richards, Mary III:41
Richards, Mitchell I:269
Richards, Morris III:454
Richards, Nathan I:376
Richards, Nathaniel I:71
Richards, Nehemiah I:484
Richards, Oliver I:550
Richards, Paul III:47
Richards, Peter I:51, 813
Richards, Philemon III:837
Richards, Philip II:184
Richards, Sally I:686
Richards, Samuel I:43, 155, 686, 869
Richards, Solomon I:523
Richards, Stephen III:581
Richards, Theodore I:779
Richards, Thomas IV:212
Richards, William I:71; II:97, 736; IV:4
Richardson, Abel I:506, 648
Richardson, Abijah I:505, 523, 538
Richardson, Abijah, 2d I:626
Richardson, Abner II:324
Richardson, Almira I:533
Richardson, Amasa I:550
Richardson, Amos III:40, 161, 610
Richardson, Asa I:505, 905
Richardson, Benj. A. I:587
Richardson, Benjamin I:648
Richardson, Caleb III:399, 750
Richardson, Charles III:60
Richardson, Daniel II:562; III:57; IV:242
Richardson, David I:761; III:307
Richardson, Ebenezer I:161, 403, 754
Richardson, Edward I:288
Richardson, Eliphalet I:702
Richardson, Enoch I:703
Richardson, Ezekiel I:649

Richardson, George II:212, 597; III:272
Richardson, Gershom II:479
Richardson, Godfrey I:991
Richardson, Hezekiah I:165
Richardson, Humphrey I:872
Richardson, Isaac II:458
Richardson, J. II:556
Richardson, Jacob IV:191
Richardson, James I:260, 403; II:487; III:40, 607; IV:15, 165
Richardson, Jason I:533, 550
Richardson, Jeremiah I:434, 991
Richardson, Jesse IV:276
Richardson, Job I:625
Richardson, Joel I:209
Richardson, John I:422, 523; II:179, 501; III:40, 609, 747, 851; IV:258
Richardson, Jonas I:712
Richardson, Joseph I:150, 255, 437, 649, 677, 779; II:324, 741; III:38
Richardson, Joseph A. I:795
Richardson, Joshua IV:176
Richardson, Josiah I:505
Richardson, Lemuel II:294
Richardson, Moses I:523
Richardson, Parris I:680
Richardson, Randolph III:840
Richardson, Richard I:523, 694; III:775, 802
Richardson, Robert I:474; II:184; III:691
Richardson, Rufus II:260, 421
Richardson, Russel II:243
Richardson, Samuel I:702; IV:222
Richardson, Seth I:402
Richardson, Stephen I:966
Richardson, Thomas I:795; IV:3, 96
Richardson, Thomas P. I:744
Richardson, Timothy I:189
Richardson, William I:353, 523, 649, 744, 894; II:324; III:40; IV:115
Richarson, Stephen I:725
Richart, Thomas II:616
Richcreek, Philip III:711; IV:299
Richer, Simeon I:315
Richey, Albert McClure II:623
Richey, Jacob II:623
Richey, John III:204, 511; IV:276
Richey, Newton II:623
Richey, Samuel II:623
Richey, Stephen III:199
Richey, Steward II:623
Richie, Abraham II:633
Richie, James III:619
Richmond, Abiezer II:431
Richmond, Abner I:151
Richmond, Amaziah I:980

Richmond, Anthony I:27
Richmond, Asa I:376
Richmond, Benjamin I:364
Richmond, Edward II:315
Richmond, Ezra I:649
Richmond, Gamaliel I:364
Richmond, George I:376
Richmond, Henry I:27
Richmond, James I:376; III:634
Richmond, John I:359
Richmond, Jonathan I:364
Richmond, Nathan I:270
Richmond, Nathaniel I:991; IV:38
Richmond, Samuel I:376
Richmond, Seth I:364
Richmond, Vail I:129
Richmond, William III:781
Richmond, Zebulon I:340
Richter, Nicholas II:126
Richtmyer, Henry II:431-32
Richy, Peter III:593
Rickard, Abner II:407
Rickard, Samuel II:431
Rickards, Benjamin I:565
Ricker, George I:240, 734
Ricker, John I:779
Ricker, John N. II:65
Ricker, Joseph I:733
Ricker, Maturian I:315
Ricker, Noah I:315
Ricker, Reuben I:229, 734
Ricker, Stephen I:240
Ricker, Timothy I:315, 733
Ricker, Tobias I:288
Ricker, Wentworth I:255
Ricketson, Jesse III:183
Rickett, Robert IV:66
Ricketts, Nathan IV:92
Ricketts, William III:398; IV:25
Rickey, Albert McClure II:623
Rickey, Benjamin II:756
Rickey, Cornelius IV:287
Rickey, Jacob II:623
Rickey, Jeremiah II:204
Rickey, John II:526
Rickey, Joseph IV:283
Rickey, Newton II:623
Rickey, Robert IV:173
Rickey, Samuel II:623
Rickey, Steward II:623
Rickhart, Leonard IV:234
Rickko, Jeremiah II:204
Rickner, Daniel III:42
Ricks, Edmund III:443
Rictor, Catherine III:41
Rictor, Christian III:41
Riddall, John I:953
Riddin, Christopher IV:280
Riddle, David I:761
Riddle, John III:291, 453, 779
Riddle, Joseph II:243
Riddle, Samuel II:597
Riddle, William III:771
Rideout, Benjamin I:278

Rider, Adam IV:214
Rider, Asa I:877
Rider, Benjamin II:534; IV:250
Rider, Daniel II:260, 383
Rider, David II:253
Rider, Giles I:474
Rider, James I:689
Rider, Jeremiah I:786
Rider, John I:198
Rider, Joseph III:286
Rider, Michael II:165
Rider, Moses I:744
Rider, Peter I:854
Rider, Phinehas I:972
Rider, Reuben III:634
Rider, Robert I:578
Rider, Timothy II:479
Ridgeway, James I:297
Ridgeway, John III:507
Ridgeway, Samuel IV:277
Ridgway, Isaac II:356
Ridinhour, John III:316
Ridley, Daniel I:209
Ridley, David I:198
Ridley, George I:209; III:530
Ridley, Samuel I:905
Ridley, William III:364
Ridlin, John IV:199
Ridout, Abraham I:240
Ridout, Stephen I:209
Ridout, William I:163
Rieley, James III:776
Riend, Christopher III:38
Rienhart, Martin IV:234
Ries, Joseph II:368
Riffee, Jacob III:789
Riffey, George III:755
Riffort, Christian II:680
Rifle, Michael III:7
Rigby, John III:414
Rigby, William IV:182
Rigdon, James III:278
Rigel, Abraham IV:141
Rigg, Hosea IV:18
Rigg, Rufus II:575
Riggan, Francis III:457
Riggan, William P. III:422
Riggins, James II:61; III:601
Riggins, Joel III:372
Riggs, Bethnel IV:254
Riggs, Charles III:285
Riggs, Daniel M. I:xvi
Riggs, Gideon IV:176
Riggs, John III:441, 454
Riggs, Jonathan II:736
Riggs, Laban I:63
Riggs, Moses I:63
Riggs, Reuben III:582
Riggs, Samuel III:588
Right, Bazel III:799
Righton, Joseph III:500
Righton, Nicholas II:487
Rigsby, Frederick III:396
Rigsby, James III:460
Rigsby, Jesse III:351
Riker, Abraham I. II:141
Riker, Gerardus II:446

Riker, James II:446
Riker, John II:519
Riker, Matthias II:446
Riker, Tunis I:173
Rilea, Richard IV:171
Riley, Charles II:324
Riley, James I:587; III:161;
  IV:289
Riley, John II:141, 394;
  III:323; IV:52
Riley, Joseph IV:269
Riley, Major I:761
Riley, Stephen III:62
Riley, Valerius III:31
Riley, William III:419; IV:276
Rimmee, Conrad II:644
Rindge, Richard I:891
Rindress, James II:551
Rines, Samuel I:240
Rinevault, William I:35
Ring, Abijah I:673
Ring, Addison I:683
Ring, Amanda I:683
Ring, Betsey I:683
Ring, Charles I:683
Ring, Hancot I:683
Ring, John Adams I:683
Ring, Jonathan I:564, 683
Ring, Mary I:683
Ring, Stephen II:141
Ring, Thomas I:80
Ring, Thomas, Sen. III:453
Ringman, Ann III:518
Ringo, Burtis III:278
Ringo, Cornelius III:291
Ringo, John III:325
Ringstorph, Philip II:386
Rinker, Abraham II:666
Ripley, Abraham I:456
Ripley, Calvin I:376
Ripley, Charles III:338
Ripley, David I:894
Ripley, Hezekiah I:150, 564,
  658
Ripley, Jacob IV:262
Ripley, Job II:225
Ripley, Joseph I:725
Ripley, Laban I:744
Ripley, Nehemiah I:151
Ripley, Noah I:649
Ripley, Pelham II:466
Ripley, Peter II:615
Ripley, Piram II:427
Ripley, Richard III:806
Ripley, William I:210, 564
Rippart, George III:26
Risdel, John II:729
Risdon, Daniel I:966
Risdon, John I:931
Risdon, Onesimus II:427
Rishell, George II:674
Rising, Abraham I:466
Rising, Ben IV:268
Rising, Harriet I:29
Rising, Josiah II:281, 458
Rising, Samuel I:29
Risley, Allen II:458

Risley, Asa I:754
Risley, David II:458
Risley, Eli II:458
Risley, Elijah II:215
Risley, George I:144
Risley, Levi I:43
Risley, Richard II:303
Risley, Samuel IV:229
Risley, Stephen II:260
Risley, William II:416
Riston, Zadoc III:13
Ritchell, William II:616
Ritchey, Esaw III:195
Ritchey, Jacob IV:257
Ritchie, John III:509
Ritchie, Nancy Hudson III:9
Ritchie, Robert II:652
Ritchie, William II:738
Ritchmyer, Hendrich II:123
Rittenhouse, Jacob II:732
Ritter, Ezra I:920
Ritter, Frederick II:416
Ritter, Henry II:416
Ritter, Killiam II:441
Ritter, Thomas III:62
Ritter, William I:695
Ritz, Matthias II:761
Riveley, Frederick II:653
Rivenbark, Frederick III:414
Rivers, Samuel III:500
Rix, James I:683
Rix, Lewis I:683
Rix, Nancy I:683
Rix, Nathan II:487
Rix, Nathaniel I:712
Rix, Peter I:587
Rixford, Henry I:626
Rixford, Joseph I:112
Rixford, Samuel II:253
Rixford, Simon II:751
Rixford, William I:744
Rlanchard, Jeremiah I:409
Rlodgett, Joshua I:715
Roach, Absalom III:819
Roach, Berdat Price III:852
Roach, Francis IV:15
Roach, Israel I:931
Roach, James III:634, 823
Roach, John I:198; III:601,
  731
Roach, Jonathan III:810
Roach, Thomas I:138
Roach, William IV:196
Roads, Anderson III:669
Roads, Eliza III:669
Roads, Robert III:669
Roaff, Peter IV:206
Roan, John II:741
Roan, Thomas III:408
Roane, James H. III:74
Roarer, Henry III:835
Roat, Christian II:441
Roath, Silas I:71
Robards, Jesse III:281
Robarsh, Peter II:221
Robarts, Freelove I:878
Robason, Daniel III:436

Robb, Hugh III:7
Robb, Samuel I:744
Robbe, John I:673
Robbing, Ephraim I:433
Robbins, Asa I:167, 269, 591
Robbins, Benjamin I:523, 648
Robbins, Brintal II:759
Robbins, Daniel I:198, 649
Robbins, Daniel, 2d I:198
Robbins, Ebenezer I:151;
II:479
Robbins, Elijah II:511
Robbins, Eliphalet I:198
Robbins, Eliza L. I:859
Robbins, Ephraim IV:87
Robbins, Evan II:324
Robbins, Ezra I:859
Robbins, Ichabod I:625
Robbins, Jacob I:505
Robbins, John I:613, 920;
III:54
Robbins, Jonathan I:218
Robbins, Joseph I:198, 648,
712; II:218
Robbins, Josiah I:744
Robbins, Luke I:626
Robbins, Luther I:269
Robbins, Moses I:927; II:23
Robbins, Oliver II:149
Robbins, Otis I:278
Robbins, Paul I:702
Robbins, Peter II:519
Robbins, Samuel I:150, 165,
210, 991; II:308
Robbins, Seth S. I:859
Robbins, Silas I:138
Robbins, Stephen I:80
Robbins, Thomas I:138, 625;
II:713
Robbins, William I:210, 564
Robbins, Zachariah I:712
Robenson, John II:616
Roberson, Isaiah II:156
Roberson, John III:94, 154
Robert, William IV:289
Roberts, Aaron I:13; III:460
Roberts, Abner III:325
Roberts, Abraham II:495
Roberts, Ambrose III:772
Roberts, Amos II:387, 656
Roberts, Ann II:188
Roberts, Archibald III:787
Roberts, Ashbel I:103
Roberts, Benjamin I:733;
III:323
Roberts, Betsy II:188
Roberts, Brittian III:427
Roberts, Charles II:188
Roberts, Cornelius II:471
Roberts, Cuff I:598
Roberts, Daniel I:103
Roberts, David I:63; III:93
Roberts, Ebenezer I:119; IV:25
Roberts, Edmund II:69; III:601
Roberts, Edward II:738;
III:237
Roberts, Elijah I:119; II:441

Roberts, Elisha II:281
Roberts, Ephraim I:779
Roberts, Ezek. I:827
Roberts, Ezekiel II:348
Roberts, Francis I:422
Roberts, George I:226, 733;
III:307
Roberts, Gideon II:736
Roberts, Giles I:434
Roberts, Henry III:219
Roberts, Isaac I:931; II:225;
III:759
Roberts, James III:47
Roberts, Jeremiah I:315
Roberts, Joel I:935
Roberts, John I:50, 625, 703,
854, 912; II:221; III:111,
219, 404, 849; IV:92, 120
Roberts, John, 2d I:102; II:47
Roberts, John, 3d I:733
Roberts, John T. I:506
Roberts, Jonathan I:725
Roberts, Joseph I:301, 465,
779; II:673
Roberts, Joshua III:429, 608
Roberts, Josiah I:894
Roberts, Judah I:112
Roberts, Levi M. II:104
Roberts, Love I:240
Roberts, Luke I:901
Roberts, Mark R. III:524
Roberts, Martin III:388
Roberts, Mourning III:319
Roberts, Nathan I:734; II:345
Roberts, Nathaniel II:458
Roberts, Noah II:324
Roberts, Norman III:303
Roberts, Patience II:188
Roberts, Paul I:315
Roberts, Philip III:288
Roberts, Reuben I:808;
III:171, 561
Roberts, Richard III:153, 683
Roberts, Robert III:513
Roberts, Rufus II:345
Roberts, Samuel I:240; II:188,
228
Roberts, Sears II:65
Roberts, Simon I:315
Roberts, Stephen II:668
Roberts, Thomas I:422; II:664;
III:138, 257, 593, 759;
IV:4, 113
Roberts, Timothy I:779, 972
Roberts, Warren II:247
Roberts, William I:151, 456;
III:42, 408-9, 497, 585;
IV:284
Roberts, William, 2d II:141
Roberts, William, 3d II:315
Roberts, William, Sen. III:414
Roberts, William, 1st II:141
Roberts, Wilson III:746
Roberts, Zachariah III:25, 47
Robertson, Andrew II:721
Robertson, Benjamin III:276
Robertson, Daniel II:393

Robertson, Daniel, 1st I:626
Robertson, David III:299
Robertson, Edward IV:117
Robertson, Ephraim I:75
Robertson, Francis I:795
Robertson, George III:658
Robertson, Hugh III:684
Robertson, Isaac III:764
Robertson, James III:93, 262,
281, 658, 741
Robertson, Jesse III:274, 555
Robertson, John II:446;
III:603, 709, 764; IV:16
Robertson, Joseph III:10, 569,
725
Robertson, Lucinda III:10
Robertson, Matthew III:320
Robertson, Mitchell III:766
Robertson, Peter I:680
Robertson, Richard III:775
Robertson, Robert II:23, 184
Robertson, Sarah Ann III:10
Robertson, Simeon II:227
Robertson, Stephen III:240
Robertson, Thomas III:195,
607
Robertson, William III:278,
502, 616, 847
Robertson, Zachariah III:225
Robeson, James III:429
Robey, Henry I:990
Robey, Joseph II:545
Robey, Richard III:837
Robey, Samuel I:664
Robey, Silas II:380
Robins, Abner I:327
Robins, Daniel I:506, 940
Robins, Enoch I:324
Robins, Isaac II:88
Robins, Jeremiah I:587
Robins, John III:591
Robins, Samuel I:579
Robins, William IV:67, 196
Robinson, Abel II:206
Robinson, Alexander II:759
Robinson, Amasa I:151
Robinson, Amos I:7, 71, 972
Robinson, Andrew I:151, 773
Robinson, Andrews I:278
Robinson, Arch. III:672
Robinson, Asher I:972
Robinson, Bartlett II:308
Robinson, Benjamin I:673;
II:286; III:202, 276, 381
Robinson, Caleb II:458
Robinson, Caroline II:25
Robinson, Carrick III:202
Robinson, Chandler II:732
Robinson, Charles III:38, 67,
666
Robinson, Daniel II:212, 382
Robinson, Daniel, 2d I:403
Robinson, David I:xiv, 786;
II:227
Robinson, Ebenezer I:376, 991
Robinson, Eber I:957
Robinson, Edmund II:369

Rogers, Jedediah II:271
Rogers, Jeremiah I:966;
III:604
Rogers, John I:198, 376, 695;
II:184, 355, 363; IV:3
Rogers, John, 2d I:210, 474
Rogers, John, 1st I:625
Rogers, Jonathan I:331, 649,
785
Rogers, Jose III:833
Rogers, Joseph I:786; II:310;
III:567; IV:228
Rogers, Josiah I:50; II:436
Rogers, Josias II:732
Rogers, Juduthun I:991
Rogers, Leonard I:144
Rogers, Levi II:411
Rogers, Lucy I:862
Rogers, M.D.L.F. II:141
Rogers, Moses II:466
Rogers, Nathaniel I:144, 578;
II:363, 401; III:516
Rogers, Nathaniel, 2d I:579
Rogers, Noadiah I:129
Rogers, Oliver I:80
Rogers, Paul II:348
Rogers, Perley II:208
Rogers, Peter I:433; IV:20
Rogers, Rhodam III:789
Rogers, Richard I:331; IV:280
Rogers, Robert I:819; III:758
Rogers, Russell P. I:13
Rogers, Samuel I:767; II:387,
583, 757; IV:250
Rogers, Simeon II:458
Rogers, Smith I:327
Rogers, Stephen I:613; II:260
Rogers, Thomas I:578, 738,
967; III:260, 445, 666
Rogers, William I:278, 403;
II:141, 421; III:38, 585;
IV:165-66
Rogers, William, Sen. III:253
Rogers, Willoughby III:538
Rogers, Zephaniah II:641
Rogerson, John III:386
Roge_s, William II:104
Rogues, Samuel I:203
Rohads, John II:56
Roheson, Isaac II:23
Rohrer, Martin IV:148
Rohrman, John II:597
Roist, Samuel Restals I:912
Roland, Jacob III:835
Roland, James III:602
Roland, Tendrel III:613
Rolf, Henry II:37
Rolf, James IV:51
Rolf, Jeremiah I:226
Rolfe, Joseph I:269
Rolfe, William I:953
Rolings, Nathaniel I:269
Roll, Isaac IV:295
Roll, Israel IV:295
Roll, Mathias IV:173
Roll, Matthias IV:295
Roll, Michael III:311

Rollf, Ephraim I:891
Rollins, Anthony N. I:995
Rollins, Daniel I:725
Rollins, Eliphalet I:226
Rollins, Jabez I:198
Rollins, James I:278
Rollins, Jeremiah I:733
Rollins, John I:198, 875
Rollins, John, 2d I:712
Rollins, Josiah I:43
Rollins, Lorrin II:458
Rollins, Moses III:707
Rollins, Robert I:878
Rolls, James II:257
Rolls, John III:736
Rolls, Zachariah I:43
Rolo, Joseph II:487
Rolstone, David III:833
Romaine, Benjamin II:446
Roman, Alexander II:149
Romer, Henry II:351
Romer, Luke II:534
Romine, John III:789
Romine, Samuel II:59
Rone, Saml. II:122
Roney, Michael II:141
Rood, Clark II:97
Rood, Eli II:386
Rood, Ira II:281
Rood, Jeremiah II:215
Rood, John I:4
Rood, Moses I:905
Rood, Rozzel II:411
Rood, Simeon II:333
Roof, John II:441
Rooker, John III:517
Rooker, Joseph II:348
Rooks, Daniel II:746
Rooksbury, Jacob III:228
Roolo, Daniel II:487
Roome, Benjamin II:271
Roome, Henry II:65
Roosa, Cornelius II:446
Roosa, Jacob J. II:534
Roosa, Johannes II:534
Roosa, John E. II:534
Root, Aaron II:425
Root, Abel II:718
Root, Amos II:421
Root, Asahel II:541
Root, Azariah IV:244
Root, Bella II:361
Root, Conrad II:120
Root, Ebenezer II:380
Root, Elias I:485
Root, Elijah I:103; II:545
Root, Erastus II:458
Root, Israel II:212, 477
Root, Joel I:340
Root, John I:991
Root, Joseph II:477
Root, Joshua II:386
Root, Josiah I:103
Root, Moses I:967
Root, Nathan I:75
Root, Nathaniel I:51, 144
Root, Nathaniel H. I:129

Root, Oliver II:427
Root, Rufus I:920
Root, Samuel I:434, 656;
II:726
Root, Seth I:43
Root, Solomon II:256
Root, Thaddeus I:343; II:243
Root, Thomas II:243
Root, William II:218
Root, Zenas I:340
Roots, Daniel I:51
Roper, David III:318
Roper, Drury III:595
Roper, George IV:9
Roper, James III:324, 438
Roper, John I:649; III:164
Roper, Silas I:626
Roper, Sylvester I:649
Ropes, William I:402
Rorer, George II:744
Rorer, John II:729
Rork, Michael III:588
Rosa, Abraham II:391
Roscrow, Henry II:91
Rose, Abner I:450
Rose, Abraham I:712
Rose, Amos II:51
Rose, Archibald III:724
Rose, Benjamin I:297; III:111
Rose, Benjamin B. III:307
Rose, David II:717
Rose, Elijah II:294
Rose, Elisha II:236
Rose, Evert II:530
Rose, Gad I:103
Rose, Isaac II:670; III:723,
740
Rose, Jacob II:340, 565;
IV:296
Rose, Jesse III:225
Rose, John II:204, 208; III:455
Rose, Joseph II:380
Rose, Lemuel II:521
Rose, Levi I:456
Rose, Matthias IV:124
Rose, Nathaniel I:376
Rose, Peter II:124, 530
Rose, Philip III:449
Rose, Prosper I:137
Rose, Richard II:32; IV:8
Rose, Russell II:686
Rose, Samuel III:435, 474
Rose, Sterling III:459
Rose, Thomas I:376
Rose, William II:363; III:330;
IV:117
Rose, Winthrop II:208
Roseboond, Garrett II:65
Rosebraugh, Elizabeth III:623
Rosebraugh, John II:623
Rosebrom, Hendrick IV:284
Rosebrough, John III:785
Rosekrans, Jacob II:343
Rosekrans, Peter II:355
Roselbrough, John II:633
Rosell, Elias II:42
Rosenteel, Jacob II:569

Roser, Abraham II:682
Rosetter, Samuel I:11
Rosetter, Timothy II:271
Ross, Adam I:403
Ross, Alexander I:613; III:259
Ross, Andrew II:17
Ross, Catherine III:41
Ross, Charles III:76
Ross, Daniel I:421; III:229
Ross, David II:348; III:41, 412
Ross, Edward II:466
Ross, Elijah I:935
Ross, Eliza III:41
Ross, Emerson I:863
Ross, Esther I:863
Ross, Ezekiel IV:234
Ross, George I:626; III:586
Ross, Horatio II:208
Ross, Isaac I:254; II:724
Ross, Jackson II:74
Ross, James I:626; II:756; III:222, 398
Ross, Jeremiah I:598
Ross, John I:753, 863; II:91, 250, 271, 615; III:204, 278, 303, 582; IV:175, 257
Ross, John E. I:863
Ross, Jonathan I:315
Ross, Joseph I:184; III:813; IV:254
Ross, Joseph N. IV:148
Ross, Lemuel I:626
Ross, Levi IV:107
Ross, Nathaniel III:228
Ross, Rebecca I:863
Ross, Reuben IV:176
Ross, Robert III:45; III:539
Ross, Robinson III:553
Ross, Rufus I:966
Ross, Samuel II:345, 537
Ross, Sarah I:863; II:197
Ross, Seth I:648, 827
Ross, Suminer I:863
Ross, Thomas I:421; II:197, 740; III:460; IV:46
Ross, Thomas N. II:141
Ross, Timothy I:403
Ross, Urana II:197
Ross, Valentine III:742
Ross, Walter III:78
Ross, William I:353, 403, 863; II:271; III:15, 395
Ross, Williamson III:434
Ross, Zephaniah I:883
Rossburgh, John II:23
Rossen, John III:407
Rossequie, Alexander I:90
Rosser, Richard III:307
Rosseter, Noah I:353
Rosseter, Timothy W. III:143
Rossetter, Bryan II:271, 560
Rossetter, Sarah II:560
Rossin, James III:814
Rossin, Reubin III:766
Rossiter, Benjamin I:112
Rossiter, Timothy I:129
Rosson, Archilaus III:613

Roth, Matthias II:703
Rothe, Thomas IV:145
Rouch, Jonas III:805
Rouley, Philander I:102
Round, Bartram II:487
Round, Samuel II:286, 466
Round, Simeon I:828
Roundey, Joseph I:403
Rounds, Amos I:364
Rounds, James IV:171
Rounds, Joseph I:315
Rounds, Jotham II:526
Rounds, Lemuel IV:171
Rounds, Nathaniel I:151
Rounds, Theodore I:240
Roundtree, Nathaniel III:289
Roundy, Benjamin I:163
Rounes, Charles IV:200
Rounsavill, John III:426
Rourke, David O. III:835
Rouse, Henry II:335
Rouse, Jacob III:259
Rouse, John II:530
Rouse, Lewis III:194, 289
Rouse, Nicholas II:141, 519
Rouse, Peter II:724
Rouse, Samuel III:259
Rouse, Simeon II:212
Rouse, Thomas II:466; IV:262
Rousk, George IV:270
Routon, James III:833
Routon, John III:163
Roux, Louis III:499
Row, Ebenezer I:165
Row, Hezekiah IV:11
Row, John I:198, 218, 920; II:534; III:289, 707
Row, Solomon I:403
Row, Webber I:240
Rowan, Benjamin III:479
Rowan, John II:658; III:374
Rowan, Robert I:xv
Rowan, Samuel III:84
Rowark, Elisha III:409
Rowden, George III:283
Rowe, Archibald I:172
Rowe, Benjamin I:172, 189; III:599
Rowe, Caleb I:198; II:271
Rowe, Charles II:431
Rowe, David II:253
Rowe, Enoch I:725
Rowe, Ezra I:128
Rowe, Isaac I:422
Rowe, Jacque II:221
Rowe, James III:323, 384
Rowe, Jesse IV:246
Rowe, John I:129, 218, 718; II:703
Rowe, Joseph II:421
Rowe, Joshua III:159
Rowe, Lazarus I:198
Rowe, Samuel I:626
Rowe, Thomas II:697
Rowe, William I:198; III:215
Rowe, Zebulon I:255
Rowel, Jonathan I:927

Rowell, Daniel IV:169
Rowell, Enoch I:703
Rowell, Israel I:725
Rowell, James I:891
Rowell, Jesse III:141
Rowell, Moses I:891
Rowell, Samuel I:725
Rowell, Thomas I:754
Rowell, William I:773
Rowen, J. I:xiv
Rowen, John I:702; II:542
Rowen, Joseph I:xii
Rowen, William II:721
Rowick, Gasper II:88
Rowland, Benjamin II:308
Rowland, Daniel I:35; II:387
Rowland, David II:466
Rowland, Henry II:635
Rowland, Hezekiah II:310
Rowland, Jack I:90
Rowland, Jesse I:35
Rowland, John II:458
Rowland, Luke II:471
Rowland, Nathan III:657
Rowland, Peter III:488
Rowland, Samuel III:263
Rowland, Sherman I:43
Rowland, Thomas I:xvi; III:534
Rowlandson, Joseph II:351
Rowlandson, Reuben II:218
Rowles, William III:771
Rowlett, John III:849
Rowlett, William III:765
Rowley, Aaron I:613
Rowley, Abijah IV:210
Rowley, Benjamin I:327
Rowley, Daniel II:407
Rowley, Eli Smith I:112
Rowley, Eliza I:856
Rowley, Joseph II:436
Rowley, Joseph L. IV:264
Rowley, Marilla I:856
Rowley, Nathan II:686
Rowley, Olive I:856
Rowley, Reuben I:856; II:641
Rowley, Seth, 2d II:308
Rowley, Seth, 1st II:308
Rowley, Silas I:103
Rowley, Thomas I:485
Rowley, Timothy II:333
Rowlin, George III:534
Rowlin, Thomas III:534
Rowlins, Aaron II:555
Rowlinson, Joseph II:351
Rowlison, William III:831
Rowntree, William III:791
Rowse, Thomas III:693
Rowsey, Edward III:82
Roxbury, Reuben III:693
Royal, John II:340
Royall, Francis III:765
Royall, Grief III:765
Royall, Jesse III:8
Royall, Tilitha III:464
Royall, William III:464
Royaltree, John III:267

495

Royce, Aaron I:694
Royce, Asa I:144
Royce, Elijah I:63, 991
Royce, Lemuel I:738
Royce, Samuel II:458
Roys, Silas I:972
Royse, Solomon III:253
Royster, Daniel III:780
Royster, Dedrich II:95
Rozell, Jeremiah II:233
Rozier, John I:912
Rozier, William III:487
Rubison, Calza IV:97
Ruble, John IV:258
Rucher, William III:161
Ruchford, William II:26
Rucker, Angus III:851
Rucker, Elliot III:337
Rucker, Elzaphen III:196
Rucker, Lemuel IV:205
Rucker, Nancy III:337
Ruckman, John II:756
Rudd, Andrew I:433
Rudd, Archer III:783
Rudd, Bezaleel II:396
Rudd, Burlingham III:616
Rudd, Nathaniel I:353
Rudd, William I:151
Ruddeau, John II:616
Ruddeel, James III:259
Rudder, John III:783
Rude, Isaac I:150
Rude, William I:367, 808
Rudeailly, Henry IV:238
Rudolph, Christopher IV:206
Rudolph, George II:575
Rudolph, Jacob II:708
Rudolph, John Christopher IV:206
Ruduback, Peter II:652
Rudy, Jacob II:761
Rue, John II:74
Rue, Richard IV:98
Ruffcorn, Simon II:656
Ruford, Frederick II:294
Rugan, John II:742, 744
Ruger, Frederick II:633
Ruger, John II:343
Rugg, Abraham II:364
Rugg, Betsey I:615
Rugg, David I:875
Rugg, Isaac II:364
Rugg, Joshua I:927
Rugg, Josiah I:615
Rugg, Martha I:615
Rugg, Moses IV:184
Rugg, Phineas II:281
Rugg, Sewal I:615
Rugg, Stephen I:598
Rugg, Thomas I:437, 695
Ruggles, Benjamin I:9
Ruggles, Bostwick I:35
Ruggles, Daniel I:649
Ruggles, Ephraim I:649
Ruggles, John I:598
Ruggles, Joseph I:505; II:396
Ruggles, Seth I:966

Ruggles, Timothy I:380
Ruich, Owen I:43
Ruland, Benjamin II:204
Ruland, Thomas II:335
Rule, Thomas III:307
Rumble, Catherine II:623
Rumble, Jacob II:623
Rumble, Rosanna II:623
Rumble, Susanna II:623
Rumblo, Thomas I:613
Rumfelt, Henry III:380
Ruminer, Daniel IV:25
Rummery, Dominicus I:302
Rumney, Stephen I:852
Rumrill, Thomas I:538
Rumsay, John I:901
Rumsdell, Ebenezer I:303
Rumsey, Aaron II:200
Rumsey, Betsey II:200
Rumsey, Charles IV:29
Rumsey, Clarinda II:200
Rumsey, David II:215
Rumsey, Eliza Ann II:200
Rumsey, John I:999; II:200
Rumsey, Maria II:200
Rumsey, William I:966
Rundell, Reuben II:548
Rundler, Nathaniel I:209
Rundlet, Jonathan I:733
Rundlet, Reuben I:753
Rundlet, Theophilus I:935
Rundlett, Jonathan I:773
Runels, Enoch I:995
Runey, John I:506
Runions, Benjamin II:563
Runkle, Henry II:355
Runnell, Joseph I:505
Runnells, A. II:90
Runnells, Samuel I:303
Runnels, Anna I:686
Runnels, Enos I:421-22
Runnels, James I:779
Runnels, Jesse III:753
Runnels, John I:686
Runnels, Miles I:779
Runnels, Paul I:686
Runnels, Peleg I:734
Runnels, Robert I:883
Runnels, Samuel I:779
Runnels, Thomas I:773
Runneon, Conrad II:659
Runsall, Valentine II:708
Runwell, Joseph I:505
Runyan, Clark II:26
Runyan, George II:658
Runyan, Hugh II:83
Runyan, Israel II:26
Runyan, John IV:282
Runyan, Richard II:83
Runyan, William II:26
Runyard, Job II:65
Runyon, John IV:236
Rupart, Adam IV:241
Rupert, George IV:246
Rusco, David I:869
Ruse, A. W. III:637
Ruse, Aaron IV:258

Rusell, Stevens II:491
Rush, John II:208; IV:115
Rush, Samuel II:361
Rush, William II:756
Rusk, Jacob II:680
Rusk, James IV:208
Russ, Epaphras II:324
Russ, Jonathan II:260
Russ, Joseph III:402
Russ, Nathan I:733
Russ, Samuel III:7
Russel, Benjamin II:495
Russel, Chandler I:538
Russel, David I:940
Russel, James III:384, 532
Russel, John I:155; II:37, 253
Russel, Levi I:210
Russel, Newton I:940
Russel, Richard III:398
Russell, Abner I:455
Russell, Absalom III:267
Russell, Alexander II:696
Russell, Amos I:505
Russell, Andrew I:226
Russell, Asa I:353
Russell, Asher IV:204
Russell, Benjamin I:177, 288, 601
Russell, Bill I:523
Russell, Buckner III:628
Russell, Calvin I:226
Russell, Charles IV:248
Russell, Cornelius I:891
Russell, Daniel I:677, 712, 779
Russell, David I:129
Russell, Eleazer II:281
Russell, Elijah IV:246
Russell, Elmore I:363
Russell, Enoch IV:261
Russell, Evan II:710
Russell, George II:11; III:558
Russell, Gideon IV:250
Russell, Henry I:422
Russell, Israel I:446
Russell, James I:402; II:664; III:476; IV:257
Russell, James G. III:154
Russell, Jedediah I:712
Russell, John I:51, 484, 801; II:179, 569; III:525, 715; IV:29, 38
Russell, Jonathan I:695; II:387
Russell, Joseph I:168, 297; II:204
Russell, Josiah II:225
Russell, Moor I:753
Russell, Moses III:601
Russell, Oliver I:555
Russell, Paul II:680
Russell, Pelatiah I:506
Russell, Philip I:434; IV:12
Russell, Philip M. II:680
Russell, Reuben I:905
Russell, Robert III:50, 745, 835
Russell, Robert S. III:276

497

Sampson, Bristoll II:684
Sampson, Colson I:579
Sampson, Crocker I:565
Sampson, Elijah I:581
Sampson, George I:992
Sampson, Gideon I:579
Sampson, Henry II:691
Sampson, Howland I:580
Sampson, Isaac III:247, 366;
IV:194
Sampson, Isaiah I:579
Sampson, James I:257
Sampson, Jonathan I:650
Sampson, Joseph III:824
Sampson, Joshua I:539
Sampson, Luther I:270
Sampson, Miles P. II:556
Sampson, Nathaniel I:981
Sampson, Peleg I:579
Sampson, Philemon I:992
Sampson, Samuel I:579;
IV:229
Sampson, Studley I:581
Sampson, Thomas I:580
Sampson, William III:298;
IV:74
Sampson, Zephaniah I:72
Sams, Samuel III:810
Samson, Ahira I:565
Samuel, Gray III:762
Samuel, James III:687
Samuel, Jeremiah III:369
Samuels, William IV:25
Sanbone, Richard I:703
Sanborn, Abigail I:687
Sanborn, Abner I:317
Sanborn, Anna C. I:687
Sanborn, Benjamin I:303, 780
Sanborn, Benjamin, 2d I:185
Sanborn, David I:713
Sanborn, Elias H.D. I:687
Sanborn, Geo. W. I:687
Sanborn, James I:734
Sanborn, Jeremiah I:780
Sanborn, Jewett I:774
Sanborn, John I:185; II:33
Sanborn, John, 2d I:185
Sanborn, Joseph I:780
Sanborn, Josiah I:780
Sanborn, Leonard I:687
Sanborn, Mary B. I:687
Sanborn, Matthew N. I:298
Sanborn, Moses I:712
Sanborn, Nathan I:680
Sanborn, Paul I:185; II:295
Sanborn, Peter I:185, 957
Sanborn, Reuben I:704
Sanborn, Richard IV:34
Sanborn, Simeon I:218
Sanborn, Solomon I:168
Sanbourne, Solomon I:168
Sanbrun, Levi II:495
Sanburn, Benjamin II:200
Sanburn, Jacob II:200
Sanburn, Ransom II:200
Sanburn, Stillwell II:200
Sandborn, Geo. W. I:687

Sanders, Avery II:383
Sanders, Benjamin I:523
Sanders, Cornelius III:615
Sanders, David I:754
Sanders, Isaac D. III:189
Sanders, James III:619, 801
Sanders, Jesse III:772
Sanders, John I:780; II:271;
III:315, 573; IV:251
Sanders, John, 1st II:238
Sanders, Jonathan II:238
Sanders, Joseph II:381
Sanders, Joshua I:973
Sanders, Obed II:238
Sanders, Philip III:415
Sanders, Reuben III:323
Sanders, Richard III:634
Sanders, Solomon I:761;
III:581
Sanders, Thomas I:91; III:38,
377, 516
Sanders, Timothy II:51
Sanders, William I:884;
II:744; III:418; IV:241
Sanders, Zachariah III:330
Sanderson, Abel I:863
Sanderson, Amaziah II:229
Sanderson, Asa I:447
Sanderson, David I:475
Sanderson, Elnathan I:341
Sanderson, Isaac I:447
Sanderson, Lucinda Z. I:863
Sanderson, Moses I:606
Sanderson, Phinehas I:991
Sanderson, Reuben I:738
Sanderson, Rufus I:298
Sanderson, S. I:659
Sanderson, Sylvanus I:466
Sandeson, Nathaniel H. I:383
Sandford, Archibald I:130
Sandford, Edward III:732
Sandford, Elisha I:130
Sandford, Ezekiel I:24
Sandford, George I:813, 820
Sandford, Jarius I:129
Sandford, Jesse I:103
Sandford, John I:51, 90
Sandford, Royal I:813
Sandford, Samuel IV:280
Sandifer, James III:236
Sandridge, Joseph III:652
Sands, Andrew II:661
Sands, Edward I:725
Sands, William III:453
Sandy, William IV:209
Sanford, D. C. I:155
Sanford, David I:353
Sanford, Ebenezer I:91
Sanford, Elihu I:64, 156
Sanford, Ezekiel II:340
Sanford, Holsey I:486
Sanford, James II:324
Sanford, John I:485
Sanford, Jonathan II:380
Sanford, Joseph I:377; II:363
Sanford, Kingsbury II:416
Sanford, Lewis II:521

Sanford, Reuben II:383
Sanford, Sala II:149
Sanford, Samuel I:91
Sanford, Solomon II:149
Sanford, Strong I:51, 156
Sanford, William II:65, 432
Sanford, Zaccheus I:51
Sanger, Daniel I:354
Sanger, David I:601
Sanhorn, Theophilus I:703
Sankee, Caesar I:921
Sanner, Tryall IV:290
Sapler, John II:756
Sapp, Jesse III:627
Sapp, Joseph II:5; III:356, 720
Sappington, Hartly IV:121
Sapplefield, Michael IV:74
Sardenzas, David III:479
Sargeant, Charles I:241
Sargeant, Daniel I:241
Sargeant, Daniel, 2d I:185
Sargeant, Ebenezer II:238
Sargeant, Jacob I:103
Sargeant, James I:423
Sargeant, John I:967
Sargeant, Moses I:973
Sargeant, Richard II:725
Sargeant, Samuel I:507
Sargeant, Solomon I:507
Sargeant, Winthrop I:422
Sargent, Benjamin I:293
Sargent, Chase I:317
Sargent, Daniel I:650
Sargent, John I:774
Sargent, Phineas I:754
Sargent, Samuel G. I:525
Sargent, Timothy I:754
Sargent, William I:719; II:185
Sarle, Thomas II:349
Sarles, Jonathan II:110
Sarles, Richard II:526
Sarles, Thaddeus II:548
Saroen, Garret II:499
Sarrete, Samuel III:537
Sarrett, Allen III:574
Sarrett, John III:592
Sartell, John I:301, 465
Sartell, Nathaniel I:506, 524
Sartin, Clayburn III:285
Sartin, Eli III:525
Sartine, James III:185
Sartwell, Sylvanus I:981
Sasater, Abner III:407
Sash, Moses I:44
Sass, Jacob III:500
Sassen, Abel III:427
Sasser, Benjamin III:412
Satterly, Samuel IV:181
Satterwhite, John S. III:219
Satterwhite, Robert III:762
Saucaw, Edm. II:561
Saunders, Abel I:44
Saunders, Abraham IV:224
Saunders, Celia I:172
Saunders, Daniel II:496;
III:770
Saunders, David III:300, 753

Saunders, Elisha I:796
Saunders, Francis IV:141
Saunders, George III:54, 762; IV:4
Saunders, Henry IV:96
Saunders, Isaac I:902
Saunders, James IV:60
Saunders, John III:786
Saunders, Jordan I:172
Saunders, Joseph I:163, 555, 835; III:85, 263
Saunders, Mary I:172
Saunders, Nathan I:172
Saunders, Nathaniel I:172; III:423
Saunders, Noah I:626
Saunders, Peter I:81, 459
Saunders, Philemon III:775
Saunders, Richard III:762
Saunders, Robert I:72; II:185
Saunders, Robert H. III:791
Saunders, Samuel I:695
Saunders, Stephen I:835
Saunders, Thomas III:834
Saunders, Uriah I:835
Saunders, Wait II:542
Saunders, William II:10; III:802
Saunderson, Reuben I:738
Saurman, Peter IV:36
Sautell, Jonas I:226
Sautell, Jonathan I:695
Savacool, William II:407
Savage, Abijah I:57
Savage, Edward II:542
Savage, Elijah D. I:163
Savage, Francis I:627
Savage, Gideon II:282, 459
Savage, Hiel II:508
Savage, Jacob I:226
Savage, Joel II:480
Savage, John II:459
Savage, Leven III:593
Savage, Roger II:480
Savage, Selah I:103
Savage, Seth I:120
Savery, Thomas I:927
Savidge, John II:680
Savory, Benjamin I:423
Savoy, Philip III:44
Sawel, John III:588
Sawin, Abner I:651
Sawin, James I:649
Sawin, Levi I:550
Sawlborne, Sherbourne I:718
Sawtell, Benjamin IV:179
Sawtell, Elnathan I:524
Sawtell, Hezekiah I:663
Sawtell, Jonathan I:631
Sawtell, Joseph, 2d I:524
Sawtell, Richard I:650
Sawtell, Solomon I:745
Sawyer, Abel I:754, 906
Sawyer, Asa I:71
Sawyer, Asahel I:113
Sawyer, Barnabas I:317
Sawyer, Barzilla I:754

Sawyer, Benjamin I:650, 744, 767
Sawyer, Calvin I:627
Sawyer, Conant I:891
Sawyer, David I:872
Sawyer, Ebenezer I:316, 875
Sawyer, Eber II:515
Sawyer, Edmund I:767
Sawyer, Eli III:529
Sawyer, Ephraim I:43, 885
Sawyer, Frederick A. I:843
Sawyer, George I:298
Sawyer, Isaac I:256
Sawyer, Jabez I:169
Sawyer, Jacob I:271, 901
Sawyer, James I:744, 878; III:613
Sawyer, John I:185, 256, 754; II:243
Sawyer, Jonathan I:754, 920
Sawyer, Joseph I:744
Sawyer, Josiah I:232, 780, 995
Sawyer, Jude I:650
Sawyer, Lewis III:574
Sawyer, Luke I:298
Sawyer, Oliver I:703
Sawyer, Paul II:212
Sawyer, Samuel I:24, 734
Sawyer, Solomon I:256
Sawyer, Stephen I:713; III:83
Sawyer, Thomas I:256
Sawyer, William I:270, 936
Sawyers, Joseph III:445
Sax, Andrew II:673
Sax, Jacob II:324
Saxson, John II:519
Saxton, Asher II:448
Saxton, Atha III:470
Saxton, James III:486
Saxton, John I:353; III:470
Saxton, Luraney III:470
Saxton, Noah III:470
Saxton, Polly III:470
Saxton, Solomon III:169
Saxton, William II:308
Saxton, Zephaniah II:508
Sayer, Nathaniel I:316; II:83
Sayere, Pierson IV:234
Sayers, Anthony II:65
Sayers, Robert III:243
Sayles, Daniel I:551
Sayles, Elisha I:828
Sayles, Ezekiel II:143
Sayles, Smith I:829
Sayles, Stukely II:459
Sayles, Sylvanus I:808
Saylor, Jacob II:681
Saylor, John II:646
Sayre, Job II:476
Sayre, John II:143
Sayre, Joseph IV:238
Sayre, Joshua II:516
Sayre, Nathan II:530
Sayre, Rauel IV:277
Sayre, William II:37
Sayres, John III:670

Sayres, Nicklin III:670
Sayres, Richard II:67
Sayres, Selee III:670
Sayres, Seley III:670
Sayres, Uzal II:65
Sayward, George I:279
Scaborn, Richard II:338
Scales, James III:449
Scales, Nathan I:524
Scales, Nathaniel III:759
Scales, Samuel I:255
Scally, William III:542
Scamel, Henry III:463
Scarborough, James III:388, 417
Scarborough, John I:151; IV:50
Scarborough, Sam'l Sr. III:460
Scarrit, James II:381
Scarritt, Nathaniel I:703
Scates, James IV:191
Sceney, Adeline II:196
Sceney, Ann II:196
Sceney, Julian II:196
Sceney, King II:196
Sceney, Maria II:196
Sceney, Theodore II:196
Schaefer, Lambert IV:260
Schamp, David II:69
Schantz, Henry II:673
Schatz, Henry II:738
Scheenhan, William IV:241
Scheib, William II:680
Scheiner, Philip II:617
Schell, George II:164
Schellenex, Abraham I:57
Schenck, Chrincyonce II:79
Schenck, Henry H. II:86
Schenck, Jacob II:707
Schenck, Koert II:79
Schenck, Ralph II:442, 564
Schenck, William II:47
Scheneman, John II:412
Schennack, Garret G. IV:291
Scherer, Philip Peter II:695
Scherlin, James III:328
Schermerhorn, Bartholomew II:511
Schermerhorn, Garret II:511
Schermerhorn, John I. II:511
Schermerhorn, Lawrence II:511
Schleppy, Jacob II:732
Schlife, John IV:182
Schlott, Adam II:761
Schmidt, Christian II:703
Schmuck, John II:761
Schneider, Jacob II:747
Schneider, John II:675
Schoff, Jacob I:942
Schofield, David II:59
Schofield, Hester II:201
Schofield, Joseph II:201
Schofield, Mary Francis II:191
Schofield, Patty II:201
Schofield, Smith II:201
Schofield, William II:191, 646

Scholfield, Jesse III:263
Scholl, John Jost II:416
Schoolcraft, Jacob II:515
Schoolcraft, John II:356, 515; III:799
Schoolcraft, Lawrence II:282
Schoolcraft, Samuel II:328
Schooler, William III:334
Schools, George III:796
Schooly, John IV:254
Schoonmaker, Henry II:233
Schoonmaker, Johannes II:534
Schoonmaker, John II:357
Schoonmaker, John Ed. II:534
Schoonover, James II:175
Schoonover, Joseph II:476
Schovil, Jacob I:51
Schrach, Andrew III:48
Schram, Frederick II:412
Schram, John II:442
Schreader, Jacob III:727
Schreeder, John II:300
Schreiner, Christopher II:616
Schreiner, John II:616
Schrimpler, Robert III:607
Schroeder, Anthony II:704
Schryver, Martinus II:534
Schultz, John III:777
Schutt, James II:534
Schutt, Solomon II:534
Schuyler, David A. II:416
Schuyler, Jeremiah II:552
Schuyler, John II:587
Schuyler, Nicholas II:315
Schuyler, Peter S. II:356
Schuyler, Reuben II:356
Schwartze, Peter I:279
Scidel, Peter II:730
Scislar, Philip III:47
Scisson, Robert III:693
Scites, Christopher II:581
Scobey, James II:308
Scoffield, Selah II:151
Scofield, Asahel II:548
Scofield, Elisha II:421
Scofield, Enos II:352, 374
Scofield, Ezra I:91
Scofield, Hait I:92
Scofield, Israel II:459
Scofield, John III:8
Scofield, Josiah W. I:91
Scofield, Nathaniel II:564
Scofield, Neazer II:508
Scofield, Pellit I:24
Scofield, Reuben I:91
Scofield, Selah II:374
Scofield, Silas II:466
Scofield, Stephen II:325
Scofield, Sylvanus II:300
Scoggins, Jonah IV:13
Scoggins, Robert III:406
Scoggins, Willis III:496
Scoggs, Samuel S. III:722
Scollay, John I:506
Scoone, George III:38
Scotland, Thomas II:617
Scott, Abel I:447

Scott, Abraham II:725
Scott, Alexander II:275; III:847; IV:62
Scott, Amasa I:470, 854; II:348
Scott, Anderson Hughes III:203
Scott, Andrew II:628, 736
Scott, Ann II:628
Scott, Anne III:202
Scott, Arthur III:596
Scott, Benjamin II:516, 542; IV:76
Scott, Buby III:202
Scott, Caleb II:230
Scott, Carolina III:202
Scott, Charles I:695, 795-96
Scott, Christopher II:737
Scott, Daniel II:508; III:392
Scott, David I:539; II:427, 714; III:202, 504, 654
Scott, Dennis III:478
Scott, Devy III:202
Scott, Drury III:214
Scott, Ebenezer I:912
Scott, Edmond Waller III:203
Scott, Edward II:185
Scott, Eleazer II:97
Scott, Eliza II:628
Scott, Eliza Green III:203
Scott, Ethiel I:883
Scott, Ezekiel II:330, 545
Scott, Francis III:205
Scott, George III:643
Scott, Gideon II:282
Scott, Henry I:947; II:562; III:202
Scott, Hezekiah I:744
Scott, Hugh III:203
Scott, Isaac IV:289
Scott, Isham III:378
Scott, James II:185, 521, 534, 628; III:38, 264, 491, 596, 634, 809
Scott, James, 2d III:7
Scott, James M. III:724
Scott, Jesse III:319
Scott, Joel IV:286
Scott, John I:28, 713, 920, 967; II:18, 169, 348, 628; III:202, 225, 272, 286, 415, 426, 495, 572, 637, 676, 847; IV:16, 80, 297, 300
Scott, John, 2d II:325
Scott, John, 3d II:286
Scott, Jonathan II:303, 643
Scott, Joseph I:43, 957; III:202, 667, 686
Scott, Laura I:28
Scott, Lemuel I:845
Scott, Margaret II:628
Scott, Merit Cowthers III:203
Scott, Micah II:687
Scott, Moses II:325, 563
Scott, Nathaniel II:281
Scott, Oliver IV:185
Scott, Philip II:421

Scott, Phineas I:447
Scott, Rebecca II:628
Scott, Reuben III:557
Scott, Richard II:617
Scott, Robert II:698, 741; III:280
Scott, Sally III:202
Scott, Samuel II:646, 750; III:55, 649; IV:30
Scott, Samuel (2) IV:30
Scott, Severn III:674
Scott, Stephen II:487
Scott, T. II:603
Scott, Thomas II:320, 616; III:280, 632
Scott, Thomas, 2d III:579
Scott, Uri I:129
Scott, William I:819; II:185, 336, 387, 472, 534, 573, 616-17, 628, 706; III:155, 189, 202, 526, 681, 783, 826; IV:16
Scott, William, 2d II:688
Scott, Zeriah II:750
Scouten, Jacob II:732
Scouter, Elias II:115
Scovel, Abijah II:295
Scovel, Ebenezer II:254
Scovel, Matthew II:459
Scovel, Stephen II:253
Scovell, Moses IV:266
Scovell, Solomon I:138
Scovil, Benjamin II:325
Scovil, John II:425
Scovil, Joseph I:120
Scovil, Samuel II:363
Scovil, Samuel, Jr. II:294
Scovill, Amasa IV:289
Scovill, Westol II:363
Scoville, Michael IV:290
Scowden, Theodorus II:714
Scrafford, George II:356
Scranton, Abraham I:120, 129
Scranton, John I:129
Scranton, Stephen I:695
Scranton, Thomas I:130
Scranton, Timothy I:63
Scranton, Torry I:129
Scribbing, William III:694
Scribner, Abel II:265
Scribner, Ebenezer I:713
Scribner, Jonathan II:383
Scribner, Nathaniel I:24
Scribner, Stephen I:270
Scribner, Thaddeus II:508
Scribner, Zadock I:902
Scripter, John I:345
Scripture, Samuel I:744
Scriven, James II:495
Scriven, William II:496
Scriven, Zebulon II:315
Scrivner, Benjamin III:619
Scroggin, Thomas C. III:279
Scroggs, Jeremiah III:426
Scroggy, Thomas II:60
Scrogs, John III:426
Scruggs, Timothy III:684

Semore, Thomas III:571
Senior, David II:629
Senior, John II:629
Senior, Margaretta II:629
Senior, Mary II:629
Senior, Rosanna II:629
Sennett, Patrick III:845
Senter, Abel I:256
Senter, Asa I:789
Senter, Moses I:780
Sephton, Richard I:795
Seranton, Stafford I:811
Serberling, Frederick II:730
Sergeant, Abel II:300
Sergeant, Amos I:506
Sergeant, Daniel I:177
Sergeant, Ebenezer II:706
Sergeant, Elijah IV:240
Sergeant, Jacob II:111
Sergeant, James I:684
Sergeant, Jane I:684
Sergeant, Jeremiah III:699
Sergeant, John G. I:684
Sergeant, Jotham I:177
Sergeant, Mary I:177, 684
Sergeant, Miriam I:177
Sergeant, Nancy I:177
Sergeant, Paul Dudley I:189
Sergeant, Robert I:735
Sergeant, Sarah I:177
Sergeant, Valentine I:734
Sergeant, William I:946;
   III:261
Sergent, Ebenezer I:761
Sergent, Jonathan I:767
Sergent, Joseph I:767
Sergent, Joshua I:761
Serjeant, James II:271
Servants, William III:236
Servess, William G. IV:132
Service, Nathaniel I:598
Sessions, Abijah I:145
Sessions, David I:184
Sessions, John III:144
Sessions, Robert I:467
Setton, William III:545
Setts, Henry II:266
Seuter, Asa I:725
Seuter, Thomas I:773
Seva, John III:133
Sever, Christopher I:565
Sever, James I:658
Severance, Abbe I:921
Severance, Abel I:718
Severance, Abigail I:687
Severance, Asa I:744
Severance, Benjamin IV:275
Severance, Caleb I:222
Severance, Ebenezer I:992
Severance, Jonathan I:780
Severance, Jon'n I:687
Severance, Joseph I:712
Severance, Joshua I:293
Severance, Mehitabel I:687
Severance, Parker I:687
Severance, Polly I:687
Severance, Sally I:687

Severance, Samuel II:641
Severn, David III:220
Severy, John I:650
Sevey, Eleakin I:241
Sevier, Abraham III:609
Sevier, James III:625
Sewall, Clement III:7, 16
Sewall, Dummer I:199
Sewall, Henry I:199, 320
Sewall, James III:18, 61;
   IV:120
Sewall, Jane III:16
Sewall, Thomas IV:210
Seward, Daniel III:282
Seward, George I:780
Seward, Jedediah I:902
Seward, John IV:4
Seward, Josiah I:695
Seward, Leverett II:115
Seward, Samuel I:744; IV:38
Seward, Silas II:208
Seward, Timothy I:129; II:204
Sewell, Charles III:49
Sewell, John III:44
Sewell, Joseph III:272
Seword, Swain II:160
Sexton, Charles IV:246
Sexton, Elijah II:381
Sexton, Ezra IV:228
Sexton, John III:297, 363
Sexton, Noble II:238
Sexton, Timothy III:539
Sexton, William III:251
Seybert, Christian III:846
Seybert, David III:61
Seydam, Abraham II:628
Seydam, Henry II:628
Seydam, Jacob II:628
Seydam, Mary II:628
Seydam, Sally Ann II:628
Seydam, Sylvester II:628
Seydam, William II:628
Seydon, Jacob II:628
Seymour, Asa I:466
Seymour, George I:44
Seymour, Gerard III:671
Seymour, Horatio I:997
Seymour, James I:91
Seymour, Joseph II:281
Seymour, Nancy III:671
Seymour, Nathan I:477, 878
Seymour, Nathaniel II:508
Seymour, Samuel I:112
Seymour, Seth I:91
Seymour, Stephen II:308
Seymour, William I:7, 927;
   II:508
Seymour, Zadock II:466
Seyner, Michael IV:177
Seypeart, Robert III:561
Shackelford, Alex. III:796
Shackelford, Dudley III:837
Shackelford, Leonard III:796
Shackelford, William III:792
Shackelton, Richard II:89
Shacklee, Peter IV:204
Shackleford, Henry III:287

Shackleford, John III:133, 667
Shackleford, Richard III:692
Shackler, Philip III:560
Shackley, Joseph I:316
Shaddy, John IV:92
Shade, Jacob III:777
Shadley, Daniel IV:266
Shadow, Deadlove II:695
Shafer, Andrew IV:258
Shafer, Henrich, Jun. II:515
Shafer, Henry II:515
Shafer, Peter III:356, 515
Shaff, Henry II:471
Shaff, William II:330
Shaffer, Adam II:702
Shaffer, Andrew IV:217
Shaffer, David III:558
Shaffer, Frederick II:669
Shaffer, George II:328
Shaffer, Jacob III:738
Shaffer, Jocob IV:207
Shaffer, John III:47, 453, 621
Shaffer, Thomas II:690
Shafford, Jesse II:407
Shaft, John II:432
Shaft, William II:169
Shaler, Ephraim IV:151
Shaler, Henry II:671
Shaler, Joseph V:160
Shall, George III:67
Shall, Henry II:416
Shandley, Jacob III:38
Shands, William, Sr. III:840
Shane, Daniel III:26
Shaner, George III:711
Shaner, Matthias II:636
Shank, Christian III:812
Shank, Manus III:370
Shankland, Alexander IV:293
Shankle, George III:434
Shanks, John III:233
Shanks, John, 2d III:235
Shannon, Archibald B. III:531
Shannon, Arthur III:217
Shannon, Baxter II:115
Shannon, George II:327;
   IV:114
Shannon, John I:774
Shannon, Robert II:711
Shannon, Thomas I:725
Shannon, William III:583
Sharewood, James II:333
Sharon, Samuel III:200
Sharp, Adam III:449
Sharp, Amos IV:241
Sharp, Andrew I:751
Sharp, Anthony II:25
Sharp, Benjamin IV:125
Sharp, Delany II:25
Sharp, Elizabeth II:25
Sharp, Gibeon I:565
Sharp, Isaac II:25, 338
Sharp, Isham III:320
Sharp, John II:142; III:180,
   196, 321, 707
Sharp, John, 2d III:263
Sharp, John, Sen. III:820

Sharp, Joseph II:25
Sharp, Reuben I:151
Sharp, Richard II:25
Sharp, Salmon II:100
Sharp, Samuel III:596
Sharp, Samuel, Sr. III:262
Sharp, Thomas III:404
Sharp, William III:229, 545
Sharp, William, 2d III:217
Sharpe, Caleb I:151
Sharpe, Daniel I:991
Sharpe, Joseph III:426
Sharpe, Josiah III:826
Sharpe, Peter II:294
Shartel, Jacob II:573
Shattock, John I:606
Shattuck, Abial I:973
Shattuck, Abraham I:738
Shattuck, Daniel II:196
Shattuck, David I:71
Shattuck, Ebenezer L. I:507
Shattuck, Elizabeth II:196
Shattuck, John II:112
Shattuck, Jonas I:165
Shattuck, Joseph I:422
Shattuck, Nathaniel I:981
Shattuck, Phedilla II:196
Shattuck, Rufus II:196
Shattuck, Samuel II:275
Shattuck, Stephen I:712
Shattuck, Thomas II:219
Shattuck, William II:196
Shaver, Henry II:356, 417
Shaver, Jacob II:466
Shaver, John II:127, 394;
   IV:36
Shaver, John F. II:295
Shaver, Paul III:799
Shaver, Peter II:387, 759
Shavers, Shadrach III:740
Shaw, Abiatha I:744
Shaw, Abraham I:315
Shaw, Alexander II:616
Shaw, Archibald III:62
Shaw, Asa I:475, 581
Shaw, Basil III:165
Shaw, Bela I:875
Shaw, Benjamin I:81, 232,
   447; III:627
Shaw, Beriah I:485
Shaw, Brackley I:580
Shaw, Charles III:789
Shaw, Chipman I:447
Shaw, Crispus I:565, 894
Shaw, Daniel II:333, 502;
   III:356
Shaw, Darling II:496
Shaw, David II:488
Shaw, Eliab I:270
Shaw, Elijah I:565, 946
Shaw, Elisha I:270
Shaw, Ephriam I:199
Shaw, Follansbee I:767
Shaw, Geo. IV:297
Shaw, George I:222, 565
Shaw, Gilman B. I:168
Shaw, Henry III:192; IV:54

Shaw, Ichabod II:668
Shaw, Jacob I:199
Shaw, James I:199, 434, 927;
   III:522; IV:33
Shaw, Jarius I:289
Shaw, John I:210, 377, 466,
   767; II:205; III:38, 163, 191;
   IV:180
Shaw, John Robert II:617
Shaw, Jonathan IV:59
Shaw, Joseph I:256, 376, 774;
   II:319; III:196, 460
Shaw, Joshua I:774
Shaw, Josiah I:485; II:230
Shaw, Lemuel I:991
Shaw, Levi I:256
Shaw, Luther I:967
Shaw, Michael III:387
Shaw, Nathaniel I:184, 289
Shaw, Nathaniel (2) I:289
Shaw, Noah I:820
Shaw, Obed I:485
Shaw, Richard I:869
Shaw, Robert, Jr. II:569
Shaw, Samuel I:317, 565;
   II:164; IV:11
Shaw, Seth I:819
Shaw, Sylvanus I:485, 921
Shaw, Thomas I:255, 725;
   III:260
Shaw, William I:241; II:228,
   233; III:576, 599
Shaw, Zachariah III:581
Shawke, Jacob IV:241
Shawn, Frederick IV:286
Shay, James II:272
Shay, John II:185
Shay, Peter II:361
Shay, Seers II:586
Shay, Timothy II:352
Shaylor, Joseph III:7
Shays, Daniel II:294
Shays, David I:901
Shea, Stephen II:598
Sheaf, George II:281
Sheaman, George III:819
Shean, Richard I:185
Shear, John L. IV:105
Shear, Matthias II:545
Shearer, David II:685
Shearer, James I:762; II:326
Shearer, William II:325
Shearin, Frederic III:457
Shearman, Daniel I:820
Shearman, Eber I:835
Shearman, Henry I:811
Shearman, Job. I:811
Shearman, John II:30
Shearman, John W. I:835
Shearman, Lodowick I:835
Shearman, Peter I:808
Shearman, Remington I:835
Shearman, Reuben I:835
Shearman, Solomon I:813
Shearman, William I:820
Shears, Peter IV:220
Shed, Daniel I:221; IV:36

Shed, David II:234
Shed, Joel I:524
Shed, John I:271, 713, 762
Shed, Jonathan I:289
Shed, Nathaniel H. I:532
Sheely, Conrad II:534
Sheerman, Richard I:680
Sheese, Peter IV:220
Sheets, John III:845
Sheets, Mathias IV:182
Shefer, Andrew IV:258
Sheffer, Tennis II:508
Sheffield, Charles II:222
Sheffield, George III:274
Sheffield, Joseph II:219
Sheffield, Nathan II:369
Sheffield, Robert I:35
Sheffield, Samuel I:811
Sheffield, Stanton I:835
Shefstall, Shefstall III:158
Shehee, John III:145
Shelby, Samuel I:71
Shelden, Elihu II:243
Shelden, Elisha II:295
Shelden, Israel I:878
Shelden, Job II:345
Shelden, Joseph III:317
Shelden, Moses I:931
Shelden, Nathaniel II:519
Sheldon, Amos I:627
Sheldon, Asa I:828
Sheldon, Cephas I:906
Sheldon, Daniel I:803
Sheldon, Elijah I:24
Sheldon, Ephraim I:465
Sheldon, Ephriam I:301, 353
Sheldon, Ezekiel II:381
Sheldon, George II:370
Sheldon, Isaac II:381
Sheldon, John I:354
Sheldon, Jonathan I:811, 936
Sheldon, Josiah I:940
Sheldon, Nathaniel I:796
Sheldon, Ptolemy II:115
Sheldon, Remembrance I:43
Sheldon, Reuben I:447
Sheldon, Roger I:835
Sheldon, Samuel I:475
Sheldon, Whiting I:343; II:262
Sheldon, William I:210, 507
Shelhamer, Philip Jacob II:747
Shell, Edward II:185
Shell, Henry II:144
Shell, Marks II:425
Shellehamer, George II:716
Shelley, Ebenezer II:542
Shelley, Samuel II:557
Shellman, John III:158
Shelly, Cyrus I:71
Shelor, Daniel III:777
Shelp, William I:91
Shelton, Edwin III:850
Shelton, John II:7, 10
Shelton, Joseph III:780
Shelton, Medley III:219
Shelton, Samuel III:307
Shelton, Wilson III:291

503

Shemer, Isaac II:740
Shenault, Benjamin III:392
Shenck, John II:79
Shenck, John H. II:75
Shenefelt, Nicholas II:645
Shepard, Amos I:120
Shepard, Asa I:152
Shepard, Benjamin IV:231
Shepard, Daniel I:120
Shepard, George I:884
Shepard, Henry II:364
Shepard, James I:598; II:387
Shepard, Joel I:447
Shepard, John II:287
Shepard, Joseph I:434; IV:290
Shepard, Samuel I:151, 954
Shepard, Silas II:330
Shepard, Simeon I:152
Shepard, Whitmore I:103
Shepard, William I:927
Shepardson, Zephaniah I:980
Sheperdson, Nathan II:315
Shephard, Daniel I:718
Shephard, Israel II:432
Shephard, Jesse I:44
Shephard, Joseph II:412
Shephard, Rufus II:381
Shephard, Stephen I:466
Shepherd, Amos I:456
Shepherd, Charles II:327;
   IV:229
Shepherd, Elisha I:891; IV:254
Shepherd, Furman II:61
Shepherd, George III:304
Shepherd, Jacob III:753;
   IV:255
Shepherd, James I:24, 210
Shepherd, John II:272, 295,
   572
Shepherd, Lewis I:185
Shepherd, Morrell I:767
Shepherd, Phinehas IV:243
Shepherd, Prestley III:190
Shepherd, Samuel I:762;
   III:634
Shepherd, Stephen I:626
Shepherd, Thomas I:13, 63;
   II:101; III:613
Shepherd, William I:210;
   IV:50, 234
Shepherdson, David III:832
Sheppard, Jonathan I:901;
   III:715
Sheppard, Joseph III:675
Sheppard, Levi I:199
Sheppard, Robert II:674
Sheppard, Valentine III:427
Shepperd, A. C. IV:99
Shepperd, A. H. III:462
Shepperd, Jonathan I:999
Sherborne, John S. I:674
Sherbourne, Thomas I:725
Sherburn, Andrew II:281
Sherburne, Benjamin II:315,
   562
Sherburne, Job I:199
Sherer, Jacob II:744

Sherer, James II:185
Sheridan, Abner III:162
Sheridan, James II:616
Sherley, John I:744
Sherley, Thomas IV:14
Sherlock, Edward IV:214
Sherman, Abiel II:164, 396
Sherman, Amos P. II:349
Sherman, Benjamin I:466
Sherman, Beriah I:972
Sherman, Caleb I:447
Sherman, Christopher I:475;
   II:750
Sherman, Darius II:496
Sherman, David I:606
Sherman, Edmund II:508
Sherman, Edward I:613
Sherman, Enoch I:931
Sherman, Ephraim I:524
Sherman, Isaac I:316; II:42,
   143
Sherman, Jabez II:537
Sherman, Jeremiah I:466
Sherman, Job II:356
Sherman, John I:365, 580,
   811; III:756
Sherman, Joseph I:301, 456,
   465, 973
Sherman, Nathan I:279
Sherman, Paul II:300
Sherman, Peleg II:487
Sherman, Peter II:564
Sherman, Renel I:973
Sherman, Reuben I:754
Sherman, Robert I:532; III:699
Sherman, Rufus I:579
Sherman, Samuel I:565; II:467
Sherman, Stephen II:442
Sherman, Thomas II:222
Sherman, Timothy I:456;
   IV:224
Sherman, William II:421
Sherman, William B. I:354
Sherod, Jordon III:437
Sherrell, George III:581
Sherrer, James III:671
Sherrer, Robert III:671
Sherrill, Abraham, Jr. II:521
Sherrill, James III:284
Sherrill, Jeremiah II:394
Sherrod, Robert III:325
Sherron, John III:460
Sherry, William III:254
Sherwill, Thomas I:725
Sherwin, Daniel I:992
Sherwin, Elnathan IV:176
Sherwin, Ohimaas IV:179
Sherwood, Abel I:91
Sherwood, Abel M. I:154
Sherwood, Adiel II:349
Sherwood, Andrew II:340
Sherwood, Asa II:219
Sherwood, Daniel I:51
Sherwood, Eliphalet I:4
Sherwood, James II:326, 333
Sherwood, Jedediah I:884
Sherwood, Joel IV:161

Sherwood, John II:233
Sherwood, Moses II:548
Sherwood, Nathan II:243
Sherwood, Nehemiah I:35;
   II:352, 519, 688
Sherwood, Philinia IV:161
Sherwood, Reuben I:92
Sherwood, Seth II:542
Sherwood, Seth N. II:534
Sherwood, Seymour II:271
Sherwood, Stratton II:228
Sherwood, Thomas I:91;
   II:142; III:38
Sherwood, William IV:161
Sherwood, Zachariah I:35
Shery, John IV:131
Shethar, John II:471
Shever, Frederick III:585
Sheverdecker, Michael IV:282
Shew, Jacob II:558
Shew, Stephen II:421
Shewell, Susan II:624
Shewell, William II:624
Shewmaker, Leonard IV:76
Shibley, John II:79
Shields, Daniel II:327, 552
Shields, David II:42, 699;
   IV:239
Shields, David L. I:456, 657
Shields, James II:349, 662
Shields, John II:726; III:572
Shields, Joshua IV:25
Shields, Tobias IV:201
Shiflet, Blan III:819
Shillingford, George II:628
Shillingford, Hiram II:628
Shillingford, James II:628
Shillingford, Michael II:628
Shilty, Christopher II:333
Shindlebowe, George III:217
Shiner, John IV:293
Shingle, Peter II:729
Shingleton, William III:707
Shinn, Isaac III:790
Shinnick, Jacob III:26
Shipe, Philip III:370
Shipherd, David I:967
Shipley, Peter IV:153
Shipley, Samuel III:236
Shipman, Abraham I:973
Shipman, Benoni I:57
Shipman, David IV:13
Shipman, George II:295
Shipman, James I:404; III:402
Shipman, John IV:254
Shipman, Samuel I:992; II:65
Shippee, Christopher I:353
Shippee, Jesse II:508
Shippee, Nathan I:434
Shippee, Samuel I:801
Shippey, Daniel II:123
Shippey, Silas I:340
Shippey, Solomon I:828
Shippey, Thomas II:219
Shippey, William I:112
Shirer, Jeremiah II:574
Shirk, Jacob II:658

Shirkee, Anthony II:210
Shirkey, John II:575
Shirley, Daniel II:688
Shirley, James III:126
Shirley, Job II:412
Shirley, John I:324
Shirley, Samuel I:735
Shirley, Thomas II:723
Shirman, Abner II:260
Shirtliff, John I:946
Shirtliff, Noah IV:280
Shirts, Mathias IV:177
Shirts, Peter II:295
Shirtz, P___r II:69
Shirtzer, Casper III:59
Shite, Peter II:127
Shitz, John II:716
Shive, Lewis II:761
Shiveley, Jacob II:673
Shiverick, Joseph I:327
Shivers, Adam II:598
Shivers, Jesse III:385
Shlife, John IV:182
Shoafler, Valentine II:729
Shoales, Abel I:17
Shobe, John Wm. III:675
Shober, John III:754
Shockey, Christian II:683
Shockler, Frederick II:674
Shockley, John III:60
Shockley, Thomas III:630
Shockney, Patrick III:47
Shoebrook, Philip III:38
Shoecraft, Jacob II:421
Shoecraft, John II:295
Shoemaker, Abr'm II:713
Shoemaker, Christian II:598
Shoemaker, Daniel II:526
Shoemaker, John, Sen. II:747
Shoemaker, Peter II:356
Shoemaker, Randal III:378
Shoemaker, Samuel II:526
Shoemaker, Thomas T. II:416
Shoemaker, William IV:246
Shoeman, Adam II:695
Shoemate, Spencer III:195
Sholes, Carey Wheeler I:72
Sholes, Jabez I:145
Sholes, Miner II:487
Shome, John II:703
Shook, Andrew III:424
Shook, Jacob II:361; III:424
Shoonover, James IV:146
Shoop, Martin II:584
Shoppe, Anthony I:531
Shores, Christian IV:63
Shores, Thomas, 2d III:772
Shores, Thomas, 1st III:772
Shores, William I:735
Shorey, Daniel I:685
Shorey, Ephraim I:685
Shorey, Jefferson I:685
Shorey, John I:734
Shorey, Samuel I:168
Short, Eli IV:5
Short, John III:220; IV:80
Short, Joshua III:223

Short, Moses I:423
Short, Patrick II:143
Short, Peter W. II:174
Short, Samuel I:813; II:488; III:649
Short, Seth I:151
Short, Silvan I:151
Short, Simeon I:998
Short, Zachariah II:534
Shorts, Nicholas II:387
Sho_t, Shubael I:905
Shots, John III:52
Shott, Richard III:678
Shottler, John II:564
Shoun, John III:285
Shoup, Henry, Sen. II:662
Shoup, Ludwig II:674
Shouse, Christian IV:196
Shout, Adam II:753
Shovell, John III:38
Shover, Francis II:658
Shover, John III:754
Shreve, Godfrey II:315
Shreve, John IV:280
Shrider, Philip II:680
Shrieves, William III:732
Shrifler, Henry II:753
Shriven, Thomas II:5
Shrohl, Jacob II:664
Shrom, Henry II:698
Shropshire, Abner III:260
Shropshire, William III:563
Shrott, Samuel II:664
Shroyer, Matthias II:643
Shruber, Frederick II:664
Shruder, John II:641
Shrupp, Henry III:47
Shryock, Christian II:637
Shryock, John III:47
Shubert, John II:680
Shuck, Jacob III:11
Shuck, Matthew III:291
Shuck, Philip IV:74
Shuckford, Samuel I:316
Shufeldt, John III:807
Shufelt, Peter II:356
Shufelt, William II:412
Shuff, Frederick II:682
Shuffield, Ephraim III:325
Shuffield, John IV:112
Shugart, Eli II:631
Shull, Peter IV:19
Shuller, Frederick II:759
Shulp, John II:476
Shultis, Jacob II:357
Shultis, Philip II:383
Shults, George II:467
Shults, Henry II:442
Shults, Matthias III:313
Shultz, Jacob II:425
Shultz, John II:572
Shultz, Michael II:695
Shumaker, Hamieen III:82
Shumaker, Zedekiah III:749
Shumate, Samuel III:792
Shumate, W. J. III:530
Shumaway, Isaac W. IV:106

Shumaway, Peter II:686
Shumway, Augustus I:856
Shumway, Benjamin I:446
Shumway, Cyrenus I:856
Shumway, Cyril I:835
Shumway, Deruses I:856
Shumway, Diadama I:856
Shumway, Elijah I:81
Shumway, John I:872, 997
Shumway, Levi I:981
Shumway, Nathan I:856
Shumway, Orsamus I:856
Shumway, Samuel I:651
Shumway, Seruses I:856
Shumway, Stephen I:475
Shundler, Robert II:685
Shup, Martin II:584
Shupe, John IV:92
Shurman, Asa I:579
Shurtleff, David I:579
Shurtleff, Gideon I:579
Shurtleff, Timothy I:936
Shurtliff, Amasa II:271
Shurtliff, Benoni I:927
Shurtliff, Eliza I:556
Shurtliff, Isaac I:556
Shurtliff, William I:185
Shuster, Andrew II:744
Shute, A. II:90
Shute, Benjamin I:773
Shute, Dan., Jr. I:659
Shute, Daniel I:659
Shute, George I:599, 719
Shute, John I:507
Shute, Thomas III:366
Shute, William II:447, 553
Shutliff, John II:185
Shuttuck, William I:112
Shutz, Adam IV:163
Shutz, Henry IV:163
Shutz, Jacob IV:163
Shutz, Lancy IV:163
Sias, John I:289
Sibberal, William IV:155
Sibery, William II:37
Sibley, Archelaus I:152
Sibley, Daniel I:651
Sibley, David I:456
Sibley, Ezra I:343; II:262
Sibley, James I:927
Sibley, John III:114, 121
Sibley, Moses I:466
Sibley, Samuel I:780
Sibliss, Thomas IV:184
Siche, Samuel I:738
Sickels, Zacharias II:356
Sickle, David II:37
Sickler, Michael II:669
Sickler, William II:356
Sickles, John II:116
Sickles, John W. II:620
Siddle, George II:606
Siddles, John II:120
Sidebottom, John III:214
Sidebottom, Joseph III:226
Sidgeley, Joseph I:279
Sidle, Peter IV:222

Sidway, James II:476
Sifert, Peter II:211
Sigle, Henry II:740
Sigler, Henry II:37
Sigman, George III:400
Sigourney, Andrew I:601
Sike, Bartlet III:574
Sikes, David I:104
Sikes, Gideon I:104
Sikes, Jacob I:967
Sikes, Nathan II:228
Sikes, Nathaniel II:394
Sikes, Thomas A. III:557
Silence, William III:56
Silk, James II:695
Silkworth, William II:534
Sill, Andrew II:488
Sill, Henry II:562
Sill, Samuel I:57
Sillaway, Daniel I:423
Sillcocks, Valentine II:37
Silley, Thomas I:713
Sillick, Abigail II:196
Sillick, Benjamin II:196
Sillick, Clarissa II:196
Silliman, Samuel II:364
Silliman, Thomas II:740
Sillimant, W. IV:296
Sills, Elisha N. I:103
Sills, Miles III:359
Sillsbury, Jonathan II:558
Silly, Benjamin I:230
Silsbe, David II:56
Silsbee, John IV:102
Silsby, David II:179
Silsby, Lazell I:786
Silver, Aaron III:588
Silver, Adeline I:863
Silver, Betsey I:863
Silver, Catherine I:388
Silver, Daniel I:423
Silver, David I:863
Silver, George III:400
Silver, Jessie I:863
Silver, John I:384, 388, 863
Silver, Sarah I:863
Silver, Sarah Abigail I:388
Silver, Susanna I:863
Silver, Zebediah I:703
Silvers, John IV:115
Silverthorn, Robert III:423
Silvester, Joel I:565
Silvester, Joseph IV:203
Silvester, Levi II:526
Silvester, Thomas I:256
Silvey, Stephen III:181
Simmers, George II:698
Simmonds, Joel IV:75
Simmonds, Joseph IV:115
Simmonds, Joshua I:525
Simmonds, Robert IV:234
Simmonds, Samuel I:168, 703
Simmons, Abner I:819
Simmons, Asa III:785
Simmons, Benjamin I:63;
  II:432
Simmons, Benoni I:793

Simmons, Ensley II:380
Simmons, Ephraim I:377
Simmons, Ezekiel II:233
Simmons, Ezra I:816
Simmons, Gideon II:432
Simmons, Ichabod I:298, 803
Simmons, Isaac I:279, 820
Simmons, Ivory II:459
Simmons, Jehu III:764
Simmons, Jeremiah III:456
Simmons, Jesse III:613
Simmons, John II:542; III:381,
  412, 821
Simmons, Joseph III:585
Simmons, Joshua I:992; II:471
Simmons, Lemuel I:579
Simmons, Libbeus I:301, 465
Simmons, Nathaniel I:580
Simmons, Peter D. II:143
Simmons, Robert II:233
Simmons, Samuel I:218
Simmons, Sanders III:402
Simmons, Sebre II:343
Simmons, Stephen IV:19
Simmons, Sylvanus II:447
Simmons, Thomas I:365, 580;
  III:7
Simmons, William III:61, 291,
  660; IV:217
Simms, James III:569
Simms, Joseph III:13
Simms, Richard IV:120
Simon, Cummy I:64
Simonds, Albert I:683
Simonds, Ashney I:103
Simonds, Benjamin I:566
Simonds, Eliza I:860
Simonds, Elizur I:860
Simonds, James I:703
Simonds, Jonathan I:683
Simonds, Joseph I:524, 940
Simonds, Joshua II:380
Simonds, Nathaniel I:703
Simonds, Rosilla I:683
Simonds, Simeon I:713
Simonds, William I:703
Simons, Aaron I:51
Simons, Andrew II:352
Simons, Arad I:754
Simons, Eli I:340
Simons, Elijah I:151
Simons, Faulkner IV:158
Simons, Isham II:480
Simons, James III:546
Simons, John II:225
Simons, Jonathan I:754
Simons, Joseph I:43, 627;
  II:230, 381
Simons, Lycus I:57-58
Simons, Nathan I:151
Simons, Reuben III:702
Simons, Simeon I:72
Simonson, Christopher II:515
Simonson, Simon II:59
Simonton, Alexander II:588
Simonton, John IV:169
Simonton, Thomas IV:217

Simonton, Walter I:185
Simpkin, Ephraim IV:240
Simpkins, Charles III:481, 809
Simpkins, Gilbert II:196
Simpkins, James III:647, 811
Simpkins, Jeremiah II:196
Simpkins, John G. IV:8
Simpkins, Robert II:357
Simpkins, Wm. II:196
Simpson, Alexander II:421;
  IV:274
Simpson, Benjamin I:316
Simpson, Charles I:447
Simpson, Edmond III:516
Simpson, Elisha III:95
Simpson, George I:681
Simpson, Henry II:88
Simpson, Hugh III:327
Simpson, Isaac II:396
Simpson, James I:423; II:387,
  508; III:755
Simpson, Jeremiah III:227
Simpson, John I:598, 673-74;
  II:143, 343; III:33, 296;
  IV:209
Simpson, Joseph II:616
Simpson, Josiah IV:203
Simpson, Lawrence III:49
Simpson, Lockey III:532
Simpson, Margaret I:175
Simpson, Peter II:142
Simpson, Rachael I:175
Simpson, Rezin III:42
Simpson, Robert III:295;
  IV:226
Simpson, Samuel I:175
Simpson, Simeon I:199
Simpson, Stephen II:725
Simpson, Thomas I:678, 780,
  981; IV:207
Simpson, William I:175, 626,
  774; IV:20, 300
Simpson, Zebadiah I:317
Simrall, Alexander IV:196
Sims, Augustus IV:16
Sims, Cuthbert II:86
Sims, Daniel II:624
Sims, Edward III:489, 765
Sims, Elizabeth II:624
Sims, James III:815
Sims, John II:668; III:569, 799
Sims, Micajah III:558
Sims, Patrick III:55
Sims, Reuben III:766
Sims, Rhodam IV:123
Sims, Samuel I:835
Sims, William I:811; III:221
Sims, William, Sen. IV:71
Simson, William III:198
Sinclair, Charles G. I:667
Sinclair, Francis I:921
Sinclair, George II:204; IV:173
Sinclair, Joshua I:229
Sinclair, Noah I:664
Sinclair, Robert IV:122
Sinclair, Samuel II:215
Sinclare, Jacob I:734

Slocum, William I:819
Slocumb, Ezekiel III:459
Slone, Philip II:295
Sloper, Henry I:754
Slote, Peter G. II:30
Slotterback, Henry II:606
Slotterbark, George II:652
Slough, Jacob II:584
Slouter, John II:496
Slover, Daniel II:74
Slover, Isaac II:74
Slover, James II:74
Slover, John II:74
Slowter, Andrew II:328
Sluyter, Cornelius II:534
Sluyter, Daniel II:534
Sly, Isaac II:23
Sly, Samuel II:300
Slye, William IV:132
Small, Andrew IV:274
Small, Anna C. I:687
Small, Daniel I:255, 303
Small, Daniel, 2d I:315
Small, Daniel, 3d I:185
Small, Edward I:687
Small, Elisha I:185
Small, Ephraim I:270
Small, Francis I:687
Small, George III:221
Small, Henry I:241
Small, James I:255; IV:251
Small, Jeremiah I:185
Small, John I:591; II:149;
  III:406
Small, Mary Jane I:687
Small, Samuel I:279, 734
Small, William I:315
Small, Zachariah I:185
Smallery, Isaac II:53
Smalley, David IV:258
Smalley, Isaiah II:310
Smalley, Reuben II:542
Smalling, Jacob II:412
Smallwood, Beane III:258
Smallwood, Elisha III:529
Smallwood, John II:40
Smallwood, Wm. III:574
Smart, Alexander III:533
Smart, Caleb I:738
Smart, Dudley I:767
Smart, Elijah I:703
Smart, Jonathan I:735
Smart, Joseph III:533
Smart, Laban IV:15
Smart, Moses I:703
Smart, Nancy III:533
Smart, Nathaniel I:713
Smart, Richard I:189
Smart, Sally III:533
Smart, Samuel I:754; III:533
Smart, Thomas III:777
Smart, William I:663
Smaw, John II:271
Smead, Darius IV:107
Smeck, Frederick II:143
Smedes, Aldert II:396
Smedley, Jedediah II:254

Smedley, Lemuel II:601
Smee, Isaac II:734
Smell, Philip III:809
Smethers, John III:310
Smick, John II:32
Smiley, David I:713
Smiley, James I:403
Smiley, Robert II:45
Smiley, Samuel II:646
Smith, Aaron I:11, 551, 663,
  695, 967; II:308; IV:9
Smith, Aaron, 2d IV:213
Smith, Abel I:91; II:247
Smith, Abel, 2d II:228
Smith, Abisha I:377
Smith, Abishai I:120
Smith, Abner I:744-45, 894;
  II:446
Smith, Abraham I:113, 271;
  II:508, 736; IV:191
Smith, Abram I:767
Smith, Abra'm II:554
Smith, Absalom IV:240
Smith, Adam II:661
Smith, Alathea I:92
Smith, Albert I:856
Smith, Alexander I:507;
  II:619, 734; III:175, 777
Smith, Allen I:129; II:222
Smith, Alpheus, Jr. I:844
Smith, Amanda II:200
Smith, Ambrose III:300
Smith, Amos I:738, 835, 957;
  II:459
Smith, Andrew I:129; II:516
Smith, Anthony I:129; II:702,
  725; IV:273
Smith, Aquilla III:196
Smith, Asa I:954, 981; II:330,
  537; IV:69
Smith, Asahel I:992
Smith, Asaph I:58
Smith, Asher I:51, 475
Smith, Augustine II:258
Smith, Augustus P. I:388
Smith, Austin II:295; III:145,
  496
Smith, Azariah I:92
Smith, Azor O. I:593
Smith, Benjamin I:91, 151,
  301, 456, 465, 695, 780,
  891;II:447; III:336, 459, 689;
  IV:19
Smith, Benjamin, 1st II:156
Smith, Benjamin, 2d I:703;
  II:236
Smith, Benjamin, 3d II:328
Smith, Benjamin N. II:399
Smith, Benoni III:764
Smith, Betsey I:360; II:619
Smith, Bezalell I:447
Smith, Bill II:459
Smith, Bird III:201
Smith, Buckner III:511
Smith, Cadwallader L. II:142
Smith, Caleb III:559
Smith, Caroline S. I:593

Smith, Cesar II:315
Smith, Charles I:92, 210, 593;
  III:378, 443, 637, 793, 825;
  IV:274
Smith, Charles, 2d I:230
Smith, Chauncey W. II:173
Smith, Chester III:26
Smith, Christian III:42
Smith, Christopher I:539, 808
Smith, Clarinda II:200
Smith, Clementina I:388
Smith, Conrad II:651, 723
Smith, Cuff I:71
Smith, Curtis II:243
Smith, Cushing I:328
Smith, Cyril I:377
Smith, Dan I:901
Smith, Daniel I:71, 129, 199,
  303, 388, 423, 507, 828;
  II:286, 416, 446, 521; III:38,
  651, 670, 790; IV:28
Smith, David I:91, 103, 129,
  163, 189, 767, 954, 981;
  II:281, 548; III:38, 371;
  IV:182, 224, 251
Smith, David, 2d II:295
Smith, David, 3d II:254
Smith, David, Sen. III:226
Smith, David, 4th II:333
Smith, David R. II:97
Smith, Deliverance II:357
Smith, Doctor II:356
Smith, Dominicus I:241
Smith, Dow II:488
Smith, Ebenezer I:91, 199,
  210, 354, 725, 811, 847,
  981; II:526; III:118; IV:297
Smith, Ebenezer, 2d II:228
Smith, Ebenezer, 3d II:229
Smith, Edmond I:13
Smith, Edward I:446, 734;
  II:295, 652, 695; III:455,
  596, 843; IV:275
Smith, Eleanor III:670
Smith, Eleazer I:551
Smith, Electa I:388
Smith, Elhawah I:44
Smith, Eli I:550
Smith, Elijah I:44, 138, 343,
  447, 829, 996; II:225, 508;
  III:47, 542, 615
Smith, Elijah, 1st II:349
Smith, Eliphalet I:91, 780;
  II:67, 361, 637
Smith, Elisha I:677; II:374,
  422, 487; IV:107
Smith, Elkanah II:496
Smith, Elnathan I:35
Smith, Enoch I:119; III:165
Smith, Enoch, 2d II:228
Smith, Enoch, 1st II:271
Smith, Enos I:447, 954
Smith, Ephraim I:256, 854,
  981; II:328, 422, 436
Smith, Esek I:936
Smith, Ezekiel I:138; III:172
Smith, Ezra II:325, 422

Smith, Fleming III:308
Smith, Francis I:695; II:570
Smith, Frederick I:138, 954;
II:515, 566; III:257
Smith, Gabriel II:545
Smith, Garnet III:597
Smith, Garret II:447
Smith, Garrett II:59
Smith, George I:35, 485, 651;
II:78; III:576, 680, 786
Smith, George, Sen. III:567
Smith, George P. III:799
Smith, George W. II:144
Smith, Gerard III:246
Smith, Gerard D. II:143
Smith, Gideon I:754; II:488,
710
Smith, Godfrey III:223, 335
Smith, Gregory II:247
Smith, Griffith II:738
Smith, Hardy III:180
Smith, Harriet I:388
Smith, Harry I:856
Smith, Heber I:11
Smith, Heman I:211; II:459
Smith, Henry I:343, 780, 856;
II:308, 338, 442, 730, 738;
III:162, 323, 332, 410, 601,
749; IV:205
Smith, Henry (2) III:749
Smith, Henry, 2d IV:52
Smith, Henry, Sr. II:721
Smith, Hezekiah I:981; II:530
Smith, Hill III:156
Smith, Hiram II:83
Smith, Ira I:130; II:530
Smith, Isaac I:35, 92, 279,
423, 525, 627, 704; II:295,
341, 407; III:173, 362, 460,
493, 764, 806
Smith, Isaac, 1st II:341
Smith, Isaac, 2d I:507, 883;
II:335
Smith, Isaac, 3d II:325
Smith, Israel I:434, 580, 651,
786; II:260, 356
Smith, Israel, 2d II:325
Smith, Ithael I:677
Smith, Ithamar II:243
Smith, Ithamer I:883
Smith, Ithamir II:467
Smith, Jabez I:91; IV:144
Smith, Jacob I:241, 598, 734,
774, 819; II:86, 238, 692;
III:733, 812; IV:97
Smith, Jacobus II:421
Smith, James I:241, 403, 485,
761, 912; II:47, 185, 200,
310, 394, 442, 530; III:30,
253, 276, 373, 463, 516,
527, 834, 838; IV:177
Smith, James, 1st II:683;
III:702
Smith, James, 2d II:683;
III:721
Smith, James A. III:694
Smith, James E. II:680

Smith, James G. II:100
Smith, James W. II:589
Smith, Jane II:619
Smith, Jaziel I:270
Smith, Jedediah I:475, 891,
999
Smith, Jeffery I:129
Smith, Jehiel II:219
Smith, Jeremiah I:120, 129,
185, 403, 734; II:250, 394,
522
Smith, Jeremy I:725
Smith, Jesse I:64, 222, 354,
403, 829; II:324; III:162
Smith, Jesse, 2d II:430
Smith, Job T. I:72
Smith, Joel I:447; II:564;
III:630
Smith, John I:11, 24, 129,
139, 156, 255, 271, 404,
466, 598, 657, 680, 734,
767, 780, 795, 808, 912,
954, 981, 999; II:23, 65,
396, 526, 542, 548, 598,
616, 707, 715, 729; III:70,
79, 88, 156, 237, 270, 284,
332, 394, 421, 456, 482,
588, 667, 765, 777, 790,
819, 821, 830; IV:28, 115,
186, 234, 240, 258
Smith, John, 1st I:57, 185,
475; II:37, 236; III:44, 581,
700
Smith, John, 2d I:43, 255,
475, 901; II:45, 265, 598,
693; III:47, 240, 253, 487,
590
Smith, John, 3d I:35, 189,
891; II:42, 213, 672; III:218,
731
Smith, John, 4th I:44, 189;
II:219; III:699
Smith, John, 4(th) II:665
Smith, John, 5th II:281;
III:736
Smith, John, 6th II:343;
III:712
Smith, John, 7th III:678
Smith, John Andrew IV:44
Smith, John C. II:515
Smith, John E. II:499
Smith, John Eli II:447
Smith, John K. I:185
Smith, John Kilby I:320
Smith, John N. IV:275
Smith, John O. C. IV:278
Smith, John P. II:394
Smith, Johnston IV:185
Smith, John V. II:143
Smith, John Noah I:7
Smith, Jonas III:843
Smith, Jonathan I:298, 340,
816, 828, 902; II:126; III:38;
IV:182, 300
Smith, Jonathan, Sr. III:460
Smith, Jonathan W. I:650
Smith, Jordan I:24

Smith, Joseph I:63, 138, 485,
674, 735, 780, 891; II:391,
530, 659, 706, 740; III:38,
286, 693, 823; IV:231
Smith, Joseph, 2d I:63, 872
Smith, Joshua I:377; II:315;
III:557
Smith, Josiah I:4, 152, 176,
565, 658, 780, 891; II:142,
310
Smith, Josiah, 2d I:43
Smith, Justin I:35
Smith, Kitty P. I:388
Smith, Laban I:130, 288
Smith, Larkin III:177
Smith, Laton III:568
Smith, Lawrence II:616
Smith, Lemuel I:103, 550;
II:459
Smith, Leonard II:759; III:137
Smith, Levi I:113, 627; II:421
Smith, Lewee I:51
Smith, Lewis I:485, 649;
II:425; III:768
Smith, Liffey I:539, 551
Smith, Louis III:424
Smith, Luther I:151; II:275
Smith, Margaret III:670
Smith, Maria A. I:593
Smith, Mark III:799
Smith, Martha D. I:593
Smith, Martin II:69; IV:103,
289
Smith, Mary Ann II:619
Smith, Massa Ara III:334
Smith, Mathew I:485
Smith, Matilda II:200
Smith, Matthew I:151
Smith, Matthias II:79
Smith, Michael II:23, 476;
III:47, 288; IV:52
Smith, Montillion I:176
Smith, Moody I:767
Smith, Moses I:72, 230;
II:176, 542, 560, 680; III:47,
253
Smith, Nahum I:627
Smith, Nahum, 3d I:627
Smith, Nancy I:360, 593
Smith, Nathan I:145, 199,
388, 524, 695, 884, 927;
II:391, 545
Smith, Nathan, 2d I:506
Smith, Nathaniel I:51, 71,
151, 199, 447, 819, 920;
II:205; III:531, 780
Smith, Nehemiah I:565; II:230
Smith, Nicholas II:422;
III:291; IV:224
Smith, Noah I:xiv, 242
Smith, Obadiah III:595;
IV:176
Smith, Obed C. I:331
Smith, Oliver I:475, 828, 927;
II:477
Smith, Orange I:27
Smith, Othniel II:233

Snow, Samuel I:828
Snow, Shubael I:341
Snow, Silas II:480
Snow, Solomon I:485
Snow, Sylvanus I:555
Snow, Timothy I:565, 906
Snow, William I:365; II:399
Snowden, Aaron III:105
Snowden, David III:274
Snowden, John II:225
Snowden, Jonathan II:156
Snyder, Adam II:656, 747
Snyder, Andrew II:534; III:26
Snyder, Anthony III:783
Snyder, Christopher II:534
Snyder, Daniel II:628
Snyder, Dieter II:747
Snyder, Elias II:534
Snyder, Elizabeth II:629
Snyder, George II:370, 629;
    IV:274
Snyder, Gotlib II:265
Snyder, Hannah II:628
Snyder, Henry II:69, 695
Snyder, John II:616, 695
Snyder, John P. II:578
Snyder, John S. II:515
Snyder, Jonathan III:160
Snyder, Ludowick II:542
Snyder, Margaretta II:629
Snyder, Peter II:628; IV:283
Snyder, William II:387; IV:134
Sockman, Henry II:723
Sockman, John III:726
Sodom, Jonathan II:299-300
Sodon, Jonathan II:352
Sofield, Joseph II:74
Sohn, David II:666
Sohn, George J. II:666
Solcum, Prince I:808
Soley, Nathaniel I:403
Solladay, John II:738
Sollers, Sabert IV:120
Solley, Thomas I:35
Solliday, Daniel II:671
Solsby, Daniel IV:72
Solstonstall, Brittain I:797
Solter, Jacob III:140
Somerly, Moses I:423
Somers, David II:67
Somers, Simon III:16
Somersett, Thomas IV:214
Somerville, James III:33
Somerville, John III:221
Somerville, William III:681
Somes, Anna I:388
Somes, Ch's I:388
Somes, John I:754
Somes, Lydia I:388
Somes, Nabby I:388
Somes, Sally I:388
Somes, Trask I:388
Somes, William I:388
Sommers, Jonathan I:185
Sommers, Leonard II:729
Son, Anthony III:113
Sonday, Adam II:710

Sones, Peter II:734
Sonner, Anthony IV:258
Soop, Conrad II:356
Soots, Frederick III:419
Sooy, Samuel II:67
Soper, A. D. II:565
Soper, Amasa I:912
Soper, Henry II:412
Soper, Jesse II:542
Soper, Oliver I:365
Soper, Prince I:902
Soper, Timothy I:103
Sopers, Richard II:78
Sorrell, Edward III:817
Sorrell, Elisha III:206
Sorrell, John III:837
Sorrell, Thomas III:844
Sorrels, John III:313
Sorter, Peter II:713
Soul, James I:185
Soul, Samuel II:325
Soule, Asa I:221
Soule, Charles II:228
Soule, Daniel I:579
Soule, Ivory I:744
Soule, Jesse I:316
Soule, Jonathan I:255
Sourcee, Francis I:199
South, Benjamin II:725
Southall, Henry III:457
Southard, Abraham I:199
Southard, Alba I:850
Southard, Henry II:86, 333
Southard, John III:440
Southard, Thomas III:705
Southart, Constant I:226
Souther, Joseph I:539
Souther, Laban I:580
Southerland, James III:511
Southerland, Philip III:713
Southern, Gipson III:483
Southern, William, Sen.
    III:453
Southgate, Elijah I:650
Southgate, Thomas I:992
Southmayd, Daniel I:121
Southward, Andrew I:64
Southward, David II:243
Southwell, Ashwell II:750
Southwick, Benjamin I:475
Southwick, David II:222, 554
Southwick, George I:423
Southworth, Abia I:466
Southworth, Addison I:860
Southworth, Alden I:860
Southworth, Edward I:579
Southworth, Elijah II:447
Southworth, George III:780
Southworth, Isaac I:967
Southworth, James I:860
Southworth, Jasher I:967
Southworth, Joseph I:475
Southworth, Lemuel I:891
Southworth, Luther I:860
Southworth, Milton I:860
Southworth, Samuel W. I:91

Southworth, William II:654;
    III:762
Soward, Richard I:242
Sowder, Christopher II:744
Sowell, Zadock III:152
Sowers, John IV:11
Sowl, David II:467
Sowl, Job I:377
Soyars, James III:852
Soyers, James III:657
Spader, Bergen IV:89
Spafford, Amos I:713
Spafford, Jacob II:407
Spafford, Jonathan I:434
Spafford, Samuel I:774
Spain, Thomas III:385
Spain, William III:443
Spaine, Clairborne III:415
Spalden, John III:804
Spaldin, Nathaniel I:828
Spalding, Abel IV:244
Spalding, Benjamin I:957
Spalding, Daniel III:62
Spalding, Ezekiel I:613
Spalding, George III:251
Spalding, Isaac I:967
Spalding, James I:607
Spalding, John II:641
Spalding, Joseph I:695, 967
Spalding, Josiah I:24
Spalding, Silas I:972
Spalding, Thaddeus I:524
Spalding, William I:297, 613
Spalding, Wright II:222
Spanbergh, Jacob II:387
Spanler, Charles III:755
Spann, Charles III:513
Spann, James III:513
Sparhawk, Timothy I:651
Sparkank, Jacob I:199
Sparks, Abraham II:244
Sparks, David I:210
Sparks, Henry III:315
Sparks, James IV:76
Sparks, John II:52, 348;
    III:459
Sparks, Josiah I:75
Sparks, Matthew III:571
Sparks, Pearl II:126
Sparks, Solomon II:701
Sparlin, John II:286
Sparling, George IV:34, 144
Sparr, Richard IV:191
Sparre, John II:739
Sparrock, Jacob I:199
Sparrow, Henry III:303
Sparrow, Jabez I:331
Sparrow, Stephen II:654
Spatz, Michael II:703
Spaulding, Aaron III:251
Spaulding, Barzilla I:957
Spaulding, Benjamin I:353
Spaulding, Darius I:972
Spaulding, Edward II:213
Spaulding, Eleazer I:222
Spaulding, Ezra I:991
Spaulding, Henry III:56

Sprague, Silas IV:106
Sprague, Stephen II:195
Sprague, Theodore II:281
Sprague, Uriah I:581
Sprague, Van II:407
Sprague, William I:199, 279;
II:374
Sprake, Samuel I:761
Sprigg, Leven III:304
Spring, Isaac B. I:485
Spring, Josiah I:218
Spring, Richard III:433
Spring, Seth I:316
Spring, Thomas I:289
Springer, Benjamin III:163
Springer, Durfee II:213
Springer, Edward II:104
Springer, Henry I:754
Springer, Jacob II:633; IV:224
Springer, John I:173, 260,
279, 820
Springer, Knight I:803
Springer, Mary I:173
Springer, Uriah II:656
Springs, Micajah III:391
Springs, Samuel III:634
Springs, Sedgwick III:401
Springstead, George II:299
Springstead, John II:499
Springstein, John II:78
Springum, John IV:204
Sproat, Robert I:279
Sproat, Thomas I:581
Sproul, William I:279
Sprouse, David IV:248
Sprout, James I:627
Sprout, Nathan I:485
Sprout, Robert I:447
Sprout, Samuel I:485
Spruance, Presley II:12
Spry, William IV:263
Spurr, Enoch I:256
Spurr, John I:808
Spyers, Richard IV:172
Squier, Ephraim I:151
Squier, John II:407
Squier, Joseph II:37
Squier, Noble II:501
Squire, Abner I:103
Squire, Asa II:301
Squire, Calvin I:103
Squire, Daniel I:35, 967
Squire, David I:24, 51
Squire, Ebenezer I:967
Squire, Elisha I:43
Squire, Ezra IV:268
Squire, Frederick II:165
Squire, Isaac I:91
Squire, Philip I:81
Squire, Samuel I:24
Squire, Sylvester I:466
Squire, Thomas I:92
Squires, Ambrose II:287
Squires, Daniel II:349
Squires, James II:700
Squires, Jesse II:387
Squires, Joel II:487

Squires, Phineas I:157
Squires, Selah II:363
Squires, Thomas I:475
St. Clair, Arthur II:598
St. Clair, Daniel II:590, 673
St. Clair, George II:95
St. Clair, James II:244
St. Clair, John II:157
St. Clair, William I:674
St. George, George III:491
St. John, Adonijah I:64
St. John, Enoch I:91
St. John, Jacob III:764
St. John, Jesse I:36, 154
St. John, John II:167
St. John, Lewis III:698
St. John, Matthew II:357
St. John, Matthias I:91
St. Johns, James III:176
Staats, Abraham J. II:459
Staats, John II:387
Staats, Philip II:164
Stabb, John II:761
Stacey, Ebenezer I:891
Stacey, John I:627, 891
Stacey, Rufus I:464
Stacey, Samuel I:872
Stacey, William II:330
Stackhouse, Amos IV:188
Stackhouse, Isaac IV:273
Stackhouse, John III:707
Stackpole, Absalom I:316
Stackweather, John I:139
Stacpole, Samuel I:734
Stacy, Aaron III:400
Stacy, Caleb I:466
Stacy, Ebenezer I:695
Stacy, Job, Jun. I:365
Stacy, John I:242; II:281
Stacy, Molton I:906
Stacy, Nathaniel I:403
Stacy, Nymphas I:486
Stacy, Thomas IV:254
Stacy, William I:241
Stadden, William II:741
Stadner, John III:667
Stafford, Aaron II:149
Stafford, Andrew II:381
Stafford, Benjamin II:401
Stafford, David II:719; III:76
Stafford, Elisha I:336
Stafford, James I:816
Stafford, James B. II:60
Stafford, Joab II:185
Stafford, Job II:111
Stafford, John I:336; II:40,
281; III:283
Stafford, Joseph II:401
Stafford, Rich'd I:336
Stafford, Samuel I:981
Stafford, Susan I:336
Stafford, Thomas II:265
Stag, Isaac II:88
Stage, Benjamin II:734
Stage, William II:330
Stagg, Abraham II:191
Stagg, Benjamin II:680

Stagg, Catherine II:191
Stagg, Daniel IV:157
Stagg, John IV:78
Stahley, Jacob II:589, 729
Staley, George II:511
Staley, Henry II:442
Staley, Matthias II:515
Staley, Peter III:794
Stalker, Peter II:387
Stalker, Robert I:403
Stall, Adam II:680
Stallard, Randolph III:766
Stalmacker, Samuel III:799
Stamey, John III:429
Stamm, George IV:9
Stamper, Jacob III:315
Stamper, Joel III:459
Stanard, Oliver II:275, 555
Stanberry, Recompence II:65
Stanberry, Wm. IV:298
Stanbro, John II:391
Stanbrough, Lemuel II:295
Stanbury, James I:835
Stanclift, Comfort II:719
Stanclift, John II:399
Stanclift, Lemuel II:719
Stanclift, Samuel II:295
Standefer, Benjamin III:568
Standeford, Samuel III:460
Standiforth, Daniel W. II:421
Standish, Amos I:152, 569
Standish, Ebenezer I:580
Standish, Samuel I:542
Standley, Isaac II:75
Standley, Jacob II:370
Standley, Spims III:617
Standley, William I:422
Standridge, James III:511
Stanert, John II:579
Stanfield, James III:601
Stanford, Abner I:695
Stanford, John I:185
Stanford, John, 2d I:210
Stanford, Moses I:341
Stanford, Samuel, Sen. III:414
Stanhope, Samuel II:407
Stanley, Adin I:270
Stanley, Betsy I:26
Stanley, Christopher III:453
Stanley, Elisha IV:109
Stanley, Esther I:26
Stanley, Frederick II:447
Stanley, Hugh III:347
Stanley, James I:241
Stanley, Joseph I:26, 754
Stanley, Moses III:687, 762
Stanley, Nathaniel I:303
Stanley, Noadiah II:526
Stanley, Page IV:112
Stanley, Polly I:26
Stanley, Real I:270
Stanley, Timothy II:381
Stanley, William III:651
Stannard, Abel I:369
Stannard, Claudius IV:243
Stannard, Eliakim II:412
Stannard, Elijah I:120

514

Stevens, Peter I:902, 967;
II:498; IV:298
Stevens, Phineas, 2d II:295
Stevens, Phinehas IV:194
Stevens, Resolvert II:499
Stevens, Reuben III:155
Stevens, Roger I:878
Stevens, Safford I:878
Stevens, Samuel I:861
Stevens, Sarah I:684
Stevens, Seth I:377
Stevens, Simeon I:967
Stevens, Simon I:613
Stevens, Smith III:667
Stevens, Solomon II:412
Stevens, Stephen I:353
Stevens, Sylvanus II:548
Stevens, Sylvester II:115
Stevens, T. H. I:156
Stevens, Thomas I:44, 112,
840; II:448; III:190
Stevens, Vincent II:702
Stevens, William I:256; II:143,
192, 685; III:756
Stevens, Zachariah I:423
Stevenson, Alexander II:633
Stevenson, Fred'k P. II:142
Stevenson, George IV:263
Stevenson, Hugh II:143
Stevenson, James III:228;
IV:289
Stevenson, John III:426
Stevenson, Nathaniel II:643
Stevenson, Obadiah IV:280
Stevenson, Peter II:542
Stevenson, William II:723
Steverns, Edward IV:272
Steward, Daniel I:241
Steward, Eliphalet II:374
Steward, John IV:280
Steward, Robert II:2
Steward, William I:912
Stewart, Aaron I:856; IV:141
Stewart, Abraham II:191;
IV:113
Stewart, Alexander III:26, 535;
IV:10
Stewart, Alfred I:859
Stewart, Allen I:936
Stewart, Amasa I:297
Stewart, Andrew II:545
Stewart, Andrews IV:151
Stewart, Ann II:191
Stewart, Archibald II:721
Stewart, Asa C. II:120
Stewart, Barney III:623
Stewart, Benjamin I:226
Stewart, Budd II:496
Stewart, Caleb I:17; III:61
Stewart, Calvin I:840
Stewart, Charles I:859; II:56,
212, 723; III:321; IV:77
Stewart, Charles, 2d II:333
Stewart, Chas. A. III:847
Stewart, Daniel I:298; IV:229
Stewart, David II:37, 616
Stewart, Ebert II:191

Stewart, Edward III:445, 751
Stewart, Elisha II:496
Stewart, Ezekiel III:309
Stewart, Finley II:185
Stewart, Francis I:884
Stewart, Geo. II:191
Stewart, George I:859; II:5,
732
Stewart, Henry I:230
Stewart, Hugh I:199; II:658;
IV:243
Stewart, Ira H. I:856
Stewart, Isaac III:63, 535
Stewart, James I:145; II:665;
III:168, 196, 419, 479, 535,
751; IV:21
Stewart, James, 2d II:665
Stewart, Jeremiah I:627
Stewart, Jesse II:394
Stewart, Joel I:703
Stewart, John I:859, 891;
II:185, 416, 487, 636; III:26,
400, 426, 500, 751, 838;
IV:240, 277
Stewart, John N. III:18
Stewart, Joseph I:58; II:508,
519
Stewart, Maxey III:724
Stewart, Moses II:394
Stewart, Nathan II:511
Stewart, Oliver II:459
Stewart, Paul I:466
Stewart, Philip III:8, 16
Stewart, Rachael III:535
Stewart, Ralph III:800
Stewart, Robert I:725; II:47,
542; III:26, 315, 563
Stewart, Samuel I:91; III:839
Stewart, Simeon III:535
Stewart, Thomas I:856; III:78
Stewart, Thomas B. II:570
Stewart, William I:151, 859;
II:247; III:59, 173, 276, 299,
552, 563, 775, 834; IV:58,
263
Stickel, Valentine II:695
Stickies, Nicholas II:387
Stickles, John II:620
Stickley, Peter II:704
Sticklin, Lot III:446
Stickney, Ancill I:423
Stickney, Benjamin I:271
Stickney, Charles I:667
Stickney, Daniel I:754
Stickney, Jeremiah I:408, 719
Stickney, Jonathan I:946
Stickney, Josiah I:403
Stickney, Levi I:725
Stickney, Paul II:295
Stickney, Reuben II:243
Stickney, Samuel I:293
Stickney, Thomas I:883
Stickney, William I:423
Stidham, Samuel III:317
Stiers, Henry IV:149
Stiff, James III:753
Stiles, Aaron II:107

Stiles, Asa II:104, 383
Stiles, Asahel I:103, 967
Stiles, Beriah II:436
Stiles, Caleb I:875
Stiles, Eli II:617
Stiles, Elijah IV:291
Stiles, Ezra I:218
Stiles, G. C. I:xii
Stiles, Gould I:967
Stiles, Hezekiah IV:254
Stiles, J. I:880
Stiles, James II:65
Stiles, Job II:641
Stiles, John I:466; III:377
Stiles, Jonah II:391
Stiles, Lewis II:357
Stiles, Lincoln I:921
Stiles, Martin II:551
Stiles, Reuben II:104
Stiles, Robert II:328
Still, Christopher II:616
Still, Ebenezer II:545
Still, Ruel II:39
Still, William III:247, 699
Stiller, John II:598
Stillings, Peter I:689
Stillings, Thomas III:15
Stillman, George III:849
Stillman, Jeremiah S. I:862
Stillman, Joseph I:103
Stillman, Nathaniel I:104
Stillman, Samuel I:11
Stillwagon, Frederick II:673
Stillwagon, Jacob II:711
Stillwagon, Philip II:739
Stillwell, Elias I:63
Stillwell, Ezekiel II:37
Stillwell, James II:173
Stillwell, Jarrat II:446
Stillwell, Joseph II:656
Stillwell, R. IV:299
Stillwell, Silas II:442
Stilman, Roger I:113
Stilson, Ebenezer II:69
Stilth, Joseph III:304
Stilwell, David IV:40
Stilwell, Jacob III:180
Stilwell, Joseph I:803
Stimmel, Isaac II:759
Stimpson, Andrew I:601
Stimpson, Thomas I:475
Stimson, David I:991
Stimson, Lemuel I:650
Stinchfield, Ephraim I:256
Stincipher, Joseph III:608
Stine, George II:511
Stine, Martin IV:234
Stine, Philip IV:74
Stingerland, Peter II:488
Stingle, George IV:93
Stinson, Elijah IV:94
Stinson, James IV:284
Stinson, John III:270, 433
Stinson, Samuel I:189
Stinson, Thomas I:210
Stinson, William II:740
Stipp, John III:260

516

Strother, George III:795
Stroud, Hampton III:113
Stroud, Isaac III:268
Stroud, Isham IV:29
Stroud, John II:401
Stroud, William, Sen. III:794
Strouel, Mathew III:93
Strough, Nicholas II:719
Strous, George II:680
Strous, Jacob II:680
Strout, Nathaniel I:168
Strout, Prince I:185
Strow, Richard I:767; III:586
Strung, John II:67
Strunk, John II:682
Struter, Nathan I:829
Struver, John II:325
Stryker, Simon II:86
Stuart, Dempsey III:684
Stuart, George II:658
Stuart, James II:356
Stuart, John III:414
Stuart, Peter I:255
Stuart, Rich'd H. III:16
Stuart, Samuel I:222
Stuart, William II:552
Stubblefield, William S.
　III:501
Stubbs, Joseph I:168
Stubbs, Lewis III:508
Stubbs, Richard I:185
Stubbs, Samuel I:199
Stubbs, Williams III:508
Stubrach, Barend II:417
Studellman, John II:680
Studer, Philip II:637
Studley, Consider I:627
Studley, John I:581
Studley, William I:581
Studthem, John III:426
Studwell, Henry II:370
Stufflebean, John III:274
Stukebury, Jacob III:539
Stull, Frederick II:692
Stull, Joseph II:516
Stultz, Adam IV:163
Stultz, Casper, Sen. III:453
Stultz, Christiana IV:163
Stultz, Elizabeth IV:163
Stultz, Jacob IV:163
Stultz, Marshall IV:163
Stultz, Susannah IV:163
Stump, Charles II:617
Stump, George IV:289
Stump, Jacob IV:206
Stump, John II:300, 616
Stump, Lewis IV:199
Stupe, Samuel II:453
Stuppleton, Jacob II:387
Sturdevant, Caleb II:254
Sturdevant, James II:519
Sturdevant, Lemuel I:957
Sturdevant, Zenas I:469
Sturdivant, Charles III:153
Sturdivant, Joel III:768
Sturdivant, Thomas II:164
Sturgeon, Peter IV:246

Sturgeon, Robert II:672
Sturges, Augustus II:243
Sturges, Benjamin I:4
Sturges, Hezekiah I:91
Sturges, Jedediah IV:254
Sturges, Jonathan I:256
Sturges, Lewis IV:266
Sturges, Moses I:35
Sturgis, Aaron II:507
Sturgis, Abram II:213
Sturgiss, Aaron II:508
Sturman, William III:561
Sturtevant, Andrew I:199
Sturtevant, Asa I:221
Sturtevant, Barze I:539
Sturtevant, Ephraim I:579
Sturtevant, Francis I:288
Sturtevant, Heman I:565
Sturtevant, Hozea I:767
Sturtevant, Isaac I:404
Sturtevant, Jesse I:189
Sturtevant, Jonathan II:526
Sturtevant, Joseph I:218
Sturtevant, Lemuel I:828
Sturtevant, Lot I:199
Sturtevant, Noah I:598
Sturtevant, Seth I:218
Sturtevant, Zebedee I:113
Stutinger, John II:674
Stutt, William II:343
Stutton, Philip IV:260
Stutts, Jacob II:75
Stvers, Simeon II:65
Styles, Henry II:704
Styvers, David II:721
Styvers, William III:215
Subbuth, William IV:209
Sublett, Abraham III:298
Suddoth, Benjamin III:612
Suddoth, William IV:209
Sudduth, Bower III:197
Sudduth, Jared III:156
Sudrick, Michael I:725
Suggan, James IV:42
Suggett, John III:321
Suggs, George III:724
Sulcer, William IV:79
Sullenheim, Henry I:703
Sullenkein, Jacob I:754
Sullinger, James III:299
Sullivan, Barnabas I:211
Sullivan, Benj. I:718
Sullivan, Cornelius III:276
Sullivan, Daniel III:400; IV:34
Sullivan, David II:357
Sullivan, George III:630
Sullivan, James III:47
Sullivan, Jeremiah II:569
Sullivan, John III:502, 731
Sullivan, Patrick III:648;
　IV:191
Sullivan, Peter III:218
Sullivan, Philip III:38
Sullivan, Pleasant III:161
Sullivant, Owen III:383
Sully, Daniel I:241
Sult, David II:687

Sumerlin, Winburn III:459
Summer, George III:507
Summer, Sylvester I:120
Summerford, William III:517
Summers, Farrell II:185
Summers, George III:693
Summers, John III:156, 278
Summers, Joseph IV:17
Summers, Peter II:721
Summers, Solomon III:57
Summers, Thomas I:260
Sumner, Adam I:846
Sumner, Clement I:551
Sumner, Darius I:650
Sumner, Ebenezer I:551, 927
Sumner, Eber II:189
Sumner, Eli I:734
Sumner, Jeremiah I:377
Sumner, John I:551
Sumner, Joseph I:649
Sumner, Robert II:508
Sumner, Samuel I:507; II:189
Sumner, Shuball II:236
Sumner, William I:57, 551
Sumner, William, 2d I:551
Sumpter, Thomas III:597
Sunborn, Jonathan I:256
Sunderland, Joseph II:734
Sunderland, Samuel I:869
Sunderlier, Daniel I:835
Surgenor, John III:446
Surls, Robert III:434
Sutch, George III:676
Suter, Jacob II:356
Sutfin, David II:472
Sutfin, William II:383
Sutherland, Daniel II:53;
　III:568
Sutherland, George II:617
Sutherland, John III:558
Sutherland, Traverse III:291
Sutherland, Walter E. III:291
Sutherland, William III:201,
　267
Sutley, James III:141
Sutphen, Richard II:515
Sutphin, Aaron II:79
Sutphin, Peter II:86
Sutphin, Richard II:74
Suts, John P. II:442
Sutterlee, Elisha II:641
Sutterlee, James II:641
Suttle, Edward III:619
Sutton, Benjamin II:286;
　III:266, 281; IV:232
Sutton, Charles III:392
Sutton, David IV:27
Sutton, Elijah III:812
Sutton, Ephraim II:656
Sutton, George III:73
Sutton, Harman II:598
Sutton, Henry II:74; IV:104
Sutton, Jacob III:54
Sutton, John I:241, 767;
　II:330; III:610, 762; IV:141
Sutton, Joseph III:679
Sutton, Peter II:32

Sutton, Richard F. III:303
Sutton, Robert III:76
Sutton, Uriah II:86
Sutton, William II:271; III:288; IV:13
Sutton, Zachariah II:333
Sutton, Zebulon IV:266
Sutts, Peter P. II:425
Suydam, Hendrick II:86
Swadle, John I:71
Swadley, Mark III:607
Swager, Adam II:642
Swager, John II:616
Swain, Anthony II:721
Swain, Benjamin I:780; II:623
Swain, David I:529
Swain, Dudley I:780
Swain, Ezra II:542
Swain, George III:753
Swain, James I:529
Swain, Jeremiah I:780
Swain, Jeroham I:992
Swain, Joseph I:912
Swain, Joseph F. I:288
Swain, Paul II:623
Swain, Phineas I:774
Swain, Richard II:65
Swain, Samuel I:289; II:23
Swaine, Edward II:616
Swallow, Andrew III:609
Swallow, John Zephaniah III:9
Swallow, Zephaniah III:9
Swan, Aaron I:384
Swan, Adin II:387
Swan, Henry II:537
Swan, James I:289
Swan, John I:138, 712
Swan, Joshua I:423
Swan, Nathan I:218
Swan, Nathaniel I:7
Swan, Thomas III:16
Swan, Timothy IV:219, 300
Swan, William III:168
Swann, Charles III:842
Swann, John II:208
Swanson, John III:459
Swanson, Levi III:310
Swart, Bartholomew II:515
Swart, Cornelius I:27
Swart, Cornelius W. I:27
Swart, David I:27
Swart, Lawrence II:488
Swartga, Henry II:639
Swarthout, Aaron II:519
Swarthout, Anthony II:519
Swartwood, Barnardius II:745
Swartwood, Daniel II:526
Swartwood, James II:526
Swartwood, John II:526
Swartwood, Joseph III:26
Swartwood, Moses II:674
Swartwout, Cornelius II:171
Swartwout, Jacobus II:476
Swartwout, Moses II:487
Swartwout, Thomas II:534
Swartwout, William II:530
Swartz, Ludwig II:761

Swartz, Philip II:747
Swartz, Phineas IV:260
Swasey, John I:388
Swasey, Lydia I:388
Swatzel, Philip III:585
Sway, George III:169
Swaze, David IV:283
Swead, Charles III:643
Swearengen, Samuel III:667
Swearingen, Thomas III:121
Swearingen, Van III:323
Swearinger, Richard C. III:399
Sweat, David III:390
Sweatman, William III:151
Sweeney, James II:23
Sweeney, John II:153
Sweeney, Joseph III:328
Sweeney, Moses III:327, 758
Sweeny, Edward II:664
Sweeny, Hugh II:650
Sweeny, Joseph II:734
Sweet, Allen III:551
Sweet, Benajah I:828
Sweet, Benjamin I:808; II:126
Sweet, Charles II:545
Sweet, Ebenezer I:270; II:101
Sweet, Freeborn II:496
Sweet, Godfrey II:164
Sweet, Isaac II:416
Sweet, Israel I:185
Sweet, James I:931
Sweet, Jeremiah I:828
Sweet, John I:627; II:381, 432
Sweet, John, 2d II:260
Sweet, John Thomas I:798
Sweet, Jonathan II:213, 436
Sweet, Joshua I:255, 434
Sweet, Reuben II:370
Sweet, Samuel I:256, 816
Sweet, Stephen I:947
Sweet, Thomas II:394
Sweet, Valentine I:828
Sweet, William I:798
Sweeten, Benjamin II:209
Sweeting, Lewis II:467
Sweeting, Nathaniel II:459
Sweetland, Benjamin I:447
Sweetland, Eben'r L. I:145
Sweetland, John I:901
Sweetland, Luke II:668
Sweetland, Stephen I:279
Sweetland, William I:377
Sweetser, Cornelius I:524
Sweetser, John I:524
Sweetser, Philip I:745
Sweetser, Stephen I:875
Sweetsere, Richard I:199
Sweezy, David II:476
Sweger, John III:790
Swem, Jesse IV:176
Swenney, John III:354
Swentzel, Frederick II:729
Swepston, John III:823
Swesy, Daniel II:753
Swetland, Benjamin II:281
Swetland, Daniel I:456
Swett, Abraham T. I:712

Swett, Cicero I:712
Swett, Daniel I:780
Swett, James I:167
Swett, John I:255; II:349
Swett, Jonathan IV:169
Swett, Stockman I:703
Swett, Thomas R. I:767
Swett, William I:166
Swift, Abraham I:331
Swift, B. II:553
Swift, Benj. I:998
Swift, Charles II:206
Swift, Enoch I:270
Swift, Heman I:448
Swift, James I:581; II:16
Swift, John II:185, 466
Swift, Joseph I:289
Swift, Joshua II:208
Swift, Nathaniel I:51
Swift, Roland II:260
Swift, Samuel III:725
Swift, Socrates IV:30
Swift, Stephen I:331
Swift, Thomas III:226
Swindle, John III:259, 592
Swing, Mathias III:419
Swingle, John, Sen. III:297
Swinington, Joseph I:927
Swink, John III:400
Swinnerton, James IV:201
Swinney, William III:318
Swinson, Jesse III:414
Swinson, Richard III:395
Swinson, Theophilus III:414
Swishelm, John II:698
Swisher, Jacob III:845
Switland, Ambrose II:325
Switz, Walter II:326
Switzen, George II:761
Switzer, Emanuel II:272
Switzon, Philip IV:248
Sword, Michael III:834
Swords, James III:184
Swords, John III:488
Swyers, Daniel IV:157
Sxton, John II:330
Sydnor, Fortunatus III:732
Sykes, Ashbel I:931
Sykes, Harry I:845
Sykes, James III:599
Sykes, John II:416; III:834
Sykes, Josiah I:437
Sylver, Samuel III:188
Sylvester, Adam I:403
Sylvester, Caleb I:524
Sylvester, Elisha I:270
Sylvester, Gershom II:256
Sylvester, H.H. I:xii
Sylvester, Job I:185
Sylvester, Joseph I:579
Sylvester, Peter I:649
Symmes, Benjamin I:494
Symmes, Ebenezer I:241
Symmes, Fanny I:494
Symmes, John I:524
Symmes, Martha S. I:494
Symmes, Mary S. I:494

Symmes, Presley IV:82
Symmes, Rispah I:494
Symmes, William I:169
Symmond, Henry IV:173
Symmonds, John IV:128
Symmonds, Levi II:295
Symmons, Sylvanus II:364
Symonds, Bowman I:593
Symonds, Clark I:593
Symonds, Daniel I:403
Symonds, George I:593
Symonds, John I:403
Symonds, Mary I:593
Symonds, Silas I:879
Symonds, Sylvester I:593
Symonds, Thomas I:288
Symonds, Zebedee I:627
Sympson, William III:285
Sype, Christopher II:695
Sype, Tobias II:761
Sypert, Henry II:680
Sypert, William L. III:531
Sypher, Anne II:201
Sypher, Daniel II:201
Sypher, Fanny II:201
Sypher, Gabriel II:201
Sypher, James II:201
Sypher, William II:201
Syphird, Matthias III:52

Taber, Gideon I:902
Taber, Humphrey I:377
Taber, Noel I:365
Taber, Philip I:359
Taber, Samuel I:820
Tabor, Benjamin I:139, 808
Tabor, Church I:947
Tabor, Henry I:808
Tabor, Ichabod I:829
Tabor, Lemuel II:422
Tabor, Pardon I:767
Tabor, Philip I:704
Tabor, Thomas I:656
Tabor, William II:309; III:79
Tabour, Church I:841; II:165
Taburn, Joel III:375
Taburn, William, Sen. III:422
Tack, Jacob III:451
Taff, George III:595
Taff, James IV:34
Taff, Peter III:719
Taft, Abel I:968
Taft, Artemas I:861, 921
Taft, Caleb IV:108
Taft, Ebenezer I:651, 981
Taft, Eleazer I:725
Taft, Enos I:652
Taft, Frederick I:652
Taft, George I:651
Taft, Israel I:652
Taft, Jonathan I:532
Taft, Joseph I:539
Taft, Joseph R. I:587
Taft, Josiah I:435
Taft, Moses I:652
Taft, Sarah Ann Esther I:861

Taft, William I:981
Taft, William P. I:861
Tafton, Elias D. I:365
Taggart, James I:713
Taggart, John I:200, 745
Taggart, Joseph I:992
Taggart, Robert I:200
Taggart, William I:669, 820
Taggert, Patrick II:599
Tague, Daniel I:475
Tailor, John I:689
Tailor, Oliver II:387
Tainter, Stephen II:412
Tait, Robert L. III:172
Talady, Solomon II:641
Talbee, Stephen I:813
Talbert, Abraham I:200
Talbert, Benjamin III:154
Talbert, John II:617
Talbert, William II:205
Talbot, Daniel I:539
Talbot, Enoch I:551
Talbot, Henry III:15
Talbot, Isham III:208
Talbot, John Q. III:110
Talbot, Joseph I:257
Talbot, Josiah I:551
Talbot, Levi III:11
Talbot, Richard IV:205
Talbot, Salas II:185
Talbott, Thomas III:327
Talbut, Ebenezer I:152
Talcot, Aaron I:44
Talcott, Abraham I:104
Talcott, Eleazer IV:290
Talcott, Justice I:145
Talcott, Phineas I:145
Taleaferro, William III:773
Talf, Matthew IV:228
Taliafero, John III:853
Taliaferro, Richard IV:240
Taliferro, John III:796
Talley, Billy III:791
Talley, Henry III:176
Talley, John III:147
Tallmadge, Benjamin I:156
Tallmadge, Joel II:526
Tallmadge, Maria I:156
Tallmadge, Samuel II:266
Tallmage, Thomas II:86
Tallman, Benjamin I:829
Tallman, James I:377
Tallman, John G. II:499
Tallman, Peter II:467; IV:231
Tallman, Rescom II:407
Tallman, Samuel I:796
Tallman, Thomas II:488
Tallman, Tunis III:796
Tallman, William II:79
Tally, John III:636
Talmadge, John I:467
Talmadge, Nathaniel I:467
Talmadge, Noah II:88
Talmage, Elisha I:139
Talmage, Samuel I:130
Talmage, Seymour II:508
Talmage, Solomon I:130

Talman, John I:841
Tamblin, John W. II:557
Tamblin, Timothy II:422
Tan-de-het-se IV:137
Tandy, Gorham I:685
Tandy, Haril I:685
Tandy, Hervey I:685
Tandy, Jonathan I:685
Tandy, Vienna D. I:685
Tandy, William I:685
Tandy, Willis III:191
Tankersley, John III:533, 599
Tankersley, Lucinda III:533
Tankersley, Washington
  III:533
Tankersley, Wm. III:533
Tann, Dreury III:836
Tannahill, James II:570
Tannehill, James III:273
Tanner, Abraham III:804
Tanner, Helyer I:928
Tanner, Jacob II:515; III:682
Tanner, John II:542
Tanner, Joseph I:796
Tanner, Michael III:405
Tanner, Nathan II:391
Tanner, Quom II:315
Tanner, Samuel III:8
Tanner, William I:152; II:185,
  660; IV:290
Tapervine, John C. I:867
Tapley, Asa I:423
Tapp, Vincent III:641
Tappan, Ebenezer I:423
Tappan, Edward I:404
Tappan, Mansfield I:954
Tappan, Peter II:560
Tappan, Samuel II:157
Tappan, William I:423
Tappen, Peter II:343
Tapper, William I:51
Tapscott, William III:285
Tar, Melcher III:416
Tarbell, David I:525
Tarbell, Isaac II:422
Tarbell, Joseph I:227
Tarbell, Thomas I:525
Tarbell, William I:507
Tarble, Benjamin I:696
Tarble, Nathan II:52
Tarbox, Samuel I:257
Tarbox, William I:404
Tarbush, Joseph II:396
Tare, Daniel B. I:423
Tare, Jabez I:423
Tare, John I:423
Tarlton, William III:427
Tarney, Matthew II:333
Tarp, John I:808
Tarr, Abraham I:279
Tarr, Charles I:175
Tarr, David I:404
Tarr, David, 2d I:404
Tarr, Joseph I:211, 279
Tarr, Leonard I:175
Tarr, Levi III:201
Tarr, Mary I:175

Teague, William III:634
Teal, Adam II:740
Teal, John II:690
Teal, Nathan II:330
Teall, Joseph II:556
Teall, Oliver II:387
Team, Adam III:512
Teaney, Daniel III:811
Teaque, Jesse II:287
Tearcot, Francis II:336
Tearney, Gilbert III:392
Teasley, Silas III:161
Teaton, Henry II:396
Tedford, John III:570
Tedford, Robert III:570
Tedrich, Michael IV:11
Teed, John II:65
Teeder, Michael II:617
Teel, Ezekiel H. II:744
Teel, Joseph II:396
Teel, Nathan II:330
Teeple, Jacob IV:63
Teerpenning, Jacobus II:535
Teerpenning, William II:535
Tefft, Caleb I:835
Tefft, Daniel I:835
Tefft, Gardiner I:835
Teft, David II:543
Telford, Alexander IV:272
Telford, Hugh III:634
Teller, Ahasuerus II:459
Teller, James L. II:157
Teller, Tobias II:447
Tellis, John, Sen. IV:200
Temmett, George II:90
Temmett, John Peter II:90
Temple, Archelaus II:641
Temple, Chauncey L. I:851
Temple, Ebenezer I:872
Temple, Enos I:755
Temple, Ephraim I:651
Temple, Eppes III:827
Temple, Frederick I:921
Temple, John I:271, 651;
   III:77
Temple, Joseph S. I:651
Temple, Josiah I:587
Temple, R. I:999
Temple, Salmon I:435
Temple, Samuel I:507
Temple, Silas I:435
Temple, Stephen I:435
Templeman, Samuel III:844
Templeton, Robert IV:71
Templeton, Thomas I:427
Tenant, Thomas III:366
Tenant, William II:664
Ten Broeck, Adam II:225
Ten Broeck, John C. II:557
Tenbroeck, Leonard II:387
Tenbroeck, Samuel II:387
Ten Brook, John C. II:325
Tench, John III:615
Tench, William III:727
Tenery, William II:633
Ten Eych, Andrew J. II:70
Ten Eych, Jeremiah II:75

Ten Eyck, Conrad II:370
Ten Eyck, Henry II:185
Ten Eyck, Jacob T. II:442
Tennant, James I:820
Tennell, George III:239
Tenney, David I:755
Tenney, Edmund I:762
Tenney, Edward III:137
Tenney, Gideon I:968
Tenney, James III:829
Tenney, Samuel I:687
Tenney, William I:687
Tennill, George III:827
Tenny, Benjamin I:921
Tenny, Joshua I:651
Tenny, Josiah I:434
Terheum, Albert II:25
Terheum, John A. II:25
Terheum, Peter II:25
Terhune, John IV:109
Terney, Henry II:681
Terney, James IV:215
Ternure, James II:499
Terrant, Eunice I:863
Terrant, Jonas I:863
Terrant, Rufus I:863
Terrell, Elihu IV:268
Terrell, Joel III:354
Terrell, William III:159
Terrence, Adam III:346
Terrence, Alexander II:282
Terrey, Thomas III:619
Terril, Presley III:252
Terrill, Ephraim I:130
Terrill, John III:208
Terrill, Nathan IV:263
Terrill, Stephen I:869
Terrill, Thomas I:486, 566
Terrill, William II:266
Terry, Asa II:275
Terry, Asaph I:104
Terry, Benjamin II:706
Terry, David I:211
Terry, Ebenezer I:104; II:381
Terry, Gideon III:713
Terry, John I:211
Terry, Joseph III:820
Terry, Martin I:407
Terry, Nathaniel I:51; III:338
Terry, Solomon II:407
Terry, Stephen I:104; III:652;
   IV:3
Terry, Thomas II:488; III:257,
   398, 749
Terry, Thomas, 2d III:309
Terry, William N. IV:109
Terry, Zeno I:460
Tersel, Jared I:130
Terson, James II:119
Terwilliger, Abraham J. II:535
Terwilliger, Ben. F. II:535
Terwilliger, Evert II:535
Terwilliger, Harmonius II:535
Terwilliger, James II:343
Terwilliger, Josiah II:381
Terwilliger, Peter V. II:535
Terwilliger, Simon H. II:381

Terwilliger, William II:343
Tesher, John I:404
Tessier, Charles II:222
Tete, James III:844
Teumey, John III:307
Tevis, Andrew III:203
Tevis, Catherine III:203
Tevis, Eliza III:203
Tevis, George III:203
Tevis, Peter III:203
Tevis, Samuel III:337
Tew, Henry I:820
Tewgood, Jonathan I:829
Thacher, John I:24
Thacher, Ambrose III:579
Thacker, Benjamin III:612
Thacker, Daniel III:773
Thacker, Nathaniel III:747
Thacker, Reuben III:659
Thacker, Sackville III:803
Thacker, William III:562
Tharp, Charles III:292
Tharp, David II:56
Tharp, Earl I:51
Tharp, John III:740
Tharp, Jonathan III:392
Tharp, Joseph I:931
Tharp, Perry III:336
Tharp, Peter II:272
Tharp, Thomas III:824
Tharpe, Thomas III:764
Thatcher, Amasa II:96
Thatcher, Amos IV:251
Thatcher, Asa I:873
Thatcher, Benjamin I:745, 993
Thatcher, Ebenezer I:328
Thatcher, Eleakim II:375
Thatcher, James I:566, 658
Thatcher, John II:750
Thatcher, John O. I:921
Thatcher, Josiah I:394
Thatcher, Lot I:581
Thatcher, Obadiah II:685
Thatcher, Peter II:364
Thatcher, Samuel II:427, 442
Thatcher, Thomas I:628
Thaxter, Gridley I:581
Thayer, Abijah I:651
Thayer, Alexander I:566
Thayer, Amos, 2d I:628
Thayer, Amos, 1st I:539
Thayer, Artimas I:477
Thayer, Asa I:435, 696
Thayer, Barnabas I:551
Thayer, Bartholomew IV:178
Thayer, Christopher I:713
Thayer, Cornelia I:682
Thayer, Daniel I:745
Thayer, David I:52
Thayer, Eli I:435
Thayer, Eliphas I:551
Thayer, Ephraim I:601
Thayer, Eseck II:750
Thayer, Ezekiel I:113; II:417
Thayer, Gideon I:627; II:427
Thayer, Henry I:745
Thayer, Isaac I:954

Thayer, Jacob I:902; II:295
Thayer, James II:732
Thayer, Jeremiah I:200
Thayer, Jerijah I:912
Thayer, Joel I:437; II:213
Thayer, John I:377, 486; II:309
Thayer, Jonathan I:486, 762
Thayer, Joseph IV:167
Thayer, Leavitt I:582
Thayer, Levi I:456
Thayer, Nathan I:539
Thayer, Nathaniel I:682
Thayer, Obadiah I:539
Thayer, Oliver II:543
Thayer, Philip I:200, 551
Thayer, Randal I:566
Thayer, Richard I:582
Thayer, Rufus I:551
Thayer, Samuel I:354, 873
Thayer, Simeon I:796, 873
Thayer, Solomon I:539, 551
Thayer, Stephen I:628
Thayer, William III:694
Thayer, William, Jr. II:160
Thayer, Zaccheus I:539
Thayer, Zachariah I:539
Theams, Jonathan III:371
Theobald, James III:282
Thew, Gilbert II:383
Thigpen, Joseph III:91
Thigphen, Gilead III:417
Thing, Jonathan I:774
Thing, Levi I:271
Thing, Nathaniel I:317
Thing, Samuel I:606
Thissell, Jeffy I:404
Thiveatt, Edward III:509
Thomas, Aaron III:435; IV:107
Thomas, Abraham IV:272
Thomas, Alex. II:617
Thomas, Alexander III:415
Thomas, Amos III:363
Thomas, Andrew I:993
Thomas, Asa II:45, 91, 707
Thomas, Beriah II:383
Thomas, Briggs I:581
Thomas, Buckner III:725
Thomas, Caleb I:64; III:186; IV:228
Thomas, Catlett III:762
Thomas, Charles I:257; III:268, 716
Thomas, Charles (2) I:257
Thomas, Cosner H. II:629
Thomas, Daniel I:139
Thomas, David I:906; II:653; IV:93
Thomas, Eli II:584
Thomas, Elijah I:354; II:230
Thomas, Elisha III:251, 307, 330
Thomas, Ellis III:61
Thomas, Enoch II:309, 629
Thomas, Ephraim II:542
Thomas, Etheldred III:172

Thomas, Evan III:790; IV:43, 78
Thomas, Ezekiel II:686
Thomas, Foxwell I:434
Thomas, Francis III:48
Thomas, Garner I:803
Thomas, George II:205; III:713
Thomas, Giles III:755
Thomas, Henry II:213, 553; III:211, 578; IV:87
Thomas, Holmes I:289
Thomas, Ichabod I:293
Thomas, Isaac I:566
Thomas, Isaac Hanway II:629
Thomas, Israel I:469, 628
Thomas, Jacob I:968; II:257; III:549
Thomas, James I:121, 567; II:711; III:270, 581, 728, 806; IV:10
Thomas, James, 2d III:728
Thomas, Jason II:480
Thomas, Jesse I:928
Thomas, John I:44, 656, 863; II:185, 233, 711; III:315, 366, 426, 515, 564, 568, 599, 848; IV:80, 240
Thomas, John A. I:13
Thomas, John T. III:209
Thomas, Jonathan I:200; IV:224
Thomas, Joseph I:257, 566, 658; II:349, 629, 685; III:597, 717, 795
Thomas, Joshua I:189, 566
Thomas, Josiah IV:297
Thomas, Leonard II:629
Thomas, Lewis I:251
Thomas, Lodowick I:407
Thomas, Lyman I:863
Thomas, Mary II:91
Thomas, Moses I:704
Thomas, Mrs. Samuel I:260
Thomas, Nancy I:863
Thomas, Nathan I:260; III:234
Thomas, Nathaniel I:581
Thomas, Nelson I:567
Thomas, Nicholas I:829
Thomas, Noah I:581
Thomas, Notley III:588
Thomas, Obadiah II:599
Thomas, Oliver II:295
Thomas, Owen IV:241
Thomas, Peleg I:993
Thomas, Philemon III:114
Thomas, Philip III:356
Thomas, Rachel II:629
Thomas, Reuben III:525
Thomas, Richard II:75; III:258
Thomas, Robert I:628; II:325; III:576
Thomas, Salmon I:486
Thomas, Samuel I:835; II:309, 488
Thomas, Sarah II:629
Thomas, Seth I:582; II:213
Thomas, Simeon I:139

Thomas, Spencer I:166
Thomas, Stephen I:863; II:282; III:528
Thomas, Thomas II:617, 759
Thomas, Willard I:435
Thomas, William I:614, 658, 902, 999; II:598, 629; III:8, 162, 446, 578, 628, 688; IV:56
Thomas, Wm. I:658
Thomason, Ezekiel III:60
Thomason, George III:433, 558
Thomas (Seneca Indian) II:98
Thomasson, John III:753, 802
Thompkins, Ichabod II:88
Thompkins, Joseph II:75
Thompkins, Phineas IV:283
Thompkins, Stephen II:65
Thompkins, Stephen N. II:361
Thompsom, Joseph III:323
Thompson, Abraham I:36; IV:215
Thompson, Alexander I:211; II:761; III:795
Thompson, Alex'r, 2d I:200
Thompson, Amherst I:354
Thompson, Amos I:551
Thompson, Ann Jane II:192
Thompson, Anthony III:273
Thompson, Asa I:354; II:432
Thompson, B. C. II:192
Thompson, Barnard III:338
Thompson, Bart'omew III:430
Thompson, Benjamin I:317, 533, 581, 719, 768; III:90, 167
Thompson, Bethiah I:533
Thompson, Betsey M. IV:161
Thompson, Burwell III:581
Thompson, C. B. IV:299
Thompson, Caesar I:614
Thompson, Charles III:430, 577
Thompson, Cornelius I:260
Thompson, Daniel II:205
Thompson, David I:64, 242; IV:26
Thompson, Ebenezer I:581; II:330
Thompson, Edward II:425
Thompson, Electrous III:89
Thompson, Elijah I:551
Thompson, Epaphras II:675
Thompson, Ephraim I:242
Thompson, Evan III:323
Thompson, Festus L. I:792
Thompson, Flanders III:486
Thompson, Francis I:891
Thompson, Frederick III:185
Thompson, George II:629; III:307, 416; IV:115
Thompson, Gideon III:325
Thompson, Henry I:113
Thompson, Herminus II:617
Thompson, Horace B. I:855
Thompson, Hudson III:623

526

Tipton, J. IV:99
Tipton, Jonathan III:609, 634
Tipton, Luke IV:259
Tipton, William III:526, 597, 659
Tipton, William, Sen. III:309
Tirrell, Benjamin I:551
Tisco, John II:59
Tisdale, Barnabas I:755
Tisdale, Benj. H I:837
Tisdale, Cudbud IV:65
Tisdale, George II:282
Tisdale, James I:539, 658
Tisdale, Joseph I:835
Tisdale, Peter C. I:658
Tise, Peter II:59
Tison, James III:140
Titcomb, John I:257
Titcomb, Michael I:404
Titlar, George II:548
Titter, Jacob III:617
Titton, John II:79
Titus, Abel I:968
Titus, Benjamin II:725
Titus, John I:843
Titus, Jonathan II:272
Titus, Joseph I:113, 377
Titus, Samuel I:271
Tncker, Abraham III:316
Tobey, Barnabas I:279
Tobey, Edward I:388
Tobey, Eliza I:388
Tobey, Isaac I:448
Tobey, John I:185
Tobey, Mary Ann I:388
Tobey, William I:279
Tobin, Isaac IV:252
Tobin, Samuel I:185
Tobin, Thomas II:721
Todd, Archibald I:365
Todd, Asa I:486
Todd, Benjamin I:456; III:615
Todd, Ichie II:488
Todd, John I:726, 762; II:300
Todd, Joseph III:303; IV:31, 109
Todd, Lewis III:417
Todd, Peter III:303
Todd, Samuel I:946; II:247; III:266
Todd, Thaddeus I:64
Todd, Thomas I:968; III:303
Todd, William II:86, 646
Todd, Yale I:25
Toland, John II:21; IV:278
Tolar, Daniel III:366
Tolar, Nehemiah III:459
Tolen, Eli III:237
Toliver, Jesse III:399
Tollen, Cornelius IV:175
Tolles, Amos I:113
Tolles, Jared I:130
Tolley, William III:307
Tolman, Benjamin I:745
Tolman, Ebenezer I:745
Tolman, John I:968
Tolman, Lyman I:992

Tolman, Peleg I:587
Tolman, Samuel I:271, 551
Tolman, Stoddard I:448
Tolman, Thomas I:894, 999
Tolman, Thos. I:1000
Tomb, David IV:123
Tomblin, James II:67
Tombs, Clifton III:655
Tombs, Joseph I:507
Tombs, William I:507
Tome, Henry II:761
Tomilson, William II:598
Tomiton, Jasper III:473
Tomkins, Amos II:38
Tomkins, Nathaniel II:309
Tomlin, Samuel IV:121
Tomlin, Wm., Sen. III:771
Tomlinson, Agur I:130
Tomlinson, Benjamin I:64
Tomlinson, Curtis I:92
Tomlinson, Eliphalet I:878
Tomlinson, George III:303
Tomlinson, Jabez I:25
Tomlinson, Jabez H. I:130
Tomlinson, Joseph II:244
Tomlinson, Nathaniel III:318
Tomlinson, Richard III:398
Tomm, Henry III:35, 59
Tompkins, Benjamin I:793
Tompkins, Gideon I:820
Tompkins, James I:803; II:412
Tompkins, John I:820
Tompkins, Jonathan II:535
Tompkins, Nathaniel I:820
Tompkins, Solomon II:333
Tompkins, Sylvanus II:549
Tompson, David I:735
Tompson, Joseph II:751
Toms, Enoch II:192
Toms, James II:370
Toms, John II:262
Toms, Mary II:192
Toms, Richard II:192
Toms, Stephen II:250
Toms, Thomas II:667
Tone, John F. I:696
Toner, James II:681
Toney, Carey IV:282
Toney, William III:522, 643
Tongate, Merideth III:193
Tonner, John III:588
Toocker, James I:58
Toocker, Philip I:58
Tood, Joseph I:423
Tooker, Joseph II:521
Toole, James III:179
Toombs, Emanuel III:764
Toombs, George III:786
Toombs, William III:762
Toomey, John III:55
Tooms, William III:762
Toon, Henry III:315
Toone, Argelon III:719
Tooney, Daniel M. III:463
Toops, Leonard II:661
Toothaker, Seth I:186
Tootheaker, George II:282

Topham, Reuben II:744
Topliff, Calvin I:781
Topliff, James I:993
Topp, George III:394
Toppan, Stephen I:424
Topping, Daniel II:256
Topping, William II:425
Toppon, Michael I:211
Torhune, Cornelius II:59
Torr, Vincent I:726
Torrance, Thomas II:154
Torrence, John IV:251
Torrence, Joseph I:928
Torrence, Thomas IV:182
Torrens, Samuel IV:73
Torrey, Bill II:526
Torrey, Haviland I:658
Torrey, Jesse II:225
Torrey, John II:260
Torrey, Jonathan I:467
Torrey, Joseph I:486; II:560
Torrey, Nathaniel B. I:884
Torrey, Philip I:581
Torrey, Reuben I:525
Torrey, Samuel I:902, 999
Torrey, William I:567, 658; II:560
Torry, Caleb II:115
Torry, Elijah I:651
Torry, Jonathan II:260
Torry, Josiah I:651
Torry, Nathaniel I:475
Torry, Oliver I:152
Torry, Timothy II:244
Torry, William II:272
Tory, Elisha I:185
Tothune, Abraham II:86
Totman, George II:391
Totman, Stephen I:566
Totten, Levi I:835
Totten, Samuel II:205
Tottenden, John I:72
Totterson, Ann II:629
Totterson, Elizabeth II:629
Totterson, Henry II:629
Totterson, Jesse II:629
Totterson, Lewis II:629
Tottingham, David I:981
Totty, Daniel, Jr. III:791
Touissant, Louis I:341
Toulong, Leander I:365
Toup, Caleb III:410
Tourge, Philip II:325
Tourgee, William I:835
Tourtelott, Abraham I:222
Tourtelott, Joseph I:152
Tourtelott, Orono I:222
Tourtelott, Reuben I:242
Tousley, Thomas I:940
Tousley, William II:244
Towb, William I:298
Tower, Abraham I:551
Tower, Augustus I:525
Tower, Bela I:581
Tower, Benjamin I:613; II:112
Tower, Calvin I:384
Tower, Elisha I:594

Tower, Hannah I:594
Tower, Jonathan I:507
Tower, Mathew I:567
Tower, Nathaniel II:750
Towers, Gideon IV:66
Towers, Isaiah II:511
Towle, Daniel I:774
Towle, Jeremiah I:200
Towle, Jonathan I:781
Towle, Josiah I:230
Towle, Nathan I:755
Towle, Reuben I:946
Towle, Thomas I:317
Towle, William I:726
Towler, Benjamin III:615
Towler, Richard III:780
Towles, Henry III:189, 804
Town, David I:906
Town, David D. I:906
Town, Edmund I:973
Town, Elisha I:973
Town, Ephraim I:906
Town, Francis I:475
Town, James I:973
Town, Jonathan I:475
Town, Joseph I:242
Town, Moses I:768
Town, Noah I:211
Town, Phinehas I:652
Town, William I:152
Town, William, 3d II:272
Town, Wm. II:349
Town, Wm. 2d II:349
Towne, Elisha I:745
Towne, Joshua I:424
Towner, Elijah II:412, 706
Towner, Ezekiel II:116
Towner, Samuel II:370
Townley, James S. II:530
Townley, Joshua II:65
Townsend, Andrew III:93
Townsend, Charles II:522, 555
Townsend, D. S. I:659
Townsend, Daniel II:185
Townsend, David I:659, 745
Townsend, David S. I:587
Townsend, George I:796, 891;
  III:573
Townsend, Isaac I:242
Townsend, James IV:229
Townsend, Jeremiah II:488
Townsend, John I:581; II:460;
  III:204
Townsend, Joseph I:185
Townsend, Joshua III:581
Townsend, Moses I:423
Townsend, Oswald III:303
Townsend, Richard II:467
Townsend, Robert I:257;
  IV:169
Townsend, Samuel III:239
Townsend, Silas I:581
Townsend, Solomon I:659
Townsend, Solomon D. I:25
Townsend, Sylvanus II:548
Townsend, Thomas III:67, 166

Townsend, William III:492,
  519; IV:83
Townshend, Abraham I:973
Townsley, Dan I:448
Townsley, Gad I:232
Townsley, Jacob I:200
Townsley, Nicanor I:696
Townsley, Thomas IV:251
Townson, John III:635
Towsend, Reuben I:651
Towser, Jeremiah II:61
Towsley, Matthew IV:269
Towsley, Nathaniel I:931
Towson, Benjamin III:202
Towson, Mary III:202
Towson, Susanna III:202
Tozer, John I:745; II:325
Tozer, Julius II:706
Tozer, Peter II:685
Tozier, William I:170
Trabue, Daniel III:253
Tracey, Calvin II:370
Tracey, Dudley I:64
Tracey, Ebenezer II:208
Tracey, Gerard III:31
Tracey, Moses I:72
Tracey, Philip III:15
Tracey, Uri II:553
Tracey, William III:743
Tracy, Ann II:194
Tracy, Charles III:270
Tracy, Cyrus I:955
Tracy, Daniel I:601
Tracy, Dill II:194
Tracy, Eleazer I:139
Tracy, Elias II:375
Tracy, Elijah I:955
Tracy, Gamaliel R. I:139
Tracy, Gilbert II:370
Tracy, James I:992
Tracy, James, Sen. III:516
Tracy, John II:194
Tracy, Levi II:472
Tracy, Lycenas II:194
Tracy, Lysanius II:194
Tracy, Moses I:24
Tracy, P. L. II:556
Tracy, Philemon I:139
Tracy, Solomon I:902; II:399;
  III:233
Tracy, Thomas I:651
Tracy, William I:72, 384;
  III:753, 778
Trader, Arthur III:790
Traffarn, Cromwell II:282
Trafford, Eliza I:388
Trafford, George I:388
Trafford, Joseph I:365
Trafton, Abial I:902
Trafton, Benjamin I:242
Trafton, Elias D. I:829
Trafton, Eliphalet I:242
Trafton, Joshua I:317
Trafton, Josiah I:242
Trafton, Samuel I:681
Trail, James III:585
Trail, Thomas III:777

Train, Isaac II:519
Train, John I:902
Train, Oliver I:434
Trainum, William III:623
Tramel, Sampson IV:83
Tranus, John II:617
Trapp, Vincent III:830
Trask, Alfred II:173
Trask, Anna I:336
Trask, Artimassa I:336
Trask, Charles I:388
Trask, Daniel I:336
Trask, Darling I:336
Trask, Ebenezer I:271
Trask, Ezra I:423
Trask, George I:173
Trask, Hannah I:388
Trask, Jefferson I:173
Trask, Jesse I:448
Trask, John I:808; II:320
Trask, John, 2d II:222
Trask, Joseph I:173
Trask, Levi I:388
Trask, Martha Mange I:388
Trask, Michael I:336
Trask, Moses I:279, 388
Trask, Nahum I:993
Trask, Nathaniel I:525
Trask, Nehemiah I:388
Trask, Obadiah I:279
Trask, Polly I:173
Trask, Retire I:992; IV:251
Trask, Roxa I:336
Trask, Rufus II:654
Trask, Ruth I:173
Trask, Samuel I:539
Trask, Sarah I:336
Trask, Thomas, Jr. I:211
Trask, Thomas T. I:388
Trask, William I:169
Traver, Adam II:535
Travers, Elijah I:507
Traverse, Abraham II:508
Travis, Arthur III:299
Travis, Asa I:696
Travis, Caroline E. II:192
Travis, Ezekiel II:185
Travis, Jacob II:185
Travis, James III:323
Travis, Jonathan II:491
Travis, Joseph II:310
Travis, Joseph D. II:192
Travis, Nathaniel II:225
Travis, Oliver I:289
Travis, Philip II:247
Travis, Robert II:548
Travis, Susan II:192
Travis, Sylvanus II:564
Travis, Thomas III:579
Travis, Uriah II:352
Travis, William IV:255
Treadway, David II:488
Treadway, Elijah I:139
Treadway, Jonathan I:869
Treadway, Robert III:621
Treadwell, Benjamin I:36
Treadwell, Cato I:36

Treadwell, Daniel I:5
Treadwell, Marsters I:219
Treadwell, Nathaniel I:404, 423
Treadwell, Reuben III:451
Treadwell, Samuel I:317
Treakwell, Abel II:549
Treasure, Richard III:356
Treat, Asbel II:370
Treat, Ashbel W. II:407
Treat, Charles II:436
Treat, Cornelius II:436
Treat, John I:58
Treat, Joseph I:58
Treat, Philo I:44
Treat, Russell I:44
Treat, Samuel I:328
Treat, Samuel P. II:250
Treat, Theodore II:309
Treat, Thomas II:399, 550
Tree, John II:361
Treece, Michael III:583
Trees, John II:661
Trefry, Edward I:423
Tremain, Nathaniel I:354
Trench, Benjamin III:76
Trench, James I:25, 58
Trenor, James III:755
Trent, Thomas III:643
Trescott, Jonathan IV:290
Trescott, Solon II:668
Trescott, William I:875
Trevett, Benjamin C. II:275
Trevett, John I:211, 803
Trevillian, Henry III:773
Trevitt, Henry IV:266
Trezvant, John III:710
Tribble, Elijah III:84
Tribble, George III:838
Tribble, James II:89
Trible, Joseph F. IV:224
Trice, James III:570
Trickey, Ephraim II:427
Trickey, John I:681, 781
Trickey, Samuel I:704
Trim, Ezra II:480
Trimble, John II:580, 740; III:288
Trimble, William III:318
Trine, George II:704
Trinkle, Christopher IV:58
Trip, Jonathan I:614
Trip, William II:282
Triplett, Betsy H. III:333
Triplett, Daniel III:830
Triplett, Hedgman III:279
Triplett, Peter II:690
Triplett, Sarah III:338
Triplett, Thomas, Jr. III:333
Triplett, Thomas, Sen. III:333
Triplett, Thos. Jr. III:637
Tripner, George II:681
Tripp, Abiel I:829
Tripp, Calvin II:295
Tripp, Consider I:799
Tripp, Ephraim I:365
Tripp, Everitt II:345

Tripp, Francis I:377
Tripp, Henry Dow II:272
Tripp, Othniel I:829
Tripp, Richard II:412
Tripp, Robert I:242
Tripplett, George III:338
Tripplett, Thomas III:338
Trisner, John III:38
Tritt, Peter II:715
Trivett, Samuel I:301, 465
Trolinger, Henry III:440
Trotter, Christopher IV:166
Trotter, John IV:166
Trotter, William III:616
Trout, Adam II:338
Trout, Anthony D. IV:74
Trout, Baltzer II:759
Trout, Jacob II:32; III:445
Trout, Michael II:317
Trout, William II:60
Troutman, Peter II:748
Trover, Andrew II:619
Trover, George II:619
Trover, John II:619
Trover, Jonathan II:619
Trover, William II:619
Trowant, Nathan I:582, 614
Trowbridge, Aaron II:295
Trowbridge, Absalom II:51
Trowbridge, Benj. H. II:662
Trowbridge, Benjamin II:272
Trowbridge, Charles D. II:196
Trowbridge, Dolly I:998
Trowbridge, Ebenezer IV:213
Trowbridge, Elihu I:51
Trowbridge, Isaac II:213
Trowbridge, James I:704
Trowbridge, John I:36
Trowbridge, Pamela II:196
Trowbridge, Samuel I:525
Trowbridge, Seth II:391
Trowbridge, Stephen I:884, 998; II:542
Trowbridge, Thomas I:92
Trowbridge, William I:652
Trowell, James III:565
Trower, Solomon III:307
Troxel, Jacob III:604
Troy, James III:809
Troyman, William III:804
Truair, Manuel I:475
Truax, Abraham C. II:357
Truax, David IV:282
Truax, Isaac II:511
Truax, Jacob I:946; II:79
Truax, John II:79, 320
True, Aaron I:279
True, Benjamin I:767
True, Daniel I:279
True, Edward I:271
True, Jabez I:768
True, James III:276
True, John I:774; III:314
True, Jonathan I:298
True, Martin III:563
True, Obadiah I:219
True, Robert IV:77

True, William I:257
True, Zebulon I:200
Trueman, Shem II:257
Truesdale, Almira I:452
Truesdale, Asa I:452
Truesdale, Darius I:452
Truesdale, Levy I:452
Truesdale, Titus I:452
Truesdale, William I:452
Truesdell, Aaron II:407
Truesdell, Hiel II:375
Truesdell, Richard II:537
Truesdell, Samuel II:352
Truex, John II:47
Trufant, David I:551
Truhitt, Stephen III:489
Truisdale, William II:387
Truisdell, Jabish II:363
Truit, William III:761
Trull, David I:384
Trull, Elijah I:968
Trull, Willard II:176, 542
Truman, John III:38
Truman, Solomon II:425
Trumble, Isaac III:832
Trumbull, Ezekiel I:52
Trumbull, John I:467; II:237, 447
Trumbull, Robert I:957
Trumbull, Samuel I:768
Trumbull, William I:227; II:442
Trump, George II:652
Trusler, James IV:71
Trusler, John IV:247
Trussell, Moses I:670, 768
Trux, John III:52
Try, Jacob IV:278
Tryer, Andrew II:664
Tryon, Amos S. II:560
Tryon, Ezra IV:225
Tryon, Isaac I:44
Tryon, Thomas I:104
Tryon, William I:44, 435; II:561
Tubbs, Annanias I:906
Tubbs, Charles II:200
Tubbs, Cyrus III:220
Tubbs, Elizabeth II:200
Tubbs, Enos II:550
Tubbs, Ezra II:315
Tubbs, Hazael II:200
Tubbs, Jacob I:219
Tubbs, John, Sen. III:91
Tubbs, Lemuel II:383
Tubbs, Nancy II:200
Tubbs, Samuel II:16, 149, 686
Tubbs, Seth I:475
Tubbs, Sidney II:200
Tubbs, Simon I:878
Tuck, Edward III:647
Tuck, Thomas III:783
Tucker, Ashbel I:955
Tucker, Athlinda R. I:360
Tucker, Benjamin I:613, 652, 954; II:327
Tucker, Daniel I:582

Tucker, David I:404; III:567
Tucker, Elisha I:152
Tucker, Ezra I:652
Tucker, George I:405; III:13, 82, 809
Tucker, Greenbury II:575
Tucker, Harbert III:161
Tucker, Henry III:790
Tucker, Isaac IV:201
Tucker, James I:81; IV:219
Tucker, John I:293, 404, 598; II:309; III:246, 261, 790; IV:84, 181
Tucker, Jonathan II:213
Tucker, Joseph I:404, 829, 921; II:222, 432
Tucker, Joshua I:651; II:233
Tucker, Josiah I:360; II:459
Tucker, Lemuel II:222
Tucker, Lydia I:360
Tucker, Morris II:496
Tucker, Nathan I:808
Tucker, Nathaniel I:404
Tucker, Reuben III:730
Tucker, Rhodes II:213
Tucker, Robert I:81; III:380
Tucker, Samuel I:279; II:215
Tucker, Seth I:651
Tucker, Shadrach III:449
Tucker, Thomas III:627, 824; IV:86
Tucker, Wait I:968
Tucker, William III:204, 762; IV:191
Tucker, Wm. I:156
Tucker, Zoeth II:537
Tudor, John II:681; III:303
Tuell, Anna III:10
Tuell, Benjamin I:829
Tuell, Lucy III:10
Tuell, Rebecca III:10
Tuell, Roderic III:10
Tuers, Jacob II:59
Tuffs, William IV:280
Tuftes, David I:404
Tufts, Ebenezer I:696
Tufts, Eliakim I:507
Tufts, Freeman I:172
Tufts, John I:172, 467
Tufts, Milton I:172
Tufts, Nathaniel I:921
Tufts, Sally I:172
Tufts, William I:172
Tufts, Zachariah I:696
Tuggle, Charles III:172
Tuggle, William III:270
Tukesbury, Thomas I:293
Tukey, William I:257
Tulbock, John L. III:522
Tull, Charles III:431
Tuller, Israel I:44
Tuller, Jacob I:44
Tuller, Joseph I:104
Tullis, Aaron IV:272
Tullock, Magnus III:570
Tull_s, Michael IV:191
Tully, Aquilla III:30

Tully, Elias I:121
Tuman, Peter IV:179
Tumer, Allen II:459
Tumey, William IV:114
Tunison, Garret II:53, 92
Tunnel, James II:626
Tunnel, Samuel Lloyd II:626
Tupper, Charles C. II:102
Tupper, Ezra I:467
Tupper, Ichabod I:456
Tupper, Reuben II:349
Tupper, Samuel I:365
Tupper, Simeon II:320
Tupper, Thomas I:435
Turball, William I:17
Turber, Nathaniel I:829
Turbyfield, William III:613
Turbyfill, John III:430
Turck, John A. II:396
Turck, William II:617
Turft, Francis IV:291
Turley, James III:759; IV:18
Turnbull, William II:327
Turner, Aaron I:835
Turner, Abiel I:219
Turner, Alexander III:656
Turner, Amasa I:850
Turner, Andrew IV:17
Turner, Asa II:375
Turner, Bates I:884
Turner, Benjamin I:755; IV:246
Turner, Bezalleel I:652
Turner, Charles I:601; II:266
Turner, Consider I:696
Turner, Daniel II:644
Turner, David I:227
Turner, Edward III:197
Turner, Elias III:736
Turner, Elijah I:354
Turner, Elisha I:566; II:397
Turner, Enoch, Jr. I:5
Turner, Ephraim I:365
Turner, Ezekiel A. IV:149
Turner, Geo. I:837
Turner, George III:334, 481; IV:297
Turner, Henry I:507; II:325
Turner, Hezekiah I:539
Turner, Isaac I:186
Turner, Jabez I:354
Turner, James II:250; III:330, 440, 632; IV:230
Turner, Jeremiah III:767
Turner, Joel I:786
Turner, John I:139, 525, 581; III:718; IV:224, 298
Turner, John B. IV:255
Turner, John T. III:636
Turner, Jonathan I:567
Turner, Joshua I:582; II:325
Turner, Julius IV:32
Turner, Lewis III:93, 802
Turner, Luther I:582
Turner, Marlbury I:566
Turner, Mary III:636; IV:298
Turner, Mason II:115

Turner, Mattiah III:348
Turner, Moses I:726, 902
Turner, Nathan I:365
Turner, Nathaniel II:295
Turner, Oliver I:289
Turner, Patrick II:681
Turner, Peter I:801; II:205, 552
Turner, Plato I:566
Turner, Robert I:279; III:166
Turner, Robin III:793
Turner, Roger III:317
Turner, Roland I:582
Turner, Samuel I:293, 879; III:400; IV:123
Turner, Samuel, 2d I:895
Turner, Selah I:145
Turner, Seth I:64, 551
Turner, Simeon I:412
Turner, Simon I:525
Turner, Smith IV:55
Turner, Solomon III:224
Turner, Starbird I:200
Turner, Stephen III:397
Turner, Stukely I:829
Turner, Thomas I:5; II:407, 681; III:486
Turner, W. R. I:xiii
Turner, William I:17, 58, 591; II:32, 149-50, 370; III:437, 749
Turner, William G. II:656
Turner, Wm II:333
Turner, Zadock I:434
Turner, Zebadee II:370
Turneur, Woodhull II:467
Turney, Aaron I:92
Turney, Abel I:93
Turney, Asa IV:251
Turney, Samuel II:32
Turnham, Thomas IV:54
Turnley, George III:525
Turnley, John III:561
Turpin, Alexander III:791
Turpin, Martin III:318
Turpin, Obadiah IV:81
Turrell, Amos I:92
Turrill, Isaac II:750
Turry, William III:667
Turvey, William II:617
Tuthill, Daniel II:459
Tuthill, David II:335
Tuthill, Jonathan II:521
Tuthill, William II:219
Tutt, Gabriel III:767
Tutterton, Benjamin III:440
Tuttle, Aaron I:13, 157
Tuttle, Abel I:456
Tuttle, Abraham I:912
Tuttle, Andrew IV:19
Tuttle, Asahel I:130
Tuttle, Caleb I:456; II:83
Tuttle, Chandler I:861
Tuttle, Clement IV:228
Tuttle, Ebenezer I:384
Tuttle, Edward I:92
Tuttle, Enos IV:63

531

Vaughan, Obadiah II:209
Vaughan, Prince II:272
Vaughan, Thomas I:476; II:633; III:515, 767
Vaughan, Vincent III:422
Vaughan, Will_am III:398
Vaughan, William I:152; III:48, 513, 689
Vaughan, Zebulon I:567
Vaughn, Absalom III:768
Vaughn, Almond III:767
Vaughn, Detedo III:656
Vaughn, James III:757
Vaughn, John II:733
Vaughn, Lewis II:617
Vaughn, William III:780
Vauhan, Samuel I:820
Vaunsdall, Cornelius IV:263
Vauscoy, Samuel II:732
Vawter, John I:xvi
Veach, Elijah III:211
Veale, James Carr IV:65
Veasey, Samuel I:271
Veasey, Simon II:121
Veatch, Elias IV:19
Veatch, Jeremiah III:295
Vedder, Albert II:198
Vedder, Albert L. II:442
Vedder, Daniel II:198
Vedder, David II:198
Vedder, Hermanus II:488
Vedder, Nancy II:198
Vedder, Rebecca II:198
Vedder, Sally II:198
Vedder, Valkert II:198
Veder, Frederick II:512
Veeder, Garret S. II:511
Veeder, Nicholas G. II:512
Veeder, Simon II:443
Veght, Henry II:87
Venable, John III:453
Venable, Joseph II:617
Venalter, James II:315
Venard, Thomas IV:291
Venard, William III:288
Vendivier, Matthew III:426
Vendrick, Peter III:409
Venner, John I:836
Verano, Peter I:946
Verback, Philip I:996
Verbryck, Ralph II:499
Verbryck, Samuel G. II:499
Verden, James IV:117
Verelass, J. Conrad II:617
Vergeson, Daniel II:219
Vergin, John I:671
Vergin, Leavitt C. I:671
Verlie, Michael II:272
Vermilgea, John II:228
Vermillion, Jesse III:834
Vermillion, Samuel III:435
Vermilyea, John, 2d II:309
Vermilyea, Philip II:272
Vermilyea, William II:370
Verner, John II:668; III:511
Vernon, Isaac III:172
Vernon, Richard III:632, 689

Verone, Joseph III:728
Verrus, John II:311
Verry, Jonathan I:58
Vervalen, Samuel II:499
Vervalin, Daniel II:397
Very, George I:405
Very, Jonathan I:408
Very, William I:405
Vesbrough, Isaac I:341
Vesey, Joshua I:774
Vest, George III:259
Vest, John III:753; IV:123
Vest, Philip H. III:765
Vest, Samuel IV:97
Via, William III:675
Viadenburgh, Wm. II:213
Viah, Gideon IV:248
Vial, Nathaniel I:378
Viall, John I:808; II:237
Viall, Nathaniel I:820, 931
Viall, Samuel I:981
Vibbard, Jesse I:44
Vibbard, John I:44
Vibbard, Timothy II:509
Vice, Nathaniel IV:28
Vick, Jesse III:393
Vick, John III:601
Vick, Joseph III:576
Vick, Joshua IV:19
Vickere, Samuel I:328
Vickers, William III:175
Vickery, Benjamin III:343
Vickery, David I:200
Vickery, Elijah I:360; II:219
Vickery, John II:338
Vickery, Lucy I:360
Vickery, Polly I:360
Vickery, Robert I:365
Vickery, Samuel I:328
Vickes, Elijah III:459
Vickory, Edward II:110
Vickory, Luke III:604
Vickory, William III:139
Vicory, John I:808
Vicory, Merifield IV:175
Videto, Joseph I:211
Viele, John II:535
Vier, John III:775
Viers, Benjamin IV:248
Vighte, Rymer II:87
Villas, Noah I:879
Viltum, Jonathan I:678
Vincal, John II:617
Vincent, Aaron III:64
Vincent, Bethuel II:741
Vincent, David I:448
Vincent, Isaac II:144
Vincent, Jeremiah II:508
Vincent, Jesse III:473
Vincent, John II:185; IV:71
Vincent, Johsua II:357
Vincent, Joshua I:448
Vincent, Levi II:38
Vincent, Thomas I:755; III:195
Vinciner, George IV:13
Vine, Solomon II:349
Viner, John I:628

Vines, Thomas III:832
Vinet, John II:222
Vineyard, William IV:133
Vining, Ebenezer II:209
Vining, Elisha I:567
Vining, George I:476
Vining, Israel I:354
Vining, John I:257
Vining, Richard II:460
Vinson, James L. II:144
Vinson, John I:551
Vinson, Thomas I:552
Vinton, Abiather I:476
Vinton, Earl D. IV:141
Vinton, John I:786, 906
Vinton, Joseph I:628
Vinton, Levi II:244
Vinton, Seth I:145
Vinzant, Barnabas III:455
Vinzant, John III:321
Violet, John IV:299
Virgil, Abijah II:341
Virgil, Asa II:309
Virginia, Jeremiah I:946
Vittilon, Samuel III:312
Vittum, William I:781
Vleit, Daniel II:89
Vleit, David II:87
Voght, Peter Christian II:352
Voice, John III:27
Voit, Joseph II:186
Vol_ntine, Stephen II:116
Voltz, Joshua III:835
Vonght, Henry C. II:549
Voorhees, Aaron II:83
Voorhees, Abraham II:87, 407
Voorhees, Albert II:756
Voorhees, Corneliuis II:83
Voorhees, David II:75
Voorhees, Isaac II:86
Voorhees, Paul II:87
Voorhees, Peter II:87
Voorhees, Peter G. II:79
Voorhes, James II:472
Voorhis, Garret IV:100
Vorhies, Abraham II:54
Vorhies, Albert II:53
Vorhies, James II:127
Vorhies, Minne L. II:24
Vorhis, Henry II:272
Voris, James II:45
Voris, John III:307
Vorse, Jesse I:64
Vory, Isaiah IV:247
Vosburg, John P. II:554
Vosburg, Peter J. II:554
Vosburgh, Abraham II:357
Vosburgh, Abraham J. II:443
Vosburgh, Jehoickim II:388
Vosburgh, Peter II:391
Vosburgh, William II:388
Vosbury, Eliakim II:399
Vose, Charles II:247
Vose, Edward I:793
Vose, Elijah I:539
Vose, Jesse I:200
Vose, John I:539

535

Walden, George III:762
Walden, Isaac II:341
Walden, Jacob I:727
Walden, James III:325
Walden, John III:281, 435, 738; IV:86
Walden, Nathan II:296
Waldo, Daniel I:152
Waldo, David II:375
Waldo, Edward I:847
Waldo, John T. III:790
Waldo, Joseph II:527
Waldo, Nathan II:407
Waldo, Zaccheus I:152
Waldon, James I:820
Waldren, John III:227
Waldren, Nathaniel II:250
Waldrepe, James III:141
Waldron, Charles III:85
Waldron, Ebenezer I:200
Waldron, Eliza II:192
Waldron, Isaac II:192
Waldron, Lewis II:192
Waldron, Nicholas II:192
Waldron, Richard II:116
Waldron, Sally II:192
Waldron, Samuel II:736; IV:109
Waldron, Samuel B. II:447
Waldron, Thomas III:365
Waldrop, John III:503
Waldrow, David I:755
Wale, Timothy IV:268
Wales, Eleazer II:433
Wales, Eliel IV:199
Wales, Jacob I:628
Wales, Jonathan I:487
Wales, Joseph I:631, 892, 998
Wales, Nathaniel I:25
Wales, Samuel I:552
Wales, Shubal I:467
Wales, Thomas I:583
Wales, Timothy I:540
Walhever, Abraham II:106
Walisee, Christian II:320
Walker, Aaron F. II:79
Walker, Aaron Grant I:615
Walker, Abel I:745
Walker, Abraham I:212, 830
Walker, Adam I:588
Walker, Andrew III:433
Walker, Benjamin I:906, 957; II:629; III:27; IV:66, 276
Walker, Bruce I:755
Walker, Buckley III:442
Walker, Calvin I:830
Walker, Charity II:629
Walker, Charles I:258; III:761
Walker, Daniel III:807
Walker, Daniel, Sen. III:179
Walker, Edward I:243, 982; II:219, 633; III:573, 688
Walker, Eliakim I:768
Walker, George I:378, 615; III:490, 568
Walker, Gordon II:296
Walker, Green III:418

Walker, Hannah II:629
Walker, Henry II:682; IV:13
Walker, Hiram I:615
Walker, Isaac II:556; III:577
Walker, James I:378, 405, 467, 476, 487, 762, 968, 981; II:256, 381; III:299, 525; IV:226
Walker, Jason I:629
Walker, Jeremiah III:115
Walker, Jesse I:714; IV:121
Walker, John I:227; II:282, 629; III:52, 461, 542, 556, 570; IV:103, 281
Walker, Joseph I:527, 629, 996; II:629, 654; III:787
Walker, Joshua III:589
Walker, Josiah I:258
Walker, Learned I:705
Walker, Lemuel I:280
Walker, M. I:655
Walker, Martha II:629
Walker, Mashah IV:298
Walker, Matthias II:266
Walker, Meshec IV:199
Walker, Moses I:378
Walker, Nathaniel I:75, 615
Walker, Needham III:406
Walker, Obadiah IV:42, 99
Walker, Oliver III:800
Walker, Paul III:410
Walker, Peter I:153; IV:166, 297
Walker, Philip III:303
Walker, Reuben III:400
Walker, Richard I:378, 540; III:537
Walker, Robert I:341, 655; III:567
Walker, Samuel I:527, 869, 932; III:556, 619, 657; IV:98, 207
Walker, Samuel C. I:164
Walker, Seth I:774
Walker, Simeon I:936
Walker, Simons I:145
Walker, Solomon II:349
Walker, Tandy III:382
Walker, Thomas I:714; III:810, 819
Walker, Timothy I:201, 540
Walker, William I:153, 170, 219, 290, 781; II:489, 575; III:410, 586, 767; IV:243
Walker, William J. III:753
Walker, William L. III:406
Walker, William T. III:826
Walker, Zaccheus I:714
Walkins, Samuel III:592
Walkly, John II:751
Walkup, George I:449
Walkup, Samuel III:303
Wall, Edward I:999
Wall, Francis I:81
Wall, Isaac II:645
Wall, Jacob III:459
Wall, James II:79

Wall, Jesse III:461
Wall, John III:744
Wall, Jonathan III:451
Wall, Joseph III:403
Wall, Peter III:823
Wall, Richard III:368, 500
Wall, William I:836; II:599; III:51; IV:80
Wallace, Andrew II:711
Wallace, Andrew (2) II:711
Wallace, Asa II:629
Wallace, Benjamin I:735
Wallace, Caesar I:735
Wallace, Charles II:711
Wallace, Charles D. II:629
Wallace, Cornelius II:467
Wallace, Ebenezer II:254
Wallace, Edward III:572
Wallace, Eli II:629
Wallace, George III:385, 464
Wallace, Hugh III:652
Wallace, Ira II:629
Wallace, James I:803; II:698; III:500, 717, 783, 794
Wallace, John I:567, 755, 762, 993; II:381; III:79; IV:48, 124
Wallace, Joseph I:714; II:602; IV:213
Wallace, Josiah I:232
Wallace, Ross IV:137
Wallace, Samuel III:455, 593
Wallace, Thomas III:484
Wallace, Webb II:629
Wallace, Weymouth I:735
Wallace, William I:75, 667; II:127, 530, 558, 727, 756, 759
Wallace, William B. III:333
Wallasie, Christian II:320
Wallen, Daniel IV:238
Wallen, Jonathan I:809
Waller, Ashbel IV:235
Waller, Daniel III:719
Waller, George II:300
Waller, Jesse IV:275
Waller, John III:242
Waller, John C. I:928
Waller, Joshua III:291
Waller, Nathaniel III:382
Waller, Thomas III:738
Waller, Walter I:846
Waller, William IV:252
Wallerath, Adolph II:443
Wallerath, Isaac II:443
Wallice, Samuel I:931
Walling, Carhart III:387
Walling, Daniel II:79
Walling, James II:45
Walling, John III:601
Walling, Joseph II:79
Walling, Philip II:145
Walling, Simeon III:309
Walling, William III:89, 589
Wallington, Charles II:599
Wallis, Benjamin III:589
Wallis, Curwin I:973

Wallis, David I:654
Wallis, Ebenezer I:654
Wallis, Henry II:407
Wallis, James III:414
Wallis, John III:378
Wallis, Matthew III:568
Wallis, Moses II:205
Wallis, Robert I:879
Wallradt, Henry II:417
Walls, Charles III:164
Walls, Francis I:736
Walls, John IV:86
Walls, Reuben III:240
Wallsworth, Elijah I:913
Walmsley, William I:36
Walpole, S. III:518
Walradt, Adolphus J. II:309
Walradt, Peter II:443
Walrath, Henry II:186
Walrath, Nicholas II:186
Walsh, James I:608; IV:166
Walsh, Mark III:39
Walsh, Thomas II:250
Walsh, William III:310
Walston, Thomas III:406
Waltamger, David II:761
Waltars, John II:698
Walter, Adam II:467
Walter, Asher II:722
Walter, Charles I:52
Walter, Christian II:489
Walter, Christopher IV:188, 297
Walter, David II:753
Walter, Henry II:83
Walter, John I:936; II:287
Walter, Martin II:287
Walters, George II:127
Walters, Jacob II:52, 704
Walters, Jacob, 2d II:721
Walters, James IV:183
Walters, John II:698; III:330; IV:109, 273, 297
Walters, Martin II:745
Walters, Peter IV:275
Walthall, Henry III:761
Walthall, Wm., Sr. III:765
Waltman, Lewis II:695
Waltman, Michael III:30
Walton, George III:27, 667
Walton, Henry II:629
Walton, Joel III:803
Walton, Josiah I:669
Walton, Martin III:613
Walton, Newell III:496
Walton, Oliver I:527
Walton, Reuben I:219
Walton, Silas II:208
Walton, Thomas II:629
Walton, Tilman III:364
Walton, William II:629, 733; III:83
Walts, Conrad II:254
Waltz, Michael II:652
Wambach, Philip II:761
Wamer, Solomon II:381
Wamire, Frederick II:300

Wamsley, David III:799
Wamsley, James III:799
Wamsley, William III:790
Wandall, David II:124
Wandall, Jacob II:352
Wandel, John II:668
Wandell, Alex. II:192
Wandell, John II:309
Wandell, Louisa II:192
Wandell, Malissa II:192
Wandell, Sally Ann II:192
Wanger, John II:145
Wann, John III:53
Wanslaw, John III:161
Wanton, William I:820
Wapples, Samuel III:847
Wapples, Seevra III:847
Ward, A. II:566
Ward, Aaron II:417
Ward, Abijah II:333
Ward, Abner I:768; II:213
Ward, Amos IV:255
Ward, Andrew III:195
Ward, Benjamin I:222, 594; III:356; IV:228
Ward, Bernard I:946
Ward, Caleb I:448; II:491
Ward, Christopher I:457-58; II:512
Ward, Daniel II:196, 272; IV:56
Ward, Daniel A. II:408
Ward, David IV:243
Ward, Dixsey III:502
Ward, Ebenezer II:467
Ward, Edward II:34
Ward, Elijah II:287
Ward, Elisha I:328, 607-8, 629, 922
Ward, Eliza I:594; II:196
Ward, Elmira II:196
Ward, Elnathan I:848
Ward, George I:161
Ward, Hannah II:198
Ward, Henry D. II:196
Ward, Hopper II:696
Ward, Ichabod I:139; II:685
Ward, Isaac II:38
Ward, Israel II:417; IV:255
Ward, Jabez I:902
Ward, Jacob II:330
Ward, James II:145, 706; III:297, 402
Ward, Jesse I:928
Ward, John II:45, 325, 397, 489, 563; III:79, 336, 453, 803; IV:30, 62, 87
Ward, John, 1st II:145
Ward, John, 2d II:345
Ward, John, 3d II:213
Ward, John L. III:457
Ward, Jonathan II:509
Ward, Joseph I:365, 540; II:681
Ward, Joshna I:553
Ward, Josiah I:669; IV:260
Ward, Kerley I:427

Ward, Laban II:198
Ward, Lawrence III:215
Ward, Luther I:982
Ward, Moses I:58
Ward, Nathan IV:215
Ward, Nehemiah I:165, 457; IV:240
Ward, Nicholas I:355
Ward, Nicholson I:820
Ward, Obadiah IV:228
Ward, R. R. II:559-60, 566
Ward, Reuben II:338
Ward, Richard R. II:560, 562
Ward, Rufus IV:263
Ward, Samuel I:487, 726; II:502, 562; III:177
Ward, Samuel C. II:66, 196
Ward, Simon I:704
Ward, Solomon II:372
Ward, Stephen I:968, 999
Ward, Thomas I:45, 201, 969; II:186, 713; III:199
Ward, Timothy IV:66
Ward, William I:654, 657; II:45; III:161, 394, 456, 503; IV:125
Ward, Zadock II:225
Ward, Zebediah IV:63
Wardell, Robert IV:34
Wardell, Samuel II:206
Warden, Benjamin II:686
Warden, Elisha III:254
Warden, Ichabod II:254
Warden, James IV:173
Warden, John II:733
Warden, Joseph I:53
Warden, Nathan II:303
Warden, Samuel III:172
Warden, Thomas I:242; II:237
Wardlaw, William III:164
Wardley, Moses I:243
Wards, Edward IV:277
Wardwell, Benjamin I:457
Wardwell, D. I:xxv
Wardwell, Ezekiel I:405
Wardwell, G., cen. II:484
Wardwell, Jacob I:36
Wardwell, Joseph I:219
Wardwell, Joshua I:406
Wardwell, Nathan I:355
Wardwell, Simon I:405
Wardwell, Stephen I:829
Wardwell, William IV:173
Ware, Amos I:653
Ware, Asa I:384
Ware, Edward III:172
Ware, Elias I:540
Ware, Emer II:188
Ware, Frederick I:921
Ware, George I:981
Ware, James I:527
Ware, Jason I:280
Ware, John I:583
Ware, John, Sen. III:409
Ware, Joseph I:491
Ware, Michael II:188
Ware, Mich'l W. II:188

537

Ware, Nathan I:279
Ware, Thomas II:84; III:814
Ware, William III:409, 489
Warefield, Ephraim II:750
Warfield, Joseph III:65
Warfield, Joshua I:435
Warfield, Reuben I:467
Warfield, Samuel I:653
Warford, Benjamin III:255
Warham, Charles III:330
Waring, Anthony II:310
Waring, Gideon II:186
Waring, Henry I:36
Waring, James I:93
Waring, Jonathan IV:255
Waring, Morton A. I:xv
Waring, Schudder II:372
Warmack, William III:204
Warmouth, Thadeus H. III:221
Warn, Benoni II:213
Warn, William II:244
Warner, Amasa II:219
Warner, Amos I:64
Warner, Benjamin I:775;
  II:363, 401
Warner, Charles II:30, 467
Warner, Cornelius II:273
Warner, Daniel I:104, 583,
  809, 931; II:472
Warner, Ebenezer I:653
Warner, Eleazer I:969
Warner, Elias I:654
Warner, George II:515
Warner, Israel II:565
Warner, Jabez J. I:941
Warner, Jehiel II:422
Warner, Jesse I:385; II:436
Warner, John I:53, 105, 113,
  801; II:489, 633
Warner, John, 2d I:9
Warner, John B. I:861
Warner, Jonathan I:487, 629;
  II:399
Warner, Loomis I:105
Warner, Mary II:629
Warner, Michael II:695
Warner, Moses I:487; II:719
Warner, Nathaniel I:424;
  II:543
Warner, Nicolas II:515
Warner, Noadiah I:476
Warner, Noah IV:168
Warner, Omri II:234
Warner, Paul I:476
Warner, Philip II:618
Warner, Phineas I:654
Warner, Richard I:105
Warner, Robert I:58
Warner, Samuel I:105, 130,
  936; II:629
Warner, Saul I:114
Warner, Selden I:139
Warner, Seth II:412
Warner, Simeon I:861
Warner, Thomas II:341
Warner, William I:628

Warren, Aaron I:243, 319;
  II:477
Warren, Abel IV:103
Warren, Abijah I:219
Warren, Abraham II:205
Warren, Archibald III:784
Warren, Ashbel I:105
Warren, Benjamin I:567
Warren, Caleb II:543
Warren, Charles I:449
Warren, Daniel I:242, 319;
  II:460
Warren, David I:848; II:315
Warren, Drury III:613
Warren, Edward IV:139
Warren, Elijah I:653; II:89
Warren, Ephraim I:628; II:282
Warren, Ezra I:755
Warren, George I:167
Warren, Hugh III:285
Warren, James, Jr. I:555
Warren, Jason II:225
Warren, Jeduthan I:653
Warren, Jesse I:93
Warren, John I:45, 809;
  II:509; III:615, 619
Warren, John, 2d I:75
Warren, John, 3d II:309
Warren, John, 1st II:325
Warren, Joseph II:244
Warren, Joshua I:318
Warren, Josiah I:714
Warren, Moses I:290; II:309;
  IV:243
Warren, Nathan I:93, 258,
  527
Warren, Nathanied I:219
Warren, Nathaniel I:139;
  II:497
Warren, Neverson I:435
Warren, Pelatiah I:201
Warren, Peter I:201
Warren, Richard I:201
Warren, Samuel III:518
Warren, Seth II:480
Warren, Silas I:653
Warren, Simpson III:496
Warren, Stephen I:355, 653
Warren, Timothy I:436
Warren, Uriah II:161
Warren, William I:629, 736;
  II:343, 565; III:268, 366,
  440; IV:28
Warren, Zenos II:502
Warrener, Aaron II:205
Warrener, Willard II:256
Warrick, Charles D. II:722
Warriner, Abner I:457
Warriner, Benj. II:244
Warriner, Gad I:467; II:244
Warriner, Stephen I:467
Warring, Solomon II:480
Warrington, William IV:255
Warthen, Isaac II:230
Warwick, Wiat III:393
Wasburn, Bildad I:582
Wasgate, David I:189

Wash, John, Sen. IV:122
Wash, William III:501
Washbourn, Abraham I:355
Washbourn, Samuel I:630
Washbourn, William I:438
Washbourne, Alden I:736
Washburn, Abial I:583
Washburn, Abner I:955
Washburn, Amos II:189
Washburn, Asa I:567
Washburn, Bazaliel I:378
Washburn, Benjamin III:323
Washburn, Ebenezer I:290
Washburn, Elijah I:762
Washburn, Ephraim I:293
Washburn, Hugh I:567
Washburn, Isaac I:378
Washburn, Isaiah I:946
Washburn, Isreal I:379
Washburn, Jonah I:955
Washburn, Joseph I:762;
  II:178
Washburn, Lemuel II:349
Washburn, Lettice I:365
Washburn, Luther II:282
Washburn, Nathan I:75
Washburn, Reuben I:1000
Washburn, Samuel II:349
Washburn, Solomon I:567
Washburn, Thomas I:583;
  III:530
Washburn, William II:215
Washburne, Eli I:704
Wason, John I:774; III:832
Wasson, James II:213
Wasson, John I:260; II:381,
  512, 552
Wasson, John (2) I:260
Wasson, Joseph IV:32
Wasson, Robert I:94
Wasson, Samuel I:260
Wasson, Thomas I:260
Wasson, William IV:248
Wa_stcott, Benjamin I:365
Watcher, Nicholas I:999
Waterbury, Enos I:93
Waterbury, John I:25, 36
Waterbury, Joseph I:105
Waterbury, William I:36, 93
Waterfield, Meshac III:724
Waterfield, Peter III:211
Waterhouse, George I:258
Waterhouse, John I:186
Waterhouse, Jonathan I:145
Waterhouse, Joseph I:257
Waterhouse, William IV:297
Waterman, Abraham I:993
Waterman, Benjamin I:829
Waterman, Calvin II:287
Waterman, Charles IV:231
Waterman, Chester II:296
Waterman, Darius II:391
Waterman, David II:449
Waterman, Edward I:830
Waterman, Elisha I:582, 993
Waterman, Ephraim I:567
Waterman, Ignatius IV:224

Waterman, Jedediah II:273, 560
Waterman, John I:816; II:309
Waterman, Joseph I:230; II:123
Waterman, Levi II:364
Waterman, Malachi I:186
Waterman, Noah I:258
Waterman, Olney I:830
Waterman, Robert I:957
Waterman, Seth I:704
Waterman, T. B. I:xiii
Waterman, William I:809, 816-17, 993-94
Waterman, Zebedee I:467
Waterous, Benjamin II:296
Waterous, Josiah II:336
Waters, Abner IV:290
Waters, Asa I:552
Waters, Benjamin II:461
Waters, Bigelow II:381
Waters, Charles II:178
Waters, Daniel II:497
Waters, David I:275
Waters, Elisha II:287
Waters, George II:599
Waters, Henry II:45
Waters, Israel II:96; IV:2, 114
Waters, Jacob IV:266
Waters, James III:550
Waters, John I:755; II:274
Waters, Joseph I:424; II:618
Waters, Judah II:489
Waters, Moses III:451
Waters, Richard I:65; III:48, 69
Waters, Thomas I:726; II:447
Waters, Thomas, Sen. IV:166
Waters, William III:676
Waters, Wilson III:61
Watford, William III:402
Watkins, Abner III:803
Watkins, Badwell I:903
Watkins, David II:287
Watkins, Edward I:745; III:825
Watkins, Ephraim II:230
Watkins, Gassaway III:44, 69
Watkins, Gilbert II:338
Watkins, John III:288, 680
Watkins, Jonathan IV:229
Watkins, Joseph III:667
Watkins, Joseph D. III:780
Watkins, Leonard III:52
Watkins, Michael I:341
Watkins, Nathan I:922
Watkins, Oliver II:480
Watkins, Robert II:230; III:761
Watkins, Seth II:545
Watkins, Spencer III:595
Watkins, Stephen I:438, 936; III:720
Watkins, Thomas III:317
Watkins, Willard I:468
Watkins, William III:632
Watkins, Zaccheus I:628
Watkins, Zachariah I:341

Watmough, John G. II:599
Watrond, Noah I:380
Watrous, Allen IV:260
Watrous, Benjamin IV:228
Watrous, John R. I:45, 157
Watrous, William I:921
Watson, Aaron I:355
Watson, Alexander II:417
Watson, Amariah IV:283
Watson, Benjamin II:643
Watson, Caleb II:325
Watson, Daniel I:726, 745
Watson, David I:727; III:285
Watson, Guy I:811
Watson, J. L. I:xiii
Watson, Jack I:81
Watson, James II:208, 635, 726
Watson, Jesse I:903; II:2
Watson, John I:25, 121, 212, 258, 735; II:208, 371; III:257, 440
Watson, John, 1st IV:88
Watson, John, 2d I:736; III:255
Watson, Jos. I:998; II:553, 557; IV:297
Watson, Joseph I:998; II:553-54, 559, 563; III:303, 325, 335, 349; IV:296
Watson, Larner III:804
Watson, Leven III:398
Watson, Levi I:114; II:309
Watson, Major II:320
Watson, Nathaniel III:607
Watson, Neal III:381
Watson, Oliver I:836
Watson, Philip III:675
Watson, Samuel I:81, 816; IV:123
Watson, Stephen I:319
Watson, Thomas I:113, 704, 811; II:2; IV:120
Watson, Titus II:325
Watson, Walter III:675
Watson, William I:902; II:618; III:303; IV:287
Watson, William, Sen. III:451
Watson, Winthrop I:781
Watsor, Evan T. III:327
Watt, James II:599
Watterman, Elijah II:388
Watterman, Gladding IV:281
Watters, Bennett Miller II:189
Watters, Eliza Ann II:189
Watters, John IV:188
Watters, Lewis Matthews II:189
Watters, Moses III:459
Watters, Samuel II:189
Watterson, Robert III:729
Wattles, Charles II:381
Wattles, Daniel II:527
Wattles, David II:228
Wattles, Mason II:272
Wattles, William II:371
Watts, Aaron IV:80

Watts, Alexander II:590
Watts, Betsey III:41
Watts, Daniel I:424
Watts, David III:509
Watts, Ganet III:91
Watts, George III:593
Watts, Jacob II:250
Watts, James III:28, 426
Watts, Jesse I:696
Watts, John I:787; II:310; III:847
Watts, Michael III:41
Watts, Peter III:323
Watts, R. K. I:xii
Watts, Rebecca III:41
Watts, Robert III:41
Watts, Stephen R. I:388
Watts, Thomas IV:104
Watts, William I:388, 614; IV:97
Watts, Wm. W. III:847
Waugh, Joseph IV:284
Waugh, Samuel I:52, 156
Waugh, T. I:xiii
Waugh, Thaddeus I:25
Way, Abner I:130
Way, Asa II:371
Way, Asa (2) II:371
Way, Durien I:140
Way, Elisha I:140
Way, Isaac I:53; IV:87
Way, John II:361
Way, Peter I:72
Way, Selah II:433
Wayland, Edward I:94
Wayland, James I:5
Wayland, Joshua III:247
Wayland, Molly I:94
Wayley, Aaron I:36
Wayson, Orpha II:623
Wayson, Thomas II:623
Wayt, William III:819
Weah, Fred. Wm. II:643
Wealey, George IV:195
Wear, Cornelius II:654
Wear, John III:616
Wear, Richard C. I:841
Weare, Jeremiah I:318
Weare, William I:44
Weasy, John II:643
Weatherbee, Amos I:993
Weatherbee, Daniel I:993
Weatherbee, Thomas I:476, 921
Weatherby, Luther I:470
Weatherford, Benj. III:719
Weatherhall, Jacob III:209
Weatherhead, Amaziah I:830
Weatherhead, Levi I:830
Weathers, Elisha III:430
Weathers, Valentine III:176
Weathers, William III:451
Weatherstine, John II:250
Weaver, Abiel I:796
Weaver, Adam II:692
Weaver, Anthony II:750
Weaver, Caleb I:809

Weaver, David II:186
Weaver, Dutee I:816
Weaver, Edward II:205
Weaver, George, 2d II:343
Weaver, George, 1st II:145
Weaver, Henry II:233, 665;
III:482
Weaver, Jacob II:631
Weaver, James III:714
Weaver, John III:27, 204, 381,
463, 630, 750; IV:300
Weaver, John G. II:150
Weaver, Joseph I:378
Weaver, Lodowick II:381
Weaver, Michael II:690; IV:97
Weaver, Nathan I:366
Weaver, Philip III:278
Weaver, Reuben I:830
Weaver, Richard I:969
Weaver, Samuel I:113; III:630
Weaver, Shadrack III:606
Weaver, Sheffel I:378
Weaver, Thomas I:75
Weaver, Timothy II:422
Weaver, William I:809;
III:443; IV:236
Webb, Abner I:152
Webb, Andrew II:381
Webb, Augustin III:263
Webb, Austin III:185
Webb, Azariah I:942
Webb, Barnabas I:583
Webb, Barruch IV:59
Webb, Benjamin II:467;
III:621
Webb, Christopher II:433
Webb, Constant I:12
Webb, Daniel I:355
Webb, David II:489; IV:300
Webb, Ebenezer I:93; II:230,
433
Webb, Edward I:186; II:145
Webb, George I:629
Webb, Isaac II:422; III:276
Webb, James I:186; III:371
Webb, Jeremiah I:809
Webb, Jesse III:418, 523, 595
Webb, John I:52, 257, 539,
588; II:408, 560; III:221,
417, 526, 599, 679
Webb, Johnson III:440
Webb, Joseph II:256, 394
Webb, Joseph, Jr. I:170
Webb, Joshua I:153; III:366
Webb, Josiah IV:290
Webb, Lewis III:328
Webb, Matthias II:741
Webb, Matthias (2) II:741
Webb, Moses I:36
Webb, Nathan II:554
Webb, Nathaniel I:212
Webb, Reynolds I:121
Webb, Robert I:803
Webb, Samuel I:583
Webb, Thomas I:539
Webb, William II:564
Webber, Asa I:272

Webber, Benjamin I:243, 406
Webber, Bradley I:467
Webber, Daniel I:189
Webber, Edward II:273
Webber, Ezekiel I:212
Webber, George I:280
Webber, John I:526; II:43
Webber, Jonathan I:242;
IV:115
Webber, Joseph I:201
Webber, Lewis I:271
Webber, Nathaniel III:48
Webber, Noah I:212
Webber, Paul I:243
Webber, Reuben I:75
Webber, Ronaldo II:433
Webber, Stephen I:318
Webber, William I:189, 508;
II:287, 641
Weber, Peter I:599
Webster, Aaron II:436
Webster, Abraham II:261
Webster, Allen II:391
Webster, Andrew IV:292
Webster, Benjamin II:361, 562
Webster, Daniel II:296
Webster, David I:941
Webster, Eleazer I:476
Webster, Eve II:562
Webster, Humphrey IV:24
Webster, Isaac II:388
Webster, Israel I:200
Webster, J. D. I:xiii
Webster, Jacob I:774
Webster, John II:460
Webster, John B. II:683
Webster, Joseph I:714, 996;
II:549
Webster, Joshua II:230
Webster, Michael IV:228
Webster, Moses I:993
Webster, Nathan II:371-72
Webster, Nathaniel I:936
Webster, Obed I:131
Webster, Richard I:775
Webster, Roswell IV:103
Webster, Samuel I:405; II:467;
IV:240
Webster, Simeon I:75
Webster, Stephen I:170, 689,
768
Webster, Stephen, 2d I:736
Webster, Thomas I:170;
IV:141
Webster, William II:375;
III:328
Wedgbare, Wm. III:377
Wedge, Stephen I:53
Wedgewood, James I:726
Wedgewood, Jesse I:317
Wedgwood, Noah I:781
Weed, Abishai I:93
Weed, Abraham II:509
Weed, Alexander II:371
Weed, Anny II:192
Weed, Benjamin I:94, 385;
II:358

Weed, Benjamin, Jr. I:5
Weed, Charles I:892; II:519
Weed, Daniel I:93
Weed, David I:93; II:192, 300
Weed, Eleazer I:94
Weed, Ephraim II:564
Weed, Ezra I:36
Weed, Gilbert II:371
Weed, Henry I:94
Weed, Isaac I:93; II:192
Weed, J. II:192
Weed, Jehiel II:303
Weed, John I:93; II:192, 394,
480
Weed, Jonas I:36
Weed, Jonathan II:394
Weed, Joseph I:736
Weed, Samued II:300
Weed, Sarah II:192
Weed, Seth I:5
Weed, Smith III:357
Weed, Stephen I:36
Weeden, Horatio III:33
Weeden, Thomas I:921
Weedman, Jacob II:618
Weedman, Peter III:509
Weedon, Augustine III:827
Weedon, Peleg I:816
Weekly, Thomas III:842
Weeks, Abisha I:328
Weeks, David I:931; III:293
Weeks, Elijah II:371
Weeks, James I:272; II:38;
III:325
Weeks, Jedediah I:727
Weeks, John I:719; III:610
Weeks, Joseph I:13, 654;
III:601
Weeks, Leonard I:736
Weeks, Levi III:477
Weeks, Martha III:671
Weeks, Mary I:175
Weeks, Micajah II:230
Weeks, Moses III:671
Weeks, Pelatiah I:243
Weeks, Samuel I:486
Weeks, Theophilus III:104
Weeks, Thomas II:282
Weeks, Uriah I:436
Weeks, Wait I:175
Weeks, William I:768
Weelright, Joseph I:318
Weems, Henry III:475
Weems, John, Sr. III:122
Weersheem, John III:95
Wees, Peter III:612
Weese, George IV:261
Weese, Michael III:545
Weider, Michael II:704
Weiderick, Francis II:585
Weightman, George IV:184
Weigle, Christopher II:639
Weinnand, Philip III:294
Weir, Edward I:614
Weir, James II:185
Weir, John II:708, 725
Weir, Joseph III:204

540

Weirick, Michael II:695
Weirick, Valentine II:652
Weise, George III:749
Weiser, John II:651; III:41
Weisner, Godfrey II:666
Weiss, Jacob II:740
Weith, Johannes II:515
Welbour, John I:528
Welch, Amos II:238
Welch, Benjamin I:884
Welch, Daniel IV:36
Welch, Dan'l III:195
Welch, Ebenezer I:932; IV:180
Welch, Edward I:895; II:185
Welch, Hopestill I:52
Welch, Isaac III:704
Welch, James III:308, 767
Welch, John I:17, 156, 719,
892; II:100, 341, 399, 509,
761; III:8, 628
Welch, John, 1st I:52
Welch, Jonas I:653
Welch, Joseph I:996; II:325;
III:453
Welch, Lemuel I:212
Welch, Michael II:56
Welch, Moses II:551
Welch, Paul I:243
Welch, Peter II:54
Welch, Robert II:325
Welch, Rossel I:261
Welch, Samuel II:233; IV:27
Welch, Solomon I:487
Welch, Sylvester, Sen. III:771
Welch, Thomas I:599; III:630
Welch, William I:211-12
Weld, Benjamin I:602
Weld, Calvin I:913
Weld, Jacob I:598
Weld, Moses I:895
Welden, Abraham I:52
Welden, Jesse IV:236
Welden, Joshua I:449
Welder, Ephraim I:318
Weldon, Joshua II:358
Weldy, George III:701
Welker, Daniel II:658
Wellborn, Elias III:157
Wellborn, Isaac III:89
Welldon, John III:99
Weller, Amos I:968
Weller, Dan II:349
Weller, Frederick II:443
Weller, John II:729
Weller, Martin I:457
Weller, Philip II:89
Welles, Nathaniel III:715
Wellington, Ebenezer I:745
Wellington, Jeduthan I:526
Wellington, Josiah I:508
Wellington, Oliver I:527
Wellkey, John I:803
Wellman, Abraham I:201;
IV:191
Wellman, Barnabas II:215
Wellman, Jacob I:762; II:309
Wellman, Oliver I:931

Wellman, Paul II:330
Wellman, Samuel I:230, 696
Wellman, Silas II:309
Wellman, Timothy I:982
Wellman, William I:121
Wells, Abner I:131
Wells, Abraham II:502
Wells, Alexander III:472
Wells, Andrew III:616
Wells, Asa II:381
Wells, Benjamin II:296, 489,
561; III:472; IV:232
Wells, Charles D. IV:257
Wells, Cornelius III:15
Wells, Daniel II:543
Wells, David I:424, 913
Wells, Duckett III:842
Wells, Ebenezer I:755
Wells, Elias II:433
Wells, Elisha I:44; II:460
Wells, Ezekiel II:719
Wells, George I:816
Wells, Gideon I:93
Wells, Henry II:564, 756
Wells, Israel IV:199
Wells, Jacob III:414
Wells, James I:105, 836;
II:185; III:27, 209
Wells, Jesse III:597
Wells, John II:161, 266, 489;
III:280, 693, 809
Wells, Jonathan I:121; II:154
Wells, Joshua I:272
Wells, Levi II:115
Wells, Littlebury III:291
Wells, Moses I:406
Wells, Nancy III:472
Wells, Nathaniel I:781; III:691
Wells, Nicholas C. I:847
Wells, Noah II:394
Wells, Oliver I:941
Wells, Paul I:875
Wells, Peter II:343, 467
Wells, Phineas I:212
Wells, Priscilla III:472
Wells, Richard III:277
Wells, Robert IV:260
Wells, Sally III:203
Wells, Samuel I:93, 895;
III:246
Wells, Silas II:417
Wells, Simeon I:105
Wells, Solomon R. III:768
Wells, Stephen I:25, 768
Wells, Thomas I:139; II:5
Wells, Thos. K. III:203
Wells, Timothy I:775; IV:187
Wells, W. B. II:561
Wells, William II:476; III:8,
299, 582; IV:160
Wells, Youngs III:335
Wells, Zachariah III:559
Welman, John I:913
Welsch, Dan'l III:195
Welsch, Michael II:618
Welsh, Crawford IV:295
Welsh, Daniel I:873

Welsh, David S. IV:263
Welsh, Isaiah III:767
Welsh, James III:294
Welsh, John I:873; II:643;
III:667, 790
Welsh, John, 2d I:72
Welsh, Jonas I:553
Welsh, Jonathan I:319
Welsh, Joseph II:653
Welsh, Matthias I:735
Welsh, Michael I:869
Welsh, Nicholas II:145
Welsh, Patrick II:681
Welsh, Robert III:583; IV:141
Welsh, Thomas I:704
Welsh, William B. IV:32
Welson, Jonathan I:301, 465
Welton, Joel I:44
Welton, Shubael II:219
Welton, Solomon I:44
Welton, Thomas III:841
Welts, Barney II:681
Welty, John III:545
Wemple, John II:512
Wemple, Myndert B. II:443
Wendall, Ahasuerus II:512
Wendell, Ann II:552
Wendell, Catherine II:552
Wendell, John H. II:205, 552
Wensel, John II:739
Wentle, John II:599
Wentworth, Alice I:687
Wentworth, Andrew I:243
Wentworth, Anna I:687
Wentworth, Benjamin I:687
Wentworth, Benning IV:284
Wentworth, Betsey I:687
Wentworth, Clark I:491
Wentworth, Daniel I:356, 892
Wentworth, Edm'd I:687
Wentworth, Edmund I:687
Wentworth, Elijah I:902
Wentworth, Enock I:189
Wentworth, Ezekiel I:687
Wentworth, Foster I:280
Wentworth, Ichabod I:170
Wentworth, Jacob I:687
Wentworth, Jedediah I:170,
592
Wentworth, Joannah I:687
Wentworth, John I:189, 687;
II:96
Wentworth, John, 2d I:227
Wentworth, Jonah W. I:140
Wentworth, Lemuel I:212
Wentworth, Levi III:247
Wentworth, Lewis I:687
Wentworth, Mary I:687
Wentworth, Moses I:687
Wentworth, Nathaniel I:553
Wentworth, Nicholas I:687
Wentworth, Patience I:687
Wentworth, Paul I:170, 230,
789
Wentworth, Phinehas I:736
Wentworth, Polly I:687
Wentworth, Richard I:319

Wentworth, Sabina I:687
Wentworth, Sally I:687
Wentworth, Samuel I:540, 689
Wentworth, Sarah I:687
Wentworth, Timothy I:319
Wentz, Frederick II:571
Wentz, John III:349
Wereham, Peter II:602
Werker, Albert Vander II:287
Werner, John II:698
Werner, Peter II:617
Wernsz, Philip II:710
Werse, Adam II:716
Wert, Anah II:282
Werts, Jacob II:639
Wertz, John II:741
Wertz, Samuel II:571
Wescoat, Daniel I:172
Wescoat, David I:172
Wescoat, Joseph II:338
Wescoat, Lucy I:172
Wescoat, Sally I:172
Wescott, Isaac I:727
Wescott, Joshua I:219
Wescott, Ziba II:237
Wesley, John III:784
Wessels, Hercules II:273
Wessinger, Ludwig II:709
Wesson, Ephraim I:936
Wesson, Isaac III:757
Wesson, James I:614
West, Aaron II:480
West, Alexander III:799
West, Amos II:296
West, Anthony II:208
West, Benjamin III:62
West, Benjamin, Sen. III:165
West, Bransford III:814
West, Caleb II:399
West, Charles I:654; II:145
West, David II:273, 388
West, Edward I:714, 973
West, Elnathan I:379
West, Frederick II:590
West, George III:615
West, Hezekiah IV:14
West, Ichabod I:341
West, Ira I:145
West, Isaac I:272
West, Jacob II:266
West, John I:406, 829; II:467,
   660; III:181, 801, 823;
   IV:77
West, Jonathan II:527
West, Joseph III:62, 513
West, Josiah II:225
West, Judah I:52
West, Leonard III:265
West, Levi III:557
West, Nathan I:379, 755;
   II:237
West, Nathaniel I:799; IV:15
West, Nathaniel Hix I:799
West, Peter I:227
West, Richard II:408
West, Samuel I:145, 667

West, Thomas I:829; II:79,
   433, 656; III:246; IV:3
West, Timothy I:787, 836
West, William II:79, 472;
   III:387, 490
West, Williim III:613
West, Willoughly, Sen. III:411
Westbrook, Aaron II:88
Westbrook, Cornelius B. II:685
Westbrook, Gideon II:745
Westbrook, James II:527
Westbrook, Richard IV:121
Westbrook, Samuel II:527
Westcot, Amos II:381
Westcott, Daniel I:93
Westcott, James II:489
Westcott, Joseph II:161
Westcott, Samuel I:45; II:61
Westcott, Thomas I:366
Westcott, Ttephen I:829
Western, Jacob I:567
Western, James II:502
Westervelt, A. II:90
Westervelt, Benjamin II:447
Westervelt, Benjamin P. II:59
Westervelt, Casparus II:83
Westervelt, Cornelius P. II:59
Westervelt, John B. II:491
Westfall, Abraham IV:177
Westfall, Cornelius IV:40
Westfall, Jacob IV:82
Westfall, John III:707
Westgate, Joseph E. I:957
Westgate, Wanton I:820
Westhaver, Godfrey IV:156
Westlake, Benjamin II:527
Westlake, Josiah II:588
Westland, Robert I:45
Westlin, Dewitt II:102
Westmoreland, Jesse III:579
Weston, Abraham I:487
Weston, Asa I:567
Weston, Benjamin III:360
Weston, C. B. I:xiv
Weston, Daniel I:186
Weston, David I:583
Weston, Edmund III:670
Weston, Eliphas I:378
Weston, Jabez I:582
Weston, James I:582; II:341;
   III:423
Weston, John IV:281
Weston, Jonathan I:527
Weston, Joseph I:186
Weston, Levi I:567
Weston, Nancy III:360
Weston, Roger I:762
Weston, Samuel I:212
Weston, Sutherick I:714
Weston, Uriah III:360
Weston, William II:208
Weston, Zachariah III:349
Westray, Daniel III:418
Wetherall, Charles I:227
Wetherbee, Abijah I:696
Wetherbee, David I:653
Wetherbee, Hezekiah I:913

Wetherbee, Isaac II:509
Wetherbee, Jacob II:349
Wetherbee, Joab I:746
Wetherbee, Simon II:349
Wetherbie, Joseph I:714
Wetherell, Samuel I:869
Wetherill, Obadiah I:298
Wetherspoon, William III:433
Wethneckt, Martin II:666
Wetmore, Bela II:472
Wetmore, Joel I:714
Wets, John II:713
Wettherell, John I:272
Wever, Adam II:254
Wever, Conrad II:729
Weyant, Peter II:590
Weygant, Tobias II:461
Weymouth, Dean I:591; III:8
Weymouth, James I:271
Weymouth, Moses I:243
Weysham, Samuel III:111
Weyson, Henry III:811
Whalen, Jeremiah II:325
Whalen, John I:385
Whalen, Joseph I:655
Whalen, Michael III:133
Whalen, Walter II:341
Whaley, Caleb J. II:154
Whaley, Edward IV:184
Whaley, Ezekiel III:380
Whaley, Hezekiah I:36
Whaley, James II:581; IV:203
Whaley, Job I:816
Whaley, Jonathan I:25
Whaley, Joseph I:811
Whaley, Reynolds II:408
Whaley, Theophilus II:282,
   489
Whaley, William III:225
Whaling, Richard II:208
Whapples, Samuel I:104
Wharf, John I:406
Wharry, Daniel II:422
Wharton, Samuel II:672
Wharton, William III:242
Wharton, Zachariah III:812
Whateley, Samuel III:132
Whatley, William B. I:598
Wheadon, Abraham I:130
Wheadon, Rufus I:999
Wheat, Amos II:476
Wheat, Joseph I:654, 704, 789
Wheat, Samuel II:371
Wheatley, Alexander III:628
Wheatley, Andrew I:875
Wheatly, Joseph IV:42
Wheaton, Benjamin I:830
Wheaton, Ephraim II:275
Wheaton, Freeman II:623
Wheaton, Jeremiah I:153
Wheaton, Jesse I:552
Wheaton, John Freeman
   II:623
Wheaton, Jonathan IV:193
Wheaton, Joseph I:378-79;
   III:13, 16
Wheaton, Reuben II:512

543

White, Archelaus I:727
White, Archibald I:921
White, Asa I:583
White, Barney II:629
White, Benjamin I:152, 201,
  583; II:460, 590; III:409, 553
White, Caleb I:486; II:702
White, Charles I:121, 201,
  319, 674; IV:258
White, Christopher I:139
White, Consider II:543
White, Cornelius I:598
White, Daniel I:145, 508,
  526-27; II:123; III:515
White, David I:652, 873, 884;
  II:213, 467, 581, 725;
  III:294, 426; IV:292
White, Ebenezer I:569; IV:217
White, Eli I:955
White, Elijah I:928; III:762
White, Elisha I:152
White, Elizabeth II:198
White, Enoch I:746
White, Ephraim I:104; II:330,
  668
White, Ezekiel III:363
White, Fortune C. II:150
White, Francis I:921; II:618
White, Galen III:303
White, George I:189; II:623;
  III:582
White, Godfrey II:433
White, Gordon III:570
White, Goven III:613
White, Hampton III:703
White, Henry I:406; II:287,
  521
White, Hezekiah II:116
White, Isa I:365
White, Isaac II:543
White, Israel II:433
White, J. M. III:107
White, Jacob IV:255
White, James I:449; II:233,
  375, 383, 585, 756; III:32,
  84, 133, 212, 363, 704
White, Jane II:623
White, Jedediah I:52
White, Jenkins II:543
White, Jeremiah III:819
White, Jesse III:156
White, Joel I:955; II:497
White, John I:212, 319, 378,
  406, 553, 599, 696, 768;
  II:38, 198, 371, 433, 521,
  629; III:363, 416, 630, 806,
  852; IV:184, 229
White, John, 1st IV:18
White, John, 2d IV:20
White, John B. III:849
White, John H. I:788
White, Jonathan I:801; II:300;
  III:39, 50
White, Joseph I:280, 318,
  508, 736; II:186, 497, 645;
  III:171, 645, 753
White, Joseph, 2d III:707

White, Joshua I:227
White, Lawrence II:391
White, Levi I:341
White, Lewis I:467
White, Luke I:438; II:502
White, Luther I:355
White, Margaretta II:623
White, Matthew N. II:186
White, Micah I:552
White, Moses I:385, 762, 788
White, Nathan I:878; III:217
White, Nathaniel II:234, 275;
  IV:93
White, Nelly II:198
White, Nichols II:56
White, Obadiah I:145
White, Oliver I:25, 928;
  II:254, 422
White, Peter III:363
White, Phebe Ann II:623
White, Philip I:58, 156, 973
White, Potter II:660
White, Reuben I:435; II:412
White, Richard III:778, 819
White, Robert I:850; II:145;
  III:630, 646, 800, 849; IV:81
White, Samuel I:152, 532,
  727, 852; II:80, 433; III:632,
  818; IV:252
White, Samuel, 2d I:457
White, Samuel, 1st I:508
White, Samuel B. III:32
White, Samuel W. III:200
White, Seth I:654; II:371
White, Silas I:583, 736
White, Simeon I:365, 796
White, Simpson I:298
White, Smith I:630
White, Solomon I:114, 696,
  788, 993
White, Stephen I:745; III:615
White, Thaddeus I:955
White, Theophilus III:381
White, Thomas I:113, 583,
  628, 821; II:696; III:253,
  308, 634; IV:29, 199, 231,
  234
White, Timothy I:379
White, Truman II:107
White, Uriah II:309
White, Vassal I:335; II:118
White, William I:xv, 58, 993;
  II:16, 160, 364, 381, 388,
  623, 693; III:363, 499, 565,
  570, 599, 852; IV:66, 172,
  213
White, William, 2d I:212;
  II:333
White, William, 3d II:219, 381
White, William C. I:726
White, William D. III:653
White, Wm. II:198
White, Wm. F. III:853
White, Zachariah I:378
Whitecar, Joseph II:61
Whitecotton, Axton III:792
Whitecotton, James III:307

Whitefield, William III:77
Whiteham, Jerry I:227
Whitehead, Armistead III:195
Whitehead, Burrell III:461
Whitehead, James II:38
Whitehead, John II:325;
  III:366
Whitehead, John H. II:27
Whitehead, Mahlon II:27
Whitehead, Nathan II:27
Whitehead, Robert IV:86
Whitehead, Samuel II:682
Whitehead, William II:300
Whitehorn, Samuel I:836
Whitehouse, Daniel I:201
Whitehouse, Ebenezer I:242
Whitehouse, James I:781
Whitehouse, John I:164, 201,
  681
Whitehouse, Jonathan I:736
Whitehouse, Samuel I:242-43
Whitehouse, Thomas I:81
Whitehurst, Arthur, Sr. III:443
Whiteley, Charles III:852
Whiteley, John II:685
Whitely, Charles III:847
Whiteman, Frederick III:621
Whiteman, Henry III:829
Whiteman, Wolley III:681
Whitemarsh, Gideon II:509
Whitemarsh, Samuel II:205
Whitemore, Timothy II:315
Whiten, Solomon I:227
Whitenack, Abraham II:87
Whiter, Jacob III:331
Whiteside, John II:543
Whiteside, William III:571
Whitfield, Solomon III:813
Whitfield, Willis III:615
Whitford, Asa II:170
Whitford, Constant II:237
Whitford, David I:811
Whitford, Stukely II:489
Whitford, Thomas I:836
Whitham, Joshua I:211
Whithington, Thomas I:365
Whitiker, Ebenezer I:755
Whiting, Aaron I:553
Whiting, Caleb I:598
Whiting, Delecta I:360
Whiting, Ebenezer II:338
Whiting, Elihu II:371
Whiting, Elijah II:296
Whiting, Elkanah I:553
Whiting, Enos II:750
Whiting, Esther I:360
Whiting, Francis III:667
Whiting, G. B. I:xii
Whiting, George B. I:xiii
Whiting, George C. I:xiii
Whiting, Harvey I:114
Whiting, Henry II:106
Whiting, Isaac II:234
Whiting, Jacob I:449
Whiting, Jason I:360
Whiting, Jason (2) I:360

Wigham, Robert II:300
Wight, Daniel M. I:587
Wight, Jabez I:892
Wight, Jonathan I:921
Wight, Lemuel I:539
Wight, Nahum I:525-26
Wight, Samuel I:830
Wight, William I:955
Wightman, John I:816
Wightman, Peleg I:817
Wigington, John III:847
Wiginton, George III:92
Wigner, Daniel IV:248
Wikes, Oliver I:816
Wikoff, Joachan III:756
Wilbar, Isaac I:583
Wilbar, Joseph II:497
Wilbeck, Abraham L. II:358
Wilbeck, Andris II:388
Wilbee, John II:79
Wilber, Benjamin II:433
Wilber, Uriel I:808
Wilborne, William III:667
Wilbur, Benjamin I:379
Wilbur, Daniel I:830
Wilbur, Francis I:820
Wilbur, Gideon II:315
Wilbur, John II:706
Wilbur, Joseph I:821
Wilbur, Josiah II:296
Wilbur, Oliver II:230
Wilbur, Samuel I:821, 830
Wilbur, Thomas I:298, 821
Wilburn, Hezekiah I:820
Wilcklow, Jacob II:535
Wilckman, Michael III:52
Wilcocks, William II:272
Wilcox, Abner I:869
Wilcox, Abraham II:345
Wilcox, Asa I:745
Wilcox, Benjamin II:460
Wilcox, Billy I:457
Wilcox, Borden II:408
Wilcox, Comfort I:787
Wilcox, Daniel I:139; II:83
Wilcox, De La Fayette IV:102
Wilcox, Edward II:433
Wilcox, Eleazer I:105
Wilcox, Elijah I:58
Wilcox, Elisha I:973
Wilcox, Ezekiel I:341
Wilcox, Ezra I:25, 131
Wilcox, Hosea IV:213
Wilcox, J. C. I:xii
Wilcox, Jacob I:105
Wilcox, James I:121, 928
Wilcox, Jared I:884
Wilcox, Jehiel I:64; IV:245
Wilcox, Joel I:863; IV:201
Wilcox, John I:272; II:275, 443, 497
Wilcox, John W. II:3
Wilcox, Jonah II:530
Wilcox, Jonathan II:461
Wilcox, Joseph I:121
Wilcox, Josiah II:244, 556; IV:243

Wilcox, Lemuel II:325, 563
Wilcox, Melona I:863
Wilcox, Nathan I:64
Wilcox, Nathaniel I:863; II:412
Wilcox, Noah I:836
Wilcox, Pardon I:821
Wilcox, Reuben II:461
Wilcox, Stephen II:215
Wilcox, Sylvanus, Jr. II:443
Wilcox, Sylvester I:836
Wilcox, Thomas I:820
Wilcox, Timothy I:913
Wilcox, William II:296
Wilcoxen, Daniel III:323
Wilcoxen, Elnathan I:93
Wilcoxen, Ephraim J. I:93
Wilcoxon, David I:36
Wilcutt, Jesse I:487
Wilcutt, Zebulon I:487
Wild, Benjamin I:318
Wild, Daniel I:527
Wild, John I:787
Wild, Jonathan I:552, 652
Wild, Jonathan (2) I:553
Wild, Levi I:552
Wild, Micah I:425
Wild, Thomas II:489
Wilday, Absalom III:152
Wilde, John I:365
Wilder, Aaron I:855, 982
Wilder, Charles II:489
Wilder, Christopher C. I:615
Wilder, Elijah I:472
Wilder, Ephraim I:615, 652
Wilder, George III:93
Wilder, Horace I:615
Wilder, Jacob I:921
Wilder, James I:652
Wilder, Jonathan I:653
Wilder, Joseph I:583
Wilder, Joshua I:982
Wilder, Levi I:922
Wilder, Luther I:745
Wilder, Martha I:615
Wilder, Nathaniel I:448
Wilder, Peter I:745; II:551
Wilder, Phineas I:653
Wilder, Reuben I:652
Wilder, Reuben W. IV:167-68
Wilder, Shubael I:486
Wilder, Thomas I:105
Wilder, Timothy I:629
Wilder, Titus I:654
Wilder, William III:461
Wilder, Willis III:171
Wildrick, Michael II:89
Wilds, Ezra I:405
Wilds, Jacob I:892
Wilds, John I:470
Wiles, Abraham III:395
Wiley, Absalom III:152
Wiley, Alexander II:408; III:565
Wiley, Andrew III:832
Wiley, Ebenezer I:332
Wiley, Henry III:323

Wiley, Isaac II:102
Wiley, James II:381; III:395
Wiley, John I:527, 873; II:83, 120, 272
Wiley, Owen II:618
Wiley, Rufus III:409
Wiley, Samuel IV:178, 272
Wiley, Thomas IV:275
Wiley, William III:577; IV:75
Wilfong, John III:352
Wilford, John C. II:115
Wilford, Lewis III:105
Wilforg, John II:739
Wilheid, Frederick III:52
Wilhelm, Baltzer II:330
Wilhelm, Frederick II:681
Wilhelm, George II:656
Wilhelm, Henry II:43
Wilhelm, Peter I:843; III:509
Wilhite, John III:315
Wilhite, Tobias III:307
Wilkelow, John II:343
Wilkenson, Benjamin III:228
Wilker, Jacob III:597
Wilkerson, David IV:57
Wilkerson, Francis III:262
Wilkerson, Richard III:18
Wilkerson, Thomas III:593; IV:291
Wilkerson, Turner III:619
Wilkerson, Young III:44
Wilkes, Samuel III:753
Wilkes, Thomas, Sen. III:507
Wilkie, Augustus III:325
Wilkin, James W. II:476
Wilkins, Amos II:287
Wilkins, Aquila I:713
Wilkins, Asa I:884
Wilkins, Edward I:222, 526
Wilkins, Elisha III:371
Wilkins, Frederick I:845
Wilkins, George IV:84
Wilkins, James II:681
Wilkins, John III:453
Wilkins, Jonathan I:713
Wilkins, Matilda I:789
Wilkins, Nathaniel III:667
Wilkins, Robert B. I:726, 789
Wilkins, Thomas III:224
Wilkins, Uriah I:973
Wilkins, William III:599
Wilkinson, Abel I:152
Wilkinson, Amos II:636
Wilkinson, Benning I:667, 755
Wilkinson, David II:178
Wilkinson, Elisha III:162
Wilkinson, Ichabod IV:173
Wilkinson, James I:735; III:430, 758
Wilkinson, John I:829; II:363, 509, 561; III:95; IV:235
Wilkinson, Joseph I:319; III:198, 309
Wilkinson, Levi II:371
Wilkinson, Malachi II:244
Wilkinson, Mott II:726
Wilkinson, Reuben II:349

546

Wilkinson, Samuel I:931; II:54
Wilkinson, Thomas I:53;
  III:691
Wilkinson, William I:829;
  II:461; III:630, 757
Wilkison, Aaron II:83
Wilkison, James II:83
Wilks, Mills III:189
Willard, Aaron I:696
Willard, Eli I:787
Willard, Elijah I:745
Willard, Elizabeth I:685
Willard, Ephraim II:215
Willard, Ezra I:298
Willard, Humphrey I:689
Willard, James IV:174
Willard, Jeremiah I:787
Willard, John I:xiv; II:408,
  565; III:686
Willard, Jonathan I:653, 786
Willard, Joseph II:417
Willard, Joseph D. I:614
Willard, Joshua I:746
Willard, Josiah II:296
Willard, Justin I:657
Willard, Lezier I:131
Willard, Moses I:685; II:205
Willard, Moses T. I:685
Willard, Nancy I:685
Willard, Peter I:629
Willard, Samuel I:457
Willard, Sarah I:685
Willard, William I:653; II:643;
  IV:17
Willbar, Joshua II:489
Willbern, Joshua III:571
Willcock, James II:66
Willcox, Gideon I:830
Willcox, James II:296
Willcox, Joseph I:941
Willcox, Nathan I:957
Willcox, Stephen II:433
Wille, Benjamin II:266
Willee, William I:689
Willen, Levin III:66
Willes, John I:81
Willet, Hartshorn II:443
Willet, Joseph II:111
Willett, Cornelius II:543
Willett, Marinus II:560
Willey, Abraham II:372
Willey, Ahimas I:341
Willey, Andrew I:719
Willey, Barzilla IV:63
Willey, Charles I:736
Willey, Ephraim I:973
Willey, Jonathan I:58, 114
Willey, Josiah I:781
Willey, Samuel I:781
William, Daniel IV:290
William, John, 2d III:56
Williama, Isaac II:345
Williams, Abel II:371
Williams, Abijah II:472
Williams, Abraham I:406;
  III:304

Williams, Alexander I:81;
  III:11, 546, 750
Williams, Amos I:243, 829
Williams, Amos A. III:27
Williams, Andrew II:225
Williams, Asa I:104, 435
Williams, Asahel I:969; II:489
Williams, Bartholomew II:425
Williams, Bastinus II:330
Williams, Benjamin I:152,
  200, 946; II:449; III:208,
  437, 597; IV:191, 248
Williams, Bennett III:242, 442
Williams, Beverly III:524
Williams, Bill II:282
Williams, Buckner III:438
Williams, Burnet IV:246
Williams, Caleb II:706; III:619
Williams, Charles I:768;
  II:581; III:56
Williams, Constant IV:64
Williams, Cornelius I:168
Williams, Daniel I:652; II:38,
  266, 391; III:635
Williams, Davenport II:461
Williams, David I:25, 104,
  355, 602; II:66, 460; III:336,
  615; IV:231
Williams, Dyer II:320
Williams, Eben II:287
Williams, Ebenezer I:72;
  II:357, 472, 561, 722
Williams, Edward IV:121
Williams, Elijah I:607, 921;
  III:281
Williams, Elisha I:105; II:530;
  III:606
Williams, Elisha S. I:602
Williams, Eliza II:192
Williams, Elizabeth IV:296
Williams, Ephraim I:830
Williams, Ezekial II:123
Williams, Fielding III:661
Williams, Frederick II:681
Williams, Frederick W. I:72
Williams, Gabriel III:720
Williams, George III:423, 471
Williams, Gerard III:278
Williams, Henry I:72, 936;
  II:66, 381, 480; III:352, 471,
  654, 809
Williams, Henry J. III:654;
  IV:3
Williams, Hickman III:550
Williams, Ichabod II:100
Williams, Isaac I:139, 508;
  II:38, 192; III:73, 283; IV:74
Williams, Isaac, 2d I:509
Williams, Jabez I:829
Williams, Jacob I:20
Williams, James I:705; II:213,
  433, 467, 549, 623; III:115,
  324, 815, 838; IV:91, 94,
  209, 226
Williams, James, 2d II:261;
  III:272; IV:178
Williams, James, 3d II:349

Williams, James M. III:823
Williams, Jeremiah III:382,
  842; IV:299
Williams, Jesse I:993
Williams, John I:212, 602,
  628, 830; II:16, 157, 300,
  352, 375, 394, 408, 422,
  460, 557, 618; III:48, 90,
  227, 324, 411, 461, 567,
  608, 675, 758, 765, 786,
  819; IV:25, 64, 153, 191,
  245, 290, 295-96
Williams, John, 1st I:843;
  II:32; IV:178
Williams, John (2) III:227
Williams, John, 2d I:913;
  II:45; III:699
Williams, John, 3d I:507
Williams, John, Sen. III:839
Williams, John B. II:146
Williams, John B., 2d II:110
Williams, John J. III:565
Williams, Jonathan I:903;
  II:66
Williams, Joseph I:139, 318,
  885; II:146, 432, 649, 685;
  III:69, 181
Williams, Joseph J. IV:14
Williams, Joshua I:189, 379
Williams, Lavi III:615
Williams, Lawrence III:278
Williams, Lemuel I:227
Williams, Levi III:11
Williams, Lewis IV:207
Williams, Lot III:41
Williams, Mary III:471
Williams, Matthew III:523,
  836
Williams, Matthias II:83;
  III:608
Williams, Miles IV:255
Williams, Morris III:670
Williams, Nathan I:152; II:497
Williams, Nathaniel II:213;
  III:27
Williams, Norman I:1000
Williams, O. H. I:xv
Williams, Obed I:52
Williams, Oliver II:145
Williams, Osborn III:44
Williams, Othaniel II:371
Williams, Pearson III:740
Williams, Peleg I:809
Williams, Peter I:139; II:357,
  509; III:92
Williams, Philip III:310
Williams, Platt II:110
Williams, Richard II:352
Williams, Robert I:72, 140,
  599, 659, 704; III:443, 542,
  704; IV:142
Williams, Samuel I:591, 654,
  704; III:438; IV:134, 259
Williams, Samuel, Sen. III:634
Williams, Sanford I:25
Williams, Sarah I:659
Williams, Sarah Jane II:623

Williams, Shadrack III:583
Williams, Silas I:487
Williams, Solomon I:139;
II:460; III:578
Williams, Stacey II:681
Williams, Stephen I:378;
III:113, 401
Williams, Stinson I:378
Williams, Thomas I:12, 341,
602, 902, 993; II:225, 599;
III:8, 211, 272, 297, 411,
435, 765, 852; IV:9, 70, 191,
268
Williams, Thomas C. III:634
Williams, Thomas P. III:446
Williams, Tobias III:619
Williams, Uriah I:72; II:282
Williams, Veach I:131
Williams, W. L. I:xii
Williams, Wareham I:139
Williams, Waring III:423
Williams, William I:94, 738;
II:24, 56, 79, 161, 205, 530,
722; III:41, 152, 184, 304,
449, 451, 518, 589, 709,
844; IV:96, 248, 278, 282
Williams, William, 2d II:327
Williams, William J. III:30
Williams, Wm. II:443
Williams, Wm. B. I:xvi
Williams, Wm., 2d II:24
Williams, Zebedee III:558
Williamson, Andw. II:620
Williamson, Calvin II:507
Williamson, Charles III:405
Williamson, Diborix III:761
Williamson, Eleazer IV:284
Williamson, Elijah III:405
Williamson, Eliza II:620
Williamson, Elizabeth III:533
Williamson, Garrett II:45
Williamson, George I:892
Williamson, Henry IV:216
Williamson, Isaac II:75
Williamson, Isaac, Sen. III:446
Williamson, Jacob II:43, 75
Williamson, James II:266,
725; III:254
Williamson, Jedediah II:521
Williamson, John II:79, 357,
521, 653; III:533, 576, 682
Williamson, Littleton III:615
Williamson, Marcus II:527
Williamson, Matthias II:66
Williamson, Nancy III:533
Williamson, Nathan I:996
Williamson, Nelson III:533
Williamson, Peter II:70
Williamson, Reuben III:533
Williamson, William II:681;
III:457, 495
Willicus, Elias II:576
Williford, Brittain III:582
Williford, Jacob III:583
Williford, Nathan III:159
Williford, Richard III:513
Williford, Willis III:373

Willigus, Elias II:576
Willing, John C. II:51
Willington, John I:653
Willington, Jonathan IV:241
Willington, Samuel I:608, 851,
982
Willis, Abisha I:487
Willis, Andrew III:59
Willis, Azarah I:476
Willis, Bailey III:740
Willis, Benjamin II:266
Willis, Betsey II:198
Willis, Britton III:311
Willis, Caleb II:461
Willis, Caty II:198
Willis, Charles I:599
Willis, Daniel I:705
Willis, Ebenezer I:435
Willis, Edmund I:973
Willis, Henry II:447
Willis, Hezekiah II:432
Willis, James I:201, 921;
III:783
Willis, Jarvis III:543
Willis, Joel I:968
Willis, John I:425, 582;
II:161; III:27, 589, 716
Willis, Jonathan I:906
Willis, Joseph I:508; II:282;
III:430
Willis, Lewis III:545
Willis, Meshach III:553
Willis, Nancy II:198
Willis, Owen II:145
Willis, Russell II:371
Willis, Sally II:198
Willis, Silas I:968
Willis, Smith III:608
Willis, Sylvanus I:993
Willis, Thomas II:447
Willis, William II:66, 198;
III:556, 810
Willis, William R. III:110
Willis, Zenas II:315
Willison, William II:371
Williston, Caleb I:921
Williston, Godfrey II:467
Williston, Ichabod I:820
Williston, Payson I:487
Willman, Benoni II:489
Willman, Jacob, Jr. I:669
Willman, John II:244
Willman, Joseph I:212
Willmore, Christop'r III:712
Willmot, Timothy I:892
Willock, John II:569
Willons, Charles III:427
Willoughby, Alexander III:295
Willoughby, Bliss II:381
Willoughby, Edlyne III:398
Willoughby, Henry III:838
Willoughby, Salmon I:946
Willoughby, Samuel I:355
Willoughby, William III:138
Wills, Conrad II:664
Wills, Daniel III:39
Wills, David III:523

Wills, James I:200-201; IV:120
Wills, John III:27
Wills, Jonathan I:892
Wills, Leonard III:164
Wills, Thomas C. III:590
Wills, William III:309
Willsie, Abraham II:489
Willsie, Henry T. II:443
Willsie, Jacob II:357-58
Willsie, William II:222
Willsly, George II:161
Willson, Andrew II:476
Willson, Asa I:946
Willson, Harvey II:194
Willson, Hugh II:320
Willson, James II:54
Willson, John II:54, 502;
III:318
Willson, Moore II:333
Willson, Richard III:48
Willson, Robert II:51
Willson, Samuel II:325, 417
Willson, W. II:194
Willson, W. B. II:194
Willson, William I:836
Willyard, Henry IV:191
Willys, Thomas I:105
Wilmarth, Amos I:449
Wilmarth, Ebenezer I:365
Wilmarth, Eliphalet I:379
Wilmarth, Ephraim I:855
Wilmarth, Jonathan I:378
Wilmarth, Joseph I:755
Wilmarth, Nathaniel I:969
Wilmarth, Samuel I:81
Wilmarth, Thomas I:366
Wilmoth, William III:165
Wilmott, Robert III:333
Wilmott, Walter I:64
Wilner, Henry II:599
Wilse, James B. II:195
Wilsey, David II:195
Wilsey, Hannah II:195
Wilsey, Isaac II:195
Wilsey, James B. II:195
Wilsey, William II:195
Wilshire, John III:826
Wilsie, James II:422
Wilson, Aaron I:746
Wilson, Abial I:45
Wilson, Abiel I:714
Wilson, Abraham I:864;
III:838
Wilson, Albert II:59
Wilson, Alexander II:215
Wilson, Alexander, 2d II:100
Wilson, Alexander, 1st II:145,
273
Wilson, Andrew II:489, 669;
III:217; IV:235
Wilson, Archibald III:376
Wilson, Artemus I:746
Wilson, Augustin III:184
Wilson, Benjamin I:653; II:79
Wilson, Charles II:27
Wilson, Daniel II:75; III:27
Wilson, Daniel S. I:113

Wilson, David I:508; II:185, 645, 696; III:59, 239
Wilson, Ebenezer II:315
Wilson, Edward I:186; III:719
Wilson, Eli B. III:821
Wilson, Eliza II:195
Wilson, Elnathan II:733
Wilson, Ephraim I:508, 654; IV:87
Wilson, Francis I:629
Wilson, Francis Walter I:864
Wilson, George II:145, 472; III:185, 799
Wilson, George C. III:27
Wilson, Gilbreath II:633
Wilson, Henry I:438, 840, 903; II:559; III:309, 500, 679
Wilson, Hosea II:5
Wilson, Irvin I:52
Wilson, Isaac I:508; II:275; IV:238
Wilson, Israel II:266
Wilson, J. C. I:xii
Wilson, James I:52, 653, 864; II:27, 102, 499; III:214, 313, 426, 568, 681; IV:29, 80, 290
Wilson, James (2) IV:290
Wilson, Jared I:552
Wilson, Jeremiah II:618; III:332
Wilson, Joab I:105
Wilson, John I:114, 152, 227, 260, 280, 359, 405, 774, 855; II:89, 383, 408, 543, 556, 635, 741, 753; III:79, 163, 345, 406, 488, 495, 572, 593, 599, 828; IV:173
Wilson, John, 1st II:213
Wilson, John, 2d II:40, 266
Wilson, John D. I:xii
Wilson, Jonathan I:153
Wilson, Joseph I:243, 507, 654; II:412, 721; III:572, 715
Wilson, Joshua III:81
Wilson, Josiah II:273; III:293
Wilson, Lucy I:864
Wilson, Luke I:913
Wilson, Matthew IV:258
Wilson, Matthew IV:204
Wilson, Michael IV:55
Wilson, Mindart II:87
Wilson, Moses I:105
Wilson, Nathan II:543
Wilson, Nathaniel I:114, 799; II:83
Wilson, Nehemiah I:36; II:641
Wilson, Newhall I:424
Wilson, Newman III:515
Wilson, Noah II:706
Wilson, Obadiah IV:199
Wilson, Paul II:325
Wilson, Richard III:749
Wilson, Richard J. II:461
Wilson, Riley II:195

Wilson, Robert I:774; II:603; III:76, 228, 294, 398, 517, 810; IV:73
Wilson, Robert, 2d II:635
Wilson, Robert, Sen. IV:273
Wilson, Robert M. II:603, 745
Wilson, Robt. M. (2d) II:745
Wilson, Sally II:195
Wilson, Samuel I:93, 696; II:489, 715; III:39, 300, 433, 438; IV:240
Wilson, Solomon I:993
Wilson, Stafford II:83
Wilson, Supply I:762
Wilson, Thaddeus I:762
Wilson, Thomas I:94, 727, 762, 813; II:186, 213, 300; III:513
Wilson, Valentine II:522
Wilson, Wallis III:807
Wilson, Walter II:496
Wilson, Warren I:755
Wilson, William I:13, 508; II 87, 89, 195, 535, 698, 736; III:192, 572, 750, 852; IV:75, 77, 219
Wilson, William, 2d III:809
Wilson, William, Sr. III:750
Wilson, Willis III:443, 644
Wilt, Frederick II:618
Wilton, George I:114
Wilton, William IV:27
Wilts, Michael II:56
Wiltsie, Isaac II:328
Wilty, James IV:246
Wiman, John I:873
Wiman, William I:932
Wimbish, James III:784
Wimbro, Thomas III:70
Wimmer, Israel IV:208
Wimmer, John IV:208
Winans, John II:273, 357
Winans, Silas II:331
Winborne, John III:438
Winch, Abijah II:401
Winch, Jason I:973
Winch, Joseph I:227
Winch, Silas I:527
Winch, William II:150
Winchel, James II:535
Winchel, Jedediah II:287
Winchel, John I:114
Winchel, Justus II:213
Winchell, William II:489
Winchester, Amanah II:397
Winchester, Amariah I:75
Winchester, Charles I:873
Winchester, Daniel III:586
Winchester, David I:745
Winchester, Elizabeth I:594
Winchester, Henry II:238
Winchester, Icha. I:594
Winchester, Jabez II:461
Winchester, Jacob B. I:656
Winchester, Jonathan I:508
Winchester, Laura I:594
Winchester, Lemuel I:424

Winchester, Richard III:286
Winchester, Silas I:222
Winchester, William I:448
Winckleblack, Henry III:810
Windfield, Henry II:88
Windolph, Jacob II:681
Windsor, Peter I:658
Windsor, Ricahrd IV:6
Wine, Jacob III:667
Wine, Rallion II:230
Winfield, Abraham II:343
Winfield, Benjamin II:535
Winfield, David III:535
Winfield, Emanuel II:472
Winfield, Harris III:840
Winfield, William II:476
Winford, Henry II:343
Winfrey, Philip III:253
Wing, Asa I:173
Wing, Bani I:982
Wing, Benjamin II:408
Wing, Daniel II:375
Wing, Dan'l I:173
Wing, David I:173
Wing, Deborah I:173
Wing, Eli I:436
Wing, Gideon I:201
Wing, Isaiah I:449
Wing, Israel I:599
Wing, James I:355
Wing, John I:173
Wing, Moses I:164, 272, 386
Wing, Nathan I:227
Wing, Parmenio I:173
Wing, William I:173
Wingard, James C. IV:141
Wingate, Daniel I:736
Wingate, Driscilla I:173
Wingate, Ebenezer I:173
Wingate, Enoch I:735
Wingate, Jeremiah I:173
Wingate, John I:201; III:217
Wingate, Jonathan I:319
Wingate, Lydiah H. I:173
Wingate, Noah I:173
Wingfield, Enoch III:332
Wingo, William III:515
Wingrove, John III:799
Winham, George IV:170
Wink, Jacob III:48
Winkler, Henry III:274
Winlock, Joseph III:337
Winn, Elisha III:77
Winn, Galanus III:89
Winn, John I:629, 653; II:145; III:59, 488, 783
Winn, Jonathan I:319
Winn, Joseph I:318
Winn, Joshua I:384
Winn, Samuel I:607
Winn, William III:796
Winn, Zachariah III:500
Winne, Aaron II:358
Winne, Cornelius II:535
Winne, Jacobus II:535
Winne, John II:412
Winne, John D. II:358

549

Winne, Peter J. II:535
Winner, Jacob IV:75
Winney, Jeremiah H. II:116
Winning, James III:672
Winningham, Joseph III:510
Winsett, Raphael III:239
Winship, Abel I:508
Winship, Ebenezer II:273
Winship, Joel II:537
Winship, John I:258, 507
Winship, Richard II:550
Winslow, Asa II:722
Winslow, Benjamin I:211
Winslow, David I:212
Winslow, Ezekiel I:212
Winslow, George I:280
Winslow, Job II:296
Winslow, John I:186
Winslow, Kenelm IV:194
Winslow, Lemuel I:583
Winslow, Oliver I:567
Winslow, Samuel I:936
Winslow, Stephen IV:228
Winson, John II:315
Winson, Samuel I:830
Winsor, John I:583
Winsor, William I:582
Winstead, Francis III:589
Winstead, Maudley III:293
Winston, Anthony III:803
Winston, Isaac II:358
Winston, Nathaniel III:615
Winston, Robt. III:709
Winston, Wm. Bobby III:709
Winter, Asa I:628
Winter, Benjamin I:704
Winter, Jacob II:111
Winter, John, Sen. II:739
Winter, Jonathan W. IV:287
Winter, Joseph I:219
Winter, Joshua I:598
Winter, Nicholas II:480
Winter, Peter II:89
Winter, Stephen IV:251
Wintercalef, Ebenezer I:535
Winters, Jacob II:169, 668
Winters, James II:690
Winters, Juvenil II:375
Winton, Joseph I:93
Winton, Nathan II:649
Wintworth, Alpheus II:282
Wipping, George I:424
Wirble, Henry III:337
Wire, Rhinheart II:695
Wire, Samuel I:64
Wisbaugh, Martin III:27
Wise, Daniel I:318, 746
Wise, Ebenezer I:705
Wise, Henry III:42
Wise, John I:808; III:186, 393
Wise, Peter III:574; IV:274
Wise, Samuel III:229
Wise, William I:65
Wisecarver, George II:725
Wiseman, Caleb III:743
Wiseman, George II:651
Wiseman, James IV:62

Wiseman, Joseph III:810
Wiseman, Thomas III:482
Wiser, Elizabeth III:41
Wiser, John III:41
Wisler, Michael II:664
Wisman, John III:671
Wisman, Julian III:671
Wisman, Paul III:671
Wisman, Polly III:671
Wisner, David II:449
Wisner, George III:573
Wisner, Samuel II:371
Wisnor, Jacob II:646
Wisong, Fiat III:755
Wisor, Michael III:694
Wisswell, Daniel I:436
Wistcoot, Thomas I:816
Wiston, William I:186
Wiswall, Samuel I:982
Wiswell, David I:922
Wiswell, Israel IV:208
Witch, James I:186
Witchell, Jacob II:51
Witcher, James III:619
Witderstein, John II:556
Witham, Andrew I:243
Witham, Bartholomew I:243
Witham, Caleb I:212
Witham, David I:172
Witham, Elijah I:736
Witham, Eliza I:172
Witham, James I:243; II:331
Witham, John I:172
Witham, John Spicer I:243
Witham, Joseph I:172
Witham, Maria I:172
Witham, Nathan I:243
Witham, Peter IV:84
Witham, Philip I:172
Witham, Rufus I:172
Witham, Samuel I:172
Witham, Thomas I:161
Withee, Zoe I:272
Wither, Uzziel I:227
Witherel, Abel I:539
Witherell, James IV:110
Witherell, John I:332
Witherell, Nathaniel I:378
Witherell, Theophilus I:607
Witherick, George II:556
Witherill, B. F. H. IV:110
Witherington, Joseph III:590
Witherington, Solomon III:409
Witherington, William III:409
Withers, James III:15, 853
Withers, Jesse III:771
Withers, Spencer III:771
Withers, Susanna III:853
Withers, William III:694
Withers, William R. III:849
Witherspoon, David III:475
Witherspoon, John III:627
Withington, Ebenezer I:552
Withington, John I:598
Withington, Lemuel I:541
Withron, James III:451
Withrow, Samuel II:723

Withy, Henry II:497
Witing, Leonard IV:104
Witler, Jonah I:140
Witley, William II:145
Witmeyer, Everard II:618
Witmore, Daniel I:230
Witney, Simon I:630
Witram, John II:618
Witt, Artemas I:696
Witt, Benjamin I:629
Witt, Bergess III:554
Witt, Earis III:601
Witt, Elisha III:274
Witt, Jacob II:748
Witt, Jesse III:642, 753
Witt, Jesse, 2d III:701
Witt, Joseph I:487
Witt, Stephen I:630
Witter, Joseph IV:187
Witter, Josiah I:884
Witters, Conrad IV:206
Wittington, Jarratt III:118
Wittington, Nathan III:508
Wittum, Rexford II:110
Witz, John II:713
Wixom, Shubael I:201
Wixon, Daniel II:491
Wizer, Michael III:694
Woddin, John II:233
Wolcot, Silas II:641
Wolcott, Benajah IV:194
Wolcott, Giles II:296
Wolcott, John II:315
Wolcott, N. K. I:655
Wolcott, Samuel II:247
Wolcott, William I:105
Wolever, Philip .III:585
Wolf, Adam II:761
Wolf, Andrew III:186
Wolf, George IV:158
Wolf, Jacob II:699
Wolf, Jesse III:195
Wolf, Levi D. I:108
Wolf, Lewis III:453
Wolf, Michael II:740; IV:177
Wolf, Peter II:730
Wolf, Seth D. I:124
Wolf, William, Sen. II:756
Wolfe, Adam IV:283
Wolfe, Christian II:618
Wolfe, David II:447
Wolfe, James III:636
Wolfen, John H. II:535
Wolfenbarger, Philip IV:210
Wolfenton, Catherine II:629
Wolfenton, John II:629
Wolfenton, Margaretta II:629
Wolfenton, Richard II:629
Wolfenton, Robert II:629
Wolfenton, Thomas II:629
Wolfinger, John II:620
Wolfinger, Magdalena II:620
Wolfinger, Margaret II:620
Wolfinger, Mary Ann II:620
Wolfinger, Sarah II:620
Wolfinger, Thomas II:620
Wolford, John III:829